Pro Android 3

Satya Komatineni
Dave MacLean
Sayed Y. Hashimi

Apress®

Pro Android 3

ISBN-13 (pbk): 978-1-4302-3222-3

ISBN-13 (electronic): 978-1-4302-3223-0

President and Publisher: Paul Manning
Lead Editor: Matthew Moodie
Technical Reviewer: Dylan Phillips
Editorial Board: Steve Anglin, Mark Beckner, Ewan Buckingham, Gary Cornell, Jonathan Gennick, Jonathan Hassell, Michelle Lowman, Matthew Moodie, Jeffrey Pepper, Frank Pohlmann, Douglas Pundick, Ben Renow-Clarke, Dominic Shakeshaft, Matt Wade, Tom Welsh
Coordinating Editor: Corbin Collins
Copy Editors: Heather Lang, Tracy Brown, Mary Behr
Compositor: MacPS, LLC
Indexer: BIM Indexing & Proofreading Services
Artist: April Milne
Cover Designer: Anna Ishchenko

Distributed to the book trade worldwide by Springer Science+Business Media, LLC., 233 Spring Street, 6th Floor, New York, NY 10013. Phone 1-800-SPRINGER, fax (201) 348-4505, e-mail orders-ny@springer-sbm.com, or visit www.springeronline.com.

For information on translations, please e-mail rights@apress.com, or visit www.apress.com.

Apress and friends of ED books may be purchased in bulk for academic, corporate, or promotional use. eBook versions and licenses are also available for most titles. For more information, reference our Special Bulk Sales–eBook Licensing web page at www.apress.com/info/bulksales.

The source code for this book is available to readers at www.apress.com.

To my brother Hari, to whom life yielded few favors.

—Satya Komatineni

To my wife, Rosie, and my son, Mike, for their support; I couldn't have done this without you. And to Max, for spending so much time at my feet keeping me company.

—Dave MacLean

To my son, Sayed-Adieb.

—Sayed Y. Hashimi

Contents at a Glance

Contents ... vi
Foreword ... xviii
About the Authors ... xix
About the Technical Reviewer ... xx
Acknowledgments ... xxi
Preface ... xxii
Chapter 1: Introducing the Android Computing Platform ... 1
Chapter 2: Setting Up Your Development Environment ... 21
Chapter 3: Understanding Android Resources ... 63
Chapter 4: Understanding Content Providers ... 89
Chapter 5: Understanding Intents ... 125
Chapter 6: Building User Interfaces and Using Controls ... 145
Chapter 7: Working with Menus ... 217
Chapter 8: Working with Dialogs ... 243
Chapter 9: Working with Preferences and Saving State ... 265
Chapter 10: Exploring Security and Permissions ... 287
Chapter 11: Building and Consuming Services ... 307
Chapter 12: Exploring Packages ... 377
Chapter 13: Exploring Handlers ... 399
Chapter 14: Broadcast Receivers and Long-Running Services ... 425
Chapter 15: Exploring the Alarm Manager ... 465
Chapter 16: Exploring 2D Animation ... 491
Chapter 17: Exploring Maps and Location-based Services ... 519
Chapter 18: Using the Telephony APIs ... 559
Chapter 19: Understanding the Media Frameworks ... 575
Chapter 20: Programming 3D Graphics with OpenGL ... 623
Chapter 21: Exploring Live Folders ... 693
Chapter 22: Home Screen Widgets ... 711
Chapter 23: Android Search ... 745
Chapter 24: Exploring Text to Speech ... 825
Chapter 25: Touch Screens ... 845
Chapter 26: Using Sensors ... 891
Chapter 27: Exploring the Contacts API ... 937
Chapter 28: Deploying Your Application: Android Market and Beyond ... 993
Chapter 29: Fragments for Tablets and More ... 1015
Chapter 30: Exploring ActionBar ... 1069
Chapter 31: Additional Topics in 3.0 ... 1097
Index ... 1141

Contents

Contents at a Glance iv
Foreword xviii
About the Authors xix
About the Technical Reviewer xx
Acknowledgments xxi
Preface xxii

Chapter 1: Introducing the Android Computing Platform 1
A New Platform for a New Personal Computer 1
Early History of Android 3
Delving Into the Dalvik VM 6
Understanding the Android Software Stack 6
Developing an End-User Application with the Android SDK 8
- Android Emulator 8
- The Android UI 9
- The Android Foundational Components 10
- Advanced UI Concepts 11
- Android Service Components 13
- Android Media and Telephony Components 13
- Android Java Packages 14

Taking Advantage of Android Source Code 18
The Sample Projects in this Book 19
Summary 20

Chapter 2: Setting Up Your Development Environment 21
Setting Up Your Environment 22
- Downloading JDK 6 22
- Downloading Eclipse 3.6 23
- Downloading the Android SDK 23
- The Tools Window 26
- Installing Android Development Tools (ADT) 26

Learning the Fundamental Components 29
View 29
Activity 29
Intent 29
Content Provider 30
Service 30
AndroidManifest.xml 30
Android Virtual Devices 30
Hello World! 31
Android Virtual Devices 37
Exploring the Structure of an Android Application 39
Analyzing the Notepad Application 42
Loading and Running the Notepad Application 42
Dissecting the Application 44
Examining the Application Lifecycle 51
Debugging Your App 54
Launching the Emulator 56
StrictMode 57
References 61
Summary 62
Chapter 3: Understanding Android Resources 63
Understanding Resources 63
String Resources 64
Layout Resources 66
Resource Reference Syntax 67
Defining Your Own Resource IDs for Later Use 69
Compiled and Uncompiled Android Resources 70
Enumerating Key Android Resources 71
Working with Arbitrary XML Resource Files 80
Working with Raw Resources 82
Working with Assets 82
Reviewing the Resources Directory Structure 83
Resources and Configuration Changes 83
Reference URLs 87
Summary 88
Chapter 4: Understanding Content Providers 89
Exploring Android's Built-in Providers 90
Architecture of Content Providers 96
Implementing Content Providers 108
Exercising the Book Provider 120
Adding A Book 120
Removing a Book 120
Getting a Count of the Books 121
Displaying the List of Books 121
Resources 122
Summary 123
Chapter 5: Understanding Intents 125
Basics of Android Intents 125
Available Intents in Android 127
Exploring Intent Composition 129
Intents and Data URIs 129

Generic Actions....130
Using Extra Information....131
Using Components to Directly Invoke an Activity....133
Understanding Intent Categories....134
Rules for Resolving Intents to Their Components....137
Exercising the ACTION_PICK....139
Exercising the GET_CONTENT Action....141
Introducing Pending Intents....142
Resources....144
Summary....144
Chapter 6: Building User Interfaces and Using Controls....145
UI Development in Android....145
Building a UI Completely in Code....147
Building a UI Completely in XML....149
Building a UI in XML With Code....150
Understanding Android's Common Controls....152
Text Controls....152
Button Controls....157
The ImageView Control....165
Date and Time Controls....167
The MapView Control....169
Understanding Adapters....170
Getting to Know SimpleCursorAdapter....171
Getting to Know ArrayAdapter....172
Using Adapters With AdapterViews....174
The Basic List Control: ListView....175
The GridView Control....183
The Spinner Control....185
The Gallery Control....187
Creating Custom Adapters....188
Other Controls in Android....194
Styles and Themes....194
Using Styles....194
Using Themes....197
Understanding Layout Managers....198
The LinearLayout Layout Manager....199
The TableLayout Layout Manager....202
The RelativeLayout Layout Manager....206
The FrameLayout Layout Manager....208
Customizing Layout for Various Device Configurations....210
Debugging and Optimizing Layouts with the Hierarchy Viewer....213
References....216
Summary....216
Chapter 7: Working with Menus....217
Understanding Android Menus....217
Creating a Menu....219
Working with Menu Groups....220
Responding to Menu Items....221
Creating a Test Harness for Testing Menus....222
Working with Other Menu Types....229
Expanded Menus....229
Working with Icon Menus....229

Working with Submenus 230
Provisioning for System Menus 231
Working with Context Menus 231
Working with Alternative Menus 234
Working with Menus in Response to Changing Data 238
Loading Menus Through XML Files 238
Structure of an XML Menu Resource File 239
Inflating XML Menu Resource Files 239
Responding to XML-Based Menu Items 240
A Brief Introduction to Additional XML Menu Tags 241
Resource 242
Summary 242

Chapter 8: Working with Dialogs 243

Using Dialogs in Android 243
Designing an Alert Dialog 244
Designing a Prompt Dialog 246
Nature of Dialogs in Android 251
Rearchitecting the Prompt Dialog 252
Working with Managed Dialogs 253
Understanding the Managed-Dialog Protocol 253
Recasting the Nonmanaged Dialog as a Managed Dialog 253
Simplifying the Managed-Dialog Protocol 255
Working with Toast 263
Resources 264
Summary 264

Chapter 9: Working with Preferences and Saving State 265

Exploring the Preferences Framework 265
Understanding ListPreference 266
Understanding CheckBoxPreference 275
Understanding EditTextPreference 277
Understanding RingtonePreference 278
Organizing Preferences 280
Manipulating Preferences Programmatically 283
Saving State with Preferences 284
Reference 285
Summary 286

Chapter 10: Exploring Security and Permissions 287

Understanding the Android Security Model 287
Overview of Security Concepts 287
Signing Applications for Deployment 288
Performing Runtime Security Checks 295
Understanding Security at the Process Boundary 295
Declaring and Using Permissions 295
Understanding and Using Custom Permissions 297
Understanding and Using URI Permissions 303
References 305
Summary 305

Chapter 11: Building and Consuming Services 307

Consuming HTTP Services 307
Using the HttpClient for HTTP GET Requests 308
Using the HttpClient for HTTP POST Requests (a Multipart Example) 310

SOAP, JSON, and XML Parsers 312
Dealing with Exceptions....313
Addressing Multithreading Issues 315
Fun With Timeouts....318
Using the HttpURLConnection....319
Using the AndroidHttpClient....319
Using Background Threads (AsyncTask)....320
Handling Configuration Changes with AsyncTasks....327
Getting Files Using DownloadManager....331
Using Android Services....337
Understanding Services in Android....338
Understanding Local Services 339
Understanding AIDL Services....346
Defining a Service Interface in AIDL 347
Implementing an AIDL Interface 349
Calling the Service from a Client Application....351
Passing Complex Types to Services 355
Real-World Example Using Services....366
Google Translate API....366
Using the Google Translate API....367
References....375
Summary 376
Chapter 12: Exploring Packages 377
Packages and Processes....377
Details of a Package Specification 377
Translating Package Name to a Process Name....378
Listing Installed Packages 378
Deleting a Package through the Package Browser....379
Revisiting the Package Signing Process....379
Understanding Digital Signatures: Scenario 1 380
Understanding Digital Signatures: Scenario 2 380
A Pattern for Understanding Digital Signatures....380
So How Do You Digitally Sign?....381
Implications of the Signing Process....381
Sharing Data Among Packages....382
The Nature of Shared User IDs....382
A Code Pattern for Sharing Data 383
Library Projects....384
What Is a Library Project?....384
Library Project Predicates....385
Creating a Library Project 387
Creating an Android Project That Uses a library 390
References....397
Summary 398
Chapter 13: Exploring Handlers.... 399
Android Components and Threading....399
Activities Run on the Main Thread 400
Broadcast Receivers run on the Main Thread....401
Services Run on the Main Thread 401
Content Provider Runs on the Main Thread 401
Implications of a Singular Main Thread 401
Thread Pools, Content Providers, External Service Components....401

Thread Utilities: Discover Your Threads 401
Handlers 403
Implications of Holding the Main Thread 404
Using a Handler to Defer Work on the Main Thread 405
A Sample Handler Source Code That Defers Work 405
Constructing a Suitable Message Object 407
Sending Message Objects to the Queue 407
Responding to the handleMessage Callback 408
Using Worker Threads 408
Invoking a Worker Thread from a Menu 409
Communicating Between the Worker and the Main Threads 410
A Quick Overview of Thread Behavior 412
Handler Example Driver classes 413
Driver Activity File 414
Layout File 417
Menu File 417
Manifest File 417
Component and Process Lifetimes 418
Activity Life Cycle 418
Service Life Cycle 420
Receiver Life Cycle 420
Provider Life Cycle 421
Instructions for Compiling the Code 421
Creating the Project from the ZIP File 421
Creating the Project from the Listings 422
References 422
Summary 423
Chapter 14: Broadcast Receivers and Long-Running Services 425
Broadcast Receivers 425
Sending a Broadcast 426
Coding a Simple Receiver: Sample Code 426
Registering a Receiver in the Manifest File 427
Sending a Test Broadcast 428
Accommodating Multiple Receivers 431
A Project for Out-of-Process Receivers 433
Using Notifications from a Receiver 434
Monitoring Notifications Through the Notification Manager 435
Sending a Notification 437
Long-Running Receivers and Services 440
Long-Running Broadcast Receiver Protocol 441
IntentService 442
IntentService Source Code 443
Extending IntentService for a Broadcast Receiver 445
Long-Running Broadcast Service Abstraction 445
A Long-Running Receiver 447
Abstracting a Wake Lock with LightedGreenRoom 449
Long-Running Service Implementation 455
Details of a Nonsticky Service 456
Details of a Sticky Service 457
A Variation of Nonsticky: Redeliver Intents 457
Specifying Service Flags in OnStartCommand 457
Picking Suitable Stickiness 457

Controlling the Wake Lock from Two Places 458
Long-Running Service Implementation....458
Testing Long Running Services 460
Instructions for Compiling the Code....461
Creating the Projects from the ZIP File 461
Creating the Project from the Listings 461
References....464
Summary 464
Chapter 15: Exploring the Alarm Manager 465
Alarm Manager Basics: Setting Up a Simple Alarm....465
Obtaining the Alarm Manager....466
Setting Up the Time for the Alarm 466
Setting Up a Receiver for the Alarm....467
Creating a PendingIntent Suitable for an Alarm....467
Setting the Alarm 468
Test Project....468
Exploring Alarm Manager Alternate Scenarios 476
Setting Off an Alarm Repeatedly....476
Cancelling an Alarm....479
Working with Multiple Alarms....480
Intent Primacy in Setting Off Alarms....484
Persistence of Alarms....487
Alarm Manager Predicates 487
References....488
Summary 489
Chapter 16: Exploring 2D Animation 491
Frame-by-Frame Animation....492
Planning for Frame-by-Frame Animation 492
Creating the Activity....493
Adding Animation to the Activity....494
Layout Animation 498
Basic Tweening Animation Types....498
Planning the Layout Animation Test Harness 499
Creating the Activity and the ListView 500
Animating the ListView 502
Using Interpolators....506
View Animation....507
Understanding View Animation....507
Adding Animation....511
Using Camera to Provide Depth Perception in 2D....514
Exploring the AnimationListener Class 515
Some Notes on Transformation Matrices 516
Resources....517
Summary 517
Chapter 17: Exploring Maps and Location-based Services 519
Understanding the Mapping Package....520
Obtaining a map-api Key from Google....520
Understanding MapView and MapActivity 522
Adding Markers Using Overlays....528
Understanding the Location Package 533
Geocoding with Android....534

Geocoding with Background Threads 538
Understanding the LocationManager Service 541
Showing Your Location Using MyLocationOverlay 549
Using Proximity Alerts 554
References 558
Summary 558
Chapter 18: Using the Telephony APIs 559
Working with SMS 559
Sending SMS Messages 559
Monitoring Incoming SMS Messages 563
Working with SMS Folders 565
Sending E-mail 567
Working with the Telephony Manager 568
Session Initiation Protocol (SIP) 571
References 574
Summary 574
Chapter 19: Understanding the Media Frameworks 575
Using the Media APIs 575
Using SD Cards 576
Playing Media 581
Playing Audio Content 581
Playing Video Content 593
Recording Media 595
Exploring Audio Recording with MediaRecorder 596
Recording Audio with AudioRecord 600
Exploring Video Recording 605
Exploring the MediaStore Class 614
Recording Audio Using an Intent 615
Adding Media Content to the Media Store 618
Triggering MediaScanner for the Entire SD Card 621
References 621
Summary 621
Chapter 20: Programming 3D Graphics with OpenGL 623
Understanding the History and Background of OpenGL 624
OpenGL ES 625
OpenGL ES and Java ME 626
M3G: Another Java ME 3D Graphics Standard 626
Fundamentals of OpenGL 627
Essential Drawing with OpenGL ES 628
Understanding OpenGL Camera and Coordinates 633
Interfacing OpenGL ES with Android 637
Using GLSurfaceView and Related Classes 638
Implementing the Renderer 638
Using GLSurfaceView from an Activity 641
Changing Camera Settings 647
Using Indices to Add Another Triangle 649
Animating the Simple OpenGL Triangle 651
Braving OpenGL: Shapes and Textures 653
Drawing a Rectangle 653
Working with Shapes 656
Working with Textures 668

Drawing Multiple Figures....674
OpenGL ES 2.0....678
Java Bindings for OpenGL ES 2.0....678
Rendering Steps....682
Understanding Shaders....682
Compiling Shaders into a Program....684
Getting Access to the Shader Program Variables....685
A Simple ES 2.0 Triangle....685
Further Reading on OpenGL ES 2.0....689
Instructions for Compiling the Code....689
References....690
Summary....691
Chapter 21: Exploring Live Folders....693
Exploring Live Folders....693
How a User Experiences Live Folders....694
Building a Live Folder....700
Instructions for Compiling the Code....709
References....710
Summary....710
Chapter 22: Home Screen Widgets....711
Architecture of Home Screen Widgets....712
What Are Home Screen Widgets?....712
User Experience with Home Screen Widgets....713
Life Cycle of a Widget....716
A Sample Widget Application....722
Defining the Widget Provider....724
Defining Widget Size....725
Widget Layout-Related Files....726
Implementing a Widget Provider....728
Implementing Widget Models....730
Implementing Widget Configuration Activity....738
Widget Limitations and Extensions....742
Resources....742
Summary....743
Chapter 23: Android Search....745
Android Search Experience....746
Exploring Android Global Search....746
Enabling Suggestion Providers for Global Search....753
Activities and Search Key Interaction....757
Behavior of Search Key on a Regular Activity....758
Behavior of an Activity that Disables Search....766
Explicitly Invoking Search Through a Menu....767
Understanding Local Search and Related Activities....771
Enabling Type-to-Search....777
Implementing a Simple Suggestion Provider....778
Planning the Simple Suggestions Provider....779
Simple Suggestions Provider Implementation Files....779
Implementing the SimpleSuggestionProvider class....780
Understanding Simple Suggestions Provider Search Activity....784
Search Invoker Activity....789
Simple Suggestion Provider User Experience....791

Implementing a Custom Suggestion Provider....796
Planning the Custom Suggestion Provider....796
SuggestURLProvider Project Implementation Files....796
Implementing the SuggestUrlProvider Class....797
Implementing a Search Activity for a Custom Suggestion Provider....807
Custom Suggestions Provider Manifest File....813
Custom Suggestion User Experience....814
Using Action Keys and Application-Specific Search Data....818
Using Action Keys in Android Search....818
Working with Application-Specific Search Context....821
Resources....822
Implications for Tablets....823
Summary....823
Chapter 24: Exploring Text to Speech....825
The Basics of Text-to-Speech Capabilities in Android....825
Using Utterances to Keep Track of Our Speech....830
Using Audio Files for Your Voice....832
Advanced Features of the TTS Engine....838
Setting Audio Streams....839
Using Earcons....839
Playing Silence....840
Choosing a Different Text-to-Speech Engine....840
Using Language Methods....840
References....842
Summary....843
Chapter 25: Touch Screens....845
Understanding MotionEvents....845
The MotionEvent Object....845
Recycling MotionEvents....857
Using VelocityTracker....857
Exploring Drag and Drop....859
Multitouch....862
Multitouch Before Android 2.2....863
Multitouch Since Android 2.2....871
Touches with Maps....871
Gestures....874
The Pinch Gesture....875
GestureDetector and OnGestureListeners....878
Custom Gestures....881
The Gestures Builder Application....882
References....889
Summary....889
Chapter 26: Using Sensors....891
What Is a Sensor?....891
Detecting Sensors....892
What Can We Know About a Sensor?....892
Getting Sensor Events....895
Issues with Getting Sensor Data....898
Interpreting Sensor Data....905
Light Sensors....905
Proximity Sensors....906

Temperature Sensors 907
Pressure Sensors 907
Gyroscope Sensors 907
Accelerometers 908
Magnetic Field Sensors 914
Using Accelerometers and Magnetic Field Sensors Together 915
Orientation Sensors 915
Magnetic Declination and GeomagneticField 922
Gravity Sensors 923
Linear Acceleration Sensors 923
Rotation Vector Sensors 923
Near Field Communication Sensors 923
References 934
Summary 935

Chapter 27: Exploring the Contacts API 937

Understanding Accounts 938
A Quick Tour of Account Screens 938
Relevance of Accounts to Contacts 942
Enumerating Accounts 943
Understanding Contacts Application 944
Show Contacts 944
Show Contact Detail 945
Edit Contact Details 946
Setting a Contact's Photo 948
Exporting Contacts 949
Various Contact Data Types 951
Understanding Contacts 952
Examining the Contents SQLite Database 952
Raw Contacts 953
Data Table 955
Aggregated Contacts 956
view_contacts 958
contact_entities_view 959
Working with the Contacts API 960
Exploring Accounts 960
Exploring Aggregated Contacts 968
Exploring Raw Contacts 977
Exploring Raw Contact Data 982
Adding a Contact and Its Details 985
Controlling Aggregation 988
Impacts of Syncing 989
References 990
Summary 991

Chapter 28: Deploying Your Application: Android Market and Beyond 993

Becoming a Publisher 994
Following the Rules 994
Developer Console 997
Preparing Your Application for Sale 1001
Testing for Different Devices 1001
Supporting Different Screen Sizes 1001
Preparing AndroidManifest.xml for Uploading 1002
Localizing Your Application 1003

Preparing Your Application Icon....1004
Considerations for Making Money From Apps....1004
Directing Users Back to the Market....1005
The Android Licensing Service....1006
Preparing Your .apk File for Uploading....1007
Uploading Your Application....1007
User Experience on Android Market....1010
Beyond Android Market....1012
References....1013
Summary....1013
Chapter 29: Fragments for Tablets and More....1015
What is a Fragment?....1015
When to Use Fragments....1016
The Structure of a Fragment....1017
A Fragment's Lifecycle....1018
Sample Fragment App Showing the Lifecycle....1024
FragmentTransactions and the Fragment Back Stack....1032
Fragment Transaction Transitions and Animations....1034
The FragmentManager....1035
Caution When Referencing Fragments....1037
ListFragments and <fragment>....1037
Invoking a Separate Activity When Needed....1041
Persistence of Fragments....1044
Understanding Dialog Fragments....1044
DialogFragment Basics....1045
DialogFragment Sample Application....1050
More Communications with Fragments....1063
Using startActivity() and setTargetFragment()....1064
Custom Animations with ObjectAnimator....1064
References....1067
Summary....1068
Chapter 30: Exploring ActionBar....1069
Anatomy of an ActionBar....1070
Tabbed Navigation Action Bar Activity....1071
Implementing Base Activity Classes....1073
Assigning Uniform Behavior for the ActionBar....1075
Implementing the Tabbed Listener....1077
Implementing the Tabbed Action Bar Activity....1078
Scrollable Debug Text View Layout....1080
Action Bar and Menu Interaction....1081
Android Manifest File....1083
Examining the Tabbed Action Bar Activity....1084
List Navigation Action Bar Activity....1084
Creating a SpinnerAdapter....1085
Creating a List Listener....1086
Setting Up a List Action Bar....1086
Making Changes to BaseActionBarActivity....1087
Making Changes to AndroidManifest.xml....1087
Examining the List Action Bar Activity....1088
Standard Navigation Action Bar Activity....1090
Standard Navigation Action Bar Activity....1090
Making Changes to BaseActionBarActivity....1091

Making Changes to AndroidManifest.xml 1092
Examining the Standard Action Bar activity....1092
References....1093
Summary 1094
Chapter 31: Additional Topics in 3.0 1097
List-Based Home Screen Widgets 1097
New Remote Views in 3.0....1098
Working with Lists in Remote Views....1099
Working Sample: Test Home Screen List Widget....1114
Testing the Test List Widget 1122
Drag and Drop....1124
Basics of Drag and Drop in 3.0 1124
Drag and Drop Sample Application....1125
Testing the Sample Drag-and-Drop Application 1137
References....1138
Summary 1139
Index 1141

Foreword

All this has happened before, and all this will happen again. Emergence Theory is the way complex systems and patterns arise out of a set of environmental interactions.

And we have been here before.

When I started programming in 1985, there were a variety of personal computers available. While I cut my teeth on an Apple II C, my friends either had Commodore 128s, Tandy CoCo 3s, or Atari computers. Each of us grew within the constraints of our own environment, but we were rarely able to share our work. When affordable IBM clones running Microsoft's DOS began to emerge, developers started to see value of the marketplace created, and rapid evolution began to occur within the DOS ecosystem. Eventually Microsoft created the dominate position in the PC market that it still enjoys today.

In 2003, when I started mobile programming, the ecosystem looked much the same as it did back in 1985. You could implement your vision in everything from Microsoft .NET CF to Java Micro Edition to BREW. But like the games I coded with my friends, our applications were isolated within our chosen ecosystem.

As 2011 dawns, by spreading the Android OS across hardware vendors, Google looks to be the Microsoft of the Mobile Space. That is likely why you have picked up this book and are reading this foreword. Either you are a student of history or, like me, you were lucky enough to live it.

Well, good news! We have worked very hard in this edition of the book to ensure you have the tools to implement the ideas rattling around in your imagination. We take you from the basics of setting up your environment through deploying to the marketplace. Of course this is a vast journey, so we mainly take you down the road most travelled. But we will provide you plenty of resources to explore on your own.

Good luck, and happy trails.

—Dylan Phillips

About the Authors

Satya Komatineni (www.satyakomatineni.com) has over 20 years of programming experience working with small and large corporations. Satya has published over 30 articles on web development using Java, .NET, and database technologies. He is a frequent speaker at industry conferences on innovative technologies and a regular contributor to the weblogs on Java.net. He is the author of AspireWeb (www.activeintellect.com/aspire), a simplified open source tool for Java web development, and the creator of Aspire Knowledge Central (www.knowledgefolders.com), an open source personal web operating system with a focus on individual productivity and publishing. Satya is also a contributing member to a number of Small Business Innovation Research Programs (SBIR). He received a bachelor's degree in electrical engineering from Andhra University, Visakhapatnam, and a master's degree in electrical engineering from the Indian Institute of Technology, New Delhi. You can contact him at satya.komatineni@gmail.com.

Dave MacLean is a software engineer and architect currently living and working in Jacksonville, Florida. Since 1980, he has programmed in many languages, developing solutions ranging from robot automation systems to data warehousing, from web self-service applications to EDI transaction processors. Dave has worked for Sun Microsystems, IBM, Trimble Navigation, General Motors, and several small companies. He graduated from the University of Waterloo in Canada with a degree in systems design engineering. Visit his blog at http://davemac327.blogspot.com or contact him at davemac327@gmail.com.

Sayed Y. Hashimi was born in Afghanistan and now resides in Jacksonville, Florida. His expertise spans the fields of health care, financials, logistics, and service-oriented architecture. In his professional career, Sayed has developed large-scale distributed applications with a variety of programming languages and platforms, including C/C++, MFC, J2EE, and .NET. He has published articles in major software journals and has written several other popular Apress titles. Sayed holds a master's degree in engineering from the University of Florida. You can reach him by visiting www.sayedhashimi.com.

Please visit the authors at their web site: www.androidbook.com.

About the Technical Reviewer

Dylan Phillips is a software engineer and architect who has been working in the mobile space for the last 10 years. With a broad range of experience ranging from J2ME to .NET Compact Framework to Android, he is incredibly excited about the opportunity presented by the broad consumer adoption of an array of Android devices. He can be reached at `mykoan@hotmail.com`, `@mykoan` on Twitter, or at lunch, in various Pho Houses around the country.

Acknowledgments

Writing this book took effort not only on the part of the authors, but also from some of the very talented staff at Apress, as well as the technical reviewer. Therefore, we would like to thank Steve Anglin, Matthew Moodie, Corbin Collins, Heather Lang, Tracy Brown, Mary Behr, and Brigid Duffy from Apress. We would also like to extend our appreciation to the technical reviewer, Dylan Phillips, for the work he did on this book. His commentary and corrections were invaluable. When searching for answers on the android developers forum, we were often helped by Dianne Hackborn, Nick Pelly, Brad Fitzpatrick, and other members of the Android Team, at all hours of the day and weekends, and to them we would like to say, "Thank you." They truly are the hardest working team in mobile. The Android community is very much alive and well and was also very helpful in answering questions and offering advice. We hope this book in some way is able to give back to the community. Finally, the authors are deeply grateful to their families for accommodating prolonged irresponsibility.

Preface

Have you ever wanted to be a Rodin? Sitting with a chisel and eroding away a block of rock to mold it to your vision? Well, mainstream programmers have kept away from the severely constrained mobile devices for fear of being unable to chisel out at a workable application. Those times have passed.

Android OS places the incredible reach of a programmable device at your door step. In this book we want to positively confirm your suspicion that Android is a great OS to program with. If you are a Java programmer, you have a great opportunity to profit from this exciting, capable, general-purpose computing platform. We are excited about Android because it is an advanced platform that introduces a number of new paradigms in framework design (even with the limitations of a mobile platform).

This is our third edition on the subject of Android, and it's our best edition yet. *Pro Android 3* is an extensive programming guide. In this edition we've refined, rewritten, and enhanced everything from *Pro Android 2* to create a thoroughly updated guide for both beginners and professionals—the result of our three years of research. We cover over 100 topics in 31 chapters. This edition covers versions 2.3 and 3.0 of Android, the optimized versions of Android for phones and tablets, respectively.

In this edition we have beefed up Android internals by covering threads, processes, long running services, broadcast receivers, and alarm managers. We cover many more UI controls in this edition. We have over 150 pages of dedicated material on 3.0, covering fragments, fragment dialogs, ActionBar, and drag and drop. We have significantly enhanced the services and sensor chapters. OpenGL has been revised to include OpenGL ES 2.0.

Concepts, Code, and Tutorials are the essence of this book. Every chapter in the book reflects this philosophy. The self-contained tutorials in each chapter are annotated with expert advice. All projects in the book are available for download for easy importing into Eclipse. We have worked hard so that the code can also be compiled right out of the book. The list of files that goes into each project are explicitly catalogued and listed in each chapter for easy reference.

The areas we cover in the book include key concepts such as resources, intents, content providers, processes, threads, UI controls, broadcast receivers, services, and long running services. We have a lot of coverage on OpenGL ES 1.0 and 2.0 for OpenGL beginners. We have a lot of coverage on text to speech, sensors, and multi-touch. We are also able to incorporate a lot of coverage on 3.0 topics that include fragments, fragment dialogs, ActionBar, and drag and drop.

Finally, in this book we went beyond basics, asked tough questions on every topic, and documented the results (see the table of contents for the extensive list of what we cover in the book). We are also actively updating the supplemental website (`www.androidbook.com`) with current and future research material on the Android SDK. As you walk through the book, if you have any questions we are only an email away for a quick response.

Chapter 1

Introducing the Android Computing Platform

Computing continues to become more and more personalized and accessible. Handheld devices have largely transformed into computing platforms. Mobile phones are no longer just for talking—they have been capable of carrying data and video for some time. Be it a phone or a tablet, the mobile device is now so capable of general-purpose computing that it's becoming more like a PC. A number of traditional PC manufacturers such as ASUS, HP, and Dell are producing devices of various form factors based on the Android OS. The battles between operating systems, computing platforms, programming languages, and development frameworks are being shifted and reapplied to mobile devices.

We are also seeing a surge in mobile programming as more and more IT applications start to offer mobile counterparts. In this book, we'll show you how to take advantage of your Java skills to write programs for devices that run on Google's Android platform (`http://developer.android.com/index.html`), an open-source platform for mobile and tablet development.

> **NOTE:** We are excited about Android because it is an advanced platform that introduces a number of new paradigms in framework design (even with the limitations of a mobile platform).

In this chapter, we'll provide an overview of Android and its SDK, give a brief overview of key packages, introduce what we are going to cover in each chapter briefly, show you how to take advantage of Android source code, and highlight the benefits of programming for the Android platform.

A New Platform for a New Personal Computer

The fact that dedicated devices such as mobile phones can now count themselves among general-computing platforms is good news for programmers (see Figure 1–1).

Starting with Android 3.0, we can officially add tablets to this list. This trend makes programming for mobile devices possible with general-purpose computing languages, which increases the range and market share for mobile applications.

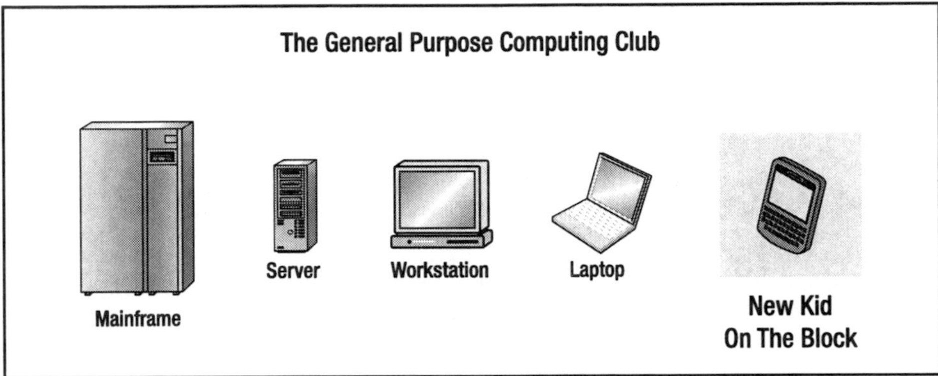

Figure 1–1. *Handheld is the new PC.*

The Android platform embraces this idea of general-purpose computing for handheld devices. It is a comprehensive platform that features a Linux-based operating system stack for managing devices, memory, and processes. Android's Java libraries cover telephony, video, speech, graphics, connectivity, UI programming, and a number of other aspects of the device.

> **NOTE:** Although built for mobile- and tablet-based devices, the Android platform exhibits the characteristics of a full-featured desktop framework. Google makes this framework available to Java programmers through a Software Development Kit (SDK) called the Android SDK. When you are working with the Android SDK, you rarely feel that you are writing to a mobile device because you have access to most of the class libraries that you use on a desktop or a server—including a relational database.

The Android SDK supports most of the Java Platform, Standard Edition (Java SE), except for the Abstract Window Toolkit (AWT) and Swing. In place of AWT and Swing, Android SDK has its own *extensive modern UI framework*. Because you're programming your applications in Java, you could expect that you need a Java Virtual Machine (JVM) that is responsible for interpreting the runtime Java byte code. A JVM typically provides the necessary optimization to help Java reach performance levels comparable to compiled languages such as C and C++. Android offers its own optimized JVM to run the compiled Java class files in order to counter the handheld device limitations such as memory, processor speed, and power. This virtual machine is called the Dalvik VM, which we'll explore in a later section "Delving into the Dalvik VM."

NOTE: The familiarity and simplicity of the Java programming language, coupled with Android's extensive class library, makes Android a compelling platform to write programs for.

Figure 1–2 provides an overview of the Android software stack. (We'll provide further details in the section "Understanding the Android Software Stack.")

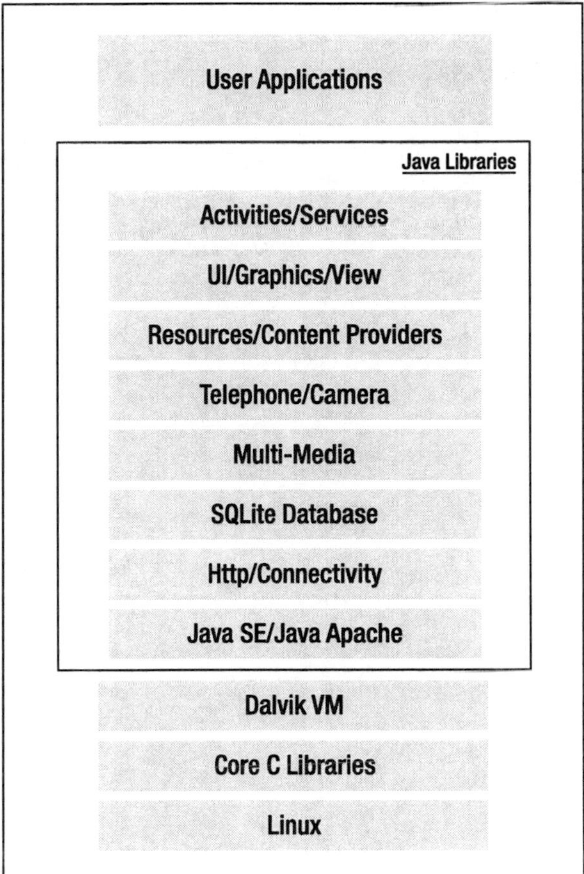

Figure 1–2. *High-level view of the Android software stack*

Early History of Android

Mobile phones use a variety of operating systems, such as Symbian OS, Microsoft's Windows Mobile, Mobile Linux, iPhone OS (based on Mac OS X), Moblin (from Intel), and many other proprietary OSes. So far, no single OS has become the de facto standard. The available APIs and environments for developing mobile applications are too restrictive and seem to fall behind when compared to desktop frameworks. In contrast, the Android platform promised openness, affordability, open-source code, and, more important, a high-end, all-in-one-place, consistent development framework.

Google acquired the startup company Android Inc. in 2005 to start the development of the Android platform (see Figure 1–3). The key players at Android Inc. included Andy Rubin, Rich Miner, Nick Sears, and Chris White.

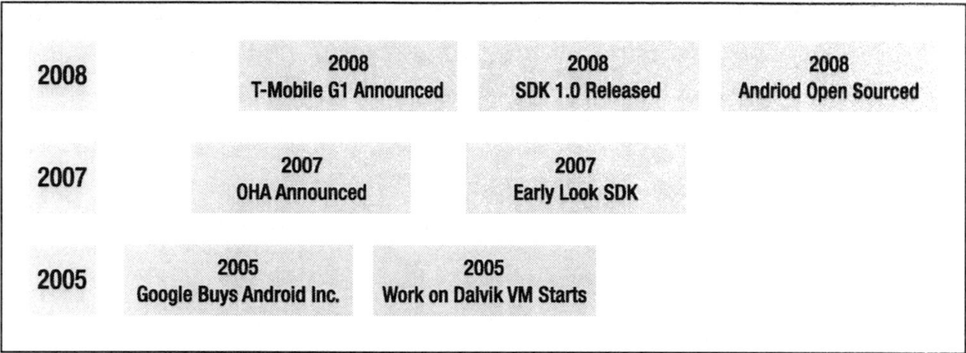

Figure 1–3. *Android early timeline*

In late 2007, a group of industry leaders came together around the Android platform to form the Open Handset Alliance (`www.openhandsetalliance.com`). Some of the alliance's prominent members as of 2009 were as follows:

- Sprint Nextel
- T-Mobile
- Motorola
- Samsung
- Sony Ericsson
- Toshiba
- Vodafone
- Google
- Intel
- Texas Instruments

As of 2011, this list has grown by multifold (over 80 in number), as you can see at the Open Handset Alliance web site.

According to the site, part of the alliance's goal is to innovate rapidly and respond better to consumer needs in the mobile space and its first key outcome was the Android platform. Android was designed to serve the needs of mobile operators, handset manufacturers, and application developers. The members have committed to release significant intellectual property through the open source Apache License, Version 2.0.

The Android SDK was first issued as an "early look" release in November 2007. In September 2008, T-Mobile announced the availability of T-Mobile G1, the first smartphone based on the Android platform. A few days after that, Google announced the availability of Android SDK Release Candidate 1.0. In October 2008, Google made the source code of the Android platform available under Apache's open source license. In late 2010, Google released Android SDK 2.3 for smartphones, code named Gingerbread, which was upgraded to 2.3.3 by March 2011. In early 2011 an optimized version of Android for tablets, Android 3.0 code named Honeycomb, was released. Motorola XOOM is one of the early tablets to carry this OS release.

When Android was released, one of its key architectural goals was to allow applications to interact with one another and reuse components from one another. This reuse not only applies to services, but also to data and the user interface (UI). As a result, the Android platform has a number of architectural features that keep this openness a reality.

Android has attracted an early following and sustained the developer momentum because of its fully developed features to exploit the cloud-computing model offered by Web resources and to enhance that experience with local data stores on the handset itself. Android's support for a relational database on the handset also played a part in early adoption.

In releases 1.0 and 1.1 (2008) Android did not support soft keyboards, requiring the devices to carry physical keys. Android fixed this issue by releasing the 1.5 SDK in April 2009, along with a number of other features, such as advanced media-recording capabilities, widgets, and live folders.

In September 2009 came release 1.6 of the Android OS and, within a month, Android 2.0 followed, facilitating a flood of Android devices in time for the 2009 Christmas season. This release introduced advanced search capabilities and text to speech.

With support for HTML 5, Android 2.0 introduces interesting possibilities for using HTML. The contact API is significantly overhauled. Support for Flash is added. More and more Android-based applications are introduced every day, as well as new types of independent online application stores. Much anticipated tablet computers based on Android can now be purchased.

In Android 2.3 the significant features include remote wiping of secure data by administrators, the ability to use camera and video in low-light conditions, WiFi hotspot, significant performance improvements, improved Bluetooth functionality, installation of applications on the SD card optionally, OpenGL ES 2.0 support, improvements in backup, improvements in search usability, Near Field Communications support for credit card processing, much improved motion and sensor support (similar to Wii), video chat, and improved Market.

The latest incarnation of Android, 3.0 is focused on tablet-based devices and much more powerful dual core processors such as Nvidia Tegra2. The main features of this release include support to use larger screen. A significantly new concept called Fragments has been introduced. This permeates the 3.0 experience. More desktop-like capabilities, such as ActionBar and Drag and Drop, have been introduced. Home screen widgets have been significantly enhanced. More UI controls are now available. In the 3D space, OpenGL has been enhanced with Renderscript to further supplement ES 2.0. It is an exciting introduction for tablets.

Delving Into the Dalvik VM

As part of Android, Google has spent a lot of time thinking about optimizing designs for low-powered handheld devices. Handheld devices lag behind their desktop counterparts in memory and speed by eight to ten years. They also have limited power for computation. The performance requirements on handsets are severe as a result, requiring handset designers to optimize everything. If you look at the list of packages in Android, you'll see that they are fully featured and extensive.

These issues led Google to revisit the standard JVM implementation in many respects. The key figure in Google's implementation of this JVM is Dan Bornstein, who wrote the Dalvik VM—Dalvik is the name of a town in Iceland. Dalvik VM takes the generated Java class files and combines them into one or more Dalvik Executable (.dex) files. It reuses duplicate information from multiple class files, effectively reducing the space requirement (uncompressed) by half from a traditional .jar file

Google has also fine-tuned the garbage collection in the Dalvik VM, but it has chosen to omit a just-in-time (JIT) compiler, in early releases. Android 2.3 has added JIT. The reports are that this can give two to five times faster raw performance at places and 10 to 20% for general-purpose applications.

Dalvik VM uses a different kind of assembly-code generation, in which it uses registers as the primary units of data storage instead of the stack. Google is hoping to accomplish 30% fewer instructions as a result. We should point out that the final executable code in Android, as a result of the Dalvik VM, is based not on Java byte code but on .dex files instead. This means you cannot directly execute Java byte code; you have to start with Java class files and then convert them to linkable .dex files.

This performance paranoia extends into the rest of the Android SDK. For example, the Android SDK uses XML extensively to define UI layouts. However, all of this XML is compiled to binary files before these binary files become resident on the devices. Android provides special mechanisms to use this XML data.

Understanding the Android Software Stack

So far we've covered Android's history and its optimization features including the Dalvik VM, and we've hinted at the Java programming stack available. In this section, we will cover the development aspect of Android. Figure 1–4 is a good place to start this discussion.

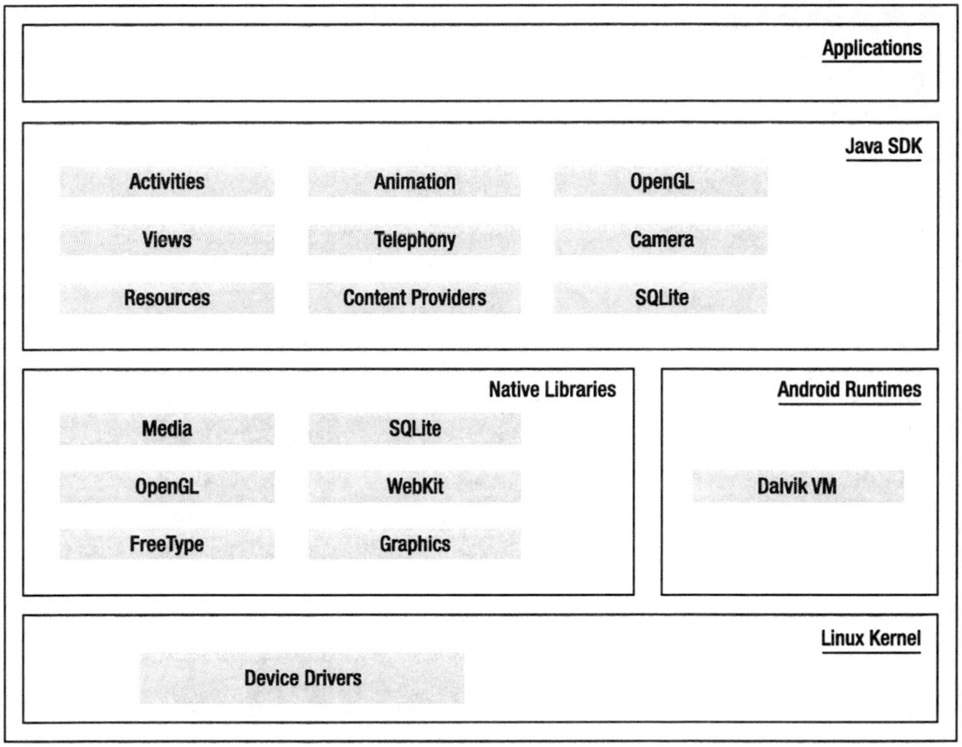

Figure 1–4. *Detailed Android SDK software stack*

At the core of the Android platform is a Linux kernel responsible for device drivers, resource access, power management, and other OS duties. The supplied device drivers include Display, Camera, Keypad, WiFi, Flash Memory, Audio, and IPC (inter-process communication). Although the core is Linux, the majority—if not all—of the applications on an Android device such as a Motorola Droid are developed in Java and run through the Dalvik VM.

Sitting at the next level, on top of the kernel, are a number of C/C++ libraries such as OpenGL, WebKit, FreeType, Secure Sockets Layer (SSL), the C runtime library (libc), SQLite, and Media. The system C library based on Berkeley Software Distribution (BSD) is tuned (to roughly half its original size) for embedded Linux-based devices. The media libraries are based on PacketVideo's (`www.packetvideo.com/`) OpenCORE. These libraries are responsible for recording and playback of audio and video formats. A library called Surface Manager controls access to the display system and supports 2D and 3D. More of these native libraries are likely to be added with new releases.

The WebKit library is responsible for browser support; it is the same library that supports Google Chrome and Apple's Safari. The FreeType library is responsible for font support. SQLite (`www.sqlite.org/`) is a relational database that is available on the device itself. SQLite is also an independent open-source effort for relational databases and not directly tied to Android. You can acquire and use tools meant for SQLite for Android databases as well.

Most of the application framework accesses these core libraries through the Dalvik VM, the gateway to the Android platform. As we indicated in the previous sections, Dalvik is optimized to run multiple instances of VMs. As Java applications access these core libraries, each application gets its own VM instance.

The Android Java API's main libraries include telephony, resources, locations, UI, content providers (data), and package managers (installation, security, and so on). Programmers develop end-user applications on top of this Java API. Some examples of end-user applications on the device include Home, Contacts, Phone, Browser, and so on.

Android also supports a custom Google 2D graphics library called Skia, which is written in C and C++. Skia also forms the core of the Google Chrome browser. The 3D APIs in Android, however, are based on an implementation of OpenGL ES from the Khronos group (`www.khronos.org`). OpenGL ES contains subsets of OpenGL that are targeted toward embedded systems.

From media perspective, the Android platform supports the most common formats for audio, video, and images. From a wireless perspective, Android has APIs to support Bluetooth, EDGE, 3G, WiFi, and Global System for Mobile Communication (GSM) telephony, depending on the hardware.

Developing an End-User Application with the Android SDK

In this section, we'll introduce you to the high-level Android Java APIs that you'll use to develop end-user applications on Android. We will briefly talk about the Android emulator, Android foundational components, UI programming, services, media, telephony, animation, and OpenGL.

Android Emulator

Android SDK ships with an Eclipse plug-in called Android Development Tools (ADT). You will use this Integrated Development Environment (IDE) tool for developing, debugging, and testing your Java applications. (We'll cover ADT in depth in Chapter 2.) You can also use the Android SDK without using ADT; you'd use command-line tools instead. Both approaches support an emulator that you can use to run, debug, and test your applications. You will not even need the real device for 90% of your application development. The full-featured Android emulator mimics most of the device features. The emulator limitations include USB connections, camera and video capture, headphones, battery simulation, Bluetooth, WiFi, NFC, and OpenGL ES 2.0.

The Android emulator accomplishes its work through an open source "processor emulator" technology called QEMU developed by Fabrice Bellard (`http://bellard.org/qemu/`). This is the same technology that allows emulation of one operating system on top of another, irrespective of the processor. QEMU allows emulation at the CPU level.

With the Android emulator, the processor is based on Advanced RISC Machine (ARM). ARM is a 32-bit microprocessor architecture based on Reduced Instruction Set Computer (RISC), in which design simplicity and speed is achieved through a reduced number of instructions in an instruction set. The emulator runs the Android version of Linux on this simulated processor.

ARM is widely used in handhelds and other embedded electronics where lower power consumption is important. Much of the mobile market uses processors based on this architecture.

You can find more details about the emulator in the Android SDK documentation at `http://developer.android.com/guide/developing/tools/emulator.html`.

The Android UI

Android uses a UI framework that resembles other desktop-based, full-featured UI frameworks. In fact, it's more modern and more asynchronous in nature. The Android UI is essentially a fourth-generation UI framework, if you consider the traditional C-based Microsoft Windows API the first generation and the C++-based MFC (Microsoft Foundation Classes) the second generation. The Java-based Swing UI framework would be the third generation, introducing design flexibility far beyond that offered by MFC. The Android UI, JavaFX, Microsoft Silverlight, and Mozilla XML User Interface Language (XUL) fall under this new type of fourth-generation UI framework, in which the UI is declarative and independently themed.

> **NOTE:** In Android, you program using a modern user interface paradigm, even though the device you're programming for happens to be a handheld.

Programming in the Android UI involves declaring the interface in XML files. You then load these XML view definitions as windows in your UI application. Even menus in your application are loaded from XML files. Screens or windows in Android are often referred to as *activities*, which comprise multiple views that a user needs in order to accomplish a logical unit of action. *Views* are Android's basic UI building blocks, and you can further combine them to form composite views called *view groups*. Views internally use the familiar concepts of canvases, painting, and user interaction. An activity hosting these composite views, which include views and view groups, is the logical replaceable UI component in Android. Android 3.0 introduced another UI concept called *fragments* to allow developers to chunk views and functionality for display on tablets. Tablets provide enough screen space for multi-pane activities, and fragments provide the abstraction for the panes.

One of the Android framework's key concepts is the lifecycle management of activity windows. Protocols are put in place so that Android can manage state as users hide, restore, stop, and close activity windows. You will get a feel for these basic ideas in Chapter 2, along with an introduction to setting up the Android development environment.

The Android Foundational Components

The Android UI framework, along with other parts of Android, relies on a new concept called an *intent*. An intent is an amalgamation of ideas such as windowing messages, actions, publish-and-subscribe models, inter-process communications, and application registries. Here is an example of using the Intent class to invoke or start a web browser:

```
public static void invokeWebBrowser(Activity activity)
{
    Intent intent = new Intent(Intent.ACTION_VIEW);
    intent.setData(Uri.parse("http://www.google.com"));
    activity.startActivity(intent);
}
```

In this example, through an intent, we are asking Android to start a suitable window to display the content of a web site. Depending on the list of browsers that are installed on the device, Android will choose a suitable one to display the site. You will learn more about intents in Chapter 5.

Android has extensive support for *resources*, which include familiar elements and files such as strings and bitmaps, as well as some not-so-familiar items such as XML-based view definitions. The framework makes use of resources in a novel way to make their usage easy, intuitive, and convenient. Here is an example where resource IDs are automatically generated for resources defined in XML files:

```
public final class R {
    public static final class attr { }
    public static final class drawable {
        public static final int myanimation=0x7f020001;
        public static final int numbers19=0x7f02000e;
    }

    public static final class id {
        public static final int textViewId1=0x7f080003;
    }
    public static final class layout {
        public static final int frame_animations_layout=0x7f030001;
        public static final int main=0x7f030002;
    }
    public static final class string {
        public static final int hello=0x7f070000;
    }
}
```

Each auto-generated ID in this class corresponds to either an element in an XML file or a whole file itself. Wherever you would like to use those XML definitions, you will use these generated IDs instead. This indirection helps a great deal when it comes to localization. (Chapter 3 covers the R.java file and resources in more detail.)

Another new concept in Android is the *content provider*. A content provider is an abstraction on a data source that makes it look like an emitter and consumer of RESTful services. The underlying SQLite database makes this facility of content providers a powerful tool for application developers. We will cover content providers in Chapter 4. In

Chapters 3, 4 and 5, we'll discuss how intents, resources, and content providers promote openness in the Android Platform.

Advanced UI Concepts

We have already pointed out that XML plays a critical role in describing the Android UI. Let's look at an example of how XML does this for a simple layout containing a text view:

```
<?xml version="1.0" encoding="utf-8"?>
<LinearLayout xmlns:android=http://schemas.android.com/apk/res/android>
<TextView android:id="@+id/textViewId"
    android:layout_width="fill_parent"
    android:layout_height="wrap_content"
    android:text="@string/hello"
    />
</LinearLayout>
```

You will use an ID generated for this XML file to load this layout into an activity window. (We'll cover this process further in Chapter 6.) Android also provides extensive support for menus (more on that in Chapter 7), from standard menus to context menus. You'll find it convenient to work with menus in Android, because they are also loaded as XML files and because resource IDs for those menus are auto-generated. Here's how you would declare menus in an XML file:

```
<menu xmlns:android="http://schemas.android.com/apk/res/android">
    <!-- This group uses the default category. -->
    <group android:id="@+id/menuGroup_Main">
        <item android:id="@+id/menu_clear"
            android:orderInCategory="10"
            android:title="clear" />
        <item android:id="@+id/menu_show_browser"
            android:orderInCategory="5"
            android:title="show browser" />
    </group>
</menu>
```

Android supports dialogs, and all dialogs in Android are asynchronous. These asynchronous dialogs present a special challenge to developers accustomed to the synchronous modal dialogs in some windowing frameworks. We'll address menus in Chapter 7 and dialogs in Chapter 8, where we'll also provide a number of mechanisms to deal with asynchronous-dialog protocols.

Android also offers support for animation as part of its UI stack based on views and drawable objects. Android supports two kinds of animation: *tweening* animation and frame-by-frame animation. Tweening is a term in animation that refers to the drawings that are *in between* the key drawings. You accomplish this with computers by changing the intermediate values at regular intervals and redrawing the surface. Frame-by-frame animation occurs when a series of frames is drawn one after the other at regular intervals. Android enables both animation approaches through animation callbacks, interpolators, and transformation matrices.

Moreover, Android allows you to define these animations in an XML resource file. Check out this example, in which a series of numbered images is played in frame-by-frame animation:

```
<animation-list xmlns:android="http://schemas.android.com/apk/res/android"
        android:oneshot="false">
    <item android:drawable="@drawable/numbers11" android:duration="50" />
  ……
    <item android:drawable="@drawable/numbers19" android:duration="50" />
 </animation-list>
```

The underlying graphics libraries support the standard transformation matrices, allowing scaling, movement, and rotation. A `Camera` object in the graphics library provides support for depth and projection, which allows 3D-like simulation on a 2D surface. (We'll explore animation further in Chapter 16.)

Android also supports 3D graphics through its implementation of the OpenGL ES 1.0 and 2.0 standards. OpenGL ES, like OpenGL, is a C-based flat API. The Android SDK, because it's a Java-based programming API, needs to use Java binding to access the OpenGL ES. Java ME has already defined this binding through Java Specification Request (JSR) 239 for OpenGL ES, and Android uses the same Java binding for OpenGL ES in its implementation. If you are not familiar with OpenGL programming, the learning curve is steep. But we've reviewed the basics here, so you'll be ready to start programming in OpenGL for Android when you complete Chapter 20. Starting in 3.0 Android has introduced a script based approach to OpenGL to supplement ES 2.0.

Android has a number of new concepts that revolve around *information at your fingertips* using the homepage. The first of these is *live folders*. Using live folders, you can publish a collection of items as a folder on the homepage. The contents of this collection change as the underlying data changes. This changing data could be either on the device or from the Internet. (We will cover live folders in Chapter 21.)

The second homepage-based idea is the *home screen widget*. Home screen widgets are used to paint information on the homepage using a UI widget. This information can change at regular intervals. An example could be the number of e-mail messages in your e-mail store. We describe home screen widgets in Chapter 22. The home screen widgets are enhanced in 3.0 to include list views that can get updated when their underlying data changes. These enhancements are covered in Chapter 31.

Integrated Android Search is the third homepage-based idea. Using integrated search you can search for content both on the device and also across the Internet. Android search goes beyond search and allows you to fire off commands through the search control. We cover Android search in Chapter 23.

Android also supports touchscreen and gestures based on finger movement on the device. Android allows you to record any random motion on the screen as a named gesture. This gesture can then be used by applications to indicate specific actions. We cover touchscreens and gestures in Chapter 25.

Sensors are now becoming a significant part of mobile experience. We cover sensors in Chapter 26.

Another necessary innovation required for a mobile device is the dynamic nature of its configurations. For instance it is very easy to change the viewing modes of a handheld between portrait and landscape. Or you may dock your handheld to become a laptop. Android 3.0 has introduced a concept called fragments to deal with these variations effectively. Chapter 29 is dedicated to fragments.

We also cover the 3.0 feature of action bars in Chapter 30. Action bars bring Android up to par with desktop menu bar paradigm. We cover drag and drop in Chapter 25 (the old way) as well as in Chapter 31 (the Android 3.0 way).

Outside of the Android SDK, there are a number of independent innovations taking place to make development exciting and easy. Some examples are XML/VM, PhoneGap, and Titanium. Titanium allows you to use HTML technologies to program the WebKit-based Android browser. We covered Titanium in the second edition of this book. However, due to time and space limitations, we are not covering Titanium in this edition.

Android Service Components

Security is a fundamental part of the Android platform. In Android, security spans all phases of the application lifecycle—from design-time policy considerations to runtime boundary checks. We cover security and permissions in Chapter 10.

In Chapter 11, we'll show you how to build and consume services in Android, specifically HTTP services. This chapter will also cover inter-process communication (communication between applications on the same device).

Location-based service is another of the more exciting components of the Android SDK. This portion of the SDK provides application developers APIs to display and manipulate maps, as well as obtain real-time device-location information. We'll cover these ideas in detail in Chapter 17.

Android Media and Telephony Components

Android has APIs that cover audio, video, and telephony components. Chapter 18 will address the telephony API. We'll cover the audio and video APIs extensively in Chapter 19. Starting with Android 2.0, Android includes the Pico Text To Speech engine. This is covered in Chapter 24.

Last but not least, Android ties all these concepts into an application by creating a single XML file that defines what an application package is. This file is called the application's manifest file (`AndroidManifest.xml`). Here is an example:

```
<?xml version="1.0" encoding="utf-8"?>
<manifest xmlns:android="http://schemas.android.com/apk/res/android"
      package="com.ai.android.HelloWorld"
      android:versionCode="1"
      android:versionName="1.0.0">
    <application android:icon="@drawable/icon" android:label="@string/app_name">
        <activity android:name=".HelloWorld"
                  android:label="@string/app_name">
```

```
            <intent-filter>
                <action android:name="android.intent.action.MAIN" />
                <category android:name="android.intent.category.LAUNCHER" />
            </intent-filter>
        </activity>
    </application>
</manifest>
```

The Android manifest file is where activities are defined, where services and content providers are registered, and where permissions are declared. Details about the manifest file will emerge throughout the book as we develop each idea.

Android Java Packages

One way to get a quick snapshot of the Android platform is to look at the structure of Java packages. Because Android deviates from the standard JDK distribution, it is important to know what is supported and what is not. Here's a brief description of the important packages that are included in the Android SDK:

> *android.app*: Implements the Application model for Android. Primary classes include `Application`, representing the start and stop semantics, as well as a number of activity-related classes, fragments, controls, dialogs, alerts, and notifications.
>
> *android.bluetooth*: Provides a number of classes to work with Bluetooth functionality. The main classes include `BluetoothAdapter`, `BluetoothDevice`, `BluetoothSocket`, `BluetoothServerSocket`, and `BluetoothClass`. You can use `BluetoothAdapter` to control the locally installed Bluetooth adapter. For example, you can enable it, disable it, and start the discovery process. The `BluetoothDevice` represents the remote Bluetooth device that you are connecting with. The two Bluetooth sockets are used to establish communication between the devices. A Bluetooth class represents the type of Bluetooth device you are connecting to.
>
> *android.content*: Implements the concepts of content providers. Content providers abstract out data access from data stores. This package also implements the central ideas around intents and Android Uniform Resource Identifiers (URIs).
>
> *android.content.pm*: Implements Package Manager-related classes. A package manager knows about permissions, installed packages, installed providers, installed services, installed components such as activities, and installed applications.
>
> *android.content.res*: Provides access to resource files both structured and unstructured. The primary classes are `AssetManager` (for unstructured resources) and `Resources`.
>
> *android.database*: Implements the idea of an abstract database. The primary interface is the `Cursor` interface.

android.database.sqlite: Implements the concepts from the android.database package using SQLite as the physical database. Primary classes are SQLiteCursor, SQLiteDatabase, SQLiteQuery, SQLiteQueryBuilder, and SQLiteStatement. However, most of your interaction is going to be with classes from the abstract android.database package.

android.gesture: This package houses all the classes and interfaces necessary to work with user-defined gestures. Primary classes are Gesture, GestureLibrary, GestureOverlayView, GestureStore, GestureStroke, GesturePoint. A Gesture is a collection of GestureStrokes and GesturePoints. Gestures are collected in a GestureLibrary. Gesture libraries are stored in a GestureStore. Gestures are named so that they can be identified as actions.

android.graphics: Contains the classes Bitmap, Canvas, Camera, Color, Matrix, Movie, Paint, Path, Rasterizer, Shader, SweepGradient, and TypeFace.

android.graphics.drawable: Implements drawing protocols and background images, and allows animation of drawable objects.

android.graphics.drawable.shapes: Implements shapes including ArcShape, OvalShape, PathShape, RectShape, and RoundRectShape.

android.hardware: Implements the physical Camera-related classes. The Camera represents the hardware camera, whereas android.graphics.Camera represents a graphical concept that's not related to a physical camera at all.

android.location: Contains the classes Address, GeoCoder, Location, LocationManager, and LocationProvider. The Address class represents the simplified XAL (Extensible Address Language). GeoCoder allows you to get a latitude/longitude coordinate given an address, and vice versa. Location represents the latitude/longitude.

android.media: Contains the classes MediaPlayer, MediaRecorder, Ringtone, AudioManager, and FaceDetector. MediaPlayer, which supports streaming, is used to play audio and video. MediaRecorder is used to record audio and video. The Ringtone class is used to play short sound snippets that could serve as ringtones and notifications. AudioManager is responsible for volume controls. You can use FaceDetector to detect people's faces in a bitmap.

android.net: Implements the basic socket-level network APIs. Primary classes include Uri, ConnectivityManager, LocalSocket, and LocalServerSocket. It is also worth noting here that Android supports HTTPS at the browser level and also at the network level. Android also supports JavaScript in its browser.

android.net.wifi: Manages WiFi connectivity. Primary classes include `WifiManager` and `WifiConfiguration`. `WifiManager` is responsible for listing the configured networks and the currently active WiFi network.

android.opengl: Contains utility classes surrounding OpenGL ES 1.0 and 2.0 operations. The primary classes of OpenGL ES are implemented in a different set of packages borrowed from JSR 239. These packages are `javax.microedition.khronos.opengles`, `javax.microedition.khronos.egl`, and `javax.microedition.khronos.nio`. These packages are thin wrappers around the Khronos implementation of OpenGL ES in C and C++.

android.os: Represents the OS services accessible through the Java programming language. Some important classes include `BatteryManager`, `Binder`, `FileObserver`, `Handler`, `Looper`, and `PowerManager`. `Binder` is a class that allows interprocess communication. `FileObserver` keeps tabs on changes to files. You use `Handler` classes to run tasks on the message thread, and `Looper` to run a message thread.

android.preference: Allows applications the ability to have users manage their preferences for that application in a uniform way. The primary classes are `PreferenceActivity`, `PreferenceScreen`, and various Preference-derived classes such as `CheckBoxPreference` and `SharedPreferences`.

android.provider: Comprises a set of prebuilt content providers adhering to the `android.content.ContentProvider` interface. The content providers include `Contacts`, `MediaStore`, `Browser`, and `Settings`. This set of interfaces and classes stores the metadata for the underlying data structures.

android.sax: Contains an efficient set of Simple API for XML (SAX) parsing utility classes. Primary classes include `Element`, `RootElement`, and a number of `ElementListener` interfaces.

android.speech: Contains constants for use with speech recognition.

android.speech.tts: Provides support for converting text to speech. The primary class is `TextToSpeech`. You will be able to take text and ask an instance of this class to queue the text to be spoken. You have access to a number of callbacks to monitor when the speech has finished, for example. Android uses the Pico TTS (Text to Speech) engine from SVOX.

android.telephony: Contains the classes `CellLocation`, `PhoneNumberUtils`, and `TelephonyManager`. A `TelephonyManager` lets you determine cell location, phone number, network operator name, network type, phone type, and Subscriber Identity Module (SIM) serial number.

android.telephony.gsm: Allows you to gather cell location based on cell towers and also hosts classes responsible for SMS messaging. This package is called GSM because Global System for Mobile Communication is the technology that originally defined the SMS data-messaging standard.

android.telephony.cdma: Provides support for CDMA telephony.

android.text: Contains text-processing classes.

android.text.method: Provides classes for entering text input for a variety of controls.

android.text.style: Provides a number of styling mechanisms for a span of text.

android.utils: Contains the classes Log, DebugUtils, TimeUtils, and Xml.

android.view: Contains the classes Menu, View, ViewGroup, and a series of listeners and callbacks.

android.view.animation: Provides support for tweening animation. The main classes include Animation, a series of interpolators for animation, and a set of specific animator classes that include AlphaAnimation, ScaleAnimation, TranslationAnimation, and RotationAnimation. Android 3.0 introduced the android.animation package, which is similar, but more broad because it can work with objects rather than just views.

android.view.inputmethod: Implements the input-method framework architecture.

android.webkit: Contains classes representing the web browser. The primary classes include WebView, CacheManager, and CookieManager.

android.widget: Contains all of the UI controls usually derived from the View class. Primary widgets include Button, Checkbox, Chronometer, AnalogClock, DatePicker, DigitalClock, EditText, ListView, FrameLayout, GridView, ImageButton, MediaController, ProgressBar, RadioButton, RadioGroup, RatingButton, Scroller, ScrollView, Spinner, TabWidget, TextView, TimePicker, VideoView, and ZoomButton.

com.google.android.maps: Contains the classes MapView, MapController, and MapActivity, essentially classes required to work with Google maps.

These are some of the critical Android-specific packages. From this list you can see the depth of the Android core platform.

NOTE: In all, the Android Java API contains more than 40 packages and more than 700 classes, and keeps growing with each release.

In addition, Android provides a number of packages in the java.* namespace. These include awt.font, io, lang, lang.annotation, lang.ref, lang.reflect, math, net, nio, nio.channels, nio.channels.spi, nio.charset, security, security.acl, security.cert, security.interfaces, security.spec, sql, text, util, util.concurrent, util.concurrent.atomic, util.concurrent.locks, util.jar, util.logging, util.prefs, util.regex, and util.zip. Android comes with these packages from the javax namespace: crypto, crypto.spec, microedition.khronos.egl, microedition.khronos.opengles, net, net.ssl, security.auth, security.auth.callback, security.auth.login, security.auth.x500, security.cert, sql, xml, and xmlparsers. In addition to these, it contains a lot of packages from org.apache.http.* as well as org.json, org.w3c.dom, org.xml.sax, org.xml.sax.ext, org.xml.sax.helpers, org.xmlpull.v1, and org.xmlpull.v1.sax2. Together, these numerous packages provide a rich computing platform to write applications for handheld devices.

Taking Advantage of Android Source Code

In the early releases of Android, documentation was a bit wanting in places. Android source code could be used to fill the gaps.

The details of the Android source distribution are published at http://source.android.com. The code was made available as open source around October 2008. One of the Open Handset Alliance's goals was to make Android a free and fully customizable mobile platform.

As indicated, Android is a platform and not just one project. You can see the scope and the number of projects at http://android.git.kernel.org/.

The source code for Android and all its projects is managed by the Git source code control system. Git (http://git.or.cz/) is an open-source source-control system designed to handle large and small projects with speed and convenience. The Linux kernel and Ruby on Rails projects also rely on Git for version control. The complete list of Android projects in the Git repository appears at http://android.git.kernel.org/.

You can download any of these projects using the tools provided by Git and described at the product's web site. Some of the primary projects include Dalvik, frameworks/base (the android.jar file), the Linux kernel, and a number of external libraries such as Apache HTTP libraries (apache-http). The core Android applications are also hosted here. Some of these core applications include: AlarmClock, Browser, Calculator, Calendar, Camera, Contacts, Email, GoogleSearch, HTML Viewer, IM, Launcher, Mms, Music, PackageInstaller, Phone, Settings, SoundRecorder, Stk, Sync, Updater, and VoiceDialer.

The Android projects also include the Provider projects. *Provider projects* are like databases in Android that wrap their data into RESTful services. These projects are CalendarProvider, ContactsProvider, DownloadProvider, DrmProvider, GoogleContactsProvider, GoogleSubscribedFeedsProvider, ImProvider, MediaProvider, SettingsProvider, Subscribed FeedsProvider, and TelephonyProvider.

As a programmer, you will be most interested in the source code that makes up the `android.jar` file. (If you'd rather download the entire platform and build it yourself, refer to the documentation available at `http://source.android.com/source/download.html`.) You can download the source for this .jar file by typing in the following URL: `http://git.source.android.com/?p=platform/frameworks/base.git;a=snapshot;h=HEAD;sf=tgz`.

This is a general-purpose URL you can use to download Git projects. On Windows, you can unzip this file using `pkzip`. Although you can download and unzip the source, it might be more convenient to just look at these files online, if you don't need to debug the source code through your IDE. Git also allows you to do this. For example, you can browse through `android.jar` source files by visiting this URL: `http://android.git.kernel.org/?p=platform/frameworks/base.git;a=summary`.

However, you have to do some work after you visit this page. Pick `grep` from the drop-down list and enter some text in the search box. Click one of the resulting file names to open that source file in your browser. This facility is convenient for a quick look-up of source code.

At times, the file you are looking for might not be in the `frameworks/base` directory or project. In that case, you need to find the list of projects and search each one step by step. The URL for this list is here: `http://android.git.kernel.org/`.

You cannot `grep` across all projects, so you will need to know which project belongs to which facility in Android. For example, the graphics-related libraries in the Skia project are available here: `http://android.git.kernel.org/?p=platform/external/skia.git;a=summary`.

The `SkMatrix.cpp` file contains the source code for a transformational matrix, which is useful in animation: `http://android.git.kernel.org/?p=platform/external/skia.git;a=blob;f=src/core/SkMatrix.cpp`.

The Sample Projects in this Book

In this book you will find many, many working sample projects. Chapters 2 through 28 were written with smartphones in mind, and as such, all projects in these chapters were tested with versions of Android up to Android 2.3. After all, there are an awful lot of Android smartphones out there.

Most if not all of the sample projects will run unchanged on Android 3.0 for tablets, although they may not look exactly as you might like. Our main purpose in developing the sample projects was to demonstrate the particular concepts and Android packages, and in some cases to show how certain features work in the older releases of Android.

These concepts can easily be applied to Android 3.0 tablet applications, and our sample applications would certainly integrate with other Android 3.0-specific features if required. But including those additional features in all our sample projects would have distracted us from focusing on the concepts we're trying to explain.

Chapters 29 through 31 are specifically about Android 3.0, so those projects were designed and tested for Android 3.0. If you have trouble with any of the sample projects, please check our website (`www.androidbook.com`) for updates, and if you are still searching for answers, please contact us by email.

Summary

In this chapter, we wanted to pique your curiosity about Android. If you are a Java programmer, you have a great opportunity to profit from this exciting capable general purpose computing platform. We welcome you to journey through the rest of the book for an in-depth understanding of the Android SDK.

Chapter 2

Setting Up Your Development Environment

The last chapter provided an overview of Android's history and hinted at concepts that will be covered in the rest of the book. At this point, you're probably eager to get your hands on some code. We'll start by showing you what you need to begin building applications with the Android software development kit (SDK) and help you set up your development environment. Next, we'll step you through a "Hello World!" application and dissect a slightly larger application after that. Then we'll explain the Android application lifecycle and end with a discussion about debugging your applications with Android Virtual Devices (AVDs).

To build applications for Android, you'll need the Java SE Development Kit (JDK), the Android SDK, and a development environment. Strictly speaking, you can develop your applications using a primitive text editor, but for the purposes of this book, we'll use the commonly available Eclipse IDE. The Android SDK requires JDK 5 or higher (we used JDK 6 for the examples) and Eclipse 3.4 or higher (we used Eclipse 3.5, also known as Galileo, and 3.6, also known as Helios).

To make your life easier, you'll want to use Android Development Tools (ADT). ADT is an Eclipse plug-in that supports building Android applications with the Eclipse IDE. In fact, we built all the examples in this book using the Eclipse IDE with the ADT tool.

The Android SDK is made up of two main parts: the tools and the packages. When you first install the SDK, all you get are the base tools. These are executables and supporting files to help you develop applications. The packages are the files specific to a particular version of Android (called a platform) or a particular add-on to a platform. The platforms include Android 1.5 through 3.0. The add-ons include the Google Maps API, the Market License Validator, and even vendor-supplied ones such as Samsung's Galaxy Tab add-on. After you install the SDK, you then use one of the tools to download and set up the platforms and add-ons. Let's get started!

Setting Up Your Environment

To build Android applications, you need to establish a development environment. In this section, we are going to walk you through downloading JDK 6, the Eclipse IDE, the Android SDK (tools and packages), and Android Development Tools (ADT). We'll also help you configure Eclipse to build Android applications.

The Android SDK is compatible with Windows (Windows XP, Windows Vista, and Windows 7), Mac OS X (Intel only), and Linux (Intel only). In this chapter, we'll show you how to set up your environment for all of these platforms (for Linux, we only cover the Ubuntu variant). We will not specifically address any platform differences in other chapters.

Downloading JDK 6

The first thing you'll need is the Java SE Development Kit. The Android SDK requires JDK 5 or higher; we developed the examples using JDK 6. For Windows, download JDK 6 from the Oracle web site (`www.oracle.com/technetwork/java/javase/downloads/index.html`) and install it. You only need the JDK, not the bundles. For Mac OS X, download the JDK from the Apple web site (`http://developer.apple.com/java/download/`), select the appropriate file for your particular version of Mac OS, and install it. You will need to register for free as an Apple developer to get the JDK, and once at the Downloads page, you'll need to click on the Java link on the right-hand side of the page. To install the JDK for Linux, open a Terminal window and try the following:

```
sudo apt-get install sun-java6-jdk
```

This should install the JDK plus any dependencies such as the Java Runtime Environment (JRE). If it doesn't, it probably means you need to add a new Software Source and then try that command again. The web page `https://help.ubuntu.com/community/Repositories/Ubuntu` explains Software Sources and how to add the connection to third party software. The process is different depending on which version of Linux you have. Once that has been done, retry the command.

With the introduction of Ubuntu 10.04 (Lucid Lynx), Ubuntu recommends using OpenJDK instead of the Oracle/Sun JDK. To install OpenJDK, try the following:

```
sudo apt-get install openjdk-6-jdk
```

If this is not found, set up the third party software as outlined previously and run the command again. All packages upon which the JDK depends will be automatically added for you. It is possible to have both OpenJDK and the Oracle/Sun JDK installed at the same time. To switch active Java between the installed versions of Java on Ubuntu, run this command at a shell prompt

```
sudo update-alternatives --config java
```

then choose which Java you want as the default.

Now that you have a Java JDK installed, it's time to set the JAVA_HOME environment variable to point to the JDK install folder. On a Windows XP machine, you can do this by going to Start ➤ My Computer, right-click to get Properties, choose the Advanced tab, and click Environment Variables. Click New to add the variable, or Edit to modify it if it already exists. The value of JAVA_HOME will be something like C:\Program Files\Java\jdk1.6.0_23. For Windows Vista and Windows 7, the steps to get to the Environment Variables screen are a little different. Go to Start ➤ Computer, right-click to get Properties, click the link for Advanced system settings and click Environment Variables. After that, follow the same instructions as for Windows XP to change the JAVA_HOME environment variable. For Mac OS X, you set JAVA_HOME in your .profile in your home directory. Edit or create your .profile file and add a line that looks like this

```
export JAVA_HOME=path_to_JDK_directory
```

where path_to_JDK_directory is probably /Library/Java/Home. For Linux, edit your .profile file and add a line like the one for Mac OS X, except that your path to Java is probably something like /usr/lib/jvm/java-6-sun or /usr/lib/jvm/java-6-openjdk. Some people prefer to use .bashrc instead of .profile; either one should work.

Downloading Eclipse 3.6

Once the JDK is installed, you can download the Eclipse IDE for Java Developers. (You don't need the edition for Java EE; it works, but it's much larger and includes things we won't need for this book.) The examples in this book use Eclipse 3.6 (on a Windows environment). You can download all versions of Eclipse from www.eclipse.org/downloads/. The Eclipse distribution is a .zip file that can be extracted just about anywhere. The simplest place to extract to on Windows is C:\ which results in a C:\eclipse folder where you'll find eclipse.exe. For Mac OS X, you can extract to Applications. For Linux, you can extract to your home directory or have your administrator put Eclipse into a common place where you can get to it. The Eclipse executable is in the eclipse folder for all platforms. You may also find and install Eclipse using Linux's Software Center for adding new applications, although this may not provide you with the latest version.

When you first start up Eclipse, it will ask you for a location for the workspace. To make things easy, you can choose a simple location such as C:\android or a directory under your home directory. If you share the computer with others, you should put your workspace folder somewhere underneath your home directory.

Downloading the Android SDK

To build applications for Android, you need the Android SDK. As stated before, the SDK comes with the base tools part, then you download the package parts that you need and/or want to use. The tools part of the SDK includes an emulator so you don't need a mobile device with the Android OS to develop Android applications. It also has a setup utility to allow you to install the packages that you want to download.

You can download the Android SDK from `http://developer.android.com/sdk`. The Android SDK ships as a .zip file, similar to the way Eclipse is distributed, so you need to unzip it to an appropriate location. For Windows, unzip the file to a convenient location (we used our C: drive), after which you should have a folder called something like `C:\android-sdk-windows` that will contain the files as shown in Figure 2–1. For Mac OS X and Linux, you can unzip the file to your home directory. You will notice that Mac OS X and Linux do not have an SDK Manager executable. The equivalent of the SDK Manager in Mac OS X and Linux is to run the tools/android program.

An alternate approach (for Windows only) is to download an installer EXE instead of the zip file, then run the installer executable. This executable will check for the Java JDK, unpack the embedded files for you, and run the SDK Manager program to help you set up the rest of the downloads.

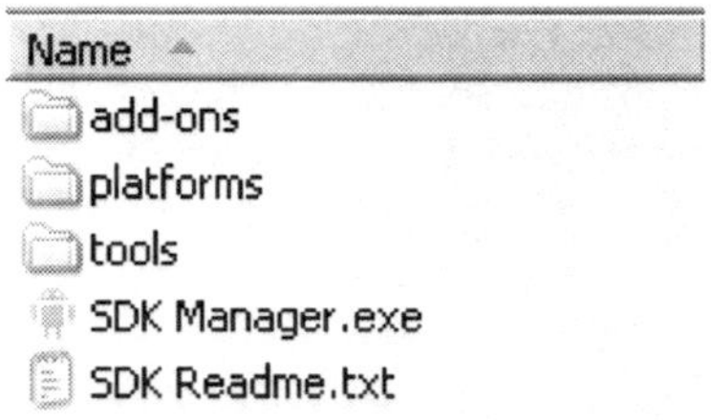

Figure 2–1. *Base contents of the Android SDK*

Whether through using the Windows installer or by executing the SDK Manager, you should install some packages next. When you first install the Android SDK it does not come with any platform versions (i.e., versions of Android). Installing platforms is pretty easy. Once you've launched the SDK Manager, choose Available Packages, choose the `https://dl-ssl.google.com/android/repository/repository.xml` source, then select the platforms and add-ons that you want, such as Android 2.3 (see Figure 2–2). You must add Android SDK platform-tools in order for your environment to work. Because we'll use it very shortly, please add at least the Android 1.6 platform.

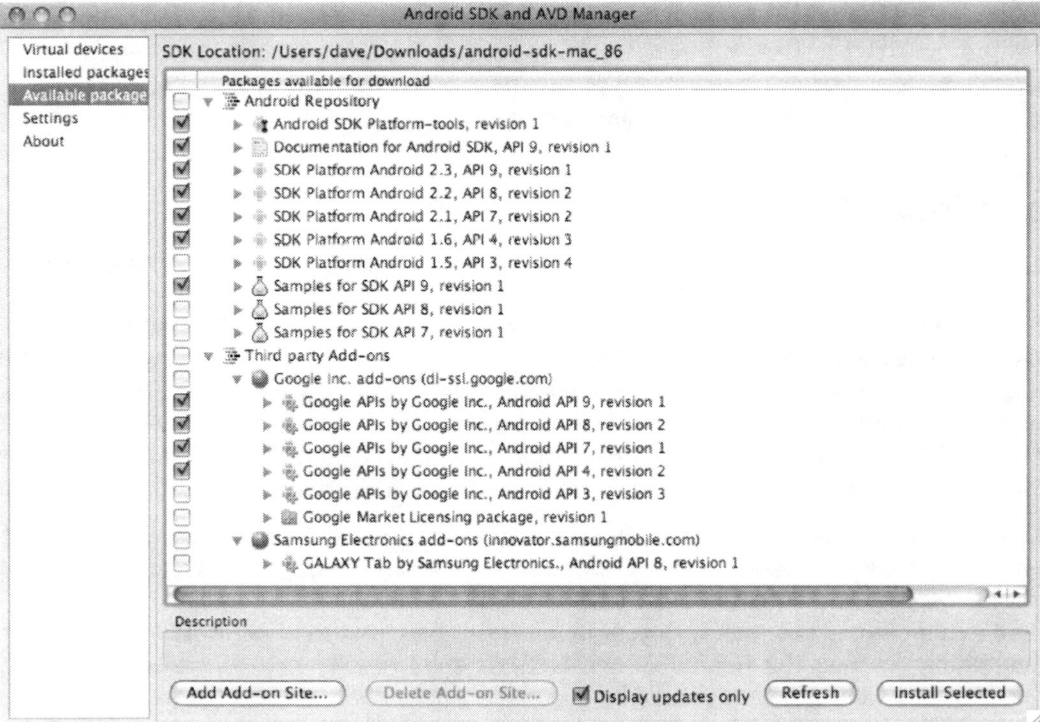

Figure 2–2. *Adding packages to the Android SDK*

Click Install Selected. You will need to click Accept for each item that you're installing, then click Install Accepted. Android will then download your packages and platforms to make them available to you. The Google APIs are add-ons for developing applications using Google Maps. You can always see the installed platforms by clicking Installed packages on the left side of this window. And you can always come back to add more packages later.

Updating Your PATH Environment Variable

The Android SDK comes with a tools directory that you'll want to have in your PATH. You also need in your PATH the platform-tools directory that you just installed. Let's add them now or, if you're upgrading, let's make sure they're correct. While you're there, you'll also add your JDK bin directory, which will make life easier later. For Windows, get back to the Environment Variables window. Edit the PATH variable and add a semi-colon (;) on the end, followed by the path to the Android SDK tools folder, followed by another semi-colon, followed by the path to the Android SDK platform-tools folder, following by another semi-colon, and then `%JAVA_HOME%\bin`. Click OK when done. For Mac OS X and Linux, edit your `.profile` file and add the Android SDK tools directory path to your PATH variable, as well as the Android SDK platform-tools directory and the `$JAVA_HOME/bin` directory. Something like the following would work for Linux:

```
export PATH=$PATH:$HOME/android-sdk-linux_x86/tools:$HOME/android-sdk-
linux_x86/platform-tools:$JAVA_HOME/bin
```

Just make sure that the path component that's pointing to the Android SDK tools directories is correct for your particular setup.

The Tools Window

Later in this book there will be times when you need to execute a command-line utility program. These programs will be part of the JDK or will be part of the Android SDK. By having these directories in your PATH, you won't need to specify the full pathnames in order to execute them, but you will need to start up a "tools window" in order to run them (we'll refer to this tools window in later chapters). The easiest way to create a tools window in Windows is to click Start ➤ Run, type in `cmd`, and click OK. For Mac OS X, choose Terminal from your Applications folder in Finder or from the Dock if it's there. For Linux, choose Terminal from the Applications ➤ Accessories menu.

One last thing while we're talking about the differences between platforms: you may need to know the IP address of your workstation later on. To do this in Windows, launch a tools window and enter the command `ipconfig`. The results will contain an entry for IPv4 (or something like that) with your IP address listed next to it. An IP address looks something like this: 192.168.1.25. For Mac OS X and Linux, launch a tools window and use the command `ifconfig`. You'll find your IP address next to a label called "inet addr". You might see a network connection called "localhost" or "lo". The IP address for this network connection is 127.0.0.1. This is a special network connection used by the operating system and is not the same as your workstation's IP address. Look for a different number for your workstation's IP address.

Installing Android Development Tools (ADT)

Now you need to install ADT, an Eclipse plug-in that helps you build Android applications. Specifically, ADT integrates with Eclipse to provide facilities for you to create, test, and debug Android applications. You'll need to use the Install New Software facility within Eclipse to perform the installation. (The instructions for upgrading ADT appear later in this section.) To get started, launch the Eclipse IDE and follow these steps:

1. Select the Help menu item and choose the Install New Software… option. (This was called Software Updates in previous versions of Eclipse.)
2. Select the Work with field, type in

   `https://dl-ssl.google.com/android/eclipse/`

   and press Return. Eclipse will contact the site and populate the list as shown in Figure 2–3.

3. You should see an entry named Developer Tools with three child nodes: Android DDMS, Android Development Tools, and Android Hierarchy Viewer. Select the parent node Developer Tools, make sure the child nodes are also selected, and click the Next button. The versions that you see could be newer than these, and that's okay. There may be additional tools here also.

4. Eclipse will ask you to verify the tools to install. Click Next again. This applies also to Android Traceview which was added in Android 3.0.

5. You will be asked to review the licenses for ADT as well as for the tools required to install ADT. Review the licenses, click "I accept...", and then click the Finish button.

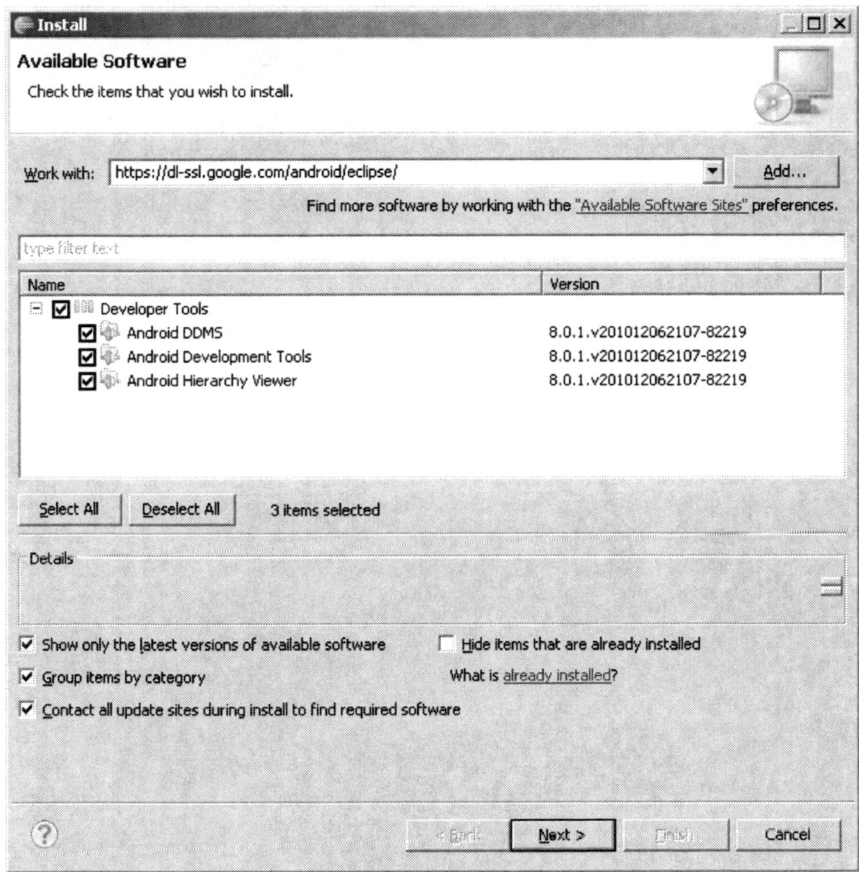

Figure 2–3. *Installing ADT using the Install New Software feature in Eclipse*

Eclipse will then download the Developer Tools and install them. You'll need to restart Eclipse for the new plug-in to show up in the IDE.

If you already have an older version of ADT in Eclipse, go to the Eclipse Help menu and choose Check for Updates. You should see the new version of ADT and be able to follow the installation instructions, picking up at step 3.

NOTE Android Hierarchy Viewer was added to the Developer Tools as of Android 2.3. Therefore, if you are doing a new install of ADT, you'll pick it up. But if you're doing an upgrade of ADT, you may not see Hierarchy Viewer in the list of tools to be upgraded. If you don't see it, once you've upgraded the rest of the ADT, go to Install New Software... and select `https://dl-ssl.google.com/android/eclipse/` from the Works With menu. The middle window should show you Android Hierarchy Viewer so you can install it separately from the rest of the ADT.

The final step to get ADT functional inside of Eclipse is to point it to the Android SDK. Within Eclipse, select the Window menu and choose Preferences. (On Mac OS X, Preferences is under the Eclipse menu.) In the Preferences dialog box, select the Android node and set the SDK Location field to the path of the Android SDK (see Figure 2–4), then click the Apply button. Note that you might see a dialog box asking if you want to send usage statistics to Google concerning the Android SDK. That decision is up to you. Click OK to close the Preferences window.

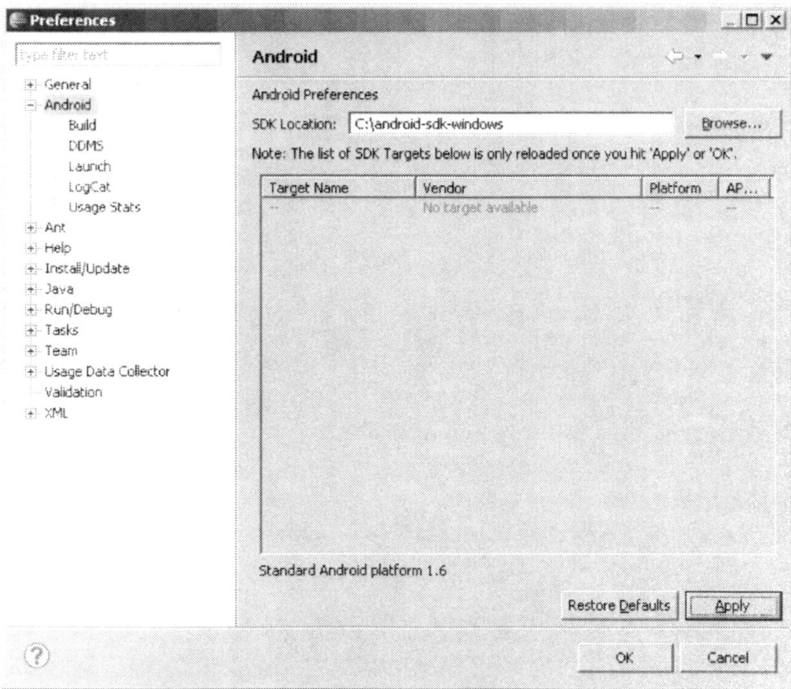

Figure 2–4. *Pointing ADT to the Android SDK*

From Eclipse, you can launch the SDK Manager. Within Eclipse, go to Window ➤ Android SDK and AVD Manager. You should see the same window show up as in Figure 2–2, although you may not see all of the options on the left side as you do when launching SDK Manager yourself.

You are almost ready for your first Android application—but first, we must briefly discuss the fundamental concepts of Android applications.

Learning the Fundamental Components

Every application framework has some key components that developers need to understand before they can begin to write applications based on the framework. For example, you would need to understand JavaServer Pages (JSP) and servlets in order to write Java 2 Platform, Enterprise Edition (J2EE) applications. Similarly, you need to understand activities, views, intents, content providers, services, and the `AndroidManifest.xml` file when you build applications for Android. We will briefly cover these fundamental concepts here and we'll discuss them in more detail throughout the book.

View

Views are user interface (UI) elements that form the basic building blocks of a user interface. A view could be a button, label, text field, or many other UI elements. If you're familiar with views in J2EE and Swing then you'll understand views in Android. Views are also used as containers for views, which means that there's usually a hierarchy of views in the UI. In the end, everything you see is a view.

Activity

An activity is a user interface concept. An activity usually represents a single screen in your application. It generally contains one or more views, but it doesn't have to. An activity is pretty much like it sounds—something that helps the user do one thing—and that one thing could be viewing data, creating data, or editing data. Most Android applications have several activities within them.

Intent

An intent generically defines an "intention" to do some work. Intents encapsulate several concepts, so the best approach to understanding them is to see examples of their use. You can use intents to perform the following tasks:

- Broadcast a message.
- Start a service.
- Launch an activity.
- Display a web page or a list of contacts.
- Dial a phone number or answer a phone call.

Intents are not always initiated by your application—they're also used by the system to notify your application of specific events (such as the arrival of a text message).

Intents can be explicit or implicit. If you simply say that you want to display a URL, the system will decide what component will fulfill the intention. You can also provide specific information about what should handle the intention. Intents loosely couple the action and action handler.

Content Provider

Data sharing among mobile applications on a device is common. Therefore, Android defines a standard mechanism for applications to share data (such as a list of contacts) without exposing the underlying storage, structure, and implementation. Through content providers, you can expose your data and have your applications use data from other applications.

Service

Services in Android resemble services you see in Windows or other platforms—they're background processes that can potentially run for a long time. Android defines two types of services: local services and remote services. Local services are components that are only accessible by the application that is hosting the service. Conversely, remote services are services that are meant to be accessed remotely by other applications running on the device.

An example of a service is a component that is used by an e-mail application to poll for new messages. This kind of service might be a local service if the service is not used by other applications running on the device. If several applications use the service, then it would be implemented as a remote service. The difference, as you'll see in Chapter 11, is in `startService()` vs. `bindService()`.

You can use existing services and also write your own services by extending the `Service` class.

AndroidManifest.xml

`AndroidManifest.xml`, which is similar to the `web.xml` file in the J2EE world, defines the contents and behavior of your application. For example, it lists your application's activities and services, along with the permissions and features the application needs to run.

Android Virtual Devices

An Android Virtual Device (AVD) allows developers to test their applications without hooking up an actual Android device (typically a phone or a tablet). AVDs can be created in various configurations to emulate different types of real devices.

Hello World!

Now you're ready to build your first Android application. You'll start by building a simple "Hello World!" program. Create the skeleton of the application by following these steps:

1. Launch Eclipse and select File ➤ New ➤ Project. In the New Project dialog box, select Android and then click Next. You will see the New Android Project dialog box, as shown in Figure 2–5. (Eclipse might have added Android Project to the New menu, so you can use it if it's there.) There's also a New Android Project button on the toolbar.

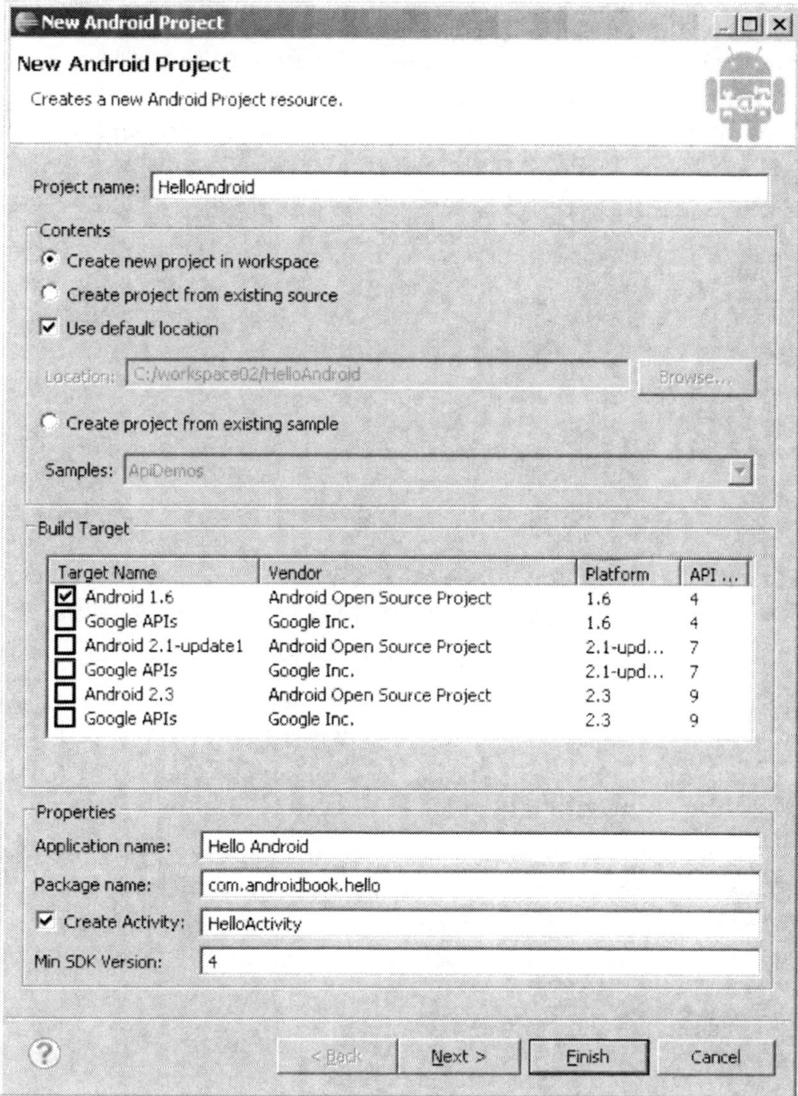

Figure 2–5. *Using the New Project wizard to create an Android application*

2. As shown in Figure 2–5, enter **HelloAndroid** as the project name. You need to distinguish this project from other projects you'll create in Eclipse, so choose a name that will make sense to you when you are looking at all the projects within your Eclipse environment. Also note that the default location for the project will be derived from the Eclipse workspace location. The New Project wizard appends the name of the new application to the workspace location. In this case, if your Eclipse workspace is `c:\android`, your new project will be at `c:\android\HelloAndroid\`.
3. Leave the Contents section alone for now, since you want to create a new project in your workspace in the default location.
4. For the Build Target, check Android 1.6, as shown in Figure 2–5. This will be the version of Android you'll use as your base for the application. You'll be able to run your application on later versions of Android, such as 2.1 and 2.3, but Android 1.6 has all the functionality you need so you'll choose it as your target. In general, it's best to choose the lowest version number that you can, since that will maximize the number of devices that can run your application.
5. Type in **Hello Android** as the application name. This is the name that will appear with your application icon, in your application's title bar, and in application lists. It should be descriptive but not too long.
6. Use **com.androidbook.hello** as the package name. Your application must have a base package name and this is it. This package name will be used as an identifier for your application and must be unique across all applications. For this reason, it's best to start the package name with a domain name that you own. If you don't own one, just be creative to ensure that your package name won't likely be used by anyone else. However, don't use a package name that starts with com.google, com.android, android or com.example as these are restricted by Google and you would not be able to upload your application to Android Market.
7. Type **HelloActivity** as the Create Activity name. You're telling Android that this activity should be the one to launch when your application starts up. You could have other activities in your application, but this is the first one the user should see when the application is started.
8. Finally, the Min SDK Version value of 4 tells Android that your application requires Android 1.6 or newer. Technically, you could specify a Min SDK Version that is less than the Build Target value. If your application calls for functionality that is not present in the older version of Android, you will need to handle that situation gracefully, but this can be done. For most applications, the Min SDK Version number will match the Build Target number.

9. Click the Finish button, which tells ADT to generate the project skeleton for you. For now, open the `HelloActivity.java` file under the `src` folder and modify the `onCreate()` method as follows:

```
/** Called when the activity is first created. */
    @Override
    public void onCreate(Bundle savedInstanceState) {
        super.onCreate(savedInstanceState);
        /** create a TextView and write Hello World! */
        TextView tv = new TextView(this);
        tv.setText("Hello World!");
        /** set the content view to the TextView */
        setContentView(tv);
    }
```

You'll probably need to add an `import android.widget.TextView;` statement to the code to get rid of the error reported by Eclipse. Save the `HelloActivity.java` file.

To run the application, you'll need to create an Eclipse launch configuration, and you'll need a virtual device on which to run it. We're going to quickly take you through these steps and come back later to more details about Android Virtual Devices (AVDs). Create the Eclipse launch configuration by following these steps:

1. Select the main Run menu, then choose the Run Configurations menu item.
2. In the Run Configurations dialog box, double-click Android Application in the left pane. The wizard will insert a new configuration named New Configuration.
3. Rename the configuration **RunHelloWorld**.
4. Click the Browse button and select the HelloAndroid project.
5. Under Launch Action, select Launch: and select com.androidbook.hello.HelloActivity from the drop-down list. The dialog should appear as shown in Figure 2–6.

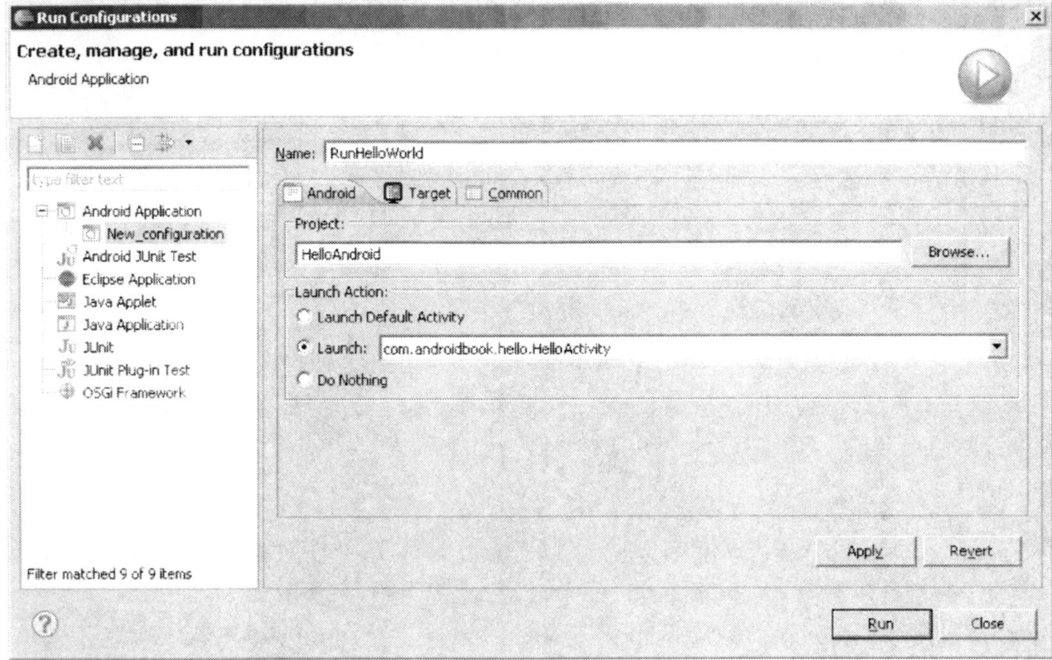

Figure 2–6. *Configuring an Eclipse launch configuration to run the "Hello World!" application*

6. Click Apply and then Run. You're almost there! Eclipse is ready to run your application, but it needs a device on which to run it. As shown in Figure 2–7, you will be warned that no compatible targets were found and asked if you'd like to create one. Click Yes.

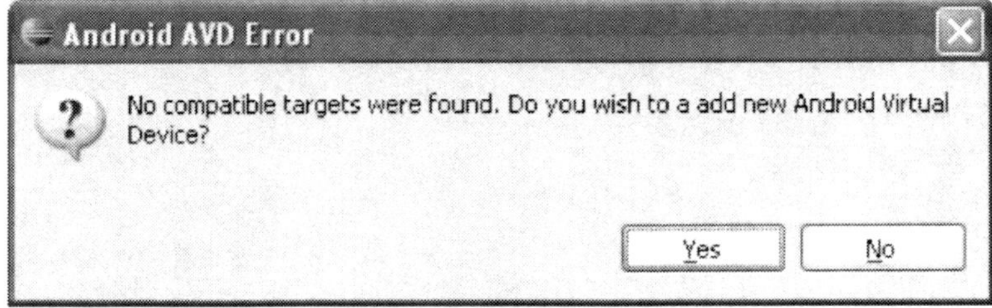

Figure 2–7. *Error message warning about targets and asking for a new AVD*

7. You'll be presented with a window that shows the existing AVDs (see Figure 2–8). Note that this is the same window you saw in Figure 2–2 when you installed packages, but now you're looking at the virtual devices. You'll need to add an AVD suitable for your new application. Click the New button.

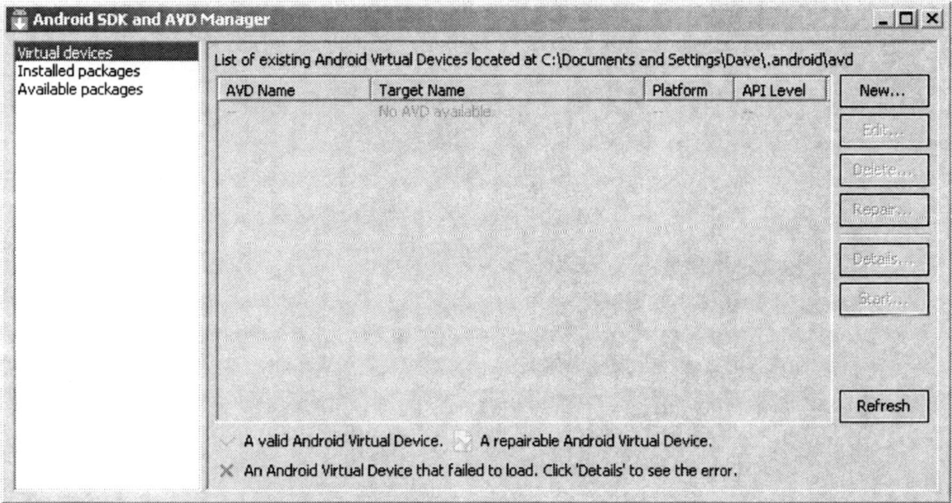

Figure 2–8. *The existing Android Virtual Devices*

8. Fill in the Create AVD form as shown in Figure 2–9. Set Name to Gingerbread, choose Android 2.3 - API Level 9 (or some other version) for the Target, set SD Card Size to 10 (for 10MB), enable Snapshots, and choose HVGA for Skin. Click Create AVD. The Manager may confirm the successful creation of your AVD. Close the Android SDK and AVD Manager window by clicking X in the upper right corner.

NOTE: You're choosing a newer version of the SDK for your Android Virtual Device, but your application could also run on an older one. This is okay because AVDs with newer SDKs can run applications that require older SDKs. The opposite, of course, would not be true: an application that requires features of a newer SDK won't run on an AVD with an older SDK.

9. Finally, select your new AVD from the bottom list. Note that you may need to click the Refresh button for any new AVDs to show up in the list. Click the OK button.

10. Eclipse will now launch the emulator with your very first Android app (see Figure 2–10)!

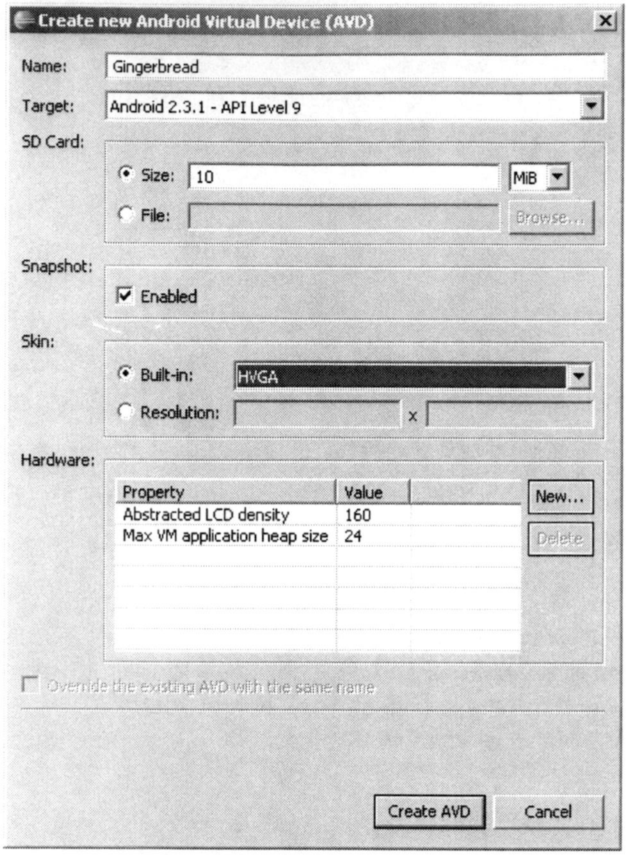

Figure 2–9. *Configuring an Android Virtual Device*

NOTE: It might take the emulator a while to emulate the device bootup process. Once the bootup process has completed, you will typically see a locked screen. Press the Menu button or drag on the unlock image to unlock the AVD. After unlocking, you should see HelloAndroidApp running in the emulator, as shown in Figure 2–10. Be aware that the emulator starts other applications in the background during the startup process, so you might see a warning or error message from time to time. If you see an error message, you can generally dismiss it to allow the emulator to go to the next step in the startup process. For example, if you run the emulator and see a message like "application abc is not responding," you can either wait for the application to start or simply ask the emulator to forcefully close the application. Generally, you should wait and let the emulator start up cleanly.

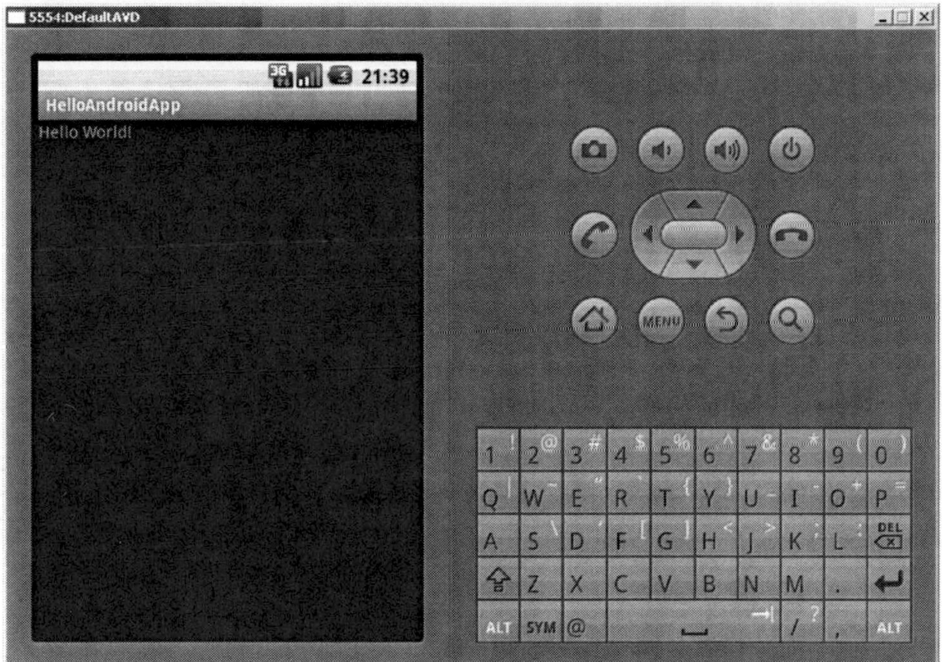

Figure 2–10. *HelloAndroidApp running in the emulator*

Now you know how to create a new Android application and run it in the emulator. Next, we'll look more closely at Android Virtual Devices, followed by a deeper dive into an Android application's artifacts and structure.

Android Virtual Devices

An AVD represents a device configuration. For example, you could have an AVD representing an older Android device running version 1.5 of the SDK with a 32MB SD card. The idea is that you create AVDs you are going to support and then point the emulator to one of those AVDs when developing and testing your application. Specifying (and changing) which AVD to use is very easy and makes testing with various configurations a snap. Earlier you saw how to create an AVD using Eclipse. You can make more AVDs in Eclipse by going to Window ➤ Android SDK and AVD Manager and clicking Virtual Devices on the left side. You can also create AVDs using the command line. Here's how.

To create an AVD, you'll use a batch file named `android` under the `tools` directory (`c:\android-sdk-windows\tools\`). `android` allows you to create a new AVD and manage existing AVDs. For example, you can view existing AVDs, move AVDs, and so on. You can see the options available for using `android` by running `android -help`. For now, let's just create an AVD.

By default, AVDs are stored under your home directory (all platforms) in a folder called `.android\AVD`. If you created an AVD for the "Hello World!" application you just created, then you will find it here. If you want to store or manipulate AVDs somewhere else, you can do that, too. For this example, let's create a folder where the AVD image will be stored, such as `c:\avd\`. The next step is to list your available Android targets using the following command inside of a tools window:

```
android list target
```

The output of this command is a list of all installed Android versions, and each item in the list has an ID. Now, run the `android` file to create the AVD. Using the tools window again, type the following command (using an appropriate path to store the AVD files for your workstation, and using an appropriate value for the `-t` ID argument based on what SDK platform targets you installed):

```
android create avd -n CupcakeMaps -t 2 -c 16M -p c:\avd\CupcakeMaps\
```

The parameters passed to the batch file are listed in Table 2–1.

Table 2–1. *Parameters Passed to the android.bat Tool*

Argument/Command	Description
`create avd`	Tells the tool to create an AVD.
`n`	The name of the AVD.
`t`	The target runtime ID. Use the `android list target` command to get the ID for each installed target.
`c`	Size of the SD card in bytes. Use K for kilobytes and M for megabytes.
`p`	The path to the generated AVD. This is optional.
`A`	Enables snapshots. This is optional. Snapshots will be explained later in the "Launching the Emulator" section.

Executing the preceding command will generate an AVD; you should see output similar to what's shown in Figure 2–11. Note that when you run the `create avd` command, you are asked if you want to create a custom hardware profile. Answer no to this question for now, but know that answering yes will then prompt you to configure many options for your AVD, such as screen size, presence of a camera, and so on.

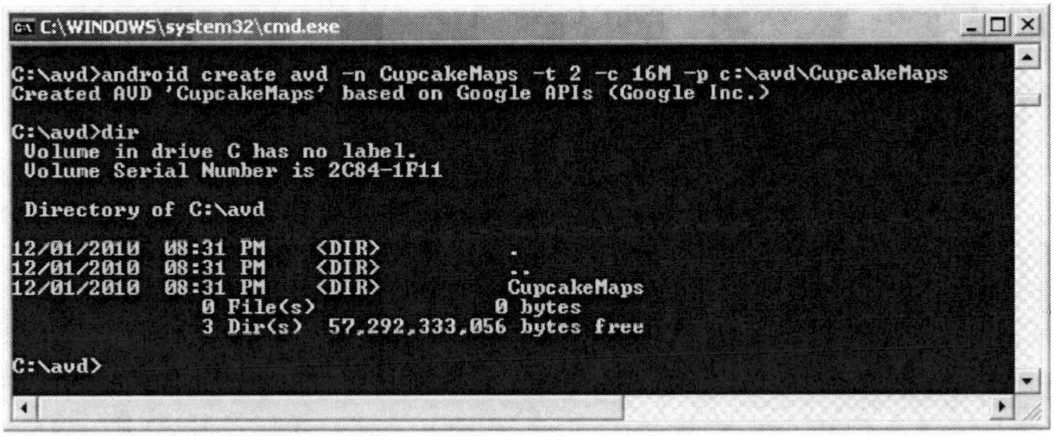

```
C:\WINDOWS\system32\cmd.exe

C:\avd>android create avd -n CupcakeMaps -t 2 -c 16M -p c:\avd\CupcakeMaps
Created AVD 'CupcakeMaps' based on Google APIs (Google Inc.)

C:\avd>dir
 Volume in drive C has no label.
 Volume Serial Number is 2C84-1F11

 Directory of C:\avd

12/01/2010  08:31 PM    <DIR>          .
12/01/2010  08:31 PM    <DIR>          ..
12/01/2010  08:31 PM    <DIR>          CupcakeMaps
               0 File(s)              0 bytes
               3 Dir(s)  57,292,333,056 bytes free

C:\avd>
```

Figure 2–11. *Creating an AVD yields this android.bat output*

Even though you specified an alternate location for CupcakeMaps using the android.bat program, there is a `CupcakeMaps.ini` file under your home directory's `.android/AVD` folder. This is a good thing because if you go back into Eclipse, and select Window ➤ Android SDK and AVD Manager, you will see all of your AVDs. You can access any of them when running your Android applications within Eclipse.

Take another look at Figure 2–4. Each version of Android has an API level. Android 1.6 has an API level of 4 and Android 2.1 has an API level of 7. These API level numbers do not correspond to the target IDs that the `android create avd` command uses for the `-t` argument. You'll always have to use the `android list target` command to get the appropriate target ID value for the `android create avd` command.

Also be aware that selecting a Google API from the SDK Target list will include mapping functionality in your AVD, while selecting Android 1.5 or later will not. We'll get into much more detail about maps in Chapter 17.

Exploring the Structure of an Android Application

Although the size and complexity of Android applications can vary greatly, their structures will be similar. Figure 2–12 shows the structure of the "Hello World!" app you just built.

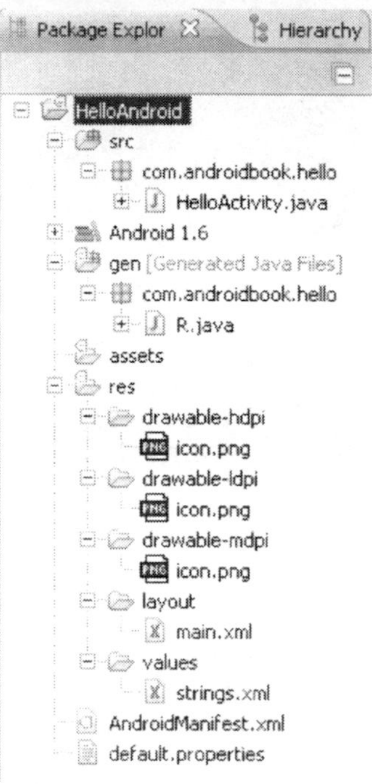

Figure 2–12. *The structure of the "Hello World!" application*

Android applications have some artifacts that are required and some that are optional. Table 2–2 summarizes the elements of an Android application.

Table 2–2. *The Artifacts of an Android Application*

Artifact	Description	Required?
`AndroidManifest.xml`	The Android application descriptor file. This file defines the activities, content providers, services, and intent receivers of the application. You can also use this file to declaratively define permissions required by the application, as well as grant specific permissions to other applications using the services of the application. Moreover, the file can contain instrumentation detail that you can use to test the application or another application.	Yes
`src`	A folder containing all of the source code of the application.	Yes
`assets`	An arbitrary collection of folders and files.	No
`res`	A folder containing the resources of the application. This is the parent folder of `drawable`, `anim`, `layout`, `menu`, `values`, `xml`, and `raw`.	Yes

Artifact	Description	Required?
`drawable`	A folder containing the images or image-descriptor files used by the application.	No
`anim`	A folder containing the XML-descriptor files that describe the animations used by the application.	No
`layout`	A folder containing views of the application. You should create your application's views by using XML descriptors rather than coding them.	No
`menu`	A folder containing XML-descriptor files for menus in the application.	No
`values`	A folder containing other resources used by the application. Examples of resources found in this folder include strings, arrays, styles, and colors.	No
`xml`	A folder containing additional XML files used by the application.	No
`raw`	A folder containing additional data—possibly non-XML data—that is required by the application.	No

As you can see from Table 2–2, an Android application is primarily made up of three pieces: the application descriptor, a collection of various resources, and the application's source code. If you put aside the `AndroidManifest.xml` file for a moment, you can view an Android app in this simple way: you have some business logic implemented in code, and everything else is a resource. This basic structure resembles the basic structure of a J2EE app, where the resources correlate to JSPs, the business logic correlates to servlets, and the `AndroidManifest.xml` file correlates to the `web.xml` file.

You can also compare J2EE's development model to Android's development model. In J2EE, the philosophy of building views is to build them using markup language. Android has also adopted this approach, although the markup in Android is XML. You benefit from this approach because you don't have to hard-code your application's views; you can modify the look and feel of the application by editing the markup.

It is also worth noting a few constraints regarding resources. First, Android supports only a linear list of files within the predefined folders under `res`. For example, it does not support nested folders under the `layout` folder (or the other folders under `res`). Second, there are some similarities between the `assets` folder and the `raw` folder under `res`. Both folders can contain raw files, but the files within `raw` are considered resources and the files within `assets` are not. So the files within `raw` will be localized, accessible through resource IDs, and so on. But the contents of the `assets` folder are considered general-purpose contents to be used without resource constraints and support. Note that because the contents of the `assets` folder are not considered resources, you can put an arbitrary hierarchy of folders and files within it. (We'll talk a lot more about resources in Chapter 3.)

> **NOTE:** You might have noticed that XML is used quite heavily with Android. We all know that XML is a bloated data format, so this begs the question, does it make sense to rely on XML when you know your target is going to be a device with limited resources? It turns out that the XML you create during development is actually compiled down to binary using the Android Asset Packaging Tool (AAPT). Therefore, when your application is installed on a device, the files on the device are stored as binary. When the file is needed at runtime, the file is read in its binary form and is not transformed back into XML. This gives you the benefits of both worlds—you get to work with XML and you don't have to worry about taking up valuable resources on the device.

Analyzing the Notepad Application

Not only have you learned how to create a new Android application and run it in the emulator, but you should also have a feel for the artifacts of an Android application. Next, we are going to look at the Notepad application that ships with the Android SDK. Notepad's complexity falls between that of the "Hello World!" app and a full-blown Android application, so analyzing its components will give you some realistic insight into Android development. This is going to be a quick run-through of the Notepad application. You may find some of these concepts difficult to grasp at this time, but don't worry; this book will go into much greater detail on all these concepts in the chapters that follow.

Loading and Running the Notepad Application

In this section, we'll show you how to load the Notepad application into the Eclipse IDE and run it in the emulator. Before we start, you should know that the Notepad application implements several use cases. For example, the user can create a new note, edit an existing note, delete a note, view the list of created notes, and so on. When the user launches the application, there aren't any saved notes yet, so the user sees an empty note list. If the user presses the Menu key, the application presents him with a list of actions, one of which allows him to add a new note. After he adds the note, he can edit or delete the note by selecting the corresponding menu option.

Follow these steps to load the Notepad sample into the Eclipse IDE:

1. Start Eclipse.
2. Go to File ➤ New ➤ Project.
3. In the New Project dialog, select Android ➤ Android Project.

4. In the New Android Project dialog, type in NotesList for the Project name, select "Create project from existing sample," then select a Build Target of Android 1.6. In the Samples menu, scroll down to the Notepad application. Note that the Notepad application is located in the `platforms\android-1.6\samples` folder of the Android SDK that you downloaded earlier. After you choose Notepad, the dialog reads the `AndroidManifest.xml` file and prepopulates the remaining fields in the New Android Project dialog box. (See Figure 2–13.)
5. Click the Finish button.

You should now see the NotesList application in your Eclipse IDE. If you see any problems reported in Eclipse for this project, try using the Clean option from the Project menu in Eclipse to clear them. To run the application, you can create a launch configuration (as you did for the "Hello World!" application), or you can simply right-click the project, choose Run As, and select Android Application. This will launch the emulator and install the application on it. After the emulator has completed loading, unlock the emulator screen so you can see your new NotesList application. Play around with the application for a few minutes to become familiar with it.

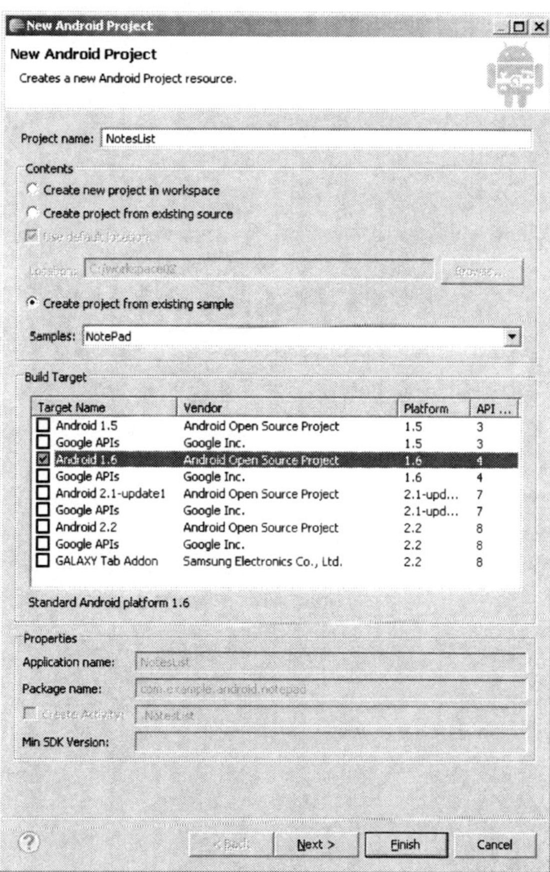

Figure 2–13. *Creating the Notepad application*

Dissecting the Application

Now let's study the contents of the application (see Figure 2–14).

As you can see, the application contains several .java files, a few .png images, three views (under the `layout` folder), and the `AndroidManifest.xml` file. If this were a command-line application, you would start looking for the class with the `Main` method. So what's the equivalent of a `Main` method in Android?

Android defines an entry-point activity, also called the top-level activity. If you look in the `AndroidManifest.xml` file, you'll find one provider and three activities. The `NotesList` activity defines an intent-filter for the action `android.intent.action.MAIN` and for the category `android.intent.category.LAUNCHER`. When an Android application is asked to run, the host loads the application and reads the `AndroidManifest.xml` file. It then looks for, and starts, an activity or activities with an intent-filter that has the `MAIN` action with a category of `LAUNCHER`, as shown here:

```
<intent-filter>
    <action android:name="android.intent.action.MAIN" />
    <category android:name="android.intent.category.LAUNCHER" />
</intent-filter>
```

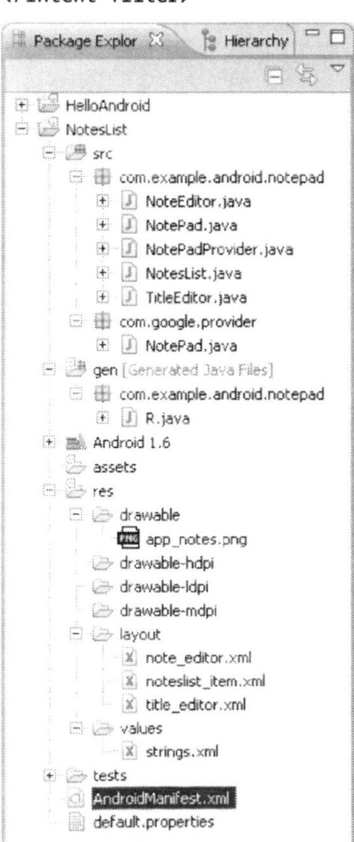

Figure 2–14. *Contents of the Notepad application*

After the host finds the activity it wants to run, it must resolve the defined activity to an actual class. It does this by combining the root package name and the activity name, which in this case becomes `com.example.android.notepad.NotesList` (see Listing 2–1).

Listing 2–1. *The AndroidManfiest.xml File*

```
<manifest xmlns:android="http://schemas.android.com/apk/res/android"
    package="com.example.android.notepad"
>
    <application android:icon="@drawable/app_notes"
        android:label="@string/app_name"
    >
        <provider android:name="NotePadProvider"
            android:authorities="com.google.provider.NotePad"
        />
        <activity android:name="NotesList" android:label="@string/title_notes_list">
            <intent-filter>
                <action android:name="android.intent.action.MAIN" />
                <category android:name="android.intent.category.LAUNCHER" />
            </intent-filter>
            <intent-filter>
                <action android:name="android.intent.action.VIEW" />
                <action android:name="android.intent.action.EDIT" />
                <action android:name="android.intent.action.PICK" />
                <category android:name="android.intent.category.DEFAULT" />
                <data android:mimeType="vnd.android.cursor.dir/vnd.google.note" />
            </intent-filter>
            <intent-filter>
                <action android:name="android.intent.action.GET_CONTENT" />
                <category android:name="android.intent.category.DEFAULT" />
                <data android:mimeType="vnd.android.cursor.item/vnd.google.note" />
            </intent-filter>
        </activity>
…
</manfiest>
```

The application's root package name is defined as an attribute of the `<manifest>` element in the `AndroidManifest.xml` file, and each activity has a name attribute.

Once the entry-point activity is determined, the host starts the activity and the `onCreate()` method is called. Let's have a look at `NotesList.onCreate()`, shown in Listing 2–2.

Listing 2–2. *The onCreate Method*

```
public class NotesList extends ListActivity {
  @Override
  protected void onCreate(Bundle savedInstanceState) {
      super.onCreate(savedInstanceState);

      setDefaultKeyMode(DEFAULT_KEYS_SHORTCUT);
      Intent intent = getIntent();
      if (intent.getData() == null) {
          intent.setData(Notes.CONTENT_URI);
      }

      getListView().setOnCreateContextMenuListener(this);
```

```
        Cursor cursor = managedQuery(getIntent().getData(), PROJECTION, null, null,
                Notes.DEFAULT_SORT_ORDER);

        SimpleCursorAdapter adapter =
            new SimpleCursorAdapter(this, R.layout.noteslist_item,
                cursor, new String[] { Notes.TITLE }, new int[] { android.R.id.text1 });
        setListAdapter(adapter);
    }
}
```

Activities in Android are usually started with an intent, and one activity can start another activity. The onCreate() method checks whether the current activity's intent has data (notes). If not, it sets the URI to retrieve the data on the intent. In Chapter 4, we'll show that Android accesses data through content providers that operate on URIs. In this case, the URI provides enough information to retrieve data from a database. The constant Notes.CONTENT_URI is defined as a static final in Notepad.java, like so:

```
public static final Uri CONTENT_URI =
         Uri.parse("content://" + AUTHORITY + "/notes");
```

The Notes class is an inner class of the Notepad class. For now, know that the preceding URI tells the content provider to get all of the notes. If the URI looked something like this

```
public static final Uri CONTENT_URI =
      Uri.parse("content://" + AUTHORITY + "/notes/11");
```

then the consuming content provider would return the note with an ID equal to 11. We will discuss content providers and URIs in depth in Chapter 4.

The NotesList class extends the ListActivity class, which knows how to display list-oriented data. The items in the list are managed by an internal ListView (a UI component), which displays the notes in the list. After setting the URI on the activity's intent, the activity registers to build the context menu for notes. If you've played with the application, you probably noticed that context-sensitive menu items are displayed depending on your selection. For example, if you select an existing note, the application displays Edit note and Edit title. Similarly, if you don't select a note, the application shows you the Add note option.

Next, you see the activity execute a managed query and get a cursor for the result. A managed query means that Android will manage the returned cursor. As part of managing the cursor, if the application has to be unloaded or reloaded, neither the application nor the activity has to worry about positioning the cursor, loading it, or unloading it. The parameters to managedQuery(), shown in Table 2–3, are interesting.

Table 2–3. *Parameters to Activity.managedQuery*

Parameter	Data Type	Description
URI	Uri	URI of the content provider
projection	String[]	The column to return (column names)
selection	String	Optional where clause
selectionArgs	String[]	The arguments to the selection, if the query contains ?s
sortOrder	String	Sort order to be used on the result set

We will discuss managedQuery() and its sibling query() later in this section and also in Chapter 4. For now, realize that a query in Android returns tabular data. The projection parameter allows you to define the columns you are interested in. You can also reduce the overall result set and sort the result set using a SQL order-by clause (such as asc or desc). Also note that an Android query must return a column named _ID to support retrieving an individual record. Moreover, you must know the type of data returned by the content provider—whether a column contains a string, int, binary, or the like.

After the query is executed, the returned cursor is passed to the constructor of SimpleCursorAdapter, which adapts records in the dataset to items in the user interface (ListView). Look closely at the parameters passed to the constructor of SimpleCursorAdapter.

```
SimpleCursorAdapter adapter =
    new SimpleCursorAdapter(this, R.layout.noteslist_item,
        cursor, new String[] { Notes.TITLE }, new int[] { android.R.id.text1 });
```

Specifically, look at the second parameter: an identifier to the view that represents the items in the ListView. As you'll see in Chapter 3, Android provides an auto-generated utility class that provides references to the resources in your project. This utility class is called the R class (which is short for resources). Its filename is R.java and you can see it in Figure 2–14. When you compile your project, the AAPT generates the R class for you from the resources defined within your res folder. For example, you could put all your string resources into the values folder and the AAPT will generate a public static identifier for each string. Android supports this generically for all of your resources. For example, in the constructor of SimpleCursorAdapter, the NotesList activity passes in the identifier of the view that displays an item from the notes list. The benefit of this utility class is that you don't have to hard-code your resources and you get compile-time reference checking. In other words, if a resource is deleted, the R class will lose the reference and any code referring to the resource will not compile.

Let's look at another important concept in Android that we alluded to earlier: the onListItemClick() method of NotesList (see Listing 2–3).

Listing 2–3. *The onListItemClick Method*

```
    @Override
    protected void onListItemClick(ListView l, View v, int position, long id) {
        Uri uri = ContentUris.withAppendedId(getIntent().getData(), id);

        String action = getIntent().getAction();
        if (Intent.ACTION_PICK.equals(action) ||
Intent.ACTION_GET_CONTENT.equals(action)) {
            setResult(RESULT_OK, new Intent().setData(uri));
        } else {
            startActivity(new Intent(Intent.ACTION_EDIT, uri));
        }
    }
```

The `onListItemClick()` method is called when a user selects a note in the UI. There are two use cases implemented by this method. In the first case, your notes list activity could be invoked via an intent so the user could select a specific note that would be returned to the calling activity. In the second case, you could be simply looking at the list of notes; upon selecting a note, your current activity will invoke an edit activity on the selected note. When a note is selected, the method creates a URI by taking the base URI and appending the selected note's ID to it. If your activity was called via an intent to either pick a note or get the content of a note, you call `setResult()` to return the URI of the selected note back to the caller. If you're the second use case, the URI is passed to `startActivity()` with a new intent. `startActivity()` is one way to start an activity: it starts an activity but doesn't report on the results of the activity after it completes. Another way to start an activity is to use `startActivityForResult()`. With this method, you can start another activity and use a callback to be notified when the activity completes so you can grab the results. For example, the activity that calls NotesList to select a note would use `startActivityForResult()` so that they get notified with the answer after your NotesList activity calls `setResult()`.

At this point, you might be wondering about user interaction with respect to activities. For example, if the running activity starts another activity, and *that* activity starts an activity (and so on), then what activity can the user work with? Can she manipulate all the activities simultaneously, or is she restricted to a single activity? Actually, activities have a defined lifecycle. They're maintained on an activity stack, with the running activity at the top. If the running activity starts another activity, the first running activity moves down the stack and the new activity is placed on the top. Activities lower in the stack can be in a paused or stopped state. A paused activity is partially or fully visible to the user; a stopped activity is not visible to the user. The system can kill paused or stopped activities if it deems that resources are needed elsewhere.

Let's move on to data persistence. The notes that a user creates are saved to an actual database on the device. Specifically, the Notepad application's backing store is a SQLite database. The `managedQuery()` method discussed earlier eventually resolves to data in a database via a content provider. Let's examine how the URI passed to `managedQuery()` results in the execution of a query against a SQLite database. Recall that the URI passed to `managedQuery()` looks like this:

```
public static final Uri CONTENT_URI =
    Uri.parse("content://" + AUTHORITY + "/notes");
```

Content URIs always have this form: content://, followed by the authority, followed by a general segment (context-specific). Because the URI doesn't contain the actual data, it somehow results in the execution of code that produces data. What is this connection? How is the URI reference resolved to code that produces data? Is the URI an HTTP service or a web service? Actually, the URI, or the authority portion of the URI, is configured in the AndroidManifest.xml file as a content provider, like so:

```
<provider android:name="NotePadProvider"
     android:authorities="com.google.provider.NotePad"/>
```

When Android sees a URI that needs to be resolved, it pulls out the authority portion of it and looks up the ContentProvider class configured for the authority. In the Notepad application, the AndroidManifest.xml file contains a class called NotePadProvider configured for the com.google.provider.NotePad authority. Listing 2–4 shows a small portion of the class.

Listing 2–4. ***The NotePadProvider Class***

```
public class NotePadProvider extends ContentProvider
{

    @Override
    public Cursor query(Uri uri, String[] projection, String selection,
         String[] selectionArgs,String sortOrder) {}

    @Override
    public Uri insert(Uri uri, ContentValues initialValues) {}

    @Override
    public int update(Uri uri, ContentValues values, String where,
        String[] whereArgs) {}

    @Override
    public int delete(Uri uri, String where, String[] whereArgs) {}

    @Override
    public String getType(Uri uri) {}

    @Override
    public boolean onCreate() {}


    private static class DatabaseHelper extends SQLiteOpenHelper {}

    @Override
        public void onCreate(SQLiteDatabase db) {}

        @Override
        public void onUpgrade(SQLiteDatabase db,
            int oldVersion, int newVersion) {
            //...
        }
    }
}
```

The NotePadProvider class extends the ContentProvider class. The ContentProvider class defines six abstract methods, four of which are CRUD (Create, Read, Update, Delete) operations. The other two abstract methods are onCreate() and getType(). Note that onCreate() is called when the content provider is created for the first time; getType() provides the MIME type for the result set (you'll see how MIME types work when you read Chapter 3).

The other interesting thing about the NotePadProvider class is the internal DatabaseHelper class, which extends the SQLiteOpenHelper class. Together, the two classes take care of initializing the Notepad database, opening and closing it, and performing other database tasks. Interestingly, the DatabaseHelper class is just a few lines of custom code (see Listing 2–5), while the Android implementation of SQLiteOpenHelper does most of the heavy lifting.

Listing 2–5. *The DatabaseHelper Class*

```
private static class DatabaseHelper extends SQLiteOpenHelper {

        DatabaseHelper(Context context) {
            super(context, DATABASE_NAME, null, DATABASE_VERSION);
        }

        @Override
        public void onCreate(SQLiteDatabase db) {
            db.execSQL("CREATE TABLE " + NOTES_TABLE_NAME + " ("
                    + Notes._ID + " INTEGER PRIMARY KEY,"
                    + Notes.TITLE + " TEXT,"
                    + Notes.NOTE + " TEXT,"
                    + Notes.CREATED_DATE + " INTEGER,"
                    + Notes.MODIFIED_DATE + " INTEGER"
                    + ");");
        }

        //…
}
```

As shown in Listing 2–5, the onCreate() method creates the Notepad table. Notice that the class's constructor calls the superclass's constructor with the name of the table. The superclass will call the onCreate() method only if the table does not exist in the database. Also notice that one of the columns in the Notepad table is the _ID column we discussed in the section "Dissecting the Application."

Now let's look at one of the CRUD operations: the insert() method shown in Listing 2–6.

Listing 2–6. *The insert() Method*

```
//…
SQLiteDatabase db = mOpenHelper.getWritableDatabase();
        long rowId = db.insert(NOTES_TABLE_NAME, Notes.NOTE, values);
        if (rowId > 0) {
            Uri noteUri = ContentUris.withAppendedId(
                    NotePad.Notes.CONTENT_URI, rowId);
            getContext().getContentResolver().notifyChange(noteUri, null);
            return noteUri;
        }
```

The `insert()` method uses its internal `DatabaseHelper` instance to access the database and then inserts a notes record. The returned row ID is then appended to the URI and a new URI is returned to the caller.

At this point, you should be familiar with how an Android application is laid out. You should be able to navigate your way around Notepad and some of the other samples in the Android SDK. You should be able to run the samples and play with them. Now let's look at the overall lifecycle of an Android application.

Examining the Application Lifecycle

The lifecycle of an Android application is strictly managed by the system, based on the user's needs, available resources, and so on. A user might want to launch a web browser, for example, but the system ultimately decides whether to start the application. Although the system is the ultimate manager, it adheres to some defined and logical guidelines to determine whether an application can be loaded, paused, or stopped. If the user is currently working with an activity, the system will give high priority to that application. Conversely, if an activity is not visible and the system determines that an application must be shut down to free up resources, it will shut down the lower-priority application.

Contrast this with the lifecycle of web-based J2EE applications. J2EE apps are loosely managed by the container they run in. For example, a J2EE container can remove an application from memory if it sits idle for a predetermined time period. But the container generally won't move applications in and out of memory based on load and/or available resources. A J2EE container will generally have sufficient resources to run lots of applications at the same time. With Android, resources are more limited so Android must have more control and power over applications.

> **NOTE:** Android runs each application in a separate process, each of which hosts its own virtual machine. This provides a protected memory environment. By isolating applications to an individual process, the system can control which application deserves higher priority. For example, a background process that's doing a CPU-intensive task can't block an incoming phone call.

The concept of application lifecycle is logical, but a fundamental aspect of Android applications complicates matters. Specifically, the Android application architecture is component- and integration-oriented. This allows a rich user experience, seamless reuse, and easy application integration, but creates a complex task for the application-lifecycle manager.

Let's consider a typical scenario. A user is talking to someone on the phone and needs to open an e-mail message to answer a question. She goes to the home screen, opens the mail application, opens the e-mail message, clicks a link in the e-mail, and answers her friend's question by reading a stock quote from a web page. This scenario would require four applications: the home application, a talk application, an e-mail application, and a browser application. As the user navigates from one application to the next, her experience is seamless. In the background, however, the system is saving and restoring application state. For instance, when the user clicks the link in the e-mail message, the system saves metadata on the running e-mail message activity before starting the browser-application activity to launch a URL. In fact, the system saves metadata on any activity before starting another so that it can come back to the activity (when the user backtracks, for example). If memory becomes an issue, the system will have to shut down a process running an activity and resume it as necessary.

Android is sensitive to the lifecycle of an application and its components. Therefore, you'll need to understand and handle lifecycle events in order to build a stable application. The processes running your Android application and its components go through various lifecycle events, and Android provides callbacks that you can implement to handle state changes. For starters, you'll want to become familiar with the various lifecycle callbacks for an activity (see Listing 2–7).

Listing 2–7. *Lifecycle Methods of an Activity*

```
protected void onCreate(Bundle savedInstanceState);
protected void onStart();
protected void onRestart();
protected void onResume();
protected void onPause();
protected void onStop();
protected void onDestroy();
```

Listing 2–7 shows the list of lifecycle methods that Android calls during the life of an activity. It's important to understand when each of the methods is called by the system in order to ensure that you implement a stable application. Note that you do not need to react to all of these methods. If you do, however, be sure to call the superclass versions as well. Figure 2–15 shows the transitions between states.

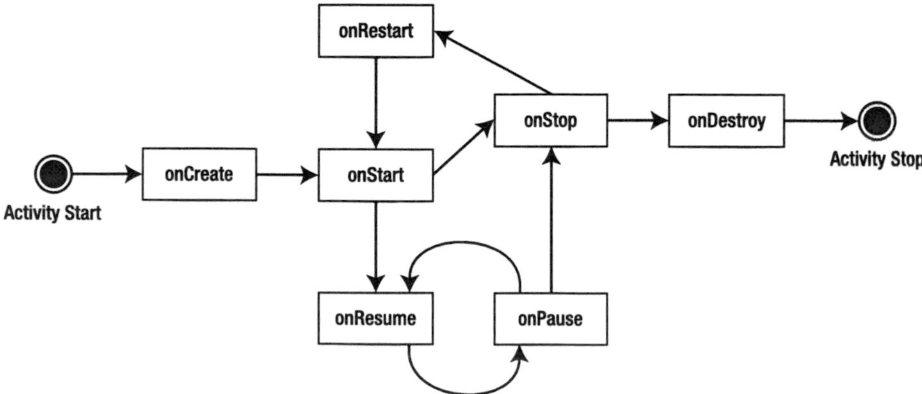

Figure 2–15. *State transitions of an activity*

The system can start and stop your activities based on what else is happening. Android calls the `onCreate()` method when the activity is freshly created. `onCreate()` is always followed by a call to `onStart()`, but `onStart()` is not always preceded by a call to onCreate() because onStart() can be called if your application was stopped. When onStart() is called, your activity is not visible to the user, but it's about to be. onResume() is called after onStart(), just when the activity is in the foreground and accessible to the user. At this point, the user can interact with your activity.

When the user decides to move to another activity, the system will call your activity's onPause() method. From onPause(), you can expect either onResume() or onStop() to be called. onResume() is called, for example, if the user brings your activity back to the foreground. onStop() is called if your activity becomes invisible to the user. If your activity is brought back to the foreground after a call to onStop(), then onRestart() will be called. If your activity sits on the activity stack but is not visible to the user, and the system decides to kill your activity, onDestroy() will be called.

The state model described for an activity appears complex, but you are not required to deal with every possible scenario. In fact, you will mostly handle onCreate(), onResume(), and onPause(). You will handle onCreate() to create the user interface for your activity. In this method, you will bind data to your widgets and wire up any event handlers for your UI components. In onPause(), you will want to persist critical data to your application's data store. It's the last safe method that will get called before the system kills your application. onStop() and onDestroy() are not guaranteed to be called, so don't rely on these methods for critical logic.

The takeaway from this discussion? The system manages your application, and it can start, stop, or resume an application component at any time. Although the system controls your components, they don't run in complete isolation with respect to your application. In other words, if the system starts an activity in your application, you can count on an application context in your activity. For example, it's possible to have global variables shared among the activities in your application. You can share a global variable by writing an extension of the android.app.Application class and then initializing the global variable in the onCreate() method (see Listing 2–8). Activities and other components in your application can then access these references with confidence when they are executing. We'll talk more about this concept in Chapter 11.

Listing 2–8. *An Extension of the Application Class*

```
public class MyApplication extends Application
{
    // global variable
    private static final String myGlobalVariable;

    @Override
    public void onCreate()
    {
        super.onCreate();
        //... initialize global variables here
        myGlobalVariable = loadCacheData();
    }

    public static String getMyGlobalVariable() {
        return myGlobalVariable;
    }

}
```

So far, we've covered the basics of creating a new Android app, running an Android app in the emulator, the basic structure of an Android app, and several of the common features you'll find in many Android apps. But we haven't shown you how to resolve problems that will occur in Android apps. In the final section of this chapter, we will discuss debugging.

Debugging Your App

After you write a few lines of code for your first application, you'll start wondering if it's possible to have a debug session while you interact with your application. The answer is yes. The Android SDK includes a host of tools that you can use for debugging purposes. These tools are integrated with the Eclipse IDE (see Figure 2–16 for a small sample).

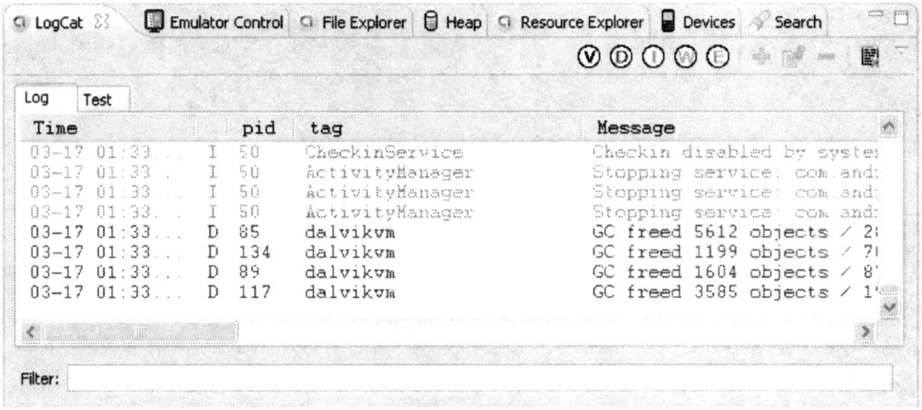

LogCat | Emulator Control | File Explorer | Heap | Resource Explorer | Devices | Search

Log | Test

Time		pid	tag	Message
03-17 01:33...	I	50	CheckinService	Checkin disabled by syste
03-17 01:33...	I	50	ActivityManager	Stopping service: com.and
03-17 01:33...	I	50	ActivityManager	Stopping service: com.and
03-17 01:33...	I	50	ActivityManager	Stopping service: com.and
03-17 01:33...	D	85	dalvikvm	GC freed 5612 objects / 2
03-17 01:33...	D	134	dalvikvm	GC freed 1199 objects / 7
03-17 01:33...	D	89	dalvikvm	GC freed 1604 objects / 8
03-17 01:33...	D	117	dalvikvm	GC freed 3585 objects / 1

Filter:

Figure 2–16. ***Debugging tools that you can use while building Android applications***

One of the tools that you'll use throughout your Android development is LogCat. This tool displays the log messages that you emit using `android.util.Log`, exceptions, `System.out.println`, and so on. While `System.out.println` works and the messages show up in the LogCat window, to log messages from your application, you'll want to use the `android.util.Log` class. This class defines the familiar informational, warning, and error methods that you can filter within the LogCat window to see just what you want to see. A sample `Log` command is:

```
Log.v("string TAG", "This is my verbose message to write to the log");
```

What's particularly nice about LogCat is that you can view log messages when you're running your application in the emulator, but you can also view log messages when you've connected a real device to your workstation and it's in debug mode. In fact, log messages are stored such that you can even retrieve the most recent messages from a device that was disconnected when the log messages were recorded. When you connect up a device to your workstation and you have the LogCat view open, you'll see the last several hundred messages.

There are two things you need to know about debugging applications on a real device. The first is that the application must be set to debuggable in the `AndroidManifest.xml` file. This involves adding android:debuggable="true" to the <application> tag. Fortunately, the ADT will set this for properly for you. When you're creating debug builds for the emulator or deploying directly from Eclipse to a device, this attribute is set to true by ADT. When you export your application to create a production version of your application, ADT knows not to set debuggable to true. Note that if you set it yourself in AndroidManifest.xml, it will stay set no matter what. The second thing to know is that the device must be put into USB Debug mode. To find this setting, go to the device's Settings screen, then choose Application, then Development. Make sure that Enable USB Debugging is checked.

While LogCat is very useful for watching log messages, you'll definitely want to have more control and more information about your application as it runs. There are two Eclipse perspectives you'll want to become familiar with: DDMS and Debug. DDMS stands for Dalvik Debug Monitor Server. This perspective gives you insight into the applications that are running on the emulator or device, the threads within an application, heap (or memory) within applications, plus a file explorer and an emulator controller so you can simulate GPS events, incoming phone calls, or SMS messages. The file explorer allows you to browse through the file system on the device, and even push or pull files between the device (or emulator) and your workstation. You can also force garbage collections, kill applications, and grab screen shots.

From within DDMS, you can select one of your running applications and connect to it for debugging. This will take you to the Debug perspective. You can also start debugging an application from the Java perspective by right-clicking on it and selecting Debug As ➤ Android Application; this will also take you to the Debug perspective. Either way, Eclipse has facilities for tracking threads, setting and clearing breakpoints in your code, inspecting variables, and stepping into or over statements. It's a powerful tool for troubleshooting application problems.

You can view the tools by selecting the DDMS or Debug perspective in Eclipse. You can also launch each tool by going to Window ➤ Show View ➤ Other ➤ Android. For example, if you want LogCat or the File Explorer in the Java perspective, you could simply do a Window ➤ Show View to add it.

You can also get detailed tracing information of your Android application by using the android.os.Debug class, which provides a start-tracing method (Debug.startMethodTracing("basename")) and a stop-tracing method (Debug.stopMethodTracing()). Android will create a trace file on the device (or emulator) on the SD card with a filename of "basename.trace". You can then copy the trace file to your workstation and view the tracer output using the traceview tool included in the Android SDK tools directory, with the trace filename as the only argument to traceview. Chapter 19 has extensive coverage of the SD card and how to pull files from it.

There are several other debugging tools you can use from a command line (or tools window). The Android Debug Bridge (adb) command allows you to install, update, and remove applications. You can start a shell on the emulator or device and from there you can run the subset of Linux commands that Android provides. For example, you can browse the file system, list processes, read the Log, even connect to SQLite databases and execute SQL commands.

Another powerful technique is to run the Emulator Console, which obviously only works with the emulator. To get started once the emulator is up and running, you'd type the following in a tools window

```
telnet localhost port#
```

where port# is where the emulator is listening. The port# is typically displayed in the emulator window title and is often a value such as 5554. Once the emulator console has launched, you type in commands to simulate GPS events, SMS messages, even battery and network status changes.

Launching the Emulator

Earlier we showed you how to launch the emulator from your project in Eclipse. In most cases, you'll want to launch the emulator first, then deploy and test your applications in a running emulator. To launch an emulator anytime, first go to the Android SDK and AVD Manager by either running the android program from the tools directory of the Android SDK or from the Window menu of Eclipse. Once in the Manager, click on Virtual devices on the left side, choose the desired AVD from the list on the right, and click Start.

When you click on the Start button, you get a Launch Options dialog (see Figure 2–17). This allows you to scale the size of the emulator's window and change the startup and shutdown options. When working with AVDs of small to medium screen devices, you will often just use the default screen size. But for large and extra-large screen sizes, such as with tablets, the default screen size may not fit nicely on the screen of your workstation. If that's the case, you can enable "Scale display to real size" and put in a value. This label is somewhat misleading, as tablets may have a different screen density than your workstation, and the emulator won't perfectly match the actual physical measurement of the emulator window on your screen. For example, on my workstation screen, when emulating a Honeycomb tablet with its 10 inch screen, a "real size" of 10 inches corresponds to a scale of .64 and a screen that is a bit larger on my workstation screen than 10 inches. Pick the value that works for you based on your screen size and screen density,

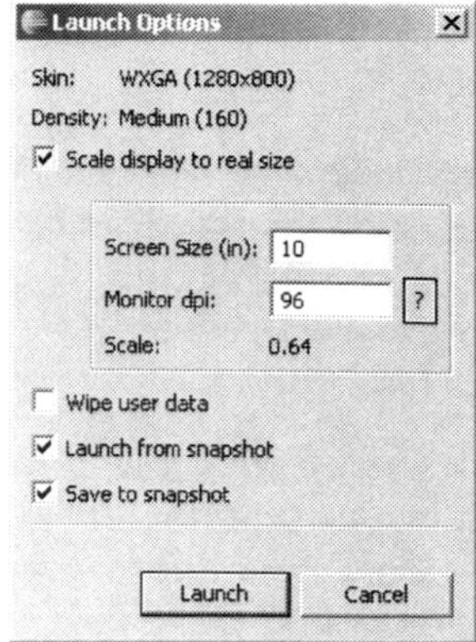

Figure 2–17. *The Launch Options dialog*

The Launch Options dialog is also where you can work with snapshots. Saving to a snapshot causes a somewhat longer delay when you exit the emulator. As the name suggests, you are writing out the current state of the emulator to a snapshot image file, which can then be used the next time you launch to avoid going through an entire Android boot-up sequence. Launching will go much faster if a snapshot is present, making the delay at save time well worth it—you basically pick up where you left off. If you want to start completely fresh, you can choose Wipe user data. You can also unselect Launch from snapshot to keep the user data and go through the boot-up sequence. Or you can create a snapshot that you like and enable *only* the Launch from snapshot option; this will reuse the snapshot over and over so your startup is fast and the shutdown is fast too, since it won't create a new snapshot image file every time it exits. The snapshot image file is stored in the same directory as the rest of the AVD image files. To use snapshots with an AVD, you must have enabled snapshots when you created the AVD.

StrictMode

Android 2.3 introduced a new debugging feature called StrictMode, and according to Google, this feature was used to make hundreds of improvements to the Google applications available for Android. So what does it do? It will report violations of policies related to threads and related to the virtual machine. If a policy violation is detected, you will get an alert, and that alert will include a stack trace to show you where your application was when the violation occurred. You can force a crash with the alert, or you can just log the alert and let your application carry on. The policy details can be difficult to determine, and we expect that Google will be adding policies as Android matures.

There are two types of policies currently available with StrictMode. The first policy relates to threads and is intended mostly to run against the main thread (also known as the UI thread). It is not good practice to do disk reads and writes from the main thread, nor is it good practice to perform network accesses from the main thread. Google has added StrictMode hooks into the disk and network code; if you enable StrictMode for one of your threads, and that thread performs disk or network access, you can be alerted. You get to choose which aspects of the ThreadPolicy you want to alert on, and you get to choose the alert method. Some of the violations you can look for include custom slow calls, disk reads, disk writes, and network accesses. For alerts, you can choose to write to LogCat, display a dialog, flash the screen, write to the DropBox log file, or crash the application. The most common choices are to write to LogCat or to crash the application. Listing 2–9 shows a sample of what it takes to set up StrictMode for thread policies.

Listing 2–9. ***Setting StrictMode's ThreadPolicy***

```
StrictMode.setThreadPolicy(new StrictMode.ThreadPolicy.Builder()
    .detectDiskReads()
    .detectDiskWrites()
    .detectNetwork()
    .penaltyLog()
    .build());
```

Note that the Builder class makes it really easy to set up StrictMode. The Builder methods that define the policy all return a reference to the Builder object, so these methods can be chained together as shown in Listing 2–9. The last method call, build(), returns a ThreadPolicy object that is the argument expected by the setThreadPolicy() method of StrictMode. Note that setThreadPolicy() is a static method so you don't need to actually instantiate a StrictMode object. Internally, setThreadPolicy() uses the current thread for the policy, so subsequent thread actions will be evaluated against the ThreadPolicy and alerted as necessary. In this sample code, the policy is defined to alert on disk reads, disk writes, and network accesses with messages to LogCat. Instead of the specific detect methods, you could use the detectAll() method instead. You can also use different or additional penalty methods, too. For instance, you could use penaltyDeath() to cause the application to crash once it has written StrictMode alert messages to LogCat (as a result of the penaltyLog() method call).

Because you enable StrictMode on a thread, once you've enabled it, you don't need to keep enabling it. Therefore, you could enable StrictMode at the beginning of your main activity's onCreate() method, which runs on the main thread, and it would then be enabled for everything that happens on that main thread. Depending on what sorts of violations you want to look for, the first activity may be soon enough to enable StrictMode. You could also enable it in your application by extending the Application class and adding StrictMode setup to the application's onCreate() method. Anything that runs on a thread could conceivably set up StrictMode, but you certainly don't need to call the setup code from everywhere; once is enough.

Similar to ThreadPolicy, StrictMode has a VmPolicy. VmPolicy can check for memory leaks if a SQLite object is finalized before it has been closed, or if any Closeable object is finalized before it has been closed. A VmPolicy is created via a similar Builder class, as shown in Listing 2–10. One difference between a VmPolicy and a ThreadPolicy is that a VmPolicy can't alert via a dialog.

Listing 2–10. *Setting StrictMode's VmPolicy*

```
StrictMode.setVmPolicy(new StrictMode.VmPolicy.Builder()
    .detectLeakedSqlLiteObjects()
    .penaltyLog()
    .penaltyDeath()
    .build());
```

Because the setup happens on a thread, StrictMode will find violations even as control flows from object to object to object. When a violation occurs, you may be surprised to realize that the code is running on the main thread, but the stack trace is there to help you follow along to uncover how it happened. You can then take steps to resolve the issue to move that code to its own background thread. Or you could decide that it's okay to leave things the way they are. It's up to you. Of course, you will probably want to turn off StrictMode when your application goes to production; you don't want it crashing on your users because of an alert.

There are a couple of ways to go about turning off StrictMode for a production application. The most straightforward way is to remove the calls, but that makes it more difficult to continue to do development on it. You could always define an application-level boolean and test it before calling the StrictMode code. Setting the value of the boolean to false just before you release your application to the world would effectively disable StrictMode. A more elegant method is to take advantage of the debug mode of the application, as defined in `AndroidManifest.xml`. One of the attributes for the `<application>` tag in this file is `android:debuggable`. This value can be set to true when you want to debug an application, and it results in the `ApplicationInfo` object getting a flag set, which you can then read in code. Listing 2–11 shows how you might use this to your advantage, so that when the application is in debug mode, StrictMode is active (and when not it's not in debug mode, StrictMode is not active).

Listing 2–11. ***Setting StrictMode Only for Debug***

```
// Return if this application is not in debug mode
ApplicationInfo appInfo = context.getApplicationInfo();
int appFlags = appInfo.flags;
if ((appFlags & ApplicationInfo.FLAG_DEBUGGABLE) != 0) {
    // Do StrictMode setup here
}
```

When developing with Eclipse, ADT sets the debuggable attribute automatically for you, which makes it even easier to manage. When you're deploying from Eclipse to the emulator or directly to a device, Eclipse will set this attribute to true, which would therefore enable StrictMode in the previous code. When you're exporting your application to create a production version, ADT will set it to false. Be aware that if you set this attribute yourself, ADT won't change it.

All of this is well and good, but it doesn't work on Android prior to version 2.3. To use StrictMode explicitly, you have to deploy to an environment running Android 2.3 or later. If you deploy to anything older than 2.3, you're going to get verify errors because this class just doesn't exist prior to Android 2.3.

To use StrictMode with older versions of Android (i.e., prior to 2.3), you can utilize reflection techniques so you can indirectly invoke StrictMode methods if they are available and fail gracefully if they are not. The simplest thing you can do is shown in Listing 2–12; you invoke a special method created just for dealing with older versions of Android.

Listing 2–12. ***Using StrictMode with Reflection***

```
try {
   Class sMode = Class.forName("android.os.StrictMode");
   Method enableDefaults = sMode.getMethod("enableDefaults");
   enableDefaults.invoke(null);
}
catch(Exception e) {
    // StrictMode not supported on this device, punt
    Log.v("StrictMode", "... not supported. Skipping...");
}
```

This determines if the StrictMode class exists, and if it does, invokes the `enableDefaults()` method on it. If StrictMode is not found, your catch block is invoked with a `ClassNotFoundException`. You shouldn't get any exceptions if StrictMode does exist, since enableDefaults() is one of its methods. The enableDefaults() method sets up StrictMode to detect everything and to write any violations to LogCat. Because this StrictMode method you're calling is a static method, you specify null as the first argument when you invoke it.

There may be times when you don't want all violations to be reported. It's perfectly fine to set up StrictMode on threads other than the main thread, and that's when you might choose to alert on less than everything. For example, you may be fine with doing disk reads on the thread you're monitoring. If this is the case, you can either not call detectDiskReads() on the Builder, or you could call detectAll(), then permitDiskReads() on the Builder. There are similar permit methods for the other policy options. But if you want to do this on Android versions prior to 2.3, is there a way? Of course there is!

If StrictMode is not available for your application, a VerifyError will be thrown if you try to access it. If you wrap StrictMode in a class and then catch the error, you can ignore when StrictMode is not available, and get it when it is. Listing 2–13 shows a sample StrictModeWrapper class that you can add to your application, and Listing 2–14 shows what the code inside your application would look like to set up StrictMode.

Listing 2–13. *Using StrictMode on pre-2.3 Android*

```
import android.content.Context;
import android.content.pm.ApplicationInfo;
import android.os.StrictMode;

public class StrictModeWrapper {
    public static void init(Context context) {
        // check if android:debuggable is set to true
        int appFlags = context.getApplicationInfo().flags;
        if ((appFlags & ApplicationInfo.FLAG_DEBUGGABLE) != 0) {
            StrictMode.setThreadPolicy(new StrictMode.ThreadPolicy.Builder()
                .detectDiskReads()
                .detectDiskWrites()
                .detectNetwork()
                .penaltyLog()
                .build());
            StrictMode.setVmPolicy(new StrictMode.VmPolicy.Builder()
                .detectLeakedSqlLiteObjects()
                .penaltyLog()
                .penaltyDeath()
                .build());
        }
    }
}
```

You can see how this is just like your code from before, except that you're combining everything you've learned so far. And finally, in order to setup StrictMode from your application, you only need to add the code shown in Listing 2–14.

Listing 2–14. *Invoking StrictMode with pre-2.3 Android*

```
try {
    StrictModeWrapper.init(this);
}
catch(Throwable throwable) {
    Log.v("StrictMode", "... is not available. Punting...");
}
```

Note that `this` is the local context of whatever object you're in, such as from within the `onCreate()` method of your main activity. The code of Listing 2–14 will work on any release of Android.

As a reader exercise, go into Eclipse and make a copy of the Notepad example from earlier in this chapter. Then add a new class under the `src` folder using the code in Listing 2–13. Within the `onCreate()` method of `NotesList.java`, add code like in Listing 2–14, then run the program on a pre-2.3 version of Android in the emulator, then on Android 2.3 or later in the emulator. When StrictMode is not available, you should see LogCat messages that indicate StrictMode is not present, but the application should continue to run well. When StrictMode is available, you should see the occasional violation messages in LogCat as you use the Notepad application.

References

Here are some helpful references to topics you may wish to explore further.

- `http://developer.motorola.com/docstools/` is the Motorola site where you can find device add-ons as well as other tools for developing Android for Motorola handsets, including the MOTODEV Studio, an alternative to Eclipse.
- `http://developer.htc.com/` is the HTC site for Android developers.
- `http://innovator.samsungmobile.com/galaxyTab.do` is the Samsung page for Android developers and includes the Android SDK add-on for the Samsung Galaxy Tab tablet device.
- `http://developer.android.com/guide/developing/tools/index.html` features developer documentation for the Android debugging tools described previously.
- `http://appinventor.googlelabs.com/about/index.html` is the site for App Inventor, another alternative IDE for creating Android applications. This one is from Google Labs and it's geared for non-programmers. Applications are laid out graphically, and so is the business logic behind the UI.
- `http://code.google.com/p/android-ui-utils/` contains links to useful tools such as Android Asset Studio, which provides an online tool for creating different types of Android icons. Note that you need to use the Chrome browser to run Android Asset Studio.

- `http://www.droiddraw.org/` is a UI designer for Android applications that uses drag-and-drop to build layouts.

Summary

In this chapter, we showed you how to set up your development environment for building Android applications. We discussed some of the basic building blocks of the Android APIs and introduced views, activities, intents, content providers, and services. We then analyzed the Notepad application in terms of the aforementioned building blocks and application components. Next, we talked about the importance of the Android application lifecycle. Finally, we introduced you to some of the Android SDK's debugging tools that integrate with the Eclipse IDE.

And so begins the foundation of your Android development. The next chapter will discuss resources in great detail.

Chapter 3

Understanding Android Resources

In Chapter 2, we gave you an overview of an Android application and a quick look at some of its underlying concepts. You also learned about the Android SDK, the Eclipse Android Development Tool (ADT) and how to run your applications on emulators identified by Android virtual devices (AVDs).

In this and the next few chapters, we'll follow that introduction with an in-depth look at Android SDK fundamentals and cover resources, content providers, and intents. These three concepts are fundamental to understanding Android programming and should place you on a solid foundation for the material in subsequent chapters.

Android depends on resources for defining UI components in a declarative manner. This declarative approach is not that dissimilar to the way HTML uses declarative tags to define its UI. In this sense, Android is quite forward thinking in its approach to UI development. Android further allows these resources to be localized. In this chapter, we will cover the variety of resources that are available in Android and how to use them.

Understanding Resources

Resources play a key role in Android architecture. A resource in Android is a file (like a music file) or a value (like the title of a dialog box) that is bound to an executable application. These files and values are bound to the executable in such a way that you can change them without recompiling the application.

Familiar examples of resources include strings, colors, and bitmaps. Instead of hard-coding strings in an application, for example, you can use their IDs instead. This indirection lets you change the text of the string resource without changing the source code.

There are many, many resource types in Android. We will cover a number of these resources in this chapter. Let's start this discussion of resources with a very common resource: a string.

String Resources

Android allows you to define strings in one or more XML resource files. These XML files containing string-resource definitions reside in the /res/values subdirectory. The names of the XML files are arbitrary, although you will commonly see the file name as strings.xml. Listing 3–1 shows an example of a string-resource file.

Listing 3–1. *Example strings.xml File*

```
<?xml version="1.0" encoding="utf-8"?>
<resources>
    <string name="hello">hello</string>
    <string name="app_name">hello appname</string>
</resources>
```

> **NOTE:** Please note that in some releases of Eclipse the <resources> node needs to be qualified with an "xmlns" specification. It doesn't seem to matter what the xmlns is pointing to as long as it is there. The following two variations of it seem to work
>
> ```
> <resources xmlns="http://schemas.android.com/apk/res/android" >
> ```
>
> or
>
> ```
> <resources xmlns="default namespace" >
> ```

When this file is created or updated, the Eclipse ADT plug-in will automatically create or update a Java class in your application's root package called R.java with unique IDs for the two string resources specified.

Notice the placement of this R.java file in the following example. We have given a high-level directory structure for a project like, say, MyProject.

```
\MyProject
   \src
         \com\mycompany\android\my-root-package
         \com\mycompany\android\my-root-package\another-package
   \gen
        \com\mycompany\android\my-root-package\R.java
   \assets
   \res
   \AndroidManifest.xml
…..etc
```

> **NOTE:** Regardless of the number of resource files, there is only one R.java file.

For the string-resource file in Listing 3–1, the updated R.java file would have the entries in Listing 3–2.

Listing 3–2. *Example of R.java*

```
package com.mycompany.android.my-root-package;
public final class R {
   ...other entries depending on your project and application

    public static final class string
   {
      ...other entries depending on your project and application

        public static final int hello=0x7f040000;
        public static final int app_name=0x7f040001;

      ...other entries depending on your project and application
    }
   ...other entries depending on your project and application
}
```

Notice, first, how R.java defines a top-level class in the root package: public static final class R. Within that outer class of R, Android defines an inner class, namely, static final class string. R.java creates this inner static class as a namespace to hold string resource IDs.

The two static final ints defined with variable names hello and app_name are the resource IDs that represent the corresponding string resources. You could use these resource IDs anywhere in the source code through the following code structure:

```
R.string.hello
```

Note that these generated IDs point to ints rather than strings. Most methods that take strings also take these resource identifiers as inputs. Android will resolve those ints to strings where necessary.

It is merely a convention that most sample applications define all strings in one strings.xml file. Android takes any number of arbitrary files as long as the structure of the XML file looks like Listing 3–1 and the files reside in the /res/values subdirectory.

The structure of this file is easy to follow. You have the root node of <resources> followed by one or more of its child elements of <string>. Each <string> element or node has a property called name that will end up as the id attribute in R.java.

To see that multiple string resource files are allowed in this subdirectory, you can place another file with the following content in the same subdirectory and call it strings1.xml (see Listing 3–3).

Listing 3–3. *Example of an Additional strings.xml File*

```
<?xml version="1.0" encoding="utf-8"?>
<resources>
    <string name="hello1">hello 1</string>
    <string name="app_name1">hello appname 1</string>
</resources>
```

The Eclipse ADT plug-in will validate the uniqueness of these IDs at compile time and place them in R.java as two additional constants: R.string.hello1 and R.string.app_name1.

Layout Resources

In Android, the view for a screen is often loaded from an XML file as a resource. These XML files are called layout resources. A *layout resource* is a key resource used in Android UI programming. Consider the code segment in Listing 3–4 for a sample Android activity.

Listing 3–4. *Using a Layout File*

```
public class HelloWorldActivity extends Activity
{
    @Override
    public void onCreate(Bundle savedInstanceState)
    {
        super.onCreate(savedInstanceState);
        setContentView(R.layout.main);
        TextView tv = (TextView)this.findViewById(R.id.text1);
        tv.setText("Try this text instead");
    }
    ...
}
```

The line setContentView(R.layout.main) points out that there is a static class called R.layout, and within that class, there is a constant called main (an integer) pointing to a View defined by an XML layout resource file. The name of the XML file is main.xml, which needs to be placed in the resources' layout subdirectory. In other words, this statement expects the programmer to create the file /res/layout/main.xml and place the necessary layout definition in that file. The contents of the main.xml layout file could look like Listing 3–5.

Listing 3–5. *Example main.xml Layout File*

```
<?xml version="1.0" encoding="utf-8"?>
<LinearLayout xmlns:android="http://schemas.android.com/apk/res/android"
    android:orientation="vertical"
    android:layout_width="fill_parent"
    android:layout_height="fill_parent"
    >
<TextView    android:id="@+id/text1"
    android:layout_width="fill_parent"
    android:layout_height="wrap_content"
    android:text="@string/hello"
    />
 <Button    android:id="@+id/b1"
    android:layout_width="fill_parent"
    android:layout_height="wrap_content"
    android:text="@string/hello"
   />
</LinearLayout>
```

The layout file in Listing 3–5 defines a root node called `LinearLayout`, which contains a `TextView` followed by a `Button`. A `LinearLayout` lays out its children vertically or horizontally—vertically, in this example.

You will need to define a separate layout file for each screen (or activity). More accurately, each layout needs a dedicated file. If you are painting two screens, you will likely need two layout files, such as `/res/layout/screen1_layout.xml` and `/res/layout/screen2_layout.xml`.

> **NOTE:** Each file in the `/res/layout/` subdirectory generates a unique constant based on the name of the file (extension excluded). With layouts, what matters is the number of files; with string resources, what matters is the number of individual string resources *inside* the files.

For example, if you have two files under `/res/layout/` called `file1.xml` and `file2.xml`, you'll have the following entries in `R.java`:

Listing 3–6. *Multiple Constants for Multiple Layout Files*

```
public static final class layout {
  .... any other files
    public static final int file1=0x7f030000;
    public static final int file2=0x7f030001;
}
```

The views defined in these layout files such as a `TextView` (see Listing 3–5) are accessible in Java code through their resource IDs generated in `R.java`:

```
TextView tv = (TextView)this.findViewById(R.id.text1);
tv.setText("Try this text instead");
```

In this example, you locate the `TextView` by using the `findViewById` method of the `Activity` class. The constant `R.id.text1` corresponds to the ID defined for the `TextView`. The `id` for the `TextView` in the layout file is as follows:

```
<TextView android:id="@+id/text1"
..
</TextView>
```

The attribute value for the `id` attribute indicates that a constant called `text1` will be used to uniquely identify this view among other views hosted by that activity. The plus sign (+) in `@+id/text1` means that the ID `text1` will be created if it doesn't exist already. There is more to this resource ID syntax. We'll talk about that next.

Resource Reference Syntax

Irrespective of the type of resource (string and layout are the two we have covered so far), all Android resources are identified (or referenced) by their `id`s in Java source code. The syntax you use to allocate an `id` to a resource in the XML file is called *resource-reference syntax*. The `id` attribute syntax in the previous example `@+id/text1` has the following formal structure:

```
@[package:]type/name
```

The type corresponds to one of the resource-type namespaces available in R.java, some of which follow:

- R.drawable
- R.id
- R.layout
- R.string
- R.attr
- R.plural
- R.array

The corresponding types in XML resource-reference syntax are as follows:

- drawable
- id
- layout
- string
- attr
- plurals
- string-array

The name part in the resource reference @[package:]type/name is the name given to the resource (for example, text1 in Listing 3–5); it also gets represented as an int constant in R.java.

If you don't specify any package in the syntax @[package:]type/name, the pair type/name will be resolved based on local resources and the application's local R.java package.

If you specify android:type/name, the reference ID will be resolved using the package android and specifically through the android.R.java file. You can use any Java package name in place of the package placeholder to locate the right R.java file to resolve the reference. Based on this information, let's analyze a examples. As you go through Listing 3–7, note that the left-hand side of the ID android:id is not part of the syntax. "android:id" is just how you allocate an ID to a control like TextView.

Listing 3–7. ***Exploring Resource Reference Syntax***

```
<TextView  android:id="text">
// Compile error, as id will not take raw text strings

<TextView  android:id="@text">
// wrong syntax. @text is missing a type name
// it should have been @id/text or @+id/text or @string/string1
// you will get an error "No Resource type specified
```

```
<TextView  android:id="@id/text">
//Error: No Resource found that matches id "text"
//Unless you have taken care to define "text" as an ID before

<TextView  android:id="@android:id/text">
// Error: Resource is not public
// indicating that there is no such id in android.R.id
// Of course this would be valid if Android R.java were to define
// an id with this name

<TextView  android:id="@+id/text">
//Success: Creates an id called "text" in the local package's R.java
```

In the syntax "`@+id/text`", the + sign has a special meaning. It tells android that the ID `text` may not already exist and, if that's the case, to create a new one and name it as `text`.

Defining Your Own Resource IDs for Later Use

The general pattern for allocating an `id` is either to create a new one or to use the one created by the Android package. However, it is possible to create `id`s beforehand and use them later in your own packages.

The line `<TextView  android:id="@+id/text">` in the preceding code segment indicates that an `id` named `text` is going to be used if one already exists. If the `id` doesn't exist, a new one is going to be created. So when might an `id` such as `text` already exist in `R.java` for it to be reused?

You might be inclined to put a constant like `R.id.text` in `R.java`, but `R.java` is not editable. Even if it were, it gets regenerated every time something gets changed, added, or deleted in the `/res/*` subdirectory.

The solution is to use a resource tag called `item` to define an `id` without attaching to any particular resource. Listing 3–8 shows an example.

Listing 3–8. *Predefining an ID*

```
<resources>
<item type="id" name="text"/>
</resources>
```

The `type` refers to the type of resource—`id` in this case. Once this `id` is in place, the `View` definition in Listing 3–9 would work.

Listing 3–9. *Reusing a Predefined ID*

```
<TextView android:id="@id/text">
..
</TextView>
```

Compiled and Uncompiled Android Resources

Android supports resources primarily through two types of files: XML files and raw files (examples of which include images, audio, and video). Even within XML files, you have seen that in some cases the resources are defined as values inside an XML file (strings, for example), and sometimes, an XML file as a whole is a resource (a layout resource file to quote).

As a further distinction within the set of XML files, you'll find two types: one gets compiled into binary format, and the other gets copied as-is to the device. The examples you have seen so far—the string resource XML files and the layout resource XML files—get compiled into binary format before becoming part of the installable package. These XML files have predefined formats where XML nodes are translated to IDs.

You can also choose some XML files to have their own free format structure; these will not get interpreted and will have resource IDs generated. However, you do want them compiled to binary formats and also have the comfort of localization. To do this, you can place these XML files in the `/res/xml/` subdirectory to have them compiled into binary format. In this case, you would use Android-supplied XML readers to read the XML nodes.

But if you place files, including XML files, in the `/res/raw/` directory instead, they don't get compiled into binary format. You must use explicit stream-based APIs to read these files. Audio and video files fall into this category.

> **NOTE:** It is worth noting that, because the `raw` directory is part of the `/res/*` hierarchy, even these raw audio and video files can take advantage of localization like all other resources.

As we mentioned in Table 2-1 in the previous chapter, resource files are housed in various subdirectories based on their type. Here are some important subdirectories in the `/res` folder and the types of resources they host:

- `anim`: Compiled animation files
- `drawable`: Bitmaps
- `layout`: UI and view definitions
- `values`: Arrays, colors, dimensions, strings, and styles
- `xml`: Compiled arbitrary XML files
- `raw`: Noncompiled raw files

The resource compiler in the Android Asset Packaging Tool (AAPT) compiles all the resources except the `raw` resources and places them all into the final `.apk` file. This file, which contains the Android application's code and resources, correlates to Java's `.jar` file ("apk" stands for "Android package"). The `.apk` file is what gets installed onto the device.

NOTE: Although the XML resource parser allows resource names such as `hello-string`, you will see a compile-time error in `R.java`. You can fix this by renaming your resource to `hello_string` (replacing the dash with an underscore).

Enumerating Key Android Resources

Now that we've been through the basics of resources, we'll enumerate some of the other key resources that Android supports, their XML representations, and the way they're used in Java code. (You can use this section as a quick reference as you write resource files for each resource.) To start with, take a quick glance at the types of resources and what they are used for (see Table 3–1).

Table 3–1. *Types of Resources*

Resource Type	Location	Description
Colors	`/res/values/any-file`	Represents color identifiers pointing to color codes. These resource IDs are exposed in `R.java` as `R.color.*`. The XML node in the file is `/resources/color`.
Strings	`/res/values/any-file`	Represents string resources. String resources allow Java-formatted strings and raw HTML in addition to simple strings. These resource IDs are exposed in `R.java` as `R.string.*`. The XML node in the file is `/resources/string`.
String arrays	`/res/values/any-file`	Represents a resource that is an array of strings. These resource IDs are exposed in `R.java` as `R.array.*`. The XML node in the file is `/resources/string-array`.
Plurals	`/res/values/any-file`	Represents a suitable collection of strings based on the value of a quantity. The quantity is a number. In various languages, the way you write a sentence depends on whether you refer to no objects, one object, few objects, or many objects. The resource IDs are exposed in `R.java` as `R.plural.*`. The XML node in the value file is `/resources/plurals`.
Dimensions	`/res/values/any-file`	Represents dimensions or sizes of various elements or views in Android. Supports pixels, inches, millimeters, density independent pixels, and scale independent pixels. These Resource ids are exposed in `R.java` as `R.dimen.*` . The XML node in the file is `/resources/dimen`.

Resource Type	Location	Description
Images	/res/drawable/multiple-files	Represents image resources. Supported images include .jpg, .gif, .png, etc. Each image is in a separate file and gets its own ID based on the file name. These resource ids are exposed in R.java as R.drawable.*. The image support also includes an image type called a stretchable image that allows portions of an image to stretch while other portions of that image stay static. The stretchable image is also known as a 9-patch file (.9.png).
Color drawables	/res/values/any-file also /res/drawable/multiple-files	Represents rectangles of colors to be used as view backgrounds or general drawables like bitmaps. This can be used in lieu of specifying a single colored bitmap as a background. In Java, this will be equivalent to creating a colored rectangle and setting it as a background for a view. The <drawable> value tag in the values subdirectory supports this. These resource IDs are exposed in R.java as R.drawable.*. The XML node in the file is /resources/drawable. Android also supports rounded rectangles and gradient rectangles through XML files placed in /res/drawable with the root XML tag of <shape>. These resource IDs are also exposed in R.java as R.drawable.*. Each file name in this case translates to a unique drawable ID.
Arbitrary XML files	/res/xml/*.xml	Android allows arbitrary XML files as resources. These files will be compiled by the AAPT compiler. These resource IDs are exposed in R.java as R.xml.*.
Arbitrary raw resources	/res/raw/*.*	Android allows arbitrary *noncompiled* binary or text files under this directory. Each file gets a unique resource ID. These resource IDs are exposed in R.java as R.raw.* .
Arbitrary raw assets	/assets/*.*/*.*	Android allows arbitrary files in arbitrary subdirectories starting at /assets subdirectory. These are not really resources, just raw files. This directory, unlike the /res resources subdirectory, allows an arbitrary depth of subdirectories. These files do not generate any resource IDs. You have to use relative pathname starting at and excluding /assets.

Each of the resources specified in this table is further elaborated in the following sections with XML and java code snippets.

NOTE: Looking at the nature of ID generation, it appears—although we haven't seen it officially stated anywhere—that there are IDs generated based on file names if those XML files are anywhere but in the /res/values subdirectory. If they are in the values subdirectory, only the contents of the files are looked at to generate the IDs.

String Arrays

You can specify an array of strings as a resource in any file under the /res/values subdirectory. You will use an XML node called string-array. This node is a child node of resources just like the string resource node. Listing 3–10 is an example of specifying an array in a resource file.

Listing 3–10. *Specifying String Arrays*

```
<resources ....>
......Other resources
<string-array name="test_array">
    <item>one</item>
    <item>two</item>
    <item>three</item>
</string-array>
......Other resources
</resources>
```

Once you have this string array resource definition, you can retrieve this array in the Java code as shown in Listing 3–11.

Listing 3–11. *Specifying String Arrays*

```
//Get access to Resources object from an Activity
Resources res = your-activity.getResources();
String strings[] = res.getStringArray(R.array.test_array);

//Print strings
for (String s: strings)
{
    Log.d("example", s);
}
```

Plurals

The resource plurals is a set of strings. These strings are various ways of saying a numerical quantity, for example, how many eggs there are in a nest. Consider an example:

```
There is 1 egg.
There are 2 eggs.
There are 0 eggs.
There are 100 eggs.
```

Notice how the sentences are identical for numbers 2, 0, and 100. However, the sentence for 1 egg is different. Android allows you to represent this variation as a `plurals` resource. Listing 3–12 shows how you would represent these two variations based on quantity in a resource file.

Listing 3–12. *Specifying String Arrays*

```
<resources…>
<plurals name="eggs_in_a_nest_text">
    <item quantity="one">There is 1 egg</item>
    <item quantity="other">There are %d eggs</item>
</plurals>
</resources>
```

Notice how the two variations are represented as two different strings under one plural. Now, you can use Java code, as shown in Listing 3–13, to use this plural to print a string given a quantity. The first parameter to `getQuantityString()` method is the plurals resource id. The second parameter selects the string to be used. When the value of the quantity is 1, we just use the string as-is. When the value is not 1, we must supply a third parameter whose value is to be placed where %d is. You must always have at least 3 parameters if you use a formatting string in your plurals resource.

Listing 3–13. *Specifying String Arrays*

```
Resources res = your-activity.getResources();
String s1 = res.getQuantityString(R.plurals.eggs_in_a_nest_text, 0,0);
String s2 = res.getQuantityString(R.plurals.eggs_in_a_nest_text, 1,1);
String s3 = res.getQuantityString(R.plurals.eggs_in_a_nest_text, 2,2);
String s4 = res.getQuantityString(R.plurals.eggs_in_a_nest_text, 10,10);
```

Given this code, each quantity will result in an appropriate string that is suitable for its plurality.

However, what other possibilities exist for the `quantity` attribute of the preceding `item` node? We strongly recommend you read the source code of `Resources.java` and `PluralRules.java` in the Android source code distribution to truly understand this. Our research link on resources at the end of this chapter has extracts from these source files.

The bottom line is that, for the `en` (English) locale, the only two possible values are `"one"` and `"other"`. This is further true for all other languages as well except for `cs` (Czech), in which case the values are `"one"` (for 1), `"few"` (for 2 to 4), and `"other"` for the rest.

More on String Resources

We covered string resources briefly in earlier sections. Let's revisit them to provide additional nuances, including HTML strings and how to substitute variables in string resources.

> **NOTE:** Most UI frameworks allow string resources. However, unlike other UI frameworks, Android offers the ability to quickly associate IDs with string resources through `R.java`, so using strings as resources is that much easier in Android.

We'll start by showing how you can define normal strings, quoted strings, HTML strings, and substitutable strings in an XML resource file (see Listing 3–14).

Listing 3–14. *XML Syntax for Defining String Resources*

```
<resources>
    <string name="simple_string">simple string</string>
    <string name="quoted_string">"quoted 'xyz' string"</string>
    <string name="double_quoted_string">\"double quotes\"</string>
    <string name="java_format_string">
          hello %2$s Java format string. %1$s again
     </string>
     <string name="tagged_string">
         Hello <b><i>Slanted Android</i></b>, You are bold.
     </string>
</resources>
```

This XML string resource file needs to be in the /res/values subdirectory. The name of the file is arbitrary.

Notice that quoted strings need to be either escaped or placed in alternate quotes. The string definitions also allow standard Java string-formatting sequences.

Android also allows child XML elements such as <b>, <i>, and other simple text-formatting HTML within the <string> node. You can use this compound HTML string to style the text before painting in a text view.

The Java examples in Listing 3–15 illustrate each usage.

Listing 3–15. *Using String Resources in Java Code*

```
//Read a simple string and set it in a text view
String simpleString = activity.getString(R.string.simple_string);
textView.setText(simpleString);

//Read a quoted string and set it in a text view
String quotedString = activity.getString(R.string.quoted_string);
textView.setText(quotedString);

//Read a double quoted string and set it in a text view
String doubleQuotedString = activity.getString(R.string.double_quoted_string);
textView.setText(doubleQuotedString);

//Read a Java format string
String javaFormatString = activity.getString(R.string.java_format_string);
//Convert the formatted string by passing in arguments
String substitutedString = String.format(javaFormatString, "Hello" , "Android");
//set the output in a text view
textView.setText(substitutedString);

//Read an html string from the resource and set it in a text view
String htmlTaggedString = activity.getString(R.string.tagged_string);
//Convert it to a text span so that it can be set in a text view
//android.text.Html class allows painting of "html" strings
//This is strictly an Android class and does not support all html tags
Spanned textSpan = android.text.Html.fromHtml(htmlTaggedString);
//Set it in a text view
textView.setText(textSpan);
```

Once you've defined the strings as resources, you can set them directly on a view such as TextView in the XML layout definition for that TextView. Listing 3–16 shows an example where an HTML string is set as the text content of a TextView.

Listing 3–16. *Using String Resources in XML*

```
<TextView android:layout_width="fill_parent"
          android:layout_height="wrap_content"
          android:gravity="center_horizontal"
          android:text="@string/tagged_string"/>
```

TextView automatically realizes that this string is an HTML string and honors its formatting accordingly, which is nice because you can quickly set attractive text in your views as part of the layout.

Color Resources

As you can with string resources, you can use reference identifiers to indirectly reference colors as well. Doing this enables Android to localize colors and apply themes. Once you've defined and identified colors in resource files, you can access them in Java code through their IDs. Whereas string-resource IDs are available under the <*your-package*>.R.string namespace, the color IDs are available under the <*your-package*>.R.color namespace.

Android also defines a base set of colors in its own resource files. These IDs, by extension, are accessible through the Android android.R.color namespace. Check out this URL to learn the color constants available in the android.R.color namespace:

http://code.google.com/android/reference/android/R.color.html

See Listing 3–17 for some examples of specifying color in an XML resource file.

Listing 3–17. *XML Syntax for Defining Color Resources*

```
<resources>
    <color name="red">#f00</color>
    <color name="blue">#0000ff</color>
    <color name="green">#f0f0</color>
    <color name="main_back_ground_color">#ffffff00</color>
</resources>
```

The entries in Listing 3–17 need to be in a file residing in the /res/values subdirectory. The name of the file is arbitrary, meaning the file name can be anything you choose. Android will read all the files and then process them and look for individual nodes such as resources and color to figure out individual IDs.

Listing 3–18 shows an example of using a color resource in Java code.

Listing 3–18. *Color Resources in Java code*

```
int mainBackGroundColor
     =  activity.getResources.getColor(R.color.main_back_ground_color);
```

Listing 3–19 shows how you would use a color resource in a view definition.

Listing 3–19. *Using Colors in View Definitions*

```
<TextView android:layout_width="fill_parent"
          android:layout_height="wrap_content"
          android:textColor="@color/red"
          android:text="Sample Text to Show Red Color"/>
```

Dimension Resources

Pixels, inches, and points are all examples of dimensions that can play a part in XML layouts or Java code. You can use these dimension resources to style and localize Android UIs without changing the source code.

Listing 3–20 shows how you can use dimension resources in XML.

Listing 3–20. *XML Syntax for Defining Dimension Resources*

```
<resources>
    <dimen name="mysize_in_pixels">1px</dimen>
    <dimen name="mysize_in_dp">5dp</dimen>
    <dimen name="medium_size">100sp</dimen>
</resources>
```

You can specify the dimensions in any of the following units:

- px: Pixels
- in: Inches
- mm: Millimeters
- pt: Points
- dp: Density-independent pixels based on a 160-dpi (pixel density per inch) screen (dimensions adjust to screen density)
- sp: Scale-independent pixels (dimensions that allow for user sizing; helpful for use in fonts)

In Java, you need to access your Resources object instance to retrieve a dimension. You can do this by calling getResources on an activity object (see Listing 3–21). Once you have the Resources object, you can ask it to locate the dimension using the dimension ID (again, see Listing 3–21).

Listing 3–21. *Using Dimension Resources in Java Code*

```
float dimen = activity.getResources().getDimension(R.dimen.mysize_in_pixels);
```

> **NOTE:** The Java method call uses Dimension (full word) whereas the R.java namespace uses the shortened version dimen to represent "dimension."

As in Java, the resource reference for a dimension in XML uses dimen as opposed to the full word "dimension" (see Listing 3–22).

Listing 3–22. *Using Dimension Resources in XML*

```
<TextView android:layout_width="fill_parent"
          android:layout_height="wrap_content"
          android:textSize="@dimen/medium_size"/>
```

Image Resources

Android generates resource IDs for image files placed in the `/res/drawable` subdirectory. The supported image types include `.gif`, `.jpg`, and `.png`. Each image file in this directory generates a unique ID from its base file name. If the image file name is `sample_image.jpg`, for example, then the resource ID generated will be `R.drawable.sample_image`.

> **CAUTION:** You'll get an error if you have two file names with the same base file name. Also, subdirectories underneath `/res/drawable` will be ignored. Any files placed under those subdirectories will not be read.

You can reference these images available in `/res/drawable` in other XML layout definitions, as shown in Listing 3–23.

Listing 3–23. *Using Image Resources in XML*

```
<Button
      android:id="@+id/button1"
      android:layout_width="fill_parent"
      android:layout_height="wrap_content"
      android:text="Dial"
      android:background="@drawable/sample_image"
/>
```

You can also retrieve the image programmatically using Java and set it yourself against a UI object like a button (see Listing 3–24).

Listing 3–24. *Using Image Resources in Java*

```
//Call getDrawable to get the image
BitmapDrawable d = activity.getResources().getDrawable(R.drawable.sample_image);

//You can use the drawable then to set the background
button.setBackgroundDrawable(d);

//or you can set the background directly from the Resource Id
button.setBackgroundResource(R.drawable.sample_image);
```

> **NOTE:** These background methods go all the way back to the `View` class. As a result, most of the UI controls have this background support.

Android also supports a special type of image called a *stretchable* image. This is a kind of `.png` where parts of the image can be specified as static and stretchable. Android provides a tool called the Draw 9-patch tool to specify these regions (you can read more about it at http://developer.android.com/guide/developing/tools/draw9patch.html).

Once the .png image is made available, you can use it as any other image. It comes in handy when used as a background for buttons where the button has to stretch itself to accommodate the text.

Color-Drawable Resources

In Android, an image is one type of a drawable resource. Android supports another drawable resource called a color-drawable resource; it's essentially a colored rectangle.

> **CAUTION:** The Android documentation seems to suggest that rounded corners are possible, but we were not successful in creating those. We have presented an alternate approach to do that instead. The documentation also suggests that the instantiated Java class is PaintDrawable, but the code returns a ColorDrawable.

To define one of these color rectangles, you define an XML element by the node name of drawable in any XML file in the /res/values subdirectory. Listing 3–25 shows a couple of color-drawable resource examples.

Listing 3–25. *XML Syntax for Defining Color-Drawable Resources*

```
<resources>
    <drawable name="red_rectangle">#f00</drawable>
    <drawable name="blue_rectangle">#0000ff</drawable>
    <drawable name="green_rectangle">#f0f0</drawable>
</resources>
```

Listings 3–26 and 3–27 show how you can use a color-drawable resource in Java and XML, respectively.

Listing 3–26. *Using Color-Drawable Resources in Java Code*

```
// Get a drawable
ColorDrawable redDrawable = (ColorDrawable)
     activity.getResources().getDrawable(R.drawable.red_rectangle);

//Set it as a background to a text view
textView.setBackgroundDrawable(redDrawable);
```

Listing 3–27. *Using Color-Drawable Resources in XML Code*

```
<TextView android:layout_width="fill_parent"
          android:layout_height="wrap_content"
          android:textAlign="center"
          android:background="@drawable/red_rectangle"/>
```

To achieve the rounded corners in your Drawable, you can use the currently undocumented <shape> tag. However, this tag needs to reside in a file by itself in the /res/drawable directory. Listing 3–28 shows how you can use the <shape> tag to define a rounded rectangle in a file called /res/drawable/my_rounded_rectangle.xml.

Listing 3–28. *Defining a Rounded Rectangle*

```
<shape xmlns:android="http://schemas.android.com/apk/res/android">
    <solid android:color="#f0600000"/>
    <stroke android:width="3dp" color="#ffff8080"/>
    <corners android:radius="13dp" />
    <padding android:left="10dp" android:top="10dp"
        android:right="10dp" android:bottom="10dp" />
</shape>
```

You can then use this drawable resource as a background of the previous text view example, as shown in Listing 3–29.

Listing 3–29. *Using a Drawable from Java Code*

```
// Get a drawable
GradientDrawable roundedRectangle =
(GradientDrawable)
activity.getResources().getDrawable(R.drawable.my_rounded_rectangle);

//Set it as a background to a text view
textView.setBackgroundDrawable(roundedRectangle);
```

NOTE: It is not necessary to cast the returned base `Drawable` to a `GradientDrawable`, but it was done to show you that this `<shape>` tag becomes a `GradientDrawable`. This information is important because you can look up the Java API documentation for this class to know the XML tags it defines.

In the end, a bitmap image in the `drawable` subdirectory will resolve to a `BitmapDrawable` class. A "drawable" resource value, such as one of the rectangles in Listing 3–29, resolves to a `ColorDrawable`. An XML file with a shape tag in it resolves to a `GradientDrawable`.

Working with Arbitrary XML Resource Files

In addition to the structured resources described so far, Android allows arbitrary XML files as resources. This approach extends the advantages of using resources to arbitrary XML files. This approach provides a quick way to reference these files based on their generated resource IDs. Second, the approach allows you to localize these resource XML files. Third, you can compile and store these XML files on the device efficiently.

XML files that need to be read in this fashion are stored under the `/res/xml` subdirectory. Listing 3–30 is an example XML file called `/res/xml/test.xml`.

Listing 3–30. *Example XML File*

```
<rootelem1>
   <subelem1>
      Hello World from an xml sub element
   </subelem1>
</rootelem1>
```

As it does with other Android XML resource files, the AAPT will compile this XML file before placing it in the application package. You will need to use an instance of XmlPullParser if you want to parse these files. You can get an instance of the XmlPullParser implementation using this code from any context (including activity):

Listing 3–31. *Reading an XML File*

```
Resources res = activity.getResources();
XmlResourceParser xpp = res.getXml(R.xml.test);
```

The returned XmlResourceParser is an instance of XmlPullParser, and it also implements java.util.AttributeSet. Listing 3–32 shows a more complete code snippet that reads the test.xml file.

Listing 3–32. *Using XmlPullParser*

```
private String getEventsFromAnXMLFile(Activity activity)
throws XmlPullParserException, IOException
{
   StringBuffer sb = new StringBuffer();
   Resources res = activity.getResources();
   XmlResourceParser xpp = res.getXml(R.xml.test);

   xpp.next();
   int eventType = xpp.getEventType();
    while (eventType != XmlPullParser.END_DOCUMENT)
    {
        if(eventType == XmlPullParser.START_DOCUMENT)
        {
           sb.append("******Start document");
        }
        else if(eventType == XmlPullParser.START_TAG)
        {
           sb.append("\nStart tag "+xpp.getName());
        }
        else if(eventType == XmlPullParser.END_TAG)
        {
           sb.append("\nEnd tag "+xpp.getName());
        }
        else if(eventType == XmlPullParser.TEXT)
        {
           sb.append("\nText "+xpp.getText());
        }
        eventType = xpp.next();
    }//eof-while
    sb.append("\n******End document");
    return sb.toString();
}//eof-function
```

In Listing 3–32, you can see how to get XmlPullParser, how to use XmlPullParser to navigate the XML elements in the XML document, and how to use additional methods of XmlPullParser to access the details of the XML elements. If you want to run this code, you must create an XML file as shown earlier and call the getEventsFromAnXMLFile function from any menu item or button click. It will return a string, which you can print out to the log stream using the Log.d debug method.

Working with Raw Resources

Android also allows raw files in addition to arbitrary XML files. These raw resources, placed in /res/raw, are raw file resources such as audio, video, or text files that require localization or references through resource IDs. Unlike the XML files placed in /res/xml, these files are not compiled but moved to the application package as they are. However, each file will have an identifier generated in R.java. If you were to place a text file at /res/raw/test.txt, you would be able to read that file using the code in Listing 3–33.

Listing 3–33. *Reading a Raw Resource*

```
String getStringFromRawFile(Activity activity)
   throws IOException
   {
      Resources r = activity.getResources();
      InputStream is = r.openRawResource(R.raw.test);
      String myText = convertStreamToString(is);
      is.close();
      return myText;
   }

   String convertStreamToString(InputStream is)
   throws IOException
   {
      ByteArrayOutputStream baos = new ByteArrayOutputStream();
      int i = is.read();
      while (i != -1)
      {
         baos.write(i);
         i = is.read();
      }
      return baos.toString();
   }
```

CAUTION: File names with duplicate base names generate a build error in the Eclipse ADT plug-in. This is the case for all resource IDs generated for resources that are based on files.

Working with Assets

Android offers one more directory where you can keep files to be included in the package: /assets. It's at the same level as /res, meaning it's not part of the /res subdirectories. The files in /assets do not generate IDs in R.java; you must specify the file path to read them. The file path is a relative path starting at /assets. You will use the AssetManager class to access these files, as shown in Listing 3–34.

Listing 3–34. *Reading an Asset*

```
//Note: Exceptions are not shown in the code
String getStringFromAssetFile(Activity activity)
{
    AssetManager am = activity.getAssets();
```

```
    InputStream is = am.open("test.txt");
    String s = convertStreamToString(is);
    is.close();
    return s;
}
```

Reviewing the Resources Directory Structure

In summary, Listing 3–35 offers a quick look at the overall resources directory structure.

Listing 3–35. *Resource Directories*

```
/res/values/strings.xml
           /colors.xml
           /dimens.xml
           /attrs.xml
           /styles.xml
    /drawable/*.png
             /*.jpg
             /*.gif
             /*.9.png
    /anim/*.xml
    /layout/*.xml
    /raw/*.*
    /xml/*.xml
/assets/*.*/*.*
```

> **NOTE:** Because it's not under the `/res` directory, only the `/assets` directory can contain an arbitrary list of subdirectories. Every other directory can only have files at the level of that directory and no deeper. This is how `R.java` generates identifiers for those files.

Resources and Configuration Changes

Resources help with localization. For example, you can have a string value that changes based on the language locale of the user. Android resources generalize this idea to any configuration of the device of which language is just one configuration choice. Another example of a configuration change is when a device is turned from a vertical position to a horizontal position. The vertical mode is called the portrait mode and the horizontal mode the landscape mode.

Android allows you to pick different sets of layouts based on this layout mode for the same resource ID. Android does this by using different directories for each configuration. An example is shown in Listing 3–36.

Listing 3–36. *Alternate Resource Directories*

```
\res\layout\main_layout.xml
\res\layout-port\main_layout.xml
\res\layout-land\main_layout.xml
```

Even though there are three separate layout files here, they all generate only one layout ID in `R.java`. This ID will look as follows:

```
R.layout.main_layout
```

However, when you retrieve the layout corresponding to this layout ID, you will get the appropriate layout suitable for that device layout.

In this example the directory extensions `-port` and `-land` are called *configuration qualifiers*. These qualifiers are *case insensitive* and separated from the resource directory name with a hyphen (`-`). Resources that you specify in these configuration qualifier directories are called *alternate resources*. The resources in resource directories with out the configuration qualifiers are called *default resources*.

The available configuration qualifiers are listed in Listing 3–37.

Listing 3–37. ***Additional Alternate Resource Directories***

- `mccAAA`: `AAA` is the mobile country code
- `mncAAA`: `AAA` is the carrier/network code
- `en-rUS`: Language and region
- `small`, `normal`, `large`, `xlarge`: Screen size
- `long`, `notlong`: Screen type
- `port`, `land`: Portrait or landscape
- `car`, `desk`: Type of docking
- `night`, `notnight`: Night or day
- `ldpi`, `mdpi`, `hdpi`, `xhdpi`, `nodpi`: Screen density
- `notouch`, `stylus`, `finger`: What kind of screen
- `keysexposed`, `keyssoft`, `keyshidden`: What kind of keyboard
- `nokeys`, `qwerty`, `12key`: How many keys
- `navexposed`, `navhidden`: Navigation keys hidden or exposed
- `nonav`, `dpad`, `trackball`, `wheel`: The type of navigation device
- `v3`, `v4`, `v7`: API level

With these qualifiers you can have resource directories such as those shown in Listing 3–38.

Listing 3–38. ***Additional Alternate Resource Directories***

```
\res\layout-mcc312-mnc222-en-rUS
\res\layout-ldpi
\res\layout-hdpi
\res\layout-car
```

You can discover your current locale by navigating to the Custom Locale application available on the device. The navigation path for this application is Home ➤ List of Applications ➤ Custom Locale.

Given a resource ID, Android uses an algorithm to pick up the right resource. You can refer to the URLs included in the "Reference URLs" section to understand more about these rules, but we will point out a few rules of thumb.

The primary rule is that these qualifiers listed in Listing 3–38 are in the order of their precedence. Consider the directories in Listing 3–39.

Listing 3–39. *Layout File Variations*

```
\res\layout\main_layout.xml
\res\layout-port\main_layout.xml
\res\layout-en\main_layout.xml
```

In Listing 3–39, the layout file `main_layout.xml` is available in two additional variations. There is one variation for the language and one variation for the layout mode. Now, let's examine what layout file will be picked up if you are viewing the device portrait mode. Even though you are in portrait mode, Android will pick the layout from the `layout-en` directory, because the language variation comes before the orientation variation in the list of configuration qualifiers. The SDK links, mentioned in the "Reference URLs" section of this chapter, clearly list all the configuration qualifiers and their precedence order.

Let's look at the precedence rules further by experimenting with a few string resources. Please note that string resources are based on individual `ids`, whereas layout resources are file-based. To test the configuration qualifier precedence with string resources, let's come up with five resource IDs that can participate in the following variations: `default`, `en`, `en_us`, `port`, and `en_port`. The five resource IDs follow:

- `teststring_all`: This ID will be in all variations of the `values` directory including the default.
- `testport_port`: This ID will be in the default and in only the `-port` variation.
- `t1_enport`: This ID will be in the default and in the `-en` and `-port` variations.
- `t1_1_en_port`: This will be in the default and only in the `-en-port` variation.
- `t2`: This will be only in the default.

Listing 3–40 shows all the variations of the `values` directory.

Listing 3–40. *String Variations Based on Configuration*

```
// values/strings.xml
<resources xmlns="http://schemas.android.com/apk/res/android">
  <string name="teststring_all">teststring in root</string>
  <string name="testport_port">testport-port</string>
  <string name="t1_enport">t1 in root</string>
```

```
  <string name="t1_1_en_port">t1_1 in root</string>
  <string name="t2">t2 in root</string>
</resources>

// values-en/strings_en.xml
<resources xmlns="http://schemas.android.com/apk/res/android">
  <string name="teststring_all">teststring-en</string>
  <string name="t1_enport">t1_en</string>
  <string name="t1_1_en_port">t1_1_en</string>
</resources>

// values-en-rUS/strings_en_us.xml
<resources xmlns="http://schemas.android.com/apk/res/android">
  <string name="teststring_all">test-en-us</string>
</resources>

// values-port/strings_port.xml
<resources xmlns="http://schemas.android.com/apk/res/android">
  <string name="teststring_all">test-en-us-port</string>
  <string name="testport_port">testport-port</string>
  <string name="t1_enport">t1_port</string>
  <string name="t1_1_en_port">t1_1_port</string>
</resources>

// values-en-port/strings_en_port.xml
<resources xmlns="http://schemas.android.com/apk/res/android">
  <string name="teststring_all">test-en-port</string>
  <string name="t1_1_en_port">t1_1_en_port</string>
</resources>
```

Listing 3–41 shows the R.java file for these.

Listing 3–41. *R.java to Support String Variations*

```
public static final class string {
    public static final int teststring_all=0x7f050000;
    public static final int testport_port=0x7f050004;
    public static final int t1_enport=0x7f050001;
    public static final int t1_1_en_port=0x7f050002;
    public static final int t2=0x7f050003;
}
```

Right off the bat, you can see that, even though we have a ton of strings defined, only five string resource IDs are generated. Now, if you retrieve these string values the behavior of each string retrieval is documented below: (the configuration we tested with is en_US and portrait mode):

- teststring_all: This ID is in all five variations of the values directory. Because it is there in all variations, the variation from the values-en-rUS directory will be picked up. Based on precedence rules, the specific language trumps the default, en, port, and en-port variations.

- testport_port: This ID is in the default and in only the -port variation. Because it is not in any value directory starting with -en, the -port will take precedence over the default, and the value from the -port variation will be picked up. If this had been in one of the -en variations, the value would have been picked up from there.
- t1_enport: This ID is in three variations: default, -en, and -port. Because this is in -en and -port at the same time, the value from -en will be picked up.
- t1_1_en_port: This is in four variations: default, -port, -en, and -en-port Because this is available in -en-port it will be picked up from -en-port ignoring default, -en, and -port
- t2: This is only in the default, so the value will be picked up from default.

Android SDK has a more detailed algorithm that you can read up on. However, the example in this section gave you the essence of it. The key is to realize the precedence of one variation over the other. We have provided a URL in the reference section for this SDK link.

Reference URLs

As you learn about Android resources, you may want to keep the following reference URLs handy. We have listed these URLs and also what you will gain from each URL....

- http://developer.android.com/guide/topics/resources/index.html: This URL is a roadmap to the documentation on resources.
- http://developer.android.com/guide/topics/resources/available-resources.html: Android documents various types of resources at this URL.
- http://developer.android.com/reference/android/content/res/Resources.html: You will find here the various methods available to read resources.
- http://developer.android.com/reference/android/R.html: You can see the resources as defined to the core Android platform.
- http://www.androidbook.com/item/3542: You will find our research on plurals, string arrays, and alternate resources, as well as links to other references.
- http://www.androidbook.com/projects: You can use this URL to download the Eclipse project that demonstrates many concepts in this chapter. The name of the file is ProAndroid3_Ch03_TestResources.zip.

Summary

Let's conclude this chapter by quickly enumerating what you have learned about resources so far. You know the types of resources supported in Android and you know how to create these resources in XML files. You know how resource IDs are generated and how to use them in Java code. You also learned that resource ID generation is a convenient scheme that simplifies resource usage in Android. Finally, you learned how to work with raw resources and assets. We have also briefly touched upon alternate resources, plurals, and string arrays.

With that, we will turn our attention to content providers in the next chapter.

Chapter 4

Understanding Content Providers

Android uses a concept called *content providers* for abstracting data into services. This idea of content providers makes data sources look like REST-enabled data providers, such as web sites. In that sense, a content provider is a wrapper around data. A SQLite database on an Android device is an example of a data source that you can encapsulate into a content provider.

> **NOTE:** REST stands for REpresentational State Transfer. It is a confounding name for a simple concept which, as web users, everyone is quite familiar with. When you type a URL in a web browser and the web server responds with HTML, you have essentially performed a REST-based "query" operation on the web server. Similarly, when you update some content using a web form, you have done a REST-based "update" on the web server (or site) and changed the state of the web server. REST is also usually contrasted with (SOAP—Simple Object Access Protocol) Web Services. You can read more about REST at the following Wikipedia entry: `http://en.wikipedia.org/wiki/Representational_State_Transfer`.

To retrieve data from a content provider or save data into a content provider, you will need to use a set of REST-like URIs. For example, if you were to retrieve a set of books from a content provider that is an encapsulation of a book database, you would need to use a URI like this:

```
content://com.android.book.BookProvider/books
```

To retrieve a specific book from the book database (book 23), you would need to use a URI like this:

```
content://com.android.book.BookProvider/books/23
```

You will see in this chapter how these URIs translate to underlying database-access mechanisms. Any application on the device can make use of these URIs to access and manipulate data. As a consequence, content providers play a significant role in sharing data between applications.

Strictly speaking, though, the content providers' responsibilities comprise more of an encapsulation mechanism than a data-access mechanism. You'll need an actual data-access mechanism such as SQLite or network access to get to the underlying data sources. So, content-provider abstraction is required only if you want to share data externally or between applications. For internal data access, an application can use any data storage/access mechanism that it deems suitable, such as the following:

- *Preferences*: A set of key/value pairs that you can persist to store application preferences
- *Files*: Files internal to applications, which you can store on a removable storage medium
- *SQLite*: SQLite databases, each of which is private to the package that creates that database
- *Network*: A mechanism that lets you retrieve or store data externally through the Internet

NOTE: Despite the number of data-access mechanisms allowed in Android, this chapter focuses on SQLite and the content-provider abstraction because content providers form the basis of data sharing, which is much more common in the Android framework compared to other UI frameworks. We'll cover the network approach in Chapter 11 and the preferences mechanism in Chapter 9.

Exploring Android's Built-in Providers

Android comes with a number of built-in content providers, which are documented in the SDK's `android.provider` Java package. You can view the list of these providers here:

`http://developer.android.com/reference/android/provider/package-summary.html`

Here are a few of the providers listed on that documentation page:

```
Browser
CallLog
Contacts
   People
   Phones
   Photos
   Groups
MediaStore
   Audio
      Albums
      Artists
      Genres
```

```
      Playlists
   Images
      Thumbnails
   Video
Settings
```

> **NOTE:** The list of providers may vary slightly, depending on the release of Android you are working with. The purpose of this list is to give you an idea of what is available, and not to serve as a definitive reference.

The top-level items are databases and the lower-level items are tables. So `Browser`, `CallLog`, `Contacts`, `MediaStore`, and `Settings` are individual SQLite databases encapsulated as providers. These SQLite databases typically have an extension of `.db` and are accessible only from the implementation package. Any access outside that package must go through the content-provider interface.

Exploring Databases on the Emulator and Available Devices

Because many content providers in Android use SQLite databases (`http://www.sqlite.org/`), you can use tools provided both by Android and by SQLite to examine the databases. Many of these tools reside in the `\android-sdk-install-directory\tools` subdirectory, others are in `\android-sdk-install-directory\platform-tools`.

> **NOTE:** Refer to Chapter 2 for information on locating the `tools` directories and invoking a command window for different operating systems. This chapter, like most of the remaining chapters, gives examples primarily on Windows platforms. As you go through this section, in which we use a number of command-line tools, you can focus on the name of the executable or the batch file and not pay as much attention to the directory the tool is in. We covered how to set the path for the tools directories on various platforms in Chapter 2.

Android uses a command-line tool called Android Debug Bridge (adb), which is found here:

```
platform-tools\adb.exe
```

adb is a special tool in the Android toolkit that most other tools go through to get to the device. However, you must have an emulator running or an Android device connected for adb to work. You can find out whether you have running devices or emulators by typing this at the command line:

```
adb devices
```

If the emulator is not running, you can start the emulator by typing this at the command line:

```
emulator.exe @avdname
```

The argument @avdname is the name of an Android Virtual Device (AVD). (We covered the need for android virtual devices and how to create them in Chapter 2.) To find out what virtual devices you already have you can run the following command:

```
android    list    avd
```

This command will list the available AVDs. If you have developed and run any Android applications through Eclipse ADT, then you will have configured at least one virtual device. The preceding command will list at least that one virtual device.

Here is an example output of that list command. (Depending on where your tools directory is and also depending on the Android release, the following printout may vary as to the path or release numbers, such as i:\android.)

```
I:\android\tools>android list avd
Available Android Virtual Devices:
    Name: avd
    Path: I:\android\tools\..\avds\avd3
  Target: Google APIs (Google Inc.)
          Based on Android 1.5 (API level 3)
    Skin: HVGA
  Sdcard: 32M
---------
    Name: titanium
    Path: C:\Documents and Settings\Satya\.android\avd\titanium.avd
  Target: Android 1.5 (API level 3)
    Skin: HVGA
```

As indicated, AVDs are covered in detail in Chapter 2.

You can also start the emulator through the Eclipse ADT plug-in. This automatically happens when you choose a program to run or debug in the emulator. Once the emulator is up and running, you can test again for a list of running devices by typing this:

```
adb devices
```

Now you should see a printout that looks like this:

```
List of devices attached
emulator-5554 device
```

You can see the many options and commands that you can run with adb by typing this at the command line:

```
adb help
```

You can also visit the following URL for many of the runtime options for adb: http://developer.android.com/guide/developing/tools/adb.html.

You can use adb to open a shell on the connected device by typing this:

```
adb shell
```

> **NOTE:** This shell is a Unix `ash`, albeit with a limited command set. You can do `ls`, for example, but `find`, `grep`, and `awk` are not available in the shell.

You can see the available command set in the shell by typing this at the shell prompt:

```
#ls    /system/bin
```

The # sign is the prompt for the shell. For brevity, we will omit this prompt in the following examples. The preceding line brings up the commands listed in Table 4–1. (Please note that we have shown these commands only as a demonstration and not for completeness. This list may be somewhat different depending on the release of Android SDK you are running.)

Table 4–1. *Available Shell Command Set*

dumpcrash	sh	date
am	hciattach	dd
dumpstate	sdptool	cmp
input	logcat	cat
itr	servicemanager	dmesg
monkey	dbus-daemon	df
pm	debug_tool	getevent
svc	flash_image	getprop
ssltest	installd	hd
debuggerd	dvz	id
dhcpcd	hostapd	ifconfig
hostapd_cli	htclogkernel	insmod
fillup	mountd	ioctl
linker	qemud	kill
logwrapper	radiooptions	ln
telnetd	toolbox	log
iftop	hcid	lsmod
mkdosfs	route	ls
mount	setprop	mkdir
mv	sleep	dumpsys
notify	setconsole	service
netstat	smd	playmp3
printenv	stop	sdutil
reboot	top	rild
ps	start	dalvikvm
renice	umount	dexopt
rm	vmstat	surfaceflinger
rmdir	wipe	app_process
rmmod	watchprops	mediaserver
sendevent	sync	system_server
schedtop	netcfg	
ping	chmod	

To see a list of root-level directories and files, you can type the following in the shell:

```
ls    -l
```

You'll need to access this directory to see the list of databases:

```
ls     /data/data
```

This directory contains the list of installed packages on the device. Let's look at an example by exploring the `com.android.providers.contacts` package:

```
ls   /data/data/com.android.providers.contacts/databases
```

This will list a database file called `contacts.db`, which is a SQLite database. (This file and path are still device and release dependent.)

> **NOTE:** We also should tell you that, in Android, databases may be created when they are accessed the first time. This means you may not see this file if you have never accessed the "contacts" application.

If there were a `find` command in the included `ash`, you could look at all the `*.db` files. But there is no good way to do this with `ls` alone. The nearest thing you can do is this:

```
ls -R /data/data/*/databases
```

With this command, you will notice that the Android distribution has the following databases (again, a bit of caution; depending on your release, this list may vary):

```
alarms.db
contacts.db
downloads.db
internal.db
settings.db
mmssms.db
telephony.db
```

You can invoke `sqlite3` on one of these databases inside the adb shell by typing this:

```
sqlite3  /data/data/com.android.providers.contacts/databases/contacts.db
```

You can exit `sqlite3` by typing this:

```
sqlite>.exit
```

Notice that the prompt for adb is # and the prompt for `sqlite3` is `sqlite>`. You can read about the various `sqlite3` commands by visiting `http://www.sqlite.org/sqlite.html`. However, we will list a few important commands here so that you don't have to make a trip to the web. You can see a list of tables by typing

```
sqlite> .tables
```

This command is a shortcut for

```
SELECT name FROM sqlite_master
WHERE type IN ('table','view') AND name NOT LIKE 'sqlite_%'
UNION ALL
SELECT name FROM sqlite_temp_master
```

```
WHERE type IN ('table','view')
ORDER BY 1
```

As you probably guessed, the table `sqlite_master` is a master table that keeps track of tables and views in the database. The following command line prints out a `create` statement for a table called `people` in `contacts.db`:

```
.schema people
```

This is one way to get at the column names of a table in SQLite. This will also print out the column data types. While working with content providers, you should note these column types because access methods depend on them.

However, it is pretty tedious to manually parse through this long `create` statement just to learn the column names and their types. There is a workaround: you can pull `contacts.db` down to your local box and then examine the database using any number of GUI tools for SQLite version 3. You can issue the following command from your OS command prompt to pull down the `contacts.db` file:

```
adb pull  /data/data/com.android.providers.contacts/databases/contacts.db ➥
c:/somelocaldir/contacts.db
```

We used a free download of Sqliteman (`http://sqliteman.com/`), a GUI tool for SQLite databases, which seemed to work fine. We experienced a few crashes, but otherwise found the tool completely usable for exploring Android SQLite databases.

Quick SQLite Primer

The following sample SQL statements could help you navigate through the SQLite databases quickly:

```
//Set the column headers to show in the tool
sqlite>.headers on

//select all rows from a table
select * from table1;

//count the number of rows in a table
select count(*) from table1;

//select a specific set of columns
select col1, col2 from table1;

//Select distinct values in a column
select distinct col1 from table1;

//counting the distinct values
select count(col1) from (select distinct col1  from table1);

//group by
select count(*), col1 from table1 group by col1;

//regular inner join
select * from table1 t1, table2 t2
where t1.col1 = t2.col1;
```

```
//left outer join
//Give me everything in t1 even though there are no rows in t2
select * from table t1 left outer join table2 t2
on t1.col1 = t2.col1
where ....
```

Architecture of Content Providers

You now know how to explore existing content providers through Android and SQLite tools. Next, we'll examine some of the architectural elements of content providers and how these content providers relate to other data-access abstractions in the industry.

Overall, the content-provider approach has parallels to the following industry abstractions:

- Web sites
- REST
- Web services
- Stored procedures

Each content provider on a device registers itself like a web site with a string (akin to a domain name, but called an *authority*). This uniquely identifiable string forms the basis of a set of URIs that this content provider can offer. This is not unlike how a web site with a domain offers a number of URLs to expose its documents or content in general.

This authority registration occurs in the `AndroidManifest.xml` file. Here are two examples of how you may register providers in `AndroidManifest.xml`:

```
<provider android:name="SomeProvider"
        android:authorities="com.your-company.SomeProvider" />

<provider android:name="NotePadProvider"
   android:authorities="com.google.provider.NotePad"
/>
```

An authority is like a domain name for that content provider. Given the preceding authority registration, these providers will honor URLs starting with that authority prefix:

```
content://com.your-company.SomeProvider/
content://com.google.provider.NotePad/
```

You see that "content providers," like a web site, has a base domain name that acts as a starting URL.

> **NOTE:** It must be noted that the providers offered by Android may not carry a fully qualified authority name. It is recommended at the moment only for third-party content providers. This is why you sometimes see that content providers are referenced with a simple word such as "contacts" as opposed to "com.google.android.contacts" (in the case of a third-party provider).

Content providers also provide REST-like URLs to retrieve or manipulate data. For the preceding registration, the URI to identify a directory or a collection of notes in the `NotePadProvider` database is

```
content://com.google.provider.NotePad/Notes
```

The URI to identify a specific note is

```
content://com.google.provider.NotePad/Notes/#
```

where # is the `id` of a particular note. Here are some additional examples of URIs that some data providers accept:

```
content://media/internal/images
content://media/external/images
content://contacts/people/
content://contacts/people/23
```

Notice here how these providers' "media" (`content://media`) and "contacts" (`content://contacts`) don't have a fully qualified structure. This is because these are not third-party providers and are controlled by Android.

Content providers exhibit characteristics of web services as well. A content provider, through its URIs, exposes internal data as a service. However, the output from the URL of a content provider is not typed data, as is the case for a SOAP–based web-service call. This output is more like a result set coming from a JDBC statement. Even there the similarities to JDBC are conceptual. We don't want to give the impression that this is the same as a JDBC ResultSet.

The caller is expected to know the structure of the rows and columns that are returned. Also, as you will see in this chapter's "Structure of Android MIME Types" section, a content provider has a built-in mechanism that allows you to determine the Multipurpose Internet Mail Extensions (MIME) type of the data represented by this URI.

In addition to resembling web sites, REST, and web services, a content provider's URIs also resemble the names of stored procedures in a database. Stored procedures present service-based access to the underlying relational data. URIs are similar to stored procedures, because URI calls against a content provider return a cursor. However, content providers differ from stored procedures in that the input to a service call in a content provider is typically embedded in the URI itself.

We've provided these comparisons to give you an idea of the broader scope of content providers.

Structure of Android Content URIs

We compared a content provider to a web site because it responds to incoming URIs. So, to retrieve data from a content provider, all you have to do is invoke a URI. The retrieved data in the case of a content provider, however, is in the form of a set of rows and columns represented by an Android `cursor` object. In this context, we'll examine the structure of the URIs that you could use to retrieve data.

Content URIs in Android look similar to HTTP URIs, except that they start with `content` and have this general form:

```
content://*/*/*
```

or

```
content://authority-name/path-segment1/path-segment2/etc…
```

Here's an example URI that identifies a note numbered 23 in a database of notes:

```
content://com.google.provider.NotePad/notes/23
```

After `content:`, the URI contains a unique identifier for the authority, which is used to locate the provider in the provider registry. In the preceding example, `com.google.provider.NotePad` is the authority portion of the URI.

`/notes/23` is the path section of the URI that is specific to each provider. The `notes` and `23` portions of the path section are called path segments. It is the responsibility of the provider to document and interpret the path section and path segments of the URIs.

The developer of the content provider usually does this by declaring constants in a Java class or a Java interface in that provider's implementation Java package. Furthermore, the first portion of the path might point to a collection of objects. For example, `/notes` indicates a collection or a directory of notes, whereas `/23` points to a specific note item.

Given this URI, a provider is expected to retrieve rows that the URI identifies. The provider is also expected to alter content at this URI using any of the state-change methods: `insert`, `update`, or `delete`.

Structure of Android MIME Types

Just as a web site returns a MIME type for a given URL (this allows browsers to invoke the right program to view the content), a content provider has an added responsibility to return the MIME type for a given URI. This allows flexibility of viewing data. Knowing what kind of data it is, you may have more than one program that knows how to handle that data. For example, if you have a text file on your hard drive, there are many editors that can display that text file. Depending on the OS, it may even give you an option of which editor to pick.

MIME types work in Android similar to how they work in HTTP. You ask a provider for the MIME type of a given URI that it supports, and the provider returns a two-part string identifying its MIME type according to the standard web MIME conventions. You can find the MIME-type standard here:

```
http://tools.ietf.org/html/rfc2046
```

According to the MIME-type specification, a MIME type has two parts: a type and a subtype. Here are some examples of well-known MIME-type pairs:

```
text/html
text/css
text/xml
text/vnd.curl
```

```
application/pdf
application/rtf
application/vnd.ms-excel
```

You can see a complete list of registered types and subtypes at the Internet Assigned Numbers Authority (IANA) web site:

```
http://www.iana.org/assignments/media-types/
```

The primary registered content types are

```
application
audio
example
image
message
model
multipart
text
video
```

Each of these primary types has subtypes. But if a vendor has proprietary data formats, the subtype name begins with vnd. For example, Microsoft Excel spreadsheets are identified by the subtype `vnd.ms-excel`, whereas `pdf` is considered a nonvendor standard and is represented as such without any vendor-specific prefix.

Some subtypes start with `x-`; these are nonstandard subtypes that don't have to be registered. They're considered private values that are bilaterally defined between two collaborating agents. Here are a few examples:

```
application/x-tar
audio/x-aiff
video/x-msvideo
```

Android follows a similar convention to define MIME types. The vnd in Android MIME types indicates that these types and subtypes are nonstandard, vendor-specific forms. To provide uniqueness, Android further demarcates the types and subtypes with multiple parts similar to a domain specification. Furthermore, the Android MIME type for each content type has two forms: one for a specific record and one for multiple records.

For a single record, the MIME type looks like this:

```
vnd.android.cursor.item/vnd.yourcompanyname.contenttype
```

For a collection of records or rows, the MIME type looks like this:

```
vnd.android.cursor.dir/vnd.yourcompanyname.contenttype
```

Here are a couple of examples:

```
//One single note
vnd.android.cursor.item/vnd.google.note

//A collection or a directory of notes
vnd.android.cursor.dir/vnd.google.note
```

> **NOTE:** The implication here is that Android natively recognizes a "directory" of items and a "single" item. As a programmer, your flexibility is limited to the subtype. For example, things like list controls rely on what is returned from a cursor as one of these MIME "main" types.

MIME types are extensively used in Android, especially in intents, where the system figures out what activity to invoke based on the MIME type of data. MIME types are invariably derived from their URIs through content providers. You need to keep three things in mind when you work with MIME types:

- The type and subtype need to be unique for what they represent. The type is pretty much decided for you, as pointed out. It is primarily a directory of items or a single item. In the context of Android, these may not be as open as you might think.
- Type and subtype need to be preceded with `vnd` if they are not standard (which is usually the case when you talk about specific records).
- They are typically name-spaced for your specific need.

To reiterate this point, the primary MIME type for a collection of items returned through an Android `cursor` should always be `vnd.android.cursor.dir`, and the primary MIME type of a single item retrieved through an Android `cursor` should be `vnd.android.cursor.item`. You have more wiggle room when it comes to the subtype, as in `vnd.google.note`; after the `vnd.` part, you are free to subtype it with anything you'd like.

Reading Data Using URIs

Now you know that to retrieve data from a content provider you need to use URIs supplied by that content provider. Because the URIs defined by a content provider are unique to that provider, it is important that these URIs are documented and available to programmers to see and then call. The providers that come with Android do this by defining constants representing these URI strings.

Consider these three URIs defined by helper classes in the Android SDK:

```
MediaStore.Images.Media.INTERNAL_CONTENT_URI
MediaStore.Images.Media.EXTERNAL_CONTENT_URI
Contacts.People.CONTENT_URI
```

The equivalent textual URI strings would be as follows:

```
content://media/internal/images
content://media/external/images
content://contacts/people/
```

The `MediaStore` provider defines two URIs and the `Contacts` provider defines one URI. If you notice, these constants are defined using a hierarchical scheme. For example, the content URI example for the contacts is pointed out as `Contacts.People.CONTENT_URI`. This is because the databases of contacts may have a lot of tables to represent the entities of a Contact. People is one of the tables or a collection. Each primary entity of a database may carry its own content URI, however, all rooted at the base authority name (such as contacts://contacts in the case of contacts provider).

NOTE: In the reference Contacts.People.CONTENT_URI, Contacts is a java package and People is a class within that package. Also note that Contacts and Contacts.People were deprecated in Android 2.0 and the new equivalent URIs are discussed in Chapter 27. However these URIs still work, especially to explain the concepts.

Given these URIs, the code to retrieve a single row of people from the contacts provider looks like this:

```
Uri peopleBaseUri = Contacts.People.CONTENT_URI;
Uri myPersonUri = Uri.withAppendedPath(Contacts.People.CONTENT_URI, "23");

//Query for this record.
//managedQuery is a method on Activity class
Cursor cur = managedQuery(myPersonUri, null, null, null);
```

Notice how the Contacts.People.CONTENT_URI is predefined as a constant in the People class. In this example, the code takes the root URI, adds a specific person ID to it, and makes a call to the managedQuery method.

As part of the query against this URI, it is possible to specify a sort order, the columns to select, and a where clause. These additional parameters are set to null in this example.

NOTE: A content provider should list which columns it supports by implementing a set of interfaces or by listing the column names as constants. However, the class or interface that defines constants for columns should also make the column types clear through a column naming convention, or comments or documentation, as there is no formal way to indicate the type of a column through constants.

Listing 4–1 shows how to retrieve a cursor with a specific list of columns from the People table of the contacts content provider, based on the previous example.

Listing 4–1. *Retrieving a Cursor from a Content Provider*

```
// An array specifying which columns to return.
string[] projection = new string[] {
    People._ID,
    People.NAME,
    People.NUMBER,
};

// Get the base URI for People table in Contacts Content Provider.
// ie. content://contacts/people/
Uri mContactsUri = Contacts.People.CONTENT_URI;

// Best way to retrieve a query; returns a managed query.
Cursor managedCursor = managedQuery( mContactsUri,
                        projection, //Which columns to return.
```

```
                    null,       // WHERE clause
                    Contacts.People.NAME + " ASC"); // Order-by clause.
```

Notice how a `projection` is merely an array of strings representing column names. So unless you know what these columns are, you'll find it difficult to create a `projection`. You should look for these column names in the same class that provides the URI, in this case the `People` class. Let's look at the other column names defined in this class:

```
CUSTOM_RINGTONE
DISPLAY_NAME
LAST_TIME_CONTACTED
NAME
NOTES
PHOTO_VERSION
SEND_TO_VOICE_MAIL
STARRED
TIMES_CONTACTED
```

You can discover more about each of these columns by looking at the SDK documentation for the `android.provider.Contacts.PeopleColumns` class, available at this URL:

`http://developer.android.com/reference/android/provider/Contacts.PeopleColumns.html`

As alluded to earlier, a database like `contacts` contains several tables, each of which is represented by a class or an interface to describe its columns and their types. Let's take a look at the package `android.providers.Contacts`, documented at the following URL:

`http://developer.android.com/reference/android/provider/Contacts.html`

You will see that this package has the following nested classes or interfaces:

```
ContactMethods
Extensions
Groups
Organizations
People
Phones
Photos
Settings
```

Each of these classes represents a table name in the `contacts.db` database, and each table is responsible for describing its own URI structure. Plus, a corresponding `Columns` interface is defined for each class to identify the column names, such as `PeopleColumns`.

Let's revisit the `cursor` that is returned: it contains zero or more records. Column names, order, and type are provider specific. However, every row returned has a default column called `_id` representing a unique ID for that row.

Using the Android Cursor

Here are a few facts about an Android cursor:

- A cursor is a collection of rows.
- You need to use `moveToFirst()` before reading any data because the cursor starts off positioned before the first row.

- You need to know the column names.
- You need to know the column types.
- All field-access methods are based on column number, so you must convert the column name to a column number first.
- The cursor is a random cursor (you can move forward and backward, and you can jump).
- Because the cursor is a random cursor, you can ask it for a row count.

An Android cursor has a number of methods that allow you to navigate through it. Listing 4–2 shows you how to check if a cursor is empty and how to walk through the cursor row by row when it is not empty.

Listing 4–2. ***Navigating Through a Cursor Using a while Loop***

```
if (cur.moveToFirst() == false)
{
   //no rows empty cursor
   return;
}

//The cursor is already pointing to the first row
//let's access a few columns
int nameColumnIndex = cur.getColumnIndex(People.NAME);
String name = cur.getString(nameColumnIndex);

//let's now see how we can loop through a cursor

while(cur.moveToNext())
{
   //cursor moved successfully
   //access fields
}
```

The assumption at the beginning of Listing 4–2 is that the cursor has been positioned before the first row. To position the cursor on the first row, we use the `moveToFirst()` method on the cursor object. This method returns `false` if the cursor is empty. We then use the `moveToNext()` method repetitively to walk through the cursor.

To help you learn where the cursor is, Android provides the following methods:

```
isBeforeFirst()
isAfterLast()
isClosed()
```

Using these methods, you can also use a `for` loop as in Listing 4–3 to navigate through the cursor instead of the `while` loop used in Listing 4–2.

Listing 4–3. ***Navigating Through a Cursor Using a for Loop***

```
//Get your indexes first outside the for loop
int nameColumn = cur.getColumnIndex(People.NAME);
int phoneColumn = cur.getColumnIndex(People.NUMBER);

//Walk the cursor now based on column indexes
```

```
for(cur.moveToFirst();!cur.isAfterLast();cur.moveToNext())
{
   String name = cur.getString(nameColumn);
   String phoneNumber = cur.getString(phoneColumn);
}
```

The index order of columns seems to be a bit arbitrary. As a result, we advise you to explicitly get the indexes first from the cursor to avoid surprises. To find the number of rows in a cursor, Android provides a method on the cursor object called `getCount()`.

Working with the where Clause

Content providers offer two ways of passing a `where` clause:

- Through the URI
- Through the combination of a `string` clause and a set of replaceable string-array arguments

We will cover both of these approaches through some sample code.

Passing a where Clause Through a URI

Imagine you want to retrieve a note whose ID is 23 from the Google notes database. You'd use the code in Listing 4–4 to retrieve a cursor containing one row corresponding to row 23 in the notes table.

Listing 4–4. *Passing SQL where Clauses Through the URI*

```
Activity someActivity;
//..initialize someActivity
String noteUri = "content://com.google.provider.NotePad/notes/23";
Cursor managedCursor = someActivity.managedQuery( noteUri,
                        projection, //Which columns to return.
                        null,       // WHERE clause
                        null); // Order-by clause.
```

We left the `where` clause argument of the `managedQuery` method `null` because, in this case, we assumed that the note provider is smart enough to figure out the `id` of the book we wanted. This `id` is embedded in the URI itself. We used the URI as a vehicle to pass the `where` clause. This becomes apparent when you notice how the notes provider implements the corresponding query method. Here is a code snippet from that query method:

```
//Retrieve a note id from the incoming uri that looks like
//content://.../notes/23
int noteId = uri.getPathSegments().get(1);

//ask a query builder to build a query
//specify a table name
queryBuilder.setTables(NOTES_TABLE_NAME);

//use the noteid to put a where clause
queryBuilder.appendWhere(Notes._ID + "=" + noteId);
```

Notice how the id of a note is extracted from the URI. The Uri class representing the incoming argument uri has a method to extract the portions of a URI after the root content://com.google.provider.NotePad. These portions are called *path segments*; they're strings between / separators such as /seg1/seg3/seg4/, and they're indexed by their positions. For the URI here, the first path segment would be 23. We then used this ID of 23 to append to the where clause specified to the QueryBuilder class. In the end, the equivalent select statement would be

```
select * from notes where _id = 23
```

NOTE: The classes Uri and UriMatcher are used to identify URIs and extract parameters from them. (We'll cover UriMatcher further in the section "Using UriMatcher to Figure Out the URIs.") SQLiteQueryBuilder is a helper class in android.database.sqlite that allows you to construct SQL queries to be executed by SQLiteDatabase on a SQLite database instance.

Using Explicit where Clauses

Now that you have seen how to use a URI to send in a where clause, consider the other method by which Android lets us send a list of explicit columns and their corresponding values as a where clause. To explore this, let's take another look at the managedQuery method of the Activity class that we used in Listing 4–4. Here's its signature:

```
public final Cursor managedQuery(Uri uri,
   String[] projection,
   String selection,
   String[] selectionArgs,
   String sortOrder)
```

Notice the argument named selection, which is of type String. This selection string represents a filter (a where clause, essentially) declaring which rows to return, formatted as a SQL where clause (excluding the WHERE itself). Passing null will return all rows for the given URI. In the selection string you can include ?s, which will be replaced by the values from selectionArgs in the order that they appear in the selection. The values will be bound as Strings.

Because you have two ways of specifying a where clause, you might find it difficult to determine how a provider has used these where clauses and which where clause takes precedence if both where clauses are utilized.

For example, you can query for a note whose ID is 23 using either of these two methods:

```
//URI method
managedQuery("content://com.google.provider.NotePad/notes/23"
,null
,null
,null
,null);
```

or

```
//explicit where clause
managedQuery("content://com.google.provider.NotePad/notes"
,null
,"_id=?"
,new String[] {23}
,null);
```

The convention is to use where clauses through URIs where applicable and use the explicit option as a special case.

Inserting Records

So far, we have talked about how to retrieve data from content providers using URIs. Now, let us turn our attention to inserts, updates, and deletes.

> Note: In explaining content providers so far, we have generously used examples from the Notepad application that Google provided as the prototypical application as part of their tutorials. However, it is not necessary to be completely familiar with that application. Even if you haven't seen the application you should be able to follow through the examples. We will, however, give you complete code for a sample provider later in this chapter.

Android uses a class called android.content.ContentValues to hold the values for a single record, which is to be inserted. ContentValues is a dictionary of key/value pairs, much like column names and their values. You insert records by first populating a record into ContentValues and then asking android.content.ContentResolver to insert that record using a URI.

> **NOTE:** You need to locate ContentResolver, because at this level of abstraction, you are not asking a database to insert a record; instead, you are asking to insert a record into a provider identified by a URI. ContentResolver is responsible for resolving the URI reference to the right provider and then passing on the ContentValues object to that specific provider.

Here is an example of populating a single row of notes in ContentValues in preparation for an insert:

```
ContentValues values = new ContentValues();
values.put("title", "New note");
values.put("note","This is a new note");

//values object is now ready to be inserted
```

You can get a reference to ContentResolver by asking the Activity class:

```
ContentResolver contentResolver = activity.getContentResolver();
```

Now, all you need is a URI to tell ContentResolver to insert the row. These URIs are defined in a class corresponding to the Notes table. In the Notepad example, this URI is

```
Notepad.Notes.CONTENT_URI
```

We can take this URI and the ContentValues we have and make a call to insert the row:

```
Uri uri = contentResolver.insert(Notepad.Notes.CONTENT_URI, values);
```

This call returns a URI pointing to the newly inserted record. This returned URI would match the following structure:

```
Notepad.Notes.CONTENT_URI/new_id
```

Adding a File to a Content Provider

Occasionally, you might need to store a file in a database. The usual approach is to save the file to disk and then update the record in the database that points to the corresponding file name.

Android takes this protocol and automates it by defining a specific procedure for saving and retrieving these files. Android uses a convention where a reference to the file name is saved in a record with a reserved column name of _data.

When a record is inserted into that table, Android returns the URI to the caller. Once you save the record using this mechanism, you also need to follow it up by saving the file in that location. To do this, Android allows ContentResolver to take the Uri of the database record and return a writable output stream. Behind the scenes, Android allocates an internal file and stores the reference to that file name in the _data field.

If you were to extend the Notepad example to store an image for a given note, you could create an additional column called _data and run an insert first to get a URI back. The following code demonstrates this part of the protocol:

```
ContentValues values = new ContentValues();
values.put("title", "New note");
values.put("note","This is a new note");

//Use a content resolver to insert the record
ContentResolver contentResolver = activity.getContentResolver();
Uri newUri = contentResolver.insert(Notepad.Notes.CONTENT_URI, values);
```

Once you have the URI of the record, the following code asks the ContentResolver to get a reference to the file output stream:

```
….
//Use the content resolver to get an output stream directly
//ContentResolver hides the access to the _data field where
//it stores the real file reference.
OutputStream outStream = activity.getContentResolver().openOutputStream(newUri);
someSourceBitmap.compress(Bitmap.CompressFormat.JPEG, 50, outStream);
outStream.close();
```

The code then uses that output stream to write to.

Updates and Deletes

So far, we have talked about queries and inserts; updates and deletes are fairly straightforward. Performing an update is similar to performing an insert, in which changed column values are passed through a ContentValues object. Here is the signature of an update method on the ContentResolver object:

```
int numberOfRowsUpdated =
activity.getContentResolver().update(
    Uri uri,
    ContentValues values,
    String whereClause,
    String[] selectionArgs )
```

The whereClause argument will constrain the update to the pertinent rows. Similarly, the signature for the delete method is

```
int numberOfRowsDeleted =
activity.getContentResolver().delete(
    Uri uri,
    String whereClause,
    String[] selectionArgs )
```

Clearly a delete method will not require the ContentValues argument because you will not need to specify the columns you want when you are deleting a record.

Almost all the calls from managedQuery and ContentResolver are directed eventually to the provider class. Knowing how a provider implements each of these methods gives us enough clues as to how those methods are used by a client. In the next section, we'll cover the implementation from scratch of an example content provider called BookProvider.

Implementing Content Providers

We've discussed how to interact with a content provider for data needs but haven't yet discussed how to write a content provider. To write a content provider, you have to extend android.content.ContentProvider and implement the following key methods:

```
query
insert
update
delete
getType
```

You'll also need to set up a number of things before implementing them. We will illustrate all the details of a content-provider implementation by describing the steps you'll need to take:

1. Plan your database, URIs, column names, and so on, and create a metadata class that defines constants for all of these metadata elements.
2. Extend the abstract class ContentProvider.
3. Implement these methods: query, insert, update, delete, and getType.

4. Register the provider in the manifest file.

Planning a Database

To explore this topic, we'll create a database that contains a collection of books. The book database contains only one table called books, and its columns are name, isbn, and author. These column names fall under metadata. You'll define this sort of relevant metadata in a Java class. This metadata-bearing Java class BookProviderMetaData is shown in Listing 4–5. Some key elements of this metadata class are highlighted.

Listing 4–5. ***Defining Metadata for Your Database: The BookProviderMetaData Class***

```
public class BookProviderMetaData
{
    public static final String AUTHORITY = "com.androidbook.provider.BookProvider";

    public static final String DATABASE_NAME = "book.db";
    public static final int DATABASE_VERSION = 1;
    public static final String BOOKS_TABLE_NAME = "books";

    private BookProviderMetaData() {}

    //inner class describing BookTable
    public static final class BookTableMetaData implements BaseColumns
    {
        private BookTableMetaData() {}
        public static final String TABLE_NAME = "books";

        //uri and MIME type definitions
        public static final Uri CONTENT_URI =
                          Uri.parse("content://" + AUTHORITY + "/books");

        public static final String CONTENT_TYPE =
                         "vnd.android.cursor.dir/vnd.androidbook.book";

        public static final String CONTENT_ITEM_TYPE =
                        "vnd.android.cursor.item/vnd.androidbook.book";

        public static final String DEFAULT_SORT_ORDER = "modified DESC";

        //Additional Columns start here.
        //string type
        public static final String BOOK_NAME = "name";

        //string type
        public static final String BOOK_ISBN = "isbn";

        //string type
        public static final String BOOK_AUTHOR = "author";

        //Integer from System.currentTimeMillis()
        public static final String CREATED_DATE = "created";

        //Integer from System.currentTimeMillis()
        public static final String MODIFIED_DATE = "modified";
    }
}
```

This BookProviderMetaData class starts by defining its authority to be com.androidbook.provider.BookProvider. We are going to use this string to register the provider in the Android manifest file. This string forms the front part of the URIs intended for this provider.

This class then proceeds to define its one table (books) as an inner BookTableMetaData class. The BookTableMetaData class then defines a URI for identifying a collection of books. Given the authority in the previous paragraph, the URI for a collection of books will look like this:

```
content://com.androidbook.provider.BookProvider/books
```

This URI is indicated by the constant

```
BookProviderMetaData.BookTableMetaData.CONTENT_URI
```

The BookTableMetaData class then proceeds to define the MIME types for a collection of books and a single book. The provider implementation will use these constants to return the MIME types for the incoming URIs.

BookTableMetaData then defines the set of columns: name, isbn, author, created (creation date), and modified (last-updated date).

> **NOTE:** You should point out your columns' data types through comments in the code.

The metadata class BookTableMetaData also inherits from the BaseColumns class that provides the standard _id field, which represents the row ID. With these metadata definitions in hand, we're ready to tackle the provider implementation.

Extending ContentProvider

Implementing our BookProvider sample content provider involves extending the ContentProvider class and overriding onCreate() to create the database and then implement the query, insert, update, delete, and getType methods. This section covers the setup and creation of the database, while the following sections deal with each of the individual methods: query, insert, update, delete, and getType. Listing 4–6 provides the complete source code for this class. Important subsections of this class are high lighted.

A query method requires the set of columns it needs to return. This is similar to a select clause that requires column names along with their as counterparts (sometimes called *synonyms*). Android uses a map object that it calls a projection map to represent these column names and their synonyms. We will need to set up this map so we can use it later in the query-method implementation. In the code for the provider implementation (see Listing 4–6), you will see this done up front as part of Project map setup.

Most of the methods we'll be implementing take a URI as an input. Although all the URIs that this content provider is able to respond to start with the same pattern, the tail ends of the URIs will be different—just like a web site. Each URI, although it starts the same, must be different to identify different data or documents. Let us illustrate this with an example:

```
Uri1: content://com.androidbook.provider.BookProvider/books
Uri2: content://com.androidbook.provider.BookProvider/books/12
```

See how the book provider needs to distinguish each of these URIs. This is a simple case. If our book provider had been housing more objects rather than just books, then there would be more URIs to identify those objects.

The provider implementation needs a mechanism to distinguish one URI from the other; Android uses a class called `UriMatcher` for this work. So we need to set up this object with all our URI variations. You will see this code in Listing 4–6 after the segment that creates a projection map. We'll further explain the `UriMatcher` class in the section "Using UriMatcher to Figure Out the URIs".

The code in Listing 4–6 then overrides the `onCreate()` method to facilitate the database creation. The source code then implements each of the `insert()`, `query()`, `update()`, `getType()`, and `delete()` methods. The code for all of this is presented in one listing (Listing 4–6), but we will explain each aspect in a separate sub section referring to this listing.

Listing 4–6. *Implementing the BookProvider Content Provider*

```
public class BookProvider extends ContentProvider
{
    //Logging helper tag. No significance to providers.
    private static final String TAG = "BookProvider";

    //Setup projection Map
    //Projection maps are similar to "as" (column alias) construct
    //in an sql statement where by you can rename the
    //columns.
    private static HashMap<String, String> sBooksProjectionMap;
    static
    {
        sBooksProjectionMap = new HashMap<String, String>();
        sBooksProjectionMap.put(BookTableMetaData._ID,
                                BookTableMetaData._ID);

        //name, isbn, author
        sBooksProjectionMap.put(BookTableMetaData.BOOK_NAME,
                                BookTableMetaData.BOOK_NAME);
        sBooksProjectionMap.put(BookTableMetaData.BOOK_ISBN,
                                BookTableMetaData.BOOK_ISBN);
        sBooksProjectionMap.put(BookTableMetaData.BOOK_AUTHOR,
                                BookTableMetaData.BOOK_AUTHOR);

        //created date, modified date
        sBooksProjectionMap.put(BookTableMetaData.CREATED_DATE,
                                BookTableMetaData.CREATED_DATE);
        sBooksProjectionMap.put(BookTableMetaData.MODIFIED_DATE,
                                BookTableMetaData.MODIFIED_DATE);
    }

    //Setup URIs
```

```
//Provide a mechanism to identify
//all the incoming uri patterns.
private static final UriMatcher sUriMatcher;
private static final int INCOMING_BOOK_COLLECTION_URI_INDICATOR = 1;
private static final int INCOMING_SINGLE_BOOK_URI_INDICATOR = 2;
static {
    sUriMatcher = new UriMatcher(UriMatcher.NO_MATCH);
    sUriMatcher.addURI(BookProviderMetaData.AUTHORITY, "books",
                      INCOMING_BOOK_COLLECTION_URI_INDICATOR);
    sUriMatcher.addURI(BookProviderMetaData.AUTHORITY, "books/#",
                      INCOMING_SINGLE_BOOK_URI_INDICATOR);

}

/**
 * Setup/Create Database
 * This class helps open, create, and upgrade the database file.
 */
private static class DatabaseHelper extends SQLiteOpenHelper {

    DatabaseHelper(Context context) {
        super(context,
            BookProviderMetaData.DATABASE_NAME,
            null,
            BookProviderMetaData.DATABASE_VERSION);
    }

    @Override
    public void onCreate(SQLiteDatabase db)
    {
        Log.d(TAG,"inner oncreate called");
        db.execSQL("CREATE TABLE " + BookTableMetaData.TABLE_NAME + " ("
                + BookTableMetaData._ID + " INTEGER PRIMARY KEY,"
                + BookTableMetaData.BOOK_NAME + " TEXT,"
                + BookTableMetaData.BOOK_ISBN + " TEXT,"
                + BookTableMetaData.BOOK_AUTHOR + " TEXT,"
                + BookTableMetaData.CREATED_DATE + " INTEGER,"
                + BookTableMetaData.MODIFIED_DATE + " INTEGER"
                + ");");
    }

    @Override
    public void onUpgrade(SQLiteDatabase db, int oldVersion, int newVersion)
    {
        Log.d(TAG,"inner onupgrade called");
        Log.w(TAG, "Upgrading database from version "
                + oldVersion + " to "
                + newVersion + ", which will destroy all old data");
        db.execSQL("DROP TABLE IF EXISTS " +
                BookTableMetaData.TABLE_NAME);
        onCreate(db);
    }
}

private DatabaseHelper mOpenHelper;

//Component creation callback
```

```
@Override
public boolean onCreate()
{
    Log.d(TAG,"main onCreate called");
    mOpenHelper = new DatabaseHelper(getContext());
    return true;
}

@Override
public Cursor query(Uri uri, String[] projection, String selection,
        String[] selectionArgs,  String sortOrder)
{
    SQLiteQueryBuilder qb = new SQLiteQueryBuilder();

    switch (sUriMatcher.match(uri)) {
    case INCOMING_BOOK_COLLECTION_URI_INDICATOR:
        qb.setTables(BookTableMetaData.TABLE_NAME);
        qb.setProjectionMap(sBooksProjectionMap);
        break;

    case INCOMING_SINGLE_BOOK_URI_INDICATOR:
        qb.setTables(BookTableMetaData.TABLE_NAME);
        qb.setProjectionMap(sBooksProjectionMap);
        qb.appendWhere(BookTableMetaData._ID + "="
                    + uri.getPathSegments().get(1));
        break;

    default:
        throw new IllegalArgumentException("Unknown URI " + uri);
    }

    // If no sort order is specified use the default
    String orderBy;
    if (TextUtils.isEmpty(sortOrder)) {
        orderBy = BookTableMetaData.DEFAULT_SORT_ORDER;
    } else {
        orderBy = sortOrder;
    }

    // Get the database and run the query
    SQLiteDatabase db = mOpenHelper.getReadableDatabase();
    Cursor c = qb.query(db, projection, selection,
               selectionArgs, null, null, orderBy);

    //example of getting a count
    int i = c.getCount();

    // Tell the cursor what uri to watch,
    // so it knows when its source data changes
    c.setNotificationUri(getContext().getContentResolver(), uri);
    return c;
}

@Override
public String getType(Uri uri)
{
    switch (sUriMatcher.match(uri)) {
```

```
        case INCOMING_BOOK_COLLECTION_URI_INDICATOR:
            return BookTableMetaData.CONTENT_TYPE;

        case INCOMING_SINGLE_BOOK_URI_INDICATOR:
            return BookTableMetaData.CONTENT_ITEM_TYPE;

        default:
            throw new IllegalArgumentException("Unknown URI " + uri);
        }
    }

    @Override
    public Uri insert(Uri uri, ContentValues initialValues)
    {
        // Validate the requested uri
        if (sUriMatcher.match(uri)
                != INCOMING_BOOK_COLLECTION_URI_INDICATOR)
        {
            throw new IllegalArgumentException("Unknown URI " + uri);
        }

        ContentValues values;
        if (initialValues != null) {
            values = new ContentValues(initialValues);
        } else {
            values = new ContentValues();
        }

        Long now = Long.valueOf(System.currentTimeMillis());

        // Make sure that the fields are all set
        if (values.containsKey(BookTableMetaData.CREATED_DATE) == false)
        {
            values.put(BookTableMetaData.CREATED_DATE, now);
        }

        if (values.containsKey(BookTableMetaData.MODIFIED_DATE) == false)
        {
            values.put(BookTableMetaData.MODIFIED_DATE, now);
        }

        if (values.containsKey(BookTableMetaData.BOOK_NAME) == false)
        {
            throw new SQLException(
               "Failed to insert row because Book Name is needed " + uri);
        }

        if (values.containsKey(BookTableMetaData.BOOK_ISBN) == false) {
            values.put(BookTableMetaData.BOOK_ISBN, "Unknown ISBN");
        }
        if (values.containsKey(BookTableMetaData.BOOK_AUTHOR) == false) {
            values.put(BookTableMetaData.BOOK_ISBN, "Unknown Author");
        }

        SQLiteDatabase db = mOpenHelper.getWritableDatabase();
        long rowId = db.insert(BookTableMetaData.TABLE_NAME,
                BookTableMetaData.BOOK_NAME, values);
```

```
    if (rowId > 0) {
        Uri insertedBookUri =
            ContentUris.withAppendedId(
                    BookTableMetaData.CONTENT_URI, rowId);
        getContext()
           .getContentResolver()
                .notifyChange(insertedBookUri, null);

        return insertedBookUri;
    }

    throw new SQLException("Failed to insert row into " + uri);
}

@Override
public int delete(Uri uri, String where, String[] whereArgs)
{
    SQLiteDatabase db = mOpenHelper.getWritableDatabase();
    int count;
    switch (sUriMatcher.match(uri)) {
    case INCOMING_BOOK_COLLECTION_URI_INDICATOR:
        count = db.delete(BookTableMetaData.TABLE_NAME,
                where, whereArgs);
        break;

    case INCOMING_SINGLE_BOOK_URI_INDICATOR:
        String rowId = uri.getPathSegments().get(1);
        count = db.delete(BookTableMetaData.TABLE_NAME,
                BookTableMetaData._ID + "=" + rowId
                + (!TextUtils.isEmpty(where) ? " AND (" + where + ')' : ""),
                whereArgs);
        break;

    default:
        throw new IllegalArgumentException("Unknown URI " + uri);
    }

    getContext().getContentResolver().notifyChange(uri, null);
    return count;
}

@Override
public int update(Uri uri, ContentValues values,
        String where, String[] whereArgs)
{
    SQLiteDatabase db = mOpenHelper.getWritableDatabase();
    int count;
    switch (sUriMatcher.match(uri)) {
    case INCOMING_BOOK_COLLECTION_URI_INDICATOR:
        count = db.update(BookTableMetaData.TABLE_NAME,
                values, where, whereArgs);
        break;

    case INCOMING_SINGLE_BOOK_URI_INDICATOR:
        String rowId = uri.getPathSegments().get(1);
        count = db.update(BookTableMetaData.TABLE_NAME,
                values, BookTableMetaData._ID + "=" + rowId
```

```
                    + (!TextUtils.isEmpty(where) ? " AND (" + where + ')' : ""),
                    whereArgs);
                break;

            default:
                throw new IllegalArgumentException("Unknown URI " + uri);
            }

            getContext().getContentResolver().notifyChange(uri, null);
            return count;
        }
    }
```

Fulfilling MIME-Type Contracts

The `BookProvider` content provider must also implement the `getType()` method to return a MIME type for a given URI. This method, like many other methods of a content provider, is overloaded with respect to the incoming URI. As a result, the first responsibility of the `getType()` method is to distinguish the type of the URI. Is it a collection of books or a single book?

As we pointed out in the previous section, we will use the `UriMatcher` to decipher this URI type. Depending on this URI, the `BookTableMetaData` class has defined the MIME-type constants to return for each URI. You can see the implementation for this method in Listing 4–6.

Implementing the Query Method

The `query` method in a content provider is responsible for returning a collection of rows depending on an incoming URI and a `where` clause.

Like the other methods, the `query` method uses `UriMatcher` to identify the URI type. If the URI type is a single-item type, the method retrieves the book ID from the incoming URI like this:

1. It extracts the path segments using `getPathSegments()`.
2. It indexes into the URI to get the first path segment, which happens to be the book ID.

The `query` method then uses the `projections` that we created up front in Listing 4–6 to identify the return columns. In the end, `query` returns the cursor to the caller. Throughout this process, the `query` method uses the `SQLiteQueryBuilder` object to formulate and execute the query (see Listing 4–6).

Implementing an Insert Method

The `insert` method in a content provider is responsible for inserting a record into the underlying database and then returning a URI that points to the newly created record.

Like the other methods, insert uses UriMatcher to identify the URI type. The code first checks whether the URI indicates the proper collection-type URI. If not, the code throws an exception (see Listing 4–6).

The code then validates the optional and mandatory column parameters. The code can substitute default values for some columns if they are missing.

Next, the code uses a SQLiteDatabase object to insert the new record and returns the newly inserted ID. In the end, the code constructs the new URI using the returned ID from the database.

Implementing an Update Method

The update method in a content provider is responsible for updating a record (or records) based on the column values passed in, as well as the where clause that is passed in. The update method then returns the number of rows updated in the process.

Like the other methods, update uses UriMatcher to identify the URI type. If the URI type is a collection, the where clause is passed through so it can affect as many records as possible. If the URI type is a single-record type, then the book ID is extracted from the URI and specified as an additional where clause. In the end, the code returns the number of records updated (see Listing 4–6). Chapter 21 fully explains the implications of this notifyChange method. Also notice how this notifyChange method enables you to announce to the world that the data at that URI has changed. Potentially, you can do the same in the insert method by saying that "…/books" has changed when a record is inserted.

Implementing a Delete Method

The delete method in a content provider is responsible for deleting a record (or records) based on the where clause that is passed in. The delete method then returns the number of rows deleted in the process.

Like the other methods, delete uses UriMatcher to identify the URI type. If the URI type is a collection type, the where clause is passed through so you can delete as many records as possible. If the where clause is null, all records will be deleted. If the URI type is a single-record type, the book ID is extracted from the URI and specified as an additional where clause. In the end, the code returns the number of records deleted (see Listing 4–6).

Using UriMatcher to Figure Out the URIs

We've mentioned the UriMatcher class several times now; let's look into it. Almost all methods in a content provider are overloaded with respect to the URI. For example, the same query() method is called whether you want to retrieve a single book or a list of multiple books. It is up to the method to know which type of URI is being requested. Android's UriMatcher utility class helps you identify the URI types.

Here's how it works: You tell an instance of UriMatcher what kind of URI patterns to expect. You will also associate a unique number with each pattern. Once these patterns are registered, you can then ask UriMatcher if the incoming URI matches a certain pattern.

As we've mentioned, our BookProvider content provider has two URI patterns: one for a collection of books and one for a single book. The code in Listing 4–7 registers both these patterns using UriMatcher. It allocates 1 for a collection of books and a 2 for a single book (the URI patterns themselves are defined in the metadata for the books table).

Listing 4–7. *Registering URI Patterns with UriMatcher*

```
private static final UriMatcher sUriMatcher;
//define ids for each uri type
private static final int INCOMING_BOOK_COLLECTION_URI_INDICATOR = 1;
private static final int INCOMING_SINGLE_BOOK_URI_INDICATOR = 2;

static {
    sUriMatcher = new UriMatcher(UriMatcher.NO_MATCH);
    //Register pattern for the books
    sUriMatcher.addURI(BookProviderMetaData.AUTHORITY
                      , "books"
                      , INCOMING_BOOK_COLLECTION_URI_INDICATOR);
    //Register pattern for a single book
    sUriMatcher.addURI(BookProviderMetaData.AUTHORITY
                     , "books/#",
                     INCOMING_SINGLE_BOOK_URI_INDICATOR);

}
```

Now that this registration is in place, you can see how UriMatcher plays a part in the query-method implementation:

```
switch (sUriMatcher.match(uri)) {
   case INCOMING_BOOK_COLLECTION_URI_INDICATOR:
   ......
   case INCOMING_SINGLE_BOOK_URI_INDICATOR:
   ......
   default:
      throw new IllegalArgumentException("Unknown URI " + uri);
}
```

Notice how the match method returns the same number that was registered earlier. The constructor of UriMatcher takes an integer to use for the root URI. UriMatcher returns this number if there are neither path segments nor authorities on the URL. UriMatcher also returns NO_MATCH when the patterns don't match. You can construct a UriMatcher with no root-matching code; in that case, Android initializes UriMatcher to NO_MATCH internally. So you could have written the code in Listing 4–7 as follows instead:

```
static {
       sUriMatcher = new UriMatcher();
       sUriMatcher.addURI(BookProviderMetaData.AUTHORITY
                         , "books"
                         , INCOMING_BOOK_COLLECTION_URI_INDICATOR);
```

```
        sUriMatcher.addURI(BookProviderMetaData.AUTHORITY
                                , "books/#",
                                INCOMING_SINGLE_BOOK_URI_INDICATOR);
}
```

Using Projection Maps

A content provider acts like an intermediary between an abstract set of columns and a real set of columns in a database, yet these column sets might differ. While constructing queries, you must map between the `where` clause columns that a client specifies and the real database columns. You set up this *projection map* with the help of the `SQLiteQueryBuilder` class.

Here is what the Android SDK documentation says about the mapping method `public void setProjectionMap(Map columnMap)` available on the `QueryBuilder` class:

> *Sets the projection map for the query. The projection map maps from column names that the caller passes into query to database column names. This is useful for renaming columns as well as disambiguating column names when doing joins. For example you could map "name" to "people.name". If a projection map is set it must contain all column names the user may request, even if the key and value are the same.*

Here is how our `BookProvider` content provider sets up the projection map:

```
sBooksProjectionMap = new HashMap<String, String>();
sBooksProjectionMap.put(BookTableMetaData._ID, BookTableMetaData._ID);

//name, isbn, author
sBooksProjectionMap.put(BookTableMetaData.BOOK_NAME
                                        , BookTableMetaData.BOOK_NAME);
sBooksProjectionMap.put(BookTableMetaData.BOOK_ISBN
                                        , BookTableMetaData.BOOK_ISBN);
sBooksProjectionMap.put(BookTableMetaData.BOOK_AUTHOR
                                        , BookTableMetaData.BOOK_AUTHOR);

//created date, modified date
sBooksProjectionMap.put(BookTableMetaData.CREATED_DATE
                                        , BookTableMetaData.CREATED_DATE);
sBooksProjectionMap.put(BookTableMetaData.MODIFIED_DATE
                                        , BookTableMetaData.MODIFIED_DATE);
```

And then the query builder uses the variable `sBooksProjectionMap` like this:

```
queryBuilder.setTables(BookTableMetaData.TABLE_NAME);
queryBuilder.setProjectionMap(sBooksProjectionMap);
```

Registering the Provider

Finally, you must register the content provider in the `Android.Manifest.xml` file using the tag structure in Listing 4–8.

Listing 4–8. *Registering A Provider*

```
<provider android:name=".BookProvider"
   android:authorities="com.androidbook.provider.BookProvider"/>
```

Exercising the Book Provider

Now that we have a book provider, we are going to show you sample code to exercise that provider. The sample code includes adding a book, removing a book, getting a count of the books, and finally displaying all the books.

Keep in mind that these are code extracts from the sample project and will not compile, as they require additional dependency files. However, we feel this sample code is valuable in demonstrating the concepts we have explored.

At the end of this chapter, we have included a link to the downloadable sample project, which you can use in your eclipse environment to compile and test.

Adding A Book

The code in Listing 4–9 inserts a new book into the book database.

Listing 4–9. *Exercising a Provider Insert*

```
public void addBook(Context context)
{
    String tag = "Exercise BookProvider";
    Log.d(tag,"Adding a book");
    ContentValues cv = new ContentValues();
    cv.put(BookProviderMetaData.BookTableMetaData.BOOK_NAME, "book1");
    cv.put(BookProviderMetaData.BookTableMetaData.BOOK_ISBN, "isbn-1");
    cv.put(BookProviderMetaData.BookTableMetaData.BOOK_AUTHOR, "author-1");

    ContentResolver cr = context.getContentResolver();
    Uri uri = BookProviderMetaData.BookTableMetaData.CONTENT_URI;
    Log.d(tag,"book insert uri:" + uri);
    Uri insertedUri = cr.insert(uri, cv);
    Log.d(tag,"inserted uri:" + insertedUri);
}
```

Removing a Book

The code in Listing 4–10 deletes the last record from the book database. See Listing 4–11 for an example of how the getCount() method in Listing 4–10 works.

Listing 4–10. *Exercising a Provider delete*

```
public void removeBook(Context context)
{
    String tag = "Exercise BookProvider";
    int i = getCount(context); //See the getCount function in Listing 4-11
    ContentResolver cr = context.getContentResolver();
```

```
    Uri uri = BookProviderMetaData.BookTableMetaData.CONTENT_URI;
    Uri delUri = Uri.withAppendedPath(uri, Integer.toString(i));
    Log.d(tag, "Del Uri:" + delUri);
    cr.delete(delUri, null, null);
    Log.d(tag, "New count:" + getCount(context));
}
```

Please note that this is a quick example to show how delete works with a URI. The algorithm to get the last URI may not be valid in all cases. However it should work if you were to add 5 records and proceed to delete them one by one from the end. In a real case you would want to display the records in a list and ask the user to pick one to delete in which case you will know the exact URI of the record.

Getting a Count of the Books

The code in Listing 4–11 gets the database cursor and counts the number of records in the cursor.

Listing 4–11. ***Counting the Records in a Table***

```
private int getCount(Context context)
{
    Uri uri = BookProviderMetaData.BookTableMetaData.CONTENT_URI;
    Activity a = (Activity)context;
    Cursor c = a.managedQuery(uri,
            null, //projection
            null, //selection string
            null, //selection args array of strings
            null); //sort order
    int numberOfRecords = c.getCount();
    c.close();
    return numberOfRecords;
}
```

Displaying the List of Books

The code in Listing 4–12 retrieves all the records in the book database.

Listing 4–12. ***Displaying a List of Books***

```
public void showBooks(Context context)
{
    String tag = "Exercise BookProvider";
    Uri uri = BookProviderMetaData.BookTableMetaData.CONTENT_URI;
    Activity a = (Activity)context;
    Cursor c = a.managedQuery(uri,
            null, //projection
            null, //selection string
            null, //selection args array of strings
            null); //sort order

    int iname = c.getColumnIndex(
        BookProviderMetaData.BookTableMetaData.BOOK_NAME);

    int iisbn = c.getColumnIndex(
```

```
        BookProviderMetaData.BookTableMetaData.BOOK_ISBN);
    int iauthor = c.getColumnIndex(
         BookProviderMetaData.BookTableMetaData.BOOK_AUTHOR);

    //Report your indexes
    Log.d(tag,"name,isbn,author:" + iname + iisbn + iauthor);

    //walk through the rows based on indexes
    for(c.moveToFirst();!c.isAfterLast();c.moveToNext())
    {
        //Gather values
        String id = c.getString(1);
        String name = c.getString(iname);
        String isbn = c.getString(iisbn);
        String author = c.getString(iauthor);

        //Report or log the row
        StringBuffer cbuf = new StringBuffer(id);
        cbuf.append(",").append(name);
        cbuf.append(",").append(isbn);
        cbuf.append(",").append(author);
        Log.d(tag, cbuf.toString());
    }

    //Report how many rows have been read
    int numberOfRecords = c.getCount(context);
    Log.d(tag,"Num of Records:" + numberOfRecords);

    //Close the cursor
    //ideally this should be done in
    //a finally block.
    c.close();
}
```

Resources

Here are some additional Android resources that can help you with the topics covered in this chapter:

- `http://developer.android.com/guide/topics/providers/content-providers.html`: You can read about Android documentation on Content Providers here.
- `http://developer.android.com/reference/android/content/ContentProvider.html`: Here is the API description for a `ContentProvider`, where you can learn about `ContentProvider` contracts.
- `http://developer.android.com/reference/android/content/UriMatcher.html`: This URL points to information that is useful for understanding `UriMatcher`.
- `http://developer.android.com/reference/android/database/Cursor.html`: This URL will help you to read data from a content provider or a database directly.

- `http://www.sqlite.org/sqlite.html`: Here is the home page of SQLite, where you can learn more about SQLite and download tools that you can use to work with SQLite databases.
- `http://www.androidbook.com/projects`: You can use this URL to download the test project dedicated for this chapter. The name of the zip file is `ProAndroid3_ch04_TestProviders.zip`.

Summary

In this chapter, you learned the nature of content URIs, MIME types, and content providers. You have learned how to use SQLite to construct providers that respond to URIs. Once your underlying data is exposed in this manner, any application on the Android platform can take advantage of it.

This ability to access and update data using URIs, irrespective of the process boundaries, falls right in step with the service-centric, cloud-computing landscape that we described in Chapter 1.

In the next chapter, we will cover intents, which get tied to content providers (among other Android components) through data URIs and URI MIME types. What you have learned in this chapter will be helpful in understanding intents, in which data URIs play a key role.

Chapter 5

Understanding Intents

Android introduced a concept called *intents* to invoke components. The list of components in Android include activities (UI components), services (background code), broadcast receivers (code that responds to broadcast messages), and content providers (code that abstracts data).

Basics of Android Intents

Although an intent is easily understood as a mechanism to invoke components, Android folds multiple ideas into the concept of an *intent*. You can use intents to invoke external applications from your application. You can use intents to invoke internal or external components from your application. You can use intents to raise events so that others can respond in a manner similar to a publish-and-subscribe model. You can use intents to raise alarms.

> **NOTE:** What is an intent? The short answer may be that an intent is an action with its associated data payload.

At the simplest level, an intent is an action that you can tell Android to perform (or *invoke*). The action Android invokes depends on what is registered for that action. Imagine you've written the following activity:

```
public class BasicViewActivity extends Activity
{
    @Override
    public void onCreate(Bundle savedInstanceState)
    {
        super.onCreate(savedInstanceState);
        setContentView(R.layout.some_view);
    }
}//eof-class
```

The layout some_view needs to point to a valid layout file in the /res/layout directory. Android then allows you to register this activity in its manifest file, making it available for other applications to invoke. The registration looks like this:

```
<activity android:name=".BasicViewActivity"
          android:label="Basic View Tests">
 <intent-filter>
   <action android:name="com.androidbook.intent.action.ShowBasicView"/>
   <category android:name="android.intent.category.DEFAULT" />
 </intent-filter>
</activity>
```

The registration here not only involves an activity but also an action that you can use to invoke that activity. The activity designer usually chooses a name for the action and specifies that action as part of an intent filter for this activity. As we go through the rest of the chapter, you will have a chance to learn more about these intent filters.

Now that you have specified the activity and its registration against an action, you can use an intent to invoke this BasicViewActivity:

```
public static void invokeMyApplication(Activity parentActivity)
{
   String actionName= "com.androidbook.intent.action.ShowBasicView";
   Intent intent = new Intent(actionName);
   parentActivity.startActivity(intent);
}
```

> **NOTE:** The general convention for an action name is *<your-package-name>*.intent.action.*YOUR_ACTION_NAME*.

Once the BasicViewActivity is invoked it has the ability to discover the intent that invoked it. Here is the BasicViewActivity code rewritten to retrieve the intent that invoked it:

```
public class BasicViewActivity extends Activity
{
    @Override
    public void onCreate(Bundle savedInstanceState)
    {
        super.onCreate(savedInstanceState);
        setContentView(R.layout.some_view);
        Intent intent = this.getIntent();
        if (intent == null)
        {
            Log.d("test tag", "This activity is invoked without an intent");
        }
    }
}//eof-class
```

Available Intents in Android

You can give intents a test run by invoking some of the applications that come with Android. The page at `http://developer.android.com/guide/appendix/g-app-intents.html` documents some of the available Google applications and the intents that invoke them.

> **NOTE:** Please note, however, that this list may change depending on the Android release.

The set of available applications could include the following:

- A browser application to open a browser window
- An application to call a telephone number
- An application to present a phone dialer so the user can enter the numbers and make a call through the UI
- A mapping application to show the map of the world at a given latitude and longitude coordinate
- A detailed mapping application that can show Google street views

Listing 5–1 has the code to invoke these applications through their published intents.

Listing 5–1. *Exercising Android's Prefabricated Applications*

```
public class IntentsUtils
{
    public static void invokeWebBrowser(Activity activity)
    {
       Intent intent = new Intent(Intent.ACTION_VIEW);
       intent.setData(Uri.parse("http://www.google.com"));
       activity.startActivity(intent);
    }
    public static void invokeWebSearch(Activity activity)
    {
       Intent intent = new Intent(Intent.ACTION_WEB_SEARCH);
       intent.setData(Uri.parse("http://www.google.com"));
       activity.startActivity(intent);
    }
    public static void dial(Activity activity)
    {
       Intent intent = new Intent(Intent.ACTION_DIAL);
       activity.startActivity(intent);
    }

    public static void call(Activity activity)
    {
       Intent intent = new Intent(Intent.ACTION_CALL);
       intent.setData(Uri.parse("tel:555-555-5555"));
       activity.startActivity(intent);
    }
```

```
    public static void showMapAtLatLong(Activity activity)
    {
        Intent intent = new Intent(Intent.ACTION_VIEW);
        //geo:lat,long?z=zoomlevel&q=question-string
        intent.setData(Uri.parse("geo:0,0?z=4&q=business+near+city"));
        activity.startActivity(intent);
    }

    public static void tryOneOfThese(Activity activity)
    {
        IntentsUtils.invokeWebBrowser(activity);
    }
}
```

You will be able to exercise this code as long you have a simple activity with a menu item to invoke `tryOneOfThese(activity)`. Creating a simple menu is easy (see Listing 5–2).

Listing 5–2. *A Test Harness to Create a Simple Menu*

```
public class MainActivity extends Activity
{
    public void onCreate(Bundle savedInstanceState)   {
        super.onCreate(savedInstanceState);

        TextView tv = new TextView(this);
        tv.setText("Hello, Android. Say hello");
        setContentView(tv);
    }
    @Override
    public boolean onCreateOptionsMenu(Menu menu)    {
        super.onCreateOptionsMenu(menu);
        int base=Menu.FIRST; // value is 1
        MenuItem item1 = menu.add(base,base,base,"Test");
        return true;
    }

    @Override
    public boolean onOptionsItemSelected(MenuItem item)   {
        if (item.getItemId() == 1)        {
            IntentUtils.tryOneOfThese(this);
        }
        else {
          return super.onOptionsItemSelected(item);
        }
        return true;
    }
}
```

NOTE: See Chapter 2 for instructions on how to make an Android project out of these files, as well as how to compile and run it. You can also read the early parts of Chapter 7 ("Menus") to see more sample code relating to menus. Or you can download the sample Eclipse project dedicated for this chapter using the URL supplied at the end of this chapter. However, when you download the sample code, this basic activity may be slightly different, but the concept remains the same. In the download sample, we also load the menus from an XML file.

Exploring Intent Composition

Another sure way to nail down an intent is to see what an intent object contains. An intent has an action, data (represented by a data URI), a key/value map of extra data elements, and an explicit class name (called a *component name*). We will explore each of these parts in turn.

> **NOTE:** When an intent carries a component name with it, it is called an *explicit* intent. When an intent doesn't carry a component name but relies on other parts such as action and data, it is called an *implicit* intent. As we go through the rest of the chapter, you will see that there are subtle differences between the two.

Intents and Data URIs

So far, we've covered the simplest of the intents, where all we need is the name of an action. The ACTION_DIAL activity in Listing 5–1 is one of these; to invoke the dialer, all we needed in that listing is the dialer's action and nothing else:

```
public static void dial(Activity activity)
{
   Intent intent = new Intent(Intent.ACTION_DIAL);
   activity.startActivity(intent);
}
```

Unlike ACTION_DIAL, the intent ACTION_CALL (again referring to Listing 5–1) that is used to make a call to a given phone number takes an additional parameter called Data. This parameter points to a URI, which, in turn, points to the phone number:

```
public static void call(Activity activity)
{
   Intent intent = new Intent(Intent.ACTION_CALL);
   intent.setData(Uri.parse("tel:555-555-5555"));
   activity.startActivity(intent);
}
```

The action portion of an intent is a string or a string constant, usually prefixed by the Java package name.

The "data" portion of an intent is not really data but a pointer to the data. This data portion is a string representing a URI. An intent's URI can contain arguments that can be inferred as data, just like a web site's URL.

The format of this URI could be specific to each activity that is invoked by that action. In this case, the CALL action decides what kind of data URI it would expect. From the URI, it extracts the telephone number.

NOTE: The invoked activity can also use the URI as a pointer to a data source, extract the data from the data source, and use that data instead. This would be the case for media such as audio, video, and images.

Generic Actions

The actions `Intent.ACTION_CALL` and `Intent.ACTION_DIAL` could easily lead us to the wrong assumption that there is a one-to-one relationship between an action and what it invokes. To disprove this, let us consider a counterexample from the `IntentUtils` code in Listing 5–1:

```
public static void invokeWebBrowser(Activity activity)
{
   Intent intent = new Intent(Intent.ACTION_VIEW);
   intent.setData(Uri.parse("http://www.google.com"));
   activity.startActivity(intent);
}
```

Note that the action is simply stated as `ACTION_VIEW`. How does Android know which activity to invoke in response to such a generic action name? In these cases, Android relies not only on the generic action name but also on the nature of the URI. Android looks at the scheme of the URI, which happens to be `http`, and questions all the registered activities to see which ones understand this scheme. Out of these, it inquires which ones can handle the `VIEW` and then invokes that activity. For this to work, the browser activity should have registered a `VIEW` intent against the data scheme of `http`. That intent declaration might look like this in the manifest file:

```
<activity......>
<intent-filter>
         <action android:name="android.intent.action.VIEW" />
        <data android:scheme="http"/>
        <data android:scheme="https"/>
</intent-filter>
</activity>
```

You can learn more about the data options by looking at the XML definition for the `data` element of the intent filter at `http://developer.android.com/guide/topics/manifest/data-element.html`. The child elements or attributes of `data` XML subnode of intent filter node include these:

```
host
mimeType
path
pathPattern
pathPrefix
port
scheme
```

`mimeType` is one attribute you'll see used often. For example, the following intent filter for the activity that displays a list of notes indicates the MIME type as a directory of notes:

```
<intent-filter>
   <action android:name="android.intent.action.VIEW" />
   <data android:mimeType="vnd.android.cursor.dir/vnd.google.note" />
</intent-filter>
```

This intent filter declaration can be read as "Invoke this activity to view a collection of notes."

The screen that displays a single note, on the other hand, declares its intent filter using a MIME type indicating a single note item:

```
<intent-filter>
   <action android:name="android.intent.action.VIEW" />
   <data android:mimeType="vnd.android.cursor.item/vnd.google.note" />
</intent-filter>
```

This intent filter declaration can be read as "Invoke this activity to view a single of note."

Using Extra Information

In addition to its primary attributes of action and data, an intent can include an additional attribute called *extras*. An extra can provide more information to the component that receives the intent. The extra data is in the form of key/value pairs: the key name typically starts with the package name, and the value can be any fundamental data type or arbitrary object as long as it implements the `android.os.Parcelable` interface. This extra information is represented by an Android class called `android.os.Bundle`.

The following two methods on an `Intent` class provide access to the extra `Bundle`:

```
//Get the Bundle from an Intent
Bundle extraBundle = intent.getExtras();

// Place a bundle in an intent
Bundle anotherBundle = new Bundle();

//populate the bundle with key/value pairs
...
//set the bundle on the Intent
intent.putExtras(anotherBundle);
```

`getExtras` is straightforward: it returns the `Bundle` that the intent has. `putExtras` checks whether the intent currently has a bundle. If the intent already has a bundle, `putExtras` transfers the additional keys and values from the new bundle to the existing bundle. If the bundle doesn't exist, `putExtras` will create one and copy the key/value pairs from the new bundle to the created bundle.

> **NOTE:** `putExtras` replicates the incoming bundle rather than referencing it. So if you were to later change the incoming bundle, you wouldn't be changing the bundle inside the intent.

You can use a number of methods to add fundamental types to the bundle. Here are some of the methods that add simple data types to the extra data:

```
putExtra(String name, boolean value);
putExtra(String name, int value);
putExtra(String name, double value);
putExtra(String name, String value);
```

And here are some not-so-simple extras:

```
//simple array support
putExtra(String name, int[] values);
putExtra(String name, float[] values);

//Serializable objects
putExtra(String name, Serializable value);

//Parcelable support
putExtra(String name, Parcelable value);

//Add another bundle at a given key
//Bundles in bundles
putExtra(String name, Bundle value);

//Add bundles from another intent
//copy of bundles
putExtra(String name, Intent anotherIntent);

//Explicit Array List support
putIntegerArrayListExtra(String name, ArrayList arrayList);
putParcelableArrayListExtra(String name, ArrayList arrayList);
putStringArrayListExtra(String name, ArrayList arrayList);
```

On the receiving side, equivalent methods starting with `get` retrieve information from the extra bundle based on key names.

The `Intent` class defines extra key strings that go with certain actions. You can discover a number of these extra-information key constants at `http://developer.android.com/reference/android/content/Intent.html#EXTRA_ALARM_COUNT`.

Let's consider a couple of example extras listed at this URL that involve sending e-mails:

- `EXTRA_EMAIL`: You will use this string key to hold a set of e-mail addresses. The value of the key is `android.intent.extra.EMAIL`. It should point to a string array of textual e-mail addresses.
- `EXTRA_SUBJECT`: You will use this key to hold the subject of an e-mail message. The value of the key is `android.intent.extra.SUBJECT`. The key should point to a string of subject.

Using Components to Directly Invoke an Activity

You've seen a couple of ways to start an activity using intents. You saw an explicit action start an activity, and you saw a generic action start an activity with the help of a data URI. Android also provides a more direct way to start an activity: you can specify the activity's ComponentName, which is an abstraction around an object's package name and class name. There are a number of methods available on the Intent class to specify a component:

```
setComponent(ComponentName name);
setClassName(String packageName, String classNameInThatPackage);
setClassName(Context context, String classNameInThatContext);
setClass(Context context, Class classObjectInThatContext);
```

Ultimately, they are all shortcuts for calling one method:

```
setComponent(ComponentName name);
```

ComponentName wraps a package name and a class name together. For example, the following code invokes the contacts activity that ships with the emulator:

```
Intent intent = new Intent();
intent.setComponent(new ComponentName(
     "com.android.contacts"
    ,"com.android.contacts.DialContactsEntryActivity");
startActivity(intent);
```

Notice that the package name and the class name are fully qualified and are used in turn to construct the ComponentName before passing to the Intent class.

You can also use the class name directly without constructing a ComponentName. Consider the BasicViewActivity code snippet again:

```
public class BasicViewActivity extends Activity
{
    @Override
    public void onCreate(Bundle savedInstanceState)
    {
        super.onCreate(savedInstanceState);
        setContentView(R.layout.some_view);
    }
}//eof-class
```

Given this, you can use the following code to start this activity:

```
Intent directIntent = new Intent(activity, BasicViewActivity.class);
activity.start(directIntent);
```

If you want any type of intent to start an activity, however, you should register the activity in the Android.Manifest.xml file like this:

```
<activity android:name=".BasicViewActivity"
          android:label="Test Activity">
```

No intent filters are necessary for invoking an activity directly through its class name or name. As explained earlier, this type of intent is called an explicit intent. Because an explicit intent specifies a fully qualified Android component to invoke, the additional parts of that intent are ignored while invoking that component.

Understanding Intent Categories

You can classify activities into categories so you can search for them based on a category name. For example, during startup Android looks for activities whose category is marked as `CATEGORY_LAUNCHER`. It then picks up these activity names and icons and places them on the home screen to launch.

Here's another example: Android looks for an activity tagged as `CATEGORY_HOME` to show the home screen during startup. Similarly, `CATEGORY_GADGET` marks an activity as suitable for embedding or reuse inside another activity.

The format of the string for a category like `CATEGORY_LAUNCHER` follows the `category` definition convention:

```
android.intent.category.LAUNCHER
```

You will need to know these text strings for `category` definitions because activities register their categories in the `AndroidManifest.xml` file as part of their activity filter definitions. Here is an example:

```
<activity android:name=".HelloWorldActivity"
          android:label="@string/app_name">
    <intent-filter>
        <action android:name="android.intent.action.MAIN" />
        <category android:name="android.intent.category.LAUNCHER" />
    </intent-filter>
</activity>
```

NOTE: Activities might have certain capabilities that restrict them or enable them, such as whether you can embed them in a parent activity. These types of activity characteristics are declared through categories.

Let's take a quick look at some predefined Android categories and how to use them (see Table 5–1).

Table 5–1. *Activity Categories and Their Descriptions*

Category Name	Description
CATEGORY_DEFAULT	An activity can declare itself as a DEFAULT activity if it wants to be invoked by implicit intents. If you don't define this category for your activity, that activity will need to be invoked explicitly every time through its class name. This is why you see activities that get invoked through generic actions or other action names use default category specification.
CATEGORY_BROWSABLE	An activity can declare itself as BROWSABLE by promising the browser that it will not violate browser security considerations when started.
CATEGORY_TAB	An activity of this type is embeddable in a tabbed parent activity.
CATEGORY_ALTERNATIVE	An activity can declare itself as an ALTERNATIVE activity for a certain type of data that you are viewing. These items normally show up as part of the options menu when you are looking at that document. For example, print view is considered an alternative to regular view.
CATEGORY_SELECTED_ALTERNATIVE	An activity can declare itself as an ALTERNATIVE activity for a certain type of data. This is similar to listing a series of possible editors for a text document or an HTML document.
CATEGORY_LAUNCHER	Assigning this category to an activity will allow it to be listed on the launcher screen.
CATEGORY_HOME	An activity of this type will be the home screen. Typically, there should be only one activity of this type. If there are more, the system will provide a prompt to pick one.
CATEGORY_PREFERENCE	This activity identifies an activity as a preference activity, so it will be shown as part of the preferences screen.
CATEGORY_GADGET	An activity of this type is embeddable in a parent activity.
CATEGORY_TEST	This is a test activity.
CATEGORY_EMBED	This category has been superseded by the GADGET category, but it's been kept for backward compatibility.

You can read the details of these activity categories at the following Android SDK URL for the Intent class: http://developer.android.com/android/reference/android/content/Intent.html#CATEGORY_ALTERNATIVE.

When you use an intent to start an activity, you can specify the kind of activity to choose by specifying a category. Or you can search for activities that match a certain category. Here is an example to retrieve a set of main activities that match the category of CATEGORY_LAUNCHER:

```
Intent mainIntent = new Intent(Intent.ACTION_MAIN, null);
mainIntent.addCategory(Intent.CATEGORY_LAUNCHER);
```

```
PackageManager pm = getPackageManager();
List<ResolveInfo> list = pm.queryIntentActivities(mainIntent, 0);
```

PackageManager is a key class that allows you to discover activities that match certain intents without invoking them. You can cycle through the received activities and invoke them as you see fit, based on the ResolveInfo API. Here is an extension to the preceding code that walks through the list of activities and invokes one of the activities if it matches a name. In the code, we have a used an arbitrary name to test it.

```
for(ResolveInfo ri: list)
{
    //ri.activityInfo.
    Log.d("test",ri.toString());
    String packagename = ri.activityInfo.packageName;
    String classname = ri.activityInfo.name;
    Log.d("test", packagename + ":" + classname);
    if (classname.equals("com.ai.androidbook.resources.TestActivity"))
    {
        Intent ni = new Intent();
        ni.setClassName(packagename,classname);
        activity.startActivity(ni);
    }
}
```

You can also start an activity based purely on an intent category such as CATEGORY_LAUNCHER:

```
public static void invokeAMainApp(Activity activity)
{
   Intent mainIntent = new Intent(Intent.ACTION_MAIN, null);
   mainIntent.addCategory(Intent.CATEGORY_LAUNCHER);
   activity.startActivity(mainIntent);
}
```

More than one activity will match the intent, so which activity will Android pick? To resolve this, Android presents a “Complete action using” dialog that lists all the possible activities so you can choose one to run.

Here is another example of using an intent to go to a home page:

```
//Go to home screen
Intent mainIntent = new Intent(Intent.ACTION_MAIN, null);
mainIntent.addCategory(Intent.CATEGORY_HOME);
startActivity(mainIntent);
```

If you don’t want to use Android’s default home page, you can write your own and declare that activity to be of category HOME. In that case, the preceding code will give you an option to open your home activity because more than one home activity is registered now:

```
//Replace the home screen with yours
<intent-filter>
   <action android:value="android.intent.action.MAIN" />
   <category android:value="android.intent.category.HOME"/>
   <category android:value="android.intent.category.DEFAULT" />
</intent-filter>
```

Rules for Resolving Intents to Their Components

So far, we have discussed a number of aspects about intents. To recap, we talked about actions, data URIs, extra data, and finally, categories. Given these aspects, Android uses multiple strategies to match intents to their target activities based on intent filters.

At the top of the hierarchy is the component name attached to an intent. If this is set, the intent is known as an explicit intent. For an explicit intent, only the component name matters; every other aspect or attribute of the intent is ignored. When a component name is not present on an intent the intent is said to be an implicit intent. The rules for resolving targets for implicit intents are numerous.

The basic rule is that an incoming intent's action, category, and data characteristics *must* match (or present) those specified in the intent filter. An intent filter, unlike an intent, can specify multiple actions, categories, and data attributes. This means the same intent filter can satisfy multiple intents, which is to say that an activity can respond to many intents. However, the meaning of "match" differs among actions, data attributes, and categories. Let's look the matching criteria for each of the parts of an implicit intent.

Action

If an intent has an action on it, the intent filter must have that action as part of its action list or not have any actions at all. So if an intent filter *doesn't define an action*, that intent filter *is a match* for any incoming intent action.

If one or more actions are specified in the intent filter, at least one of the actions must match the incoming intents action.

Data

If no data characteristics are specified in an intent filter, it does not match an incoming intent that carries any data or data attribute. This means it will only look for intents that have no data specified at all.

Lack of data and lack of action (in the filter) works the opposite. If there is no action in the filter, every thing is a match. If there is no datain the filter, every bit of data in the intent is a mismatch.

Data Type

For a data type to match, the incoming intent's data type must be one of the data types that is specified in the intent filter. The data type in the intentmust be present in the intent filter.

The incoming intents data type is determined in one of two ways. First, if the data URI is a content or file URI, the content provider or android will figure out the type. The second way is to look at the explicit data type of the intent. For this to work, the incoming intent should not have a data URI set, because this is automatically taken care of when `setType` is called on the intent.

Android also allows as part of its mime type specification to have an asterisk (*) as its subtype to cover all possible subtypes.

Also, the data type is case sensitive.

Data Scheme

For a data scheme to match, the incoming intent data scheme must be one of those specified in the intent filter. In other words, the incoming data scheme must be present in the intent filter.

The incoming intents scheme is the first part of the data URI. On an intent, there is no method to set the scheme. It is purely derived from the intent data URI that looks like `http://www.somesite.com/somepath`.

If the data scheme of the incoming intent URI is `content:` or `file:`, it is considered a match irrespective of the intent filter scheme, domain, and path. According to the SDK, this is so because every component is expected to know how to read data from content or file URLs, which are essentially local. In other words, all components are expected to support these two types of URLs.

The scheme is also case sensitive.

Data Authority

If there are no authorities in the filter, you have a match for any incoming data URI authority (or domain name). If an authority is specified in the filter, for example, `www.somesite.com`, then one scheme and one authority should match the incoming intents data URI.

For example, if we specify `www.somesite.com` as the authority in the intent filter and the scheme as `https`, the intent will fail to match `http://www.somesite.com/somepath` as `http` is not indicated as the supporting scheme.

The authority is case sensitive as well.

Data Path

No data paths in the intent filter means a match for any incoming data URI's path. If a path is specified in the filter, for example, `somepath`, one scheme, one authority, and one data path should match the incoming intent's data URI.

In other words scheme, authority, and path work together to validate an incoming intent URI such as `http://www.somesite.com/somepath`. So `path`, `authority`, and `scheme` work not in isolation but together.

The path, too, is case sensitive.

Intent Categories

Every category in the incoming intent must be present in the filter category list. Having more categories in the filter is OK. If a filter *doesn't have any categories*, it will match *only with an intent that doesn't have any* categories mentioned.

However, there is a caveat. Android treats all *implicit* intents passed to `startActivity()` as if they contained at least one category: `android.intent.category.DEFAULT`. The code in `startActivity()` will search only for those activities that have `DEFAULT` category defined if the incoming intent is an implicit intent. So every activity that wants to be invoked through an implicit intent must include the default category in its filters.

Even if an activity doesn't have the default category in its intent filter, if you know its explicit component names, you will be able to start it like the launcher does. If you explicitly search for matching intents yourself without having a default category as a search criteria, you will be able to start those activities that way.

In that sense this `DEFAULT` category is an artifact of the `startActivity` implementation and not an inherent behavior of filters.

There is an additional wrinkle because Android states that the default category is unnecessary if the activity is intended to be invoked only from launcher screens. So these activities tend to have only `MAIN` and `LAUNCHER` categories as part of their filters. However, the `DEFAULT` category can be optionally specified for these activities as well.

Exercising the ACTION_PICK

So far, we have exercised intents or actions that mainly invoke another activity without expecting a result back. Let's look at an action that is a bit more involved, where it returns a value after being invoked. `ACTION_PICK` is one such generic action.

The idea of `ACTION_PICK` is to start an activity that displays a list of items. The activity then should allow a user to pick one item from that list. Once the user picks the item, the activity should return the URI of the picked item to the caller. This allows reuse of the UI's functionality to select items of a certain type.

You should indicate the collection of items to choose from using a MIME type that points to an Android content cursor. The MIME type of this URI should look similar to the following:

```
vnd.android.cursor.dir/vnd.google.note
```

It is the responsibility of the activity to retrieve the data from the content provider based on the URI. This is also the reason that data should be encapsulated into content providers where possible.

For actions that return data like this, we cannot use `startActivity()`, because `startActivity()` does not return a result. `startActivity()` cannot return a result, because it opens the new activity as a modal dialog in a separate thread and leaves the main thread for attending events. In other words, `startActivity()` is an asynchronous call with no callbacks to indicate what happened in the invoked activity. If you want to return data, you can use a variation of `startActivity()` called `startActivityForResult()`, which comes with a callback.

Let's look at the signature of the `startActivityForResult()` method from the `Activity` class:

```
public void startActivityForResult(Intent intent, int requestCode)
```

This method launches an activity from which you would like a result. When this activity exits, the source activity's `onActivityResult()` method will be called with the given `requestCode`. The signature of this callback method is

```
protected void onActivityResult(int requestCode, int resultCode, Intent data)
```

`requestCode` is what you passed in to the `startActivityForResult()` method. The `resultCode` can be `RESULT_OK`, `RESULT_CANCELED`, or a custom code. The custom codes should start at `RESULT_FIRST_USER`. The `Intent` parameter contains any additional data that the invoked activity wants to return. In the case of `ACTION_PICK`, the returned data in the intent points to the data URI of a single item.

Listing 5–3 demonstrates invoking an activity that sends a result back.

> **NOTE:** The code in Listing 5–3 assumes that you have installed the NotePad sample project from the Android SDK distribution. We have included a link at the end of this chapter that gives you directions on how to download the NotePad sample if you don't have it in the SDK already.

Listing 5–3. *Returning Data After Invoking an Action*

```
public class SomeActivity extends Activity
{
.....
.....
public static void invokePick(Activity activity)
{
  Intent pickIntent = new Intent(Intent.ACTION_PICK);
  int requestCode = 1;
  pickIntent.setData(Uri.parse(
     "content://com.google.provider.NotePad/notes"));
  activity.startActivityForResult(pickIntent, requestCode);
}

protected void onActivityResult(int requestCode
     ,int resultCode
     ,Intent outputIntent)
{
  //This is to inform the parent class (Activity)
  //that the called activity has finished and the baseclass
  //can do the necessary clean up
  super.onActivityResult(requestCode, resultCode, outputIntent);
  parseResult(this, requestCode, resultCode, outputIntent);
}
public static void parseResult(Activity activity
     , int requestCode
     , int resultCode
```

```
        , Intent outputIntent)
{
    if (requestCode != 1)
    {
     Log.d("Test", "Some one else called this. not us");
            return;
    }
    if (resultCode != Activity.RESULT_OK)
    {
      Log.d(Test, "Result code is not ok:" + resultCode);
              return;
    }
    Log.d("Test", "Result code is ok:" + resultCode);
    Uri selectedUri = outputIntent.getData();
    Log.d("Test", "The output uri:" + selectedUri.toString());

    //Proceed to display the note
    outputIntent.setAction(Intent.ACTION_VIEW);
    startActivity(outputIntent);
}
```

The constants RESULT_OK, RESULT_CANCELED, and RESULT_FIRST_USER are all defined in the Activity class. The numerical values of these constants are

```
RESULT_OK = -1;
RESULT_CANCELED = 0;
RESULT_FIRST_USER = 1;
```

To make the PICK functionality work, the implementer that is responding should have code that explicitly addresses the needs of a PICK. Let's look at how this is done in the Google sample NotePad application. When the item is selected in the list of items, the intent that invoked the activity is checked to see whether it's a PICK intent. If it is, the data URI is set in a new intent and returned through setResult():

```
@Override
protected void onListItemClick(ListView l, View v, int position, long id) {
    Uri uri = ContentUris.withAppendedId(getIntent().getData(), id);

    String action = getIntent().getAction();
    if (Intent.ACTION_PICK.equals(action) ||
              Intent.ACTION_GET_CONTENT.equals(action))
   {
        // The caller is waiting for us to return a note selected by
        // the user.  They have clicked on one, so return it now.
        setResult(RESULT_OK, new Intent().setData(uri));
    } else {
        // Launch activity to view/edit the currently selected item
        startActivity(new Intent(Intent.ACTION_EDIT, uri));
    }
}
```

Exercising the GET_CONTENT Action

ACTION_GET_CONTENT is similar to ACTION_PICK. In the case of ACTION_PICK, you are specifying a URI that points to a collection of items, such as a collection of notes. You will expect the action to pick one of the notes and return it to the caller. In the case of ACTION_GET_CONTENT, you indicate to Android that you need an item of a particular MIME type. Android searches for either activities that can create one of those items or activities that can choose from an existing set of items that satisfy that MIME type.

Using ACTION_GET_CONTENT, you can pick a note from a collection of notes supported by the NotePad application using the following code:

```
public static void invokeGetContent(Activity activity)
{
      Intent pickIntent = new Intent(Intent.ACTION_GET_CONTENT);
      int requestCode = 2;
      pickIntent.setType("vnd.android.cursor.item/vnd.google.note");
      activity.startActivityForResult(pickIntent, requestCode);
}
```

Notice how the intent type is set to the MIME type of a single note. Contrast this with the ACTION_PICK code in the following snippet, where the input is a data URI:

```
public static void invokePick(Activity activity)
{
  Intent pickIntent = new Intent(Intent.ACTION_PICK);
  int requestCode = 1;
  pickIntent.setData(Uri.parse(
     "content://com.google.provider.NotePad/notes"));
  activity.startActivityForResult(pickIntent, requestCode);
}
```

For an activity to respond to ACTION_GET_CONTENT, the activity has to register an intent filter indicating that the activity can provide an item of that MIME type. Here is how the SDK's NotePad application accomplishes this:

```
<activity android:name="NotesList" android:label="@string/title_notes_list">
……
<intent-filter>
    <action android:name="android.intent.action.GET_CONTENT" />
    <category android:name="android.intent.category.DEFAULT" />
    <data android:mimeType="vnd.android.cursor.item/vnd.google.note" />
      </intent-filter>
……
</activity>
```

The rest of the code for responding to onActivityResult() is identical to the previous ACTION_PICK example. If there are multiple activities that can return the same MIME type, Android will show you the chooser dialog to let you pick an activity.

Introducing Pending Intents

Android has a variation on an intent called a pending intent. In this variation, Android allows a component to store an intent for future use in a location from which it can be invoked again. For example, in an alarm manager, you want to start a service when the alarm goes off. Android does this by creating a wrapper pending intent around an intent and storing it away so that even if the calling process dies off, the intent can be dispatched to its target. At the time of the pending intent creation, Android stores enough information about the originating process so that security credentials can be checked at the time of dispatch or invocation.

Let's see how we can go about creating a pending intent.

```
Intent regularIntent;
PendingIntent pi = PendingIntent.getActivity(context, 0, regularIntent,...);
```

> **NOTE:** The second argument to the `PendingIntent.getActivity()` method is called `requestCode` and in this example we are setting it to zero. This argument is used to distinguish two pending intents when their underlying intents are the same. This aspect is talked in much more detail in Chapter 15 where we talk about pending intents in the context of alarm managers.

There are a couple of odd things here when it comes to the naming of the method `PendingActivity.getActivity()`.What is the role of an activity here? Second, why don't we call `create` for creating a pending intent but instead use `get`?

To understand the first point, we have to dig a bit into the usage of a regular intent. A regular intent can be used to start an activity or a service or invoke a broadcast receiver. (You will learn about services and broadcast receivers later in this book). The nature of using an intent to call these different sorts of components is different. To accommodate this, an Android context (a superclass of `Activity`) provides three distinct methods. These are

```
startActivty(intent)
startService(intent)
sendBroadcast(intent)
```

Given these variations, if we were to store an intent to be reused later, how would Android know whether to start an activity, start a service, or start a broadcast reciever due to a broadcast? This is why we have to explicitly specify the purpose for which we are creating the pending intent when it's created, and it explains the following three separate methods:

```
PendingIntent.getActivity(context, 0, intent, ...)
PendingIntent.getService(context, 0, intent, ...)
PendingIntent.getBroadcast(context, 0, intent, ...)
```

Now to explain the "get" part. Android stores away intents and reuses them. If you ask for a pending intent using the same intent object twice, you get the same pending intent. This becomes a bit clear if you see the full signature of the `PendingIntent.getActivity()` method. Here it is:

```
PendingIntent.getActivity(Context context, //originating context
     int requestCode, //1,2, 3, etc
     Intent intent, //original intent
     int flags ) //flags
```

If your goal is to get a different copy of the pending intent, you have to supply a different `requestCode`. This need is explained in much greater detail when we cover alarm managers in Chapter 15. Two "intents" are considered identical if their internal parts match except for the extra bundle.

The flags indicate what to do if there is an existing pending intent—whether to return a null, overwrite extras, and so on. See the following URL to see more detail about the possible flags:

`http://developer.android.com/reference/android/app/PendingIntent.html`

Usually, you can pass a zero for `requestCode` and flags to get the default behavior.

Resources

Here are some useful links to further strengthen your understanding of this chapter:

- `http://developer.android.com/reference/android/content/Intent.html`: You will find the overview of intents at this URL. You will discover here well-known actions, extras, and so on.
- `http://developer.android.com/guide/appendix/g-app-intents.html`: This URL lists the intents for a set of Google applications. Here, you will see here how to invoke Browser, Map, Dialer, and Google Street View.
- `http://developer.android.com/reference/android/content/IntentFilter.html`: This URL talks about intent filters and is useful when you are registering intent filters.
- `http://developer.android.com/guide/topics/intents/intents-filters.html`: This URL goes into the resolution rules of intent filters.
- `http://developer.android.com/resources/samples/get.html`: You can use this URL to download the sample code for NotePad application. You will need this sample project loaded to test some of the intents.
- `http://developer.android.com/resources/samples/NotePad/index.html`: You can use this URL to browse the source code online for the NotePad application.
- `http://www.openintents.org/`: This URL points to a web effort to collect open intents from various vendors.
- `http://www.androidbook.com/projects`: You can use this URL to download the test project dedicated for this chapter. The name of the ZIP file is `ProAndroid3_ch05_TestIntents.zip`.

Summary

In this chapter, we have identified important elements about an Android intent. We have explored various scenarios in which intents can be used, and we showed you the relationship between intents and content URIs. We explained how you can use intents to invoke activities that return results as well. We also introduced pending intents, which we will explore further when we use them in Chapters 15 and 22.

Chapter 6

Building User Interfaces and Using Controls

Thus far, we have covered the fundamentals of Android but have not touched the user interface (UI). In this chapter, we are going to discuss user interfaces and controls. We will begin by discussing the general philosophy of UI development in Android, then we'll describe the common UI controls that ship with the Android SDK. We will also discuss layout managers and view adapters. We will conclude by discussing the Hierarchy Viewer tool—a tool used to debug and optimize Android UIs.

UI Development in Android

UI development in Android is fun. It's fun because it's relatively easy. With Android, we have a simple-to-understand framework with a limited set of out-of-the-box controls. The available screen area is generally limited. Android also takes care of a lot of the heavy lifting normally associated to designing and building quality UIs. This, combined with the fact that the user usually wants to do one specific action, allows us to easily build a good user interface to deliver a good user experience.

The Android SDK ships with a host of controls that you can use to build user interfaces for your application. Similar to other SDKs, the Android SDK provides text fields, buttons, lists, grids, and so on. In addition, Android provides a collection of controls that are appropriate for mobile devices.

At the heart of the common controls are two classes: `android.view.View` and `android.view.ViewGroup`. As the name of the first class suggests, the `View` class represents a general-purpose `View` object. The common controls in Android ultimately extend the `View` class. `ViewGroup` is also a view, but contains other views too. `ViewGroup` is the base class for a list of layout classes. Android, like Swing, uses the concept of layouts to manage how controls are laid out within a container view. Using layouts, as we'll see, makes it easy for us to control the position and orientation of the controls in our user interfaces.

You can choose from several approaches to build user interfaces in Android. You can construct user interfaces entirely in code. You can also define user interfaces in XML. You can even combine the two—define the user interface in XML and then refer to it, and modify it, in code. To demonstrate this, we are going to build a simple user interface using each of these three approaches.

Before we get started, let's define some nomenclature. In this book and other Android literature, you will find the terms *view*, *control*, *widget*, *container*, and *layout* in discussions regarding UI development. If you are new to Android programming or UI development in general, you might not be familiar with these terms. We'll briefly describe them before we get started (see Table 6–1).

Table 6–1. *UI Nomenclature*

Term	Description
View, Widget, Control	Each of these represents a user interface element. Examples include a button, a grid, a list, a window, a dialog box, and so on. The terms "view," "widget," and "control" are used interchangeably in this chapter.
Container	This is a view used to contain other views. For example, a grid can be considered a container because it contains cells, each of which is a view.
Layout	This is a visual arrangement of containers and views and can include other layouts.

Figure 6–1 shows a screenshot of the application that we are going to build. Next to the screenshot is the layout hierarchy of the controls and containers in the application.

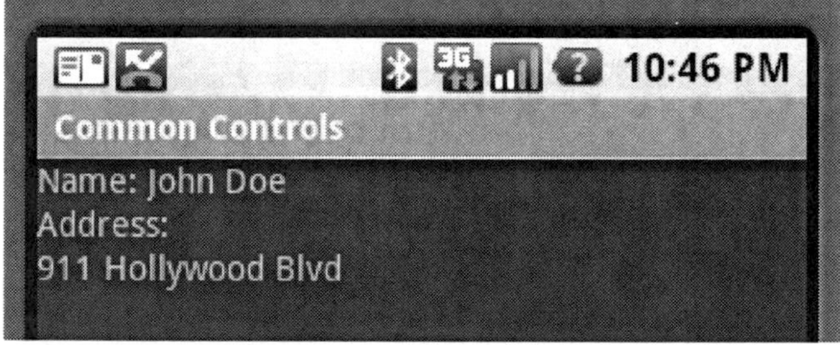

Figure 6–1. *The user interface and layout of an activity*

We will refer to this layout hierarchy as we discuss the sample programs. For now, know that the application has one activity. The user interface for the activity is composed of three containers: a container that contains a person's name, a container that contains the address, and an outer parent container for the child containers.

Building a UI Completely in Code

The first example, Listing 6–1, demonstrates how to build the user interface entirely in code. To try this out, create a new Android project with an activity named `MainActivity` and then copy the code from Listing 6–1 into your `MainActivity` class.

NOTE: We will give you a URL at the end of the chapter which you can use to download projects from this chapter. This will allow you to import these projects into your Eclipse directly, instead of copying and pasting code.

Listing 6–1. *Creating a Simple User Interface Entirely in Code*

```
package com.androidbook.controls;
import android.app.Activity;
import android.os.Bundle;
import android.view.ViewGroup.LayoutParams;
import android.widget.LinearLayout;
import android.widget.TextView;
public class MainActivity extends Activity
{
    private LinearLayout nameContainer;

    private LinearLayout addressContainer;

    private LinearLayout parentContainer;

    /** Called when the activity is first created. */
    @Override
    public void onCreate(Bundle savedInstanceState)
    {
        super.onCreate(savedInstanceState);

        createNameContainer();

        createAddressContainer();

        createParentContainer();

        setContentView(parentContainer);
    }

    private void createNameContainer()
    {
        nameContainer = new LinearLayout(this);

        nameContainer.setLayoutParams(new LayoutParams(LayoutParams.FILL_PARENT,
                LayoutParams.WRAP_CONTENT));
        nameContainer.setOrientation(LinearLayout.HORIZONTAL);

        TextView nameLbl = new TextView(this);
        nameLbl.setText("Name: ");

        TextView nameValue = new TextView(this);
        nameValue.setText("John Doe");
```

```
        nameContainer.addView(nameLbl);
        nameContainer.addView(nameValue);
    }

    private void createAddressContainer()
    {
        addressContainer = new LinearLayout(this);

        addressContainer.setLayoutParams(new LayoutParams(LayoutParams.FILL_PARENT,
                LayoutParams.WRAP_CONTENT));
        addressContainer.setOrientation(LinearLayout.VERTICAL);

        TextView addrLbl = new TextView(this);
        addrLbl.setText("Address:");

        TextView addrValue = new TextView(this);
        addrValue.setText("911 Hollywood Blvd");

        addressContainer.addView(addrLbl);
        addressContainer.addView(addrValue);
    }

    private void createParentContainer()
    {
        parentContainer = new LinearLayout(this);

        parentContainer.setLayoutParams(new LayoutParams(LayoutParams.FILL_PARENT,
                LayoutParams.FILL_PARENT));
        parentContainer.setOrientation(LinearLayout.VERTICAL);

        parentContainer.addView(nameContainer);
        parentContainer.addView(addressContainer);
    }
}
```

As shown in Listing 6–1, the activity contains three `LinearLayout` objects. As we mentioned earlier, layout objects contain logic to position objects within a portion of the screen. A `LinearLayout`, for example, knows how to lay out controls either vertically or horizontally. Layout objects can contain any type of view—even other layouts.

The `nameContainer` object contains two `TextView` controls: one for the label `Name:` and the other to hold the actual name (i.e., John Doe). The `addressContainer` also contains two `TextView` controls. The difference between the two containers is that the `nameContainer` is laid out horizontally and the `addressContainer` is laid out vertically. Both of these containers live within the `parentContainer`, which is the root view of the activity. After the containers have been built, the activity sets the content of the view to the root view by calling `setContentView(parentContainer)`. When it comes time to render the user interface of the activity, the root view is called to render itself. The root view then calls its children to render themselves, and the child controls call their children, and so on, until the entire user interface is rendered.

As shown in Listing 6–1, we have several `LinearLayout` controls. Two of them are laid out vertically and one is laid out horizontally. The `nameContainer` is laid out horizontally.

This means the two TextView controls appear side by side horizontally. The addressContainer is laid out vertically, which means that the two TextView controls are stacked one on top of the other. The parentContainer is also laid out vertically, which is why the nameContainer appears above the addressContainer. Note a subtle difference between the two vertically laid-out containers, addressContainer and parentContainer: parentContainer is set to take up the entire width and height of the screen.

```
parentContainer.setLayoutParams(new LayoutParams(LayoutParams.FILL_PARENT,
        LayoutParams.FILL_PARENT));
```

And addressContainer wraps its content vertically:

```
addressContainer.setLayoutParams(new LayoutParams(LayoutParams.FILL_PARENT,
        LayoutParams.WRAP_CONTENT));
```

Said another way, WRAP_CONTENT means that the view should take just the space it needs in that dimension and no more, up to what the containing view will allow. For the addressContainer, this means the container will take two lines vertically, because that's all it needs.

Building a UI Completely in XML

Now let's build the same user interface in XML (see Listing 6–2). Recall from Chapter 3 that XML layout files are stored under the resources (/res/) directory within a folder called layout. To try out this example, create a new Android project in Eclipse. By default, you will get an XML layout file named main.xml, located under the res/layout folder. Double-click main.xml to see the contents. Eclipse will display a visual editor for your layout file. You probably have a string at the top of the view that says "Hello World, MainActivity!" or something like that. Click the main.xml tab at the bottom of the view to see the XML of the main.xml file. This reveals a LinearLayout and a TextView control. Using either the Layout or main.xml tab, or both, re-create Listing 6–2 in the main.xml file. Save it.

Listing 6–2. *Creating a User Interface Entirely in XML*

```
<?xml version="1.0" encoding="utf-8"?>
<LinearLayout xmlns:android="http://schemas.android.com/apk/res/android"
    android:orientation="vertical" android:layout_width="fill_parent"
    android:layout_height="fill_parent">
    <!-- NAME CONTAINER -->
    <LinearLayout xmlns:android="http://schemas.android.com/apk/res/android"
        android:orientation="horizontal" android:layout_width="fill_parent"
        android:layout_height="wrap_content">

            <TextView  android:layout_width="wrap_content"
        android:layout_height="wrap_content" android:text="Name:" />

            <TextView android:layout_width="wrap_content"
        android:layout_height="wrap_content" android:text="John Doe" />

    </LinearLayout>

    <!-- ADDRESS CONTAINER -->
```

```
    <LinearLayout xmlns:android="http://schemas.android.com/apk/res/android"
        android:orientation="vertical" android:layout_width="fill_parent"
        android:layout_height="wrap_content">

            <TextView android:layout_width="fill_parent"
        android:layout_height="wrap_content" android:text="Address:" />

            <TextView android:layout_width="fill_parent"
        android:layout_height="wrap_content" android:text="911 Hollywood Blvd." />
    </LinearLayout>

</LinearLayout>
```

Under your new project's src directory, there is a default .java file containing an Activity class definition. Double-click that file to see its contents. Notice the statement setContentView(R.layout.main). The XML snippet shown in Listing 6–2, combined with a call to setContentView(R.layout.main), will render the same user interface as before when we generated it completely in code. The XML file is self-explanatory, but note that we have three container views defined. The first LinearLayout is the equivalent of our parent container. This container sets its orientation to vertical by setting the corresponding property like this: android:orientation="vertical". The parent container contains two LinearLayout containers, which represent the nameContainer and addressContainer.

Running this application will produce the same UI as our previous example application. The labels and values will be displayed as shown in Figure 6–1.

Building a UI in XML With Code

Listing 6–2 is a contrived example. It doesn't make any sense to hard-code the values of the TextView controls in the XML layout. Ideally, we should design our user interfaces in XML and then reference the controls from code. This approach enables us to bind dynamic data to the controls defined at design time. In fact, this is the recommended approach. It is fairly easy to build layouts in XML and then use code to populate the dynamic data.

Listing 6–3 shows the same user interface with slightly different XML. This XML assigns IDs to the TextView controls so that we can refer to them in code.

Listing 6–3. *Creating a User Interface in XML with IDs*

```
<?xml version="1.0" encoding="utf-8"?>
<LinearLayout xmlns:android="http://schemas.android.com/apk/res/android"
    android:orientation="vertical" android:layout_width="fill_parent"
    android:layout_height="fill_parent">
    <!-- NAME CONTAINER -->
    <LinearLayout xmlns:android="http://schemas.android.com/apk/res/android"
        android:orientation="horizontal" android:layout_width="fill_parent"
        android:layout_height="wrap_content">

            <TextView android:layout_width="wrap_content"
        android:layout_height="wrap_content" android:text="@string/name_text" />
```

```
        <TextView android:id="@+id/nameValue"
    android:layout_width="wrap_content" android:layout_height="wrap_content" />

  </LinearLayout>

  <!-- ADDRESS CONTAINER -->
  <LinearLayout xmlns:android="http://schemas.android.com/apk/res/android"
      android:orientation="vertical" android:layout_width="fill_parent"
      android:layout_height="wrap_content">

        <TextView android:layout_width="fill_parent"
    android:layout_height="wrap_content" android:text="@string/addr_text" />

        <TextView android:id="@+id/addrValue"
    android:layout_width="fill_parent" android:layout_height="wrap_content" />
  </LinearLayout>

</LinearLayout>
```

In addition to adding the IDs to the TextView controls that we want to populate from code, we also have label TextView controls that we're populating with text from our strings resource file. These are the TextViews without IDs that have an android:text attribute. As you may recall from Chapter 3, the actual strings for these TextViews will come from our strings.xml file in the /res/values folder. Listing 6–4 shows what our strings.xml file might look like.

Listing 6–4. *Our strings.xml File for Listing 6–3*

```
<?xml version="1.0" encoding="utf-8"?>
<resources>
    <string name="app_name">Common Controls</string>
    <string name="name_text">Name:</string>
    <string name="addr_text">Address:</string>
</resources>;
```

The code in Listing 6–5 demonstrates how you can obtain references to the controls defined in the XML to set their properties. You might put this into your onCreate() method for your Activity.

Listing 6–5. *Referring to Controls in Resources at Runtime*

```
setContentView(R.layout.main);

TextView nameValue = (TextView)findViewById(R.id.nameValue);
nameValue.setText("John Doe");
TextView addrValue = (TextView)findViewById(R.id.addrValue);
addrValue.setText("911 Hollywood Blvd.");
```

The code in Listing 6–5 is straightforward, but note that we load the resource, by calling setContentView(R.layout.main), before calling findViewById()—we cannot get references to views if they have not been loaded yet.

The developers of Android have done a nice job of making just about every aspect of a control settable via XML or code. It's usually a good idea to set the control's attributes in the XML layout file rather than using code. However, there will be lots of times when you need to use code, such as setting a value to be displayed to the user.

FILL_PARENT vs. MATCH_PARENT

The constant FILL_PARENT was deprecated in Android 2.2 and replaced with MATCH_PARENT. This was strictly a name change though. The value of this constant is still –1. Similarly for XML layouts, "fill_parent" was replaced with "match_parent". So what value do you use? Instead of FILL_PARENT or MATCH_PARENT, you could simply use the value –1, and you'd be fine. However, this isn't very easy to read, and you don't have an equivalent unnamed value to use with your XML layouts. There's a better way.

Depending on which Android APIs you need to use in your application, you can either build your application against a version of Android before 2.2 and rely on forward compatibility or build your application against version 2.2 or later of Android and set the minSdkVersion to the lowest version of Android your application will run on. For example, if you only need APIs that existed in Android 1.6, build against Android 1.6, and use FILL_PARENT and "fill_parent". Your application should run with no problems in all later versions of Android including 2.2 and beyond. If you need APIs from Android 2.2 or later, go ahead and build against that version of Android, use MATCH_PARENT "match_parent" and set minSdkVersion to the something older, for example "4" (for Android 1.6). You can still deploy an Android application built in Android 2.2 to an older version of Android, but you'll have to take care of the classes and/or methods that aren't in the earlier releases of the Android SDK. There are ways around this, such as using reflection or creating wrapper classes to handle differences in Android versions. We won't cover that here though.

Understanding Android's Common Controls

We will now start our discussion of the common controls in the Android SDK. We'll start with text controls and then discuss buttons, check boxes, radio buttons, lists, grids, date and time controls, and a map-view control. We will also talk about layout controls.

Text Controls

Text controls are likely to be the first type of control that you'll work with in Android. Android has a complete, but not overwhelming, set of text controls. In this section, we are going to discuss the TextView, EditText, AutoCompleteTextView, and MultiCompleteTextView controls. Figure 6–2 shows the controls in action.

Figure 6–2. *Text controls in Android*

TextView

You've already seen a simple XML specification for a `TextView` control, in Listing 6–3, and how to handle `TextViews` in code in Listing 6–4. Notice how we specified the ID, width, height and value of the text in XML and how we set the value using the `setText()` method. The `TextView` control knows how to display text but does not allow editing. This might lead you to conclude that the control is essentially a dummy label. Not true. The `TextView` control has a few interesting properties that make it very handy. If you know that the content of the `TextView` is going to contain a web URL or an e-mail address, for example, you can set the `autoLink` property to `"email|web",` and the control will find and highlight any email addresses and URLs. Moreover, when the user clicks on one of these highlighted items, the system will take care of launching the email application with the email address, or a browser with the URL. In XML, this attribute would be inside the `TextView` tag and would look something like this:

```
<TextView   ...     android:autoLink="email|web"    ...    />
```

where you specify a pipe-delimited set of values including "web", "email", "phone" or "map", or use "none" (the default) or "all". If you want to set autoLink behavior in code instead of using XML, the corresponding method call is `setAutoLinkMask()`. You would pass it an int representing the combination of values sort of like before, such as Linkify.EMAIL_ADDRESSES|Linkify.WEB_ADDRESSES. To achieve this functionality, TextView is utilizing the android.text.util.Linkify class. Listing 6–6 shows an example of auto-linking with code.

Listing 6–6. *Using Linkify on Text in a TextView*

```
TextView tv =(TextView)this.findViewById(R.id.tv);
tv.setAutoLinkMask(Linkify.ALL);
tv.setText("Please visit my website, http://www.androidbook.com
or email me at davemac327@gmail.com.");
```

Notice that we set the auto-link options on our TextView before we set the text. This is important because setting the auto-link options after setting the text won't affect the existing text. Because we're using code to add hyperlinks to our text, our XML for the TextView in Listing 6–6 does not require any special attributes and can look as simple as this:

```
<TextView android:id="@+id/tv" android:layout_width="wrap_content"
  android:layout_height="wrap_content"/>
```

If you want to, you can invoke the static addLinks() method of the Linkify class to find and add links to the content of any TextView or any Spannable on demand. Instead of using setAutoLinkMask(), we could have done the following *after* setting the text:

```
Linkify.addLinks(tv, Linkify.ALL);
```

Clicking a link will cause the default intent to be called for that action. For example, clicking a web URL will launch the browser with the URL. Clicking a phone number will launch the phone dialer, and so on. The Linkify class can perform this work right out of the box.

Linkify can also detect custom patterns you want to look for, decide if they are a match for something you decide needs to be clickable, and set up how to fire an intent to make a click turn into some sort of action. We won't go into those details here, but know that these things can be done.

There are many more features of TextView to explore, from font attributes to minLines and maxLines and many more. These are fairly self-explanatory, and you are encouraged to experiment to see how you might be able to use them. Although you should keep in mind that some functionality in the TextView class is not applicable to a read-only field, the functionality is there for the subclasses of TextView, one of which we will cover next.

EditText

The EditText control is a subclass of TextView. As suggested by the name, the EditText control allows for text editing. EditText is not as powerful as the text-editing controls that you find on the Internet, but users of Android-based devices probably won't type documents—they'll type a couple paragraphs at most. Therefore, the class has limited but appropriate functionality and may even surprise you. For example, one of the most significant properties of an EditText is the inputType. You can set the inputType property to textAutoCorrect have the control correct common misspellings. You can set it to textCapWords to have the control capitalize words. There are other options to expect only phone numbers or passwords.

There are older, now deprecated, ways of specifying capitalization, multiline text and other features. If these are specified without an inputType property, they can be read, but if inputType is specified at all, these older properties are ignored.

The old default behavior of the EditText control is to display text on one line and expand as needed. In other words, if the user types past the first line, another line will appear, and so on. You could, however, force the user to a single line by setting the singleLine property to true. In this case, the user will have to continue typing on the same line. With inputType, if you don't specify textMultiLine, the EditText will default to single line only. So if you want the old default behavior of multiline typing, you need to specify inputType with textMultiLine.

One of the nice features of EditText is that you can specify hint text. This text will be displayed slightly faded and disappears as soon as the user starts to type text. The purpose of the hint is to let the user know what is expected in this field, without the user having to select and erase default text. In XML, this attribute is android:hint="your hint text here" or android:hint="@string/your_hint_name", where your_hint_name is a resource name of a string to be found in /res/values/strings.xml. In code, you would call the setHint() method with either a CharSequence or a resource Id.

AutoCompleteTextView

The AutoCompleteTextView control is a TextView with auto-complete functionality. In other words, as the user types in the TextView, the control can display suggestions for selection. Listing 6–7 demonstrates the AutoCompleteTextView control with XML and with the corresponding code.

Listing 6–7. *Using an AutoCompleteTextView Control*

```
<AutoCompleteTextView android:id="@+id/actv"
    android:layout_width="fill_parent"  android:layout_height="wrap_content" />


AutoCompleteTextView actv = (AutoCompleteTextView) this.findViewById(R.id.actv);

ArrayAdapter<String> aa = new ArrayAdapter<String>(this,
                android.R.layout.simple_dropdown_item_1line,
                new String[] {"English", "Hebrew", "Hindi", "Spanish", "German", "Greek"
});

actv.setAdapter(aa);
```

The AutoCompleteTextView control shown in Listing 6–7 suggests a language to the user. For example, if the user types **en**, the control suggests English. If the user types **gr**, the control recommends Greek, and so on.

If you have used a suggestion control or a similar auto-complete control, you know that controls like this have two parts: a text-view control and a control that displays the suggestion(s). That's the general concept. To use a control like this, you have to create the control, create the list of suggestions, tell the control the list of suggestions, and possibly tell the control how to display the suggestions. Alternatively, you could create a second control for the suggestions and then associate the two controls.

Android has made this simple, as is evident from Listing 6–7. To use an `AutoCompleteTextView`, you can define the control in your layout file and reference it in your activity. You then create an adapter class that holds the suggestions and define the ID of the control that will show the suggestion (in this case, a simple list item). In Listing 6–7, the second parameter to the `ArrayAdapter` tells the adapter to use a simple list item to show the suggestion. The final step is to associate the adapter with the `AutoCompleteTextView`, which you do using the `setAdapter()` method. Don't worry about the adapter for the moment; we'll cover those later in this chapter.

MultiAutoCompleteTextView

If you have played with the `AutoCompleteTextView` control, you know that the control offers suggestions only for the *entire* text in the text view. In other words, if you type a sentence, you don't get suggestions for each word. That's where `MultiAutoCompleteTextView` comes in. You can use the `MultiAutoCompleteTextView` to provide suggestions as the user types. For example, Figure 6–2 shows that the user typed the word **English** followed by a comma, and then **Ge**, at which point the control suggested **German**. If the user were to continue, the control would offer additional suggestions.

Using the `MultiAutoCompleteTextView` is like using the `AutoCompleteTextView`. The difference is that you have to tell the control where to start suggesting again. For example, in Figure 6–2, you can see that the control can offer suggestions at the beginning of the sentence and after it sees a comma. The `MultiAutoCompleteTextView` control requires that you give it a tokenizer that can parse the sentence and tell it whether to start suggesting again. Listing 6–8 demonstrates using the `MultiAutoCompleteTextView` control with the XML and then the Java code.

Listing 6–8. ***Using the MultiAutoCompleteTextView Control***

```
<MultiAutoCompleteTextView android:id="@+id/mactv"
    android:layout_width="fill_parent"  android:layout_height="wrap_content" />


MultiAutoCompleteTextView mactv = (MultiAutoCompleteTextView) this
                .findViewById(R.id.mactv);
ArrayAdapter<String> aa2 = new ArrayAdapter<String>(this,
                android.R.layout.simple_dropdown_item_1line,
new String[] {"English", "Hebrew", "Hindi", "Spanish", "German", "Greek" });

mactv.setAdapter(aa2);

mactv.setTokenizer(new MultiAutoCompleteTextView.CommaTokenizer());
```

The only significant differences between Listings 6–7 and 6–8 are the use of `MultiAutoCompleteTextView` and the call to the `setTokenizer()` method. Because of the `CommaTokenizer` in this case, after a comma is typed into the `EditText` field, the field will again make suggestions using the array of strings. Any other characters typed in will not trigger the field to make suggestions. So even if you were to type **French Spani** the partial word "Spani" would not trigger the suggestion because it did not follow a comma. Android provides another tokenizer for e-mail addresses called `Rfc822Tokenizer`. You can always create your own tokenizer if you want to.

Button Controls

Buttons are common in any widget toolkit, and Android is no exception. Android offers the typical set of buttons as well as a few extras. In this section, we will discuss three types of button controls: the basic button, the image button, and the toggle button. Figure 6–3 shows a UI with these controls. The button at the top is the basic button, the middle button is an image button, and the last one is a toggle button.

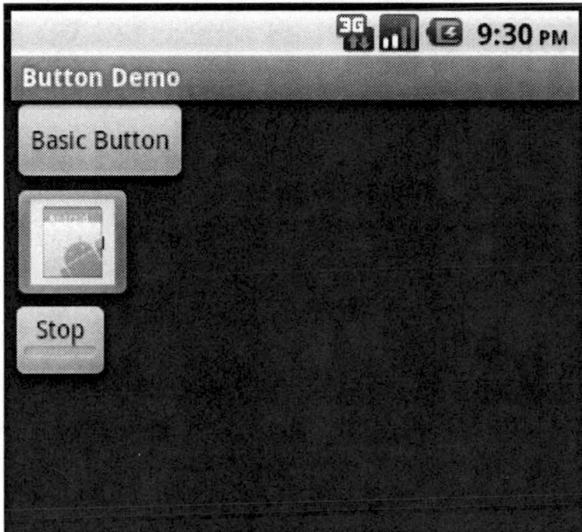

Figure 6–3. *Android button controls*

Let's get started with the basic button.

The Button Control

The basic button class in Android is `android.widget.Button`. There's not much to this type of button, beyond how you use it to handle click events. Listing 6–9 shows a fragment of an XML layout for the `Button` control, plus some Java that we might set up in the `onCreate()` method of our activity. Our basic button would look like the top button in Figure 6–3.

Listing 6–9. *Handling Click Events on a Button*

```
<Button android:id="@+id/ccbtn1"
    android:text="@string/basicBtnLabel"
    android:layout_width="fill_parent"
    android:layout_height="wrap_content" />
```

```
Button btn = (Button)this.findViewById(R.id.ccbtn1);
btn.setOnClickListener(new OnClickListener()
{
     public void onClick(View v)
     {
        Intent intent = new Intent(Intent.ACTION_VIEW,
                             Uri.parse("http://www.androidbook.com"));
        startActivity(intent);
     }
});
```

Listing 6–9 shows how to register for a button-click event. You register for the on-click event by calling the `setOnClickListener()` method with an `OnClickListener`. In Listing 6–9, an anonymous listener is created on the fly to handle click events for `btn`. When the button is clicked, the `onClick()` method of the listener is called and, in this case, launches the browser to our web site.

Since Android SDK 1.6, there is an easier way to set up a click handler for your button or buttons. Listing 6–10 shows the XML for a `Button` where you specify an attribute for the handler, plus the Java code that is the click handler.

Listing 6–10. *Setting Up a Click Handler for a Button*

```
<Button  ...   android:onClick="myClickHandler"   ...  />

    public void myClickHandler(View target) {
        switch(target.getId()) {
        case R.id.ccbtn1:
        …
```

The handler method will be called with target set to the `View` object representing the button that was pressed. Notice how the switch statement in the click handler method uses the resource IDs of the buttons to select the logic to run. Using this method means you won't have to explicitly create each `Button` object in your code, and you can reuse the same method across multiple buttons. This makes things easier to understand and maintain. This works with the other button types as well. But it won't work in Android 1.5 or below. You won't get an error message; you just won't get any action from clicking your buttons.

The ImageButton Control

Android provides an image button via `android.widget.ImageButton`. Using an image button is similar to using the basic button (see Listing 6–11). Our image button would look like the middle button in Figure 6–3.

Listing 6–11. *Using an ImageButton*

```
<ImageButton android:id="@+id/imageBtn"
    android:layout_width="wrap_content" android:layout_height="wrap_content"
    android:onClick="myClickHandler"
    android:src="@drawable/icon"  />

ImageButton btn = (ImageButton)this.findViewById(R.id.imageBtn);
btn.setImageResource(R.drawable.icon);
```

Here we've created the image button in XML and set the button's image from a drawable resource. The image file for the button must exist under /res/drawable. In our case, we're simply reusing the Android icon for the button. We also show in Listing 6–11 how you can set the button's image dynamically by calling setImageResource() method on the button and passing it a resource ID. Note that you only need to do one or the other. You don't need to specify the button image in both the XML file and in code.

One of the nice features of an image button is that you can specify a transparent background for the button. The result will be a clickable image that acts like a button but can look like whatever you want it to look like.

Because your image may be something very different than a standard button, you can customize how the button looks in the two other states it can be in when used in your UI. Besides appearing as normal, buttons can have focus, and they can be pressed. Having *focus* simply means that the button is currently where events will go. You can direct focus to a button using the arrow keys on the keypad or D-pad for example. *Pressed* means that the button's appearance changes when it has been pressed but before the user has let go. To tell Android what the three images are for our button, and which one is which, we set up a selector. This is a simple XML file that resides in the /res/drawable folder of our project. This is somewhat counterintuitive, since this is an XML file and not an image file, yet that is where the selector file must go. The content of a selector file will look like Listing 6–12.

Listing 6–12. *Using a Selector with an ImageButton*

```
<?xml version="1.0" encoding="utf-8"?>
    <selector xmlns:android="http://schemas.android.com/apk/res/android">
     <item android:state_pressed="true"
           android:drawable="@drawable/button_pressed" /> <!-- pressed -->
     <item android:state_focused="true"
           android:drawable="@drawable/button_focused" /> <!-- focused -->
     <item android:drawable="@drawable/icon" /> <!-- default -->
    </selector>
```

There are several things to note about the selector file. First, you do not specify a <resources> tag like in values XML files. Second, the order of the button images is important. Android will test each item in the selector to see if it matches, and you want the normal image to be used only if the button is not pressed and if the button does not have focus. If the normal image was listed first, it would always match and be selected even if the button is pressed or has focus. Of course, the drawables you refer to must exist in the /res/drawables folder. Last, in the definition of your button in the layout XML file, you want to set the android:src property to the selector XML file as if it were a regular drawable, like so:

```
<Button   ...    android:src="@drawable/imagebuttonselector"    ...   />
```

The ToggleButton Control

The ToggleButton control, like a check box or a radio button, is a two-state button. This button can be in either the On or Off state. As shown in Figure 6–3, the ToggleButton's default behavior is to show a green bar when in the On state and a grayed-out bar when in the Off state. Moreover, the default behavior also sets the button's text to On when it's in the On state and Off when it's in the Off state. You can modify the text for the ToggleButton if On/Off is not appropriate for your application. For example, if you have a background process that you want to start and stop via a ToggleButton, you could set the button's text to Stop and Run by using android:textOn and android:textOff properties.

Listing 6–13 shows an example. Our toggle button is the bottom button in Figure 6–3, and it is in the On position, so the label on the button says "Stop".

Listing 6–13. *The Android ToggleButton*

```
<ToggleButton android:id="@+id/cctglBtn"
        android:layout_width="wrap_content"
        android:layout_height="wrap_content"
        android:text="Toggle Button"
        android:textOn="Stop"
        android:textOff="Run"/>
```

Because ToggleButtons have on and off text as separate attributes, the android:text attribute of a ToggleButton is not really used. It's available because it has been inherited (from TextView, actually), but in this case, you don't need to use it.

The CheckBox Control

The CheckBox control is another two-state button that allows the user to toggle its state. The difference is that, for many situations, the users don't view it as a button that invokes immediate action. From Android's point of view however, it is a button. and you can do anything with a check box that you can do with a button.

In Android, you can create a check box by creating an instance of android.widget.CheckBox. See Listing 6–14 and Figure 6–4.

Listing 6–14. *Creating Check Boxes*

```
<LinearLayout xmlns:android="http://schemas.android.com/apk/res/android"
        android:orientation="vertical" android:layout_width="fill_parent"
        android:layout_height="fill_parent">

<CheckBox android:id="@+id/chickenCB"  android:text="Chicken" android:checked="true"
    android:layout_width="wrap_content" android:layout_height="wrap_content" />

<CheckBox android:id="@+id/fishCB"  android:text="Fish"
    android:layout_width="wrap_content" android:layout_height="wrap_content" />

<CheckBox android:id="@+id/steakCB"  android:text="Steak" android:checked="true"
    android:layout_width="wrap_content" android:layout_height="wrap_content" />

</LinearLayout>
```

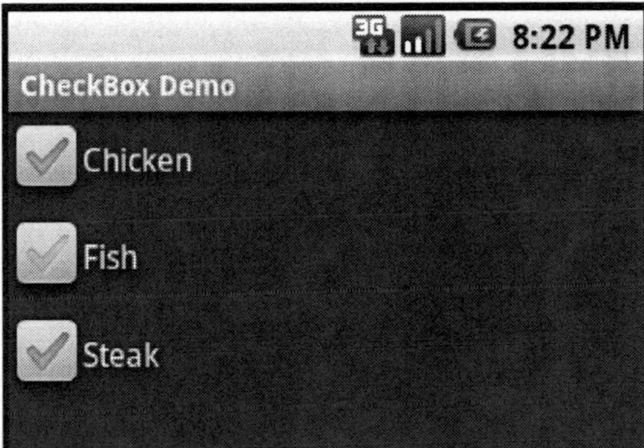

Figure 6–4. *Using the CheckBox control*

You manage the state of a check box by calling setChecked() or toggle(). You can obtain the state by calling isChecked().

If you need to implement specific logic when a check box is checked or unchecked, you can register for the on-checked event by calling setOnCheckedChangeListener() with an implementation of the OnCheckedChangeListener interface. You'll then have to implement the onCheckedChanged() method, which will be called when the check box is checked or unchecked. Listing 6–15 show some code that deals with a CheckBox.

Listing 6–15. *Using CheckBoxes in Code*

```
public class CheckBoxActivity extends Activity {
        /** Called when the activity is first created. */
        @Override
        public void onCreate(Bundle savedInstanceState) {
            super.onCreate(savedInstanceState);
            setContentView(R.layout.checkbox);

            CheckBox fishCB = (CheckBox)findViewById(R.id.fishCB);

            if(fishCB.isChecked())
                fishCB.toggle();     // flips the checkbox to unchecked if it was
checked

            fishCB.setOnCheckedChangeListener(
                        new CompoundButton.OnCheckedChangeListener() {

                @Override
                public void onCheckedChanged(CompoundButton arg0, boolean isChecked) {
                    Log.v("CheckBoxActivity", "The fish checkbox is now "
                            + (isChecked?"checked":"not checked"));
                }});
        }
}
```

The nice part of setting up the OnCheckedChangeListener is that you are passed the new state of the CheckBox button. You could instead use the OnClickListener technique like we used with basic buttons. When the onClick() method is called, you would need to determine yourself the new state of the button by casting it appropriately and then calling isChecked() on it. Similarly, Listing 6–16 shows what this code might look like if we added android:onClick="myClickHandler" to the XML definition of our CheckBox buttons (remember, this is only supported in Android 1.6 and later).

Listing 6–16. *Using CheckBoxes in Code with android:onClick*

```
    public void myClickHandler(View view) {
        switch(view.getId()) {
        case R.id.steakCB:
            Log.v("CheckBoxActivity", "The steak checkbox is now " +
                    (((CheckBox)view).isChecked()?"checked":"not checked"));
        }
    }
```

The RadioButton Control

RadioButton controls are an integral part of any UI toolkit. A radio button gives the users several choices and forces them to select a single item. To enforce this single-selection model, radio buttons generally belong to a group, and each group is forced to have only one item selected at a time.

To create a group of radio buttons in Android, first create a RadioGroup, and then populate the group with radio buttons. Listing 6–17 and Figure 6–5 show an example.

Listing 6–17. *Using Android RadioButton Widgets*

```
<LinearLayout xmlns:android="http://schemas.android.com/apk/res/android"
        android:orientation="vertical" android:layout_width="fill_parent"
        android:layout_height="fill_parent">

<RadioGroup     android:id="@+id/rBtnGrp" android:layout_width="wrap_content"
            android:layout_height="wrap_content"  android:orientation="vertical" >

    <RadioButton     android:id="@+id/chRBtn" android:text="Chicken"
            android:layout_width="wrap_content"  android:layout_height="wrap_content"/>

    <RadioButton  android:id="@+id/fishRBtn" android:text="Fish" android:checked="true"
            android:layout_width="wrap_content"  android:layout_height="wrap_content"/>

    <RadioButton android:id="@+id/stkRBtn" android:text="Steak"
            android:layout_width="wrap_content"  android:layout_height="wrap_content"/>

</RadioGroup>

</LinearLayout>
```

In Android, you implement a radio group using android.widget.RadioGroup and a radio button using android.widget.RadioButton.

Figure 6–5. *Using radio buttons*

Note that the radio buttons within the radio group are, by default, unchecked to begin with, although you can set one to checked in the XML definition, as we did with Fish above. To set one of the radio buttons to the checked state programmatically, you can obtain a reference to the radio button and call `setChecked()`:

```
RadioButton rbtn = (RadioButton)this.findViewById(R.id.stkRBtn);
rbtn.setChecked(true);
```

You can also use the `toggle()` method to toggle the state of the radio button. As with the `CheckBox` control, you will be notified of `on-checked` or `on-unchecked` events if you call the `setOnCheckedChangeListener()` with an implementation of the `OnCheckedChangeListener` interface. There is a slight difference here though. This is actually a different class than before. This time, it's technically the `RadioGroup.OnCheckedChangeListener` class, whereas before it was the `CompoundButton.OnCheckedChangeListener` class.

The `RadioGroup` can also contain views other than the radio button. For example, Listing 6–18 adds a `TextView` after the last radio button. Also note that a radio button lies outside the radio group.

Listing 6–18. *A RadioGroup with More Than Just RadioButtons*

```
<LinearLayout xmlns:android="http://schemas.android.com/apk/res/android"
        android:orientation="vertical"  android:layout_width="fill_parent"
        android:layout_height="fill_parent">

<RadioButton android:id="@+id/anotherRadBtn"  android:text="Outside"
            android:layout_width="wrap_content"  android:layout_height="wrap_content"/>

<RadioGroup android:id="@+id/radGrp"
            android:layout_width="wrap_content"  android:layout_height="wrap_content">

      <RadioButton android:id="@+id/chRBtn"  android:text="Chicken"
            android:layout_width="wrap_content"  android:layout_height="wrap_content"/>

      <RadioButton android:id="@+id/fishRBtn"  android:text="Fish"
```

```
            android:layout_width="wrap_content"  android:layout_height="wrap_content"/>

        <RadioButton android:id="@+id/stkRBtn"  android:text="Steak"
            android:layout_width="wrap_content"  android:layout_height="wrap_content"/>

        <TextView android:text="My Favorite"
            android:layout_width="wrap_content"  android:layout_height="wrap_content"/>

</RadioGroup>
</LinearLayout>
```

Listing 6–18 shows that you can have non-RadioButton controls inside a radio group. You should also know that the radio group can only enforce single-selection on the radio buttons within its own container. That is, the radio button with ID anotherRadBtn will not be affected by the radio group shown in Listing 6–18 because it is not one of the group's children.

You can manipulate the RadioGroup programmatically. For example, you can obtain a reference to a radio group and add a radio button (or other type of control). Listing 16–19 demonstrates this concept.

Listing 6–19. ***Adding a RadioButton to a RadioGroup in Code***

```
RadioGroup radGrp = (RadioGroup)findViewById(R.id.radGrp);
RadioButton newRadioBtn = new RadioButton(this);
newRadioBtn.setText("Pork");
radGrp.addView(newRadioBtn);
```

Once a user has checked a radio button within a radio group, the user cannot uncheck it by clicking it again. The only way to clear all radio buttons within a radio group is to call the clearCheck() method on the RadioGroup programmatically.

Of course, you want to do something interesting with the RadioGroup. You probably don't want to poll each RadioButton to determine if it's checked or not. Fortunately, the RadioGroup has several methods to help you out. We demonstrate those with Listing 16–20. The XML for this code is in Listing 6–18.

Listing 6–20. ***Using a RadioGroup Programmatically***

```
public class RadioGroupActivity extends Activity {
        protected static final String TAG = "RadioGroupActivity";

        /** Called when the activity is first created. */
        @Override
        public void onCreate(Bundle savedInstanceState) {
            super.onCreate(savedInstanceState);
            setContentView(R.layout.radiogroup);

            RadioGroup radGrp = (RadioGroup)findViewById(R.id.radGrp);

            int checkedRadioButtonId = radGrp.getCheckedRadioButtonId();

            radGrp.setOnCheckedChangeListener(new RadioGroup.OnCheckedChangeListener() {
                @Override
                public void onCheckedChanged(RadioGroup arg0, int id) {
                    switch(id) {
                    case -1:
```

```
                    Log.v(TAG, "Choices cleared!");
                    break;
                case R.id.chRBtn:
                    Log.v(TAG, "Chose Chicken");
                    break;
                case R.id.fishRBtn:
                    Log.v(TAG, "Chose Fish");
                    break;
                case R.id.stkRBtn:
                    Log.v(TAG, "Chose Steak");
                    break;
                default:
                    Log.v(TAG, "Huh?");
                    break;
                }
            }});
    }
}
```

We can always get the currently checked RadioButton using `getCheckedRadioButtonId()`, which returns the resource Id of the checked item, or –1 if nothing is checked (possible if there's no default and the user hasn't chosen one yet). We showed this in our `onCreate()` method previously, but in reality, you'd want to use it at the appropriate time to read the user's current choice. We can also set up a listener to be notified immediately when the user chooses one of the `RadioButtons`. Notice that the `onCheckedChanged()` method takes a `RadioGroup` parameter, allowing you to use the same `OnCheckedChangeListener` for multiple `RadioGroups`. You may have noticed the switch option of –1. This will occur if the `RadioGroup` is cleared through code.

The ImageView Control

One of the basic controls we haven't covered yet is the `ImageView` control. This is used to display an image, where the image can come from a file, content provider or a resource such as a drawable. You can even specify just a color, and the `ImageView` will display that color. Listing 6–21 shows some XML examples of `ImageViews`, followed by some code that shows how to create an `ImageView`.

Listing 6–21. *ImageViews in XML and in Code*

```
<ImageView android:id="@+id/image1"
  android:layout_width="wrap_content"  android:layout_height="wrap_content"
  android:src="@drawable/icon" />

<ImageView android:id="@+id/image2"
  android:layout_width="125dip"  android:layout_height="25dip"
  android:src="#555555" />

<ImageView android:id="@+id/image3"
  android:layout_width="wrap_content"  android:layout_height="wrap_content" />

<ImageView android:id="@+id/image4"
  android:layout_width="wrap_content"  android:layout_height="wrap_content"
  android:src="@drawable/manatee02"
  android:scaleType="centerInside"
```

```
    android:maxWidth="35dip"  android:maxHeight="50dip"
    />


ImageView imgView = (ImageView)findViewById(R.id.image3);

imgView.setImageResource( R.drawable.icon );

imgView.setImageBitmap(BitmapFactory.decodeResource(
            this.getResources(), R.drawable.manatee14) );

imgView.setImageDrawable(
            Drawable.createFromPath("/mnt/sdcard/dave2.jpg") );

imgView.setImageURI(Uri.parse("file://mnt/sdcard/dave2.jpg"));
```

In this example, we have four images defined in XML. The first is simply the icon for our application. The second is a gray bar that is wider than it is tall. The third definition does not specify an image source in the XML, but we have an ID associated to this one (`image3`) that we can use from our code to set the image. The fourth image is another of our drawable image files where we not only specify the source of the image file but also set the maximum dimensions of the image on the screen and define what to do if the image is larger than our maximum size. In this case, we tell the `ImageView` to center and scale the image so it fits inside the size we specified.

In the Java code of Listing 6–21 we show several ways to set the image of `image3`. We first of course must get a reference to the ImageView by finding it using its resource ID. The first setter method, `setImageResource()`, simply uses the image's resource ID to locate the image file to supply the image for our `ImageView`. The second setter uses the `BitmapFactory` to read in an image resource into a `Bitmap` object and then sets the `ImageView` to that `Bitmap`. Note that we could have done some modifications to the `Bitmap` before applying it to our `ImageView`, but in our case, we used it as is. In addition, the `BitmapFactory` has several methods of creating a `Bitmap`, including from a byte array and an `InputStream`. You could use the `InputStream` method to read an image from a web server, create the `Bitmap` image, and then set the `ImageView` from there.

The third setting uses a `Drawable` for our image source. In this case, we're showing the source of the image coming from the SD card. You'll need to put some sort of image file out on the SD card with the proper name for this to work for you. Similar to `BitmapFactory`, the `Drawable` class has a few different ways to construct `Drawables`, including from an XML stream.

The final setter method takes the URI of an image file and uses that as the image source. For this last call, please don't think that you can use any image URI as the source. This method is really only intended to be used for local images on the device, not for images that you might find through HTTP. To use Internet-based images as the source for your `ImageView`, you'd most likely use `BitmapFactory` and an `InputStream`.

Date and Time Controls

Date and time controls are quite common in many widget toolkits. Android offers several date- and time-based controls, some of which we'll discuss in this section. Specifically, we are going to introduce the DatePicker, the TimePicker, the DigitalClock, and the AnalogClock controls.

The DatePicker and TimePicker Controls

As the names suggest, you use the DatePicker control to select a date and the TimePicker control to pick a time. Listing 6–22 and Figure 6–6 show examples of these controls.

Listing 6–22. *The DatePicker and TimePicker Controls in XML*

```
<LinearLayout xmlns:android="http://schemas.android.com/apk/res/android"
        android:orientation="vertical"
        android:layout_width="fill_parent"
        android:layout_height="fill_parent">

  <TextView android:id="@+id/dateDefault"
    android:layout_width="fill_parent" android:layout_height="wrap_content" />

  <DatePicker android:id="@+id/datePicker"
    android:layout_width="wrap_content" android:layout_height="wrap_content" />

  <TextView android:id="@+id/timeDefault"
    android:layout_width="fill_parent" android:layout_height="wrap_content" />

  <TimePicker android:id="@+id/timePicker"
    android:layout_width="wrap_content" android:layout_height="wrap_content" />

</LinearLayout>
```

Figure 6–6. *The DatePicker and TimePicker UIs*

If you look at the XML layout, you can see that defining these controls is quite easy. As with any other control in the Android toolkit, you can access the controls programmatically to initialize them or to retrieve data from them. For example, you can initialize these controls as shown in Listing 6–23.

Listing 6–23. *Initializing the DatePicker and TimePicker with Date and Time, Respectively*

```
    public void onCreate(Bundle savedInstanceState) {
        super.onCreate(savedInstanceState);
        setContentView(R.layout.datetimepicker);

        TextView dateDefault = (TextView)findViewById(R.id.dateDefault);
        TextView timeDefault = (TextView)findViewById(R.id.timeDefault);

        DatePicker dp = (DatePicker)this.findViewById(R.id.datePicker);
        // The month, and just the month, is zero-based. Add 1 for display.
        dateDefault.setText("Date defaulted to " + (dp.getMonth() + 1) + "/" +
                dp.getDayOfMonth() + "/" + dp.getYear());
        // And here, subtract 1 from December (12) to set it to December
        dp.init(2008, 11, 10, null);

        TimePicker tp = (TimePicker)this.findViewById(R.id.timePicker);

        java.util.Formatter timeF = new java.util.Formatter();
        timeF.format("Time defaulted to %d:%02d", tp.getCurrentHour(),
                        tp.getCurrentMinute());
        timeDefault.setText(timeF.toString());

        tp.setIs24HourView(true);
        tp.setCurrentHour(new Integer(10));
        tp.setCurrentMinute(new Integer(10));
    }
}
```

Listing 6–23 sets the date on the `DatePicker` to December 10, 2008. Note that for the month, the internal value is zero-based, which means that January is 0, and December is 11. For the `TimePicker`, the number of hours and minutes is set to 10. Note also that this control supports 24–hour view. If you do not set values for these controls, the default values will be the current date and time as known to the device.

Finally, note that Android offers versions of these controls as modal windows, such as `DatePickerDialog` and `TimePickerDialog`. These controls are useful if you want to display the control to the user and force the user to make a selection. We'll cover dialogs in more detail in Chapter 8.

The DigitalClock and AnalogClock Controls

Android also offers DigitalClock and AnalogClock controls (see Figure 6–7).

Figure 6–7. *Using the AnalogClock and DigitalClock*

As shown, the digital clock supports seconds in addition to hours and minutes. The analog clock in Android is a two-handed clock, with one hand for the hour indicator and the other hand for the minute indicator. To add these to your layout, use the XML as shown in Listing 6–24.

Listing 6–24. Adding a DigitalClock or an AnalogClock in XML

```
<DigitalClock
  android:layout_width="wrap_content" android:layout_height="wrap_content" />

<AnalogClock
  android:layout_width="wrap_content" android:layout_height="wrap_content" />
```

These two controls are really just for displaying the current time, as they don't let you modify the date or time. In other words, they are controls whose only capability is to display the current time. Thus, if you want to change the date or time, you'll need to stick to the DatePicker/TimePicker or DatePickerDialog/TimePickerDialog. The nice part about these two clocks, though, is that they will update themselves without you having to do anything. That is, the seconds tick away in the DigitalClock, and the hands move on the AnalogClock without anything extra from us.

The MapView Control

The com.google.android.maps.MapView control can display a map. You can instantiate this control either via XML layout or code, but the activity that uses it must extend

MapActivity. MapActivity takes care of multithreading requests to load a map, perform caching, and so on.

Listing 6–25 shows an example instantiation of a MapView.

Listing 6–25. *Creating a MapView Control via XML Layout*

```
<LinearLayout xmlns:android="http://schemas.android.com/apk/res/android"
        android:orientation="vertical" android:layout_width="fill_parent"
        android:layout_height="fill_parent">

    <com.google.android.maps.MapView
        android:layout_width="fill_parent"
        android:layout_height="fill_parent"
        android:enabled="true"
        android:clickable="true"
        android:apiKey="myAPIKey"
        />

</LinearLayout>
```

We'll discuss the MapView control in detail in Chapter 17, when we discuss location-based services. This is also where you'll learn how to obtain your own mapping API key.

Understanding Adapters

Before we get into the details of list controls of Android, we need to talk about adapters. List controls are used to display collections of data. But instead of using a single type of control to manage both the display and the data, Android separates these two responsibilities into list controls and adapters. List controls are classes that extend android.widget.AdapterView and include ListView, GridView, Spinner, and Gallery (see Figure 6–8).

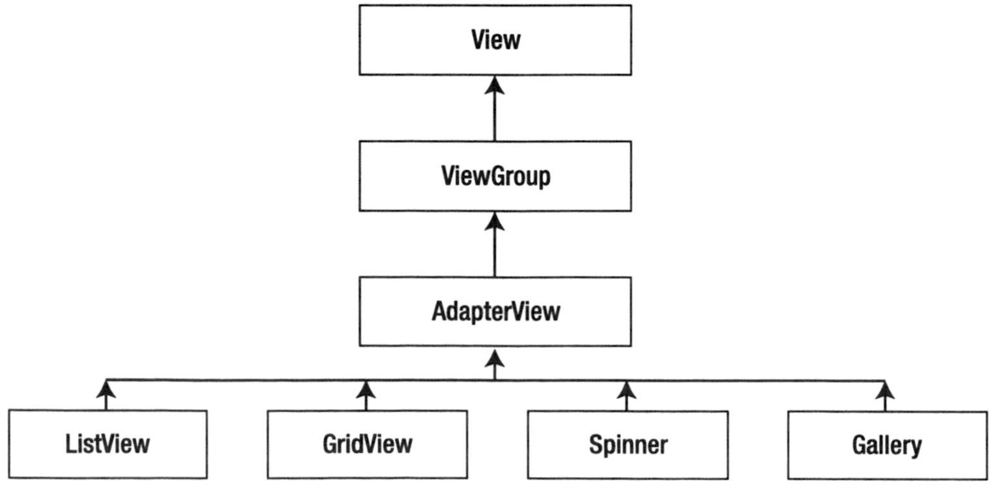

Figure 6–8. *AdapterView class hierarchy*

AdapterView itself actually extends android.widget.ViewGroup, which means that ListView, GridView, and so on are container controls. In other words, list controls contain collections of child views. The purpose of an adapter is to manage the data for an AdapterView, and to provide the child views for it. Let's see how this works by examining the SimpleCursorAdapter.

Getting to Know SimpleCursorAdapter

The SimpleCursorAdapter is depicted in Figure 6–9.

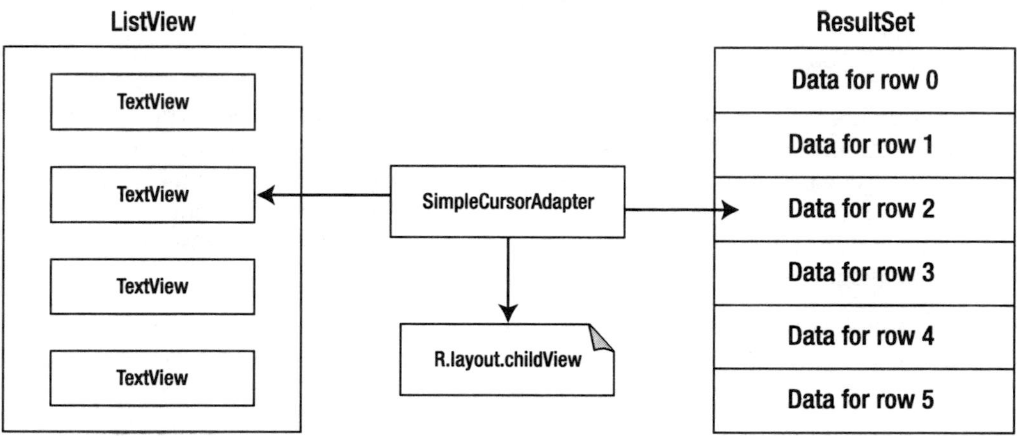

Figure 6–9. *The SimpleCursorAdapter*

This is a very important picture to understand. On the left-hand side is the AdapterView; in this example, it is a ListView made up of TextView children. On the right-hand side is the data; in this example, it's represented as a result set of data rows that came from a query against a content provider.

To map the data rows to the ListView, the SimpleCursorAdapter needs to have a child layout resource ID. The child layout must describe the layout for each of the data elements from the right-hand side that should be displayed on the left-hand side. A layout in this case is just like the layouts we've been working with for our activities, but it only needs to specify the layout of a single row of our ListView. For example, if you have a result set of information from the Contacts content provider, and you only want to display each contact name in your ListView, you would need to provide a layout to describe what the name field should look like. If you wanted to display the name and an image from the result set in each row of the ListView, your layout must say how to display the name and the image.

This does not mean you must provide a layout specification for every field in your result set, nor does it mean you must have a piece of data in your result set for everything you want to include in each row of the ListView. For example, we'll show you in a bit how you can have check boxes in your ListView for selecting rows, and those check boxes don't need to be set from data in a result set. We'll also show you how to get to data in the result set that is not part of the ListView. And while we've just talked about

ListViews, TextViews, cursors, and result sets, please keep in mind that the adapter concept is more general than this. The left-hand side can be a gallery, and the right-hand side can be a simple array of images. But let's keep things fairly simple for now and look at SimpleCursorAdapter in more detail.

The constructor of SimpleCursorAdapter looks like this:

```
SimpleCursorAdapter(Context context, int childLayout, Cursor c, String[] from, int[] to)
```

This adapter converts a row from the cursor to a child view for the container control. The definition of the child view is defined in an XML resource (childLayout parameter). Note that because a row in the cursor might have many columns, you tell the SimpleCursorAdapter which columns you want to select from the row by specifying an array of column names (using the from parameter).

Similarly, because each column you select must be mapped to a View in the layout, you must specify the IDs in the to parameter. There's a one-to-one mapping between the column that you select and a View that displays the data in the column, so the from and to parameter arrays must have the same number of elements. As we mentioned before, the child view could contain other types of views; they don't have to be TextViews. You could use an ImageView for example.

There is a careful collaboration going on between the ListView and our adapter. When the ListView wants to display a row of data, it calls the getView() method of the adapter, passing in the position to specify the row of data to be displayed. The adapter responds by building the appropriate child view using the layout that was set in the adapter's constructor and by pulling the data from the appropriate record in the result set. The ListView, therefore, doesn't have to deal with how the data exists on the adapter side; it only needs to call for child views as needed. This is a critical point, as it means our ListView doesn't necessarily need to create every child view for every data row. It really only needs to have as many child views as are necessary for what's visible in the display window. If only ten rows are being displayed, technically the ListView only needs to have ten child layouts instantiated, even if there are hundreds of records in our result set. In reality, more than ten child layouts get instantiated, as Android usually keeps extras on hand to make it faster to bring a new row to visibility. The conclusion you should reach is that the child views managed by the ListView can be recycled. We'll talk more about that a little later.

Figure 6–9 reveals some flexibility in using adapters. Because the list control uses an adapter, you can substitute various types of adapters based on your data and child view. For example, if you are not going to populate an AdapterView from a content provider or database, you don't have to use the SimpleCursorAdapter. You can opt for an even "simpler" adapter—the ArrayAdapter.

Getting to Know ArrayAdapter

The ArrayAdapter is the simplest of the adapters in Android. It specifically targets list controls and assumes that TextView controls represent the list items (i.e., the child views). Creating a new ArrayAdapter can look as simple as this:

```
ArrayAdapter<String> adapter = new ArrayAdapter<String>(this,
                android.R.layout.simple_list_item_1,
                new string[]{"Dave","Satya","Dylan"});
```

We still pass the context (i.e., this), and a childLayout resource ID. But instead of passing a from array of data field specifications, we pass in an array of strings as the actual data. We don't pass a cursor or a to array of View resource IDs. The assumption here is that our child layout consists of a single TextView, and that's what the ArrayAdapter will use as the destination for the strings that are in our data array.

Now we're going to introduce a nice shortcut for the childLayout resource ID. Instead of creating our own layout file for the list items, we can take advantage of predefined layouts in Android. Notice that the prefix on the resource for the child layout resource ID is android.. Instead of looking in our local /res directory, Android looks in its own. You can browse to this folder by navigating to the Android SDK folder and looking under platforms/<android-version>/data/res/layout. There you'll find simple_list_item_1.xml and can see inside that it defines a simple TextView. That TextView is what our ArrayAdapter will use to create a view (in its getView() method) to give to the ListView. Feel free to browse through these folders to find predefined layouts for all sorts of uses. We'll be using more of these later.

ArrayAdapter has other constructors. If the childLayout is not just a simple TextView, you can pass in the row layout resource ID, plus the resource ID of the TextView to receive the data. When you don't have a ready-made array of strings to pass in, you can use the createFromResource() method. Listing 6–26 shows an example in which we create an ArrayAdapter for a spinner.

Listing 6–26. *Creating an ArrayAdapter from a String-Resource File*

```
<Spinner android:id="@+id/spinner"
    android:layout_width="wrap_content"  android:layout_height="wrap_content" />


Spinner spinner = (Spinner) findViewById(R.id.spinner);

ArrayAdapter<CharSequence> adapter = ArrayAdapter.createFromResource(this,
        R.array.planets, android.R.layout.simple_spinner_item);

adapter.setDropDownViewResource(android.R.layout.simple_spinner_dropdown_item);

spinner.setAdapter(adapter);


<?xml version="1.0" encoding="utf-8"?>
<!-- This file is /res/values/planets.xml -->
<resources>
  <string-array name="planets">
    <item>Mercury</item>
    <item>Venus</item>
    <item>Earth</item>
    <item>Mars</item>
    <item>Jupiter</item>
    <item>Saturn</item>
    <item>Uranus</item>
```

```
    <item>Neptune</item>
  </string-array>
</resources>
```

Listing 6–26 has three parts to it. The first part is the XML layout for a spinner. The second Java part shows how you can create an ArrayAdapter whose data source is defined in a string resource file. Using this method allows you to not only externalize the contents of the list to an XML file but also use localized versions. We'll talk about spinners a little later, but for now, know that a spinner has a view to show the currently selected value, plus a list view to show the values that can be selected from. It's basically a drop-down menu. The third part of Listing 6–26 is the XML resource file called /res/values/planets.xml, which is read in to initialize the ArrayAdapter.

Worth mentioning is that the ArrayAdapter allows for dynamic modifications to the underlying data. For example, the add() method will append a new value on the end of the array. The insert() method will add a new value at a specified position within the array. And remove() takes an object out of the array. You can also call sort() to reorder the array. Of course, once you've done this, the data array is out of sync with the ListView, so that's when you call the notifyDataSetChanged() method of the adapter. This method will resync the ListView with the adapter.

The following list summarizes the adapters that Android provides:

- ArrayAdapter<T>: This is an adapter on top of a generic array of arbitrary objects. It's meant to be used with a ListView.
- CursorAdapter: This adapter, also meant to be used in a ListView, provides data to the list via a cursor.
- SimpleAdapter: As the name suggests, this adapter is a simple adapter. It is generally used to populate a list with static data (possibly from resources).
- ResourceCursorAdapter: This adapter extends CursorAdapter and knows how to create views from resources.
- SimpleCursorAdapter: This adapter extends ResourceCursorAdapter and creates TextView/ImageView views from the columns in the cursor. The views are defined in resources.

We've covered enough of adapters to start showing you some real examples of working with adapters and with list controls (also known as AdapterViews). Let's get to it.

Using Adapters With AdapterViews

Now that you've been introduced to adapters, it is time to put them to work for us, providing data for list controls. In this section, we're going to first cover the basic list control, the ListView. Then, we'll describe how to create your own custom adapter, and finally, we'll describe the other types of list controls: GridViews, spinners, and the gallery.

The Basic List Control: ListView

The ListView control displays a list of items vertically. That is, if we've got a list of items to view and the number of items extends beyond what we can currently see in the display, we can scroll to see the rest of the items. You generally use a ListView by writing a new activity that extends android.app.ListActivity. ListActivity contains a ListView, and you set the data for the ListView by calling the setListAdapter() method. As we described previously, adapters link list controls to the data and help prepare the child views for the list control. Items in a ListView can be clicked to take immediate action or selected to act on the set of selected items later. We're going to start really simple and then add functionality as we go.

Displaying Values in a ListView

Figure 6–10 shows a ListView control in its simplest form.

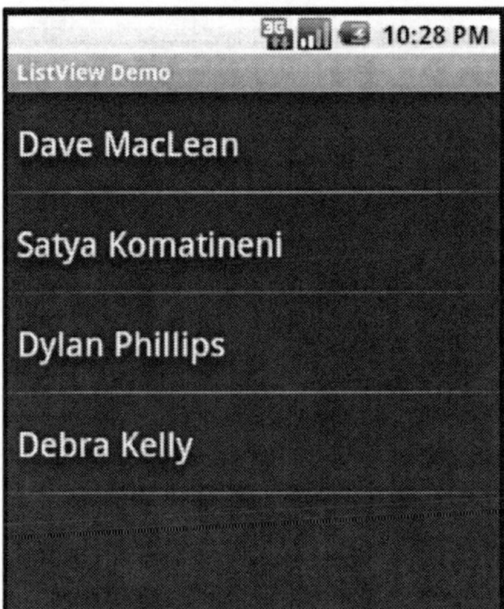

Figure 6–10. *Using the ListView control*

For this exercise, we will fill the entire screen with the ListView, so we don't even need to specify a ListView in our main layout XML file. Listing 6–27 shows the Java code for our ListActivity.

Listing 6–27. *Adding Items to a ListView*

```
public class ListViewActivity extends ListActivity
{
    @Override
    protected void onCreate(Bundle savedInstanceState)
    {
        super.onCreate(savedInstanceState);

        Cursor c = managedQuery(People.CONTENT_URI,
                        null, null, null, People.NAME);
```

```
        String[] cols = new String[] {People.NAME};
        int[]    views = new int[]   {android.R.id.text1};

        SimpleCursorAdapter adapter = new SimpleCursorAdapter(this,
                        android.R.layout.simple_list_item_1,
                        c, cols, views);
        this.setListAdapter(adapter);
    }
}
```

Listing 6–27 creates a ListView control populated with the list of contacts on the device. In our example, we query the device for the list of contacts. For demonstration purposes, we're selecting all fields from Contacts (i.e., using the first null parameter in the managedQuery() method), and we're sorting on the People.NAME field (using the final parameter in the managedQuery() method). We then create a projection (cols) to select only the names of the contacts for our ListView—a projection defines the columns that we are interested in. Next, we provide the corresponding resource ID array (views) to map the name column (People.NAME) to a TextView control (android.R.id.text1). After that, we create a cursor adapter and set the list's adapter. The adapter class has the smarts to take the rows in the data source and pull out the name of each contact to populate the user interface.

There's one more thing we need to do to make this work. Because this demonstration is accessing the phone's contacts database, we need to ask permission to do so. This security topic will be covered in more detail in Chapter 10, so for now, we'll just walk you through getting our ListView to show up. Double-click the AndroidManifest.xml file for this project, and click the Permissions tab. Click the Add button, choose Uses Permission, and click OK. Scroll down the Name list until you get to android.permission.READ_CONTACTS. Your Eclipse window should look like the one shown in Figure 6–11. Then, save the AndroidManifest.xml file. Now, you can run this application in the emulator. You might need to add some contacts using the Contacts application before any names will show up in this example application.

You'll notice that the onCreate() method does not set the content view of the activity. Instead, because the base class ListActivity contains a ListView already, it just needs to provide the data for the ListView. We've used a couple of shortcuts in this example, the first being that we've taken advantage of our ListActivity supplying the main layout. We're also using an Android-provided layout for our child view (resource ID android.R.layout.simple_list_item_1), which contains an Android-provided TextView (resource ID android.R.id.text1). All in all, pretty simple to set up.

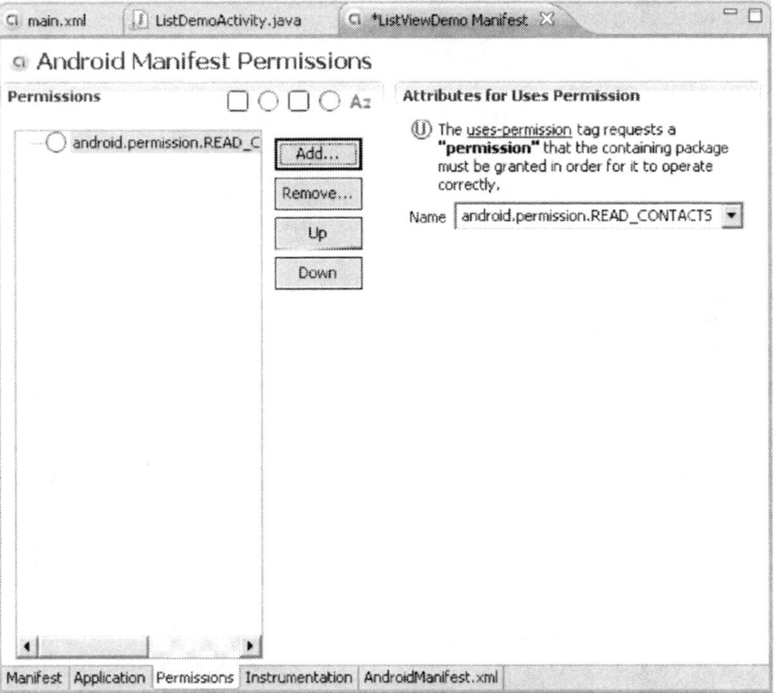

Figure 6–11. *Modifying AndroidManifest.xml so our application will run*

Clickable Items in a ListView

Of course, once you run this example, you'll see that you're able to scroll up and down the list to see all your contact names, but that's about it. What if we want to do something a little more interesting with this example, like launch the Contact application when a user clicks one of the items in our `ListView`? Listing 6–28 shows a modification to our example to accept user input.

Listing 6–28. *Accepting User Input on a ListView*

```
public class ListViewActivity2 extends ListActivity implements OnItemClickListener
{
    @Override
    protected void onCreate(Bundle savedInstanceState)
    {
        super.onCreate(savedInstanceState);

        ListView lv = getListView();

        Cursor c = managedQuery(People.CONTENT_URI,
                null, null, null, People.NAME);

        String[] cols = new String[]{People.NAME};
        int[]   views = new int[]   {android.R.id.text1};

        SimpleCursorAdapter adapter = new SimpleCursorAdapter(this,
```

```
                android.R.layout.simple_list_item_1,
                c, cols, views);
        this.setListAdapter(adapter);
        lv.setOnItemClickListener(this);
    }

    @Override
    public void onItemClick(AdapterView<?> adView, View target, int position, long id) {
        Log.v("ListViewActivity", "in onItemClick with " + ((TextView) target).getText()
+
                ". Position = " + position + ". Id = " + id);
        Uri selectedPerson = ContentUris.withAppendedId(
                People.CONTENT_URI, id);
        Intent intent = new Intent(Intent.ACTION_VIEW, selectedPerson);
        startActivity(intent);
    }
}
```

Our activity is now implementing the `OnItemClickListener` interface, which means we'll receive a callback when the user clicks on something in our `ListView`. As you can see by our `onItemClick()` method, we get a lot of information about what was clicked, including the view receiving the click, the position of the clicked item in the `ListView`, and the ID of the item according to our adapter. Because we know that our `ListView` is made up of `TextViews`, we assume that we received a `TextView` and cast accordingly before calling the `getText()` method to retrieve the contact's name. The position value represents where this item is in relation to the overall list of items in the `ListView`, and it's zero-based. Therefore, the first item in the list is at position 0.

The ID value depends entirely on the adapter and the source of the data. In our example, we happen to be querying the Contacts content provider, so the ID according to this adapter is the `_ID` of the record from the content provider. But your data source in other situations may not be from a content provider, so you should not think that you can always create a URI as we've done in this example. If we were using an `ArrayAdapter` that had read its values from a resource XML file, the ID given to us is very likely the position of the value in the data array and could, in fact, be exactly the same as the position value.

When we discussed `ArrayAdapters` before, we mentioned the `notifyDataSetChanged()` method to have the adapter update the `ListView` if the data has changed. Try this little experiment with our current example. Click one of your contacts, which should launch the Contacts application. Now, edit the contact by changing the name of the contact; click Done, and click the Back button so you're back to our example application. You should see that the name of that contact in your `ListView` has automatically been updated. How cool is that? Through the `SimpleCursorAdapter` and the Contacts content provider, our `ListView` has been updated for us. With `ArrayAdapters`, however, you will need to invoke the `notifyDataSetChanged()` method yourself.

That was pretty easy to do. We generated our own `ListView` of contact names, and by clicking a name, we launched the Contacts application for the selected person. But what if we want to select a bunch of names first and then do something with the subset of people? For the next example application, we're going to modify the layout of a list item to include a check box, and we're going to add a button to the user interface to then act on the subset of selected items.

Adding Other Controls With a ListView

If you want additional controls in your main layout, you can provide your own layout XML file, put in a `ListView`, and add other desired controls. For example, you could add a button below the `ListView` in the UI to submit an action on the selected items, as shown in Figure 6–12.

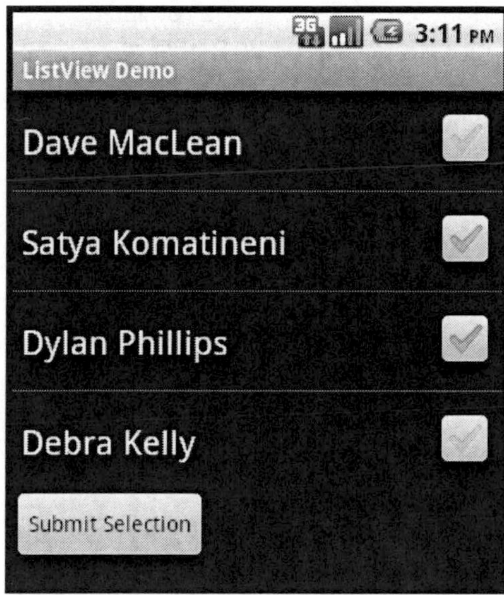

Figure 6–12. *An additional button that lets the user submit the selected item(s)*

The main layout for this example is in Listing 6–29, and it contains the user interface definition of the activity—the `ListView` and the `Button`.

Listing 6–29. *Overriding the ListView Referenced by ListActivity*

```
<?xml version="1.0" encoding="utf-8"?>
<!-- This file is at /res/layout/list.xml -->
<LinearLayout xmlns:android="http://schemas.android.com/apk/res/android"
    android:orientation="vertical"
    android:layout_width="fill_parent"  android:layout_height="fill_parent">

    <ListView android:id="@android:id/list"
            android:layout_width="fill_parent"  android:layout_height="0dip"
            android:layout_weight="1" />

    <Button android:id="@+id/btn" android:onClick="doClick"
           android:layout_width="wrap_content"  android:layout_height="wrap_content"
           android:text="Submit Selection" />

</LinearLayout>
```

Notice the specification of the ID for the ListView. We've had to use "@android:id/list", because the ListActivity expects to find a ListView in our layout with this name. If we had relied on the default ListView that ListActivity would have created for us, it would have this ID.

The other thing to note is the way we have to specify the height of the ListView in LinearLayout. We want our button to appear on the screen at all times no matter how many items are in our ListView, and we don't want to be scrolling all the way to the bottom of the page just to find the button. To accomplish this, we set the layout_height to 0 and then use layout_weight to say that this control should take up all available room from the parent container. This trick allows room for the button and retains our ability to scroll the ListView. We'll talk more about layouts and weights later in this chapter.

The activity implementation would then look like Listing 6–30.

Listing 6–30. ***Reading User Input from the ListActivity***

```
public class ListViewActivity3 extends ListActivity
{
    private static final String TAG = "ListViewActivity3";
    private ListView lv = null;
    private Cursor cursor = null;
    private int idCol = -1;
    private int nameCol = -1;
    private int notesCol = -1;

    @Override
    protected void onCreate(Bundle savedInstanceState)
    {
        super.onCreate(savedInstanceState);
        setContentView(R.layout.list);

        lv = getListView();

        cursor = managedQuery(People.CONTENT_URI,
                        null, null, null, People.NAME);

        String[] cols = new String[]{People.NAME};
        idCol = cursor.getColumnIndex(People._ID);
        nameCol = cursor.getColumnIndex(People.NAME);
        notesCol = cursor.getColumnIndex(People.NOTES);

        int[] views = new int[]{android.R.id.text1};

        SimpleCursorAdapter adapter = new SimpleCursorAdapter(this,
                android.R.layout.simple_list_item_multiple_choice,
                cursor, cols, views);

        this.setListAdapter(adapter);

        lv.setChoiceMode(ListView.CHOICE_MODE_MULTIPLE);
    }

    public void doClick(View view) {
        int count=lv.getCount();
```

```
        SparseBooleanArray viewItems = lv.getCheckedItemPositions();
        for(int i=0; i<count; i++) {
            if(viewItems.get(i)) {
                cursor.moveToPosition(i);
                long id = cursor.getLong(idCol);
                String name = cursor.getString(nameCol);
                String notes = cursor.getString(notesCol);
                Log.v(TAG, name + " is checked. Notes: " + notes +
                        ". Position = " + i + ". Id = " + id);
            }
        }
    }
}
```

Now, we're back to calling `setContentView()` to set the user interface for the activity. And within the setup of the adapter, we're passing another of the Android-provided views for a `ListView` line item (`android.R.layout.simple_list_item_multiple_choice`), which results in each row having a `TextView` and a `CheckBox`. If you look inside this layout file, you will see another subclass of `TextView`, this one called `CheckedTextView`. This special type of `TextView` is intended for use with `ListView`s. See, we told you there were some interesting things in that Android layout folder! You will see that the ID of the `CheckedTextView` is `text1`, which is what we needed to pass in our views array to the constructor of the `SimpleCursorAdapter`.

Because we want the user to be able to select our rows, we set the choice mode to `CHOICE_MODE_MULTIPLE`. By default, the choice mode is `CHOICE_MODE_NONE`. The other possible value is `CHOICE_MODE_SINGLE`. If you wanted to use that choice mode for this example, you would want to use a different layout, most likely `android.R.layout.simple_list_item_single_choice`.

In this example, we've implemented a basic button that calls the `doClick()` method of our activity. To keep things simple, we just want to write out to LogCat the names of the items that were checked by the user. The good news is that the solution is pretty easy; the bad news is that Android has evolved so the best solution depends on which version of Android you're targeting. The `ListView` solution we've shown here has worked since Android 1 (although we took the Android 1.6 shortcut on the button callback). That is, the `getCheckedItemPositions()` method is old, yet still works. The return value is an array that can tell you if an item has been checked or not. So we iterate through the array. `viewItems.get(i)` will return true if the corresponding row in our `ListView` has been checked. Our data is accessible through the cursor. So instead of looking up data in the `ListView`, we look up data in the cursor. The `ListView` will tell us is where in the adapter to look.

When we get a position number from the `ListView` that has been checked, we can use the cursor's `moveToPosition()` method to prepare to read the data. There's another method that does nearly the same thing, the `getItemAtPosition()` method of the `ListView`. In our case, the object returned from `getItemAtPosition()` would turn out to be a `CursorWrapper` object. As we said before, in other situations, we might get some other type of object. It's only because we're working with a content provider that we would get a `CursorWrapper` here. You have to understand your data source and your adapter to know what to expect.

We can then use our Cursor (or CursorWrapper if we went with that) to retrieve the data that is connected to our ListView row. Notice how, in our example, we can retrieve not only the name of the contact but notes as well, even though we never mapped notes to the ListView. When we set up the cursor for our adapter, we selected all available fields. In practice, you won't need all fields, so you should restrict your query to just the fields you're going to use. But this is a case where we query for more fields than we need for display in the ListView, so we can get easy access to the other fields in our button callback.

Another Way to Read Selections From a ListView

Android 1.6 introduced another method for retrieving a list of the checked rows from a ListView: getCheckItemIds(). Then in Android 2.2, this method was deprecated and replaced with getCheckedItemIds(). It was a subtle name change, but the way you use the method is basically the same. Also, the way you deal with contacts changed in Android 2.2. For our next example, we'll use Android 2.2 features to show how our example might look. Listing 6–31 shows the Java code. For the XML layout of list.xml, we can continue to use the same file as found in Listing 6–29.

Listing 6–31. *Another Way of Reading User Input From the ListActivity*

```
public class ListViewActivity4 extends ListActivity
{
    private static final String TAG = "ListViewActivity4";
    private static final Uri CONTACTS_URI = ContactsContract.Contacts.CONTENT_URI;
    private SimpleCursorAdapter adapter = null;
    private ListView lv = null;

    @Override
    protected void onCreate(Bundle savedInstanceState)
    {
        super.onCreate(savedInstanceState);
        setContentView(R.layout.list);

        lv = getListView();

        String[] projection = new String[] {ContactsContract.Contacts._ID,
                ContactsContract.Contacts.DISPLAY_NAME};
        Cursor c = managedQuery(CONTACTS_URI,
                        projection, null, null, ContactsContract.Contacts.DISPLAY_NAME);

        String[] cols = new String[] {ContactsContract.Contacts.DISPLAY_NAME};
        int[]    views = new int[]       {android.R.id.text1};

        adapter = new SimpleCursorAdapter(this,
                android.R.layout.simple_list_item_multiple_choice,
                c, cols, views);

        this.setListAdapter(adapter);

        lv.setChoiceMode(ListView.CHOICE_MODE_MULTIPLE);
    }
```

```
    public void doClick(View view) {
        if(!adapter.hasStableIds()) {
            Log.v(TAG, "Data is not stable");
            return;
        }
        long[] viewItems = lv.getCheckedItemIds();
        for(int i=0; i<viewItems.length; i++) {
            Uri selectedPerson = ContentUris.withAppendedId(
                    CONTACTS_URI, viewItems[i]);

            Log.v(TAG, selectedPerson.toString() + " is checked.");
        }
    }
}
```

In this example application, when we click the button, our callback calls the method getCheckedItemIds(). Whereas in our last example, we got an array of positions of the checked items in the ListView, this time we get an array of IDs of the records from the adapter that have been checked in the ListView. We can bypass the ListView and the cursor now, because the IDs can be used with the content provider to take whatever action we desire. In our example, we simply construct a URI that represents the specific record from the Contacts content provider, and we write that URI to LogCat. We could have operated on the data using the content provider directly. This technique works equally well using the older Contacts content provider and the Android 1.6 getCheckItemIds() method.

Something else we've done differently in this example is to only select a couple of columns when we created our Cursor. This is the normal practice since you do not want to read more data than is necessary. The last thing to point out from this example is that the method getCheckedItemIds() requires that the underlying data in the adapter is stable. Therefore, it is highly recommended that you call hasStableIds() on the adapter before calling getCheckedItemIds() on the ListView. In our example, we took a shortcut and simply logged the fact and returned. In reality, you'd want to do something more intelligent, like maybe initiate a background thread to do retries and throw up a dialog indicating that you're doing processing.

We've shown you how to work with ListViews from a variety of scenarios. We've shown that adapters do a lot of the work to support a ListView. Next, we'll cover the other types of list controls, starting with the GridView.

The GridView Control

Most widget toolkits offer one or more grid-based controls. Android has a GridView control that can display data in the form of a grid. Note that although we use the term "data" here, the contents of the grid can be text, images, and so on.

The GridView control displays information in a grid. The usage pattern for the GridView is to define the grid in the XML layout (see Listing 6–32) and then bind the data to the grid using an android.widget.ListAdapter. Don't forget to add the uses-permission tag to the AndroidManifest.xml file to make this example work.

Listing 6–32. *Definition of a GridView in an XML Layout and Associated Java Code*

```
<?xml version="1.0" encoding="utf-8"?>
<!-- This file is at /res/layout/gridview.xml -->
<GridView xmlns:android="http://schemas.android.com/apk/res/android"
    android:id="@+id/dataGrid"
    android:layout_width="fill_parent"
    android:layout_height="fill_parent"
    android:padding="10px"
    android:verticalSpacing="10px"
    android:horizontalSpacing="10px"
    android:numColumns="auto_fit"
    android:columnWidth="100px"
    android:stretchMode="columnWidth"
    android:gravity="center"
    />


public class GridViewActivity extends Activity
{
    @Override
    protected void onCreate(Bundle savedInstanceState)
    {
        super.onCreate(savedInstanceState);
        setContentView(R.layout.gridview);

        GridView gv = (GridView)findViewById(R.id.gridview);

        Cursor c = managedQuery(People.CONTENT_URI,
                        null, null, null, People.NAME);

        String[] cols = new String[] {People.NAME};
        int[]    views = new int[]      {android.R.id.text1};

        SimpleCursorAdapter adapter = new SimpleCursorAdapter(this,
                android.R.layout.simple_list_item_1,
                c, cols, views);

        gv.setAdapter(adapter);
    }
}
```

Listing 6–32 defines a simple GridView in an XML layout. The grid is then loaded into the activity's content view. The generated UI is shown in Figure 6–13.

Figure 6–13. *A GridView populated with contact information*

The grid shown in Figure 6–13 displays the names of the contacts on the device. We have decided to show a `TextView` with the contact names, but you could easily generate a grid filled with images or other controls. We've again taken advantage of predefined layouts in Android. In fact, this example looks very much like Listing 6–27 except for a few important differences. First, our `GridViewActivity` extends `Activity`, not `ListActivity`. Second, we must call `setContentView()` to set the layout for our `GridView`; there are no default views to fall back on. And finally, to set the adapter we call `setAdapter()` on the `GridView` object instead of calling `setListAdapter()` on `Activity`.

You've no doubt noticed that the adapter used by the grid is a `ListAdapter`. Lists are generally one-dimensional, whereas grids are two-dimensional. We can conclude, then, that the grid actually displays list-oriented data. And it turns out that the list is displayed by rows. That is, the list goes across the first row, then across the second row, and so on.

As before, we have a list control that works with an adapter to handle the data management, and the generation of the child views. The same techniques we used before should work just fine with `GridView`s. One exception is in terms of making selections. There is no way to specify multiple choices in a `GridView`, like we did in Listing 6–30.

The Spinner Control

The `Spinner` control is like a drop-down menu. It is typically used to select from a relatively short list of choices. If the choice list is too long for the display, a scrollbar is automatically added for you. You can instantiate a `Spinner` via XML layout as simply as this:

```
<Spinner
    android:id="@+id/spinner"  android:prompt="@string/spinnerprompt"
    android:layout_width="wrap_content"  android:layout_height="wrap_content" />
```

While a spinner is technically a list control, it will appear to you more like a simple `TextView` control. In other words, only one value will be displayed when the spinner is at rest. The purpose of the spinner is to allow the user to choose from a set of predetermined values: when the user clicks the small arrow, a list is displayed, and the user is expected to pick a new value. Populating this list is done in the same way as the other list controls, that is, with an adapter. Because a spinner is often used like a drop-down menu, it is common to see the adapter get the list choices from a resource file. An example that sets up a spinner using a resource file is shown in Listing 6–33. Notice the new attribute called `android:prompt` for setting a prompt at the top of the list to choose from. The actual text for our spinner prompt is in our `/res/values/strings.xml` file. As you should expect, the `Spinner` class has a method for setting the prompt in code as well.

Listing 6–33. *Code to Create a Spinner From a Resource File*

```
public class SpinnerActivity extends Activity {
    /** Called when the activity is first created. */
    @Override
    public void onCreate(Bundle savedInstanceState) {
        super.onCreate(savedInstanceState);
        setContentView(R.layout.spinner);

        Spinner spinner = (Spinner)findViewById(R.id.spinner);

        ArrayAdapter<CharSequence> adapter = ArrayAdapter.createFromResource(this,
                R.array.planets, android.R.layout.simple_spinner_item);

        adapter.setDropDownViewResource(android.R.layout.simple_spinner_dropdown_item);

        spinner.setAdapter(adapter);
    }
}
```

You may recall seeing the `planets.xml` file in Listing 6–26. We show in this example how a `Spinner` control is created; the adapter is set up and then associated to the spinner. See Figure 6–14 for what this looks like in action.

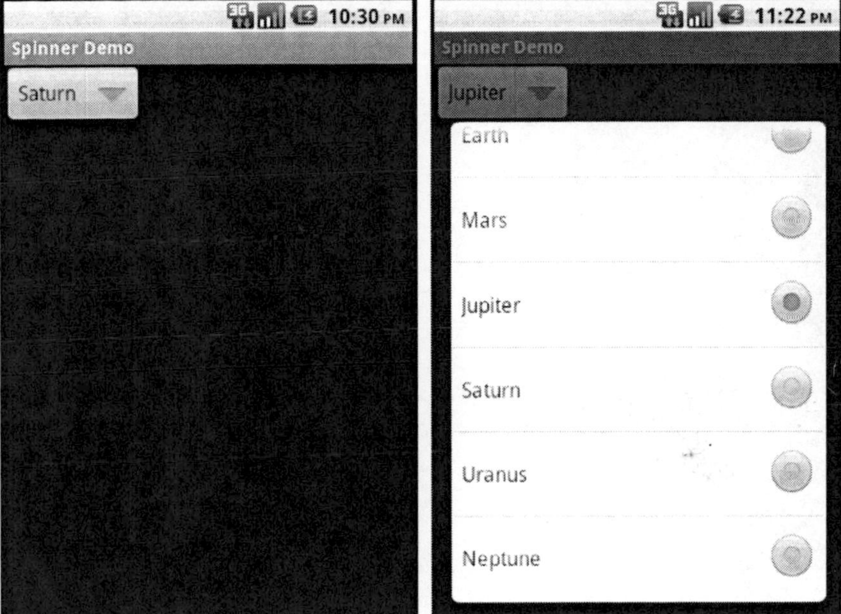

Figure 6–14. *A spinner for choosing a planet*

One of the differences from our earlier list controls is that we've got an extra layout to contend with when working with a spinner. The left-hand side of Figure 6–14 shows the normal mode of a spinner, where the current selection is shown. In this case, the current selection is Saturn. Next to the word is a downward-pointing arrow indicating that this control is a spinner and can be used to pop up a list to select a different value. The first layout, supplied as a parameter to the `ArrayAdapter.createFromResource()` method, defines how the spinner looks in normal mode. On the right-hand side of Figure 6–14, we show the spinner in the pop-up list mode, waiting for the user to choose a new value. The layout for this list is set using the `setDropDownViewResource()` method. Again in this example, we're using Android-provided layouts for these two needs, so if you want to inspect the definition of either of these layouts, you can visit the Android `res/layout` folder. And of course, you can specify your own layout definition for either of these to get the effect you want.

The Gallery Control

The `Gallery` control is a horizontally scrollable list control that always focuses at the center of the list. This control generally functions as a photo gallery in touch mode. You can instantiate a `Gallery` either via XML layout or code:

```
<Gallery
    android:id="@+id/gallery"
    android:layout_width="fill_parent"
    android:layout_height="wrap_content"
/>
```

The Gallery control is typically used to display images, so your adapter is likely going to be specialized for images. We'll show you a custom image adapter in next section on custom adapters. Visually, a Gallery looks like Figure 6–15.

Figure 6–15. *A gallery with images of manatees*

Creating Custom Adapters

Standard adapters in Android are easy to use, but they have some limitations. To address this, Android provides an abstract class called BaseAdapter that you can extend if you need a custom adapter. You would use a custom adapter if you had special data-management needs or if you wanted more control over how to display child views. You might also use a custom adapter to improve performance by using caching techniques. We're going to show you how to build a custom adapter next.

Listing 6–34 shows what the XML layout and the Java code could look like for a custom Adapter. For this next example, our adapter is going to deal with images of manatees, so we'll call it ManateeAdapter. We're going to create it inside of an activity as well.

Listing 6–34. *Our Custom Adapter: ManateeAdapter*

```
<?xml version="1.0" encoding="utf-8"?>
<!-- This file is at /res/layout/gridviewcustom.xml -->
<GridView xmlns:android="http://schemas.android.com/apk/res/android"
    android:id="@+id/gridview"
    android:layout_width="fill_parent"
    android:layout_height="fill_parent"
```

```
    android:padding="10dip"
    android:verticalSpacing="10dip"
    android:horizontalSpacing="10dip"
    android:numColumns="auto_fit"
    android:gravity="center"
    />
```

```
public class GridViewCustomAdapter extends Activity
{
    @Override
    protected void onCreate(Bundle savedInstanceState)
    {
        super.onCreate(savedInstanceState);
        setContentView(R.layout.gridviewcustom);

        GridView gv = (GridView)findViewById(R.id.gridview);

        ManateeAdapter adapter = new ManateeAdapter(this);

        gv.setAdapter(adapter);
    }

    public static class ManateeAdapter extends BaseAdapter {
        private static final String TAG = "ManateeAdapter";
        private static int convertViewCounter = 0;
        private Context mContext;
        private LayoutInflater mInflater;

        static class ViewHolder {
            ImageView image;
        }

        private int[] manatees = {
                R.drawable.manatee00, R.drawable.manatee01, R.drawable.manatee02,
                R.drawable.manatee03, R.drawable.manatee04, R.drawable.manatee05,
                R.drawable.manatee06, R.drawable.manatee07, R.drawable.manatee08,
                R.drawable.manatee09, R.drawable.manatee10, R.drawable.manatee11,
                R.drawable.manatee12, R.drawable.manatee13, R.drawable.manatee14,
                R.drawable.manatee15, R.drawable.manatee16, R.drawable.manatee17,
                R.drawable.manatee18, R.drawable.manatee19, R.drawable.manatee20,
                R.drawable.manatee21, R.drawable.manatee22, R.drawable.manatee23,
                R.drawable.manatee24, R.drawable.manatee25, R.drawable.manatee26,
                R.drawable.manatee27, R.drawable.manatee28, R.drawable.manatee29,
                R.drawable.manatee30, R.drawable.manatee31, R.drawable.manatee32,
                R.drawable.manatee33 };

        private Bitmap[] manateeImages = new Bitmap[manatees.length];
        private Bitmap[] manateeThumbs = new Bitmap[manatees.length];

        public ManateeAdapter(Context context) {
            Log.v(TAG, "Constructing ManateeAdapter");
            this.mContext = context;
            mInflater = LayoutInflater.from(context);

            for(int i=0; i<manatees.length; i++) {
                manateeImages[i] = BitmapFactory.decodeResource(
```

```
                    context.getResources(), manatees[i]);
            manateeThumbs[i] = Bitmap.createScaledBitmap(manateeImages[i],
                    100, 100, false);
        }
    }

    @Override
    public int getCount() {
        Log.v(TAG, "in getCount()");
        return manatees.length;
    }

    public int getViewTypeCount() {
        Log.v(TAG, "in getViewTypeCount()");
        return 1;
    }

    public int getItemViewType(int position) {
        Log.v(TAG, "in getItemViewType() for position " + position);
        return 0;
    }

    @Override
    public View getView(int position, View convertView, ViewGroup parent) {
        ViewHolder holder;

        Log.v(TAG, "in getView for position " + position +
                ", convertView is " +
                ((convertView == null)?"null":"being recycled"));

        if (convertView == null) {
            convertView = mInflater.inflate(R.layout.gridimage, null);
            convertViewCounter++;
            Log.v(TAG, convertViewCounter + " convertViews have been created");

            holder = new ViewHolder();
            holder.image = (ImageView) convertView.findViewById(R.id.gridImageView);

            convertView.setTag(holder);
        } else {
            holder = (ViewHolder) convertView.getTag();
        }

        holder.image.setImageBitmap( manateeThumbs[position] );

        return convertView;
    }

    @Override
    public Object getItem(int position) {
        Log.v(TAG, "in getItem() for position " + position);
        return manateeImages[position];
    }

    @Override
    public long getItemId(int position) {
        Log.v(TAG, "in getItemId() for position " + position);
```

```
            return position;
        }
    }
}
```

When you run this application, you should see a display that looks like Figure 6–16.

Figure 6–16. *A gridview with images of manatees*

There is a lot to explain in this example, even though it looks relatively simple. We'll start with our `Activity` class, which looks a lot like the ones we've been working with throughout this section of the chapter. There's a main layout from `gridviewcustom.xml`, which contains just a `GridView` definition. We need to get a reference to the `GridView` from inside the layout, so we define and set `gv`. We instantiate our `ManateeAdapter`, passing it our context, and we set the adapter on our `GridView`. This is pretty standard stuff so far, although you've no doubt noticed that our custom adapter doesn't use nearly as many parameters as pre-defined adapters when being created. This is mainly because we're in complete control over this particular adapter, and we're using it with only this application. If we were making this adapter more general, we would most likely be setting more parameters. But let's keep going.

Our job inside an adapter is to manage the passing of data into Android `View` objects. The `View` objects will be used by the list control (a `GridView` in this case). The data comes from some data source. In the earlier examples, the data came via a cursor object that was passed into the adapter. In our custom case here, our adapter knows all about the data and where it comes from. The list control will ask for things so it knows how to build the user interface. It is also kind enough to pass in views for recycling when it has a view it no longer needs. It may seem a bit strange to think that our adapter must know how to construct views, but in the end, it all makes sense.

When we instantiate our custom adapter `ManateeAdapter`, it is customary to pass in the context and for the adapter to hold onto it. It is often very useful to have it available when needed. The second thing we want to do in our adapter is to hang onto the inflater. This will help performance when we need to create a new view to return to the list control. The third thing that is typical in an adapter is to create a `ViewHolder` object, to contain the `View` objects for the data we are managing. For this example, we are simply storing an `ImageView`, but if we had additional fields to deal with, we would add them into the definition of `ViewHolder`. For example, if we had a `ListView` where each row contained an `ImageView` and two `TextViews`, our `ViewHolder` would have an `ImageView` and two `TextViews`.

Because we're dealing with images of manatees in this adapter, we set up an array of their resource IDs to be used during construction to create bitmaps. We also define an array of bitmaps to use as our data list.

As you can see from our `ManateeAdapter` constructor, we save the context, create and hang onto an inflater, and then, we iterate through the image resource IDs and build an array of bitmaps. This bitmap array will be our data.

As you learned previously, setting the adapter will cause our `GridView` to call methods on the adapter to set itself up with data to display. For example, gv will call the adapter's `getCount()` method to determine how many objects there are for displaying. It will also call the `getViewTypeCount()` method to determine how many different types of views could be displayed within the `GridView`. For our purposes in this example, we set this to 1. However, if we had a `ListView` and wanted to put separators in between regular rows of data, we would have two types of views and would need to return 2 from `getViewTypeCount()`. You could have as many different view types as you like, as long as you appropriately return the correct count from this method. Related to this method is `getItemViewType()`. We just said that we could have more than one type of view to return from the adapter. But to keep things simpler, `getItemViewType()` needs to return only an integer value to indicate which of our view types is at a particular position in the data. Therefore, if we had two types of views to return, `getItemViewType()` would need to return either 0 or 1 to indicate which type. If we have three types of views, this method needs to return 0, 1, or 2.

If our adapter is dealing with separators in a `ListView`, it must treat the separators as data. That means there is a position in the data that is taken up by a separator. When `getView()` is called by a list control to retrieve the appropriate view for that position, `getView()` will need to return a separator as a view instead of regular data as a view. And when asked in `getItemViewType()` for the view type for that position, we need to return the appropriate integer value that we've decided matches that view type. The other thing you should do if using separators is to implement the `isEnabled()` method. This should return true for list items and false for separators because separators should not be selectable or clickable.

The most interesting method in ManateeAdapter is the getView() method call. Once gv has determined how many items are available, it starts to ask for the data. Now, we can talk about recycling of views. A list control can only show as many child views on the display as will fit. That means there's no point in calling getView() for every piece of data in the adapter; it only makes sense to call getView() for as many items as can be displayed. As gv gets child views back from the adapter, it is determining how many will fit on the display. Once the display is full of child views, gv can stop calling getView().

If you look at LogCat after starting up this example application, you will see the various calls, but you will also see that getView() stops getting called before all images have been requested. If you start scrolling up and down the GridView, you will see more calls to getView() in LogCat, and you will notice that, once we've created a certain number of child views, getView() is being called with convertView set to something, not null. This means we're now recycling child views—and that's very good for performance.

If we get a nonnull convertView value from gv in getView(), it means gv is recycling that view. By reusing the view passed in, we avoid having to inflate an XML layout, and we avoid having to find the ImageView. By linking a ViewHolder object to the View that we return, we can be much faster at recycling the view next time it comes back to us. All we have to do in getView() is reacquire the ViewHolder, and assign the right data into the view.

For this example, we wanted to show that the data placed into the view is not necessarily exactly what exists in the data. The createScaledBitmap() method is creating a smaller version of the data for display purposes. The point is that our list control does not call the getItem() method. This method would be called by our other code that wants to do something with the data if the user acts on the list control. Once again, for any adapter, it is very important that you understand what it is doing. You don't necessarily want to rely on data in the view from the list control, as created by getView() in the adapter. Sometimes, you will need to call the adapter's getItem() method to get the actual data to be operated on. And sometimes, as we did in the earlier ListView examples, you'll want to go to a cursor for the data. It all depends on the adapter and where the data is ultimately coming from. Although we used the createScaledBitmap() method in our example, Android 2.2 introduced another class that might have been helpful here: ThumbnailUtils. This class has some static methods for generating thumbnail images from bitmaps and videos.

The last thing to point out from this example is the getItemId() method call. In our earlier examples with ListViews and contacts, the item ID was the _ID value from the content provider. For this example, we don't really need to use anything other than position for the item ID. The whole point of item IDs is to provide a mechanism to refer to the data separately from its position. This is especially true when the data has a life away from this adapter, as existed with our contacts. When we have this kind of direct control over the data, as we do with our images of manatees, and we understand how to get to the actual data in our application, it is a common shortcut to simply use position as the item ID. This is particularly true in our case, since we don't even allow adding or removal of data.

Other Controls in Android

There are many, many controls in Android that you can use. We've covered quite a few so far, and more will be covered in later chapters (such as `MapView` in Chapter 17, `VideoView` and `MediaController` in Chapter 19, and `GLSurfaceView` in Chapter 20). You will find that the other controls, because they're all descended from `View`, have a lot in common what the ones we've covered here. For now, we'll just mention a few of the controls you might want to explore further on your own.

`ScrollView` is a control for setting up a `View` container with a vertical scrollbar. This is really useful when you just have too much to fit onto a single screen. See this chapter's "References" section for a link to a blog post from Romain Guy on how to use this.

The `ProgressBar` and `RatingBar` controls are like sliders, the first to show the progress of some operation visually (perhaps a file download or music playing) and the second to show a rating scale of stars.

The `Chronometer` control is a timer that counts up. There's a `CountDownTimer` class if you want something to help you display a countdown timer, but it's not a `View` class.

`WebView` is a very special View for displaying HTML. It can do a lot more than that, including handling cookies and JavaScript and linking to Java code in your application. But before you go implementing a web browser inside your application, you should carefully consider simply invoking the on-device web browser to let it do all that heavy lifting.

That completes our introduction of controls in this chapter. We'll now move on to styles and themes for modifying the look and feel of our controls and then to layouts for arranging our controls on screens.

Styles and Themes

Android provides several ways to alter the style of views in your application. We'll first cover using markup tags in strings, then how to use spannables to change specific visual attributes of text. But what if you want to control how things look using a common specification for several views or across an entire activity or application? We'll discuss Android styles and themes to show you how.

Using Styles

Sometimes, you want to highlight or style a portion of the `View`'s content. You can do this statically or dynamically. Statically, you can apply markup directly to the strings in your string resources, for example:

```
<string name="styledText"><i>Static</i> style in a <b>TextView</b>.</string>
```

You can then reference it in your XML or from code. Note that you can use the following HTML tags with string resources: `<i>`, `<b>`, and `<u>` for italics, bold and underlined respectively as well as `<sup>` (superscript), `<sub>` (subscript), `<strike>` (strike-through),

<big>, <small>, and <monospace>. You can even nest these to get, for example, small superscripts. This works not just in TextViews but also in other views, like buttons. Figure 6–17 shows what styled and themed text looks like, using many of the examples in this section.

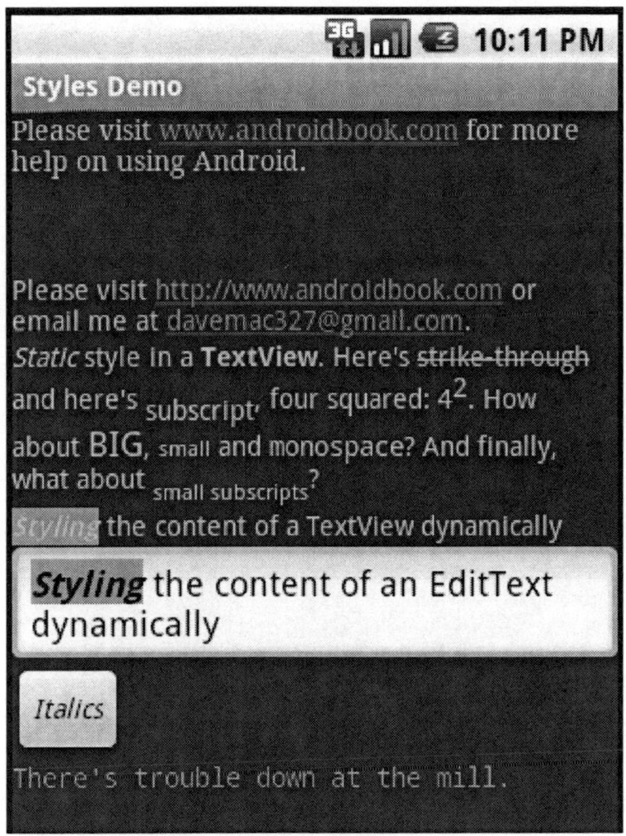

Figure 6–17. *Examples of styles and themes*

Styling a TextView control's content programmatically requires a little additional work but allows for much more flexibility (see Listing 6–35), because you can style it at runtime. This flexibility can only be applied to a spannable though, which is how EditText normally manages the internal text, whereas TextView does not normally use Spannable. Spannable is basically a String that you can apply styles to. To get a TextView to store text as a spannable, you can call setText() this way:

```
tv.setText("This text is stored in a Spannable", TextView.BufferType.SPANNABLE);
```

Then, when you call tv.getText(), you'll get a spannable.

As shown in Listing 6–35, you can get the content of the EditText (as a Spannable object) and then set styles to portions of the text. The code in the listing sets the text styling to bold and italics and sets the background to red. You can use all of the styling options as we have with the HTML tags as described previously, and then some.

Listing 6–35. *Applying Styles to the Content of an EditText Dynamically*

```
EditText et =(EditText)this.findViewById(R.id.et);
et.setText("Styling the content of an EditText dynamically");
Spannable spn = (Spannable) et.getText();
spn.setSpan(new BackgroundColorSpan(Color.RED), 0, 7,
            Spannable.SPAN_EXCLUSIVE_EXCLUSIVE);
spn.setSpan(new StyleSpan(android.graphics.Typeface.BOLD_ITALIC),
            0, 7, Spannable.SPAN_EXCLUSIVE_EXCLUSIVE);
```

These two techniques for styling only work on the one view they're applied to. Android provides a style mechanism to define a common style to be reused across views, as well as a theme mechanism, which basically applies a style to an entire activity or the entire application. To begin with, we need to talk about styles.

A *style* is a collection of View attributes that is given a name so you can refer to that collection by its name and assign that style by name to views. For example, Listing 6–36 shows a resource XML file, saved in /res/values, that we could use for all error messages.

Listing 6–36. *Defining a Style to Be Used Across Many Views*

```
<?xml version="1.0" encoding="utf-8"?>
<resources>
    <style name="ErrorText">
        <item name="android:layout_width">fill_parent</item>
        <item name="android:layout_height">wrap_content</item>
        <item name="android:textColor">#FF0000</item>
        <item name="android:typeface">monospace</item>
    </style>
</resources>
```

The size of the view is defined as well as the font color (i.e., red) and typeface. Notice how the name attribute of the item tag is the XML attribute name we used in our layout XML files, and the value of the item tag no longer requires double quotes. We can now use this style for an error TextView as shown in Listing 6–37.

Listing 6–37. *Using a Style in a View*

```
<TextView  android:id="@+id/errorText"
    style="@style/ErrorText"
    android:text="No errors at this time"
    />
```

It is important to note that the attribute name for style in this View definition does not start with android:. Watch out for this, as everything else seems to use android: except for the style. When you've got many views in your application that share a style, changing that style in one place is much simpler; you only need to modify the style's attributes in the one resource file. You can, of course, create many different styles for various controls. Buttons could share a common style, for example, that's different from the common style for text in menus.

One really nice aspect of styles is that you can set up a hierarchy of them. We could define a new style for really bad error messages and base it on the style of ErrorText. Listing 6–38 shows how this might look.

Listing 6–38. *Defining a Style From a Parent Style*

```
<?xml version="1.0" encoding="utf-8"?>
<resources>
    <style name="ErrorText.Danger" >
        <item name="android:textStyle">bold</item>
    </style>
</resources>
```

This example shows that we can simply name our child style using the parent style as a prefix to the new style name. Therefore, ErrorText.Danger is a child of ErrorText and inherits the style attributes of the parent. It then adds a new attribute for textStyle. This can be continued again and again to create a whole tree of styles.

As was the case for adapter layouts, Android provides a large set of styles that we can use. To specify an Android-provided style, use syntax like this:

```
style="@android:style/TextAppearance"
```

This style sets the default style for text in Android. To locate the master Android styles.xml file, visit the Android SDK/platforms/<android-version>/data/res/values/ folder. Inside this file, you will find quite a few styles that are ready made for you to use or extend. Here's a word of caution about extending the Android-provided styles: the previous method of using a prefix won't work with Android-provided styles. Instead, you must use the parent attribute of the style tag, like this:

```
<style name="CustomTextAppearance" parent="@android:style/TextAppearance">
    <item  ... your extensions go here ...    />
</style>
```

You don't always have to pull in an entire style on your view. You could choose to borrow just a part of the style instead. For example, if you want to set the color of the text in your TextView to a system style color, you could do the following:

```
<EditText id="@+id/et2"
    android:layout_width="fill_parent"  android:layout_height="wrap_content"
    android:textColor="?android:textColorSecondary"
    android:text="@string/hello_world" />
```

Notice that in this example, the name of the textColor attribute value starts with the ? character instead of the @ character. The ? character is used so Android knows to look for a style value in the current theme. Because we see ?android, we look in the Android system theme for this style value.

Using Themes

One problem with styles is that you need to add an attribute specification of style="@style/..." to every view definition that you want it to apply to. If you have some style elements you want applied across an entire activity, or across the whole application, you should use a theme instead. A *theme* is really just a style applied broadly, but in terms of defining a theme, it's exactly like a style. In fact, themes and styles are fairly interchangeable, as you can extend a theme into a style or refer to a style as a theme. Typically, only the names give a hint as to whether a style is intended to be used as a style or a theme.

To specify a theme for an activity or an application, you would add an attribute to the `<activity>` or `<application>` tag in the `AndroidManifest.xml` file for your project. The code might look like one of these:

```
<activity android:theme="@style/MyActivityTheme">
<application android:theme="@style/MyApplicationTheme">
<application android:theme="@android:style/Theme.NoTitleBar">
```

You can find the Android-provided themes in the same folder as the Android-provided styles, with the themes in a file called `themes.xml`. When you look inside the themes file, you will see a large set of styles defined, with names that start with `"Theme"`. You will also notice that within the Android-provided themes and styles, there is a lot of extending going on, which is why you end up with styles called `"Theme.Dialog.AppError"` for example.

This concludes our discussion of the Android control set. As we mentioned in the beginning of the chapter, building user interfaces in Android requires you to master two things: the control set and the layout managers. In the next section, we are going to discuss the Android layout managers.

Understanding Layout Managers

Android offers a collection of view classes that act as containers for views. These container classes are called *layouts* (or *layout managers*), and each implements a specific strategy to manage the size and position of its children. For example, the `LinearLayout` class lays out its children either horizontally or vertically, one after the other. All layout managers derive from the `View` class, therefore you can nest layout managers inside of one another.

The layout managers that ship with the Android SDK are defined in Table 6–2.

Table 6–2. *Android Layout Managers*

Layout Manager	Description
`LinearLayout`	Organizes its children either horizontally or vertically
`TableLayout`	Organizes its children in tabular form
`RelativeLayout`	Organizes its children relative to one another or to the parent
`FrameLayout`	Allows you to dynamically change the control(s) in the layout

We will discuss these layout managers in the sections that follow. The layout manager called `AbsoluteLayout` has been deprecated and will not be covered in this book.

The LinearLayout Layout Manager

The LinearLayout layout manager is the most basic. This layout manager organizes its children either horizontally or vertically based on the value of the orientation property. We've used LinearLayout in several of our examples so far. Listing 6–39 shows LinearLayout with a horizontal configuration.

Listing 6–39. *LinearLayout with a Horizontal Configuration*

```
<LinearLayout xmlns:android="http://schemas.android.com/apk/res/android"
    android:orientation="horizontal"
    android:layout_width="fill_parent"  android:layout_height="wrap_content">

    <!-- add children here-->

</LinearLayout>
```

You can create a vertically oriented LinearLayout by setting the value of orientation to vertical. Because layout managers can be nested, you could, for example, construct a vertical layout manager that contained horizontal layout managers to create a fill-in form, where each row had a label next to an EditText control. Each row would be its own horizontal layout, but the rows as a collection would be organized vertically.

Understanding Weight and Gravity

The orientation attribute is the first important attribute recognized by the LinearLayout layout manager. Other important properties that can affect size and position of child controls are weight and gravity. You use *weight* to assign size importance to a control relative to the other controls in the container. Suppose a container has three controls: one has a weight of 1, while the others have a weight of 0. In this case, the control whose weight equals 1 will consume the empty space in the container. *Gravity* is essentially alignment. For example, if you want to align a label's text to the right, you would set its gravity to right. There are quite a few possible values for gravity, including left, center, right, top, bottom, center_vertical, clip_horizontal, and still others. See the web pages in the "References" section for details on these and the other values of gravity.

NOTE: Layout managers extend android.widget.ViewGroup, as do many control-based container classes such as ListView. Although the layout managers and control-based containers extend the same class, the layout manager classes strictly deal with the sizing and position of controls and not user interaction with child controls. For example, compare the LinearLayout to the ListView control. On the screen, they look similar in that both can organize children vertically. But the ListView control provides APIs for the user to make selections, while the LinearLayout does not. In other words, the control-based container (ListView) supports user interaction with the items in the container, whereas the layout manager (LinearLayout) addresses sizing and positioning only.

Now let's look at an example involving the weight and gravity properties (see Figure 6–18).

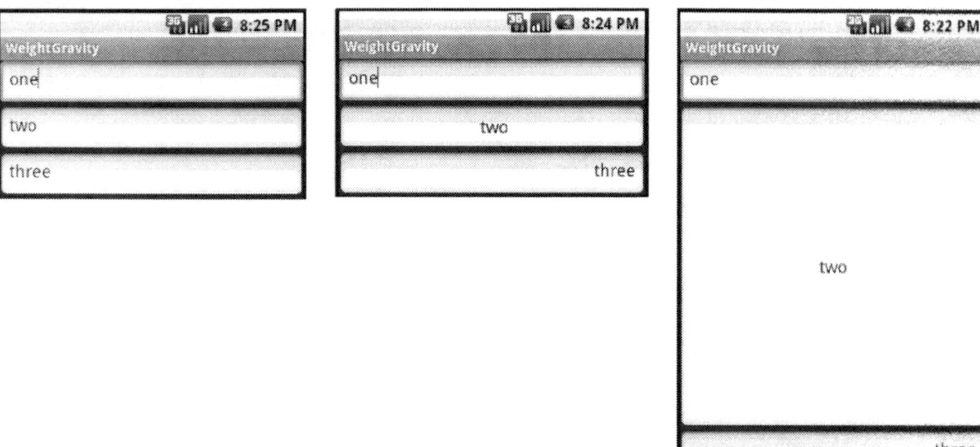

Figure 6–18. *Using the LinearLayout layout manager*

Figure 6–18 shows three user interfaces that utilize `LinearLayout`, with different weight and gravity settings. The UI on the left uses the default settings for weight and gravity. The XML layout for this first user interface is shown in Listing 6–40.

Listing 6–40. *Three Text Fields Arranged Vertically in a LinearLayout, Using Default Values for Weight and Gravity*

```
<LinearLayout xmlns:android="http://schemas.android.com/apk/res/android"
    android:orientation="vertical" android:layout_width="fill_parent"
    android:layout_height="fill_parent">

    <EditText android:layout_width="fill_parent"
        android:layout_height="wrap_content"
        android:text="one"/>
    <EditText android:layout_width="fill_parent"
        android:layout_height="wrap_content"
        android:text="two"/>
    <EditText android:layout_width="fill_parent"
        android:layout_height="wrap_content"
        android:text="three"/>
</LinearLayout>
```

The user interface in the center of Figure 6–18 uses the default value for weight but sets `android:gravity` for the controls in the container to `left`, `center`, and `right`, respectively. The last example sets the `android:layout_weight` attribute of the center component to 1.0 and leaves the others to the default value of 0.0 (see Listing 6–41). By setting the weight attribute to 1.0 for the middle component and leaving the weight attributes for the other two components at 0.0, we are specifying that the center component should take up all the remaining white space in the container and that the other two components should remain at their ideal size.

Similarly, if you want two of the three controls in the container to share the remaining white space among them, you would set the weight to 1.0 for those two and leave the third one at 0.0. Finally, if you want the three components to share the space equally, you'd set all of their weight values to 1.0. Doing this would expand each text field equally.

Listing 6–41. *LinearLayout with Weight Configurations*

```
<LinearLayout xmlns:android="http://schemas.android.com/apk/res/android"
    android:orientation="vertical" android:layout_width="fill_parent"
    android:layout_height="fill_parent">

    <EditText android:layout_width="fill_parent" android:layout_weight="0.0"
    android:layout_height="wrap_content" android:text="one"
    android:gravity="left"/>

    <EditText android:layout_width="fill_parent" android:layout_weight="1.0"
    android:layout_height="wrap_content" android:text="two"
    android:gravity="center"/>

    <EditText android:layout_width="fill_parent" android:layout_weight="0.0"
    android:layout_height="wrap_content" android:text="three"
    android:gravity="right"
    />
</LinearLayout>
```

android:gravity vs. android:layout_gravity

Note that Android defines two similar gravity attributes: `android:gravity` and `android:layout_gravity`. Here's the difference: `android:gravity` is a setting used by the view, whereas `android:layout_gravity` is used by the container (`android.view.ViewGroup`). For example, you can set `android:gravity` to `center` to have the text in the `EditText` centered within the control. Similarly, you can align an `EditText` to the far right of a `LinearLayout` (the container) by setting `android:layout_gravity="right"`. See Figure 6–19 and Listing 6–42.

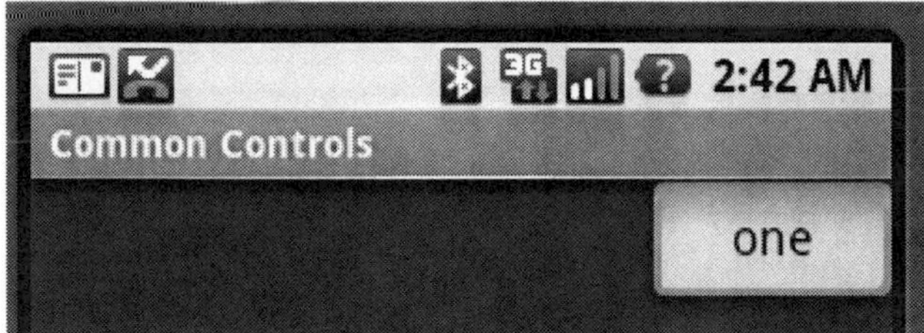

Figure 6–19. *Applying gravity settings*

Listing 6–42. *Understanding the Difference Between android:gravity and android:layout_gravity*

```
<LinearLayout xmlns:android="http://schemas.android.com/apk/res/android"
    android:orientation="vertical" android:layout_width="fill_parent"
    android:layout_height="fill_parent">

    <EditText android:layout_width="wrap_content" android:gravity="center"
    android:layout_height="wrap_content" android:text="one"
 android:layout_gravity="right"/>
</LinearLayout>
```

As shown in Figure 6–19, the text is centered within the EditText, which is aligned to the right of the LinearLayout.

The TableLayout Layout Manager

The TableLayout layout manager is an extension of LinearLayout. This layout manager structures its child controls into rows and columns. Listing 6–43 shows an example.

Listing 6–43. *A Simple TableLayout*

```
<?xml version="1.0" encoding="utf-8"?>
<TableLayout xmlns:android="http://schemas.android.com/apk/res/android"
    android:layout_width="fill_parent"  android:layout_height="fill_parent">

  <TableRow>
    <TextView android:text="First Name:"
        android:layout_width="wrap_content"  android:layout_height="wrap_content" />

    <EditText android:text="Edgar"
        android:layout_width="wrap_content"  android:layout_height="wrap_content" />
  </TableRow>

  <TableRow>
    <TextView android:text="Last Name:"
        android:layout_width="wrap_content"  android:layout_height="wrap_content" />

    <EditText android:text="Poe"
        android:layout_width="wrap_content"  android:layout_height="wrap_content" />
  </TableRow>

</TableLayout>
```

To use this layout manager, you create an instance of TableLayout and place TableRow elements within it. These TableRow elements contain the controls of the table. The user interface for Listing 6–43 is shown in Figure 6–20.

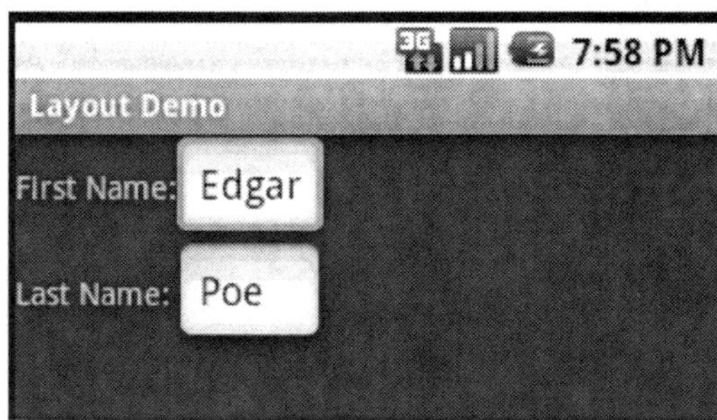

Figure 6–20. *The TableLayout layout manager*

Because the contents of a TableLayout are defined by rows as opposed to columns, Android determines the number of columns in the table by finding the row with the most cells. For example, Listing 6–44 creates a table with two rows where one row has two cells and the other has three cells (see Figure 6–21). In this case, Android creates a table with two rows and three columns. The last column of the first row is an empty cell.

Listing 6–44. *An Irregular Table Definition*

```
<TableLayout xmlns:android="http://schemas.android.com/apk/res/android"
    android:layout_width="fill_parent"  android:layout_height="fill_parent">

  <TableRow>
    <TextView android:text="First Name:"
        android:layout_width="wrap_content"  android:layout_height="wrap_content" />

    <EditText android:text="Edgar"
        android:layout_width="wrap_content"  android:layout_height="wrap_content" />
  </TableRow>

  <TableRow>
    <TextView android:text="Last Name:"
        android:layout_width="wrap_content"  android:layout_height="wrap_content" />

    <EditText android:text="Allen"
        android:layout_width="wrap_content"  android:layout_height="wrap_content" />

    <EditText android:text="Poe"
        android:layout_width="wrap_content"  android:layout_height="wrap_content" />
  </TableRow>

</TableLayout>
```

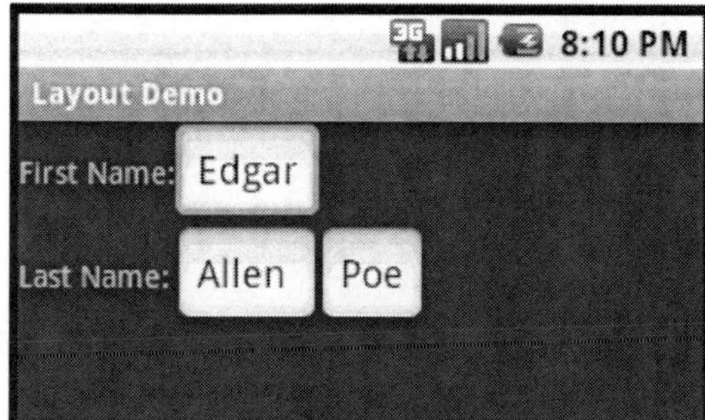

Figure 6–21. *An irregular TableLayout*

In Listings 6–43 and 6–44, we populated the TableLayout with TableRow elements. Although this is the usual pattern, you can place any android.widget.View as a child of the table. For example, Listing 6–45 creates a table where the first row is an EditText (see Figure 6–22).

Listing 6–45. *Using an EditText Instead of a TableRow*

```
<?xml version="1.0" encoding="utf-8"?>
<TableLayout xmlns:android="http://schemas.android.com/apk/res/android"
    android:layout_width="fill_parent"  android:layout_height="fill_parent"
    android:stretchColumns="0,1,2" >

  <EditText android:text="Fullname:"
        android:layout_width="wrap_content"  android:layout_height="wrap_content" />

  <TableRow>
    <TextView android:text="Edgar"
```

```
        android:layout_width="wrap_content"  android:layout_height="wrap_content" />

    <TextView android:text="Allen"
        android:layout_width="wrap_content"  android:layout_height="wrap_content" />

    <TextView android:text="Poe"
        android:layout_width="wrap_content"  android:layout_height="wrap_content" />
  </TableRow>

</TableLayout>
```

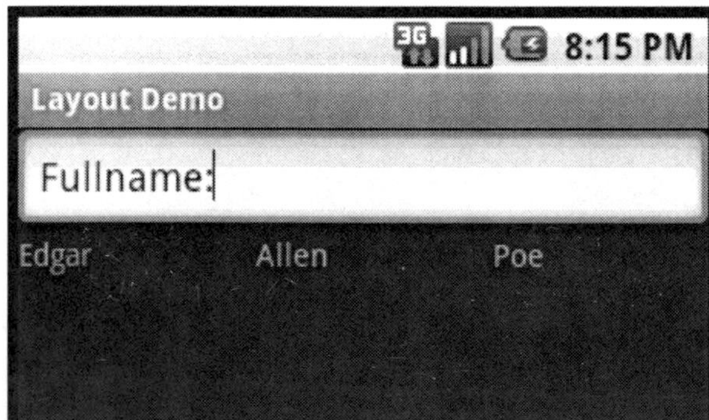

Figure 6–22. *EditText as a child of a TableLayout*

The user interface for Listing 6–45 is shown in Figure 6–22. Notice that the `EditText` takes up the entire width of the screen, even though we have not specified this in the XML layout. That's because children of `TableLayout` always span the entire row. In other words, children of `TableLayout` can specify `android:layout_width="wrap_content"` (as we did with `EditText`), but it won't affect actual layout—they are forced to accept `fill_parent`. They can, however, set `android:layout_height`.

Because the content of a table is not always known at design time, `TableLayout` offers several attributes that can help you control the layout of a table. For example, Listing 6–45 sets the `android:stretchColumns` property on the `TableLayout` to `"0,1,2"`. This gives a hint to the `TableLayout` that columns `0`, `1`, and `2` can be stretched if required, based on the contents of the table. If we had not used `stretchColumns` in Listing 6–45, we would have seen `"EdgarAllenPoe"` all squished together. Technically, the second row takes up the entire width, but the three `TextViews` do not spread across.

Similarly, you can set `android:shrinkColumns` to wrap the content of a column or columns if other columns require more space. You can also set `android:collapseColumns` to make columns invisible. Note that columns are identified with a zero-based indexing scheme.

`TableLayout` also offers `android:layout_span`. You can use this property to have a cell span multiple columns. This field is similar to the HTML `colspan` property.

At times, you might also need to provide spacing within the contents of a cell or a control. The Android SDK supports this via `android:padding` and its siblings. `android:padding` lets you control the space between a view's outer boundary and its content (see Listing 6–46).

Listing 6–46. *Using android:padding*

```
<LinearLayout xmlns:android="http://schemas.android.com/apk/res/android"
    android:orientation="vertical" android:layout_width="fill_parent"
    android:layout_height="fill_parent">

    <EditText android:text="one"
    android:layout_width="wrap_content"  android:layout_height="wrap_content"
    android:padding="40px" />
</LinearLayout>
```

Listing 6–46 sets the padding to `40px`. This creates 40 pixels of white space between the `EditText` control's outer boundary and the text displayed within it. Figure 6–23 shows the same `EditText` with two different padding values. The UI on the left does not set any padding, while the one on the right sets `android:padding="40px"`.

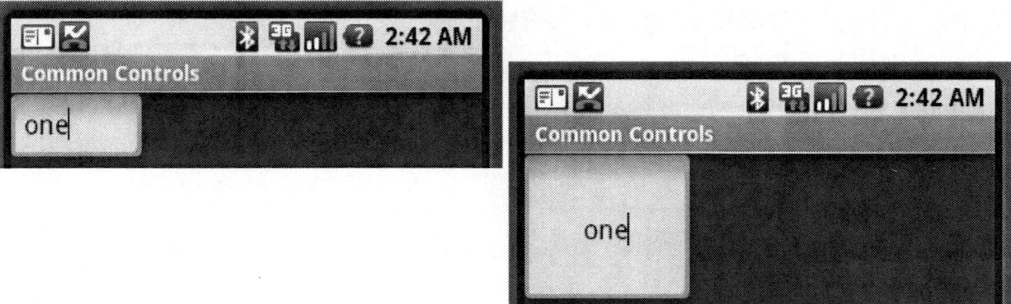

Figure 6–23. *Utilizing padding*

`android:padding` sets the padding for all sides: left, right, top, and bottom. You can control the padding for each side by using `android:leftPadding`, `android:rightPadding`, `android:topPadding`, and `android:bottomPadding`.

Android also defines `android:layout_margin`, which is similar to `android:padding`. In fact, `android:padding/android:layout_margin` is analogous to `android:gravity/android:layout_gravity`, but one is for a view, and the other is for a container.

Finally, the padding value is always set as a dimension type. Android supports the following dimension types:

- *Pixels*: Abbreviated as `px`. This dimension represents physical pixels on the screen.
- *Inches*: Abbreviated as `in`. This dimension represents real inches on the screen.
- *Millimeters*: Abbreviated as `mm`. This dimension represents real millimeters on the screen.
- *Points*: Abbreviated as `pt`. A point is equal to 1/72 of an inch.

- *Density-independent pixels*: Abbreviated as dip or dp, this dimension type uses a 160-dp screen as a frame of reference and then maps that to the actual screen. For example, a screen with a 160-pixel width would map 1 dip to 1 pixel.
- *Scale-independent pixels*: Abbreviated as sp, this dimension type is generally used with font types. It will take the user's preferences and font size into account to determine actual size.

Note that the preceding dimension types are not specific to padding—any Android field that accepts a dimension value (such as android:layout_width or android:layout_height) can accept these types.

The RelativeLayout Layout Manager

Another interesting layout manager is the RelativeLayout. As the name suggests, this layout manager implements a policy where the controls in the container are laid out relative to either the container or another control in the container. Listing 6–47 and Figure 6–24 show an example.

Listing 6–47. *Using a RelativeLayout Layout Manager*

```
<RelativeLayout xmlns:android="http://schemas.android.com/apk/res/android"
        android:layout_width="fill_parent"
        android:layout_height="wrap_content">

<TextView android:id="@+id/userNameLbl"
        android:layout_width="fill_parent"  android:layout_height="wrap_content"
        android:text="Username: "
        android:layout_alignParentTop="true" />

<EditText android:id="@+id/userNameText"
        android:layout_width="fill_parent"  android:layout_height="wrap_content"
        android:layout_below="@id/userNameLbl" />

<TextView android:id="@+id/pwdLbl"
        android:layout_width="fill_parent"  android:layout_height="wrap_content"
        android:layout_below="@id/userNameText"
        android:text="Password: " />

<EditText android:id="@+id/pwdText"
        android:layout_width="fill_parent"  android:layout_height="wrap_content"
        android:layout_below="@id/pwdLbl" />

<TextView android:id="@+id/pwdCriteria"
        android:layout_width="fill_parent"  android:layout_height="wrap_content"
        android:layout_below="@id/pwdText"
        android:text="Password Criteria... " />

<TextView android:id="@+id/disclaimerLbl"
        android:layout_width="fill_parent"  android:layout_height="wrap_content"
        android:layout_alignParentBottom="true"
        android:text="Use at your own risk... " />
```

```
</RelativeLayout>
```

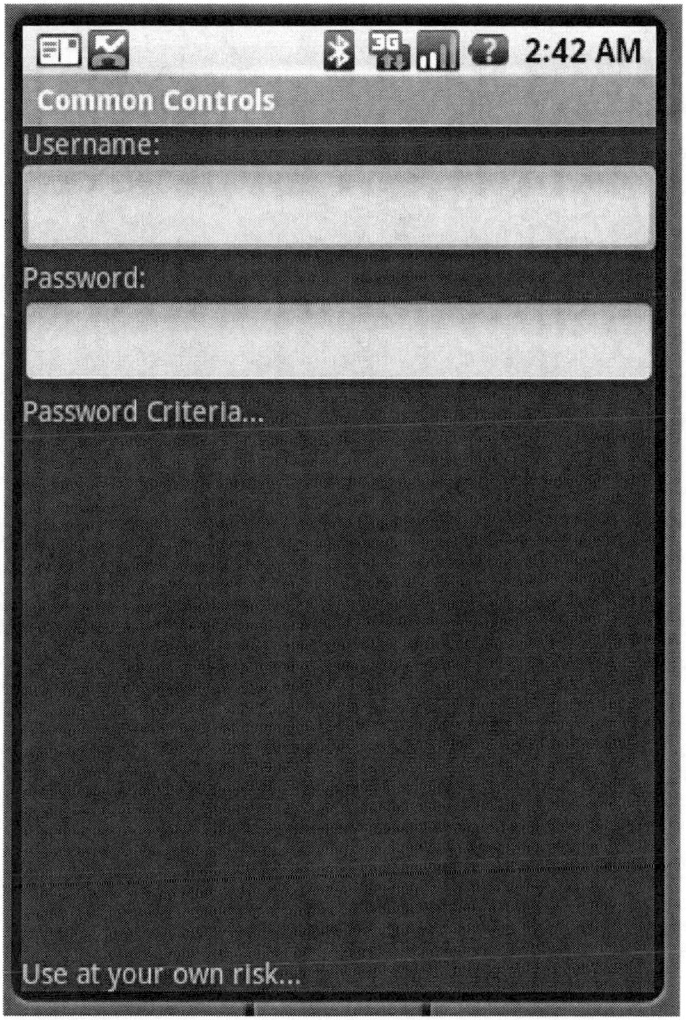

Figure 6–24. *A UI laid out using the RelativeLayout layout manager*

As shown, the user interface looks like a simple login form. The username label is pinned to the top of the container, because we set `android:layout_alignParentTop` to `true`. Similarly, the Username input field is positioned below the Username label because we set `android:layout_below`. The Password label appears below the Username label, and the Password input field appears below the Password label. The disclaimer label is pinned to the bottom of the container because we set `android:layout_alignParentBottom` to `true`.

Besides these three layout attributes, you can also specify `layout_above`, `layout_toRightOf`, `layout_toLeftOf`, `layout_centerInParent`, and several more. Working with `RelativeLayout` is fun due to its simplicity. In fact, once you start using it, it'll become your favorite layout manager—you'll find yourself going back to it over and over again.

The FrameLayout Layout Manager

The layout managers that we've discussed so far implement various layout strategies. In other words, each one has a specific way that it positions and orients its children on the screen. With these layout managers, you can have many controls on the screen at one time, each taking up a portion of the screen. Android also offers a layout manager that is mainly used to display a single item—the `FrameLayout` layout manager. You mainly use this utility layout class to dynamically display a single view, but you can populate it with many items, setting one to visible while the others are invisible. Listing 6–48 demonstrates using a `FrameLayout`.

Listing 6–48. *Populating FrameLayout*

```
<?xml version="1.0" encoding="utf-8"?>
<FrameLayout xmlns:android="http://schemas.android.com/apk/res/android"
    android:id="@+id/frmLayout"
    android:layout_width="fill_parent"  android:layout_height="fill_parent">

     <ImageView
        android:id="@+id/oneImgView" android:src="@drawable/one"
        android:scaleType="fitCenter"
        android:layout_width="fill_parent"  android:layout_height="fill_parent"/>
    <ImageView
        android:id="@+id/twoImgView" android:src="@drawable/two"
        android:scaleType="fitCenter"
        android:layout_width="fill_parent"  android:layout_height="fill_parent"
        android:visibility="gone" />

</FrameLayout>


public class FrameLayoutActivity extends Activity{
    private ImageView one = null;
    private ImageView two = null;
    @Override
    protected void onCreate(Bundle savedInstanceState) {
        super.onCreate(savedInstanceState);
        setContentView(R.layout.listing6_48);

        one = (ImageView)findViewById(R.id.oneImgView);
        two = (ImageView)findViewById(R.id.twoImgView);

        one.setOnClickListener(new OnClickListener(){

            public void onClick(View view) {
                two.setVisibility(View.VISIBLE);

                view.setVisibility(View.GONE);
            }});

        two.setOnClickListener(new OnClickListener(){
```

```
            public void onClick(View view) {
                one.setVisibility(View.VISIBLE);

                view.setVisibility(View.GONE);
            }});
    }
}
```

Listing 6–48 shows the layout file as well as the onCreate() method of the activity. The idea of the demonstration is to load two ImageView objects in the FrameLayout, with only one of the ImageView objects visible at a time. In the UI, when the user clicks the visible image, we hide one image and show the other one.

Look at Listing 6–48 more closely now, starting with the layout. You can see that we define a FrameLayout with two ImageView objects (an ImageView is a control that knows how to display images). Notice that the second ImageView's visibility is set to gone, making the control invisible. Now, look at the onCreate() method. In the onCreate() method, we register listeners to click events on the ImageView objects. In the click handler, we hide one ImageView and show the other one.

As we said earlier, you generally use FrameLayout when you need to dynamically set the content of a view to a single control. Although this is the general practice, the control will accept many children, as we demonstrated. Listing 6–48 adds two controls to the layout but has one of the controls visible at a time. FrameLayout, however, does not force you to have only one control visible at a time. If you add many controls to the layout, FrameLayout will simply stack the controls, one on top of the other, with the last one on top. This can create an interesting UI. For example, Figure 6–25 shows a FrameLayout control with two ImageView objects that are visible. You can see that the controls are stacked, and that the top one is partially covering the image behind it.

Another interesting aspect of the FrameLayout is that if you add more than one control to the layout, the size of the layout is computed as the size of the largest item in the container. In Figure 6–25, the top image is actually much smaller than the image behind it, but because the size of the layout is computed based on the largest control, the image on top is stretched.

Also note that if you put many controls inside a FrameLayout with one or more of them invisible to start, you might want to consider using setMeasureAllChildren(true) on your FrameLayout. Because the largest child dictates the layout size, you'll have a problem if the largest child is invisible to begin with. That is, when it becomes visible, it will be only partially visible. To ensure that all items get rendered properly, call setMeasureAllChildren() and pass it a value of true. The equivalent XML attribute for FrameLayout is android:measureAllChildren="true".

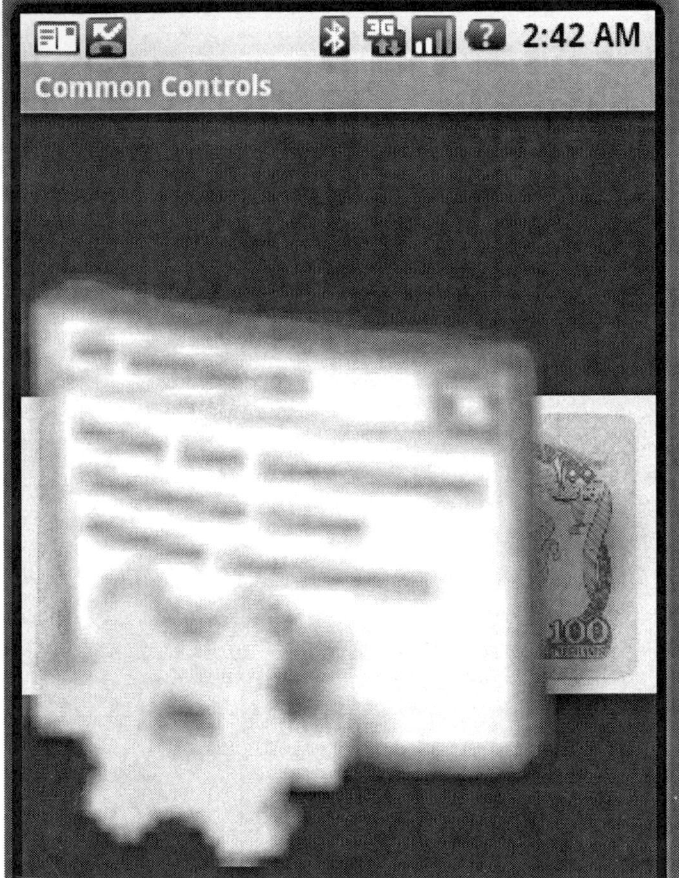

Figure 6–25. *FrameLayout with two ImageView objects*

Customizing Layout for Various Device Configurations

By now, you know very well that Android offers a host of layout managers that help you build user interfaces. If you've played around with the layout managers we've discussed, you know that you can combine the layout managers in various ways to obtain the look and feel you want. Even with all the layout managers, building UIs—and getting them right—can be a challenge. This is especially true for mobile devices. Users and manufacturers of mobile devices are getting more and more sophisticated, and that makes the developer's job even more challenging.

One of the challenges is building a UI for an application that displays in various screen configurations. For example, what would your UI look like if your application were displayed in portrait versus landscape mode? If you haven't run into this yet, your mind is probably racing right now, wondering how to deal with this common scenario. Interestingly, and thankfully, Android provides some support for this use case.

Here's how it works: when building a layout, Android will find and load layouts from specific folders based on the configuration of the device. A device can be in one of three configurations: portrait, landscape, or square (square is rare). To provide different layouts for the various configurations, you have to create specific folders for each configuration from which Android will load the appropriate layout. As you know, the default layout folder is located at `res/layout`. To support the portrait display, create a folder called `res/layout-port`. For landscape, create a folder called `res/layout-land`. And for a square, create one called `res/layout-square`.

A good question at this point is, "With these three folders, do I need the default layout folder (`res/layout`)?" Generally, yes. Realize that Android's resource-resolution logic looks in the configuration-specific directory first. If Android doesn't find a resource there, it goes to the default layout directory. Therefore, you should place default layout definitions in `res/layout` and the customized versions in the configuration-specific folders.

Note that the Android SDK does not offer any APIs for you to programmatically specify which configuration to load—the system simply selects the folder based on the configuration of the device. You can, however, set the orientation of the device in code, for example, using the following:

```
import android.content.pm.ActivityInfo;
…
setRequestedOrientation(ActivityInfo.SCREEN_ORIENTATION_LANDSCAPE);
```

This forces your application to appear on the device in landscape mode. Go ahead and try it out in one of your earlier projects. Add the code to your `onCreate()` method of an Activity, run it in the emulator, and see your application sideways.

The layout is not the only resource that is configuration driven, and other qualifiers of the device configuration are taken into account when finding the resource to use. The entire contents of the `res` folder can have variations for each configuration. For example, to have different drawables loaded for each configuration, create folders for `drawable-port`, `drawable-land`, and `drawable-square`. But Android gets even more powerful than that. The complete list of qualifiers that can be used when finding resources is shown in Table 6–3.

Table 6–3. *Qualifiers for Resources*

Qualifier	Description
MCC and MNC	Mobile country code and mobile network code
Language and region	The two-letter language code in lowercase; could also add `-r` and an uppercase two-letter region code
Screen dimensions	Gives rough idea of screen size; values: `small`, `normal`, `large` and `xlarge`
Wider/taller screens	Related to aspect ratio; values: `long` and `notlong`
Screen orientation	Values: `land`, `port`, and `square`
Screen pixel density	Approximate densities; values: `ldpi` (near 120), `mdpi` (near 160), `hdpi` (near 240) and `xhdpi` (near 320). Android may scale to fit resources found in these, unless the resource is under `nodpi`.
Touch screen type	Values: `finger`, `notouch`, and `stylus`
Keyboard	State of the keyboard; values: `keysexposed`, `keyshidden`, and `keyssoft`
Text input	Values: `nokeys`, `qwerty`, and `12key` (numeric)
Non-touch-screen navigation	Values: `dpad`, `nonav`, `trackball`, and `wheel`
SDK version	Values: `v4` (SDK 1.6), `v7` (SDK 2.1), etc.

For more details on these qualifiers, please see the following Android web page:

`http://developer.android.com/guide/topics/resources/providing-resources.html#table2`

These qualifiers can be used in many combinations to get whatever behavior you desire. A resource directory name would use zero or one of each of these qualifier values, separated by dashes, in order. For example, this is technically a valid drawable resource directory name (although not recommended):

```
drawable-mcc310-en-rUS-large-long-port-mdpi-stylus-keyssoft-qwerty-dpad-v3
```

but so are these:

```
drawable-en-rUS-land (images for English in US in landscape mode)
values-fr  (strings in French)
```

Regardless of how many qualifiers you're using for resources in your application, remember that in your code, you still only refer to the resource as `R.resource_type.name` without any qualifiers. For example, if you have lots of different variations of your layout file `main.xml` in several different qualified resource directories, your code will still refer to `R.layout.main`. Android takes care of finding the appropriate `main.xml` for you.

This concludes our discussion about building UIs. In the next section, we are going to introduce you to the Hierarchy Viewer tool. This tool will help you debug and optimize your user interfaces.

Debugging and Optimizing Layouts with the Hierarchy Viewer

The Android SDK ships with a host of tools that you can use to make your development life a lot easier. Because we are on the topic of user interface development, it makes sense for us to discuss the Hierarchy Viewer tool. This tool, shown in Figure 6–26, allows you to debug your user interfaces from a layout perspective.

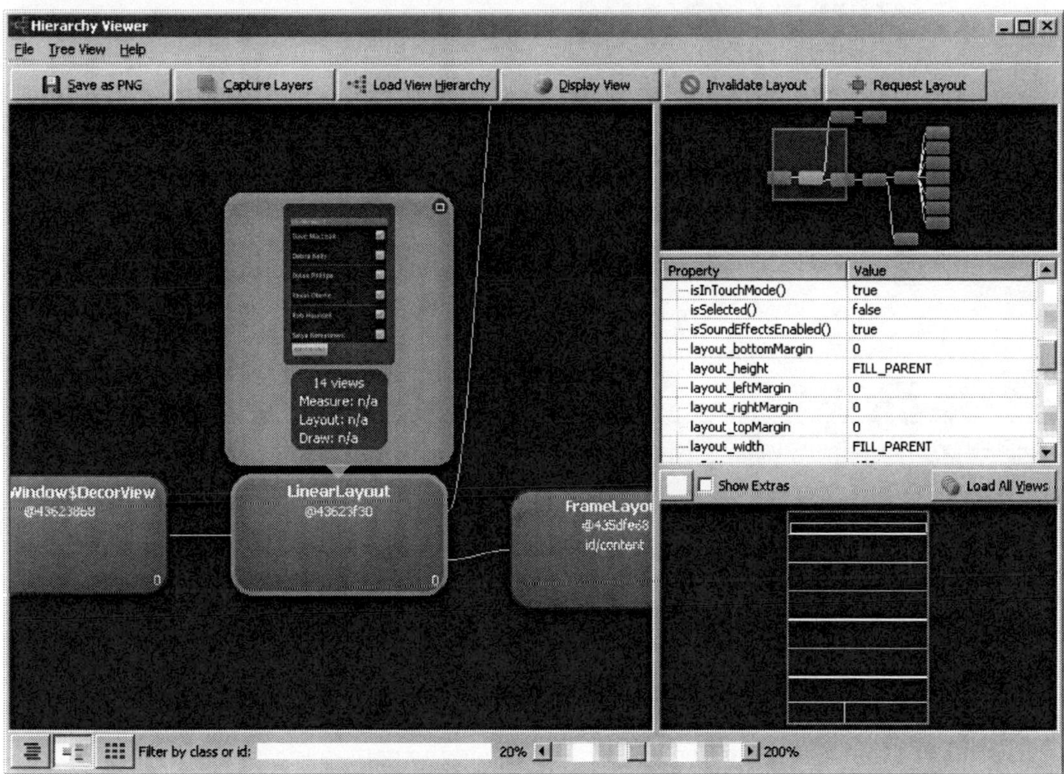

Figure 6–26. *The layout view of the Hierarchy Viewer tool*

As shown in Figure 6–26, the Hierarchy Viewer shows the hierarchy of views in the form of a tree. The idea is this: you load a layout into the tool and then inspect the layout to determine possible layout problems and/or try to optimize the layout so that you minimize the number of views (for performance reasons).

To debug your UIs, run your application in the emulator, and browse to the UI that you want to debug. Then, go to the Android SDK `/tools` directory to start the Hierarchy Viewer tool. On a Windows installation, you'll see a batch file called hierarchyviewer.bat in the /tools directory. When you run the batch file, you'll see the Hierarchy Viewer's Devices screen (see Figure 6–27).

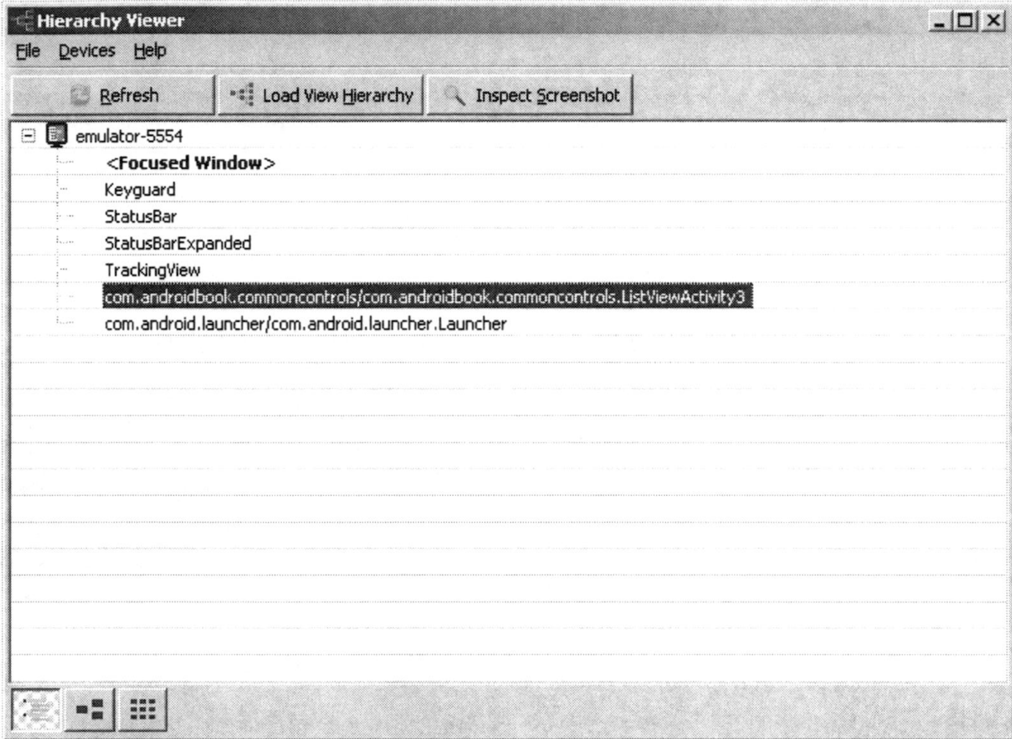

Figure 6–27. *The Hierarchy Viewer's Devices screen*

The Devices screen displays the set of devices (emulators, in this case) running on the machine. When you expand a device, the list of windows in the selected device appears below. To view the hierarchy of views for a particular window, select that window (typically the fully qualified name of your activity prefixed with the application's package name), and click the Load View Hierarchy button.

In the View Hierarchy screen, you'll see that window's hierarchy of views in the left pane (see Figure 6–26). When you select a view element in the left pane, you can see the properties of that element in the properties view to the right, and you can see the location of the view, relative to the other views, in the wire frame pane to the right. The selected view will be highlighted with a red border. By seeing all of the views in use, you can hopefully find ways to reduce the number of views and thereby make the application perform faster.

Figure 6–27 shows three buttons in the lower left corner of the Hierarchy Viewer tool. The left button displays the tree view that we explained earlier. The middle button is the View Hierarchy screen. The right button displays the current layout in pixel perfect view, but only after you've initialized the pixel perfect view using the Inspect Screenshot button at the top of this tool. This view is interesting in that you get a pixel-by-pixel representation of your layouts (see Figure 6–28). There are several items of interest on this screen. On the left-hand side is a navigator view of all of the window's components. If you click one of the components, it will be highlighted with a red border in the middle view. The crosshairs in the right-hand view allow you to direct what shows up in the view in the middle in the loupe (a *loupe* is a small magnifier used by jewelers and watchmakers). The zoom control allows you to zoom in even closer in the loupe. The loupe also shows the exact location of the selected pixel in (x, y) coordinates as well as the color value of that pixel.

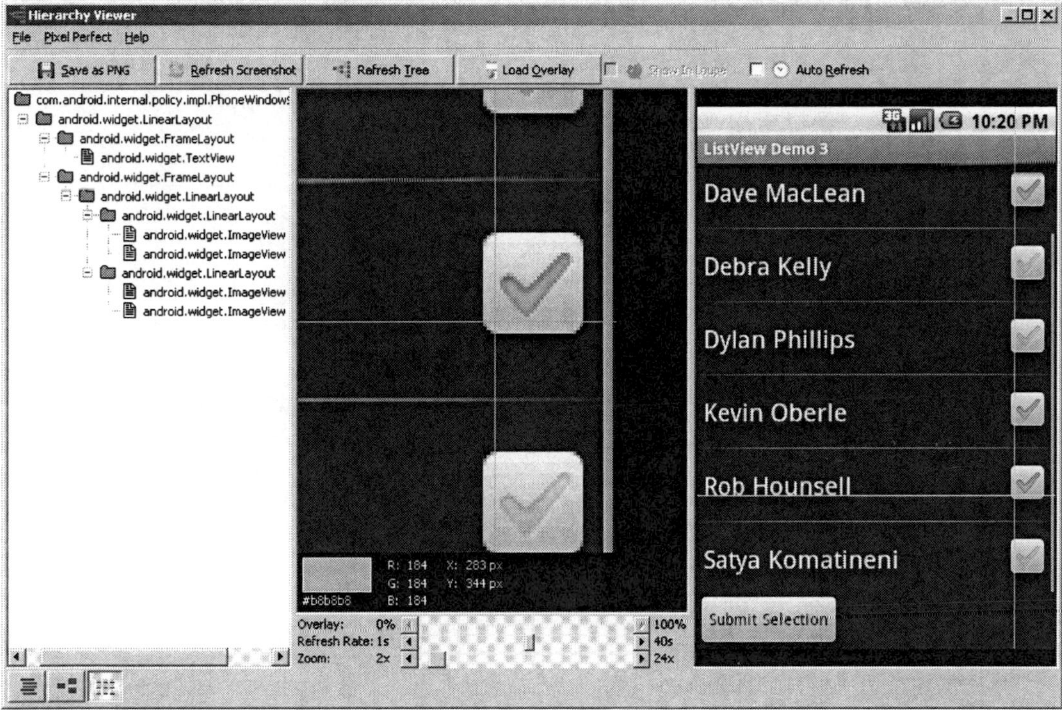

Figure 6–28. *Pixel Perfect mode of the Hierarchy Viewer*

The last very interesting features of this screen are the Load Overlay button and the Overlay slider. You can load an image file (perhaps a new mockup of the screen you're developing) behind the displayed screen to compare that image file to your current one and use the Overlay slider to make it more or less visible. The image comes in anchored to the lower-left corner. By default, the image is not shown in the loupe, but selecting the check box will make it show up there.

When Android 2.3 was released, the Hierarchy Viewer also became available for use within Eclipse. There are new perspectives called Hierarchy View and Pixel Perfect, each with a set of views for their various features. These function pretty much like the executable that we covered earlier. Chapter 2 covered installing the Hierarchy Viewer into Eclipse if you need help finding it.

With tools like these, you have a vast amount of control over the look and feel of your application.

References

Here are some helpful references to topics you may wish to explore further.

- `http://www.androidbook.com/projects`. Look here for a list of downloadable projects related to this book. For this chapter look for a ZIP file called ProAndroid3_Ch06_Controls.zip. This ZIP file contains all projects from this chapter, listed in separate root directories. There is also a README.TXT file that describes exactly how to import projects into Eclipse from one of these ZIP files.
- `http://developer.android.com/reference/android/widget/LinearLayout.html#attr_android:gravity`: This is the reference page describing different values for `gravity` when used with a `LinearLayout`.
- `www.curious-creature.org/2010/08/15/scrollviews-handy-trick`: This blog post from Romain Guy (of the Android team) explains how to use the `ScrollView` properly.
- `http://developer.android.com/resources/articles/index.html`: This page contains several technical articles called "Layout Tricks," and these are well worth reading. They get into performance aspects of designing and building user interfaces in Android. Look for other articles in this list related to building user interfaces.

Summary

At this point, you should have a good overview of the controls that are available in the Android SDK. You should also be familiar with Android's adapters, as well as its layout managers. Given a potential screen requirement, you should be able to quickly identify the controls and layout managers that you'll use to build the screen.

In the next chapter, we'll take user interface development further—we are going to discuss menus.

Chapter 7

Working with Menus

The Android SDK offers extensive support for menus. In this chapter, you'll learn to work with several of the menu types that Android supports: regular menus, submenus, context menus, icon menus, secondary menus, and alternative menus. Android 3.0 introduced something called an action bar that integrates well with menu items. This action bar and menu interaction is covered in chapter 30.

In Android, menus, in addition to being Java objects, are also represented as resources. Because they are resources, the Android SDK allows you to load menus from XML files, like other resources. Android generates resource IDs for each of the loaded menu items. We will cover these XML menu resources in detail in this chapter. We will also show you how to take advantage of auto-generated resource IDs for all types of menu items.

Understanding Android Menus

Whether you've worked with Swing in Java, with Windows Presentation Foundation (WPF) in Windows, or with any other UI framework, you've no doubt worked with menus.

The key class in Android menu support is `android.view.Menu`. Every activity in Android is associated with one menu object of this type, which can contain a number of menu items and submenus.

Menu items are represented by `android.view.MenuItem`. Submenus are represented by `android.view.SubMenu`. These relationships are graphically represented in Figure 7–1. Strictly speaking, this is not a class diagram but a structural diagram designed to help you visualize the relationships between various menu-related classes and functions.

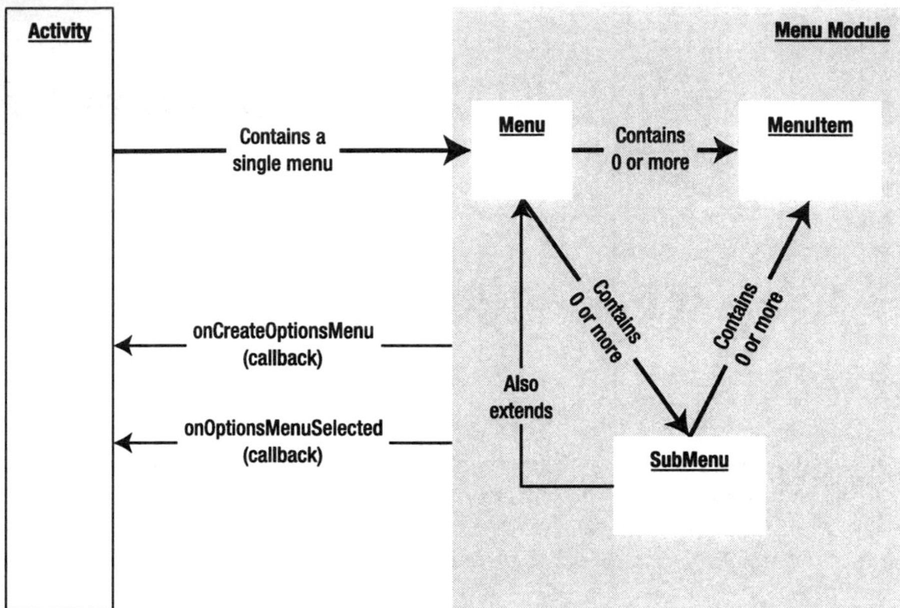

Figure 7–1. *Structure of Android menu related classes*

Figure 7–1 illustrates that a Menu object contains a set of menu items.

A menu item carries a name (title), a menu item ID, and a sort order (referred to as just "order" in the SDK), and an ID (or number). You use these order IDs to specify the order of menu items within a menu. For example, if one menu item carries an order number of 4 and another menu item carries a order number of 6, the first menu item will appear above the second menu item in the menu.

Some of these menu order number ranges are reserved for certain kinds of menus. Secondary menu items, which are considered less important than others, start at 0x30000 and are defined by the constant Menu.CATEGORY_SECONDARY. Other types of menu categories—such as system menus, alternative menus, and container menus—have different order-number ranges.

System menu items start at 0x20000 and are defined by the constant Menu.CATEGORY_SYSTEM. Alternative menu items start at 0x40000 and are defined by the constant Menu.CATEGORY_ALTERNATIVE. Container menu items start at 0x10000 and are defined by the constant Menu.CATEGORY_CONTAINER. By looking at the values for these constants, you can see the order in which they'll appear in the menu. (We'll discuss these various types of menu items in the "Working with Other Menu Types" section.)

You can group menu items together by assigning each one a group ID, which is an attribute of the menu item object. Multiple menu items that carry the same group ID are considered part of the same group.

Figure 7–1 also shows two callback methods that you can use to create and respond to menu items: onCreateOptionsMenu and onOptionsItemSelected. We will cover these next.

Creating a Menu

In the Android SDK, you don't need to create a menu object from scratch. Because an activity is associated with a single menu, Android creates this single menu for that activity and passes it to the onCreateOptionsMenu callback method of the activity class. (As the name of the method indicates, menus in Android are also known as *options menus*.) This method allows you to populate the single passed-in menu with a set of menu items (see Listing 7–1).

Listing 7–1. *Signature for the onCreateOptionsMenu Method*

```
@Override
public boolean onCreateOptionsMenu(Menu menu)
{
    // populate menu items
    .....
   ...return true;
}
```

Once the menu items are populated, the code should return true to make the menu visible. If this method returns false, the menu is invisible. The code in Listing 7–2 shows how to add three menu items using a single group ID along with incremental menu item IDs and order IDs.

Listing 7–2. *Adding Menu Items*

```
@Override
public boolean onCreateOptionsMenu(Menu menu)
{
   //call the base class to include system menus
   super.onCreateOptionsMenu(menu);

   menu.add(0           // Group
         ,1             // item id
         ,0             //order
         ,"append");    // title

   menu.add(0,2,1,"item2");
   menu.add(0,3,2,"clear");

   //It is important to return true to see the menu
   return true;
}
```

You should also call the base class implementation of this method to give the system an opportunity to populate the menu with system menu items. To keep these system menu items separate from other kinds of menu items, Android adds the system menu items starting at 0x20000. (As we mentioned before, the constant Menu.CATEGORY_SYSTEM defines the starting ID for these system menu items. In all releases so far, Android has not added any system menus.)

The first parameter required for adding a menu item is the group ID (an integer). The second parameter is the menu item ID, which is sent back to the callback function when that menu item is chosen. The third argument represents the order ID.

The last argument is the name or title of the menu item. Instead of free text, you can use a string resource through the `R.java` constants file. The group, menu item, and order IDs are all optional; you can use `Menu.NONE` if you don't want to specify any of those.

Working with Menu Groups

Now, let us show you how to work with menu groups. Listing 7–3 shows how you would add two groups of menus: Group 1 and Group 2.

Listing 7–3. ***Using Group IDs to Create Menu Groups***

```
@Override
public boolean onCreateOptionsMenu(Menu menu)
{
   //Group 1
   int group1 = 1;
   menu.add(group1,1,1,"g1.item1");
   menu.add(group1,2,2,"g1.item2");

   //Group 2
   int group2 = 2;
   menu.add(group2,3,3,"g2.item1");
   menu.add(group2,4,4,"g2.item2");

   return true; // it is important to return true
}
```

Notice how the menu item IDs and the order IDs are independent of the groups. So what good is a group, then? Well, Android provides a set of methods on the `android.view.Menu` class that are based on group IDs. You can manipulate a group's menu items using these methods:

```
removeGroup(id)
setGroupCheckable(id, checkable, exclusive)
setGroupEnabled(id,boolean enabled)
setGroupVisible(id,visible)
```

`removeGroup` removes all menu items from that group, given the group ID. You can enable or disable menu items in a given group using the `setGroupEnabled` method. Similarly, you can control the visibility of a group of menu items using `setGroupVisible`.

`setGroupCheckable` is a bit interesting. You can use this method to show a check mark on a menu item when that menu item is selected. When applied to a group, it will enable this functionality for all menu items within that group. If this method's `exclusive` flag is set, only one menu item within that group is allowed to go into a checked state. The other menu items will remain unchecked.

You now know how to populate an activity's main menu with a set of menu items and group them according to their nature. Next, we will show you how to respond to these menu items.

Responding to Menu Items

There are multiple ways of responding to menu item clicks in Android. You can use the onOptionsItemSelected method of the activity class; you can use stand-alone listeners, or you can use intents. We will cover each of these techniques in this section.

Responding to Menu Items through onOptionsItemSelected

When a menu item is clicked, Android calls the onOptionsItemSelected callback method on the Activity class (see Listing 7–4).

Listing 7–4. *Signature and Body of the onOptionsItemSelected Method*

```
@Override
public boolean onOptionsItemSelected(MenuItem item)
{
   switch(item.getItemId()) {
      .....
   }
   //for items handled
   return true;

   //for the rest
   ...return super.onOptionsItemSelected(item);
}
```

The key pattern here is to examine the menu item ID through the getItemId() method of the MenuItem class and do what's necessary. If onOptionsItemSelected() handles a menu item, it returns true. The menu event will not be further propagated. For the menu item callbacks that onOptionsItemSelected() doesn't deal with, onOptionsItemSelected() should call the parent method through super.onOptionsItemSelected. The default implementation of the onOptionsItemSelected() method returns false so that the normal processing can take place. Normal processing includes alternative means of invoking responses for a menu click.

Responding to Menu Items through Listeners

You usually respond to menus by overriding onOptionsItemSelected; this is the recommended technique for better performance. However, a menu item allows you to register a listener that could be used as a callback.

This approach is a two-step process. In the first step, you implement the OnMenuClickListener interface. Then, you take an instance of this implementation and pass it to the menu item. When the menu item is clicked, the menu item will call the onMenuItemClick() method of the OnMenuClickListener interface (see Listing 7–5).

Listing 7–5. *Using a Listener as a Callback for a Menu Item Click*

```
//Step 1
public class MyResponse implements OnMenuClickListener
{
```

```
        //some local variable to work on
        //...
        //Some constructors
        @override
        boolean onMenuItemClick(MenuItem item)
        {
           //do your thing
           return true;
        }
}

//Step 2
MyResponse myResponse = new MyResponse(...);
menuItem.setOnMenuItemClickListener(myResponse);
...
```

The onMenuItemClick method is called when the menu item has been invoked. This code executes as soon as the menu item is clicked, even before the onOptionsItemSelected method is called. If onMenuItemClick returns true, no other callbacks will be executed—including the onOptionsItemSelected callback method. This means that the listener code takes precedence over the onOptionsItemSelected method.

Using an Intent to Respond to Menu Items

You can also associate a menu item with an intent by using the MenuItem's method setIntent(intent). By default, a menu item has no intent associated with it. But when an intent *is* associated with a menu item, and nothing else handles the menu item, then the default behavior is to invoke the intent using startActivity(intent). For this to work, all the handlers—especially the onOptionsItemSelected method—should call the parent class's onOptionsItemSelected() method for those items that are not handled. Or you could look at it this way: the system gives onOptionsItemSelected an opportunity to handle menu items first (followed by the listener, of course). This is assuming there is no listener directly associated with that menu item, if it is, then the listener will override the rest.

If you don't override the onOptionsItemSelected method, the base class in the Android framework will do what's necessary to invoke the intent on the menu item. But if you do override this method and you're not interested in this menu item, you must call the parent method, which, in turn, facilitates the intent invocation. So here's the bottom line: either don't override the onOptionsItemSelected method, or override it and invoke the parent for the menu items that you are not handling.

Creating a Test Harness for Testing Menus

That's pretty straightforward so far. You have learned how to create menus and how to respond to them through various callbacks. Now, we'll show you a sample activity to exercise these menu APIs that you have already learned.

NOTE: We have included a URL at the end of this chapter to download this project so that you can set it up in Eclipse development environment.

The goal of this exercise is to create a simple activity with a text view in it. The text view will act like a debugger. As we invoke menus, we will write out the invoked menu item name and ID to this text view. The finished Menus application will look like the one shown in Figure 5–2.

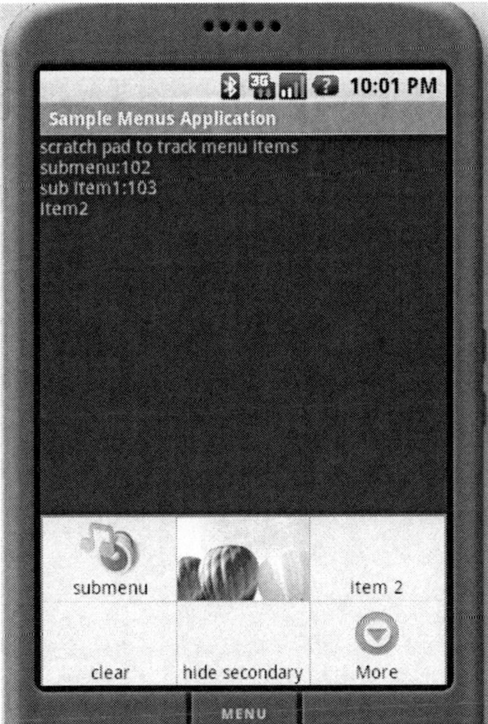

Figure 7–2. *Sample Menus application*

Figure 7–2 shows two things of interest: the menu and the text view. The menu appears at the bottom. You will not see it, though, when you start the application; you must click the Menu button on the emulator or the device in order to see the menu. The second point of interest is the text view that lists the debug messages near the top of the screen. As you click through the available menu items, the test harness logs the menu item names in the text view. If you click the "clear" menu item, the program clears the text view.

NOTE: Figure 7–2 does not necessarily represent the beginning state of the sample application. We have presented it here to illustrate the menu types that we'll cover in this chapter.

Follow these steps to implement the test harness:

1. Create an XML layout file that contains the text view.
2. Create an Activity class that hosts the layout defined in step 1.
3. Set up the menu.
4. Add some regular menu items to the menu.
5. Add some secondary menu items to the menu.
6. Respond to the menu items.
7. Modify the AndroidManifest.xml file to show the application's proper title.

We will cover each of these steps in the following sections and provide the necessary source code to assemble the test harness.

Creating an XML Layout

Step 1 involves creating a simple XML layout file with a text view in it (see Listing 7–6). You could load this file into an activity during its startup.

Listing 7–6. *XML Layout File for the Test Harness*

```
<?xml version="1.0" encoding="utf-8"?>
<LinearLayout xmlns:android="http://schemas.android.com/apk/res/android"
    android:orientation="vertical"
    android:layout_width="fill_parent"
    android:layout_height="fill_parent"
    >
<TextView android:id="@+id/textViewId"
    android:layout_width="fill_parent"
    android:layout_height="wrap_content"
    android:text="Debugging Scratch Pad"
    />
</LinearLayout>
```

Creating an Activity

Step 2 dictates that you create an activity, which is also quite a simple. Assuming that the layout file in step 1 is available at \res\layout\main.xml, you can use that file through its resource ID to populate the activity's view (see Listing 7–7).

Listing 7–7. *Menu Test Harness Activity Class*

```
public class SampleMenusActivity extends Activity {

   //Initialize this in onCreateOptions
   Menu myMenu = null;

    @Override
    public void onCreate(Bundle savedInstanceState) {
        super.onCreate(savedInstanceState);
```

```
        setContentView(R.layout.main);
    }
```

For brevity, we have not included the import statements. In Eclipse, you can automatically populate the import statements by pulling up the context menu in the editor and selecting Source Organize Imports. You can also use the short cut Ctrl + Shift + O.

Setting Up the Menu

Now that you have a view and an activity, you can move on to step 3: overriding the onCreateOptionsMenu and setting up the menu programmatically (see Listing 7–8).

Listing 7–8. *Setting Up the Menu Programmatically*

```
@Override
public boolean onCreateOptionsMenu(Menu menu)
{
   //call the parent to attach any system level menus
   super.onCreateOptionsMenu(menu);

   this.myMenu = menu;

   //add a few normal menus
   addRegularMenuItems(menu);

   //add a few secondary menus
   add5SecondaryMenuItems(menu);

   //it must return true to show the menu
   //if it is false menu won't show
   return true;
}
```

The code in Listing 7–8 first calls the parent onCreateOptionsMenu to give the parent an opportunity to add any system-level menus.

> **NOTE:** In all releases of the Android SDK so far, the onCreateOptionsMenu method does not add new menu items. However, a future release might, so it is a good practice to call the parent.

The code then remembers the Menu object in order to manipulate it later for demonstration purposes. After that, the code proceeds to add a few regular menu items and a few secondary menu items.

Adding Regular Menu Items

Now comes step 4, adding a few regular menu items to the menu. The code for addRegularMenuItems appears in Listing 7–9.

Listing 7–9. *The addRegularMenuItems Function*

```
private void addRegularMenuItems(Menu menu)
{
   int base=Menu.FIRST; // value is 1

   menu.add(base,base,base,"append");
   menu.add(base,base+1,base+1,"item 2");
   menu.add(base,base+2,base+2,"clear");

   menu.add(base,base+3,base+3,"hide secondary");
   menu.add(base,base+4,base+4,"show secondary");

   menu.add(base,base+5,base+5,"enable secondary");
   menu.add(base,base+6,base+6,"disable secondary");

   menu.add(base,base+7,base+7,"check secondary");
   menu.add(base,base+8,base+8,"uncheck secondary");
}
```

The `Menu` class defines a few convenience constants, one of which is `Menu.FIRST`. You can use this as a baseline number for menu IDs and other menu-related sequential numbers. Notice how you can peg the group ID at `base` and increment only the sort order and menu item IDs. In addition, the code adds a few specific menu items, such as `"hide secondary"` and `"enable secondary"`, to demonstrate some of the menu concepts.

Adding Secondary Menu Items

Let's now add a few secondary menu items to perform step 5 (see Listing 7–10). Secondary menu items, as mentioned earlier, start at 0x30000 and are defined by the constant `Menu.CATEGORY_SECONDARY`. Their sort order IDs are higher than regular menu items, so they appear after the regular menu items in a menu. Note that the sort order is the only thing that distinguishes a secondary menu item from a regular menu item. In all other aspects, a secondary menu item works and behaves like any other menu item.

Listing 7–10. *Adding Secondary Menu Items*

```
private void add5SecondaryMenuItems(Menu menu)
{
   //Secondary items are shown just like everything else
   int base=Menu.CATEGORY_SECONDARY;

   menu.add(base,base+1,base+1,"sec. item 1");
   menu.add(base,base+2,base+2,"sec. item 2");
   menu.add(base,base+3,base+3,"sec. item 3");
   menu.add(base,base+3,base+3,"sec. item 4");
   menu.add(base,base+4,base+4,"sec. item 5");
}
```

Responding to Menu Item Clicks

Now that the menus are set up, we move on to step 6, responding to them. When a menu item is clicked, Android calls the onOptionsItemSelected callback method of the Activity class by passing a reference to the clicked menu item. You then use the getItemId() method on the MenuItem to see which item it is.

It is not uncommon to see either a switch statement or a series of if and else statements calling various functions in response to menu items. Listing 7–11 shows this standard pattern of responding to menu items in the onOptionsItemSelected callback method. (You will learn a slightly better way of doing the same thing in the "Loading Menus Through XML Files" section, where you will have symbolic names for these menu item IDs.)

Listing 7–11. *Responding to Menu Item Clicks*

```
@Override
public boolean onOptionsItemSelected(MenuItem item)     {
   if (item.getItemId() == 1)       {
       appendText("\nhello");
   }
   else if (item.getItemId() == 2)       {
      appendText("\nitem2");
   }
   else if (item.getItemId() == 3)       {
      emptyText();
   }
   else if (item.getItemId() == 4)       {
      //hide secondary
      this.appendMenuItemText(item);
      this.myMenu.setGroupVisible(Menu.CATEGORY_SECONDARY,false);
   }
   else if (item.getItemId() == 5)       {
      //show secondary
      this.appendMenuItemText(item);
      this.myMenu.setGroupVisible(Menu.CATEGORY_SECONDARY,true);
   }
   else if (item.getItemId() == 6)       {
      //enable secondary
      this.appendMenuItemText(item);
      this.myMenu.setGroupEnabled(Menu.CATEGORY_SECONDARY,true);
   }
   else if (item.getItemId() == 7)       {
      //disable secondary
      this.appendMenuItemText(item);
      this.myMenu.setGroupEnabled(Menu.CATEGORY_SECONDARY,false);
   }
   else if (item.getItemId() == 8)       {
      //check secondary
      this.appendMenuItemText(item);
      myMenu.setGroupCheckable(Menu.CATEGORY_SECONDARY,true,false);
   }
   else if (item.getItemId() == 9)       {
      //uncheck secondary
      this.appendMenuItemText(item);
      myMenu.setGroupCheckable(Menu.CATEGORY_SECONDARY,false,false);
```

```
        }
        else        {
           this.appendMenuItemText(item);
        }
        //should return true if the menu item
        //is handled
        return true;
    }
```

Listing 7–11 also exercises operations on menus at the group level; calls to these methods are highlighted in bold. The code also logs the details about the clicked menu item to the TextView. Listing 7–12 shows some utility functions to write to the TextView. Notice an additional method on a MenuItem to get its title.

Listing 7–12. *Utility Functions to Write to the Debug TextView*

```
//Given a string of text append it to the TextView
    private void appendText(String text)    {
          TextView tv = (TextView)this.findViewById(R.id.textViewId);
          tv.setText(tv.getText() + text);
    }

//Given a menu item append its title to the TextView
    private void appendMenuItemText(MenuItem menuItem)    {
       String title = menuItem.getTitle().toString();
       TextView tv = (TextView)this.findViewById(R.id.textViewId);
          tv.setText(tv.getText() + "\n" + title);
    }
//Empty the TextView of its contents
    private void emptyText()    {
          TextView tv = (TextView)this.findViewById(R.id.textViewId);
          tv.setText("");
    }
```

Tweaking the AndroidManifest.xml File

Your final step in the process of creating the test harness is to update the application's AndroidManifest.xml file. This file, which is automatically created for you when you create a new project, is available in your project's root directory.

This is the place where you register the Activity class (such as SampleMenusActivity) and where you specify a title for the activity. We called this activity Sample Menus Application, as shown in Figure 7–2. See this entry highlighted in Listing 7–13.

Listing 7–13. *The AndroidManifest.xml File for the Test Harness*

```
<?xml version="1.0" encoding="utf-8"?>
<manifest xmlns:android="http://schemas.android.com/apk/res/android"
      package="your-package-name-goes-here "
      android:versionCode="1"
      android:versionName="1.0.0">
    <application android:icon="@drawable/icon" android:label="Sample Menus">
        <activity android:name=".SampleMenusActivity"
                  android:label="Sample Menus Application">
            <intent-filter>
                <action android:name="android.intent.action.MAIN" />
```

```
            <category android:name="android.intent.category.LAUNCHER" />
        </intent-filter>
    </activity>
  </application>
</manifest>
```

Using the code we've provided, you should be able to quickly construct this test harness for experimenting with menus. We showed you how to create a simple activity initialized with a text view and then how to populate and respond to menus. Most menus follow this basic yet functional pattern. You can use Figure 7–2 as a guide for what kind of UI to expect when you are finished with the exercise, but as we pointed out, what you see might not exactly (but mostly will) match the figure because we haven't yet shown you how to add the icon menus. Your UI might differ slightly even after you add the icon menus, because your images might differ from the images we used.

Working with Other Menu Types

So far we've covered some of the simpler, although quite functional, menu types. As you walk through the SDK, you will see that Android also supports icon menus, submenus, context menus, and alternative menus. Out of these, alternative menus are unique to Android. We will cover all of these menu types in this section.

Expanded Menus

Recall from Figure 7–2 that the sample application displays a menu item called "More" at the bottom-right corner of the menu. We didn't show you how to add this menu item in any of the sample code, so where does it come from?

If an application has more menu items than it can display on the main screen, Android shows the More menu item to allow the user to see the rest. This menu, called an *expanded menu*, shows up automatically when there are too many menu items to display in the limited amount of space. But the expanded menu has a limitation: it cannot accommodate icons. Users who click More will see a resultant menu that omits icons.

Working with Icon Menus

Now that we've hinted at icon menus, let's talk about them in more detail. Android supports not only text, but also images or icons as part of its menu repertoire. You can use icons to represent your menu items instead of and in addition to text. But note a few limitations when it comes to using icon menus. First, as you saw in the previous paragraph, you can't use icon menus for expanded menus. Second, icon menu items do not support menu item check marks. Third, if the text in an icon menu item is too long, it will be truncated after a certain number of characters, depending on the size of the display. (This last limitation applies to text-based menu items also.)

Creating an icon menu item is straightforward. You create a regular text-based menu item as before, then you use the `setIcon` method on the `MenuItem` class to set the image.

You'll need to use the image's resource ID, so you must generate it first by placing the image or icon in the /res/drawable directory. For example, if the icon's file name is balloons, then the resource ID will be R.drawable.balloons.

Here is some sample code that demonstrates this:

```
//add a menu item and remember it so that you can use it
//subsequently to set the icon on it.
MenuItem item8 = menu.add(base,base+8,base+8,"uncheck secondary");
item8.setIcon(R.drawable.balloons);
```

As you add menu items to the menu, you rarely need to keep a local variable returned by the menu.add method. But in this case, you need to remember the returned object so you can add the icon to the menu item. The code in this example also demonstrates that the type returned by the menu.add method is MenuItem.

The icon will show as long as the menu item is displayed on the main application screen. If it's displayed as part of the expanded menu, the icon will not show, just the text. The menu item displaying an image of balloons in Figure 7–2 is an example of an icon menu item.

Working with Submenus

Let's take a look at Android's submenus now. Figure 7–1 points out the structural relationship of a SubMenu to a Menu and a MenuItem. A Menu object can have multiple SubMenu objects. Each SubMenu object is added to the Menu object through a call to the Menu.addSubMenu method (see Listing 7–14). You add menu items to a submenu the same way that you add menu items to a menu. This is because SubMenu is also derived from a Menu object. However, you cannot add additional submenus to a submenu.

Listing 7–14. *Adding Submenus*

```
private void addSubMenu(Menu menu)
{
   //Secondary items are shown just like everything else
   int base=Menu.FIRST + 100;
   SubMenu sm = menu.addSubMenu(base,base+1,Menu.NONE,"submenu");
   sm.add(base,base+2,base+2,"sub item1");
   sm.add(base,base+3,base+3, "sub item2");
   sm.add(base,base+4,base+4, "sub item3");

    //submenu item icons are not supported
   item1.setIcon(R.drawable.icon48x48_2);

   //the following is ok however
   sm.setIcon(R.drawable.icon48x48_1);

   //This will result in runtime exception
    //sm.addSubMenu("try this");
}
```

> **NOTE:** SubMenu, as a subclass of the Menu object, continues to carry the addSubMenu method. The compiler won't complain if you add a submenu to another submenu, but you'll get a runtime exception if you try to do it.

The Android SDK documentation also suggests that submenus do not support icon menu items. When you add an icon to a menu item and then add that menu item to a submenu, the menu item will ignore that icon, even if you don't see a compile-time or runtime error. However, the submenu itself can have an icon.

Provisioning for System Menus

Most Windows applications come with menus such as File, Edit, View, Open, Close, and Exit. These menus are called system menus. The Android SDK suggests that the system could insert a similar set of menus when an options menu is created. However, current releases of the Android SDK do not populate any of these menus as part of the menu-creation process. It is conceivable that these system menus might be implemented in a subsequent release. The documentation suggests that programmers make provisions in their code so that they can accommodate these system menus when they become available. You do this by calling the `onCreateOptionsMenu` method of the parent, which allows the system to add system menus to a group identified by the constant `CATEGORY_SYSTEM`.

Working with Context Menus

Users of desktop programs are no doubt familiar with context menus. In Windows applications, for example, you can access a context menu by right-clicking a UI element. Android supports the same idea of context menus through an action called a *long click*. A long click is a mouse click held down slightly longer than usual on any Android view.

On handheld devices such as cell phones, mouse clicks are implemented in a number of ways, depending on the navigation mechanism. If your phone has a wheel to move the cursor, a press of the wheel would serve as the mouse click. Or if the device has a touch pad, a tap or a press would be equivalent to a mouse click. Or you might have a set of arrow buttons for movement and a selection button in the middle; clicking that button would be equivalent to clicking the mouse. Regardless of how a mouse click is implemented on your device, if you hold the mouse click a bit longer you will realize the long click.

A context menu differs structurally from the standard options menu that we've been discussing (see Figure 7–3). Context menus have some nuances that options menus don't have.

Figure 7–3 shows that a context menu is represented as a `ContextMenu` class in the Android menu architecture. Just like a `Menu`, a `ContextMenu` can contain a number of menu items. You will use the same set of `Menu` methods to add menu items to the context menu. The biggest difference between a Menu and a ContextMenu boils down to the ownership of the menu in question. An activity owns a regular options menu, whereas a view owns a context menu. This is to be expected, because the long clicks that activate context menus apply to the *view* being clicked. So an activity can have only one options menu but many context menus. Because an activity can contain multiple views, and each view can have its own context menu, an activity can have as many context menus as there are views.

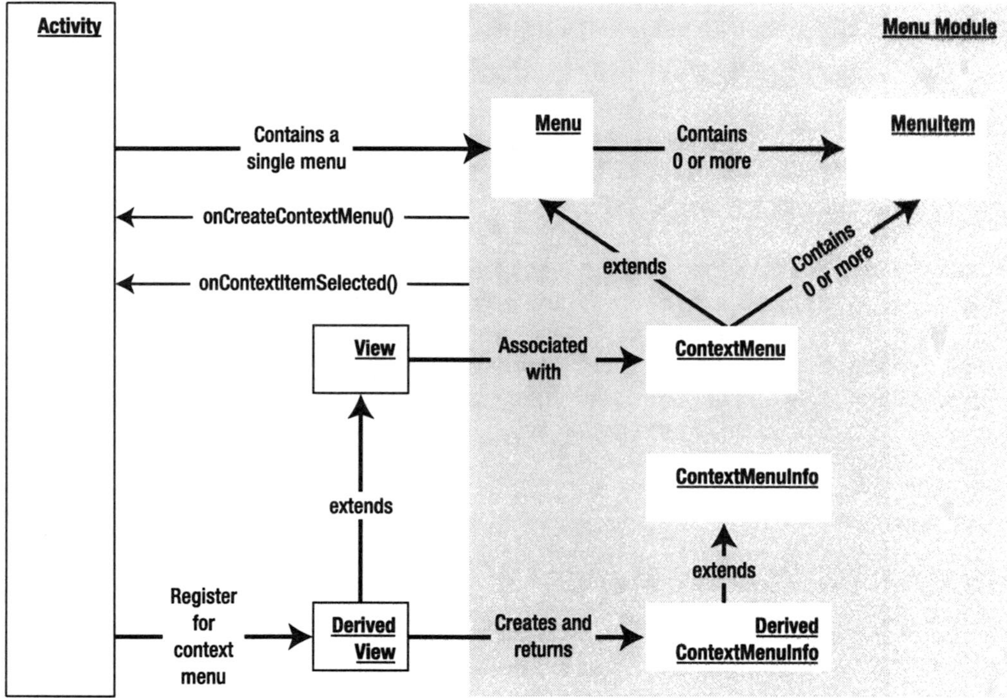

Figure 7–3. *Activities, views, and context menus*

Although a context menu is owned by a view, the method to populate context menus resides in the Activity class. This method is called activity.onCreateContextMenu(), and its role resembles that of the activity.onCreateOptionsMenu() method. This callback method also carries with it the view for which the context menu items are to be populated.

There is one more notable wrinkle to the context menu. Whereas the onCreateOptionsMenu() method is automatically called for every activity, this is not the case with onCreateContextMenu(). A view in an activity does not *have* to own a context menu. You can have three views in your activity, for example, but perhaps you want to enable context menus for only one view and not the others. If you want a particular view to own a context menu, you must register that view with its activity specifically for the purpose of owning a context menu. You do this through the activity.registerForContextMenu(view) method, which we'll discuss in the section "Registering a View for a Context Menu."

Now note the ContextMenuInfo class shown in Figure 7–3. An object of this type is passed to the onCreateContextMenu method. This is one way for the view to pass additional information to this method. For a view to do this, it needs to override the getContextViewInfo() method and return a derived class of ContextMenuInfo with additional methods to represent the additional information. You might want to look at the source code for android.view.View to fully understand this interaction.

NOTE: Per the Android SDK documentation, context menus do not support shortcuts, icons, or submenus.

Now that you know the general structure of the context menus, let's look at some sample code that demonstrates each of the steps to implement a context menu:

1. Register a view for a context menu in an activity's onCreate() method.
2. Populate the context menu using onCreateContextMenu(). You must complete step 1 before this callback method is invoked by Android.
3. Respond to context menu clicks.

Registering a View for a Context Menu

The first step in implementing a context menu is to register a view for the context menu in an activity's onCreate() method. If you were to use the menu test harness introduced in this chapter, you could register the TextView for a context menu in that test harness by using the code in Listing 7–15. You would first find the TextView and then call registerForContextMenu on the activity using the TextView as an argument. This will set up the TextView for context menus.

Listing 7–15. ***Registering a TextView for a Context Menu***

```
@Override
public void onCreate(Bundle savedInstanceState) {
    super.onCreate(savedInstanceState);
    setContentView(R.layout.main);

    TextView tv = (TextView)this.findViewById(R.id.textViewId);
    registerForContextMenu(tv);
}
```

Populating a Context Menu

Once a view like the TextView in this example is registered for context menus, Android will call the onCreateContextMenu() method with this view as the argument. This is where you can populate the context menu items for that context menu. The onCreateContextMenu() callback method provides three arguments to work with.

The first argument is a preconstructed ContextMenu object, the second is the view (such as the TextView) that generated the callback, and the third is the ContextMenuInfo class that we covered briefly while discussing Figure 7–3. For a lot of simple cases, you can just ignore the ContextMenuInfo object. However, some views might pass extra information through this object. In those cases, you will need to cast the ContextMenuInfo class to a subclass and then use the additional methods to retrieve the additional information.

Some examples of classes derived from ContextMenuInfo include AdapterContextMenuInfo and ExpandableContextMenuInfo. Views that are tied to database cursors in Android use the AdapterContextMenuInfo class to pass the row ID within that view for which the context menu is being displayed. In a sense, you can use this class to further clarify the object underneath the mouse click, even within a given view.

Listing 7–16 demonstrates the onCreateContextMenu() method.

Listing 7–16. *The onCreateContextMenu() Method*

```
@Override
public void onCreateContextMenu(ContextMenu menu, View v, ContextMenuInfo menuInfo)
{
        menu.setHeaderTitle("Sample Context Menu");
        menu.add(200, 200, 200, "item1");
}
```

Responding to Context Menu Items

The third step in our implementation of a context menu is responding to context menu clicks. The mechanism of responding to context menus is similar to the mechanism of responding to options menus. Android provides a callback method similar to onOptionsItemSelected() called onContextItemSelected(). This method, like its counterpart, is also available on the Activity class. Listing 7–17 demonstrates onContextItemSelected().

Listing 7–17. *Responding to Context Menus*

```
@Override
 public boolean onContextItemSelected(MenuItem item)
{
     if (item.getitemId() = some-menu-item-id)
     {
        //handle this menu item
        return true;
     }
… other exception processing
}
```

Working with Alternative Menus

So far, you have learned to create and work with menus, submenus, and context menus. Android introduces a new concept called *alternative menus*, which allow alternative menu items to be part of menus, submenus, and context menus. Alternative menus allow multiple applications on Android to use one another. These alternative menus are part of the Android interapplication communication or usage framework.

Specifically, alternative menus allow one application to include menus from another application. When the alternative menus are chosen, the target application or activity will be launched with a URL to the data needed by that activity. The invoked activity will then use the data URL from the intent that is passed. To understand alternative menus well, you must first understand content providers, content URIs, content MIME types, and intents (see Chapters 4 and 5).

The general idea here is this: imagine you are writing a screen to display some data. Most likely, this screen will be an activity. On this activity, you will have an options menu that allows you to manipulate or work with the data in a number of ways. Also assume for a moment that you are working with a document or a note that is identified by a URI and a corresponding MIME type. What you want to do as a programmer is anticipate that the device will eventually contain more programs that will know how to work with this data or display this data. You want to give this new set of programs an opportunity to display their menu items as part of the menu that you are constructing for this activity.

To attach alternative menu items to a menu, follow these steps while setting up the menu in the `onCreateOptionsMenu` method:

1. Create an intent whose data URI is set to the data URI that you are showing at the moment.
2. Set the category of the intent as `CATEGORY_ALTERNATIVE`.
3. Search for activities that allow operations on data supported by this type of URI.
4. Add intents that can invoke those activities as menu items to the menu.

These steps tell us a lot about the nature of Android applications, so we'll examine each one. As we know now, attaching the alternative menu items to the menu happens in the `onCreateOptionsMenu` method:

```
@Override public boolean onCreateOptionsMenu(Menu menu)
{
}
```

Let's now figure out what code makes up this function. We first need to know the URI for the data we might be working on in this activity. You can get the URI like this:

```
this.getIntent().getData()
```

This works because the `Activity` class has a method called `getIntent()` that returns the data URI for which this activity is invoked. This invoked activity might be the main activity invoked by the main menu; in that case, it might not have an intent and the `getIntent()`method will return `null`. In your code, you will have to guard against this situation.

Our goal now is to find out the other programs that know how to work with this kind of data. We do this search using an intent as an argument. Here's the code to construct that intent:

```
Intent criteriaIntent = new Intent(null, getIntent().getData());
intent.addCategory(Intent.CATEGORY_ALTERNATIVE);
```

Once we construct the intent, we will also add a category of actions that we are interested in. Specifically, we are interested only in activities that can be invoked as part of an alternative menu. We are ready now to tell the Menu object to search for matching activities and add them as menu options (see Listing 7–18).

Listing 7–18. ***Populating a Menu with Alternative Menu Items***

```
// Search for, and populate the menu with matching Activities.
menu.addIntentOptions(
     Menu.CATEGORY_ALTERNATIVE,   // Group
     Menu.CATEGORY_ALTERNATIVE,   // Any unique IDs we might care to add.
     Menu.CATEGORY_ALTERNATIVE,   // order
     this.getComponentName(),     // Name of the activity class displaying
                                  // the menu--here, it's this class.
                                    //variable "this" points to activity
     null,                          // No specifics.
     criteriaIntent,                // Previously created intent that
                                    // describes our requirements.
     0,                             // No flags.
     null);                         // returned menu items
```

Before going through this code line by line, we'll explain what we mean by the term "matching activities." A *matching activity* is an activity that's capable of handling a URI that it has been given. Activities typically register this information in their manifest files using URIs, actions, and categories. Android provides a mechanism that lets you use an Intent object to look for the matching activities given these attributes.

Now, let's look closely at Listing 7–18. The method addIntentOptions on the Menu class is responsible for looking up the activities that match an intent's URI and category attributes. Then, the method adds these activities to the menu under the right group with the appropriate menu item and sort order IDs. The first three arguments deal with this aspect of the method's responsibility. In Listing 7–18, we start off with the Menu.CATEGORY_ALTERNATIVE as the group under which the new menu items will be added. We also use this same constant as the starting point for the menu item and order IDs.

The next argument points to the fully qualified component name of the activity that this menu is part of. The code uses a method from the Activity class called getComponentName(). A *component name* is simply the name of the package and the name of the class, and this component name is needed because when a new menu item is added, that menu item will need to invoke the target activity. To do that, the system needs the source activity that started the target activity. The next argument is an array of intents that you should use as a filter on the returned intents. We have used "null" in the example.

The next argument points to criteriaIntent, which we just constructed. This is the search criteria we want to use. The argument after that is a flag such as Menu.FLAG_APPEND_TO_GROUP to indicate whether to append to the set of existing menu items in this group or replace them. The default value is 0, which indicates that the menu items in the menu group should be replaced.

The last argument in Listing 7–18 is an array of menu items that are added. You could use these added menu item references if you want to manipulate them in some manner after adding them.

All of this is well and good. But a few questions remain unanswered. For example, what will be the names of the added menu items? The Android documentation is silent about this, so we snooped around the source code to see what this function is actually doing behind the scenes (refer to Chapter 1 to see how to get to Android's source code).

As it turns out, the `Menu` class is only an interface, so we can't see any implementation source code for it. The class that implements the `Menu` interface is called `MenuBuilder`. Listing 7–19 shows the source code of a relevant method, `addIntentOptions`, from the `MenuBuilder` class (we're providing the code for your reference; we won't explain it line by line).

Listing 7–19. ***MenuBuilder.addIntentOptions Method***

```
public int addIntentOptions(int group, int id, int categoryOrder,
                            ComponentName caller,
                            Intent[] specifics,
                            Intent intent, int flags,
                            MenuItem[] outSpecificItems)
{
    PackageManager pm = mContext.getPackageManager();
    final List<ResolveInfo> lri =
            pm.queryIntentActivityOptions(caller, specifics, intent, 0);
    final int N = lri != null ? lri.size() : 0;

    if ((flags & FLAG_APPEND_TO_GROUP) == 0) {
        removeGroup(group);
    }

    for (int i=0; i<N; i++) {
        final ResolveInfo ri = lri.get(i);
        Intent rintent = new Intent(
            ri.specificIndex < 0 ? intent : specifics[ri.specificIndex]);
        rintent.setComponent(new ComponentName(
                ri.activityInfo.applicationInfo.packageName,
                ri.activityInfo.name));
 final MenuItem item = add(group, id, categoryOrder,
                        ri.loadLabel(pm));
        item.setIntent(rintent);
        if (outSpecificItems != null && ri.specificIndex >= 0) {
            outSpecificItems[ri.specificIndex] = item;
        }
    }
    return N;
}
```

Note the line in Listing 7–19 highlighted in bold; this portion of the code constructs a menu item. The code delegates the work of figuring out a menu title to the `ResolveInfo` class. The source code of the `ResolveInfo` class shows us that the intent filter that declared this intent should have a title associated with it. Here is an example:

```
<intent-filter android:label="Menu Title ">
    …….
```

```
    <category android:name="android.intent.category.ALTERNATE" />
    <data android:mimeType="some type data" />
</intent-filter>
```

The label value of the intent filter ends up serving as the menu name. You can look at the Android NotePad example to see this behavior.

Working with Menus in Response to Changing Data

So far, we've talked about static menus—you set them up once, and they don't change dynamically according to what's onscreen. If you want to create dynamic menus, use the onPrepareOptionsMenu method that Android provides. This method resembles onCreateOptionsMenu except that it gets called every time a menu is invoked. You should use onPrepareOptionsMenu, for example, if you want to disable some menus or menu groups based on the data you are displaying. You might want to keep this in mind as you design your menu functionality.

We need to cover one more important aspect of menus before moving on to dialogs. Android supports the creation of menus using XML files. The next high-level topic is dedicated to exploring this XML menu support in Android.

Loading Menus Through XML Files

Up until this point, we've created all our menus programmatically. This is not the most convenient way to create menus, because for every menu, you have to provide several IDs and define constants for each of those IDs. You'll no doubt find this tedious.

Instead, you can define menus through XML files, which is possible in Android because menus are also resources. The XML approach to menu creation offers several advantages, such as the ability to name menus, order them automatically, and give them IDs. You can also get localization support for the menu text.

Follow these steps to work with XML-based menus:

1. Define an XML file with menu tags.
2. Place the file in the /res/menu subdirectory. The name of the file is arbitrary, and you can have as many files as you want. Android automatically generates a resource ID for this menu file.
3. Use the resource ID for the menu file to load the XML file into the menu.
4. Respond to the menu items using the resource IDs generated for each menu item.

We will talk about each of these steps and provide corresponding code snippets in the following sections.

Structure of an XML Menu Resource File

First, we'll look at an XML file with menu definitions (see Listing 7–20). All menu files start with the same high-level menu tag followed by a series of group tags. Each of these group tags corresponds to the menu item group we talked about at the beginning of the chapter. You can specify an ID for the group using the @+id approach. Each menu group will have a series of menu items with their menu item IDs tied to symbolic names. You can refer to the Android SDK documentation for all the possible arguments for these XML tags.

Listing 7–20. *An XML File with Menu Definitions*

```
<menu xmlns:android="http://schemas.android.com/apk/res/android">
    <!-- This group uses the default category. -->
    <group android:id="@+id/menuGroup_Main">

        <item android:id="@+id/menu_testPick"
            android:orderInCategory="5"
            android:title="Test Pick" />
        <item android:id="@+id/menu_testGetContent"
            android:orderInCategory="5"
            android:title="Test Get Content" />
        <item android:id="@+id/menu_clear"
            android:orderInCategory="10"
            android:title="clear" />
        <item android:id="@+id/menu_dial"
            android:orderInCategory="7"
            android:title="dial" />
        <item android:id="@+id/menu_test"
            android:orderInCategory="4"
            android:title="@+string/test" />
        <item android:id="@+id/menu_show_browser"
            android:orderInCategory="5"
            android:title="show browser" />
    </group>
</menu>
```

The menu XML file in Listing 7–20 has one group. Based on the resource ID definition @+id/menuGroup_main, this group will be automatically assigned a resource ID called menuGroup_main in the R.java resource ID file. Similarly, all the child menu items are allocated menu item IDs based on their symbolic resource ID definitions in this XML file.

Inflating XML Menu Resource Files

Let's assume that the name of this XML file is my_menu.xml. You will need to place this file in the /res/menu subdirectory. Placing the file in /res/menu automatically generates a resource ID called R.menu.my_menu.

Now, let's look at how you can use this menu resource ID to populate the options menu. Android provides a class called android.view.MenuInflater to populate Menu objects from XML files. We will use an instance of this MenuInflater to make use of the R.menu.my_menu resource ID to populate a menu object:

```
@Override
public boolean onCreateOptionsMenu(Menu menu)
{
   MenuInflater inflater = getMenuInflater(); //from activity
   inflater.inflate(R.menu.my_menu, menu);

   //It is important to return true to see the menu
   return true;

}
```

In this code, we first get the MenuInflater from the Activity class and then tell it to inflate the menu XML file into the menu directly.

Responding to XML-Based Menu Items

You haven't yet seen the specific advantage of this approach—it becomes apparent when you start responding to the menu items. You respond to XML menu items the way you respond to menus created programmatically, but with a small difference. As before, you handle the menu items in the onOptionsItemSelected callback method. This time, you will have some help from Android's resources (see Chapter 3 for details on resources). As we mentioned in the section "Structure of an XML Menu Resource File," Android not only generates a resource ID for the XML file but also generates the necessary menu item IDs to help you distinguish between the menu items. This is an advantage in terms of responding to the menu items because you don't have to explicitly create and manage their menu item IDs.

To further elaborate on this, in the case of XML menus, you don't have to define constants for these IDs and you don't have to worry about their uniqueness because resource ID generation takes care of that. The following code illustrates this:

```
private void onOptionsItemSelected (MenuItem item)
{
   this.appendMenuItemText(item);
   if (item.getItemId() == R.id.menu_clear)
   {
       this.emptyText();
    }
   else if (item.getItemId() == R.id.menu_dial)
   {
        //do something
   }
   else if (item.getItemId() == R.id.menu_testPick)
   {
        //do something
   }
  else if (item.getItemId() == R.id.menu_testGetContent)
   {
        //do something
   }
   else if (item.getItemId() == R.id.menu_show_browser)
   {
        //do something
    }
```

```
    ......etc
}
```

Notice how the menu item names from the XML menu resource file have automatically generated menu item IDs in the R.id space.

A Brief Introduction to Additional XML Menu Tags

As you construct your XML files, you will need to know the various XML tags that are possible. You can quickly get this information by examining the API demonstrations that come with the Android SDK. These Android API demonstrations include a series of menus that help you explore all aspects of Android programming. If you look at the /res/menu subdirectory, you will find a number of XML menu samples. We'll briefly cover some key tags here.

Group Category Tag

In an XML file, you can specify the category of a group by using the menuCategory tag:

```
<group android:id="@+id/some_group_id "
        android:menuCategory="secondary">
```

Checkable Behavior Tags

You can use the checkableBehavior tag to control checkable behavior at a group level:

```
<group android:id="@+id/noncheckable_group"
       android:checkableBehavior="none">
```

You can use the checked tag to control checkable behavior at an item level:

```
<item android:id=".."
      android:title="..."
      android:checked="true" />
```

Tags to Simulate a Submenu

A submenu is represented as a menu element under a menu item:

```
<item android:title="All without group">
       <menu>
                 <item...>
       </menu>
</item>
```

Menu Icon Tag

You can use the icon tag to associate an image with a menu item:

```
<item android:id=".. "
       android:icon="@drawable/some-file" />
```

Menu Enabling/Disabling Tag

You can enable and disable a menu item using the enabled tag:

```
<item android:id=".. "
        android:enabled="true"
       android:icon="@drawable/some-file" />
```

Menu Item Shortcuts

You can set a shortcut for a menu item using the alphabeticShortcut tag:

```
<item android:id="… "
       android:alphabeticShortcut="a"
      …
  </item>
```

Menu Visibility

You can control a menu item's visibility using the visible flag:

```
<item android:id="… "
       android:visible="true"
      …
</item>
```

Resource

As you learn and work with Android Menus, you may want to keep the following URL handy. This URL points to the downloadable project for this chapter.

- http://www.androidbook.com/projects: You can use this URL to download the test project dedicated for this chapter. The name of the ZIP file is ProAndroid3_ch07_TestMenus.zip.

Summary

This chapter has explained how to work with various types of Android menus: regular menus, context menus, alternative menus, and XML-based menus. A number of subsequent chapters such as 8 (Dialogs), 16 (2D Animation), and 20 (OpenGL) use XML menus to test the functionality presented in those chapters. Finally the 3.0 specific action bar and menu interaction is covered in Chapter 30.

Chapter 8

Working with Dialogs

Android SDK offers extensive support for dialogs. Dialogs that are explicitly supported in Android include the alert, pick list, single choice, multiple choice, progress, time picker, and date picker dialogs. (This list could vary depending on the Android release.) Android also supports custom dialogs for other needs. The primary focus of this chapter is not to cover each of these dialogs but to cover the underlying architecture of Android dialogs. Android 3.0 has added dialogs based on fragments. This aspect of dialogs is covered in the fragments Chapter 29. Fragment based dialogs are expected to gradually replace the traditional dialogs that are covered here. However these dialogs are not yet deprecated and still the norm on phones.

Dialogs in Android are asynchronous, which provides flexibility. However, if you are accustomed to a programming framework where dialogs are primarily synchronous (such as Microsoft Windows, or JavaScript dialogs in web pages), you might find asynchronous dialogs a bit unintuitive.

After giving you the basics of creating and using Android dialogs, we will provide an intuitive abstraction that will make working with asynchronous dialogs easier. We will then use this abstraction to implement a few sample dialogs. We also provide a link to a downloadable project at the end of this chapter in the References section. You can use this download to experiment with the code and the concepts presented in this chapter.

Using Dialogs in Android

If you are coming from an environment where dialogs are synchronous (especially modal dialogs), you need to think differently with Android dialogs. Dialogs in Android are asynchronous. Not only that but they are also *managed*; that is, they are reused between multiple invocations, perhaps to help improve performance.

Designing an Alert Dialog

We will begin the discussion with alert dialogs. Alert dialogs commonly contain simple messages about validating forms or sometimes (rightly or wrongly) for debugging. Consider the following debug example that you often find in HTML pages:

```
if (validate(field1) == false)
{
   //indicate that formatting is not valid through an alert dialog
   showAlert("What you have entered in field1 doesn't match required format");
   //set focus to the field
   //..and continue
}
```

You would likely program this dialog in JavaScript through the `alert` JavaScript function, which displays a simple synchronous dialog box containing a message and an OK button. After the user clicks the OK button, the flow of the program continues. This dialog is considered modal as well as synchronous because the next line of code will not be executed until the `alert` function returns.

This type of alert dialog proves useful for debugging. But Android offers no such direct function or dialog. Instead, it supports an alert-dialog builder, a general-purpose facility for constructing and working with alert dialogs. So you can build an alert dialog yourself using the `android.app.AlertDialog.Builder` class. You can use this builder class to construct dialogs that allow users to perform the following tasks:

- Read a message and respond with Yes or No.
- Pick an item from a list.
- Pick multiple items from a list.
- View the progress of an application.
- Choose an option from a set of options.
- Respond to a prompt before continuing the program.

We will show you how to build one of these dialogs and invoke that dialog from a menu item. This approach, which applies to any of these dialogs, consists of these steps:

1. Construct a `Builder` object.
2. Set parameters for the display such as the number of buttons, the list of items, and so on.
3. Set the callback methods for the buttons.
4. Tell the `Builder` to build the dialog. The type of dialog that's built depends on what you've set on the `Builder` object.
5. Use `dialog.show()` to show the dialog.

Listing 8–1 shows the code that implements these steps.

Listing 8–1. *Building and Displaying an Alert Dialog*

```
public class Alerts
{
   public static void showAlert(String message, Context ctx)
   {
   //Create a builder
      AlertDialog.Builder builder = new AlertDialog.Builder(ctx);
      builder.setTitle("Alert Window");

   //add buttons and listener
     EmptyOnClickListener el = new EmptyOnClickListener();
      builder.setPositiveButton("Ok", el);

   //Create the dialog
      AlertDialog ad = builder.create();

   //show
      ad.show();
   }
}

public class EmptyOnClickListener
implements android.content.DialogInterface.OnClickListener {
   public void onClick(DialogInterface v, int buttonId)
   {
   }
}
```

You can invoke the code in Listing 8–1 by creating a menu item in a suitable test activity (such as the downloadable sample project) and responding to it using this code:

```
if (item.getItemId() == R.id.menu_simple_alert)
{
    Alerts.showAlert("Simple Sample Alert", this);
}
```

The result could (depending on your test activity) look like the screen shown in Figure 8–1.

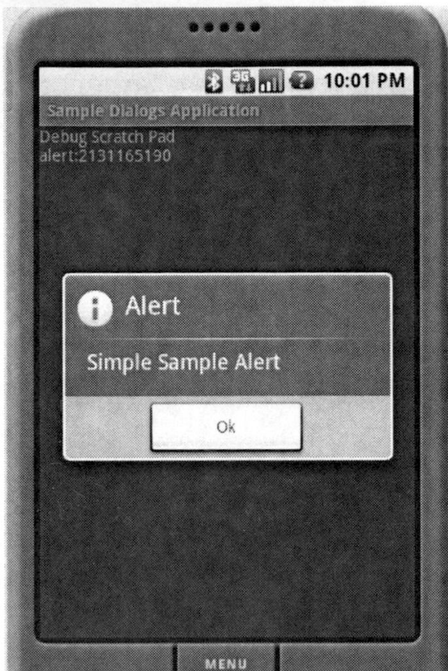

Figure 8–1. *A simple alert dialog*

The code for this simple alert dialog is straightforward (as shown in Listing 8–1 and the code snippet that appears after it). Even the listener part is easy to understand. Essentially, we do nothing when the button is clicked.

It is worth noting, however, that the listener is passed a reference to a `DialogInterface`. This reference points to the actual dialog on which this callback is invoked. This interface supports a number of constants used by the dialog classes, a number of callback interfaces and also two key methods. These methods are

```
cancel()
dismiss()
```

Usually, you don't need to call these methods as the button clicks automatically invoke them as necessary. If you want to react to these method calls, you can register their corresponding callbacks. Refer to the SDK documentation on `DialogInterface` for a complete list of callback methods available.

In Listing 8–1, we just created an empty listener to register against the OK button. The only odd part is that you don't use a `new` to create the dialog; instead, you set parameters and ask the alert-dialog builder to create it.

Designing a Prompt Dialog

Now that you've successfully created a simple alert dialog, let's tackle an alert dialog that's more: the prompt dialog. Another JavaScript staple, the prompt dialog shows the user a hint or question and asks for input via an edit box. The prompt dialog returns that string to the program so it can continue. This will be a good example to study because it features a number of facilities provided by the `Builder` class and allows us to examine the synchronous, asynchronous, modal, and nonmodal nature of Android dialogs.

Here are the steps you need to take in order to create a prompt dialog:

1. Come up with a layout view for your prompt dialog.
2. Load the layout into a `View` class.
3. Construct a `Builder` object.
4. Set the view in the `Builder` object.
5. Set the buttons along with their callbacks to capture the entered text.
6. Create the dialog using the alert-dialog builder.
7. Show the dialog

Now, we'll show you the code for each step.

XML Layout File for the Prompt Dialog

When we show the prompt dialog, we need to show a prompt `TextView` followed by an edit box where a user can type a reply. Listing 8–2 contains the XML layout file for the prompt dialog. If you call this file `prompt_layout.xml`, you need to place it in the `/res/layout` subdirectory to produce a resource ID called `R.layout.prompt_layout`.

Listing 8–2. *The prompt_layout.xml File*

```
<LinearLayout xmlns:android="http://schemas.android.com/apk/res/android"
    android:layout_width="fill_parent"
    android:layout_height="wrap_content"
    android:orientation="vertical">

    <TextView
        android:id="@+id/promptmessage"
        android:layout_height="wrap_content"
        android:layout_width="wrap_content"
        android:layout_marginLeft="20dip"
        android:layout_marginRight="20dip"
        android:text="Your text goes here"
        android:gravity="left"
        android:textAppearance="?android:attr/textAppearanceMedium" />

    <EditText
        android:id="@+id/editText_prompt"
        android:layout_height="wrap_content"
        android:layout_width="fill_parent"
        android:layout_marginLeft="20dip"
        android:layout_marginRight="20dip"
        android:scrollHorizontally="true"
        android:autoText="false"
        android:capitalize="none"
```

```
        android:gravity="fill_horizontal"
        android:textAppearance="?android:attr/textAppearanceMedium" />

</LinearLayout>
```

Setting Up an Alert-Dialog Builder with a User View

Let's combine steps 2 through 4 from our instructions to create a prompt dialog: loading the XML view and setting it up in the alert-dialog builder. Android provides a class called `android.view.LayoutInflater` to create a `View` object from an XML layout definition file. We will use an instance of the `LayoutInflater` to populate the view for our dialog based on the XML layout file (see Listing 8–3).

Listing 8–3. *Inflating a Layout into a Dialog*

```
LayoutInflater li = LayoutInflater.from(activity);
//the 'activity' variable is a reference to your activity or context
View view = li.inflate(R.layout.prompt_layout, null);

//get a builder and set the view
AlertDialog.Builder builder = new AlertDialog.Builder(ctx);
builder.setTitle("Prompt");
builder.setView(view);
```

In Listing 8–3, we get the `LayoutInflater` using the static method `LayoutInflater.from(ctx)` and then use the `LayoutInflater` object to inflate the XML to create a `View` object. We then configure an alert-dialog builder with a title and the view that we just created.

Setting Up Buttons and Listeners

We now move on to step 5, setting up buttons. You need to provide OK and Cancel buttons, so the user can respond to the prompt. If the user clicks Cancel, the program doesn't need to read any text for the prompt. If the user clicks OK, the program gets the value from the text and passes it back to the activity.

To set up these buttons, you need a listener to respond to these callbacks. We will give you the code for the listener in the "Prompt Dialog Listener" section, but first examine the button setup in Listing 8–4, which continues on from Listing 8–3.

Listing 8–4. *Setting Up OK and Cancel Buttons*

```
    //add buttons and listener
    PromptListener pl = new PromptListener(view);
    builder.setPositiveButton("OK", pl);
    builder.setNegativeButton("Cancel", pl);
```

The code in Listing 8–4 assumes that the name of the listener class is `PromptListener`. We have registered this listener against each button. The `PromptListener` class takes the layout view we constructed in Listing 8–3. When you examine the class in a little while, you will notice that the `view` variable is used to identify the text controls and retrieve what the user has entered.

Creating and Showing the Prompt Dialog

Finally, we finish up with steps 6 and 7, creating and showing the prompt dialog. That's easy to do once you have the alert-dialog builder (see Listing 8–5).

Listing 8–5. *Telling the Alert-Dialog Builder to Create the Dialog*

```
//get the dialog
AlertDialog ad = builder.create();
ad.show();

//return the prompt
return pl.getPromptReply();
```

The last line uses the listener to return the reply for the prompt. Now, as promised, we'll show you the code for the `PromptListener` class.

Prompt Dialog Listener

The prompt dialog interacts with an activity through a listener callback class called `PromptListener`. The class has one callback method called `onClick`, and the button ID that is passed to `onClick` identifies what type of button is clicked. The rest of the code is easy to follow (see Listing 8–6). When the user enters text and clicks the OK button, the value of the text is transferred to the `promptReply` field. Otherwise, the value stays `null`. Notice how we have used the edit text control ID (`editText_prompt`) from the prompt dialog layout identified in Listing 8–2

Listing 8–6. *PromptListener, the Listener Callback Class*

```
public class PromptListener
implements android.content.DialogInterface.OnClickListener
{
   // local variable to return the prompt reply value
   private String promptReply = null;

   //Keep a variable for the view to retrieve the prompt value
   View promptDialogView = null;

   //Take in the view in the constructor
   public PromptListener(View inDialogView)   {
         promptDialogView = inDialogView;
   }

   //Call back method from dialogs
   public void onClick(DialogInterface v, int buttonId)   {
         if (buttonId == DialogInterface.BUTTON_POSITIVE)      {
              //ok button
              promptReply = getPromptText();
      }
      else      {
         //cancel button
         promptReply = null;
      }
   }
```

```
    //Just an access method for what is in the edit box
    private String getPromptText()   {
        EditText et =  (EditText)
        promptDialogView.findViewById(R.id.editText_prompt);
        return et.getText().toString();
    }
    public String getPromptReply() { return promptReply; }
}
```

Putting It All Together

Now that we have explained each piece of code that goes into a prompt dialog, we'll present it in one place so you can use it to test the dialog (see Listing 8–7). We have excluded the `PromptListener` class, because it appears separately in Listing 8–6.

Listing 8–7. *Code to Test the Prompt Dialog*

```
public class Alerts
{
    public static String prompt(String message, Context ctx)
    {
        //load some kind of a view
        LayoutInflater li = LayoutInflater.from(ctx);
        View view = li.inflate(R.layout.prompt_layout, null);

        //get a builder and set the view
        AlertDialog.Builder builder = new AlertDialog.Builder(ctx);
        builder.setTitle("Prompt");
        builder.setView(view);

        //add buttons and listener
        PromptListener pl = new PromptListener(view);
        builder.setPositiveButton("OK", pl);
        builder.setNegativeButton("Cancel", pl);

        //get the dialog
        AlertDialog ad = builder.create();

        //show
        ad.show();

        return pl.getPromptReply();
    }
}
```

You can invoke the code in Listing 8–7 by creating a menu item in a suitable test harness and responding to that menu item using this code:

```
if (item.getItemId() == R.id.your_menu_item_id)
{
     String  reply = Alerts.showPrompt("Your text goes here", this);
}
```

The result would look like the screen shown in Figure 8–2.

Figure 8–2. *A simple prompt dialog*

After writing all this code, however, you will notice that the prompt dialog always returns `null` even if the user enters text into it. As it turns out, in the following code the `show()` method will invoke the dialog asynchronously:

```
ad.show() //dialog.show
return pl.getPromptReply(); // listener.getpromptReply()
```

This means the `getPromptReply()` method (see Listing 8–6) gets called for the prompt value before the user has time to enter text, and click the OK button. This fallacy in our code takes us to the heart of the nature of Android dialogs.

Nature of Dialogs in Android

As we've mentioned, displaying dialogs in Android is an asynchronous process. Once a dialog is shown, the main thread that invoked the dialog returns and continues to process the rest of the code. This doesn't mean that the dialog isn't modal. The dialog is still modal. The mouse clicks apply only to the dialog, while the parent activity goes back to its message loop.

On some windowing systems, modal dialogs behave a bit differently. The caller is blocked until the user provides a response through the dialog. (This block can be a virtual block instead of a real block.) On the Windows operating system, the message-dispatching thread starts dispatching to the dialog and suspends dispatching to the parent window. When the dialog closes, the thread returns to the parent window. This makes the call synchronous.

Such an approach might not work for a handheld device, where unexpected events on the device are more frequent, and the main thread needs to respond to those events. To accomplish this level of responsiveness, Android returns the main thread to its message loop right away.

The implication of this model is that you cannot have a simple dialog where you ask for a response and wait for it before moving on. In fact, your programming model for dialogs must differ and incorporate callbacks.

Rearchitecting the Prompt Dialog

Let's revisit the problematic code in the previous prompt dialog implementation:

```
if (item.getItemId() == R.id.your_menu_id)
{
    String  reply = Alerts.showPrompt("Your text goes here", this);
}
```

As we have proven, the value of the string variable `reply` will be `null`, because the prompt dialog initiated by `Alerts.showPrompt()` is incapable of returning a value on the same thread. The only way you can accomplish this is to have the activity implement the callback method directly and not rely on the `PromptListener` class. You do this in the `Activity` class by implementing the `OnClickListener`:

```
public class SampleActivity extends Activity
implements android.content.DialogInterface.OnClickListener
{
..... other code

if (item.getItemId() == R.id.your_menu_id)
{
    Alerts.showPrompt("Your text goes here", this);
}
.....
public void onClick(DialogInterface v, int buttonId)
{
       //figure out a way here to read the reply string from the dialog
}
```

As you can see from this `onClick` callback method, you can correctly read the variables from the instantiated dialog because the user will have closed the dialog by the time this method is called.

It is perfectly legitimate to use dialogs this way. However, Android provides a supplemental mechanism to optimize performance by introducing *managed dialogs*—dialogs that are reused between multiple invocations. You'll still need to use callbacks when you work with managed dialogs, though. In fact, everything you've learned in implementing the prompt dialog will help you work with managed dialogs and understand the motivation behind them. These managed dialogs also allow Android to manage the state of a dialog between multiple invocations as long as the activity's view state is intact.

Working with Managed Dialogs

Android follows a managed-dialog protocol to promote the reuse of previously created dialog instances rather than creating new dialogs in response to actions. In this section, we will talk about the details of the managed-dialog protocol and show you how to implement the alert dialog as a managed dialog. However, in our view, the managed-dialog protocol makes using dialogs tedious. We will subsequently develop a small framework to abstract out most of this protocol to make it easier to work with managed dialogs.

Understanding the Managed-Dialog Protocol

The primary goal of the managed-dialog protocol is to reuse a dialog if it's invoked a second time, or subsequently. It is similar to using object pools in Java. The managed-dialog protocol consists of these steps:

1. Assign a unique ID to each dialog you want to create and use. Suppose one of the dialogs is tagged as 1.
2. Tell Android to show a dialog called 1.
3. Android checks whether the current activity already has a dialog tagged as 1. If the dialog exists, Android shows it without re-creating it. Android calls the `onPrepareDialog()` function before showing the dialog for cleanup purposes.
4. If the dialog doesn't exist, Android calls the `onCreateDialog()` method by passing the dialog ID (1, in this case).
5. You, as the programmer, need to override the `onCreateDialog()` method. You must create the dialog using the alert-dialog builder and return it. But before creating the dialog, your code needs to determine which dialog ID needs to be created. You'll need a switch statement to figure this out.
6. Android shows the dialog.
7. The dialog invokes callbacks dialog buttons are clicked.

Let's use this protocol to re-implement our non-managed alert dialog as a managed alert dialog.

Recasting the Nonmanaged Dialog as a Managed Dialog

We will follow each of the steps laid out to reimplement the alert dialog. Let's start by defining a unique ID for this dialog in the context of a given activity:

```
//unique dialog id
private static final int DIALOG_ALERT_ID = 1;
```

That is simple enough. We have just created an ID to represent a dialog to orchestrate the callbacks. This ID will allow us to do the following in response to a menu item:

```
someactivity.showDialog(this.DIALOG_ALERT_ID);
```

The Android SDK method showDialog triggers a call to the onCreateDialog() method of the activity class. Android is smart enough not to call onCreateDialog() multiple times. When this method is called, we need to create the dialog and return it to Android. Android then keeps the created dialog internally for reuse purposes. Here is the sample code to create the dialog based on a unique ID:

```
public class SomeActivity extends Activity {
...
    @Override
    protected Dialog onCreateDialog(int id) {
        switch (id) {
            case DIALOG_ALERT_ID:
               return createAlertDialog();
        }
        return null;
    }

    private Dialog createAlertDialog()
    {
       AlertDialog.Builder builder = new AlertDialog.Builder(this);
       builder.setTitle("Alert");
       builder.setMessage("some message");
       EmptyOnClickListener emptyListener = new EmptyOnClickListener();
       builder.setPositiveButton("Ok", emptyListener );
       AlertDialog ad = builder.create();
       return ad;
    }
```

Notice how onCreateDialog() has to figure out the incoming ID to identify a matching dialog. createAlertDialog() itself is kept in a separate function and parallels the alert-dialog creation described in the previous sections. This code also uses the same EmptyOnClickListener that was used when we worked with the alert dialog.

Because the dialog is created only once, you need a mechanism if you want to change something in the dialog every time you show it. You do this through the onPrepareDialog() callback method:

```
    @Override
    protected void onPrepareDialog(int id, Dialog dialog) {
        switch (id) {
        case DIALOG_ALERT_ID:
           prepareAlertDialog(dialog);
        }
    }

    private void prepareAlertDialog(Dialog d)    {
       AlertDialog ad = (AlertDialog)d;
       //change something about this dialog
    }
```

With this code in place, showDialog(1) will work. Even if you were to invoke this method multiple times, your onCreateMethod method would get called only once. You can follow the same protocol to redo the prompt dialog.

Responding to dialog callbacks is work, but the managed-dialog protocol adds even more work. After looking at the managed-dialog protocol, we got the idea to abstract out the protocol and rearrange it in such a way that it accomplishes two goals:

- Moving the dialog identification and creation out of the activity class
- Concentrating the dialog creation and response in a dedicated dialog class

In the next subsection, we will go through the design of this framework and then use it to re-create both the alert and prompt dialogs.

Simplifying the Managed-Dialog Protocol

As you've probably noticed, working with managed alert dialogs can become messy and can pollute the mainline code. If we abstract out this protocol into a simpler protocol, the new protocol could look like this:

1. Create an instance of a dialog you want by using new and keeping it as a local variable. Call this dialog1.
2. Show the dialog using dialog1.show().
3. Implement one method in the activity called dialogFinished().
4. In the dialogFinished() method, read attributes from dialog1 such as dialog1.getValue1().

Under this scheme, showing a managed alert dialog will look like this:

```
….class MyActivity ….
{
 //new dialog
   ManagedAlertDialog  mad = new ManagedAlertDialog("message", …, .. );

  ….some menu method
  if (item.getItemId() == R.id.your_menu_id)
  {
  //show dialog
    mad.show();
  }
  …..
  //access the mad dialog for internals if you want
  dialogFinsihed()
  {
    ….
  //use values from dialog
     mad.getA();
     mad.getB();
  }
}
```

We think this is a far simpler model to work with dialogs. The clear advantages of this approach are as follows:

- You don't have to assign or remember arbitrary dialog IDs.
- You don't have to pollute the mainline activity code with dialog creation.
- You can use derived dialog objects directly to access values.

How does the principle of this abstraction work? As a first step, we abstract out the creation of a dialog and the preparation of that dialog into a class that identifies a base dialog. We call this interface `IDialogProtocol`. This dialog interface also has a `show()` method on it directly. These dialogs are collected and kept in a registry in the base class for an activity, and they use their IDs as keys. The base activity will demultiplex the `onCreate`, `onPrepare`, and `onClick` calls based on their IDs and reroute them to the dialog class. This architecture is illustrated in Figure 8–3.

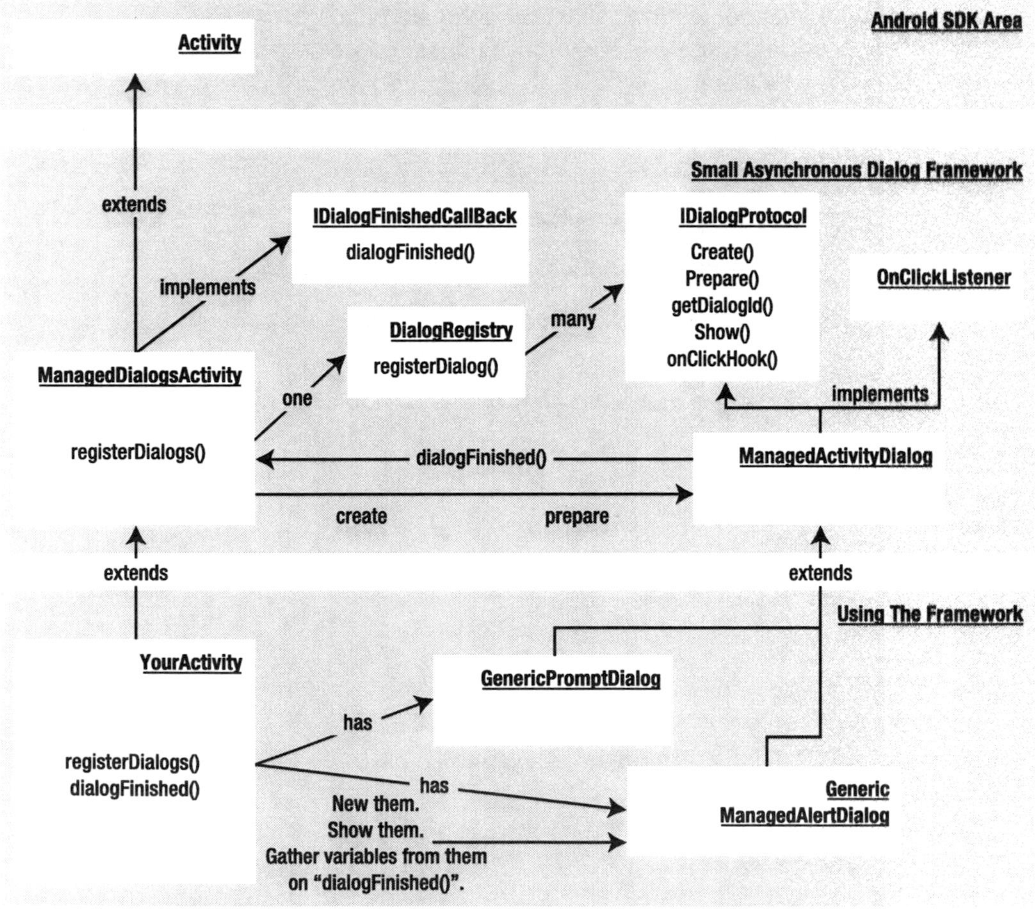

Figure 8–3. *A simple managed-dialog framework*

Listing 8–8 illustrates the utility of this framework. Source code for the key classes (including GenericPromptDialog and GenericManagedAlertDialog) are presented subsequently in this chapter. However, we haven't included driver class in full, just the highlights in Listing 8–8. You can use the download URL in this chapter's "References" section to see this class driving the various dialogs mentioned in this chapter.

Listing 8–8. *The Abstraction of the Managed-Dialog Protocol*

```
public class MainActivity extends ManagedDialogsActivity
{
   //dialog 1
   private GenericManagedAlertDialog gmad =
      new GenericManagedAlertDialog(this,1,"InitialValue");

   //dialog 2
   private GenericPromptDialog gmpd =
      new GenericPromptDialog(this,2,"InitialValue");

   //menu items to start the dialogs
   if (item.getItemId() == R.id.your_menu_id1)
   {
      gmad.show();
   }
   else if (item.getItemId() == R.id.your_menu_id2)
   {
       gmpd.show();
   }

   //dealing with call backs
   public void dialogFinished(ManagedActivityDialog dialog, int buttonId)
   {
      if (dialog.getDialogId() == gmpd.getDialogId())
      {
         //Assuming "gmpd" has an access method for the reply string
         String replyString = gmpd.getReplyString();
      }
   }
}
```

To make use of this framework, you start by extending ManagedDialogsActivity. Then, you instantiate the dialogs you need, each of which derives from ManagedActivityDialog. In a menu-item response, you can simply run the show() method on these dialogs. The dialogs themselves take the necessary parameters up front in order to be created and shown. Although we are passing a dialog ID, we don't need to remember those IDs anymore. You could even abstract out these IDs completely if you'd like.

Now, we'll explore each of the classes shown in Figure 8–3. You can also see these listings in the download for this chapter. If you are meaning to compile this code, we strongly recommend downloading that project. If you choose not to, the majority of the code to reconstruct a project is all here; you may have to fill in the gaps.

IDialogProtocol

The IDialogProtocol interface defines what it means to be a managed dialog. Responsibilities of a managed dialog include creating the dialog and preparing it every time it is shown. It also makes sense to delegate the show functionality to the dialog itself. A dialog also must recognize button clicks and call the respective parent of the dialog closure. The following interface code represents these ideas as a set of functions:

```
public interface IDialogProtocol
{
    public Dialog create();
    public void prepare(Dialog dialog);
    public int getDialogId();
    public void show();
    public void onClickHook(int buttonId);
}
```

ManagedActivityDialog

The abstract class ManagedActivityDialog provides the common implementation for all the dialog classes wanting to implement the IDialogProtocol interface. It leaves the create and prepare functions to be overridden by the base classes but provides implementations for the rest of the IDialogProtocol methods. ManagedActivityDialog also informs the parent activity that the dialog has finished after responding to a button-click event. It uses the template-hook pattern and allows the derived classes to specialize the hook method onClickHook. This class is also responsible for redirecting the show() method to the parent activity, thereby providing a more natural implementation for show(). You can use the ManagedActivityDialog class as the base class for all your new dialogs (see Listing 8–9).

Listing 8–9. *The ManagedActivityDialog Class*

```
public abstract class ManagedActivityDialog implements IDialogProtocol
    ,android.content.DialogInterface.OnClickListener

{
    private ManagedDialogsActivity mActivity;
    private int mDialogId;
    public ManagedActivityDialog(ManagedDialogsActivity a, int dialogId)
    {
        mActivity = a;
        mDialogId = dialogId;
    }
    public int getDialogId()
    {
        return mDialogId;
    }
    public void show()
    {
        mActivity.showDialog(mDialogId);
    }
    public void onClick(DialogInterface v, int buttonId)
    {
        onClickHook(buttonId);
```

```
            this.mActivity.dialogFinished(this, buttonId);
        }
    }
```

DialogRegistry

The DialogRegistry class is responsible for two things. It keeps a mapping between the dialog IDs and the actual dialog (factory) instances. It also translates the generic onCreate and onPrepare calls to the specific dialogs using the ID-to-object mapping. The ManagedDialogsActivity uses the DialogRegistry class as a repository to register new dialogs (see Listing 8–10).

Listing 8–10. *The DialogRegistry Class*

```
public class DialogRegistry
{
   SparseArray<IDialogProtocol> idsToDialogs
                                 = new SparseArray();

   public void registerDialog(IDialogProtocol dialog)
   {
      idsToDialogs.put(dialog.getDialogId(),dialog);
   }

   public Dialog create(int id)
   {
      IDialogProtocol dp = idsToDialogs.get(id);
      if (dp == null) return null;

      return dp.create();
   }
   public void prepare(Dialog dialog, int id)
   {
      IDialogProtocol dp = idsToDialogs.get(id);
      if (dp == null)
      {
         throw new RuntimeException("Dialog id is not registered:" + id);
      }
      dp.prepare(dialog);
   }
}
```

ManagedDialogsActivity

The ManagedDialogsActivity class acts as a base class for your activities that support managed dialogs. It keeps a single instance of DialogRegistry to keep track of the managed dialogs identified by the IDialogProtocol interface. It allows the derived activities to register their dialogs through the registerDialogs() function. As shown in Figure 8–3, it is also responsible for transferring the create and prepare semantics to the respective dialog instance by locating that dialog instance in the dialog registry. Finally, it provides the callback method dialogFinished for each dialog in the dialog registry (see Listing 8–11).

Listing 8–11. *The ManagedDialogsActivity Class*

```
public class ManagedDialogsActivity extends Activity
             implements IDialogFinishedCallBack
{
   //A registry for managed dialogs
    private DialogRegistry dr = new DialogRegistry();

    public void onCreate(Bundle savedInstanceState) {
        super.onCreate(savedInstanceState);
        this.registerDialogs();
    }

    protected void registerDialogs()
    {
       // does nothing
       // have the derived classes override this method
       // to register their dialogs
       // example:
       // registerDialog(this.DIALOG_ALERT_ID_3, gmad);

    }
    public void registerDialog(IDialogProtocol dialog)
    {
       this.dr.registerDialog(dialog);
    }

    @Override
    protected Dialog onCreateDialog(int id) {
              return this.dr.create(id);
    }
    @Override
    protected void onPrepareDialog(int id, Dialog dialog) {
             this.dr.prepare(dialog, id);
    }

   public void dialogFinished(ManagedActivityDialog dialog, int buttonId)
   {
      //nothing to do
      //have derived classes override this
   }
}
```

IDialogFinishedCallBack

The `IDialogFinishedCallBack` interface allows the `ManagedActivityDialog` class to tell the parent activity that the dialog has finished and that the parent activity can call methods on the dialog to retrieve parameters. Usually, a `ManagedDialogsActivity` implements this interface and acts as a parent activity to the `ManagedActivityDialog` (see Listing 8–12).

Listing 8–12. *The IDialogFinishedCallBack Interface*

```
public interface IDialogFinishedCallBack
{
      public static int OK_BUTTON = -1;
```

```
        public static int CANCEL_BUTTON = -2;
        public void dialogFinished(ManagedActivityDialog dialog, int buttonId);
}
```

GenericManagedAlertDialog

GenericManagedAlertDialog is the alert-dialog implementation; it extends ManagedActivityDialog. This class is responsible for creating the actual alert dialog using the alert-dialog builder. It also carries all the information it needs as local variables. Because GenericManagedAlertDialog implements a simple alert dialog, it does nothing in the onClickHook method. The key thing to note is that when you use this approach, GenericManagedAlertDialog encapsulates all pertinent information in one place (see Listing 8–13). That keeps the mainline code in the activity squeaky clean.

Listing 8–13. *The GenericManagedAlertDialog Class*

```
public class GenericManagedAlertDialog extends ManagedActivityDialog
{
   private String alertMessage = null;
   private Context ctx = null;
   public GenericManagedAlertDialog(ManagedDialogsActivity inActivity,
                            int dialogId,
                            String initialMessage)
   {
      super(inActivity,dialogId);
      alertMessage = initialMessage;
      ctx = inActivity;
   }
   public Dialog create()
   {
       AlertDialog.Builder builder = new AlertDialog.Builder(ctx);
       builder.setTitle("Alert");
       builder.setMessage(alertMessage);
       builder.setPositiveButton("Ok", this );
       AlertDialog ad = builder.create();
       return ad;
   }

   public void prepare(Dialog dialog)
   {
       AlertDialog ad = (AlertDialog)dialog;
       ad.setMessage(alertMessage);
   }
   public void setAlertMessage(String inAlertMessage)
   {
      alertMessage = inAlertMessage;
   }
   public void onClickHook(int buttonId)
   {
      //nothing to do
      //no local variables to set
   }
}
```

GenericPromptDialog

The GenericPromptDialog class encapsulates all the needs of a prompt dialog by extending the ManagedActivityDialog class and providing the necessary create and prepare methods (see Listing 8–14). You can also see that it saves the reply text in a local variable so that the parent activity can get to it in the dialogFinished callback method.

Listing 8–14. *The GenericPromptDialog Class*

```
public class GenericPromptDialog extends ManagedActivityDialog
{
   private String mPromptMessage = null;
   private View promptView = null;
   String promptValue = null;

   private Context ctx = null;
   public GenericPromptDialog(ManagedDialogsActivity inActivity,
         int dialogId,
         String promptMessage)
   {
      super(inActivity,dialogId);
      mPromptMessage = promptMessage;
      ctx = inActivity;
   }
   public Dialog create()
   {
       LayoutInflater li = LayoutInflater.from(ctx);
       promptView = li.inflate(R.layout.promptdialog, null);
       AlertDialog.Builder builder = new AlertDialog.Builder(ctx);
       builder.setTitle("prompt");
       builder.setView(promptView);
       builder.setPositiveButton("OK", this);
       builder.setNegativeButton("Cancel", this);
       AlertDialog ad = builder.create();
       return ad;
   }

   public void prepare(Dialog dialog)
   {
      //nothing for now
   }
   public void onClickHook(int buttonId)
   {
      if (buttonId == DialogInterface.BUTTON1)
      {
         //ok button
         String promptValue = getEnteredText();
      }
   }
   private String getEnteredText()
   {
      EditText et =
         (EditText)
         promptView.findViewById(R.id.editText_prompt);
      String enteredText = et.getText().toString();
      Log.d("xx",enteredText);
```

```
        return enteredText;
    }
}
```

The framework presented here needs to be adjusted somewhat when activities are recreated when the device configuration changes. The primary change involves recreating dialog objects using the save instance and restore instance methods. As these dialogs are going to be superceded by fragment based dialogs (covered in chapter 29) we haven't provided the necessary changes to persist these dialogs across device configuration changes.

Working with Toast

We have started off the chapter indicating how "alert" messages are used commonly for debugging JavaScript on error pages. If you are pressed to use a similar approach for infrequent debug messages you can use the `Toast` object in Android.

A `Toast` is like an alert dialog that has a message and displays for a certain amount of time and goes away. So it can be said that it is a transient alert message.

Listing 8–15 shows an example of how you can show a message using `Toast`.

Listing 8–15. *Using Toast for Debugging*

```
//Create a function to wrap a message as a toast
//show the toast
public void reportToast(String message)
{
    String s = tag + ":" + message;
    Toast mToast = Toast.makeText(activity, s, Toast.LENGTH_SHORT);
    mToast.show();
    Log.d(tag,message);
}

//You can invoke the function above
//multiple times if needed as below
private void testToast()
{
    reportToast("Message1");
    reportToast("Message2");
    reportToast("Message3");
}
```

The `makeText()` method in Listing 8–14 can take not only an activity but any context object, such as the one passed to a broadcast receiver or a service for example. This extends the use of `Toast` to outside of activities.

Resources

- http://developer.android.com/guide/topics/ui/dialogs.html: This Android SDK document is an excellent introduction to working with Android dialogs. You will find here an explanation of how to use managed dialogs and various examples of available dialogs.
- http://developer.android.com/reference/android/content/DialogInterface.html: At this URL, you will see the many constants defined for dialogs.
- http://developer.android.com/reference/android/app/Dialog.html: You can discover a number of methods available on a **Dialog** object at this URL.
- http://developer.android.com/reference/android/app/AlertDialog.Builder.html: This URL is the API documentation URL for the **AlertDialog** builder class.
- http://developer.android.com/reference/android/app/ProgressDialog.html: This is API documentation URL for **ProgressDialog**.
- http://developer.android.com/reference/android/app/DatePickerDialog.html: This is API documentation URL for **DatePickerDialog**.
- http://developer.android.com/reference/android/app/TimePickerDialog.html: This is API documentation URL for **TimePickerDialog**.
- http://developer.android.com/resources/tutorials/views/hello-datepicker.html: This is an Android tutorial for using the date picker dialog.
- http://developer.android.com/resources/tutorials/views/hello-timepicker.html: This is an Android tutorial for using the time picker dialog.
- http://www.androidbook.com/item/3540: You can use this URL to download the test project dedicated for this chapter. The name of the ZIP file is ProAndroid3_ch08_SampleDialogs.zip. We also have examples of the date and time picker dialog in the download.

Summary

In this chapter, you saw that dialogs present a special challenge in Android. We showed you the implications of asynchronous dialogs and presented an abstraction to simplify the managed dialogs. Please refer to chapter 29 to see how dialogs work with the introduction of fragments in 3.0. As the fragments API is being made available for previous releases of Android you may want to use the fragment dialogs as your preferred dialog implementation approach.

Chapter 9

Working with Preferences and Saving State

Like many other SDKs, Android supports preferences. It tracks preferences for users of an application as well as the application itself. For example, a user of Microsoft Outlook might set a preference to view e-mail messages a certain way, and Microsoft Outlook itself has some default preferences that are configurable by users. But even though Android theoretically tracks preferences for both users and the application, it does not differentiate between the two. The reason for this is that Android applications run on a device that is generally not shared among several users; people don't often share cell phones. So Android refers to preferences with the term *application preferences*, which encompasses both the user's preferences and the application's default preferences.

When you see Android's preferences support for the first time, you'll likely be impressed. Android offers a robust and flexible framework for dealing with preferences. It provides simple APIs that hide the reading and persisting of preferences, as well as prebuilt user interfaces that you can use to let the user make preference selections. Because of the power built in to the Android preferences framework, we can also use preferences for more general-purpose storing of application state, to allow our application to pick up where it left off for example, should our application go away and come back later. We will explore all of these features in the sections that follow.

Exploring the Preferences Framework

Before we dig into Android's preferences framework, let's establish a scenario that would require the use of preferences and then explore how we would go about addressing it. Suppose you are writing an application that provides a facility to search for airline flights. Moreover, suppose that the application's default setting is to display flights based on the lowest cost, but the user can set a preference to always sort flights by the least number of stops or by a specific airline. How would you go about doing that?

Understanding ListPreference

Obviously, you would have to provide a UI for the user to view the list of sort options. The list would contain radio buttons for each option, and the default (or current) selection would be preselected. To solve this problem with the Android preferences framework requires very little work. First, you would create a preferences XML file to describe the preference and then use a prebuilt activity class that knows how to show and persist preferences. Listing 9–1 shows the details.

> **NOTE:** We will give you a URL at the end of the chapter which you can use to download projects of this chapter. This will allow you to import these projects into your Eclipse directly.

Listing 9–1. *The Flight-Options Preferences XML File and Associated Activity Class*

```
<?xml version="1.0" encoding="utf-8"?>
<!-- This file is /res/xml/flightoptions.xml -->
<PreferenceScreen
        xmlns:android="http://schemas.android.com/apk/res/android"
    android:key="flight_option_preference"
    android:title="@string/prefTitle"
    android:summary="@string/prefSummary">

  <ListPreference
    android:key="@string/selected_flight_sort_option"
    android:title="@string/listTitle"
    android:summary="@string/listSummary"
    android:entries="@array/flight_sort_options"
    android:entryValues="@array/flight_sort_options_values"
    android:dialogTitle="@string/dialogTitle"
    android:defaultValue="@string/flight_sort_option_default_value" />

</PreferenceScreen>


package com.androidbook.preferences.sample;

import android.os.Bundle;
import android.preference.PreferenceActivity;

public class FlightPreferenceActivity extends PreferenceActivity
{
    @Override
    protected void onCreate(Bundle savedInstanceState) {
        super.onCreate(savedInstanceState);
        addPreferencesFromResource(R.xml.flightoptions);
    }
}
```

Listing 9–1 contains an XML fragment that represents the flight-option preference setting. The listing also contains an activity class that loads the preferences XML file. Let's start with the XML. Android provides an end-to-end preferences framework. This means that the framework lets you define your preferences, display the setting(s) to the user, and persist the user's selection to the data store. You define your preferences in

XML under /res/xml/. To show preferences to the user, you write an activity class that extends a predefined Android class called android.preference.PreferenceActivity and use the addPreferencesFromResource() method to add the resource to the activity's resource collection. The framework takes care of the rest (displaying and persisting).

In this flight scenario, you create a file called flightoptions.xml at /res/xml/flightoptions.xml. You then create an activity class called FlightPreferenceActivity that extends the android.preference.PreferenceActivity class. Next, you call addPreferencesFromResource(), passing in R.xml.flightoptions. Note that the preference resource XML points to several string resources. To ensure compilation, you need to add several string resources to your project. We will show you how to do that shortly. For now, have a look at the UI generated by Listing 9–1 (see Figure 9–1).

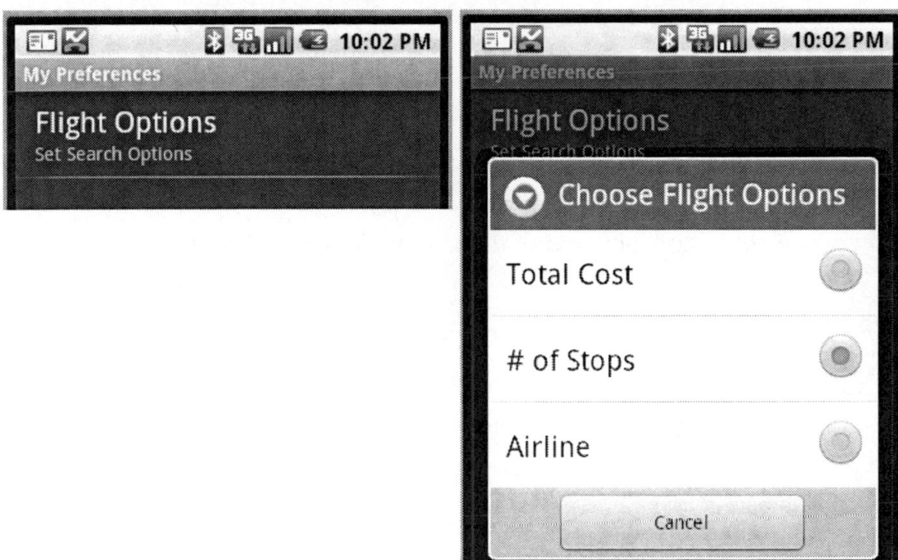

Figure 9–1. *The flight-options preference UI*

Figure 9–1 contains two views. The view on the left is called a *preference screen* and the UI on the right is a *list preference*. When the user selects Flight Options, the Choose Flight Options view appears as a modal dialog with radio buttons for each option. The user selects an option, which immediately saves that option and closes the view. When the user returns to the options screen, the view reflects the saved selection from before.

The XML code in Listing 9–1 defines PreferenceScreen and then creates ListPreference as a child. For PreferenceScreen, you set three properties: key, title, and summary. key is a string you can use to refer to the item programmatically (similar to how you use android:id); title is the screen's title (Flight Options); and summary is a description of the screen's purpose, shown below the title in a smaller font (Set Search Options, in this case). For the list preference, you set the key, title, and summary, as well as attributes for entries, entryValues, dialogTitle, and defaultValue. Table 9–1 summarizes these attributes.

Table 9–1. *A Few Attributes of android.preference.ListPreference*

Attribute	Description
android:key	A name or key for the option (such as selected_flight_sort_option).
android:title	The title of the option.
android:summary	A short summary of the option.
android:entries	The text of the items in the list that the option can be set to.
android:entryValues	Defines the key, or value, for each item. Note that each item has some text and a value. The text is defined by entries and the values are defined by entryValues.
android:dialogTitle	The title of the dialog—used if the view is shown as a modal dialog.
android:defaultValue	The default value of the option from the list of items.

To finish getting our example to work, add or modify the files as indicated in Listing 9–2.

Listing 9–2. *Setting Up the Rest of the Project for Our Example*

```
<?xml version="1.0" encoding="utf-8"?>
<!-- This file is /res/values/arrays.xml -->
<resources>
<string-array name="flight_sort_options">
    <item>Total Cost</item>
    <item># of Stops</item>
    <item>Airline</item>
</string-array>
<string-array name="flight_sort_options_values">
    <item>0</item>
    <item>1</item>
    <item>2</item>
</string-array>
</resources>


<?xml version="1.0" encoding="utf-8"?>
<!-- This file is /res/values/strings.xml -->
<resources>
    <string name="app_name">Preferences Demo</string>
    <string name="prefTitle">My Preferences</string>
    <string name="prefSummary">Set Flight Option Preferences</string>
    <string name="flight_sort_option_default_value">1</string>
    <string name="dialogTitle">Choose Flight Options</string>
    <string name="listSummary">Set Search Options</string>
    <string name="listTitle">Flight Options</string>
    <string name="selected_flight_sort_option">
        selected_flight_sort_option</string>
    <string name="menu_prefs_title">Settings</string>
```

```
</resources>


<?xml version="1.0" encoding="utf-8"?>
<!-- This file is /res/menu/mainmenu.xml -->
<menu xmlns:android="http://schemas.android.com/apk/res/android">
    <item android:id="@+id/menu_prefs"
        android:title="@string/menu_prefs_title"
    />
</menu>


<?xml version="1.0" encoding="utf-8"?>
<!-- This file is /res/layout/main.xml -->
<LinearLayout xmlns:android="http://schemas.android.com/apk/res/android"
    android:orientation="vertical"
    android:layout_width="fill_parent"
    android:layout_height="fill_parent"
    >

<TextView android:text="" android:id="@+id/text1"
    android:layout_width="fill_parent"
    android:layout_height="wrap_content"
    />

</LinearLayout>


// This file is MainActivity.java
import android.app.Activity;
import android.content.Intent;
import android.content.SharedPreferences;
import android.os.Bundle;
import android.view.Menu;
import android.view.MenuInflater;
import android.view.MenuItem;
import android.widget.TextView;

public class MainActivity extends Activity {
    private TextView tv = null;
    private Resources resources;

    /** Called when the activity is first created. */
    @Override
    public void onCreate(Bundle savedInstanceState) {
        super.onCreate(savedInstanceState);
        setContentView(R.layout.main);

        resources = this.getResources();

        tv = (TextView)findViewById(R.id.text1);

        setOptionText();
    }

    @Override
    public boolean onCreateOptionsMenu(Menu menu)
```

```
    {
       MenuInflater inflater = getMenuInflater();
       inflater.inflate(R.menu.mainmenu, menu);
       return true;
    }

    @Override
    public boolean onOptionsItemSelected (MenuItem item)
    {
       if (item.getItemId() == R.id.menu_prefs)
       {
           // Launch to our preferences screen.
           Intent intent = new Intent()
                   .setClass(this,
              com.androidbook.preferences.sample.FlightPreferenceActivity.class);
           this.startActivityForResult(intent, 0);
       }
       return true;
    }

    @Override
    public void onActivityResult(int reqCode, int resCode, Intent data)
    {
        super.onActivityResult(reqCode, resCode, data);
        setOptionText();
    }

    private void setOptionText()
    {
        SharedPreferences prefs =
                PreferenceManager.getDefaultSharedPreferences(this);
//      This is the other way to get to the shared preferences:
//      SharedPreferences prefs = getSharedPreferences(
//              "com.androidbook.preferences.sample_preferences", 0);
        String option = prefs.getString(
                resources.getString(R.string.selected_flight_sort_option),
                resources.getString(R.string.flight_sort_option_default_value));
        String[] optionText = resources.getStringArray(R.array.flight_sort_options);

        tv.setText("option value is " + option + " (" +
                optionText[Integer.parseInt(option)] + ")");
    }
}


<?xml version="1.0" encoding="utf-8"?>
<!-- This file is AndroidManifest.xml -->
<manifest xmlns:android="http://schemas.android.com/apk/res/android"
      package="com.androidbook.preferences.sample"
      android:versionCode="1"
      android:versionName="1.0">
    <application android:icon="@drawable/icon"
          android:label="@string/app_name">
        <activity android:name=".MainActivity"
                  android:label="@string/app_name">
            <intent-filter>
              <action android:name="android.intent.action.MAIN" />
```

```
                <category android:name="android.intent.category.LAUNCHER"/>
            </intent-filter>
        </activity>

        <activity android:name=".FlightPreferenceActivity"
                android:label="@string/prefTitle">
            <intent-filter>
                <action android:name=
 "com.androidbook.preferences.sample.intent.action.FlightPreferences" />
                <category
                    android:name="android.intent.category.PREFERENCE" />
            </intent-filter>
        </activity>

    </application>
    <uses-sdk android:minSdkVersion="4" />

</manifest>
```

After making these changes and running this application, you will first see a simple text message that says "option value is 1 (# of Stops)". Click the Menu button and then Settings to get to the `PreferenceActivity`. Click the back arrow when you're finished, and you will see any changes to the option text immediately.

The first file we added was `/res/values/arrays.xml`. This file contains the two string arrays that we need to implement the option choices. The first array holds the text to be displayed, and the second holds the values that we'll get back in our method calls, plus the value that gets stored in the preferences XML file. For our purposes, we chose to use array index values 0, 1, and 2 for `flight_sort_options_values`. We could use any value that helps us run the application. If our option was numeric in nature (for example a countdown timer starting value), then we could have used values such as 60, 120, 300, and so on. The values don't need to be numeric at all as long as they make sense to the developer; the user doesn't see these values unless you choose to expose them. The user only sees the text from the first string array `flight_sort_options`.

As we said earlier, the Android framework also takes care of persisting preferences. For example, when the user selects a sort option, Android stores the selection in an XML file within the application's `/data` directory (see Figure 9–2).

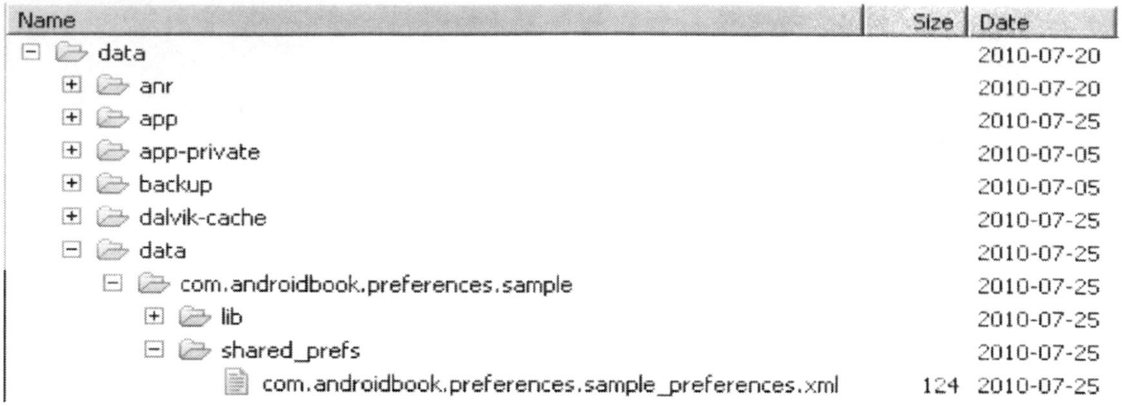

Name	Size	Date
data		2010-07-20
anr		2010-07-20
app		2010-07-25
app-private		2010-07-05
backup		2010-07-05
dalvik-cache		2010-07-25
data		2010-07-25
com.androidbook.preferences.sample		2010-07-25
lib		2010-07-25
shared_prefs		2010-07-25
com.androidbook.preferences.sample_preferences.xml	124	2010-07-25

Figure 9–2. *Path to an application's saved preferences*

The actual file path is `/data/data/[PACKAGE_NAME]/shared_prefs/[PACKAGE_NAME]_preferences.xml`. Listing 9–3 shows the `com.androidbook.preferences.sample_preferences.xml` file for our example.

Listing 9–3. *Saved Preferences for Our Example*

```
<?xml version='1.0' encoding='utf-8' standalone='yes' ?>
<map>
    <string name="selected_flight_sort_option">1</string>
</map>
```

You can see that for a list preference, the preferences framework persists the selected item's value using the list's key attribute. Note also that the selected item's *value* is stored—not the text. A word of caution here: because the preferences XML file is only storing the value and not the text, should you ever upgrade your application and change the text of the options or add items to the string arrays, any value stored in the preferences XML file should still line up with the appropriate text after the upgrade. The preferences XML file is kept during the application upgrade. If the preferences XML file had a "1" in it, and that meant "# of Stops" before the upgrade, it should still mean "# of Stops" after the upgrade.

The next file we touched was `/res/values/strings.xml`. We added several strings for our titles, summaries, and menu items. There are two strings to pay particular attention to. The first is `flight_sort_option_default_value`. We set the default value to `1` to represent "# of Stops" in our example. It is usually a good idea to choose a default value for each option. If you don't choose a default value and no value has yet been chosen, the methods that return the value of the option will return `null`. Your code would have to deal with null values in this case. The other interesting string is `selected_flight_sort_option`. Strictly speaking, the user is not going to see this string, so we don't need to put it inside of `strings.xml` to provide alternate text for other languages. However, because this string value is a key used in the method call to retrieve the value, by creating an ID out of it, we can ensure at compile time that we didn't make a typographical error on the key's name.

The third file we added was /res/menu/mainmenu.xml. We're assuming that you'd like to access the preferences view through a menu and not through a button. This file represents our application's menu.

The fourth file we touched was /res/layout/main.xml. This is our main UI for this application. So far, we've covered how to maintain the preferences, through the use of a special activity class PreferenceActivity. But you want to use preferences in your main activity, not a PreferenceActivity. Therefore, we need a way to get to the preferences from another activity. For this example, the layout is a simple TextView to display the current value of our flight preferences option.

Next up is the source code for our MainActivity. This is a basic activity that gets a reference to the preferences and a handle to the TextView and then calls a method to read the current value of our option to set it into the TextView. We set up our menu and the menu callback. Within the menu callback, we launch an Intent for the FlightPreferenceActivity. Launching an intent for our preferences is the best way to get to the preferences screen. You could use a menu or use a button to fire the intent. We'll not repeat this code for later examples, but you would do the same thing with them, except that you'd use the appropriate activity class name. When the preferences Intent returns to us, we call the setOptionText() method to update our TextView.

There are two ways to get a handle to the preferences:

- The easiest is what we show in the example, that is, to call PreferenceManager.getDefaultSharedPreferences(this). The this argument is the context for finding the default shared preferences, and the method will use the package name of this to determine the file name and location of the preferences file, which happens to be the one created by our PreferenceActivity, since they share the same package name.
- The other way to get a handle to a preferences file is to use the getSharedPreferences() method call, passing in a file name argument as well as a mode argument. In Listing 9–2, we show this way, but it's been commented out. Notice that you only specify the base part of the file name, not the path and not the file name extension. The mode argument controls permissions to our XML preferences file. In our preceding example, the mode argument wouldn't affect anything because the file is only created within the PreferenceActivity, which sets the default permissions of MODE_PRIVATE (i.e., zero). We'll discuss the mode argument later in the sections on saving state.

Inside of setOptionText(), with a reference to the preferences, you call the appropriate methods to retrieve the preference values. In our example, we call getString(), because we know we're retrieving a string value from the preferences. The first argument is the string value of the option key. We noted before that using an ID ensures that we haven't made any typographical errors while building our application. We could also have simply used the string "selected_flight_sort_option" for the first argument, which you might want to do because you want to keep applications as small and fast as possible. For the second argument, you specify a default value in case the value can't be found in the preferences XML file. When your application runs for the very first time, you don't have a preferences XML file, so without specifying a value for the second argument, you'll always get null the first time. This is true even though you've specified a default value for the option in the ListPreference specification in flightoptions.xml. In our example, we set a default value in XML, and we used a resource ID to do it, so the code in setOptionText() can be used to read the value of the resource ID for the default value. Note that if we had not used an ID for the default value, it would be a lot tougher to read it directly from the ListPreference. By sharing a resource ID between the XML and our code, we have only one place in which to change the default value (that is, in strings.xml).

In addition to displaying the value of the preference, we also display the text of the preference. We're taking a shortcut in our example, because we used array indices for the values in flight_sort_options_values. By simply converting the value to an int, we know which string to read from flight_sort_options. Had we used some other set of values for flight_sort_options_values, we would need to determine the index of the element that is our preference and then turn around and use that index to grab the text of our preference from flight_sort_options.

The final file to be touched for our example is AndroidManifest.xml. Because we now have two activities in our application, we need two activity tags. The first one is a standard activity of category LAUNCHER. The second one is for a PreferenceActivity, so we set the action name according to convention for intents, and we set the category to PREFERENCE. We probably don't want the PreferenceActivity showing up on the Android page with all our other applications, which is why we chose not to use LAUNCHER for it. You would need to make similar changes to AndroidManifest.xml if you were to add other preferences screens.

We showed one way to read a default value for a preference in code. Android provides another way that is a bit more elegant. In onCreate(), we could have done the following instead:

```
PreferenceManager.setDefaultValues(this, R.xml.flightoptions, false);
```

Then in setOptionText(), we could have done this to read the option value:

```
String option = prefs.getString(
        resources.getString(R.string.selected_flight_sort_option), null);
```

The first call will use flightoptions.xml to find the default values and generate the preferences XML file for us using the default values. If we already have an instance of the SharedPreferences object in memory, it will update that too. The second call will then find a value for selected_flight_sort_option, because we took care of loading defaults first.

After running this code the first time, if you look in the shared_prefs folder, you will see the preferences XML file even if the preferences screen has not yet been invoked. You will also see another file called _has_set_default_values.xml. This tells your application that the preferences XML file has already been created with the default values. The third argument to setDefaultValues(), that is, false, indicates that you only want the defaults set in the preferences XML file if it hasn't been done before. If you choose `true` instead, you'll always reset the preferences XML file with default values. Android remembers this information through the existence of this new XML file. If the user has selected new preference values, and you choose `false` for the third argument, the user preferences won't be overwritten the next time this code runs. Notice that now we don't need to provide a default value in the `getString()` method call, since we should always get a value from the preferences XML file.

If you need a reference to the preferences from inside of an activity that extends `PreferenceActivity`, you could do it this way:

```
SharedPreferences prefs = getPreferenceManager().getDefaultSharedPreferences(this);
```

We showed you how to use the `ListPreference` view; now, let's examine the other UI elements within the Android preferences framework. Namely, let's talk about the `CheckBoxPreference` view, the `EditTextPreference` view, and the `RingtonePreference` view.

Understanding CheckBoxPreference

You saw that the `ListPreference` preference displays a list as its UI element. Similarly, the `CheckBoxPreference` preference displays a check box widget as its UI element.

To extend the flight search example application, suppose you want to let the user set the list of columns to see in the result set. This preference displays the available columns and allows the user to choose the desired columns by marking the corresponding check boxes. The user interface for this example is shown in Figure 9–3, and the preferences XML file is shown in Listing 9–4.

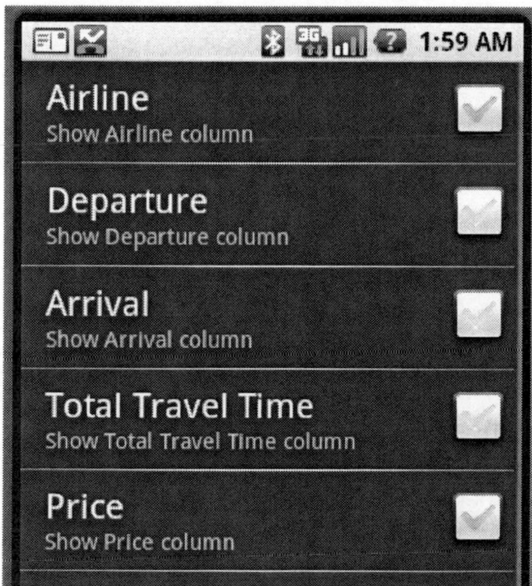

Figure 9–3. *The user interface for the check box preference*

Listing 9–4. *Using CheckBoxPreference*

```
<?xml version="1.0" encoding="utf-8"?>
<!-- This file is /res/xml/chkbox.xml -->
    <PreferenceScreen
        xmlns:android="http://schemas.android.com/apk/res/android"
                android:key="flight_columns_pref"
                android:title="Flight Search Preferences"
                android:summary="Set Columns for Search Results">
        <CheckBoxPreference
                android:key="show_airline_column_pref"
                android:title="Airline"
                android:summary="Show Airline column" />
        <CheckBoxPreference
                android:key="show_departure_column_pref"
                android:title="Departure"
                android:summary="Show Departure column" />
        <CheckBoxPreference
                android:key="show_arrival_column_pref"
                android:title="Arrival"
                android:summary="Show Arrival column" />
         <CheckBoxPreference
                android:key="show_total_travel_time_column_pref"
                android:title="Total Travel Time"
                android:summary="Show Total Travel Time column" />
        <CheckBoxPreference
                android:key="show_price_column_pref"
                android:title="Price"
                android:summary="Show Price column" />

</PreferenceScreen>


// CheckBoxPreferenceActivity.java


import android.os.Bundle;
import android.preference.PreferenceActivity;

public class CheckBoxPreferenceActivity extends PreferenceActivity
{
    @Override
    protected void onCreate(Bundle savedInstanceState) {
        super.onCreate(savedInstanceState);
        addPreferencesFromResource(R.xml.chkbox);
    }
}
```

Listing 9–4 shows the preferences XML file, `chkbox.xml`, and a simple activity class that loads it using `addPreferencesFromResource()`. As you can see, the UI has five check boxes, each of which is represented by a `CheckBoxPreference` node in the preferences XML file. Each of the check boxes also has a key, which—as you would expect—is ultimately used to persist the state of the UI element when it comes time to save the selected preference. With `CheckBoxPreference`, the state of the preference is saved when the user sets the state. In other words, when the user checks or unchecks the preference control, its state is saved. Listing 9–5 shows the preference data store for this example.

Listing 9–5. *The Preferences Data Store for the Check Box Preference*

```
<?xml version='1.0' encoding='utf-8' standalone='yes' ?>
<map>
    <boolean name="show_total_travel_time_column_pref" value="false" />
    <boolean name="show_price_column_pref" value="true" />
    <boolean name="show_arrival_column_pref" value="false" />
    <boolean name="show_airline_column_pref" value="true" />
    <boolean name="show_departure_column_pref" value="false" />
</map>
```

Again, you can see that each preference is saved through its key attribute. The data type of the CheckBoxPreference is a boolean, which contains a value of either true or false: true to indicate the preference is selected, and false to indicate otherwise. To read the value of one of the check box preferences, you would get access to the shared preferences and call the getBoolean() method, passing the key of the preference:

```
boolean option = prefs.getBoolean("show_price_column_pref", false);
```

One other useful feature of CheckBoxPreference is that you can set different summary text depending on whether or not it's checked. The XML attributes are summaryOn and summaryOff. Now, let's have a look at the EditTextPreference.

Understanding EditTextPreference

The preferences framework also provides a free-form text preference called EditTextPreference. This preference allows you to capture raw text rather than ask the user to make a selection. To demonstrate this, let's assume you have an application that generates Java code for the user. One of the preference settings of this application might be the default package name to use for the generated classes. Here, you want to display a text field to the user for setting the package name for the generated classes. Figure 9–4 shows the UI, and Listing 9–6 shows the XML.

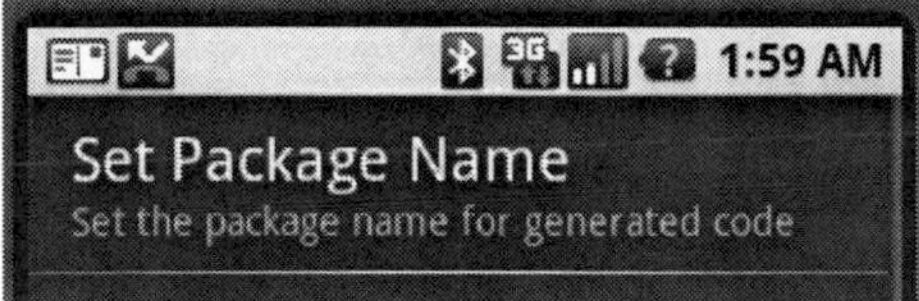

Figure 9–4. *Using the EditTextPreference*

Listing 9–6. *An Example of an EditTextPreference*

```
<?xml version="1.0" encoding="utf-8"?>
<!-- This file is /res/xml/packagepref.xml -->
<PreferenceScreen
        xmlns:android="http://schemas.android.com/apk/res/android"
                android:key="package_name_screen"
                android:title="Package Name"
                android:summary="Set package name">

        <EditTextPreference
                android:key="package_name_preference"
                android:title="Set Package Name"
                android:summary="Set the package name for generated code"
                android:dialogTitle="Package Name" />

</PreferenceScreen>

// EditTextPreferenceActivity.java

import android.os.Bundle;
import android.preference.PreferenceActivity;

public class EditTextPreferenceActivity extends PreferenceActivity{

    @Override
    protected void onCreate(Bundle savedInstanceState) {
        super.onCreate(savedInstanceState);

        addPreferencesFromResource(R.xml.packagepref);
    }
}
```

You can see that Listing 9–6 defines `PreferenceScreen` with a single `EditTextPreference` instance as a child. The generated UI for the listing features the `PreferenceScreen` on the left and the `EditTextPreference` on the right (see Figure 9–4). When Set Package Name is selected, the user is presented with a dialog to input the package name. When the OK button is clicked, the preference is saved to the preference store.

As with the other preferences, you can obtain the `EditTextPreference` from your activity class by using the preference's key. Once you have the `EditTextPreference`, you can manipulate the actual `EditText` by calling `getEditText()`—if, for example, you want to apply validation, preprocessing, or postprocessing on the value that the user types in the text field. To get the text of the `EditTextPreference`, just use the `getText()` method.

Now, let's look at the preferences framework's `RingtonePreference`.

Understanding RingtonePreference

`RingtonePreference` deals specifically with ringtones. You'd use it in an application that gives the user an option to select a ringtone as a preference. Figure 9–5 shows the UI of the `RingtonePreference` example, and Listing 9–7 shows the XML.

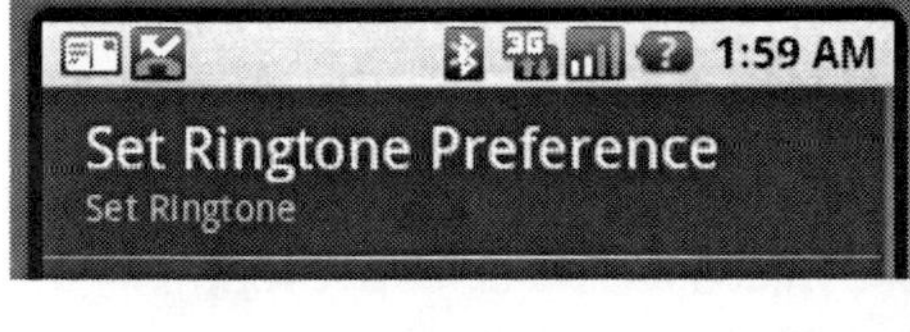

Figure 9–5. *The RingtonePreference example UI*

Listing 9–7. *Defining a RingtonePreference Preference*

```
<?xml version="1.0" encoding="utf-8"?>
<!-- This file is /res/xml/ringtone.xml -->
<PreferenceScreen
        xmlns:android="http://schemas.android.com/apk/res/android"
                android:key="ringtone_option_preference"
                android:title="My Preferences"
                android:summary="Set Ring Tone Preferences">
    <RingtonePreference
        android:key="ring_tone_pref"
        android:title="Set Ringtone Preference"
        android:showSilent="true"
        android:ringtoneType="alarm"
        android:summary="Set Ringtone" />
</PreferenceScreen>

// RingtonePreferenceActivity.java

import android.os.Bundle;
import android.preference.PreferenceActivity;

public class RingtonePreferenceActivity extends PreferenceActivity
{
    @Override
    protected void onCreate(Bundle savedInstanceState) {
        super.onCreate(savedInstanceState);
        addPreferencesFromResource(R.xml.ringtone);
    }
}
```

When the user selects Set Ringtone Preference, the preferences framework displays a ListPreference containing the ringtones on the device (see Figure 9–5). The user can select a ringtone and then choose OK or Cancel. If OK is clicked, the selection is persisted to the preference store. Note that, with the ringtones, the value stored in the preference store is the URI of the selected ringtone—unless a user selects Silent, in which case the stored value is an empty string. An example URI looks like this:

```
<string name="ring_tone_pref">content://media/internal/audio/media/26</string>
```

NOTE: If the emulator is short on ringtones, you can add some yourself. Copy music files to your SD card. Then, go to the Android Music Player application and choose a music file. Click the Menu button, and click "Use as ringtone". We'll be teaching you how to copy files to the SD card in Chapter 19.

Finally, the RingtonePreference shown in Listing 9–7 follows the same pattern as the other preferences you've defined thus far. The difference here is that you set a few different attributes, including showSilent and ringtoneType. You can use showSilent to include the silent ringtone in the ringtone list and ringtoneType to restrict the types of ringtones displayed in the list. Possible values for this property include ringtone, notification, alarm, and all.

Organizing Preferences

The preferences framework provides some support for you to organize your preferences into categories. If you have a lot of preferences, for example, you can build a view that shows high-level categories of preferences. Users could then drill down into each category to view and manage preferences specific to that group.

You can implement something like this in one of two ways. You can introduce nested PreferenceScreen elements within the root PreferenceScreen, or you can use PreferenceCategory elements to get a similar result. Figure 9–6 and Listing 9–8 show how to implement the first technique, grouping preferences by using nested PreferenceScreen elements.

The view on the left of Figure 9–6 displays two preference screens, one with the title Meats and the other with the title Vegetables. Clicking a group takes you to the preferences within that group. Listing 9–8 shows how to create nested screens.

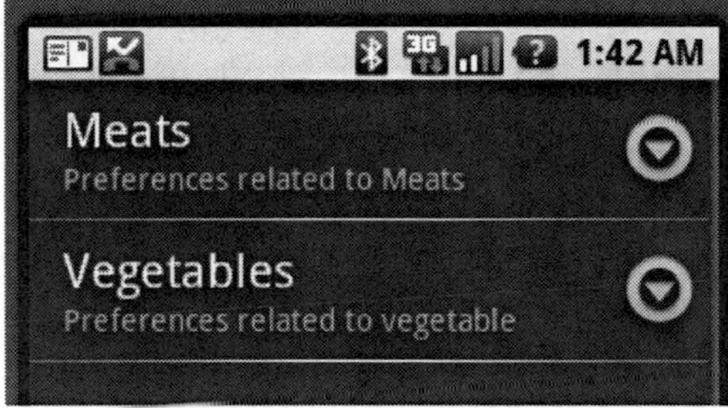

Figure 9–6. *Creating groups of preferences by nesting PreferenceScreen elements*

Listing 9–8. *Nesting PreferenceScreen Elements to Organize Preferences*

```
<?xml version="1.0" encoding="utf-8"?>
<PreferenceScreen
        xmlns:android="http://schemas.android.com/apk/res/android"
                android:key="using_categories_in_root_screen"
                android:title="Categories"
                android:summary="Using Preference Categories">

    <PreferenceScreen
        xmlns:android="http://schemas.android.com/apk/res/android"
                android:key="meats_screen"
                android:title="Meats"
                android:summary="Preferences related to Meats">

        <CheckBoxPreference
                android:key="fish_selection_pref"
                android:title="Fish"
                android:summary="Fish is great for the healthy" />
        <CheckBoxPreference
                android:key="chicken_selection_pref"
                android:title="Chicken"
                android:summary="A common type of poultry" />
        <CheckBoxPreference
                android:key="lamb_selection_pref"
                android:title="Lamb"
                android:summary="Lamb is a young sheep" />

    </PreferenceScreen>
    <PreferenceScreen
```

```
        xmlns:android="http://schemas.android.com/apk/res/android"
                android:key="vegi_screen"
                android:title="Vegetables"
                android:summary="Preferences related to vegetable">
        <CheckBoxPreference
                android:key="tomato_selection_pref"
                android:title="Tomato "
                android:summary="It's actually a fruit" />
        <CheckBoxPreference
                android:key="potato_selection_pref"
                android:title="Potato"
                android:summary="My favorite vegetable" />

    </PreferenceScreen>

</PreferenceScreen>
```

You create the groups in Figure 9–6 by nesting `PreferenceScreen` elements within the root `PreferenceScreen`. Organizing preferences this way is useful if you have a lot of preferences and you're concerned about having the users scroll to find the preference they are looking for. If you don't have a lot of preferences but still want to provide high-level categories for your preferences, you can use `PreferenceCategory`, which is the second technique we mentioned. Figure 9–7 and Listing 9–9 show the details.

Figure 9–7. *Using PreferenceCategory to organize preferences*

Figure 9–7 shows the same groups we used in our previous example, but now organized with preference categories. The only difference between the XML in Listing 9–9 and the XML in Listing 9–8 is that you create a `PreferenceCategory` for the nested screens rather than nest `PreferenceScreen` elements.

Listing 9–9. *Creating Categories of Preferences*

```
<?xml version="1.0" encoding="utf-8"?>
<PreferenceScreen
        xmlns:android="http://schemas.android.com/apk/res/android"
                android:key="using_categories_in_root_screen"
                android:title="Categories"
                android:summary="Using Preference Categories">

    <PreferenceCategory
        xmlns:android="http://schemas.android.com/apk/res/android"
                android:key="meats_category"
                android:title="Meats"
                android:summary="Preferences related to Meats">

        <CheckBoxPreference
                android:key="fish_selection_pref"
                android:title="Fish"
                android:summary="Fish is great for the healthy" />
        <CheckBoxPreference
                android:key="chicken_selection_pref"
                android:title="Chicken"
                android:summary="A common type of poultry" />
        <CheckBoxPreference
                android:key="lamb_selection_pref"
                android:title="Lamb"
                android:summary="Lamb is a young sheep" />

    </PreferenceCategory>
    <PreferenceCategory
        xmlns:android="http://schemas.android.com/apk/res/android"
                android:key="vegi_category"
                android:title="Vegetables"
                android:summary="Preferences related to vegetable">
        <CheckBoxPreference
                android:key="tomato_selection_pref"
                android:title="Tomato "
                android:summary="It's actually a fruit" />
        <CheckBoxPreference
                android:key="potato_selection_pref"
                android:title="Potato"
                android:summary="My favorite vegetable" />

    </PreferenceCategory>

</PreferenceScreen>
```

Manipulating Preferences Programmatically

It goes without saying that you might need to access the actual preference controls programmatically. For example, what if you need to provide the `entries` and `entryValues` for the `ListPreference` at runtime? You can define and access preference controls similarly to the way you define and access controls in layout files and activities. For example, to access the list preference defined in Listing 9–1, you would call the `findPreference()` method of `PreferenceActivity`, passing the preference's key (note the similarity to findViewById()). You would next cast the control to ListPreference and then go about manipulating the control. For example, if you want to set the entries of the ListPreference view, call the setEntries() method, and so on. Listing 9–10 shows what this might look like with a simple example of using code to setup the preference.

Listing 9–10. *Setting ListPreference Values Programmatically*

```
public class FlightPreferenceActivity extends PreferenceActivity
{
    @Override
    protected void onCreate(Bundle savedInstanceState) {
        super.onCreate(savedInstanceState);
        addPreferencesFromResource(R.xml.flightoptions);

        ListPreference listpref = (ListPreference) findPreference(
                                                "selected_flight_sort_option");

        listpref.setEntryValues(new String[] {"0","1","2"});
        listpref.setEntries(new String[] {"Food", "Lounge", "Frequent Flier Program"});
    }
}
```

Saving State with Preferences

Preferences are great for allowing users to customize applications to their liking, but we can use the Android preference framework for more than that. When your application needs to keep track of some data between invocations of the application, preferences are one way to accomplish the task. We've already talked about content providers for maintaining data. We could use custom files on the SD card. We can also use preference files and code.

The Activity class has a getPreferences(int mode) method. This, in reality, simply calls getSharedPreferences() with the class name of the activity as the tag plus the mode as passed in. The result is an activity-specific preferences file that you can use to store data about this activity across invocations. A simple example of how you could use this is in Listing 9–11.

Listing 9–11. *Using Preferences to Save State for an Activity*

```
        final String INITIALIZED = "initialized";
        SharedPreferences myPrefs = getPreferences(MODE_PRIVATE);

        boolean hasPreferences = myPrefs.getBoolean(INITIALIZED, false);
        if(hasPreferences) {
                Log.v("Preferences", "We've been called before");
                // Read other values as desired from preferences file...
                someString = myPrefs.getString("someString", "");
        }
        else {
                Log.v("Preferences", "First time ever being called");
                // Set up initial values for what will end up
                // in the preferences file
                someString = "some default value";
        }
```

```
// Later when ready to write out values
Editor editor = myPrefs.edit();
editor.putBoolean(INITIALIZED, true);
editor.putString("someString", someString);
// Write other values as desired
editor.commit();
```

What this code does is acquire a reference to preferences for our activity class and check for the existence of a boolean "preference" called `initialized`. We write "preference" in double quotation marks because this value is not something the user is going to see or set; it's merely a value that we want to store in a preferences file for use next time. If we get a value, the preferences file exists, so our application must have been called before. We could then read other values out of the preferences file.

To write values to the preferences file, we must first get a preferences `Editor`. We can then put values into preferences and commit those changes when we're finished. Note that, behind the scenes, Android is managing a `SharedPreferences` object that is truly shared. Ideally, there is never more than one `Editor` active at a time. But it is very important to call the `commit()` method so that the `SharedPreferences` object and the preferences XML file get updated.

You can access, write, and commit values anytime to your preferences file. Possible uses for this include writing out high scores for a game or recording when the application was last run. You can also use the `getSharedPreferences()` call with different names to manage separate sets of preferences, all within the same application or even the same activity.

We've used `MODE_PRIVATE` for mode in our examples thus far. The other possible values of mode are `MODE_WORLD_READABLE` and `MODE_WORLD_WRITEABLE`. These modes are used when creating the preferences XML file to set the file permissions accordingly. Because the preferences files are stored within your application's data directory, and therefore not accessible to other applications, you only need to use `MODE_PRIVATE`.

Reference

Here is a helpful reference to a topic you may wish to explore further.

- `http://www.androidbook.com/projects`. Look here for a list of downloadable projects related to this book. For this chapter look for a ZIP file called ProAndroid3_Ch09_Preferences.zip. This ZIP file contains all projects from this chapter, listed in separate root directories. There is also a README.TXT file that describes exactly how to import projects into Eclipse from one of these ZIP files.

Summary

In this chapter, we talked about managing preferences in Android. We showed you how to use `ListPreference`, `CheckBoxPreference`, `EditTextPreference`, and `RingtonePreference`. We also talked about how to organize preferences into groups and programmatically manipulate preferences. Last, we showed you how to use the preferences framework to save and restore information from an activity across invocations.

Chapter 10

Exploring Security and Permissions

In this chapter, we are going to talk about Android's application-security model, which is a fundamental part of the Android platform. In Android, security spans all phases of the application life cycle—from design-time policy considerations to runtime boundary checks. You'll learn Android's security architecture and understand how to design secure applications.

Let's get started with the Android security model.

Understanding the Android Security Model

In this first section, we're going to cover security during the deployment and execution of the application. With respect to deployment, Android applications have to be signed with a digital certificate in order for you to install them onto a device. With respect to execution, Android runs each application within a separate process, each of which has a unique and permanent user ID (assigned at install time). This places a boundary around the process and prevents one application from having direct access to another's data. Moreover, Android defines a declarative permission model that protects sensitive features (such as the contact list).

In the next several sections, we are going to discuss these topics. But before we get started, let's provide an overview of some of the security concepts that we'll refer to later.

Overview of Security Concepts

Android requires that applications be signed with a digital certificate. One of the benefits of this requirement is that an application cannot be updated with a version that was not published by the original author. If we publish an application, for example, then you cannot update our application with your version (unless, of course, you somehow obtain our certificate). That said, what does it mean for an application to be signed? And what is the process of signing an application?

You sign an application with a digital certificate. A *digital certificate* is an artifact that contains information about you, such as your company name, address, and so on. A few important attributes of a digital certificate include its signature and public/private key. A public/private key is also called a *key pair*. Note that although you use digital certificates here to sign `.apk` files, you can also use them for other purposes (such as encrypted communication). You can obtain a digital certificate from a trusted certificate authority (CA) and you can also generate one yourself using tools such as the `keytool`, which we'll discuss shortly. Digital certificates are stored in keystores. A *keystore* contains a list of digital certificates, each of which has an alias that you can use to refer to it in the keystore.

Signing an Android application requires three things: a digital certificate, an `.apk` file, and a utility that knows how to apply a digital signature to the `.apk` file. As you'll see, we use a free utility that is part of the Java Development Kit (JDK) distribution called the `jarsigner`. This utility is a command-line tool that knows how to sign a `.jar` file using a digital certificate.

Now, let's move on and talk about how you can sign an `.apk` file with a digital certificate.

Signing Applications for Deployment

To install an Android application onto a device, you first need to sign the Android package (`.apk` file) using a digital certificate. The certificate, however, can be self-signed—you do not need to purchase a certificate from a certificate authority such as VeriSign.

Signing your application for deployment involves three steps. The first step is to generate a certificate using `keytool` (or a similar tool). The second step involves using the `jarsigner` tool to sign the `.apk` file with the generated certificate. The third step aligns portions of your application on memory boundaries for more efficient memory usage when running on a device. Note that during development, the ADT plug-in for Eclipse takes care of everything for you: signing your `.apk` file and doing the memory alignment, before deploying onto the emulator or a device.

Generating a Self-Signed Certificate Using the Keytool

The `keytool` utility manages a database of private keys and their corresponding X.509 certificates (a standard for digital certificates). This utility ships with the JDK and resides under the JDK `bin` directory. If you followed the instructions in Chapter 2 regarding changing your `PATH`, the JDK `bin` directory should already be in your `PATH`.

In this section, we'll show you how to generate a keystore with a single entry, which you'll later use to sign an Android `.apk` file. To generate a keystore entry, do the following:

1. Create a folder to hold the keystore, for example `c:\android\release\`.
2. Open a tools window, and execute the `keytool` utility with the parameters shown in Listing 10–1 (see Chapter 2 for details of what we mean by a "tools window").

Listing 10–1. *Generating a Keystore Entry Using the keytool Utility*

```
keytool -genkey -v -keystore "c:\android\release\release.keystore"
-alias androidbook -storepass paxxword -keypass paxxword -keyalg RSA
-validity 14000
```

All of the arguments passed to the `keytool` are summarized in Table 10–1.

Table 10–1. *Arguments Passed to the keytool Utility*

Argument	Description
`genkey`	Tells `keytool` to generate a public/private key pair.
`v`	Tells `keytool` to emit verbose output during key generation.
`keystore`	Path to the keystore database (in this case, a file). The file will be created if necessary.
`alias`	A unique name for the keystore entry. This alias is used later to refer to the keystore entry.
`storepass`	The password for the keystore.
`keypass`	The password used to access the private key.
`keyalg`	The algorithm.
`validity`	The validity period.

`keytool` will prompt you for the passwords listed in Table 10–1 if you do not provide them on the command line. If you are not the sole user of your computer, it would be safer to not specify `-storepass` and `-keypass` on the command line, but rather type them in when prompted by `keytool`. The command in Listing 10–1 will generate a keystore database file in your keystore folder. The database will be a file named `release.keystore`. The `validity` of the entry will be 14,000 days (or approximately 38 years)—which is a long time from now. You should understand the reason for this. The Android documentation recommends that you specify a validity period long enough to surpass the entire lifespan of the application, which will include many updates to the application. It recommends that the validity be at least 25 years. Moreover, if you plan to publish the application on Android Market (`http://www.android.com/market/`), your certificate will need to be valid through at least October 22, 2033. Android Market checks each application when uploaded to make sure it will be valid at least until then. Because your updates must match what you used in the beginning, make sure you safeguard your keystore file! If you lose it and you can't re-create it, you won't be able to update your application, and you'll have to issue a whole new application instead.

Going back to the keytool, the argument alias is a unique name given to the entry in the keystore database; you will use this name later to refer to the entry. When you run the keytool command in Listing 10–1, keytool will ask you a few questions (see Figure 10–1) and then generate the keystore database and entry.

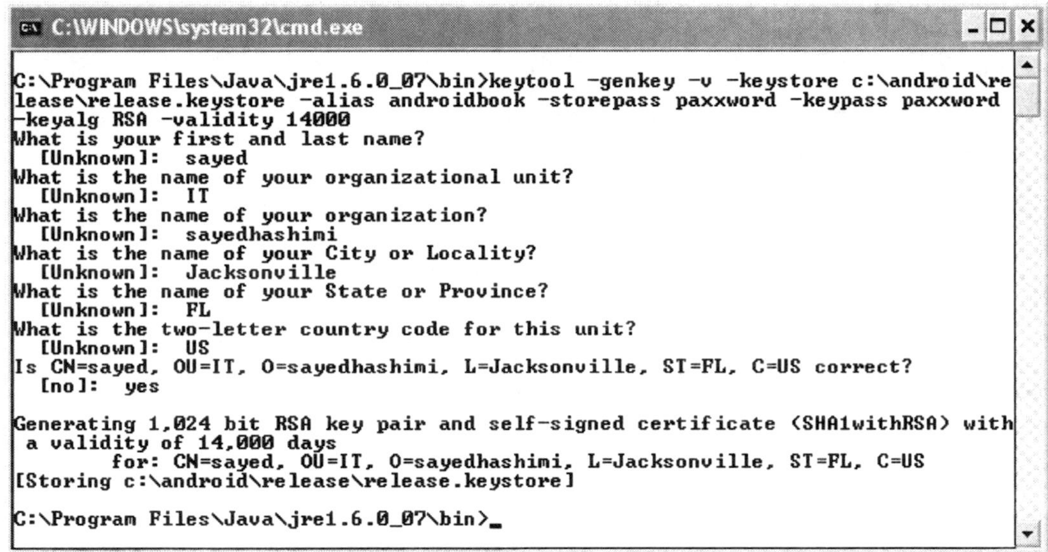

Figure 10–1. *Additional questions asked by keytool*

Once you have a keystore file for your production certificates, you can reuse this file to add more certificates. Just use keytool again and specify your existing keystore file.

The Debug Keystore and the Development Certificate

We mentioned that the ADT plug-in for Eclipse takes care of setting up a development keystore for you. However, the default certificate used for signing during development cannot be used for production deployment onto a real device. This is partly because the ADT–generated development certificate is only valid for 365 days, which clearly does not get you past October 22, 2033. So what happens on the three hundred sixty-sixth day of development? You'll get a build error. Your existing applications should still run, but to build a new version of an application, you need to generate a new certificate. The easiest way to do this is to delete the existing debug.keystore file, and as soon as it is needed again, the ADT will generate a new file and certificate valid for another 365 days.

To find your debug.keystore file, open the Preferences screen of Eclipse and go to Android ➤ Build. The debug certificate's location will be displayed in the "Default debug keystore" field, as shown in Figure 10–2 (see Chapter 2 if you have trouble finding the Preferences menu).

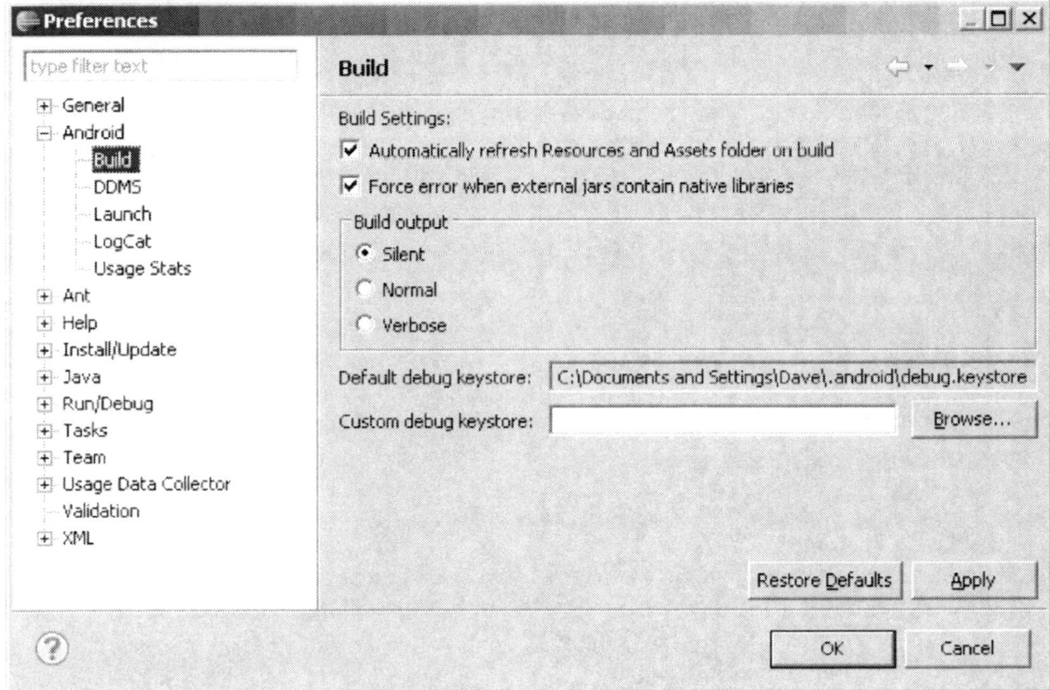

Figure 10–2. ***The debug certificate's location***

Of course, now that you've got a new development certificate, you cannot update your existing applications in AVDs or on devices using a new development certificate. Eclipse will provide messages in the Console telling you to uninstall the existing application first using `adb`, which you can certainly do. If you have a lot of your applications installed onto an AVD, you may feel it is easier to simply re-create the AVD, so it does not contain any of your applications and you can start fresh. To avoid this problem a year from now, you could generate your own `debug.keystore` file with whatever validity period you desire. Obviously, it needs to have the same file name and be in the same directory as the file that ADT would create. The certificate alias is `androiddebugkey` and the `storepass` and `keypass` are both `"android"`. ADT sets the first and last name on the certificate as `"Android Debug"`, the organizational unit as `"Android"` and the two-letter country code as `"US"`. You can leave the organization, city, and state values as `"Unknown"`.

If you acquired a `map-api` key from Google using the old debug certificate, you will need to get a new `map-api` key to match the new debug certificate. We'll cover `map-api` keys in Chapter 17.

Now that you have a digital certificate that you can use to sign your production `.apk` file, you need to use the `jarsigner` tool to do the signing. Here's how to do that.

Using the Jarsigner Tool to Sign the .apk File

The `keytool` utility described in the previous section created a digital certificate, which is one of the parameters for the `jarsigner` tool. The other parameter for `jarsigner` is the actual Android package to be signed. To generate an Android package, you need to use the Export Unsigned Application Package utility in the ADT plug-in for Eclipse. You access the utility by right-clicking an Android project in Eclipse, selecting Android Tools, and selecting Export Unsigned Application Package. Running the Export Unsigned Application Package utility will generate an `.apk` file that will not be signed with the debug certificate. To see how this works, run the Export Unsigned Application Package utility on one of your Android projects and store the generated `.apk` file somewhere. For this example, we'll use the keystore folder we created earlier, and generate an `.apk` file called `c:\android\release\myappraw.apk`.

With the `.apk` file and the keystore entry, run the `jarsigner` tool to sign the `.apk` file (see Listing 10–2). Use the full path names to your keystore file and `.apk` file as appropriate when you run this.

Listing 10–2. *Using jarsigner to Sign the .apk File*

```
jarsigner -keystore "PATH TO YOUR release.keystore FILE" -storepass paxxword
-keypass paxxword  "PATH TO YOUR RAW APK FILE" androidbook
```

To sign the `.apk` file, you pass the location of the keystore, the keystore password, the private-key password, the path to the `.apk` file, and the alias for the keystore entry. The `jarsigner` will then sign the `.apk` file with the digital certificate from the keystore entry. To run the `jarsigner` tool, you will need to either open a tools window (as explained in Chapter 2) or open a command or Terminal window and either navigate to the JDK `bin` directory or ensure that your JDK `bin` directory is on the system path. For security reasons, it is safer to leave off the password arguments to the command, and simply let `jarsigner` prompt you as necessary for passwords. Figure 10–3 shows what the `jarsigner` tool invocation looks like.

As we pointed out earlier, Android requires that an application be signed with a digital signature to prevent a malicious programmer from updating your application with his version. For this to work, Android requires that updates to an application be signed with the same signature as the original. If you sign the application with a different signature, Android treats them as two different applications. So we remind you again, be careful with your keystore file so it's available to you later when you need to provide an update to your application.

```
C:\WINDOWS\system32\cmd.exe
08/15/2010  03:44 PM             8,588 weightgravityraw.apk
               8 File(s)         85,001 bytes
               2 Dir(s)  51,236,655,104 bytes free

C:\android\release>jarsigner -keystore "release.keystore" weightgravityraw.apk androidbook
Enter Passphrase for keystore:

C:\android\release>
```

Figure 10–3. *Using jarsigner*

Aligning Your Application with zipalign

You want your application to be as memory efficient as possible when running on a device. If your application contains uncompressed data (perhaps certain image types or data files) at runtime, Android can map this data straight into memory using the `mmap()` call. For this to work, though, the data must be aligned on a 4-byte memory boundary. The CPUs in Android devices are 32-bit processors, and 32 bits equals 4 bytes. The `mmap()` call makes the data in your `.apk` file look like memory, but if the data is not aligned on a 4-byte boundary, it can't do that and extra copying of data must occur at runtime. The `zipalign` tool, found in the Android SDK tools directory, looks through your application and moves slightly any uncompressed data not already on a 4-byte memory boundary to a 4-byte memory boundary. You may see the file size of your application increase slightly but not significantly. To perform an alignment on your `.apk` file, use this command in a tools window (see also Figure 10–4):

```
zipalign -v 4 infile.apk outfile.apk
```

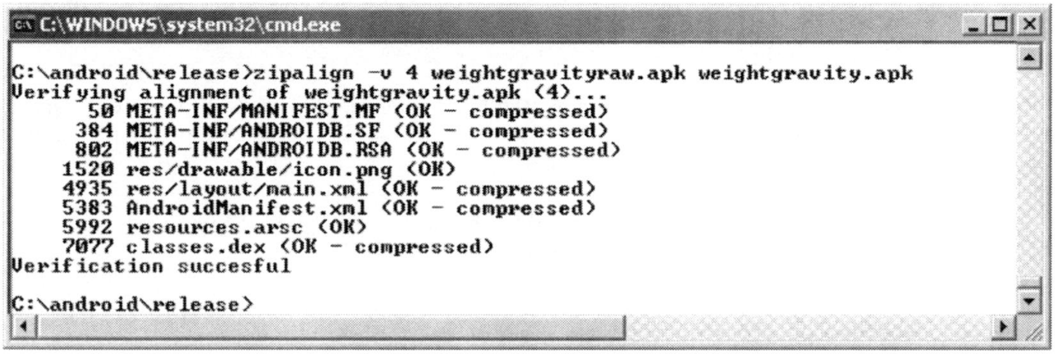

```
C:\WINDOWS\system32\cmd.exe
C:\android\release>zipalign -v 4 weightgravityraw.apk weightgravity.apk
Verifying alignment of weightgravity.apk (4)...
      50 META-INF/MANIFEST.MF (OK - compressed)
     384 META-INF/ANDROIDB.SF (OK - compressed)
     802 META-INF/ANDROIDB.RSA (OK - compressed)
    1520 res/drawable/icon.png (OK)
    4935 res/layout/main.xml (OK - compressed)
    5383 AndroidManifest.xml (OK - compressed)
    5992 resources.arsc (OK)
    7077 classes.dex (OK - compressed)
Verification succesful

C:\android\release>
```

Figure 10–4. *Using zipalign*

Note that `zipalign` does not modify the input file, so this is why we chose to use "raw" as part of our file name when exporting from Eclipse. Now, our output file has an appropriate name for deployment. If you need to overwrite an existing `outfile.apk` file you can use the `-f` option. Also note that `zipalign` performs a verification of the alignment when you create your aligned file. To verify that an existing file is properly aligned, use `zipalign` in the following way:

```
zipalign -c -v 4 filename.apk
```

It is very important that you align *after* signing; otherwise, signing could cause things to go back out of alignment. This does not mean your application would crash, but it could use more memory than it needs to.

In Eclipse, you may have noticed a menu choice under Android Tools called Export Signed Application Package. This launches what is called the export wizard, and it does all of the previous steps for you, prompting only for the path to your keystore file, key alias, the passwords and the name of your output .apk file. It will even create a new keystore or new key if you need one. You may find it easier to use the wizard, or you may prefer to script the steps yourself to operate on an exported unsigned application package. Now that you know how each works, you can decide which is better for you.

Once you have signed and aligned an .apk file, you can install it onto the emulator manually using the adb tool. As an exercise, start the emulator. One way to do this, which we haven't discussed yet, is to go to the Window menu of Eclipse and select Android SDK and AVD Manager. A window will be displayed showing your available AVDs. Select the one you want to use for your emulator and click on the Start button. The emulator will start without copying over any of your development projects from Eclipse. Now, open a tools window, and run the adb tool with the install command:

```
adb install "PATH TO APK FILE GOES HERE"
```

This may fail for a couple of reasons, but the most likely are that the debug version of your application was already installed on the emulator, giving you a certificate error, or the release version of your application was already installed on the emulator, giving you an already exists error. In the first case, you can uninstall the debug application with this command:

```
adb uninstall packagename
```

Note that the argument to uninstall is the application's package name and not the .apk file name. The package name is defined in the AndroidManifest.xml file of the installed application.

For the second case, you can use this command, where -r says to reinstall the application while keeping its data on the device (or emulator):

```
adb install -r "PATH TO APK FILE GOES HERE"
```

Now, let's see how signing affects the process of updating an application.

Installing Updates to an Application and Signing

Earlier, we mentioned that a certificate has an expiration date and that Google recommends you set expiration dates far into the future, to account for a lot of application updates. That said, what happens if the certificate does expire? Would Android still run the application? Fortunately, yes—Android tests the certificate's expiration only at install time. Once your application is installed, it will continue to run even if the certificate expires.

But what about updates? Unfortunately, you will not be able to update the application once the certificate expires. In other words, as Google suggests, you need to make sure the life of the certificate is long enough to support the entire life of the application. If a certificate does expire, Android will not install an update to the application. The only choice left will be for you to create another application—an application with a different package name—and sign it with a new certificate. So as you can see, it is critical for you to consider the expiration date of the certificate when you generate it.

Now that you understand security with respect to deployment and installation, let's move on to runtime security in Android.

Performing Runtime Security Checks

Runtime security in Android happens at the process and operation levels. At the process level, Android prevents one application from directly accessing another application's data. It does this by running each application within a different process and under a unique and permanent user ID. At the operational level, Android defines a list of protected features and resources. For your application to access this information, you have to add one or more permission requests to your `AndroidManifest.xml` file. You can also define custom permissions with your application.

In the sections that follow, we will talk about process-boundary security and how to declare and use predefined permissions. We will also discuss creating custom permissions and enforcing them within your application. Let's start by dissecting Android security at the process boundary.

Understanding Security at the Process Boundary

Unlike your desktop environment, where most of the applications run under the same user ID, each Android application generally runs under its own unique ID. By running each application under a different ID, Android creates an isolation boundary around each process. This prevents one application from directly accessing another application's data.

Although each process has a boundary around it, data sharing between applications is obviously possible but has to be explicit. In other words, to get data from another application, you have to go through the components of that application. For example, you can query a content provider of another application, you can invoke an activity in another application, or—as you'll see in Chapter 11—you can communicate with a service of another application. All of these facilities provide methods for you to share information between applications, but they do so in an explicit manner because you don't directly access the underlying database, files, and so on.

Android's security at the process boundary is clear and simple. Things get interesting when we start talking about protecting resources (such as contact data), features (such as the device's camera), and our own components. To provide this protection, Android defines a permission scheme. Let's dissect that now.

Declaring and Using Permissions

Android defines a permission scheme meant to protect resources and features on the device. For example, applications, by default, cannot access the contacts list, make phone calls, and so on. To protect the user from malicious applications, Android requires applications to request permissions if they need to use a protected feature or resource. As you'll see shortly, permission requests go in the manifest file. At install time, the APK installer either grants or denies the requested permissions based on the signature of the `.apk` file and/or feedback from the user. If permission is not granted, any attempt to execute or access the associated feature will result in a permission failure.

Table 10–2 shows some commonly used features and the permissions they require. Although you are not yet familiar with all the features listed, you will learn about them later (either in this chapter or in subsequent chapters).

Table 10–2. *Features and Resources and the Permissions They Require*

Feature/Resource	Required Permission	Description
Camera	`android.permission.CAMERA`	Enables you to access the device's camera.
Internet	`android.permission.INTERNET`	Enables you to make a network connection.
User's contact data	`android.permission.READ_CONTACTS` `android.permission.WRITE_CONTACTS`	Enables you to read from or write to the user's contact data.
User's calendar data	`android.permission.READ_CALENDAR` `android.permission.WRITE_CALENDAR`	Enables you to read from or write to the user's calendar data.
Record audio	`android.permission.RECORD_AUDIO`	Enables you to record audio.
Wi-Fi location information	`android.permission.ACCESS_COARSE_LOCATION`	Enables you to access coarse-grained location information from Wi-Fi and cell towers.
GPS location information	`android.permission.ACCESS_FINE_LOCATION`	Enables you to access fine-grained location information. This includes GPS location information. It is also sufficient for Wi-Fi and cell towers.
Battery information	`android.permission.BATTERY_STATS`	Enables you to obtain battery-state information.
Bluetooth	`android.permission.BLUETOOTH`	Enables you to connect to paired Bluetooth devices.

For a complete list of permissions, see the following URL:

`http://developer.android.com/reference/android/Manifest.permission.html`

Application developers can request permissions by adding entries to the `AndroidManifest.xml` file. For example, Listing 10–3 asks to access the camera on the device, to read the list of contacts, and to read the calendar.

Listing 10–3. *Permissions in AndroidManifest.xml*

```
<manifest … >
    <application>
        …
    </application>
```

```
    <uses-permission android:name="android.permission.CAMERA" />
    <uses-permission android:name="android.permission.READ_CONTACTS"/>
    <uses-permission android:name="android.permission.READ_CALENDAR" />
</manifest>
```

Note that you can either hard-code permissions in the `AndroidManifest.xml` file or use the manifest editor. The manifest editor is wired up to launch when you open (double-click) the manifest file. The manifest editor contains a drop-down list that has all of the permissions preloaded to prevent you from making a mistake. As shown in Figure 10–5, you can access the permissions list by selecting the Permissions tab in the manifest editor.

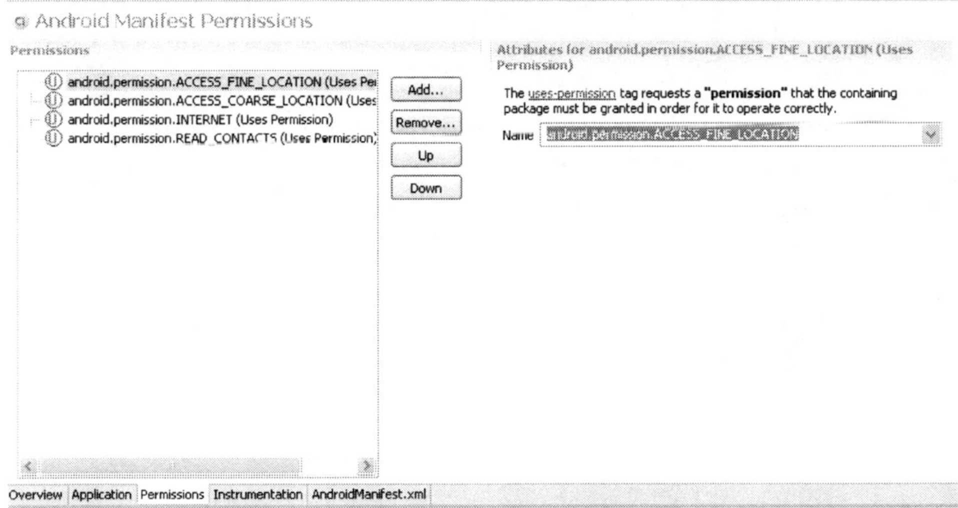

Figure 10–5. *The Android manifest editor tool in Eclipse*

You now know that Android defines a set of permissions that protects a set of features and resources. Similarly, you can define, and enforce, custom permissions with your application. Let's see how that works.

Understanding and Using Custom Permissions

Android allows you to define custom permissions with your application. For example, if you wanted to prevent certain users from starting one of the activities in your application, you could do that by defining a custom permission. To use custom permissions, you first declare them in your `AndroidManifest.xml` file. Once you've defined a permission, you can then refer to it as part of your component definition. We'll show you how this works.

Let's create an application containing an activity that not everyone is allowed to start. Instead, to start the activity, a user must have a specific permission. Once you have the application with a privileged activity, you can write a client that knows how to call the activity.

> **NOTE:** We will give you a URL at the end of the chapter which you can use to download projects of this chapter. This will allow you to import these projects into your Eclipse directly.

First, create the project with the custom permission and activity. Open the Eclipse IDE, and select New ➤ New Project ➤ Android Project. This will open the New Android Project dialog box. Enter **CustomPermission** as the project name, select the "Create new project in workspace" radio button, and mark the "Use default location" check box. Enter **Custom Permission** as the application name, **com.cust.perm** as the package name, **CustPermMainActivity** as the activity name, and select a Build Target. Click the Finish button to create the project. The generated project will have the activity you just created, which will serve as the default (main) activity. Let's also create a *privileged activity*—an activity that requires a special permission. In the Eclipse IDE, go to the `com.cust.perm` package, create a class named **PrivActivity** whose superclass is `android.app.Activity`, and copy the code shown in Listing 10–4.

Listing 10–4. *The PrivActivity Class*

```
package com.cust.perm;

import android.app.Activity;
import android.os.Bundle;
import android.view.ViewGroup.LayoutParams;
import android.widget.LinearLayout;
import android.widget.TextView;

public class PrivActivity extends Activity
{
    @Override
    public void onCreate(Bundle savedInstanceState) {
        super.onCreate(savedInstanceState);
        LinearLayout view = new LinearLayout(this);

        view.setLayoutParams(new LayoutParams(
                LayoutParams.FILL_PARENT, LayoutParams.WRAP_CONTENT));
        view.setOrientation(LinearLayout.HORIZONTAL);

        TextView nameLbl = new TextView(this);

        nameLbl.setText("Hello from PrivActivity");
        view.addView(nameLbl);

        setContentView(view);
    }
}
```

As you can see, `PrivActivity` does not do anything miraculous. We just want to show you how to protect this activity with a permission and then call it from a client. If the client succeeds, you'll see the text "Hello from PrivActivity" on the screen. Now that you have an activity you want to protect, you can create the permission for it.

To create a custom permission, you have to define it in the `AndroidManifest.xml` file. The easiest way to do this is to use the manifest editor. Double-click the

AndroidManifest.xml file, and select the Permissions tab. In the Permissions window, click the Add button, choose Permission, and click the OK button. The manifest editor will create an empty new permission for you. Populate the new permission by setting its attributes as shown in Figure 10–6. Fill in the fields on the right-hand side, and if the label on the left-hand side still says just Permission, click it and it should update with the name from the right-hand side.

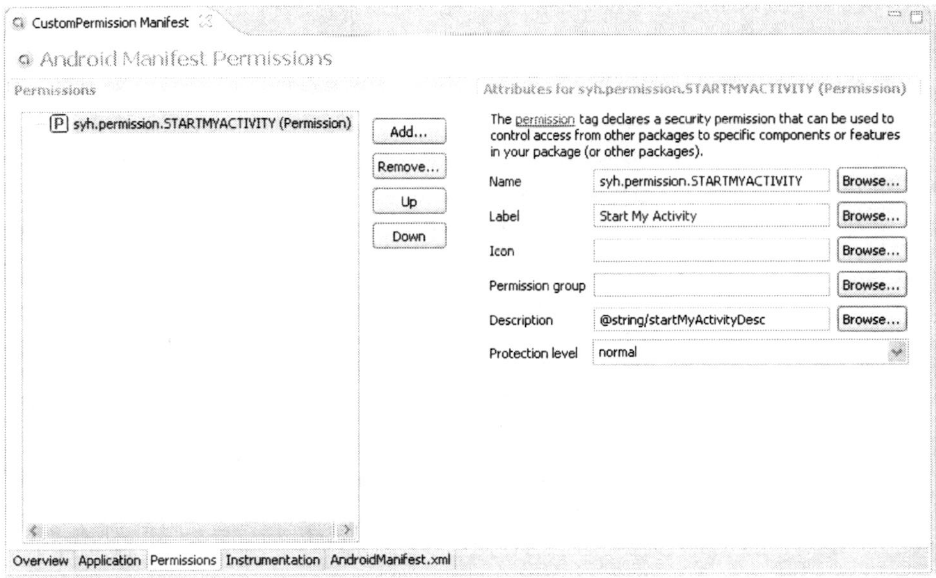

Figure 10–6. *Declaring a custom permission using the manifest editor*

As shown in Figure 10–6, each permission has a name, a label, an icon, a permission group, a description, and a protection level. Table 10–3 defines these properties.

Now, you have a custom permission. Next, you want to tell the system that the PrivActivity activity should be launched only by applications that have the syh.permission.STARTMYACTIVITY permission. You can set a required permission on an activity by adding the android:permission attribute to the activity definition in the AndroidManifest.xml file. For you to be able to launch the activity, you'll also need to add an intent-filter to the activity. Update your AndroidManifest.xml file with the content from Listing 10–5.

Table 10–3. *Attributes of a Permission*

Attribute	Required?	Description
android:name	Yes	Name of the permission. You should generally follow the Android naming scheme (*.permission.*).
android:protectionLevel	Yes	Defines the potential for risk associated with the permission. Must be one of the following values: normal dangerous signature signatureOrSystem Depending on the protection level, the system might take different action when determining whether to grant the permission or not. normal signals that the permission is low risk and will not harm the system, the user, or other applications. dangerous signals that the permission is high risk, and that the system will likely require input from the user before granting this permission. signature tells Android that the permission should be granted only to applications that have been signed with the same digital signature as the application that declared the permission. signatureOrSystem tells Android to grant the permission to applications with the same signature or to the Android package classes. This protection level is for very special cases involving multiple vendors needing to share features through the system image.
android:permissionGroup	No	You can place permissions into a group, but for custom permissions, you should avoid setting this property. If you really want to set this property, use this instead: android.permission-group.SYSTEM_TOOLS
android:label	No	Although it's not required, use this property to provide a short description of the permission.
android:description	No	Although it's not required, you should use this property to provide a more useful description of what the permission is for and what it protects.
android:icon	No	Permissions can be associated with an icon out of your resources (such as @drawable/myicon).

Listing 10–5. *The AndroidManifest.xml File for the Custom-Permission Project*

```
<?xml version="1.0" encoding="utf-8"?>
<manifest xmlns:android="http://schemas.android.com/apk/res/android"
      package="com.cust.perm"
      android:versionCode="1"
      android:versionName="1.0.0">
    <application android:icon="@drawable/icon" android:label="@string/app_name">
        <activity android:name=".CustPermMainActivity"
                  android:label="@string/app_name">
            <intent-filter>
                <action android:name="android.intent.action.MAIN" />
```

```
                <category android:name="android.intent.category.LAUNCHER" />
            </intent-filter>
        </activity>
    <activity android:name="PrivActivity"
android:permission="syh.permission.STARTMYACTIVITY">
        <intent-filter>
                <action android:name="android.intent.action.MAIN" />
        </intent-filter>
    </activity>
</application>

<permission
android:protectionLevel="normal"
android:label="Start My Activity"
android:description="@string/startMyActivityDesc"
android:name="syh.permission.STARTMYACTIVITY"></permission>

    <uses-sdk android:minSdkVersion="4" />
</manifest>
```

Listing 10–5 requires that you add a string constant named `startMyActivityDesc` to your string resources. To ensure compilation of Listing 10–5, add the following string resource to the `res/values/strings.xml` file:

```
<string name="startMyActivityDesc">Allows starting my activity</string>
```

Now, run the project in the emulator. Although the main activity does not do anything, you want the application installed on the emulator before you write a client for the privileged activity.

Let's write a client for the privileged activity. In the Eclipse IDE, click New ➤ Project ➤ Android Project. Enter **ClientOfCustomPermission** as the project name, select the "Create new project in workspace" radio button, and mark the "Use default location" check box. Set the application name to **Client Of Custom Permission**, the package name to **com.client.cust.perm**, the activity name to **ClientCustPermMainActivity**, and select a Build Target. Click the Finish button to create the project.

Next, you want to write an activity that displays a button you can click to call the privileged activity. Copy the layout shown in Listing 10–6 to the `main.xml` file in the project you just created.

Listing 10–6. ***Main.xml File for the Client Project***

```
<?xml version="1.0" encoding="utf-8"?>
<LinearLayout xmlns:android="http://schemas.android.com/apk/res/android"
    android:orientation="vertical"
    android:layout_width="fill_parent"    android:layout_height="fill_parent"  >

    <Button android:id="@+id/btn"    android:text="Launch PrivActivity"
    android:layout_width="wrap_content"    android:layout_height="wrap_content"
    android:onClick=”doClick”  />
</LinearLayout>
```

As you can see, the XML layout file defines a single button whose text reads "Launch PrivActivity." Now, let's write an activity that will handle the button-click event and launch the privileged activity. Copy the code from Listing 10–7 to your ClientCustPermMainActivity class.

Listing 10–7. *The Modified ClientCustPermMainActivity Activity*

```
package com.client.cust.perm;
// This file is ClientCustPermMainActivity.java

import android.app.Activity;
import android.content.Intent;
import android.os.Bundle;
import android.view.View;

public class ClientCustPermMainActivity extends Activity {
    @Override
    public void onCreate(Bundle savedInstanceState) {
        super.onCreate(savedInstanceState);
        setContentView(R.layout.main);
    }

    public void doClick(View view) {
                Intent intent = new Intent();
                intent.setClassName("com.cust.perm","com.cust.perm.PrivActivity");
                startActivity(intent);
    }
}
```

As shown in Listing 10–7, when the button is invoked, you create a new intent, and then set the class name of the activity you want to launch. In this case, you want to launch com.cust.perm.PrivActivity in the com.cust.perm package.

The only thing missing at this point is a uses-permission entry, which you add into the manifest file to tell the Android runtime that you need the syh.permission.STARTMYACTIVITY to run. Replace your client project's manifest file with that shown in Listing 10–8.

Listing 10–8. *The Client Manifest File*

```
<?xml version="1.0" encoding="utf-8"?>
<manifest xmlns:android="http://schemas.android.com/apk/res/android"
      package="com.client.cust.perm"
      android:versionCode="1"
      android:versionName="1.0.0">
    <application android:icon="@drawable/icon"
                 android:label="@string/app_name">
        <activity android:name=".ClientCustPermMainActivity"
                  android:label="@string/app_name">
            <intent-filter>
              <action android:name="android.intent.action.MAIN" />
              <category android:name="android.intent.category.LAUNCHER" />
            </intent-filter>
        </activity>
    </application>

    <uses-permission android:name="syh.permission.STARTMYACTIVITY" />
    <uses-sdk android:minSdkVersion="4" />
</manifest>
```

As shown in Listing 10–8, we added a `uses-permission` entry to request the custom permission required to start the `PrivActivity` we implemented in the custom-permission project.

With that, you should be able to deploy the client project to the emulator and then select the Launch PrivActivity button. When the button is invoked, you should see the text "Hello from PrivActivity."

After you successfully call the privileged activity, remove the `uses-permission` entry from your client project's manifest file and redeploy the project to the emulator. Once it's deployed, confirm that you get an error when you invoke the button to launch the privileged activity. Note that LogCat will display a permission-denial exception.

Now you know how custom permissions work in Android. Obviously, custom permissions are not limited to activities. In fact, you can apply both predefined and custom permissions to Android's other types of components as well. We'll explore an important one next: URI permissions.

Understanding and Using URI Permissions

Content providers (discussed in Chapter 3) often need to control access at a finer level than all or nothing. Fortunately, Android provides a mechanism for this. Think about e-mail attachments. The attachment may need to be read by another activity to display it. But the other activity should not get access to all of the e-mail data and does not need access even to all attachments. This is where URI permissions come in.

Passing URI Permissions in Intents

When invoking another activity and passing a URI, your application can specify that it is granting permissions to the URI being passed. But before your application can do this, it needs permission itself to the URI, and the URI content provider must cooperate and allow the granting of permissions to another activity. The code to invoke an activity with granting of permissions looks like Listing 10–9, which is actually from the Android Email program where it is launching an activity to view an email attachment.

Listing 10–9. *Code to Launch an Activity with Granting of Permission*

```
try {
    Intent intent = new Intent(Intent.ACTION_VIEW);
    intent.setData(contentUri);
    intent.addFlags(Intent.FLAG_GRANT_READ_URI_PERMISSION);
    startActivity(intent);
} catch (ActivityNotFoundException e) {
    mHandler.attachmentViewError();
    // TODO: Add a proper warning message (and lots of upstream cleanup to prevent
    // it from happening) in the next release.
}
```

The attachment is specified by `contentUri`. Notice how the intent is created with the action `Intent.ACTION_VIEW`, and the data is set using `setData()`. The flag is set to grant read permission of the attachment to whatever activity will match on the intent. This is where the content provider comes into play. Just because an activity has read permission to content doesn't mean it can pass along that permission to some other activity that does not have the permission already. The content provider must allow it as well. As Android finds a matching intent filter on an activity, it consults with the content provider to make sure that permissions can be granted. In essence, the content provider is being asked to allow access to this new activity to the content specified by the URI. If the content provider refuses then a `SecurityException` is thrown, and the operation fails. In Listing 10–9, this particular application is not checking for a `SecurityException`, because the developer is not expecting any refusals to grant permission. That's because the attachment content provider is part of the Email application! There is a possibility though that no activity can be found to handle the attachment, so that is the only `Exception` being watched for. In the case where the activity being called to process the URI already has permission to access that URI, the content provider does not get to deny access. That is, the calling activity can grant permission, and if the activity on the receiving end of the intent already has the necessary permissions for `contentURI`, the called activity will be allowed to proceed with no problems.

In addition to `Intent.FLAG_GRANT_READ_URI_PERMISSION`, there is a flag for write permissions: `Intent.FLAG_GRANT_WRITE_URI_PERMISSION`. It is possible to specify both in an `Intent`. Also, these flags can apply to `Services` and `BroadcastReceivers` as well as `Activities` since they can receive intents too.

Specifying URI Permissions in Content Providers

So how does a content provider specify URI permissions? It does so in the `AndroidManifest.xml` file in one of two ways.

- First, in the `<provider>` tag, the `android:grantUriPermissions` attribute can be set to either `true` or `false`. If `true`, any content from this content provider can be granted. If `false`, the second way of specifying URI permissions can happen, or the content provider can decide not to let anyone else grant permissions at all.
- The second way to allow granting of permissions is to specify it with child tags of `<provider>`. The child tag is `<grant-uri-permission>`, and you can have more than one within `<provider>`. `<grant-uri-permission>` has three possible attributes:
    - Using the `android:path` attribute, you can specify a complete path which will then have permissions that are grantable.
    - Similarly, `android:pathPrefix` specifies the beginning of a URI path
    - `android:pathPattern` allows wildcards (i.e., the asterisk, *, character) to specify a path.

As we stated before, the granting entity must also have appropriate permissions to the content before being allowed to grant them to some other entity. Content providers have additional ways of controlling access to their content, through the `android:readPermission` attribute of the `<provider>` tag, the `android:writePermission` attribute and the `android:permission` attribute (a convenient way to specify both read and write permissions with one permission `String` value). The value for any of these three attributes is a `String` that represents the permission a caller must have in order to read or write with this content provider. Before an activity could grant read permission to a content URI, that activity must have read permission first, as specified by either the `android:readPermission` attribute or the `android:permission` attribute. The entity wanting these permissions would declare them in their manifest file with the `<uses-permissions>` tag.

References

Here are some helpful references to topics you may wish to explore further:

- http://www.androidbook.com/projects. Look here for a list of downloadable projects related to this book. For this chapter look for a zip file called ProAndroid3_Ch10_Security.zip. This zip file contains all projects from this chapter, listed in separate root directories. There is also a README.TXT file that describes exactly how to import projects into Eclipse from one of these zip files.
- `http://developer.android.com/guide/topics/security/security.html`: This URL is a reference to the *Android Developer's Guide* section on *Security and Permissions*. It provides an overview with links to lots of references pages.
- `http://developer.android.com/guide/publishing/app-signing.html`: This URL is a reference to the *Android Developer's Guide* section on *Signing Your Applications*.
- `http://android.git.kernel.org/?p=platform/packages/apps/Email.git;a=blob_plain;f=src/com/android/email/activity/MessageView.java`: This URL is the source code from the stock Android Email application, where a `FLAG_GRANT_READ_URI_PERMISSION` is used. You can see how the Android team implements URI permissions by browsing in the source code for this application.

Summary

In this chapter, you learned that Android requires all applications to be signed with a digital certificate. We discussed ensuring build-time security with the emulator and Eclipse, as well as signing an Android package for release. We also talked about runtime security; you learned that the Android installer requests the permissions your application needs at install time. We also showed you how to define the permissions required by your application and how to create your own custom permissions. Finally, we covered how content providers can control access to their content and how they allow entities to grant permissions to other entities that could be called on to perform operations on content from the content provider, without giving that helper entity permissions to *all* content from the content provider.

In the next chapter, we'll talk about building and consuming services in Android.

Chapter 11

Building and Consuming Services

The Android Platform provides a complete software stack. This means you get an operating system and middleware, as well as working applications (such as a phone dialer). Alongside all of this, you have an SDK that you can use to write applications for the platform. Thus far, we've seen that we can build applications that directly interact with the user through a user interface. We have not, however, discussed background services or the possibilities of building components that run in the background.

In this chapter, we are going to focus on building and consuming services in Android. First we'll discuss consuming HTTP services, and then we'll cover a nice way to do simple background tasks, and finally we'll discuss interprocess communication—that is, communication between applications on the same device. Then we'll go one step further and build a working example application that integrates with Google's Translate API.

Consuming HTTP Services

Android applications and mobile applications in general are small apps with a lot of functionality. One of the ways that mobile apps deliver such rich functionality on such a small device is that they pull information from various sources. For example, most Android smartphones come with the Maps application, which provides sophisticated mapping functionality. We, however, know that the application is integrated with the Google Maps API and other services, which provide most of the sophistication.

That said, it is likely that the applications you write will also leverage information from other applications and APIs. A common integration strategy is to use HTTP. For example, you might have a Java servlet available on the Internet that provides services you want to leverage from one of your Android applications. How do you do that with Android? Interestingly, the Android SDK ships with a variation of Apache's `HttpClient` (`http://hc.apache.org/httpclient-3.x/`), which is universally used within the J2EE space. The Android version has been modified for Android, but the APIs are very similar to the APIs in the J2EE version.

The Apache `HttpClient` is a comprehensive HTTP client. Although it offers full support for the HTTP protocol, you will likely utilize only HTTP GET and POST. In this section, we will discuss using the `HttpClient` to make HTTP GET and HTTP POST calls.

Using the HttpClient for HTTP GET Requests

Here's one of the general patterns for using the `HttpClient`:

1. Create an `HttpClient` (or get an existing reference).
2. Instantiate a new HTTP method, such as `PostMethod` or `GetMethod`.
3. Set HTTP parameter names/values.
4. Execute the HTTP call using the `HttpClient`.
5. Process the HTTP response.

Listing 11–1 shows how to execute an HTTP GET using the `HttpClient`.

> **NOTE:** We give you a URL at the end of the chapter which you can use to download projects from this chapter. This will allow you to import these projects into your Eclipse directly. Also, because the code attempts to use the Internet, you will need to add `android.permission.INTERNET` to your manifest file when making HTTP calls using the `HttpClient`.

Listing 11–1. *Using HttpClient and HttpGet: HttpGetDemo.java*

```
import java.io.BufferedReader;
import java.io.IOException;
import java.io.InputStreamReader;
import org.apache.http.HttpResponse;
import org.apache.http.client.HttpClient;
import org.apache.http.client.methods.HttpGet;
import org.apache.http.impl.client.DefaultHttpClient;
import android.app.Activity;
import android.os.Bundle;

public class HttpGetDemo extends Activity {
    /** Called when the activity is first created. */
    @Override
    public void onCreate(Bundle savedInstanceState) {
        super.onCreate(savedInstanceState);
        setContentView(R.layout.main);

        BufferedReader in = null;
        try {

            HttpClient client = new DefaultHttpClient();
            HttpGet request = new HttpGet("http://code.google.com/android/");
```

```
            HttpResponse response = client.execute(request);

            in = new BufferedReader(
                    new InputStreamReader(
                        response.getEntity().getContent()));

            StringBuffer sb = new StringBuffer("");
            String line = "";
            String NL = System.getProperty("line.separator");
            while ((line = in.readLine()) != null) {
                sb.append(line + NL);
            }
            in.close();

            String page = sb.toString();
            System.out.println(page);
        } catch (Exception e) {
            e.printStackTrace();
        } finally {
            if (in != null) {
                try {
                    in.close();
                } catch (IOException e) {
                    e.printStackTrace();
                }
            }
        }
    }
}
```

The HttpClient provides abstractions for the various HTTP request types, such as HttpGet, HttpPost, and so on. Listing 11–1 uses the HttpClient to get the contents of the http://code.google.com/android/ URL. The actual HTTP request is executed with the call to client.execute(). After executing the request, the code reads the entire response into a string object. Note that the BufferedReader is closed in the finally block, which also closes the underlying HTTP connection.

For our example we embedded the HTTP logic inside of an activity, but we don't need to be within the context of an activity to use HttpClient. You can use it from within the context of any Android component or use it as part of a standalone class. In fact, you really shouldn't use HttpClient directly within an activity, since a web call could take a while to complete and cause the activity to be force closed. We'll cover that topic later in this chapter. For now we're going to cheat a little so we can focus on how to make HttpClient calls.

The code in Listing 11–1 executes an HTTP request without passing any HTTP parameters to the server. You can pass name/value parameters as part of the request by appending name/value pairs to the URL, as shown in Listing 11–2.

Listing 11–2. *Adding Parameters to an HTTP GET Request*

```
HttpGet request = new HttpGet("http://somehost/WS2/Upload.aspx?one=valueGoesHere");
client.execute(request);
```

When you execute an HTTP GET, the parameters (names and values) of the request are passed as part of the URL. Passing parameters this way has some limitations. Namely, the length of a URL should be kept below 2,048 characters. If you have more than this amount of data to submit, you should use HTTP POST instead. The POST method is more flexible and passes parameters as part of the request body.

Using the HttpClient for HTTP POST Requests (a Multipart Example)

Making an HTTP POST call is very similar to making an HTTP GET call (see Listing 11–3).

Listing 11–3. *Making an HTTP POST Request with the HttpClient*

```
HttpClient client = new DefaultHttpClient();
HttpPost request = new HttpPost(
        "http://192.165.13.37/services/doSomething.do");
List<NameValuePair> postParameters = new ArrayList<NameValuePair>();
postParameters.add(new BasicNameValuePair("first",
        "param value one"));
postParameters.add(new BasicNameValuePair("issuenum", "10317"));
postParameters.add(new BasicNameValuePair("username", "dave"));
UrlEncodedFormEntity formEntity = new UrlEncodedFormEntity(
        postParameters);
request.setEntity(formEntity);
HttpResponse response = client.execute(request);
```

The code in Listing 11–3 would replace the 3 lines in Listing 11–1 where the HttpGet is used. Everything else could stay the same. To make an HTTP POST call with the `HttpClient`, you have to call the `execute()` method of the `HttpClient` with an instance of `HttpPost`. When making HTTP POST calls, you generally pass URL-encoded name/value form parameters as part of the HTTP request. To do this with the `HttpClient`, you have to create a list that contains instances of `NameValuePair` objects and then wrap that list with a `UrlEncodedFormEntity` object. The `NameValuePair` wraps a name/value combination and the `UrlEncodedFormEntity` class knows how to encode a list of `NameValuePair` objects suitable for HTTP calls (generally POST calls). After you create a `UrlEncodedFormEntity`, you can set the entity type of the `HttpPost` to the `UrlEncodedFormEntity` and then execute the request.

In Listing 11–3, we created an `HttpClient` and then instantiated the `HttpPost` with the URL of the HTTP endpoint. Next, we created a list of `NameValuePair` objects and populated it with several name/value parameters. We then created a `UrlEncodedFormEntity` instance, passing the list of `NameValuePairobjects` to its constructor. Finally, we called the `setEntity()` method of the POST request and then executed the request using the `HttpClient` instance.

HTTP POST is actually much more powerful than this. With an HTTP POST, we can pass simple name/value parameters, as shown in Listing 11–3, as well as complex parameters such as files. HTTP POST supports another request-body format known as a *multipart POST*. With this type of POST, you can send name/value parameters as before, along with arbitrary files. Unfortunately, the version of `HttpClient` shipped with

Android does not directly support multipart POST. To do multipart POST calls, you need to get three additional Apache open source projects: Apache Commons IO, Mime4j, and HttpMime. You can download these projects from the following web sites:

- *Commons IO*: `http://commons.apache.org/io/`
- *Mime4j*: `http://james.apache.org/mime4j/`
- *HttpMime*: `http://hc.apache.org/downloads.cgi` (inside of HttpClient)

Alternatively, you can visit this site to download all of the required .jar files to do multipart POST with Android:

`http://www.apress.com/book/view/1430226595`

Listing 11–4 demonstrates a multipart POST using Android.

Listing 11–4. ***Making a Multipart POST Call***

```
import java.io.ByteArrayInputStream;
import java.io.InputStream;
import org.apache.commons.io.IOUtils;
import org.apache.http.HttpResponse;
import org.apache.http.client.HttpClient;
import org.apache.http.client.methods.HttpPost;
import org.apache.http.entity.mime.MultipartEntity;
import org.apache.http.entity.mime.content.InputStreamBody;
import org.apache.http.entity.mime.content.StringBody;
import org.apache.http.impl.client.DefaultHttpClient;

import android.app.Activity;

public class TestMultipartPost extends Activity
{
    public void executeMultipartPost() throws Exception
    {
        try {
            InputStream is = this.getAssets().open("data.xml");
            HttpClient httpClient = new DefaultHttpClient();
            HttpPost postRequest =
              new HttpPost("http://mysomewebserver.com/services/doSomething.do");

            byte[] data = IOUtils.toByteArray(is);

            InputStreamBody isb = new InputStreamBody(new
                    ByteArrayInputStream(data), "uploadedFile");
            StringBody sb1 = new StringBody("some text goes here");
            StringBody sb2 = new StringBody("some text goes here too");

            MultipartEntity multipartContent = new MultipartEntity();
            multipartContent.addPart("uploadedFile", isb);
            multipartContent.addPart("one", sb1);
            multipartContent.addPart("two", sb2);

            postRequest.setEntity(multipartContent);
            HttpResponse response =httpClient.execute(postRequest);
            response.getEntity().getContent().close();
        } catch (Throwable e)
        {
```

```
            // handle exception here
        }
    }
}
```

NOTE: The multipart example uses several .jar files that are not included as part of the Android runtime. To ensure that the .jar files will be packaged as part of your .apk file, you need to add them as external .jar files in Eclipse. To do this, right-click your project in Eclipse, select Properties, choose Java Build Path, select the Libraries tab, and then select Add External JARs.

Following these steps will make the .jar files available during compile time as well as runtime.

To execute a multipart POST, you need to create an `HttpPost` and call its `setEntity()` method with a `MultipartEntity` instance (rather than the `UrlEncodedFormEntity` we created for the name/value parameter form post). `MultipartEntity` represents the body of a multipart POST request. As shown, you create an instance of a `MultipartEntity` and then call the `addPart()` method with each part. Listing 11–4 adds three parts to the request: two string parts and an XML file.

Finally, if you are building an application that requires you to pass a multipart POST to a web resource, you'll likely have to debug the solution using a dummy implementation of the service on your local workstation. When you're running applications on your local workstation, normally you can access the local machine by using `localhost` or IP address `127.0.0.1`. With Android applications, however, you will not be able to use `localhost` (or `127.0.0.1`) because the emulator will be its own `localhost`. You don't want to point this client to a service on the Android device, you want to point to your workstation. To refer to your development workstation from the application running in the emulator, you'll have to use your workstation's IP address. (Refer back to Chapter 2 if you need help figuring out what your workstation's IP address is.) You will need to modify Listing 11–4 by substituting the IP address with the IP address of your workstation.

SOAP, JSON, and XML Parsers

What about SOAP? There are lots of SOAP-based web services on the Internet, but to date, Google has not provided direct support in Android for calling SOAP web services. Google instead prefers REST-like web services, seemingly to reduce the amount of computing required on the client device. However, the tradeoff is that the developer must do more work to send data and to parse the returned data. Ideally, you will have some options for how you can interact with your web services. Some developers have used the kSOAP2 developer kit to build SOAP clients for Android. We won't be covering that approach, but it's out there if you're interested.

NOTE: The original kSOAP2 source is located here: `http://ksoap2.sourceforge.net/`. The open source community has (thankfully!) contributed a version of kSOAP2 for Android, and you can find out more about it here: `http://code.google.com/p/ksoap2-android/`.

One approach that's been used successfully is to implement your own services on the Internet, which can talk SOAP (or whatever) to the destination service. Then your Android application only needs to talk to your services, and you now have complete control. If the destination services change, you might be able to handle that without having to update and release a new version of your application. You'd only have to update the services on your server. A side benefit of this approach is that you could more easily implement a paid subscription model for your application. If a user lets their subscription lapse, you can turn them off at your server.

Android *does* have support for JavaScript Object Notation (JSON). This is a fairly common method of packaging data between a web server and a client. The JSON parsing classes make it very easy to unpack data from a response so your application can act on it. We'll show you some JSON code later in this chapter when we learn about the Google Translate API.

Android also has a couple of XML parsers which you can use to interpret the responses from the HTTP calls. The main one (`XMLPullParser`) was covered in chapter 3.

Dealing with Exceptions

Dealing with exceptions is part of any program, but software that makes use of external services (such as HTTP services) must pay additional attention to exceptions because the potential for errors is magnified. There are several types of exceptions that you can expect while making use of HTTP services. These are transport exceptions, protocol exceptions, and timeouts. You should understand when these exceptions could occur.

Transport exceptions can occur due to a number of reasons, but the most likely scenario with a mobile device is poor network connectivity. Protocol exceptions are exceptions at the HTTP protocol layer. These include authentication errors, invalid cookies, and so on. You can expect to see protocol exceptions if, for example, you have to supply login credentials as part of your HTTP request but fail to do so. Timeouts, with respect to HTTP calls, come in two flavors: connection timeouts and socket timeouts. A connection timeout can occur if the `HttpClient` is not able to connect to the HTTP server—if, for example, the server is not available. A socket timeout can occur if the `HttpClient` fails to receive a response within a defined time period. In other words, the `HttpClient` was able to connect to the server, but the server failed to return a response within the allocated time limit.

Now that you understand the types of exceptions that might occur, how do you deal with them? Fortunately, the `HttpClient` is a robust framework that takes most of the burden off your shoulders. In fact, the only exception types that you'll have to worry about are the ones that you'll be able to manage easily. The `HttpClient` takes care of transport exceptions by detecting transport issues and retrying requests (which works very well with this type of exception). Protocol exceptions are exceptions that can generally be flushed out during development. Timeouts are the most likely exceptions that you'll have to deal with. A simple and effective approach to dealing with both types of timeouts—connection timeouts and socket timeouts—is to wrap the `execute()`

method of your HTTP request with a try/catch and then retry if a failure occurs. This is demonstrated in Listing 11–5.

Listing 11–5. ***Implementing a Simple Retry Technique to Deal with Timeouts***

```
import java.io.BufferedReader;
import java.io.IOException;
import java.io.InputStreamReader;
import java.net.URI;

import org.apache.http.HttpResponse;
import org.apache.http.client.HttpClient;
import org.apache.http.client.methods.HttpGet;
import org.apache.http.impl.client.DefaultHttpClient;

public class TestHttpGet {

    public String executeHttpGetWithRetry() throws Exception {
        int retry = 3;

        int count = 0;
        while (count < retry) {
            count += 1;
            try {
                String response = executeHttpGet();
                /**
                 * if we get here, that means we were successful and we
                 * can stop.
                 */
                return response;
            } catch (Exception e) {
                /**
                 * if we have exhausted our retry limit
                 */
                if (count < retry) {
                    /**
                     * we have retries remaining, so log the message
                     * and go again.
                     */
                    System.out.println(e.getMessage());
                } else {
                    System.out.println("all retries failed");
                    throw e;
                }
            }
        }
        return null;
    }

    public String executeHttpGet() throws Exception {
        BufferedReader in = null;
        try {
            HttpClient client = new DefaultHttpClient();
            HttpGet request = new
                    HttpGet("http://code.google.com/android/");
            HttpResponse response = client.execute(request);
            in = new BufferedReader(
                        new InputStreamReader(
```

```
                                        response.getEntity().getContent()));

            StringBuffer sb = new StringBuffer("");
            String line = "";
            String NL = System.getProperty("line.separator");
            while ((line = in.readLine()) != null) {
                sb.append(line + NL);
            }
            in.close();

            String result = sb.toString();
            return result;
        } finally {
            if (in != null) {
                try {
                    in.close();
                } catch (IOException e) {
                    e.printStackTrace();
                }
            }
        }
    }
}
```

The code in Listing 11–5 shows how you can implement a simple retry technique to recover from timeouts when making HTTP calls. The listing shows two methods: one that executes an HTTP GET (`executeHttpGet()`), and another that wraps this method with the retry logic (`executeHttpGetWithRetry()`). The logic is very simple. We set the number of retries we want to attempt to 3, and then we enter a `while` loop. Within the loop, we execute the request. Note that the request is wrapped with a `try/catch` block, and in the `catch` block we check whether we have exhausted the number of retry attempts.

When using the `HttpClient` as part of a real-world application, you need to pay some attention to multithreading issues that might come up. Let's delve into these now.

Addressing Multithreading Issues

The examples we've shown so far created a new `HttpClient` for each request. In practice, however, you should probably create one `HttpClient` for the entire application and use that for all of your HTTP communication. With one `HttpClient` servicing all of your HTTP requests, you should also pay attention to multithreading issues that could surface if you make simultaneous requests through the same `HttpClient`. Fortunately, the `HttpClient` provides facilities that make this easy—all you have to do is create the `DefaultHttpClient` using a `ThreadSafeClientConnManager`, as shown in Listing 11–6.

Listing 11–6. *Creating an HttpClient for Multithreading: CustomHttpClient.java*

```
import org.apache.http.HttpVersion;
import org.apache.http.client.HttpClient;
import org.apache.http.conn.ClientConnectionManager;
import org.apache.http.conn.params.ConnManagerParams;
import org.apache.http.conn.scheme.PlainSocketFactory;
import org.apache.http.conn.scheme.Scheme;
import org.apache.http.conn.scheme.SchemeRegistry;
```

```
import org.apache.http.conn.ssl.SSLSocketFactory;
import org.apache.http.impl.client.DefaultHttpClient;
import org.apache.http.impl.conn.tsccm.ThreadSafeClientConnManager;
import org.apache.http.params.BasicHttpParams;
import org.apache.http.params.HttpConnectionParams;
import org.apache.http.params.HttpParams;
import org.apache.http.params.HttpProtocolParams;
import org.apache.http.protocol.HTTP;

public class CustomHttpClient {
    private static HttpClient customHttpClient;

    /** A private Constructor prevents instantiation */
    private CustomHttpClient() {
    }

    public static synchronized HttpClient getHttpClient() {
        if (customHttpClient == null) {
            HttpParams params = new BasicHttpParams();
            HttpProtocolParams.setVersion(params, HttpVersion.HTTP_1_1);
            HttpProtocolParams.setContentCharset(params,
                    HTTP.DEFAULT_CONTENT_CHARSET);
            HttpProtocolParams.setUseExpectContinue(params, true);
            HttpProtocolParams.setUserAgent(params,
"Mozilla/5.0 (Linux; U; Android 2.2.1; en-us; Nexus One Build/FRG83) AppleWebKit/533.1
(KHTML, like Gecko) Version/4.0 Mobile Safari/533.1"
            );

            ConnManagerParams.setTimeout(params, 1000);

            HttpConnectionParams.setConnectionTimeout(params, 5000);
            HttpConnectionParams.setSoTimeout(params, 10000);

            SchemeRegistry schReg = new SchemeRegistry();
            schReg.register(new Scheme("http",
                            PlainSocketFactory.getSocketFactory(), 80));
            schReg.register(new Scheme("https",
                            SSLSocketFactory.getSocketFactory(), 443));
            ClientConnectionManager conMgr = new
                            ThreadSafeClientConnManager(params,schReg);

            customHttpClient = new DefaultHttpClient(conMgr, params);
        }
        return customHttpClient;
    }

    public Object clone() throws CloneNotSupportedException {
        throw new CloneNotSupportedException();
    }
}
```

If your application needs to make more than a few HTTP calls, you should create an HttpClient that services all your HTTP requests. The simplest way to do this is to create a singleton class that can be accessed from anywhere in the application, as we've shown here. This is a fairly standard Java pattern in which we synchronize access to a getter method, and that getter method returns the one and only HttpClient object for the singleton, creating it the first time as necessary.

Now, take a look at the getHttpClient() method of CustomHttpClient. This method is responsible for creating our singleton HttpClient. We set some basic parameters, some timeout values, and the schemes that our HttpClient will support (i.e., HTTP and HTTPS). Notice that when we instantiate the DefaultHttpClient(), we pass in a ClientConnectionManager. The ClientConnectionManager is responsible for managing HTTP connections for the HttpClient. Because we want to use a single HttpClient for all the HTTP requests (requests which could overlap if we're using threads), we create a ThreadSafeClientConnManager.

We also show you a simpler way of collecting the response from the HTTP request, using a BasicResponseHandler. The code for our activity that uses our CustomHttpClient is in Listing 11–7.

Listing 11–7. *Using Our CustomHttpClient: HttpActivity.java*

```
import java.io.IOException;
import org.apache.http.client.HttpClient;
import org.apache.http.client.methods.HttpGet;
import org.apache.http.impl.client.BasicResponseHandler;
import org.apache.http.params.HttpConnectionParams;
import org.apache.http.params.HttpParams;
import android.app.Activity;
import android.os.Bundle;
import android.util.Log;

public class HttpActivity extends Activity
{
    private HttpClient httpClient;
    @Override
    public void onCreate(Bundle savedInstanceState)
    {
        super.onCreate(savedInstanceState);
        setContentView(R.layout.main);

        httpClient = CustomHttpClient.getHttpClient();
        getHttpContent();
    }

    public void getHttpContent()
    {
        try {
            HttpGet request = new HttpGet("http://www.google.com/");
            String page = httpClient.execute(request,
                    new BasicResponseHandler());
            System.out.println(page);
        } catch (IOException e) {
            // covers:
            //      ClientProtocolException
            //      ConnectTimeoutException
            //      ConnectionPoolTimeoutException
            //      SocketTimeoutException
            e.printStackTrace();
        }
```

```
    }
}
```

For this sample application, we do a simple HTTP get of the Google home page. We also use a BasicResponseHandler object to take care of rendering the page as a big String, which we then write out to LogCat. As you can see, adding a BasicResponseHandler to the execute() method is very easy to do.

You may be tempted to take advantage of the fact that each Android application has an associated Application object. By default, if you don't define a custom application object, Android uses android.app.Application. Here's the interesting thing about the application object: there will always be exactly one application object for your application, and all of your components can access it (using the global context object). It is possible to extend the Application class and add functionality such as our CustomHttpClient. However, in our case there is really no reason to do this within the Application class itself, and you will be much better off not messing with the Application class when you can simply create a separate singleton class to handle this type of need.

Fun With Timeouts

There are other terrific advantages to setting up a single HttpClient for our application to use. We can modify the properties of it in one place, and everyone can take advantage of it. For example, if we want to setup common timeout values for our HTTP calls, we can do that when creating our HttpClient by calling the appropriate setter functions against our HttpParams object. Please refer to Listing 11–6 and the getHttpClient() method. Notice that there are three timeouts we can play with. The first is a timeout for the connection manager, and it defines how long we should wait to get a connection out of the connection pool managed by the connection manager. In our example, we set this to 1 second. About the only time we might ever have to wait is if all connections from the pool are in use. The second timeout value defines how long we should wait to make a connection over the network to the server on the other end. Here, we used a value of 2 seconds. And lastly, we set a socket timeout value to 4 seconds to define how long we should wait to get data back for our request.

Corresponding to the three timeouts described previously, we could get these three exceptions: ConnectionPoolTimeoutException, ConnectTimeoutException or SocketTimeoutException. All three of these exceptions are subclasses of IOException, which we've used in our HttpActivity instead of catching each subclass exception separately.

If you investigate each of the parameter-setting classes that we used in getHttpClient(), you might discover even more parameters that you would find useful.

We've described for you how to set up a common pool of HTTP connections for use across your application. And the implication is that every time you need to use a connection, the various settings will apply to your particular needs. But what if you want different settings for a particular message? Thankfully, there's an easy way to do that as well. We showed you how to use an HttpGet or an HttpPost object to describe the request to be made across the network. In a similar way to how we set HttpParams on our HttpClient, you can set HttpParams on both HttpGet and HttpPost objects. The settings you apply at the message level will override the settings at the HttpClient level without changing the HttpClient settings. Listing 11–8 shows what this might look like if we wanted to have a socket timeout of 1 minute instead of 4 seconds for one particular request. You would use these lines in place of the lines in the try block of getHttpContent() in Listing 11–7.

Listing 11–8. *Overriding the Socket Timeout at the Request Level*

```
HttpGet request = new HttpGet("http://www.google.com/");
HttpParams params = request.getParams();
HttpConnectionParams.setSoTimeout(params, 60000);   // 1 minute
request.setParams(params);
String page = httpClient.execute(request,
                     new BasicResponseHandler());
System.out.println(page);
```

Using the HttpURLConnection

Android provides another way to deal with HTTP services, and that is using the java.net.HttpURLConnection class. This is not unlike the HttpClient classes we've just covered, but HttpURLConnection tends to require more statements to get things done. Your choice of which to use depends on what you are comfortable with.

Using the AndroidHttpClient

Android 2.2 introduced a new subclass of HttpClient called AndroidHttpClient. The idea behind this class is to make things easier for the developer of Android apps by providing default values and logic appropriate for Android apps. For example, the timeout values for the connection and the socket (i.e., operation) default to 20 seconds each. The connection manager defaults to the ThreadSafeClientConnManager. For the most part, it is interchangeable with the HttpClient we used in the previous examples. There are a few differences though that you should be aware of.

- To create an AndroidHttpClient, you invoke the static newInstance() method of the AndroidHttpClient class, like this:

```
AndroidHttpClient httpClient = AndroidHttpClient.newInstance("my-http-agent-string");
```

- Notice that the parameter to the newInstance() method is an HTTP agent string. In Android's default browser, you might see a string such as the following but you can use whatever you want:

```
Mozilla/5.0 (Linux; U; Android 2.1; en-us; ADR6200 Build/ERD79) AppleWebKit/530.17
(KHTML, like Gecko) Version/ 4.0 Mobile Safari/530.17
```

- When `execute()` is called on this client, you must be in a thread separate from the main UI thread. This means that you'll get an exception if you simply attempt to replace our previous `HttpClient` with an `AndroidHttpClient`. It is bad practice to make HTTP calls from the main UI thread, so `AndroidHttpClient` won't let you. We'll be covering threading issues in the next section.
- You must call `close()` on the `AndroidHttpClient` instance when you are done with it. This is so memory can be freed up properly.
- There are some handy static methods for dealing with compressed responses from a server, including
  - `modifyRequestToAcceptGzipResponse(HttpRequest request)`
  - `getCompressedEntity(byte[] data, ContentResolver resolver)`
  - `getUngzippedContent(HttpEntity entity)`

Once you've acquired an instance of the `AndroidHttpClient`, you cannot modify any parameter settings in it, nor can you add any parameter settings to it (such as the HTTP protocol version for example). Your options are to override settings within the `HttpGet` object as shown previously or to not use the `AndroidHttpClient`.

This concludes our discussion of using HTTP services with the `HttpClient`. In the sections that follow, we will turn our focus to another interesting part of the Android Platform: writing background/long-running services. Although not immediately obvious, the processes of making HTTP calls and writing Android services are linked in that you will do a lot of integration from within Android services. Take, for example, a simple mail-client application. On an Android device, this type of application will likely be composed of two pieces: one that will provide the UI to the user, and another to poll for mail messages. The polling will likely have to be done within a background service. The component that polls for new messages will be an Android service, which will in turn use the `HttpClient` to perform the work.

> **NOTE:** For a great tutorial on using `HttpClient` and these other concepts, please check out the Apache site at http://hc.apache.org/httpcomponents-client-ga/tutorial/html/.

Using Background Threads (AsyncTask)

So far in our examples, we've been using the main thread of the activity to do our HTTP calls. While we may get lucky and get fast response times to every call, our network connection and the Internet are not always so speedy. Since the main thread of an activity is used mainly to process events from the user (button clicks and so on) and perform updates to the user interface, we should use a background thread to do work that could take a while. Android forces us into this position because if the main thread does not handle something within 5 seconds, an Application Not Responding (ANR) condition will be triggered, which ruins the user's experience by displaying a nasty dialog box asking the user to confirm that the current application should be terminated (also known as a force close). We'll get into the details of the main thread and the 5 second time limit in Chapter 13, but for now, just know that we can't tie up the main thread for long.

If all you want to do is some computing, with no updates required to the user interface, you could use a simple Thread object to offload some processing from the main thread. This technique won't work, however, if you need to do updates to the user interface. And that's because the Android user interface toolkit is not thread safe, so it should always be updated only from the main thread.

If you intend to update the user interface in any way as a result of your background thread, you should seriously consider using an AsyncTask. The AsyncTask provides a convenient way of backgrounding some processing that wishes to update the user interface. The AsyncTask takes care of creating a background thread for us where the work will get done, as well as providing callbacks that will run on the main thread to allow easy access to the user interface element (i.e., views). The callbacks can fire before, during, and after our background thread has run.

For example, consider the problem of grabbing an image from a network server to display in our application. Perhaps the image needs to be created on the fly. We cannot guarantee how long it will take the image to be returned to us, so we really need to use a background thread for the job.

Listing 11–9 shows a simple implementation of an AsyncTask that will do the job for us. We'll talk about that and then show you the layout file and the Java code for an activity that can call this AsyncTask.

Listing 11–9. *AsyncTask for Downloading an Image: DownloadImageTask.java*

```
import java.io.IOException;
import org.apache.http.HttpResponse;
import org.apache.http.client.HttpClient;
import org.apache.http.client.methods.HttpGet;
import org.apache.http.params.BasicHttpParams;
import org.apache.http.params.HttpConnectionParams;
import org.apache.http.params.HttpParams;
import org.apache.http.util.EntityUtils;
import android.app.Activity;
import android.content.Context;
import android.graphics.Bitmap;
import android.graphics.BitmapFactory;
import android.os.AsyncTask;
import android.util.Log;
import android.widget.ImageView;
import android.widget.TextView;

public class DownloadImageTask extends AsyncTask<String, Integer, Bitmap> {
    private Context mContext;

    DownloadImageTask(Context context) {
        mContext = context;
    }
```

```
protected void onPreExecute() {
    // We could do some setup work here before doInBackground() runs
}

protected Bitmap doInBackground(String... urls) {
    Log.v("doInBackground", "doing download of image");
    return downloadImage(urls);
}

protected void onProgressUpdate(Integer... progress) {
    TextView mText = (TextView)
            ((Activity) mContext).findViewById(R.id.text);
    mText.setText("Progress so far: " + progress[0]);
}

protected void onPostExecute(Bitmap result) {
    if(result != null) {
        ImageView mImage = (ImageView)
            ((Activity) mContext).findViewById(R.id.image);
        mImage.setImageBitmap(result);
    }
    else {
        TextView errorMsg = (TextView)
            ((Activity) mContext).findViewById(R.id.errorMsg);
        errorMsg.setText("Problem downloading image. Please try again later.");
    }
}

private Bitmap downloadImage(String... urls)
{
  HttpClient httpClient = CustomHttpClient.getHttpClient();
  try {
    HttpGet request = new HttpGet(urls[0]);
    HttpParams params = new BasicHttpParams();
    HttpConnectionParams.setSoTimeout(params, 60000);   // 1 minute
    request.setParams(params);

    publishProgress(25);

    HttpResponse response = httpClient.execute(request);

    publishProgress(50);

    byte[] image = EntityUtils.toByteArray(response.getEntity());

    publishProgress(75);

    Bitmap mBitmap = BitmapFactory.decodeByteArray(
                        image, 0, image.length);

    publishProgress(100);

    return mBitmap;
  } catch (IOException e) {
    // covers:
    //      ClientProtocolException
    //      ConnectTimeoutException
```

```
        //      ConnectionPoolTimeoutException
        //      SocketTimeoutException
        e.printStackTrace();
      }
      return null;
    }
}
```

Because AsyncTask is abstract, you need to customize it by extending it, which we do with the class DownloadImageTask. We're going to use a constructor that takes a reference to the calling context, which, in our case, will be the calling activity. We'll use that context to get to the activity's views. We'll also reuse the CustomHttpClient class from before.

There are four steps to an AsyncTask:

1. Do any setup work in the onPreExecute() method. This method executes on the main thread.
2. Run a background thread with doInBackground(). Thread creation is all handled for us behind the scenes. This code runs in a separate background thread.
3. Update progress using publishProgress() and onProgressUpdate(). publishProgress() gets called from within the code of doInBackground(), while onProgressUpdate() is executed in the main thread as a result of the call to publishProgress(). With these two methods, the backgrounded thread is able to communicate with the main thread while it is executing, so status updates can be made in the user interface before the backgrounded thread has completed its work.
4. Update the user interface in onPostExecute() with the results. This method executes in the main thread.

Steps 1 and 3 are optional. In our example, we chose not to do any initialization in onPreExecute(), but we did utilize the progress updating as in step 3. The main work of the background thread is done in the downloadImage() method called from doInBackground(). The downloadImage() method takes a URL and uses our HttpClient to execute an HttpGet request and response. Notice that we're now able to set a timeout of 60 seconds without worrying about getting any ANRs. You can see in the code where the progress is updated during the steps of setting up the HttpClient connection, executing the HTTP request, converting the image response to a byte array and then building a Bitmap object from it. When downloadImage() returns back to doInBackground() and doInBackground() returns, Android takes care of taking our return value and passing it to onPostExecute(). Once the Bitmap has been passed to onPostExecute(), it is safe to update our ImageView with it, since onPostExecute() runs on the main thread of our activity. But what if we got some sort of exception while doing the download? If we do not get an image back from our HTTP call but get an exception instead, our Bitmap will be null. We can detect that fact in onPostExecute() and display an error message instead of attempting to set the ImageView to a Bitmap. Of course, we could take other action if we know that our download failed.

Please keep in mind that the only code that does not run on the main thread is the code from `doInBackground()`. So be careful not to work with the UI within the `doInBackground()` method, since that is where you could get into trouble. Do not, for instance, call methods from `doInBackground()` that modify the UI elements. Only touch UI elements in `onPreExecute()`, `onProgressUpdate()`, and `onPostExecute()`.

Let's fill out our latest example with the layout XML file and the Java code for our activity in Listings 11–10 and 11–11 respectively.

Listing 11–10. *Layout for Calling our AsyncTask: /res/layout/main.xml*

```
<?xml version="1.0" encoding="utf-8"?>
<LinearLayout xmlns:android="http://schemas.android.com/apk/res/android"
    android:layout_width="fill_parent"
    android:layout_height="fill_parent"
    android:orientation="vertical"
    >
<LinearLayout
    android:layout_width="fill_parent"
    android:layout_height="wrap_content"
    android:orientation="horizontal"
    >
  <Button android:id="@+id/button"  android:text="Get Image"
    android:layout_width="wrap_content"
    android:layout_height="wrap_content"
    android:onClick="doClick"
    />
  <TextView android:id="@+id/text"
    android:layout_width="wrap_content"
    android:layout_height="wrap_content"
    />
</LinearLayout>
<TextView android:id="@+id/errorMsg"  android:textColor="#ff0000"
    android:layout_width="wrap_content"
    android:layout_height="wrap_content"
    />
<ImageView  android:id="@+id/image"
    android:layout_width="fill_parent"  android:layout_height="0dip"
    android:layout_weight="1" />
</LinearLayout>
```

Listing 11–11. *Activity for Calling our AsyncTask: HttpActivity.java*

```
import android.app.Activity;
import android.os.AsyncTask;
import android.os.Bundle;
import android.util.Log;
import android.view.View;

public class HttpActivity extends Activity {
    private DownloadImageTask diTask;

    @Override
    public void onCreate(Bundle savedInstanceState)
    {
        super.onCreate(savedInstanceState);
        setContentView(R.layout.main);
    }
```

```
    public void doClick(View view) {
        if(diTask != null) {
            AsyncTask.Status diStatus = diTask.getStatus();
            Log.v("doClick", "diTask status is " + diStatus);
            if(diStatus != AsyncTask.Status.FINISHED) {
                Log.v("doClick", "... no need to start a new task");
                return;
            }
            // Since diStatus must be FINISHED, we can try again.
        }
        diTask = new DownloadImageTask(this);

diTask.execute("http://chart.apis.google.com/chart?&cht=p&chs=460x250&chd=t:15.3,20.3,0.
2,59.7,4.5&chl=Android%201.5%7CAndroid%201.6%7COther*%7CAndroid%202.1%7CAndroid%202.2&ch
co=c4df9b,6fad0c");
    }
}
```

When you run this sample and click the button, you should see a display like Figure 11–1.

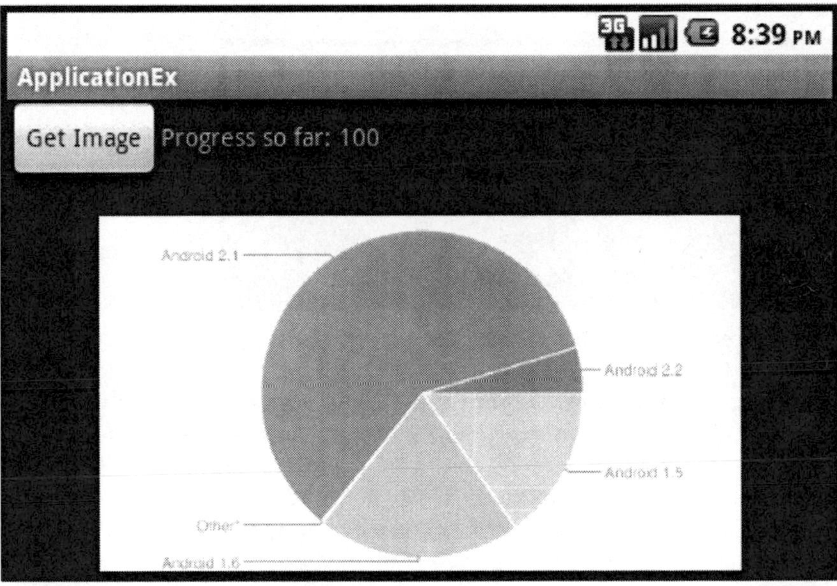

Figure 11–1. *Using AsyncTask to download an image (the Android device chart as of August 2, 2010)*

The layout is pretty straightforward. We have a button with a text message next to it. This text will be our progress message. Underneath that, we have room for an error message, whose text will be colored red. And finally, we have a place for our image.

Within our button callback method doClick(), we need to instantiate a new instance of our customized AsyncTask class and call the execute() method. This is the pattern you would use also. Instantiate an extension of AsyncTask, and call the execute() method. For our example, we're calling a Google charts service that takes data values and label names and creates a chart image for us, returning it as a PNG image. But before we launch our task, we really should check to see if a task is already running. If the user double-clicks the button, we could end up with two backgrounded tasks. Fortunately, the AsyncTask class allows us to check its status. If `doTask` is not `null`, there's a possibility that we have a running task. So we check the status of our AsyncTask. If it's anything but `FINISHED`, the task is either `RUNNING` or `PENDING` and about to run. Therefore, we only want to drop through and create a new AsyncTask if we have a task and it is already `FINISHED`. Of course, if the previous AsyncTask was able to successfully download the image, we might not want to download it again. But for our example, we'll go ahead and get it again.

While our sample application runs, you should notice the progress message updating after pressing the button and then the image appears. The button goes from a pressed state back to the normal state *before* the progress message starts to change. This is an important observation, since it means our main thread has returned to managing the user interface while our download is underway.

Just for fun, go into the URL string for the Google charts call, and make a change that will cause an error situation. Now, run the application again. You should see a result similar to Figure 11–2.

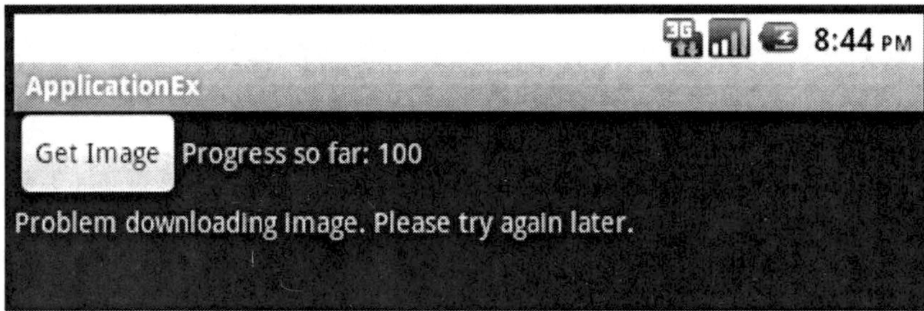

Figure 11–2. ***Communicating exceptions back to the user interface with AsyncTask***

Here are a few more things to know about AsyncTasks. Once we've instantiated our extension of AsyncTask and launched the `execute()` method, our main thread goes back to executing. But we still have a reference to the task and can operate on it from the main thread. For example, we could call `cancel()` to kill it. We could call `isCancelled()` to see if it's been cancelled. We might want to modify our logic in `onPostExecute()` to deal with those cancellations. And AsyncTask has two forms of `get()` where we could get the result from `doInBackground()` instead of letting `onPostExecute()` do our work. One form of `get()` blocks, while the other uses a timeout value to prevent the calling thread from waiting too long.

An AsyncTask can only be run once. Therefore, if you do keep a reference to an AsyncTask, do not call `execute()` more than once on it. You will get an exception if you do. You are free to create new instances of your AsyncTask, but each of those instances can only be executed once. That's why we create a new `DownloadImageTask` every time we need one.

Handling Configuration Changes with AsyncTasks

But there's one more big thing to realize about AsyncTasks. In our example previously, our AsyncTask won't work if the activity that launched it gets destroyed and re-created. This is a really big thing. Obviously, if our onPostExecute() callback executes against the original activity, but that activity has been replaced in our application with a new one, our AsyncTask will be updating views that are no longer visible to the user. How is it possible that an activity will be destroyed and re-created? Actually, it happens all the time. Any time the configuration of the device is changed, for example, when the device is rotated from portrait to landscape mode, our activity will be destroyed and re-created.

Remember that when Android is creating the user interface, it uses the configuration of the device to figure out which layouts and resources to use. This is rather complicated, so the easiest and quickest thing for Android to do is to destroy the current activity and re-create it with the new configuration. Fortunately, all is not lost, especially our AsyncTask. Because our AsyncTask is running in a separate thread within our application, it is still there when our new activity comes into being. What we need to do is reconnect the two, so our AsyncTask can find the views on the new activity. There is a callback and a method on an activity to make this work for us, and they are onRetainNonConfigurationInstance() and getLastNonConfigurationInstance() respectively. Basically, what these two do is pass an object from our old activity to our new one.

Listing 11–12. *Our New HttpActivity.java That Handles Reconfiguration*

```
import android.app.Activity;
import android.os.AsyncTask;
import android.os.Bundle;
import android.util.Log;
import android.view.View;

public class HttpActivity extends Activity {
    private DownloadImageTask diTask;

    @Override
    public void onCreate(Bundle savedInstanceState)
    {
        super.onCreate(savedInstanceState);
        setContentView(R.layout.main);

        // The following checks to see if we're restarting with a
        // backgrounded AsyncTask. If so, re-establish the connection.
        // Also, since the image did not get saved across the
        // destroy/create cycle, if the AsyncTask has finished,
        // grab the downloaded image again from the AsyncTask.
        if( (diTask =
            (DownloadImageTask)getLastNonConfigurationInstance())
              != null)
        {
            diTask.setContext(this);  // Give my AsyncTask the new
                                      // Activity reference
            if(diTask.getStatus() == AsyncTask.Status.FINISHED)
                diTask.setImageInView();
        }
```

```
    }

    public void doClick(View view) {
        if(diTask != null) {
            AsyncTask.Status diStatus = diTask.getStatus();
            Log.v("doClick", "diTask status is " + diStatus);
            if(diStatus != AsyncTask.Status.FINISHED) {
                Log.v("doClick", "... no need to start a new task");
                return;
            }
            // Since diStatus must be FINISHED, we can try again.
        }
          diTask = new DownloadImageTask(this);

diTask.execute("http://chart.apis.google.com/chart?&cht=p&chs=460x250&chd=t:15.3,20.3,0.
2,59.7,4.5&chl=Android%201.5%7CAndroid%201.6%7COther*%7CAndroid%202.1%7CAndroid%202.2&ch
co=c4df9b,6fad0c");
    }

    // This gets called before onDestroy(). We want to pass forward
    // a reference to our AsyncTask.
    @Override
    public Object onRetainNonConfigurationInstance() {
        return diTask;
    }
}
```

This looks a lot like our HttpActivity from Listing 11–11, except that this time we call getLastNonConfigurationInstance() to see if we have a DownloadImageTask object waiting for us from an old instance of HttpActivity. If we do find one, we need to give it a new reference to the activity, so it can find the new views. See Listing 11–13 for the code of our new DownloadImageTask. Once we've set the new context in our DownloadImageTask, we check to see if the task has finished, as it might have done while HttpActivity was being re-created. If so, we use the setImageInView() method to update our image—more on this a bit later.

You should notice that our button handler, doClick(), is exactly the same as before. But now, we have an implementation of the onRetainNonConfigurationInstance() callback, which only needs to return an object to be passed forward. In our case, we only care about our DownloadImageTask so that's all we need to pass. If we needed to pass more stuff forward, we would need to construct an object to hold it all and then pass that. These are basic Java objects, so we don't need to worry about serialization or parcels (more on parcels later in this chapter). We're merely passing our AsyncTask into the future so we can reconnect with it then.

Listing 11–13. *Our New DownloadImageTask.java That Handles Reconfiguration*

```
import java.io.IOException;
import org.apache.http.HttpResponse;
import org.apache.http.client.HttpClient;
import org.apache.http.client.methods.HttpGet;
import org.apache.http.params.BasicHttpParams;
import org.apache.http.params.HttpConnectionParams;
import org.apache.http.params.HttpParams;
import org.apache.http.util.EntityUtils;
```

```
import android.app.Activity;
import android.content.Context;
import android.graphics.Bitmap;
import android.graphics.BitmapFactory;
import android.os.AsyncTask;
import android.util.Log;
import android.widget.ImageView;
import android.widget.TextView;

public class DownloadImageTask extends AsyncTask<String, Integer, Bitmap> {
    private Context mContext;  // reference to the calling Activity
    int progress = -1;
    Bitmap downloadedImage = null;

    DownloadImageTask(Context context) {
        mContext = context;
    }

    // Called from main thread to re-connect
    protected void setContext(Context context) {
        mContext = context;
        if(progress >= 0) {
            publishProgress(this.progress);
        }
    }

    protected void onPreExecute() {
        progress = 0;
        // We could do some other setup work
        // here before doInBackground() runs
    }

    protected Bitmap doInBackground(String... urls) {
        Log.v("doInBackground", "doing download of image...");
        return downloadImage(urls);
    }

    protected void onProgressUpdate(Integer... progress) {
        TextView mText = (TextView)
                ((Activity) mContext).findViewById(R.id.text);
        mText.setText("Progress so far: " + progress[0]);
    }

    protected void onPostExecute(Bitmap result) {
        if(result != null) {
            downloadedImage = result;
            setImageInView();
        }
        else {
            TextView errorMsg = (TextView)
                ((Activity) mContext).findViewById(R.id.errorMsg);
            errorMsg.setText("Problem downloading image. Please try later.");
        }
    }

    public Bitmap downloadImage(String... urls)
    {
```

```
            HttpClient httpClient = CustomHttpClient.getHttpClient();
            try {
              HttpGet request = new HttpGet(urls[0]);
              HttpParams params = new BasicHttpParams();
              HttpConnectionParams.setSoTimeout(params, 60000);   // 1 minute
              request.setParams(params);

              setProgress(25);

              HttpResponse response = httpClient.execute(request);

              setProgress(50);

              sleepFor(5000);    // five second sleep

              byte[] image = EntityUtils.toByteArray(response.getEntity());

              setProgress(75);

              Bitmap mBitmap = BitmapFactory.decodeByteArray(image, 0,
                                     image.length);

              setProgress(100);

              return mBitmap;
            } catch (IOException e) {
              // covers:
              //      ClientProtocolException
              //      ConnectTimeoutException
              //      ConnectionPoolTimeoutException
              //      SocketTimeoutException
              e.printStackTrace();
            }
            return null;
          }

          private void setProgress(int progress) {
              this.progress = progress;
              publishProgress(this.progress);
          }

          protected void setImageInView() {
              if(downloadedImage != null) {
                  ImageView mImage = (ImageView)
                      ((Activity) mContext).findViewById(R.id.image);
                  mImage.setImageBitmap(downloadedImage);
              }
          }

          private void sleepFor(long msecs) {
              try {
                  Thread.sleep(msecs);
              } catch (InterruptedException e) {
                  Log.v("sleep", "interrupted");
              }
          }
      }
```

Go ahead and run this example. We've added a delay of 5 seconds to our AsyncTask to allow you time to rotate the screen while the background task is running. To rotate the emulator, press Ctrl+F11 on your workstation's keyboard. You should see our UI rotate and then correct itself. Each time it rotates, the image disappears (if it was visible) and reappears as our code runs. Feel free to rotate at different times of operation to see the effects. You might even want to go back to the earlier AsyncTask example, add a delay step, and experiment with rotation to see that it does *not* behave as a user would want. Now, let's dig into the new code to see how it works.

This time our AsyncTask extension class is a little bit different.

There are a couple of things that happen in a configuration change that we have to handle. First of all, you need to know that our AsyncTask needs to be given a new reference to the activity so it will be able to update the appropriate views, both in `onProgressUpdate()` and in `onPostExecute()`. When our old activity got destroyed, our old reference to it became useless. We need a new reference. We would need a reference to the new activity in `onPreExecute()` also if we did something in there with the user interface. We now have a method called `setContext()` to let the activity update its context with us, so we'll be able to find the views when we need them.

Second, we're handling the progress updates a little differently. We hang onto a progress member that we can refer to in our `setContext()` method as well as in our `setProgress()` method. We now call `setProgress()` at the appropriate places of our `downloadImage()` method. When we reconnect from the new activity, we want to immediately display the current progress, so we do a `publishProgress()` call in `setContext()`.

Third, images are not maintained across the destroy/create cycle. If our activity is re-created before our AsyncTask finishes, we'll be fine, since `onPostExecute()` will set our new bitmap. But, if our AsyncTask finished long ago, and then we rotate the device, our activity will be re-created, but our image will not get set. We could again download the image from the server, but in our example, we chose to hang onto the bitmap using a new member called `downloadedImage` and provide a new protected method called `setImageInView()` to reattach the bitmap to the `ImageView`. As was said before, you do not want to hang onto a user interface element such as a `View` inside of the AsyncTask. That is why we keep the bitmap and not the `ImageView`. We do not want to leak memory through references to views on the old activity.

Getting Files Using DownloadManager

Under certain circumstances, your application may need to download a large file to the device. Because this can take awhile, and because the procedure can be standardized, Android 2.3 introduced a special class just to manage this type of operation: DownloadManager. The purpose of the DownloadManager is to satisfy a DownloadManager Request by using a background thread to download a large file to a local location on the device. It is possible to configure the DownloadManager to provide a notification of the download to the user.

In our next sample application, we use the DownloadManager to pull down one of the Android SDK ZIP files. This sample project will have the following files

- `res/layout/main.xml` (Listing 11–14)
- `MainActivity.java` (Listing 11–15)
- `AndroidManifest.xml` (Listing 11–16)

Listing 11–14. *Using DownloadManager: /res/layout/main.xml*

```
<?xml version="1.0" encoding="utf-8"?>
<LinearLayout xmlns:android="http://schemas.android.com/apk/res/android"
    android:orientation="vertical"
    android:layout_width="fill_parent"
    android:layout_height="fill_parent" >
  <Button android:onClick="doClick" android:text="Start"
    android:layout_width="wrap_content"
    android:layout_height="wrap_content" />
  <TextView  android:id="@+id/tv"
    android:layout_width="fill_parent"
    android:layout_height="wrap_content" />
</LinearLayout>
```

Our layout is a simple one with a button and a text view. The button will cause the download to start, and we'll display some messages in the text view to indicate the beginning and end of the download. The user interface looks like Figure 11–3.

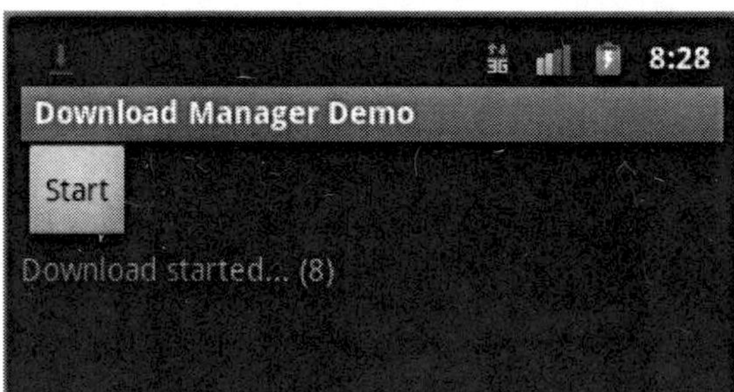

Figure 11–3. *User Interface of our DownloadManagerDemo Sample Application*

Our next listing has the Java code for this application.

Listing 11–15. *Using DownloadManager: MainActivity.java*

```
import android.app.Activity;
import android.app.DownloadManager;
import android.content.BroadcastReceiver;
import android.content.Context;
import android.content.Intent;
import android.content.IntentFilter;
import android.net.Uri;
import android.os.Bundle;
import android.util.Log;
import android.view.View;
import android.widget.TextView;

public class MainActivity extends Activity {
```

```
    protected static final String TAG = "DownloadMgr";
    private DownloadManager dMgr;
    private TextView tv;
    private long downloadId;

    /** Called when the activity is first created. */
    @Override
    public void onCreate(Bundle savedInstanceState) {
        super.onCreate(savedInstanceState);
        setContentView(R.layout.main);

        tv = (TextView)findViewById(R.id.tv);
    }

    @Override
    protected void onResume() {
        super.onResume();
        dMgr = (DownloadManager) getSystemService(DOWNLOAD_SERVICE);
    }

    public void doClick(View view) {
        DownloadManager.Request dmReq = new DownloadManager.Request(
            Uri.parse(
                "http://dl-ssl.google.com/android/repository/" +
                "platform-tools_r01-linux.zip"));
        dmReq.setTitle("Platform Tools");
        dmReq.setDescription("Download for Linux");
        dmReq.setAllowedNetworkTypes(DownloadManager.Request.NETWORK_MOBILE);

        IntentFilter filter = new
IntentFilter(DownloadManager.ACTION_DOWNLOAD_COMPLETE);
        registerReceiver(mReceiver, filter);

        downloadId = dMgr.enqueue(dmReq);

        tv.setText("Download started... (" + downloadId + ")");
    }

    public BroadcastReceiver mReceiver = new BroadcastReceiver() {
        public void onReceive(Context context, Intent intent) {
            Bundle extras = intent.getExtras();
            long doneDownloadId =
                extras.getLong(DownloadManager.EXTRA_DOWNLOAD_ID);
            tv.setText(tv.getText() + "\nDownload finished (" +
                doneDownloadId + ")");
            if(downloadId == doneDownloadId)
                Log.v(TAG, "Our download has completed.");
        }
    };

    @Override
    protected void onPause() {
        super.onPause();
        unregisterReceiver(mReceiver);
        dMgr = null;
    }
}
```

The code for this application is very straightforward. First we initialize our main view, and then we get a reference to the text view. Within our onResume() method, we get a reference to the DOWNLOAD_SERVICE service. Note that we de-reference this service in onPause(). Our button click method doClick() creates a new DownloadManager.Request object using the path to the ZIP file we want to download. We also set the title, description, and allowed network type for the download. There are a few more options to choose from; see the documentation for details.

Simply for demonstration purposes, we chose to use the mobile network for downloading, but you can also choose just WiFi (using NETWORK_WIFI instead of NETWORK_MOBILE) or you can OR the two values together to allow either. By default both networks are allowed for download, which means for our sample application we only want to use the mobile network for downloading, even if WiFi is available.

Once we've set up our request object, we create a filter for a broadcast receiver and we register it. We'll get to our broadcast receiver code shortly. By registering the receiver, we'll be notified when any download has completed. This means we need to keep track of the ID of our request, which is returned when we call enqueue() on our DownloadManager. Finally, we update the status message in our UI to indicate that a download has started.

For this application to work, we need to specify a couple of permissions, as shown in our AndroidManifest.xml file in Listing 11–16, to allow our application to access the Internet and to be able to write the file to the SD card. What's strange about Android 2.3 is that if you don't specify the permissions as indicated in Listing 11–16, you'll get an error message that complains about not having the ACCESS_ALL_DOWNLOADS permission, which you don't even need for this example.

Listing 11–16. *Using DownloadManager: AndroidManifest.xml*

```
<?xml version="1.0" encoding="utf-8"?>
<manifest xmlns:android="http://schemas.android.com/apk/res/android"
      package="com.androidbook.services.download"
      android:versionCode="1"
      android:versionName="1.0">
    <application android:icon="@drawable/icon" android:label="@string/app_name">
        <activity android:name=".MainActivity"
                  android:label="@string/app_name">
            <intent-filter>
                <action android:name="android.intent.action.MAIN" />
                <category android:name="android.intent.category.LAUNCHER" />
            </intent-filter>
        </activity>

    </application>
    <uses-sdk android:minSdkVersion="9" />

<uses-permission android:name="android.permission.INTERNET" />
<uses-permission android:name="android.permission.WRITE_EXTERNAL_STORAGE" />
</manifest>
```

When you run this application, it should show the button. Clicking the button will initiate the download operation and show the message as in Figure 11–3. Notice that there's a download icon in the notification bar in the upper left corner of the screen. If you were to drag down on the download icon, you would see a notification window that looks like Figure 11–4.

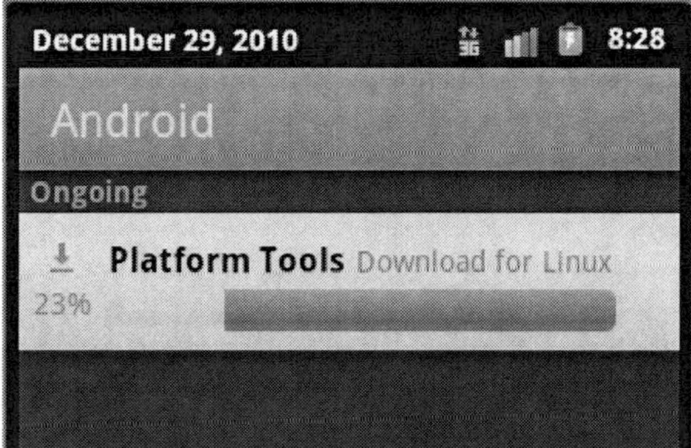

Figure 11–4. *Downloads in the Notification List*

The notification is the download occurring in the background. Once the download has completed, this notification item will be cleared, and we'll see an additional message in our application, as shown in Figure 11–5.

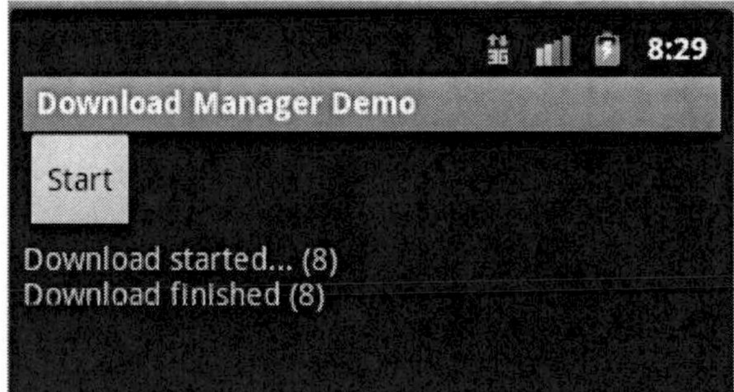

Figure 11–5. *Application shows download is complete*

In our broadcast receiver, we interrogate the intent to find out if the download that completed was ours or not. If it is, we update our status message in the UI, and that's all we're doing. Remember that we cannot do much processing in our broadcast receiver because we must return from `onReceive()` quickly. For example, we could instead invoke a service to process the file that was downloaded. Within that service, we could call something like Listing 11–17 to get to the file contents.

Listing 11–17. *Reading a Downloaded File*

```
try {
    ParcelFileDescriptor pfd = dMgr.openDownloadedFile(doneDownloadId);
    // Now we have a read-only handle to the downloaded file
    // Proceed to read the file...
} catch (FileNotFoundException e) {
    e.printStackTrace();
}
```

One way to locate the downloaded file is to use the `DownloadManager` service, and we need to specify the download ID to get the appropriate file. This was shown in Listing 11–17. The `DownloadManager` class takes care of resolving the download ID to the actual file. While our example downloads a file to the public area on the SD card, you can in fact download a file to the application's private data area on the SD card, using one of the `setDestination*()` methods of `DownloadManager.Request`.

`DownloadManager` has its own application that you can also access to see downloaded files. From the application menu on the Android device or emulator, look for the icon as shown in Figure 11–6.

Figure 11–6. *The Downloads application icon*

You can use the Downloads application to also get to downloaded files. Go ahead and try it now. When you launch the Downloads application, you'll see a screen that looks like Figure 11–7. Actually, it won't have the menu along the bottom until you click in a checkbox to select a specific download, as we did before taking the screen shot.

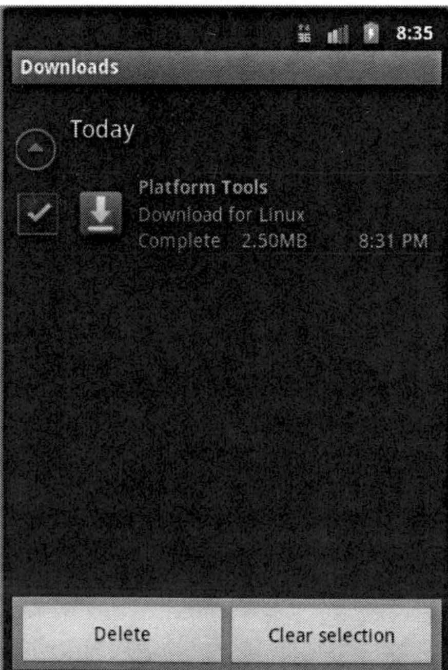

Figure 11–7. *The Downloads application*

The DownloadManager contains a content provider for the download file information. The Downloads application is simply accessing this content provider to show the list of available downloads to the user. This means you can also interrogate the content provider within your application to get information about downloads. To do that, you would use a DownloadManager.Query object, and DownloadManager's query() method. There aren't very many options for searching however. You can search by download ID (one or more), or you can search by download status. The result from the query() method is a Cursor object which can be used to interrogate rows from the DownloadManager content provider. The columns available are listed in the documentation for DownloadManager, and include things like the local Uri of the downloaded file, the number of bytes, the media type of the file, the download status, and several others. When you access the content provider in this way, you need to add the ACCESS_ALL_DOWNLOADS permission to your AndroidManifest.xml file.

Finally, you can use DownloadManager's remove() method to cancel a download, although this does not remove the file if it has been downloaded.

We've shown you how to operate with HTTP-based services, and we showed you how to manage the interface to those services using a special class called AsyncTask. The typical use case of an AsyncTask is some operation that will last for a time, but not for a long time, and where the conclusion of that operation should directly affect the user interface in some way. But what if we wanted to run some background processing that lasted longer than a short while, or what if we wanted to invoke some non-UI functionality that exists in another application? For these needs, Android provides services. We will discuss them next.

Using Android Services

Android supports the concept of services. Services are components that run in the background, without a user interface. You can think of these components as similar to Windows services or Unix daemons. Similar to these types of services, Android services can be always available but don't have to be actively doing something. More importantly, Android services can have life cycles separate from activities. When an activity pauses, stops, or gets destroyed, there may be some processing that you want to continue. Services are good for that too.

Android supports two types of services: local services and remote services. A *local service* is a service that is only accessible to the application that is hosting it, and it is not accessible from other applications running on the device. Generally, these types of services simply support the application that is hosting the service. A *remote service* is accessible from other applications on the device in addition to the application hosting the service. Remote services define themselves to clients using Android Interface Definition Language (AIDL). We're going to talk about both of these types of services, although in the next few chapters, we're going deep into local services. Therefore, we will introduce them here but not spend that much time on them. We'll cover remote services in more detail in this chapter.

Understanding Services in Android

The Android `Service` class is a wrapper of sorts for code that has service-like behavior. Unlike the AsyncTask we covered earlier, a `Service` object does not create its own threads automatically. For a `Service` object to use threads, the developer must make it happen. This means that without adding threading to a service, the code of the service will run on the main thread. If our service is performing operations that will complete quickly, this won't be a problem. If our service might run for a while, we definitely want to involve threading. Keep in mind there is nothing wrong with using AsyncTasks to do threading within services.

Android supports the concept of a service for two reasons.

- First, to allow you to implement background tasks easily
- Second, to allow you to do interprocess communication between applications running on the same device

These two reasons correspond to the two types of services that Android supports: local services and remote services. An example of the first case might be a local service implemented as part of an e-mail application. The service could handle the sending of a new e-mail to the e-mail server, complete with attachments and retries. As this could take a while to complete, a service is a nice way of wrapping up that functionality so the main thread can kick it off and get back to the user. Plus, if the e-mail activity goes away, you still want the sent e-mails to be delivered. An example of the second case, as we'll see later, is a language translation application. Suppose you have several applications running on a device, and you need a service to accept text that needs to be translated from one language to another. Rather than repeat the logic in every application, you could write a remote translation service and have the applications talk to the service.

There are some important differences between local services and remote services. Specifically, if a service is strictly used by the components in the same process, the clients must start the service by calling `Context.startService()`. This type of service is a local service, because its purpose is, generally, to run background tasks for the application that is hosting the service. If the service supports the `onBind()` method, it's a remote service that can be called via interprocess communication (`Context.bindService()`). We also call remote services *AIDL-supporting services* because clients communicate with the service using AIDL.

Although the interface of `android.app.Service` supports both local and remote services, it's not a good idea to provide one implementation of a service to support both types. The reason for this is that each type of service has a predefined life cycle; mixing the two, although allowed, can cause errors.

Now, we can begin a detailed examination of the two types of services. We will start by talking about local services and then discuss remote services (AIDL-supporting services). As mentioned before, local services are services that are called only by the application that hosts them. Remote services are services that support a remote procedure call (RPC) mechanism. These services allow external clients, on the same device, to connect to the service and use its facilities.

> **NOTE:** The second type of service in Android is known by several names: remote service, AIDL-supporting service, AIDL service, external service, and RPC service. These terms all refer to the same type of service—one that's meant to be accessed remotely by other applications running on the device.

Understanding Local Services

Local services are services that are started via `Context.startService()`. Once started, these types of services will continue to run until a client calls `Context.stopService()` on the service or the service itself calls `stopSelf()`. Note that when `Context.startService()` is called and the service has not already been created, the system will instantiate the service and call the service's `onStartCommand()` method. Keep in mind that calling `Context.startService()` after the service has been started (that is, while it exists) will not result in another instance of the service, but will reinvoke the running service's `onStartCommand()` method. Here are a couple of examples of local services:

- A service to monitor sensor data from the device and do analysis, issuing alerts if a certain condition is realized. This service might run constantly.
- A task-executor service that lets your application's activities submit jobs and queue them for processing. This service might only run for the duration of the operation to submit the job.

Listing 11–18 demonstrates a local service by implementing a service that executes background tasks. We'll end up with four artifacts required to create and consume the service: `BackgroundService.java` (the service itself), `main.xml` (a layout file for the activity), `MainActivity.java` (an activity class to call the service), and `AndroidManifest.xml`. Listing 11–18 only contains `BackgroundService.java`. We'll dissect this code first and then move on to the other three. This implementation requires Android 2.0 or later.

Listing 11–18. ***Implementing a Local Service: BackgroundService.java***

```
import android.app.Notification;
import android.app.NotificationManager;
import android.app.PendingIntent;
import android.app.Service;
import android.content.Intent;
import android.os.IBinder;
import android.util.Log;

public class BackgroundService extends Service
{
    private static final String TAG = "BackgroundService";
```

```
private NotificationManager notificationMgr;
private ThreadGroup myThreads = new ThreadGroup("ServiceWorker");

@Override
public void onCreate() {
    super.onCreate();

    Log.v(TAG, "in onCreate()");
    notificationMgr =(NotificationManager)getSystemService(
          NOTIFICATION_SERVICE);
    displayNotificationMessage("Background Service is running");
}

@Override
public int onStartCommand(Intent intent, int flags, int startId) {
    super.onStartCommand(intent, flags, startId);

    int counter = intent.getExtras().getInt("counter");
    Log.v(TAG, "in onStartCommand(), counter = " + counter +
            ", startId = " + startId);

    new Thread(myThreads, new ServiceWorker(counter),
        "BackgroundService")
            .start();

    return START_STICKY;
}

class ServiceWorker implements Runnable
{
    private int counter = -1;
    public ServiceWorker(int counter) {
        this.counter = counter;
    }

    public void run() {
        final String TAG2 = "ServiceWorker:" +
            Thread.currentThread().getId();
        // do background processing here... we'll just sleep...
        try {
            Log.v(TAG2, "sleeping for 10 seconds. counter = " +
                counter);
            Thread.sleep(10000);
            Log.v(TAG2, "... waking up");
        } catch (InterruptedException e) {
            Log.v(TAG2, "... sleep interrupted");
        }
    }
}

@Override
public void onDestroy()
{
    Log.v(TAG, "in onDestroy(). Interrupting threads and cancelling notifications");
    myThreads.interrupt();
    notificationMgr.cancelAll();
    super.onDestroy();
```

```
    }

    @Override
    public IBinder onBind(Intent intent) {
        Log.v(TAG, "in onBind()");
        return null;
    }

    private void displayNotificationMessage(String message)
    {
        Notification notification =
            new Notification(R.drawable.emo_im_winking,
                message, System.currentTimeMillis());

        notification.flags = Notification.FLAG_NO_CLEAR;

        PendingIntent contentIntent =
            PendingIntent.getActivity(this, 0,
                new Intent(this, MainActivity.class), 0);

        notification.setLatestEventInfo(this, TAG, message,
            contentIntent);

        notificationMgr.notify(0, notification);
    }
}
```

The structure of a `Service` object is somewhat similar to an activity. There is an `onCreate()` method where you can do initialization, and an `onDestroy()` where you do cleanup. Prior to Android 2.0, a service had an `onStart()` method, and since 2.0 it's called `onStartCommand()`. The difference between the two is the addition of a flags parameter, which is used to specify to the service that an intent is being redelivered or that the service should restart. We're using the `onStartCommand()` version for our example. Services don't pause or resume the way activities do so we don't see `onPause()` or `onResume()` methods. Because this is a local service, we won't be binding to it, but since `Service` requires an implementation of the `onBind()` method, we provide one that simply returns null.

Going back to our `onCreate()` method, we don't need to do much except to notify the user that this service has been created. We do this using the `NotificationManager`. You've probably noticed the notification bar at the top left of an Android screen. By pulling down on this, the user can view messages of importance, and by clicking on notifications can act on the notifications, which usually means returning to some activity related to the notification. With services, since they can be running, or at least existing, in the background without a visible activity, there has to be some way for the user to get back in touch with the service, perhaps to turn it off. Therefore, we create a Notification object, populate it with a `PendingIntent`, which will get us back to our control activity, and we post it. This all happens in the `displayNotificationMessage()` method. One more thing we really need to do is set a flag on our Notification object so the user can't clear it from the list. We really need that Notification to exist as long as our service exists so we set `Notification.FLAG_NO_CLEAR` to keep it in the Notifications list until we clear it ourselves from our service's onDestroy() method. The method we used in onDestroy() to clear our notification is cancelAll() on the NotificationManager.

There's another thing you need to have for this example to work. You'll need to create a drawable named emo_im_winking and place it within your project's drawable folder. A good source of drawables for this demonstration purpose is to look under the Android platform folder at Android SDK/platforms/<version>/data/res/drawable where <version> is the version you're interested in. Unfortunately, you can't refer to Android system drawables from your code the way you can with layouts, so you'll need to copy what you want over to your project's drawables folder. If you choose a different drawable file for your example, just go ahead and rename the resource Id in the constructor for the Notification.

When an intent is sent into our service using startService(), onCreate() is called if necessary, and our onStartCommand() method is called to receive the caller's intent. In our case, we're not going to do anything special with it, except to unpack the counter and use it to start a background thread. In a real-world service, we would expect any data to be passed to us via the intent, and this could include Uris for example. Notice the use of a ThreadGroup when creating the Thread. This will prove to be useful later when we want to get rid of our background threads. Also notice the startId parameter. This is set for us by Android, and is a unique identifier of the service calls since this service was started.

Our ServiceWorker class is a typical runnable and is where the work happens for our service. In our particular case, we're simply logging some messages and sleeping. We're also catching any interruptions and logging them. One thing we're not doing is manipulating the user interface. We're not updating any views for example. Since we're not on the main thread anymore, we cannot touch the UI directly. There are ways for our ServiceWorker to effect changes in the user interface, and we'll get into those details in the next few chapters.

The last item to pay attention to in our BackgroundService is the onDestroy() method. This is where we perform the cleanup. For our example, we want to get rid of the threads we created earlier, if any are still around. If we don't do this, they could simply hang around and take up memory. Second, we want to get rid of our notification message. Since our service is going away, there's no longer any need for the user to get to the activity to get rid of it. In a real-world application, however, we might want to keep our workers working. If our service is sending e-mails, we certainly don't want to simply kill off the threads. Our example is overly simple, since we imply through the use of the interrupt() method that you can easily kill off background threads. In reality, however, the most you can do is interrupt. This won't necessarily kill off a thread though. There are deprecated methods for killing threads, but you should not use these. They can cause memory and stability problems for you and your users. Interrupting works in our example, because we're doing sleeps, which can be interrupted.

It's worthwhile taking a look at the ThreadGroup class since it provides ways for you to get access to your threads. We created a single ThreadGroup object within our service and then used that when creating our individual threads. Within our onDestroy() method of the service, we simply interrupt() on the ThreadGroup and it issues an interrupt to each thread in the ThreadGroup.

So there you have the makings of a simple local service. Before we show you the code for our activity, Listing 11–19 shows the XML layout file for our user interface.

Listing 11–19. *Implementing a Local Service: main.xml*

```
<?xml version="1.0" encoding="utf-8"?>
<!-- This file is /res/layout/main.xml -->
<LinearLayout xmlns:android="http://schemas.android.com/apk/res/android"
    android:orientation="vertical"
    android:layout_width="fill_parent"
    android:layout_height="fill_parent"
    >
<Button  android:id="@+id/startBtn"
    android:layout_width="wrap_content"
    android:layout_height="wrap_content"
    android:text="Start Service"  android:onClick="doClick" />
<Button  android:id="@+id/stopBtn"
    android:layout_width="wrap_content"
    android:layout_height="wrap_content"
    android:text="Stop Service"  android:onClick="doClick" />

</LinearLayout>
```

We're going to show two buttons on the user interface, one to do startService() and the other to do stopService(). We could have chosen to use a ToggleButton, but then you would not be able to call startService() multiple times in a row. This is an important point. There is not a one-to-one relationship between startService() and stopService(). When stopService() is called, the service object will be destroyed, and all threads created from all startServices() should also go away. For our example, we require a minSdkVersion of 5 since we're using the newer onStartCommand() instead of the older onStart(). Therefore, we can also take advantage of the android:onClick attribute of the Button tag in our layout XML file. Now, let's look at the code for our activity in Listing 11–20.

Listing 11–20. *Implementing a Local Service: MainActivity.java*

```
// MainActivity.java
import android.app.Activity;
import android.content.Intent;
import android.os.Bundle;
import android.util.Log;
import android.view.View;

public class MainActivity extends Activity
{
    private static final String TAG = "MainActivity";
    private int counter = 1;

    @Override
    public void onCreate(Bundle savedInstanceState)
    {
        super.onCreate(savedInstanceState);
        setContentView(R.layout.main);
```

```
    }

    public void doClick(View view) {
        switch(view.getId()) {
        case R.id.startBtn:
            Log.v(TAG, "Starting service... counter = " + counter);
            Intent intent = new Intent(MainActivity.this,
                    BackgroundService.class);
            intent.putExtra("counter", counter++);
            startService(intent);
            break;
        case R.id.stopBtn:
            stopService();
        }
    }

    private void stopService() {
        Log.v(TAG, "Stopping service...");
        if(stopService(new Intent(MainActivity.this,
                    BackgroundService.class)))
            Log.v(TAG, "stopService was successful");
        else
            Log.v(TAG, "stopService was unsuccessful");
    }

    @Override
    public void onDestroy()
    {
        stopService();
        super.onDestroy();
    }
}
```

Our `MainActivity` looks a lot like other activities you've seen. There's a simple `onCreate()` to set up our user interface from the `main.xml` layout file. There's a `doClick()` method to handle the button callbacks. In our example, we're calling `startService()` when the Start Service button is pressed, and we're calling `stopService()` when the Stop Service button is pressed. When we start the service, we want to pass in some data, which we do via the intent. We chose to pass the data in the Extras bundle, but we could have added it using `setData()` if we had a URI. When we stop the service, we check to see the return result. It should normally be true, but if the service was not running, we could get a return of false. Lastly, when our activity dies, we want to stop the service so we also stop the service in our `onDestroy()` method. There's one more item to discuss, and that's the `AndroidManifest.xml` file, which we show in Listing 11–21.

Listing 11–21. *Implementing a Local Service: AndroidManifest.xml*

```
<?xml version="1.0" encoding="utf-8"?>
<manifest xmlns:android="http://schemas.android.com/apk/res/android"
      package="com.androidbook.services.simplelocal"
      android:versionCode="1"
      android:versionName="1.0">
    <application android:icon="@drawable/icon"
            android:label="@string/app_name">
        <activity android:name=".MainActivity"
```

```
            android:label="@string/app_name"
            android:launchMode="singleTop" >
        <intent-filter>
          <action android:name="android.intent.action.MAIN" />
          <category android:name="android.intent.category.LAUNCHER" />
        </intent-filter>
      </activity>
      <service android:name="BackgroundService"/>
  </application>
  <uses-sdk android:minSdkVersion="5" />

</manifest>
```

In addition to our regular `<activity>` tags in the manifest file, we now have a `<service>` tag. Because this is a local service that we're calling explicitly using the class name, we don't need to put much into the `<service>` tag. All that is required is the name of our service. But there is one other thing to point out about this manifest file. Our service creates a notification so that the user can get back to our `MainActivity` if, for example, the user pressed the Home key on `MainActivity` without stopping the service.

The `MainActivity` is still there; it's just not visible. One way to get back to the `MainActivity` is to click the notification that our service created. What we don't want to have happen is for a new `MainActivity` to be created in addition to our existing, invisible `MainActivity`. To prevent this from happening, we set an attribute in our manifest file for `MainActivity` called `android:launchMode`, and we set it to `singleTop`. This will help ensure that the existing invisible `MainActivity` will be brought forward and displayed, rather than creating another `MainActivity`.

When you run this application, you will see our two buttons. By clicking the Start Service button, you will be instantiating the service and calling `onStartCommand()`. Our code logs several messages to LogCat, so you can follow along. Go ahead and click Start Service several times in a row, even quickly. You will see threads created to handle each request. You'll also notice that the value of counter is passed along through to each `ServiceWorker` thread. When you press the Stop Service button, our service will go away, and you'll see the log messages from our `MainActivity`'s `stopService()` method, from our `BackgroundService`'s `onDestroy()` method, and possibly from `ServiceWorker` threads if they got interrupted.

You should also notice the notification message when the service has been started. With the service running, go ahead and press the Back button from our `MainActivity` and notice that the notification message disappears. This means our service has gone away also. To restart our `MainActivity`, click Start Service to get the service going again. Now, press the Home button. Our `MainActivity` disappears from view, but the notification remains, meaning our service is still in existence. Go ahead and click the notification, and you'll again see our `MainActivity`.

Note that our example uses an activity to interface with the service, but any component in your application can use the service. This includes other services, activities, generic classes, and so on. Also note that our service does not stop itself; it relies on the activity to do that for it. There are some methods available to a service to allow the service to stop itself, namely `stopSelf()` and `stopSelfResult()`.

Our BackgroundService is a typical example of a service that is used by the components of the application that is hosting the service. In other words, the application that is running the service is also the only consumer. Because the service does not support clients from outside its process, the service is a local service. And because it's a local service, as opposed to a remote service, it returns null in the bind() method. Therefore, the only way to bind to this service is to call Context.startService(). The critical methods of a local service are onCreate(), onStartCommand(), stop*(), and onDestroy().

There's another option with a local service, and that is for the case where you'll only have one instance of the service with one background thread. In this case, in the onCreate() method of the BackgroundService, we could create a thread that does the service's heavy lifting. We could create and start the thread in onCreate() rather than onStartCommand(). We could do this because onCreate() is called only once, and we want the thread to be created only once during the life of the service. One thing we wouldn't have in onCreate(), though, is the content of the intent passed by startService(). If we need that, we might as well use the pattern as described previously, and we'd just know that onStartCommand() should only be called once.

This concludes our introduction to local services. Remember that we'll get into more details of local services in subsequent chapters. Let's move on to AIDL services—the more complicated type of service.

Understanding AIDL Services

In the previous section, we showed you how to write an Android service that is consumed by the application that hosts the service. Now, we are going to show you how to build a service that can be consumed by other processes via remote procedure call (RPC). As with many other RPC-based solutions, in Android you need an interface definition language (IDL) to define the interface that will be exposed to clients. In the Android world, this IDL is called Android Interface Definition Language (AIDL). To build a remote service, you do the following:

1. Write an AIDL file that defines your interface to clients. The AIDL file uses Java syntax and has an .aidl extension. Use the same package name inside your AIDL file as the package for your Android Project.
2. Add the AIDL file to your Eclipse project under the src directory. The Android Eclipse plug-in will call the AIDL compiler to generate a Java interface from the AIDL file (the AIDL compiler is called as part of the build process).
3. Implement a service and return the interface from the onBind() method.
4. Add the service configuration to your AndroidManifest.xml file. The sections that follow show you how to execute each step.

Defining a Service Interface in AIDL

To demonstrate an example of a remote service, we are going to write a stock-quoter service. This service will provide a method that takes a ticker symbol and returns the stock value. To write a remote service in Android, the first step is to define the service interface definition in an AIDL file. Listing 11–22 shows the AIDL definition of `IStockQuoteService`. This file goes into the same place as a regular Java file would for your `StockQuoteService` project.

Listing 11–22. *The AIDL Definition of the Stock-Quoter Service*

```
// This file is IStockQuoteService.aidl
package com.androidbook.services.stockquoteservice;
interface IStockQuoteService
{
        double getQuote(String ticker);
}
```

The `IStockQuoteService` accepts the stock-ticker symbol as a string and returns the current stock value as a double. When you create the AIDL file, the Android Eclipse plug-in runs the AIDL compiler to process your AIDL file (as part of the build process). If your AIDL file compiles successfully, the compiler generates a Java interface suitable for RPC communication. Note that the generated file will be in the package named in your AIDL file—`com.androidbook.services.stockquoteservice`, in this case.

Listing 11–23 shows the generated Java file for our `IStockQuoteService` interface. The generated file will be put into the gen folder of our Eclipse project.

Listing 11–23. *The Compiler-Generated Java File*

```
  /*
 * This file is auto-generated.  DO NOT MODIFY.
 * Original file: C:\\android\\StockQuoteService\\src\\com\\androidbook\\➥
services\\stockquoteservice\\IStockQuoteService.aidl
 */
package com.androidbook.services.stockquoteservice;
import java.lang.String;
import android.os.RemoteException;
import android.os.IBinder;
import android.os.IInterface;
import android.os.Binder;
import android.os.Parcel;
public interface IStockQuoteService extends android.os.IInterface
{
/** Local-side IPC implementation stub class. */
public static abstract class Stub extends android.os.Binder implements ➥
com.androidbook.services.stockquoteservice.IStockQuoteService
{
private static final java.lang.String DESCRIPTOR = ➥
"com.androidbook.services.stockquoteservice.IStockQuoteService";
/** Construct the stub at attach it to the interface. */
public Stub()
{
this.attachInterface(this, DESCRIPTOR);
}
/**
```

```
 * Cast an IBinder object into an IStockQuoteService interface,
 * generating a proxy if needed.
 */
public static com.androidbook.services.stockquoteservice.IStockQuoteService ➥
asInterface(android.os.IBinder obj)
{
if ((obj==null)) {
return null;
}
android.os.IInterface iin = (android.os.IInterface)obj.queryLocalInterface(DESCRIPTOR);
if (((iin!=null)&&(iin instanceof
com.androidbook.services.stockquoteservice.IStockQuoteService))) {
return ((com.androidbook.services.stockquoteservice.IStockQuoteService)iin);
}
return ((com.androidbook.services.stockquoteservice.IStockQuoteService)iin);
}
return new
com.androidbook.services.stockquoteservice.IStockQuoteService.Stub.Proxy(obj);
}
public android.os.IBinder asBinder()
{
return this;
}
@Override public boolean onTransact(int code, android.os.Parcel data,➥
     android.os.Parcel reply, int flags) throws android.os.RemoteException
{
switch (code)
{
case INTERFACE_TRANSACTION:
{
reply.writeString(DESCRIPTOR);
return true;
}
case TRANSACTION_getQuote:
{
data.enforceInterface(DESCRIPTOR);
java.lang.String _arg0;
_arg0 = data.readString();
double _result = this.getQuote(_arg0);
reply.writeNoException();
reply.writeDouble(_result);
return true;
}
}
return super.onTransact(code, data, reply, flags);
}
private static class Proxy implements
        com.androidbook.services.stockquoteservice.IStockQuoteService
{
private android.os.IBinder mRemote;
Proxy(android.os.IBinder remote)
{
mRemote = remote;
}
public android.os.IBinder asBinder()
{
return mRemote;
```

```
}
public java.lang.String getInterfaceDescriptor()
{
return DESCRIPTOR;
}
public double getQuote(java.lang.String ticker) throws android.os.RemoteException
{
android.os.Parcel _data = android.os.Parcel.obtain();
android.os.Parcel _reply = android.os.Parcel.obtain();
double _result;
try {
_data.writeInterfaceToken(DESCRIPTOR);
_data.writeString(ticker);
mRemote.transact(Stub.TRANSACTION_getQuote, _data, _reply, 0);
_reply.readException();
_result = _reply.readDouble();
}
finally {
_reply.recycle();
_data.recycle();
}
return _result;
}
}
static final int TRANSACTION_getQuote = (IBinder.FIRST_CALL_TRANSACTION + 0);
}
public double getQuote(java.lang.String ticker) throws android.os.RemoteException;
}
```

Note the following important points regarding the generated classes:

- The interface we defined in the AIDL file is implemented as an interface in the generated code (that is, there is an interface named IStockQuoteService).
- A static final abstract class named Stub extends android.os.Binder and implements IStockQuoteService. Note that the class is an abstract class.
- An inner class named Proxy implements the IStockQuoteService that proxies the Stub class.
- The AIDL file must reside in the package where the generated files are supposed to be (as specified in the AIDL file's package declaration).

Now, let's move on and implement the AIDL interface in a service class.

Implementing an AIDL Interface

In the previous section, we defined an AIDL file for a stock-quoter service and generated the binding file. Now, we are going to provide an implementation of that service. To implement the service's interface, we need to write a class that extends android.app.Service and implements the IStockQuoteService interface. The class we are going to write will call StockQuoteService. To expose the service to clients, our

StockQuoteService will need to provide an implementation of the onBind() method, and we'll need to add some configuration information to the AndroidManifest.xml file. Listing 11–24 shows an implementation of the IStockQuoteService interface. This file also goes into the src folder of the StockQuoteService project.

Listing 11–24. *The IStockQuoteService Service Implementation*

```
// StockQuoteService.java
import android.app.Service;
import android.content.Intent;
import android.os.IBinder;
import android.os.RemoteException;
import android.util.Log;

public class StockQuoteService extends Service
{
    private static final String TAG = "StockQuoteService";
    public class StockQuoteServiceImpl extends IStockQuoteService.Stub
    {
        @Override
        public double getQuote(String ticker) throws RemoteException
        {
            Log.v(TAG, "getQuote() called for " + ticker);
            return 20.0;
        }
    }

    @Override
    public void onCreate() {
        super.onCreate();
        Log.v(TAG, "onCreate() called");
    }

    @Override
    public void onDestroy()
    {
        super.onDestroy();
        Log.v(TAG, "onDestroy() called");
    }

    @Override
    public IBinder onBind(Intent intent)
    {
        Log.v(TAG, "onBind() called");
        return new StockQuoteServiceImpl();
    }
}
```

The StockQuoteService.java class in Listing 11–24 resembles the local BackgroundService we created earlier, but without the NotificationManager. The important difference is that we now implement the onBind() method. Recall that the Stub class generated from the AIDL file was an abstract class and that it implemented the IStockQuoteService interface. In our implementation of the service, we have an inner class that extends the Stub class called StockQuoteServiceImpl. This class serves as the remote-service implementation, and an instance of this class is returned from the onBind() method. With that, we have a functional AIDL service, although external clients cannot connect to it yet.

To expose the service to clients, we need to add a service declaration in the AndroidManifest.xml file, and this time, we need an intent filter to expose the service. Listing 11–25 shows the service declaration for the StockQuoteService. The <service> tag is a child of the <application> tag.

Listing 11–25. *Manifest Declaration for the IStockQuoteService*

```
<?xml version="1.0" encoding="utf-8"?>
<manifest xmlns:android="http://schemas.android.com/apk/res/android"
      package="com.androidbook.services.stockquoteservice"
      android:versionCode="1"
      android:versionName="1.0">
    <application android:icon="@drawable/icon"
        android:label="@string/app_name">
      <service android:name="StockQuoteService">
        <intent-filter>
                <action
android:name="com.androidbook.services.stockquoteservice.IStockQuoteService" />
        </intent-filter>
      </service>
    </application>
    <uses-sdk android:minSdkVersion="4" />
</manifest>
```

As with all services, we define the service we want to expose with a <service> tag. For an AIDL service, we also need to add an <intent-filter> with an <action> entry for the service interface we want to expose.

With this in place, we have everything we need to deploy the service. When you are ready to deploy the service application from Eclipse, just go ahead and choose Run As the way you would for any other application. Eclipse will comment in the Console that this application has no Launcher, but it will deploy the app anyway, which is what we want. Let's now look at how we would call the service from another application (on the same device, of course).

Calling the Service from a Client Application

When a client talks to a service, there must be a protocol or contract between the two. With Android, the contract is in our AIDL file. So the first step in consuming a service is to take the service's AIDL file and copy it to your client project. When you copy the AIDL file to the client project, the AIDL compiler creates the same interface-definition file that was created when the service was implemented (in the service-implementation project). This exposes to the client all of the methods, parameters, and return types on the service. Let's create a new project and copy the AIDL file.

1. Create a new Android project named StockQuoteClient. Use a different package name, such as com.androidbook.stockquoteclient. Use MainActivity for the Create Activity field.

2. Create a new Java package in this project named `com.androidbook.services.stockquoteservice` in the `src` directory.

3. Copy the `IStockQuoteService.aidl` file from the `StockQuoteService` project to this new package. Note that after you copy the file to the project, the AIDL compiler will generate the associated Java file.

The service interface that you regenerate serves as the contract between the client and the service. The next step is to get a reference to the service so we can call the `getQuote()` method. With remote services, we have to call the `bindService()` method rather than the `startService()` method. Listing 11–26 shows an activity class that acts as a client of the `IStockQuoteService` service. Listing 11–27 contains the layout file for the activity.

Listing 11–26 shows our `MainActivity.java` file. Realize that the package name of the client activity is not that important—you can put the activity in any package you'd like. However, the AIDL artifacts that you create are package-sensitive because the AIDL compiler generates code from the contents of the AIDL file.

Listing 11–26. *A Client of the IStockQuoteService Service*

```
// This file is MainActivity.java
import com.androidbook.services.stockquoteservice.IStockQuoteService;
import android.app.Activity;
import android.content.ComponentName;
import android.content.Context;
import android.content.Intent;
import android.content.ServiceConnection;
import android.os.Bundle;
import android.os.IBinder;
import android.os.RemoteException;
import android.util.Log;
import android.view.View;
import android.widget.Button;
import android.widget.Toast;
import android.widget.ToggleButton;

public class MainActivity extends Activity {
    private static final String TAG = "StockQuoteClient";
    private IStockQuoteService stockService = null;
    private ToggleButton bindBtn;
    private Button callBtn;

    /** Called when the activity is first created. */
    @Override
    public void onCreate(Bundle savedInstanceState) {
        super.onCreate(savedInstanceState);
        setContentView(R.layout.main);

        bindBtn = (ToggleButton)findViewById(R.id.bindBtn);
        callBtn = (Button)findViewById(R.id.callBtn);
    }

    public void doClick(View view) {
        switch(view.getId()) {
```

```
        case R.id.bindBtn:
            if(((ToggleButton) view).isChecked()) {
                bindService(new Intent(
                    IStockQuoteService.class.getName()),
                    serConn, Context.BIND_AUTO_CREATE);
            }
            else {
                unbindService(serConn);
                callBtn.setEnabled(false);
            }
            break;
        case R.id.callBtn:
            callService();
            break;
        }
    }

    private void callService() {
        try {
            double val = stockService.getQuote("ANDROID");
            Toast.makeText(MainActivity.this,
                    "Value from service is " + val,
                    Toast.LENGTH_SHORT).show();
        } catch (RemoteException ee) {
            Log.e("MainActivity", ee.getMessage(), ee);
        }
    }

    private ServiceConnection serConn = new ServiceConnection() {

        @Override
        public void onServiceConnected(ComponentName name,
            IBinder service)
        {
            Log.v(TAG, "onServiceConnected() called");
            stockService = IStockQuoteService.Stub.asInterface(service);
            bindBtn.setChecked(true);
            callBtn.setEnabled(true);
        }

        @Override
        public void onServiceDisconnected(ComponentName name) {
            Log.v(TAG, "onServiceDisconnected() called");
            bindBtn.setChecked(false);
            callBtn.setEnabled(false);
            stockService = null;
        }
    };

    protected void onDestroy() {
        Log.v(TAG, "onDestroy() called");
        if(callBtn.isEnabled())
            unbindService(serConn);
        super.onDestroy();
    }
}
```

The activity displays our layout, and grabs a reference to the Call Service button so we can properly enable it when the service is running, and disable it when the service is stopped. When the user clicks the Bind button, the activity calls the bindService() method. Similarly, when the user clicks UnBind, the activity calls the unbindService() method. Notice that three parameters are passed to the bindService() method: the name of the AIDL service, a ServiceConnection instance, and a flag to autocreate the service.

Listing 11–27. *The IStockQuoteService Service Client Layout*

```
<?xml version="1.0" encoding="utf-8"?>
<!-- This file is /res/layout/main.xml -->
<LinearLayout xmlns:android="http://schemas.android.com/apk/res/android"
    android:orientation="vertical"
    android:layout_width="fill_parent"
    android:layout_height="fill_parent" >

<ToggleButton android:id="@+id/bindBtn"
    android:layout_width="wrap_content"
    android:layout_height="wrap_content"
    android:textOff="Bind"  android:textOn="Unbind"
    android:onClick="doClick" />

<Button android:id="@+id/callBtn"
    android:layout_width="wrap_content"
    android:layout_height="wrap_content"
    android:text="Call Service"  android:enabled=”false”
    android:onClick="doClick" />
</LinearLayout>
```

With an AIDL service, you need to provide an implementation of the ServiceConnection interface. This interface defines two methods: one called by the system when a connection to the service has been established and one called when the connection to the service has been destroyed. In our activity implementation, we define a private anonymous member that implements the ServiceConnection for the IStockQuoteService. When we call the bindService() method, we pass in the reference to this member. When the connection to the service is established, the onServiceConnected() callback is invoked, and we then obtain a reference to the IStockQuoteService using the Stub and we enable the Call Service button.

Note that the bindService() call is an asynchronous call. It is asynchronous because the process or service might not be running and thus might have to be created or started. And we cannot wait on the main thread for the service to start. Because bindService() is asynchronous, the platform provides the ServiceConnection callback, so we know when the service has been started and when the service is no longer available.

Please notice the onServiceDisconnected() callback. This does *not* get invoked when we unbind from the service. It is only invoked if the service crashes. If it does, we should not think that we're still connected, and we might need to reinvoke the bindService() call. That is why we change the status of our buttons in the UI when this callback is invoked. But notice we said "we might need to reinvoke the bindService() call." Android could restart our service for us and invoke our onServiceConnected() callback.

You can try this yourself by running the client, binding to the service, and using DDMS to do a Stop on the Stock Quote Service application.

When you run this example, watch the log messages in LogCat to get a feel for what is going on behind the scenes.

Now you know how to create and consume an AIDL interface. Before we move on and complicate matters further, let's review what it takes to build a simple local service versus an AIDL service. A local service is a service that does not support `onBind()`—it returns `null` from `onBind()`. This type of service is accessible only to the components of the application that is hosting the service. You call local services by calling `startService()`.

On the other hand, an AIDL service is a service that can be consumed both by components within the same process and by those that exist in other applications. This type of service defines a contract between itself and its clients in an AIDL file. The service implements the AIDL contract, and clients bind to the AIDL definition. The service implements the contract by returning an implementation of the AIDL interface from the `onBind()` method. Clients bind to an AIDL service by calling `bindService()`, and they disconnect from the service by calling `unbindService()`.

In our service examples thus far, we have strictly dealt with passing simple Java primitive types. Android services actually support passing complex types, too. This is very useful, especially for AIDL services, because you might have an open-ended number of parameters that you want to pass to a service, and it's unreasonable to pass them all as simple primitives. It makes more sense to package them as complex types and then pass them to the service.

Let's see how we can pass complex types to services.

Passing Complex Types to Services

Passing complex types to and from services requires more work than passing Java primitive types. Before embarking on this work, you should get an idea of AIDL's support for nonprimitive types:

- AIDL supports `String` and `CharSequence`.
- AIDL allows you to pass other AIDL interfaces, but you need to have an `import` statement for each AIDL interface you reference (even if the referenced AIDL interface is in the same package).
- AIDL allows you to pass complex types that implement the `android.os.Parcelable` interface. You need to have an `import` statement in your AIDL file for these types.

- AIDL supports `java.util.List` and `java.util.Map`, with a few restrictions. The allowable data types for the items in the collection include Java primitive, `String`, `CharSequence`, or `android.os.Parcelable`. You do not need `import` statements for `List` or `Map`, but you do need them for the `Parcelables`.
- Nonprimitive types, other than `String`, require a directional indicator. Directional indicators include `in`, `out`, and `inout`. `in` means the value is set by the client; `out` means the value is set by the service; and `inout` means both the client and service set the value.

The `Parcelable` interface tells the Android runtime how to serialize and deserialize objects during the marshalling and unmarshalling process. Listing 11–28 shows a `Person` class that implements the `Parcelable` interface.

Listing 11–28. *Implementing the Parcelable Interface*

```
// This file is Person.java
package com.androidbook.services.stock2;
import android.os.Parcel;
import android.os.Parcelable;

public class Person implements Parcelable {
    private int age;
    private String name;
    public static final Parcelable.Creator<Person> CREATOR =
        new Parcelable.Creator<Person>()
    {
        public Person createFromParcel(Parcel in) {
            return new Person(in);
        }

        public Person[] newArray(int size) {
            return new Person[size];
        }
    };

    public Person() {
    }

    private Person(Parcel in) {
        readFromParcel(in);
    }

    @Override
    public int describeContents() {
        return 0;
    }

    @Override
    public void writeToParcel(Parcel out, int flags) {
        out.writeInt(age);
        out.writeString(name);
    }

    public void readFromParcel(Parcel in) {
```

```
        age = in.readInt();
        name = in.readString();
    }

    public int getAge() {
        return age;
    }

    public void setAge(int age) {
        this.age = age;
    }

    public String getName() {
        return name;
    }

    public void setName(String name) {
        this.name = name;
    }
}
```

To get started on implementing this, create a new Android Project in Eclipse called `StockQuoteService2`. For Create Activity use a name of `MainActivity`, and use a package of `com.androidbook.services.stock2`. Then add the `Person.java` file above to the `com.androidbook.services.stock2` package of our new project.

The `Parcelable` interface defines the contract for hydration and dehydration of objects during the marshalling/unmarshalling process. Underlying the `Parcelable` interface is the `Parcel` container object. The `Parcel` class is a fast serialization/deserialization mechanism specially designed for interprocess communication within Android. The class provides methods that you use to flatten your members to the container and to expand the members back from the container. To properly implement an object for interprocess communication, we have to do the following:

1. Implement the `Parcelable` interface. This means that you implement `writeToParcel()` and `readFromParcel()`. The write method will write the object to the parcel and the read method will read the object from the parcel. Note that the order in which you write properties must be the same as the order in which you read them.

2. Add a `static final` property to the class with the name `CREATOR`. The property needs to implement the `android.os.Parcelable.Creator<T>` interface.

3. Provide a constructor for the `Parcelable` that knows how to create the object from the `Parcel`.

4. Define a `Parcelable` class in an `.aidl` file that matches the `.java` file containing the complex type. The AIDL compiler will look for this file when compiling your AIDL files. An example of a `Person.aidl` file is shown in Listing 11–29. This file should be in the same place as `Person.java`.

NOTE: Seeing `Parcelable` might have triggered the question, why is Android not using the built-in Java serialization mechanism? It turns out that the Android team came to the conclusion that the serialization in Java is far too slow to satisfy Android's interprocess-communication requirements. So the team built the `Parcelable` solution. The `Parcelable` approach requires that you explicitly serialize the members of your class, but in the end, you get a much faster serialization of your objects.

Also realize that Android provides two mechanisms that allow you to pass data to another process. The first is to pass a bundle to an activity using an intent, and the second is to pass a `Parcelable` to a service. These two mechanisms are not interchangeable and should not be confused. That is, the `Parcelable` is not meant to be passed to an activity. If you want to start an activity and pass it some data, use a Bundle. `Parcelable` is meant to be used only as part of an AIDL definition.

Listing 11–29. *An Example of Person.aidl File*

```
// This file is Person.aidl
package com.androidbook.services.stock2;
parcelable Person;
```

You will need an .aidl file for each `Parcelable` in your project. In this case, we have just one `Parcelable`, which is `Person`. You may notice that you don't get a `Person.java` file created in the gen folder. This is to be expected. We already have this file from when we created it previously.

Now, let's use the `Person` class in a remote service. To keep things simple, we will modify our `IStockQuoteService` to take an input parameter of type `Person`. The idea is that clients will pass a `Person` to the service to tell the service who is requesting the quote. The new `IStockQuoteService.aidl` looks like Listing 11–30.

Listing 11–30. *Passing Parcelables to Services*

```
// This file is IStockQuoteService.aidl
package com.androidbook.services.stock2;
import com.androidbook.services.stock2.Person;

interface IStockQuoteService
{
    String getQuote(in String ticker,in Person requester);
}
```

The `getQuote()` method now accepts two parameters: the stock's ticker symbol and a `Person` object to specify who is making the request. Note that we have directional indicators on the parameters because the parameters include nonprimitive types and that we have an `import` statement for the `Person` class. The `Person` class is also in the same package as the service definition (`com.androidbook.services.stock2`).

The service implementation now looks like Listing 11–31, with the layout in Listing 11–32.

Listing 11–31. *The StockQuoteService2 Implementation*

```
package com.androidbook.services.stock2;
// This file is StockQuoteService2.java

import android.app.Notification;
import android.app.NotificationManager;
import android.app.PendingIntent;
import android.app.Service;
import android.content.Intent;
import android.os.IBinder;
import android.os.RemoteException;

public class StockQuoteService2 extends Service
{
    private NotificationManager notificationMgr;

    public class StockQuoteServiceImpl extends IStockQuoteService.Stub
    {
        public String getQuote(String ticker, Person requester)
                throws RemoteException {
            return "Hello " + requester.getName() +
                "! Quote for " + ticker + " is 20.0";
        }
    }

    @Override
    public void onCreate() {
        super.onCreate();

        notificationMgr =
          (NotificationManager)getSystemService(NOTIFICATION_SERVICE);

        displayNotificationMessage(
              "onCreate() called in StockQuoteService2");
    }

    @Override
    public void onDestroy()
    {
        displayNotificationMessage(
              "onDestroy() called in StockQuoteService2");
        // Clear all notifications from this service
        notificationMgr.cancelAll();
        super.onDestroy();
    }

    @Override
    public IBinder onBind(Intent intent)
    {
        displayNotificationMessage(
              "onBind() called in StockQuoteService2");
        return new StockQuoteServiceImpl();
    }

    private void displayNotificationMessage(String message)
    {
        Notification notification =
```

```
                new Notification(R.drawable.emo_im_happy,
                    message, System.currentTimeMillis());

            PendingIntent contentIntent =
                PendingIntent.getActivity(this, 0,
                    new Intent(this, MainActivity.class), 0);

            notification.setLatestEventInfo(this,
                "StockQuoteService2", message,
                contentIntent);

            notification.flags = Notification.FLAG_NO_CLEAR;

            notificationMgr.notify(R.id.app_notification_id, notification);
        }
    }
```

Listing 11–32. *The StockQuoteService2 Layout*

```
<?xml version="1.0" encoding="utf-8"?>
<!-- This file is /res/layout/main.xml -->
<LinearLayout xmlns:android="http://schemas.android.com/apk/res/android"
    android:orientation="vertical"
    android:layout_width="fill_parent"
    android:layout_height="fill_parent" >
<TextView
    android:layout_width="fill_parent"
    android:layout_height="wrap_content"
    android:text="This is where the service could ask for help." />
</LinearLayout>
```

The differences between this implementation and the previous one are that we brought back the notifications, and we now return the stock value as a string and not a double. The string returned to the user contains the name of the requester from the Person object, which demonstrates that we read the value sent from the client and that the Person object was passed correctly to the service.

There are a few other things that need to be done to make this work:

1. Find the emo_im_happy.png image file from under Android SDK/platforms/android-2.1/data/res/drawable-mdpi, and copy it to the /res/drawable directory of our project. Or change the name of the resource in the code, and put whatever image you want in the drawables folder.

2. Add a new <item type="id" name="app_notification_id"/> tag to the /res/values/strings.xml file

3. We need to modify the application in the AndroidManifest.xml file as shown in Listing 11–33.

Listing 11–33. *Modified <application> in AndroidManifest.xml File for StockQuoteService2*

```
<?xml version="1.0" encoding="utf-8"?>
<manifest xmlns:android="http://schemas.android.com/apk/res/android"
      package="com.androidbook.services.stock2"
      android:versionCode="1"
      android:versionName="1.0">
```

```
    <application android:icon="@drawable/icon"
            android:label="@string/app_name">
        <activity android:name=".MainActivity"
                android:label="@string/app_name"
                android:launchMode="singleTop" >
            <intent-filter>
                <action android:name="android.intent.action.MAIN" />
            </intent-filter>
        </activity>
      <service android:name="StockQuoteService2">
        <intent-filter>
            <action android:name="com.androidbook.services.stock2.IStockQuoteService" />
        </intent-filter>
      </service>
    </application>
    <uses-sdk android:minSdkVersion="7" />
</manifest>
```

While it is OK to use the dot notation for our `android:name=".MainActivity"` attribute, it is not OK to use dot notation inside of our `<action>` tag inside the service's `<intent-filter>` tag. We need to spell it out; otherwise, our client will not find the service specification.

Last, we'll use the default `MainActivity.java` file that simply displays a basic layout with a simple message. We showed you earlier how to launch to the activity from a notification. This activity would serve that purpose also in real life, but for this example, we'll keep that part simple. Now that we have our service implementation, let's create a new Android project called `StockQuoteClient2`. Use `com.dave` for the package and `MainActivity` for the activity name. To implement a client that passes the `Person` object to the service, we need to copy everything that the client needs from the service project to the client project. In our previous example, all we needed was the `IStockQuoteService.aidl` file. Now, we also need to copy the `Person.java` and `Person.aidl` files, because the `Person` object is now part of the interface. After you copy these three files to the client project, modify `main.xml` according to Listing 11–34, and modify `MainActivity.java` according to Listing 11–35. Or simply import this project from the source code on our website.

Listing 11–34. *Updated main.xml for StockQuoteClient2*

```
<?xml version="1.0" encoding="utf-8"?>
<!-- This file is /res/layout/main.xml -->
<LinearLayout xmlns:android="http://schemas.android.com/apk/res/android"
    android:orientation="vertical"
    android:layout_width="fill_parent"
    android:layout_height="fill_parent" >

<ToggleButton android:id="@+id/bindBtn"
    android:layout_width="wrap_content"
    android:layout_height="wrap_content"
    android:textOff="Bind"  android:textOn="Unbind"
    android:onClick="doClick" />

<Button android:id="@+id/callBtn"
    android:layout_width="wrap_content"
    android:layout_height="wrap_content"
```

```
    android:text="Call Service" android:enabled="false"
    android:onClick="doClick" />
</LinearLayout>>
```

Listing 11–35. *Calling the Service with a Parcelable*

```
package com.dave;
// This file is MainActivity.java
import android.app.Activity;
import android.content.ComponentName;
import android.content.Context;
import android.content.Intent;
import android.content.ServiceConnection;
import android.os.Bundle;
import android.os.IBinder;
import android.os.RemoteException;
import android.util.Log;
import android.view.View;
import android.widget.Button;
import android.widget.Toast;
import android.widget.ToggleButton;

import com.androidbook.services.stock2.IStockQuoteService;
import com.androidbook.services.stock2.Person;

public class MainActivity extends Activity {

    protected static final String TAG = "StockQuoteClient2";
    private IStockQuoteService stockService = null;
    private ToggleButton bindBtn;
    private Button callBtn;

    /** Called when the activity is first created. */
    @Override
    public void onCreate(Bundle savedInstanceState) {
        super.onCreate(savedInstanceState);
        setContentView(R.layout.main);

        bindBtn = (ToggleButton)findViewById(R.id.bindBtn);
        callBtn = (Button)findViewById(R.id.callBtn);
    }

    public void doClick(View view) {
        switch(view.getId()) {
        case R.id.bindBtn:
            if(((ToggleButton) view).isChecked()) {
                bindService(new Intent(
                    IStockQuoteService.class.getName()),
                    serConn, Context.BIND_AUTO_CREATE);
            }
            else {
                unbindService(serConn);
                callBtn.setEnabled(false);
            }
            break;
        case R.id.callBtn:
            callService();
            break;
```

```
        }
    }

    private void callService() {
        try {
            Person person = new Person();
            person.setAge(47);
            person.setName("Dave");
            String response = stockService.getQuote("ANDROID", person);
            Toast.makeText(MainActivity.this,
                        "Value from service is "+response,
                        Toast.LENGTH_SHORT).show();
        } catch (RemoteException ee) {
            Log.e("MainActivity", ee.getMessage(), ee);
        }
    }

    private ServiceConnection serConn = new ServiceConnection() {

        @Override
        public void onServiceConnected(ComponentName name,
            IBinder service)
        {
            Log.v(TAG, "onServiceConnected() called");
            stockService = IStockQuoteService.Stub.asInterface(service);
            bindBtn.setChecked(true);
            callBtn.setEnabled(true);
        }

        @Override
        public void onServiceDisconnected(ComponentName name) {
            Log.v(TAG, "onServiceDisconnected() called");
            bindBtn.setChecked(false);
            callBtn.setEnabled(false);
            stockService = null;
        }
    };

    protected void onDestroy() {
        if(callBtn.isEnabled())
            unbindService(serConn);
        super.onDestroy();
    }
}
```

This is now ready to run. Remember to send over the service to the emulator before you send over the client to run. The user interface should look like Figure 11–8.

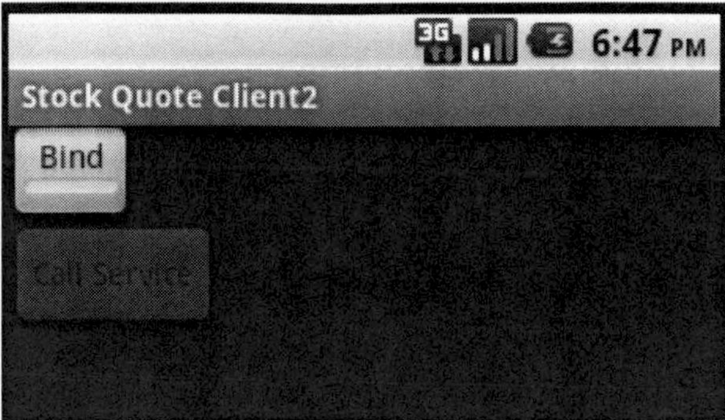

Figure 11–8. *User Interface of StockQuoteClient2*

Let's take a look at what we've got. As before, we bind to our service, then we can invoke a service method. The `onServiceConnected()` method is where we get told that our service is running, so we can then enable the Call Service button so the button can invoke the `callService()` method. As shown, we create a new `Person` object and set its `Age` and `Name` properties. We then execute the service and display the result from the service call. The result looks like Figure 11–9.

Figure 11–9. *Result from calling the service with a Parcelable*

Notice that when the service is called you get a notification in the status bar. This is coming from the service itself. We briefly touched on Notifications earlier as a way for a service to communicate to the user. Normally, services are in the background and do not display any sort of UI. But what if a service needs to interact with the user? While tempting to think that a service can invoke an activity, a service should *never* invoke an activity directly. A service should instead create a notification, and the notification should be how the user gets to the desired activity. This was shown in our last exercise. We defined a simple layout and activity implementation for our service. When we created the notification within the service, we set the activity in the notification. The user can click the notification, and it will take the user to our activity that is part of this service. This will allow the user to interact with the service.

Notifications are saved so that you can get to them by pulling up the Menu on the Android Home page and clicking Notifications. A user can also drag down from the notification icon in the status bar to see them. Note the use of the `setLatestEventInfo()` method call and the fact that we reuse the same ID for every message. This combination means that we are updating the one and only notification every time, rather than creating new notification entries. Therefore, if you go to the Notifications screen in Android after clicking on Bind, Call Again, and Unbind a few times, you will only see one message in Notifications, and it will be the last one sent by the `BackgroundService`. If we used different IDs, we could have multiple notification messages, and we could update each one separately. Notifications can also be set with additional user "prompts" such as sound, lights, and/or vibration.

It is also useful to see the artifacts of the service project and the client that calls it (see Figure 11–10).

Figure 11–10. *The artifacts of the service and the client*

Figure 11–10 shows the Eclipse project artifacts for the service (left) and the client (right). Note that the contract between the client and the service consists of the AIDL artifacts and the `Parcelable` objects exchanged between the two parties. This is the reason that we see `Person.java`, `IStockQuoteService.aidl`, and `Person.aidl` on both sides. Because the AIDL complier generates the Java interface, stub, proxy, and so on from the AIDL artifacts, the build process creates the `IStockQuoteService.java` file on the client side when we copy the contract artifacts to the client project.

Now, you know how to exchange complex types between services and clients. Let's briefly touch on another important aspect of calling services: synchronous versus asynchronous service invocation.

All of the calls that you make on services are synchronous. This brings up the obvious question, do you need to implement all of your service calls in a worker thread? Not necessarily. On most other platforms, it's common for a client to use a service that is a complete black box, so the client would have to take appropriate precautions when making service calls. With Android, you will likely know what is in the service (generally because you wrote the service yourself), so you can make an informed decision. If you know that the method you are calling is doing a lot of heavy lifting, you should consider using a secondary thread to make the call. If you are sure that the method does not have any bottlenecks, you can safely make the call on the UI thread. If you conclude that it's best to make the service call within a worker thread, you can create the thread and then call the service. You can then communicate the result to the UI thread.

Real-World Example Using Services

So far in this chapter, we've showed you various ways to call HTTP services and to implement Android services. In this section, we will show you how to translate text from one language to another using Android services and the Google Translate API, which is an HTTP-based service over the Internet—but first, some background on the Google Translate API.

Google Translate API

Translating from one language to another is not something that will fit very well on a mobile device. The number of words in English alone is hundreds of thousands, even possibly more than a million (depending on how you define "English"). Loading languages and rules onto a mobile device to allow translation between arbitrary pairs of languages is just not feasible, yet.

Google has supplied an API on the Internet that does translations. It takes a string of text and a pair of language specifications, one for the source and one for the destination, and it converts the text from the source language to the destination language. There is a catch though. The original intent of this service was to be called from web sites, not mobile devices. The Terms of Use for the Google AJAX Language API (as it is formally known) does not have a version for Android devices, like the Google Maps API Terms of Use does. To read the Terms of Use for the AJAX Language API, go here:

`http://code.google.com/apis/ajaxlanguage/terms.html`

While it is not entirely clear that Google intends for Android developers to use this API, in fact, a demonstration of this API was given at Google I/O in May 2009 using an Android application! Perhaps by the time you read this Google will have a separate Terms of Use for Android for the AJAX Language API, or perhaps the existing terms will have been updated to make it clearer how Google intends for it to be used with Android. There's also a version 2 of this Translate API in Google Labs, so watch that for developments. In the meantime, you have a couple of options. One, you could go ahead and use the AJAX Language API directly from your Android application, as we will show you next.

Two, you could access the AJAX Language API using a web server that you control, like a proxy to the AJAX Language API. Your application would interface with your web server, and your web server would make the calls to the AJAX Language API. With your own web server in the middle, it becomes much easier to disable the access to the AJAX Language API from your application, since you control a chokepoint between them. Of course, there may not be much you can do to allow your application to continue to work if you can't use the Google service anymore. At a minimum, you could build in some sort of response to your application that indicates that the service is no longer available from Google, in order to provide a suitable message to the user. In the former case, if Google asks that you stop using the AJAX Language API, you really won't be able to do much about it; your application has been distributed to devices, and unless you've built in some way to make them stop using the API, they will continue to try to do so.

Google has the right to disable your access, but this could be somewhat difficult for it to do. Google did not state in the Terms of Use that you need to use an API key to use the AJAX Language API, although the Developer Documentation (`http://code.google.com/apis/ajaxlanguage/documentation/`) states that you *must* use a `REFERER` and you *should* use an API key. Without these, your requests will appear anonymously from the users' devices, and Google would have no way of contacting you if there is some problem with your use of the API. We've chosen to set the `REFERER` header value in our example (see the `Translator.java` code), but we skipped the API key part. If you want to send an API key value to the AJAX Language API, you will first need to acquire one from Google. Note that you should not reuse your Maps API key for the AJAX APIs. To register for an AJAX API key, you only need submit the URL of your web site (the exact same one you used as your `REFERER`) and agree to the Terms of Use. With the new API key in hand, you would add it to the AJAX API URL with the following snippet:

```
&key=Your_API_key_goes_here_with_no_quotation_marks
```

If you decide to pass an API key to an AJAX API, the `REFERER` must be set to the same URL that you used to create the API key, or some sub-page of that URL. Otherwise, you will not get results back.

Using the Google Translate API

For the rest of this section, we will help you build an application that calls the Google AJAX Language API directly. Up to this point in the book, we've shown you all the individual components you need to get translations into your application. Now, we'll bring them all together. For this example, we're going to create an application with an `EditText` for the input, that uses spinners to select the languages to translate to and from, has a read-only EditText for the translated output, invokes a service over the Internet, and uses a service to isolate the UI from logic that might take a while to succeed. One of the extras we need to include in this application is the Jakarta Commons Lang project, specifically to unescape XML entity codes into Unicodes for display. We'll cover how to do that too after the code listings. Refer to Figure 11–11 to see what it looks like.

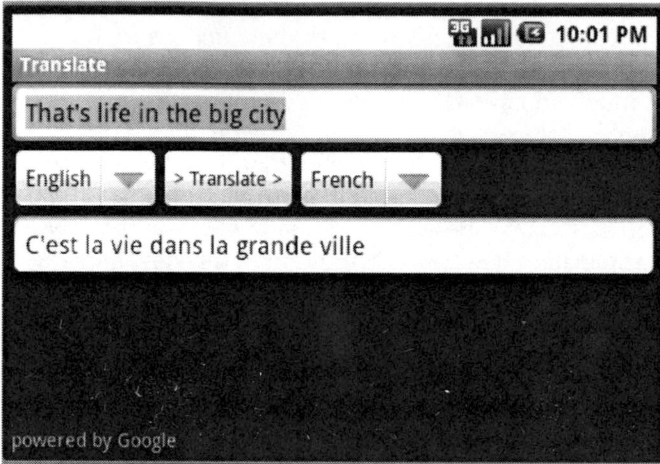

Figure 11–11. *The Translate Demo UI*

For the code, we have the following files:

- `/res/layout/main.xml` (Listing 11–36)
- `/res/values/strings.xml` (Listing 11–37)
- `/res/values/arrays.xml` (Listing 11–38)
- ITranslate.aidl under /src (Listing 11–39)
- MainActivity.java (Listing 11–40)
- TranslateService.java (Listing 11–41) handles service semantics
- Translator.java (Listing 11–42) where the actual Google service is called
- AndroidManifest.xml (Listing 11–43)

For this sample application, we chose to use the HttpURLConnection class instead of the HttpClient as before, so you could see how this other class is used in a real application.

Listing 11–36. *XML and Java to Implement a Translation Demonstration*

```
<?xml version="1.0" encoding="utf-8"?>
<!-- This file is /res/layout/main.xml -->
<RelativeLayout xmlns:android="http://schemas.android.com/apk/res/android"
    android:orientation="vertical"
    android:layout_height="fill_parent"
    android:layout_width="fill_parent">

    <EditText android:id="@+id/input"  android:hint="@string/input"
        android:layout_height="wrap_content"
        android:layout_width="fill_parent" />
```

```
    <Spinner android:id="@+id/from"
        android:layout_weight="1"
        android:layout_width="wrap_content"
        android:layout_height="wrap_content"
        android:layout_below="@id/input"
        android:prompt="@string/prompt" />

    <Button android:id="@+id/translateBtn"
        android:text="@string/translateBtn"
        android:layout_weight="1"
        android:layout_width="wrap_content"
        android:layout_height="wrap_content"
        android:layout_below="@id/input"
        android:layout_toRightOf="@id/from"
        android:enabled="false" />

    <Spinner android:id="@+id/to"
        android:layout_weight="1"
        android:layout_width="wrap_content"
        android:layout_height="wrap_content"
        android:layout_below="@id/input"
        android:layout_toRightOf="@id/translateBtn"
        android:prompt="@string/prompt" />

    <EditText android:id="@+id/translation"
        android:hint="@string/translation"
        android:layout_height="wrap_content"
        android:layout_width="fill_parent"
        android:editable="false"
        android:layout_below="@id/from" />

    <TextView android:id="@+id/poweredBy"
        android:text="powered by Google"
        android:layout_width="wrap_content"
        android:layout_height="wrap_content"
        android:layout_alignParentBottom="true" />

</RelativeLayout>
```

Listing 11–37. *String Resources for our Translation Application*

```
<?xml version="1.0" encoding="utf-8"?>
<!-- This file is /res/values/strings.xml -->
<resources>
    <string name="translateBtn">>  Translate  ></string>
    <string name="input">Enter the text to translate</string>
    <string name="translation">The translation will appear here</string>
    <string name="prompt">Choose a language</string>
</resources>
```

Listing 11–38. *Array Resources for our Translation Application*

```
<?xml version="1.0" encoding="utf-8"?>
<!-- This file is /res/values/arrays.xml -->
<resources>
<string-array name="languages">
    <item>Chinese</item>
    <item>English</item>
```

```
    <item>French</item>
    <item>German</item>
    <item>Japanese</item>
    <item>Spanish</item>
</string-array>
<string-array name="language_values">
    <item>zh</item>
    <item>en</item>
    <item>fr</item>
    <item>de</item>
    <item>ja</item>
    <item>es</item>
</string-array>
</resources>
```

Listing 11–39. *Translation Service AIDL file*

```
// This file is ITranslate.aidl under /src
interface ITranslate {
    String translate(in String text, in String from, in String to);
}
```

Listing 11–40. *Main Translation Application: MainActivity.java*

```
// This file is MainActivity.java
import android.app.Activity;
import android.content.ComponentName;
import android.content.Context;
import android.content.Intent;
import android.content.ServiceConnection;
import android.os.Bundle;
import android.os.Handler;
import android.os.IBinder;
import android.util.Log;
import android.view.View;
import android.view.View.OnClickListener;
import android.widget.ArrayAdapter;
import android.widget.Button;
import android.widget.EditText;
import android.widget.Spinner;
import android.widget.TextView;

public class MainActivity extends Activity implements OnClickListener {
    static final String TAG = "Translator";
    private EditText inputText = null;
    private TextView outputText = null;
    private Spinner fromLang = null;
    private Spinner toLang = null;
    private Button translateBtn = null;
    private String[] langShortNames = null;
    private Handler mHandler = new Handler();

    private ITranslate mTranslateService;

    private ServiceConnection mTranslateConn = new ServiceConnection() {
        public void onServiceConnected(ComponentName name,
                IBinder service) {
            mTranslateService = ITranslate.Stub.asInterface(service);
            if (mTranslateService != null) {
```

```
                translateBtn.setEnabled(true);
            } else {
                translateBtn.setEnabled(false);
                Log.e(TAG, "Unable to acquire TranslateService");
            }
        }

        public void onServiceDisconnected(ComponentName name) {
            translateBtn.setEnabled(false);
            mTranslateService = null;
        }
    };

    @Override
    protected void onCreate(Bundle icicle) {
        super.onCreate(icicle);

        setContentView(R.layout.main);
        inputText = (EditText) findViewById(R.id.input);
        outputText = (EditText) findViewById(R.id.translation);
        fromLang = (Spinner) findViewById(R.id.from);
        toLang = (Spinner) findViewById(R.id.to);

        langShortNames = getResources()
                .getStringArray(R.array.language_values);

        translateBtn = (Button) findViewById(R.id.translateBtn);
        translateBtn.setOnClickListener(this);

        ArrayAdapter<?> fromAdapter =
            ArrayAdapter.createFromResource(this,
                R.array.languages, android.R.layout.simple_spinner_item);
        fromAdapter.setDropDownViewResource(
                android.R.layout.simple_dropdown_item_1line);
        fromLang.setAdapter(fromAdapter);
        fromLang.setSelection(1); // English

        ArrayAdapter<?> toAdapter =
            ArrayAdapter.createFromResource(this,
                R.array.languages,android.R.layout.simple_spinner_item);
        toAdapter.setDropDownViewResource(
                android.R.layout.simple_dropdown_item_1line);
        toLang.setAdapter(toAdapter);
        toLang.setSelection(3); // German

        inputText.selectAll();

        Intent intent = new Intent(Intent.ACTION_VIEW);
        bindService(intent, mTranslateConn, Context.BIND_AUTO_CREATE);
    }

    @Override
    protected void onDestroy() {
        super.onDestroy();
        unbindService(mTranslateConn);
    }
```

```
    public void onClick(View v) {
        if (inputText.getText().length() > 0) {
            doTranslate();
        }
    }

    private void doTranslate() {
        mHandler.post(new Runnable() {
            public void run() {
                String result = "";
                try {
                    int fromPosition =
                            fromLang.getSelectedItemPosition();
                    int toPosition = toLang.getSelectedItemPosition();
                    String input = inputText.getText().toString();
                    if(input.length() > 5000)
                        input = input.substring(0,5000);
                    Log.v(TAG,"Translating from " +
                        langShortNames[fromPosition] + " to " +
                        langShortNames[toPosition]);
                    result = mTranslateService.translate(input,
                        langShortNames[fromPosition],
                        langShortNames[toPosition]);
                    if (result == null) {
                        throw new Exception("Failed to get a translation");
                    }
                    outputText.setText(result);
                    inputText.selectAll();
                } catch (Exception e) {
                    Log.e(TAG, "Error: " + e.getMessage());
                }
            }
        });
    }
}
```

Listing 11–41. *Translation Service Java file: TranslateService.java*

```
// This file is TranslateService.java
import android.app.Service;
import android.content.Intent;
import android.os.IBinder;
import android.util.Log;

public class TranslateService extends Service {
    public static final String TAG = "TranslateService";

    private final ITranslate.Stub mBinder = new ITranslate.Stub() {
        public String translate(String text, String from, String to) {
            try {
                return Translator.translate(text, from, to);
            } catch (Exception e) {
                Log.e(TAG, "Failed to translate: " + e.getMessage());
                return null;
            }
        }
    };
```

```
    @Override
    public IBinder onBind(Intent intent) {
        return mBinder;
    }
}
```

Listing 11–42. *Translation Function Java file*

```
// This file is Translator.java
import java.io.BufferedReader;
import java.io.InputStream;
import java.io.InputStreamReader;
import java.net.HttpURLConnection;
import java.net.URL;
import java.net.URLEncoder;

import org.apache.commons.lang.StringEscapeUtils;
import org.json.JSONObject;
import android.util.Log;

public class Translator {
    private static final String ENCODING = "UTF-8";
    private static final String URL_BASE =
"http://ajax.googleapis.com/ajax/services/language/translate?v=1.0&langpair=";
    private static final String INPUT_TEXT = "&q=";
    private static final String MY_SITE = "http://my.website.com";
    private static final String TAG = "Translator";

    public static String translate(String text, String from, String to) throws Exception
{
        try {
            StringBuilder url = new StringBuilder();
            url.append(URL_BASE).append(from).append("%7C").append(to);
            url.append(INPUT_TEXT).append(
                URLEncoder.encode(text, ENCODING));

            HttpURLConnection conn = (HttpURLConnection)
                new URL(url.toString()).openConnection();
            conn.setRequestProperty("REFERER", MY_SITE);
            conn.setDoInput(true);
            conn.setDoOutput(true);
            try {
                InputStream is= conn.getInputStream();
                String rawResult = makeResult(is);

                JSONObject json = new JSONObject(rawResult);
                String result =
                    ((JSONObject)json.get("responseData"))
                    .getString("translatedText");
                return (StringEscapeUtils.unescapeXml(result));
            } finally {
                conn.getInputStream().close();
                if(conn.getErrorStream() != null)
                    conn.getErrorStream().close();
            }
        } catch (Exception ex) {
            throw ex;
        }
```

```
    }

    private static String makeResult(InputStream inputStream) throws Exception {
        StringBuilder outputString = new StringBuilder();
        try {
            String string;
            if (inputStream != null) {
                BufferedReader reader =
                    new BufferedReader(
                        new InputStreamReader(inputStream, ENCODING));
                while (null != (string = reader.readLine())) {
                    outputString.append(string).append('\n');
                }
            }
        } catch (Exception ex) {
            Log.e(TAG, "Error reading translation stream.", ex);
        }
        return outputString.toString();
    }
}
```

Listing 11–43. *Translation Application AndroidManifest.xml*

```
<?xml version="1.0" encoding="utf-8"?>
<!-- This file is AndroidManifest.xml -->
<manifest xmlns:android="http://schemas.android.com/apk/res/android"
      package="com.androidbook.translation"
      android:versionName="1.0"
      android:versionCode="1" >

  <application android:label="Translate"
      android:icon="@drawable/icon">

      <activity android:name="MainActivity" android:label="Translate">
         <intent-filter>
            <action android:name="android.intent.action.MAIN" />
            <category android:name="android.intent.category.DEFAULT" />
            <category android:name="android.intent.category.LAUNCHER" />
         </intent-filter>
      </activity>

      <service android:name="TranslateService" android:label="Translate">
         <intent-filter>
            <action android:name="android.intent.action.VIEW" />
            <category android:name="android.intent.category.DEFAULT" />
         </intent-filter>
      </service>
  </application>
  <uses-permission android:name="android.permission.INTERNET" />
</manifest>
```

Before this example will build properly, we need to provide a helper class. The Jakarta Commons Lang project has a class called `StringEscapeUtils` that we would like to use to convert the result string from the AJAX Language API into something human-readable. The AJAX Language API can give us back XML entities representing certain special characters. For example, an apostrophe would come back as `'`. We want to display those special characters properly to the user. That's where the Commons Lang project comes in. The location of Jakarta Commons Lang is here:

```
http://commons.apache.org/lang/
```

Go to the Jakarta Commons Lang web site, and find and download the `commons-lang` ZIP (or TAR) file that contains the JAR file. Unpack it so you can get to the JAR file for the next step. Within Eclipse, you're going to select the project, right-click and choose Build Path > Configure Build Path. Click the Libraries tab and then Add External JARs. Navigate to the `commons-lang` JAR file, and add it. Now, click OK to finish adding the JAR file to the project. Your application should build to completion. Go ahead and try it out. If the application doesn't fit too well in portrait mode, try using the Ctrl+F11 trick to switch the emulator to landscape mode. If you doubt any of the results that you get back, go to this site to compare your results with Google's:

```
http://www.google.com/uds/samples/language/translate.html
```

There are several items we'd like to draw your attention to. Due to the Terms of Use, this example includes a "powered by Google" string on the UI. Also due to the Terms of Use, the strings you pass must not exceed 5,000 characters, so we cut them off if that happens. You'd likely want to do something a little different there, such as breaking the text into manageable chunks of text to pass to the API so you don't lose anything. We've intentionally kept the list of languages short just to make this application manageable, but feel free to add additional languages to the string arrays to do more translations. However, be aware that the Droid fonts may not have every character for every language that the translator can translate. If you see strangeness in the results, you might suspect that you've got a font problem. It is possible to acquire additional fonts to alleviate this, but we won't be covering fonts in this chapter. The response from the API is structured using JSON. Therefore, we use JSON to parse the response into our result string. Note that JSON is provided as part of Android, so we didn't need to grab it from the Internet to include it as an external jar file.

One of the features of the AJAX Language API is that you don't have to tell it what the input language is. The API will make an attempt at guessing the input language. If you want to take this approach, you can choose to leave off the input language in the URL that you pass, and instead immediately follow the `langpair=` with `%7C`. This would be handy when you're not sure what language will be provided to you, however, without a sufficient amount of text passed to it, the API may not guess correctly.

References

Here are some helpful references to topics you may wish to explore further.

- `http://www.androidbook.com/projects`. Look here for a list of downloadable projects related to this book. For this chapter look for a ZIP file called ProAndroid3_Ch11_Services.zip. This ZIP file contains all projects from this chapter, listed in separate root directories. There is also a README.TXT file that describes exactly how to import projects into Eclipse from one of these ZIP files.

- `http://hc.apache.org/httpcomponents-client-ga/tutorial/html/`. This site has great tutorials on using the `HttpClient` classes, including authentication and the use of cookies.

Summary

This chapter was all about services. We talked about consuming external HTTP services using the Apache `HttpClient` and about writing background services. With regard to using the `HttpClient`, we showed you how to do HTTP `GET` calls and HTTP `POST` calls. We also showed you how to do multipart `POST`s.

The second part of this chapter dealt with writing services in Android. Specifically, we talked about writing local services and remote services. We said that local services are services that are consumed by the components (such as activities) in the same process as the service. Remote services are services whose clients are outside the process hosting the services.

Chapter 12

Exploring Packages

In Chapters 1 through 11, we covered the basics of the Android platform. However, these chapters detailed the happy path through Android. In the next few chapters, starting with this one (Chapters 12, 13, 14, and 15), we will cover the next grain of detail around the core of Android.

We will start that exploration by looking under the hood of Android packages, the Android package signing process, sharing data between packages, and Android library projects. You will understand the Linux process context in which an .apk file runs. You will see how multiple .apk files can share data and resources given that context.

Although you were introduced to signing Android package files in Chapter 10, in this chapter, you will learn the meaning, implication, and use of signed JAR files. In the context of data sharing, we will also look at Android library projects to see how they work and if they could be used for resource and code sharing.

Let's start this discussion by going back to the basics of an .apk file, as it forms the basis for an Android process.

Packages and Processes

As you have witnessed in previous chapters when you develop an application in Android, you end up with an .apk file. You then sign this .apk file and deploy it to the device. Let's learn a little bit more about Android packages.

Details of a Package Specification

Each .apk file is uniquely identified by its root package name which is specified in its manifest file. Here is an example of a package definition that we will be using for this chapter (the package name is highlighted):

```
<manifest xmlns:android="http://schemas.android.com/apk/res/android"
      package="com.androidbook.library.testlibraryapp"
      ...>
      ...rest of the xml nodes
</manifest>
```

If you were the developer of this package and signed it and installed on the device, no one else other than you can update this package. The package name is tied to the signature with which it is signed. Subsequently, a developer with a different signature cannot sign and install a package with the same fully qualified Java package name.

Translating Package Name to a Process Name

Android uses the package name as the name of the process under which to run the components of this package. Android also allocates a unique user ID for this package process to run under. This allocated user ID is essentially an ID for the underlying Linux OS. You can discover this information by looking at the details of the installed package.

Listing Installed Packages

On the emulator you can see a list of installed packages by navigating to the package browser using the path Home ➤ Dev Tools ➤ Package Browser. (Note that you may or may not find a similar package browser on a real device. This could also change based on the Android release.)

Once you see the list of packages, you can highlight a package for a particular application such as, say, a browser and click it. This will bring up a package detail screen that looks like Figure 12–1.

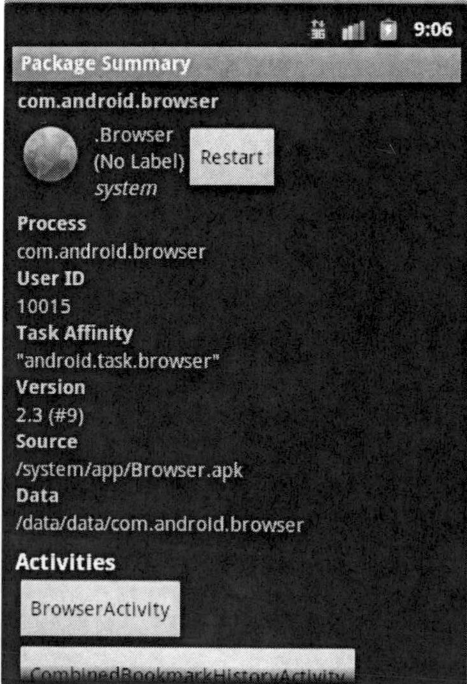

Figure 12–1. *Android package details*

Figure 12–1 shows the name of the process as indicated by the Java package name in the manifest file and the unique user ID allocated to this package. In the case of the browser, the manifest file would have indicated its package name as `com.android.browser` (reflected by the attribute process in Figure 12–1).

Any resources created by this process or package will be secured under that Linux user ID. This screen also lists the components inside this package. Examples of components are activities, services, and broadcast receivers.

Deleting a Package through the Package Browser

While we are on the subject of the package browser, we'd like to point out that you can also delete the package from the emulator using the following steps in the package browser mentioned in the previous section:

1. Highlight the package.
2. Click Menu.
3. Click "delete package" to delete a package.

Because a process is tied to a package name, and a package name is tied to its signature, signatures play a role in securing the data belonging to a package. To fully understand the implications of this, let's investigate the nature of the package signing process.

Revisiting the Package Signing Process

In Chapter 10, we introduced the mechanics of signing an application prior to installing on the device. However, we haven't explored the need and implications of the package signing process.

For example, when we download an application and install it on Windows or other operating systems, we doesn't need to sign it. How come signing is mandated on an Android device? What does the signing process really mean? What does it ensure? Are there any real-world parallels to the signing process that we can quickly relate to? We will explore these questions in this section.

As packages are installed on to a device, it is necessary that each installed package has a unique or distinct Java package name. If you try to install a new package with an existing name, the device will disallow the installation until the previous package is removed. To allow this type of package upgrading, you must ensure that the same application publisher is associated with that package. This is done with digital signatures. After going through the following sections of this chapter, you will see that the signing process ensures that, as a developer, you reserve that package name for you through your digital signature.

Let's walk through a couple of scenarios so you can fully understand and internalize digital signatures.

Understanding Digital Signatures: Scenario 1

Imagine you are a wine collector located in a very un-wine-like place, like the Sahara. Furthermore, say wine makers around the world are sending you wine casks to archive or sell.

As a wine collector, you notice that each cask and the wine inside it has a specific hue and color that is distinct from others. On further investigation, you find out that if two casks or the wine inside them have the same hue, it *always* comes from the same wine maker. On digging further, you find out that each vintner has a secret hue recipe that is kept locked up in a cellar and never revealed. This explained why each wine is different and why two wines with the same hue *must* come from the same wine maker. Of course, this identification by no means reveals the identity of the wine maker—just that the vintner is distinct and unique.

The hue becomes a signature of the wine maker, like a family stamp, and the wine maker hides the signature from everyone else.

An important distinction in this example is that there is no way for you, as a collector, to know *which* wine maker sent a particular shipment of wine—there is no name or address associated with that signature. Even if there were, it is quite possible that a wine maker could send wine that appeared to come from another's address. In that case, you can therefore assume that the two wine caskets, which have the same address but different hues, are from two different wine makers resident at the same address.

Understanding Digital Signatures: Scenario 2

Let's consider another scenario for naturally occurring signatures. When you visit a foreign land, you turn on the radio and hear many songs. You can tell there are different singers, and you can identify each separately but not know who they are or know their names. This is self-signing (in this case with their vocal chords). When a friend of yours tells you of a singer and associates that singer with a voice you have heard, it is analogous to third-party signing.

One singer can imitate another's voice to confuse or trick the listener. However, it is far, far harder to emulate a digital signature because of the mathematical algorithms that are used to encode signatures.

A Pattern for Understanding Digital Signatures

When we talk about someone signing a JAR file, that JAR file is uniquely "colored" and can be distinguished from other set of JAR files. However, there is no way to identify the source developer or company with authenticity. Such JAR files are called self-signed JAR files.

To know the *source*, you need a third-party company that the wine collector trusts tell us that the color red comes from Company1. Now, every time we see "color-red", we know that the wine is from Company1. These are called third-party-signed JAR files. These are useful in your browsers to tell you that you are downloading a file from Company 1 or installing an application manufactured by Company 1 (authoritatively).

So How Do You Digitally Sign?

Digital signatures, which follow similar semantics explained in the scenarios above, are technically implemented through what is called a public/private key encryption. Mathematics can be applied to generate two numbers whereby if you encode with the first number (the private key), only the second number (the public key) can decrypt it. These keys are asymmetric. Even if everyone knows the public key there is no way they can encrypt a message that the public key can decrypt. Only its matching private key can do that.

Let consider the idea of public and private keys in the context of the wine example.

A wine maker who wants to distinguish wine through digital signatures, as opposed to hues, creates a code (hue) for her casket using the private key. Because the private key is used to generate the `code (hue)`, only a corresponding public key can decrypt the code.

The wine maker then boldly writes down the public key name and the encrypted code on top of the cask, or transfers the public key once through a courier.

When you, the wine collector, take that public key and successfully unravel the encrypted code, you know that the public key is correct and the message is only encrypted by the wine maker who wrote the public key. In this scenario, even if another imposter wine maker copies the public key of the real wine maker and writes it on a casket, the imposter will not possess the ability to write a secret message that the public key will decrypt.

In essence the public key becomes the signature of the wine maker. Even if someone else were to claim the public key, that person wouldn't be able to produce a message that could be decrypted with the public key.

With this comparison of digital signatures with real signatures, we have established a parallel to help you grasp and internalize digital signatures. We already covered, in Chapter 10, the mechanics of using the JDK-based `keytool` and `jarsigner` commands to accomplish the signing process.

Implications of the Signing Process

We now can see that we cannot have two distinct signatures for the same package name. Signatures are sometimes referred to as public key infrastructure (PKI) certificates. More accurately stated, you would use a PKI certificate to sign a bundle, a JAR file, or a DLL or an application.

The PKI certificate is tied to the package name to ensure that two developers cannot install a package that carries the same package name. However, the same certificate can be used to sign any number of packages. In other words *one* PKI certificate supports *many* packages. This relationship is one-to-many. However *one* package has *one, and only one,* signature through its PKI certificate. A developer then protects the private key of a certificate with a password.

These facts are important not only for new releases of the same package but also to share data between packages when the packages are signed with the same signature.

Sharing Data Among Packages

In previous chapters, we established that each package runs in its own process. All assets that are installed or created through this package belong to the user whose ID is assigned to the package. You also know that Android allocates a unique Linux-based user ID to run that package. In Figure 12–1, you can see what this user ID look like. According to the Android SDK documentation

> *"This user ID is assigned when the application is installed on the device, and remains constant for the duration of its life on that device. Any data stored by an application will be assigned that application's user ID, and not normally accessible to other packages. When creating a new file with `getSharedPreferences(String, int)`, `openFileOutput(String, int)`, or `openOrCreateDatabase(String, int, SQLiteDatabase.CursorFactory)`, you can use the `MODE_WORLD_READABLE` and/or* `MODE_WORLD_WRITEABLE` *flags to allow any other package to read/write the file. When setting these flags, the file is still owned by your application, but it's global read and/or write permissions have been set appropriately so any other application can see it."*

If your intention is to allow a set of cooperating applications that depend on a common set of data you have an option to explicitly specify a user ID that is unique to you and common for your needs. This shared user ID is also defined in the manifest file, similar to the definition of a package name. Listing 12–1 shows an example.

Listing 12–1. *Shared User ID Declaration*

```
<manifest xmlns:android="http://schemas.android.com/apk/res/android"
      package="com.androidbook.somepackage"
      sharedUserId="com.androidbook.mysharedusrid"
      ...
>
...the rest of the xml nodes
</manifest>
```

The Nature of Shared User IDs

Multiple applications can specify the same shared user id if they share the same signature (Signed with the same PKI certificate). Having a shared user ID allows multiple applications to share data and even run in the same process. To avoid the duplication of a shared user ID, use a convention similar to naming a Java class. Here are some examples of shared user IDs found in the Android system

```
"android.uid.system"
"android.uid.phone"
```

NOTE: There have been some reports in Android-related news groups that a shared ID must be specified as a raw string and not a string resource.

As a note of caution, if you are planning on using shared user IDs, the recommendation is to use them from the start. Otherwise, they don't work well when you upgrade your application from a nonshared user ID to one with a shared ID. One of the cited reasons is that Android will not run chown on the old resources because of the user ID change. Therefore, we strongly advised that you

- Use a shared user ID from the start if needed.
- Don't change a user ID once it's in use.

A Code Pattern for Sharing Data

This section explores the opportunities we have when two applications want to share resources and data. As you know, the resources and data of each package are owned and protected by that package's context during run time. It is no surprise then that you need access to the context of the package that you want to share the resources or data from.

Android provides an API called createPackageContext() to help with this. You can use the createPackageContext() API on any existing context object (such as your activity) to get a reference to the target context that you want to interact with. Listing 12–1 provides an example (this is an example only to show you the usage and not intended to be compiled).

Listing 12–2. *Using the createPackageContext() API*

```
//Identify package you want to use
String targetPackageName="com.androidbook.samplepackage1";

//Decide on an appropriate context flag
int flag=Context.CONTEXT_RESTRICTED;

//Get the target context through one of your activities
Activity myContext = ......;
Context targetContext =
        myContext.createPackageContext(targetPackageName, flag);

//Use context to resolve file paths
Resources res = targetContext.getResources();
File path = targetContext.getFilesDir();
```

Notice how we are able to get a reference to the context of a given package name such as `com.androidbook.samplepackage1`. This `targetContext` in Listing 12–2 is identical to the context that is passed to the target application when that application is launched. As the name of the method indicates (in its "create" prefix), each call returns a new context object. However, the documentation assures us that this returned context object is designed to be lightweight.

This API is applicable irrespective of whether or not you have a shared user ID. If you share the user ID, it is well and good. If you don't share a user ID, the target application would need to declare its resources accessible to the outside users.

`createPackageContext()` uses one of three flags:

- If the flag is `CONTEXT_INCLUDE_CODE`, Android allows you to load the target application code into the current process. That code will then run as yours. This will succeed only if both packages have the same signature and a shared user ID. If the shared user IDs don't match, using this flag will result in a security exception.
- If the flag is `CONTEXT_RESTRICTED`, we still should be able to access the resource paths without going to the extreme case of requesting a code load.
- If the flag is `CONTEXT_IGNORE_SECURITY`, the certificates are ignored and the code is loaded but however it will run under your user ID. The documentation as a consequence suggests severe caution if you were to use this flag.

Now, we know how packages, signatures, and shared user IDs can be used in concert in controlling access to what applications own and create.

Library Projects

As we talk through sharing code and resources one question worth asking is, will the idea of a "library" project help? To investigate this, we first understand what library projects are, how to create them, and how these projects are used.

What Is a Library Project?

Starting with the ADT 0.9.7 Eclipse plug-in, Android supports the idea of library projects. A library project is a collection of Java code and resources that look like a regular project but never ends up in an `.apk` file by itself. Instead the code and resources of a library project become part of another project and get compiled into that main project's `.apk` file.

Library Project Predicates

Here are some facts about these library projects:

- A library project can have its own package name
- A library project will not be compiled into its own .apk file and instead gets absorbed into an .apk file of the project that uses this as a dependency.
- A library project can use other JAR files.
- A library project cannot be made into a JAR file by itself.
- Eclipse ADT will merge a library project into the main referenced project and compiles them together as part of the main project compilation.
- Both the library project and the main project can access the resources from the library project through their respective R.java files.
- You can have duplicate resource IDs between main project and a library project. Resource IDs from the main project will take precedence over those in the library project.
- If you would like to distinguish resource ids between the two projects, you can use different resource prefixes, such as lib_ for the library project resources.
- A main project can reference any number of library projects.
- You can set precedence for the library projects to see whose resources are more important.
- Components, such as an activity, of a library need to be defined in the target main project manifest file. When done so, the component name from the library package must be fully qualified with the library package name.
- It is not necessary to define the components in a library manifest file although it may be a good practice to know quickly what components it supports.
- Creating a library project starts with creating a regular Android project and then choosing the Is Library flag in its properties window.
- You can set the dependent library projects for a main project through project properties screen as well.
- Clearly being a library project, many main projects can include that library project.

- Library feature is available in ADT 0.9.7, SDK tools version r6 or higher, Android 2.1 or up.
- One library project cannot reference another library project as of this release although there seem to be a desire to do so in future releases
- Library project cannot support AIDL files.
- A library project does not support sharable assets directory.

Let's explore library projects by creating a library project and a main project. The goal of this sample project is to do the following:

1. Create a simple activity in a library project.
2. Create a menu for the activity in step 1 by defining some menu resources.
3. Create a main project activity that uses the library project as a dependency.
4. Create an activity in the main project from step 3.
5. Create a menu for the main activity in step 4.
6. Have a menu item from the main activity invoke the activity from the library project.

Once these projects created here is the activity from the main project (the activity from step 4, Figure 12–2).

Figure 12–2. *A sample activity with menus in a main project*

When you click on the **invoke lib** menu item from the main project activity, you will see the activity shown in Figure 12–3 served from the library project.

Figure 12–3. *A sample activity from the Library project*

The menus in this library activity come from resources of the library project. Clicking these menus simply logs a message on the screen that a particular menu item is clicked. Let's start the exercise by creating a library project first.

Creating a Library Project

This sample library project will have the following files:

- `TestLibActivity.java` (Listing 12–3)
- `layout/lib_main.xml` (Listing 12–4)
- `menu/lib_main_menu.xml` (Listing 12–5)
- `AndroidManifest.xml` (Listing 12–6)

These files should be sufficient to create your own Android library project and are shown in the following listings.

NOTE: We will give you a URL at the end of the chapter that you can use to download projects of this chapter. This will allow you to import these projects into your Eclipse directly.

Listing 12–3. *Sample Library Project Activity: TestLibActivity.java*

```
package com.androidbook.library.testlibrary;

//...basic imports here
//use CTRL-SHIFT-O to have eclipse generate
//necessary imports

public class TestLibActivity extends Activity
{
    public static final String tag="TestLibActivity";
    @Override
    public void onCreate(Bundle savedInstanceState) {
        super.onCreate(savedInstanceState);
        setContentView(R.layout.lib_main);
    }
    @Override
    public boolean onCreateOptionsMenu(Menu menu) {
        super.onCreateOptionsMenu(menu);
        MenuInflater inflater = getMenuInflater(); //from activity
        inflater.inflate(R.menu.lib_main_menu, menu);
        return true;
    }
    @Override
    public boolean onOptionsItemSelected(MenuItem item) {
        appendMenuItemText(item);
        if (item.getItemId() == R.id.menu_clear){
                this.emptyText();
                return true;
        }
        return true;
    }
    private TextView getTextView(){
        return (TextView)this.findViewById(R.id.text1);
    }
    public void appendText(String abc){
        TextView tv = getTextView();
        tv.setText(tv.getText() + "\n" + abc);
    }
    private void appendMenuItemText(MenuItem menuItem){
       String title = menuItem.getTitle().toString();
       TextView tv = getTextView();
       tv.setText(tv.getText() + "\n" + title);
    }
    private void emptyText(){
          TextView tv = getTextView();
          tv.setText("");
    }
}
```

Listing 12–4 shows the supporting layout file for this activity: just a single text view that is used to write out the name of the menu item clicked.

Listing 12–4. *Sample Library Project Layout File: layout/lib_main.xml*

```
<?xml version="1.0" encoding="utf-8"?>
<LinearLayout xmlns:android="http://schemas.android.com/apk/res/android"
    android:orientation="vertical"
```

```
    android:layout_width="fill_parent"
    android:layout_height="fill_parent"
    >
<TextView
    android:id="@+id/text1"
    android:layout_width="fill_parent"
    android:layout_height="wrap_content"
    android:text="Your debug will appear here "
    />
</LinearLayout>
```

Listing 12–5 provides the menu file to support the menus shown in the library activity of Figure 12–3.

Listing 12–5. *Library Project Menu File: Menu/lib_main_menu.xml*

```
<menu xmlns:android="http://schemas.android.com/apk/res/android">
    <!-- This group uses the default category. -->
    <group android:id="@+id/menuGroup_Main">
        <item android:id="@+id/menu_clear"
             android:title="clear" />
        <item android:id="@+id/menu_testlib_1"
            android:title="Lib Test Menu1" />
        <item android:id="@+id/menu_testlib_2"
            android:title="Lib Test Menu2" />
    </group>
</menu>
```

And the manifest file for the library project is contained in Listing 12–6.

Listing 12–6. *Library Project Manifest File: AndroidManifest.xml*

```
<?xml version="1.0" encoding="utf-8"?>
<manifest xmlns:android="http://schemas.android.com/apk/res/android"
      package="com.androidbook.library.testlibrary"
      android:versionCode="1"
      android:versionName="1.0.0">
    <uses-sdk android:minSdkVersion="3" />
    <application android:icon="@drawable/icon"
         android:label="Test Library Project">
        <activity android:name=".TestLibActivity"
                  android:label="Test Library Activity">
        </activity>
    </application>
</manifest>
```

As pointed out in the library project predicates section, the activity definition in the library project manifest file is merely for documentation and executionally optional.

Once these files are assembled you start by creating a regular Android project. Once the project is set up, right-click the project name, and click the properties context menu to show the properties dialog for the library project. This dialog is shown in Figure 12–4. (The available build targets in this figure may vary with your version of the Android SDK.) Simply select Is Library from this dialog to set up this project as a library project.

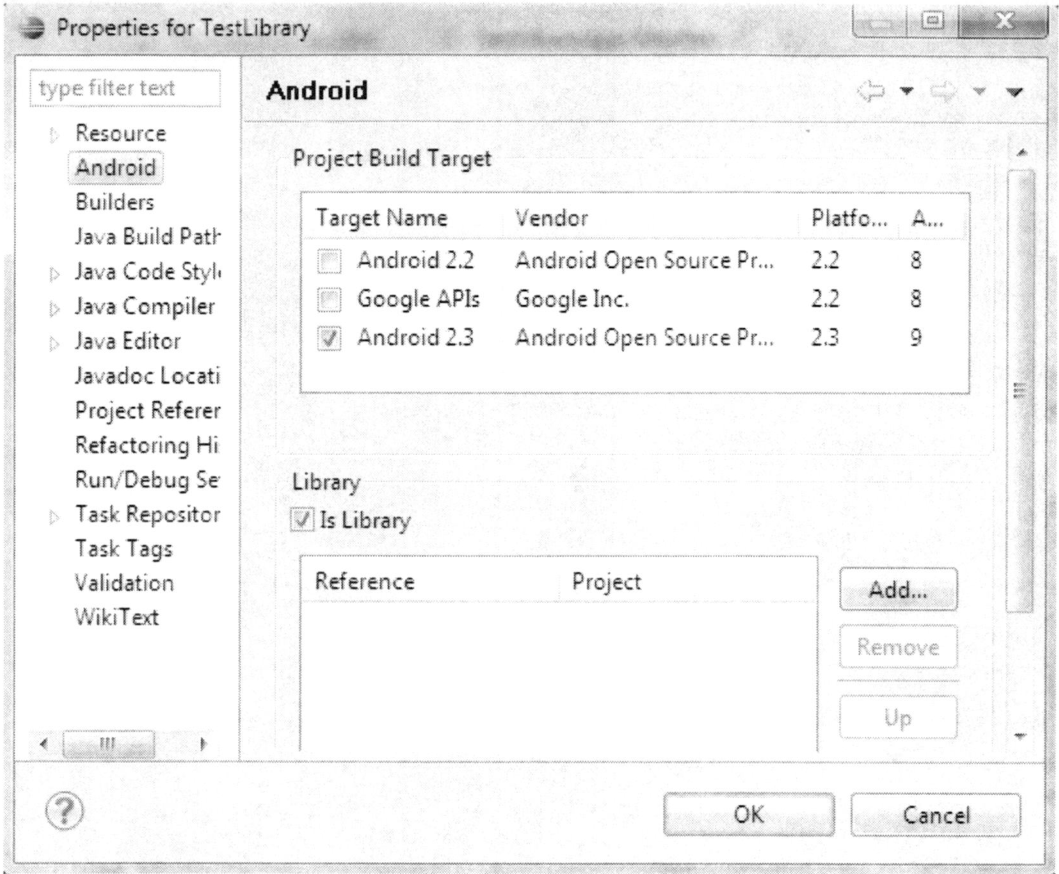

Figure 12–4. *Designating a project as a library project*

With that, we have completed creating a library project. Let's see now how to create an application project that can use this library project.

Creating an Android Project That Uses a library

We will use a similar set of files to create an application project and then go on to use the library project from above as a dependency. Here is the list of files we will be using to create the main project:

- `TestAppActivity.java` (Listing 12–7)
- `layout/main.xml` (Listing 12–8)
- `menu/main_menu.xml` (Listing 12–9)
- `AndroidManifest.xml` (Listing 12–10)

Listing 12–7 shows `TestAppActivity.java`.

Listing 12–7. *Main Project Activity Code: TestAppActivity.java*

```
package com.androidbook.library.testlibraryapp;
import com.androidbook.library.testlibrary.*;
//...other imports

public class TestAppActivity extends Activity
{
    public static final String tag="TestAppActivity";
    @Override
    public void onCreate(Bundle savedInstanceState) {
        super.onCreate(savedInstanceState);
        setContentView(R.layout.main);
    }
    @Override
    public boolean onCreateOptionsMenu(Menu menu) {
        super.onCreateOptionsMenu(menu);
        MenuInflater inflater = getMenuInflater(); //from activity
        inflater.inflate(R.menu.main_menu, menu);
        return true;
    }
    @Override
    public boolean onOptionsItemSelected(MenuItem item) {
        appendMenuItemText(item);
        if (item.getItemId() == R.id.menu_clear)
        {
                this.emptyText();
                return true;
        }
        if (item.getItemId() == R.id.menu_library_activity){
                this.invokeLibActivity(item.getItemId());
                return true;
        }
        return true;
    }
    private void invokeLibActivity(int mid)
    {
        Intent intent = new Intent(this,TestLibActivity.class);
        intent.putExtra("com.ai.menuid", mid);
        startActivity(intent);
    }
    private TextView getTextView(){
        return (TextView)this.findViewById(R.id.text1);
    }
    public void appendText(String abc){
        TextView tv = getTextView();
        tv.setText(tv.getText() + "\n" + abc);
    }
    private void appendMenuItemText(MenuItem menuItem){
       String title = menuItem.getTitle().toString();
       TextView tv = getTextView();
       tv.setText(tv.getText() + "\n" + title);
    }
    private void emptyText(){
          TextView tv = getTextView();
          tv.setText("");
    }
}
```

Please note that, after creating this file, you may get a compile error on the reference to the activity class that is in the library project. This will not go away until your read a bit further and discover how to specify the previous library project as a dependency of the application project.

The corresponding layout file to support the activity is in Listing 12–8.

Listing 12–8. *Main Project layout file: layout/main.xml*

```
<?xml version="1.0" encoding="utf-8"?>
<LinearLayout xmlns:android="http://schemas.android.com/apk/res/android"
    android:orientation="vertical"
    android:layout_width="fill_parent"
    android:layout_height="fill_parent"
    >
<TextView
    android:id="@+id/text1"
    android:layout_width="fill_parent"
    android:layout_height="wrap_content"
    android:text="Debug Text Will Appear here"
    />
</LinearLayout>
```

The Java code in the main project activity (Listing 12–7) is using a menu item called `R.id.menu_library_activity` to invoke the `TestLibActivity`. Here is the code extracted from the Java file (Listing 12–7):

```
private void invokeLibActivity(int mid)
{
    Intent intent = new Intent(this,TestLibActivity.class);
    //Pass the menu id as an intent extra
    //incase if the lib activity wants it.
    intent.putExtra("com.androidbook.library.menuid", mid);
    startActivity(intent);
}
```

Notice how we have used `TestLibActivity.class` as if it is a local class, except that we have imported the Java classes from the library package:

```
import com.androidbook.library.testlibrary.*;
```

And the menu file is in Listing 12–9.

Listing 12–9. *Main Project Menu File: menu/main_menu.xml*

```
<menu xmlns:android="http://schemas.android.com/apk/res/android">
    <!-- This group uses the default category. -->
    <group android:id="@+id/menuGroup_Main">
        <item android:id="@+id/menu_clear"
             android:title="clear" />
        <item android:id="@+id/menu_library_activity"
         android:title="invoke lib" />
    </group>
</menu>
```

The manifest file to complete the project creation is shown in Listing 12–10.

Listing 12–10. *Main Project Manifest File: AndroidManifest.xml*

```
<?xml version="1.0" encoding="utf-8"?>
<manifest xmlns:android="http://schemas.android.com/apk/res/android"
      package="com.androidbook.library.testlibraryapp"
      android:versionCode="1"
      android:versionName="1.0.0">
    <application android:icon="@drawable/icon" android:label="Test Library App">
        <activity android:name=".TestAppActivity"
                  android:label="Test Library App">
            <intent-filter>
                <action android:name="android.intent.action.MAIN" />
                <category android:name="android.intent.category.LAUNCHER" />
            </intent-filter>
        </activity>
        <activity android:name=
"com.androidbook.library.testlibrary.TestLibActivity"
                  android:label="Test Library Activity"/>
    </application>
    <uses-sdk android:minSdkVersion="3" />
</manifest>
```

In this main application manifest file, notice how we have defined the activity `TestLibActivity` from the library project. We have also used the fully qualified package name for the activity definition. Also notice that the package names for the library project could be different from the main application project.

Once you have set up an Android project with these files, you can use the following project properties dialogue (see Figure 12–5) to indicate that this main project depends on the library project that was created earlier.

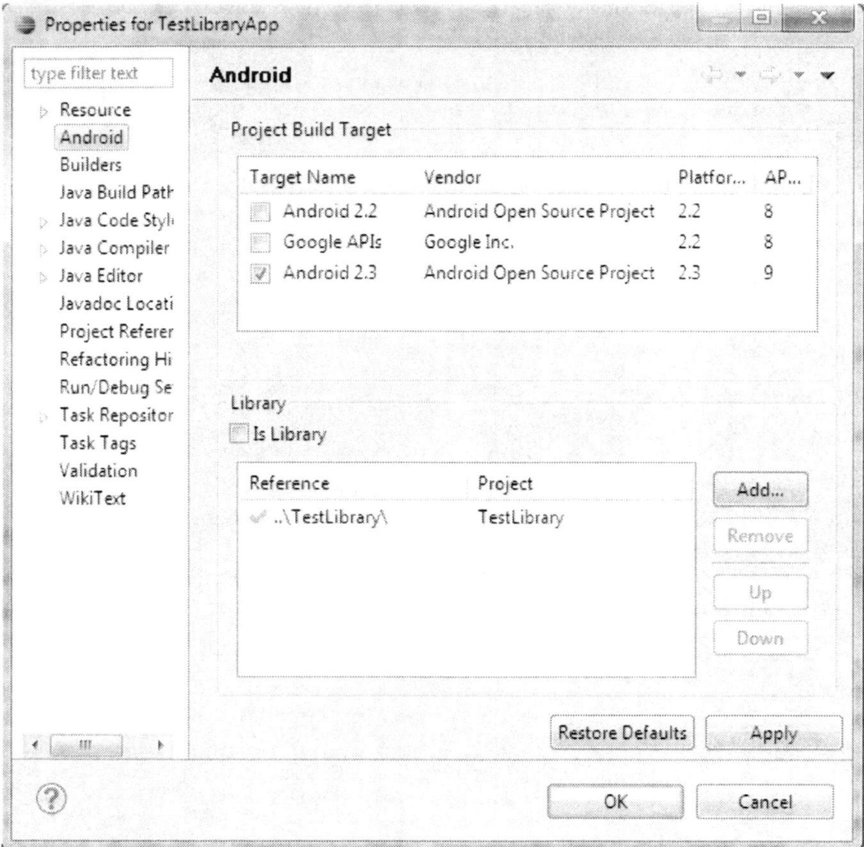

Figure 12–5. *Declaring a library project dependency*

Notice the Add button in the dialogue. You can use this to add the library in Figure 12–5 as a reference. You don't need to do anything else.

Once this step is done, the library project usually shows up as an additional node (in addition to being a library project by itself) under the main application project. Figure 12–6 illustrates this.

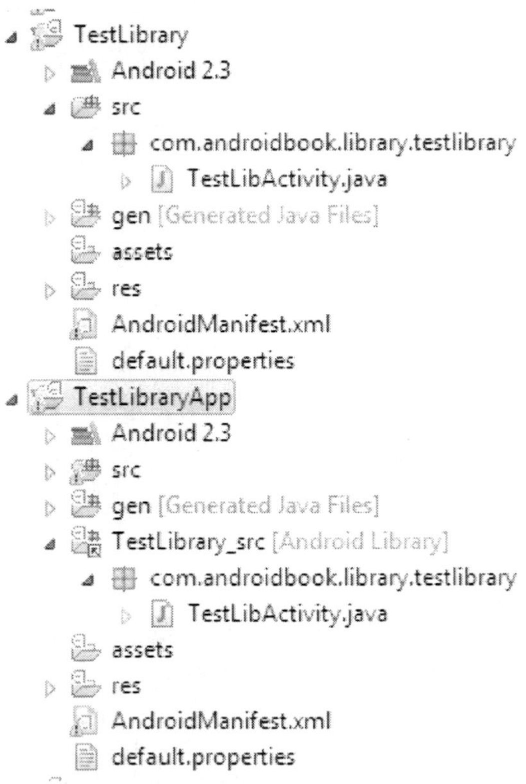

Figure 12–6. ***Absorbed library project in the main project view***

Notice the node that said [Android Library] and the replicated/referenced Java source files. Notice the structure of this node. It is named by concatenating the name of the library project, an underscore, and the name of the corresponding source directory under the library project. This scheme allows for any number of arbitrary source directories under the library project. This is the primary difference between ADT 0.9.8 and the more recent ADT releases.

If you were to change the source files belonging to the library project under the application project, you are actually changing them in the library project as well. Sometimes, you don't see this subnode. You may want to restart Eclipse in such a case. In any case, if it works, you should see this extra node.

Android does another interesting thing with `R.java` files. Consider Figure 12–7.

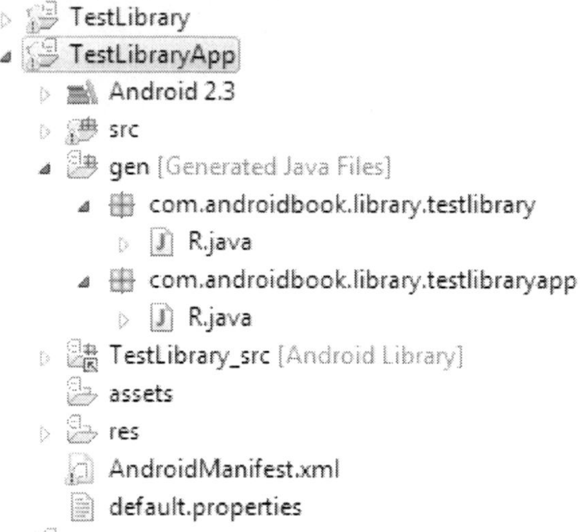

Figure 12–7. *Replicated resources in R.java*

First Android generates one `R.java` file in the library project for the resources belonging to the library project. Android also generates another `R.java` file for the resources in the main Java project. This is to be expected—two projects, two `R.java` files.

However, the interesting thing is that Android creates the resource IDs for the library resources in the `R.java` file of the main application as well. This means the programmer can use the `R.id.` syntax for IDs of the `R.java` file belonging to the main application (please note that `R.java` is automatically generated, so the numbers such as 0x7f02000 in Listing 12–11 may be different in your project).

Listing 12–11. *Redefined Shared Resource IDs in the Main Project R.java File*

```
public final class R {
    public static final class attr {
    }
    public static final class drawable {
        public static final int icon=0x7f020000;
        public static final int robot=0x7f020001;
    }
    public static final class id {
        public static final int menuGroup_Main=0x7f060001;
        public static final int menu_clear=0x7f060002;
        public static final int menu_library_activity=0x7f060005;
        public static final int menu_testlib_1=0x7f060003;
        public static final int menu_testlib_2=0x7f060004;
        public static final int text1=0x7f060000;
    }
    public static final class layout {
        public static final int lib_main=0x7f030000;
        public static final int main=0x7f030001;
    }
    public static final class menu {
        public static final int lib_main_menu=0x7f050000;
        public static final int main_menu=0x7f050001;
```

```
    }
    public static final class string {
        public static final int app_name=0x7f040001;
        public static final int hello=0x7f040000;
    }
}
```

Notice that the resources identified with lib_ are now available in the main application's R.java as well. This means the library project will have one resource constant for lib_, and the main project will have another resource constant for the same lib_ resource.

Both projects in their Java code can refer to this resource by using the R.some-id. The value of the constant may be the same, but you will have that resource ID available in both Java namespaces: the library package namespace and the main project package namespace.

Also, pay attention to the menu names: lib_main_menu and main_menu. We would be in a real pickle if we names these two menu resource files the same but had different menu items inside them. The bottom line is that the resources are aggregated and available in one place for the main application. Pay special attention to the resources that are at the file level, such as menus and layouts, and the IDs that are generated for internal items of those resource files.

Now that you understand library projects, are we any closer to answering the shared data questions posed before considering them?

As you can see, library projects are compile-time constructs. Clearly, any resources that belong to the library get absorbed and merged into the main project. There is not a question of sharing at run time, as there is just one package file with the name of the main package. One suggestion often mentioned is that you can potentially develop free versions and paid versions of an application by both versions sharing a library.

References

Here are some useful links to further strengthen your understanding of this chapter:

- http://developer.android.com/guide/publishing/app-signing.html: This reference is really a good read for information about signing .apk files.
- http://java.sun.com/j2se/1.3/docs/tooldocs/win32/keytool.html: This site offers excellent documentation on keytool, jarsigner, and the signing process itself.
- http://www.androidbook.com/item/3493: Author's notes, including a conceptual model, on understanding what it means to sign a JAR file.

- http://www.androidbook.com/item/3279: This site compiles our research on understanding Android packages. You will see how to sign .apk files, further links to how to share data between packages, more on shared user ID, and instructions to install and uninstall packages.
- http://developer.android.com/guide/developing/eclipse-adt.html#libraryProject: Read this article to understand library projects.
- http://www.androidbook.com/projects: Look here for a list of downloadable projects related to this book. For this chapter, look for a file called ProAndroid3_Ch12_TestAndroidLibraries.zip. This ZIP file contains both projects in this chapter in separate root directories, so you can import them into Eclipse ADT.

Summary

In this chapter, we covered working with packages and processes, sharing code and data among packages, and creating Android library projects. You learned that signatures play an important security role in assigning ownership to packages.

This chapter lays the foundation for the next chapter, where we talk about components that are housed in a package process and (primarily) run on its main thread. We will talk about how to optimally co-opt the main thread via handlers and subthreads so that an Android application can run smoothly.

Chapter 13

Exploring Handlers

We showed in Chapter 12 that each package runs in its own process. In this chapter, we will explain the organization of threads within this process. This will lead us to why we need handlers.

Most code in an Android application runs in the context of a component such as an Activity or a Service. We will show how these components of an application interact with threads. Most of the time there is only one thread running in an Android process called the main thread. We will talk about the implications of sharing this main thread among various components. Primarily, this can lead to Application Not Responding (ANR) messages (the "A" stands for "application" and not "Annoying") . We will show you how you can use handlers, messages, and threads to break the dependency on the main thread when long running operations are needed.

We will start this chapter by looking at the components of an Android application and the thread context they run under.

Android Components and Threading

As you have gathered by now from many of the previous chapters, an Android process has four primary components. These are

- `Activity`
- `Service`
- `ContentProvider` (often referred as just a provider)
- `BroadcastReceiver` (often referred as just a receiver)

Most code you write in an Android application is part of one of these components or called by one of these components. Each of these components gets its own XML node under an application node specification in the Android project manifest file. To repaint, here are these nodes

```
<application>
     <activity/>
     <service/>
     <receiver/>
     <provider/>
</application>
```

With some exceptions Android uses the same thread to process (or run through) code in these components. This thread is called the main thread of the application. When these components are called, the call can be either a synchronous call, such as when you call a content provider for data, or a deferred one through a message queue, such as when you invoke functionality by calling a start service.

Figure 13–1 describes the relationship between threads and these four components. The goal of this diagram is to show how threads weave through the Android framework and its components. We explore aspects of this diagram in the next few subsections.

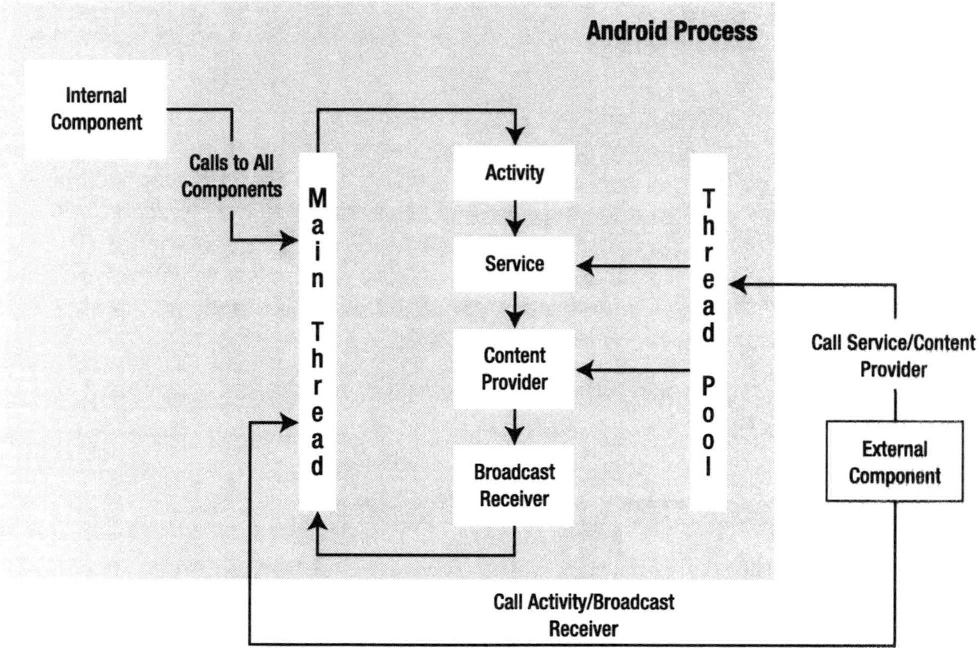

Figure 13–1. *Android Components and Threading Framework*

Activities Run on the Main Thread

As indicated in Figure 13–1 the main thread does the heavy lifting. It runs through all the components. Moreover, it does this through a message queue. For example, as you select menus or buttons on the device screen, the device will translate these actions as messages and drop them on to the main queue of the process that is in focus. The main thread sits in a loop and processes each message. If any message takes more than 5 seconds or so, Android throws an ANR message.

Broadcast Receivers run on the Main Thread

Similarly, in response to a menu item, if you were to invoke a broadcast message, Android again drops a message on the main queue of the package process in which the registered receiver is to be invoked from. The main thread will come around to that message at a later time to invoke the receiver. The main thread does the work for a broadcast receiver as well. If the main thread is busy responding to a menu action, the broadcast receiver will have to wait until the main thread gets freed up.

Services Run on the Main Thread

The same is true with a service. When you start a local service with `startService` from a menu item, a message is dropped on to the main queue, and the main thread will come around to process it via the service code.

Content Provider Runs on the Main Thread

Calls to a local content provider are slightly different. A content provider still runs on the main thread, but a call to it is synchronous and does not use message queues.

Implications of a Singular Main Thread

You may ask, "why is it important whether most code in an Android application runs on the main thread or otherwise?" Because the main thread has the responsibility to get back to its queue so that UI events are responded to. As a consequence, one should not hold up the main thread. If there is something that is going to take longer than 5 seconds you should get that done in a separate thread or defer it by asking the main thread to come back to it when it is freed up from other processing. As it turns out doing work in a separate thread is not as simple as it initially appears. We will return to that again later in this chapter and also next chapter, but let's talk about the thread pool that is identified in Figure 13–1.

Thread Pools, Content Providers, External Service Components

When external clients or components outside of the process makes a call to the content provider for data, then that call is allocated a thread from a thread pool. The same is true with external clients connecting to services.

Thread Utilities: Discover Your Threads

After much talk on main threads and worker threads, it is quite instructive to use the following utility class in Listing 13–1 to figure out which thread is running your part of the code. You can then verify what we have covered so far by monitoring the logcat and see which thread ID is being printed.

Listing 13–1. *Thread Utilities*

```
//utils.java
public class Utils
{
   public static long getThreadId() {
      Thread t = Thread.currentThread();
      return t.getId();
   }

   public static String getThreadSignature(){
      Thread t = Thread.currentThread();
      long l = t.getId();
      String name = t.getName();
      long p = t.getPriority();
      String gname = t.getThreadGroup().getName();
      return (name
            + ":(id)" + l
            + ":(priority)" + p
            + ":(group)" + gname);
   }

   public static void logThreadSignature(){
      Log.d("ThreadUtils", getThreadSignature());
   }

   public static void sleepForInSecs(int secs){
      try{
         Thread.sleep(secs * 1000);
      } catch(InterruptedException x){
         throw new RuntimeException("interrupted",x);
      }
   }
   //The following two methods are used by worker threads
   //that we will introduce later.
   public static Bundle getStringAsABundle(String message){
       Bundle b = new Bundle();
       b.putString("message", message);
       return b;
    }
    public static String getStringFromABundle(Bundle b){
        return b.getString("message");
    }
}
```

If you use the logThreadSignature(), you can see which thread is executing the code. You can also use the sleep() method to see what happens if you pause the main thread and thereby disallow it to process the message queue.

We have briefly referred to the idea of deferring work on a main thread if needed. This is done through handlers. Handlers are extensively used throughout Android so that the main UI thread is not held up. They also play a role in communicating with the main thread from other spawned worker threads. Let's look at what handlers are and how they function in the next section.

Handlers

A *handler* is a mechanism to drop a message on the main queue (more precisely, the queue attached to the thread on which the handler is instantiated) so that the message can be processed at a later point in time by the main thread. The message that is dropped has an internal reference pointing to the handler that dropped it.

When the main thread gets around to processing that message, it invokes the handler that dropped the message through a callback method on the handler object. This callback method is called `handleMesage`. Figure 13–2 presents this relationship between handlers, messages, and the main thread.

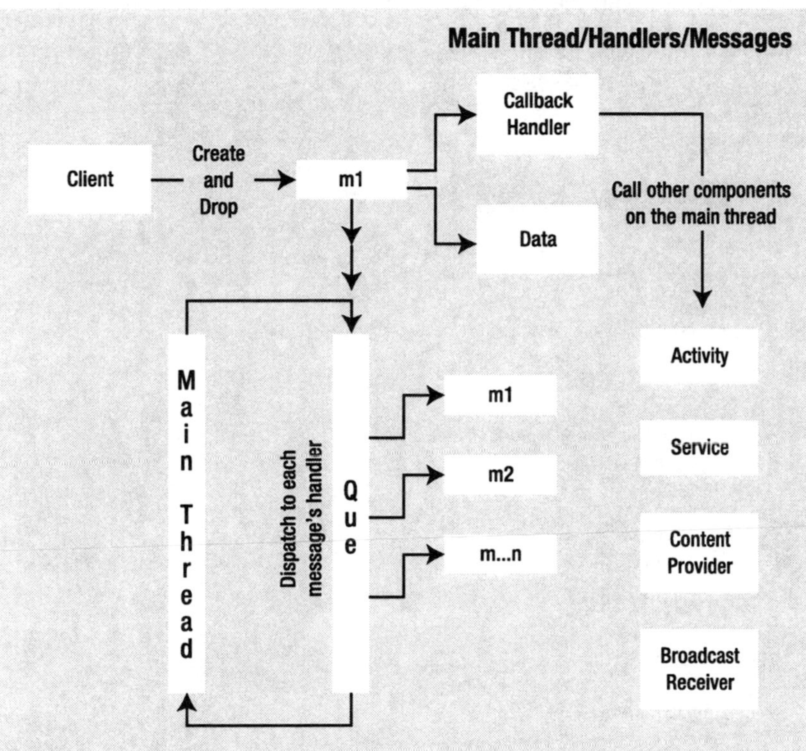

Figure 13–2. *Handler, Message, Message Queue Relationship*

Figure 13–2 illustrates the key players that work together when we talk about handlers. These key players are

- Main thread
- Main thread queue

- Handler
- Message

Out of these four, we are not exposed to the main thread or the queue directly. We primarily deal with the Handler object and the Message object. Even between these two, the Handler object coordinates most of the work.

Despite the importance of a Handler in this interaction, you should also note that, although a handler allows us to drop a message on to the queue, it is the message that actually holds a reference back to the handler. The Message object also holds a data structure that can be passed back to the handler. In Figure 13–2, the Message object is depicting this relationship by showing reference to a Data object.

Because of this seemingly inverted relationship between a handler and a message, and also the fact that the main thread and its queue are hidden from the programmer, a handler is best understood by an example.

For the example, we will have a menu item that invokes a function, and that function, in turn, performs an action five times at one-second intervals and reports back to the invoking activity each time.

Implications of Holding the Main Thread

If we don't mind holding up the main thread, we could have coded the preceding scenario like the pseudo code in Listing 13–2

Listing 13–2. *Holding Up the Main Thread with a Sleep Method*

```
public class SomeActivity
{
    ....other methods

    void respondToMenuItem()
    {
        //Prove that we are on the main thread
        Utils.logThreadSignature();

        for (int i=0;i<5;i++)
        {
            sleepFor(1000);// put main thread to sleep for 1 sec
            dosomething();
            SomeTextView.setText("did something");
         }
    }
}
```

This will satisfy the requirement of the use case. However, if we do this, we *are* holding up the main thread, and we are guaranteed to have an ANR.

Using a Handler to Defer Work on the Main Thread

We can use a handler to avoid the ANR in the previous example. Pseudo code to do this via a handler will look like Listing 13–3.

Listing 13–3. *Instantiating a Handler From Main Thread*

```
void respondToMenuItem()
{
    SomeHandlerDerivedFromHandler myHandler =
                new SomeHandlerDerivedFromHandler();
    myHandler.doDeferredWork(); //invoke a function in 1 sec intervals
}
```

Now, the call respondToMenuItem() will allow the main thread to go back to its loop. The instantiated handler knows that it is invoked on the main thread and hooks itself up to the queue. The method doDeferredWork() will schedule work so that the main thread can get back to this work once it is free. So how does it do that? Here are the steps for implementing this function:

1. Construct a message object so that it can be dropped off on the queue.
2. Send the message object to the queue so that it can invoke a callback in 1 second.
3. Respond to the handleMessage() callback from the main thread.

To investigate this protocol, let's see the actual source code for a proper handler. The code in Listing 13–4 demonstrates this handler, which is called DeferWorkHandler.

In the pseudo code in Listing 13–3, the indicated handler SomeHandlerDerivedFromHandler is equivalent to DeferWorkHandler. Similarly, the indicated method doDeferredWork() is implemented on the DeferWorkHandler in Listing 13–4.

A Sample Handler Source Code That Defers Work

Before we explain each of the steps in the previous section, the code for DeferWorkHandler is presented in Listing 13–4. Keep in mind that the source code for the main driver activity that invokes this handler is given later in this chapter.

This parent driver activity is indicated as the variable parentActivity in Listing 13–4. This variable is not critical for understanding this code, and it is primarily used to report the status of the work that is occurring in the handler.

Listing 13–4. *DeferWorkHandler Source Code*

```
public class DeferWorkHandler extends Handler
{
    public static final String tag = "DeferWorkHandler";

    //Keep track of how many times we sent the message
    private int count = 0;
```

```
    //A parent driver activity we can use
    //to inform of status.
    private TestHandlersDriverActivity parentActivity = null;

    //During construction we take in the parent
    //driver activity.
    public DeferWorkHandler(TestHandlersDriverActivity inParentActivity){
        parentActivity = inParentActivity;
    }
    @Override
    public void handleMessage(Message msg)
    {
        String pm = new String(
                "message called:" + count + ":" +
                msg.getData().getString("message"));

        Log.d(tag,pm);
        this.printMessage(pm);

        if (count > 5)
        {
            return;
        }
        count++;
        sendTestMessage(1);
    }
    public void sendTestMessage(long interval)
    {
        Message m = this.obtainMessage();
        prepareMessage(m);
        this.sendMessageDelayed(m, interval * 1000);
    }
    public void doDeferredWork()
    {
        count = 0;
        sendTestMessage(1);
    }
    public void prepareMessage(Message m)
    {
        Bundle b = new Bundle();
        b.putString("message", "Hello World");
        m.setData(b);
        return ;
    }
    //This method just prints a message
    //in a text box in the parent activity.
    //You can see this method in Listing 13-9
    private void printMessage(String xyz)
    {
        parentActivity.appendText(xyz);
    }
}
```

Let's look at the primary aspects of this source code.

Constructing a Suitable Message Object

As we have indicated before, when the DeferWorkHandler is constructed, it already knows how to hook itself up to the main queue, because it inherited that property from the base Handler class. The base handler offers a series of methods to send messages to the queue to be responded later.

sendMessage() and sendMessageDelayed() are two examples of these send methods. sendMessageDelayed(), which we used in the example, allows us to drop a message on the main queue with a given amount of time delay.

When you call sendMessage() or sendMessageDelayed(), you will need an instance of the Message object. It is best that you ask the handler to give it to you, because when the handler returns the Message object, it hides itself in the belly of the Message. That way, when the main thread comes along, it knows which handler to call based solely on the message.

In Listing 13–4, the message is obtained using the following code:

```
Message m = this.obtainMessage();
```

The variable this refers to the handler object instance. As the name indicates, the method does not create a new message but instead gets one from a global message pool. At a later point, once this message is processed, it will be recycled. The method obtainMessage() has the variations listed in Listing 13–5

Listing 13–5. ***Constructing a Message Through a Handler***

```
obtainMessage();
obtainMessage(int what);
obtainMessage(int what, Object object);
obtainMessage(int what, int arg1, int arg2)
obtainMessage(int what, int arg1, int arg2, Object obj);
```

Each method variation sets the corresponding fields on the message object. There are some restrictions on the Object object argument when the message crosses process boundaries. In such cases, it needs to be parcellable. It is much safer and compatible in such cases to use the setData() method explicitly on the message object, which takes a bundle. In Listing 13–4, we have used setData(). You are encouraged to use the arg1 or arg2 instead if what you are intending to pass are simple indicators that can be accommodated with integer values.

The argument what allows you to dequeue message or enquire if there are messages of this type in the queue. See the operations on the Handler class for more details. This chapter's "References" section has a URL for the API documentation of the Handler class.

Sending Message Objects to the Queue

Once we obtain a message from the handler, we can optionally modify the data contents of that message. In our example, we have used the setData() function by passing it a bundle object. Once we have categorized or identified the data of the message, we can send the message to the queue through sendMessage() or sendMessageDelayed(). Once these methods are called, the main thread will return to attending the queue.

Responding to the handleMessage Callback

The class DeferWorkHandler is derived from Handler. Once the messages are delivered to the queue, the handler sits and waits (figuratively speaking) until the main thread retrieves those messages and calls the handler's handleMessage().

If you want to see this handler and main thread interaction more clearly, you can write a logcat message when you are sending the message and in the handleMessage() callback. You will notice the time stamps differ as the main thread would have taken a few more milliseconds to come back to the handleMessage() method.

This is also a good way to know that both the sendMessage() and the handleMessage() run on the main thread. You can use the Utils.logThreadSignature() method (see Listing 13–1) to illustrate this.

In our example, each handleMessage(), after processing one message, sends another message to the queue so that it can be called again. It does this five times, and when the counter reaches five, it quits sending messages to the queue.

In our example of a handler, DeferWorkHandler (as indicated earlier) also takes the parent activity as an input so that it can report back any information using the methods provided by that activity.

Using Worker Threads

When we use a handler like the one in the previous section, the code is still executed on the main thread. Each call to handleMessage() still should return within the time stipulations of the main thread (in other words, each message invocation should complete in less than five seconds to avoid Android Not Responding). If your goal is to extend that time of execution further, you will need to start a separate thread, keep the thread running until it finishes the work, and allow for that subthread to report back to the main activity, which is running on the main thread. This type of a subthread is often called a *worker thread*.

It is a no-brainer to start a separate thread while responding to a menu item. However, the clever trick is to allow the worker thread to post a message to the queue of the main thread that something is happening and that the main thread should look at it when it gets to that message.

A reasonable solution that involves a worker thread is as follows:

1. Create a handler in the main thread while responding to the menu item. Keep it aside. Unlike in the earlier section, we will not use this handler to send messages to defer work.

2. Create a separate thread (a worker thread) that does the actual work. Pass the handler from step 1 to the worker thread.

3. The worker thread code can now do the actual work for longer than 5 seconds and, while doing it, can call the handler to send status messages to communicate with the main thread

4. These status messages now get processed by the main thread, because the handler belonged to the main thread. The main thread can process these messages while the worker thread is doing its work.

Let's show you some sample code for a menu item that starts the process for a worker thread

Invoking a Worker Thread from a Menu

The code in Listing 13–6 illustrates a function called `testThread()` that can be invoked in response to a menu item on the main thread.

Listing 13–6. *Instantiating a Sub Thread from a Main Thread*

```
//Keep a couple of local variables
//so that they are not recreated with every menu click
//in your activity

//Holds a pointer to the handler
Handler statusBackHandler = null;

//An instance of the thread
Thread workerThread = null;

//this method will be invoked by a menu
private void testThread()
{
    if (statusBackHandler == null)
    {
        //Menu item was never clicked before
        //The classes refered here are listed later in the chapter
        statusBackHandler = new ReportStatusHandler(this);
        workerThread = new Thread(new WorkerThreadRunnable(statusBackHandler));
        workerThrread.start();
        return;
    }

    //Thread is already there
    if (workerThread.getState() != Thread.State.TERMINATED)
    {
        Log.d(tag, "thread is new or alive, but not terminated");
    }
    else
    {
        Log.d(tag, "thread is likely dead. starting now");
        //you have to create a new thread.
        //no way to resurrect a dead thread.
```

```
            workerThread = new Thread(new WorkerThreadRunnable(statusBackHandler));
            workerThread.start();
        }
    }
```

The code looks a bit roundabout, but the crux of the code is

```
            statusBackHandler = new ReportStatusHandler(this);
            workerThread = new Thread(new WorkerThreadRunnable(statusBackHandler));
            workerThread.start();
```

Basically, we have created a handler (one that is responsible for reporting the status), passed it to the worker thread, and started the worker thread. The extra code in Listing 13–6 is there so that, if we were to press the menu item twice or thrice while the thread is doing its work and not terminated, we won't create another thread and handler.

Communicating Between the Worker and the Main Threads

We will now cover the classes ResportStatusHandler and WorkerThreadRunnable. We didn't present them earlier because we wanted to drive the understanding using top-down approach, where we plan and tell you what is required a high level and then go into the details of how each concept is executed.

WorkerThreadRunnable Implementation

Let's see now what the worker thread is doing through the WorkerThreadRunnable class. The source code for the WorkerThreadRunnable class is in Listing 13–7. Take a quick look at this listing, especially the comments in the code, to get a feel for what it might be doing. Following the listing we will explain the key concepts.

Listing 13–7. *Worker Thread Implementation*

```
//Primary Responsibilities
//1. Do the work
//2. Inform the parent activty
public class WorkerThreadRunnable implements Runnable
{
    //the handler to communicate with the main thread
    //Set this in the constructor
    Handler statusBackMainThreadHandler = null;

    public WorkerThreadRunnable(Handler h)
    {
        statusBackMainThreadHandler = h;
    }

    //usual debug tag
    public static String tag = "WorkerThreadRunnable";
    public void run()
    {
        Log.d(tag,"start execution");
        //see which thread is running this code
        //The following method is from Listing 13-1
        //It prints out the thread id and name
```

```
        Utils.logThreadSignature();

        //Tell parent that the worker thread has
        //started working
        informStart();
        for(int i=1;i <= 5;i++)
        {
            //In the real world instead of sleeping
            //work will be done here.
            Utils.sleepForInSecs(1);
              //Report back the work is progressing
            informMiddle(i);
        }
        informFinish();
    }

    public void informMiddle(int count)
    {
        Message m = this.statusBackMainThreadHandler.obtainMessage();
        m.setData(Utils.getStringAsABundle("done:" + count));
        this.statusBackMainThreadHandler.sendMessage(m);
    }

    public void informStart()
    {
        Message m = this.statusBackMainThreadHandler.obtainMessage();
        m.setData(Utils.getStringAsABundle("starting run"));
        this.mainThreadHandler.sendMessage(m);
    }
    public void informFinish()
    {
        Message m = this.statusBackMainThreadHandler.obtainMessage();
        m.setData(Utils.getStringAsABundle("Finishing run"));
        this.statusBackMainThreadHandler.sendMessage(m);
    }
}
```

There are two important things in Listing 13–7. In the `run()` method, we put the thread to sleep for 1 second and call the inform methods to tell the main thread whether the worker thread is at the beginning, middle, or end of the processing.

We have also included a call to the `Utils.logThreadSignature()` to identify the thread.

However, in the real world, instead of the sleep() method, this code will be calling a useful function for as longs as necessary. You can think of sleep() as simulating a work item that takes that many seconds.

ReportStatusHandler Implementation

All of the inform methods in Listing 13–7 create an appropriate string message and send it to the main thread through the `ReportStatusHandler`, which is shown in Listing 13–8.

Listing 13–8. *Sending Status to the Main Thread*

```
public class ReportStatusHandler extends Handler
{
```

```
    public static final String tag = "ReportStatusHandler";

    //Remember the parent activity so that
    //so that we can incorm it of the progress
    private TestHandlersDriverActivity
                parentTestHandlersDriverActivity = null;

    public ReportStatusHandler(
                TestHandlersDriverActivity inParentActivity){
        parentTestHandlersDriverActivity = inParentActivity;
    }

    @Override
    public void handleMessage(Message msg)
    {
        //Get string data from the message
        String pm = Utils.getStringFromABundle(msg.getData());
        Log.d(tag,pm);
        //Tell the parent activity that something happened
        this.printMessage(pm);
        //Assert that this runs on the main thread
        Utils.logThreadSignature();
    }

    private void printMessage(String xyz){
        parentTestHandlersDriverActivity.appendText(xyz);
    }
}
```

The code in this class is straightforward. When this handler receives the `handleMessage()`, it tells the parent driver activity that the worker thread has sent a status string through the appendText() method. The parent activity can choose whatever is necessary for that message. In our case, we just log it to the activity screen.

So far, we have demonstrated the following with handler examples:

Through `DeferWorkHandler`handler examples:

- Through `DeferWorkHandler`, we have showed how the main thread can schedule a message (or messages) to be processed at a later time (or deferred). This technique can also be used to do repetitive processing without using a timer or alarm manager.

- Through `ReportStatusHandler` and a `WorkerThread`, we have showed how you can start a separate worker thread and have that worker thread communicate back to the main UI through a handler.

A Quick Overview of Thread Behavior

As we started a thread in response to a menu item, it is natural to worry if we need to stop it as well. A thread automatically stops when it finishes the `run()` method. In fact, we are advised not to stop a running thread externally, as it might kill the work in the middle. The recommendation is to set a flag so that the thread will recognize that flag and gracefully exit the `run()` method.

It is also worth noting the various states of a thread to understand thread behavior. A thread has the following states:

- *New thread*: Someone has created it (`alive=false`).
- *Runnable*: Someone called a start on it (`alive=true`).
- *Not runnable*: Sleeping, suspending, waiting, called, or blocking on I/O (`alive=true`).
- *Dead*: When `stop()` is called or `run()` exits (`alive=false`).

The `isAlive()` method on a thread tells us that the thread has been started but not stopped. This means that the thread is in either `runnable` or `not-runnable` state. If it returns `false`, the thread could be a new thread or a dead thread.

As you work with threads, you may want to be mindful of the thread states.

Handler Example Driver classes

So far, we have presented the source code for the following classes:

- `DeferWorkHandler.java`: This has the ability to defer functionality (see Listing 13–4).
- `ReportStatusHandler.java`: This is a communication vehicle for a worker thread (see Listing 13–8).
- `WorkerThreadRunnable.java`: This is a worker thread implementation (see Listing 13–7).
- `Utils.java`: This contains a few thread utilities (see Listing 13–1).

It is time we present you with the full source code of the driver activity class that responds to menu items and invokes the functionality we have discussed. We will also give you the source code for the menu resource and manifest files so that you have all the classes necessary to create a project and play with the concepts.

As you try to compile these files, note that the listings do not include the package name or import statements. It is easy to re-create the import statements using Eclipse. While you have the source file open in Eclipse, press Ctrl+Shift+O, and Eclipse will fill in the necessary imports.

As far as the package name goes, you can view the manifest file to see what package name is used for this application. You will need to put that package name at the top of the Java source files. As all these files are designed to be in the same package, you can even change the package name to suit your needs and use that package name in the manifest file subsequently.

Note: You can also download the prebuilt project ZIP file using a link in this chapter's "References" section. The name of the ZIP file will be ProAndroid3_Ch13_`TestHandlers.zip`. To create a project, unzip this file, and import the project into your eclipse ADT environment.

Again, the list of additional files you need to compile is as follows:

- `TestHandlersDriverActivity.java`: Main driver activity (see Listing 13–9)
- `layout/main.xml`: Layout file for `TestHandlersDriverActivity` (see Listing 13–10)
- `res/menu/main_menu.xml`: Menu to invoke handlers (see Listing 13–11)
- `AndroidManifest.xml`: The usual manifest file (see Listing 13–12)

The following sections explain these files one by one.

Driver Activity File

Here is the first of these files, `TestHandlersDriverActivity.java`. This class is a simple activity with a text view in it. The text view will list the menu items that are clicked. There is one menu item to test the deferred handler and one menu item to test the worker thread. The messages from the worker thread are also logged to this text view.

This class also includes a list of the activity life cycle methods toward the end. This is because we will be examining the behavior of the main thread and its queue with respect to an activity's life cycle. The code is in Listing 13–9.

Listing 13–9. *Test Activity to Test Handlers and Worker Threads*

```
public class TestHandlersDriverActivity extends Activity
{
    public static final String tag="TestHandlersDriverActivity";
    @Override
    public void onCreate(Bundle savedInstanceState) {
        super.onCreate(savedInstanceState);
        setContentView(R.layout.main);
    }
    @Override
    public boolean onCreateOptionsMenu(Menu menu)
    {
        super.onCreateOptionsMenu(menu);
            MenuInflater inflater = getMenuInflater(); //from activity
            inflater.inflate(R.menu.main_menu, menu);
        return true;
    }
    @Override
    public boolean onOptionsItemSelected(MenuItem item)
    {
        appendMenuItemText(item);
        if (item.getItemId() == R.id.menu_clear)
```

```
    {
        this.emptyText();
        return true;
    }
    if (item.getItemId() == R.id.menu_test_thread)
    {
        this.testThread();
        return true;
    }
    if (item.getItemId() == R.id.menu_test_defered_handler)
    {
        this.testDeferedHandler();
        return true;
    }
    return true;
}

private TextView getTextView(){
    return (TextView)this.findViewById(R.id.text1);
}
public void appendText(String abc){
    TextView tv = getTextView();
    tv.setText(tv.getText() + "\n" + abc);
}
private void appendMenuItemText(MenuItem menuItem){
   String title = menuItem.getTitle().toString();
   TextView tv = getTextView();
   tv.setText(tv.getText() + "\n" + title);
}
private void emptyText(){
      TextView tv = getTextView();
      tv.setText("");
}

private DeferWorkHandler th = null;
private void testDeferedHandler()
{
    if (th == null)
    {
        th = new DeferWorkHandler(this);
        this.appendText("Creating a new handler");
    }
    this.appendText(
            "Starting to do deferred work by sending messages");
    th.doDeferredWork();
}

Handler statusBackHandler = null;
Thread workerThread = null;
private void testThread()
{
    if (statusBackHandler == null)
    {
        statusBackHandler = new ReportStatusHandler(this);
        workerThread =
            new Thread(
                    new WorkerThreadRunnable(statusBackHandler));
```

```
        }
        if (workerThread.getState() != Thread.State.TERMINATED)
        {
            Log.d(tag, "thread is new or alive, but not terminated");
        }
        else
        {
            Log.d(tag, "thread is likely dead. starting now");
            //you have to create a new thread.
            //no way to resurrect a dead thread.
            workerThread =
                new Thread(
                        new WorkerThreadRunnable(statusBackHandler));
            workerThread.start();
        }
    }

//The following lifecycle methods are included to see the behavior
//deferred messages and the nature of the worker thread as the activity
//goes through various life stages

    @Override
    protected void onPause() {
        Log.d(tag,"onpause. I may be partially or fully invisible");
        this.appendText("onpause");
        super.onPause();
    }
    @Override
    protected void onStop() {
        Log.d(tag,"onstop. I am fully invisible");
        this.appendText("onstop");
        super.onStop();
    }
    @Override
    protected void onDestroy() {
        Log.d(tag,"ondestroy. about to be removed.");
        super.onDestroy();
    }
    @Override
    protected void onRestart() {
        Log.d(tag,"onRestart. UI controls are there.");
        super.onRestart();
    }
    @Override
    protected void onStart() {
        Log.d(tag,"onStart. UI may be partially visible.");
        super.onStart();
    }
    @Override
    protected void onResume() {
        Log.d(tag,"onResume. UI fully visible.");
        super.onResume();
    }
}
```

Layout File

Listing 13–10 shows the layout file (layout/main.xml). This is a simple layout file to support the activity in Listing 13–9. As stated before that listing, it contains a single text view with an instruction to click the menu to start things off.

Listing 13–10. *Layout File*

```
<?xml version="1.0" encoding="utf-8"?>
<LinearLayout xmlns:android="http://schemas.android.com/apk/res/android"
    android:orientation="vertical"
    android:layout_width="fill_parent"
    android:layout_height="fill_parent"
    >
<TextView
    android:id="@+id/text1"
    android:layout_width="fill_parent"
    android:layout_height="wrap_content"
    android:text="Click Menu to see available options"
    />
</LinearLayout>
```

Menu File

The supporting menu file, menu/main_menu.xml, is shown in Listing 13–11. This is the menu file to support the activity in Listing 13–9. As stated in that activity, this menu file declares three menu items. One clears the text view as you work with menu items. We then have two primary menu items: menu_test_defered_handler invokes DeferWorkHandler, and menu_test_thread spawns the worker thread and works through ReportStatusHandler.

Listing 13–11. *Menu Items to Invoke Handler and Subthread Code*

```
<menu xmlns:android="http://schemas.android.com/apk/res/android">
    <!-- This group uses the default category. -->
    <group android:id="@+id/menuGroup_Main">
        <item android:id="@+id/menu_clear"
         android:title="clear" />

        <item android:id="@+id/menu_test_thread"
            android:title="Test Worker Thread" />

        <item android:id="@+id/menu_test_defered_handler"
            android:title="Defered Handler" />
    </group>
</menu>
```

Manifest File

Listing 13–12 contains the manifest file to complete the list of source files (manifest.xml). This manifest file is simple as well, pointing to the single activity of Listing 13–9 (the main driver activity).

Listing 13–12. *AndroidManifest File*

```
<manifest xmlns:android="http://schemas.android.com/apk/res/android"
      package="com.androidbook.handlers"
      android:versionCode="1"
      android:versionName="1.0.0">
    <application android:icon="@drawable/icon" android:label="Test Handlers">
        <activity android:name=".TestHandlersDriverActivity"
                  android:label="Test Handlers">
            <intent-filter>
                <action android:name="android.intent.action.MAIN" />
                <category android:name="android.intent.category.LAUNCHER" />
            </intent-filter>
        </activity>
</application>
    <uses-sdk android:minSdkVersion="3" />
</manifest>
```

The manifest file includes a reference to the Android application icon. You can use the project ZIP file that is referenced at the end of this chapter to get this file, or you can use any icon file you may have from other projects.

Component and Process Lifetimes

If you have looked carefully the `TestHandlersDriverActivity` test activity (see Listing 13–9), you have seen that we included the activity life cycle methods. We did so to show you what will happen as the activity gets hidden and shown. What would happen to the messages that are pending in the main queue? What would happen to the worker thread that is executing?

We will explain what happens by considering the life cycle of each of the Android components.

Although we discuss the component life cycles here, please note that this is not a full discussion of those life cycles. The activity life cycle is already described with the help of a diagram in Chapter 2. Similarly, the service life cycle is elaborated on in Chapter 11. The discussion here is limited to addressing only those aspects that affect message processing and worker threads.

Activity Life Cycle

We will start with the `Activity` component. Figure 13–3 shows the activity life cycle with respect to its visibility and lifetime (the state transitions of an activity between its life cycle methods are described in Chapter 2).

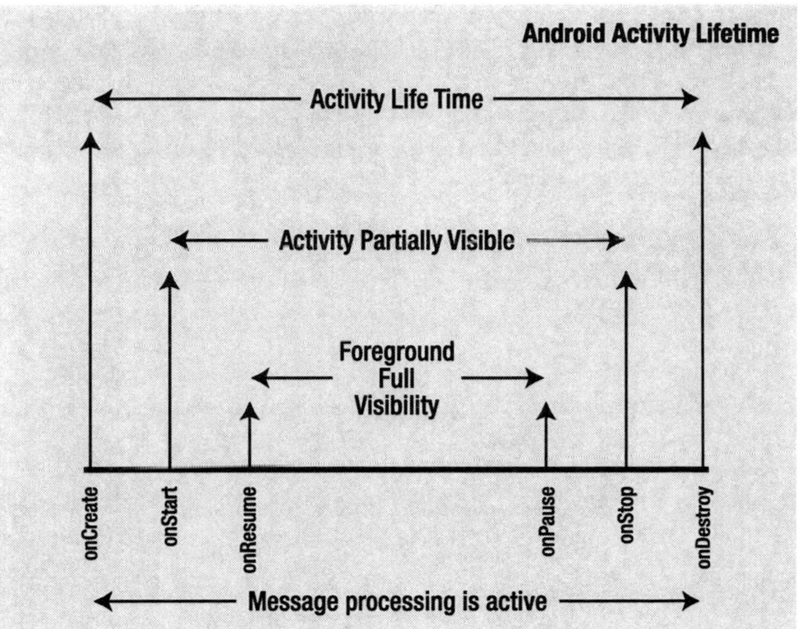

Figure 13–3. *Activity Life Cycle*

Once an activity comes to life (due to a start), it is fully visible, partially visible, or completely hidden. You can detect each boundary through callback methods.

An activity calls `onPause` when it is moving into partially visible state. It then may call the `onStop` method when it goes into the completely hidden state. Finally, when the process is taken out, its `onDestory` method is called. When the `onDestory` method is called, the view state is destroyed right after the call. Prior to that, the view state is still intact.

When an activity is moving into full visibility state its `onResume` is called. When it is moving out of the invisible state, it first calls `onStart` and then `onResume` (or it may call `onStop` if the activity gets hidden again). Between `onResume` and `onPause` the activity is in fully visible state.

Although an application may be partially or fully invisible, the message queue will still be active and so will your worker thread. You can see this by monitoring the activity life cycle methods shown in Listing 13–9. You can see that messages from the worker thread and the handler are still active when `OnPause` and `OnStop` are called.

You can test this hypothesis by clicking the home button when you are on this activity. Doing so will send this activity to the background and invokes `OnPause` , `OnStop`, and maybe even `OnDestroy` . You will see the messages all the way until `OnDestroy` is called (assuming you have sent that many messages).

If the process is not active when an activity is requested, it will be started and brought to life. Under low-memory conditions or when the application is completely hidden and nothing else is going on in that process, Android will remove the process.

> **Note:** The key thing to know is that if an activity is stopped for any of these needs, it will not automatically be brought back to life. A user has to explicitly invoke the activity either by clicking it or through other indirect means, such as starting another activity that results in invoking this activity. The only time an activity is stopped and started automatically is when the device configuration changes (such as going from portrait to landscape). As you can imagine, this can happen quite often as a phone is moved from vertical to horizontal and back.

Service Life Cycle

A service component acts differently from an activity in one primary respect—a service component is fundamentally sticky. Android makes every effort to keep a service running. Even if the service process is reclaimed due to memory conditions, it will be restarted if there are pending messages. We will go into lot more detail of this interaction in the next chapter when we discuss broadcast receivers and long-running services.

However, a common thing to a service component and an activity component is that they both can be taken down under low-memory conditions. Android will try its best to keep a service running, but even still, there are no guarantees it will run to completion.

> **Note:** Services and activities should be coded such that they can be gracefully stopped through `onDestroy` when they have worker threads running and doing work for them.

Receiver Life Cycle

Broadcast receivers use a call-and-be-gone model. The process hosting the broadcast receiver will be around only for the lifetime of the receiver and no longer. Also, the broadcast receiver runs on the main thread, and it has a hard 10-second timeframe to finish its work. You have to follow a pretty roundabout protocol to accomplish more complicated and time-consuming work in a broadcast receiver. This, indeed, is the topic of next chapter. But briefly, if you have a broadcast receiver that takes longer than 10 seconds, you will need to follow a protocol such as the following:

1. Get hold of a wakelock in the receiver code (no later) so that the device is at least partially awake.
2. Issue a `startService()` call so that the process is tagged as sticky and restartable, if needed, and hangs around.
3. Note that you cannot do the work in the service directly, because it would take more than 10 seconds and that would hold up the main thread. This is because the service also runs on the main thread.
4. Start a worker thread from the service

5. Have the worker thread post a message through a handler to the service or issue a `stopService()` call on the service.

As promised, we will go through this protocol in lot more detail in the next chapter. In fact, the solution relies heavily on handlers. You will see lot of sample code as well to make these ideas concrete.

Provider Life Cycle

Content providers are another story. Clients both internal and external interact with a content provider synchronously. For external clients, content providers use a thread pool to satisfy this requirement. Like broadcast receivers, content providers do not have a particular life cycle. They get started when needed and stay around as long as the process stays around. Even though they are synchronous for external clients, they will run not on the main thread but on a thread pool of the process that they reside in, similar to a web client and a web server. The client thread will wait until the call comes back. When there are on clients around, the process gets reclaimed as per the reclamation rules of a process, depending on what other components are defined and active in that process.

Instructions for Compiling the Code

There are primarily eight files in the project for this chapter. We strongly suggest that you download the ZIP file using the URL provided in the "References" section, though you can compile it using the code listings in this chapter as well.

Creating the Project from the ZIP File

The steps to create this chapter's project from the ZIP file follow:

1. Download the ZIP file.
2. Select the File ➤ Import menu option from Eclipse.
3. Then, choose General ➤ Existing Projects into Workspace.
4. Next, choose "Select root directory".
5. Choose "Copy projects into work space".
6. You may need to choose the right API level once the project is in place by selecting Project properties ➤ Android and picking the right build target.

Creating the Project from the Listings

Instead, if you want to build the project from the listings in this chapter, the steps are as follows; the files are listed in the "Handler Example Driver Classes" section of this chapter:

1. Create a new project by selecting File ➤ New project ➤ Android ➤ Android Project.
2. Pick a name, and choose "Create new project in work space".
3. Give the application the name Test Handlers.
4. Pick an API level.
5. Use a package name like `com.androidbook.handlers`.
6. Pick `minsdk version : 3`.
7. Choose `TestHandlersDriverActivity` as your activity, and click Finish.
8. Android will create a number of resource files and probably (depending on your release) a single source file.
9. Create or update these files based on the code listings in this chapter.
10. For Java files, when you copy the listings, put the package name at the top of each file before copying it. Then, press Ctrl+Shift+O to fill in the imports.

Please note that, in this process, you will need to make adjustments to the code to get it compiled and provide any missing pieces. You can refer to the ZIP file to fill in the gaps.

References

As you learn about the topics in this chapter, you may want to keep the following reference URLs handy; we have also indicated what you will gain from each URL:

- `http://developer.android.com/reference/android/os/Handler.html`: This URL is a reference to the Handler API. You will see here method signatures for how to construct a handler, obtain a message, override `handleMessage()` and `sendMessage()`, and so on.
- `http://developer.android.com/reference/android/os/Message.html`: This URL is a reference to the Message API. Although you use this API less as equivalent functions are available on the handler API, it is good to know the underpinnings of a message by looking at this API. We recommend taking a look at this API reference.

- http://developer.android.com/guide/topics/fundamentals.html#lcycles: You can read about component life cycles in more detail. This primarily explains activity and service life cycles and a bit about broadcast receivers. This resource is quite silent about content providers.
- http://www.science.uva.nl/ict/ossdocs/java/tutorial/java/threads/states.html: This is a very zippy, and necessary, introduction to threads.
- http://www.netmite.com/android/mydroid/1.6/frameworks/base/core/java/android/app/IntentService.java: This shows an excellent use of handlers by core Android code in implementing the `IntentService` class. This is a reference to the source code listing of `IntentService.java`. With the background information provided in this chapter, we strongly urge you to go over this source code of `IntentService` as an exercise to solidify your understanding of threads in Android.
- http://www.androidbook.com/item/3514: This is one of the author's research on long-running services.
- http://www.androidbook.com/projects: You can see a list of downloadable projects from this book referenced here. For this chapter, look for a ZIP file named `ProAndroid3_Ch13_TestHandlers.zip`.

Summary

In this chapter, we explored various components of an Android process and how the main thread coordinates them. We showed how handlers and threads can be used to extend the reach of a main thread, as well as how a main thread must return in 5 seconds to avoid ANR messages. This rule applies to broadcast receivers as well, except that the limit for a broadcast receiver is 10 seconds.

We talked about component life cycles and how they impact both main threads and subthreads. This knowledge is essential to understand the intricacies of these components and what needs to be done for performing long-running operations.

The next chapter is dedicated to working with broadcast receivers and performing long-running operations. What we have covered in this chapter will help you to understand the next chapter.

Chapter 14

Broadcast Receivers and Long-Running Services

Through previous chapters, you have been exposed to activities, content providers, and services. We haven't talked much about broadcast receivers, so we will do that in this chapter.

We'll show you first how to invoke a simple broadcast receiver and then extend the idea to invoking multiple broadcast receivers. We will also explore how broadcast receivers can reside in processes outside of the client processes. We will demonstrate how a broadcast receiver can send notification messages via the notification manager.

We will talk about the 10-second limit on a broadcast receiver to respond before the system throws "application not responding" (ANR) messages and suggest known mechanisms to work around this. We will develop a framework where you can start viewing a long-running service as a special abstraction of a broadcast intent, and finally, we'll talk about wake locks in the context of long running services.

Let's start this extensive coverage on broadcast receivers by starting with coding a simple broadcast receiver.

Broadcast Receivers

In Chapter 13, we talked about broadcast receiver being another component of an Android process, along with activities, content providers, and services. As the name indicates, a broadcast receiver is a component that can respond to a broadcast message sent by a client. The message itself is an Android broadcast intent, and a broadcast message can be received by more than one receiver.

A component such as an activity or a service (or anything that is eventually implementing the `Context` class) wanting to broadcast an event (intent) uses the `sendBroadCast()` method available on the `Context` class. The argument to this method is an intent.

Receiving components of the broadcast intent will need to inherit from a Receiver class available in the Android SDK. These receiving components (broadcast receivers) then need to be registered in the manifest file as a receiver that is interested in the broadcast intent.

> **NOTE:** You can register receivers at run time as well without mentioning them in the manifest file. Please note that we are not covering that aspect in this chapter, and we recommended that you see the API documentation URL indicated in the "References" section of this chapter for further information.

Sending a Broadcast

Listing 14–1 shows sample code, taken from an activity class, that sends a broadcast. This code creates an intent with a unique, specific action, puts an extra message on it, and calls the sendBroadcast() Method. Putting an extra message on the intent is optional; many times, receiving an intent is sufficient for a receiver, and an extra is not needed.

Listing 14–1. *Broadcasting an Intent*

```
private void testSendBroadcast(Activity activty)
{
    //Create an intent with an action
    String uniqueActionString = "com.androidbook.intents.testbc";
    Intent broadcastIntent = new Intent(uniqueActionString);
    broadcastIntent.putExtra("message", "Hello world");
    activity.sendBroadcast(broadcastIntent);
}
```

In the code in Listing 14–1, the action is an arbitrary identifier that is suitable for your needs. To make this action string unique, you may want to use a namespace similar to a Java class. Now, let's look at how we can respond to this broadcast intent.

Coding a Simple Receiver: Sample Code

Listing 14–2 shows how you can code a receiver to respond to the broadcasted intent in Listing 14–1.

Listing 14–2. *Sample Receiver Code*

```
public class TestReceiver extends BroadcastReceiver
{
    private static final String tag = "TestReceiver";
    @Override
    public void onReceive(Context context, Intent intent)
    {
        Utils.logThreadSignature(tag);
        Log.d("TestReceiver", "intent=" + intent);
        String message = intent.getStringExtra("message");
        Log.d(tag, message);
    }
}
```

Creating a broadcast receiver is quite simple. Just extend the `BroadcastReceiver` class and override the `onReceive()` method. We are able to see the intent in the receiver and extract the message from it. If the broadcast intent doesn't have an extra that is called "message," it will return a null. In our example, because we know that we are setting that extra, we haven't checked for a null value. Once we retrieve the extra, we are just logging the retrieved message.

We have included a utility method in our test receiver that allows you to log the signature of the thread that is running the receiver code. As we use the `Utils` class often in this chapter, we introduce the source code of `Utils.java` in Listing 14–3.

Listing 14–3. *Utils Class Definition*

```
public class Utils
{
    public static long getThreadId()
    {
        Thread t = Thread.currentThread();
        return t.getId();
    }
    public static String getThreadSignature()
    {
        Thread t = Thread.currentThread();
        long l = t.getId();
        String name = t.getName();
        long p = t.getPriority();
        String gname = t.getThreadGroup().getName();
        return (name + ":(id)" + l + ":(priority)" + p
                + ":(group)" + gname);
    }
    public static void logThreadSignature(String tag)
    {
        Log.d(tag, getThreadSignature());
    }
    public static void sleepForInSecs(int secs)
    {
        try
        {
            Thread.sleep(secs * 1000);
        }
        catch(InterruptedException x)
        {
            throw new RuntimeException("interrupted",x);
        }
    }
}
```

Once we have the receiver code available, from Listing 14–2, we need to register it in the manifest file as a receiver.

Registering a Receiver in the Manifest File

Listing 14–4 shows how you can declare your receiver as the recipient of the intent whose action is `com.androidbook.intents.testbc`.

Listing 14–4. *Receiver Definition in the Manifest File*

```
<manifest>
<application>
...
<activity .....>
...
<receiver android:name=".TestReceiver">
    <intent-filter>
        <action android:name="com.androidbook.intents.testbc"/>
    </intent-filter>
</receiver>
...
</application>
</manifest>
```

The receiver element is a child node of the application element like the other component nodes. This is all you need to test your receiver. We'll now the list of files that you can use to make a project to test this.

Before you eagerly copy and paste (or worse, hand type) these source files, note that we have included a URL in the "References" section at the end of this chapter where you can download importable projects for this chapter.

Sending a Test Broadcast

The needed files and their corresponding listings are as follows:

- TestBCRActivity.java: A sample activity to kick off the broadcast receiver (BCR) (Listing 14–5)
- layout/main.xml: A simple text layout for debug messages that is used as the layout for the TestBCRActivity (Listing 14–6)
- menu/main_menu.xml: The menu to start the broadcast again used by the TestBCRActivity (Listing 14–7)
- TestReceicer.java: A sample receiver (already presented in Listing 14–2)
- Utils.java: A few threading utilities (already presented in Listing 14–3)
- AndriudManifest.xml: The manifest file to with the project and the file in which the receiver and the activity are defined (Listing 14–8)

We have already presented some of the files used for this project, so we will present now the rest of the files. Listing 14–5 contains the activity file TestBCRActivity that invokes the menu item that sends the broadcast. The menu call is highlighted.

Listing 14–5. *Broadcasting Activity Client*

```
public class TestBCRActivity extends Activity
{
    public static final String tag="TestBCRActivity";
    @Override
    public void onCreate(Bundle savedInstanceState) {
```

```
        super.onCreate(savedInstanceState);
        setContentView(R.layout.main);
    }
    @Override
    public boolean onCreateOptionsMenu(Menu menu){
        super.onCreateOptionsMenu(menu);
        MenuInflater inflater = getMenuInflater(); //from activity
        inflater.inflate(R.menu.main_menu, menu);
        return true;
    }
    @Override
    public boolean onOptionsItemSelected(MenuItem item){
        appendMenuItemText(item);
        if (item.getItemId() == R.id.menu_clear){
            this.emptyText();
            return true;
        }
        if (item.getItemId() == R.id.menu_send_broadcast){
            this.testSendBroadcast();
            return true;
        }
        return true;
    }
    private TextView getTextView(){
        return (TextView)this.findViewById(R.id.text1);
    }
    private void appendMenuItemText(MenuItem menuItem){
       String title = menuItem.getTitle().toString();
       TextView tv = getTextView();
       tv.setText(tv.getText() + "\n" + title);
    }
    private void emptyText(){
          TextView tv = getTextView();
          tv.setText("");
    }
    private void testSendBroadcast()
    {
        //Print out what your running thread id is
        Utils.logThreadSignature(tag);

        //Create an intent with an action
        Intent broadcastIntent = new Intent("com.androidbook.intents.testbc");
        //load up the intent with a message
        //you want to broadcast
        broadcastIntent.putExtra("message", "Hello world");

        //send out the broadcast
        //there may be multiple receivers receiving it
        this.sendBroadcast(broadcastIntent);

        //Log a message after sending the broadcast
        //This message should appear first in the log file
        //before the log messages from the broadcast
        //because they all run on the same thread
        Log.d(tag,"after send broadcast from main menu");
    }
}
```

The layout file to support theTestBCRActivity is shown in Listing 14–6 and its corresponding view in Figure 14–1.

Listing 14–6. *Layout file*

```
<!-- layout/main.xml -->
<LinearLayout xmlns:android="http://schemas.android.com/apk/res/android"
    android:orientation="vertical"
    android:layout_width="fill_parent"
    android:layout_height="fill_parent"
    >
<TextView
    android:id="@+id/text1"
    android:layout_width="fill_parent"
    android:layout_height="wrap_content"
    android:text="Your debug will appear here"
    />
</LinearLayout>
```

Here is the menu file.

Listing 14–7. *Menu Resource File*

```
<!-- menu/main_menu.xml -->
<menu xmlns:android="http://schemas.android.com/apk/res/android">
    <group android:id="@+id/menuGroup_Main">
        <item android:id="@+id/menu_clear"
        android:title="clear" />
        <item android:id="@+id/menu_send_broadcast"
            android:title="broadcast" />
    </group>
</menu>
```

> **NOTE:** You can find the full source code for TestReceiver.java in Listing 14–2 and for Utils.java in Listing 14–3.

Listing 14–8 contains the manifest file source code.

Listing 14–8. *AndroidManifest File*

```
<manifest xmlns:android="http://schemas.android.com/apk/res/android"
      package="com.androidbook.bcr"
      android:versionCode="1"
      android:versionName="1.0.0">
    <application android:icon="@drawable/icon" android:label="Test Broadcast Receiver">
        <activity android:name=".TestBCRActivity"
                  android:label="Test Broadcast Receiver">
            <intent-filter>
                <action android:name="android.intent.action.MAIN" />
                <category android:name="android.intent.category.LAUNCHER" />
            </intent-filter>
        </activity>
    <receiver android:name=".TestReceiver">
       <intent-filter>
        <action android:name="com.androidbook.intents.testbc"/>
       </intent-filter>
    </receiver>
```

```
</application>
    <uses-sdk android:minSdkVersion="3" />
</manifest>
```

Once you compile and run this project you will see an activity and a menu that look like the following

Figure 14–1. *A sample activity with a menu to test a broadcast*

Once you click the broadcast menu item, you will see that TestReceiver in Listing 14–2 will be invoked, and logcat will show the helloworld message that was loaded into the broadcast intent by the activity.

Accommodating Multiple Receivers

The idea of a broadcast is that there is a possibility for more than one receiver. So let's replicate TestReceiver (see Listing 14–2) as TestReceiver2 and see if both get invoked. The code for TestReceiver2 is presented in Listing 14-9.

Listing 14–9. *Test Receiver 2*

```
public class TestReceiver2 extends BroadcastReceiver
{
    private static final String tag = "TestReceiver2";
    @Override
    public void onReceive(Context context, Intent intent)
    {
        Utils.logThreadSignature(tag);
        Log.d(tag, "intent=" + intent);
        String message = intent.getStringExtra("message");
        Log.d(tag, message);
    }
}
```

Once you have this code, you can add this receiver to the manifest file in Listing 14–8 using the definition below

Listing 14–10. *TestReceiver2 Definition in the Manifest File*

```
<receiver android:name=".TestReceiver2">
    <intent-filter>
        <action android:name="com.androidbook.intents.testbc"/>
    </intent-filter>
</receiver>
```

Now, if you invoke the broadcast menu item again from Figure 14–1, you will see `helloworld` message in `logcat` from both receivers.

You will also see that these receivers are called in the order defined in the manifest. Another thing you can test is to see what thread these broadcast receivers run under. The method call `Utils.logThreadSignature(tag)` will have printed the running thread signature. You will realize that this indeed is the main thread.

Also, you will see that the log messages that were placed before and after the `sendBroadcast()` in the `testSendBroadcast()` (see Listing 14–5) will both have been printed before the receiver messages and with the same thread signature.

This proves that the main thread is going around and attending to the broadcast receivers at a later time from the message queue. So the `sendBroadcast()` is clearly an asynchronous message that lets the main thread get to back to its queue.

To see further proof, you can hold up the main thread a bit longer so that the time stamps are clearly demarcated. Let's write another receiver that delays the main thread by sleeping a little while. The source code for such a time delay receiver is presented in Listing 14–11.

Listing 14–11. *A Receiver with a Time Delay*

```
/*
 * This receiver is introduced to see
 * how the main thread schedules broad cast receivers
 *
 * it helps answer such questions as
 * 1. Do they get invoked in the order they are specificed?
 * 2. Do they get invoked one after the other? or do they get invoked parallel
 *
```

```
 * The time delay here shows that the main thread
 * gets halted for those many secs. You can see this
 * in the Log.d output
 */
public class TestTimeDelayReceiver extends BroadcastReceiver
{
    private static final String tag = "TestTimeDelayReceiver";
    @Override
    public void onReceive(Context context, Intent intent)
    {
        Utils.logThreadSignature(tag);
        Log.d(tag, "intent=" + intent);
        Log.d(tag, "going to sleep for 2 secs");
        Utils.sleepForInSecs(2);
        Log.d(tag, "wake up");
        String message = intent.getStringExtra("message");
        Log.d(tag, message);
    }
}
```

Now, if you insert this receiver as the second receiver in the manifest file, you can see the traversal of the main thread through the main logic and the broadcast receiver's logic. In `logcat`, you will see that the first receiver is executed first. Then, the second receiver is invoked, and the main thread waits there for 2 seconds and proceeds with the third receiver. Moreover, you will see that all receivers get invoked only after the `sendbroadcast()` call returns.

You can add the receiver definition file in Listing 14–12 to the manifest file in Listing 14–8 to test the time delay receiver.

Listing 14–12. *Time Delay Receiver definition in the manifest file*

```
<receiver android:name=".TestTimeDelayReceiver">
    <intent-filter>
        <action android:name="com.androidbook.intents.testbc"/>
    </intent-filter>
</receiver>
```

A Project for Out-of-Process Receivers

The intention of a broadcast is more likely that the process responding to it is an unknown one and a separate one from the client process. Let's proactive by creating another `.apk` file and registering a receiver in that package against the same event broadcast in Figure 14–1.

Here are the files needed to create this separate stand-alone project; again, you can always use the project downloads URL a t the end of this chapter to download importable projects:

- `StandaloneReceiver.java`: A simple receiver (Listing 14–11)
- `AndroidManifest.xml`: A manifest file (Listing 14–12)
- `Utils.java`: The same file as from the previous project (Listing 14–4)

This is a headless project without any activity to speak of, and as a result, it is quite clean and requires no activities or layout files. The sample receiver that belongs to this stand-alone process is shown in Listing 14–13. We will call this appropriately `StandaloneReceiver`.

Listing 14–13. *A Receiver Example in its Own Process*

```
public class StandaloneReceiver extends BroadcastReceiver
{
    private static final String tag = "Standalone Receiver";
    @Override
    public void onReceive(Context context, Intent intent)
    {
        Utils.logThreadSignature(tag);
        Log.d(tag, "intent=" + intent);
        String message = intent.getStringExtra("message");
        Log.d(tag, message);
    }
}
```

Again, nothing's special here—just a regular receiver. The manifest file that registers this receiver is in Listing 14–14.

Listing 14–14. *AndroidManifest File That Has Just the Receiver*

```
<manifest xmlns:android="http://schemas.android.com/apk/res/android"
      package="com.androidbook.salbcr"
      android:versionCode="1"
      android:versionName="1.0.0">

<application android:icon="@drawable/icon"
               android:label="Standalone Broadcast Receiver">

    <receiver android:name=".StandaloneReceiver">
       <intent-filter>
          <action android:name="com.androidbook.intents.testbc"/>
       </intent-filter>
    </receiver>
</application>
<uses-sdk android:minSdkVersion="3" />
</manifest>
```

With just these two files and the `Utils.java` file borrowed from the previous project, you can create the stand-alone project and deploy. Now, if you go to the screen shown in Figure 14–1 from project 1 and invoke the `broadcast` menu item, you will see that the standalone receiver will output to `logcat` like the other receivers from Project 1.

Using Notifications from a Receiver

Broadcast receivers often need to communicate to the user about something that happened or a status, and this is done by alerting the user through a notification icon in the systemwide notification bar. We will show you, in this section, how to create a notification from a broadcast receiver, send it, and view it through the notification manager.

Monitoring Notifications Through the Notification Manager

Android shows icons of notifications as alerts in the notification area. The notification area is located at the top of device in a strip that looks like Figure 14–2. The look and placement of the notification area may change based on whether the device is a tablet or a phone and may at times also change based on Android release.

Figure 14–2. *Android notification icon status bar*

When we deliver a notification, the notification will appear in this area shown Figure 14–2 as an icon. The notification icon is illustrated in Figure 14–3.

Figure 14–3. *Status bar showing a notification icon*

Figure 14–3 is illustrating both the notification area and an activity, in addition to the notification icon. For an activity, we just happened to be sitting in an application that is issuing the broadcast. It can be any activity or even the home page.

The notification icon is an indicator to the user that something needs to be observed. To see the full notification, you have to hold a finger on the icon and drag the title strip shown in Figure 14–2 down like a curtain. This will expand the notification area, as shown in Figure 14–4.

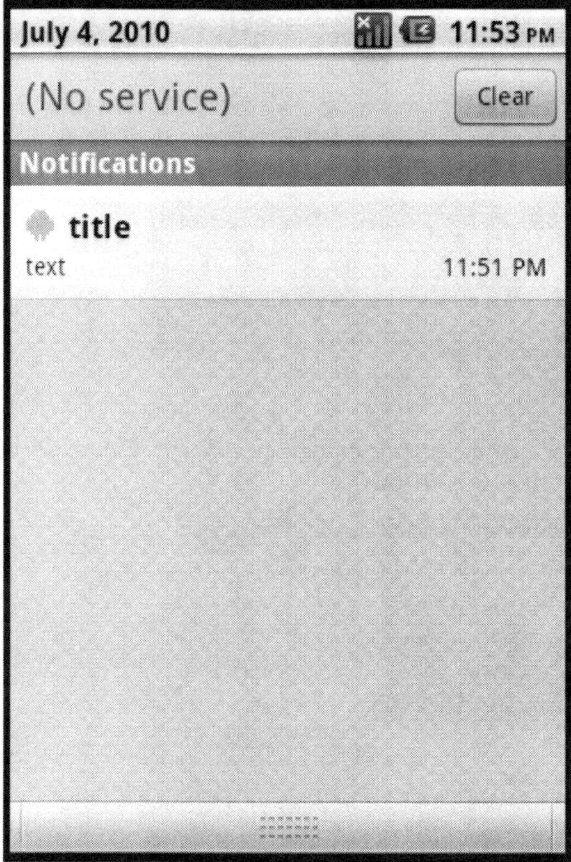

Figure 14–4. *Expanded notification view*

In the expanded view of the notification in Figure 14–4 you get to see the details supplied to the notification. You can also click a notification detail to fire off the intent to bring up the full application of which the notification could be a part. In our upcoming example, we have used an intent to kick off the browser.

As you can also see from Figure 14–4, you can use this view to clear notifications.

You can also reach the notification detail view shown in Figure 14–4 from the menu of the home page. Figure 14–5 shows the available menu on the home page of the emulator. Depending on the device and the Android release, this homepage menu may differ.

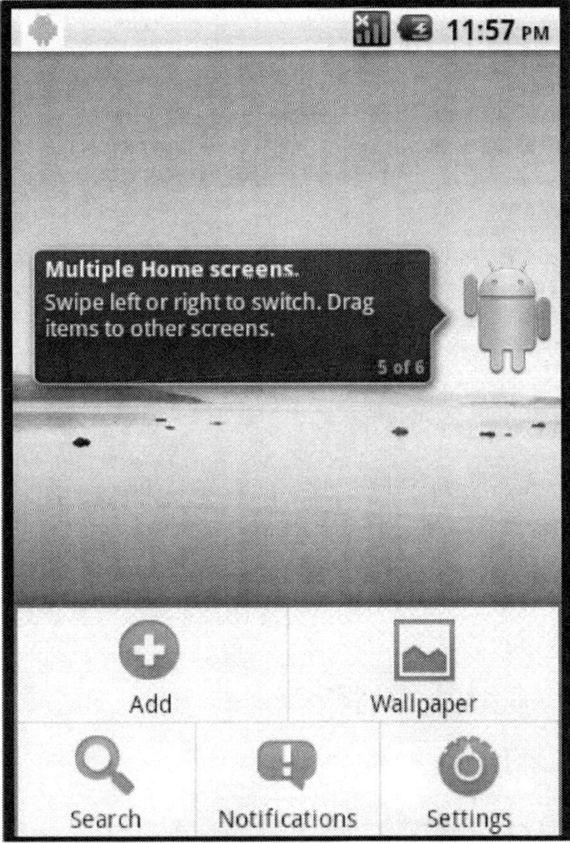

Figure 14–5. *The Notifications menu item from home menu*

Clicking the Notifications icon in Figure 14–5 will bring up the notification screen in Figure 14–4.

Let's see now how to generate a notification icon like the one illustrated in Figures 14–3 and 14–4.

Sending a Notification

Let's get started. The process of sending a notification has the following three steps:

1. Create a suitable notification.
2. Get access to the notification manager.
3. Send the notification to the notification manager.

When you create a notification, you'll need to ensure that it had the following basic parts:

- An icon to display

- A ticker text like "hello world"
- The time when it is delivered

Once you have a notification object constructed with these details, you get the notification manager by asking the context to give you a system service named `Context.NOTIFICATION_SERVICE`. Once you have the notification manager call the notify method on that object to send the notification.

Listing 14–15 presents the source code for a broadcast receiver that sends the notification shown in Figures 14–3 and 14–4.

Listing 14–15. *A Receiver That Sends a Notification*

```
public class NotificationReceiver extends BroadcastReceiver
{
    private static final String tag = "Notification Receiver";
    @Override
    public void onReceive(Context context, Intent intent)
    {
        Utils.logThreadSignature(tag);
        Log.d(tag, "intent=" + intent);
        String message = intent.getStringExtra("message");
        Log.d(tag, message);
        this.sendNotification(context, message);
    }
    private void sendNotification(Context ctx, String message)
    {
        //Get the notification manager
        String ns = Context.NOTIFICATION_SERVICE;
        NotificationManager nm =
            (NotificationManager)ctx.getSystemService(ns);

        //Create Notification Object
        int icon = R.drawable.robot;
        CharSequence tickerText = "Hello";
        long when = System.currentTimeMillis();

        Notification notification =
            new Notification(icon, tickerText, when);

        //Set ContentView using setLatestEvenInfo
        Intent intent = new Intent(Intent.ACTION_VIEW);
        intent.setData(Uri.parse("http://www.google.com"));
        PendingIntent pi = PendingIntent.getActivity(ctx, 0, intent, 0);
        notification.setLatestEventInfo(ctx, "title", "text", pi);

        //Send notification
        //The first argument is a unique id for this notification.
        //This id allows you to cancel the notification later
        nm.notify(1, notification);
    }
}
```

In the source code in Listing 14–13, we have referenced to an alert icon called `R.draawable.robot`. You can create your own alert icon and drop it into the `res/drawable` subdirectory and name it `robot` with a proper image extension. Or you can refer to the downloadable ZIP file for this project (a URL is included in the "References" section).

When you create a notification with the basic parameters (icon, text, time) and send it to the notification manager, it looks like it is not sufficient (the first part of creating the notification in Listing 14–13). You will also have to set up something called a content view for that notification using the method

```
setLatestEventInfo(...)
```

The content view of a notification is displayed when the notification is expanded. This is what you see in Figure 14–4. Typically, the content view needs to be a `RemoteViews` object. However, we don't pass a content view directly to the `setLatestEventInfo` method. This `setLatestEventInfo()` method is a shortcut for setting the standard predefined content view using a title and the text to display.

This method `setLatestEventInfo()` also takes a pending intent, called a content intent, that gets fired when this expanded view is clicked. Look back at Listing 14–15 to see what parameters we have used to pass to this method.

You also have an option to create a remote view yourself and set it as the content view, without using `setLatestEventInfo()` .

The steps for using remote views for a content view of a notification follow:

1. Create a layout file.
2. Create a `RemoteViews` object using the package name and the layout file ID.
3. Call set methods on the `RemoteViews` to set text, icons, and so on.
4. Call `setContentView()` on the notification object before sending it to the notification manager.

Keep in mind that only the following limited set of controls may participate in a remote view as of Android release 2.2.:

- `FrameLayout`
- `LinearLayout`
- `RelativeLayout`
- `AnalogClock`
- `Button`
- `Chronometer`
- `ImageButton`
- `ImageView`
- `ProgressBar`
- `TextView`

Refer to Chapter 22 to learn more about constructing these remote views as widget views on the homepage are essentially remote views. See chapter 31 to see an updated list of possible RemoteViews in releases 2.3 and 3.0.

The code in Listing 14–15 creates a notification and uses the `setLatestEventInfo()` to set the implicit content view (through title and text) and the intent to fire (in our case, this intent is the browser intent).

Long-Running Receivers and Services

So far we have covered the happy path of broadcast receivers where the execution of a broadcast receiver is unlikely to take more than 10 seconds. As it turns out, the problem space becomes a bit complicated if we want to perform tasks that take longer than 10 seconds.

To understand why, let's quickly review a few facts about broadcast receivers:

- A broadcast receiver like other components of an Android process runs on the main thread.
- Holding up the code in a broadcast receiver will hold up the main thread and will result in ANR.
- The time limit on a broadcast receiver is 10 seconds compared to 5 seconds for an activity. It is a bit more lenient and a touch of a reprieve, but the limit is still there.
- The process hosting the broadcast receiver will start and terminate along with the broadcast receiver execution. In other words, the process will not stick around after the broadcast receiver's `onReceive()` method returns. Of course, this is assuming that the process contains only the broadcast receiver. If the process contains other components, such as activities or services, that are already running, then the lifetime of the process takes these component life cycles into account as well.
- Unlike a service process, a broadcast receiver process will not get restarted.
- If a broadcast receiver were to start a separate thread and return to the main thread, Android will assume that the work is complete and will shut down the process even if there are threads running bringing those threads to abrupt stop.
- Android acquires a partial wake lock when invoking a broadcast service and releases it when it returns from the service in the main thread. A wake lock is a mechanism and an API class available in the SDK to keep the device from going to sleep or wake it up if it is already asleep.

Given these predicates how can one execute longer running code in response to a broadcast event?

Long-Running Broadcast Receiver Protocol

The answer lies in resolving the following:

- We will clearly need a separate thread so that the main thread can get back and avoid ANR messages.
- To stop Android from killing the process and hence the worker thread, we need to tell Android that this process contains a component, such as a service, with a life cycle. So we need to create or start that service. The service itself cannot directly do the work for more than 5 seconds because that happens on the main thread, so the service needs to start a worker thread and let the main thread go.
- For the duration of the worker thread's execution, we need to hold on to the partial wake lock so that the device won't go to sleep. A partial wake lock will allow the device to run code without turning on the screen and so on, which allows for longer battery life.
- The partial wake lock must be obtained in the main line code of the receiver; otherwise, it will be too late. For example, you cannot do this in the service, because it may be too late between the `startService()` being issued by the broadcast receiver and the `onStartCommand()` of a service that begin execution.
- Because we are creating a service, the service itself can be brought down and brought back up because low memory conditions. If this happens, we need to acquire the wake lock again.
- When the worker thread started by `onStartCommand()` completes its work, it needs to tell the service to stop so that it can be put to bed and not brought back to life by Android.
- It is also possible that more than one broadcast event can occur. Given that, we need to be cautious about how many worker threads we need to spawn.

Given these facts, the recommended protocol for extending the life of a broadcast receiver is as follows:

1. Get a (static) partial wake lock in the `onReceive()` method of the broadcast receiver. The partial wake lock needs to be static to allow communication between the broadcast receiver and the service. There is no other way of passing a reference of the wake lock to the service, as the service is invoked through a default constructor that takes no parameters.
2. Start a local service so that the process won't be killed.
3. In the service, start a worker thread to do the work. Do not do the work in the `onStart()` method of the service. If you do, you are basically holding up the main thread again.

4. When the worker thread is done, tell the service to stop itself either directly or through a handler.

5. Have the service turn of the static wake lock. To repeat, a static wake lock is the only way to communicate between a service and its invoker, in this case the broadcast service, because there is no way to pass wake lock reference to the service

IntentService

Recognizing the need for a service to not hold up the main thread, Android has provided a utility local service implementation called `IntentService` to offload work to a worker thread so that the main thread can be released after scheduling the work to the subthread. Under this scheme, when you do a `startService()` on an `IntentService`, the `IntentService` will queue that request to a sub thread using a looper and a handler so that a derived method of the `IntentService` is called to do the actual work.

Here is what the API documentation for an `IntentService` says:

> *IntentService is a base class for Services that handle asynchronous requests (expressed as Intents) on demand. Clients send requests through startService(Intent) calls; the service is started as needed, handles each Intent in turn using a worker thread, and stops itself when it runs out of work. This "work queue processor" pattern is commonly used to offload tasks from an application's main thread. The IntentService class exists to simplify this pattern and take care of the mechanics. To use it, extend IntentService and implement onHandleIntent(Intent). IntentService will receive the Intents, launch a worker thread, and stop the service as appropriate. All requests are handled on a single worker thread -- they may take as long as necessary (and will not block the application's main loop), but only one request will be processed at a time.*

This idea of `IntentService` can be clearly demonstrated using a simple example, as in Listing 14–16. You extend the `IntentService` and provide what you want to do in the `onHandleIntent()` method.

Listing 14–16. *Using IntentService*

```
public class MyService extends IntentService
{
    protected abstract void onHandleIntent(Intent intent)
    {
        Utils.logThreadSignature("MyService");
        //do the work i n this sub thread
        //and return
    }
}
```

Once you have a service like this, you can register this service in the manifest file and use client code to invoke this service as `context.startService(new Intent(MyService.class))`. This invocation will result in a call to the `onHandleIntent()` in Listing 14–16.

You will notice that the `logThreadSignature()` method will print the ID of the worker thread and not the main thread (remember that this is just pseudo code; we will present the real code soon).

IntentService Source Code

In Chapter 13, we covered the main thread and the role of handlers. In that context, it is very instructive to study the source code of the `IntentService` to see how handlers and the main thread are used in conjunction with a long running service that utilizes a worker thread. Let's now consider the source code of `IntentService` (taken from the source code distribution of Android) in Listing 14–17.

Listing 14–17. ***IntentService Souce Code***

```
public abstract class IntentService extends Service {
    private volatile Looper mServiceLooper;
    private volatile ServiceHandler mServiceHandler;
    private String mName;

    private final class ServiceHandler extends Handler {
        public ServiceHandler(Looper looper) {
            super(looper);
        }
        @Override
        public void handleMessage(Message msg) {
            onHandleIntent((Intent)msg.obj);
            stopSelf(msg.arg1);
        }
    }

    public IntentService(String name) {
        super();
        mName = name;
    }
    @Override
    public void onCreate() {
        super.onCreate();
        HandlerThread thread =
          new HandlerThread("IntentService[" + mName + "]");
        thread.start();

        mServiceLooper = thread.getLooper();
        mServiceHandler = new ServiceHandler(mServiceLooper);
    }

    @Override
    public void onStart(Intent intent, int startId) {
        super.onStart(intent, startId);
        Message msg = mServiceHandler.obtainMessage();
```

```
        msg.arg1 = startId;
        msg.obj = intent;
        mServiceHandler.sendMessage(msg);
    }
    @Override
    public void onDestroy() {
        mServiceLooper.quit();
    }
    @Override
    public IBinder onBind(Intent intent) {
        return null;
    }
    protected abstract void onHandleIntent(Intent intent);
}
```

Let's step through an explanation of this code:

1. Create a separate worker thread in the `onCreate()` method of the service. Typically, you will have started worker threads in the `onStartCommand` method of a service. However, that would have resulted in multiple worker threads, one for each `startService`. IntentService wants to do this by having a single worker thread that services all of the `startService` invocations, so we set up the worker thread in the `onCreate` method, which is invoked only once.

2. Set up a looper (and thereby a queue to receive and dispatch messages) on that worker thread. This allows the same worker thread to respond to many messages one by one instead of creating a new worker thread for each request

3. Establish a handle on the worker thread so that the main thread of the service can drop a message via the handler. We need this worker thread, because every time a client uses a `startService()` that call goes to the main thread of the `IntentService`, and we don't want to hold up the main thread of the `IntentService`. We need a mechanism to queue this request so that the worker thread can process it when it becomes available. This is feasible by having the main thread hold a handler for the worker thread. Notice the `onStart()` method that runs on the main thread. If you want to prove this, just override this method and call its parent while you log the thread signature. You will see that the `onStart()` runs on the main thread and the `onHandleMessage()` runs on the secondary worker thread.

4. Finally, when the `onHandleIntent()` returns the handler will call `stopSelf()` of the service. This `stopSelf()` will succeed in stopping the service if there are no pending messages. The `stopSelf()` method is reference counted. This means even if you call it multiple times, there must be an equal number of `startService` invocations. This is why we are able to call `stopSelf()` after handling every `startService` invocation.

Extending IntentService for a Broadcast Receiver

From the perspective of a broadcast receiver an IntentService is a wonderful thing. It lets us execute long-running code with out blocking the main thread. So can we use the `IntentService` for the needs of a long running operation? Yes and No.

Yes, because the `IntentService` does two things: First, it keeps the process running because it is a service. And second, it lets the main thread go and avoids related ANR messages.

To understand the "no" answer, you need to better understand the wake locks. When a broadcast receiver is invoked, especially through an alarm manager, the device may not be on. So the alarm manager partially turns on the device (just enough to run the code without any UI) by making a call to the power manager and requesting a wake lock. And this wake lock gets released as soon as the broadcast receiver returns.

This leaves the `IntentService` invocation with out a wake lock, so the device may go to sleep before the actual code runs. However `IntentService`, being a general-purpose extension to a service, it does not acquire a wake lock.

So we need further props on top of an `IntentService`. We need an abstraction.

Mark Murphy has created a variant of the `IntentService` called `WakefulIntentService` that keeps the semantics of using an `IntentService` but also acquires the wake lock and releases it properly under a variety of conditions. You can look at its implementation at `http://github.com/commonsguy/cwac-wakeful`.

Long-Running Broadcast Service Abstraction

`WakefulIntentService` is a fine abstraction. However, we want to go a step further so that our abstraction parallels the method of extending `IntentService` as in Listing 14–14 and does everything that an `IntentService` does but also provides the following additional benefits:

1. Acquire and release wake locks (similar to `WakefulIntentService`).
2. Pass the original intent that was passed to the broadcast receiver to the overridden method `onHandleIntent`. This allows us to largely hide the broadcast receiver.
3. Deal with a service being restarted.
4. Allow a uniform way to deal with the wake lock for multiple receivers and multiple services in the same process.

We will call this abstract class `ALongRunningNonStickyBroadcastService`. As the name suggests, we want this service to allow for long-running work. It will also be specifically built for a broadcast receiver. This service will also be nonsticky (we will explain this concept later in the chapter, but briefly, this indicates that Android will not start the service if there are no messages in the queue). To allow for the behavior of an IntentService, it will extend the IntentService and override the onHandleIntent method.

Combining these ideas, the abstract ALongRunningNonStickyBroadcastService service will have signature that looks like Listing 14–18.

Listing 14–18. *Long-Running Service Abstract Idea*

```
public abstract class ALongRunningNonStickyBroadcastService
extends IntentService
{
...other implementation detials
   protected abstract void
   handleBroadcastIntent(Intent broadcastIntent);
...other implementation details

}
```

The implementation details for this ALongRunningNonStickyBroadcastService are quite involved, and we will cover them later, as soon as we explain why we are going after this type of service. We want to demonstrate first the utility and simplicity of having it.

Once we have this abstract class, the MyService example in Listing 14–16 can be rewritten as in Listing 14–19.

Listing 14–19. *Long-Running Service Sample Usage*

```
public class MyService extends ALongRunningNonStickyBroadcastService
{
    protected abstract void handleBroadcastIntent(Intent broadcastIntent)
    {
        Utils.logThreadSignature("MyService");
        //do the work here
        //and return
    }
}
```

As you can see, you can extend this new long running service class (just like IntentService and WakefulIntentService) and override a single method and do very little to nothing in the broadcast receiver. Your work will be done in a worker thread (thanks to IntentService) without blocking the main thread.

Listing 14–19 is a simple example demonstrating the concept. Let's now turn to a more complete implementation that implements a long-running service that can run for 60 seconds in response to a broadcast event (proving that we can run for more than 10 seconds and avoid an ANR message). We will call this service appropriately Test60SecBCRService ("BCR" stands for broadcast receiver), and its implementation is shown in Listing 14–20.

Listing 14–20. *Test60SecBCRService*

```
public class Test60SecBCRService
extends ALongRunningNonStickyBroadcastService
{
   public static String tag = "Test60SecBCRService";
   //Required by IntentService to pass the classname
```

```
    public Test60SecBCRService(){
        super("com.androidbook.service.Test60SecBCRService");
    }

    /*
     * Perform long running operations in this method.
     * This is executed in a separate thread.
     */
    @Override
    protected void handleBroadcastIntent(Intent broadcastIntent)
    {
        Utils.logThreadSignature(tag);
        Log.d(tag,"Sleeping for 60 secs");
        Utils.sleepForInSecs(60);
        String message =
            broadcastIntent.getStringExtra("message");
        Log.d(tag,"Job completed");
        Log.d(tag,message);
    }
}
```

As you can see, this code successfully simulates doing work for 60 seconds and still avoids the ANR message. You may be wondering at this point why you won't be able to compile this class, as we didn't give you the implementation of the abstract long-running service class. That is true. Just wait until you completely understand all the pieces of this example, and in the course of the explanation, you will see the implementation code for all the classes. We also have given specific instructions to compile this example later, in addition to giving you a URL where you can download the project in the "References" section.

A Long-Running Receiver

Once we have the long-running service in Listing 14–20, we need to be able to invoke the service from a broadcast receiver.

The first goal of a long-running broadcast receiver is to delegate the work to a long-running service. To do this, the long-running receiver will need the class name of the long-running service to invoke it.

The second goal for this long-running receiver is to acquire a wake lock if we want to ensure the code will continue to run when the receiver returns.

The third goal for the long-running receiver is to transfer the original intent that the broadcast receiver is invoked on to the service. We will do this by sticking the original intent as a parcellable in the intent extras. We will use `original_intent` as the name for this extra. The long-running service then extracts `original_intent` and passes it to the overridden method of the long-running service (you will see this later in the implementation of the long-running service). This facility, thus, gives the impression that the long-running service is indeed an extension of the broadcast receiver.

Although we could instruct every long-running receiver to do these two things every time, it is better that we abstract out these and provide a base class. The long-running receiver abstraction will then use the derived class to supply the name of the long-running service (LRS) class through an abstract method called `getLRSClass()`.

Before we let you go on to the implementation of this abstraction, we have to talk a little bit about the direction we took on wake locks. Wake locks need to be coordinated between the broadcast receiver and the corresponding service they invoke. Although the idea is simple, in the implementation, we need to worry about many places and conditions where this needs to happen. So we have conceptually abstracted the wake lock out using a concept called `LightedGreenRoom`. We will present this class later, but for now, treat this as just a wake lock that you turn on and off.

Putting these needs together, the source code for the implementation of the abstract class `ALongRunningReceiver` is in Listing 14–21.

Listing 14–21. *ALongRunningReceiver*

```
public abstract class  ALongRunningReceiver
extends BroadcastReceiver
{
    private static final String tag = "ALongRunningReceiver";
    @Override
    public void onReceive(Context context, Intent intent)
    {
       Log.d(tag,"Receiver started");
       //LightedGreenRoom abstracts the Android WakeLock
       //to keep the device partially on.
       //In short this is equivalent to turning on
       //or acquiring the wakelock.
       LightedGreenRoom.setup(context);
       startService(context,intent);
       Log.d(tag,"Receiver finished");
    }
    private void startService(Context context, Intent intent)
    {
       Intent serviceIntent = new Intent(context,getLRSClass());
       serviceIntent.putExtra("original_intent", intent);
       context.startService(serviceIntent);
    }
    /*
     * Override this methode to return the
     * "class" object belonging to the
     * nonsticky service class.
     */
    public abstract Class getLRSClass();
}
```

Once this abstraction is available, you'll need a receiver that works hand in hand with the 60-second long-running service in Listing 14–16. Such a receiver is provided in Listing 14–22.

Listing 14–22. *A Sample Long Running Broadcase Receiver, Test60SecBCR*

```
public class Test60SecBCR
extends ALongRunningReceiver
{
   @Override
```

```
    public Class getLRSClass()
    {
        Utils.logThreadSignature("Test60SecBCR");
        return Test60SecBCRService.class;
    }
}
```

Just like the service abstraction in Listings 14–19 and 14–20, the code in Listing 14–22 uses an abstraction for the broadcast receiver. The receiver abstraction starts the service indicated by the service class returned by the `getLRSClass()` method.

Thus far, we have demonstrated why we needed the two important abstractions to implement long-running services invoked by broadcast receivers, namely:

- `ALongRunningNonStickyBroadcastService`
- `ALongRunningReceiver`

However, we have postponed showing the implementation for one of these classes due to the level of detail involved. We also have not presented the implementation of a common class, `LightedGreenRoom`, that both these abstractions use. We are now at a point to explain and present the code for these two remaining classes. We will start first with the common class `LightedGreenRoom`.

Abstracting a Wake Lock with LightedGreenRoom

As mentioned earlier the primary purpose of the `LightedGreenRoom` abstraction is to simplify the interaction with the wake lock, and a wake lock is used to keep the device from being turned off. Listing 14–23 shows how a wake lock is used typically as stated in the SDK.

Listing 14–23. *Wakelock API*

```
//Get access to the power manager service
PowerManager pm =
    (PowerManager)inCtx.getSystemService(Context.POWER_SERVICE);

//Get hold of a wake lock
PowerManager.WakeLock wl =
    pm.newWakeLock(PowerManager.PARTIAL_WAKE_LOCK, tag);

//Acquire the wake lock
wl.acquire();

//do some work
//while this work is being done the device will be on partially

//release the wakelock
wl.release();
```

Given this interaction, the broadcast receiver is supposed acquire the lock, and when the long-running service is finished, it needs to release the lock. However, there is no good way to pass the wake lock variable to the service from the broadcast receiver. The only way the service knows about this wake lock is to use a static or application-level variable.

Another difficulty in acquiring and releasing a wake lock is the reference count. So as a broadcast receiver is invoked multiple times, if the invocations overlap, there are going to be multiple calls to acquire the wake lock. Similarly, there are going to be multiple calls to release. If number of acquire and release calls don't match, we will end up with a wake lock that is at worst keep the device on for far longer than needed. Also, when the service is no longer needed and the garbage collection runs, if the wake lock counts are mismatched, there will be a run time exception in the LogCat.

These issues have prompted us to do our best to abstract the wake lock to ensure proper usage.

> **NOTE:** Now that you are aware of issues and the need for wake locks, you are encouraged to tinker with `LightedGreenRoom` and replace it with another class if you find that to be simpler. This disclaimer is to reassure you that there is no magic about `LightedGreenRoom` and that it is quite simple at its heart.

We will now explain the conceptual thought that went into seeing the wake lock as `LightedGreenRoom`.

A Lighted Green Room

Let's start with a green room, which is a room that allows visitors. The room starts out dark, and the first one to enter turns on the lights. Subsequent visitors have no effect if the lights are already on. The last visitor to leave will turn off the lights. It is called a "green room" because it uses energy efficiently. The enter and leave methods need to be synchronized to keep their states, as they could happen between multiple threads.

So what, then, is a lighted green room? Unlike a green room that starts with lights off, a lighted green room starts with lights on, even before the first visitor arrives. We can assume that, with lights off, a visitor cannot find the way to the green room. This relates to the fact that if a device is off no service even can run. Still, the last one to leave will turn off the lights. This is useful for a broadcast receiver, because it needs to turn on the lights first and then transfer to the service.

Starting a service is considered equivalent to a visitor coming in. Stopping a service equates to a visitor leaving the room. Please note that you need to distinguish between the *creation* of a service and *starting* a service. Creation and destruction happen only once per service, whereas starting and stopping can happen many times.

There could be, and typically is, a time delay between setting up the wakelock (the lighted green room) in the receiver and starting the service, essentially a call to `onStartCommand` (having the first visitor enter the room).

Because a `wakelock` is reference counted, if a service is to be taken down because of low-memory conditions, we would like to explicitly release the locks. If you were to use the same lighted green room to serve multiple services, you may want to track the last service to be destroyed and release the locks only once that service is finished.

To allow for this pattern, we will create a client. Each service will register with the lighted green room as a client so that its destroy method will work.

On top of that, we need to keep track of "**enter**" and "**leave**" of each "startService".

Lighted Green Room Implementation

Combining all the concepts from the last section, the implementation of a lighted green room looks like Listing 14–24. Please note that this seemed to work well with our limited testing. Please tinker with it and adjust it to your needs, as it is quite difficult for us to consider each possibility that might exist in your development environment. (In other words, think of this example as experimental.)

Listing 14–24. *Lighted Green Room Implementation*

```
public class LightedGreenRoom
{
   //debug tag
   private static String tag="LightedGreenRoom";

   //Keep count of visitors to know the last visitor.
   //On destory set the count to zero to clear the room.
   private int count;

   //Needed to create the wake lock
   private Context ctx = null;

   //Our switch
   PowerManager.WakeLock wl = null;

   //Multi-client support
   private int clientCount = 0;

   /*
    * This is expected to be a singleton.
    * One could potentially make the constructor
    * private.
    */
   public LightedGreenRoom(Context inCtx)
   {
      ctx = inCtx;
      wl = this.createWakeLock(inCtx);
   }

   /*
    * Setting up the green room using a static method.
    * This has to be called before calling any other methods.
    * what it does:
    *      1. Instantiate the object
    *      2. acquire the lock to turn on lights
    * Assumption:
    *      It is not required to be synchronized
```

```
 *       because it will be called from the main thread.
 *       (Could be wrong. need to validate this!!)
 */
private static LightedGreenRoom s_self = null;

public static void setup(Context inCtx)
{
   if (s_self == null)
   {
      Log.d(LightedGreenRoom.tag,"Creating green room and lighting it");
      s_self = new LightedGreenRoom(inCtx);
      s_self.turnOnLights();
   }
     }
     public static boolean isSetup()
{
   return (s_self != null) ? true: false;
}

/*
 * The methods "enter" and "leave" are
 * expected to be called in tandem.
 *
 * On "enter" increment the count.
 *
 * Do not turn the lights or off
 * as they are already turned on.
 *
 * Just increment the count to know
 * when the last visitor leaves.
 *
 * This is a synchronized method as
 * multiple threads will be entering and leaving.
 *
 */
synchronized public int enter()
{
   count++;
   Log.d(tag,"A new visitor: count:" + count);
   return count;
}
/*
 * The methods "enter" and "leave" are
 * expected to be called in tandem.
 *
 * On "leave" decrement the count.
 *
 * If the count reaches zero turn off the lights.
 *
 * This is a synchronized method as
 * multiple threads will be entering and leaving.
 *
 */
synchronized public int leave()
{
   Log.d(tag,"Leaving room:count at the call:" + count);
   //if the count is already zero
```

```
        //just leave.
        if (count == 0)
        {
           Log.w(tag,"Count is zero.");
           return count;
        }
        count--;
        if (count == 0)
        {
           //Last visitor
           //turn off lights
           turnOffLights();
        }
        return count;
     }
  synchronized public int getCount()
     {
        return count;
     }

     /*
      * acquire the wake lock to turn the lights on
      * it is upto other synchronized methods to call
      * this at the appropriate time.
      */
     private void turnOnLights()
     {
        Log.d(tag, "Turning on lights. Count:" + count);
        this.wl.acquire();
     }

     /*
      * Release the wake lock to turn the lights off.
      * it is upto other synchronized methods to call
      * this at the appropriate time.
      */
     private void turnOffLights()
     {
        if (this.wl.isHeld())
        {
           Log.d(tag,"Releasing wake lock. No more visitors");
           this.wl.release();
        }
     }
     /*
      * Standard code to create a partial wake lock
      */
     private PowerManager.WakeLock createWakeLock(Context inCtx)
     {
        PowerManager pm =
           (PowerManager)inCtx.getSystemService(Context.POWER_SERVICE);

        PowerManager.WakeLock wl = pm.newWakeLock
             (PowerManager.PARTIAL_WAKE_LOCK, tag);
        return wl;
     }
```

```
private int registerClient()
{
   Utils.logThreadSignature(tag);
   this.clientCount++;
   Log.d(tag,"registering a new client:count:" + clientCount);
   return clientCount;
}

private int unRegisterClient()
{
   Utils.logThreadSignature(tag);
   Log.d(tag,"un registering a new client:count:" + clientCount);
   if (clientCount == 0)
   {
      Log.w(tag,"There are no clients to unregister.");
      return 0;
   }
   //clientCount is not zero
   clientCount--;
   if (clientCount == 0)
   {
      emptyTheRoom();
   }
   return clientCount;
}
synchronized public void emptyTheRoom()
{
   Log.d(tag, "Call to empty the room");
   count = 0;
   this.turnOffLights();
}
//*************************************************
//*  static members: Purely helper methods
//*   Delegates to the underlying singleton object
//*************************************************
public static int s_enter()
{
   assertSetup();
   return s_self.enter();
}
public static int s_leave()
{
   assertSetup();
   return s_self.leave();
}
//Dont directly call this method
//probably will be deprecated.
//Call register and unregister client methods instead
public static void ds_emptyTheRoom()
{
   assertSetup();
   s_self.emptyTheRoom();
   return;
}
public static void s_registerClient()
{
   assertSetup();
```

```
        s_self.registerClient();
        return;
    }
    public static void s_unRegisterClient()
    {
        assertSetup();
        s_self.unRegisterClient();
        return;
    }
    private static void assertSetup()
    {
        if (LightedGreenRoom.s_self == null)
        {
            Log.w(LightedGreenRoom.tag,"You need to call setup first");
            throw new RuntimeException("You need to setup GreenRoom first");
        }
    }
}
```

A reasonable approach for the broadcast receiver and the service to communicate with each other is through a static variable. Instead of making the wakelock static, we have made the entire LightedGreenRoom a static instance. However, every other variable inside LightedGreenRoom stays local and nonstatic.

Every public method of LightedGreenRoom is also exposed as a static method for convenience. You can choose, instead, to get rid of the static methods and directly call the single object instance of LightedGreenRoom.

Long-Running Service Implementation

Now that the LightedGreenRoom implementation is finished, we are almost ready to present the long-running service abstraction. However, we have to take one more detour to explain the lifetime of a service and how it relates to the implementation of onStartCommand. This is the method that is ultimately responsible for starting the worker thread and the semantics of a service.

You know that the broadcast receiver invokes the service using a startService call and that this call will result in calling the onStartCommand method of the service. The lifetime of the service is controlled by what this method returns.

To understand what happens in this method, you need a detailed background on the nature of local services. We have covered the basics of local services in Chapter 11, and now we need to dig a bit deeper.

When a service is started, it gets created first and its onStartCommand method is called. Android has enough provisions to keep this process in memory so that the service can serve incoming client requests.

There is a difference between a service process being in memory and running. A service runs only in response to startService, which calls its onStartCommand method. Just because this method is not executing doesn't mean the service process is not in memory. Sometimes, people refer to this as service running even though it is just sitting there and claiming some resources but not actually executing anything. This is what typically means when Android claims that it keeps the service running.

In fact, if a `startService` call, resulting in an `onStartCommand`, takes more than 5 to 10 seconds, this will result in ANR message and could kill the process hosting the service. Without a worker thread, a service cannot run for longer than 10 seconds. So you should distinguish between a service that's available and one that's running.

Android does its best to keep a service available in memory. However, under demanding memory conditions, Android may choose to reclaim the process and call the `onDestory()` method of the service. Android tries to do this when the service is not executing its `onCreate()`, `onStart()`, or `onDestroy()` methods.

However, unlike an activity that is shut down, a service is scheduled to restart again when resources are available if there are pending `startService` intents in the queue. The service will be woken up and the next intent delivered to it via `onStartCommand()`. Of course, `onCreate()` will be called when the service is brought back. Because services are restarted all the time ,it is reasonable to think that, unlike activity and other components, a service component is *fundamentally a sticky component*.

Details of a Nonsticky Service

What is a nonsticky service then?

Let's talk about a situation when a service is not automatically restarted. After a client calls `startservice`, the service is created and `OnStartCommand` is called to do its work. This service will not be automatically restarted if a client explicitly calls `stopservice`.

This `stopservice`, depending on how many clients are still connected, can move the service into a stopped state, at which time the service's `onDestroy` method is called and the service life cycle is complete. Once a service has been stopped like this by its last client, the service will not be brought back.

This protocol works well when everything happens as per design, where start and stop methods are called and executed in sequence and without a miss.

Prior to Android 2.0, devices have seen a lot of services hanging around and claiming resources even though there was no work to be done, meaning Android brought the services back into memory even though there were no messages in the queue. This would have happened when `stopService` was not invoked either because of an exception or because the process is taken out between `onStartCommand` and `stopService`.

Android 2.0 introduced a solution so that we can indicate that, if there are no pending intents, it shouldn't bother restarting the service. This is ok because whoever started the service to do the work will call it again such as the alarm manager. This is done by returning the nonsticky flag (`Service.START_NOT_STICKY`) from `onStartCommand` .

However, nonsticky is not really that nonsticky. Remember, even if we mark the service as nonsticky, if there are pending intents, Android will bring the service back to life. This setting applies only when there are no pending intents.

Details of a Sticky Service

What does it mean for a service to be really sticky then?

The sticky flag (`Service.START_STICKY`) means that Android should restart the service even if there are no pending intents. When the service is restarted, call `onCreate` and `onStartCommand` with a null intent. This will give the service an opportunity, if need be, to call `stopself` if that is appropriate. The implication is that a service that is sticky needs to deal with null intents on restarts.

A Variation of Nonsticky: Redeliver Intents

Local services in particular follow a pattern where `onstart` and `stopself` are called in pairs. A client calls `onstart`. The service, when it finishes that work, calls `stopself`. You can see this clearly in the implementation of `IntentService` utility class in Listing 14–15.

If a service takes, say, 30 minutes to complete a task, it will not call `stopself` for 30 minutes. Meanwhile, the service is reclaimed. If we use the nonsticky flag, the service will not wake up, and we would never have called `stopself`.

Many times, this is OK. However, if you want to make sure if these two calls happen for sure, you can tell Android to not to unque the `start` event until `stopself` is called. This ensures that, when the service is reclaimed, there is always a pending event unless the `stopself` is called. This is called `redeliver` mode, and it can be indicated in reply to the `onStartCommand` method by returning the `Service.START_REDELIVER` flag.

Specifying Service Flags in OnStartCommand

Interestingly, stickiness is tied to `onStartCommand`, and not to `onCreate`, for a service. This is a bit odd, because so far, we have been talking about a service being in `sticky`, `nonsticky`, or `redeliver mode` as if these were service-level attributes. However, this determination for the nature of a service is made based on the return value from `OnStartCommand`. Wonder what the goal here is? We do too. Because, for the same service instance `OnStartCommand` is called many times, once for each `startservice`. What if the method returns different flags indicating different service behaviors? Perhaps the best guess is that the last returned value is what determines.

Picking Suitable Stickiness

Given the combination of possible service behaviors, what type of service is suitable for a long-running broadcast receiver? We believe a simple, nonsticky service, which just assumes the service will stop if there are no pending messages in the queue, will do. We are finding it hard to think that there is a use case for sticky long-running broadcast receivers, especially if we want to use `IntentService`, which expects the service to stop if there are no pending intents.

You will see this conclusion in the implementation of our long-running service abstraction in the upcoming Listing 14–19, where we have returned the nonsticky flag.

Controlling the Wake Lock from Two Places

Before presenting the source code for the long-running service, let's talk about the responsibilities of the service regarding keeping the device on.

When the service code is running, we should have the partial wake lock in effect. To do this, when the service is created, we need to turn on the wake lock by creating the lighted green room. You might say that this is done by the broadcast receiver, which is true. However, the service may be woken up by itself, in which case we would have missed the setup of the lighted room. So we need to control the wake lock from both places.

The long-running broadcast receiver code in Listing 14–18 initializes the wake lock using `LightedGreenRoom.setup()`. We will do the same in the service creation callback.

In addition to setting up the lighted green room, our service needs to register itself as a client to the lighted green room. This allows for clean up when the service component gets destroyed through `onDestroy()`.

Long-Running Service Implementation

Now that you have the background on `IntentService`, service start flags, and the lighted green room, we're ready to take a look at the long-running service in Listing 14–25.

Listing 14–25. *A Long-Running Service*

```
public abstract class ALongRunningNonStickyBroadcastService
extends IntentService
{
    public static String tag = "ALongRunningBroadcastService";
    protected abstract void
    handleBroadcastIntent(Intent broadcastIntent);

    public ALongRunningNonStickyBroadcastService(String name){
        super(name);
    }
    /*
     * This method can be invoked under two circumstances
     * 1. When a broadcast receiver issues a "startService"
     * 2. when android restarts it due to pending "startService" intents.
     *
     * In case 1, the broadcast receiver has already
     * setup the "lightedgreenroom".
     *
```

```
     * In case 2, we need to do the same.
     */
    @Override
    public void onCreate()
    {
        super.onCreate();

        //Set up the green room
        //The setup is capable of getting called multiple times.
        LightedGreenRoom.setup(this.getApplicationContext());

        //It is possible that there are more than one service
        //of this type is running.
        //Knowing the number will allow us to clean up
        //the locks in ondestroy.
        LightedGreenRoom.s_registerClient();
    }
    @Override
    public int onStartCommand(Intent intent, int flag, int startId)
    {
        //Call the IntetnService "onstart"
        super.onStart(intent, startId);

        //Tell the green room there is a visitor
        LightedGreenRoom.s_enter();

        //mark this as non sticky
        //Means: Don't restart the service if there are no
        //pending intents.
        return Service.START_NOT_STICKY;
    }
    /*
     * Note that this method call runs
     * in a secondary thread setup by the IntentService.
     *
     * Override this method from IntentService.
     * Retrieve the original broadcast intent.
     * Call the derived class to handle the broadcast intent.
     * finally tell the ligthed room that you are leaving.
     * if this is the last visitor then the lock
     * will be released.
     */
    @Override
    final protected void onHandleIntent(Intent intent)
    {
        try
        {
            Intent broadcastIntent
            = intent.getParcelableExtra("original_intent");
            handleBroadcastIntent(broadcastIntent);
        }
        finally
        {
            LightedGreenRoom.s_leave();
        }
    }
    /*
```

```
     * If Android reclaims this process,
     * this method will release the lock
     * irrespective of how many visitors there are.
     */
    @Override
    public void onDestroy() {
        super.onDestroy();
        LightedGreenRoom.s_unRegisterClient();
    }

}
```

Clearly, this class extends IntentService and gets all the benefits of a worker thread as set up by IntentService. In addition, it specializes the IntentService further so that it is set up as a non-sticky service. From a developer's perspective, the primary method to focus on is the abstract handleBroadcastIntent() method.

Testing Long Running Services

To test this code, you will need to add these additional files to your project:

- LightedGreenRoom.java (Listing 14–24)
- ALongRunningNonStickyBroadcastService (Listing 14–25)
- ALongRunningReceiver.java (Listing 14–21)
- Test60SecBCR.java (Listing 14–22)
- Test60SecBCRService.java (Listing 14–20)
- An updated manifest file with the 60–second receiver and the service (Listing 14–14)

The Java source code files can be found previously in the chapter, let's now look at the additional entries you need in the manifest file shown in Listing 14–26.

Listing 14–26. ***The Long-Running Receiver and Service Definition***

```
<manifest…>
……
<application….>
<receiver android:name=".Test60SecBCR">
    <intent-filter>
       <action android:name="com.androidbook.intents.testbc"/>
    </intent-filter>
</receiver>
<service android:name=".Test60SecBCRService"/>
</application>
…..
<uses-permission android:name="android.permission.WAKE_LOCK"/>
</manifest>
```

Also notice that you will need the wake lock permission to run this long-running receiver abstraction.

Instructions for Compiling the Code

This chapter has two projects. One to test the broadcast receiver (Let's call it TestBCR) and one to test the stand-alone receivers, including the long-running receiver and service (let's call it StandaloneBCR). Both these project are zipped up and available in the download file; the URL for this is listed in the "References" section. We strongly suggest that you download the ZIP file and unzip it to see these projects individually.

Creating the Projects from the ZIP File

The steps to create the projects from the zip file follow:

1. Download the ZIP file.
2. Unzip the file to see two root directories, one for each project. For each project, do the following:
    a. From the File/Import menu in Eclipse, choose General/Existing Projects into Workspace.
    b. Choose "select root directory".
    c. Choose "copy projects into work space".
    d. You may need to choose the right API level once the project is in place by selecting "project properties/android" and picking the right build target

Once you build the projects, deploy both of them into the emulator. The stand-alone project is a headless project with just receivers and services. The TestBCR project has a simple activity that triggers the single broadcast intent which is responded by receivers inside the TestBCR project and the receivers from the stand-alone BCR project.

Creating the Project from the Listings

Here are the list of files you need for each project and how to create those projects from the listings in this chapter.

TestBCR Project files

These are the files you should need for TestBCR:

- `TestBCRActivity.java` (Listing 14–5)
- `TestReceiver.java` (Listing 14–2)
- `TestReceiver2.java` (Listing 14–9)
- `TestTimeDelayReceiver.java` (Listing 14–11)
- `Utils.java` (Listing 14–3)

- /res/layout/main.xml (Listing 14–6)
- /res/menu/main_menu.xml (Listing 14–7)
- manifest.xml (Listing 14–8)

If you need any other files you may have to look at the project in the zip file or fill them in yourself. These may be simple things like default icons or string values. Once you have the receivers, you will also need to register them in the manifest file shown in Listing 14–8.

You can build this project from the preceding list of files using the following approach:

1. Create a new project by choosing File ➤ new project ➤ Android ➤ Android Project.
2. Pick a name, and choose "create new project in workspace".
3. Supply an application name, such as TestBCR. The application name really doesn't matter, as it is the package name that counts.
4. Pick an API level.
5. Use the package name com.androidbook.bcr.
6. Pick any minsdk version, for example 3.
7. Choose your activity as TestBCRActivity, and click Finish
8. Android will create a number of resource files and probably (depending on your release) a single source file.
9. Create, update, or delete these files based Listings 14–2 through 14–11.
10. For Java files, when you copy the listings from here, put the package name at the top of the file first. Then use Ctrl+Shift+O for filling in the imports.

Please note that, in this process, you will need to make adjustments to the code to get it compiled and to provide any missing pieces. You can refer to the ZIP file to fill in the gaps.

Stand-Alone BCR Project Files

These are the stand-alone project files:

- ALongRunningNonStickyBroadcastService.java (Listing 14–25)
- ALongRunningReceiver.java (Listing 14–21)
- LightedGreenRoom.java (Listing 14–24)
- NotificationReceiver.java (Listing 14–15)
- StandaloneReceiver.java (Listing 14–13)

- `Test60SecBCR.java` (Listing 14–22)
- `Test60SecBCRService.java` (Listing 14–20)
- `Utils.java` (Listing 14–3)
- `manifest.xml` (Listing 14–14, 14–26)

Because this project is a headless project, you will not need the layout files or the menu resource files. You can build this project from this list of files using the following approach:

1. Create a new project by selecting File ➤ New Project ➤ Android➤ Android Project.
2. Pick a name, and choose "create new project in work space".
3. Give the application a name, such as TestStandaloneBCR. An application name really doesn't matter; it is the package name that counts.
4. Pick an API level.
5. Use the package name `com.androidbook.salbcr`.
6. Pick any minsdk version, for example, 3.
7. Don't choose any activity.
8. Android will create a number of resource files and probably (depending on your Android release) no source files. But it will create a Java package.
9. Create, update, and delete these files based on the listings noted at the beginning of this section.
10. For Java files, when you copy the listings, put the package name at the top of the file first. Then use Ctrl+Shift+O to fill in the imports.

Please note that, in this process, you will need to make adjustments to the code to get it compiled and provide any missing pieces. You can refer to the ZIP file to fill in the gaps.

References

Here are some helpful references to topics you may wish to explore further:

- http://developer.android.com/reference/android/content/BroadcastReceiver.html: This is a link for the BroadcastReceiver API. In this chapter, we have covered the most basic version of a broadcast receiver. You will find at this link more about ordered broadcasts and a little bit about its life cycle.
- http://developer.android.com/reference/android/app/Service.html: This is a link for the Service API. This reference is especially good to have while working with long-running services.
- http://developer.android.com/reference/android/app/NotificationManager.html: This is a link for the Notification Manager API.
- http://developer.android.com/reference/android/app/Notification.html: This is a link for the Notification API. You will see here the various options available for working with a notification, such as content views and sound effects.
- http://developer.android.com/reference/android/widget/RemoteViews.html: This is a link for the RemoteViews API. RemoteViews are used to construct custom detailed views of notifications.
- http://www.androidbook.com/item/3514: The authors' research on long-running services can be found here.
- http://www.androidbook.com/projects: Here, you can see a list of downloadable projects from this book. For this chapter, look for a ZIP file named ProAndroid3_Ch14_TestReceivers.zip.

Summary

We have covered important ground in this chapter: broadcast receivers, notifications, wake locks, and long-running services. This chapter also has brought together the essence of what you learned in Chapters 12 and 13.

We have shown the basics of broadcast receiver usage and lifetimes and how they work in the same process as well as outside. We showed how you can co-opt services to extend the lifetime of a broadcast receiver. Finally, we tinkered with the IntentService to give you a pattern that you can further tailor for your own needs of long-running services.

In Chapter 15, we will go over using alarm manager to invoke broadcast receivers.

Chapter 15

Exploring the Alarm Manager

In Android, you can use the alarm manager to trigger events. These events can be at a specific time or at regular intervals. We will start the chapter with the basics of the alarm manager where we set a simple alarm. We will then cover setting an alarm that repeats, cancelling an alarm, the role of pending intents (specifically the role their uniqueness plays), and setting multiple alarms. By the end of the chapter, you will have learned both the basics and the practical nitty-gritty of the Android alarm manager.

Alarm Manager Basics: Setting Up a Simple Alarm

We will start the chapter setting an alarm at a particular time and have it call a broadcast receiver. Once the broadcast receiver is invoked, we can use the information from Chapter 14 to perform both simple and long running operations in that broadcast receiver.

The steps we follow for this exercise are

1. Get access to the alarm manager.
2. Come up with a time to set the alarm.
3. Create a receiver to be invoked.
4. Create a pending intent that can be passed to the alarm manager to invoke the receiver.
5. Use the time from step 2 and the pending intent from step 4 to set the alarm.
6. Watch the logcat for messages coming from the invoked receiver from step 3.

Obtaining the Alarm Manager

Getting access to the alarm manager is simple and is illustrated in Listing 15–1.

Listing 15–1. *Getting an Alarm Manager*

```
AlarmManager am =
    (AlarmManager)
         mContext.getSystemService(Context.ALARM_SERVICE);
```

In Listing 15–1, the variable mContext refers to a context object. For example, if you are invoking this code from an activity menu, the context variable is the activity.

Setting Up the Time for the Alarm

To set the alarm for a particular date and time, you will need an instance in time identified by a Java Calendar object. Listing 15–2 contains a Java file (one we will use later to set up a project) that has some utilities to work with the Calendar object.

Listing 15–2. *A Few Useful Calendar Utilities*

```
public class Utils {
    public static Calendar getTimeAfterInSecs(int secs) {
        Calendar cal = Calendar.getInstance();
        cal.add(Calendar.SECOND,secs);
        return cal;
    }
    public static Calendar getCurrentTime(){
        Calendar cal = Calendar.getInstance();
        return cal;
    }
    public static Calendar getTodayAt(int hours){
        Calendar today = Calendar.getInstance();
        Calendar cal = Calendar.getInstance();
        cal.clear();

        int year = today.get(Calendar.YEAR);
        int month = today.get(Calendar.MONTH);
        //represents the day of the month
        int day = today.get(Calendar.DATE);
        cal.set(year,month,day,hours,0,0);
        return cal;
    }
    public static String getDateTimeString(Calendar cal){
        SimpleDateFormat df = new SimpleDateFormat("MM/dd/yyyy hh:mm:ss");
        df.setLenient(false);
        String s = df.format(cal.getTime());
        return s;
    }
}
```

From this list of utilities, we will use the function getTimeAfterInSecs(), as shown in Listing 15–3 , to look for a time instance that is 30 seconds from now.

Listing 15–3. *Obtaining a Time Instance*

```
Calendar cal = Utils.getTimeAfterInSecs(30);
```

Setting Up a Receiver for the Alarm

Now, we need a receiver to set against the alarm. A simple receiver is shown in Listing 15–4.

Listing 15–4. *TestReceiver to Test Alarm Broadcasts*

```
public class TestReceiver extends BroadcastReceiver
{
    private static final String tag = "TestReceiver";
    @Override
    public void onReceive(Context context, Intent intent)
    {
        Log.d("TestReceiver", "intent=" + intent);
        String message = intent.getStringExtra("message");
        Log.d(tag, message);
    }
}
```

You will need to register this receiver in the manifest file using the corresponding <receiver> tag, as shown in Listing 15–5.

Listing 15–5. *Registering a Broadcast Receiver*

```
<receiver android:name=".TestReceiver"/>
```

Creating a PendingIntent Suitable for an Alarm

Once we have a receiver, we can set up a PendingIntent, which is needed to set the alarm. We start off by creating an intent to invoke the TestReceiver in Listing 15–4. This intent creation is shown in Listing 15–6.

Listing 15–6. *Creating an Intent Pointing to TestReceiver*

```
Intent intent =
    new Intent(mContext, TestReceiver.class);
intent.putExtra("message", "Single Shot Alarm");
```

The variable mContext is the activity context from which you are going to be using to invoke this functionality. We have used the TestReceiver class directly (instead of using an intent filter against an intent action as we did in Chapter 14 for receivers). We also have an opportunity to load the intent with extras while creating this intent.

Once we have this regular intent pointing to a receiver, we need to create a pending intent that is necessary to pass to an alarm manager. Listing 15–7contains an example of creating a PendingIntent from the intent in Listing 15–6.

Listing 15–7. *Creating a Pending Intent*

```
PendingIntent pi =
    PendingIntent.getBroadcast(
      mContext,    //context
```

```
    1,              //request id, used for disambiguating this intent
    intent,         //intent to be delivered
    0);             //pending intent flags
```

Notice that we have asked the `PendingIntent` class to construct a pending intent that is suitable for a broadcast explicitly. The other variations of this follow:

```
PendingIntent.getActivity() //useful to start an activity
PendingIntent.getService() //useful to start a service
```

We will discuss the `request id` argument, which we set to 1, in greater detail later in this chapter. Briefly, it is used to separate two intent objects that are similar.

The pending intent flags have little to no influence on the alarm manager. Our recommendation is to use no flags at all and use `0` for their values. These flags are typically useful in controlling the lifetime of the pending intent. However, in this case, the lifetime is maintained by the alarm manager. For example to cancel a pending intent, you ask the alarm manager to cancel it.

Setting the Alarm

Once we have the time instance in milliseconds as a `Calendar` object and the pending intent pointing to the receiver, we can set up an alarm by calling the `set()` method of the alarm manager, as illustrated in Listing 15–8.

Listing 15–8. *Alarm Manager Set Method*

```
alarmManager.set(AlarmManager.RTC_WAKEUP,
        calendarObject.getTimeInMillis(),
        pendintIntent);
```

If you use `RTC_WAKEUP`, the alarm will wake up the device. Or you can use `RTC` in its place to deliver the intent when the device wakes up.

The time specified by the second argument is the instance in time specified by the `calendarObject` that we have created earlier (see Listing 15–3). This time is in milliseconds since 1970. This also coincides with the Java `Calendar` object default.

Once this method is called, the alarm manager will invoke the `TestReceiver` in Listing 15–4 in 30 seconds from now.

Test Project

Let's create a test project to demonstrate the code introduced so far.

> **NOTE:** We have given a URL at the end of the chapter that you can use to download projects of this chapter and import them into Eclipse directly.

To create this project we will need the following files:

TestAlarmsDriverActivity.java: This is the activity to set alarms (Listing 15–12).

SendAlarmOnceTester.java: This is the main class for exercising the functionality of sending an alarm once. There will be more similar testers that test the new functionality that will be introduced (Listing 15–11).

BaseTester.java: This base class allows testers such as SendAlarmOnceTester to report back results through the interface IReportBack (Listing 15–10).

IReportBack.java: This small interface helper for BaseTester.java takes debug messages and passes them to the driver activity (Listing 15–9).

TestReceiver.java: This is the java class that gets invoked when the alarm goes off. This class was presented in a previous listing (Listing 15–4).

Utils.java: These date/time/calendar utilities were already presented in a (Listing 15–2).

/res/menu/main_menu.xml: This is the menu file for the driver activity (Listing 15–13).

/res/layout/main.xml: This is the layout file for the driver activity (Listing 15–14).

AndroidManifest.xml: This is the very familiar manifest file required by every Android project. (Listing 15–15)

We will present each of the files in turn, starting with the base classes, which allow us to coordinate between the driver activity and the various testers that test individual alarm functionality. The first of these, IReportBack, is presented in Listing 15–9.

Listing 15–9. *IReportBack.java*

```
//IReportBack.java
package com.androidbook.alarms;

/*
 * An interface implemented typically by an activity
 * so that a worker class can report back
 * on what happened.
 */
public interface IReportBack
{
   public void reportBack(String tag, String message);
}
```

As indicated in the comments, this interface is used by a tester class to pass a message to the driver activity. You will see this clearly when you notice the code in its inherited subclasses, such as SendAlarmOnceTester.java (Listing 15–11).

All testers like SendAlarmOnceTester inherit from BaseTester. The source code for BaseTester.java is in Listing 15–10.

Listing 15–10. *BaseTester.java*

```
//BaseTester.java
package com.androidbook.alarms;
import android.content.Context;public class BaseTester
{
    protected IReportBack mReportTo;
    protected Context mContext;
    public BaseTester(Context ctx, IReportBack target)
    {
        mReportTo = target;
        mContext = ctx;
    }
}
```

This is a simple helper class that provides two things for the derived tester classes such as SendAlarmOnceTester: a context to be used by its methods where necessary and an activity that implements the IReportBack interface to log messages.

With IReportBack and BaseTester in place, we're ready for the code for SendAlarmOnceTester.java, the class that tests sending a single alarm event (see Listing 15–11).

Listing 15–11. *A File to Test Sending an Alarm Once*

```
// SendAlarmOnceTester.java
package com.androidbook.alarms;
import java.util.Calendar;
import android.app.AlarmManager;
import android.app.PendingIntent;
import android.content.Context;
import android.content.Intent;

public class SendAlarmOnceTester extends BaseTester
{
    private static String tag = "SendAlarmOnceTester";
    SendAlarmOnceTester(Context ctx, IReportBack target)
    {
        super(ctx, target);
    }

    /*
     * An alarm can invoke a broadcast request
     * at a specified time.
     * The name of the broadcast receiver is explicitly
     * specified in the intent.
     */
    public void sendAlarmOnce()
    {
        //Get the instance in time that is 30secs from now
        Calendar cal = Utils.getTimeAfterInSecs(30);

        //If you want to point to 11:00 hours today.
        //Calendar cal = Utils.getTodayAt(11);
```

```
        //Print to the debug view that we are
        //scheduling at a specific time
        String s = Utils.getDateTimeString(cal);
        mReportTo.reportBack(tag, "Schdeduling alarm at: " + s);

        //Get an intent to invoke a receiver
        //TestReceiver class
        Intent intent =
            new Intent(mContext, TestReceiver.class);
        intent.putExtra("message", "Single Shot Alarm");

        PendingIntent pi =
            PendingIntent.getBroadcast(
              mContext,         //context
              1,                //request id, used for disambiguating this intent
              intent,           //intent to be delivered
              PendingIntent.FLAG_ONE_SHOT);  //pending intent flags

        // Schedule the alarm!
        AlarmManager am =
            (AlarmManager)
                 mContext.getSystemService(Context.ALARM_SERVICE);

        am.set(AlarmManager.RTC_WAKEUP,
                cal.getTimeInMillis(),
                pi);
    }
}
```

The intent of the class `SendAlarmOnceTester` is to send an alarm once so that it invokes a broadcast receiver. You see this done in the method `sendAlarmOnce()` in Listing 15–11. The TestReceiver that is used as the target for the alarm is in Listing 15–4, so every aspect of `sendAlarmOnce()` is already discussed in the prior section. Listing 15–11 is merely putting together the code that we have covered already.

Let's now look at the driver activity responsible for invoking the `sendAlarmOnce()` method. The source code for this activity is in Listing 15–12. This main activity of the test project invokes the menus to test the various alarm scenarios we have discussed and will discuss in this chapter. However to start, we have just enough code to invoke the single menu item that we talked about. We will add code to respond to additional menus as we go along.

The `onCreate()` method of `TestAlarmsDriverActivity` (Listing 15–12) instantiates a `SendAlarmOnceTester` to transfer the menu actions to. Notice that the activity passes itself as both the `IReportBack` variable and the Context variable to the `SendAlarmOnceTester` constructor. This class also implements the `IReportBack` interface and updates the debug view with the passed in text (notice the highlighted `reportBack` method in Listing 15–12).

Listing 15–12. *A Sample Activity to Test Setting Alarms*

```
// TestAlarmsDriverActivity.java
package com.androidbook.alarms;
import android.app.Activity;
import android.os.Bundle;
```

```
import android.util.Log;
import android.view.Menu;
import android.view.MenuInflater;
import android.view.MenuItem;
import android.widget.TextView;

public class TestAlarmsDriverActivity extends Activity
implements IReportBack
{
    public static final String tag="TestAlarmsDriverActivity";
    private SendAlarmOnceTester alarmTester = null;
    /** Called when the activity is first created. */
    @Override
    public void onCreate(Bundle savedInstanceState) {
        super.onCreate(savedInstanceState);
        setContentView(R.layout.main);
        alarmTester = new SendAlarmOnceTester(this,this);
    }

    @Override
    public boolean onCreateOptionsMenu(Menu menu)
    {
        //call the parent to attach any system level menus
        super.onCreateOptionsMenu(menu);
        MenuInflater inflater = getMenuInflater(); //from activity
        inflater.inflate(R.menu.main_menu, menu);
        return true;
    }

    @Override
    public boolean onOptionsItemSelected(MenuItem item)
    {
        appendMenuItemText(item);
        if (item.getItemId() == R.id.menu_clear)
        {
            this.emptyText();
            return true;
        }
        if (item.getItemId() == R.id.menu_alarm_once)
        {
            alarmTester.sendAlarmOnce();
            return true;
        }
        //You will add more menus later here
        return true;
    }
    //Inherited function from IReportBack
    public void reportBack(String tag, String message)
    {
        this.appendText(tag + ":" + message);
        Log.d(tag,message);
    }

    //Simple utility functions to work the debug view
    //of this activity
    private TextView getTextView() {
        return (TextView)this.findViewById(R.id.text1);
```

```
    }
    private void appendMenuItemText(MenuItem menuItem){
       String title = menuItem.getTitle().toString();
       TextView tv = getTextView();
       tv.setText(tv.getText() + "\n" + title);
    }
    private void emptyText(){
          TextView tv = getTextView();
          tv.setText("");
    }
    private void appendText(String s){
       TextView tv = getTextView();
       tv.setText(tv.getText() + "\n" + s);
       Log.d(tag,s);
    }
}
```

As you can see from the `TestAlarmsDriverActivity` activity, it responds to a couple of menu items. The corresponding `menu.xml` file is in Listing 15–13. In this listing, we have also included one time the additional test cases we will handle. As the presence of these menu items will not stop you from compiling this first exercise, we have included them here one time.

Listing 15–13. *Menu Items to Test Various Alarm Manager Scenarios*

```
<!-- /res/menu/main_menu.xml -->
<menu xmlns:android="http://schemas.android.com/apk/res/android">
    <!-- This group uses the default category. -->
    <group android:id="@+id/menuGroup_Main">
        <item android:id="@+id/menu_alarm_once"
            android:title="Alarm Once" />
        <item android:id="@+id/menu_alarm_repeated"
            android:title="Alarm Repeat" />
        <item android:id="@+id/menu_alarm_cancel"
            android:title="Cancel Alarms" />
        <item android:id="@+id/menu_alarm_multiple"
            android:title="Multiple Alarms" />
        <item android:id="@+id/menu_alarm_distinct_intents"
            android:title="Distinct Intents" />
        <item android:id="@+id/menu_alarm_intent_primacy"
            android:title="Intent Primacy" />

        <item android:id="@+id/menu_clear"
             android:title="clear" />
    </group>
</menu>
```

Listing 15–14 contains the layout file to go with the driver activity `TestAlarmsDriverActivity` (Listing 15–12).The location of this file is /res/layout/main.xml.

Listing 15–14. *Layout File for TestAlaramsDriverActivity*

```
<?xml version="1.0" encoding="utf-8"?>
<!-- /res/layout/main.xml -->
<LinearLayout xmlns:android="http://schemas.android.com/apk/res/android"
    android:orientation="vertical"
```

```
    android:layout_width="fill_parent"
    android:layout_height="fill_parent"
    >
<TextView
    android:id="@+id/text1"
    android:layout_width="fill_parent"
    android:layout_height="wrap_content"
    android:text="@string/hello"
    />
</LinearLayout>
```

Listing 15–15 is the manifest file for this project.

Listing 15–15. *Alarm Manager Test Program Manifest File*

```
<?xml version="1.0" encoding="utf-8"?>
<!-- AndroidManifest.xml  -->
<manifest xmlns:android="http://schemas.android.com/apk/res/android"
      package="com.androidbook.alarms"
      android:versionCode="1"
      android:versionName="1.0.0">
    <application android:icon="@drawable/icon" android:label="Test Alarms">
        <activity android:name=".TestAlarmsDriverActivity"
                  android:label="Test Alarms">
            <intent-filter>
                <action android:name="android.intent.action.MAIN" />
                <category android:name="android.intent.category.LAUNCHER" />
            </intent-filter>
        </activity>
    <receiver android:name=".TestReceiver">
        <intent-filter>
            <action android:name="com.androidbook.intents.testbc"/>
        </intent-filter>
    </receiver>
</application>
    <uses-sdk android:minSdkVersion="3" />
</manifest>
```

To work with an alarm manager, there are no specific entries needed in the manifest file other than the receiver. The receiver definition is highlighted in the manifest file listing 15–15. Once you build this project and fire it off, you will see an activity and menu structure like the one shown in Figures 15–1 and 15–2.

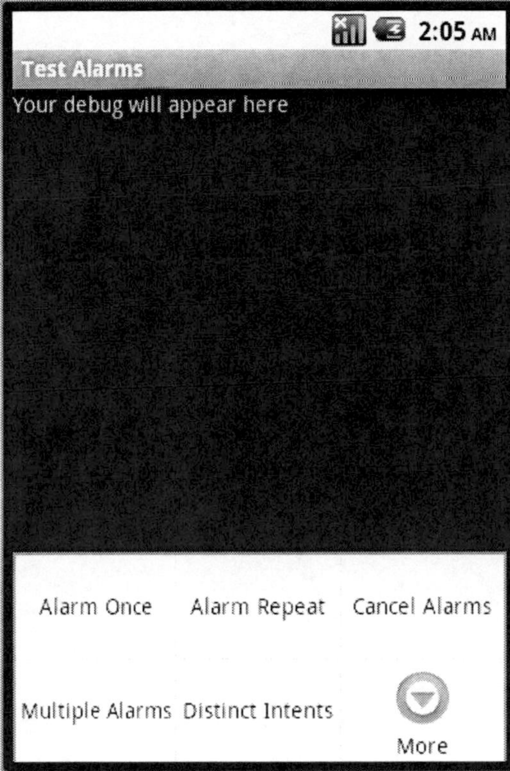

Figure 15–1. *A sample activity to test the alarm manager*

A portion of the available menu items are shown in Figure 15–1. To see the other menu items click the More icon to see the rest of the menus. This view is illustrated in Figure 15–2.

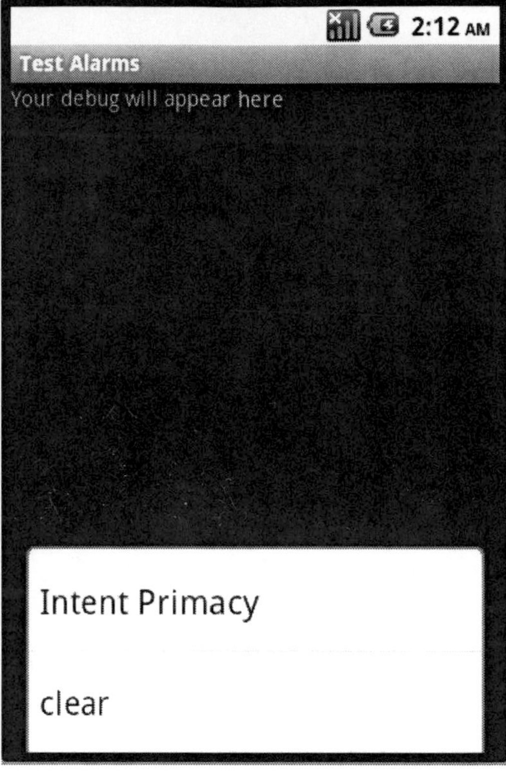

Figure 15–2. *Expanded menus for our sample activity*

Now, if you select the Alarm Once menu item from Figure 15–1, you will execute the code in `sendAlarmOnce()` of Listing 15–11. This will set the alarm to go off in 30 seconds from now. `TestReceiver` will then log messages to LogCat.

Exploring Alarm Manager Alternate Scenarios

Now that we have explained the basics of setting an alarm, we will now cover a few additional scenarios, such as setting off an alarm repeatedly and cancelling alarms. We will also show you exception conditions that you may run into while using the alarm manager.

Setting Off an Alarm Repeatedly

We have already covered how to set a simple one-time alarm, so let's now consider how we can set an alarm that goes of repeatedly. To understand this, see the code in Listing 15–16. This is another tester similar to the `SendOnceAlarmTester()` and implements a method called `sendRepeatingAlarm()` to test sending an alarm repeatedly

Listing 15–16. *Setting a Repeating Alarm*

```
// SendRepeatingAlarmTester.java
package com.androidbook.alarms;
import java.util.Calendar;
import android.app.AlarmManager;
import android.app.PendingIntent;
import android.content.Context;
import android.content.Intent;

public class SendRepeatingAlarmTester
extends SendAlarmOnceTester
{
    private static String tag = "SendRepeatingAlarmTester";
    SendRepeatingAlarmTester(Context ctx, IReportBack target)
    {
        super(ctx, target);
    }

    /*
     * An alarm can invoke a broadcast request
     * starting at a specified time and at
     * regular intervals.
     *
     * Uses the same intent as above
     * but a distinct request id to avoid conflicts
     * with the single shot alarm above.
     *
     * Uses getDistinctPendingIntent() utility.
     */
    public void sendRepeatingAlarm()
    {
        Calendar cal = Utils.getTimeAfterInSecs(30);
        //Calendar testcal = Utils.getTodayAt(11);
        String s = Utils.getDateTimeString(cal);
        this.mReportTo.reportBack(tag,
            "Schdeduling Repeating alarm in 5 sec interval starting at: " + s);

        //Get an intent to invoke the receiver
        Intent intent =
            new Intent(this.mContext, TestReceiver.class);
        intent.putExtra("message", "Repeating Alarm");

        PendingIntent pi = this.getDistinctPendingIntent(intent, 2);
        // Schedule the alarm!
        AlarmManager am =
            (AlarmManager)
                this.mContext.getSystemService(Context.ALARM_SERVICE);

        am.setRepeating(AlarmManager.RTC_WAKEUP,
                cal.getTimeInMillis(),
                5*1000, //5 secs
                pi);
    }

    protected PendingIntent getDistinctPendingIntent
                            (Intent intent, int requestId)
```

```
    {
        PendingIntent pi =
            PendingIntent.getBroadcast(
              mContext,     //context
              requestId,     //request id
              intent,         //intent to be delivered
              0);
        return pi;
    }
}
```

Key elements of the code in Listing 15–16 are highlighted. The repeating alarm is set by invoking the `setRepeating()` method on the alarm manager object. One of the inputs to this method is a pending intent pointing to a receiver. We have used the same intent that was used in the `SendAlarmOnceTester` pointing to the `TestReceiver` broadcast receiver.

However, when we made a pending intent out of it, we have used a unique request code, such as 2. If we don't do this, we will see a bit of odd behavior. Say you click the menu item for repeating alarm first. This would schedule the alarm to go off repeatedly and call `TestReceiver`. Say this repeating alarm starts in 30 seconds. Now, you go ahead and click the menu item Alarm Once. This will schedule the alarm to go off just one time in 30 seconds and call the same `TestReceiver`.

If both these menu items worked, we would have seen both types of alarms go off. However, you will notice that the alarm will go off only one time. To make this work right, you have to use a different `requestcode` on the pending intent. We will go into the reasoning for `requestcode` in the "Primacy of PendingIntent" section.

Compiling Code for This Example

To test this portion of the code, you will need to add/change a couple of files in the project.

First, you will need to add the file listed in Listing 15–16 as a new source file called `SendRepeatingAlarmTester.java`.

Then, you need to change the driver activity `TestAlarmsDriverActivity` in Listing 15–12 in a couple of places.

Replace the following lines

```
private SendAlarmOnceTester alarmTester = null;
...
alarmTester = new SendAlarmOnceTester(this,this);
```

with

```
private SendRepeatingAlarmTester alarmTester = null;
...
alarmTester = new SendRepeatingAlarmTester(this,this);
```

Add the following code to respond to the menu:

```
if (item.getItemId() == R.id.menu_alarm_repeated)
{
```

```
    alarmTester.sendRepeatingAlarm();
    return true;
}
```

With these changes in place, you can use Figure 15–1 to invoke the Alarm Repeat menu item to test this exercise. You will see the results of this test in LogCat. Next, let's look at how to cancel a repeating alarm.

Cancelling an Alarm

To help you understand how to cancel an alarm, we'll use another tester called CancelRepeatingAlarmTester (see Listing 15–17).

Listing 15–17. ***Cancelling a Repeating Alarm***

```
// CancelRepeatingAlarmTester.java
package com.androidbook.alarms;
import android.app.AlarmManager;
import android.app.PendingIntent;
import android.content.Context;
import android.content.Intent;

public class CancelRepeatingAlarmTester
extends SendRepeatingAlarmTester
{
    private static String tag = "CancelRepeatingAlarmTester";
    CancelRepeatingAlarmTester(Context ctx, IReportBack target) {
        super(ctx, target);
    }
    /*
     * An alarm can be stopped by canceling the intent.
     * You will need to have a copy of the intent
     * to cancel it.
     *
     * The intent needs to have the same signature
     * and request id.
     */
    public void cancelRepeatingAlarm()
    {
        //Get an intent to invoke
        //TestReceiver class
        Intent intent =
            new Intent(this.mContext, TestReceiver.class);

        //To cancel, extra is not necessary to be filled in
        //intent.putExtra("message", "Repeating Alarm");

        PendingIntent pi = this.getDistinctPendingIntent(intent, 2);

        // Schedule the alarm!
        AlarmManager am =
            (AlarmManager)
               this.mContext.getSystemService(Context.ALARM_SERVICE);
        am.cancel(pi);
        this.mReportTo.reportBack(tag,"You shouldn't see alarms again");
    }
}
```

To cancel an alarm, we have to construct a pending intent first and then pass it to the alarm manager as an argument to the cancel() method.

However, you must pay attention to make sure that the pendingintent is constructed the exact same way when setting the alarm, including the request code and targeted receiver. Examine the source code for getDistinctPendingIntent() in Listing 15–16 to see how the request code is used with PendingIntent.getBroadcast()—you can ignore the intent extras in Listing 15–17 because intent extras don't play a role in cancelling that intent.

Compiling code for this example

Before you can test this portion of the code, you will need to add/change a couple of files in the project.

First, you will need to add the new file listed in Listing 15–17 as a new source file called CancelRepeatingAlarmTester.java.

Then, you need to change the driver activity TestAlarmsDriverActivity in Listing 15–12 in a couple of places as outlined below.

Replace the following lines

```
private SendAlarmOnceTester alarmTester = null;
…
alarmTester = new SendAlarmOnceTester(this,this);
```

with

```
private CancelRepeatingAlarmTester alarmTester = null;
…
alarmTester = new CancelRpeatingAlarmTester(this,this);
```

Add the following code to respond to the menu:

```
if (item.getItemId() == R.id.menu_alarm_cancel)
{
  alarmTester.cancelRepeatingAlarm();
  return true;
}
```

You can test this functionality by first selecting the Alarm Repeat menu item (see Figure 15–1). This will start updating the logcat every 5 seconds. Now, if you click the Cancel Alarms menu item, the messages will stop.

Working with Multiple Alarms

When it comes to setting multiple alarms pointing to the same receiver, in our opinion, there is a bit of unintuitive behavior attached to alarm managers—if you invoke an alarm pointing to a particular receiver multiple times, only the last invocation takes effect.

To explain this behavior, first examine the tester we have prepared in Listing 15–18. There are two methods in this listing. The first one, scheduleSameIntentMultipleTimes(), schedules the same Intent multiple times. The second function, scheduleDistinctIntents(), does the same but distinguishes the intents with the aid of the request ID.

Listing 15–18. *Working with Multiple Alarms*

```
//ScheduleIntentMultipleTimesTester.java
package com.androidbook.alarms;
import java.util.Calendar;
import android.app.AlarmManager;
import android.app.PendingIntent;
import android.content.Context;
import android.content.Intent;

public class ScheduleIntentMultipleTimesTester
extends CancelRepeatingAlarmTester
{
    private static String tag = "ScheduleIntentMultipleTimesTester";
    ScheduleIntentMultipleTimesTester(Context ctx, IReportBack target){
        super(ctx, target);
    }
    /*
     * Same intent cannot be scheduled multiple times.
     * If you do, only the last one will take affect.
     *
     * Notice you are using the same request id.
     */
    public void scheduleSameIntentMultipleTimes()
    {
        //Get multiple time instances
        Calendar cal = Utils.getTimeAfterInSecs(30);
        Calendar cal2 = Utils.getTimeAfterInSecs(35);
        Calendar cal3 = Utils.getTimeAfterInSecs(40);
        Calendar cal4 = Utils.getTimeAfterInSecs(45);

        //Print to the debug view that we are
        //scheduling at a specific time
        String s = Utils.getDateTimeString(cal);
        mReportTo.reportBack(tag, "Schdeduling alarm at: " + s);

        //Get an intent to invoke a receiver
        Intent intent =
            new Intent(mContext, TestReceiver.class);
        intent.putExtra("message", "Same intent multiple times");

        PendingIntent pi = this.getDistinctPendingIntent(intent, 1);

        // Schedule this same intent multiple times
        AlarmManager am =
            (AlarmManager)
                 mContext.getSystemService(Context.ALARM_SERVICE);

        am.set(AlarmManager.RTC_WAKEUP,
                cal.getTimeInMillis(),
                pi);

        am.set(AlarmManager.RTC_WAKEUP,
                cal2.getTimeInMillis(),
```

```
                pi);
        am.set(AlarmManager.RTC_WAKEUP,
                cal3.getTimeInMillis(),
                pi);
        am.set(AlarmManager.RTC_WAKEUP,
                cal4.getTimeInMillis(),
                pi);
    }
    /*
     * Same intent can be scheduled multiple times
     * if you change the request id on the pending intent.
     * Request id identifies an intent as a unique intent.
     */
    public void scheduleDistinctIntents()
    {
        //Get the instance in time that is
        //30 secs from now.
        Calendar cal = Utils.getTimeAfterInSecs(30);
        Calendar cal2 = Utils.getTimeAfterInSecs(35);
        Calendar cal3 = Utils.getTimeAfterInSecs(40);
        Calendar cal4 = Utils.getTimeAfterInSecs(45);

        //If you want to point to 11:00 hours today.
        //Calendar cal = Utils.getTodayAt(11);

        //Print to the debug view that we are
        //scheduling at a specific time
        String s = Utils.getDateTimeString(cal);
        mReportTo.reportBack(tag, "Schdeduling alarm at: " + s);

        //Get an intent to invoke
        //TestReceiver class
        Intent intent =
            new Intent(mContext, TestReceiver.class);
        intent.putExtra("message", "Schedule distinct alarms");

        //Schedule the same intent but with different req ids.
        AlarmManager am =
            (AlarmManager)
                 mContext.getSystemService(Context.ALARM_SERVICE);

        am.set(AlarmManager.RTC_WAKEUP,
                cal.getTimeInMillis(),
                getDistinctPendingIntent(intent,1));

        am.set(AlarmManager.RTC_WAKEUP,
                cal2.getTimeInMillis(),
                getDistinctPendingIntent(intent,2));
        am.set(AlarmManager.RTC_WAKEUP,
                cal3.getTimeInMillis(),
                getDistinctPendingIntent(intent,3));
        am.set(AlarmManager.RTC_WAKEUP,
                cal4.getTimeInMillis(),
                getDistinctPendingIntent(intent,4));
    }
}
```

In the code of method `scheduleSameIntentMultipleTimes` (), we have taken the same intent and scheduled it four times. You will see that when you test this by selecting the Multiple Alarms menu item: only the last alarm was fired, and none of the previous ones were.

The recommended way to fix this is to change the code so that each pending intent has a different request ID. This is why we have a function `getDistinctPendingIntent` (), which quickly creates pending intents based on request ID. Listing 15–16 shows the source code for this function.

You can fix the duplicate intent problem by looking at the `scheduleDistinctIntents()` method of Listing 15–18. Here, we have varied the request ID, so the `TestReceiver` will get called multiple times, and you will see the evidence of this in LogCat.

When you create a pending intent, the Android development team strongly recommends that you keep the following in mind:

Don't uniquely create pending intents randomly in multiplicity. Pay attention if you are creating a lot of unique pending intents varying the request ID or any other aspect of an intent.

A pending intent is expected to be able to be quickly re-created by the sender so that it can be cancelled.This implies there is a natural order to creating a pending intent. Ideally, the parameters that are used to create an intent should be unique. If they are not and if you need to use request IDs to make the intent unique, remember the request IDs you have used to create the pending intents. You will need them when you intent to cancel the pending intents later.

Without a request ID, two pending intents point to the same intent as long as their key attributes are the same. Intent extras are not considered for intent equivalence.

The get methods for a pending intent usually locate an existing pending intent rather than creating a new one.

Pending intents typically should point to a specific class or component.

Compiling Code for This Example

Before you can test this portion of the code, you will need to add/change a couple of files in the project.

First, you will need to add the file listed in Listing 15–18 as a new source file called `CancelRepeatingAlarmTester.java`.

Then, you need to change the driver activity `TestAlarmsDriverActivity` in Listing 15–12 in a couple of places.

Replace the following lines

```
private SendAlarmOnceTester alarmTester = null;
...
alarmTester = new SendAlarmOnceTester(this,this);
```

with

```
private ScheduleIntentMultipleTimesTester alarmTester = null;
...
alarmTester = new ScheduleIntentMultipleTimesTester (this,this);
```

Add the following code to respond to the two menu items in this example:

```
if (item.getItemId() == R.id.menu_alarm_multiple)
{
    alarmTester.scheduleSameIntentMultipleTimes();
    return true;
}
if (item.getItemId() == R.id.menu_alarm_distinct_intents)
{
    alarmTester.scheduleDistinctIntents();
    return true;
}
```

Once you can make these code changes and compile, you can test the functionality of this exercise by using the two menu items Multiple Alarms and Distinct Intents. You will see the result of these menu items in LogCat.

Intent Primacy in Setting Off Alarms

We have mentioned a number of times so far that if you set alarms on the same type of intent, only the last alarm will take effect. Let's explore the reason behind this. Throughout the code examples, you might think that we are setting an alarm on the alarm manager. At least, that is the impression the API is giving us by exposing the following method:

```
alarmManager.set(time, intent);
```

However, assume we do the following:

```
alarmManager.set(time1, intent1);
alarmManager.setRepeated(time2, interval,  intent1);
```

You might have expected that the `intent1` object would just be a passive receiver and get invoked by both the alarms. However, in practice only the last `set` method counts. This is as if we are doing a set on the intent as in the following example:

```
intent1.set(...)
intent1.setRepeated(..)
```

In this case, it probably makes sense that you have just one intent object and one alarm against it and that if you set it multiple times you are resetting the previous alarm, just like an alarm clock on your desk.

This idea is tested using the tester listed in Listing 15–19. The method of interest in this listing is `alarmIntentPrimacy()`.

Listing 15–19. *Code to Test Intent Primacy*

```
//AlarmIntentPrimacyTester.java
package com.androidbook.alarms;
import java.util.Calendar;
import android.app.AlarmManager;
import android.app.PendingIntent;
import android.content.Context;
import android.content.Intent;

public class AlarmIntentPrimacyTester
extends ScheduleIntentMultipleTimesTester
{
    private static String tag = "AlarmIntentPrimacyTester";
    AlarmIntentPrimacyTester(Context ctx, IReportBack target){
        super(ctx, target);
    }
    /*
     * It is not the alarm that matters
     * but the pending intent.
     * Even with a repeating alarm for an intent,
     * if you schedule the same intent again
     * for one time, the later one takes affect.
     *
     * It is as if you are setting the
     * alarm on an existing intent multiple
     * times and not the other way around.
     */
    public void alarmIntentPrimacy()
    {
        Calendar cal = Utils.getTimeAfterInSecs(30);
        String s = Utils.getDateTimeString(cal);
        this.mReportTo.reportBack(tag,
            "Schdeduling Repeating alarm in 5 sec interval starting at: " + s);

        //Get an intent to invoke
        //TestReceiver class
        Intent intent =
            new Intent(this.mContext, TestReceiver.class);
        intent.putExtra("message", "Repeating Alarm");

        PendingIntent pi = getDistinctPendingIntent(intent,0);
        AlarmManager am =
            (AlarmManager)
                this.mContext.getSystemService(Context.ALARM_SERVICE);

        this.mReportTo.reportBack(tag,"Setting a repeat alarm 5 secs duration");
        am.setRepeating(AlarmManager.RTC_WAKEUP,
                cal.getTimeInMillis(),
                5*1000, //5 secs
                pi);

        this.mReportTo.reportBack(tag,"Setting a onetime alarm on the same intent");
        am.set(AlarmManager.RTC_WAKEUP,
                cal.getTimeInMillis(),
                pi);
        this.mReportTo.reportBack(tag,
             "The later alarm, one time one, takes precedence");
```

```
    }
}
```

Compiling Code for This Example

Before you can test this portion of the code, you will need to add/change a couple of files in the project.

First, you will need to add the file listed in Listing 15–19 as a new source file called `AlarmIntentPrimacyTester.java`.

Then, you need to change the driver activity `TestAlarmsDriverActivity` in Listing 15–12 in a couple of places.

Replace the following lines

```
private SendAlarmOnceTester alarmTester = null;
…
alarmTester = new SendAlarmOnceTester(this,this);
```

with

```
private AlarmIntentPrimacyTester alarmTester = null;
…
alarmTester = new AlarmIntentPrimacyTester (this,this);
```

Add the following code to respond to the menu item:

```
if (item.getItemId() == R.id.menu_alarm_intent_primacy)
{
    alarmTester.alarmIntentPrimacy();
    return true;
}
```

Once you make these code changes and compile, you can test the functionality of this exercise using the Intent Primacy menu item. You will see the result of these menu items in LogCat where the later alarm overwrites the previous one.

Why does the later alarm replace the prior one if set on the same intent?

Many folks in the Android developer group pointed out that two intents are really the will result in the same `PendingIntent` object if their attributes are the same. Setting those intents as targets for multiple alarms is like setting multiple alarm times on the same intent.

However, what is really happening becomes obvious when we look at the source code of the `AlarmManagerService` (this is an implementation of the `IAlarmManager` interface). Listing 15–20 contains the code segment that is used to set an alarm (all sets ultimately flow through this code).

Listing 15–20. ***AlarmManagerService implementation Extract from Android Source***

```
    public void setRepeating(int type, long triggerAtTime, long interval,
            PendingIntent operation) {
        if (operation == null) {
            Slog.w(TAG, "set/setRepeating ignored because there is no intent");
            return;
        }
        synchronized (mLock) {
```

```
            Alarm alarm = new Alarm();
            alarm.type = type;
            alarm.when = triggerAtTime;
            alarm.repeatInterval = interval;
            alarm.operation = operation;

            // Remove this alarm if already scheduled.
            removeLocked(operation);

            if (localLOGV) Slog.v(TAG, "set: " + alarm);

            int index = addAlarmLocked(alarm);
            if (index == 0) {
                setLocked(alarm);
            }
        }
    }
```

Notice that, in the middle of a set method, the code is calling `removeLocked(operation)`, where the `operation` argument is the `PendingIntent`. This essentially removes the previous alarm. In fact, when we call `cancel(pendingIntent)`, it ends up calling the same `removeLocked(pendingIntent)`.

In essence, the SDK chose to cancel the previous alarms and keep only the latest for that particular pending intent. If you want to do otherwise, you will need to qualify the pending intent with a request ID. This also becomes clear when we take a closer look at the `cancel()` API, which just takes the `PendingIntent` object. If the relationship between an alarm and a `PendingIntent` is not unique, what would be the meaning of cancelling an alarm based on a `PendingIntent` and nothing else?

Of course, you can also use this feature to your advantage if your goal is to cancel any previous alarms and set a new one for that particular receiver.

Persistence of Alarms

One final note on alarms is they are not persisted across device reboots. This means you will need to persist the alarm settings and pending intents in a persistent store and reregister them based on device reboot broadcast messages, and possibly time-change messages (e.g., `android.intent.action.BOOT_COMPLETED`, `ACTION_TIME_CHANGED`, `ACTION_TIMEZONE_CHANGED`).

Alarm Manager Predicates

Let's conclude the chapter by providing a quick summary of the facts surrounding alarms, pending intents, and the alarm manager:

Pending intents are intents kept in a pool and reused. You cannot new a pending intent. You really locate a pending intent with an option to reuse, update, and so on.

An intent is uniquely distinguished by its action, data URI, and category. The details of this uniqueness is specified in the filterEquals() API of the intent class.

A pending intent is further qualified (in addition to the base intent it depended on) by the request code.

Alarms and pending intents (even intents for that matter) are not independent. A given pending intent cannot be used for multiple alarms. The last alarm will override the previous alarms

Alarms are not persistent across boots. Whatever alarms you have set through the alarm manager will be lost when the device reboots.

You will need to persist alarm parameters yourself if you would like to retain them beyond device reboots. You will need to listen to broadcast boot event and time-change events to reset these alarms as needed.

The implication of the intent-based cancel API is that, when you use or persist alarms, you will also need to persist intents so that those alarms can be cancelled at a later time when needed.

References

The following references are useful to support material of this chapter. Especially note the last reference URL of this section, which allows you to download projects developed for this chapter.

http://developer.android.com/reference/android/app/AlarmManager.html: This is the alarm manager API. You will see here signatures for methods like set, setrepeating, and cancel.

http://developer.android.com/reference/android/app/PendingIntent.html: This site explains how to construct a pending intent. Don't pay too much attention to the pending intent flags; they are not that critical to the alarm manager.

http://www.androidbook.com/item/1040. You will see quick examples and some references to working with date and time classes here.

http://download.oracle.com/docs/cd/E17476_01/javase/1.4.2/docs/api/java/util/Calendar.html. You can use this resource to better understand how to work with the Calendar object.

http://www.androidbook.com/projects. You can see a list of downloadable projects from this book referenced here. For this chapter, look for a ZIP file named ProAndroid3_Ch15_TestAlarmManager.zip.

Summary

In this chapter, we used the alarm manager to run code at a given time and at specific intervals. This facility is important for updating home screen widgets and other time-sensitive operations. We also pointed out the odd things about the alarm manager and showed you how to work around those issues.

Chapter 16

Exploring 2D Animation

Animation allows an object on a screen to change its color, position, size, or orientation over time. Animation capabilities in Android are practical, fun, and simple, and they are used frequently.

Android 2.3 and prior release support three types of animation: frame-by-frame animation, which occurs when a series of frames is drawn one after the other at regular intervals; layout animation, in which you animate views inside a container view such as lists and tables; and view animation, in which you animate any general-purpose view. The latter two types fall into the category of tweening animation, which involves the drawings in between the key drawings.

NOTE: Android 3.0 enhanced animation by introducing the ability to animate the properties of UI elements. Some of these features, especially as they apply to the new concept of fragments, are covered in Chapter 29. As this chapter is completed prior to the release of 3.0, due to time constraints we cover in this chapter only 2.3 features. Chapter 29 covers a few of the 3.0 animation features.

Another way of explaining tweening animation is to say that it is *not* frame-by-frame animation. If you are able to accomplish animating a figure without repeating frames, you are primarily doing tweening animation. For example, if a figure is at location A now and will be at location B in 4 seconds, we can change the location every second and redraw the same figure. This will make the figure look like it is moving from A to B.

The idea is that knowing the beginning and ending states of a drawing allows an artist to vary certain aspect of the drawing in time. This varying aspect could be color, position, size, or some other element. With computers, you accomplish this kind of animation by changing the intermediate values at regular intervals and redrawing the surface.

In this chapter, we will cover frame-by-frame, layout, and view animation using working examples and in-depth analysis.

NOTE: We have given a URL at the end of the chapter that you can use to download projects from this chapter and import these projects into Eclipse directly.

Frame-by-Frame Animation

Frame-by-frame animation is the simple process of showing a series of images in succession at quick intervals so that the final effect is that of an object moving or changing. This is how movie projectors work. We'll explore an example in which we'll design an image and save that image as a number of distinct images, where each one differs slightly from the others. Then, we will take the collection of those images and run them through the sample code to simulate animation.

Planning for Frame-by-Frame Animation

Before you start writing code, you first need to plan the animation sequence using a series of drawings. As an example of this planning exercise, Figure 16–1 shows a set of same-sized circles with a colored ball on each of the circles placed at a different position. You can create a series of these pictures showing the circle at the same size and position with the colored ball at different points along the circle's border. Once you save seven or eight of these frames, you can use animation to suggest that the colored ball is moving around the circle.

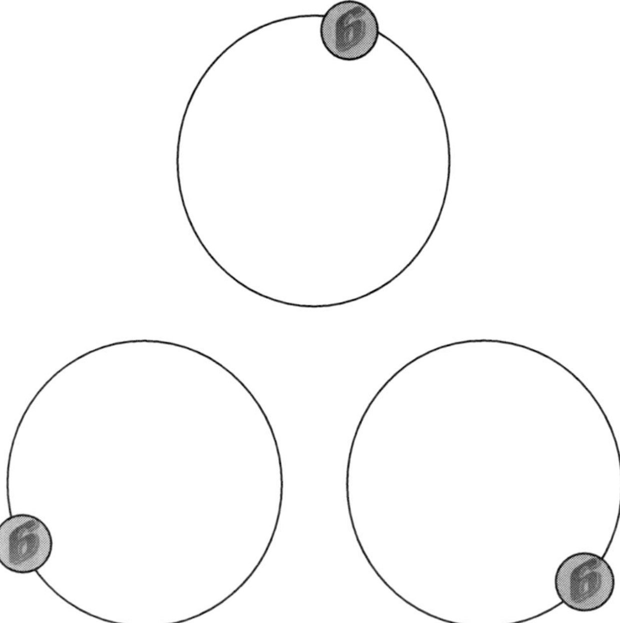

Figure 16–1. *Designing your animation before coding it*

Give the image a base name of `colored-ball`, and store eight of these images in the `/res/drawable` subdirectory so that you can access them using their resource IDs. The name of each image will have the pattern `colored-ballN`, where `N` is the digit representing the image number. When you have finished with the animation, you want it to look like Figure 16–2.

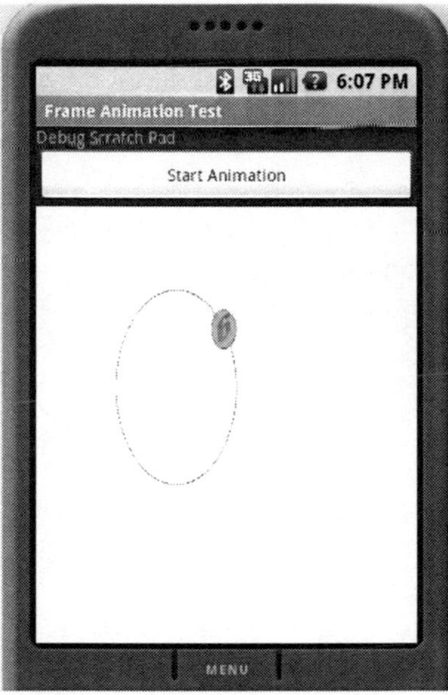

Figure 16–2. *A frame-by-frame animation test harness*

The primary area in this activity is used by the animation view. We have included a button to start and stop the animation to observe its behavior. We have also included a debug scratch pad at the top, so you can write any significant events to it as you experiment with this program. Let's see now how we could create the layout for such an activity.

Creating the Activity

Start by creating the basic XML layout file in the `/res/layout` subdirectory (see Listing 16–1).

Listing 16–1. *XML Layout File for the Frame Animation Example*

```
<?xml version="1.0" encoding="utf-8"?>
<!—filename: /res/layout/frame_animations_layout.xml -->
<LinearLayout xmlns:android="http://schemas.android.com/apk/res/android"
    android:orientation="vertical"
    android:layout_width="fill_parent"
    android:layout_height="fill_parent"
    >
<TextView android:id="@+id/textViewId1"
    android:layout_width="fill_parent"
    android:layout_height="wrap_content"
    android:text="Debug Scratch Pad"
```

```
    />
<Button
   android:id="@+id/startFAButtonId"
    android:layout_width="fill_parent"
    android:layout_height="wrap_content"
    android:text="Start Animation"
/>
<ImageView
        android:id="@+id/animationImage"
        android:layout_width="fill_parent"
      android:layout_height="wrap_content"
        />
</LinearLayout>
```

The first control is the debug-scratch text control, which is a simple `TextView`. You then add a button to start and stop the animation. The last view is the `ImageView`, where you will play the animation. Once you have the layout, create an activity to load this view (see Listing 16–2).

Listing 16–2. *Activity to Load the ImageView*

```
public class FrameAnimationActivity extends Activity
{
    @Override
    public void onCreate(Bundle savedInstanceState)
    {
        super.onCreate(savedInstanceState);
        setContentView(R.layout.frame_animations_layout);
    }
}
```

You will be able to run this activity from any menu item you might have in your current application by executing the following code:

```
Intent intent = new Intent(inActivity,FrameAnimationActivity.class);
inActivity.startActivity(intent);
```

At this point, you will see an activity that looks like the one in Figure 16–3.

Adding Animation to the Activity

Now that you have the activity and layout in place, we'll show you how to add animation to this sample. In Android, you accomplish frame-by-frame animation through a class in the graphics package called `AnimationDrawable`. You can tell from its name that it is like any other drawable that can work as a background for any view (for example, the background bitmaps are represented as `Drawables`). This class, `AnimationDrawable`, in addition to being a `Drawable`, can take a list of other `Drawable` resources (like images) and render them at specified intervals. This class is really a thin wrapper around the animation support provided by the basic `Drawable` class.

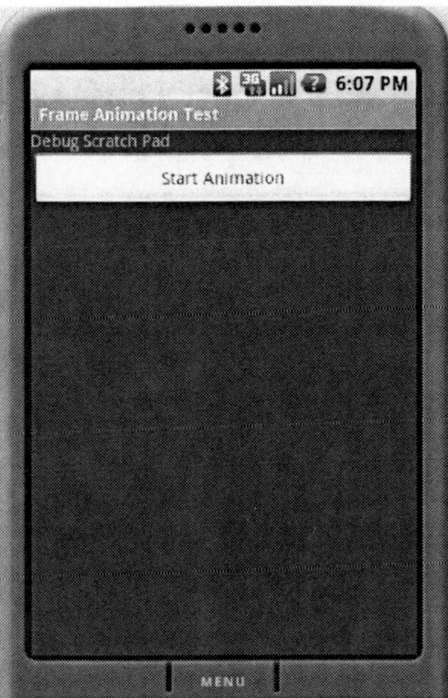

Figure 16–3. *Frame-by-frame animation activity*

> **TIP:** The `Drawable` class enables animation by asking its container or view to invoke a `Runnable` class that essentially redraws the `Drawable` using a different set of parameters. Note that you don't need to know these internal implementation details to use the `AnimationDrawable` class. But if your needs are more complex, you can look at the `AnimationDrawable` source code for guidance in writing your own animation protocols.

To make use of the `AnimationDrawable` class, start with a set of `Drawable` resources (for example, a set of images) placed in the `/res/drawable` subdirectory. In our case, these will be the eight similar, but slightly different, images that we talked about in the "Planning for Frame-by-Frame Animation" section. You will then construct an XML file that defines the list of frames (see Listing 16–3). This XML file will need to be placed in the `/res/drawable` subdirectory as well.

Listing 16–3. *XML File Defining the List of Frames to Be Animated*

```
<animation-list xmlns:android="http://schemas.android.com/apk/res/android"
android:oneshot="false">
   <item android:drawable="@drawable/colored_ball1" android:duration="50" />
   <item android:drawable="@drawable/colored_ball2" android:duration="50" />
   <item android:drawable="@drawable/colored_ball3" android:duration="50" />
   <item android:drawable="@drawable/colored_ball4" android:duration="50" />
   <item android:drawable="@drawable/colored_ball5" android:duration="50" />
   <item android:drawable="@drawable/colored_ball6" android:duration="50" />
   <item android:drawable="@drawable/colored_ball7" android:duration="50" />
   <item android:drawable="@drawable/colored_ball8" android:duration="50" />
</animation-list>
```

NOTE: As you prepare this list of images, we have to draw attention to some limitations of the AnimationDrawable class. This class loads all images into memory before it starts animation. When we tested this in the Android 2.3 emulator, a set of images greater than six exceeds the memory limitations allocated for each application. Depending on your test bed, you may need to restrict how many frames you have. To overcome this limitation, you will need to directly use the animation capabilities of Drawable and roll your own solution. Unfortunately, we haven't covered the Drawable class in detail in this edition of this book. Please check www.androidbook.com, as we intend to post an update soon.

Each frame points to one of the colored-ball images you have assembled through their resource IDs. The animation-list tag essentially gets converted into an AnimationDrawable object representing the collection of images. You then need to set this Drawable as a background resource for our ImageView in the sample. Assuming that the file name for this XML file is frame_animation.xml and that it resides in the /res/drawable subdirectory, you can use the following code to set the AnimationDrawable as the background of the ImageView:

```
view.setBackGroundResource(Resource.drawable.frame_animation);
```

With this code, Android realizes that the resource ID Resource.drawable.frame_animation is an XML resource and accordingly constructs a suitable AnimationDrawable Java object for it before setting it as the background. Once this is set, you can access this AnimationDrawable object by doing a get on the view object like this:

```
Object  backgroundObject = view.getBackground();
AnimationDrawable ad = (AnimationDrawable)backgroundObject;
```

Once you have the AnimationDrawable object, you can use its start() and stop() methods to start and stop the animation. Here are two other important methods on this object:

```
setOneShot();
addFrame(drawable, duration);
```

The setOneShot() method runs the animation once and then stops. The addFrame() method adds a new frame using a Drawable object and sets its display duration. The functionality of the addFrame() method resembles that of the XML tag android:drawable.

Put this all together to get the complete code for our frame-by-frame animation test harness (see Listing 16–4).

Listing 16–4. *Complete Code for the Frame-by-Frame Animation Test Harness*

```
public class FrameAnimationActivity extends Activity {
    @Override
    public void onCreate(Bundle savedInstanceState)
    {
        super.onCreate(savedInstanceState);
        setContentView(R.layout.frame_animations_layout);
```

```
        this.setupButton();
    }

    private void setupButton()
    {
       Button b = (Button)this.findViewById(R.id.startFAButtonId);
       b.setOnClickListener(
             new Button.OnClickListener(){
                public void onClick(View v)
                {
                   parentButtonClicked(v);
                }
             });
    }
    private void parentButtonClicked(View v)
    {
       animate();
    }
    private void animate()
    {
        ImageView imgView =
          (ImageView)findViewById(R.id.animationImage);
        imgView.setVisibility(ImageView.VISIBLE);
        imgView.setBackgroundResource(R.drawable.frame_animation);

        AnimationDrawable frameAnimation =
           (AnimationDrawable) imgView.getBackground();

        if (frameAnimation.isRunning())
        {
            frameAnimation.stop();
        }
        else
        {
            frameAnimation.stop();
            frameAnimation.start();
        }
    }
}//eof-class
```

The `animate()` method locates the `ImageView` in the current activity and sets its background to the `AnimationDrawable` identified by the resource `R.drawable.frame_animation`. The code then retrieves this object and performs the animation. The Start/Stop button is set up such that if the animation is running, clicking the button will stop it; if the animation is in a stopped state, clicking the button will start it.

Note that, if you set the `OneShot` parameter of the animation list to `true`, the animation will stop after executing once. However, there is no clear-cut way to know when that happens. Although the animation ends when it plays the last picture, you have no callback telling you when it finishes. Because of this, there isn't a direct way to invoke another action in response to the completed animation.

That drawback aside, you can bring great visual effects to bear by drawing a number of images in succession through the simple process of frame-by-frame animation.

Layout Animation

Like frame-by-frame animation, layout animation is pretty simple. As the name suggests, layout animation is dedicated to certain types of views laid out in a particular manner. For instance, you'll use layout animation with `ListView` and `GridView`, which are two commonly used layout controls in Android. Specifically, you'll use layout animation to add visual effects to the way each item in a `ListView` or `GridView` is displayed. In fact, you can use this type of animation on all controls derived from a `ViewGroup`.

Unlike frame-by-frame animation, layout animation is not achieved through repeating frames. Instead, it is achieved by changing the various properties of a view over time. Every view in Android has a transformation matrix that maps the view to the screen. By changing this matrix in a number of ways, you can accomplish scaling, rotation, and movement (translation) of the view. By changing the transparency of the view from `0` to `1`, for example, you can accomplish what is called an alpha animation.

Basic Tweening Animation Types

These are the basic tweening animation types in a bit more detail:

- *Scale animation*: You use this type of animation to make a view smaller or larger either along the x axis or on the y axis. You can also specify the pivot point around which you want the animation to take place.
- *Rotate animation*: You use this to rotate a view around a pivot point by a certain number of degrees.
- *Translate animation*: You use this to move a view along the x axis or the y axis.
- *Alpha animation*: You use this to change the transparency of a view.

You can define these animations as XML files in the `/res/anim` subdirectory. Listing 16–5 shows a quick sample of how one of these animations can be declared in an XML file

Listing 16–5. ***A Scale Animation Defined in an XML File at*** *`/res/anim/scale.xml`*

```
<set xmlns:android="http://schemas.android.com/apk/res/android"
android:interpolator="@android:anim/accelerate_interpolator">
   <scale
         android:fromXScale="1"
         android:toXScale="1"
         android:fromYScale="0.1"
         android:toYScale="1.0"
         android:duration="500"
         android:pivotX="50%"
         android:pivotY="50%"
         android:startOffset="100" />
</set>
```

All of the parameter values associated with these animation XML definitions have a "from" and a "to" flavor because you must specify the starting and ending values for the animation.

Each animation also allows duration and a time interpolator as arguments. We'll cover interpolators at the end of the section on layout animation, but for now, know that interpolators determine the rate of change of the animated argument during animation.

Once you have this declarative animation file, you can associate this animation with a layout to animate the layout's constituent views.

NOTE: This is a good place to point out that each of these animations is represented as a Java class in the `android.view.animation` package. The Java documentation for each of these classes describes not only its Java methods but also the allowed XML arguments for each type of animation.

Now that you have enough background on animation types and understand a little bit about layout animation, let's design an example.

Planning the Layout Animation Test Harness

You can test all the layout-animation concepts we've covered using a simple `ListView` set in an activity. Once you have a `ListView`, you can attach an animation to it so that each list item will go through that animation.

Assume you have a scale animation in mind that makes a view grow from zero to its original size on the y axis. Visually this is equivalent to a line of text starting as a horizontal line and become fatter to grow to its actual font size.

You can attach such an animation to a `ListView`. When this happens, the `ListView` will animate each item in that list using this animation.

You can set some additional parameters that extend the basic animation, such as animating the list items from top to bottom or from bottom to top. You specify these parameters through an intermediate class that acts as a mediator between the individual animation XML file and the list view.

You can define both the individual animation and the mediator in XML files in the `/res/anim` subdirectory. Once you have the mediator XML file, you can use that file as an input to the `ListView` in its XML layout definition. Once you have this basic setup working, you can start altering the individual animations to see how they impact the `ListView` display.

Before we embark on this exercise, let us show you what the `ListView` will look like after the animation completes (see Figure 16–4).

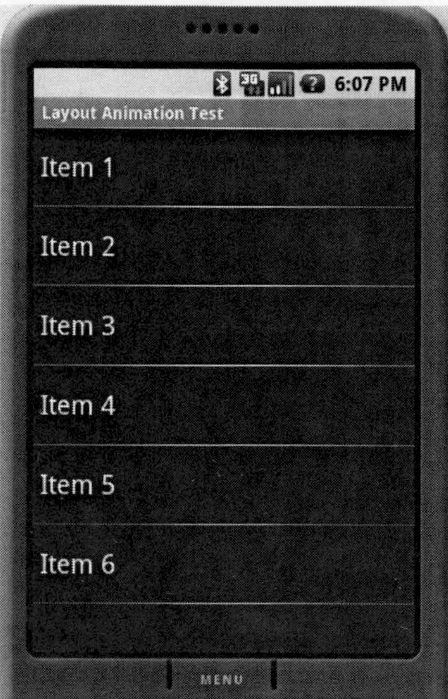

Figure 16–4. *The ListView we will animate*

Creating the Activity and the ListView

Start by creating an XML layout for the `ListView` in Figure 16–4 so you can load that layout in a basic activity. Listing 16–6 contains a simple layout with a `ListView` in it. You will need to place this file in the `/res/layout` subdirectory. Assuming the file name is `list_layout.xml`, your complete file will reside in `/res/layout/list_layout.xml`.

Listing 16–6. *XML Layout File Defining the ListView*

```
<?xml version="1.0" encoding="utf-8"?>
<!-- filename: /res/layout/list_layout.xml -->
<LinearLayout xmlns:android="http://schemas.android.com/apk/res/android"
    android:orientation="vertical"
    android:layout_width="fill_parent"
    android:layout_height="fill_parent"
    >

    <ListView
        android:id="@+id/list_view_id"
        android:layout_width="fill_parent"
        android:layout_height="fill_parent"
        />
</LinearLayout>
```

Listing 16–6 shows a simple `LinearLayout` with a single `ListView` in it. However, we should take this opportunity to mention one point about the `ListView` definition that is somewhat tangentially related to this chapter. If you happen to work through the

Notepad examples and other Android examples, you'll see that the ID for a ListView is usually specified as @android:id/list. As we discussed in Chapter 3, the resource reference @android:id/list points to an ID that is predefined in the android namespace. The question is, when do we use this android:id vs. our own ID such as @+id/list_view_id?

You will need to use @android:id/list only if the activity is a ListActivity. A ListActivity assumes that a ListView identified by this predetermined ID is available for loading. In this case, you're using a general-purpose activity rather than a ListActivity, and you are going to explicitly populate the ListView yourself. As a result, there are no restrictions on the kind of ID you can allocate to represent this ListView. However, you do have the option of also using @android:id/list because it doesn't conflict with anything as there is no ListActivity in sight.

This surely is a digression, but it's worth noting as you create your own ListViews outside a ListActivity. Now that you have the layout needed for the activity, you can write the code for the activity to load this layout file so you can generate your UI (see Listing 16–7).

Listing 16–7. *Code for the Layout-Animation Activity*

```
public class LayoutAnimationActivity extends Activity
{
    @Override
    public void onCreate(Bundle savedInstanceState)
    {
        super.onCreate(savedInstanceState);
        setContentView(R.layout.list_layout);
        setupListView();
    }
    private void setupListView()
    {
          String[] listItems = new String[] {
                "Item 1", "Item 2", "Item 3",
                "Item 4", "Item 5", "Item 6",
          };

          ArrayAdapter listItemAdapter =
               new ArrayAdapter(this
                       ,android.R.layout.simple_list_item_1
                       ,listItems);
          ListView lv = (ListView)this.findViewById(R.id.list_view_id);
          lv.setAdapter(listItemAdapter);
    }
}
```

Some of the code in Listing 16–7 is obvious, and some is not. The first part of the code simply loads the view based on the generated layout ID R.layout.list_layout. Our goal is to take the ListView from this layout and populate it with six text items. These text items are loaded into an array. You'll need to set a data adapter into a ListView so that the ListView can show those items.

To create the necessary adapter, you will need to specify how each item will be laid out when the list is displayed. You specify the layout by using a predefined layout in the base Android framework. In this example, this layout is specified as follows:

```
android.R.layout.simple_list_item_1
```

The other possible view layouts for these items include

```
simple_list_item_2
simple_list_item_checked
simple_list_item_multiple_choice
simple_list_item_single_choice
```

You can refer to the Android documentation to see how each of these layouts looks and behaves. You can now invoke this activity from any menu item in your application using the following code:

```
Intent intent = new Intent(inActivity,LayoutAnimationActivity.class);
inActivity.startActivity(intent);
```

However, as with any other activity invocation, you will need to register the LayoutAnimationActivity in the AndroidManifest.xml file for the preceding intent invocation to work. Here is the code for it:

```
<activity android:name=".LayoutAnimationActivity"
        android:label="View Animation Test Activity"/>
```

Animating the ListView

Now that you have the test harness ready (see Listings 16–6 and 16–7), you'll learn how to apply scale animation to this ListView. Take a look at how this scale animation is defined in an XML file (see Listing 16–8).

Listing 16–8. *Defining Scale Animation in an XML File*

```
<set xmlns:android="http://schemas.android.com/apk/res/android"
android:interpolator="@android:anim/accelerate_interpolator">
   <scale
         android:fromXScale="1"
         android:toXScale="1"
         android:fromYScale="0.1"
         android:toYScale="1.0"
         android:duration="500"
         android:pivotX="50%"
         android:pivotY="50%"
         android:startOffset="100" />
</set>
```

As indicated earlier, these animation-definition files reside in the /res/anim subdirectory.

Let's break down these XML attributes into plain English.

The from and to scales point to the starting and ending magnification factors. The magnification starts at 1 and stays at 1 on the x axis. This means the list items will not grow or shrink on the x axis.

On the y axis, however, the magnification starts at `0.1` and grows to `1.0`. In other words, the object being animated starts at one-tenth of its normal size and then grows to reach its normal size.

The scaling operation will take `500` milliseconds to complete.

The center of action is halfway (`50%`) in both x and y directions.

The `startOffset` value refers to the number of milliseconds to wait before starting the animation.

The parent node of scale animation points to an animation set that could allow more than one animation to be in effect. We will cover one of those examples as well, but for now, there is only one animation in this set.

Name this file `scale.xml`, and place it in the `/res/anim` subdirectory. You are not yet ready to set this animation XML as an argument to the `ListView`; the `ListView` first requires another XML file that acts as a mediator between itself and the animation set. The XML file that describes that mediation is shown in Listing 16–9.

Listing 16–9. ***Definition for a Layout-Controller XML File***

```
<layoutAnimation xmlns:android="http://schemas.android.com/apk/res/android"
        android:delay="30%"
        android:animationOrder="reverse"
        android:animation="@anim/scale" />
```

You will also need to place this XML file in the `/res/anim` subdirectory. For our example, assume that the file name is `list_layout_controller`. Once you look at this definition, you can see why this intermediate file is necessary.

This XML file specifies that the animation in the list should proceed in reverse, and that the animation for each item should start with a 30 percent delay with respect to the total animation duration. This XML file also refers to the individual animation file, `scale.xml`. Also notice that instead of the file name, the code uses the resource reference `@anim/scale`.

Now that you have the necessary XML input files, we'll show you how to update the `ListView` XML definition to include this animation XML as an argument. First, review the XML files you have so far:

```
// individual scale animation
/res/anim/scale.xml

// the animation mediator file
/res/anim/list_layout_controller.xml

// the activity view layout file
/res/layout/list_layout.xml
```

With these files in place, you need to modify the XML layout file `list_layout.xml` to have the `ListView` point to the `list_layout_controller.xml` file (see Listing 16–10).

Listing 16–10. *The Updated Code for the `list_layout.xml` File*

```
<?xml version="1.0" encoding="utf-8"?>
<LinearLayout xmlns:android="http://schemas.android.com/apk/res/android"
    android:orientation="vertical"
    android:layout_width="fill_parent"
    android:layout_height="fill_parent"
    >
    <ListView
        android:id="@+id/list_view_id"
        android:persistentDrawingCache="animation|scrolling"
        android:layout_width="fill_parent"
        android:layout_height="fill_parent"
        android:layoutAnimation="@anim/list_layout_controller" />
        />
</LinearLayout>
```

The changed lines are highlighted in bold. `android:layoutAnimation` is the key tag, which points to the mediating XML file that defines the layout controller using the XML tag `layoutAnimation` (see Listing 16–9). The `layoutAnimation` tag, in turn, points to the individual animation, which in this case is the scale animation defined in `scale.xml`.

Android also recommends setting the `persistentDrawingCache` tag to optimize for animation and scrolling. Refer to the Android SDK documentation for more details on this tag.

When you update the `list_layout.xml` file, as shown in Listing 16–10, Eclipse's ADT plug-in will automatically recompile the package taking this change into account. If you were to run the application now, you would see the scale animation take effect on the individual items. We have set the duration to `500` milliseconds so that you can observe the scale change clearly as each item is drawn.

Now, you're in a position to experiment with different animation types. You'll try alpha animation next. To do this, create a file called `/res/anim/alpha.xml`, and populate it with the content from Listing 16–11.

Listing 16–11. *The alpha.xml File to Test Alpha Animation*

```
<alpha xmlns:android="http://schemas.android.com/apk/res/android"
       android:interpolator="@android:anim/accelerate_interpolator"
       android:fromAlpha="0.0" android:toAlpha="1.0" android:duration="1000" />
```

Alpha animation is responsible for controlling the fading of color. In this example, you are asking the alpha animation to go from invisible to full color in 1,000 milliseconds, or 1 second. Make sure the duration is 1 second or longer; otherwise, the color change is hard to notice.

Every time you want to change the animation of an individual item like this, you will need to change the mediator XML file (see Listing 16–9) to point to this new animation file. Here is how to change the animation from scale animation to alpha animation:

```
<layoutAnimation xmlns:android="http://schemas.android.com/apk/res/android"
        android:delay="30%"
        android:animationOrder="reverse"
        android:animation="@anim/alpha" />
```

The changed line in the `layoutAnimation` XML file is highlighted. Let's now try an animation that combines a change in position with a change in color gradient. Listing 16–12 shows the sample XML for this animation.

Listing 16–12. *Combining Translate and Alpha Animations Through an Animation Set*

```
<set xmlns:android="http://schemas.android.com/apk/res/android"
android:interpolator="@android:anim/accelerate_interpolator">
    <translate android:fromYDelta="-100%" android:toYDelta="0"
android:duration="500" />
    <alpha android:fromAlpha="0.0" android:toAlpha="1.0"
android:duration="500" />
</set>
```

Notice how we have specified two animations in the animation set. The translate animation will move the text from top to bottom in its currently allocated display space. The alpha animation will change the color gradient from invisible to visible as the text item descends into its slot. The duration setting of `500` will allow the user to perceive the change in a comfortable fashion. Of course, you will have to change the `layoutAnimation` mediator XML file again with a reference to this file name. Assuming the file name for this combined animation is `/res/anim/translate_alpha.xml`, your `layoutAnimation` XML file will look like this:

```
<layoutAnimation xmlns:android="http://schemas.android.com/apk/res/android"
        android:delay="30%"
        android:animationOrder="reverse"
        android:animation="@anim/translate_alpha" />
```

Let's now look at how to use rotate animation (see Listing 16–13).

Listing 16–13. *Rotate Animation XML File*

```
<rotate xmlns:android="http://schemas.android.com/apk/res/android"
       android:interpolator="@android:anim/accelerate_interpolator"
       android:fromDegrees="0.0"
      android:toDegrees="360"
      android:pivotX="50%"
      android:pivotY="50%"
      android:duration="500" />
```

The code in Listing 16–13 will spin each text item in the list one full circle around the midpoint of the text item. The duration of `500` milliseconds is a good amount of time for the user to perceive the rotation. As before, to see this effect you must change the layout controller XML file and the `ListView` XML layout file and then rerun the application.

Now, we've covered the basic concepts in layout animation, where we start with a simple animation file and associate it with a `ListView` through an intermediate `layoutAnimation` XML file. That's all you need to do to see the animated effects. However, we need to talk about one more thing with regard to layout animation: interpolators.

Using Interpolators

Interpolators tell an animation how a certain property, such as a color gradient, changes over time. Will it change in a linear or exponential fashion? Will it start quickly but slow down toward the end? Consider the alpha animation that we introduced in Listing 16–11:

```
<alpha xmlns:android="http://schemas.android.com/apk/res/android"
       android:interpolator="@android:anim/accelerate_interpolator"
       android:fromAlpha="0.0" android:toAlpha="1.0" android:duration="1000" />
```

The animation identifies the interpolator it wants to use—`accelerate_interpolator`, in this case. There is a corresponding Java object that defines this interpolator. Also, note that we've specified this interpolator as a resource reference. This means there must be a file corresponding to the `anim/accelerate_interpolator` that describes what this Java object looks like and what additional parameters it might take. That indeed is the case. Look at the XML file definition for `@android:anim/accelerate_interpolator`:

```
<accelerateInterpolator
  xmlns:android="http://schemas.android.com/apk/res/android"
  factor="1" />
```

You can see this XML file in the following subdirectory within the Android package:

```
/res/anim/accelerate_interpolator.xml
```

The `accelerateInterpolator` XML tag corresponds to a Java object with this name:

```
android.view.animation.AccelerateInterpolator
```

You can look up the Java documentation for this class to see what XML tags are available. This interpolator's goal is to provide a multiplication factor given a time interval based on a hyperbolic curve. The source code for the interpolator illustrates this:

```
public float getInterpolation(float input)
{
   if (mFactor == 1.0f)
   {
      return (float)(input * input);
   }
   else
   {
      return (float)Math.pow(input, 2 * mFactor);
   }
}
```

Every interpolator implements this `getInterpolation` method differently. In this case, if the interpolator is set up so that the factor is `1.0`, it will return the square of the factor. Otherwise, it will return a power of the input that is further scaled by the factor. So if the factor is `1.5`, you will see a cubic function instead of a square function.

The supported interpolators include

```
AccelerateDecelerateInterpolator
AccelerateInterpolator
CycleInterpolator
DecelerateInterpolator
LinearInterpolator
```

```
AnticipateInterpolator
AnticipateOvershootInterpolator
BounceInterpolator
OvershootInterpolator
```

To see how flexible these interpolators can be, take a quick look at the `BounceInterpolator` which bounces the object (that is, moves it back and forth) toward the end of the following animation:

```
public class BounceInterpolator implements Interpolator {
    private static float bounce(float t) {
        return t * t * 8.0f;
    }

    public float getInterpolation(float t) {
        t *= 1.1226f;
        if (t < 0.3535f) return bounce(t);
        else if (t < 0.7408f) return bounce(t - 0.54719f) + 0.7f;
        else if (t < 0.9644f) return bounce(t - 0.8526f) + 0.9f;
        else return bounce(t - 1.0435f) + 0.95f;
    }
}
```

You can find the behavior of these interpolators described at the following URL:

`http://developer.android.com/reference/android/view/animation/package-summary.html`

The Java documentation for each of these classes also points out the XML tags available to control them. However, the description of what each interpolator does is hard to figure out from the documentation. The best approach is to try it out in an example and see the effect produced. You can also use this URL to search the online source code:

`http://android.git.kernel.org/?p=platform%2Fframeworks%2Fbase.git&a=search&h=HEAD&st=grep&s=BounceInterpolator`

This concludes our section on layout animation. We will now move to the third section on view animation, in which we'll discuss animating a view programmatically.

View Animation

Now that you're familiar with frame-by-frame animation and layout animation, you're ready to tackle view animation—the most complex of the three animation types. View animation allows you to animate any arbitrary view by manipulating the transformation matrix that is in place for displaying the view.

Understanding View Animation

When a view is displayed on a presentation surface in Android, it goes through a transformation matrix. In graphics applications, you use transformation matrices to transform a view in some way. The process involves taking the input set of pixel coordinates and color combinations and translating them into a new set of pixel coordinates and color combinations. At the end of a transformation, you will see an altered picture in terms of size, position, orientation, or color.

You can achieve all of these transformations mathematically by taking the input set of coordinates and multiplying them in some manner using a transformation matrix to arrive at a new set of coordinates. By changing the transformation matrix, you can impact how a view will look.

A matrix that *doesn't* change the view when you multiply with it is called an identity matrix. You typically start with an identity matrix and apply a series of transformations involving size, position, and orientation. You then take the final matrix and use that matrix to draw the view.

Android exposes the transformation matrix for a view by allowing you to register an animation object with that view. The animation object will have a callback that lets it obtain the current matrix for a view and change it in some manner to arrive at a new view. We will go through this process now.

Let's start by planning an example for animating a view. You'll begin with an activity where you'll place a `ListView` with a few items, similar to the way you began the example in the "Layout Animation" section. You will then create a button at the top of the screen to start the `ListView` animation when clicked (see Figure 16–5). Both the button and the `ListView` appear, but nothing has been animated yet. You'll use the button to trigger the animation.

When you click the Start Animation button in this example, you want the view to start small in the middle of the screen and gradually become bigger until it consumes all the space that is allocated for it. We'll show you how to write the code to make this happen. Listing 16–14 shows the XML layout file that you can use for the activity.

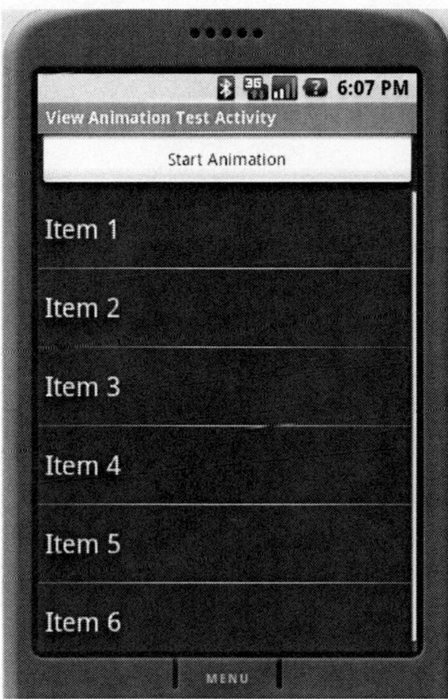

Figure 16–5. *The view-animation activity*

Listing 16–14. *XML Layout File for the View-Animation Activity*

```
<?xml version="1.0" encoding="utf-8"?>
<!-- This file is at /res/layout/list_layout.xml -->
<LinearLayout xmlns:android="http://schemas.android.com/apk/res/android"
    android:orientation="vertical"
    android:layout_width="fill_parent"
    android:layout_height="fill_parent"
    >
<Button
   android:id="@+id/btn_animate"
    android:layout_width="fill_parent"
    android:layout_height="wrap_content"
    android:text="Start Animation"
/>
<ListView
     android:id="@+id/list_view_id"
     android:persistentDrawingCache="animation|scrolling"
     android:layout_width="fill_parent"
     android:layout_height="fill_parent"
 />
</LinearLayout>
```

Notice that the file location and the file name are embedded at the top of the XML file for your reference. This layout has two parts: the first is the button named `btn_animate` to animate a view, and the second is the `ListView`, which is named `list_view_id`.

Now that you have the layout for the activity, you can create the activity to show the view and set up the Start Animation button (see Listing 16–15).

Listing 16–15. *Code for the View-Animation Activity, Before Animation*

```
public class ViewAnimationActivity extends Activity {

    @Override
    public void onCreate(Bundle savedInstanceState)
    {
        super.onCreate(savedInstanceState);
        setContentView(R.layout.list_layout);
        setupListView();
        this.setupButton();
    }
    private void setupListView()
    {
         String[] listItems = new String[] {
               "Item 1", "Item 2", "Item 3",
               "Item 4", "Item 5", "Item 6",
         };

         ArrayAdapter listItemAdapter =
             new ArrayAdapter(this
                     ,android.R.layout.simple_list_item_1
                     ,listItems);
         ListView lv = (ListView)this.findViewById(R.id.list_view_id);
         lv.setAdapter(listItemAdapter);
    }
    private void setupButton()
    {
       Button b = (Button)this.findViewById(R.id.btn_animate);
       b.setOnClickListener(
           new Button.OnClickListener(){
             public void onClick(View v)
             {
                //animateListView();
             }
           });
    }
}
```

The code for the view-animation activity in Listing 16–15 closely resembles the code for the layout-animation activity in Listing 16–7. We have similarly loaded the view and set up the ListView to contain six text items. We've set up the button in such a way that it would call animateListView() when clicked. But for now, comment out that part until you get this basic example running.

You can invoke this activity as soon as you register it in the AndroidManifest.xml file:

```
<activity android:name=".ViewAnimationActivity"
        android:label="View Animation Test Activity">
```

Once this registration is in place, you can invoke this view-animation activity from any menu item in your application by executing the following code:

```
Intent intent = new Intent(this, ViewAnimationActivity.class);
startActivity(intent);
```

When you run this program, you will see the UI as laid out in Figure 16–5.

Adding Animation

Our aim in this example is to add animation to the ListView shown in Figure 16–5. To do that, you need a class that derives from android.view.animation.Animation. You then need to override the applyTransformation method to modify the transformation matrix. Call this derived class ViewAnimation. Once you have the ViewAnimation class, you can do something like this on the ListView class:

```
ListView lv = (ListView)this.findViewById(R.id.list_view_id);
lv.startAnimation(new ViewAnimation());
```

Let us go ahead and show you the source code for ViewAnimation and discuss the kind of animation we want to accomplish (see Listing 16–16).

Listing 16–16. *Code for the ViewAnimation Class*

```
public class ViewAnimation extends Animation
{
  @Override
  public void initialize(int width, int height,
                         int parentWidth,
                         int parentHeight)
    {
        super.initialize(width, height, parentWidth, parentHeight);
        setDuration(2500);
        setFillAfter(true);
        setInterpolator(new LinearInterpolator());
    }
  @Override
  protected void
  applyTransformation(float interpolatedTime, Transformation t)
    {
        final Matrix matrix = t.getMatrix();
        matrix.setScale(interpolatedTime, interpolatedTime);
    }
}
```

The initialize method is a callback method that tells us about the dimensions of the view. This is also a place to initialize any animation parameters you might have. In this example, we have set the duration to be 2,500 milliseconds (2.5 seconds). We have also specified that we want the animation effect to remain intact after the animation completes by setting FillAfter to true. Plus, we've indicated that the interpolator is a linear interpolator, meaning that the animation changes in a gradual manner from start to finish. All of these properties come from the base android.view.animation.Animation class.

The main part of the animation occurs in the applyTransformation method. The Android framework will call this method again and again to simulate animation. Every time Android calls the method, interpolatedTime has a different value. This parameter changes from 0 to 1 depending on where you are in the 2.5-second duration that you set during initialization. When interpolatedTime is 1, you are at the end of the animation.

Our goal, then, is to change the transformation matrix that is available through the transformation object called t in the applyTransformation method. You will first get the matrix and change something about it. When the view gets painted, the new matrix will take effect. You can find the kinds of methods available on the Matrix object by looking up the API documentation for android.graphics.Matrix:

http://developer.android.com/reference/android/graphics/Matrix.html

In Listing 16–16, here is the code that changes the matrix:

```
matrix.setScale(interpolatedTime, interpolatedTime);
```

The setScale method takes two parameters: the scaling factor in the x direction and the scaling factor in the y direction. Because the interpolatedTime goes between 0 and 1, you can use that value directly as the scaling factor.

So when you start the animation, the scaling factor is 0 in both x and y directions. Halfway through the animation, this value will be 0.5 in both x and y directions. At the end of the animation, the view will be at its full size because the scaling factor will be 1 in both x and y directions. The end result of this animation is that the ListView starts out tiny and grows into full size.

Listing 16–17 shows the complete source code for the ViewAnimationActivity that includes the animation.

Listing 16–17. *Code for the View-Animation Activity, Including Animation*

```
public class ViewAnimationActivity extends Activity {

    @Override
    public void onCreate(Bundle savedInstanceState)
    {
        super.onCreate(savedInstanceState);
        setContentView(R.layout.list_layout);
        setupListView();
        this.setupButton();
    }
    private void setupListView()
    {
         String[] listItems = new String[] {
               "Item 1", "Item 2", "Item 3",
               "Item 4", "Item 5", "Item 6",
         };

         ArrayAdapter listItemAdapter =
             new ArrayAdapter(this
                     ,android.R.layout.simple_list_item_1
                     ,listItems);
         ListView lv = (ListView)this.findViewById(R.id.list_view_id);
         lv.setAdapter(listItemAdapter);
    }
    private void setupButton()
    {
       Button b = (Button)this.findViewById(R.id.btn_animate);
       b.setOnClickListener(
           new Button.OnClickListener(){
             public void onClick(View v)
             {
                animateListView();
```

```
            }
        });
    }
    private void animateListView()
    {
       ListView lv = (ListView)this.findViewById(R.id.list_view_id);
       lv.startAnimation(new ViewAnimation());
    }
}
```

When you run the code in Listing 16–17, you will notice something odd. Instead of uniformly growing larger from the middle of the screen, the `ListView` grows larger from the top-left corner. The reason is that the origin for the matrix operations is at the top-left corner. To get the desired effect, you first have to move the whole view so that the view's center matches the animation center (top-left). Then, you apply the matrix and move the view back to the previous center.

The code rewriting Listing 16–16 for doing this, is shown in Listing 16–18 with key elements highlighted.

Listing 16–18. *View Animation using preTranslate and postTranslate*

```
public class ViewAnimation extends Animation {
    float centerX, centerY;
    public ViewAnimation3(){}

    @Override
    public void initialize(int width, int height, int parentWidth, int parentHeight) {
        super.initialize(width, height, parentWidth, parentHeight);
        centerX = width/2.0f;
        centerY = height/2.0f;
        setDuration(2500);
        setFillAfter(true);
        setInterpolator(new LinearInterpolator());
    }
    @Override
    protected void applyTransformation(float interpolatedTime, Transformation t) {
        final Matrix matrix = t.getMatrix();
        matrix.setScale(interpolatedTime, interpolatedTime);
        matrix.preTranslate(-centerX, -centerY);
        matrix.postTranslate(centerX, centerY);
    }
}
```

The `preTranslate` and `postTranslate` methods set up a matrix before the scale operation and after the scale operation. This is equivalent to making three matrix transformations in tandem. The following code

```
        matrix.setScale(interpolatedTime, interpolatedTime);
        matrix.preTranslate(-centerX, -centerY);
        matrix.postTranslate(centerX, centerY);
```

is equivalent to

```
move to a different center
scale it
move to the original center
```

You will see this pattern of pre and post applied again and again. You can also accomplish this result using other methods on the Matrix class, but this technique is the most common—plus, it's succinct. We will, however, cover these other methods toward the end of this section.

More important, the Matrix class allows you not only to scale a view but also to move it around through translate methods and change its orientation through rotate methods. You can experiment with these methods and see what the resulting animation looks like. In fact, the animations presented in the preceding "Layout Animation" section are all implemented internally using the methods on this Matrix class.

Using Camera to Provide Depth Perception in 2D

The graphics package in Android provides another animation-related—or more accurately, transformation-related—class called Camera. You can use this class to provide depth perception by projecting a 2D image moving in 3D space onto a 2D surface. For example, you can take our ListView and move it back from the screen by 10 pixels along the z axis and rotate it by 30 degrees around the y axis. Listing 16–19 is an example of manipulating the matrix using Camera.

Listing 16–19. *Using Camera*

```
...
public class ViewAnimation extends Animation {
    float centerX, centerY;
    Camera camera = new Camera();
    public ViewAnimation1(float cx, float cy){
        centerX = cx;
        centerY = cy;
    }
    @Override
    public void initialize(int width, int height, int parentWidth, int parentHeight) {
        super.initialize(width, height, parentWidth, parentHeight);
        setDuration(2500);
        setFillAfter(true);
        setInterpolator(new LinearInterpolator());
    }
    @Override
    protected void applyTransformation(float interpolatedTime, Transformation t) {
        applyTransformationNew(interpolatedTime,t);
    }
    protected void applyTransformationNew(float interpolatedTime, Transformation t)
    {
        final Matrix matrix = t.getMatrix();
        camera.save();
        camera.translate(0.0f, 0.0f, (1300 - 1300.0f * interpolatedTime));
        camera.rotateY(360 * interpolatedTime);
        camera.getMatrix(matrix);

        matrix.preTranslate(-centerX, -centerY);
        matrix.postTranslate(centerX, centerY);
        camera.restore();
    }
}
```

This code animates the ListView by first placing the view 1,300 pixels back on the z axis and then bringing it back to the plane where the z coordinate is 0. While doing this, the code also rotates the view from 0 to 360 degrees around the y axis. Let's see how the code relates to this behavior by looking at the following method:

```
camera.translate(0.0f, 0.0f, (1300 - 1300.0f * interpolatedTime));
```

This method tells the camera object to translate the view such that when interpolatedTime is 0 (at the beginning of the animation), the z value will be 1300. As the animation progresses, the z value will get smaller and smaller until the end, when the interpolatedTime becomes 1 and the z value becomes 0.

The method camera.rotateY(360 * interpolatedTime) takes advantage of 3D rotation around an axis by the camera. At the beginning of the animation, this value will be 0. At the end of the animation, it will be 360.

The method camera.getMatrix(matrix) takes the operations performed on the Camera so far and imposes those operations on the matrix that is passed in. Once the code does that, the matrix has the translations it needs to get the end effect of having a Camera. Now the Camera is out of the picture (no pun intended) because the matrix has all the operations embedded in it. Then, you do the pre and post on the matrix to shift the center and bring it back. At the end, you set the Camera to its original state that was saved earlier.

When you plug this code into our example, you will see the ListView arriving from the center of the view in a spinning manner toward the front of the screen, as we intended when we planned our animation.

As part of our discussion about view animation, we showed you how to animate any view by extending an Animation class and then applying it to a view. In addition to letting you manipulate matrices (both directly and through a Camera class), the Animation class lets you detect various stages in an animation. We will cover this next.

Exploring the AnimationListener Class

Android uses a listener interface called AnimationListener to monitor animation events (see Listing 16–20). You can listen to these animation events by implementing the AnimationListener interface and setting that implementation against the Animation class implementation.

Listing 16–20. *An Implementation of the AnimationListener Interface*

```
public class ViewAnimationListener
implements Animation.AnimationListener {

    public ViewAnimationListener(){}

    public void onAnimationStart(Animation animation)
    {
        Log.d("Animation Example", "onAnimationStart");
    }
    public void onAnimationEnd(Animation animation)
```

```
    {
        Log.d("Animation Example", "onAnimationEnd");
    }
    public void onAnimationRepeat(Animation animation)
    {
        Log.d("Animation Example", "onAnimationRepeat");
    }
}
```

The `ViewAnimationListener` class just logs messages. You can update the `animateListView` method in the view-animation example (see Listing 16–17) to take the animation listener into account:

```
private void animateListView()
{
   ListView lv = (ListView)this.findViewById(R.id.list_view_id);
   ViewAnimation animation = new ViewAnimation();
   animation.setAnimationListener(new ViewAnimationListener());
   lv.startAnimation(animation);
}
```

Some Notes on Transformation Matrices

As you have seen in this chapter, matrices are key to transforming views and animations. We will now briefly explore some key methods of the `Matrix` class. These are the primary operations on a matrix:

```
matrix.reset();
matrix.setScale();
matrix.setTranslate()
matrix.setRotate();
matrix.setSkew();
```

The first operation resets a matrix to an identity matrix, which causes no change to the view when applied. `setScale` is responsible for changing size; `setTranslate` is responsible for changing position to simulate movement, and `setRotate` is responsible for changing orientation. `setSkew` is responsible for distorting a view.

You can concatenate matrices or multiply them together to compound the effect of individual transformations. Consider the following example, where `m1`, `m2`, and `m3` are identity matrices:

```
m1.setScale();
m2.setTranlate()
m3.concat(m1,m2)
```

Transforming a view by `m1` and then transforming the resulting view with `m2` is equivalent to transforming the same view by `m3`. Note that `set` methods replace the previous transformations, and that `m3.concat(m1,m2)` is different from `m3.concat(m2,m1)`.

You have already seen the pattern used by `preTranslate` and `postTranslate` methods to affect matrix transformation. In fact, `pre` and `post` methods are not unique to `translate`, and you have versions of `pre` and `post` for every one of the `set` transformation methods. Ultimately, a `preTranslate` such as `m1.preTranslate(m2)` is equivalent to

```
m1.concat(m2,m1)
```

In a similar manner, the method `m1.postTranslate(m2)` is equivalent to

```
m1.concat(m1,m2)
```

By extension, the following code

```
matrix.setScale(interpolatedTime, interpolatedTime);
matrix.preTranslate(-centerX, -centerY);
matrix.postTranslate(centerX, centerY);
```

is equivalent to

```
Matrix matrixPreTranslate = new Matrix();
matrixPreTranslate.setTranslate(-centerX, -centerY);

Matrix matrixPostTranslate = new Matrix();
matrixPostTranslate.setTranslate(cetnerX, centerY);

matrix.concat(matrixPreTranslate,matrix);
matrix.postTranslate(matrix,matrixpostTranslate);
```

Resources

Here are some useful links to further strengthen your understanding of this chapter:

- `http://developer.android.com/reference/android/view/animation/package-summary.html`: You can discover various animation-related APIs here, including interpolators.
- `http://developer.android.com/guide/topics/resources/animation-resource.html`: You will find XML tags for various animation types here.
- `http://www.androidbook.com/projects`: You can use this URL to download test projects dedicated for this chapter. The names of the zip files are `ProAndroid3_ch16_SampleFrameAnimation.zip`, `ProAndroid3_ch16_SampleLayoutAnimation.zip`, and `ProAndroid3_ch16_SampleViewAnimation.zip`.

Summary

In this chapter, we showed you a fun way to enhance UI programs by extending them with animation capabilities. We covered all major types of animation supported by Android, including frame-by-frame animation, layout animation, and view animation. We also covered supplemental animation concepts such as interpolators and transformation matrices.

Now that you have this background, we encourage you to go through the API samples that come with the Android SDK to examine the sample XML definitions for a variety of animations. We will also return to animation briefly in Chapter 20, when you'll see how to draw and animate using OpenGL. See chapter 29 for a brief overview of property based animation applied to fragments.

Chapter 17

Exploring Maps and Location-based Services

In this chapter, we are going to talk about maps and location-based services. Location-based services comprise one of the more exciting pieces of the Android SDK. This portion of the SDK provides APIs to let application developers display and manipulate maps, obtain real-time device-location information, and take advantage of other exciting features.

The location-based services facility in Android sits on two pillars: the mapping and location-based APIs. Each of these APIs is isolated with respect to its own package. For example, the mapping package is `com.google.android.maps`, and the location package is `android.location`. The mapping APIs in Android provide facilities for you to display a map and manipulate it. For example, you can zoom and pan; you can change the map mode (from satellite view to street view, for example); you can add custom data to the map, and so on. The other end of the spectrum is Global Positioning System (GPS) data and real-time location data, both of which are handled by the location package.

These APIs often reach across the Internet to invoke services from Google servers. Therefore, you will usually need to have Internet connectivity for these to work. In addition, Google has Terms of Service that you must agree to before you can develop applications with these Android Maps API services. Read the terms carefully; Google places some restrictions on what you can do with the service data. For example, you can use location information for users' personal use, but certain commercial uses are restricted, as are applications involving automated control of vehicles. The terms will be presented to you when you sign up for a map-api key.

In this chapter, we'll go through each of these packages. We'll start with the mapping APIs and show you how to use maps with your applications. As you'll see, mapping in Android boils down to using the `MapView` UI control and the `MapActivity` class in addition to the mapping APIs, which integrate with Google Maps. We will also show you how to place custom data onto the maps that you display and how to show the current location of the device on a map. After talking about maps, we'll delve into location-based services, which extend the mapping concepts. We will show you how to use the Android

Geocoder class and the LocationManager service. We will also touch on threading issues that surface when you use these APIs.

Understanding the Mapping Package

As we mentioned, the mapping APIs comprise one of the components of Android's location-based services. The mapping package contains everything you'll need to display a map on the screen, handle user interaction with the map (such as zooming), display custom data on top of the map, and so on. The first step to working with this package is to display a map. To do that, you'll use the MapView view class. Using this class, however, requires some preparation work. Specifically, before you can use the MapView, you'll need to get a map-api key from Google. The *map-api key* enables Android to interact with Google Maps services to obtain map data. The next section explains how to obtain a map-api key.

Obtaining a map-api Key from Google

The first thing to understand about the map-api key is that you'll actually need two keys: one for development with the emulator and another for production (on devices). The reason for this is that the certificate used to obtain the map-api key will differ between development and production (as we discussed in Chapter 10).

For example, during development, the ADT plug-in generates the .apk file and deploys it to the emulator. Because the .apk file must be signed with a certificate, the ADT plug-in uses the debug certificate during development. For production deployment, you'll likely use a self-signed certificate to sign your .apk file. The good news is that you can obtain one map-api key for development and another for production, and it's then easy to swap the keys before exporting the production build.

To obtain a map-api key, you need the certificate that you'll use to sign your application (in the case of the emulator, the debug certificate). You'll get the MD5 fingerprint of your certificate, and then you'll enter it on Google's web site to generate an associated map-api key.

First, you must locate your debug certificate, which is generated and maintained by Eclipse. You can find the exact location using the Eclipse IDE. From Eclipse's Preferences menu, go to Android ➤ Build. The debug certificate's location will be displayed in the "Default debug keystore" field, as shown in Figure 17–1. (See Chapter 2 if you have trouble finding the Preferences menu.)

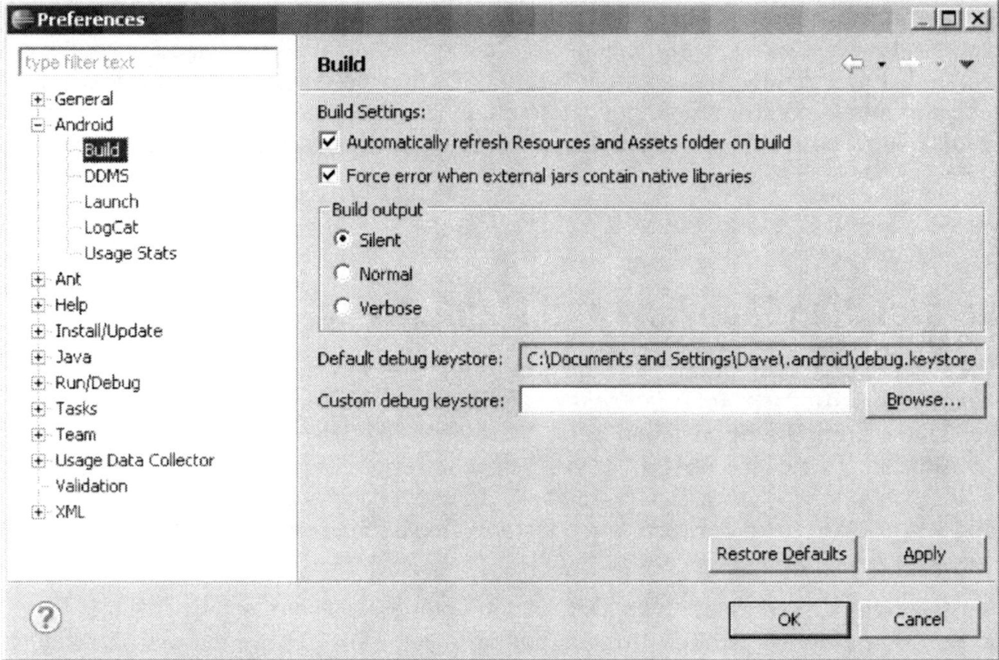

Figure 17–1. *The debug certificate's location*

To extract the MD5 fingerprint, you can run the keytool with the -list option, as shown here:

```
keytool -list -alias androiddebugkey -keystore
"FULL PATH OF YOUR debug.keystore FILE" -storepass android -keypass android
```

Note that the alias of the debug store is androiddebugkey. Similarly, the keystore password is android, and the private key password is also android. When you run this command, the keytool provides the fingerprint (see Figure 17–2).

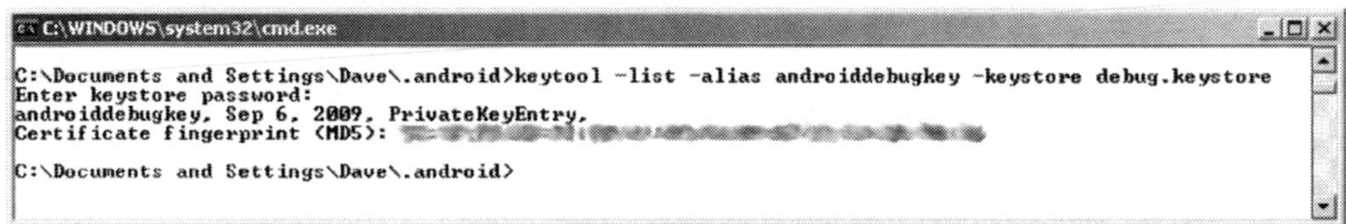

Figure 17–2. *The keytool output for the list option (actual fingerprint smudged on purpose)*

Now, paste your certificate's MD5 fingerprint in the appropriate field on this Google site:

http://code.google.com/android/maps-api-signup.html

Read through the Terms of Service. If you agree to the terms, click the Generate API Key button to get a corresponding map-api key from the Google Maps service. The map-api key is active immediately, so you can start using it to obtain map data from Google. Note that you will need a Google account to obtain a map-api key; when you try to generate the map-api key, you will be prompted to log in to your Google account.

Remember from Chapter 10 that when your debug certificate expires, so too will your development map-api key. If you change your debug certificate, you'll need to repeat these steps, with the new debug certificate, to get a new development map-api key. This is good motivation for creating a debug certificate that lasts longer than the default one year. See Chapter 10 for more details on creating a debug certificate that lasts a long time.

Now, let's start playing with maps.

Understanding MapView and MapActivity

A lot of the mapping technology in Android relies on the `MapView` UI control and an extension of `android.app.Activity` called `MapActivity`. The `MapView` and `MapActivity` classes take care of the heavy lifting when it comes to displaying and manipulating a map in Android. One of the things that you'll have to remember about these two classes is that they have to work together. Specifically, to use a `MapView`, you need to instantiate it within a `MapActivity`. In addition, when instantiating a `MapView`, you need to supply the map-api key.

If you instantiate a `MapView` using an XML layout, you need to set the `android:apiKey` property. If you create a `MapView` programmatically, you have to pass the map-api key to the `MapView` constructor. Finally, because the underlying data for the map comes from Google Maps, your application will need permission to access the Internet. This means you need at least the following permission request in your `AndroidManifest.xml` file:

```
<uses-permission android:name="android.permission.INTERNET" />
```

Listing 17–1 shows in bold the entries required in AndroidManifest.xml to make a map application work.

Listing 17–1. *Tags Needed in AndroidManifest.xml for a Map Application*

```
<?xml version="1.0" encoding="utf-8"?>
<manifest xmlns:android="http://schemas.android.com/apk/res/android"
      package="com.androidbook"
      android:versionCode="1"
      android:versionName="1.0">
    <application android:icon="@drawable/icon"
                 android:label="@string/app_name">
        <uses-library android:name="com.google.android.maps" />
        <activity android:name=".MapViewDemoActivity"
                  android:label="@string/app_name">
          <intent-filter>
             <action android:name="android.intent.action.MAIN" />
             <category android:name="android.intent.category.LAUNCHER" />
          </intent-filter>
        </activity>
    </application>
    <uses-permission android:name="android.permission.INTERNET"/>
    <uses-sdk android:minSdkVersion="4" />
</manifest>
```

There's another modification you need to make to the AndroidManifest.xml file. The definition of your map application needs to reference a mapping library (this line was also included in Listing 17–1). With the prerequisites out of the way, have a look at Figure 17–3.

Figure 17–3. *A MapView control in street-view mode*

Figure 17–3 shows an application that displays a map in street-view mode. The application also demonstrates how you can zoom in, zoom out, and change the map's view mode. The XML layout is shown in Listing 17–2.

> **NOTE:** We will give you a URL at the end of the chapter which you can use to download projects of this chapter. This will allow you to import these projects into your Eclipse directly.

Listing 17–2. *XML Layout of the MapView Demonstration*

```
<?xml version="1.0" encoding="utf-8"?>
<!-- This file is /res/layout/mapview.xml -->
<LinearLayout xmlns:android="http://schemas.android.com/apk/res/android"
    android:orientation="vertical" android:layout_width="fill_parent"
    android:layout_height="fill_parent">

    <LinearLayout
        xmlns:android="http://schemas.android.com/apk/res/android"
        android:orientation="horizontal"
        android:layout_width="fill_parent"
        android:layout_height="wrap_content">

        <Button android:id="@+id/zoomin"
            android:layout_width="wrap_content"
            android:layout_height="wrap_content" android:text="+"
```

```
            android:onClick="myClickHandler" android:padding="12px" />

        <Button android:id="@+id/zoomout"
            android:layout_width="wrap_content"
            android:layout_height="wrap_content" android:text="-"
            android:onClick="myClickHandler" android:padding="12px" />

        <Button android:id="@+id/sat"
            android:layout_width="wrap_content"
            android:layout_height="wrap_content" android:text="Satellite"
            android:onClick="myClickHandler" android:padding="8px" />

        <Button android:id="@+id/street"
            android:layout_width="wrap_content"
            android:layout_height="wrap_content" android:text="Street"
            android:onClick="myClickHandler" android:padding="8px" />

        <Button android:id="@+id/traffic"
            android:layout_width="wrap_content"
            android:layout_height="wrap_content" android:text="Traffic"
            android:onClick="myClickHandler" android:padding="8px" />

        <Button android:id="@+id/normal"
            android:layout_width="wrap_content"
            android:layout_height="wrap_content" android:text="Normal"
            android:onClick="myClickHandler" android:padding="8px" />

    </LinearLayout>

    <com.google.android.maps.MapView
        android:id="@+id/mapview" android:layout_width="fill_parent"
        android:layout_height="wrap_content" android:clickable="true"
        android:apiKey="YOUR MAP API KEY GOES HERE" />

</LinearLayout>
```

As shown in Listing 17–2, a parent `LinearLayout` contains a child `LinearLayout` and a `MapView`. The child `LinearLayout` contains the buttons shown at the top of Figure 17–3. Also note that you need to update the `MapView` control's `android:apiKey` value with the value of your own map-api key.

The code for our sample mapping application is shown in Listing 17–3.

Listing 17–3. ***The MapActivity Extension Class That Loads the XML Layout***

```
// This file is MapViewDemoActivity.java
import android.os.Bundle;
import android.view.View;

import com.google.android.maps.MapActivity;
import com.google.android.maps.MapView;

public class MapViewDemoActivity extends MapActivity
{
    private MapView mapView;

    @Override
    protected void onCreate(Bundle savedInstanceState) {
```

```
        super.onCreate(savedInstanceState);
        setContentView(R.layout.mapview);

        mapView = (MapView)findViewById(R.id.mapview);
    }

    public void myClickHandler(View target) {
        switch(target.getId()) {
        case R.id.zoomin:
            mapView.getController().zoomIn();
            break;
        case R.id.zoomout:
            mapView.getController().zoomOut();
            break;
        case R.id.sat:
            mapView.setSatellite(true);
            break;
        case R.id.street:
            mapView.setStreetView(true);
            break;
        case R.id.traffic:
            mapView.setTraffic(true);
            break;
        case R.id.normal:
            mapView.setSatellite(false);
            mapView.setStreetView(false);
            mapView.setTraffic(false);
            break;
        }
        // The following line should not be required but it is,
        // at least up until Froyo (Android 2.2)
        mapView.postInvalidateDelayed(2000);
    }

    @Override
    protected boolean isLocationDisplayed() {
        return false;
    }

    @Override
    protected boolean isRouteDisplayed() {
        return false;
    }
}
```

As shown in Listing 17–3, displaying the `MapView` using `onCreate()` is no different from displaying any other control. That is, you set the content view of the UI to a layout file that contains the `MapView`, and that takes care of it. Surprisingly, supporting zoom features is also fairly easy. To zoom in or out, you use the `MapController` class of the `MapView`. Do this by calling `mapView.getController()` and then calling the appropoiate `zoomIn()` or `zoomOut()` method. Zooming this way produces a one-level zoom; users need to repeat the action to increase the amount of magnification or reduction.

You'll also find it straightforward to offer the ability to change view modes. The `MapView` supports several modes:

- Map is the default mode.
- Street view mode places a layer on top of the map that puts blue outlines on roads for which street-level images are available for viewing. These images were taken from cameras mounted on vehicles that drove around the streets. Note, however, that the `MapView` control does not display street view images. To view those street-level images, you will need a separate view control. This will be covered in greater detail in Chapter 25.
- Satellite mode shows aerial photographs of the map, so you can see the actual tops of buildings, trees, roads, and so on.
- Traffic mode shows traffic information on the map with colored lines to represent traffic that is moving well as opposed to traffic that is backed up. Note that traffic mode is supported on a limited number of major highways and roads.

To change modes, you must call the appropriate setter method with `true.` In some cases, setting one mode will turn off another. For example, you can't have street view mode on at the same time as traffic mode, so setting traffic mode on automatically turns off street view mode. To turn off a mode, set that mode to `false`. We'll be talking about `Overlays` in just a bit, but for now, know that the traffic mode and the street view mode do *not* use `Overlays`.

> **NOTE:** The statement `mapView.postInvalidateDelayed(2000)` is used to work around an issue with street view and traffic modes of the map. The issue is with the way threads are used internally to fetch the data for displaying the street view blue lines and traffic lines. See Android Issue 10317 for more information at http://code.google.com/p/android/issues/detail?id=10317.

To make the map move sideways, set the attribute `android:clickable="true"` for the `MapView` in XML; otherwise, users will only be able to zoom in and out, not laterally. You can also set this in code using the `setClickable(true)` method call on your `mapView`.

The final things to mention from this example are the two methods `isLocationDisplayed()` and `isRouteDisplayed()`. The documentation for these methods says their use is required by the Google Terms of Service, although when requesting a Maps API key, there is no mention of these methods in those Terms of Service. I'm no lawyer, but I'd recommend implementing these methods. Your application is obligated to respond with `true` or `false` to indicate to the map server whether or not the current device location is being displayed or if any route information is being displayed, such as driving directions.

You'll probably agree that the amount of code required to display a map and to implement zoom and mode changes is minimal with Android (see Listing 17–3). However, there's an even easier way to implement zoom controls. Take a look at the XML layout and code shown in Listing 17–4.

Listing 17–4. *Zooming Made Easier*

```
<?xml version="1.0" encoding="utf-8"?>
<!-- This file is /res/layout/mapview.xml -->
<RelativeLayout xmlns:android="http://schemas.android.com/apk/res/android"
        android:orientation="vertical" android:layout_width="fill_parent"
        android:layout_height="fill_parent">

    <com.google.android.maps.MapView android:id="@+id/mapview"
            android:layout_width="fill_parent"
            android:layout_height="wrap_content"
            android:clickable="true"
            android:apiKey="YOUR MAP API KEY GOES HERE"
            />
</RelativeLayout>

public class MapViewDemoActivity extends MapActivity
{
    private MapView mapView;
    @Override
    protected void onCreate(Bundle savedInstanceState) {
        super.onCreate(savedInstanceState);

        setContentView(R.layout.mapview);
        mapView = (MapView)findViewById(R.id.mapview);

        mapView.setBuiltInZoomControls(true);
    }

    @Override
    protected boolean isLocationDisplayed() {
        return false;
    }

    @Override
    protected boolean isRouteDisplayed() {
        return false;
    }
}
```

The difference between Listing 17–4 and Listing 17–3 is that we changed the XML layout for our view to use `RelativeLayout`. We removed all the zoom controls and view mode controls. The magic in this example is in the code and not the layout. The `MapView` already has controls that allow you to zoom in and out. All you have to do is turn them on using the `setBuiltInZoomControls()` method. Figure 17–4 shows the `MapView`'s default zoom controls.

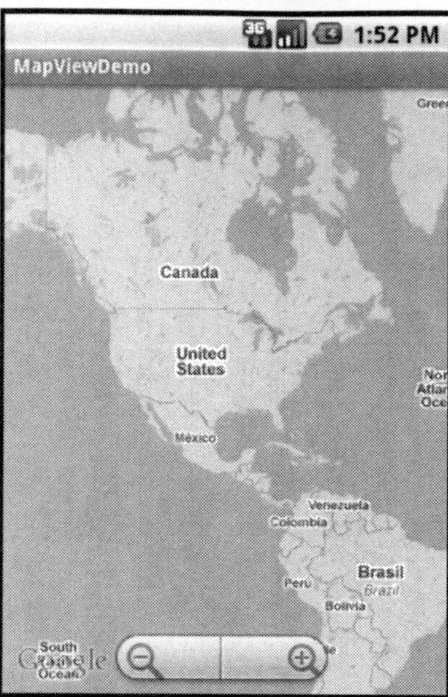

Figure 17–4. *The MapView's built-in zoom controls*

Now, let's discuss how to add custom data to the map.

Adding Markers Using Overlays

Google Maps provides a facility that allows you to place custom data on top of the map. You can see an example of this if you search for pizza restaurants in your area: Google Maps places pushpins, or balloon markers, to indicate each location. Google Maps provides this facility by allowing you to add a layer on top of the map. Android provides several classes that help you to add layers to a map. The key class for this type of functionality is `Overlay`, but you can use an extension of this class called `ItemizedOverlay`. Listing 17–5 shows an example of the Java code. The layout XML file from Listing 17–4 can be used for this project as well.

Listing 17–5. *Marking Up a Map Using ItemizedOverlay*

```
import java.util.ArrayList;
import java.util.List;

import android.graphics.Canvas;
import android.graphics.drawable.Drawable;
import android.os.Bundle;
import android.widget.LinearLayout;

import com.google.android.maps.GeoPoint;
import com.google.android.maps.ItemizedOverlay;
import com.google.android.maps.MapActivity;
import com.google.android.maps.MapView;
import com.google.android.maps.OverlayItem;

public class MappingOverlayActivity extends MapActivity {
```

```
private MapView mapView;

@Override
protected void onCreate(Bundle savedInstanceState) {
    super.onCreate(savedInstanceState);

    setContentView(R.layout.mapview);

    mapView = (MapView) findViewById(R.id.mapview);
    mapView.setBuiltInZoomControls(true);

    Drawable marker=getResources().getDrawable(R.drawable.mapmarker);
    marker.setBounds( (int) (-marker.getIntrinsicWidth()/2),
                            -marker.getIntrinsicHeight(),
                            (int) (marker.getIntrinsicWidth()/2),
                            0);

    InterestingLocations funPlaces =
                new InterestingLocations(marker);
    mapView.getOverlays().add(funPlaces);

    GeoPoint pt = funPlaces.getCenterPt();
    int latSpan = funPlaces.getLatSpanE6();
    int lonSpan = funPlaces.getLonSpanE6();
    Log.v("Overlays", "Lat span is " + latSpan);
    Log.v("Overlays", "Lon span is " + lonSpan);

    MapController mc = mapView.getController();
    mc.setCenter(pt);
    mc.zoomToSpan((int)(latSpan*1.5), (int)(lonSpan*1.5));
}

@Override
protected boolean isLocationDisplayed() {
    return false;
}

@Override
protected boolean isRouteDisplayed() {
    return false;
}

class InterestingLocations extends ItemizedOverlay {
    private ArrayList<OverlayItem> locations =
            new ArrayList<OverlayItem>();
    private GeoPoint center = null;

    public InterestingLocations(Drawable marker)
    {
        super(marker);

        // create locations of interest
        GeoPoint disneyMagicKingdom =
            new GeoPoint((int)(28.418971*1000000),
                         (int)(-81.581436*1000000));
        GeoPoint disneySevenLagoon =
            new GeoPoint((int)(28.410067*1000000),
                         (int)(-81.583699*1000000));
```

```
            locations.add(new OverlayItem(disneyMagicKingdom ,
                          "Magic Kingdom", "Magic Kingdom"));
            locations.add(new OverlayItem(disneySevenLagoon ,
                          "Seven Seas Lagoon", "Seven Seas Lagoon"));

            populate();
        }

        //  We added this method to find the middle point of the cluster
        //  Start each edge on its opposite side and move across with
        //  each point. The top of the world is +90, the bottom -90,
        //  the west edge is -180, the east +180
        public GeoPoint getCenterPt() {
            if(center == null) {
                int northEdge = -90000000;   // i.e., -90E6 microdegrees
                int southEdge = 90000000;
                int eastEdge = -180000000;
                int westEdge = 180000000;
                Iterator<OverlayItem> iter = locations.iterator();
                while(iter.hasNext()) {
                    GeoPoint pt = iter.next().getPoint();
                    if(pt.getLatitudeE6() > northEdge)
                        northEdge = pt.getLatitudeE6();
                    if(pt.getLatitudeE6() < southEdge)
                        southEdge = pt.getLatitudeE6();
                    if(pt.getLongitudeE6() > eastEdge)
                        eastEdge = pt.getLongitudeE6();
                    if(pt.getLongitudeE6() < westEdge)
                        westEdge = pt.getLongitudeE6();
                }
                center = new GeoPoint((int)((northEdge +southEdge)/2),
                        (int)((westEdge + eastEdge)/2));
            }
            return center;
        }

        @Override
        public void draw(Canvas canvas, MapView mapView, boolean shadow)
        {
            // Hide the shadow by setting shadow to false
            super.draw(canvas, mapView, shadow);
        }

        @Override
        protected OverlayItem createItem(int i) {
            return locations.get(i);
        }

        @Override
        public int size() {
            return locations.size();
        }

    }
}
```

Listing 17–5 demonstrates how you can overlay markers onto a map. The example places two markers: one at Disney's Magic Kingdom and another at Disney's Seven Seas Lagoon, both near Orlando, Florida (see Figure 17–5).

> **NOTE:** To run this demonstration, you'll need to get a drawable to serve as your map marker. This image file must be saved into your `/res/drawable` folder so that the resource ID reference in the `getDrawable()` call matches the file name you choose for your image file. If possible, make the area surrounding your marker transparent. Some sample markers are provided with the source code for this chapter.

In order for you to add markers onto a map, you have to create and add an extension of `com.google.android.maps.Overlay` to the map. The `Overlay` class itself cannot be instantiated, so you'll have to extend it or use one of the extensions. In our example, we have implemented `InterestingLocations`, which extends `ItemizedOverlay`, which in turn extends `Overlay`. The `Overlay` class defines the contract for an overlay, and `ItemizedOverlay` is a handy implementation that makes it easy for you to create a list of locations that can be marked on a map.

The general usage pattern is to extend the `ItemizedOverlay` class and add your items—interesting locations—in the constructor. After you instantiate your points of interest, you call the `populate()` method of `ItemizedOverlay`. The `populate()` method is a utility that caches any `OverlayItems`. Internally, the class calls the `size()` method to determine the number of overlay items and then enters a loop, calling `createItem(i)` for each item. In the `createItem` method, you return the already-created item given the index in the array.

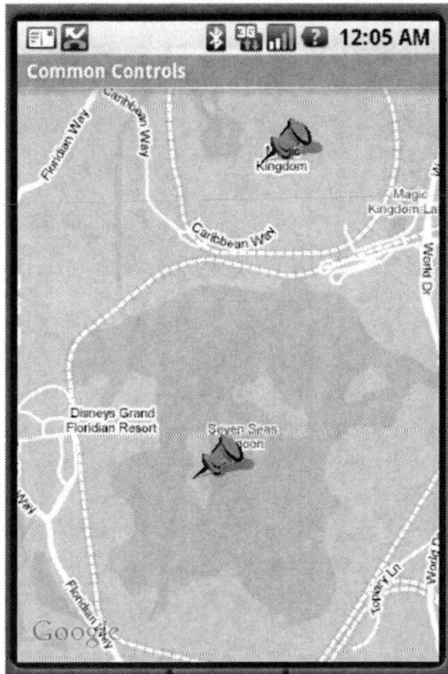

Figure 17–5. *MapView with markers*

As Listing 17–5 shows, you simply create the points and call populate() to show markers on a map. The Overlay contract manages the rest. To make it all work, the onCreate() method of the activity creates the InterestingLocations instance, passing in the Drawable that's used as a default for the markers. Then, onCreate() adds the InterestingLocations instance to the overlay collection (mapView.getOverlays().add()).

The Drawable you choose needs to be prepared for use with an ItemizedOverlay. The Maps API needs to know where the (0, 0) point is on the Drawable. This point will be used to mark the exact spot on the map that the marker is supposed to represent. You can do this yourself using the setBounds() method of the Drawable class as shown in our example. The arguments represent the left, top, right, and bottom coordinates and we can use the getIntrinsicHeight() and getIntrinsicWidth() methods to figure out how tall and wide our Drawable is.

In our example, the (0, 0) coordinate would be halfway across the bottom edge. Remember that the coordinate system starts from the left and increases as you go right, and from the top increasing as you go down. Therefore, our top coordinate must be less than the 0 at the bottom, so is negative.

Android provides a couple of convenience methods in the ItemizedOverlay class to set bounds on Drawables. They are boundCenterBottom() and boundCenter(). The first method acts on our Drawable in the exact same way that we did, resulting in (0, 0) being halfway across the bottom edge of the Drawable. The second method would put (0, 0) in the very center of the Drawable. A common practice is to use one of these methods as the first call in your constructor. We could have done the following instead of using setBounds() earlier:

```
public InterestingLocations(Drawable marker)
{
    super(boundCenterBottom(marker));
    [ … ]
```

You'll also notice that we can use any size or shape Drawable we want. One thing that makes our markers look good is to use the transparent color around the shape we want. The bubbles you're used to seeing on Google Maps are not square, and because they use a transparent color around them, you can see the map where there is no marker. This is also good because the Maps API will paint a shadow of your marker onto the map, and you want your shadow to be your shape and not a rectangle (OK, really a parallelogram).

But what if you don't want a shadow? No problem. Simply override the draw() method of your ItemizedOverlay extension class and set shadow to false when calling the parent's draw() method. Check out the draw() method in our example. We mentioned that the Drawable used to create the ItemizedOverlay is the default marker. Each OverlayItem can instead have a unique marker by using its setMarker() method with some other Drawable. You could set the unique markers when instantiating the OverlayItems, or you could set them later. We'll revisit markers in Chapter 25 when we cover touch screens, and show you how to have even more fun with markers.

Now that the overlay is associated to our map, we still need to move into the right position to actually see the markers in the display. To do this, we need to set the center of the displayed map to a point. The getCenter() method of the ItemizedOverlay class returns the first ranked point, not the center point, as you might expect. An ItemizedOverlay will sort the points it contains, and it will choose one to be first. Therefore, to find the center of the points, we implemented our own getCenterPt() method to iterate through the points and find the center. The setCenter() method of the mapview's controller sets the center of what's displayed, and we pass it our calculated center point.

MapController's setZoom() method sets how high we are above the map. It takes a value from 1 to 21, where 21 is zoomed in as close as we can go, and 1 is as far away as we can go. But because we're not exactly sure what value to use here to see all our points at once, we use the zoomToSpan() method of the MapController. We need to pass in the height and width of the rectangle that contains all our points. Fortunately, ItemizedOverlay has two methods to tell us the height and width of that rectangle, to give us our latitude span, getLatSpanE6(), and our longitude span, getLonSpanE6(), respectively; we can then use these values with zoomToSpan(). Notice that we chose to expand our rectangle by a factor of 1.5, so our points are not right at the edges of the map when displayed.

Another interesting aspect of Listing 17–5 is the creation of the OverlayItem(s). To create an OverlayItem, you need an object of type GeoPoint. The GeoPoint class represents a location by its latitude and longitude, in micro degrees. In our example, we obtained the latitude and longitude of Magic Kingdom and Seven Seas Lagoon using geocoding sites on the Web. (As you'll see shortly, you can use geocoding to convert an address to a latitude/longitude pair, for example.) We then converted the latitude and longitude to micro degrees—because the APIs operate on micro degrees—by multiplying by 1,000,000 and performing a cast to an integer.

So far, we've shown you how to place markers on a map. But overlays are not restricted to showing pushpins or balloons. They can be used to do other things. For example, we could show animations of products moving across maps, or we could show symbols such as weather fronts or thunderstorms.

All in all, you'll agree that placing markers on a map couldn't be easier. Or could it? We don't have a database of latitude/longitude pairs, but we're guessing that we'll need to somehow create one or more GeoPoints using a real address. That's when you can use the Geocoder class, which is part of the location package that we'll discuss next.

Understanding the Location Package

The android.location package provides facilities for location-based services. In this section, we are going to discuss two important pieces of this package: the Geocoder class and the LocationManager service. We'll start with Geocoder.

Geocoding with Android

If you are going to do anything practical with maps, you'll likely have to convert an address (or location) to a latitude/longitude pair. This concept is known as *geocoding*, and the `android.location.Geocoder` class provides this facility. In fact, the `Geocoder` class provides both forward and backward conversion—it can take an address and return a latitude/longitude pair, and it can translate a latitude/longitude pair into a list of addresses. The class provides the following methods:

- `List<Address> getFromLocation(double latitude, double longitude, int maxResults)`
- `List<Address> getFromLocationName(String locationName, int maxResults, double lowerLeftLatitude, double lowerLeftLongitude, double upperRightLatitude, double upperRightLongitude)`
- `List<Address> getFromLocationName(String locationName, int maxResults)`

It turns out that computing an address is not an exact science because of the various ways a location can be described. For example, the `getFromLocationName()` methods can take the name of a place, the physical address, an airport code, or simply a well-known name for the location. Thus, the methods return a list of addresses and not a single address. Because the methods return a list, you are encouraged to limit the result set by providing a value for `maxResults` that ranges between `1` and `5`. Now, let's consider an example.

Listing 17–6 shows the XML layout and corresponding code for the user interface shown in Figure 17–6. To run the example, you'll need to update the listing with your own map-api key.

Listing 17–6. ***Working with the Android Geocoder Class***

```
<?xml version="1.0" encoding="utf-8"?>
<!-- This file is /res/layout/geocode.xml -->
<RelativeLayout xmlns:android="http://schemas.android.com/apk/res/android"
        android:layout_width="fill_parent"
        android:layout_height="fill_parent">

        <LinearLayout android:layout_width="fill_parent"
            android:layout_alignParentBottom="true"
            android:layout_height="wrap_content"
            android:orientation="vertical" >

            <EditText android:layout_width="fill_parent"
                android:id="@+id/location"
                android:layout_height="wrap_content"
                android:text="White House"/>

            <Button android:id="@+id/geocodeBtn"
                android:layout_width="wrap_content"
                android:layout_height="wrap_content"
                android:onClick="doClick" android:text="Find Location"/>
        </LinearLayout>
```

```
    <com.google.android.maps.MapView
            android:id="@+id/geoMap" android:clickable="true"
            android:layout_width="fill_parent"
            android:layout_height="320px"
            android:apiKey="YOUR MAP API KEY GOES HERE"
            />

</RelativeLayout>


package com.androidbook.maps.geocoding;

import java.io.IOException;
import java.util.List;

import android.location.Address;
import android.location.Geocoder;
import android.os.Bundle;
import android.view.View;
import android.widget.Button;
import android.widget.EditText;

import com.google.android.maps.GeoPoint;
import com.google.android.maps.MapActivity;
import com.google.android.maps.MapView;

public class GeocodingDemoActivity extends MapActivity
{
    Geocoder geocoder = null;
    MapView mapView = null;

    @Override
    protected boolean isLocationDisplayed() {
        return false;
    }

    @Override
    protected boolean isRouteDisplayed() {
        return false;
    }

    @Override
    protected void onCreate(Bundle savedInstanceState)
    {
        super.onCreate(savedInstanceState);

        setContentView(R.layout.geocode);
        mapView = (MapView)findViewById(R.id.geoMap);
        mapView.setBuiltInZoomControls(true);

        // lat/long of Jacksonville, FL
        int lat = (int)(30.334954*1000000);
        int lng = (int)(-81.5625*1000000);
        GeoPoint pt = new GeoPoint(lat,lng);
        mapView.getController().setZoom(10);
        mapView.getController().setCenter(pt);
```

```
        geocoder = new Geocoder(this);
    }

    public void doClick(View arg0) {
        try {
            EditText loc = (EditText)findViewById(R.id.location);
            String locationName = loc.getText().toString();

            List<Address> addressList =
                    geocoder.getFromLocationName(locationName, 5);
            if(addressList!=null && addressList.size()>0)
            {
                int lat =
                    (int)(addressList.get(0).getLatitude()*1000000);
                int lng =
                    (int)(addressList.get(0).getLongitude()*1000000);

                GeoPoint pt = new GeoPoint(lat,lng);
                mapView.getController().setZoom(15);
                mapView.getController().setCenter(pt);
            }
        } catch (IOException e) {
            e.printStackTrace();
        }
    }
}
```

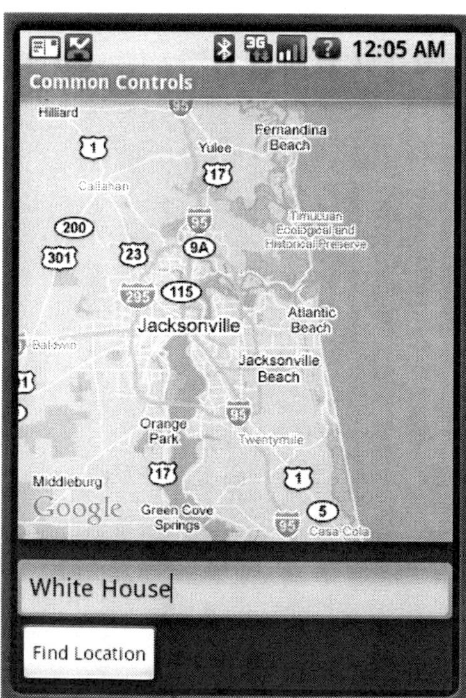

Figure 17–6. *Geocoding to a point given the location name*

To demonstrate the uses of geocoding in Android, type the name or address of a location in the `EditText` field, and then click the Find Location button. To find the address of a location, we call the `getFromLocationName()` method of `Geocoder`. The location can be an address or a well-known name such as "White House." Geocoding can be a timely operation, so we recommend that you limit the results to five, as the Android documentation suggests.

The call to `getFromLocationName()` returns a list of addresses. The sample application takes the list of addresses and processes the first one if any were found. Every address has a latitude and longitude, which you use to create a `GeoPoint`. You then get the map controller and navigate to the point. The zoom level can be set to an integer between 1 and 21, inclusive. As you move from 1 toward 21, the zoom level increases by a factor of 2. We could have presented a dialog to display multiple found locations if we wanted to, but for now, we'll just display the first location returned to us.

In our example application, we only read the latitude and longitude of our returned `Address`. In fact, there can be a ton of data about `Addresses` returned to us, including the location's common name, street, city, state, postal/zip code, country, and even phone number and web site URL.

> **NOTE:** Location-based services do not use micro degrees like the Maps API does. Forgetting to convert from one to the other is a common cause of errors. To pass a `Location`'s latitude and longitude to a Maps API method, you must multiply by 1,000,000 first.

You should understand a few points with respect to geocoding:

- First, a returned address is not always an exact address. Obviously, because the returned list of addresses depends on the accuracy of the input, you need to make every effort to provide an accurate location name to the `Geocoder`.
- Second, whenever possible, set the `maxResults` parameter to a value between `1` and `5`.
- Finally, you should seriously consider doing the geocoding operation in a different thread from the UI thread. There are two reasons for this. The first is obvious: the operation is time-consuming, and you don't want the UI to hang while you do the geocoding causing Android to kill your activity. The second reason is that, with a mobile device, you always need to assume that the network connection can be lost and that the connection is weak. Therefore, you need to handle input/output (I/O) exceptions and timeouts appropriately. Once you have computed the addresses, you can post the results to the UI thread. Let's investigate this a bit more.

Geocoding with Background Threads

Using background threads to handle time-consuming operations is very common. The general pattern is to handle a UI event (such as a button click) to initiate a timely operation. From the event handler, you create a new thread to execute the work, and then you start the new thread. The UI thread returns to the user interface to handle the interaction with the user while the background thread works. After the background thread completes, a part of the UI might have to be updated, or the user might have to be notified. The background thread does not update the UI directly; instead, the background thread notifies the UI thread to update itself. Listing 17–7 demonstrates this idea using geocoding. We'll use the same `geocode.xml` file as before. We can also use the same `AndroidManifest.xml` file as before.

Listing 17–7. *Geocoding in a Separate Thread*

```
package com.androidbook.maps.geocodingthreads;

import java.io.IOException;
import java.util.List;

import android.app.AlertDialog;
import android.app.Dialog;
import android.app.ProgressDialog;
import android.location.Address;
import android.location.Geocoder;
import android.os.Bundle;
import android.os.Handler;
import android.os.Message;
import android.view.View;
import android.widget.EditText;

import com.google.android.maps.GeoPoint;
import com.google.android.maps.MapActivity;
import com.google.android.maps.MapView;

public class GeocodingDemoActivity extends MapActivity
{
    Geocoder geocoder = null;
    MapView mapView = null;
    ProgressDialog progDialog=null;
    List<Address> addressList=null;
    @Override
    protected boolean isRouteDisplayed() {
        return false;
    }

    @Override
    protected void onCreate(Bundle icicle) {
        super.onCreate(icicle);

        setContentView(R.layout.geocode);
        mapView = (MapView)findViewById(R.id.geoMap);
        mapView.setBuiltInZoomControls(true);

        // lat/long of Jacksonville, FL
        int lat = (int)(30.334954*1000000);
```

```
        int lng = (int)(-81.5625*1000000);
        GeoPoint pt = new GeoPoint(lat,lng);
        mapView.getController().setZoom(10);
        mapView.getController().animateTo(pt);

        geocoder = new Geocoder(this);
    }

    public void doClick(View view) {
        EditText loc = (EditText)findViewById(R.id.location);
        String locationName = loc.getText().toString();

        progDialog = ProgressDialog.show(GeocodingDemoActivity.this,
                   "Processing...", "Finding Location...", true, false);

        findLocation(locationName);
    }

    private void findLocation(final String locationName)
    {
        Thread thrd = new Thread()
        {
            public void run()
            {
                try {
                    // do background work
                    addressList =
                        geocoder.getFromLocationName(locationName, 5);
                    //send message to handler to process results
                    uiCallback.sendEmptyMessage(0);

                } catch (IOException e) {
                    e.printStackTrace();
                }
            }
        };
        thrd.start();
    }

    // ui thread callback handler
    private Handler uiCallback = new Handler()
    {
        @Override
        public void handleMessage(Message msg)
        {
            // tear down dialog
            progDialog.dismiss();

            if(addressList!=null && addressList.size()>0)
            {
                int lat =
                   (int)(addressList.get(0).getLatitude()*1000000);
                int lng =
                   (int)(addressList.get(0).getLongitude()*1000000);
                GeoPoint pt = new GeoPoint(lat,lng);
                mapView.getController().setZoom(15);
                mapView.getController().animateTo(pt);
```

```
            }
            else
            {
                Dialog foundNothingDlg = new
                    AlertDialog.Builder(GeocodingDemoActivity.this)
                          .setIcon(0)
                          .setTitle("Failed to Find Location")
                          .setPositiveButton("Ok", null)
                          .setMessage("Location Not Found...")
                          .create();
                foundNothingDlg.show();
            }
        }
    };
}
```

Listing 17–7 is a modified version of the example in Listing 17–6. The difference is that, now, in the `doClick()` method, you display a progress dialog and call `findLocation()` (see Figure 17–7). `findLocation()` then creates a new thread and calls the `start()` method, which ultimately results in a call to the thread's `run()` method. In the `run()` method, you use the `Geocoder` class to search for the location. When the search is done, you must post the message to something that knows how to interact with the UI thread, because you need to update the map. Android provides the `android.os.Handler` class for this purpose. From the background thread, call the `uiCallback.sendEmptyMessage(0)` to have the UI thread process the results from the search. In our case, we don't need to actually send any content in the message, since the data is being shared through the `addressList`. The code calls the handler's callback, which dismisses the dialog, and then looks at the `addressList` returned by the `Geocoder`. After that, the callback updates the map with the result or displays an alert dialog to indicate that the search returned nothing. The UI for this example is shown in Figure 17–7.

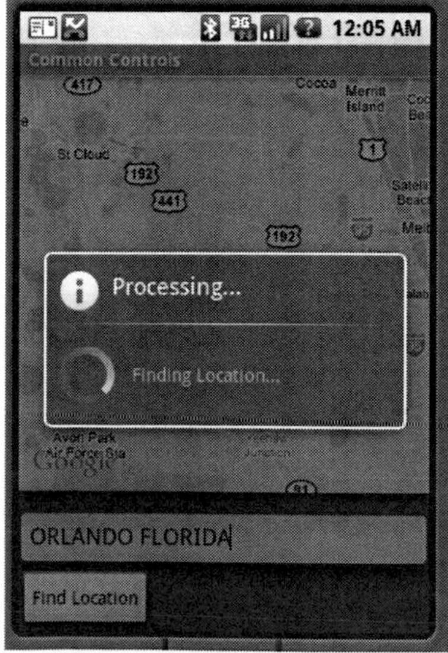

Figure 17–7. *Showing a progress window during long operations*

Understanding the LocationManager Service

The LocationManager service is one of the key services offered by the android.location package. This service provides two things: a mechanism for you to obtain the device's geographical location and a facility for you to be notified (via an intent) when the device enters a specified geographical location.

In this section, you are going to learn how the LocationManager service works. To use the service, you must first obtain a reference to it. Listing 17–8 shows a simple usage of the LocationManager service.

Listing 17–8. *Using the LocationManager Service*

```
package com.androidbook.maps.locationmanager;

import java.util.List;

import android.app.Activity;
import android.content.Context;
import android.location.Location;
import android.location.LocationManager;
import android.os.Bundle;

public class LocationManagerDemoActivity extends Activity
{

    @Override
    protected void onCreate(Bundle savedInstanceState)
    {
        super.onCreate(savedInstanceState);

        LocationManager locMgr = (LocationManager)
            this.getSystemService(Context.LOCATION_SERVICE);

        Location loc =
            locMgr.getLastKnownLocation(LocationManager.GPS_PROVIDER);

        List<String> providerList = locMgr.getAllProviders();
    }
}
```

The LocationManager service is a system-level service. System-level services are services that you obtain from the context using the service name; you don't instantiate them directly. The android.app.Activity class provides a utility method called getSystemService() that you can use to obtain a system-level service. As shown in Listing 17–8, you call getSystemService() and pass in the name of the service you want, in this case, Context.LOCATION_SERVICE.

The LocationManager service provides geographical location details by using location providers. Currently, there are three types of location providers:

- *GPS* providers use a Global Positioning System to obtain location information.

- *Network* providers use cell-phone towers or Wi-Fi networks to obtain location information.
- The *passive* provider is like a location update sniffer, and it passes to your application location updates that are requested by other applications, without your application having to specifically request any location updates. Of course, if no one else is requesting location updates, you won't get any either.

The `LocationManager` class can provide the device's last known location via the `getLastKnownLocation()` method. Location information is obtained from a provider, so the method takes as a parameter the name of the provider you want to use. Valid values for provider names are `LocationManager.GPS_PROVIDER`, `LocationManager.NETWORK_PROVIDER`, and `LocationManager.PASSIVE_PROVIDER`. In order for your application to successfully get location information, it must have the appropriate permissions in the `AndroidManifest.xml` file. `android.permission.ACCESS_FINE_LOCATION` is required for GPS and for passive providers, while `android.permission.ACCESS_COARSE_LOCATION` or `android.permission.ACCESS_FINE_LOCATION` can be used for network providers, depending on what you need. For instance, assume your application will use GPS or network data for location updates. Since you need `ACCESS_FINE_LOCATION` for GPS, you've also satisfied permissions for network access, so you do not need to also specify `ACCESS_COARSE_LOCATION`. If you're only going to use the network provider, you could get by with only `ACCESS_COARSE_LOCATION` in the manifest file.

Calling `getLastKnownLocation()` returns an `android.location.Location` instance, or `null` if no location is available. The `Location` class provides the location's latitude and longitude, the time the location was computed, and possibly the device's altitude, speed, and bearing. A `Location` object can also tell you which provider it came from using `getProvider()`, which will be either `GPS_PROVIDER` or `NETWORK_PROVIDER`. If you're getting location updates via the `PASSIVE_PROVIDER`, remember that you're only really sniffing location updates, so all updates are ultimately from either GPS or the network.

Because the `LocationManager` operates on providers, the class provides APIs to obtain providers. For example, you can get all of the known providers by calling `getAllProviders()`. You can obtain a specific provider by calling `getProvider()`, passing the name of the provider as an argument (such as `LocationManager.GPS_PROVIDER`). One thing to watch out for is that `getAllProviders()` will return providers that you may not have access to or that are currently disabled. Fortunately, you are able to determine the status of providers using other methods, such as `isProviderEnabled(String providerName)` or `getProviders(boolean enabledOnly)`, which you could call with a value of `true` to get only providers you are able to use immediately.

There's another way to get a suitable provider, and that is to use the `getProviders(Criteria criteria, boolean enabledOnly)` method of `LocationManager`. By specifying criteria for location updates, and by setting `enabledOnly` to true so you get providers that are enabled and ready to go, you can get a list of provider names returned to you without having to know the specifics of which provider you got. This could be more portable, since a device may have a custom LocationProvider that meets your needs without you having to know about it in advance. The Criteria object can be set with parameters that include accuracy level and the need for information about speed, bearing, altitude, cost, and power requirements. If no providers meet your criteria, a null list will be returned, allowing you to either bail out or relax the criteria and try again.

How to Enable Location Providers

You might think there's a simple API to enable a location provider (such as GPS) if it's not turned on when your application runs. Unfortunately this is not the case. To get a location service turned on, the user must do that from within the Settings screens of their device. Your application can make this a lot simpler for the user by launching that particular Settings screen. The location settings source screen is really just an activity, and this activity is set up to respond to an intent. So all your application needs to do is request an activity using the correct intent. The code you might use looks like this:

```
startActivityForResult(new Intent(
    android.provider.Settings.ACTION_LOCATION_SOURCE_SETTINGS), 0);
```

Remember that to handle a response, you must implement the onActivityResult() callback in your activity (covered in Chapter 5). And also keep in mind that while you hope the user turns on a location provider such as GPS, they may not. You will need to check again to see if the user has enabled a location provider, and take appropriate action based on the result.

What Can You Do With a Location?

As mentioned before, Locations can tell you the latitude and longitude, when the Location was computed, the provider that computed this Location, and optionally the altitude, speed, bearing and accuracy level. Depending on the provider where the Location came from, there could be extra information as well. For example, if the Location came from a GPS provider, there is an extras Bundle that will tell you how many satellites were used to compute the Location. The optional values may or may not be present, depending on the provider. To know if a Location has one of these values, the Location class provides a set of has. . .() methods that return a boolean value, for example hasAccuracy(). Before relying on the return value of getAccuracy(), it would be wise to call hasAccuracy() first.

The Location class has some other useful methods, including a static method distanceBetween(), which will return the shortest distance between two Locations. Another distance-related method is distanceTo(), which will return the shortest distance between the current Location object and the Location object passed to the method. Note that distances are in meters and that the distance calculations take into account the curvature of the Earth. But also be aware that the distances are not provided in terms of the distance you would have to go by car, for example.

If you want to get driving directions, or driving distances, you will need to have your beginning and ending Locations, but to do the calculations, you will likely need to use the Google Maps JavaScript API services. For example, there is a Google Directions API, similar to the Google Translate API covered in Chapter 11.The Directions API would allow your application to show how to get from your beginning to your ending location.

Sending Location Updates to Your Application During Development

When doing development testing, LocationManager needs location information, and the emulator doesn't have access to GPS or cell towers. In order for you to test your LocationManager service application in the emulator, you manually send location updates from Eclipse. Listing 17–9 shows a simple example to illustrate how to do this.

Listing 17–9. *Registering for Location Updates*

```
package com.androidbook.location.update;

import android.app.Activity;
import android.content.Context;
import android.location.Location;
import android.location.LocationListener;
import android.location.LocationManager;
import android.os.Bundle;
import android.widget.Toast;

public class LocationUpdateDemoActivity extends Activity
{
    LocationManager locMgr = null;
    LocationListener locListener = null;

    @Override
    public void onCreate(Bundle savedInstanceState)
    {
        super.onCreate(savedInstanceState);

        locMgr = (LocationManager)
            getSystemService(Context.LOCATION_SERVICE);

        locListener = new LocationListener()
        {
            public void  onLocationChanged(Location location)
            {
                if (location != null)
                {
                    Toast.makeText(getBaseContext(),
                        "New location latitude [" +
                        location.getLatitude() +
                        "] longitude [" +
                        location.getLongitude()+"]",
                        Toast.LENGTH_SHORT).show();
                }
            }

            public void  onProviderDisabled(String provider)
            {
```

```
            }

            public void  onProviderEnabled(String provider)
            {
            }

            public void  onStatusChanged(String provider,
                            int status, Bundle extras)
            {
            }
        };
    }

    @Override
    public void onResume() {
        super.onResume();

        locMgr.requestLocationUpdates(
            LocationManager.GPS_PROVIDER,
            0,              // minTime in ms
            0,              // minDistance in meters
            locListener);
    }

    @Override
    public void onPause() {
        super.onPause();
        locMgr.removeUpdates(locListener);
    }
}
```

We're not displaying a user interface for this example, so the standard initial layout XML file will do. This is also why we don't need to extend a MapActivity for this application, since we're not displaying any maps.

One of the primary uses of the LocationManager service is to receive notifications of the device's location. Listing 17–9 demonstrates how you can register a listener to receive location-update events. To register a listener, you call the requestLocationUpdates() method, passing the provider type as one of the parameters. When the location changes, the LocationManager calls the onLocationChanged() method of the listener with the new Location. It is very important that you remove any registrations for location updates at the appropriate time. In our example, we do registration in onResume(), and we remove that registration in onPause(). If we aren't going to be around to do anything with location updates, we should tell the provider not to send them. There's also the possibility that our activity could be destroyed (for example, if the user rotates their device and our activity is restarted), in which case our old activity could still exist, be receiving updates, displaying them with Toast, and taking up memory.

In our example, we set the minTime and minDistance to zero. This tells the LocationManager to send us updates as often as possible. These are not desired settings in real life, but we use them here to make the demonstrations run better. (In real life, you would not want the hardware trying to figure out our current position so often, as this drains the battery.) Set these values appropriately for the situation, trying to minimize how often you truly need to be notified of a change in position.

A new tool was introduced to you in Listing 17–9: the Toast widget. This is a handy device that allows you to briefly display a small pop-up view to the user. It appears to hover over the existing view and then goes away by itself. You can lengthen how long it hovers by using `LENGTH_LONG` instead of `LENGTH_SHORT`.

To test this in the emulator, you can use the Dalvik Debug Monitor Service (DDMS) perspective that ships with the ADT plug-in for Eclipse. The DDMS UI provides a screen for you to send the emulator a new location (see Figure 17–8).

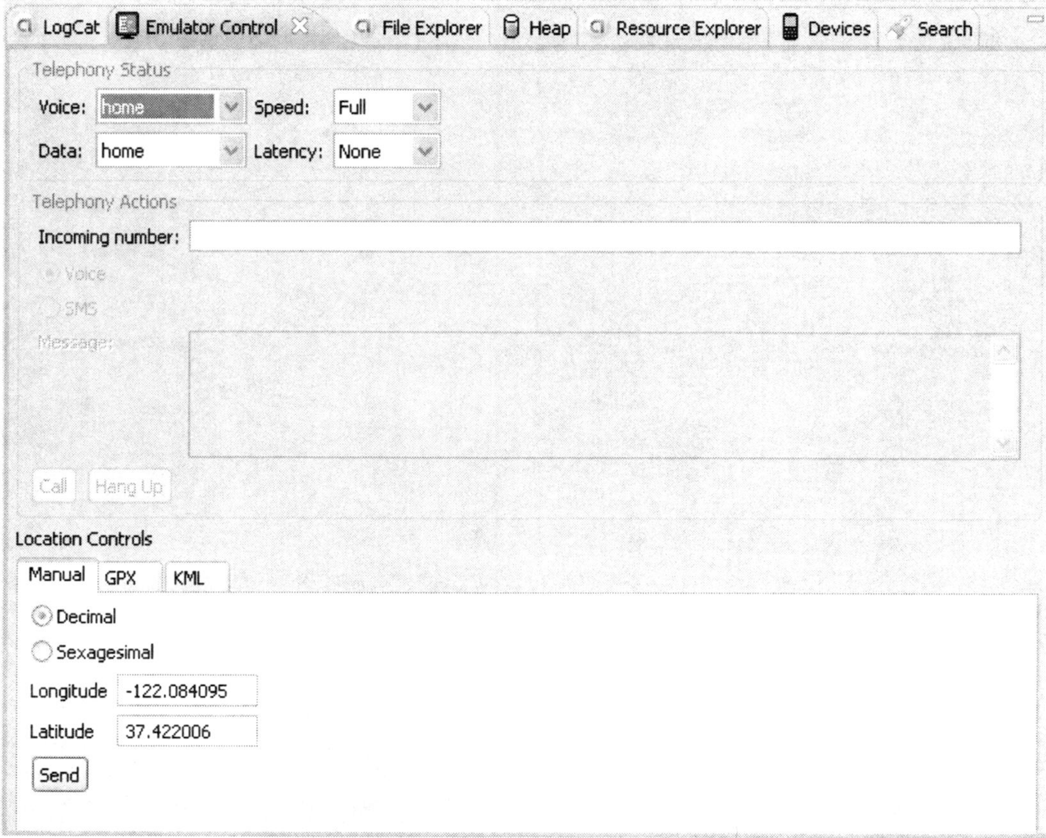

Figure 17–8. *Using the DDMS UI in Eclipse to send location data to the emulator*

To get to the DDMS in Eclipse, use Window ➤ Open Perspective ➤ DDMS. The Emulator Control view should already be there for you, but if not, use Window ➤ Show View ➤ Other ➤ Android ➤ Emulator Control to make it visible in this perspective. You may need to scroll down in the emulator control to find the location controls. As shown in Figure 17–8, the Manual tab in the DDMS user interface allows you to send a new GPS location (latitude/longitude pair) to the emulator. Sending a new location will fire the `onLocationChanged()` method on the listener, which will result in a message to the user conveying the new location.

You can send location data to the emulator using several other techniques, as shown in the DDMS user interface (see Figure 17–8). For example, the DDMS interface allows you to submit a GPS Exchange Format (GPX) file or a Keyhole Markup Language (KML) file. You can obtain sample GPX files from these sites:

- `http://www.topografix.com/gpx_resources.asp`
- `http://tramper.co.nz/?view=gpxFiles`
- `http://www.gpxchange.com/`

Similarly, you can use the following KML resources to obtain or create KML files:

- `http://bbs.keyhole.com/`
- `http://code.google.com/apis/kml/documentation/kml_tut.html`

NOTE: Some sites provide KMZ files. These are zipped KML files, so simply unzip them to get to the KML file. Some KML files need to have their XML namespace values altered in order to play properly in DDMS. If you have trouble with a particular KML file, make sure it has this:

`<kml xmlns="http://earth.google.com/kml/2.x">`.

You can upload a GPX or KML file to the emulator and set the speed at which the emulator will play back the file (see Figure 17–9). The emulator will then send location updates to your application based on the configured speed. As Figure 17–9 shows, a GPX file contains points, shown in the top part, and paths, shown in the bottom part. You can't play a point, but when you click a point, it will be sent to the emulator. You click a path, and then the Play button will be enabled so you can play the points.

NOTE: There have been reports that not all GPX files are understandable by the emulator control. If you attempt to load a GPX file and nothing happens, try a different file from a different source.

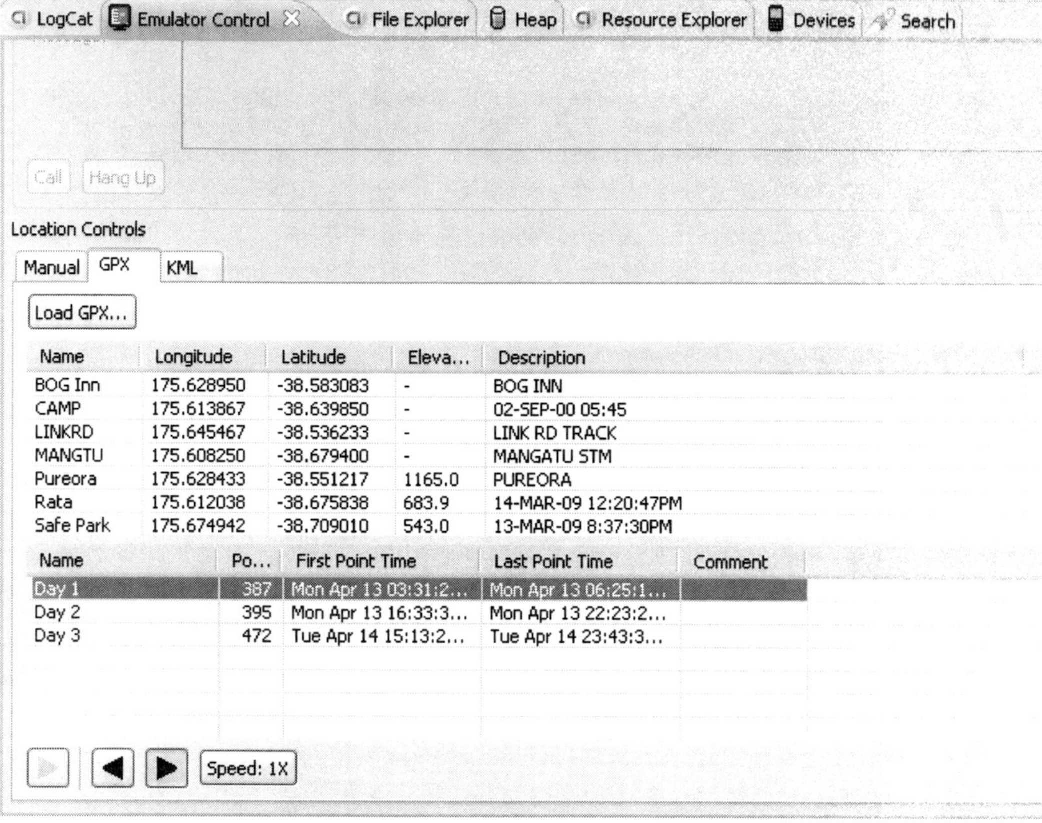

Figure 17–9. *Uploading GPX and KML files to the emulator for playback*

Listing 17–9 includes some additional methods for `LocationListener` we haven't mentioned yet. They are the callbacks `onProviderDisabled()`, `onProviderEnabled()`, and `onStatusChanged()`. For our sample, we did not do anything with these, but in your application, you could be notified when a location provider, such as gps, is disabled or enabled by the user, or when a status changes with one of the location providers. Statuses include `OUT_OF_SERVICE`, `TEMPORARILY_UNAVAILABLE`, and `AVAILABLE`. Even if a provider is enabled, it does not mean that it will be sending any location updates, and you can tell that using statuses. Note that `onProviderDisabled()` will be invoked immediately if a `requestLocationUpdates()` is called for a disabled provider.

Sending Location Updates From the Emulator Console

Eclipse has some easy to use tools for sending location updates to your application, but there's another way to do it. Remember from Chapter 2 that to launch the emulator console, you use the following command from a tools window:

```
telnet localhost emulator_port_number
```

where emulator_port_number is the number associated to the instance of the AVD that's already running, displayed in the title bar of the emulator window. Once you're connected, you can use the geo fix command to send in location updates. To send in latitude/longitude coordinates with altitude (altitude is optional), use this form of the command:

```
geo fix lon lat [ altitude ]
```

For example, the following command will send the location of Jacksonville, Florida to your application with an altitude of 120 meters.

```
geo fix  -81.5625  30.334954  120
```

Please pay careful attention to the order of the arguments to the geo fix command. Longitude is the *first* argument, and latitude is the second.

Alternate Ways of Getting Location Updates

Earlier we showed you how to get location updates sent to your activity using the requestLocationUpdates() method of the LocationManager. There are actually several different signatures of this method, including ones that use a PendingIntent. This gives you the ability to direct location updates to services or broadcast receivers. You can also direct location updates to other Looper threads instead of the main thread, giving you lots of flexibility for your application, although some of these methods are only available since Android 2.3.

Showing Your Location Using MyLocationOverlay

A common use for GPS and maps is to show users where they are. Fortunately, Android makes this easy to do by supplying a special overlay called MyLocationOverlay. By adding this overlay to your MapView, you can quite easily add a blinking blue dot to your map showing where the LocationManager service says the device is.

For this example, we're going to combine a bunch of concepts together into one application. Using Listing 17–10, we can modify our previous example by updating the main.xml and MyLocationDemoActivity.java files. Or simply create a new project from the existing source of Chapter 17. Don't forget to put your Map API key into your manifest file.

Listing 17–10. *Using MyLocationOverlay*

```
<?xml version="1.0" encoding="utf-8"?>
<!-- This file is /res/layout/main.xml -->
<RelativeLayout
        xmlns:android="http://schemas.android.com/apk/res/android"
        android:layout_width="fill_parent"
        android:layout_height="fill_parent">

    <com.google.android.maps.MapView
        android:id="@+id/geoMap" android:clickable="true"
        android:layout_width="fill_parent"
        android:layout_height="fill_parent"
```

```
        android:apiKey="YOUR MAP API KEY GOES HERE"
        />

</RelativeLayout>


package com.androidbook.location.myoverlay;

import android.os.Bundle;
import com.google.android.maps.MapActivity;
import com.google.android.maps.MapController;
import com.google.android.maps.MapView;
import com.google.android.maps.MyLocationOverlay;

public class MyLocationDemoActivity extends MapActivity {

    MapView mapView = null;
    MapController mapController = null;
    MyLocationOverlay whereAmI = null;

    @Override
    protected boolean isLocationDisplayed() {
        return whereAmI.isMyLocationEnabled();
    }

    @Override
    protected boolean isRouteDisplayed() {
        return false;
    }

    /** Called when the activity is first created. */
    @Override
    public void onCreate(Bundle savedInstanceState) {
        super.onCreate(savedInstanceState);
        setContentView(R.layout.main);

        mapView = (MapView)findViewById(R.id.geoMap);
        mapView.setBuiltInZoomControls(true);

        mapController = mapView.getController();
        mapController.setZoom(15);

        whereAmI = new MyLocationOverlay(this, mapView);
        mapView.getOverlays().add(whereAmI);
        mapView.postInvalidate();
    }

    @Override
    public void onResume()
    {
        super.onResume();
        whereAmI.enableMyLocation();
        whereAmI.runOnFirstFix(new Runnable() {
            public void run() {
                mapController.setCenter(whereAmI.getMyLocation());
            }
        });
```

```
    }

    @Override
    public void onPause()
    {
        super.onPause();
        whereAmI.disableMyLocation();
    }
}
```

Notice that, in this example, `isLocationDisplayed()` will return true if we are now showing the current location of the device on a map.

Once you launch this application in the emulator, you need to start sending it location updates before it gets very interesting. To do this, go to the DDMS Emulator Control view in Eclipse as described earlier in this section:

1. You need to find a sample GPX file from somewhere on the Internet. The sites listed earlier for GPX files have lots of them. Just pick one, and download it to your workstation.
2. Load this file into the emulator control using the Load GPX button on the GPX tab under Location Controls.
3. Select a path from the bottom list, and click the play button (the green arrow). Notice the Speed button also. This should start sending a stream of location updates to the emulator, which will be picked up by your application.
4. Click the Speed button to make the updates happen more often.

Figure 17–10 shows what your screen might look like.

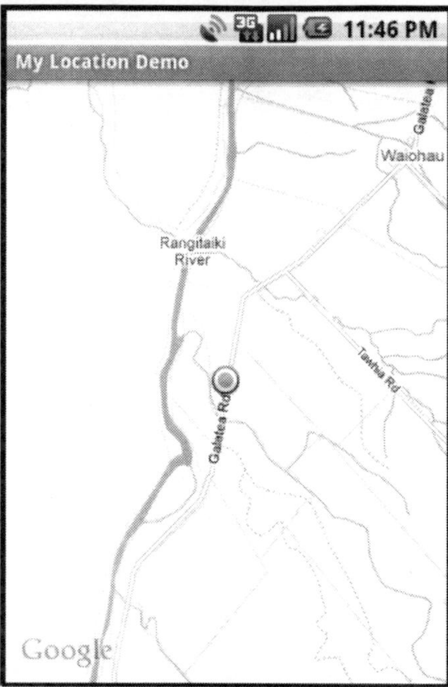

Figure 17–10. *Displaying Our Current Location with MyLocationOverlay*

The preceding code is very straightforward. After setting up the basics of a `MapView`, turning on the zoom controls and zooming in close, we create the `MyLocationOverlay` overlay. We add the new overlay to the `MapView` and call `postInvalidate()` on the `MapView`, so the new overlay will appear on the screen. Without this last call, the overlay will be created, but it will not show up.

Remember that our application will call `onResume()` even when it's just starting up, as well as after waking up. Therefore, we want to enable location tracking in `onResume()` and disable it in `onPause()`. There's no sense in draining the battery with location requests if we're not going to be around to consume them. In addition to enabling location requests in `onResume()`, we also want to jump to where we're at right now. The `MyLocationOverlay` class has a helpful method for this: `runOnFirstFix()`. This method allows us to set up code that will run as soon as we have a location at all. This could be immediately, because we've got a last location, or it could be later when we get something from `GPS_PROVIDER`, `NETWORK_PROVIDER`, or `PASSIVE_PROVIDER`. When we have a fix, we center on it. After that, we don't need to do anything ourselves, because the `MyLocationOverlay` is getting location updates and putting the blinking blue dot in that location. If the blue dot gets close to the edge of the map, the map will recenter itself so the blue dot is back in the middle of the screen.

Customizing MyLocationOverlay

You might have noticed that you are able to zoom in and out while the location updates are occurring, and you can even pan away from the current location. This could be a good thing or a bad thing depending on your point of view. If you pan away and don't remember where you are, it will be difficult to find yourself again unless you zoom way out and look for the blue dot. The recentering trick only works if the blue dot gradually approaches the edge of the map on its own. Once you've panned away so the blue dot is no longer visible, it won't put itself back into view. This situation can also occur if the blue dot jumps off the map without coming close to the edge first.

If you want the current location to always be displayed near the center of the screen, we need to make sure we keep animating to the current location, and we can do that relatively easily. For the next version of this exercise we'll reuse everything in our MyLocationDemo project except for a very small change to our `Activity`, and we're going to add a new class to our package, an extension of `MyLocationOverlay`, so we can tweak its behavior just a bit. The new extension of `MyLocationOverlay` is shown in Listing 17–11.

Listing 17–11. *Extending MyLocationOverlay and Keeping Our Location in View*

```
package com.androidbook.location.myoverlay;

import android.content.Context;
import android.location.Location;

import com.google.android.maps.GeoPoint;
import com.google.android.maps.MapView;
import com.google.android.maps.MyLocationOverlay;

public class MyCustomLocationOverlay extends MyLocationOverlay {
    MapView mMapView = null;

    public MyCustomLocationOverlay(Context ctx, MapView mapView) {
        super(ctx, mapView);
        mMapView = mapView;
    }

    public void onLocationChanged(Location loc) {
        super.onLocationChanged(loc);
        GeoPoint newPt = new GeoPoint((int) (loc.getLatitude()*1E6),
                (int) (loc.getLongitude()*1E6));
        mMapView.getController().animateTo(newPt);
    }
}
```

The only thing we need to change from Listing 17–10 is to use `MyCustomLocationOverlay` instead of `MyLocationOverlay` in our activity's `onCreate()` method, like so:

```
whereAmI = new MyCustomLocationOverlay(this, mapView);
```

Go ahead and run this in the emulator, and then send it new locations through the emulator control. If you're sending in a stream of location updates using a GPX file, you'll notice that the blue dot is always moved to the center of the map. Even if you pan completely away from the blue dot, the map returns to show it in the center.

Using Proximity Alerts

We mentioned earlier that the LocationManager can notify you when the device enters a specified geographical location. The method to set this up is addProximityAlert() from the LocationManager class. Basically, you tell the LocationManager that you want an Intent to be fired when the location of the device goes into, or leaves, a circle of a certain radius with a center at a latitude/longitude position. The Intent can trigger a BroadcastReceiver or a Service to be called, or an Activity to be started. There is also an optional time limit placed on the alert, so it could time out before the Intent fires.

Internally, the code for this method registers listeners for both the GPS and network providers and sets up location updates for once per second and a minDistance of 1 meter. You don't have any way to override this behavior or set parameters. Therefore, if you leave this running for a long time, you could end up draining the battery very quickly. If the screen goes to sleep, proximity alerts will only be checked once every 4 minutes, but again, you have no control over the time duration here.

It could be much better to do your own thing to decide if the device is within a certain distance of a latitude/longitude position using the techniques we've shown you in this chapter. For example, if you maintain a list of locations that you want to check against, you could measure the distance from the current location to each location in the list. Depending on how far away you are, you could decide to wait quite a while before checking the current location again. For example, if the nearest location is 100 miles away and we want to know when we're within 300 meters, clearly, we don't need to check in 1 second from now.

If you do wish to use this method though, we'll show you how. Listing 17–12 shows the Java code for our main Activity, as well as the BroadcastReceiver that will receive the broadcasts.

Listing 17–12. *Setting up a Proximity Alert with a BroadcastReceiver*

```
// This file is ProximityActivity.java
package com.androidbook.location.proximity;

import android.app.Activity;
import android.app.PendingIntent;
import android.content.Intent;
import android.content.IntentFilter;
import android.location.LocationManager;
import android.net.Uri;
import android.os.Bundle;

public class ProximityActivity extends Activity {
    private final String PROX_ALERT =
        "com.androidbook.intent.action.PROXIMITY_ALERT";
    private ProximityReceiver proxReceiver = null;
    private LocationManager locMgr = null;
    PendingIntent pIntent1 = null;
    PendingIntent pIntent2 = null;

    /** Called when the activity is first created. */
    @Override
```

```
    public void onCreate(Bundle savedInstanceState) {
        super.onCreate(savedInstanceState);

        locMgr = (LocationManager)
                 this.getSystemService(LOCATION_SERVICE);

        double lat = 30.334954;      // Coordinates for Jacksonville, FL
        double lon = -81.5625;
        float radius = 5.0f * 1609.0f; // 5 miles x 1609 meters per mile

        String geo = "geo:"+lat+","+lon;

        Intent intent = new Intent(PROX_ALERT, Uri.parse(geo));
        intent.putExtra("message", "Jacksonville, FL");

        pIntent1 = PendingIntent.getBroadcast(getApplicationContext(), 0,
                intent, PendingIntent.FLAG_CANCEL_CURRENT);

        locMgr.addProximityAlert(lat, lon, radius, -1L, pIntent1);

        lat = 28.54;         // Coordinates for Orlando, FL
        lon = -81.38;
        geo = "geo:"+lat+","+lon;

        intent = new Intent(PROX_ALERT, Uri.parse(geo));
        intent.putExtra("message", "Orlando, FL");

        pIntent2 = PendingIntent.getBroadcast(getApplicationContext(), 0,
                intent, PendingIntent.FLAG_CANCEL_CURRENT);

        locMgr.addProximityAlert(lat, lon, radius, -1L, pIntent2);

        proxReceiver = new ProximityReceiver();

        IntentFilter iFilter = new IntentFilter(PROX_ALERT);
        iFilter.addDataScheme("geo");

        registerReceiver(proxReceiver, iFilter);
    }

    protected void onDestroy() {
        super.onDestroy();
        unregisterReceiver(proxReceiver);
        locMgr.removeProximityAlert(pIntent1);
        locMgr.removeProximityAlert(pIntent2);
    }
}

// This file is ProximityReceiver.java
package com.androidbook.location.proximity;

import android.content.BroadcastReceiver;
import android.content.Context;
import android.content.Intent;
import android.location.LocationManager;
import android.os.Bundle;
```

```
import android.util.Log;

public class ProximityReceiver extends BroadcastReceiver {

    private static final String TAG = "ProximityReceiver";

    @Override
    public void onReceive(Context arg0, Intent intent) {
        Log.v(TAG, "Got intent");
        if(intent.getData() != null)
            Log.v(TAG, intent.getData().toString());
        Bundle extras = intent.getExtras();
        if(extras != null) {
            Log.v(TAG, "Message: " + extras.getString("message"));
            Log.v(TAG, "Entering? " +
              extras.getBoolean(LocationManager.KEY_PROXIMITY_ENTERING));
        }
    }
}
```

Because we're not actually displaying any positions on a map, we do not need to use a `MapActivity`, the Google Map APIs library, or a target. However, we do need to add a permission to our manifest file for `android.permission.ACCESS_FINE_LOCATION`, because the `LocationManager` will be attempting to use the GPS provider. It also attempts to use the network provider, but since we already require `ACCESS_FINE_LOCATION`, we're covered permissionwise. We register our `BroadcastReceiver` in code in the `onCreate()` method, so we do not need to set up a receiver in the manifest file. If you put the receiver into a separate application, then you *would* need to add an entry in that manifest file for the receiver. For our sample in Listing 17–12, it could look like the manifest snippet in Listing 17–13.

Listing 17–13. *AndroidManifest.xml snippet for a BroadcastReceiver for a Proximity Alert*

```
<application … >

    <receiver android:name=".ProximityReceiver">
        <intent-filter>
            <action android:name="com.androidbook.android.intent.PROXIMITY_ALERT" />
            <data android:scheme="geo" />
        </intent-filter>
    </receiver>
</application>
```

The proximity alert capability in Android works by receiving a `PendingIntent` object, the coordinates of our latitude/longitude point of interest, the radius (in meters) around that point that we want to check, and a time duration for how long to check. These arguments are all passed in using the `addProximityAlert()` method of `LocationManager`. The `PendingIntent` contains an `Intent` that will be the thing fired if the device either enters, or leaves, the circle we've defined. For our sample, we've chosen to use a broadcast intent, so we called the `getBroadcast()` method of the `PendingIntent` class, passing in our application's context plus our `Intent` that contains the alert action and the `Uri` of our `Location` point. If the device enters or leaves our circle of interest, our `Intent` will be broadcast to any receivers registered to receive it.

We chose not to set a timeout for our alerts, using a value of -1L for the duration. If you want to set a timeout, this value would be the number of milliseconds LocationManager waits before giving up and deleting your PendingIntent. You will not be notified if LocationManager deletes it before it fires.

For our sample, we get a reference to the LocationManager, create our first Intent and PendingIntent, and then we call addProximityAlert() to set up our first alert. Later, when our Intent fires, the only thing the LocationManager will add to it (in extras) is a boolean that says whether we're entering or leaving the circle. It does not add the current latitude/longitude position of the device, nor the latitude/longitude that we used in the call to addProximityAlert(). Therefore, in order for us to know which Location we're near in our BroadcastReceiver, we've added some data to our Intent, which is the latitude/longitude of our Location of interest. For fun, we've also added a message, in extras, with the description of this Location. We could have added doubles for the latitude and longitude if it would help on the receiving end.

After adding our first alert, we set up a second alert in the same fashion as before. Finally, we register a BroadcastReceiver to receive our Intents when they are broadcast by the LocationManager. We use an IntentFilter with both the alert as the action, and geo as the scheme. We need both things so we catch the broadcasts, because the broadcasts contain data; we could catch broadcasts without specifying a scheme if the broadcasts did not contain any data. The last thing we need to do is make sure we clean up after ourselves in the onDestroy() method, by unregistering our receiver and removing our proximity alerts from LocationManager using our saved PendingIntents. This is why we keep references to our PendingIntents, so we can remove the alerts later.

Our ProximityReceiver class is very simple. Upon receiving a broadcast message, it looks for information to print out in LogCat. Here is where you can see the extra data that LocationManager inserts for us, to tell us if we're entering or leaving the circle.

When you start up this sample application in the emulator, you'll see a blank screen with our application title. Now, you can send in location updates, using either the DDMS Emulator Control screen, or the emulator console with the geo fix command. When you send in locations such that you've transitioned across the edge of one of our circles (i.e., either the five-mile circle around Jacksonville or the five-mile circle around Orlando), you should see messages in LogCat from our BroadcastReceiver. Figure 17–11 shows what your LogCat window might look like once you've sent in some location updates that trigger the broadcasts.

Log

tag	Message
ActivityManager	Start proc com.androidbook.location.proximity for activity com.androidbook.location.proximity/.Pr
dalvikvm	LinearAlloc 0x0 used 638596 of 5242880 (12%)
ddm-heap	Got feature list request
LocationManager	Constructor: service = android.location.ILocationManager$Stub$Proxy@43d07da8
LocationManager	addProximityAlert: latitude = 30.334954, longitude = -81.5625, radius = 8045.0, expiration = 2000
GpsLocationProvider	setMinTime 1000
GpsLocationProvider	startNavigating
LocationManager	addProximityAlert: latitude = 28.54, longitude = -81.38, radius = 8045.0, expiration = 60000, int
ActivityManager	Displayed activity com.androidbook.location.proximity/.ProximityActivity: 2164 ms (total 2164 ms)
dalvikvm	GC freed 540 objects / 46120 bytes in 126ms
dalvikvm	GC freed 1860 objects / 108208 bytes in 147ms
GpsLocationProvider	TTFF: 17381
ProximityReceiver	Got intent
ProximityReceiver	geo:28.54,-81.38
ProximityReceiver	Message: Orlando, FL
ProximityReceiver	Entering? true

Figure 17–11. *LogCat window with messages from our BroadcastReceiver*

Because these are broadcasts, we cannot rely on the order in which they are received. For example, if we're inside the Orlando circle and we jump inside the Jacksonville circle, we could receive the broadcast that says we're inside the Jacksonville circle *before* we get the broadcast that says we left the Orlando circle.

Since we're dealing with `Locations`, we're using the `geo` scheme for the URI, which is one of the known schemes and quite perfect for passing latitude and longitude information. You should note that the structure of the `geo` URI puts latitude before longitude, but when we use the `geo fix` command in our emulator console, we put longitude before latitude. This can trip you up if you're not paying attention, and you could end up spending a lot of time trying to debug your application when the problem is simply the order in which you're sending in location updates. You could always use a GPX or KML file to send in locations and preselect locations for testing where your circle will overlap with the path from that file.

Our sample application is very simple. In a real application, the `BroadcastReceiver` could do notifications or start a service. Instead of a broadcast, `PendingIntent` could be for an activity or a service, even in some other application. Our application could be a mentioned service instead.

References

Here are some helpful references to topics you may wish to explore further.

- `http://www.androidbook.com/projects`. Look here for a list of downloadable projects related to this book. For this chapter look for a zip file called ProAndroid3_Ch17_Maps.zip. This zip file contains all projects from this chapter, listed in separate root directories. There is also a README.TXT file that describes exactly how to import projects into Eclipse from one of these zip files.

Summary

In this chapter, we discussed maps and location-based services. We talked at length about using the `MapView` control and the `MapActivity` class. We started with the basics of the map and then showed you how to utilize overlays to place markers on maps. We even showed you how to geocode and handle geocoding in background threads. We talked about the `LocationManager` class, which provides detailed location information through providers and allows us to display the current location of the device on a map. Last, we showed you how to use proximity alerts.

In the next chapter, we'll talk about the telephony services of Android.

Chapter 18

Using the Telephony APIs

Many Android devices are smartphones, but so far, we haven't talked about how to program applications that use phone features. In this chapter, we will show you how to send and receive Short Message Service (SMS) messages. We will also touch on several other interesting aspects of the telephony APIs in Android, including the Session Initiation Protocol (SIP) functionality. SIP is an IETF standard for implementing Voice over Internet Protocol (VoIP) where the user can make telephone-like calls over the Internet. SIP can also handle video.

Working with SMS

SMS stands for Short Message Service, but it's commonly called *text messaging*. The Android SDK supports sending and receiving text messages. We'll start by discussing various ways to send SMS messages with the SDK.

Sending SMS Messages

To send a text message from your application, you need to add the `android.permission.SEND_SMS` permission to your manifest file and then use the `android.telephony.SmsManager` class. See Listing 18-1 for the layout XML file and the Java code for this example. If you need to see where the permission goes in the manifest XML file, you can sneak ahead to Listing 18-2.

> **NOTE:** We will give you a URL at the end of the chapter which you can use to download projects of this chapter. This will allow you to import these projects into your Eclipse directly.

Listing 18-1. *Sending SMS (Text) Messages*

```
<?xml version="1.0" encoding="utf-8"?>
<!-- This file is /res/layout/main.xml -->
<LinearLayout xmlns:android="http://schemas.android.com/apk/res/android"
    android:orientation="vertical"
    android:layout_width="fill_parent"
```

```
    android:layout_height="fill_parent">

    <LinearLayout
        xmlns:android="http://schemas.android.com/apk/res/android"
        android:orientation="horizontal"
        android:layout_width="fill_parent"
        android:layout_height="wrap_content">

        <TextView android:layout_width="wrap_content"
            android:layout_height="wrap_content"
            android:text="Destination Address:" />

        <EditText android:id="@+id/addrEditText"
            android:layout_width="fill_parent"
            android:layout_height="wrap_content"
            android:phoneNumber="true"
            android:text="9045551212" />

    </LinearLayout>

    <LinearLayout
        xmlns:android="http://schemas.android.com/apk/res/android"
        android:orientation="vertical"
        android:layout_width="fill_parent"
        android:layout_height="wrap_content">

        <TextView android:layout_width="wrap_content"
            android:layout_height="wrap_content"
            android:text="Text Message:" />

        <EditText android:id="@+id/msgEditText"
            android:layout_width="fill_parent"
            android:layout_height="wrap_content"
            android:text="hello sms" />

    </LinearLayout>

    <Button android:id="@+id/sendSmsBtn"
        android:layout_width="wrap_content"
        android:layout_height="wrap_content"
        android:text="Send Text Message"
        android:onClick="doSend" />

</LinearLayout>


// This file is TelephonyDemo.java
import android.app.Activity;
import android.os.Bundle;
import android.telephony.SmsManager;
import android.view.View;
import android.widget.EditText;
import android.widget.Toast;

public class TelephonyDemo extends Activity
{
    @Override
```

```
    protected void onCreate(Bundle savedInstanceState) {
        super.onCreate(savedInstanceState);
        setContentView(R.layout.main);
    }

    public void doSend(View view) {
        EditText addrTxt =
              (EditText) findViewById(R.id.addrEditText);

        EditText msgTxt =
              (EditText) findViewById(R.id.msgEditText);

        try {
            sendSmsMessage(
                addrTxt.getText().toString(),
                msgTxt.getText().toString());
            Toast.makeText(this, "SMS Sent",
                    Toast.LENGTH_LONG).show();
        } catch (Exception e) {
            Toast.makeText(this, "Failed to send SMS",
                    Toast.LENGTH_LONG).show();
            e.printStackTrace();
        }
    }

    @Override
    protected void onDestroy() {
        super.onDestroy();
    }

    private void sendSmsMessage(String address,String message)throws Exception
    {
        SmsManager smsMgr = SmsManager.getDefault();
        smsMgr.sendTextMessage(address, null, message, null, null);
    }
}
```

The example in Listing 18-1 demonstrates sending SMS text messages using the Android SDK. Looking at the layout snippet first, you can see that the user interface has two `EditText` fields: one to capture the SMS recipient's destination address (the phone number) and another to hold the text message. The user interface also has a button to send the SMS message, as shown in Figure 18-1.

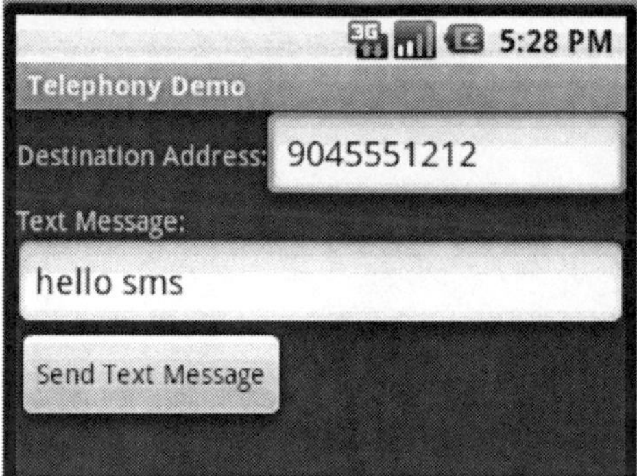

Figure 18-1. *The UI for the SMS example*

The interesting part of the sample is the `sendSmsMessage()` method. The method uses the `SmsManager` class's `sendTextMessage()` method to send the SMS message. Here's the signature of `SmsManager.sendTextMessage()`:

```
sendTextMessage(String destinationAddress, String smscAddress,
    String textMsg, PendingIntent sentIntent,
    PendingIntent deliveryIntent);
```

In this example, you populate only the destination address and the text-message parameters. You can, however, customize the method so it doesn't use the default SMS center (the address of the server on the cellular network that will dispatch the SMS message). You can also implement a customization in which pending intents are broadcast when the message is sent (or failed) and when a delivery notification has been received.

There are two main steps to sending an SMS message, sending and delivering. As each step is reached, if provided by your application, a pending intent is broadcast. You can put whatever you want into the pending intent, such as the action, but the result code passed to your `BroadcastReceiver` will be specific to SMS sending or delivery. Also, you may get extra data related to radio errors or status reports depending on the implementation of the SMS system.

Without pending intents your code can't tell if the text message was sent successfully or not. While testing though you can. If you launch this sample application in an emulator and launch *another* instance of an emulator (either from the command line or from the Eclipse Window ➤ Android SDK and AVD Manager screen), you can use the port number of the other emulator as the destination address. The port number is the number that appears in the emulator window title bar; it's usually something like 5554. After clicking the Send Text Message button, you should see a notification appear in the other emulator indicating that your text message has been received on the other side.

The `SMSManager` class provides two other ways to send SMS messages:

- `sendDataMessage()` takes an additional argument to specify a port number and, instead of a `String` message, takes a byte array.

- sendMultipartTextMessage() allows for sending text messages when the whole message is larger than is allowed in the SMS specification. sendMultipartTextMessage() method takes an array of Strings, but note that it also then takes an optional array of pending intents for both sending and delivery. The SMSManager class provides a divideMessage() method to help split up big messages into multiple parts.

All in all, sending an SMS message is about as simple as it gets with Android. Realize that, with the emulator, your SMS messages are not actually sent to their destinations. You can, however, assume success if the sendTextMessage() method returns without an exception. As shown in Listing 18-1, you can use the Toast class to display a message in the UI to indicate whether the SMS message was sent successfully.

Sending SMS messages is only half the story. Now, we'll show you how to monitor incoming SMS messages.

Monitoring Incoming SMS Messages

We're going to use the same application that you just created to send SMS messages, and we're going to add a BroadcastReceiver to listen for the action android.provider.Telephony.SMS_RECEIVED. This action is broadcast by Android when an SMS message is received by the device. When we register our receiver, our application will be notified whenever an SMS message is received. The first step in monitoring incoming SMS messages is to request permission to receive them. To do that, we must add the android.permission.RECEIVE_SMS permission to the manifest file. To implement the receiver, we must write a class that extends android.content.BroadcastReceiver and then register the receiver in the manifest file. Listing 18-2 includes both the AndroidManifest.xml file and our receiver class. Notice that both permissions are present in the manifest file because we still need the send permission for the activity we created above.

Listing 18-2. ***Monitoring SMS Messages***

```
<?xml version="1.0" encoding="utf-8"?>
<!-- This file is AndroidManifest.xml -->
<manifest xmlns:android="http://schemas.android.com/apk/res/android"
    package="com.androidbook.telephony" android:versionCode="1"
    android:versionName="1.0">
    <application android:icon="@drawable/icon"
            android:label="@string/app_name">
        <activity android:name=".TelephonyDemo"
                android:label="@string/app_name">
          <intent-filter>
            <action android:name="android.intent.action.MAIN" />
            <category android:name="android.intent.category.LAUNCHER" />
          </intent-filter>
        </activity>
        <receiver android:name="MySMSMonitor">
          <intent-filter>
            <action
```

```
                android:name="android.provider.Telephony.SMS_RECEIVED"/>
            </intent-filter>
        </receiver>

    </application>
    <uses-sdk android:minSdkVersion="4" />

    <uses-permission android:name="android.permission.SEND_SMS"/>
    <uses-permission android:name="android.permission.RECEIVE_SMS"/>

</manifest>


// This file is MySMSMonitor.java
import android.content.BroadcastReceiver;
import android.content.Context;
import android.content.Intent;
import android.telephony.SmsMessage;
import android.util.Log;

public class MySMSMonitor extends BroadcastReceiver
{
    private static final String ACTION =
                "android.provider.Telephony.SMS_RECEIVED";
    @Override
    public void onReceive(Context context, Intent intent)
    {
        if(intent!=null && intent.getAction()!=null &&
                ACTION.compareToIgnoreCase(intent.getAction())==0)
        {
            Object[] pduArray= (Object[]) intent.getExtras().get("pdus");
            SmsMessage[] messages = new SmsMessage[pduArray.length];
            for (int i = 0; i<pduArray.length; i++) {
                messages[i] = SmsMessage.createFromPdu(
                                    (byte[])pduArray [i]);
                Log.d("MySMSMonitor", "From: " +
                        messages[i].getOriginatingAddress());
                Log.d("MySMSMonitor", "Msg: " +
                        messages[i].getMessageBody());
            }
            Log.d("MySMSMonitor","SMS Message Received.");
        }
    }
}
```

The top portion of Listing 18-2 is the manifest definition for the `BroadcastReceiver` to intercept SMS messages. The SMS monitor class is `MySMSMonitor`. The class implements the abstract `onReceive()` method, which is called by the system when an SMS message arrives. One way to test the application is to use the Emulator Control view in Eclipse. Run the application in the emulator, and go to Window ➤ Show View ➤ Other ➤ Android ➤ Emulator Control. The user interface allows you to send data to the emulator to emulate receiving an SMS message or phone call. As shown in Figure 18-2, you can send an SMS message to the emulator by populating the "Incoming number" field and selecting the SMS radio button. Next, type some text in the Message field, and click the Send button. Doing this sends an SMS message to the emulator and invokes your BroadcastReceiver's onReceive() method.

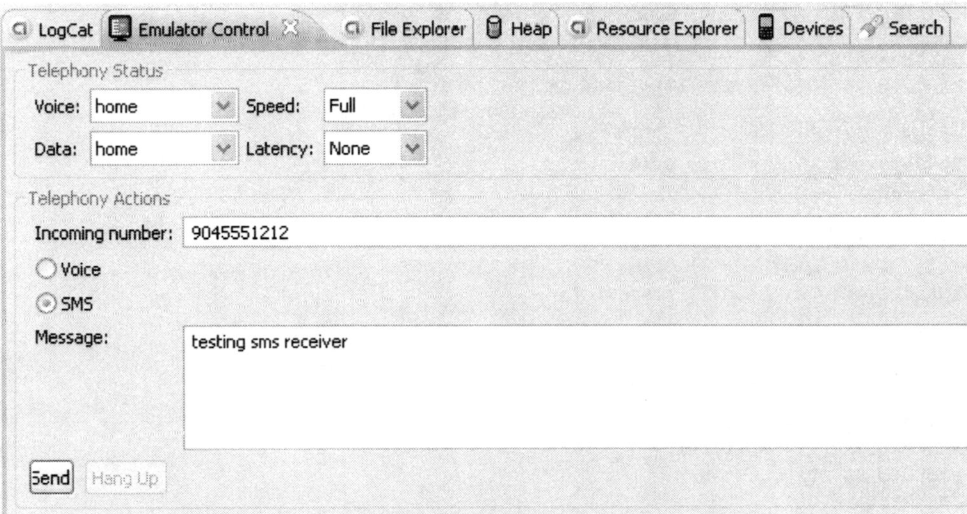

Figure 18-2. *Using the Emulator Control UI to send SMS messages to the emulator*

The onReceive() method will have the broadcast intent, which will contain the SmsMessage in the bundle property. You can extract the SmsMessage by calling intent.getExtras().get("pdus"). This call returns an array of objects defined in Protocol Description Unit (PDU) mode—an industry-standard way of representing an SMS message. You can then convert the PDUs to Android SmsMessage objects, as shown in Listing 18-2. As you can see, you get the PDUs as an object array from the intent. You then construct an array of SmsMessage objects, equal to the size of the PDU array. Finally, you iterate over the PDU array and create SmsMessage objects from the PDUs by calling SmsMessage.createFromPdu(). What you do after reading the incoming message must be quick. A broadcast receiver gets high priority in the system, but its task must be finished quickly, and it does not get put into the foreground for the user to see. Therefore, your options are limited. You should not do any direct UI work. Issuing a notification is fine, as is starting a service to continue work there. Once the onReceive() method completes, the hosting process of the onReceive() method could get killed at any time. Starting a service is OK, but binding to one is not, since that would require your process to exist for a while, which might not happen. For more information on BroadcastReceivers, please see Chapter 14.

Now, let's continue our discussion about SMS by looking at how you can work with various SMS folders.

Working with SMS Folders

Accessing the SMS inbox is another common requirement. To get started, you need to add read SMS permission (android.permission.READ_SMS) to the manifest file. Adding this permission gives you the ability to read from the SMS inbox.

To read SMS messages, you need to execute a query on the SMS inbox, as shown in Listing 18-3.

Listing 18-3. ***Displaying the Messages from the SMS Inbox***

```
<?xml version="1.0" encoding="utf-8"?>
<!-- This file is /res/layout/sms_inbox.xml -->
<LinearLayout xmlns:android="http://schemas.android.com/apk/res/android"
    android:orientation="vertical"
    android:layout_width="fill_parent"
    android:layout_height="fill_parent" >

  <TextView android:id="@+id/row"
    android:layout_width="fill_parent"
    android:layout_height="fill_parent"/>

</LinearLayout>


// This file is SMSInboxDemo.java
import android.app.ListActivity;
import android.database.Cursor;
import android.net.Uri;
import android.os.Bundle;
import android.widget.ListAdapter;
import android.widget.SimpleCursorAdapter;

public class SMSInboxDemo extends ListActivity {

    private ListAdapter adapter;
    private static final Uri SMS_INBOX =
            Uri.parse("content://sms/inbox");

    @Override
    public void onCreate(Bundle bundle) {
        super.onCreate(bundle);
        Cursor c = getContentResolver()
                .query(SMS_INBOX, null, null, null, null);
        startManagingCursor(c);
        String[] columns = new String[] { "body" };
        int[]      names = new int[]    { R.id.row };
        adapter = new SimpleCursorAdapter(this, R.layout.sms_inbox,
                c, columns, names);

        setListAdapter(adapter);
    }
}
```

Listing 18-3 opens the SMS inbox and creates a list in which each item contains the body portion of an SMS message. The layout portion of Listing 18-3 contains a simple `TextView` that will hold the body of each message in a list item. To get the list of SMS messages, you create a URI pointing to the SMS inbox (`content://sms/inbox`) and then execute a simple query. You then filter on the body of the SMS message and set the list adapter of the `ListActivity`. After executing the code from Listing 18-3, you'll see a list of SMS messages in the inbox. Make sure you generate a few SMS messages using the Emulator Control before running the code on the emulator.

Because you can access the SMS inbox, you would expect to be able to access other SMS-related folders, such as the sent or draft folder. The only difference between accessing the inbox and accessing the other folders is the URI you specify. For example, you can access the sent folder by executing a query against `content://sms/sent`. Following is the complete list of SMS folders and the URI for each folder:

- *All*: `content://sms/all`
- *Inbox*: `content://sms/inbox`
- *Sent*: `content://sms/sent`
- *Draft*: `content://sms/draft`
- *Outbox*: `content://sms/outbox`
- *Failed*: `content://sms/failed`
- *Queued*: `content://sms/queued`
- *Undelivered*: `content://sms/undelivered`
- *Conversations*: `content://sms/conversations`

Android combines MMS and SMS and allows you to access content providers for both at the same time, using an AUTHORITY of `mms-sms`. Therefore, you can access a URI such as this:

```
content://mms-sms/conversations
```

Sending E-mail

Now that you've seen how to send SMS messages in Android, you might assume that you can access similar APIs to send e-mail. Unfortunately, Android does not provide APIs for you to send e-mail. The general consensus is that users don't want an application to start sending e-mail on their behalf without them knowing about it. Instead, to send e-mail, you have to go through a registered e-mail application. For example, you could use `ACTION_SEND` to launch the e-mail application, as shown in Listing 18-4.

Listing 18-4. *Launching the E-mail Application Via an Intent*

```
Intent emailIntent=new Intent(Intent.ACTION_SEND);

String subject = "Hi!";
String body = "hello from android....";

String[] recipients = new String[]{"aaa@bbb.com"};
emailIntent.putExtra(Intent.EXTRA_EMAIL, recipients);

emailIntent.putExtra(Intent.EXTRA_SUBJECT, subject);
emailIntent.putExtra(Intent.EXTRA_TEXT, body);
emailIntent.setType("message/rfc822");
```

```
startActivity(emailIntent);
```

This code launches the default e-mail application and allows the user to decide whether to send the e-mail or not. Other "extras" that you can add to an email intent include EXTRA_CC and EXTRA_BCC.

Let's assume you want to send an e-mail attachment with your message. To do this, you would use something like the following, where the Uri is a reference to the file you want as the attachment:

```
emailIntent.putExtra(Intent.EXTRA_STREAM,
    Uri.fromFile(new File(myFileName)));
```

Next, we'll talk about the telephony manager.

Working with the Telephony Manager

The telephony APIs also include the telephony manager (android.telephony.TelephonyManager), which you can use to obtain information about the telephony services on the device, get subscriber information, and register for telephony state changes. A common telephony use case requires that an application execute business logic on incoming phone calls. For example, a music player might pause itself for an incoming call and resume when the call has been completed. The easiest way to listen for phone state changes is to implement a broadcast receiver on "android.intent.action.PHONE_STATE". You could do this in the same way we listened for incoming SMS messages above. The other way is to use the TelephonyManager.In this section, we are going to show you how to register for telephony state changes and how to detect incoming phone calls. Listing 18-4 shows the details.

Listing 18-5. *Using the Telephony Manager*

```
<?xml version="1.0" encoding="utf-8"?>
<!-- This file is res/layout/main.xml -->
<LinearLayout xmlns:android="http://schemas.android.com/apk/res/android"
    android:orientation="vertical"
    android:layout_width="fill_parent"
    android:layout_height="fill_parent"
    >
<Button
    android:id="@+id/callBtn"
    android:layout_width="wrap_content"
    android:layout_height="wrap_content"
    android:text="Place Call"
    android:onClick="doClick"
    />
<TextView
    android:id="@+id/textView"
    android:layout_width="fill_parent"
    android:layout_height="fill_parent"
    />
</LinearLayout>
```

```
// This file is PhoneCallActivity.java
package com.androidbook.phonecall.demo;

import android.app.Activity;
import android.content.Context;
import android.content.Intent;
import android.net.Uri;
import android.os.Bundle;
import android.telephony.PhoneStateListener;
import android.telephony.TelephonyManager;
import android.view.View;
import android.widget.TextView;

public class PhoneCallActivity extends Activity {
    private TelephonyManager teleMgr = null;
    private MyPhoneStateListener myListener = null;
    private String logText = "";
    private TextView tv;

    @Override
    protected void onCreate(Bundle savedInstanceState)
    {
        super.onCreate(savedInstanceState);
        setContentView(R.layout.main);

        tv = (TextView)findViewById(R.id.textView);

        teleMgr =
                (TelephonyManager)getSystemService(Context.TELEPHONY_SERVICE);
        myListener = new MyPhoneStateListener();
    }

    protected void onResume() {
        super.onResume();
        teleMgr.listen(myListener, PhoneStateListener.LISTEN_CALL_STATE);
    }

    protected void onPause() {
        super.onPause();
        teleMgr.listen(myListener, PhoneStateListener.LISTEN_NONE);
    }

    public void doClick(View target) {
        Intent intent = new Intent(Intent.ACTION_VIEW,
                Uri.parse("tel:5551212"));
        startActivity(intent);
    }

    class MyPhoneStateListener extends PhoneStateListener
    {
        @Override
        public void onCallStateChanged(int state, String incomingNumber)
        {
            super.onCallStateChanged(state, incomingNumber);

            switch(state)
            {
```

```
                case TelephonyManager.CALL_STATE_IDLE:
                    logText = "call state idle...incoming number is["+
                                incomingNumber + "]\n" + logText;
                    break;
                case TelephonyManager.CALL_STATE_RINGING:
                    logText = "call state ringing...incoming number is["+
                                incomingNumber + "]\n" + logText;
                    break;
                case TelephonyManager.CALL_STATE_OFFHOOK:
                    logText = "call state Offhook...incoming number is["+
                                incomingNumber + "]\n" + logText;
                    break;
                default:
                    logText = "call state [" + state +
                                "]incoming number is[" +
                                incomingNumber + "]\n" + logText;
                    break;
            }
            tv.setText(logText);
        }
    }
}
```

When working with the telephony manager, be sure to add the android.permission.READ_PHONE_STATE permission to your manifest file, so you can access phone state information. As shown in Listing 18-5, you get notified about phone state changes by implementing a PhoneStateListener and calling the listen() method of the TelephonyManager. When a phone call arrives, or the phone state changes, the system will call your PhoneStateListener's onCallStateChanged() method with the new state. As you will see when you try this out, the incoming phone number is only available when the state is CALL_STATE_RINGING. You write a message to the screen in this example, but your application could implement custom business logic in its place, such as pausing the playback of audio or video. To emulate incoming phone calls, you can use Eclipse's Emulator Control UI, the same one you used to send SMS messages (see Figure 18-2) but choose Voice instead of SMS.

Notice that we tell the TelephonyManager to stop sending us updates in onPause(). It is always important to turn off messages when our activity is being paused. Otherwise, the TelephonyManager could keep a reference to our object and prevent it from being cleaned up later.

This example deals with only one of the phone states that are available for listening. Check out the documentation on PhoneStateListener for others, including for example LISTEN_MESSAGE_WAITING_INDICATOR. When dealing with phone state changes, you might also need to get the subscriber's (user's) phone number. TelephonyManager.getLine1Number() will return that for you.

You may be wondering if it's possible to answer a phone via code. Unfortunately, at this time, the Android SDK does not provide a way to do this, even though the documentation implies that you can fire off an intent with an action of ACTION_ANSWER. In practice, this approach does not yet work, although you may want to check to see if this has been fixed since the time of this writing.

Similarly, you may want to place an outbound phone call via code. Here, you will find things easier. The simplest way to make an outbound call is to invoke the Dialer application via an intent with code such as the following:

```
Intent intent = new Intent(Intent.ACTION_CALL, Uri.parse("tel:5551212"));
startActivity(intent);
```

Note that for this to actually dial, your application will need the `android.permission.CALL_PHONE` permission. Otherwise, when your application attempts to invoke the Dialer application, you will get a `SecurityException`. To do dialing without this permission, change the action of the intent to `Intent.ACTION_VIEW`, which will cause the Dialer application to appear with your desired number to dial, but the user will need to press the Send button to initiate the call.

One other thing to keep in mind when dealing with phone features in your application is that other applications could very well respond to incoming phone calls and cause your activity to pause. In that case, you'll stop receiving notifications, although you will get an immediate notification when your `onResume()` method is called again and you reregister with the `TelephonyManager`. Be prepared for that when deciding what to do in your handler for phone state notifications.

Session Initiation Protocol (SIP)

Android 2.3 (Gingerbread) introduced new features to support SIP, in the android.net.sip package. SIP is an Internet Engineering Task Force (IETF) standard for orchestrating the sending of voice and video over a network connection to link people together in calls. This technology is sometimes called Voice over IP (VoIP), but note that there is more than one way to do VoIP. Skype for instance, uses a proprietary protocol to do their VoIP, and is incompatible with SIP. SIP is also not the same as Google Voice. Google Voice does not (as of this writing) support SIP directly, although there are ways to integrate Google Voice with a SIP provider to tie things together. Google Voice sets up a new telephone number for you, that you can then connect with other phones such as your home, work or mobile phone. Some SIP providers will generate a telephone number that can be used with Google Voice, but in this case Google Voice does not really know that the number is for a SIP account. A search of the Internet will reveal quite a few SIP providers, many with reasonable calling rates, and some that are free.

It is important to note that the SIP standard does not address passing audio and video data over a network. SIP is only involved in setting up, and tearing down, the direct connections between devices to allow audio and video data to flow. Client computer programs use SIP, as well as audio and video codecs and other libraries, to setup the calls between users. Other standards often involved with SIP calls include the Real-time Transport Protocol (RTP), Real-time Streaming Protocol (RTSP) and Session Description Protocol (SDP).

Users can make SIP calls from desktop computers without incurring long distance charges. The computer program can just as easily be running on a mobile device such as an Android smartphone or tablet. SIP computer programs are often called "soft phones". The real advantage of a soft phone on a mobile device occurs when the device is connecting to the Internet using Wi-Fi, so that the user is not using any wireless minutes but is still able to make or receive a call. On the receiving end, a soft phone must have registered its location and capabilities with a SIP provider so the provider's SIP server can respond to invite requests to setup the direct connection. If the receiver's soft phone is not available, the SIP server can direct the inbound request to a voicemail account for example.

Google provides a demonstration application for SIP, called SipDemo. We'd like to explore that application with you now, and help you understand how it works. Certain aspects are not obvious if you are new to SIP. If you'd like to experiment with SipDemo, you're probably going to need a physical Android device that supports SIP. This is because the Android emulators, as of this writing, do not support SIP (or Wi-Fi for that matter). There are some attempts on the Internet to make SIP work in the emulator, and by the time you read this, some may be easy to implement and robust. To play with SipDemo you will also need to get a SIP account from a SIP provider. You will need to have your SIP ID, SIP domain name (or proxy), and your SIP password. These will be plugged into the SipDemo application's preferences screen to be used by the application. Lastly, you will need a Wi-Fi connection from your device to the Internet. If you don't want to actually experiment with SipDemo on a device, you should still be able to understand the rest of this section. The SipDemo looks like Figure 18-3.

Figure 18-3. *The SipDemo application with the Menu showing*

To load SipDemo as a new project into Eclipse, use the New Android Project wizard, but click the "Create project from existing sample" option, choose Android 2.3 or higher in the Build Target section, then use the drop down Samples menu to choose SipDemo. Click Finish and Eclipse will create the new project for you. You can run this project with no changes to it, but as mentioned before, it won't do anything unless the device supports SIP, Wi-Fi is enabled, you've got a SIP account somewhere, you've used the Menu button to edit your SIP info, and you use the Menu button to initiate a call. You will need some other SIP account to call to test out the application. Pressing the big microphone image on the screen allows you to talk to the other side. This demo application can also receive an incoming call. Now let's talk about the inner workings of the android.net.sip package.

The android.net.sip package has four basic classes: SipManager, SipProfile, SipSession and SipAudioCall. SipManager is at the core of this package, and provides access to the rest of the SIP functionality. You invoke the static newInstance() method of SipManager to get a SipManager object. With a SipManager object, you can then get a SipSession for most SIP activity, or you can get a SipAudioCall for an audio-only call. This means Google has provided features in the android.net.sip package above what standard SIP provides, namely the ability to setup an audio call.

SipProfile is used to define the SIP accounts that will be talking to each other. This does not point directly to an end user's device, but rather the SIP account at a SIP provider. The servers will assist in the rest of the details to setup actual connections.

A SipSession is where the magic happens. Setting up a session includes your SipProfile so your application can make itself known to your SIP provider's server. You also pass a SipSession.Listener instance which is going to be notified when things are happening. Once you've setup a SipSession object, your application is ready to make calls to another SipProfile, or to receive incoming calls. The listener has a bunch of callbacks so your application can properly deal with the changing states of the session.

As of Honeycomb, the easiest thing to do is use SipAudioCall. The logic is all there to hook up the microphone and the speaker to the data streams so that you can carry on a conversation with the other side. There are lots of methods on SipAudioCall for managing mute, hold, and so on. All of the audio pieces are also handled for you. For anything more than that, you have work to do. The SipSession class has the makeCall() method for placing an outbound call. The main parameter is the session description (as a String). This is where things require more work. Building a session description requires formatting according to the Session Description Protocol (SDP) mentioned earlier. Understanding a received session description means parsing it according to SDP. The standards documentation for SDP is here: http://tools.ietf.org/html/rfc4566, and unfortunately, the Android SDK does not provide any support for SDP. Thanks to some very kind people, there are a couple of free SIP applications for Android that have built this capability. They are sipdroid (`http://code.google.com/p/sipdroid/`) and csipsimple (`http://code.google.com/p/csipsimple/`).

We haven't even started talking about the codecs for managing video streams between SIP clients, although sipdroid has this capability. Other aspects of SIP that are very appealing are the ability to setup conference calls among more than two people. These topics are beyond the scope of this book, but we hope you can appreciate what SIP can do for you.

Note that SIP applications will need at a minimum the android.permission.USE_SIP and android.permission.INTERNET permissions in order to function properly. Additional permissions will be needed if you use SipAudioCall. It is also a good idea to add the following tag to your AndroidManifest.xml file, as a child of <manifest>, so that your application will only be installable on devices that have hardware support for SIP:

```
<uses-feature android:name="android.hardware.sip.voip" />
```

References

Here are some helpful references to topics you may wish to explore further.

- http://www.androidbook.com/projects. Look here for a list of downloadable projects related to this book. For this chapter look for a zip file called ProAndroid3_Ch18_Telephony.zip. This zip file contains all projects from this chapter, listed in separate root directories. There is also a README.TXT file that describes exactly how to import projects into Eclipse from one of these zip files.
- http://en.wikipedia.org/wiki/Session_Initiation_Protocol. The Wikipedia page for SIP.
- http://tools.ietf.org/html/rfc3261. This is the official IETF standard for Session Initiation Protocol (SIP).
- http://tools.ietf.org/html/rfc4566. This is the official IETF standard for Session Description Protocol (SDP).
- http://code.google.com/p/sipdroid/, http://code.google.com/p/csipsimple/. Two open source applications for Android that implement SIP clients.

Summary

In this chapter, we talked about the Android telephony APIs. Specifically, we showed you how to send text messages, how to monitor incoming text messages, and how to access the various SMS folders on the device. We covered the TelephonyManager class. And we concluded with an overview of the Session Initiation Protocol (SIP) feature set introduced with Android 2.3.

Chapter 19

Understanding the Media Frameworks

Now we are going to explore a very interesting part of the Android SDK: the media frameworks. We will show you how to play and record audio and video, from a variety of sources. We'll also cover how to take photos with the camera. Any discussion of media would be incomplete without explaining secure digital (SD) cards and how to work with them, since you'll use SD cards often to read and write media files.

Using the Media APIs

Android supports playing audio and video content under the `android.media` package. In this chapter, we are going to explore the media APIs from this package.

At the heart of the `android.media` package is the `android.media.MediaPlayer` class. The `MediaPlayer` class is responsible for playing both audio and video content. The content for this class can come from the following sources:

- *Web*: You can play content from the Web via a URL.
- *.apk file*: You can play content that is packaged as part of your .apk file. You can package the media content as a resource or as an asset (within the `assets` folder).
- *SD card*: You can play content that resides on the device's SD card.

The MediaPlayer is capable of decoding quite a few different content formats, including 3GPP (.3gp), MP3 (.mp3), MIDI (.mid and others), Ogg Vorbis (.ogg), PCM/WAVE (.wav), and MPEG-4 (.mp4). As of Android 3.0, HTTP live streaming and M3U playlists are also supported. For a complete list of supported media formats, go to `http://developer.android.com/guide/appendix/media-formats.html`.

Using SD Cards

Before we get into creating and using our different types of media, let's look at how to work with SD cards. SD cards are used in Android phones for storing lots of user data, usually media content such as pictures, audio, and video. They are basically pluggable memory chips that keep their data even when they lose power. On a real phone, the SD card plugs into a memory slot and is accessible to the device. Many devices have one slot, and it's not expected that you will replace the SD card. On some devices, you can have multiple cards, switching among them with your device, and you can use them across different devices. Fortunately for us, the Android emulator can simulate SD cards, using space on your workstation's hard drive as if it were a plug-in SD card.

When you created your first Android Virtual Device (AVD) in Chapter 2, you specified a size for an SD card, which made it available to your application when you ran it in the emulator. If you look inside the AVD directory that was created, you will see a file called `sdcard.img` with the file size you specified. We didn't use the SD card then, but we'll be using it in this chapter.

As a developer, once you have an SD card, you can use the Android tools within Eclipse to push media files (or any other files) to the SD card. You can also use the Android Debug Bridge (`adb`) utility to push or pull files to and from an SD card. The `adb` utility is located in the tools subdirectory of the Android SDK; it is easy to get to from a tools window, as described in Chapter 2.

You already know how to get an SD card by creating an AVD. And, of course, you could create lots of AVDs that are the same except for the size of the SD card. Here's the other way to go: the Android SDK tools bundle contains a utility called `mksdcard` that can create an SD card image. Actually, the utility creates a formatted file that is used as an SD card. To use this utility, first find or create a folder for the image file, at `c:\Android\sdcard\`, for example. Then open a tools window and run a command like the following, using an appropriate path to the SD card image file:

```
mksdcard 256M c:\Android\sdcard\sdcard.img
```

This example command creates an SD card image at `c:\Android\sdcard\` with the file name `sdcard.img`. The size of the SD card will be 256MB. To specify other sizes, you can use K for kilobytes, but G doesn't work yet for gigabytes, so you'll need to specify multiples of 1024M to get gigabyte sizes. You can also simply specify an integer value representing the total number of bytes. Also note that the Android emulator won't work with SD card sizes below 8MB.

The Android Development Tools (ADT) in Eclipse offers a way to specify extra command-line arguments when launching the emulator. To find the field for the emulator options, go to the Preferences window of Eclipse, then choose Android ➤ Launch. In theory, you could add `-sdcard "PATH_TO_YOUR_SD_CARD_IMAGE_FILE"` here and it would override the SD card file path for your AVD. But this hasn't worked for a few Android releases now, and you always get the SD card image file that was created along with the AVD. The most reliable way to use a separate SD card with your AVD is to launch the emulator from the command line and specify the SD card image to use there. From within a Tools window (to see how to get a Tools window, refer to Chapter 2) the following command launches a named AVD but uses the specified SD card image file instead of the SD card image file that was created with the AVD:

```
emulator -avd AVDName -sdcard "PATH_TO_YOUR_SD_CARD_IMAGE_FILE"
```

When your SD card is first created, there are no files on it. You can add files by using the File Explorer tool in Eclipse. Start the emulator and wait until the emulator initializes. Then go to either the Java, Debug, or DDMS perspectives in Eclipse and look for the File Explorer tab, as shown in Figure 19–1.

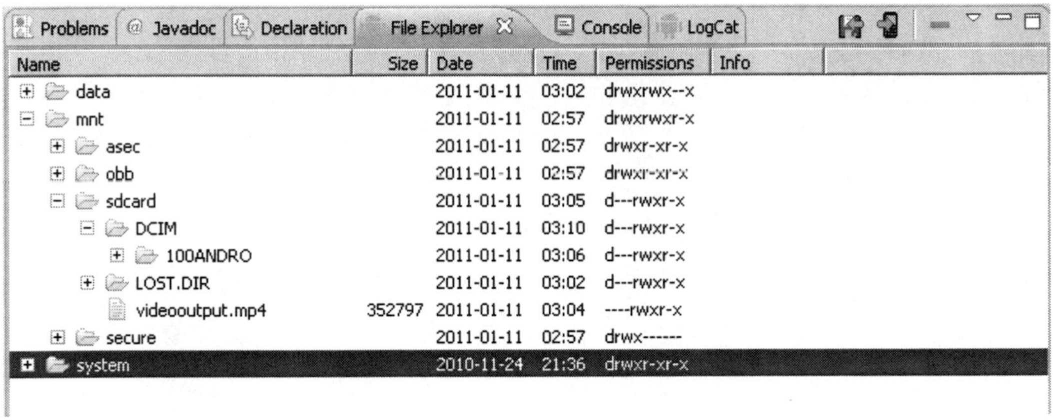

Problems | Javadoc | Declaration | File Explorer | Console | LogCat

Name	Size	Date	Time	Permissions	Info
data		2011-01-11	03:02	drwxrwx--x	
mnt		2011-01-11	02:57	drwxrwxr-x	
asec		2011-01-11	02:57	drwxr-xr-x	
obb		2011-01-11	02:57	drwxr-xr-x	
sdcard		2011-01-11	03:05	d---rwxr-x	
DCIM		2011-01-11	03:10	d---rwxr-x	
100ANDRO		2011-01-11	03:06	d---rwxr-x	
LOST.DIR		2011-01-11	03:02	d---rwxr-x	
videooutput.mp4	352797	2011-01-11	03:04	----rwxr-x	
secure		2011-01-11	02:57	drwx------	
system		2010-11-24	21:36	drwxr-xr-x	

Figure 19–1. *The File Explorer view*

If the File Explorer is not shown, you can bring it up by going to Window ➤ Show View ➤ Other ➤ Android and selecting File Explorer. Or, you can show the Dalvik Debug Monitor Service (DDMS) perspective by going to Window ➤ Open Perspective ➤ Other ➤ DDMS. The File Explorer view is by default on the DDMS perspective. The list of available views in Eclipse for Android is shown in Figure 19–2.

To push a file onto the SD card, select the sdcard folder in the File Explorer and choose the button with the right-facing arrow (at the top right-hand corner) pointing into what looks like a phone. This launches a dialog box that lets you select a file. Select the file that you want to upload to the SD card. The button next to it looks like a left arrow pointing into a floppy disk. Choose this button for pulling a file from the device onto your workstation, after selecting the file you want to pull from within the File Explorer.

If the File Explorer displays an empty view, you either don't have the emulator running, Eclipse has disconnected from the emulator, or the AVD that you are running in the emulator is not selected under the Devices tab shown in. To get a Devices tab, follow the same procedure as above for the File Explorer. Devices should also be available by default on the DDMS perspective.

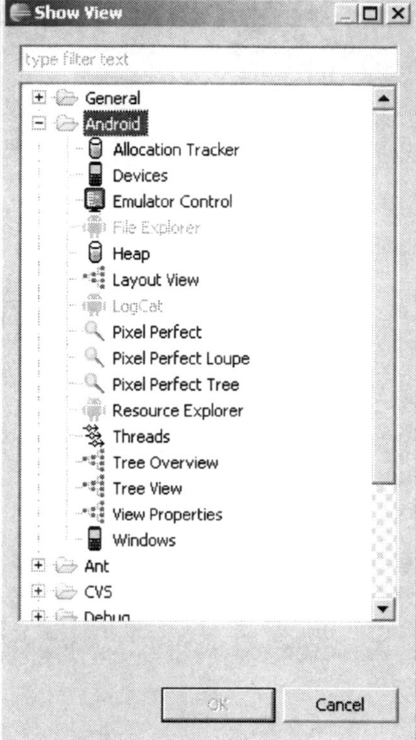

Figure 19–2. *Enabling Android views*

The other way to move files onto and off of the SD card is to use the adb utility. To try this, open a tools window, then type a command such as

```
adb push c:\path_to_my_file\filename /mnt/sdcard/newfile
```

This will push a file from your workstation to the SD card. Note that the device always uses forward slashes to separate directories. Use whatever directory separator character is appropriate for your workstation for the file that's being pushed, and use an appropriate path for the file on your workstation. Conversely, the following command will pull a file from the SD card to your workstation:

```
adb pull /mnt/sdcard/devicefile c:\path_to_where_its_going\filename
```

One of the nice features of this command is that it will create directories as needed, in either direction (push or pull), to get the file to the desired destination. Unfortunately, you cannot use adb to copy multiple files at the same time. You must do each file separately.

NOTE: Until Android 2.2, the SD card was most likely at /sdcard. Since Android 2.2, the SD card is most likely at /mnt/sdcard, however, there is a symbolic link called /sdcard that points to /mnt/sdcard for backward compatibility.

You may have noticed a directory on the SD card called DCIM. This is the Digital Camera Images directory. It is an industry standard to put a DCIM directory within the root directory of an SD card that's used for digital images. It's also an industry standard to put a directory underneath DCIM that represents a camera, in the format 123ABCDE—three digits followed by five letters. The emulator creates a directory called 100ANDRO under DCIM, but makers of digital cameras, and Android phone makers, can call this directory whatever they want. The emulator—and some Android phones—has a directory called Camera under the DCIM directory, but this isn't compliant with the standard. Nevertheless, you may find image files under Camera and you may find them under 100ANDRO, or you may find some other directory under DCIM where image files are stored.

Unfortunately, there is not a method call to tell you which directory might be used underneath the DCIM directory for Camera pictures. There are a couple of methods though to tell you where the top of the SD card is. The first is Environment.getExternalStorageDirectory() and it returns a File object for the top-level directory for the SD card. On pre-Android 2.2 devices, this was most likely /sdcard, but not on all devices. With Android 2.2, most devices will have /mnt/sdcard. It is much better to use this Environment method than to assume you know the name of the SD card's root directory. The other method we will describe next.

Since Android 2.2 (a.k.a. Froyo), there are some new constants available in the Environment class for locating directories, and there's also a new method in this class for locating directories. Previously, the SD card was a bit of a free-for-all, with no standardized directory names other than DCIM. With Froyo, there are several standardized directory names, as described in Table 19–1. The third column is the directory name used in the emulator, where the top of the SD card will most likely be /mnt/sdcard (may vary by device). The variance in directories is why you should always use an Environment method to find the desired directory on the SD card.

Table 19–1. *The Standardized Directories of the SD card*

Directory Constant	Description	Directory in Emulator from Top of SD Card
DIRECTORY_ALARMS	When Android looks for audio files to use for alarms, it looks in this standard directory.	Alarms
DIRECTORY_DCIM	Industry standard directory to look for pictures and video taken using the Camera.	DCIM
DIRECTORY_DOWNLOADS	Standard directory to hold files the user has downloaded.	Download (note: not plural)
DIRECTORY_MOVIES	When Android looks for movie files for the user, it looks in this standard directory.	Movies

Directory Constant	Description	Directory in Emulator from Top of SD Card
DIRECTORY_MUSIC	When Android looks for audio files to use as regular music for the user to listen to, it looks in this standard directory.	Music
DIRECTORY_NOTIFICATIONS	When Android looks for audio files to use for notifications, it looks in this standard directory.	Notifications
DIRECTORY_PICTURES	When Android looks for image files not taken by the Camera, it looks in this standard directory.	Pictures
DIRECTORY_PODCASTS	When Android looks for audio files to use as podcasts, it looks in this standard directory.	Podcasts
DIRECTORY_RINGTONES	When Android looks for audio files to use for ringtones, it looks in this standard directory.	Ringtones

The new method for locating directories is `Environment.getExternalStoragePublicDirectory(String type)`, where the type parameter is one of the constants from Table 19–1. This method returns a `File` object representing the requested directory. This method doesn't exist on older devices (older than Froyo), and even on newer devices you may find you need to accommodate differences. For example, Samsung has devices with two SD cards, so these methods are not sufficient to figure out all external storage on those.

And finally, a word about security. With the introduction of Android SDK 1.6, you need to add this permission to your manifest file in order for your application to be able to write to the SD card:

```
<uses-permission android:name="android.permission.WRITE_EXTERNAL_STORAGE" />
```

However, applications written for the older Android SDKs are not required to request this permission. That means that if your application's `minSdkVersion` is less than 4 (corresponding to Android SDK 1.6), you do not need to add this tag to your `AndroidManifest.xml` file, even if you're running on a device that supports a newer Android SDK. Therefore, when you are creating an application, if you choose a Build Target of Android 1.6 or later (`minSdkVersion` of 4 or higher) and you want to be able to write to the SD card, make sure you add the previous tag to your manifest file. If your Build Target is Android 1.5, you do not need this tag. Now that you know the basics of SD cards, let's get into audio.

Playing Media

To get started, we'll show you how to build a simple application that plays an MP3 file located on the Web (see Figure 19–3). After that, we will talk about using the `setDataSource()` method of the `MediaPlayer` class to play content from the .apk file or the SD card. `MediaPlayer` isn't the only way to play audio though, so we'll also cover the `SoundPool` class, as well as `JetPlayer`, `AsyncPlayer`, and for the lowest level of working with audio, the `AudioTrack` class. Next, we will discuss some of the shortfalls of the `MediaPlayer` class. Finally, we'll see how to play video content.

Playing Audio Content

Figure 19–3 shows the user interface for our first example. This application will demonstrate some of the fundamental uses of the `MediaPlayer` class, such as starting, pausing, restarting, and stopping the media file. Look at the layout for the application's user interface.

Figure 19–3. *The user interface for the media application*

The user interface consists of a `LinearLayout` with four buttons: one to start the player, one to pause the player, one to restart the player and one to stop the player. The code and layout file for the application are shown in Listing 19–1. We're going to assume you're building against Android 2.2 or later for this example, since we're using the `getExternalStoragePublicDirectory()` method of Environment. If you want to build this against an older version of Android, simply use `getExternalStorageDirectory()` instead, and adjust where you put the media files so your application will find them.

> **NOTE:** See the "References" section at the end of this chapter for the URL from which you can import these projects into your Eclipse directly, instead of copying and pasting code.

Listing 19–1. *The layout and code for the media application*

```
<?xml version="1.0" encoding="utf-8"?>
<!-- This file is /res/layout/main.xml -->
<LinearLayout xmlns:android="http://schemas.android.com/apk/res/android"
    android:layout_width="fill_parent"
    android:layout_height="fill_parent"
    android:orientation="vertical" >

  <Button android:id="@+id/startPlayerBtn"
    android:layout_width="fill_parent"
    android:layout_height="wrap_content"
    android:text="Start Playing Audio" android:onClick="doClick" />

  <Button android:id="@+id/pausePlayerBtn"
    android:layout_width="fill_parent"
    android:layout_height="wrap_content"
    android:text="Pause Player" android:onClick="doClick" />

  <Button android:id="@+id/restartPlayerBtn"
    android:layout_width="fill_parent"
    android:layout_height="wrap_content"
    android:text="Restart Player" android:onClick="doClick" />

  <Button android:id="@+id/stopPlayerBtn"
    android:layout_width="fill_parent"
    android:layout_height="wrap_content"
    android:text="Stop Player" android:onClick="doClick" />
</LinearLayout>


// This file is MainActivity.java
import android.app.Activity;
import android.content.res.AssetFileDescriptor;
import android.media.MediaPlayer;
import android.os.Bundle;
import android.os.Environment;
import android.util.Log;
import android.view.View;

public class MainActivity extends Activity
{
    static final String AUDIO_PATH =
     "http://www.androidbook.com/akc/filestorage/android/documentfiles/3389/play.mp3";
//    Environment.getExternalStoragePublicDirectory(
//        Environment.DIRECTORY_MUSIC) +
//        "/music_file.mp3";
//    Environment.getExternalStoragePublicDirectory(
//        Environment.DIRECTORY_MOVIES) +
//        " /movie.mp4";

    private MediaPlayer mediaPlayer;
    private int playbackPosition=0;

    /** Called when the activity is first created. */
    @Override
    public void onCreate(Bundle savedInstanceState) {
        super.onCreate(savedInstanceState);
```

```
        setContentView(R.layout.main);
    }

    public void doClick(View view) {
        switch(view.getId()) {
        case R.id.startPlayerBtn:
            try {
            // Only have one of these play methods uncommented
                playAudio(AUDIO_PATH);
//              playLocalAudio();
//              playLocalAudio_UsingDescriptor();
            } catch (Exception e) {
                e.printStackTrace();
            }
            break;
        case R.id.pausePlayerBtn:
            if(mediaPlayer != null && mediaPlayer.isPlaying()) {
                playbackPosition = mediaPlayer.getCurrentPosition();
                mediaPlayer.pause();
            }
            break;
        case R.id.restartPlayerBtn:
            if(mediaPlayer != null && !mediaPlayer.isPlaying()) {
                mediaPlayer.seekTo(playbackPosition);
                mediaPlayer.start();
            }
            break;
        case R.id.stopPlayerBtn:
            if(mediaPlayer != null) {
                mediaPlayer.stop();
                playbackPosition = 0;
            }
            break;
        }
    }

    private void playAudio(String url) throws Exception
    {
        killMediaPlayer();

        mediaPlayer = new MediaPlayer();
        mediaPlayer.setDataSource(url);
        mediaPlayer.prepare();
        mediaPlayer.start();
    }

    private void playLocalAudio() throws Exception
    {
        mediaPlayer = MediaPlayer.create(this, R.raw.music_file);
        // calling prepare() is not required in this case
        mediaPlayer.start();
    }

    private void playLocalAudio_UsingDescriptor() throws Exception {

        AssetFileDescriptor fileDesc = getResources().openRawResourceFd(
                        R.raw.music_file);
```

```
        if (fileDesc != null) {

            mediaPlayer = new MediaPlayer();
            mediaPlayer.setDataSource(fileDesc.getFileDescriptor(),
                    fileDesc.getStartOffset(), fileDesc.getLength());

            fileDesc.close();

            mediaPlayer.prepare();
            mediaPlayer.start();
        }
    }

    @Override
    protected void onDestroy() {
        super.onDestroy();
        killMediaPlayer();
    }

    private void killMediaPlayer() {
        if(mediaPlayer!=null) {
            try {
                mediaPlayer.release();
            }
            catch(Exception e) {
                e.printStackTrace();
            }
        }
    }
}
```

In this first scenario, you are playing an MP3 file from a web address. Therefore, you will need to add android.permission.INTERNET to your manifest file. Listing 19–1 shows that the MainActivity class contains three members: a final string that points to the URL of the MP3 file, a MediaPlayer instance, and an integer member called playbackPosition. Our onCreate() method just sets up the user interface from our layout XML file. In the button-click handler, when the Start Playing Audio button is pressed, the playAudio() method is called. In the playAudio() method, a new instance of the MediaPlayer is created and the data source of the player is set to the URL of the MP3 file. The prepare() method of the player is then called to prepare the media player for playback, and then the start() method is called to start playback.

Now look at the code for the Pause Player and Restart Player buttons. You can see that when the Pause Player button is selected, you get the current position of the player by calling getCurrentPosition(). You then pause the player by calling pause(). When the player has to be restarted, you call seekTo(), passing in the position obtained earlier from getCurrentPosition(), and then call start().

The MediaPlayer class also contains a stop() method. Note that if you stop the player by calling stop(), you need to call prepare() before calling start() again. Conversely, if you call pause(), you can call start() again without having to prepare the player. Also, be sure to call the release() method of the media player once you are done using it. In this example, you do this as part of the killMediaPlayer() method.

Listing 19–1 shows you how to play an audio file located on the Web. The MediaPlayer class also supports playing media local to your .apk file. Listing 19–2 shows how to reference and play back a file from the /res/raw folder of your .apk file. Go ahead and add the raw folder under /res if it's not already there in the Eclipse project. Then copy the mp3 file of your choice into /res/raw with the file name music_file.mp3.

Listing 19–2. *Using the MediaPlayer to play back a file local to your application*

```
private void playLocalAudio()throws Exception
{
    mediaPlayer = MediaPlayer.create(this, R.raw.music_file);
    // calling prepare() is not required in this case
    mediaPlayer.start();
}
```

If you need to include an audio or video file with your application, you should place the file in the /res/raw folder. You can then get a MediaPlayer instance for the resource by passing in the resource ID of the media file. You do this by calling the static create() method, as shown in Listing 19–2. Note that the MediaPlayer class also provides static create() methods that you can use to get a MediaPlayer rather than instantiating one yourself. For example, in Listing 19–2 you call the create() method, but you could instead call the constructor MediaPlayer(Context context,int resourceId). Using the static create() methods is preferable, because they hide the creation of the MediaPlayer, and this includes invoking the prepare() method for you. However, as you will see shortly, at times you will not have a choice between these two options—you will have to instantiate the default constructor if your media content cannot be located via a resource ID or a URL.

Understanding the setDataSource Method

In Listing 19–2, we called the create() method to load the audio file from a raw resource. With this approach, you don't need to call setDataSource(). Alternatively, if you instantiate the MediaPlayer yourself using the default constructor, or if your media content is not accessible through a resource ID or a URL, you'll need to call setDataSource().

The setDataSource() method has overloaded versions that you can use to customize the data source for your specific needs. For example, Listing 19–3 shows how you can load an audio file from a raw resource using a FileDescriptor.

Listing 19–3. *Setting the MediaPlayer's data source using a FileDescriptor*

```
private void playLocalAudio_UsingDescriptor() throws Exception {

    AssetFileDescriptor fileDesc = getResources().openRawResourceFd(
            R.raw.music_file);
    if (fileDesc != null) {

        mediaPlayer = new MediaPlayer();
        mediaPlayer.setDataSource(fileDesc.getFileDescriptor(), fileDesc
                .getStartOffset(), fileDesc.getLength());

        fileDesc.close();
```

```
            mediaPlayer.prepare();
            mediaPlayer.start();
        }
    }
```

Listing 19–3 assumes that it's within the context of an activity. As shown, you call the getResources() method to get the application's resources and then use the openRawResourceFd() method to get a file descriptor for an audio file within the /res/raw folder. You then call the setDataSource() method using the AssetFileDescriptor, the starting position to begin playback, and the ending position. You can also use this version of setDataSource() if you want to play back a specific portion of an audio file. If you always want to play the entire file, you can call the simpler version of setDataSource(FileDescriptor desc), which does not require the initial offset and length.

Using one of the setDataSource() methods with the FileDescriptor can also be handy if you want to feed a media file located within your application's /data directory. For security reasons, the media player does not have access to an application's /data directory, but your application can open the file and then feed the (opened) FileDescriptor to setDataSource(). Realize that the application's /data directory resides in the set of files and folders under /data/data/*APP_PACKAGE_NAME*/. You can get access to this directory by calling the appropriate method from the Context class, rather than hard-coding the path. For example, you can call getFilesDir() on Context to get the current application's files directory. Currently, this path looks like this: /data/data/*APP_PACKAGE_NAME*/files. Similarly, you can call getCacheDir() to get the application's cache directory. Your application will have read and write permission on the contents of these folders, so you can create files dynamically and feed them to the player. Finally, if you use FileDescriptor, as shown in Listing 19–3, be sure to close the handle after calling setDataSource().

Observe that an application's /data directory differs greatly from its /res/raw folder. The /res/raw folder is physically part of the .apk file, and it is static—that is, you cannot modify the .apk file dynamically. The contents of the /data directory, on the other hand, are dynamic.

We have one more source for audio content to talk about: the SD card. Earlier we showed you how to put content onto the SD card. Using it with MediaPlayer is pretty easy. In our example above, we used setDataSource() to access content on the Internet by passing in a URL for an MP3 file. If you've got an audio file on your SD card, you can use the same setDataSource() method but instead pass it the path to your audio file on the SD card. For example, if you put an MP3 file in the standard Music directory and called the file music_file.mp3, you could modify the AUDIO_PATH variable and it would play, like so:

```
static final String AUDIO_PATH =
Environment.getExternalStoragePublicDirectory(
    Environment.DIRECTORY_MUSIC) +
    "/music_file.mp3";
```

Use SoundPool for Simultaneous Track Playing

MediaPlayer is an essential tool in our media toolbox, but it only handles one audio or video file at a time. What if we want to play more than one audio track simultaneously? One way is to create multiple MediaPlayers and work with them at the same time. If you only have a small amount of audio to play, and you want snappy performance, Android has the SoundPool class to help you. Behind the scenes, SoundPool uses MediaPlayer but we don't get access to the MediaPlayer API, just the SoundPool API.

One of the other differences between MediaPlayer and SoundPool is that SoundPool is designed to work with local media files only. That is, you can load audio from resources files, files elsewhere using file descriptors, or files using a pathname. There are several other nice features that SoundPool provides, such as the ability to loop an audio track, pause and resume individual audio tracks, or pause and resume all audio tracks.

There are some downsides to SoundPool though. There is an overall audio buffer size for all of the tracks that a SoundPool will manage, and it's not very large. In fact, it's 1MB. This might seem large when you look at mp3 files that are only a few KB in size. But SoundPool expands the audio in memory to make the playback fast and easy. The size of an audio file in memory depends on the bit rate, number of channels (stereo vs. mono), sample rate, and length of the audio. If you have trouble getting your sounds loaded into a SoundPool, you could try playing with these parameters of your source audio file to make the audio smaller in memory.

We're going to show you an example application that loads and plays animal sounds. One of the sounds is of crickets and it plays constantly in the background. The other sounds play at different intervals of time. Sometimes all you hear are crickets; other times you will hear several animals all at the same time. We'll also put a button in the user interface to allow for pausing and resuming. Listing 19–4 shows our layout XML file and the Java code of our Activity. Your best bet is to download this from our website, in order to get the sound files as well as the code. See the "References" section at the end of this chapter for information on how to locate the downloadable source code.

Listing 19–4. *Playing Audio with a SoundPool*

```
<?xml version="1.0" encoding="utf-8"?>
<LinearLayout xmlns:android="http://schemas.android.com/apk/res/android"
    android:orientation="vertical"
    android:layout_width="fill_parent"  android:layout_height="fill_parent"
    >
<ToggleButton android:id="@+id/button"
    android:textOn="Pause"  android:textOff="Resume"
    android:layout_width="wrap_content"  android:layout_height="wrap_content"
    android:onClick="doClick" android:checked="true" />
</LinearLayout>


// This file is MainActivity.java
import java.io.IOException;
import android.app.Activity;
import android.content.Context;
import android.content.res.AssetFileDescriptor;
import android.media.AudioManager;
```

```
import android.media.SoundPool;
import android.os.Bundle;
import android.os.Handler;
import android.util.Log;
import android.view.View;
import android.widget.ToggleButton;

public class MainActivity extends Activity implements SoundPool.OnLoadCompleteListener {
    private static final int SRC_QUALITY = 0;
    private static final int PRIORITY = 1;
    private SoundPool soundPool = null;
    private AudioManager aMgr;

    private int sid_background;
    private int sid_roar;
    private int sid_bark;
    private int sid_chimp;
    private int sid_rooster;

    @Override
    public void onCreate(Bundle savedInstanceState) {
        super.onCreate(savedInstanceState);
        setContentView(R.layout.main);
    }

    @Override
    protected void onResume() {
        soundPool = new SoundPool(5, AudioManager.STREAM_MUSIC,
                SRC_QUALITY);
        soundPool.setOnLoadCompleteListener(this);

        aMgr =
            (AudioManager)this.getSystemService(Context.AUDIO_SERVICE);

        sid_background = soundPool.load(this, R.raw.crickets, PRIORITY);

        sid_chimp = soundPool.load(this, R.raw.chimp, PRIORITY);
        sid_rooster = soundPool.load(this, R.raw.rooster, PRIORITY);
        sid_roar = soundPool.load(this, R.raw.roar, PRIORITY);

        try {
            AssetFileDescriptor afd =
                    this.getAssets().openFd("dogbark.mp3");
            sid_bark = soundPool.load(afd.getFileDescriptor(),
                            0, afd.getLength(), PRIORITY);
            afd.close();
        } catch (IOException e) {
            e.printStackTrace();
        }
        //sid_bark = soundPool.load("/mnt/sdcard/dogbark.mp3", PRIORITY);

        super.onResume();
    }

    public void doClick(View view) {
        switch(view.getId()) {
        case R.id.button:
            if(((ToggleButton)view).isChecked()) {
```

```
                soundPool.autoResume();
            }
            else {
                soundPool.autoPause();
            }
            break;
        }
    }

    @Override
    protected void onPause() {
        soundPool.release();
        soundPool = null;
        super.onPause();
    }

    @Override
    public void onLoadComplete(SoundPool sPool, int sid, int status) {
        Log.v("soundPool", "sid " + sid + " loaded with status " +
                status);

        final float currentVolume =
            ((float)aMgr.getStreamVolume(AudioManager.STREAM_MUSIC)) /
            ((float)aMgr.getStreamMaxVolume(AudioManager.STREAM_MUSIC));

        if(status != 0)
            return;
        if(sid == sid_background) {
            if(sPool.play(sid, currentVolume, currentVolume,
                    PRIORITY, -1, 1.0f) == 0)
                Log.v("soundPool", "Failed to start sound");
        } else if(sid == sid_chimp) {
            queueSound(sid, 5000, currentVolume);
        } else if(sid == sid_rooster) {
            queueSound(sid, 6000, currentVolume);
        } else if(sid == sid_roar) {
            queueSound(sid, 12000, currentVolume);
        } else if(sid == sid_bark) {
            queueSound(sid, 7000, currentVolume);
        }
    }

    private void queueSound(final int sid, final long delay,
        final float volume)
    {
        new Handler().postDelayed(new Runnable() {
            @Override
            public void run() {
                if(soundPool == null) return;
                if(soundPool.play(sid, volume, volume,
                        PRIORITY, 0, 1.0f) == 0)
                    Log.v("soundPool", "Failed to start sound (" + sid +
                          ")");
                queueSound(sid, delay, volume);
            }}, delay);
    }
}
```

The structure of this example is fairly straightforward. We have a user interface with a single ToggleButton on it. We'll use this to pause and resume the active audio streams. When our app starts, we create our SoundPool and load it up with audio samples. When the samples are properly loaded, we start playing them. The crickets sound plays in a never-ending loop while the other samples play after a delay, then set themselves up to play again after the same delay. By choosing different delays we get a somewhat random effect of sounds on top of sounds.

Creating a SoundPool requires three parameters

- The first is the maximum number of samples that the SoundPool will play simultaneously. This is not how many samples the SoundPool can hold.
- The second parameter is which audio stream the samples will play on. The typical value is AudioManager.STREAM_MUSIC, but SoundPool can be used for alarms or ringtones. See the AudioManager reference page for the complete list of audio streams.
- The SRC_QUALITY value should just be set to 0 when creating the SoundPool.

The code demonstrates several different load() methods of SoundPool. The most basic is to load an audio file from /res/raw as a resource. We use this method for the first four audio files. Then we show how you could load an audio file from the /assets directory of the application. This load() method also takes parameters that specify the offset and the length of the audio to load. This would allow us to use a single file with multiple audio samples in it, pulling out just what we want to use. Finally, we show in comments how you might access an audio file from the SD card. Up through Android 3.0, the PRIORITY parameter should just be 1.

For our example, we chose to use some of the features introduced in Android 2.2, specifically the onLoadCompleteListener interface for our Activity, and the autoPause() and autoResume() methods in our button callback.

When loading sound samples into a SoundPool, we must wait until they are properly loaded before we can start playing them. Within our onLoadComplete() callback, we check the status of the load, and, depending on which sound it is, we then set it up to play. If the sound is the crickets, we play with looping turned on (a value of -1 for the fifth parameter). For the others, we queue the sound up to play after a short period of time. The time values are in milliseconds. Note the setting of the volume. Android provides the AudioManager to let us know the current volume setting. We also get the maximum volume setting from AudioManager so we can calculate a volume value for play() that is between 0 and 1 (as a float). The play() method actually takes a separate volume value for the left and right channels, but we just set both to the current volume. Again, PRIORITY should just be set to 1. The last parameter on the play() method is for setting the playback rate. This value should be between 0.5 and 2.0, with 1.0 being normal.

Our queueSound() method uses a Handler to basically set up an event into the future. Our Runnable will run after the delay period has elapsed. We check to be sure we still have a SoundPool to play from, then we play the sound once, and schedule the same sound to play again after the same interval as before. Because we call queueSound() with different sound Ids and different delays, the effect is a somewhat random playing of animal sounds.

When you run this example, you'll hear crickets, a chimp, a rooster, a dog and a roar (a bear, we think). The crickets are constantly chirping while the other animals come and go. One nice thing about SoundPool is that it lets us play multiple sounds at the same time with no real work on our part. Also, we're not taxing the device too badly, since the sounds were decoded at load time, and we simply need to feed the sounds bits to the hardware.

If you click the button, the crickets will stop, as will any other animal sound currently being played. However, the autoPause() method does not prevent new sounds from being played. You'll hear the animal sounds again within seconds (except for the crickets). Because we've been queuing up sounds into the future, we will still hear those sounds. In fact, SoundPool does not have a way to stop all sounds now and in the future. You'll need to handle stopping on your own. The crickets will only come back if we click the button again to resume the sounds. But even then, we might have lost the crickets since SoundPool will throw out the oldest sound to make room for newer sounds if the maximum number of simultaneously playing samples is reached.

Playing Sounds with JetPlayer

SoundPool is not too bad a player, but the memory limitations can make it difficult to get the job done. An alternative when you need to play simultaneous sounds is JetPlayer. Tailored for games, JetPlayer is a very flexible tool for playing lots of sounds, and for coordinating those sounds with user actions. The sounds are defined using MIDI (short for Musical Instrument Digital Interface).

JetPlayer sounds are created using a special JETCreator tool. This tool is provided under the Android SDK tools directory, although you'll also need to install Python in order to use it. The resulting JET file can be read into your application, and the sounds set up for playback. The whole process is somewhat involved, and beyond the scope of this book, so we'll just point you to more information in the "References" section at the end of this chapter.

Playing Background Sounds with AsyncPlayer

If all you want is some audio played, and you don't want to tie up the current thread, the AsyncPlayer may be what you're looking for. The audio source is passed as a Uri to this class, so the audio file could be local or remote over the network. This class automatically creates a background thread to handle getting the audio and starting the playback. Because it is asynchronous, you won't know exactly when the audio will start. Nor will you know when it ends, or even if it's still playing. You can however call stop()

to get the audio to stop playing. If you call play() again before the previous audio has finished playing, the previous audio will immediately stop and the new audio will begin at some time in the future when everything has been set up and fetched. This is a very simple class that provides an automatic background thread. Listing 19–5 shows how your code should look to implement this.

Listing 19–5. *Playing audio with AsyncPlayer*

```
    private static final String TAG = "AsyncPlayerDemo";
    private AsyncPlayer mAsync = null;

[ ... ]

        mAsync = new AsyncPlayer(TAG);
        mAsync.play(this, Uri.parse("file://" + "/perry_ringtone.mp3"),
                false, AudioManager.STREAM_MUSIC);

[ ... ]

    @Override
    protected void onPause() {
        mAsync.stop();
        super.onPause();
    }
```

Low-level Audio Playback Using AudioTrack

So far we've been dealing with audio from files, be they local files or remote files. If you want to get down to a lower level, perhaps to play audio from a stream, you need to investigate the AudioTrack class. Besides the usual methods like play() and pause(), AudioTrack provides methods for writing bytes to the audio hardware. This class gives you the most control over audio playback, but it is much more complicated than the audio classes discussed so far in this chapter. We'll be showing a sample application a little later in this chapter that uses the AudioRecord class. The AudioRecord class is very much like the AudioTrack class, so to get a better understanding of the AudioTrack class, please refer to the AudioRecord sample later on.

Understanding the MediaPlayer Oddities

In general, the MediaPlayer is very systematic, so you need to call operations in a specific order to initialize a media player properly and prepare it for playback. The following list summarizes some of the oddities of using the media APIs:

- Once you set the data source of a MediaPlayer, you cannot easily change it to another one—you'll have to create a new MediaPlayer or call the reset() method to reinitialize the state of the player.
- After you call prepare(), you can call getCurrentPosition(), getDuration(), and isPlaying() to get the current state of the player. You can also call the setLooping() and setVolume() methods after the call to prepare().

- After you call `start()`, you can call `pause()`, `stop()`, and `seekTo()`.
- Every `MediaPlayer` creates a new thread, so be sure to call the `release()` method when you are done with the media player. The `VideoView` takes care of this in the case of video playback, but you'll have to do it manually if you decide to use `MediaPlayer` instead of `VideoView`.

This concludes our discussion about playing audio content. Now we'll turn our attention to playing video. As you will see, referencing video content is similar to referencing audio content.

Playing Video Content

In this section, we are going to discuss video playback using the Android SDK. Specifically, we will discuss playing a video from a web server and playing one from an SD card. As you can imagine, video playback is a bit more involved than audio playback. Fortunately, the Android SDK provides some additional abstractions that do most of the heavy lifting.

> **NOTE:** Playing back video in the emulator is not very reliable. If it works, great. But if it doesn't, try running on a device instead. Because the emulator must use only software to run video, it can have a very hard time keeping up with video, and you could get unexpected results.

Playing video requires more effort than playing audio, because there's a visual component to take care of in addition to the audio. To take some of the pain away, Android provides a specialized view control called `android.widget.VideoView` that encapsulates creating and initializing the `MediaPlayer`. To play video, you create a `VideoView` widget in your user interface. You then set the path or Uri of the video and fire the `start()` method. Listing 19–6 demonstrates video playback in Android.

Listing 19–6. *Playing video using the Media APIs*

```
<?xml version="1.0" encoding="utf-8"?>
<!-- This file is /res/layout/main.xml -->
<LinearLayout
 android:layout_width="fill_parent" android:layout_height="fill_parent"
 xmlns:android="http://schemas.android.com/apk/res/android">

    <VideoView  android:id="@+id/videoView"
        android:layout_width="200px"  android:layout_height="200px" />

</LinearLayout>


// This file is MainActivity.java
import android.app.Activity;
import android.net.Uri;
import android.os.Bundle;
import android.widget.MediaController;
```

```
import android.widget.VideoView;

public class MainActivity extends Activity {
    /** Called when the activity is first created. */
    @Override
    protected void onCreate(Bundle savedInstanceState) {
        super.onCreate(savedInstanceState);
        this.setContentView(R.layout.main);

        VideoView videoView =
               (VideoView)this.findViewById(R.id.videoView);
        MediaController mc = new MediaController(this);
        videoView.setMediaController(mc);
        videoView.setVideoURI(Uri.parse(
              "http://www.androidbook.com/akc/filestorage/android/" +
               "documentfiles/3389/movie.mp4"));
 /* videoView.setVideoPath(
    Environment.getExternalStoragePublicDirectory(
    Environment.DIRECTORY_MOVIES) +
    "/movie.mp4");
 */
        videoView.requestFocus();
        videoView.start();
    }
}
```

Listing 19–6 demonstrates video playback of a file located on the Web at `www.androidbook.com/akc/filestorage/android/documentfiles/3389/movie.mp4`, which means the application running the code will need to request the `android.permission.INTERNET` permission. All of the playback functionality is hidden behind the `VideoView` class. In fact, all you have to do is feed the video content to the video player. The user interface of the application is shown in Figure 19–4.

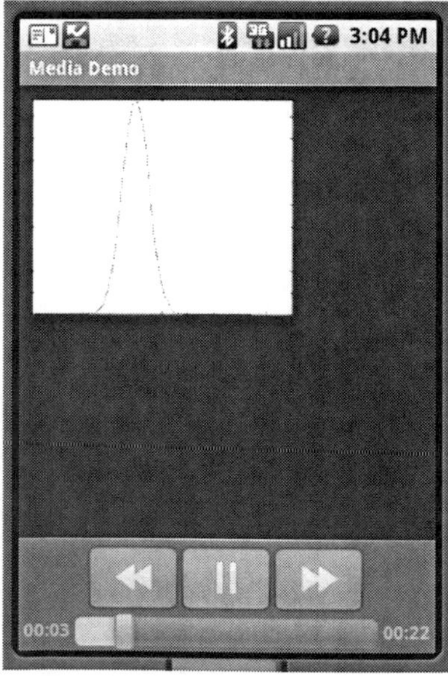

Figure 19–4. *The video playback UI with media controls enabled*

When this application runs, you will see the button controls along the bottom of the screen for about three seconds, and then they disappear. You get them back by clicking anywhere within the video frame. When we were doing playback of audio content, we only needed to display the button controls to start, pause, and restart the audio. We did not need a view component for the audio itself. With video, of course, we need button controls as well as something to view the video in. For this example, we're using a VideoView component to display the video content. But instead of creating our own button controls (which we could still do if we chose to), we create a MediaController that provides the buttons for us. As shown in Figure 19–4 and Listing 19–6, you set the VideoView's media controller by calling setMediaController() to enable the play, pause, and seek-to controls. If you want to manipulate the video programmatically with your own buttons, you can call the start(), pause(), stopPlayback(), and seekTo() methods.

Keep in mind that we're still using a MediaPlayer in this example—we just don't see it. You can in fact "play" videos directly in MediaPlayer. If you go back to the example from Listing 19–1, put a movie file on your SD card, and plug in the movie's file path in AUDIO_PATH, you will find that it plays the audio quite nicely even though you can't see the video.

While MediaPlayer has a setDataSource() method, VideoView does not. VideoView instead uses the setVideoPath() or setVideoURI() methods. Assuming you put a movie file onto your SD card, you change the code from Listing 19–6 to comment out the setVideoURI() call and uncomment the setVideoPath() call, adjusting the path to the movie file as necessary. When you run the application again, you will now hear *and see* the video in the VideoView. Technically, we could have called setVideoURI() with the following to get the same effect as setVideoPath():

```
videoView.setVideoURI(Uri.parse("file://" +
    Environment.getExternalStoragePublicDirectory(
    Environment.DIRECTORY_MOVIES) + "/movie.mp4"));
```

You might have noticed that VideoView does not have a method to read data from a file descriptor as MediaPlayer did. You may also have noticed that MediaPlayer has a couple of methods for adding a SurfaceHolder to a MediaPlayer (a SurfaceHolder is like a view port for images or video). If you need to display video from under your application's private data folder (i.e., under /data/data/...), you will need to use MediaPlayer and a SurfaceHolder rather than the VideoView class. One of the MediaPlayer methods is create(Context context, Uri uri, SurfaceHolder holder) and the other is setDisplay(SurfaceHolder holder).

Now let's explore recording media.

Recording Media

As we've shown, there are many ways to play media from within Android. For recording, there are fewer options. The main workhorse of recording is the MediaRecorder class, which is used for both audio and video. In this section, we'll show you how to use MediaRecorder for both types of media. The other class for recording audio is AudioRecord, and we'll demonstrate this with another sample application. Sometimes you don't want to write code to accomplish something when an existing application can do it for you. So we'll also show you how to fire off an intent to record audio, as well as to capture still camera images using the Camera application.

Exploring Audio Recording with MediaRecorder

The Android media framework supports recording audio. One way you record audio is through the `android.media.MediaRecorder` class. In this section, we'll show you how to build an application that records audio content and then plays the content back. The user interface of the application is shown in Figure 19–5.

Figure 19–5. *The user interface of the audio-recorder example*

As shown in Figure 19–5, the application contains four buttons: two to control recording, and two to start and stop playback of the recorded content. Listing 19–7 shows the layout file and activity class for the UI.

Listing 19–7. *Media recording and playback in Android*

```
<?xml version="1.0" encoding="utf-8"?>
<!-- This file is /res/layout/record.xml -->
<LinearLayout xmlns:android="http://schemas.android.com/apk/res/android"
    android:orientation="vertical"
    android:layout_width="fill_parent"
    android:layout_height="fill_parent">

  <Button android:id="@+id/beginBtn"  android:text="Begin Recording"
    android:layout_width="fill_parent"
    android:layout_height="wrap_content"
    android:onClick="doClick" />

  <Button android:id="@+id/stopBtn"  android:text="Stop Recording"
    android:layout_width="fill_parent"
```

```
    android:layout_height="wrap_content"
    android:onClick="doClick" />

  <Button android:id="@+id/playRecordingBtn"
    android:text="Play Recording"
    android:layout_width="fill_parent"
    android:layout_height="wrap_content"
    android:onClick="doClick" />

  <Button android:id="@+id/stopPlayingRecordingBtn"
    android:text="Stop Playing Recording"
    android:layout_width="fill_parent"
    android:layout_height="wrap_content"
    android:onClick="doClick" />

</LinearLayout>


// RecorderActivity.java
import java.io.File;
import android.app.Activity;
import android.media.MediaPlayer;
import android.media.MediaRecorder;
import android.os.Bundle;
import android.os.Environment;
import android.view.View;

public class RecorderActivity extends Activity {
    private MediaPlayer mediaPlayer;
    private MediaRecorder recorder;
    private String OUTPUT_FILE;

    @Override
    protected void onCreate(Bundle savedInstanceState) {
        super.onCreate(savedInstanceState);
        setContentView(R.layout.record);

        OUTPUT_FILE = Environment.getExternalStorageDirectory() +
                        "/recordaudio3.3gpp";
    }

    public void doClick(View view) {
        switch(view.getId()) {
        case R.id.beginBtn:
            try {
                beginRecording();
            } catch (Exception e) {
                e.printStackTrace();
            }
            break;
        case R.id.stopBtn:
            try {
                stopRecording();
            } catch (Exception e) {
                e.printStackTrace();
            }
            break;
```

```
            case R.id.playRecordingBtn:
                try {
                    playRecording();
                } catch (Exception e) {
                    e.printStackTrace();
                }
                break;
            case R.id.stopPlayingRecordingBtn:
                try {
                    stopPlayingRecording();
                } catch (Exception e) {
                    e.printStackTrace();
                }
                break;
            }
        }

        private void beginRecording() throws Exception {
            killMediaRecorder();

            File outFile = new File(OUTPUT_FILE);

            if(outFile.exists()) {
                outFile.delete();
            }
            recorder = new MediaRecorder();
            recorder.setAudioSource(MediaRecorder.AudioSource.MIC);
            recorder.setOutputFormat(MediaRecorder.OutputFormat.THREE_GPP);
            recorder.setAudioEncoder(MediaRecorder.AudioEncoder.AMR_NB);
            recorder.setOutputFile(OUTPUT_FILE);
            recorder.prepare();
            recorder.start();
        }

        private void stopRecording() throws Exception {
            if (recorder != null) {
                recorder.stop();
            }
        }

        private void killMediaRecorder() {
            if (recorder != null) {
                recorder.release();
            }
        }

        private void killMediaPlayer() {
            if (mediaPlayer != null) {
                try {
                    mediaPlayer.release();
                } catch (Exception e) {
                    e.printStackTrace();
                }
            }
        }

        private void playRecording() throws Exception {
```

```
        killMediaPlayer();

        mediaPlayer = new MediaPlayer();
        mediaPlayer.setDataSource(OUTPUT_FILE);

        mediaPlayer.prepare();
        mediaPlayer.start();
    }

    private void stopPlayingRecording() throws Exception {
        if(mediaPlayer != null) {
            mediaPlayer.stop();
        }
    }

    @Override
    protected void onDestroy() {
        super.onDestroy();

        killMediaRecorder();
        killMediaPlayer();
    }
}
```

Before we jump into Listing 19–7, you'll need to add the following permission to your manifest file in order to record audio:

```
<uses-permission android:name="android.permission.RECORD_AUDIO" />
```

As discussed earlier in the section on SD cards, if your application's `minSdkVersion` is 4 or later, you will also need to add a `uses-permission` tag for `"android.permission.WRITE_EXTERNAL_STORAGE"`. Finally, if you are going to try this out with the emulator, you'll need to provide a microphone input on your workstation.

If you look at the `onCreate()` method in Listing 19–7, you'll see that the only thing we need to do there is create the file pathname for our output audio file. Our `doClick()` method uses the standard pattern of switching on which button was pressed, and we invoke the appropriate function call to perform each desired action. The `beginRecording()` method handles recording. To record audio, you must create an instance of `MediaRecorder` and set the audio source, output format, audio encoder, and output file.

Up until Android SDK 1.6, the only supported audio source was the microphone. Android SDK 1.6 added three more audio sources available, all related to phone calls. You can record the entire call (`MediaRecorder.AudioSource.VOICE_CALL`), the uplink side only (`MediaRecorder.AudioSource.VOICE_UPLINK`), or the downlink side only (`MediaRecorder.AudioSource.VOICE_DOWNLINK`). The uplink side of a call would be the voice of the phone's user. The downlink side of the call would be sounds coming from the other end of the call.

With Android SDK 2.1, two more audio sources were added: `CAMCORDER` and `VOICE_RECOGNITION`. The `CAMCORDER` audio source would be a camera-related microphone, otherwise this option will use the default main microphone of the device. The `VOICE_RECOGNITION` microphone is one tuned to doing voice recognition, otherwise this option also will use the default main microphone of the device. The phrase “tuned to doing voice recognition” means that the audio stream will be as raw as possible, with no extra audio modifications in between the microphone and your application. For example, some HTC devices have Auto Gain Control (AGC) on the microphone, so using that audio source for voice recognition will be problematic. The VOICE_RECOGNITION audio source bypasses this extra processing for better results doing voice recognition.

The most common output format for audio is 3rd Generation Partnership Project (3GPP). Prior to Andorid 2.3.3 (Gingerbread) you must set the encoder to AMR_NB, which signifies the Adaptive Multi-Rate (AMR) narrowband audio codec, as this is the only supported audio encoder. As of Anddroid 2.3.3, you can also use AMR_WB (wideband) and AAC (Advanced Audio Coding) as audio encoders. The recorded audio in our example is written to the SD card as a file named recordoutput.3gpp. Note that Listing 19–7 assumes that you’ve created an SD card image and that you’ve pointed the emulator to the SD card. If you have not done this, refer to the section “Using SD Cards” for details on setting this up.

There are some additional methods to the MediaRecorder that you might find useful. In order to limit the length and size of audio recordings, the methods setMaxDuration(int length_in_ms) and setMaxFileSize(long length_in_bytes) can be used. You would set the maximum length of the recording, in milliseconds, or the maximum length of the recording file, in bytes, to stop recording when these limits are reached. These were both introduced with Android 1.5 so they are available on pretty much any device you can record audio with.

Recording Audio with AudioRecord

So far, you’ve seen how to record audio directly to a file. But what if you want to do some processing on the audio data before it goes to a file? Or what if you don’t even want to send the audio to a file? Android provides a class called AudioRecord for just these purposes. When you set up an AudioRecord object, Android will ensure that audio data is written to the internal buffer of the AudioRecord, and then your application can do whatever it wants with the audio data. Listing 19–8 shows an Activity for reading and processing audio using an AudioRecord. There is no user interface for this Activity, as we’ll just be writing log messages to LogCat. The AndroidManifest.xml is not shown, but you will need to add an Android permission for android.permission.RECORD_AUDIO for this to work.

Listing 19–8. ***Recording raw audio with AudioRecord***

```
import android.app.Activity;
import android.media.AudioFormat;
import android.media.AudioRecord;
import android.media.MediaRecorder;
import android.os.Bundle;
import android.util.Log;

public class MainActivity extends Activity {
    protected static final String TAG = "AudioRecord";
    private int mAudioBufferSize;
```

```
    private int mAudioBufferSampleSize;
    private AudioRecord mAudioRecord;
    private boolean inRecordMode = false;

    public void onCreate(Bundle savedInstanceState) {
        super.onCreate(savedInstanceState);

        initAudioRecord();
    }

    @Override
    public void onResume() {
        super.onResume();
        Log.v(TAG, "Resuming...");
        inRecordMode = true;
        Thread t = new Thread(new Runnable() {

            @Override
            public void run() {
                getSamples();
            }
        });
        t.start();
    }

    protected void onPause() {
        Log.v(TAG, "Pausing...");
        inRecordMode = false;
        super.onPause();
    }

    @Override
    protected void onDestroy() {
        Log.v(TAG, "Destroying...");
        if(mAudioRecord != null) {
            mAudioRecord.release();
            Log.v(TAG, "Released AudioRecord");
        }
        super.onDestroy();
    }

    private void initAudioRecord() {
        try {
            int sampleRate = 8000;
            int channelConfig = AudioFormat.CHANNEL_IN_MONO;
            int audioFormat = AudioFormat.ENCODING_PCM_16BIT;
            mAudioBufferSize =
                    2 * AudioRecord.getMinBufferSize(sampleRate,
                    channelConfig, audioFormat);
            mAudioBufferSampleSize = mAudioBufferSize / 2;
            mAudioRecord = new AudioRecord(
                    MediaRecorder.AudioSource.MIC,
                    sampleRate,
                    channelConfig,
                    audioFormat,
                    mAudioBufferSize);
            Log.v(TAG, "Setup of AudioRecord okay. Buffer size = " +
```

```
                    mAudioBufferSize);
            Log.v(TAG, "   Sample buffer size = " +
                    mAudioBufferSampleSize);
        } catch (IllegalArgumentException e) {
            e.printStackTrace();
        }

        int audioRecordState = mAudioRecord.getState();
        if(audioRecordState != AudioRecord.STATE_INITIALIZED) {
            Log.e(TAG, "AudioRecord is not properly initialized");
            finish();
        }
        else {
            Log.v(TAG, "AudioRecord is initialized");
        }
    }

    private void getSamples() {
        if(mAudioRecord == null) return;

        short[] audioBuffer = new short[mAudioBufferSampleSize];

        mAudioRecord.startRecording();

        int audioRecordingState = mAudioRecord.getRecordingState();
        if(audioRecordingState != AudioRecord.RECORDSTATE_RECORDING) {
            Log.e(TAG, "AudioRecord is not recording");
            finish();
        }
        else {
            Log.v(TAG, "AudioRecord has started recording...");
        }

        while(inRecordMode) {
            int samplesRead = mAudioRecord.read(
                            audioBuffer, 0, mAudioBufferSampleSize);
            Log.v(TAG, "Got samples: " + samplesRead);
            Log.v(TAG, "First few sample values: " +
                    audioBuffer[0] + ", " +
                    audioBuffer[1] + ", " +
                    audioBuffer[2] + ", " +
                    audioBuffer[3] + ", " +
                    audioBuffer[4] + ", " +
                    audioBuffer[5] + ", " +
                    audioBuffer[6] + ", " +
                    audioBuffer[7] + ", " +
                    audioBuffer[8] + ", " +
                    audioBuffer[9] + ", "
                    );
        }

        mAudioRecord.stop();
        Log.v(TAG, "AudioRecord has stopped recording");
    }
}
```

Our sample application is fairly straightforward. We start by initializing our AudioRecord. This requires choosing the audio source, the frequency of sampling, the channel configuration (mono, stereo, left, right, and the like), the audio encoding format, and the internal buffer size. For the audio source, you'll choose from the set of options as defined in MediaRecorder.AudioSource. One word of caution here: not all devices have implemented VOICE_CALL since that acts like two inputs instead of one. For the sample frequency, you should choose one of the standard values, such as 8000, 16000, 44100, 22050, or 11025 Hz. The channel configuration should be chosen from the CHANNEL* values described in AudioFormat. The encoding format will be either ENCODING_PCM_8BIT or ENCODING_PCM_16BIT. Note that your choice here will affect the kind of values you'll get back as raw audio data. If you don't need the precision of 16 bit, go with 8 bit—you'll use less memory and go faster. The documentation says that only the sample frequency of 44100 is guaranteed to work on all devices, but ironically the emulator only supports 8000 Hz, CHANNEL_IN_MONO and ENCODING_PCM_8BIT.

The AudioRecord class has a static helper method called getMinBufferSize(), which will take your desired parameter settings and return to you the minimum-sized buffer that you should specify to properly initialize your AudioRecord. This buffer is not directly accessible to you, but AudioRecord needs to have enough room internally to store audio data while you're processing the audio data you've retrieved previously. You can certainly go with the minimum size value, or you could bump it up a little. You definitely should not attempt to set a buffer size less than what is recommended by this helper method. In our sample, we chose a buffer size twice what the minimum is. You'll get an IllegalArgumentException if your parameters are not acceptable to the AudioRecord. For example, if you try a sample frequency value that is not supported on this hardware, you'll get this exception. Unfortunately, there is no convenient method to get a list of supported sample frequencies, so your only recourse is to try a desired sample frequency, and if you get the exception, try another sample frequency until you find one that works.

As a last check within our initialize method, we make sure that our AudioRecord is properly initialized. Now we're ready to read audio samples.

We've chosen to turn on our sampling in the onResume() method of our Activity, and turn off sampling in onPause(). We do not want to tie up our main UI thread with sampling, so we create a separate thread to do the audio sampling in. We also set a boolean (inRecordMode) so we can tell our thread to stop sampling. Within the getSamples() method, we create our own buffer for the audio data. As mentioned before, we cannot directly access the internal audio data buffer of our AudioRecord, so we read into our sample buffer. Note that the size of our buffer is audioBufferSampleSize, not audioBufferSize. We're only reading the sample size so that's all we need in our buffer. We tell the AudioRecord to start recording, we check that the state has changed to RECORDING, and then we start looping on reads. These are blocking reads, but we're in a separate thread, so it's okay. As the AudioRecord gets to our sample size of data, our read returns so we can process that audio sample.

Meanwhile, the AudioRecord will be collecting additional audio data for us for the next time we call read. We only have a certain amount of time to do our processing before the AudioRecord's internal buffer fills up, so we definitely want to be careful not to do too much. Depending on what you want to do with the data, you could simply stop recording and start again later. In our sample, we simply report in LogCat that we got samples, and we display the first 10 values. As you run this sample application, make different sounds into the microphone to see the values change in LogCat.

Our looping continues until the boolean inRecordMode goes to false, which happens when the application is being hidden or is being killed.

While perusing the documentation on AudioRecord, you may notice some callback interfaces. These allow you to set up listeners on either reaching a marker within the audio stream, or triggering a periodic callback every so often. We modified our sample above by adding the statements in Listing 19–9. For the complete source code of this project, please see our web site.

Listing 19–9. ***Recording Raw Audio with AudioRecord and Callbacks***

```
    // This code goes inside of our Activity class
    public OnRecordPositionUpdateListener mListener = new
OnRecordPositionUpdateListener() {

        public void onPeriodicNotification(AudioRecord recorder) {
            Log.v(TAG, "in onPeriodicNotification");
        }

        public void onMarkerReached(AudioRecord recorder) {
            Log.v(TAG, "in onMarkerReached");
            inRecordMode = false;
        }
    };


    // These statements go inside of initAudioRecord() after the
    // creation of mAudioRecord and before the check of the state
    // of mAudioRecord.
        mAudioRecord.setNotificationMarkerPosition(10000);
        mAudioRecord.setPositionNotificationPeriod(1000);
        mAudioRecord.setRecordPositionUpdateListener(mListener);
```

Notice how the listener has two separate callback methods. The first one is called every time we read 1,000 frames of audio, which we set up in our initialization method. This frame count is independent of our sample size buffer. While we may be reading 1,600 frames at a time, the first callback is invoked every 1,000 frames. We could therefore see our callback invoked twice within one read loop. The second callback is called when our absolute frame count is reached. In our sample application we set this to 10,000 frames, and when this count is reached, we turn off recording by setting the boolean to false. If we had only logged a message and not turned off recording, we would not have seen this callback invoked again no matter how many frames were read in the future. The marker is relative to when startRecording() is called on the AudioRecord.

Exploring Video Recording

Since the introduction of Android SDK 1.5, you can capture video using the media framework. This works in a similar way to recording audio and, in fact, recorded video usually includes an audio track. There is one big exception with video, however. Beginning with Android SDK 1.6, recording video requires that you preview the camera images onto a Surface object. In basic applications this is not much of an issue, since the user probably wants to be viewing what the camera sees . For more sophisticated applications, however, this could be a problem. If your application doesn't need to show the video feed to the user as it happens, you still need to provide a Surface object so the camera can preview the video. We expect this requirement will be relaxed in future versions of the Android SDK, so that applications could work directly with the video buffers without having to copy to a UI component as well. For now, though, we'll have to work with a Surface and we'll show you how to do this. This sample application is a bit long, so we've broken it down into pieces so we can describe what the pieces do as we go along. You'll most likely want to import this project into Eclipse after downloading from our web site. See the "References" section at the end of this chapter for instructions on how to do that. We start with the layout for our application in Listing 19–10.

Listing 19–10. *Record Video's XML layout*

```
<?xml version="1.0" encoding="utf-8"?>
<!-- This file is /res/layout-land/main.xml -->
<LinearLayout xmlns:android="http://schemas.android.com/apk/res/android"
    android:layout_width="fill_parent"  android:layout_height="fill_parent"
     android:orientation="horizontal" >
  <LinearLayout
    android:orientation="vertical" android:layout_width="wrap_content"
    android:layout_height="wrap_content">

    <Button android:id="@+id/initBtn"
        android:layout_width="wrap_content"  android:layout_height="wrap_content"
        android:text="Initialize Recorder"  android:onClick="doClick"
        android:enabled="false" />

    <Button android:id="@+id/beginBtn"
        android:layout_width="wrap_content"  android:layout_height="wrap_content"
        android:text="Begin Recording"  android:onClick="doClick"
        android:enabled="false" />

    <Button android:id="@+id/stopBtn"
        android:layout_width="wrap_content"  android:layout_height="wrap_content"
        android:text="Stop Recording"  android:onClick="doClick" />

    <Button android:id="@+id/playRecordingBtn"
        android:layout_width="wrap_content"  android:layout_height="wrap_content"
        android:text="Play Recording"  android:onClick="doClick" />

    <Button android:id="@+id/stopPlayingRecordingBtn"
        android:layout_width="wrap_content" android:layout_height="wrap_content"
        android:text="Stop Playing"  android:onClick="doClick" />
  </LinearLayout>
  <LinearLayout android:orientation="vertical"
        android:layout_width="fill_parent" android:layout_height="fill_parent" >
```

```
    <TextView android:id="@+id/recording" android:text=" "
        android:textColor="#FF0000"
        android:layout_width="wrap_content"
        android:layout_height="wrap_content" />
    <VideoView android:id="@+id/videoView"
        android:layout_width="250dip"  android:layout_height="200dip" />
  </LinearLayout>
</LinearLayout>
```

The result of this layout will look like Figure 19–6. This image was snapped during a recording of video on a real device, looking at Eclipse on the workstation.

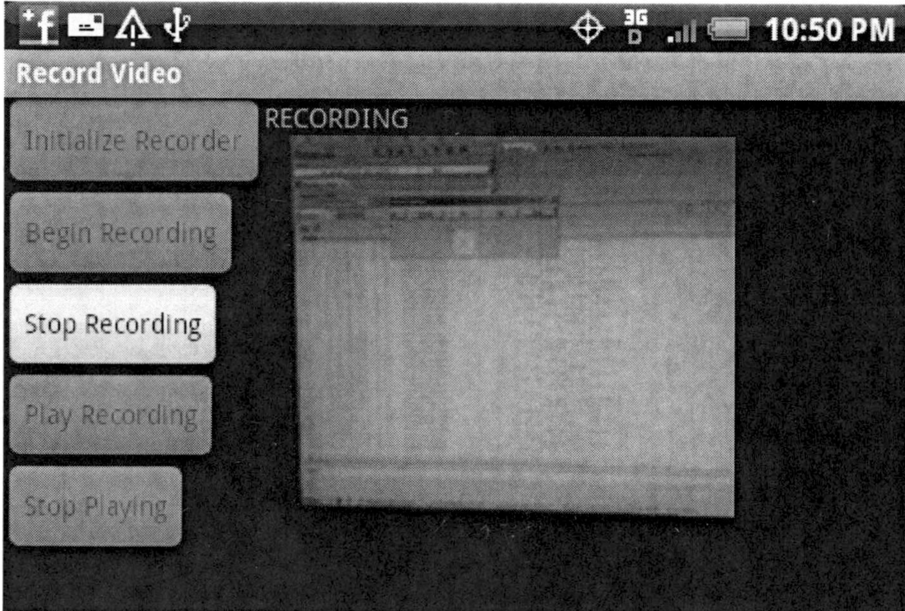

Figure 19–6. *The Record Video UI*

The layout is composed of two LinearLayouts side-by-side in a containing LinearLayout. On the left are five buttons that our application will enable and disable as the demonstration progresses. On the right is the main VideoView, and above it is the RECORDING message, which turns on when the application is actually recording video. As you've probably figured out, we've forced this application to be in landscape mode by setting the `android:screenOrientation="landscape"` attribute in the `<activity>` tag in AndroidManifest.xml. Let's start exploring this application with the MainActivity, as shown in Listing 19–11.

Listing 19–11. *Record Video's MainActivity*

```
public class MainActivity extends Activity implements
        SurfaceHolder.Callback, OnInfoListener, OnErrorListener {

    private static final String TAG = "RecordVideo";
    private MediaRecorder mRecorder = null;
    private String mOutputFileName;
    private VideoView mVideoView = null;
```

```
    private SurfaceHolder mHolder = null;
    private Button mInitBtn = null;
    private Button mStartBtn = null;
    private Button mStopBtn = null;
    private Button mPlayBtn = null;
    private Button mStopPlayBtn = null;
    private Camera mCamera = null;
    private TextView mRecordingMsg = null;

    /** Called when the activity is first created. */
    @Override
    public void onCreate(Bundle savedInstanceState) {
        super.onCreate(savedInstanceState);
        Log.v(TAG, "in onCreate");
        setContentView(R.layout.main);

        mInitBtn = (Button) findViewById(R.id.initBtn);
        mStartBtn = (Button) findViewById(R.id.beginBtn);
        mStopBtn = (Button) findViewById(R.id.stopBtn);
        mPlayBtn = (Button) findViewById(R.id.playRecordingBtn);
        mStopPlayBtn = (Button) findViewById(R.id.stopPlayingRecordingBtn);
        mRecordingMsg = (TextView) findViewById(R.id.recording);

        mVideoView = (VideoView)this.findViewById(R.id.videoView);
    }
        // The rest of this class is in the listings that will follow.
}
```

We're using a standard activity for this application, but we're also implementing three interfaces. The first interface, SurfaceHolder.Callback, is used to receive an indication of when the Surface is ready for displaying a video image. The Surface in our case comes from the VideoView. We also want to be told if there are any messages coming from our MediaRecorder, which is why we implement both OnInfoListener and OnErrorListener. The methods of these interfaces will be coming up shortly.

There are several member fields for our activity that we'll need later, and we initialize several of them in the `onCreate()` method. For now we're only showing a comment where the rest of the MainActivity class goes. Those class methods will be covered in the subsequent listings, starting with Listing 19–12 where we show our standard `onResume()` and `onPause()` methods.

Listing 19–12. *Record Video's Resume and Pause code*

```
    @Override
    protected void onResume() {
        Log.v(TAG, "in onResume");
        super.onResume();
        mInitBtn.setEnabled(false);
        mStartBtn.setEnabled(false);
        mStopBtn.setEnabled(false);
        mPlayBtn.setEnabled(false);
        mStopPlayBtn.setEnabled(false);
        if(!initCamera())
            finish();
    }
```

```
@Override
protected void onPause() {
    Log.v(TAG, "in onPause");
    super.onPause();
    releaseRecorder();
    releaseCamera();
}
```

NOTE: Listing 19–12 contains methods of our MainActivity class; we've only separated them into different listings to make it easier to follow along. The same is true of the rest of the listings for the Record Video application.

These are pretty standard methods. In onResume() we simply set our buttons to their initialized state, and then we initialize the camera (that method is coming up next). In onPause() we need to release both our MediaRecorder and Camera. This way, anytime our application goes out of view, recording will stop and the camera is released so another application can use it. If the user comes back to our application, things will restart and the user will be able to record video again. Next up, in Listing 19–13, is the initialization code for the camera, the Surface.Callback callbacks, plus the release methods for both Camera and the MediaRecorder.

Listing 19–13. ***Record Video's initCamera() and release methods***

```
private boolean initCamera() {
    try {
        mCamera  = Camera.open();
        Camera.Parameters camParams = mCamera.getParameters();
        mCamera.lock();
        //mCamera.setDisplayOrientation(90);
        // Could also set other parameters here and apply using:
        //mCamera.setParameters(camParams);

        mHolder = mVideoView.getHolder();
        mHolder.addCallback(this);
        mHolder.setType(SurfaceHolder.SURFACE_TYPE_PUSH_BUFFERS);
    }
    catch(RuntimeException re) {
        Log.v(TAG, "Could not initialize the Camera");
        re.printStackTrace();
        return false;
    }
    return true;
}

@Override
public void surfaceCreated(SurfaceHolder holder) {
    Log.v(TAG, "in surfaceCreated");

    try {
        mCamera.setPreviewDisplay(mHolder);
        mCamera.startPreview();
    } catch (IOException e) {
        Log.v(TAG, "Could not start the preview");
```

```
            e.printStackTrace();
        }
        mInitBtn.setEnabled(true);
    }

    @Override
    public void surfaceDestroyed(SurfaceHolder holder) {
        Log.v(TAG, "in surfaceDestroyed");
    }

    @Override
    public void surfaceChanged(SurfaceHolder holder, int format, int width,
            int height) {
        Log.v(TAG, "surfaceChanged: Width x Height = " + width + "x" + height);
    }

    private void releaseRecorder() {
        if(mRecorder != null) {
            mRecorder.release();
            mRecorder = null;
        }
    }

    private void releaseCamera() {
        if(mCamera != null) {
            try {
                mCamera.reconnect();
            } catch (IOException e) {
                e.printStackTrace();
            }
            mCamera.release();
            mCamera = null;
        }
    }
```

The `initCamera()` method is called to set up our access to the device's camera. It's the beginning of everything. For this sample application, we are using the default parameters of the Camera, but we could easily get the current parameter values, update them, and write them back. The commented code shows where you could change the camera's behavior and appearance. Once the camera is set, we grab the SurfaceHolder where the video images will appear.

The `surfaceCreated()` callback is where we give the camera object a place to show the current view, in other words, the camera preview. Once the preview has been started we can enable the button to initialize the MediaRecorder. The camera preview is a very useful feature that allows the user to see what the camera sees before it starts recording. Whether you're doing video recording or still photography, you would most likely do a preview and it would be done this way for either case.

For completeness, we've shown the `releaseRecorder()` and `releaseCamera()` methods. These get called in onPause() as was shown in Listing 19–12.

At this point in our application, we've set up the camera, initialized our buttons and are showing a preview of what the camera sees. Now the user can start clicking on buttons, although the only one that is enabled at the start is the Initialize Recorder button. When a button is pressed, the code in Listing 19–14 executes. Each of the five actions corresponding to each button is provided in this listing. As each action executes, the buttons will enable and disable appropriately for the next action. For example, once the recorder has been initialized, the Initialize Recorder button is disabled and the Begin Recording button is enabled.

Listing 19–14. *Record Video's Button processing code*

```
public void doClick(View view) {
    switch(view.getId()) {
    case R.id.initBtn:
        initRecorder();
        break;
    case R.id.beginBtn:
        beginRecording();
        break;
    case R.id.stopBtn:
        stopRecording();
        break;
    case R.id.playRecordingBtn:
        playRecording();
        break;
    case R.id.stopPlayingRecordingBtn:
        stopPlayingRecording();
        break;
    }
}

private void initRecorder() {
    if(mRecorder != null) return;

    mOutputFileName = Environment.getExternalStorageDirectory() +
                                "/videooutput.mp4";

    File outFile = new File(mOutputFileName);
    if(outFile.exists()) {
        outFile.delete();
    }

    try {
        mCamera.stopPreview();
        mCamera.unlock();
        mRecorder = new MediaRecorder();
        mRecorder.setCamera(mCamera);

        mRecorder.setAudioSource(MediaRecorder.AudioSource.CAMCORDER);
        mRecorder.setVideoSource(MediaRecorder.VideoSource.CAMERA);
        mRecorder.setOutputFormat(MediaRecorder.OutputFormat.MPEG_4);
        mRecorder.setVideoSize(176, 144);
        mRecorder.setVideoFrameRate(15);
        mRecorder.setVideoEncoder(MediaRecorder.VideoEncoder.MPEG_4_SP);
        mRecorder.setAudioEncoder(MediaRecorder.AudioEncoder.AMR_NB);
        mRecorder.setMaxDuration(7000); // limit to 7 seconds
        mRecorder.setPreviewDisplay(mHolder.getSurface());
        mRecorder.setOutputFile(mOutputFileName);

        mRecorder.prepare();
```

```
            Log.v(TAG, "MediaRecorder initialized");
            mInitBtn.setEnabled(false);
            mStartBtn.setEnabled(true);
        }
        catch(Exception e) {
            Log.v(TAG, "MediaRecorder failed to initialize");
            e.printStackTrace();
        }
    }

    private void beginRecording() {
        mRecorder.setOnInfoListener(this);
        mRecorder.setOnErrorListener(this);
        mRecorder.start();
        mRecordingMsg.setText("RECORDING");
        mStartBtn.setEnabled(false);
        mStopBtn.setEnabled(true);
    }

    private void stopRecording() {
        if (mRecorder != null) {
            mRecorder.setOnErrorListener(null);
            mRecorder.setOnInfoListener(null);
            try {
                mRecorder.stop();
            }
            catch(IllegalStateException e) {
                // This can happen if the recorder has already stopped.
                Log.e(TAG, "Got IllegalStateException in stopRecording");
            }
            releaseRecorder();
            mRecordingMsg.setText("");
            releaseCamera();
            mStartBtn.setEnabled(false);
            mStopBtn.setEnabled(false);
            mPlayBtn.setEnabled(true);
        }
    }

    private void playRecording() {
        MediaController mc = new MediaController(this);
        mVideoView.setMediaController(mc);
        mVideoView.setVideoPath(mOutputFileName);
        mVideoView.start();
        mStopPlayBtn.setEnabled(true);
    }

    private void stopPlayingRecording() {
        mVideoView.stopPlayback();
    }
```

The `initRecorder()` method is where a lot of our setup happens. The recorder needs to know where to record to, so we provide a file path name. We delete the file if it already exists. Notice how we then stop the preview of the camera, unlock it, then we turn around and connect it to the `MediaRecorder`? The camera is somewhat sensitive to locking and unlocking, and sometimes you need to lock the camera to prevent others from getting to it, and other times you need to unlock it so you can do what you want to with it. This is one of those times when you need to unlock it to connect it to the MediaRecorder. Once the camera is connected, which we do first, we proceed to set the rest of the MediaRecorder attributes, including audio source and video source. But wait, didn't we just connect the camera to the recorder? Well, yes we did. But we still need to set the video source explicitly. By setting the camera in the recorder, we avoid having to destroy the Camera object only to have the recorder object build a new one. We also set the audio and video encoders and a path to the output file on the SD card before calling the prepare() method. The prepare() method comes at the end and gets us ready to actually record something. We end this method by enabling the Begin Recording button.

The beginRecording() method is fairly straightforward by comparison. It adds the listeners, calls start(), then sets the recording message string and changes the buttons. When this method reaches the end, our application should be recording video and the red RECORDING message should be displayed, like it was in Figure 19–6.

The stopRecording() method is a little more complicated, in part because it could be called from more than one place. We'll get to the second place in a bit, but for now assume that the Stop Recording button has triggered this method. If we still have a valid recorder, we disable the callbacks then call stop(). Since it is possible that stop() could be called on a recorder that is already stopped, we handle the exception that says we tried to stop a recorder that was already stopped. Then we release the recorder and the camera, and set the RECORDING message to blank. Finally, the buttons change to switch from recording to playback.

The playRecording() method is also straightforward. We grab a MediaController for our VideoView, point it to our new file, then call start(). Our stopPlayingRecording() method is even simpler; we just stop the playback of the video. When we're in playback mode, it's harmless to click the Play button when the video is already playing, or click Stop when the video is stopped.

We mentioned before that the recording action can be stopped from more than one place. One of the settings on the recorder was a maximum duration of seven seconds. This means that recording will stop after seven seconds and our info callback will get called. Let's take a look at these now in Listing 19–15.

Listing 19–15. ***Record Video's Info Callbacks***

```
    @Override
    public void onInfo(MediaRecorder mr, int what, int extra) {
        Log.i(TAG, "got a recording event");
        if(what == MediaRecorder.MEDIA_RECORDER_INFO_MAX_DURATION_REACHED) {
            Log.i(TAG, "...max duration reached");
            stopRecording();
            Toast.makeText(this, "Recording limit has been reached. Stopping the
recording",
                    Toast.LENGTH_SHORT).show();
        }
    }

    @Override
    public void onError(MediaRecorder mr, int what, int extra) {
```

```
            Log.e(TAG, "got a recording error");
            stopRecording();
            Toast.makeText(this, "Recording error has occurred. Stopping the recording",
                    Toast.LENGTH_SHORT).show();
        }
    }
```

These two callbacks are very similar. The only difference between them is the circumstances under which they are called. In the onInfo() method, the messages are not considered errors. onInfo() could be called because we reached the maximum recording time, or the maximum file size, if we set either of these options on the recorder. For onError(), the documentation doesn't say specifically why this might be called, but it could be because the recorder runs out of space where the video file is being written. If onInfo() was called because we hit our time limit, or if we got some sort of recording error, we will stop recording.

As before when recording audio, we need to set the same permissions for audio (android.permission.RECORD_AUDIO) and the SD card (android.permission.WRITE_EXTERNAL_STORAGE), and now we need to add permission to access the camera (android.permission.CAMERA). For completeness, the AndroidManifest.xml file is shown in Listing 19–16. You'll notice that we force the orientation of our application to be landscape which is why our layout file is in /res/layout-land/main.xml.

Listing 19–16. Record Video's AndroidManifest.xml file

```
<?xml version="1.0" encoding="utf-8"?>
<manifest xmlns:android="http://schemas.android.com/apk/res/android"
      package="com.androidbook.record.video"
      android:versionCode="1"
      android:versionName="1.0">
    <application android:icon="@drawable/icon" android:label="@string/app_name">
        <activity android:name=".MainActivity"
                  android:label="@string/app_name"
                  android:screenOrientation="landscape">
            <intent-filter>
                <action android:name="android.intent.action.MAIN" />
                <category android:name="android.intent.category.LAUNCHER" />
            </intent-filter>
        </activity>
    </application>
    <uses-sdk android:minSdkVersion="4" />

<uses-permission android:name="android.permission.WRITE_EXTERNAL_STORAGE"/>
<uses-permission android:name="android.permission.RECORD_AUDIO"/>
<uses-permission android:name="android.permission.CAMERA"/>
</manifest>
```

Camera and Camcorder Profiles

In Listing 19–14, you saw in the initRecorder() method a series of very specific settings for the video recorder. The question is, how can you know what the capabilities of the device are that your application is running on? Prior to Android 2.2 there really wasn't a good answer to this question. The stock Camera application that comes with Android uses an undocumented SystemProperties class. Therefore, prior to Android 2.2 you had to choose values that would work on the devices you wanted to target. This was less than satisfying, especially as better cameras became available on the newer devices. To rectify this situation, Android 2.2 introduced a couple of new classes: CameraProfile and CamcorderProfile. These classes are simply containers for the camera attributes that you care about. While CameraProfile only has one value (JPEG Encoding Quality Parameter), CamcorderProfile tells you about the frame rate, frame size (height and width), and other video and audio parameters. Not only that, but the MediaRecorder class can accept a CamcorderProfile to set the various video recording values that a CamcorderProfile contains. You just have to be careful to call the setProfile() method after setting the video and audio sources, and before setting the output file.

With the introduction of Android 2.3, methods that deal with cameras now may have an alternate method that will accept a camera identifier. Before Android 2.3, most devices only had one camera and it usually faced the back of the device. With the newer devices with front-facing cameras in addition to back-facing cameras, code needs a way to specify which camera it wants to be dealing with. For example, in the Camera class, the open() method will return a Camera object for the back-facing camera, if one exists. There is an open(int cameraid) method that returns a specific camera, allowing your application to use the front-facing camera if one exists. To determine how many cameras are available and which one is which, the Camera.getNumberOfCameras() method will return the camera count, and Camera.getCameraInfo() will return information about a specific camera including in which direction it faces.

Exploring the MediaStore Class

So far, we've dealt with media by directly instantiating classes to play and record media within our own application. One of the great things about Android is that you can access other applications to do work for you. The MediaStore class provides an interface to the media that is stored on the device, both internally and externally.

MediaStore also provides APIs for you to act on the media. These include mechanisms for you to search the device for specific types of media, intents for you to record audio and video to the store, ways for you to establish playlists, and more. Note that this class was part of the older SDKs, but it has been greatly improved since the 1.5 release.

Because the MediaStore class supports intents for you to record audio and video, and the MediaRecorder class does recording also, an obvious question is: when do you use MediaStore versus MediaRecorder? As you saw with the preceding video-capture example and the audio-recording examples, MediaRecorder enables you to set various options on the source of the recording. These options include the audio/video input source, video frame rate, video frame size, output formats, and so on. MediaStore does not provide this level of granularity, but if you don't need it, you may find it easier to go through the MediaStore's intents. More important, content created with the MediaRecorder is not automatically available to other applications that are looking at the media store. If you use `MediaRecorder`, you might want to add the recording to the media store using the `MediaStore` APIs, so it might be simpler just to use `MediaStore` in the first place. Another significant difference is that calling MediaStore through an intent does not require your application to request permissions to record audio, or access the camera, or to write to the SD card. Your application is invoking a separate activity, and that other activity must have permission to record audio, access the camera, and write to the SD card. The `MediaStore` activities already have these permissions. Therefore, your application doesn't have to. So, let's see how we can leverage the `MediaStore` APIs.

Recording Audio Using an Intent

As we've seen, recording audio was easy, but its gets much easier if you use an intent from the `MediaStore`. Listing 19–17 demonstrates how to use an intent to record audio.

Listing 19–17. *Using an Intent to record audio*

```
<?xml version="1.0" encoding="utf-8"?>
<!-- This file is /res/layout/main.xml -->
<LinearLayout xmlns:android="http://schemas.android.com/apk/res/android"
    android:orientation="vertical"
    android:layout_width="fill_parent"
    android:layout_height="fill_parent" >
 <Button android:id="@+id/recordBtn"
    android:text="Record Audio"
    android:layout_width="wrap_content"
    android:layout_height="wrap_content" />
</LinearLayout>


import android.app.Activity;
import android.content.Intent;
import android.net.Uri;
import android.os.Bundle;
import android.util.Log;
import android.view.View;
import android.view.View.OnClickListener;
import android.widget.Button;

public class UsingMediaStoreActivity extends Activity {
    @Override
    protected void onCreate(Bundle savedInstanceState) {
        super.onCreate(savedInstanceState);

        setContentView(R.layout.main);

        Button btn = (Button)findViewById(R.id.recordBtn);
        btn.setOnClickListener(new OnClickListener(){

            @Override
            public void onClick(View view) {

                startRecording();
```

```
            }});
    }

    public void startRecording() {
        Intent intt =
            new Intent("android.provider.MediaStore.RECORD_SOUND");
        startActivityForResult(intt, 0);
    }

    @Override
    protected void onActivityResult(int requestCode, int resultCode, Intent data) {

        switch (requestCode) {
        case 0:
            if (resultCode == RESULT_OK) {
                Uri recordedAudioPath = data.getData();
                Log.v("Demo", "Uri is " + recordedAudioPath.toString());
            }
        }
    }
}
```

Listing 19–17 creates an intent requesting the system to begin recording audio. The code launches the intent against an activity by calling `startActivityForResult()`, passing the intent and the `requestCode`. When the requested activity completes, `onActivityResult()` is called with the `requestCode`. As shown in `onActivityResult()`, we look for a `requestCode` that matches the code that was passed to `startActivityForResult()` and then retrieve the Uri of the saved media by calling `data.getData()`. You could then feed the Uri to an intent to listen to the recording if you wanted to. The UI for Listing 19–17 is shown in Figure 19–7.

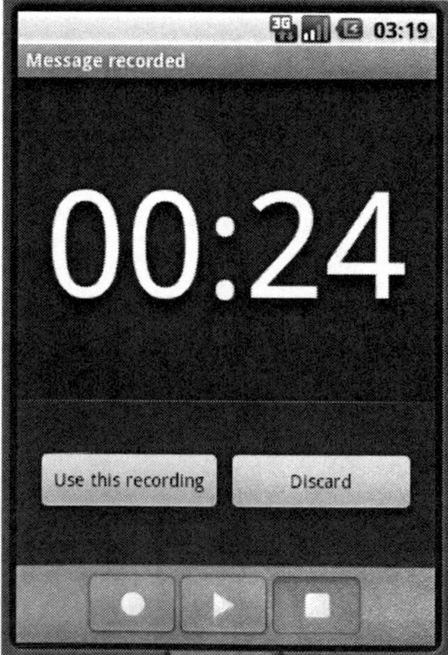

Figure 19–7. *Built-in audio recorder before and after a recording*

Figure 19–7 shows two screenshots. The image on the left displays the audio recorder during recording, and the image on the right shows the activity UI after the recording has been stopped.

Similar to the way it provides an intent for audio recording, the MediaStore also provides an intent for you to take a picture. Listing 19–18 demonstrates this.

Listing 19–18. *Launching an intent to take a picture*

```
<?xml version="1.0" encoding="utf-8"?>
<!-- This file is /res/layout/main.xml -->
<LinearLayout xmlns:android="http://schemas.android.com/apk/res/android"
    android:orientation="vertical"
    android:layout_width="fill_parent"
    android:layout_height="fill_parent" >
  <Button android:id="@+id/btn"  android:text="Take Picture"
      android:layout_width="wrap_content"
      android:layout_height="wrap_content"
      android:onClick="captureImage" />

</LinearLayout>


import android.app.Activity;
import android.content.ContentValues;
import android.content.Intent;
import android.net.Uri;
import android.os.Bundle;
import android.provider.MediaStore;
import android.provider.MediaStore.Images.Media;
import android.view.View;
import android.view.View.OnClickListener;
import android.widget.Button;

public class MainActivity extends Activity {

    Uri myPicture = null;

    @Override
    public void onCreate(Bundle savedInstanceState) {
        super.onCreate(savedInstanceState);
        setContentView(R.layout.main);

        setRequestedOrientation(ActivityInfo.SCREEN_ORIENTATION_LANDSCAPE);
    }

    public void captureImage(View view)
    {
        ContentValues values = new ContentValues();
        values.put(Media.TITLE, "My demo image");
        values.put(Media.DESCRIPTION, "Image Captured by Camera via an Intent");

        myPicture = getContentResolver().insert(Media.EXTERNAL_CONTENT_URI, values);

        Intent i = new Intent(MediaStore.ACTION_IMAGE_CAPTURE);
        i.putExtra(MediaStore.EXTRA_OUTPUT, myPicture);
```

```
        startActivityForResult(i, 0);
    }

    @Override
    protected void onActivityResult(int requestCode, int resultCode, Intent data) {
        if(requestCode==0 && resultCode==Activity.RESULT_OK)
        {
            // Now we know that our myPicture Uri
            // refers to the image just taken
        }
    }
}
```

The activity class shown in Listing 19–18 defines the `captureImage()` method. In this method, an intent is created where the action name of the intent is set to `MediaStore.ACTION_IMAGE_CAPTURE`. When this intent is launched, the camera application is brought to the foreground and the user takes a picture. Because we created the Uri in advance, we can add additional details about the picture before the camera takes it. This is what the `ContentValues` class does for us. Additional attributes can be added to `values` besides `TITLE` and `DESCRIPTION`. Look up `MediaStore.Images.ImageColumns` in the Android reference for a complete list. After the picture is taken, our `onActivityResult()` callback is called. In our example, we've used the media content provider to create a new file. We could also have created a new Uri from a new file on the SD card, as shown here:

```
myPicture = Uri.fromFile(new
File(Environment.getExternalStoragePublicDirectory(DIRECTORY_DCIM) +
"/100ANDRO/imageCaptureIntent.jpg"));
```

However, creating a Uri this way does not so easily allow us to set attributes about the image, such as TITLE and DESCRIPTION. There is another way to invoke the camera intent in order to take a picture. If we do not pass any Uri at all with the intent, we will get a bitmap object returned to us in the intent argument for `onActivityResult()`. The problem with this approach is that by default, the bitmap will be scaled down from the original size, apparently because the Android team does not want you to receive a large amount of data from the camera activity back to your activity. The bitmap will have a size of 50k. To get the Bitmap object, you'd do something like this inside of `onActivityResult()`:

```
Bitmap myBitmap = (Bitmap) data.getExtras().get("data");
```

`MediaStore` also has a video-capture intent that behaves similarly. You can use `MediaStore.ACTION_VIDEO_CAPTURE` to capture video.

Adding Media Content to the Media Store

One of the other features provided by Android's media framework is the ability to add information about content to the media store via the `MediaScannerConnection` class. In other words, if the media store doesn't know about some new content, we use a `MediaScannerConnection` to tell the media store about the new content. Then that content can be served up to others. Let's see how this works (see Listing 19–19).

Listing 19–19. *Adding a File to the MediaStore*

```
<?xml version="1.0" encoding="utf-8"?>
<!-- This file is /res/layout/main.xml -->
<LinearLayout
  xmlns:android="http://schemas.android.com/apk/res/android"
  android:orientation="vertical"
  android:layout_width="fill_parent"
  android:layout_height="wrap_content">

  <EditText android:id="@+id/fileName"  android:hint="Enter new filename"
    android:layout_width="fill_parent"
    android:layout_height="wrap_content" />

  <Button android:id="@+id/scanBtn"  android:text="Add file"
    android:layout_width="wrap_content"
    android:layout_height="wrap_content"
    android:onClick="startScan" />

</LinearLayout>


import java.io.File;
import android.app.Activity;
import android.content.Intent;
import android.media.MediaScannerConnection;
import android.media.MediaScannerConnection.MediaScannerConnectionClient;
import android.net.Uri;
import android.os.Bundle;
import android.util.Log;
import android.view.View;
import android.widget.EditText;
import android.widget.Toast;

public class MediaScannerActivity extends Activity implements
MediaScannerConnectionClient
{
    private EditText editText = null;
    private String filename = null;
    private MediaScannerConnection conn;

    @Override
    protected void onCreate(Bundle savedInstanceState) {
        super.onCreate(savedInstanceState);
        setContentView(R.layout.main);

        editText = (EditText)findViewById(R.id.fileName);
    }

    public void startScan(View view)
    {
        if(conn!=null) {
            conn.disconnect();
        }

        filename = editText.getText().toString();

        File fileCheck = new File(filename);
```

```
        if(fileCheck.isFile()) {
            conn = new MediaScannerConnection(this, this);
            conn.connect();
        }
        else {
            Toast.makeText(this,
                "That file does not exist",
                Toast.LENGTH_SHORT).show();
        }
    }

    @Override
    public void onMediaScannerConnected() {
        conn.scanFile(filename, null);
    }

    @Override
    public void onScanCompleted(String path, Uri uri) {
        try {
            if (uri != null) {
                Intent intent = new Intent(Intent.ACTION_VIEW);
                intent.setData(uri);
                startActivity(intent);
            }
            else {
                Log.e("MediaScannerDemo", "That file is no good");
            }
        } finally {
            conn.disconnect();
            conn = null;
        }
    }
}
```

Listing 19–19 shows an activity class that adds a file to the `MediaStore`. If the add is successful, the added file is displayed to the user via an intent. What happens behind the scenes is that the file is inspected by the `MediaScanner` to determine what type of file it is and other relevant details about it. We could have given the `MediaScanner` the MIME type of our file as the second argument to `scanFile()`. If `MediaScanner` can't determine what the type of the file is by the extension, it won't get added. If the file belongs in the `MediaStore`, a database entry is made into the media provider database. The file itself doesn't move. But now the media provider knows about this file. If you added an image file, you can now open the Gallery application and see it. If you added a music file, it will now show up in the Music application.

If you want to see inside the media provider's database, open a tools window, launch `adb shell`, and then navigate on the device to `/data/data/com.android.providers.media/databases`. There you will find databases, one of which is `internal.db`. There could be external database files there also, corresponding to one or more SD cards. Since you can use multiple SD cards with an Android phone, there could also be multiple external database files there. You can use the sqlite3 utility to inspect the tables in these databases. There are tables for audio, images, and video. See Chapter 4 for more information on using sqlite3.

Triggering MediaScanner for the Entire SD Card

In the previous example, we used the `MediaScanner` to look at a single, specific file. This is fine if you want to add a single file. But what if you want to rename a file, or delete a file, and you want the `MediaStore` to be updated? Fortunately, there's a very simple way to trigger this to happen. If you execute the following inside your application, it will be picked up by the `MediaScanner`, which will rescan the entire SD card:

```
sendBroadcast(new Intent(Intent.ACTION_MEDIA_MOUNTED,
    Uri.parse("file://" +
    Environment.getExternalStorageDirectory())));
```

As an exercise, go ahead and create a simple application that just does this command in the `onCreate()`.

This concludes our discussion of the media APIs. We hope you'll agree that playing and recording media content is not too difficult with Android.

References

Here are some helpful references to topics you may wish to explore further.

- `www.androidbook.com/projects`. Look here for a list of downloadable projects related to this book. For the projects in this chapter, look for a zip file called `ProAndroid3_Ch19_Media.zip`. This zip file contains all projects from this chapter, listed in separate root directories. There is also a `README.TXT` file that describes exactly how to import projects into Eclipse from one of these zip files.
- `http://developer.android.com/guide/topics/media/jet/jetcreator_manual.html`. This is the user manual for the JETCreator tool. You would use this to create a JET sound file to be played using the JetPlayer. JETCreator is only available for Windows and Mac OS. To see JetPlayer in action, load the JetBoy sample project from the Android SDK into Eclipse, build it and run it. FYI: the Fire button is the center DPAD key.

Summary

In this chapter, we talked about the Android media framework. We showed you how to play audio and video. We also showed you how to record audio and video, both directly and via intents.

In the next chapter, we are going to turn our attention to 3D graphics by discussing how to use OpenGL with your Android applications.

Chapter 20

Programming 3D Graphics with OpenGL

In this chapter, we will talk extensively about working with the OpenGL ES graphics API on the Android Platform. OpenGL ES is a version of OpenGL that is optimized for embedded systems and other low-powered devices such as mobile phones.

The Android Platform supports OpenGL ES 1.0 and OpenGL ES 2.0. The OpenGL ES 2.0 is available only from API level 8 corresponding to Android SDK release 2.2. As of this writing, there are some issues with using Java bindings to OpenGL ES 2.0. See the notes and recommendations on OpenGL ES 2.0 in a separate section towards the end of this chapter. The primary issue is the lack of support for OpenGL ES 2.0 in the emulator. Android 3.0 has strengthened the opportunities for OpenGL by introducing Renderscript. Renderscript is meant for better performance by allowing to run native code programmed in a "c" like language. This code even may be executed on the GPU (Graphical Processing Unit). Renderscript is also designed to allow for cross-platform compatibility. When performance is not critical, programmers are still advised to use the Java bindings for much of the OpenGL work. Due to time limitations we didn't cover the Renderscript in this edition of the book. We have provided a reference URL to a Renderscript (from Google) programming guide at the end of this chapter.

The Android SDK distribution comes with a number of OpenGL ES samples. However, the documentation on how to get started with OpenGL ES is minimal to nonexistent in the SDK. The underlying assumption is that OpenGL ES is an open standard that programmers can learn from outside of Android. As a result, Android online OpenGL resources and the Android OpenGL code samples assume you're already familiar with OpenGL.

In this chapter, we will help you with these minor roadblocks. With few OpenGL prerequisites, by the end of this chapter, you'll be comfortable with programming in OpenGL. We will do this by introducing almost no mathematics (unlike many OpenGL books).

In the first section of the chapter, we'll provide an overview of OpenGL, OpenGL ES, and some competing standards.

In the second section, we will explain the theory behind OpenGL. This is a critical section to read if you are new to OpenGL. In this section, we will cover OpenGL coordinates, its idea of a camera, and the essential OpenGL ES drawing APIs.

In the third section, we will explain how you interact with the OpenGL ES API on Android. This section covers `GLSurfaceView` and the `Renderer` interface and how they work together to draw using OpenGL. In one of our simple examples, we will draw a simple triangle to show how drawing is impacted by changing the OpenGL scene setup APIs.

> **NOTE:** The OpenGL camera concept is similar but distinct from the `Camera` class in Android's graphics package, which you learned about in Chapter 6. Whereas Android's `Camera` object from the graphics package simulates 3D-like viewing capabilities by projecting a 2D view moving in 3D space, the OpenGL camera is a paradigm that represents a virtual viewing point. In other words, it models a real-world scene through the viewing perspective of an observer looking through a camera. You'll learn more in the subsection "Understanding the Camera and Coordinates" under "Using OpenGL ES." Both cameras are still separate from the handheld device's physical camera that you use to take pictures or shoot video.

In the fourth section, we will take you a bit deeper into OpenGL ES and introduce the idea of shapes. We will also cover textures and show you how to draw multiple figures during a single `draw` method. We will then cover the support for OpenGL ES 2.0 by briefly introducing OpenGL shaders and a quick sample. Please note up front that OpenGL ES 2.0 can only be tested on a real device.

We conclude the chapter with a list of resources we found as we researched material for this chapter.

So, let's look into the history and background of OpenGL!

Understanding the History and Background of OpenGL

OpenGL (originally called Open Graphics Library) is a 2D and 3D graphics API that was developed by Silicon Graphics, Inc. (SGI) for its UNIX workstations. Although SGI's version of OpenGL has been around for a long time, the first standardized spec of OpenGL emerged in 1992. Now widely adopted on all operating systems, the OpenGL standard forms the basis of much of the gaming, computer-aided design (CAD), and even virtual reality (VR) industries.

The OpenGL standard is currently being managed by an industry consortium called The Khronos Group (`www.khronos.org`), founded in 2000 by companies such as NVIDIA, Sun Microsystems, ATI Technologies, and SGI. You can learn more about the OpenGL spec at the consortium's web site at:

`www.khronos.org/opengl/`

The official documentation page for OpenGL is available here:

```
www.opengl.org/documentation/
```

As you can see from this documentation page, you have access to books and online resources dedicated to OpenGL. Of these, the gold standard is *OpenGL Programming Guide: The Official Guide to Learning OpenGL, Version 1.1*, also known as the "red book" of OpenGL. You can find an online version of this book here:

```
www.glprogramming.com/red/
```

This book is quite good and quite readable. We did have some difficulty, however, unraveling the nature of *units* and *coordinates* that are used to draw. We'll try to clarify these important ideas regarding what you draw and what you see in OpenGL. These ideas center on setting up the OpenGL camera and a *viewing box*, also known as a *viewing volume* or *frustum*.

OpenGL ES

The Khronos Group is also responsible for two additional standards that are tied to OpenGL: OpenGL ES, and the EGL Native Platform Graphics Interface (known simply as EGL). As we mentioned, OpenGL ES is a smaller version of OpenGL intended for embedded systems.

> **NOTE:** Java Community Process is also developing an object-oriented abstraction for OpenGL for mobile devices called Mobile 3D Graphics API (M3G). We will give you a brief introduction to M3G in the subsection "M3G: Another Java ME 3D Graphics Standard."

The EGL standard is essentially an enabling interface between the underlying operating system (OS) and the rendering APIs offered by OpenGL ES. Because OpenGL and OpenGL ES are general-purpose interfaces for drawing, each OS needs to provide a standard hosting environment for OpenGL and OpenGL ES to interact with. Android SDK, starting with the 1.5 release, hides these platform specifics quite well. You will learn about this in the second section titled "Interfacing OpenGL ES with Android."

The target devices for OpenGL ES include cell phones, appliances, and even vehicles. Because OpenGL ES has to be much smaller than OpenGL, many convenient functions have been removed. For example, drawing rectangles is not directly supported in OpenGL ES; you have to draw two triangles to make a rectangle.

As you start exploring Android's support for OpenGL, you'll focus primarily on OpenGL ES and its bindings to the Android OS through Java and EGL. You can find the documentation for OpenGL ES here:

```
www.khronos.org/opengles/documentation/opengles1_0/html/index.html
```

We kept returning to this reference as we developed this chapter because it identifies and explains each OpenGL ES API and describe the arguments for each. You'll find these APIs similar to Java APIs, and we'll introduce you to the key ones in this chapter.

OpenGL ES and Java ME

OpenGL ES, like OpenGL, is a C-based, flat API. Because the Android SDK is a Java-based programming API, you need a Java binding to OpenGL ES. Java ME has already defined this binding through JSR 239: Java Binding for the OpenGL ES API. JSR 239 itself is based on JSR 231, which is a Java binding for OpenGL 1.5. JSR 239 could have been strictly a subset of JSR 231, but it's not because it must accommodate some extensions to OpenGL ES that are not in OpenGL 1.5.

You can find the documentation for JSR 239 here:

http://java.sun.com/javame/reference/apis/jsr239/

This reference will give you a sense of the APIs available in OpenGL ES. It also provides valuable information about the following packages:

```
javax.microedition.khronos.egl

javax.microedition.khronos.opengles

java.nio
```

The nio package is necessary because the OpenGL ES implementations take only byte streams as inputs for efficiency reasons. This nio package defines many utilities to prepare native buffers for use in OpenGL. You will see some of these APIs in action in the "glVertexPointer and Specifying Drawing Vertices" subsection under "Using OpenGL ES."

You can find documentation (although quite minimal) of the Android SDK's support for OpenGL at the following URL:

http://developer.android.com/guide/topics/graphics/opengl.html

On this page, the documentation indicates that the Android implementation mostly parallels JSR 239 but warns that it might diverge from it in a few places.

M3G: Another Java ME 3D Graphics Standard

JSR 239 is merely a Java binding on a native OpenGL ES standard. As mentioned briefly in the "OpenGL ES" subsection, Java provides another API to work with 3D graphics on mobile devices: M3G. This object-oriented standard is defined in JSR 184 and JSR 297, the latter being more recent. As per JSR 184, M3G serves as a lightweight, object-oriented, interactive 3D graphics API for mobile devices.

The object-oriented nature of M3G separates it from OpenGL ES. For details, visit the home page for JSR 184 at the following URL:

www.jcp.org/en/jsr/detail?id=184

The APIs for M3G are available in the Java package named

```
javax.microedition.m3g.*;
```

M3G is a higher-level API compared to OpenGL ES, so it should be easier to learn. However, the jury is still out on how well it will perform on handhelds. As of now, Android does not support M3G.

So far, we have laid out the options available in the OpenGL space for handheld devices. We have talked about OpenGL ES and also briefly about the M3G standard. We will now focus on understanding the fundamentals of OpenGL.

Fundamentals of OpenGL

This section will help you understand the concepts behind OpenGL and the OpenGL ES API. We'll explain all the key APIs. To supplement the information from this chapter, you might want to refer to the "Resources" section towards the end of this chapter. The resources there include the red book, JSR 239 documentation, and The Khronos Group API reference.

> **NOTE:** As you start using the OpenGL resources, you'll notice that some of the APIs are not available in OpenGL ES. This is where The Khronos Group's *OpenGL ES Reference Manual* comes in handy.

We will cover the following APIs in a fair amount of detail because they're central to understanding OpenGL and OpenGL ES:

- `glVertexPointer`
- `glDrawElements`
- `glColor`
- `glClear`
- `gluLookAt`
- `glFrustum`
- `glViewport`

As we cover these APIs, you'll learn how to

- Use the essential OpenGL ES drawing APIs.
- Clear the palette.
- Specify colors.
- Understand the OpenGL camera and coordinates.

Essential Drawing with OpenGL ES

In OpenGL, you draw in 3D space. You start out by specifying a series of points, also called vertices. Each of these points will have three values: one for the x coordinate, one for the y coordinate, and one for the z coordinate.

These points are then joined together to form a shape. You can join these points into a variety of shapes called *primitive shapes*, which include points, lines, and triangles in OpenGL ES. Note that in OpenGL, primitive shapes also include rectangles and polygons. As you work with OpenGL and OpenGL ES, you will continue to see differences whereby the latter has fewer features than the former. Here's another example: OpenGL allows you to specify each point separately, whereas OpenGL ES allows you to specify them only as a series of points in one fell swoop. However, you can often simulate OpenGL ES's missing features through other, more primitive features. For instance, you can draw a rectangle by combining two triangles.

OpenGL ES offers two primary methods to facilitate drawing:

```
glVertexPointer
glDrawElements
```

> **NOTE**: We'll use the terms "API" and "method" interchangeably when we talk about the OpenGL ES APIs.

You use `glVertexPointer` to specify a series of points or vertices, and you use `glDrawElements` to draw them using one of the primitive shapes mentioned earlier. We'll describe these methods in more detail, but first let's go over some nomenclature around the OpenGL API names.

The names of OpenGL APIs all begin with `gl`. Following `gl` is the method name. The method name is followed by an optional number such as `3`, which points to either the number of dimensions—such as `(x,y,z)`—or the number of arguments. The method name is then followed by a data type such as `f` for float. (You can refer to any of the OpenGL online resources to learn the various data types and their corresponding letters.)

There's one more convention. If a method takes an argument either as a byte (`b`) or a float (`f`), then the method will have two names: one ending with `b`, and one ending with `f`.

Let's now look at each of the two drawing-related methods, starting with `glVertexPointer`.

glVertexPointer and Specifying Drawing Vertices

The `glVertexPointer` method is responsible for specifying an array of points to be drawn. Each point is specified in three dimensions, so each point will have three values: x, y, and z. Listing 20–1 shows how to specify three points in an array.

Listing 20–1. *Vertex Coordinates Example for an OpenGL Triangle*

```
float[] coords = {
      -0.5f, -0.5f, 0,    //p1: (x1,y1,z1)
       0.5f, -0.5f, 0,    //p2: (x1,y1,z1)
       0.0f,  0.5f, 0     //p3: (x1,y1,z1)
};
```

The structure in Listing 20–1 is a contiguous set of floats kept in a Java-based float array. Don't worry about typing or compiling this code anywhere yet—our goal at this point is just to give you an idea of how these OpenGL ES methods work. We will give you the working examples and code when we develop a test harness later to draw simple figures. We have also given you a link to a downloadable project in the reference section at the end of this chapter.

In Listing 20–1, you might be wondering what units are used for the coordinates in points `p1`, `p2`, and `p3`. The short answer is, as you model your 3D space, these coordinate units can be anything you'd like. But subsequently you will need to specify something called a *bounding volume* (or *bounding box*) that quantifies these coordinates.

For example, you can specify the bounding box as a cube with 5-inch sides or a cube with 2-inch sides. These coordinates are also known as *world coordinates* because you are conceptualizing your world independent of the physical device's limitations. We will explain these coordinates more in the subsection "Understanding the Camera and Coordinates." For now, assume that you are using a cube that is 2 units across all its sides and centered at (x=0,y=0,z=0). In other words, the center is at the center of the cube and the sides of the cube are 1 unit apart from the center.

> **NOTE**: The terms *bounding volume, bounding box, viewing volume, viewing box,* and *frustum* all refer to the same concept: the pyramid-shaped 3D volume that determines what is visible onscreen. You'll learn more in the "glFrustum and the Viewing Volume" subsection under "Understanding the Camera and Coordinates."

You can also assume that the origin is at the center of the visual display. The z axis will be negative going into the display (away from you) and positive coming out of the display (toward you); x will go positive as you move right and negative as you move left. However, these coordinates will also depend on the direction from which you are viewing the scene.

To draw the points in Listing 20–1, you need to pass them to OpenGL ES through the `glVertexPointer` method. For efficiency reasons, however, `glVertexPointer` takes a native buffer that is language-agnostic rather than an array of Java floats. For this, you need to convert the Java-based array of floats to an acceptable C-like native buffer. You'll need to use the `java.nio` classes to convert the float array into the native buffer. Listing 20–2 shows an example of using `nio` buffers.

Listing 20–2. *Creating NIO Float Buffers*

```
jva.nio.ByteBuffer vbb = java.nio.ByteBuffer.allocateDirect(3 * 3 * 4);
vbb.order(ByteOrder.nativeOrder());
java.nio.FloatBuffer mFVertexBuffer = vbb.asFloatBuffer();
```

In Listing 20–2, the byte buffer is a buffer of memory ordered into bytes. Each point has three floats because of the three axes, and each float is 4 bytes. So together you get `3 * 4` bytes for each point. Plus, a triangle has three points. So you need `3 * 3 * 4` bytes to hold all three float points of a triangle.

Once you have the points gathered into a native buffer, you can call `glVertexPointer`, as shown in Listing 20–3.

Listing 20–3. *glVertexPointer API Definition*

```
glVertexPointer(
       // Are we using (x,y) or (x,y,z) in each point
       3,
       // each value is a float value in the buffer
       GL10.GL_FLOAT,
       // Between two points there is no space
      0,
      // pointer to the start of the buffer
      mFVertexBuffer);
```

Let's talk about the arguments of `glVertexPointer` method. The first argument tells OpenGL ES how many dimensions there are in a point or a vertex. In this case, we specified `3` for x, y, and z. You could also specify `2` for just x and y. In that case, z would be zero. Note that this first argument is not the number of points in the buffer, but the number of dimensions used. So if you pass 20 points to draw a number of triangles, you will not pass `20` as the first argument; you would pass `2` or `3`, depending on the number of dimensions used.

The second argument indicates that the coordinates need to be interpreted as floats. The third argument, called a `stride`, points to the number of bytes separating each point. In this case, it is zero because one point immediately follows the other. Sometimes you can add color attributes as part of the buffer after each point. If you want to do so, you'd use a `stride` to skip those as part of the vertex specification. The last argument is the pointer to the buffer containing the points.

Now that you know how to set up the array of points to be drawn, let's see how to draw this array of points using the `glDrawElements` method.

glDrawElements

Once you specify the series of points through `glVertexPointer`, you use the `glDrawElements` method to draw those points with one of the primitive shapes that OpenGL ES allows. Note that OpenGL is a state machine. It remembers the values set by one method when it invokes the next method in a cumulative manner. So you don't need to explicitly pass the points set by `glVertexPointer` to `glDrawElements`. `glDrawElements` will implicitly use those points. Listing 20–4 shows an example of this method with possible arguments.

Listing 20–4. *Example of glDrawElements*

```
glDrawElements(
        // type of shape
        GL10.GL_TRIANGLE_STRIP,
        // Number of indices
        3,
       // How big each index is
       GL10.GL_UNSIGNED_SHORT,
       // buffer containing the 3 indices
       mIndexBuffer);
```

The first argument indicates the type of geometrical shape to draw: `GL_TRIANGLE_STRIP` signifies a triangle strip. Other possible options for this argument are points only (`GL_POINTS`), line strips (`GL_LINE_STRIP`), lines only (`GL_LINES`), line loops (`GL_LINE_LOOP`), triangles only (`GL_TRIANGLES`), and triangle fans (`GL_TRIANGLE_FAN`).

The concept of a `STRIP` in `GL_LINE_STRIP` and `GL_TRIANGLE_STRIP` is to add new points while making use of the old ones. By doing so, you can avoid specifying all the points for each new object. For example, if you specify four points in an array, you can use strips to draw the first triangle out of (1,2,3) and the second one out of (2,3,4). Each new point will add a new triangle. (Refer to the OpenGL red book for more details.) You can also vary these parameters to see how the triangles are drawn as you add new points.

The idea of a `FAN` in `GL_TRIANGLE_FAN` applies to triangles where the first point is used as a starting point for all subsequent triangles. So you're essentially making a fan- or circle-like object with the first vertex in the middle. Suppose you have six points in your array: (1,2,3,4,5,6). With a `FAN`, the triangles will be drawn at (1,2,3), (1,3,4), (1,4,5), and (1,5,6). Every new point adds an extra triangle, similar to the process of extending a fan or unfolding a pack of cards.

The rest of the arguments of `glDrawElements` involve the method's ability to let you reuse point specification. For example, a square contains four points. Each square can be drawn as a combination of two triangles. If you want to draw two triangles to make up the square, do you have to specify six points? No. You can specify only four points and refer to them six times to draw two triangles. This process is called *indexing into the point buffer*.

Here is an example:

```
Points: (p1, p2, p3, p4)
Draw indices (p1, p2, p3,    p2,p3,p4)
```

Notice how the first triangle comprises `p1, p2, p3` and the second one comprises `p2, p3, p4`. With this knowledge, the second argument of `glDrawElements` identifies how many indices there are in the index buffer.

The third argument to `glDrawElements` (see Listing 20–4) points to the type of values in the index array, whether they are unsigned shorts (`GL_UNSIGNED_SHORT`) or unsigned bytes (`GL_UNSIGNED_BYTE`).

The last argument of `glDrawElements` points to the index buffer. To fill up the index buffer, you need to do something similar to what you did with the vertex buffer. Start with a Java array and use the `java.nio` package to convert that array into a native buffer.

Listing 20–5 shows some sample code that converts a short array of {0,1,2} into a native buffer suitable to be passed to glDrawElements.

Listing 20–5. *Converting Java Array to NIO Buffers*

```
//Figure out how you want to arrange your points
short[] myIndecesArray = {0,1,2};

//get a short buffer
java.nio.ShortBuffer mIndexBuffer;

//Allocate 2 bytes each for each index value
ByteBuffer ibb = ByteBuffer.allocateDirect(3 * 2);
ibb.order(ByteOrder.nativeOrder());
mIndexBuffer = ibb.asShortBuffer();

//stuff that into the buffer
for (int i=0;i<3;i++)
{
   mIndexBuffer.put(myIndecesArray[i]);
}
```

Now that you've seen mIndexBuffer at work in Listing 20–5, you can revisit Listing 20–4 and better understand how the index buffer is created and manipulated.

> **NOTE**: Rather than create any new points, the index buffer merely indexes into the array of points indicated through the glVertexPointer. This is possible because OpenGL remembers the assets set by the previous calls in a stateful fashion.

Now we'll look at two commonly used OpenGL ES methods: glClear and glColor.

glClear

You use the glClear method to erase the drawing surface. Using this method, you can reset the color, depth, and the type of stencils used. You specify which element to reset by the constant that you pass in: GL_COLOR_BUFFER_BIT, GL_DEPTH_BUFFER_BIT, or GL_STENCIL_BUFFER_BIT.

The color buffer is responsible for the pixels that are visible, so clearing it is equivalent to erasing the surface of any colors. The depth buffer is related to the pixels that are visible in a 3D scene, with depth referring to how far or close the object is.

The stencil buffer is a bit advanced to cover here, except to say this: you use it to create visual effects based on some dynamic criteria, and you use glClear to erase it.

> **NOTE**: A stencil is a drawing template that you can use to replicate a drawing many times. For example, if you are using Microsoft Office Visio, all the drawing templates that you save as *.vss files are stencils. In the noncomputer drawing world, you create a stencil by cutting out a

pattern in a sheet of paper or some other flat material. Then you can paint over that sheet and remove it, creating the impression that results in a replication of that drawing. What you see depends on what stencil or stencils are active. Clearing all of them will make everything drawn visible.

For your purposes, you can use this code to clear the color buffer:

```
//Clear the surface of any color
gl.glClear(gl.GL_COLOR_BUFFER_BIT);
```

Now let's talk about attaching a default color to what gets drawn.

glColor

You use `glColor` to set the default color for the subsequent drawing that takes place. In the following code segment, the method `glColor4f` sets the color to red:

```
//Set the current color
glColor4f(1.0f, 0, 0, 0.5f);
```

Recall the discussion about method nomenclature: `4f` refers to the four arguments that the method takes, each of which is a float. The four arguments are components of red, green, blue, and alpha (color gradient). The starting values for each are (1,1,1,1). In this case, the color has been set to red with half a gradient (specified by the last alpha argument).

Although we have covered the basic drawing APIs, we still need to address a few things regarding the coordinates of the points that you specify in 3D space. The next subsection explains how OpenGL models a real-world scene through the viewing perspective of an observer looking through a camera.

Understanding OpenGL Camera and Coordinates

As you draw in 3D space, you ultimately must project the 3D view onto a 2D screen—much like capturing a 3D scene using a camera in the real world. This symbolism is formally recognized in OpenGL, so many concepts in OpenGL are explained in terms of a camera.

As you will see in this section, the part of your drawing that becomes visible depends on the location of the camera, the direction of the camera lens, the orientation of the camera (such as upside down or tilted), the zoom level, and the size of the capturing "film."

These aspects of projecting a 3D picture onto a 2D screen are controlled by three methods in OpenGL:

- `gluLookAt` controls the direction of the camera.
- `glFrustum` controls the viewing volume or zoom or the distance (from and to) you care about.

`glViewport` controls the size of the screen or the size of the camera's film.

You won't be able to program anything in OpenGL unless you understand the implications of these three APIs. Let's elaborate on the camera symbolism further to explain how these three APIs affect what you see on an OpenGL screen. We will start with `gluLookAt`.

gluLookAt and the Camera Symbolism

Imagine you are taking photographs of a landscape involving flowers, trees, streams, and mountains. You arrive at a meadow; the scene that lies before you is equivalent to what you would like to draw in OpenGL. You can make these drawings big, like the mountains, or small, like the flowers—as long as they are all proportional to one another. The coordinates you'll use for these drawings, as we hinted at earlier, are called *world coordinates*. Under these coordinates, you can establish a line to be 4 units long on the x axis by setting your points as (0,0,0) to (4,0,0).

As you prepare to take a photograph, you find a spot to place your tripod. Then you hook up the camera to the tripod. The location of your camera—not the tripod, but the camera itself—becomes the origin of your camera in the world. So you will need to take a piece of paper and write down this location, which is called the *eye point*.

If you don't specify an eye point, the camera is located at (0,0,0), which is the exact center of your screen. Usually you want to step away from the origin so that you can see the (x,y) plane that is sitting at the origin of z = 0. For argument's sake, suppose you position the camera at (0,0,5). This would move the camera off your screen toward you by 5 units.

You can refer to Figure 20–1 to visualize how the camera is placed.

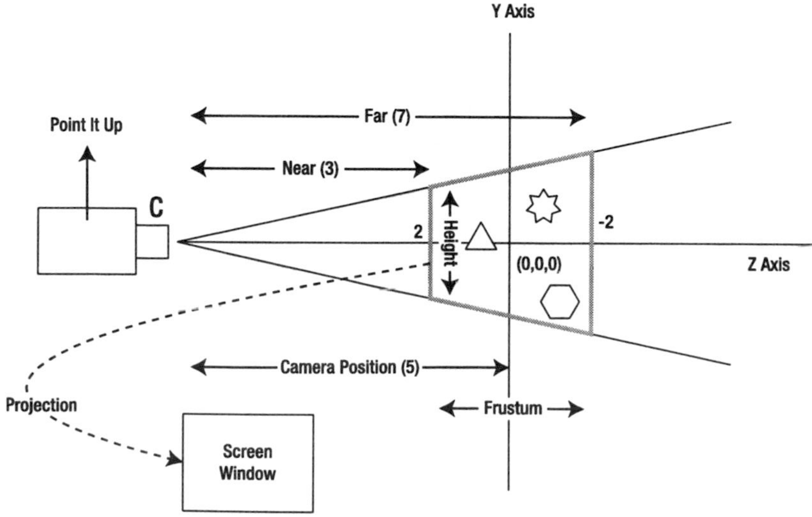

Figure 20–1. *OpenGL viewing concepts using the camera analogy*

Looking at Figure 20–1 you might wonder why the axes in the figure are y and z and not x and y. This is because we use the convention that the OpenGL camera looks down on the z axis if your normal plane of scene is the xy plane. This convention works fine because we usually associate the z axis as the axis of depth.

Once you place the camera, you start looking ahead or forward to see which portion of the scene you want to capture. You will position the camera in the direction you are looking. This far-off point that you are looking at is called a *view point* or a *look-at point*. This point specification is really a specification of the direction. If you specify your view point as (0,0,0), then the camera is looking along the z axis toward the origin from a distance of 5 units, assuming the camera is positioned at (0,0,5). You can see this in Figure 20–1 where the camera is looking down the z axis.

Imagine further that there is a rectangular building at the origin. You want to look at it not in a portrait fashion, but in a landscape fashion. What do you have to do? You obviously can leave the camera in the same location and still point it toward the origin, but now you need to turn the camera by 90 degrees (similar to tilting your head to see sideways). This is the *orientation* of the camera, as the camera is fixed at a given eye point and looking at a specific look-at point or direction. This orientation is called the *up vector*.

The up vector simply identifies the orientation of the camera (up, down, left, right, or at an angle). This orientation of the camera is also specified using a point. Imagine a line from the origin—not the camera origin, but the world-coordinate origin—to this point. Whatever angle this line subtends in three dimensions at the origin is the orientation of camera.

For example, an up vector for a camera might look like (0,1,0) or even (0,15,0), both of which would have the same effect. The point (0,1,0) is a point away from the origin along the y axis going up. This means you position the camera upright. If you use (0,-1,0), you would position the camera upside down. In both cases, the camera is still at the same point (0,0,5) and looking at the same origin (0,0,0). You can summarize these three coordinates like this:

> (0,0,5): Eye point (location of the camera)
>
> (0,0,0): Look-at point (direction the camera is pointing)
>
> (0,1,0): Up vector (whether the camera is up, down, or slanted)

You will use the `gluLookAt` method to specify these three points—the eye point, the look-at point, and the up vector, like so:

```
gluLookAt(gl, 0,0,5,    0,0,0,   0,1,0);
```

The arguments are as follows: the first set of coordinates belongs to the eye point, the second set of coordinates belongs to the look-at point, and the third set of coordinates belongs to the up vector with respect to the origin.

Let's now look at the viewing volume.

glFrustum and the Viewing Volume

You might have noticed that none of the points describing the camera position using `gluLookAt` deal with size. They deal only with positioning, direction, and orientation. How can you tell the camera where to focus? How far away is the subject you are trying to capture? How wide and how tall is the subject area? You use the OpenGL method `glFrustum` to specify the area of the scene that you are interested in.

If you were to imagine yourself sitting at a play, then the stage is your viewing volume. You really don't need to know what happens outside of that stage. However, you do care about the dimensions of this stage because you want to observe all that goes on upon/inside that stage.

Think of the scene area as bounded by a box, also called the *frustum* or *viewing volume* (this is the area marked by the bold border in the middle of Figure 20–1). Anything inside the box is captured, and anything outside the box is clipped and ignored. So how do you specify this viewing box? You first decide on the *near point*, or the distance between the camera and the beginning of the box. Then you can choose a *far point*, which is the distance between the camera and the end of the box. The distance between the near and far points along the z axis is the depth of the box. If you specify a near point of 50 and a far point of 200, then you will capture everything between those points and your box depth will be 150. You will also need to specify the left side of the box, the right side of the box, the top of the box, and the bottom of the box along the imaginary *ray* that joins the camera to the look-at point.

In OpenGL, you can imagine this box in one of two ways. One is called a *perspective projection*, which involves the frustum we've been talking about. This view, which simulates a natural camera-like function, involves a pyramidal structure in which the far plane serves as the base and the camera serves as the apex. The near plane cuts off the top of the pyramid, forming the frustum between the near plane and the far plane.

The other way to imagine the box involves thinking of it as a cube. This second scenario is called *orthographic projection* and is suited for geometrical drawings that need to preserve sizes despite the distance from the camera.

Listing 20–6 shows how to specify the frustum for our example.

Listing 20–6. ***Specifying a Frustum through glFrustum***

```
//calculate aspect ratio first
float ratio = (float) w / h;

//indicate that we want a perspective projection
glMatrixMode(GL10.GL_PROJECTION);

//Specify the frustum: the viewing volume
gl.glFrustumf(
    -ratio,     // Left side of the viewing box
    ratio,      // right side of the viewing box
    1,          // top of the viewing box
    -1,         // bottom of the viewing box
    3,          // how far is the front of the box from the camera
    7);         // how far is the back of the box from the camera
```

Because we set the top to `1` and bottom to `-1` in the preceding code (Listing 20–6), we have set the front height of the box to 2 units. We specify the sizes for the left and right sides of the frustum by using proportional numbers, taking into account the window's aspect ratio. This is why this code uses the window height and width to figure out the proportion. The code also assumes the area of action to be between `3` and `7` units along the z axis. Anything drawn outside these coordinates, relative to the camera, won't be visible.

Because we set the camera at (0,0,5) and pointing toward (0,0,0), 3 units from the camera toward the origin will be (0,0,2) and 7 units from the camera will be (0,0,-2). This leaves the origin plane right in the middle of your 3D box.

So now we've identified the size of our viewing volume. There's one more important API and it maps these sizes to the screen: `glViewport`.

glViewport and Screen Size

`glViewport` is responsible for specifying the rectangular area on the screen onto which the viewing volume will be projected. This method takes four arguments to specify the rectangular box: the x and y coordinates of the lower-left corner, followed by the width and height. Listing 20–7 is an example of specifying a view as the target for this projection.

Listing 20–7. *Defining a ViewPort through glViewPort*

```
glViewport(0,             // lower left "x" of the rectangle on the screen
           0,             // lower left "y" of the rectangle on the screen
           width,         // width of the rectangle on the screen
           height);       // height of the rectangle on the screen
```

If our window or view size is 100 pixels in height and the frustum height is 10 units, then every logical unit of 1 in the world coordinates translates to 10 pixels in screen coordinates.

So far we have covered some important introductory concepts in OpenGL. Understanding these OpenGL fundamentals is useful for learning how to write Android OpenGL code. With these prerequisites behind us, we'll now discuss what is needed to call the OpenGL ES APIs that we have learned in this section.

Interfacing OpenGL ES with Android

OpenGL ES, as indicated, is a standard that is supported by a number of platforms. At the core, it's a C-like API that addresses all of the OpenGL drawing chores. However, each platform and OS is different in the way it implements displays, screen buffers, and the like. These OS-specific aspects are left to each operating system to figure out and document. Android is no different.

Starting with its 1.5 SDK, Android simplified the interaction and initialization process necessary to start drawing in OpenGL. This support is provided in the package `android.opengl`. The primary class that provides much of this functionality is `GLSurfaceView`, and it has an internal interface called `GLSurfaceView.Renderer`. Knowing these two entities is sufficient to make a substantial headway with OpenGL on Android.

Using GLSurfaceView and Related Classes

Starting with 1.5 of the SDK, the common usage pattern for using OpenGL is quite simplified. (Refer to the first edition of this book to see the Android 1.0–approach.) Here are the typical steps to draw using these classes:

1. Implement the Renderer interface.
2. Provide the Camera settings needed for your drawing in the implementation of the renderer.
3. Provide the drawing code in the `onDrawFrame` method of the implementation.
4. Construct a `GLSurfaceView`.
5. Set the renderer implemented in steps 1 to 3 in the `GLSurfaceView`.
6. Indicate whether you want animation or not to the `GLSurfaceView`.
7. Set the `GLSurfaceView` in an Activity as the content view. You can also use this view wherever you can use a regular view.

Let's start with how to implement the renderer interface.

Implementing the Renderer

The signature of the Renderer interface is shown in Listing 20–8.

Listing 20–8. *The Renderer Interface*

```
public static interface GLSurfaceView.Renderer
{
   void onDrawFrame(GL10 gl);
   void onSurfaceChanged(GL10 gl, int width, int height);
   void onSurfaceCreated(GL10 gl, EGLConfig config);
}
```

The main drawing happens in the `onDrawFrame()` method. Whenever a new surface is created for this view, the `onSurfaceCreated()` method is called. We can call a number of OpenGL APIs such as dithering, depth control, or any others that can be called outside of the immediate `onDrawFrame()` method.

Similarly, when a surface changes, such as the width and height of the window, the onSurfaceChanged() method is called. We can set up our camera and viewing volume here.

Even in the onDrawFrame() method there are lot of things that may be common for our specific drawing context. We can take advantage of this commonality and abstract these methods in another level of abstraction called an AbstractRenderer, which will have only one method that is left unimplemented called draw().

Listing 20–9 shows the code for the AbstractRenderer.

Listing 20–9. *The AbstractRenderer*

```
//filename: AbstractRenderer.java
import android.opengl.*;
//…Use Eclipse to resolve other imports
public abstract class AbstractRenderer
implements android.opengl.GLSurfaceView.Renderer
{
    public void onSurfaceCreated(GL10 gl, EGLConfig eglConfig) {
        gl.glDisable(GL10.GL_DITHER);
        gl.glHint(GL10.GL_PERSPECTIVE_CORRECTION_HINT,
                GL10.GL_FASTEST);
        gl.glClearColor(.5f, .5f, .5f, 1);
        gl.glShadeModel(GL10.GL_SMOOTH);
        gl.glEnable(GL10.GL_DEPTH_TEST);
    }

    public void onSurfaceChanged(GL10 gl, int w, int h) {
        gl.glViewport(0, 0, w, h);
        float ratio = (float) w / h;
        gl.glMatrixMode(GL10.GL_PROJECTION);
        gl.glLoadIdentity();
        gl.glFrustumf(-ratio, ratio, -1, 1, 3, 7);
    }

    public void onDrawFrame(GL10 gl)
    {
        gl.glDisable(GL10.GL_DITHER);
        gl.glClear(GL10.GL_COLOR_BUFFER_BIT | GL10.GL_DEPTH_BUFFER_BIT);
        gl.glMatrixMode(GL10.GL_MODELVIEW);
        gl.glLoadIdentity();
        GLU.gluLookAt(gl, 0, 0, -5, 0f, 0f, 0f, 0f, 1.0f, 0.0f);
        gl.glEnableClientState(GL10.GL_VERTEX_ARRAY);
        draw(gl);
    }
    protected abstract void draw(GL10 gl);
}
```

Having this abstract class is very useful, as it allows us to focus on just the drawing methods. We'll use this class to create a SimpleTriangleRenderer class; Listing 20–10 shows the source code.

Listing 20–10. *SimpleTriangleRenderer*

```
//filename: SimpleTriangleRenderer.java
public class SimpleTriangleRenderer extends AbstractRenderer
```

```
{
   //Number of points or vertices we want to use
    private final static int VERTS = 3;

    //A raw native buffer to hold the point coordinates
    private FloatBuffer mFVertexBuffer;

    //A raw native buffer to hold indices
    //allowing a reuse of points.
    private ShortBuffer mIndexBuffer;

    public SimpleTriangleRenderer(Context context)
    {
        ByteBuffer vbb = ByteBuffer.allocateDirect(VERTS * 3 * 4);
        vbb.order(ByteOrder.nativeOrder());
        mFVertexBuffer = vbb.asFloatBuffer();

        ByteBuffer ibb = ByteBuffer.allocateDirect(VERTS * 2);
        ibb.order(ByteOrder.nativeOrder());
        mIndexBuffer = ibb.asShortBuffer();

        float[] coords = {
                -0.5f, -0.5f, 0, // (x1,y1,z1)
                 0.5f, -0.5f, 0,
                 0.0f,  0.5f, 0
        };
        for (int i = 0; i < VERTS; i++) {
            for(int j = 0; j < 3; j++) {
                mFVertexBuffer.put(coords[i*3+j]);
            }
        }
        short[] myIndecesArray = {0,1,2};
        for (int i=0;i<3;i++)
        {
           mIndexBuffer.put(myIndecesArray[i]);
        }
        mFVertexBuffer.position(0);
        mIndexBuffer.position(0);
    }

   //overriden method
    protected void draw(GL10 gl)
    {
       gl.glColor4f(1.0f, 0, 0, 0.5f);
       gl.glVertexPointer(3, GL10.GL_FLOAT, 0, mFVertexBuffer);
        gl.glDrawElements(GL10.GL_TRIANGLES, VERTS,
                GL10.GL_UNSIGNED_SHORT, mIndexBuffer);
    }
}
```

Although there seems to be a lot of code here, most of it is used to define the vertices and then translate them to NIO buffers from Java buffers. Otherwise, the `draw` method is just three lines: set the color, set the vertices, and draw.

NOTE: Although we are allocating memory for NIO buffers, we never release them in our code. So who releases these buffers? How does this memory affect OpenGL?

According to our research, the java.nio package allocates memory space outside of the Java heap that can be directly used by such systems as OpenGL, File I/O, etc. The `nio` buffers are actually Java objects that eventually point to the native buffer. These `nio` objects are garbage collected. When they are garbage collected, they go ahead and delete the native memory. Java programs don't have to do anything special to free the memory.

However, the `gc` won't get fired unless memory is needed in the Java heap. This means you can run out of native memory and `gc` may not realize it. The Internet offers many examples on this subject where an out of memory exception will trigger a `gc` and then it's possible to inquire if memory is now available due to `gc` having been invoked.

Under ordinary circumstances—and this is important for OpenGL—you can allocate the native buffers and not worry about releasing allocated memory explicitly because that is done by the `gc`.

Now that we have a sample renderer, let's see how we can supply this renderer to a GLSurfaceView and have it show up in an Activity.

Using GLSurfaceView from an Activity

Listing 20–11 shows a typical activity that uses a GLSurfaceView along with a suitable renderer.

Listing 20–11. *A Simple OpenGLTestHarness Activity*

```
public class OpenGLTestHarnessActivity extends Activity {
   private GLSurfaceView mTestHarness;
    @Override
    protected void onCreate(Bundle savedInstanceState) {
        super.onCreate(savedInstanceState);
        mTestHarness = new GLSurfaceView(this);
        mTestHarness.setEGLConfigChooser(false);
        mTestHarness.setRenderer(new SimpleTriangleRenderer(this));
        mTestHarness.setRenderMode(GLSurfaceView.RENDERMODE_WHEN_DIRTY);
        //mTestHarness.setRenderMode(GLSurfaceView.RENDERMODE_CONTINUOUSLY);
        setContentView(mTestHarness);
    }
    @Override
    protected void onResume()    {
        super.onResume();
        mTestHarness.onResume();
    }
    @Override
    protected void onPause() {
        super.onPause();
        mTestHarness.onPause();
    }
}
```

Let's explain the key elements of this source code. Here is the code that instantiates the GLSurfaceView:

```
        mTestHarness = new GLSurfaceView(this);
```

We then tell the view that we don't need a special EGL config chooser and the default will work by doing the following:

```
        mTestHarness.setEGLConfigChooser(false);
```

Then we set our renderer as follows:

```
        mTestHarness.setRenderer(new SimpleTriangleRenderer(this));
```

Next, we use one of these two methods to allow for animation or not:

```
mTestHarness.setRenderMode(GLSurfaceView.RENDERMODE_WHEN_DIRTY);
//mTestHarness.setRenderMode(GLSurfaceView.RENDERMODE_CONTINUOUSLY);
```

If we choose the first line, the drawing is going to be called only once or, more accurately, whenever it needs to be drawn. If we choose the second option, our drawing code will be called repeatedly so that we can animate our drawings.

That's all there is to interfacing with OpenGL on Android.

Now we have all the pieces necessary to test this drawing. We have the activity in Listing 20–11, we have the abstract renderer in Listing 20–9, and the SimpleTriangleRenderer (Listing 20–10) itself. All we have to do is invoke the Activity class through any of our menu items using the following:

```
private void invokeSimpleTriangle()
{
      Intent intent = new Intent(this,OpenGLTestHarnessActivity.class);
      startActivity(intent);
}
```

Of course, we will have to register the activity in the Android manifest file, like so:

```
   <activity android:name=".OpenGLTestHarnessActivity"
                 android:label="OpenGL Test Harness"/>
```

Although it's perfectly reasonable to design a standalone activity like the OpenGLTestHarnessActivity in Listing 20–11, we would like to propose an alternative that fits this chapter much better.

This need comes from the fact that we have a number of demos in this chapter. If we were to design a separate activity for each demo, we would end up with lot of code that looks very similar to what we have in Listing 20–11 and does not elucidate over and above. In addition, each of those activities needs to be registered in the manifest file.

With this in mind, let's create a unified activity that allows us to test all OpenGL ES 1.0 demos. The code is in Listing 20–12. It may look extensive compared to the activity listed in 20–11; however, if you look at the menu response for R.id.mid_opengl_simpletriangle, you'll see that we are doing essentially the same thing. As more menu options are implemented, we'll have more if statements, one each for the type of demo.

The other menu options will be explored as we go through the chapter. After Listing 20–12, we'll present the menu .xml file followed by an explanation of this multipurpose activity in a bit more detail.

Listing 20–12. *MultiviewTestHarness Activity*

```
//filename: MultiViewTestHarnessActivity.java
public class MultiViewTestHarnessActivity extends Activity {
   private GLSurfaceView mTestHarness;
    @Override
    protected void onCreate(Bundle savedInstanceState) {
        super.onCreate(savedInstanceState);

        mTestHarness = new GLSurfaceView(this);
        mTestHarness.setEGLConfigChooser(false);

        Intent intent = getIntent();
        int mid = intent.getIntExtra("com.ai.menuid", R.id.mid_OpenGL_Current);
        if (mid == R.id.mid_OpenGL_SimpleTriangle)
        {
            mTestHarness.setRenderer(new SimpleTriangleRenderer(this));
            mTestHarness.setRenderMode(GLSurfaceView.RENDERMODE_WHEN_DIRTY);
            setContentView(mTestHarness);
            return;
        }
        if (mid == R.id.mid_OpenGL_Current)
        {
                //Call someother OpenGL Renderer
                //and
                //return;
        }
        //otherwise do this
        mTestHarness.setRenderer(new SimpleTriangleRenderer(this));
        mTestHarness.setRenderMode(GLSurfaceView.RENDERMODE_CONTINUOUSLY);
        setContentView(mTestHarness);
        return;
    }
    @Override
    protected void onResume()    {
        super.onResume();
        mTestHarness.onResume();
    }
    @Override
    protected void onPause() {
        super.onPause();
        mTestHarness.onPause();
    }
}
```

The menu file in Listing 20–13 supports the code in Listing 20–12. This file is called res/menu/main_menu.xml. We went ahead and created all the possible menu items for all the demos of this chapter.

Listing 20–13. *Main Menu File*

```
<menu xmlns:android="http://schemas.android.com/apk/res/android">
    <!-- This group uses the default category. -->
    <group android:id="@+id/menuGroup_Main">
```

```
        <item android:id="@+id/mid_OpenGL_SimpleTriangle"
            android:title="Simple Triangle" />

        <item android:id="@+id/mid_OpenGL_SimpleTriangle2"
            android:title="Two Triangles" />

        <item android:id="@+id/mid_OpenGL_AnimatedTriangle"
            android:title="Animated Triangle" />

        <item android:id="@+id/mid_rectangle"
            android:title="Rectangle" />

        <item android:id="@+id/mid_square_polygon"
            android:title="Square polygon" />

        <item android:id="@+id/mid_polygon"
            android:title="Polygon" />

        <item android:id="@+id/mid_textured_square"
            android:title="Textured Square" />

        <item android:id="@+id/mid_textured_polygon"
            android:title="Textured Polygon" />

        <item android:id="@+id/mid_multiple_figures"
            android:title="Multiple Figures" />

        <item android:id="@+id/mid_OpenGL_Current"
            android:title="Current" />

        <item android:id="@+id/mid_es20_triangle"
            android:title="ES20 Triangle" />
    </group>
</menu>
```

By looking at the menu .xml file, we can anticipate the type of OpenGL renderers that will be demonstrated. If we return to the multiview activity in Listing 20–12, we'll notice that the activity is switching the renderer based on the menu IDs defined in this menu .xml file.

How does the multiview activity get the menu ID? This is done by the following code snippet (taken from Listing 20–12):

```
Intent intent = getIntent();
int mid = intent.getIntExtra("com.ai.menuid",
                    R.id.mid_OpenGL_Current);
```

This code snippet is asking the intent that is responsible for invoking this activity if there is an extra called "com.ai.menuid." If it's not present, then the code should use a menu id called "mid_opengl_current" as the default menu ID.

Who puts this extra in the intent? Where is the invoking driver activity? This invoking driver activity is presented in Listing 20–14.

Listing 20–14. *TestOpenGLMainDriver Activity*

```
public class TestOpenGLMainDriverActivity extends Activity {
    /** Called when the activity is first created. */
    @Override
    public void onCreate(Bundle savedInstanceState) {
        super.onCreate(savedInstanceState);
        setContentView(R.layout.main);
    }
    @Override
    public boolean onCreateOptionsMenu(Menu menu){
        super.onCreateOptionsMenu(menu);
        MenuInflater inflater = getMenuInflater(); //from activity
        inflater.inflate(R.menu.main_menu, menu);
        return true;
    }
    @Override
    public boolean onOptionsItemSelected(MenuItem item)
    {
        this.invokeMultiView(item.getItemId());
        return true;
    }
    private void invokeMultiView(int mid)
    {
        Intent intent =
       new Intent(this,MultiViewTestHarnessActivity.class);
        intent.putExtra("com.ai.menuid", mid);
        startActivity(intent);
    }
}
```

We need a layout file to complete and compile this activity. This layout file is in Listing 20–15.

Listing 20–15. *TestOpenGLMainDriver Activity Layout File (layout/main.xml)*

```
<?xml version="1.0" encoding="utf-8"?>
<LinearLayout xmlns:android="http://schemas.android.com/apk/res/android"
    android:orientation="vertical"
    android:layout_width="fill_parent"
    android:layout_height="fill_parent"
    >
<TextView
    android:layout_width="fill_parent"
    android:layout_height="wrap_content"
    android:text="A Simple Main Activity. Click Menu to Proceed"
    />
</LinearLayout>
```

Of course, nothing moves in Android without a manifest file. The manifest file is given in Listing 20–16.

Listing 20–16. *AndroidManifest File*

```
<manifest xmlns:android="http://schemas.android.com/apk/res/android"
      package="com.androidbook.OpenGL"
      android:versionCode="1"
      android:versionName="1.0.0">
    <application android:icon="@drawable/icon"
```

```
            android:label="OpenGL Test Harness"
            android:debuggable="true">
        <activity android:name=".TestOpenGLMainDriverActivity"
                android:label="OpenGL Test Harness">
            <intent-filter>
                <action android:name="android.intent.action.MAIN" />
                <category android:name="android.intent.category.LAUNCHER" />
            </intent-filter>
        </activity>

        <activity android:name="MultiViewTestHarnessActivity"
                android:label="OpenGL MultiView Test Harness"/>
    </application>
    <uses-sdk android:minSdkVersion="3" />
</manifest>
```

To summarize, we need the following files to compile and run our program:

TestOpenGLMainDriverActivity.java (Main driver activty; Listing 20–14)

AbstractRenderer.java (Listing 20–9)

SimpleTriangleRenderer.java (Listing 20–10)

MultiViewTestHarnessActivity.java (Listing 20–12)

res/menu/main_menu.xml (Menu file; Listing 20–13)

layout/main.xml (Layout file; Listing 20–15)

Once we compile and run the program, we'll see the driver activity show up. We can click on the menu to see the possible menus, as shown in Figure 20–2.

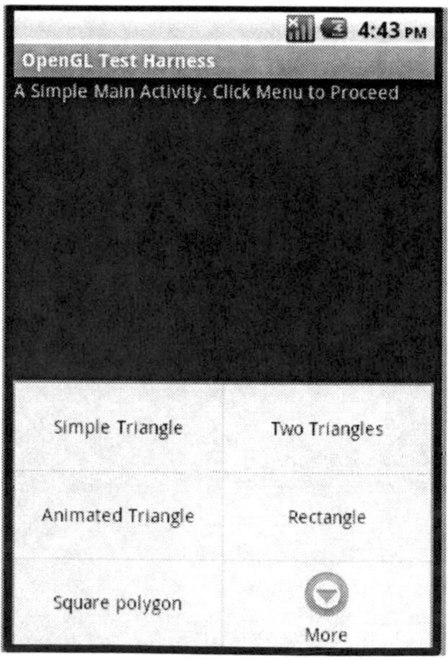

Figure 20–2. *OpenGL test harness driver*

Now if you click the "Simple Triangle" menu item, you will see the triangle like the one in Figure 20–3.

Figure 20–3. *A simple OpenGL triangle*

Changing Camera Settings

To understand the OpenGL coordinates better, let's experiment with the camera-related methods and see how they affect the triangle that we drew in Figure 20–3. Remember that these are the points of our triangle: `(-0.5,-0.5,0    0.5,-0.5,0      0,0.5,0)`. With these points, the following three camera-related methods as used in `AbstractRenderer` (Listing 20–9) yielded the triangle as it appears in Figure 20–3:

```
//Look at the screen (origin) from 5 units away from the front of the screen
GLU.gluLookAt(gl, 0,0,5,    0,0,0,   0,1,0);

//Set the height to 2 units and depth to 4 units
gl.glFrustumf(-ratio, ratio, -1, 1, 3, 7);

//normal window stuff
gl.glViewport(0, 0, w, h);
```

Now suppose you change the camera's up vector toward the negative y direction, like this:

```
GLU.gluLookAt(gl, 0,0,5,    0,0,0,   0,-1,0);
```

If you do this, you'll see an upside-down triangle (Figure 20–4). If you want to make this change, you can find the method to change in the `AbstractRenderer.java` file (Listing 20–9).

Figure 20–4. *A triangle with the camera upside down*

Now let's see what happens if we change the frustum, (also called the viewing volume or box). The following code increases the viewing box's height and width by a factor of 4 (see Figure 20–1 to understand these dimensions). If you recall, the first four arguments of `glFrustum` points to the front rectangle of the viewing box. By multiplying each value by 4, we have scaled the viewing box four times, like so:

```
gl.glFrustumf(-ratio * 4, ratio * 4, -1 * 4, 1 *4, 3, 7);
```

With this code, the triangle we see shrinks because the triangle stays at the same units while our viewing box has grown (Figure 20–5). This method call appears in the `AbstractRenderer.java` class (see Listing 20–9).

Figure 20–5. *A triangle with a viewing box that is four times bigger*

Using Indices to Add Another Triangle

We'll conclude these simple triangle examples by inheriting from the AbstractRenderer class and creating another triangle simply by adding an additional point and using indices. Conceptually, we'll define the four points as (-1,-1,   1,-1,   0,1,   1,1). And we'll ask OpenGL to draw these as (0,1,2   0,2,3). Listing 20–17 shows the code that does this (notice that we changed the dimensions of the triangle).

Listing 20–17. *The SimpleTriangleRenderer2 Class*

```
//filename: SimpleTriangleRenderer2.java
public class SimpleTriangleRenderer2 extends AbstractRenderer
{
    private final static int VERTS = 4;
    private FloatBuffer mFVertexBuffer;
    private ShortBuffer mIndexBuffer;

    public SimpleTriangleRenderer2(Context context)
    {
        ByteBuffer vbb = ByteBuffer.allocateDirect(VERTS * 3 * 4);
        vbb.order(ByteOrder.nativeOrder());
        mFVertexBuffer = vbb.asFloatBuffer();

        ByteBuffer ibb = ByteBuffer.allocateDirect(6 * 2);
        ibb.order(ByteOrder.nativeOrder());
        mIndexBuffer = ibb.asShortBuffer();
```

```
        float[] coords = {
                -1.0f, -1.0f, 0, // (x1,y1,z1)
                 1.0f, -1.0f, 0,
                 0.0f,  1.0f, 0,
                 1.0f,  1.0f, 0
        };
        for (int i = 0; i < VERTS; i++) {
            for(int j = 0; j < 3; j++) {
                mFVertexBuffer.put(coords[i*3+j]);
            }
        }
    short[] myIndecesArray = {0,1,2,    0,2,3};
        for (int i=0;i<6;i++)
        {
           mIndexBuffer.put(myIndecesArray[i]);
        }
        mFVertexBuffer.position(0);
        mIndexBuffer.position(0);
    }

    protected void draw(GL10 gl)
    {
       gl.glColor4f(1.0f, 0, 0, 0.5f);
       gl.glVertexPointer(3, GL10.GL_FLOAT, 0, mFVertexBuffer);
   gl.glDrawElements(GL10.GL_TRIANGLES, 6, GL10.GL_UNSIGNED_SHORT,
                                                        mIndexBuffer);
    }
}
```

Once this SimpleTriangleRenderer2 class is in place, we can add the if condition code in Listing 20–18 to the MultiViewTestHarness in Listing 20–12.

Listing 20–18. *Using SimpleTriangleRenderer2*

```
        if (mid == R.id.mid_OpenGL_SimpleTriangle2)
        {
            mTestHarness.setRenderer(new SimpleTriangleRenderer2(this));
            mTestHarness.setRenderMode(GLSurfaceView.RENDERMODE_WHEN_DIRTY);
            setContentView(mTestHarness);
            return;
        }
```

After we add this code, we can run the program again and choose the menu option "Two Triangles" to see the two triangles drawn out (see Figure 20–6). Notice how the design of the MultiviewTestHarness saved us from creating a new activity and registering that activity in the manifest file. We will continue this pattern of adding additional if clauses for the subsequent renderers.

Figure 20–6. *Two triangles with four points*

Animating the Simple OpenGL Triangle

We can easily accommodate OpenGL animation by changing the rendering mode on the GLSurfaceView object. Listing 20–19 shows the sample code.

Listing 20–19. *Specifying Continuous-Rendering Mode*

```
//get a GLSurfaceView
GLSurfaceView openGLView;

//Set the mode to continuous draw mode
openGLView.setRenderingMode(GLSurfaceView.RENDERMODE_CONTINUOUSLY);
```

Note that we're showing how to change the rendering mode here because we had specified RENDERMODE_WHEN_DIRTY in the previous section (see Listing 20-18). As mentioned, RENDERMODE_CONTINUOUSLY is the default setting, so animation is enabled by default.

Once the rendering mode is continuous, it is up to the renderer's onDraw method to do what's necessary to affect animation. To demonstrate this, let's use the triangle drawn in the previous example (see Listing 20–10 and Figure 20–3) and rotate it in a circular fashion.

AnimatedSimpleTriangleRenderer

The `AnimatedSimpleTriangleRenderer` class is very similar to the `SimpleTriangleRenderer` (see Listing 20–10), except for what happens in the `onDraw` method. In this method, we set a new rotation angle every four seconds. As the image gets drawn repeatedly, we'll see the triangle spinning slowly. Listing 20–20 contains the complete implementation of the `AnimatedSimpleTriangleRenderer` class.

Listing 20–20. ***AnimatedSimpleTriangleRenderer Source Code***

```
//filename: AnimatedSimpleTriangleRenderer.java
public class AnimatedSimpleTriangleRenderer extends AbstractRenderer
{
   private int scale = 1;
   //Number of points or vertices we want to use
    private final static int VERTS = 3;

    //A raw native buffer to hold the point coordinates
    private FloatBuffer mFVertexBuffer;

    //A raw native buffer to hold indices
    //allowing a reuse of points.
    private ShortBuffer mIndexBuffer;

    public AnimatedSimpleTriangleRenderer(Context context)
    {
        ByteBuffer vbb = ByteBuffer.allocateDirect(VERTS * 3 * 4);
        vbb.order(ByteOrder.nativeOrder());
        mFVertexBuffer = vbb.asFloatBuffer();

        ByteBuffer ibb = ByteBuffer.allocateDirect(VERTS * 2);
        ibb.order(ByteOrder.nativeOrder());
        mIndexBuffer = ibb.asShortBuffer();

        float[] coords = {
                -0.5f, -0.5f, 0, // (x1,y1,z1)
                 0.5f, -0.5f, 0,
                 0.0f,  0.5f, 0
        };
        for (int i = 0; i < VERTS; i++) {
            for(int j = 0; j < 3; j++) {
                mFVertexBuffer.put(coords[i*3+j]);
            }
        }
        short[] myIndecesArray = {0,1,2};
        for (int i=0;i<3;i++)
        {
           mIndexBuffer.put(myIndecesArray[i]);
        }
        mFVertexBuffer.position(0);
        mIndexBuffer.position(0);
    }

   //overridden method
    protected void draw(GL10 gl)
    {
```

```
        long time = SystemClock.uptimeMillis() % 4000L;
        float angle = 0.090f * ((int) time);

        gl.glRotatef(angle, 0, 0, 1.0f);

        gl.glColor4f(1.0f, 0, 0, 0.5f);
        gl.glVertexPointer(3, GL10.GL_FLOAT, 0, mFVertexBuffer);
         gl.glDrawElements(GL10.GL_TRIANGLES, VERTS,
                GL10.GL_UNSIGNED_SHORT, mIndexBuffer);
    }
}
```

Once this AnimatedSimpleTriangleRenderer class is in place, we can add the if condition code in Listing 20–21 to the MultiViewTestHarness in Listing 20–12.

Listing 20–21. *Using AnimatedSimpleTriangleRenderer*

```
if (mid == R.id.mid_OpenGL_AnimatedTriangle)
{
        mTestHarness.setRenderer(new AnimatedSimpleTriangleRenderer(this));
        setContentView(mTestHarness);
        return;
}
```

After we add this code, we can run the program again and choose the menu option "Animated Triangle" to see the triangle in Figure 20–3 spinning.

Braving OpenGL: Shapes and Textures

In the examples shown thus far, we have specified the vertices of a triangle explicitly. This approach becomes inconvenient as soon as we start drawing squares, pentagons, hexagons, and the like. For these, we'll need higher-level object abstractions such as shapes and even scene graphs, where the shapes decide what their coordinates are. Using this approach, we will show you how to draw any polygon with any number of sides anywhere in your geometry.

In this section, we will also cover OpenGL textures. Textures allow you to attach bitmaps and other pictures to surfaces in your drawing. We will take the polygons that we know how to draw now and attach some pictures to them. We will follow this up with another critical need in OpenGL: drawing multiple figures or shapes using the OpenGL drawing pipeline.

These fundamentals should take you a bit closer to starting to create workable 3D figures and scenes.

Drawing a Rectangle

Before going on to the idea of shapes, let's strengthen our understanding of drawing with explicit vertices by drawing a rectangle using two triangles. This will also lay the groundwork for extending a triangle to any polygon.

We already have enough background to understand the basic triangle, so here's the code for drawing a rectangle (Listing 20–22), followed by some brief commentary.

Listing 20–22. ***Simple Rectangle Renderer***

```
public class SimpleRectangleRenderer extends AbstractRenderer
{
   //Number of points or vertices we want to use
    private final static int VERTS = 4;

    //A raw native buffer to hold the point coordinates
    private FloatBuffer mFVertexBuffer;

    //A raw native buffer to hold indices
    //allowing a reuse of points.
    private ShortBuffer mIndexBuffer;

    public SimpleRectangleRenderer(Context context)
    {
        ByteBuffer vbb = ByteBuffer.allocateDirect(VERTS * 3 * 4);
        vbb.order(ByteOrder.nativeOrder());
        mFVertexBuffer = vbb.asFloatBuffer();

        ByteBuffer ibb = ByteBuffer.allocateDirect(6 * 2);
        ibb.order(ByteOrder.nativeOrder());
        mIndexBuffer = ibb.asShortBuffer();

        float[] coords = {
                -0.5f, -0.5f, 0, // (x1,y1,z1)
                 0.5f, -0.5f, 0,
                 0.5f,  0.5f, 0,
                -0.5f,  0.5f, 0,
        };

        for (int i = 0; i < VERTS; i++) {
            for(int j = 0; j < 3; j++) {
                mFVertexBuffer.put(coords[i*3+j]);
            }
        }
        short[] myIndecesArray = {0,1,2,0,2,3};
        for (int i=0;i<6;i++)
        {
           mIndexBuffer.put(myIndecesArray[i]);
        }
        mFVertexBuffer.position(0);
        mIndexBuffer.position(0);
    }

   //overriden method
    protected void draw(GL10 gl)
    {
       gl.glColor4f(1.0f, 0, 0, 0.5f);
       gl.glVertexPointer(3, GL10.GL_FLOAT, 0, mFVertexBuffer);
       gl.glDrawElements(GL10.GL_TRIANGLES, 6,
                GL10.GL_UNSIGNED_SHORT, mIndexBuffer);
    }
}
```

Notice that the approach for drawing a rectangle is quite similar to that for a triangle. We have specified four vertices instead of three. Then we have used indices as here:

```
short[] myIndecesArray = {0,1,2,0,2,3};
```

We have reused the numbered vertices (0 through 3) twice so that each three vertices make up a triangle. So (0,1,2) makes up the first triangle and (0,2,3) makes up the second triangle. Drawing these two triangles using the `GL_TRIANGLES` primitives will draw the necessary rectangle.

Once this rectangle renderer class is in place, we can add the `if` condition code in Listing 20–23 to the `MultiViewTestHarness` in Listing 20–12.

Listing 20–23. *Using SimpleRectangleRenderer*

```
if (mid == R.id.mid_rectangle)
{
      mTestHarness.setRenderer(new SimpleRectangleRenderer(this));
      mTestHarness.setRenderMode(GLSurfaceView.RENDERMODE_WHEN_DIRTY);
      setContentView(mTestHarness);
      return;
}
```

After we add this code, we can run the program again and choose the menu option "Rectangle" to see the rectangle in Figure 20–7.

Figure 20–7. *OpenGL rectangle drawn with two triangles*

Working with Shapes

This method of explicitly specifying vertices to draw can be tedious. For example, if you want to draw a polygon of 20 sides, then you need to specify 20 vertices, with each vertex requiring up to three values. That's a total of 60 values. It's just not workable.

A Regular Polygon as a Shape

A better approach to draw figures like triangles or squares is to define an abstract polygon by defining some aspects of it, such as the origin and radius, and then have that polygon give us the vertex array and the index array (so that we can draw individual triangles) in return. We named this class RegularPolygon. Once we have this kind of object, we can use it as shown in Listing 20–24 to render various regular polygons.

Listing 20–24. *Using a RegularPolygon Object*

```
//A polygon with 4 sides and a radious of 0.5
//and located at (x,y,z) of (0,0,0)
 RegularPolygon square = new RegularPolygon(0,0,0,0.5f,4);

//Let the polygon return the vertices
 mFVertexBuffer = square.getVertexBuffer();

//Let the polygon return the triangles
 mIndexBuffer = square.getIndexBuffer();

//you will need this for glDrawElements
numOfIndices = square.getNumberOfIndices();

//set the buffers to the start
  this.mFVertexBuffer.position(0);
  this.mIndexBuffer.position(0);

//set the vertex pointer
  gl.glVertexPointer(3, GL10.GL_FLOAT, 0, mFVertexBuffer);

//draw it with the given number of Indices
 gl.glDrawElements(GL10.GL_TRIANGLES, numOfIndices,
         GL10.GL_UNSIGNED_SHORT, mIndexBuffer);
```

Notice how we have obtained the necessary vertices and indices from the shape square. Although we haven't abstracted this idea of getting vertices and indices to a basic shape, it is possible that RegularPolygon could be deriving from such a basic shape that defines an interface for this basic contract. Listing 20–25 shows an example.

Listing 20–25. *Shape Interface*

```
public interface Shape
{
   FloatBuffer            getVertexBuffer();
   ShortBuffer            getIndexBuffer();
   int                          getNumberofIndices();
}
```

We will leave this idea of defining a base interface for a shape as food for thought for your own work. For now, we have built these methods out directly into the RegularPolygon.

Implementing the RegularPolygon Shape

As indicated, this RegularPolygon has the responsibility of returning what is needed to draw using OpenGL: vertices. First, we need a mechanism to define what this shape is and where it is in the geometry.

For a regular polygon, there are a number of ways of doing this. In our approach, we have defined the regular polygon using the number of sides and the distance from the center of the regular polygon to one of its vertices. We called this distance the radius, because the vertices of a regular polygon fall on the perimeter of a circle whose center is also the center of the regular polygon. So the radius of such a circle and the number of sides will tell us the polygon we want. By specifying the coordinates of the center, we also know where to draw the polygon in our geometry.

The responsibility of this RegularPolygon class is to give us the coordinates of all the vertices of the polygon, given its center and radius. Again, there may be a number of ways of doing this. Whatever mathematical method you choose to employ (based on middle school or high school math), as long as you return the vertices, you're good to go.

For our approach, we started with the assumption that the radius is 1 unit. We figured out the angles for each line connecting the center to each vertex of the polygon. We kept these angles in an array. For each angle, we calculated the x-axis projection and called this the "x multiplier array." (We used "multiplier array" because we started out with a unit of radius.) When we know the real radius, we will multiply these values with the real radius to get the real x coordinate. These real x coordinates are then stored in an array called "x array." We do the same for the y-axis projections.

Now that you have an idea of what needs to happen in the implementation of the RegularPolygon, we'll give you the source code that addresses these responsibilities. Listing 20–26 shows all the code for the RegularPolygon in one place. (Please note that the source code is several pages long.) To make the process of going through it less cumbersome, we have highlighted the function names and provided inline comments at the beginning of each function.

We define the key functions in a list that follows Listing 20–26. The important thing here is to figure out the vertices and return. If this is too cryptic, it shouldn't be hard to write your own code to get the vertices. You'll also note that this code also has functions that deal with texturing. We'll explain these texture functions in the "Working with Textures" section.

Listing 20–26. *Implementing a RegularPolygon Shape*

```
public class RegularPolygon
{
   //Space to hold (x,y,z) of the center: cx,cy,cz
   //and the radius "r"
   private float       cx, cy, cz, r;
```

```
private int         sides;

//coordinate array: (x,y) vertex points
private float[] xarray = null;
private float[] yarray = null;

//texture arrray: (x,y) also called (s,t) points
//where the figure is going to be mapped to a texture bitmap
private float[] sarray = null;
private float[] tarray = null;

//**********************************************
// Constructor
//**********************************************
public RegularPolygon(float incx, float incy, float incz, // (x,y,z) center
                   float inr, // radius
                   int insides) // number of sides
{
   cx = incx;
   cy = incy;
   cz = incz;
   r = inr;
   sides = insides;

   //allocate memory for the arrays
   xarray = new float[sides];
   yarray = new float[sides];

   //allocate memory for texture point arrays
   sarray = new float[sides];
   tarray = new float[sides];

   //calculate vertex points
   calcArrays();

  //calculate texture points
   calcTextureArrays();
}

//**********************************************
//Get and convert the vertex coordinates
//based on origin and radius.
//Real logic of angles happen inside getMultiplierArray() functions
//**********************************************
private void calcArrays()
{
  //Get the vertex points assuming a circle
  //with a radius of "1" and located at "origin" zero
   float[] xmarray = this.getXMultiplierArray();
   float[] ymarray = this.getYMultiplierArray();

   //calc xarray: get the vertex
   //by adding the "x" portion of the origin
   //multiply the coordinate with radius (scale)
   for(int i=0;i<sides;i++)
   {
      float curm = xmarray[i];
```

```
        float xcoord = cx + r * curm;
        xarray[i] = xcoord;
    }
    this.printArray(xarray, "xarray");

    //calc yarray: do the same for y coordinates
    for(int i=0;i<sides;i++)
    {
        float curm = ymarray[i];
        float ycoord = cy + r * curm;
        yarray[i] = ycoord;
    }
    this.printArray(yarray, "yarray");

}
//**********************************************
//Calculate texture arrays
//See Texture subsection for more discussion on this
//very similar approach.
//Here the polygon has to map into a space
//that is a square
//**********************************************
private void calcTextureArrays()
{
    float[] xmarray = this.getXMultiplierArray();
    float[] ymarray = this.getYMultiplierArray();

    //calc xarray
    for(int i=0;i<sides;i++)
    {
        float curm = xmarray[i];
        float xcoord = 0.5f + 0.5f * curm;
        sarray[i] = xcoord;
    }
    this.printArray(sarray, "sarray");

    //calc yarray
    for(int i=0;i<sides;i++)
    {
        float curm = ymarray[i];
        float ycoord = 0.5f +  0.5f * curm;
        tarray[i] = ycoord;
    }
    this.printArray(tarray, "tarray");
}

//**********************************************
//Convert the java array of vertices
//into an nio float buffer
//**********************************************
public FloatBuffer getVertexBuffer()
{
     int vertices = sides + 1;
     int coordinates = 3;
     int floatsize = 4;
     int spacePerVertex = coordinates * floatsize;
```

```
        ByteBuffer vbb = ByteBuffer.allocateDirect(spacePerVertex * vertices);
        vbb.order(ByteOrder.nativeOrder());
        FloatBuffer mFVertexBuffer = vbb.asFloatBuffer();

        //Put the first coordinate (x,y,z:0,0,0)
        mFVertexBuffer.put(cx); //x
        mFVertexBuffer.put(cy); //y
        mFVertexBuffer.put(0.0f); //z

        int totalPuts = 3;
        for (int i=0;i<sides;i++)
        {
            mFVertexBuffer.put(xarray[i]); //x
            mFVertexBuffer.put(yarray[i]); //y
            mFVertexBuffer.put(0.0f); //z
            totalPuts += 3;
        }
        Log.d("total puts:",Integer.toString(totalPuts));
      return mFVertexBuffer;
    }

    //**********************************************
    //Convert texture buffer to an nio buffer
    //**********************************************
    public FloatBuffer getTextureBuffer()
    {
        int vertices = sides + 1;
        int coordinates = 2;
        int floatsize = 4;
        int spacePerVertex = coordinates * floatsize;

         ByteBuffer vbb = ByteBuffer.allocateDirect(spacePerVertex * vertices);
         vbb.order(ByteOrder.nativeOrder());
         FloatBuffer mFTextureBuffer = vbb.asFloatBuffer();

         //Put the first coordinate (x,y (s,t):0,0)
         mFTextureBuffer.put(0.5f); //x or s
         mFTextureBuffer.put(0.5f); //y or t

         int totalPuts = 2;
         for (int i=0;i<sides;i++)
         {
            mFTextureBuffer.put(sarray[i]); //x
            mFTextureBuffer.put(tarray[i]); //y
             totalPuts += 2;
         }
         Log.d("total texture puts:",Integer.toString(totalPuts));
      return mFTextureBuffer;
    }

    //**********************************************
    //Calculate indices forming multiple triangles.
    //Start with the center vertex which is at 0
    //Then count them in a clockwise direction such as
    //0,1,2,  0,2,3, 0,3,4 and so on.
    //**********************************************
    public ShortBuffer getIndexBuffer()
```

```
{
   short[] iarray = new short[sides * 3];
     ByteBuffer ibb = ByteBuffer.allocateDirect(sides * 3 * 2);
     ibb.order(ByteOrder.nativeOrder());
     ShortBuffer mIndexBuffer = ibb.asShortBuffer();
     for (int i=0;i<sides;i++)
     {
        short index1 = 0;
        short index2 = (short)(i+1);
        short index3 = (short)(i+2);
        if (index3 == sides+1)
        {
           index3 = 1;
        }
        mIndexBuffer.put(index1);
        mIndexBuffer.put(index2);
        mIndexBuffer.put(index3);

        iarray[i*3 + 0]=index1;
        iarray[i*3 + 1]=index2;
        iarray[i*3 + 2]=index3;
     }
     this.printShortArray(iarray, "index array");
     return mIndexBuffer;
}
//*********************************************
//This is where you take the angle array
//for each vertex and calculate their projection multiplier
//on the x axis
//*********************************************
private float[] getXMultiplierArray()
{
   float[] angleArray = getAngleArrays();
   float[] xmultiplierArray = new float[sides];
   for(int i=0;i<angleArray.length;i++)
   {
      float curAngle = angleArray[i];
      float sinvalue = (float)Math.cos(Math.toRadians(curAngle));
      float absSinValue = Math.abs(sinvalue);
      if (isXPositiveQuadrant(curAngle))
      {
         sinvalue = absSinValue;
      }
      else
      {
         sinvalue = -absSinValue;
      }
      xmultiplierArray[i] = this.getApproxValue(sinvalue);
   }
   this.printArray(xmultiplierArray, "xmultiplierArray");
   return xmultiplierArray;
}

//*********************************************
//This is where you take the angle array
//for each vertex and calculate their projection multiplier
//on the y axis
```

```
//**********************************************
private float[] getYMultiplierArray() {
   float[] angleArray = getAngleArrays();
   float[] ymultiplierArray = new float[sides];
   for(int i=0;i<angleArray.length;i++) {
      float curAngle = angleArray[i];
      float sinvalue = (float)Math.sin(Math.toRadians(curAngle));
      float absSinValue = Math.abs(sinvalue);
      if (isYPositiveQuadrant(curAngle)) {
         sinvalue = absSinValue;
      }
      else {
         sinvalue = -absSinValue;
      }
      ymultiplierArray[i] = this.getApproxValue(sinvalue);
   }
   this.printArray(ymultiplierArray, "ymultiplierArray");
   return ymultiplierArray;
}

//**********************************************
//This function may not be needed
//Test it yourself and discard it if you dont need
//**********************************************
private boolean isXPositiveQuadrant(float angle) {
   if ((0 <= angle) && (angle <= 90))  { return true;    }
   if ((angle < 0) && (angle >= -90))   { return true;    }
   return false;
}
//**********************************************
//This function may not be needed
//Test it yourself and discard it if you dont need
//**********************************************
private boolean isYPositiveQuadrant(float angle) {
   if ((0 <= angle) && (angle <= 90)) { return true; }
   if ((angle < 180) && (angle >= 90)) {return true;}
   return false;
}
//**********************************************
//This is where you calculate angles
//for each line going from center to each vertex
//**********************************************
private float[] getAngleArrays() {
   float[] angleArray = new float[sides];
   float commonAngle = 360.0f/sides;
   float halfAngle = commonAngle/2.0f;
   float firstAngle = 360.0f - (90+halfAngle);
   angleArray[0] = firstAngle;

   float curAngle = firstAngle;
   for(int i=1;i<sides;i++)
   {
      float newAngle = curAngle - commonAngle;
      angleArray[i] = newAngle;
      curAngle = newAngle;
   }
   printArray(angleArray, "angleArray");
```

```
      return angleArray;
   }

   //**********************************************
   //Some rounding if needed
   //**********************************************
   private float getApproxValue(float f) {
      return (Math.abs(f) < 0.001) ? 0 : f;
   }
   //**********************************************
   //Return how many Indices you will need
   //given the number of sides
   //This is the count of number of triangles needed
   //to make the polygon multiplied by 3
   //It just happens that the number of triangles is
   // same as the number of sides
   //**********************************************
   public int getNumberOfIndices() {
      return sides * 3;
   }
   public static void test() {
      RegularPolygon triangle = new RegularPolygon(0,0,0,1,3);
   }
   private void printArray(float array[], String tag) {
      StringBuilder sb = new StringBuilder(tag);
      for(int i=0;i<array.length;i++) {
         sb.append(";").append(array[i]);
      }
      Log.d("hh",sb.toString());
   }
   private void printShortArray(short array[], String tag) {
      StringBuilder sb = new StringBuilder(tag);
      for(int i=0;i<array.length;i++) {
         sb.append(";").append(array[i]);
      }
      Log.d(tag,sb.toString());
   }
}
```

Here are the key elements in the code:

Constructor: The constructor of a `RegularPolygon` takes as input the coordinates of the center, the radius, and the number of sides.

getAngleArrays: This method is a key method that is responsible for calculating the angles of each spine of the regular polygon with the assumption that one of the sides of the polygon is parallel to the x-axis.

getXMultiplierArray and *getYMultiplierArray*: These methods take the angles from `getAngleArrays` and project them to the x-axis and y-axis to get the corresponding coordinates, assuming the spine is a unit in length.

calcArrays: This method uses the getXMultiplierArray and the getYMultiplierArray to take each vertex and scales them to match the specified radius and specified origin. At the end of this method, the RegularPolygon will have the right coordinates, albeit in Java float arrays.

getVertexBuffer: This method then takes the Java float coordinate arrays and populates NIO-based buffers that are needed by the OpenGL draw methods.

getIndexBuffer: This method takes the vertices that are gathered and orders them such that each triangle will contribute to the final polygon.

The other methods that deal with textures follow a very similar pattern and will make more sense when we explain the textures in the next section. We have also included some print functions to print the arrays for debugging purposes.

Rendering a Square Using RegularPolygon

Now that we have looked at the basic building blocks, let's see how we could draw a square using a RegularPolygon of four sides. Listing 20–27 shows the code for the SquareRenderer.

Listing 20–27. *SquareRenderer*

```
public class SquareRenderer extends AbstractRenderer
{
    //A raw native buffer to hold the point coordinates
    private FloatBuffer mFVertexBuffer;

    //A raw native buffer to hold indices
    //allowing a reuse of points.
    private ShortBuffer mIndexBuffer;

    private int numOfIndices = 0;

    private int sides = 4;

    public SquareRenderer(Context context)
    {
        prepareBuffers(sides);
    }

    private void prepareBuffers(int sides)
    {
        RegularPolygon t = new RegularPolygon(0,0,0,0.5f,sides);
        //RegularPolygon t = new RegularPolygon(1,1,0,1,sides);
        this.mFVertexBuffer = t.getVertexBuffer();
        this.mIndexBuffer = t.getIndexBuffer();
        this.numOfIndices = t.getNumberOfIndices();
        this.mFVertexBuffer.position(0);
        this.mIndexBuffer.position(0);
    }
```

```
    //overriden method
     protected void draw(GL10 gl)
     {
         prepareBuffers(sides);
        gl.glVertexPointer(3, GL10.GL_FLOAT, 0, mFVertexBuffer);
        gl.glDrawElements(GL10.GL_TRIANGLES, this.numOfIndices,
                GL10.GL_UNSIGNED_SHORT, mIndexBuffer);
     }
}
```

This code should be fairly obvious. We have derived it from the `AbstractRenderer` (see Listing 20–9) and overrode the `draw` method and used the `RegularPolygon` to draw out a square.

Once this square renderer class is in place, we can add the `if` condition code in Listing 20–28 to the `MultiViewTestHarness` in Listing 20–12.

Listing 20–28. *Using SimpleRectangleRenderer*

```
if (mid == R.id.mid_square_polygon)
{
     mTestHarness.setRenderer(new SquareRenderer(this));
     mTestHarness.setRenderMode(GLSurfaceView.RENDERMODE_WHEN_DIRTY);
     setContentView(mTestHarness);
     return;
}
```

After we add this code, we can run the program again and choose the menu option "Square Polygon" to see the square in Figure 20–8.

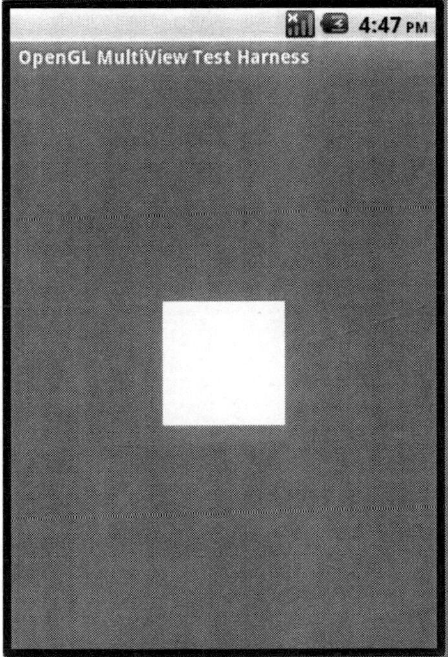

Figure 20–8. *A square drawn as a regular polygon*

Animating RegularPolygons

Now that we have explored the basic idea of drawing a shape generically through RegularPoygon, let's get a bit sophisticated. Let's see if we can use an animation where we start with a triangle and end up with a circle by using a polygon whose sides increase every four seconds or so. The code for this is in Listing 20–29.

Listing 20–29. *PolygonRenderer*

```
public class PolygonRenderer extends AbstractRenderer
{
   //Number of points or vertices we want to use
    private final static int VERTS = 4;

    //A raw native buffer to hold the point coordinates
    private FloatBuffer mFVertexBuffer;

    //A raw native buffer to hold indices
    //allowing a reuse of points.
    private ShortBuffer mIndexBuffer;

    private int numOfIndices = 0;

    private long prevtime = SystemClock.uptimeMillis();

    private int sides = 3;

    public PolygonRenderer(Context context)
    {
prepareBuffers(sides);
    }

    private void prepareBuffers(int sides)
    {
         RegularPolygon t = new RegularPolygon(0,0,0,1,sides);
this.mFVertexBuffer = t.getVertexBuffer();
        this.mIndexBuffer = t.getIndexBuffer();
        this.numOfIndices = t.getNumberOfIndices();
        this.mFVertexBuffer.position(0);
        this.mIndexBuffer.position(0);
    }

   //overriden method
    protected void draw(GL10 gl)
    {
        long curtime = SystemClock.uptimeMillis();
        if ((curtime - prevtime) > 2000)
        {
           prevtime = curtime;
           sides += 1;
           if (sides > 20)
           {
              sides = 3;
           }
```

```
            this.prepareBuffers(sides);
        }
gl.glColor4f(1.0f, 0, 0, 0.5f);
        gl.glVertexPointer(3, GL10.GL_FLOAT, 0, mFVertexBuffer);
        gl.glDrawElements(GL10.GL_TRIANGLES, this.numOfIndices,
                GL10.GL_UNSIGNED_SHORT, mIndexBuffer);
    }
}
```

All we are doing in this code is changing the `sides` variable every four seconds. The animation comes from the way the `Renderer` is registered with the surface view.

Once we have this renderer available, we will need to add the code in Listing 20–30 to the MultiviewTestHarness code.

Listing 20–30. ***Menu Item for testing a polygon***

```
if (mid == R.id.mid_polygon)
{
      mTestHarness.setRenderer(new PolygonRenderer(this));
      setContentView(mTestHarness);
      return;
}
```

If we run the program again and choose the menu item "Polygon," we'll see a set of transforming polygons whose sides continue to increase. It is instructive to see the progress of the polygons over time. Figure 20–9 shows a hexagon toward the beginning of the cycle.

Figure 20–9. ***Hexagon at the beginning of the polygon drawing cycle***

Figure 20–10 shows it towards the end of the cycle.

Figure 20–10. *A circle drawn as a regular polygon*

You can extend this idea of abstract shapes to more complex shapes and even to a scene graph where it consists of a number of other objects that are defined through some type of XML and then renders them in OpenGL using those instantiated objects.

Let's now move on to textures to see how we can integrate the idea of sticking wallpapers to the surfaces we have drawn so far, such as squares and polygons.

Working with Textures

Textures are another core topic in OpenGL. OpenGL textures have a number of nuances. We will cover only the fundamentals in this chapter so that you can get started with OpenGL textures. Use the resources provided at the end of this chapter to dig further into textures.

Understanding Textures

An OpenGL Texture is a bitmap that you paste on a surface in OpenGL. (In this chapter, we will cover only surfaces.) For example, you can take the image of a postage stamp and stick it on a square so that the square looks like a postage stamp. Or you can take the bitmap of a brick and paste it on a rectangle and repeat the brick image so that the rectangle looks like a wall of bricks.

The process of attaching a texture bitmap to an OpenGL surface is similar to the process of pasting a piece of wallpaper (in the shape of a square) on the side of a regularly or irregularly shaped object. The shape of the surface doesn't matter as long as you choose a paper that is large enough to cover it.

However, to align the paper so that the image is correctly lined up, you have to take each vertex of the shape and exactly mark it on the wallpaper so that the wallpaper and the object's shape are in lockstep. If the shape is odd and has a number of vertices, each vertex needs to be marked on your paper as well.

Another way of looking at this is to envision that you lay the object on the ground face up and put the wallpaper on top of it and rotate the paper until the image is aligned in the right direction. Now poke holes in the paper at each vertex of the shape. Remove the paper and see where the holes are and note their coordinates on the paper, assuming the paper is calibrated. These coordinates are called *texture coordinates*.

Normalized Texture Coordinates

One unresolved or unstated detail is the size of the object and the paper. OpenGL uses a normalized approach to resolve this. OpenGL assumes that the paper is always a 1 × 1 square with its origin at (0,0) and the top right corner is at (1,1). Then OpenGL wants you to shrink your object surface so that it fits within these 1 × 1 boundaries. So the burden is on the programmer to figure out the vertices of the object surface in a 1 × 1 square.

In the design of our `RegularPolygon` from Listing 20–26, we drew a polygon using a similar approach where we assumed it was a circle of 1 unit radius. Then we figured out where each vertex is. If we assume that that circle is inside a 1 × 1 square, then that square could be our paper. So figuring out texture coordinates is very similar to figuring out the polygon vertex coordinates. This is why Listing 20–26 has the following function to calculate the texture coordinates:

```
calcTextureArray()
getTextureBuffer()
```

If you notice, every other function is common between `calcTextureArrays` and `calcArrays` methods. This commonality between vertex coordinates and texture coordinates is important to note when you are learning OpenGL.

Abstracting Common Texture Handling

Once you understand this mapping between texture coordinates and vertex coordinates and can figure out the coordinates for the texture map, the rest is simple enough. (Nothing in OpenGL can be boldly stated as "quite simple!") Subsequent work involves loading the texture bitmap into memory and giving it a texture ID so that you can reuse this texture again. Then, to allow for multiple textures loaded at the same time, you have a mechanism to set the current texture by specifying an ID. During a drawing pipeline, you will specify the texture coordinates along with the drawing coordinates. Then you draw.

Because the process of loading textures is fairly common, we have abstracted out this process by inventing an abstract class called `SingleAbstractTextureRenderer` that inherits from `AbstractRenderer`.

Listing 20–31 shows the source code that abstracts out all the set-up code for a single texture.

Listing 20–31. *Abstracting Single Texturing Support*

```
public abstract class AbstractSingleTexturedRenderer
extends AbstractRenderer
{
   int mTextureID;
   int mImageResourceId;
   Context mContext;
   public AbstractSingleTexturedRenderer(Context ctx,
                                         int imageResourceId) {
      mImageResourceId = imageResourceId;
      mContext = ctx;
   }

    public void onSurfaceCreated(GL10 gl, EGLConfig eglConfig) {
        super.onSurfaceCreated(gl, eglConfig);
        gl.glEnable(GL10.GL_TEXTURE_2D);
        prepareTexture(gl);
    }
    private void prepareTexture(GL10 gl)
    {
        int[] textures = new int[1];
        gl.glGenTextures(1, textures, 0);

        mTextureID = textures[0];
        gl.glBindTexture(GL10.GL_TEXTURE_2D, mTextureID);

        gl.glTexParameterf(GL10.GL_TEXTURE_2D, GL10.GL_TEXTURE_MIN_FILTER,
                GL10.GL_NEAREST);
        gl.glTexParameterf(GL10.GL_TEXTURE_2D,
                GL10.GL_TEXTURE_MAG_FILTER,
                GL10.GL_LINEAR);

        gl.glTexParameterf(GL10.GL_TEXTURE_2D, GL10.GL_TEXTURE_WRAP_S,
                GL10.GL_CLAMP_TO_EDGE);
        gl.glTexParameterf(GL10.GL_TEXTURE_2D, GL10.GL_TEXTURE_WRAP_T,
                GL10.GL_CLAMP_TO_EDGE);

        gl.glTexEnvf(GL10.GL_TEXTURE_ENV, GL10.GL_TEXTURE_ENV_MODE,
                GL10.GL_REPLACE);

        InputStream is = mContext.getResources()
                .openRawResource(this.mImageResourceId);
        Bitmap bitmap;
        try {
            bitmap = BitmapFactory.decodeStream(is);
        } finally {
            try {
                is.close();
            } catch(IOException e) {
```

```
                // Ignore.
            }
        }

        GLUtils.texImage2D(GL10.GL_TEXTURE_2D, 0, bitmap, 0);
        bitmap.recycle();
    }

    public void onDrawFrame(GL10 gl)
    {
        gl.glDisable(GL10.GL_DITHER);
        gl.glTexEnvx(GL10.GL_TEXTURE_ENV, GL10.GL_TEXTURE_ENV_MODE,
                GL10.GL_MODULATE);

        gl.glClear(GL10.GL_COLOR_BUFFER_BIT | GL10.GL_DEPTH_BUFFER_BIT);
        gl.glMatrixMode(GL10.GL_MODELVIEW);
        gl.glLoadIdentity();
        GLU.gluLookAt(gl, 0, 0, -5, 0f, 0f, 0f, 0f, 1.0f, 0.0f);

        gl.glEnableClientState(GL10.GL_VERTEX_ARRAY);

        gl.glEnableClientState(GL10.GL_TEXTURE_COORD_ARRAY);

        gl.glActiveTexture(GL10.GL_TEXTURE0);
        gl.glBindTexture(GL10.GL_TEXTURE_2D, mTextureID);
        gl.glTexParameterx(GL10.GL_TEXTURE_2D, GL10.GL_TEXTURE_WRAP_S,
                GL10.GL_REPEAT);
        gl.glTexParameterx(GL10.GL_TEXTURE_2D, GL10.GL_TEXTURE_WRAP_T,
                GL10.GL_REPEAT);

        draw(gl);
    }
}
```

In this code, the single texture (a bitmap) is loaded and prepared in the `onSurfaceCreated` method. The code for `onDrawFrame`, just like the `AbstractRenderer`, sets up the dimensions of our drawing space so that our coordinates make sense. Depending on your situation, you may want to change this code to figure out your own optimal viewing volume.

Note how the constructor takes a texture bitmap which it prepares for later use. Depending on how many textures you have, you can craft your abstract classes accordingly.

As shown in Listing 20–31, the following APIs that revolve around textures are required:

> *glGenTextures*: This OpenGL method is responsible for generating unique IDs for textures so that those textures can be referenced later. Once we load the texture bitmap through `GLUtils.texImage2D`, we bind that texture to a specific ID. Until a texture is bound to an ID generated by `glGenTextures`, the ID is just an ID. The OpenGL literature refers to these integer IDs as *texture names*.
>
> *glBindTexture*: We use this OpenGL method to bind the currently loaded texture to a texture ID obtained from `glGenTextures`.

glTexParameter: There are many optional parameters we can set when we apply texture. This API allows us to define what these options are. Some examples include GL_REPEAT, GL_CLAMP etc. For example, GL_REPEAT allows us to repeat the bitmap many times if the size of the object is larger. A complete list of these parameters can be found at www.khronos.org/opengles/documentation/opengles1_0/html/glTexParameter.html.

glTexEnv: Some of the other texture-related options are specified through the glTexEnv method. Some example values include GL_DECAL, GL_MODULATE, GL_BLEND, GL_REPLACE, etc. For example, in the case of GL_DECAL, texture covers the underlying object. GL_MODULATE, as the name indicates, modulates the underlying colors instead of replacing them. Refer to the following URL for a complete list of the options for this API: www.khronos.org/opengles/documentation/opengles1_0/html/glTexEnv.html.

GLUtils.texImage2D: This is an Android API that allows us to load the bitmap for texturing purposes. Internally, this API calls the glTexImage2D of the OpenGL.

glActiveTexture: This sets a given texture ID as the active structure.

glTexCoordpointer: This OpenGL method is used to specify the texture coordinates. Each coordinate must match the coordinate specified in the glVertexPointer.

You can read up on most of these APIs from the OpenGL ES reference available at

www.khronos.org/opengles/documentation/opengles1_0/html/index.html

Drawing Using Textures

Once the bitmap is loaded and set up as a texture, we should be able to utilize the RegularPolygon and use the texture coordinates and vertex coordinates to draw a regular polygon along with the texture. Listing 20–32 shows the actual drawing class that draws a textured square.

Listing 20–32. ***TexturedSquareRenderer***

```
public class TexturedSquareRenderer extends AbstractSingleTexturedRenderer
{
   //Number of points or vertices we want to use
    private final static int VERTS = 4;

    //A raw native buffer to hold the point coordinates
    private FloatBuffer mFVertexBuffer;

    //A raw native buffer to hold the point coordinates
    private FloatBuffer mFTextureBuffer;

    //A raw native buffer to hold indices
```

```
    //allowing a reuse of points.
    private ShortBuffer mIndexBuffer;

    private int numOfIndices = 0;

    private int sides = 4;

    public TexturedSquareRenderer(Context context)
    {
       super(context,com.androidbook.OpenGL.R.drawable.robot);
       prepareBuffers(sides);
    }

    private void prepareBuffers(int sides)
    {
       RegularPolygon t = new RegularPolygon(0,0,0,0.5f,sides);
       this.mFVertexBuffer = t.getVertexBuffer();
       this.mFTextureBuffer = t.getTextureBuffer();
       this.mIndexBuffer = t.getIndexBuffer();
       this.numOfIndices = t.getNumberOfIndices();
       this.mFVertexBuffer.position(0);
       this.mIndexBuffer.position(0);
       this.mFTextureBuffer.position(0);

    }

   //overriden method
    protected void draw(GL10 gl)
    {
        prepareBuffers(sides);
        gl.glEnable(GL10.GL_TEXTURE_2D);
        gl.glVertexPointer(3, GL10.GL_FLOAT, 0, mFVertexBuffer);
        gl.glTexCoordPointer(2, GL10.GL_FLOAT, 0, mFTextureBuffer);
        gl.glDrawElements(GL10.GL_TRIANGLES, this.numOfIndices,
                GL10.GL_UNSIGNED_SHORT, mIndexBuffer);
    }
}
```

As you can see, most of the heavy lifting is carried out the by abstract textured renderer class and the RegularPolygon calculated the texture mapping vertices (see Listing 20–26).

Once we have this renderer available, we will need to add the code in Listing 20–33 to MultiviewTestHarness in Listing 20–12 to test the textured square.

Listing 20–33. *Responding to Textured Square Menu Item*

```
if (mid == R.id.mid_textured_square)
{
      mTestHarness.setRenderer(new TexturedSquareRenderer(this));
      mTestHarness.setRenderMode(GLSurfaceView.RENDERMODE_WHEN_DIRTY);
      setContentView(mTestHarness);
      return;
}
```

Now if we run the program again and choose the menu item "Textured Square," we will see the textured square drawn as shown In Figure 20–11

Figure 20–11. *A textured square*

Drawing Multiple Figures

Every example in this chapter so far has involved drawing a simple figure following a standard pattern. The pattern is: set up the vertices, load the texture, set up texture coordinates, and draw a single figure. What happens if we want to draw two figures? What if we want to draw a triangle using traditional means of specifying vertices and then a polygon using shapes such as the `RegularPolygon`? How do we specify combined vertices? Do we have to specify the vertices one time for both objects and then call the draw method?

As it turns out, between two `draw()` calls of the Android OpenGL Renderer interface, OpenGL allows us to issue multiple `glDraw` methods. Between these multiple `glDraw` methods, we can set up fresh vertices and textures. All of these drawing methods will then go to the screen once the `draw()` method completes.

There is another trick we can use to draw multiple figures with OpenGL. Consider the polygons we have created so far. These polygons have the capability to render themselves at any origin by taking the origin as an input. As it turns out, OpenGL can do this natively where it allows us to specify a `RegularPolygon` always at (0,0,0) and have the "translate" mechanism of OpenGL move it off of the origin to the desired position. We can do the same again with another polygon and translate it to a different position, thereby drawing two polygons at two different places on the screen.

Listing 20–34 demonstrates these ideas by drawing the textured polygon multiple times.

Listing 20–34. *Textured Polygon Renderer*

```
public class TexturedPolygonRenderer extends AbstractSingleTexturedRenderer
{
   //Number of points or vertices we want to use
    private final static int VERTS = 4;

    //A raw native buffer to hold the point coordinates
    private FloatBuffer mFVertexBuffer;

    //A raw native buffer to hold the point coordinates
    private FloatBuffer mFTextureBuffer;

    //A raw native buffer to hold indices
    //allowing a reuse of points.
    private ShortBuffer mIndexBuffer;

    private int numOfIndices = 0;

    private long prevtime = SystemClock.uptimeMillis();
   private int sides = 3;

    public TexturedPolygonRenderer(Context context)
    {
       super(context,com.androidbook.OpenGL.R.drawable.robot);
prepareBuffers(sides);
    }

    private void prepareBuffers(int sides)
    {
    RegularPolygon t = new RegularPolygon(0,0,0,0.5f,sides);
this.mFVertexBuffer = t.getVertexBuffer();
    this.mFTextureBuffer = t.getTextureBuffer();
    this.mIndexBuffer = t.getIndexBuffer();
    this.numOfIndices = t.getNumberOfIndices();
    this.mFVertexBuffer.position(0);
    this.mIndexBuffer.position(0);
    this.mFTextureBuffer.position(0);
    }

   //overriden method
    protected void draw(GL10 gl)
    {
        long curtime = SystemClock.uptimeMillis();
        if ((curtime - prevtime) > 2000)
        {
           prevtime = curtime;
           sides += 1;
           if (sides > 20)
           {
              sides = 3;
           }
            this.prepareBuffers(sides);
        }
        gl.glEnable(GL10.GL_TEXTURE_2D);

        //Draw once to the left
        gl.glVertexPointer(3, GL10.GL_FLOAT, 0, mFVertexBuffer);
```

```
        gl.glTexCoordPointer(2, GL10.GL_FLOAT, 0, mFTextureBuffer);

        gl.glPushMatrix();
        gl.glScalef(0.5f, 0.5f, 1.0f);
        gl.glTranslatef(0.5f,0, 0);
        gl.glDrawElements(GL10.GL_TRIANGLES, this.numOfIndices,
               GL10.GL_UNSIGNED_SHORT, mIndexBuffer);

        //Draw again to the right
        gl.glPopMatrix();
        gl.glPushMatrix();
        gl.glScalef(0.5f, 0.5f, 1.0f);
        gl.glTranslatef(-0.5f,0, 0);
        gl.glDrawElements(GL10.GL_TRIANGLES, this.numOfIndices,
               GL10.GL_UNSIGNED_SHORT, mIndexBuffer);
        gl.glPopMatrix();
    }
}
```

This example demonstrates the following concepts:

- Drawing using shapes.
- Drawing multiple shapes using transformation matrices.
- Providing textures.
- Providing animation.

The main code in Listing 20–34 responsible for drawing multiple times is in the method `draw()`. We have highlighted corresponding lines in that method. Note that inside one `draw()` invocation we have called `glDrawElements` twice. Each of these times we set up the drawing primitives independent of the other time.

One more point to clarify is the use of transformation matrices. Every time `glDrawElements()` is called, it uses a specific transformation matrix. If we were to change this to alter the position of the figure (or any other aspect of the figure), we would need to set it back to the original so that the next drawing could correctly draw. This is accomplished through the push and pop operations provided on the OpenGL matrices.

Once we have this renderer available, we will need to add the code in Listing 20–35 to MultiviewTestHarness in Listing 20–12 to test the drawing of multiple figures.

Listing 20–35. ***Responding to Multiple Figures Menu Item***

```
if (mid == R.id.mid_multiple_figures)
{
      mTestHarness.setRenderer(new TexturedPolygonRenderer(this));
      mTestHarness.setRenderMode(GLSurfaceView.RENDERMODE_CONTINUOUSLY);
      setContentView(mTestHarness);
      return;
}
```

If we run the program again and choose the menu item "Multiple Figures," we will see two sets of changing polygons drawn (as shown in Figure 20–12) at the beginning of the animation. (Note that we have set the render mode to continuous.)

Figure 20–12. *A pair of textured polygons*

Figure 20–13 shows the same exercise in the middle of the animation.

Figure 20–13. *A pair of textured circles*

This concludes another important concept in OpenGL. This section showed how to accumulate a number of different figures or scenes and draw them in tandem so that the end result forms a fairly complex OpenGL scene.

Next, we'll talk about Android support for OpenGL ES 2.0.

OpenGL ES 2.0

The good news is that Android not only supports OpenGL ES 2.0 but also provides Java bindings to the API starting with Android 2.2 (or API Level 8). However, keep the following restrictions in mind:

OpenGL ES 2.0 is not supported yet on the emulator.

OpenGL ES 2.0 is significantly different for a beginner, and most OpenGL books are coming out with new editions to cover this aspect of OpenGL. The programmability demanded by OpenGL ES 2.0 on the GPU (Graphics Processing Unit) puts a lot of complexity on the emulator. As a result, it's not even clear when Android will support OpenGL ES 2.0 on the emulator

The only way to test/learn OpenGL ES 2.0 on Android SDK is to use a real device. Most of the devices are in the process of getting upgraded to Android 2.2. However, it's possible that there will be a number of devices that won't support OpenGL ES 2.0

OpenGL ES 2.0 is a very different animal than OpenGL ES 1.x. It is not backward compatible. For beginners, it is most different in its initialization and learning how to draw the simplest of drawings.

It would take many pages to cover OpenGL ES 2.0 thoroughly. Instead, we will present you the basic initialization needed to get started with ES 2.0. Once you have this basic harness, you can consult the references at the end of this chapter to apply the OpenGL ES 2.0 into this framework.

The power of OpenGL ES 2.0 comes from the ability to write programs for the GPU that get compiled at run time and interpret how to draw vertices and fragments. These programs are called shaders. Unfortunately these shaders are necessary even for the simplest of OpenGL ES 2.0 programs. In that sense understanding shaders is mandatory for OpenGL ES 2.0.

Learning the OpenGL Shader Language is necessary to learn OpenGL ES 2.0. We have included a number of references at the end of this chapter to help you with this.

Java Bindings for OpenGL ES 2.0

The Java bindings for this API on Android are available in the package `android.opengl.GLES20`. All the functions of this class are static and correspond to the respective C APIs in the Khronos spec. (The URL can be found in the references section)

The GLSurfaceView and the corresponding Renderer abstraction introduced in the book for OpenGL ES 1.0 are also applicable to OpenGL ES 2.0. We will cover this soon. The documentation for this aspect is in the API documentation for the function `GLSurfaceView.setEGLContextClientVersion`.

First, let's see how to figure out if the device or the emulator supports this version of OpenGL ES 2.0 by using the code in Listing 20–36.

Listing 20–36. *Detecting OpenGL ES 2.0 Availability*

```
 private boolean detectOpenGLES20() {
        ActivityManager am =
            (ActivityManager) getSystemService(Context.ACTIVITY_SERVICE);
        ConfigurationInfo info = am.getDeviceConfigurationInfo();
        return (info.reqGlEsVersion >= 0x20000);
}
```

Once you have this function (`detectOpenGLES20`), you can start using the GLSurfaceView, as shown in Listing 20–37, in your activity.

Listing 20–37. *Using GLSurfaceView for OpenGL ES 2.0*

```
        if (detectOpenGLES20())
        {
            GLSurfaceView glview = new GLSurfaceView(this);
            // glview.setEGLConfigChooser(false);
            glview.setEGLContextClientVersion(2);

            glview.setRenderer(new YourGLES20Renderer(this));
            glview.setRenderMode(GLSurfaceView.RENDERMODE_WHEN_DIRTY);
            setContentView(glview);
        }
```

Notice how the `GLSurfaceView` is configured to use OpenGL ES 2.0 by setting the client version to "2". Then the class `YourGLESRenderer` will be similar to the `Renderer` classes introduced in this chapter. However, in the body of the renderer class, you will be using the `GLES20` APIs instead of the `GL10` APIs.

In the example we are going to develop, this renderer class is called `ES20SimpleTriangleRenderer`. We will introduce this class shortly. But let's first look at the activity class in Listing 20–38 that combines code snippets from Listing 20–36 and Listing 20–37.

Listing 20–38. *OpenGL20MultiViewTestHarness Activity*

```
public class OpenGL20MultiViewTestHarnessActivity extends Activity
{
   final String tag="es20";
   private GLSurfaceView mTestHarness;
    @Override
    protected void onCreate(Bundle savedInstanceState) {
        super.onCreate(savedInstanceState);

        if (detectOpenGLES20())
        {
            mTestHarness = new GLSurfaceView(this);
            //DO NOT call the followign function
```

```
            //mTestHarness.setEGLConfigChooser(false);
            mTestHarness.setEGLContextClientVersion(2);
        }
        else
        {
            throw new RuntimeException("20 not supported");
        }

        Intent intent = getIntent();
        int mid = intent.getIntExtra("com.ai.menuid", R.id.MenuId_OpenGL15_Current);
        if (mid == R.id.mid_es20_triangle)
        {
            mTestHarness.setRenderer(new ES20SimpleTriangleRenderer(this));
            mTestHarness.setRenderMode(GLSurfaceView.RENDERMODE_WHEN_DIRTY);
            setContentView(mTestHarness);
            return;
        }
        return;
    }
    private boolean detectOpenGLES20() {
        ActivityManager am =
            (ActivityManager) getSystemService(Context.ACTIVITY_SERVICE);
        ConfigurationInfo info = am.getDeviceConfigurationInfo();
        return (info.reqGlEsVersion >= 0x20000);
    }
    @Override
    protected void onResume()    {
        super.onResume();
        mTestHarness.onResume();
    }
    @Override
    protected void onPause() {
        super.onPause();
        mTestHarness.onPause();
    }
}
```

The ES 2.0 test harness activity in Listing 20–38 is very similar to the test harness we presented for ES 1.x in Listing 20–12. You may be wondering why can't we just use that one and create a different menu option. Two reasons have prompted us to go in this direction.

The first one is we're not sure if we can reuse the `SurfaceView` between ES 1.x and ES 2.x menu invocations. We just want to be safe.

The second reason is that the way we initialize is different, so we don't want to confuse the code by combining both into one class. For example, for ES 2.0 initialization we check the supported ES version, etc.; such code would have clouded the simpler ES 1.x initialization in Listing 20–12.

Otherwise, the motivation for this ES 2.x test harness is identical to that of the ES1.x test harness.

To be able to use OpenGL ES 2.0 features in our activities such as the one in Listing 20–38, we need to include the following <uses-feature> as a child of the application node (see Listing 20–39).

Listing 20–39. *Using OpenGL ES 2.0 Feature*

```
<application…>
……other nodes
 <uses-feature android:glEsVersion="0x00020000" />
 </application>
```

As we will be able to test OpenGL ES 2.0 applications only on a real device, we need to specify our application as debuggable using the debuggable attribute of the application node, as shown in Listing 20–40.

Listing 20–40. *Specifying a Debuggable Application*

```
 <application android:icon="@drawable/icon"
              android:label="OpenGL Test Harness"
              android:debuggable="true">
```

To be able to invoke the ES 2.0 test harness activity, we will need to change the driver activity in Listing 20–14 so that it looks like the code in Listing 20–41.

Listing 20–41. *New Main Driver Activity*

```
public class TestOpenGLMainDriverActivity extends Activity {
    /** Called when the activity is first created. */
    @Override
    public void onCreate(Bundle savedInstanceState) {
        super.onCreate(savedInstanceState);
        setContentView(R.layout.main);
    }
    @Override
    public boolean onCreateOptionsMenu(Menu menu){
        super.onCreateOptionsMenu(menu);
        MenuInflater inflater = getMenuInflater(); //from activity
        inflater.inflate(R.menu.main_menu, menu);
        return true;
    }
    @Override
    public boolean onOptionsItemSelected(MenuItem item)
    {
        if (item.getItemId() >= R.id.mid_es20_triangle)
        {
            this.invoke20MultiView(item.getItemId());
            return true;
        }
        this.invokeMultiView(item.getItemId());
        return true;
    }
    private void invokeMultiView(int mid)
    {
        Intent intent = new Intent(this,MultiViewTestHarnessActivity.class);
        intent.putExtra("com.ai.menuid", mid);
        startActivity(intent);
    }
    private void invoke20MultiView(int mid)
```

```
        {
            Intent intent = new Intent(this,OpenGL20MultiViewTestHarnessActivity.class);
            intent.putExtra("com.ai.menuid", mid);
            startActivity(intent);
        }
    }
```

We have inserted two code additions in Listing 20–41: an additional method to invoke the OpenGL20MultiViewTestHarnessActivity that we invoke if the menu ID is above or equal to the "mid_es20_triangle". The thought is that this menu item will start off the demos for ES 2.0. However, we have only one demo of ES 2.0 at this time.

Rendering Steps

Rendering a figure in OpenGL ES 2.0 requires the following steps:

1. Write shader programs that run on the GPU to extract such things as drawing coordinates and model/view/projection matrices from the client memory and draw them. There is no counterpart to this in OpenGL ES 1.0. In a simplistic sense, this is an additional level of indirection before the vertices are drawn and surfaces painted.
2. Compile the source code of shaders from step 1on the GPU.
3. Link the compiled units in step 2 into a program object that can be used at drawing time.
4. Retrieve address handlers from the program in step 3 so that data can be set into those pointers.
5. Define your vertex buffers.
6. Define your model view matrices (this is done through such things as setting the frustum, camera position, etc.; it's very similar to how it's done in OpenGL ES 1.1).
7. Pass the items from step 5 and 6 to the program through the handlers.
8. Finally, draw.

We will examine each of the steps through code snippets and then present a working renderer paralleling the `SimpleTriangleRenderer` that was presented as part of the OpenGL ES 1.0. Let's start with the key difference of OpenGL ES 2.0, namely shaders.

Understanding Shaders

Even the simplest of drawings in OpenGL ES 2.0 requires program segments called *shaders*. These shaders form the core of OpenGL ES 2.0. We will explain the minimum necessary to accomplish drawing of a simple triangle; we advise you to read the resources listed in the reference section at the end of this chapter.

Any drawing that involves vertices is carried out by *vertex shaders*. Any drawing that involves a fragment, the space between vertices, is carried out by *fragment shaders*. So a vertex shader is concerned with only vertex points. However, a fragment shader deals with every pixel.

Listing 20–42 is an example of a vertex shader program segment.

Listing 20–42. *A Simple Vertex Shader*

```
uniform mat4 uMVPMatrix;
attribute vec4 aPosition;
void main() {
  gl_Position = uMVPMatrix * aPosition;
}
```

This program is written in the shading language. The first line indicates that the variable uMVPMatrix is an input variable to the program and it is of type mat4 (a 4x4 matrix). It is also qualified as a uniform variable because this matrix variable applies to all the vertices and not to any specific vertex.

In contrast, the variable aPosition is a vertex attribute that deals with the position of the vertex (coordinates). It is identified as an attribute of the vertex and is specific to a vertex. The other attributes of a vertex include color, texture, etc. This aPosition variable is a 4 point vector as well. Now the program itself, Listing 20–42, is taking the coordinate position of the vertex and transforming it using a Model View Projection (MVP) matrix (which will be set by the calling program) and multiplying the coordinate position of the vertex to arrive at a final position identified by the reserved gl_Position of the vertex shader.

This vertex shader program is responsible for drawing or positioning the vertices. The calling program, for example, will set the buffer for the vertices of a triangle, for instance, as follows in Listing 20–43.

Listing 20–43. *Setting Data for the Vertices*

```
GLES20.glVertexAttribPointer(positionHandle, 3, GLES20.GL_FLOAT, false,
              TRIANGLE_VERTICES_DATA_STRIDE_BYTES, mFVertexBuffer);
```

The vertex buffer is the last argument of this GLES 20 method. This looks very much like the glVertexPointer in OpenGL 1.0 except for the first argument, which is identified as positionHandle. This argument points to the aPostion input attribute variable from the vertex shader program in Listing 20–42. You get this handle using code similar to the following:

```
positionHandle = GLES20.glGetAttribLocation(shaderProgram, "aPosition");
```

Essentially, you are asking the shader program to give a handle to an input variable and go from there. The shaderProgram itself needs to be constructed by passing the shader code segments to the GPU and compiling them and linking them. To make a program where you can start to draw, you also need a fragment shader. Listing 20–44 is an example of a fragment shader.

Listing 20–44. *Example of a Fragment Shader*

```
void main() {
   gl_FragColor = vec4(1.0, 0.0, 0.0, 1.0);
}
```

Again, we take the reserved variable `gl_FragColor` and hardcode it to the color red. Instead of hardcoding it to red as in Listing 20–44, we can pass these color values all the way from the user program through the vertex shader to the fragment shader. This is a bit out of scope for this chapter but is clearly demonstrated in many of the indicated reference materials on OpenGL ES 2.0

These shader programs are mandatory to start drawing.

Compiling Shaders into a Program

Once we have the shader program segments as seen in Listing 20–42 and 20–44, we can use the code in Listing 20–45 to compile and load a shader program.

Listing 20–45. *Compiling and Loading a Shader Program*

```
private int loadShader(int shaderType, String source) {
    int shader = GLES20.glCreateShader(shaderType);
    if (shader != 0) {
        GLES20.glShaderSource(shader, source);
        GLES20.glCompileShader(shader);
        int[] compiled = new int[1];
        GLES20.glGetShaderiv(shader, GLES20.GL_COMPILE_STATUS, compiled, 0);
        if (compiled[0] == 0) {
            Log.e(TAG, "Could not compile shader " + shaderType + ":");
            Log.e(TAG, GLES20.glGetShaderInfoLog(shader));
            GLES20.glDeleteShader(shader);
            shader = 0;
        }
    }
    return shader;
}
```

In this code segment, the `shadertype` is one of `GLES20.GL_VERTEX_SHADER` or `GLES20.GL_FRAGMENT_SHADER`. The variable `source` will need to point to a string containing the source, such as those shown in Listing 20–42 and 20–44.

Listing 20–46 shows how the function `loadShader` (from Listing 20–45) is utilized in constructing the program object.

Listing 20–46. *Creating a Program and Getting Variable Handles*

```
private int createProgram(String vertexSource, String fragmentSource) {
    int vertexShader = loadShader(GLES20.GL_VERTEX_SHADER, vertexSource);
    if (vertexShader == 0) {
        return 0;
    }
    Log.d(TAG,"vertex shader created");
    int pixelShader = loadShader(GLES20.GL_FRAGMENT_SHADER, fragmentSource);
    if (pixelShader == 0) {
```

```
            return 0;
        }
        Log.d(TAG,"fragment shader created");
        int program = GLES20.glCreateProgram();
        if (program != 0) {
            Log.d(TAG,"program created");
            GLES20.glAttachShader(program, vertexShader);
            checkGlError("glAttachShader");
            GLES20.glAttachShader(program, pixelShader);
            checkGlError("glAttachShader");
            GLES20.glLinkProgram(program);
            int[] linkStatus = new int[1];
            GLES20.glGetProgramiv(program, GLES20.GL_LINK_STATUS, linkStatus, 0);
            if (linkStatus[0] != GLES20.GL_TRUE) {
                Log.e(TAG, "Could not link program: ");
                Log.e(TAG, GLES20.glGetProgramInfoLog(program));
                GLES20.glDeleteProgram(program);
                program = 0;
            }
        }
        return program;
    }
```

Getting Access to the Shader Program Variables

Once the program is set up, the program's handle can be used to get handles for the input variables required by the shaders. Listing 20–47 shows how.

Listing 20–47. *Getting Vertex and Uniform Handles*

```
int maPositionHandle =
     GLES20.glGetAttribLocation(mProgram, "aPosition");
int muMVPMatrixHandle =
    GLES20.glGetUniformLocation(mProgram, "uMVPMatrix");
```

A Simple ES 2.0 Triangle

We now have covered all the basics necessary to put together a framework similar to the one we created for OpenGL 1.0. We will now put together an abstract renderer which will encapsulate all the initialization work (such as creating shaders, programs, etc.). Listing 20–48 shows the code.

Listing 20–48. *ES20AbstractRenderer*

```
public abstract class ES20AbstractRenderer
implements android.opengl.GLSurfaceView.Renderer
{
   public static String TAG = "ES20AbstractRenderer";

   private float[] mMMatrix = new float[16];
   private float[] mProjMatrix = new float[16];
   private float[] mVMatrix = new float[16];
   private float[] mMVPMatrix = new float[16];

   private int mProgram;
```

```
private int muMVPMatrixHandle;
private int maPositionHandle;

public void onSurfaceCreated(GL10 gl, EGLConfig eglConfig)
{
       prepareSurface(gl,eglConfig);
}
public void prepareSurface(GL10 gl, EGLConfig eglConfig)
{
    Log.d(TAG,"preparing surface");
    mProgram = createProgram(mVertexShader, mFragmentShader);
    if (mProgram == 0) {
        return;
    }
    Log.d(TAG,"Getting position handle:aPosition");
    maPositionHandle = GLES20.glGetAttribLocation(mProgram, "aPosition");
    checkGlError("glGetAttribLocation aPosition");
    if (maPositionHandle == -1) {
        throw new RuntimeException("Could not get attrib location for aPosition");
    }
    Log.d(TAG,"Getting matrix handle:uMVPMatrix");
    muMVPMatrixHandle = GLES20.glGetUniformLocation(mProgram, "uMVPMatrix");
    checkGlError("glGetUniformLocation uMVPMatrix");
    if (muMVPMatrixHandle == -1) {
        throw new RuntimeException("Could not get attrib location for uMVPMatrix");
    }
}
 public void onSurfaceChanged(GL10 gl, int w, int h)
 {
     Log.d(TAG,"surface changed. Setting matrix frustum: projection matrix");
     GLES20.glViewport(0, 0, w, h);
     float ratio = (float) w / h;
     Matrix.frustumM(mProjMatrix, 0, -ratio, ratio, -1, 1, 3, 7);
 }
 public void onDrawFrame(GL10 gl)
 {
     Log.d(TAG,"set look at matrix: view matrix");
     Matrix.setLookAtM(mVMatrix, 0, 0, 0, -5, 0f, 0f, 0f, 0f, 1.0f, 0.0f);

     Log.d(TAG,"base drawframe");
     GLES20.glClearColor(0.0f, 0.0f, 1.0f, 1.0f);
     GLES20.glClear( GLES20.GL_DEPTH_BUFFER_BIT | GLES20.GL_COLOR_BUFFER_BIT);

     GLES20.glUseProgram(mProgram);
     checkGlError("glUseProgram");

     draw(gl,this.maPositionHandle);
 }
 private int createProgram(String vertexSource, String fragmentSource) {
     int vertexShader = loadShader(GLES20.GL_VERTEX_SHADER, vertexSource);
     if (vertexShader == 0) {
         return 0;
     }
        Log.d(TAG,"vertex shader created");
     int pixelShader = loadShader(GLES20.GL_FRAGMENT_SHADER, fragmentSource);
     if (pixelShader == 0) {
         return 0;
```

```
        }
        Log.d(TAG,"fragment shader created");
        int program = GLES20.glCreateProgram();
        if (program != 0) {
            Log.d(TAG,"program created");
            GLES20.glAttachShader(program, vertexShader);
            checkGlError("glAttachShader");
            GLES20.glAttachShader(program, pixelShader);
            checkGlError("glAttachShader");
            GLES20.glLinkProgram(program);
            int[] linkStatus = new int[1];
            GLES20.glGetProgramiv(program, GLES20.GL_LINK_STATUS, linkStatus, 0);
            if (linkStatus[0] != GLES20.GL_TRUE) {
                Log.e(TAG, "Could not link program: ");
                Log.e(TAG, GLES20.glGetProgramInfoLog(program));
                GLES20.glDeleteProgram(program);
                program = 0;
            }
        }
        return program;
    }
    private int loadShader(int shaderType, String source) {
        int shader = GLES20.glCreateShader(shaderType);
        if (shader != 0) {
            GLES20.glShaderSource(shader, source);
            GLES20.glCompileShader(shader);
            int[] compiled = new int[1];
            GLES20.glGetShaderiv(shader, GLES20.GL_COMPILE_STATUS, compiled, 0);
            if (compiled[0] == 0) {
                Log.e(TAG, "Could not compile shader " + shaderType + ":");
                Log.e(TAG, GLES20.glGetShaderInfoLog(shader));
                GLES20.glDeleteShader(shader);
                shader = 0;
            }
        }
        return shader;
    }
    private final String mVertexShader =
        "uniform mat4 uMVPMatrix;\n" +
        "attribute vec4 aPosition;\n" +
        "void main() {\n" +
        "  gl_Position = uMVPMatrix * aPosition;\n" +
        "}\n";

    private final String mFragmentShader =
        "void main() {\n" +
        "  gl_FragColor = vec4(0.5, 0.25, 0.5, 1.0);\n" +
        "}\n";

    protected void checkGlError(String op) {
        int error;
        while ((error = GLES20.glGetError()) != GLES20.GL_NO_ERROR) {
            Log.e(TAG, op + ": glError " + error);
            throw new RuntimeException(op + ": glError " + error);
        }
    }
    protected void setupMatrices()
```

```
    {
        Matrix.setIdentityM(mMMatrix, 0);
        Matrix.multiplyMM(mMVPMatrix, 0, mVMatrix, 0, mMMatrix, 0);
        Matrix.multiplyMM(mMVPMatrix, 0, mProjMatrix, 0, mMVPMatrix, 0);
        GLES20.glUniformMatrix4fv(muMVPMatrixHandle, 1, false, mMVPMatrix, 0);
    }
    protected abstract void draw(GL10 gl, int positionHandle);
}
```

Much of this code is an aggregation of the ideas introduced previously, except for one detail. The function `setupMatrices` demonstrates how the `Matrix` class is used to combine multiple matrices into a single matrix called `mMVPMatrix` by multiplying other matrices, starting with an Identity matrix.

So the variable `mMMatrix` is an Identity matrix. The variable `mVMatrix` is obtained by using the eyepoint API or the look-at point of the camera. The Projection matrix `mProjMatrix` is obtained by using the frustum specification. Both these concepts, the eye point and the frustum, are identical to the concepts covered in OpenGL ES 1.0. The MVP matrix is just a multiplication of these matrices. Finally, the call `glUniformMatrix4fv` sets this up as a variable in the vertex shader so that the vertex shader can multiply each vertex position with this matrix to get the final position (see Listing 20–42).

Listing 20–49 shows the code for `GS20SimpleTriangleRenderer` that extends the abstract renderer and the minimum necessary to define the points and draw.

Listing 20–49. ***ES20SimpleTriangleRenderer***

```
public class ES20SimpleTriangleRenderer extends ES20AbstractRenderer
{
    //A raw native buffer to hold the point coordinates
    private FloatBuffer mFVertexBuffer;
    private static final int FLOAT_SIZE_BYTES = 4;
    private final float[] mTriangleVerticesData = {
            // X, Y, Z
            -1.0f, -0.5f, 0,
            1.0f, -0.5f, 0,
            0.0f,  1.11803399f, 0 };

    public ES20SimpleTriangleRenderer(Context context)
    {
        ByteBuffer vbb = ByteBuffer.allocateDirect(mTriangleVerticesData.length
                * FLOAT_SIZE_BYTES);
        vbb.order(ByteOrder.nativeOrder());
        mFVertexBuffer = vbb.asFloatBuffer();
        mFVertexBuffer.put(mTriangleVerticesData);
        mFVertexBuffer.position(0);
    }

    protected void draw(GL10 gl, int positionHandle)
    {
        GLES20.glVertexAttribPointer(positionHandle, 3, GLES20.GL_FLOAT, false,
                0, mFVertexBuffer);
        checkGlError("glVertexAttribPointer maPosition");
        GLES20.glEnableVertexAttribArray(positionHandle);
        checkGlError("glEnableVertexAttribArray maPositionHandle");
```

```
        this.setupMatrices();
        GLES20.glDrawArrays(GLES20.GL_TRIANGLES, 0, 3);
        checkGlError("glDrawArrays");
    }
}
```

Now if we invoke the activity in Listing 20–38, we will see a triangle drawn to the dimension specified. To do this, we will need the following additional files:

ES20AbstractRenderer.java (Listing 20–48)

ES20SimpleTriangleRenderer.java (Listing 20–49)

OpenGL20MultiveTestHarnessActivity.java (Listing 20–38)

Once we have these files compiled, we can run the program again and chose the menu option "ES20 Triangle." This will display a single triangle very similar to that in Figure 20–3.

However, as suggested, it will not work on the emulator. You have to hook up a real device to eclipse to test this. We tested it using the first Motorola Droid from Verizon. The directions to hook up a device are covered in the second chapter of this book. We have also included a URL in the reference section where we intend to update our notes to cover a variety of devices.

Further Reading on OpenGL ES 2.0

The "References" section can help you with resources on OpenGL ES 2.0. Once you get a feel for these shader programs, the background on OpenGL 1.0, and the few starting points on OpenGL ES 2.0, you can follow the samples in the Android SDK to make headway when you have suitable hardware.

Finally, we have included all of the sample code for the OpenGL ES 20 triangle in the downloadable project. The triangle has all the steps needed for OpenGL ES 2.0.

Instructions for Compiling the Code

The best way to play around with the code listed in this chapter is to download the ZIP file dedicated for this chapter. The URL for this file is listed in the "References" section. Every class file listed here is in the ZIP file. If you want to write your program directly from the listings, we have included all files here. There may be few resources wanting such as the starting icon, etc. If you are not sure how to hook those up, download the ZIP file.

References

We have found the following resources useful in understanding and working with OpenGL:

Android's `android.opengl` package reference URL: `http://developer.android.com/reference/android/opengl/GLSurfaceView.html`.

The Khronos Group's OpenGL ES Reference Manual. `www.khronos.org/opengles/documentation/opengles1_0/html/index.html`.

OpenGL Programming Guide (the red book). `www.glprogramming.com/red/`. Although this online reference is handy, it stops at OpenGL 1.1. You will need to buy the 7th edition for information on the recent stuff including OpenGL shaders.

The following is a very good article on texture mapping from Microsoft: `http://msdn.microsoft.com/en-us/library/ms970772(printer).aspx`.

You can find very insightful course material on OpenGL from Wayne O. Cochran from Washington State University at this URL: `http://ezekiel.vancouver.wsu.edu/~cs442/`.

Documentation for JSR 239 (Java Binding for the OpenGL ES API) is at `http://java.sun.com/javame/reference/apis/jsr239/`.

The man pages at khronos.org for OpenGL ES 2.0 are useful as a reference but not a guide. `www.khronos.org/opengles/sdk/docs/man/`.

Understanding shading language is essential to understand the new OpenGL direction including the OpenGL ES 2.0. `www.opengl.org/documentation/glsl/`

OpenGL Shading Language, 3rd Edition, Randi J Rost, etc. We haven't personally read this book but it seems promising.

GLES20 API reference from the Android SDK. `http://developer.android.com/reference/android/opengl/GLES20.html`

GLSurfaceView Reference. `http://developer.android.com/reference/android/opengl/GLSurfaceView.html#setEGLContextClientVersion(int)`

You can find one of the authors of this book's research on OpenGL here: `http://www.androidbook.com/akc/display?url=NotesIMPTitlesURL&ownerUserId=satya&folderName=OpenGL&order_by_format=news`.

You can find one of the authors of this book's research on OpenGL textures here: `http://www.androidbook.com/item/3190`.

How to run Android applications on the device from Eclipse ADB. `http://www.androidbook.com/item/3574`

Download the test project dedicated for this chapter at www.androidbook.com/projects. The name of the ZIP file is ProAndroid3_ch20_TestOpenGL.zip.

Summary

We have covered a lot of ground in OpenGL—especially if you are new to OpenGL programming. We would like to think that this is a great introductory chapter on OpenGL, not only for Android but any other OpenGL system.

In this chapter, you learned the fundamentals of OpenGL. You learned the Android-specific API that allows you to work with OpenGL standard APIs. You played with shapes and textures, and you learned how to use the drawing pipeline to draw multiple figures. You were introduced to OpenGL ES 2.0, its shading language, the basic differences from OpenGL 1.0, and a set of references to further explore OpenGL ES 2.0.

Chapter 21

Exploring Live Folders

Live folders, introduced in SDK 1.5, allow developers to expose content providers such as contacts, notes, and media on the device's default opening screen (which we will refer to as the device's *home page*). When a content provider such as Android's contacts content provider is exposed as a live folder on the home page, this live folder will be able to refresh itself as contacts are added, deleted, or modified in the contacts database. We will explain what these live folders are, how to implement them, and how to make them "live."

Exploring Live Folders

A live folder in Android is to a content provider what an RSS reader is to a publishing web site. We said in Chapter 4 that content providers are similar to web sites that provide information based on URIs. As web sites proliferated, each publishing its information in a unique way, there was a need to aggregate information from multiple sites so that a user could follow the developments through a single reader. RSS saw a common pattern among disparate sets of information. Having a common pattern allows for the design of a reader that can read any content, as long as the content has a uniform structure.

Live folders are not that different in concept. As an RSS reader provides common interface to published web site content, a live folder defines a common interface to a content provider in Android. As long as the content provider or a wrapper to the content provider can satisfy this protocol, Android can create a live folder icon on the device's home page to represent that content provider. When a user clicks this live folder icon, the system will contact the content provider. The content provider is then expected to return a cursor. According to the live folder contract, this cursor must have a predefined set of columns. This cursor is then visually presented through a `ListView` or a `GridView`.

Based on this common format idea, live folders work like this:

1. First, you create an icon on the home page representing a collection of rows coming from a content provider. You make this connection by specifying a URI along with the icon.

2. When a user clicks that icon, the system takes the URI and uses it to call the content provider. The content provider returns a collection of rows through a cursor.

3. As long as this cursor has the columns expected by the live folder (such as name, description, and the program to invoke when that row is clicked), the system will present these rows as a `ListView` or a `GridView`.

4. Because the `ListViews` and `GridViews` are capable of updating their data when the underlying data store changes, these views are called *live*—hence the name *live folders*.

Two key principles are at work in live folders. The first principle is that the column names are common across cursors. This principle allows Android to treat all cursors targeted for live folders the same way. The second principle is that the Android views know how to look for any updates in the underlying cursor data and change themselves accordingly. This second principle is not unique to live folders; in fact, it's natural to all views in the Android UI, especially those views that rely on cursors.

Now that we have presented the idea of what live folders are, we'll systematically explore the live-folder framework. We will do that in two main sections. In the first main section, we will examine the overall end user experience of a live folder. This should further clarify live folders.

In the second main section, we will show you how to build a live folder correctly so that it is actually live. It does take some extra work to make a live folder "live," so we will explore this not-so-obvious aspect of live folders.

How a User Experiences Live Folders

Live folders are exposed to end users through the device's home page. Users make use of live folders by performing steps similar to the following:

1. Access the device's home page.

2. Go to the context menu of the home page. You can see the context menu by long-clicking on an empty space on the home page.

3. Locate a context menu option called Folders and click it to see the live folders that might be available.

4. From the list, choose and click the live folder name you want to expose on the home page. This creates an icon on the home page representing the chosen live folder.

5. Click the live folder icon that was created in step 4 to bring up the rows of information (the data represented by that live folder) in a `ListView` or a `GridView`.

6. Click one of the rows to invoke the application that knows how to display that row of data.
7. Use further menu options displayed by that application to view or manipulate a desired item. You can also use that application's menu options to create any new items allowed by that application.
8. Note that the live folder display automatically reflects any changes to the item or set of items.

We'll walk you through these steps, illustrating them with screenshots. We will start with step 1: a typical Android home page (see Figure 21–1). Note that this home page may look a bit different depending on the Android release and the device you are using.

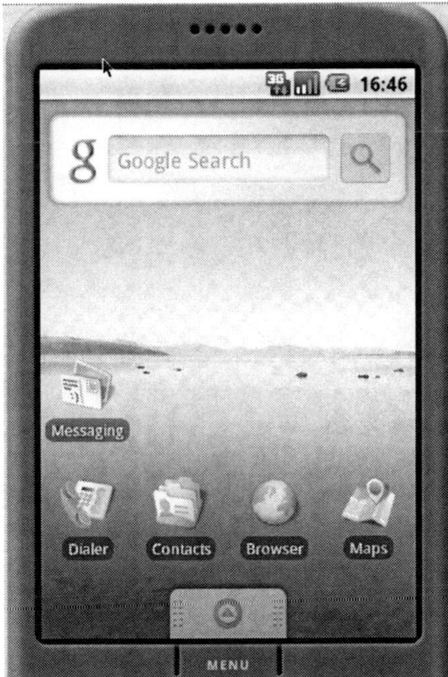

Figure 21–1. *Android home page*

If you long-click this home page, you will see its context menu (see Figure 21–2).

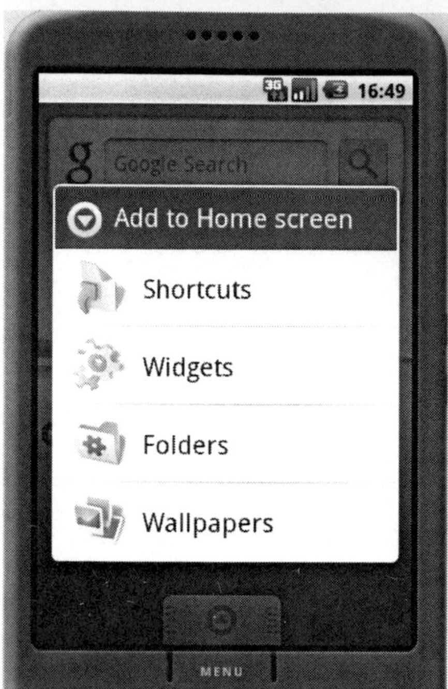

Figure 21–2. *Context menu on the Android home page*

If you click the Folders option, Android will open another menu showing the live folders that are available (see Figure 21–3). We will build a live folder in the next section, but for now, assume that the live folder we want has already been built and is called "New live folder" (see Figure 21–3).

> **NOTE:** If you want to walk through this exercise prior to developing it, you can download the project for this chapter and install it on your emulator. See the "References" section for the URL to download. Also, you need to use the contacts application that come with the SDK and is available on the emulator in order to add a few contacts. Once you download and import the project into Eclipse, run it in the emulator to install it as a live folder. Once it is installed on the emulator, it will show up as an option in Figure 21-3.

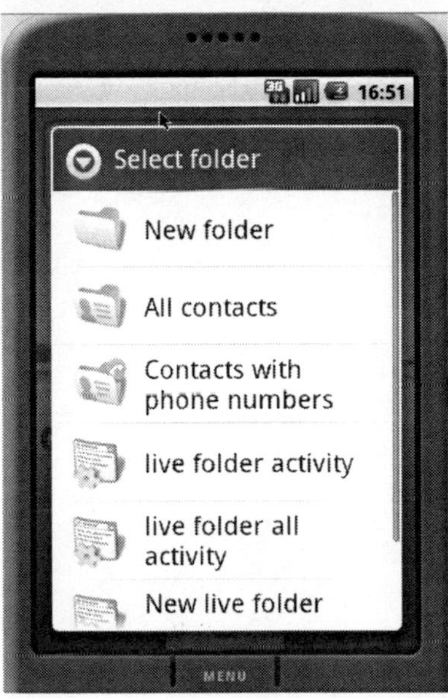

Figure 21–3. *Viewing the list of available live folders*

If you click the New live folder option, Android creates an icon on the home page representing the live folder. In our example, the name of this folder will be "Contacts LF," short for "Contacts Live Folder" (see Figure 21–4). This live folder will display contacts from the contacts database. During the implementation of the live folder we will show you how the name "Contacts LF" is specified.

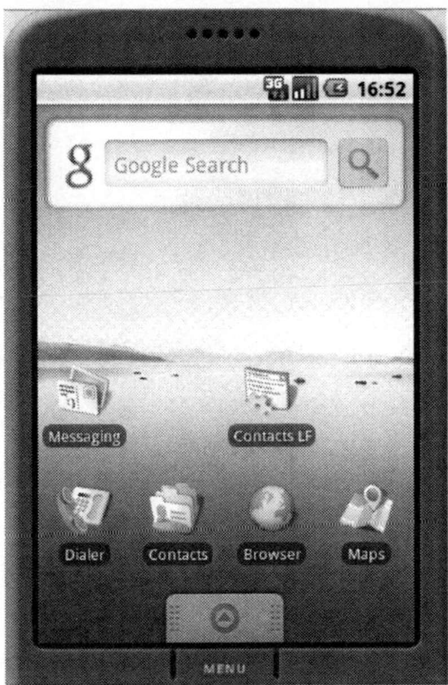

Figure 21–4. *The live folder icon on the home page*

You will see in the next section that an activity is responsible for creating the Contacts LF folder. For now, as far as the user experience is concerned, you can click the Contacts LF icon to see a list of contacts displayed in a `ListView` (see Figure 21–5). Again, depending on the release of Android, this list may be presented differently.

Figure 21–5. *Showing live folder contacts*

Depending on the number of contacts you have, this list might look different. You can click one of the contacts to display its details (see Figure 21–6). Note that because the details of this contact are presented by the contact application, the appearance is also dependent on the Android release.

Figure 21–6. *Opening a live folder contact*

You can click the Menu button at the bottom to see how you can manipulate that individual contact (see Figure 21–7). The options available here are also presented by the contact application. Again, the appearance is release- and device-dependent.

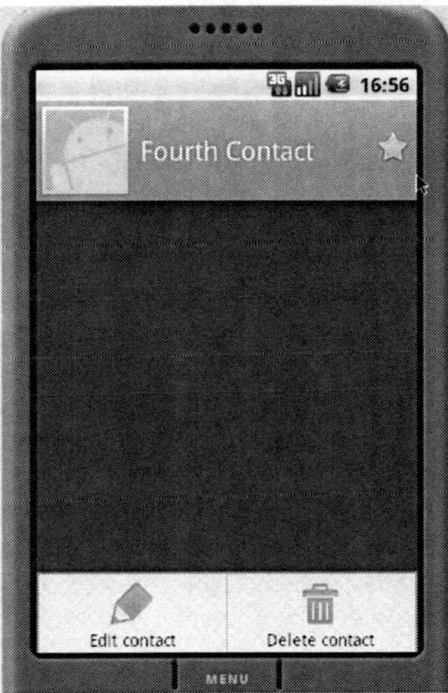

Figure 21–7. *Menu options for an individual contact*

If you choose to edit the contact, you will see the (release dependent) screen shown in Figure 21–8.

Figure 21–8. *Editing contact details*

To see the "live" aspect of this live folder, you can update the first name or last name of the contact. Then, when you go back to the live folder view of Contacts LF, you will see those changes reflected. You can do this by clicking the Back button repeatedly until you see the Contacts LF folder.

Building a Live Folder

Now that you know all about live folders and their relevance, we will show you how to build one. To build a live folder, you need two things: an activity and a dedicated content provider. Android uses the *label* of this activity to populate the list of available live folders, as in Figure 21–3. Android also invokes this activity to get a URI that will be invoked to get a list of rows to display.

The URI supplied by the activity should point to the dedicated content provider that is responsible for returning the rows. The content provider returns these rows through a well-defined cursor. We call the cursor *well defined* because the cursor is expected to have a known predefined set of column names.

Typically, you package these two entities in an application and then deploy that application onto the device. You will also need some supporting files to make it all work. We will explain and demonstrate these ideas using a sample, which contains the following files:

`AndroidManifest.xml`: This file defines which activity needs to be called to create the definition for a live folder.

`AllContactsLiveFolderCreatorActivity.java`: This activity is responsible for supplying the definition for a live folder that can display all contacts in the contacts database.

`MyContactsProvider.java`: This content provider will respond to the live folder URI that will return a cursor of contacts. This provider internally uses the contacts content provider that ships with Android.

`MyCursor.java`: This is a specialized cursor that knows how to perform a `requery` when underlying data changes.

`BetterCursorWrapper.java`: This file is needed by `MyCursor` to orchestrate the `requery`.

We'll describe each of these files to give you a detailed understanding of how live folders work.

AndroidManifest.xml

You're already familiar with `AndroidManifest.xml`; it's the same file that is needed for all Android applications. The live folders section of the file, which is demarcated with a comment, indicates that we have an activity called `AllContactsLiveFolderCreatorActivity` that is responsible for creating the live folder (see Listing 21–1). This fact is expressed through the declaration of an intent whose action is android.intent.action.CREATE_LIVE_FOLDER.

The label of this activity, "New live folder," will show up in the context menu of the home page (see Figure 21–3). As we explained in the "How a User Experiences Live Folders" section, you can get to the context menu of the home page by long-clicking the home page.

Listing 21–1. ***AndroidManifest.xml File for a Live Folder Definition***

```
<?xml version="1.0" encoding="utf-8"?>
<manifest xmlns:android="http://schemas.android.com/apk/res/android"
      package="com.androidbook.livefolders"
      android:versionCode="1"
      android:versionName="1.0">
    <application android:icon="@drawable/icon" android:label="@string/app_name">

       <!-- LIVE FOLDERS -->
        <activity
            android:name=".AllContactsLiveFolderCreatorActivity"
            android:label="New live folder "
            android:icon="@drawable/icon">

            <intent-filter>
                <action android:name="android.intent.action.CREATE_LIVE_FOLDER" />
                <category android:name="android.intent.category.DEFAULT" />
            </intent-filter>
        </activity>

      <provider android:authorities="com.androidbook.livefolders.contacts"
      android:multiprocess="true"
            android:name=".MyContactsProvider" />

    </application>
    <uses-sdk android:minSdkVersion="3" />
    <uses-permission android:name="android.permission.READ_CONTACTS"/>
</manifest>
```

Another notable point of the code in Listing 21–1 is the provider declaration, which is anchored at the URI content://com.androidbook.livefolders.contacts and serviced by the provider class MyContactsProvider. This provider is responsible for providing a cursor to populate the ListView that opens when the corresponding live-folder icon is clicked (Figure 21–5). The live folder activity AllContactsLiveFolderCreatorActivity needs to know what this URI is and return it to Android when it is invoked. Android invokes this activity when the live folder name is chosen to create a live folder icon on the home page.

According to the live folder protocol, the CREATE_LIVE_FOLDER intent will allow the home page's context menu to show the AllContactsLiveFolderCreatorActivity as an option titled "New live folder" (see Figure 21–3). Clicking this menu option will create an icon on the home page, as shown in Figure 21–4.

It is the responsibility of AllContactsLiveFolderCreatorActivity to define this icon, which will consist of an image and a label. In our case, the code in

AllContactsLiveFolderCreatorActivity specifies this label as Contacts LF (see Listing 21–2). So let's take a look at the source code for this live folder creator.

AllContactsLiveFolderCreatorActivity.java

The AllContactsLiveFolderCreatorActivity class has one responsibility: to serve as the generator or creator of a live folder (see Listing 21–2). Think of it as a template for the live folder. Every time this activity is invoked (through the Folders option in the home page's context menu), it results in a live folder on the home page.

This activity accomplishes its task by telling the invoker—the home page or live folder framework, in this case—the name of the live folder, the image to use for the live folder icon, the URI where the data is available, and the display mode (list or grid). The framework, in turn, is responsible for creating the live folder icon on the home page.

> **NOTE:** For all the contracts needed by a live folder, see the Android SDK documentation for the android.provider.LiveFolders class.

Listing 21–2. ***AllContactsLiveFolderCreatorActivity Source Code***

```
public class AllContactsLiveFolderCreatorActivity extends Activity
{
    @Override
    protected void onCreate(Bundle savedInstanceState)
    {
        super.onCreate(savedInstanceState);

        final Intent intent = getIntent();
        final String action = intent.getAction();

        if (LiveFolders.ACTION_CREATE_LIVE_FOLDER.equals(action))   {
             setResult(RESULT_OK,
                  createLiveFolder(MyContactsProvider.CONTACTS_URI,
                           "Contacts LF",
                           R.drawable.icon)
                  );
        }
        else   {
            setResult(RESULT_CANCELED);
        }
        finish();
    }

    private Intent createLiveFolder(Uri uri, String name, int icon)
    {
        final Intent intent = new Intent();
        intent.setData(uri);
        intent.putExtra(LiveFolders.EXTRA_LIVE_FOLDER_NAME, name);
        intent.putExtra(LiveFolders.EXTRA_LIVE_FOLDER_ICON,
                Intent.ShortcutIconResource.fromContext(this, icon));
        intent.putExtra(LiveFolders.EXTRA_LIVE_FOLDER_DISPLAY_MODE,
                LiveFolders.DISPLAY_MODE_LIST);
```

```
        return intent;
    }
}
```

The createLiveFolder method essentially sets values on the intent that invoked it. When this intent is returned to the caller, the caller will know the following:

- The live folder name
- The image to use for the live folder icon
- The display mode: list or grid
- The data or content URI to invoke for data

This information is sufficient to create the live folder icon shown in Figure 21–4. When a user clicks this icon, the system will call the URI to retrieve data. It is up to the content provider identified by this URI to provide the standardized cursor. We'll now show you the code for that content provider: the MyContactsProvider class.

MyContactsProvider.java

MyContactsProvider has the following responsibilities:

1. Identify the incoming URI that looks like content://com.androidbook.livefolders.contacts/contacts.
2. Make an internal call to the Android-supplied contacts content provider identified by content://contacts/people/. (Pay attention to the Contacts application that came with Android SDK and adjust this URL as it may change with a release.)
3. Read every row from the cursor and map it back to a cursor like MatrixCursor with proper column names required by the live folder framework.
4. Wrap the MatrixCursor in another cursor so that the requery on this wrapped cursor will make calls to the contacts content provider when needed.

The code for MyContactsProvider is shown in Listing 21–3. Significant items are highlighted based on the responsibilities listed above. The code is explained after the listing.

Listing 21–3. *MyContactsProvider Source Code*

```
public class MyContactsProvider extends ContentProvider
{
    public static final String AUTHORITY =
       "com.androidbook.livefolders.contacts";

    //Uri that goes as input to the livefolder creation
    public static final Uri CONTACTS_URI =
       Uri.parse("content://" + AUTHORITY + "/contacts");

    //To distinguish this URI
    private static final int TYPE_MY_URI = 0;
    private static final UriMatcher URI_MATCHER;
```

```
static{
  URI_MATCHER = new UriMatcher(UriMatcher.NO_MATCH);
  URI_MATCHER.addURI(AUTHORITY, "contacts", TYPE_MY_URI);
}
@Override
public boolean onCreate() {
    return true;
}
@Override
public int bulkInsert(Uri arg0, ContentValues[] values) {
  return 0; //nothing to insert
}
//Set of columns needed by a LiveFolder
//This is the live folder contract

private static final String[] CURSOR_COLUMNS = new String[]{

  BaseColumns._ID,
  LiveFolders.NAME,
  LiveFolders.DESCRIPTION,
  LiveFolders.INTENT,
  LiveFolders.ICON_PACKAGE,
  LiveFolders.ICON_RESOURCE
};

//In case there are no rows
//use this stand in as an error message
//Notice it has the same set of columns of a live folder
private static final String[] CURSOR_ERROR_COLUMNS = new String[]{
  BaseColumns._ID,
  LiveFolders.NAME,
  LiveFolders.DESCRIPTION
};
//The error message row
private static final Object[] ERROR_MESSAGE_ROW =
     new Object[]
     {
      -1, //id
      "No contacts found", //name
      "Check your contacts database" //description
     };

//The error cursor to use
private static MatrixCursor sErrorCursor =
     new MatrixCursor(CURSOR_ERROR_COLUMNS);
static {
  sErrorCursor.addRow(ERROR_MESSAGE_ROW);
}

//Columns to be retrieved from the contacts database

private static final String[] CONTACTS_COLUMN_NAMES =
new String[]{

  ContactsContract.Contacts._ID,
  ContactsContract.Contacts.DISPLAY_NAME,
  ContactsContract.Contacts.TIMES_CONTACTED,
  ContactsContract.Contacts.STARRED
```

```
};

public Cursor query(Uri uri, String[] projection, String selection,
        String[] selectionArgs, String sortOrder)
{
   //Figure out the uri and return error if not matching
  int type = URI_MATCHER.match(uri);
  if(type == UriMatcher.NO_MATCH){
    return sErrorCursor;
  }
  Log.i("ss", "query called");
  try
  {
   MatrixCursor mc = loadNewData(this);
    mc.setNotificationUri(getContext().getContentResolver(),
          Uri.parse("content://contacts/people/"));
    MyCursor wmc = new MyCursor(mc,this);
    return wmc;
  }
  catch (Throwable e){
    return sErrorCursor;
  }
}

public static MatrixCursor loadNewData(ContentProvider cp)
{
   MatrixCursor mc = new MatrixCursor(CURSOR_COLUMNS);
    Cursor allContacts = null;
    try
    {
       allContacts = cp.getContext().getContentResolver().query(
          ContactsContract.Contacts.CONTENT_URI,
          CONTACTS_COLUMN_NAMES,
          null, //row filter
          null,
          ContactsContract.Contacts.DISPLAY_NAME); //order by

       while(allContacts.moveToNext())
       {
         String timesContacted = "Times contacted: "+allContacts.getInt(2);
         Object[] rowObject = new Object[]
         {
             allContacts.getLong(0),              //id
             allContacts.getString(1),            //name
             timesContacted,                      //description
             Uri.parse("content://contacts/people/"
                       +allContacts.getLong(0)),  //intent
             cp.getContext().getPackageName(),    //package
             R.drawable.icon                      //icon
         };
         mc.addRow(rowObject);
       }
      return mc;
    }
    finally {
       allContacts.close();
    }
```

```
    }
    @Override
    public String getType(Uri uri)
    {
      //indicates the MIME type for a given URI
      //targeted for this wrapper provider
      //This usually looks like
      // "vnd.android.cursor.dir/vnd.google.note"
      return ContactsContract.Contacts.CONTENT_TYPE;
    }

    public Uri insert(Uri uri, ContentValues initialValues) {
      throw new UnsupportedOperationException(
            "no insert as this is just a wrapper");
    }
    @Override
    public int delete(Uri uri, String selection, String[] selectionArgs) {
        throw new UnsupportedOperationException(
        "no delete as this is just a wrapper");
    }
    public int update(Uri uri, ContentValues values,
            String selection, String[] selectionArgs)
   {
        throw new UnsupportedOperationException(
        "no update as this is just a wrapper");
    }
}
```

Note how the set of columns required by a live folder are initialized in Listing 21–3 and repeated in Listing 21-4 for immediate reference .

Listing 21–4. *Columns Needed to Fulfill the Live Folder Contract*

```
    private static final String[] CURSOR_COLUMNS = new String[]
    {
      BaseColumns._ID,
      LiveFolders.NAME,
      LiveFolders.DESCRIPTION,
      LiveFolders.INTENT,
      LiveFolders.ICON_PACKAGE,
      LiveFolders.ICON_RESOURCE
    };
```

Most of these fields are self-explanatory, except for the INTENT item. If you look at Figure 21–5, you will see that NAME relates to the title of the item in the list. The DESCRIPTION will be underneath the NAME in the same list item.

The INTENT field is actually a string field pointing to the URI of the item in the content provider. Android will use a VIEW action by using this URI when a user clicks on that item. That is why this string field is called an INTENT field, because internally Android will derive the INTENT from the string URI.

The last two fields relate to the icon that is displayed as part of the list. Again, refer to Figure 21–5 to see the icons. Study Listing 21–3 to see how these columns are provided values from the contacts database.

Also note that the MyContactsContentProvider (the wrapper content provider) executes the code from Listing 21–5 to tell the underlying cursor that it needs to watch for any data changes.

Listing 21–5. *Registering a URI with a Cursor*

```
MatrixCursor mc = loadNewData(this);
mc.setNotificationUri(getContext().getContentResolver(),
                     Uri.parse("content://contacts/people/"));
```

The function loadNewData() retrieves a set of contacts from the contact provider and creates MatrixCursor, which has the columns shown in Listing 21–4. The code then instructs the MatrixCursor to register itself with the ContentResolver so that the ContentResolver can alert the cursor when the data pointed to by the URI (content://contacts/people) changes in any manner.

You should find it interesting that the URI to watch is not the URI of our MyContactsProvider content provider, but the URI of the Android-supplied content provider for contacts. This is because MyContactsProvider is just a wrapper for the "real" content provider. So this cursor needs to watch the underlying content provider instead of the wrapper.

It is also important that we wrap the MatrixCursor in our own cursor, as shown in Listing 21–6.

Listing 21–6. *Wrapping a Cursor*

```
MatrixCursor mc = loadNewData(this);
mc.setNotificationUri(getContext().getContentResolver(),
              Uri.parse("content://contacts/people/"));
MyCursor wmc = new MyCursor(mc,this);
```

To understand why we need to wrap the cursor, we need to examine how views operate to update changed content. A content provider, like Contacts, typically tells a cursor that it needs to watch for changes by registering a URI as part of implementing the query method. This is done through cursor.setNotificationUri. The cursor then will register this URI and all its children URIs with the content provider. Then when an insert or delete happens on the content provider, the code for the insert and delete operations needs to raise an event signifying a change to the data in the rows identified by a particular URI.

This will trigger the cursor to get updated via requery, and the view will update accordingly. Unfortunately, the MatrixCursor is not geared for this requery. SQLiteCursor is geared for it, but we can't use SQLiteCursor here because we're mapping the columns to a new set of columns.

To accommodate this restriction, we have wrapped the MatrixCursor in a cursor wrapper and overridden the requery method to drop the internal MatrixCursor and create a new one with the updated data. To elaborate further, every time data changes, we want to get a new MatrixCursor. However, to the Android LiveFolder framework we return only the wrapped outer cursor. This will tell the live folder framework that there is only one cursor, but underneath we are coming up with new cursors as data changes.

This is illustrated in the following two classes.

MyCursor.java

Notice how MyCursor is initialized with a MatrixCursor in the beginning (see Listing 21–7). On requery, MyCursor will call back the provider to return a MatrixCursor. Then the new MatrixCursor will replace the old one by using the set method.

> **NOTE:** We could have done this by overriding the requery of the MatrixCursor, but that class does not provide a way to clear the data and start all over again. So this is a reasonable workaround. (Note that MyCursor extends BetterCursorWrapper, which we'll discuss next.)

Listing 21–7. *MyCursor Source Code*

```
public class MyCursor extends BetterCursorWrapper
{
   private ContentProvider mcp = null;

    public MyCursor(MatrixCursor mc, ContentProvider inCp)
    {
        super(mc);
        mcp = inCp;
    }
    public boolean requery()
    {
       MatrixCursor mc = MyContactsProvider.loadNewData(mcp);
       this.setInternalCursor(mc);
       return super.requery();
    }
}
```

Now let's look at the BetterCursorWrapper class to get an idea of how to wrap a cursor.

BetterCursorWrapper.java

The BetterCursorWrapper class (see Listing 21–8) is very similar to the CursorWrapper class in the Android database framework. But we need the BetterCursorWrapper to contain two things that CursorWrapper lacks. First, CursorWrapper doesn't have a set method to replace the internal cursor from the requery method. Second, CursorWrapper is not a CrossProcessCursor. Live folders need a CrossProcessCursor as opposed to a plain cursor because live folders work across process boundaries.

Listing 21–8. *BetterCursorWrapper Source Code*

```
public class BetterCursorWrapper implements CrossProcessCursor
{
   //Holds the internal cursor to delegate methods to
   protected CrossProcessCursor internalCursor;

   //Constructor takes a crossprocesscursor as an input
   public BetterCursorWrapper(CrossProcessCursor inCursor)
   {
      this.setInternalCursor(inCursor);
   }
```

```
    //You can reset in one of the derived class's methods
    public void setInternalCursor(CrossProcessCursor inCursor)
    {
       internalCursor = inCursor;
    }

    //All delegated methods follow
    public void fillWindow(int arg0, CursorWindow arg1) {
       internalCursor.fillWindow(arg0, arg1);
    }
    // ..... other delegated methods
}
```

We haven't shown you the entire `BetterCursorWrapper` class in Listing 21-8, but you can easily use Eclipse to generate the rest of it. Once you have this partial class loaded into Eclipse, place your cursor on the variable named `internalCursor`. Right-click and choose Source ➤ Generate Delegated Methods. Eclipse will then populate the rest of the class for you. Once Eclipse generates the delegated methods, you will need to delegate all methods to the internal cursor class as we have done for the `fillWindow` method in Listing 21-8. (If you don't want to go through this process, you can see this file in the download project for this chapter.)

Now you have all the classes you need to build, deploy, and run the sample live folder project through Eclipse. Because no activity class is registered as a MAIN category, you won't see any UI show up when you deploy this project, but you will see a message in the Eclipse console that the project is successfully installed.

Let's conclude this section on live folders by showing you what happens when you access the live folder.

Exercising Live Folders

Once you have all these files for the live folder project ready, you can build them and deploy them to the emulator. You are now ready to make use of the live folder that we have constructed.

Navigate to the device's home page; it should look like the screen in Figure 21–1. Follow the steps outlined at the beginning of the "How a User Experiences Live Folders" section. Specifically, locate the live folder you created and create the live folder icon shown in Figure 21–4. Click the Contacts LF live folder icon, and you will see the contact list populated with contacts (Figure 21–5).

Instructions for Compiling the Code

The best way to play around with the code listed in this chapter is to download the ZIP file dedicated for this chapter. The URL for this file is listed in the "References" section. Every class file listed in this chapter is in the downloadable ZIP file.

Unlike a number of projects in this book, this project does not have an activity that gets started when you run it in the emulator. However, you can see in the console of Eclipse that the package is installed successfully.

References

We have found the following resources useful in understanding and working with Live Folders:

> This URL documents the `LiveFolders` class.
> `http://developer.android.com/reference/android/provider/LiveFolders.html`
>
> This article documents how to use the contacts API. You will need this as the live folder in this chapter uses the contacts underneath.
> `http://developer.android.com/resources/articles/contacts.html`
>
> You can download the test project dedicated for this chapter from `www.androidbook.com/projects`. The name of the zip file is `ProAndroid3_ch21_TestLiveFolders.zip`.

Summary

Live folders provide an innovative single-click mechanism to display changing data on the home page. The data can be virtually anything as long as it can be laid out as a set of rows displayed in a list. All the data needs to have is a sense of how to identify and describe itself through name and description. Almost any data element will meet this requirement since most data can be named and described in some manner. It also helps if there is an activity that can display that data when clicked for further details through the live folder. This data can be local, such as contacts, or even Internet-based, such as a summary of blogs.

In this chapter, we have explained the nuances of live folder cursors and what mechanisms you will need to use if you wish to expose already-existing content providers as sources for live folders. We explained the need for cursor wrappers and showed you how to register with a `ContentResolver` to receive data updates.

In the next chapter, we will introduce you to another home page innovation called Home Screen Widgets.

Chapter 22

Home Screen Widgets

In this chapter, we will cover Android's home screen widgets in detail. Home screen widgets, like live folders (covered in Chapter 21), offer one more way of presenting frequently changing information on the home screen of Android. From a high-level perspective, home screen widgets are disconnected views (albeit populated with data) that are displayed on the home screen. The data content of these views is updated at regular intervals by background processes.

For example, an e-mail home screen widget might alert you to the number of outstanding e-mails to be read. The widget may just show you the number of e-mails and not the messages themselves. Clicking the e-mail count may then take you to the activity that displays actual e-mails. These could even be external e-mail sources such as Yahoo, Gmail, or Hotmail, as long as the device has a way to access the counts through HTTP or other connectivity mechanisms.

> **NOTE:** Android 3.0 has enhanced support for home screen widgets. These enhancements are covered in Chapter 31.

We will divide this chapter into three sections. In the first section, we will introduce home screen widgets and their architecture. We will describe how Android uses `RemoteViews` for showing widgets, and co-opts broadcast receivers to update those `RemoteViews`. You will learn how to create activities to configure widgets on the home screen and discover the relationship between services and widgets. At the end of this section, you will have a clear understanding of the architecture and life cycle of home screen widgets.

In the second section, we will show you how to design and develop a home screen widget and annotate the code. You will learn how to define widgets to Android and how to write broadcast receivers to update these widgets. We will show you how to manage widget state through shared preferences and how to write an activity to configure widgets.

In the third section, we will talk about suitability, limitations, and broader guidelines for working with widgets. We will, in addition, discuss the scope and applicability of widgets. We will also offer design suggestions to write widgets that require far more frequent updates.

We will conclude the chapter with a collection of widget related programming resources.

Architecture of Home Screen Widgets

Let's start our discussion of home screen widgets architecture by considering what home screen widgets are in greater detail.

What Are Home Screen Widgets?

Home screen widgets are views that can be displayed on a home page and updated frequently. As a view, a widget's look and feel is defined through a layout XML file. For a widget, in addition to the layout of the view, you will need to define how much space the view of the widget will need on the home screen.

A widget definition also includes a couple of Java classes that are responsible for initializing the view and updating it frequently. These Java classes are responsible for managing the life cycle of the widget on the home screen. These classes respond when the widget is dragged onto the home page and when the widget is uninstalled by dragging it to the trash can.

> **NOTE:** The view and the corresponding Java classes are architected in such a way that they are disconnected from each other. For example, any Android service or activity can retrieve the view using its layout ID, populate that view with data (just like populating a template), and send it to the home screen. Once the view is sent to the home screen, it is dislodged from the underlying Java code.

At a minimum, a widget definition contains the following:

- A view layout to be displayed on the home screen, along with how big it should be to fit on a home page. Keep in mind that this is just the view without any data. It will be the responsibility of a Java class to update the view.
- A timer that specifies the frequency of updates.
- A Java class called a *widget provider* that can respond to timer updates in order to alter the view in some fashion by populating with data.

Once a widget is defined and the Java classes are provided, the widget will be available for use. We'll give you an overview of such a defined widget is used in practice.

User Experience with Home Screen Widgets

Home screen widget functionality in Android allows you to choose a preprogrammed widget to be placed on the home screen. When placed, the widget will allow you to configure it using an activity (defined as part of the widget package), if necessary. It is important to understand this interaction before actually going into the details how a widget is programmed.

In other words, we want you to experience how one would use a widget before programming one.

We are going to walk you through a widget called Birthday Widget that we have created for this chapter. We will present the source code for it later in the chapter. First, we are going to use this widget as an example for our walk through. As a consequence of source code coming later, we need your consideration to read along and follow the pictures and not look for this widget on your screen. If you follow the provided figures and explanation, you will know the nature and behavior of the birthday widget which will make things clear when we code it subsequently.

Let's start this tour by locating the widget we want and creating an instance of it on the home screen.

Creating a Widget Instance on the Home Screen

To access the available widget list you need to long-click on the home page. This will bring up the home screen context menu as shown in Figure 22–1.

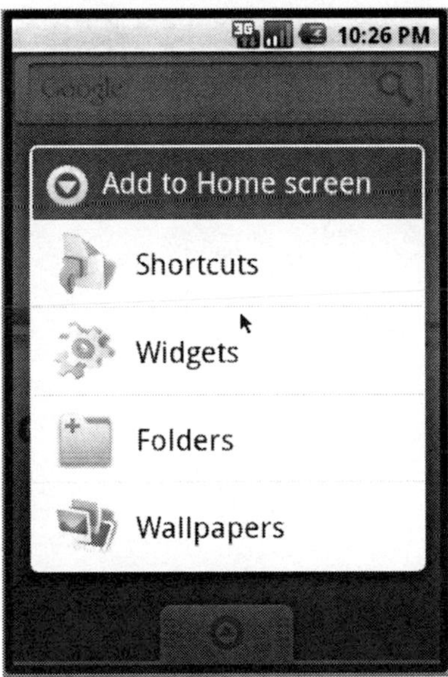

Figure 22–1. *Home screen context menu*

If you choose widgets from this list, you will be shown another screen that is a pick list of available widgets as shown in Figure 22–2.

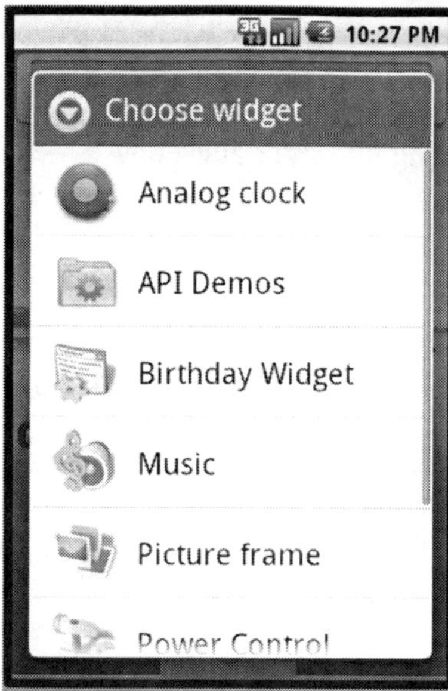

Figure 22–2. *Home screen widget pick list*

Most of these widgets come as part of Android. Depending on the release of Android you are looking at, these may vary. In this list, the widget named Birthday Widget is the widget that we designed for this exercise. If you choose that widget, it will create a corresponding widget instance on the home screen that looks like the example Birthday Widget shown in Figure 22–3.

Figure 22–3. *An example birthday widget*

This birthday widget will indicate in its header the name of a person, how many days away this person's birthday is, the date of the birthday, and a link to buy gifts.

You may be wondering how the name of the person and the date of birth were configured? What if you want two of instances of this widget, each with the name and date of birth for a different person. This is where the widget configurator activity comes into play and is the topic we are covering next.

> **NOTE:** The view that is created on the home page for this widget definition is called a *widget instance*. The implication is that you can create more than one instance of this widget definition.

Understanding Widget Configurator

A widget definition optionally includes a specification of an activity called a widget configurator activity. When you choose a widget from the home page widget pick list to create the widget instance, Android invokes the corresponding widget configuration activity. This activity is something you need to write, which is then responsible for configuring the widget instance.

In the case of our birthday widget, this configuration activity will prompt you for the name of the person and the upcoming birth date as shown in Figure 22–4. It is the responsibility of the configurator to save this information in a persistent place so that when an update is called on the widget provider, the widget provider will be able to locate this information and update the view with proper values which are set by the configurator.

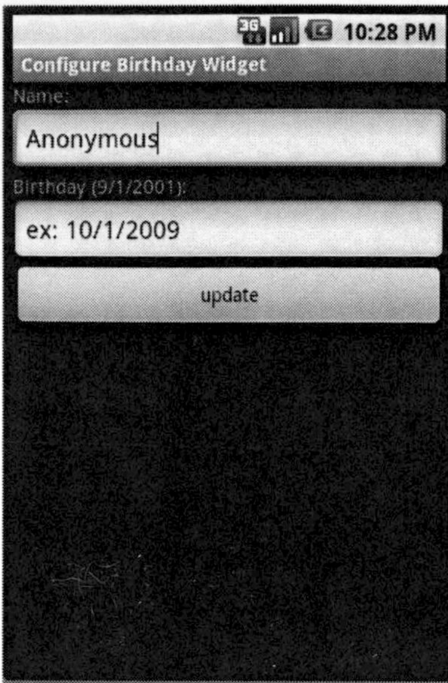

Figure 22–4. *Birthday widget configurator activity*

> **NOTE:** When a user chooses to create two birthday widget instances on the home screen, the configurator activity will be called twice (once for each widget instance).

Internally, Android keeps track of the widget instances by allocating them an ID. This ID is passed to the Java callbacks and to the configurator Java class so that initial configuration and updates can be directed to the right instance. In Figure 22–3, in the later part of the string `satya:3`, the `3` is the widget ID—or, more accurately, the widget instance ID. The widget itself is identified by its java component name (which is itself the class name and the package that the widget class is in); "Widget ID" and "widget instance ID" are interchangeably used in this chapter and refer to the widget instance ID. We have included the widget instance ID in Figure 22–3 to illustrate the point.

With this overview of a widget, we will now examine the life cycle of a widget in greater detail.

Life Cycle of a Widget

We have mentioned the widget definition a few times so far. We have also briefly talked about the role of Java classes. In this section, we will lay out both these ideas in a lot more detail and examine the life cycle of a widget.

The life cycle of a widget has the following phases:

1. Widget definition
2. Widget instance creation
3. `onUpdate()` (when the time interval expires)
4. Responses to clicks (on the widget view on the home screen)
5. Widget deletion (from the home screen)
6. Uninstallation

We will go through each of these phases in detail now.

Widget Definition Phase

The life cycle of a widget starts with the definition of the widget view. This definition tells Android to show the widget name in the widget pick list (Figure 22–2) invoked from the home page. You will need two things to complete this definition: a Java class that implements the `AppWidgetProvider` and a layout view for the widget.

You start off this widget definition with the following entry in the android manifest file where you specify the `AppWidgetProvider` (Listing 22–1).

Listing 22–1. *Widget Definition in Android Manifest File*

```
<manifest..>
<application>
....
   <receiver android:name=".BDayWidgetProvider">
      <meta-data android:name="android.appwidget.provider"
             android:resource="@xml/bday_appwidget_provider" />
      <intent-filter>
           <action android:name="android.appwidget.action.APPWIDGET_UPDATE" />
      </intent-filter>
   </receiver>
   ...
   <activity>
      .....
   </activity>
<application>
</manifest>
```

This definition indicates that there is a broadcast receiver Java class called `BDayWidgetProvider` (as you will see, this inherits from the Android core class `AppWidgetProvider` from the widget package) that receives broadcast messages intended for application widget updates.

> **NOTE:** Android delivers the update messages as broadcast messages based on the frequency of the time interval.

The widget definition in Listing 22–1 also points to an xml file in the /res/xml directory that, in turn, specifies the widget view and the update frequency, as shown in Listing 22–2.

Listing 22–2. *Widget View Definition in Widget Provider Information XML File*

```
<appwidget-provider xmlns:android="http://schemas.android.com/apk/res/android"
    android:minWidth="150dp"
    android:minHeight="120dp"
    android:updatePeriodMillis="43200000"
    android:initialLayout="@layout/bday_widget"
    android:configure="com.ai.android.BDayWidget.ConfigureBDayWidgetActivity"
    >
</appwidget-provider>
```

This XML file is called the App widget provider information file. Internally, this gets translated to the AppWidgetProviderInfo Java class. This file identifies the width and height of the layout to be 150dp and 120dp respectively. This definition file also indicates the update frequency to be 12 hours translated to milliseconds. The definition also points to a layout file (Listing 22–7) that describes what the widget view looks like (see Figure 22–5).

However, note that the layout for these widget views is restricted to contain only certain types of view elements. The views allowed in a widget layout fall under a class of views called RemoteViews, and only certain types of child views are allowed for these remote views. The allowed subview elements are shown in Listing 22–3.

Listing 22–3. *Allowed View Controls in RemoteViews*

```
FrameLayout
LinearLayout
RelativeLayout

AnalogClock
Button
Chronometer
ImageButton
ImageView
ProgressBar
TextView
```

This list may grow with each release. The primary reason for restricting what is allowed in a remote view is that these views are disconnected from the processes that actually control them. These widget views are hosted by an application like the Home application. The controllers for these views are background processes that get invoked by timers. For this reason, these views are called remote views. There is a corresponding Java class called RemoteViews that allows access to these views. In other words, programmers do not have direct access to these views to call methods on them. You have access to these views only through the RemoteViews (like a gatekeeper).

We will cover the relevant methods of a RemoteViews class when we explore the example in the next main section. For now, remember that only a limited set of views is allowed in the widget layout file (see Listing 22–3).

The widget definition (Listing 22–2) also includes a specification of the configuration activity that needs to be invoked when the user creates a widget instance. This configuration activity in Listing 22–2 is the `ConfigureBDayWidgetActivity`. This activity is like any other Android activity with a number of form fields. The form fields are used to collect the information needed by a widget instance.

Widget Instance Creation Phase

Once all the XML pieces needed by a widget definition are in place and all the widget Java classes are available, let's see what happens when a user chooses the widget name in the widget pick list (see Figure 22–2) to create a widget instance. Android invokes the configurator activity (see Figure 22–3) and expects that configurator activity to do the following:

1. Receive the widget instance ID from the invoking intent that started the configurator.
2. Prompt the user through a set of form fields to collect the widget-instance-specific information.
3. Persist the widget instance information so that subsequent calls to widget `update` have access to this information.
4. Prepare to display the widget view for the first time by retrieving the widget view layout and create a `RemoteViews` object with it.
5. Call methods on the `RemoteViews` object to set values on individual view objects, such as text and images.
6. Also use the `RemoteViews` object to register any `onClick` events on any of the subviews of the widget
7. Tell the `AppWidgetManager` to paint the `RemoteViews` on the home screen using the instance ID of that widget
8. Return the widget ID and close.

Notice that the first painting of the widget in this case is done by the configurator and not `AppWidgetProvider's` `onUpdate()` method.

> **NOTE:** The configurator activity is optional. If the configurator activity is not specified, the call goes directly to the `onUpdate()` of the `AppWidgetProvider`. It is up to `onUpdate()` to update the view.

Android will repeat this process for each widget instance that the user creates. Also note that there is no direct documented support for restricting the user to a single widget instance.

Besides invoking the configurator activity, Android also invokes the `onEnabled` callback of the `AppWidgetProvider`. Let us briefly consider the callbacks on an `AppWidgetProvider` class by taking a look at the shell of our BDayWidgetProvider (see Listing 22–4). We will examine the complete listing of this file later in Listing 22–9.

Listing 22–4. *A Widget Provider Shell*

```
public class BDayWidgetProvider extends AppWidgetProvider
{
    public void onUpdate(Context context,
                        AppWidgetManager appWidgetManager,
                        int[] appWidgetIds){}

    public void onDeleted(Context context, int[] appWidgetIds){}
    public void onEnabled(Context context){}
    public void onDisabled(Context context) {}
}
```

The onEnabled() callback method indicates that there is at least one instance of the widget up and running on the home screen. This means a user must have dropped the widget on the home page at least once. In this call, you will need to enable receiving messages for this component (you will see this in Listing 22–9). In Android, classes are sometimes referred to as components, especially when they form a reusable unit such as an activity, a service, or a broadcast receiver. In this case, the base class AppWidgetProvider is a broadcast receiver component; we can enable or disable it to receive broadcast messages.

The onDeleted() callback method is called when a user drags the widget instance view to the trash can. This is where you will need to delete any persistence values you are holding for that widget instance.

The onDisabled() callback method is called after the last widget instance is removed from the home screen. This happens when a user drags the last instance of a widget to the trash. You should use this method to unregister your interest in receiving any broadcast messages intended for this component (you will see this in Listing 22–9).

The onUpdate() callback method is called every time the timer specified in Listing 22–2 expires. This method is also called the very first time the widget instance is created if there is no configurator activity. If there is a configurator activity, this method is not called at the creation of a widget instance. This method will subsequently be called when the timer expires at the frequency indicated.

onUpdate Phase

Once the widget instance shows up on the home screen, the next significant event is the expiration of the timer. As indicated, Android will call the onUpdate() in response to that timer. The onUpdate() is called is through a broadcast receiver. This means the corresponding Java process in which the onUpdate() is defined will be loaded and will remain alive until the end of that call. Once the call returns, the process will be ready to be taken down.

It is also recommended that you use a mechanism such as a long-running broadcast receiver as documented in Chapter 14 if your response is going to take more than 10 seconds to work. If you do not, you will get an ANR (Android Not Responding) error.

Either way, once you have the necessary data available to update the widget in onUpdate() method, you can invoke the AppWidgetManager to paint the remote view. If you were to invoke a long-running service to do the update instead, you would need to pass the widget ID as extra data to the intent that starts the service.

This goes to show that the AppWidgetProvider class is stateless and may even be incapable of maintaining static variables between invocations. This is because the Java process containing this broadcast receiver class could be taken down and reconstructed between two invocations resulting in re-initialization of static variables.

As a result, you will need to come up with a scheme to remember state if that is required. When the updates are not too frequent, such as every few seconds, it is quite reasonable to save the state of the widget instance in a persistent store such as a file, shared preferences, or a SQLite database. In the next example, we will use shared preferences as the persistence API.

> **WARNING:** To save power, Google strongly recommends that the duration of the updates be more than an hour, so the device won't wake up too often. Google also warns that, in future releases, a restriction of 30 minutes or more may be enforced.

For durations that are shorter, such as only seconds, you need to call this onUpdate() method yourself by using the facilities in the AlarmManager class. When you use the AlarmManager, you also have the option not to call onUpdate() but, instead, do the work of onUpdate() in alarm callbacks. Refer to Chapter 15 for working with alarm manager.

This is what you typically need to do in an onUpdate() method:

1. Make sure the configurator has finished its work; otherwise, just return. This should not be problem in releases 2.0 and above, where the duration is expected to be longer. Otherwise, it is possible that the onUpdate() will be called before the user has finished configuring the widget in the configurator.
2. Retrieve the persisted data for that widget instance.
3. Retrieve the widget view layout, and create a RemoteViews object with it.
4. Call methods on the RemoteViews to set values on individual view objects such as text and images.
5. Register any onClick events on any of the views by using pending intents.
6. Tell the AppWidgetManager to paint the RemoteViews using the instance ID.

As you can see, there is a lot of overlap between what a configurator does initially and what the onUpdate() method does. You may want to reuse this functionality between the two places.

Widget View Mouse Click Event Callbacks

As stated, the `onUpdate()` method keeps the widget views up to date. The widget view and subelements in that view could have callbacks registered for a mouse click. Typically, the `onUpdate()` method uses a pending intent to register an action for an event like a mouse click. This action could then start a service or start an activity such as opening up a browser.

This invoked service or activity can then communicate back with the view, if needed, using the widget instance ID and the `AppWidgetManager`. Hence, it is important that the pending intent carries with it the widget instance ID.

Deleting a Widget Instance

Another distinct event that can happen to a widget instance is that it can get deleted. To do this, a user has to tap the widget on the home screen. This will enable the trash can to show at the bottom of the home screen. The user can then drag the widget instance to the trash can to delete the widget instance from the screen.

Doing so calls the `onDelete()` method of the widget provider. If you have saved any state information for this widget instance, you will need to delete that data in this `onDelete` method.

Android also calls `onDisable()` if the widget instance that is just deleted is the last of the widget instances of this type. You will use this callback to clean up any persistence attributes that are stored for all widget instances and also unregister for callbacks from the widget `onUpdate()` broadcasts (see Listing 22–9).

Uninstalling Widget Packages

That is the complete life cycle of a widget. We will move on to the next section by briefly mentioning the need to clean up the widgets if you are planning to uninstall and install a new release of your `.apk` file containing these widgets.

It is recommended that you remove or delete all widget instances before trying to uninstall the package. Follow the directions in the "Deleting a Widget Instance" section to delete each widget instance until none remains.

Then, you can uninstall and install the new release. This is especially important if you are using the Eclipse ADT to develop your widgets, because during the development time, ADT tries to do this every time you run the application. So, between runs, make sure you remove the widget instances.

A Sample Widget Application

So far, we have covered the theory and approach behind widgets. Let us use that knowledge to create the sample widget whose behavior has been used as the example to explain widget architecture. We will develop, test, and deploy this now-familiar birthday widget.

Each birthday widget instance will show a name, the date of the next birthday, and how many days from today until the birthday. It will also create an onClick area where you can click to buy gifts. This click will open a browser and take you to http://www.google.com.

The layout of the finished widget should look like Figure 22–5.

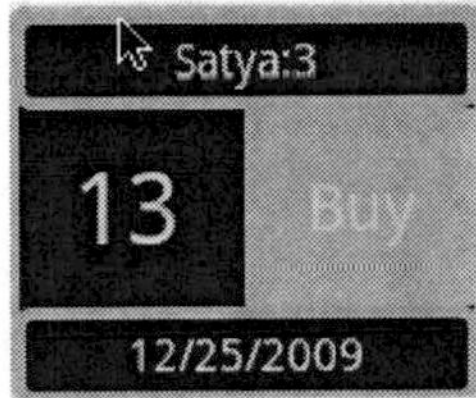

Figure 22–5. *Birthday widget look and feel*

The implementation of this widget consists of the following widget-related files. Depending on the source Java package you would like to use, the Java files will be under the src subdirectory followed by a directory structure that you would use for your Java packages. For brevity and space, we have used ellipses (. . .) to indicate those subdirectories.

- AndroidManifest.xml //: Where the AppWidgetProvider is defined (see Listing 22–5)
- res/xml/bday_appwidget_provider.xml //: Widget dimensions and layout (see Listing 22–6)
- res/layout/bday_widget.xml //: The widget layout (see Listing 22–7)
- res/drawable/box1.xml //: Provides boxes for sections of the widget layout (see Listing 22–8)
- src/.../BDayWidgetProvider //: Implementation of the AppWidgetProvider class (see Listing 22–9)

The implementation also contains the following files to manage the state of a widget:

- src/.../IWidgetModelSaveContract //: Contract for saving a widget model (see Listing 22–10)
- src/.../APrefWidgetModel //: Abstract preference-based widget model (see Listing 22–11)
- src/.../BDayWidgetModel //: Widget model holding the data for a widget view (see Listing 22–12)
- src/.../Utils.java //: A few utility classes (see Listing 22–13)

In addition, the implementation has the following files for the widget configuration activity:

- `src/.../ConfigureBDayWidgetActivity.java //`: Configuration activity (see Listing 22–14)
- `layout/edit_bday_widget.xml //`: Layout for taking the name and birthday (see Listing 22–15)

We will walk through each file and explain any additional concepts that bear further consideration. At the end of this section, you can also copy and paste these files to create and test the birthday widget in your own environment.

Defining the Widget Provider

Definition of a widget starts in the Android application manifest file. This is where you specify the widget provider, widget configuration activity, and a pointer to another XML file that further defines the widget layout.

For the birthday widget, you can see all of these highlighted in the following Android manifest file (see Listing 22–5). Notice the definition of `BDayAppWidgetProvider` as a broadcast receiver and also the definition for the configuration activity `ConfigureBDayWidgetActivity`.

Listing 22–5. *Android Manifest File for BDayWidget Sample Application*

```
<?xml version="1.0" encoding="utf-8"?>
<manifest xmlns:android="http://schemas.android.com/apk/res/android"
      package="com.ai.android.BDayWidget"
      android:versionCode="1"
      android:versionName="1.0.0">
    <application android:icon="@drawable/icon" android:label="Birthday Widget">
<!--
*********************************************************************
*  Birthday Widget Provider Receiver
*********************************************************************
 -->
   <receiver android:name=".BDayWidgetProvider">
      <meta-data android:name="android.appwidget.provider"
            android:resource="@xml/bday_appwidget_provider" />
      <intent-filter>
           <action android:name="android.appwidget.action.APPWIDGET_UPDATE" />
      </intent-filter>
   </receiver>
<!--
*********************************************************************
*  Birthday Provider Confiurator Activity
*********************************************************************
 -->
   <activity android:name=".ConfigureBDayWidgetActivity"
                 android:label="Configure Birthday Widget">
       <intent-filter>
           <action android:name="android.appwidget.action.APPWIDGET_CONFIGURE" />
       </intent-filter>
```

```
    </activity>

    </application>
    <uses-sdk android:minSdkVersion="3" />
</manifest>
```

NOTE: The receiver node is a sibling node to the activity node, if you are familiar with the manifest file. It is also the immediate child of the application node.

The application label identifier by "Birthday Widget" in the following line

```
<application android:icon="@drawable/icon" android:label="Birthday Widget">
```

is what shows up in the widget pick list (see Figure 22–2) of the home page. If you are creating a widget definition for the first time, make sure the following line is replicated exactly:

```
<meta-data android:name="android.appwidget.provider"
```

The specification "android.appwidget.provider" is Android specific and should be mentioned as such; the same is true the lines below:

```
<intent-filter>
    <action android:name="android.appwidget.action.APPWIDGET_UPDATE" />
</intent-filter>
```

Finally, the configuration activity definition is like any other normal activity, except that it needs to declare itself as capable of responding to APPWIDGET_CONFIGURE actions.

Defining Widget Size

Although the Android manifest file defines the widget provider, the additional details of the widget are provided in a separate XML file. The additional details include the size of the widget, the layout file name for the widget, the update time period, and the configuration activity component (or class) name.

This additional XML file is indicated by the android:resource node of the previous widget provider definition (see Listing 22–5). Listing 22–6 shows that widget provider information file (/res/xml/bday_appwidget_provider.xml).

Listing 22–6. *Widget View Definition for BDayWidget*

```
<!-- res/xml/bday_appwidget_provider.xml -->
<appwidget-provider xmlns:android="http://schemas.android.com/apk/res/android"
    android:minWidth="150dp"
    android:minHeight-"120dp"
    android:updatePeriodMillis="4320000"
    android:initialLayout="@layout/bday_widget"
    android:configure="com.ai.android.BDayWidget.ConfigureBDayWidgetActivity"
    >
</appwidget-provider>
```

This file indicates to Android the width and height that you want in pixels. However, Android will round them to the nearest cell. Android organizes its home screen area into a matrix of cells; each cell carries 74 density-independent pixels (dp) in width and height. Android recommends that you specify your width and height in multiples of these cells minus 2 pixels (to adjust for rounding etc.).

This file also indicates how often the `onUpdate()` needs to be called. Android highly recommends that this value be no more than a few times a day. You can put a value of 0 to indicate never to call the update. This is useful when you want to control your own updates through the `Alarm Manager` class.

The initial layout attribute points to the actual layout of the widget (see Listing 22–7). Finally, the `configure` attribute points to the configuration activity class. This class needs to be fully qualified in its definition.

Let us examine the actual layout for the widget now.

Widget Layout-Related Files

From the previous section and Listing 22–6, you can see that the layout of a widget is defined in a layout file. This layout file is just like any other layout file for a view in Android.

However, to guide standardization around widgets, Android published a set of widget design guidelines. You can access these guidelines at

`http://developer.android.com/guide/practices/ui_guidelines/widget_design.html`

In addition to the guidelines, this link has a set of view backgrounds that you can use to improve the look and feel of your widgets. In this example, we took a different route and used the traditional approach of view layouts with background shapes instead.

Widget Layout File

Listing 22–7 shows the layout file we used to produce the widget layout shown in Figure 22–5.

Listing 22–7. *Widget View Layout Definition for BDayWidget*

```
<!-- res/layout/bday_widget.xml -->
<?xml version="1.0" encoding="utf-8"?>
<LinearLayout xmlns:android="http://schemas.android.com/apk/res/android"
    android:orientation="vertical"
    android:layout_width="150dp"
    android:layout_height="120dp"
    android:background="@drawable/box1"
    >
<TextView
    android:id="@+id/bdw_w_name"
    android:layout_width="fill_parent"
    android:layout_height="30dp"
    android:text="Anonymous"
```

```
    android:background="@drawable/box1"
    android:gravity="center"
    />
<LinearLayout xmlns:android="http://schemas.android.com/apk/res/android"
    android:orientation="horizontal"
    android:layout_width="fill_parent"
    android:layout_height="60dp"
    >
   <TextView
       android:id="@+id/bdw_w_days"
       android:layout_width="wrap_content"
       android:layout_height="fill_parent"
       android:text="0"
       android:gravity="center"
       android:textSize="30sp"
       android:layout_weight="50"
       />
   <TextView
      android:id="@+id/bdw_w_button_buy"
       android:layout_width="wrap_content"
       android:layout_height="fill_parent"
       android:textSize="20sp"
       android:text="Buy"
       android:layout_weight="50"
       android:background="#FF6633"
       android:gravity="center"
   />
</LinearLayout>
<TextView
    android:id="@+id/bdw_w_date"
    android:layout_width="fill_parent"
    android:layout_height="30dp"
    android:text="1/1/2000"
    android:background="@drawable/box1"
    android:gravity="center"
    />
</LinearLayout>
```

This layout uses nested `LinearLayout` nodes to get the desired effect. Some of the controls also use a shape definition file called `box1.xml` to define the borders.

Widget Background Shape File

The code for this shape definition is shown in Listing 22–8 (this file should be in the `/res/drawable` subdirectory).

Listing 22–8. *A Boundary Box Shape Definition*

```
<!-- res/drawable/box1.xml -->
<shape xmlns:android="http://schemas.android.com/apk/res/android">
    <stroke android:width="4dp" android:color="#888888" />
    <padding android:left="2dp" android:top="2dp"
            android:right="2dp" android:bottom="2dp" />
    <corners android:radius="4dp" />
</shape>
```

We have used this layout approach because it is quite handy not only for widgets but also for your other layouts.

You may want to build an activity and test these layouts separately before actually testing them with your widget (at least, that is what we did). It took us a number of trials to get the look and feel right. It can be tedious to attempt to experiment directly with widgets; every time you run the application, you have to delete the widgets, uninstall, install, and then drag them back to the home page.

The files discussed so far complete the XML definitions needed by a typical widget. Let us see now how we will respond to the life cycle events of widgets by examining the widget provider class.

Implementing a Widget Provider

As part of widget architecture, we have talked about the responsibilities of a widget provider class. A widget provider needs to implement the following broadcast receiver callback methods.

- onUpdate()
- onDelete()
- onEnable()
- onDisable()

The Java code in Listing 22–9 demonstrates the implementation of each of these methods.

Listing 22–9. *Sample Widget Provider: BDayWidgetProvider*

```
///src/<your-package>/BDayWidgetProvider.java
public class BDayWidgetProvider extends AppWidgetProvider
{
    private static final String tag = "BDayWidgetProvider";
    public void onUpdate(Context context,
                         AppWidgetManager appWidgetManager,
                         int[] appWidgetIds)  {
        final int N = appWidgetIds.length;
        for (int i=0; i<N; i++)
        {
            int appWidgetId = appWidgetIds[i];
            updateAppWidget(context, appWidgetManager, appWidgetId);
        }
    }

public void onDeleted(Context context, int[] appWidgetIds)
{
     final int N = appWidgetIds.length;
     for (int i=0; i<N; i++)
     {
        BDayWidgetModel bwm =
                BDayWidgetModel.retrieveModel(context, appWidgetIds[i]);
        bwm.removePrefs(context);
```

```
        }
}
    @Override
    public void onReceive(Context context, Intent intent) {
        final String action = intent.getAction();
        if (AppWidgetManager.ACTION_APPWIDGET_DELETED.equals(action)) {
            Bundle extras = intent.getExtras();
            final int appWidgetId = extras.getInt
                             (AppWidgetManager.EXTRA_APPWIDGET_ID,
                              AppWidgetManager.INVALID_APPWIDGET_ID);

            if (appWidgetId != AppWidgetManager.INVALID_APPWIDGET_ID) {
                this.onDeleted(context, new int[] { appWidgetId });
            }
        }
        else {
            super.onReceive(context, intent);
        }
    }

    public void onEnabled(Context context) {
       BDayWidgetModel.clearAllPreferences(context);
        PackageManager pm = context.getPackageManager();
        pm.setComponentEnabledSetting(
                new ComponentName("com.ai.android.BDayWidget",
                       ".BDayWidgetProvider"),
                PackageManager.COMPONENT_ENABLED_STATE_ENABLED,
                PackageManager.DONT_KILL_APP);
    }

    public void onDisabled(Context context) {
        BDayWidgetModel.clearAllPreferences(context);
        PackageManager pm = context.getPackageManager();
        pm.setComponentEnabledSetting(
                new ComponentName("com.ai.android.BDayWidget",
                       ".BDayWidgetProvider"),
                PackageManager.COMPONENT_ENABLED_STATE_DISABLED,
                PackageManager.DONT_KILL_APP);
    }

    private void updateAppWidget(Context context,
                           AppWidgetManager appWidgetManager,
                            int appWidgetId) {
       BDayWidgetModel bwm = BDayWidgetModel.retrieveModel(context, appWidgetId);
       if (bwm == null) {
          return;
       }
       ConfigureBDayWidgetActivity
                      .updateAppWidget(context, appWidgetManager, bwm);
   }
}
```

Refer to the “Architecture of Home Screen Widgets” section to see what needs to happen in each of these methods. For the birthday widget, all these methods in turn make use of methods from the BDayWidgetModel class. Some of these methods are removePrefs(), retrievePrefs(), and clearAllPreferences().

The BDayWidgetModel class is used to encapsulate the state of our birthday widget instances (we will cover this class in the next section). To understand this widget provider class, all you need to know is that we are using a model class to retrieve data needed for this widget instance. This data is kept in preferences, which is why the methods are named removePrefs(), retrievePrefs(), and clearAllPreferences(). The names might make more sense if Android had substituted Data for Prefs resulting in removeData(), retrieveData(), and clearAllData(). Anyway that translation is just to make a point, and you will not find methods named with Data() suffix.

As indicated, the update method is called for all the widget instances. This method must update all the widget instances. The widget instances are passed in as an array of IDs. For each id, the onUpdate() method will locate the corresponding widget instance model and call the same method that is used by the configurator activity (see Listing 22–14) to display the retrieved widget model.

In the onDelete() method, we have instantiated a BDayWidgetModel and then asked it to remove itself from the preferences persistence store.

In the onEnabled() method, because it is called only once when the first instance comes into play, we have cleared all persistence of the widget models so that we start with a clean slate. We do the same in the onDisabled() method so that no memory of widget instances exists.

In the onEnabled() method, we enable the widget provider component so that it can receive broadcast messages. In the onDisabled() method, we disable the component so that it won't look for any broadcast messages.

NOTE: The onReceive() method is a special case. Prior to release 1.6, there was a bug where onDelete() was not being called. Google provided a workaround by explicitly providing an onReceive() method. In release 1.6 and up, you will not need this method; the same method from the base class is sufficient.

By employing the idea of widget models, the code stays clean. We'll explore the widget models and their implementation next.

Implementing Widget Models

What is a widget model? The widget model is not an Android concept. If you are familiar with traditional UI programming, you will recall the concept of Model, View Controller (MVC) architecture, where the model holds data needed by a view; the view is responsible for display; and the controller is responsible for mediating between the view and the model.

Although Android SDK does not mandate a specific approach, we have used the MVC idea to simplify widget programming. In this approach, for every widget instance view, you will have an equivalent Java class that is a widget model. This model will have all the methods that can supply the needed data for the widget instances.

In addition to supplying the data, we have created some base classes for these models so that they know how to save and retrieve themselves from a persistent store such as shared preferences. We will go through the model class hierarchy and show you how we use shared preferences to store and retrieve data. You can refer to Chapter 9 to read more about preferences.

Interface for a Widget Model

We will start this discussion with an interface that acts as a contract for a widget model so that the widget model can declare the fields to be saved in a persistent data base. The contract also defines how to set a field when that field is retrieved from a database. The interface, in addition, provides an `init()` callback so that it is called when a model is newly retrieved from the database and before being passed on to a requesting client.

Listing 22–10 shows the source code for the widget contract interface.

Listing 22–10. *Saving Widget State: The Contract*

```
//filename: src/…/IWidgetModelSaveContract.java
public interface IWidgetModelSaveContract
{
    public String getPrefname();
    public void setValueForPref(String key, String value);

    //return key value pairs you want to be saved
    public Map<String,String> getPrefsToSave();

    //gets called after restore
    public void init();
}
```

This interface is designed in such a way that a derived abstract class will provide an implementation using a specific persistence store. As mentioned before, we will use the shared preferences facility of Android as the persistence store. As the name of this interface indicates, it is purely a save contract. The clients such as the `BDayWidgetProvider` will still rely on the most-often derived class of this interface for specific methods.

The implementer of this interface will need to provide the name of a preference file in response to the method `getPrefname()`. This preference file is then used to save the key/value pairs obtained from `getPrefsToSave()`. In an inverse operation (`setValueForPref()`), the derived class is asked to set its internal value given a key and value restored from the preferences store.

Finally, the method `init()` is called on the derived class to indicate that the values have been restored from the persistent store or any other initializations that could happen.

NOTE: Please remember that, in a real-world application, you would structure this inheritance a bit differently; you would probably use a delegation mechanism for reuse instead of inheritance. However, this inheritance hierarchy will work well for our test case to demonstrate widget models.

Let us consider now the abstract implementation that stores the data fields of a widget as shared preferences.

Abstract Implementation of a Widget Model

All the code that is responsible for interacting with a persistent store is implemented in the `APrefWidgetModel` class (see Listing 22–11). The `Pref` in this class stands for "preference," because this class uses the `SharedPrferences` facility of Android to store the widget model data.

In addition, this class represents the idea of a basic widget. The field `id` represents the instance ID of the widget. This class always needs a constructor that takes the widget instance ID as an argument to accommodate the instance ID requirement.

Let's take a look at the source code of this class in Listing 22–11. Key methods of this class are highlighted.

Listing 22–11. *Implementing Widget Saves Through Shared Preferences*

```
//filename: /src/…/APrefWidgetModel.java
public abstract class APrefWidgetModel
implements IWidgetModelSaveContract
{
   private static String tag = "AWidgetModel";

   public int iid;
   public APrefWidgetModel(int instanceId) {
      iid = instanceId;
   }
  //abstract methods
   public abstract String getPrefname();
   public abstract void init();
   public Map<String,String> getPrefsToSave(){   return null;}

    public void savePreferences(Context context){
      Map<String,String> keyValuePairs = getPrefsToSave();
      if (keyValuePairs == null){
         return;
      }
      //going to save some values
      SharedPreferences.Editor prefs =
         context.getSharedPreferences(getPrefname(), 0).edit();

      for(String key: keyValuePairs.keySet()){
         String value = keyValuePairs.get(key);
         savePref(prefs,key,value);
```

```
    }
    //finally commit the values
    prefs.commit();
}

private void savePref(SharedPreferences.Editor prefs,
                      String key, String value) {
    String newkey = getStoredKeyForFieldName(key);
    prefs.putString(newkey, value);
}
private void removePref(SharedPreferences.Editor prefs, String key) {
    String newkey = getStoredKeyForFieldName(key);
    prefs.remove(newkey);
}
protected String getStoredKeyForFieldName(String fieldName){
    return fieldName + "_" + iid;
}
public static void clearAllPreferences(Context context, String prefname) {
    SharedPreferences prefs=context.getSharedPreferences(prefname, 0);
    SharedPreferences.Editor prefsEdit = prefs.edit();
    prefsEdit.clear();
    prefsEdit.commit();
}

public boolean retrievePrefs(Context ctx) {
    SharedPreferences prefs = ctx.getSharedPreferences(getPrefname(), 0);
    Map<String,?> keyValuePairs = prefs.getAll();
    boolean prefFound = false;
    for (String key: keyValuePairs.keySet()){
        if (isItMyPref(key) == true){
            String value = (String)keyValuePairs.get(key);
            setValueForPref(key,value);
            prefFound = true;
        }
    }
    return prefFound;
}
public void removePrefs(Context context) {
    Map<String,String> keyValuePairs = getPrefsToSave();
    if (keyValuePairs == null){
        return;
    }
    //going to save some values
     SharedPreferences.Editor prefs =
        context.getSharedPreferences(getPrefname(), 0).edit();

     for(String key: keyValuePairs.keySet()){
        removePref(prefs,key);
     }
     //finally commit the values
     prefs.commit();
}
private boolean isItMyPref(String keyname) {
    if (keyname.indexOf("_" + iid) > 0){
        return true;
    }
    return false;
```

```
    }
    public void setValueForPref(String key, String value) {
       return;
    }
}
```

Let us see how the key methods of this class are implemented. We'll start by saving the widget model attributes in a shared preferences file:

```
public void savePreferences(Context context)
{
     Map<String,String> keyValuePairs = getPrefsToSave();
     if (keyValuePairs == null){ return; }

    //going to save some values
    SharedPreferences.Editor prefs =
    context.getSharedPreferences(getPrefname(), 0).edit();

   for(String key: keyValuePairs.keySet()){
         String value = keyValuePairs.get(key);
          savePref(prefs,key,value);
   }
   //finally commit the values
   prefs.commit();
}
```

This method starts off by asking the derived classes to return a map of key/value pairs, where the keys are the attributes of the model, and values are string representations of those attribute values. It will then ask the android `context` to get hold of a `SharedPreferences` file through `context.getSharedPreferences()`. This API needs a unique name for this package. The derived model is responsible for supplying this.

Once we get the shared preferences, by following the Android documentation, we will ask to get an editable version of the shared preferences. Then, we update the preferences one by one. Once that is complete, we run the `commit()` method, so the preferences are persisted.

Read the API references and Chapter 9 for more information about the `SharedPreferences` and the `SharedPreferences.Editor` classes; the "Resources" section of this chapter has URLs pointing out where this information is. It is also worth noting that these shared preference files are XML files and can be found in the data directory of the package.

Because we have used a single file to store data for all widget instances, we need a way to distinguish field names among multiple widget instances. For example, if we have two widget instances named 1 and 2, we will need two keys to store the `Name` attribute so that there is a `name_1` and `name_2`. We do this translation in the following method:

```
protected String getStoredKeyForFieldName(String fieldName) {
    return fieldName + "_" + iid;
}
```

The derived class also uses this method to examine which field to update when it is called with a `setValue()` method.

Implementation of a Widget Model for Birthday Widget

Ultimately the most-often derived class in this hierarchy of widget models is responsible for actually maintaining all the fields needed by the view. It relies on its base classes to store and retrieve. We have designed this most-often derived class in such a way that the clients that are dealing with these models directly deal with the most-often derived class, as this is the class that is most pertinent to them.

For example, when a widget instance is first created by the configurator activity, the configurator activity instantiates one of these classes and fills up its values and asks to save itself.

This class, because of the needs of the view, maintains three fields:

- `name`: Name of the person
- `bday`: The date the next birthday falls on
- `url`: The URL to go to for buying gifts

The class then has a calculated attribute called `howManyDays`, which represents the number of days from today to the date of the next birthday.

You will also notice that this class is responsible for fulfilling the save contract. These methods are as follows:

```
public void setValueForPref(String key, String value);
public String getPrefname();
public Map<String,String> getPrefsToSave();
```

Listing 22–12 lays out the code that orchestrates all of this.

Listing 22–12. *BDayWidgetModel: Implementing a State Model*

```
//filename: /src/…/BDayWidgetModel.java
public class BDayWidgetModel extends APrefWidgetModel
{
   private static String tag="BDayWidgetModel";

   // Provide a unique name to store date
   private static String BDAY_WIDGET_PROVIDER_NAME=
      "com.ai.android.BDayWidget.BDayWidgetProvider";

   // Variables to paitn the widget view
   private String name = "anon";
   private static String F_NAME = "name";

   private String bday = "1/1/2001";
   private static String F_BDAY = "bday";

   private String url="http://www.google.com";

   // Constructor/gets/sets
   public BDayWidgetModel(int instanceId){
      super(instanceId);
   }
   public BDayWidgetModel(int instanceId, String inName, String inBday){
```

```
        super(instanceId);
        name=inName;
        bday=inBday;
    }
     public void init(){}
     public void setName(String inname){name=inname;}
     public void setBday(String inbday){bday=inbday;}

     public String getName(){return name;}
     public String getBday(){return bday;}

     public long howManyDays(){
        try       {
           return Utils.howfarInDays(Utils.getDate(this.bday));
        }
        catch(ParseException x){
           return 20000;
        }
     }

    //Implement save contract

     public void setValueForPref(String key, String value){
        if (key.equals(getStoredKeyForFieldName(BDayWidgetModel.F_NAME))){
           this.name = value;
           return;
        }
        if (key.equals(getStoredKeyForFieldName(BDayWidgetModel.F_BDAY))){
           this.bday = value;
           return;
        }
     }
    public String getPrefname()   {
       return BDayWidgetModel.BDAY_WIDGET_PROVIDER_NAME;
    }

    //return key value pairs you want to be saved
    public Map getPrefsToSave()   {
       Map map
       = new HashMap();
       map.put(BDayWidgetModel.F_NAME, this.name);
       map.put(BDayWidgetModel.F_BDAY, this.bday);
       return map;
    }
    public String toString()   {
       StringBuffer sbuf = new StringBuffer();
       sbuf.append("iid:" + iid);
       sbuf.append("name:" + name);
       sbuf.append("bday:" + bday);
       return sbuf.toString();
    }
    public static void clearAllPreferences(Context ctx){
       APrefWidgetModel.clearAllPreferences(ctx,
               BDayWidgetModel.BDAY_WIDGET_PROVIDER_NAME);
    }

    public static BDayWidgetModel retrieveModel(Context ctx, int widgetId){
```

```
        BDayWidgetModel m = new BDayWidgetModel(widgetId);
        boolean found = m.retrievePrefs(ctx);
        return found ? m:null;
    }
}
```

As you can see, this class uses a couple of date-related utilities. We will show you the source code for these utilities before moving on to explaining the widget configuration activity implementation.

A Few Date-Related Utilities

Listing 22–13 contains a utility class that is used to work with dates. It takes a date string and validates if it is a valid date. It also calculates how far a date is from today. The code is self-explanatory. We have included it here for completeness.

Listing 22–13. *Date Utilities*

```
public class Utils
{
    private static String tag = "Utils";
    public static Date getDate(String dateString)
    throws ParseException {
        DateFormat a = getDateFormat();
        Date date = a.parse(dateString);
        return date;
    }
    public static String test(String sdate){
        try {
            Date d = getDate(sdate);
            DateFormat a = getDateFormat();
            String s = a.format(d);
            return s;
        }
        catch(Exception x){
            return "problem with date:" + sdate;
        }
    }
    public static DateFormat getDateFormat(){
        SimpleDateFormat df = new SimpleDateFormat("MM/dd/yyyy");
        //DateFormat df = DateFormat.getDateInstance(DateFormat.SHORT);
        df.setLenient(false);
        return df;
    }

    //valid dates: 1/1/2009, 11/11/2009,
    //invalid dates: 13/1/2009, 1/32/2009
    public static boolean validateDate(String dateString){
        try {
            SimpleDateFormat df = new SimpleDateFormat("MM/dd/yyyy");
            df.setLenient(false);
            Date date = df.parse(dateString);
            return true;
        }
        catch(ParseException x) {
            return false;
```

```
        }
    }
    public static long howfarInDays(Date date){
        Calendar cal = Calendar.getInstance();
        Date today = cal.getTime();
        long today_ms = today.getTime();
        long target_ms = date.getTime();
        return (target_ms - today_ms)/(1000 * 60 * 60 * 24);
    }
}
```

Now, let's look at the implementation of the configuration activity that we have talked about already.

Implementing Widget Configuration Activity

In the "Architecture of Home Screen Widgets" section, we explained the role of configuration activity and its responsibilities. For the birthday widget example, these responsibilities are implemented in an activity class called `ConfigureBDayWidgetActivity`. You can see the source code for this class in Listing 22–14.

This class collects the name of the person and the next birthday. It then creates a `BDayWidgetModel` and stores it in shared preferences. It also has a function that knows how to transfer the `BDayWidgetModel` to a corresponding widget view.

Listing 22–14. *Implementing a Configurator Activity*

```
public class ConfigureBDayWidgetActivity extends Activity
{
    private static String tag = "ConfigureBDayWidgetActivity";
    private int mAppWidgetId = AppWidgetManager.INVALID_APPWIDGET_ID;

     /** Called when the activity is first created. */
     @Override
     public void onCreate(Bundle savedInstanceState) {
         super.onCreate(savedInstanceState);
         setContentView(R.layout.edit_bday_widget);
         setupButton();

         Intent intent = getIntent();
         Bundle extras = intent.getExtras();
         if (extras != null) {
             mAppWidgetId = extras.getInt(
                     AppWidgetManager.EXTRA_APPWIDGET_ID,
                     AppWidgetManager.INVALID_APPWIDGET_ID);
         }

     }

     private void setupButton(){
        Button b = (Button)this.findViewById(R.id.bdw_button_update_bday_widget);
        b.setOnClickListener(
              new Button.OnClickListener(){
                 public void onClick(View v)
                 {
```

```
                parentButtonClicked(v);
            }
        });

    }
    private void parentButtonClicked(View v){
        String name = this.getName();
        String date = this.getDate();
        if (Utils.validateDate(date) == false){
            this.setDate("wrong date:" + date);
            return;
        }
        if (this.mAppWidgetId == AppWidgetManager.INVALID_APPWIDGET_ID){
            return;
        }
        updateAppWidgetLocal(name,date);
        Intent resultValue = new Intent();
        resultValue.putExtra(AppWidgetManager.EXTRA_APPWIDGET_ID, mAppWidgetId);
        setResult(RESULT_OK, resultValue);
        finish();
    }
    private String getName(){
         EditText nameEdit = (EditText)this.findViewById(R.id.bdw_bday_name_id);
         String name = nameEdit.getText().toString();
         return name;
    }
    private String getDate(){
         EditText dateEdit = (EditText)this.findViewById(R.id.bdw_bday_date_id);
         String dateString = dateEdit.getText().toString();
         return dateString;
    }
    private void setDate(String errorDate){
         EditText dateEdit = (EditText)this.findViewById(R.id.bdw_bday_date_id);
         dateEdit.setText("error");
         dateEdit.requestFocus();
    }
    private void updateAppWidgetLocal(String name, String dob){
        BDayWidgetModel m = new BDayWidgetModel(mAppWidgetId,name,dob);
        updateAppWidget(this,AppWidgetManager.getInstance(this),m);
        m.savePreferences(this);
    }

    public static void updateAppWidget(Context context,
            AppWidgetManager appWidgetManager,
            BDayWidgetModel widgetModel)
   {
       RemoteViews views = new RemoteViews(context.getPackageName(),
                   R.layout.bday_widget);

       views.setTextViewText(R.id.bdw_w_name
          , widgetModel.getName() + ":" + widgetModel.iid);

       views.setTextViewText(R.id.bdw_w_date
             , widgetModel.getBday());

       //update the name
       views.setTextViewText(R.id.bdw_w_days,Long.toString(widgetModel.howManyDays()));
```

```
        Intent defineIntent = new Intent(Intent.ACTION_VIEW,
              Uri.parse("http://www.google.com"));
        PendingIntent pendingIntent =
           PendingIntent.getActivity(context,
                    0 /* no requestCode */,
                    defineIntent,
                    0 /* no flags */);
        views.setOnClickPendingIntent(R.id.bdw_w_button_buy, pendingIntent);

      // Tell the widget manager
      appWidgetManager.updateAppWidget(widgetModel.iid, views);
   }
}
```

If you look at the code for the function `updateAppWidgetLocal()`, you will notice that it is the function that creates and stores the model. It then uses the function `updateAppWidget()` to display it. It is worth noting how this function `updateAppWidget()` uses a pending intent to register a callback. The pending intent takes a primary intent such as

```
        Intent defineIntent = new Intent(Intent.ACTION_VIEW,
              Uri.parse("http://www.google.com"));
```

and creates a pending intent to start an activity. In contrast, a pending intent can be used to start a service as well. It is also noteworthy that this function works with `RemoteViews` and `AppWidgetManager`. Notice that this function accomplishes the following tasks:

- Obtaining `RemoteViews` from the layout
- Setting text values on the `RemoteViews`
- Registering a pending intent through `RemoteViews`
- Invoking the `AppWidgetManager` to send the `RemoteViews` to the widget
- Returning at the end with a result

> **NOTE:** The static function `udpateAppWidget` can be called from anywhere as long as you know the widget ID. This suggests that you can update a widget from anywhere on your device and from any process, both visual and nonvisual.

It is also important that you use the following code to end the activity:

```
Intent resultValue = new Intent();
resultValue.putExtra(AppWidgetManager.EXTRA_APPWIDGET_ID, mAppWidgetId);
setResult(RESULT_OK, resultValue);
finish();
```

Notice how we are passing the widget ID back to the caller. This is how `AppWidgetManager` knows that the configurator activity is completed for that widget instance.

Let us conclude this discussion of widget configuration by presenting the form layout for the widget configuration activity in Listing 22–15. This view is pretty straightforward: it has a couple of text boxes and edit controls with an update button. You can also see this visually in Figure 22–4.

Listing 22–15. *Layout Definition for Configurator Activity*

```
<!-- res/layout/edit_bday_widget.xml -->
<?xml version="1.0" encoding="utf-8"?>
<LinearLayout xmlns:android="http://schemas.android.com/apk/res/android"
   android:id="@+id/root_layout_id"
    android:orientation="vertical"
    android:layout_width="fill_parent"
    android:layout_height="fill_parent"
    >
<TextView
   android:id="@+id/bdw_text1"
    android:layout_width="fill_parent"
    android:layout_height="wrap_content"
    android:text="Name:"
    />
<EditText
    android:id="@+id/bdw_bday_name_id"
    android:layout_width="fill_parent"
    android:layout_height="wrap_content"
    android:text="Anonymous"
   />
<TextView
    android:id="@+id/bdw_text2"
    android:layout_width="fill_parent"
    android:layout_height="wrap_content"
    android:text="Birthday (9/1/2001):"
    />
<EditText
    android:id="@+id/bdw_bday_date_id"
    android:layout_width="fill_parent"
    android:layout_height="wrap_content"
    android:text="ex: 10/1/2009"
   />
<Button
    android:id="@+id/bdw_button_update_bday_widget"
    android:layout_width="fill_parent"
    android:layout_height="wrap_content"
    android:text="update"
/>
</LinearLayout>
```

This concludes our discussion on implementing a sample widget. As part of this exercise, we have demonstrated the following:

- Defining a widget
- Responding to widget callbacks
- Providing a configuration activity for the widget
- Showing the use of RemoteViews

- Providing a framework for state management
- Designing a pleasing layout for a widget

With that, we will proceed by offering a few guidelines for widgets.

Widget Limitations and Extensions

Android home widgets appear simple when you first look at them. However, they have many nuances that need to be looked at when you start writing widgets that are a bit off the beaten path.

If your widget doesn't require any state management and doesn't need to be invoked more than a few times a day, you have a widget that is very simple to write.

The next level of widget is one where you will need to manage the state but it is invoked infrequently, like the one we have shown here. These types of widget can benefit from a state management framework. We have shown in this chapter a bare-bones state management framework. We assume that more sophisticated ones will be available or that you could write one that is more robust and flexible.

The next level of widgets must be invoked at the levels of seconds and milliseconds. For these widgets, you will need to rig your own update calls using the `Alarm Manager`. You will also likely need a service to manage state frequently, rather than relying on a persistent framework. For example, if you were to write a widget for a `StopWatch`, you would need to have a timer that counts at least every second, and you would also need to keep track of your counters, which implies state.

Another factor to consider is that the `RemoteViews` on which the widget view framework relies have no mechanism to edit directly on a widget (at least none that is documented). `RemoteViews` also put restrictions on what kinds of views and layouts can be used. You don't have direct control of the views, only control through the methods supplied by the `RemoteViews` class.

Based on the current design and intentions of widgets, Google seems to expect that the widgets mostly fall under category 1 or 2. There is lot of opportunity to expand the widget framework in coming releases.

Resources

As we prepared material for this chapter, we found the following resources to be useful, and we present them here in the order of their utility:

- The official Android SDK documentation on app widgets is available at `http://developer.android.com/guide/topics/appwidgets/index.html`.
- You will need to understand the `SharedPreferences` API for managing state. The URL for this class is `http://developer.android.com/reference/android/content/SharedPreferences.html`.

- Related to shared preferences is the SharedPreferences.Editor API. This is available at http://developer.android.com/reference/android/content/SharedPreferences.Editor.html.
- Use the following link from Android to design pleasing widget layouts: http://developer.android.com/guide/practices/ui_guidelines/widget_design.html.
- You will need to understand the RemoteViews API to paint and manipulate widget views. This API is available at http://developer.android.com/reference/android/widget/RemoteViews.html.
- The widgets themselves are managed by a widget manager class. You can explore the API for this class at http://developer.android.com/reference/android/appwidget/AppWidgetManager.html.
- If you are in a hurry to borrow some code to get started on widgets, you can use the following URL, where one of our co-authors' gathers useful code snippets: http://www.androidbook.com/item/3300
- You can also find at the following link the research notes that were used in writing this chapter: http://www.androidbook.com/item/3299
- At http://www.androidbook.com/projects, you can download the test project dedicated for this chapter. The name of the ZIP file is ProAndroid3_ch22_TestWidgets.zip.

Summary

We had fun in this chapter exploring the possibilities provided by Android home screen widgets. These widgets are simple ideas that could benefit user experience considerably.

We have covered the theory behind widgets and given you a working example to illustrate the nuances. We have elaborated the need for widget models and widget state management, and qe hope that the state management code we presented can be used for your own widgets. Finally, we have touched on the design issues and limitations of widgets. See Chapter 31 for substantially more coverage of widgets in Android 3.0

Chapter 23

Android Search

In the last two chapters, 21 and 22, we introduced two home screen-based Android innovations. In Chapter 21, we explained how live folders can reside on the home page and provide quick access to changing data in content providers. In Chapter 22, we explored home screen widgets that provide snapshots of information on the home screen.

Continuing with the theme of *information at your fingertips*,we will now cover the Android search framework. The Android search framework is extensive. Even though Android search appears to be available only on the home screen of the device, its influence can be extended to activities in your application.

We will start this chapter with a tour of the Android search facility. We will demonstrate global search, search suggestions, suggestion rewriting, and searching the Web. We will show how to include and exclude local applications from participating in global search.

Following the usability tour, we will explore how activities in your applications integrate with the search key. We will work with activities that are not explicitly programmed for search, and we will examine an activity that disables search. We will explore a topic called type-to-search that can be used by activities in applications to invoke search. We will also show you an activity that explicitly invokes search through a menu item.

The key to Android search extensibility is a concept called a *suggestion provider*. We will explore this concept and write a simple suggestion provider by inheriting from a base suggestion provider available in Android.

However, you often will need to write a custom suggestions provider from scratch. We will discuss this, which will take us to the core of the Android search architecture.

Finally, we will cover two advanced topics and show how you can use action keys available on a device to invoke custom actions using search suggestions. We will also describe how you can pass application-specific data to search when it is invoked. We will conclude the chapter with a list of references.

Android Search Experience

Search capabilities in Android extend the familiar web-based Google search bar to search both device-based local content and Internet-based external content. You can also use this search mechanism to invoke applications directly from the search bar on the home page. Android makes these features possible by providing a search framework that allows local applications to participate.

Android search protocol is simple. It involves a single search box to let users enter search data. This is true whether you are using the global search box on the home page or searching through your own application: you use the same search box.

As the user enters text, Android takes the text and passes it to various applications that have registered to respond to search. Applications will respond by returning a collection of responses. Android aggregates these responses from multiple applications and presents them as a list of possible *suggestions*.

When the user clicks on one of these responses, Android invokes the application that presented the suggestion. In this sense, Android search is a federated search among a set of participating applications.

Although the overall idea is simple, the details of the search protocol are extensive. We will cover these details through working samples later in this chapter. In this first section, we will explore the search from a user's perspective.

Exploring Android Global Search

As we explore Android search, although not a prerequisite, we recommend that you also go through the "search" chapter in the Android users guide. We have provided a link to the latest online Android users guide in the references section.

> **NOTE:** As we were writing the book the Android releases went from 2.0 to 2.2 to 2.3 and 3.0. With each release, although the underlying API hasn't changed, the UI experience has changed slightly. The screen shots here in this chapter are from 2.2 emulator. Although we have tested the code on 2.3 and 3.0, we haven't replicated the screenshots from those releases. Where applicable we have indicated the differences in text. Depending on the Android release you have, it should not be too hard to figure out the equivalent UI functionality. Take search settings for example. In each release the place to invoke the search settings screen has changed. But the search settings screen looks the same. So we appreciate if you can keep this discrepancy in mind as you go through this chapter.

You can't miss search on an Android device; it is usually displayed on the home page, as shown in Figure 23–1. This search box is also referred to as the Quick Search Box (QSB). In some releases of Android, or depending on the device manufacturer/carrier, one may not see this search box by default on the home screen. However, you are sure to see the QSB if you click the search button on the device. Or in devices that don't have physical keys (such as tablets), you may see yet another obvious mechanism to invoke QSB. Do check with the user guide or manual for that version of Android.

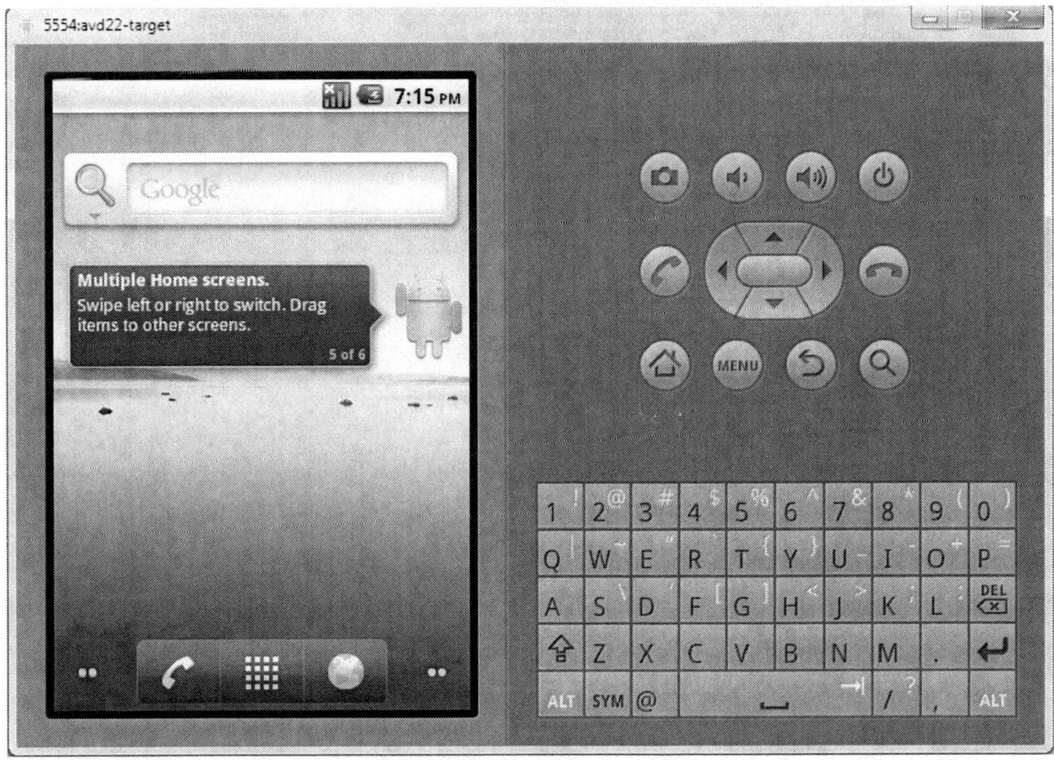

Figure 23–1. *Android home page with QSB widget and key pad*

Because QSB is implemented as a widget (see to Chapter 22 for more on widgets) you can drag and drop the search widget on to the home screen if it is not already on the home page. You can also remove the QSB from the home page by dragging it to the trash can. Of course you can redrag it from the widgets screen again.

You can directly type into the QSB to start your search. An interesting side effect of QSB being a widget is that shifting focus to the QSB on the home page will basically launch you into global search activity (see Figure 23–2), whereby you leave the home page context. Figure 23–2 is captured in Android release 2.2. It looks identical in Android release 2.3.

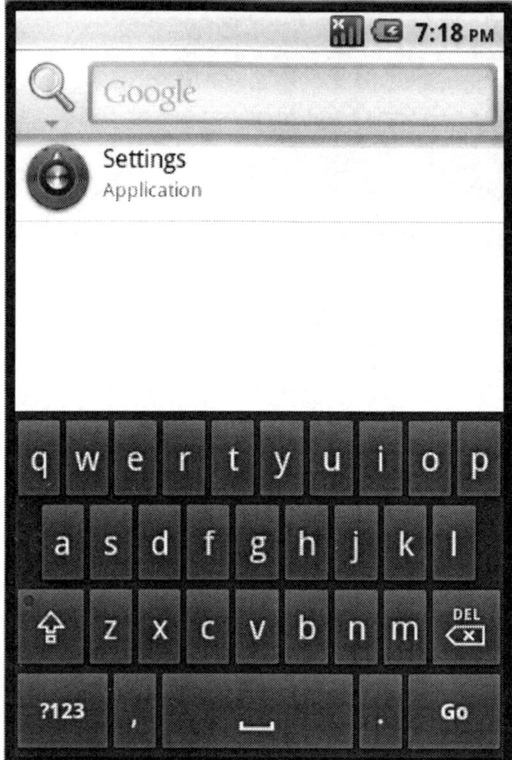

Figure 23–2. *Global search activity spawned off from the Home search widget*

As indicated you can also invoke the search by clicking on the Search action key. Action keys are the set of buttons that are shown in Figure 23–1 on the right hand side. The search key in the set is indicated by the magnifying glass.

Much like the HOME key, you can click the search key any time, irrespective of the application that is visible. However, when an application is in focus there is an opportunity for the application to specialize the search, which we will go into later. This customized search is called a *local search.* The more general, common, and non-customized search is called a *global search*.

> **NOTE:** When the search key is pressed when an application is in focus, it is up to the application to allow or disallow both local and global searches. In releases prior to 2.0 the default action is to allow the global search. In releases 2.2 and 2.3 the default behavior is to disable global search. This means when an activity is in focus the user has to click the home key first and then click the search key.

Prior to release 2.2, Android global search box did not distinguish between individual search suggestion providers (or search applications). Starting in 2.2, Android Search allows you to pick a particular search context (synonymous with a suggestion provider).

You can do this by clicking the left hand side icon of the QSB. This will open up a selection of the individual search applications that are providing searches. This is shown in Figure 23–3 for Android release 2.2. For Android release 2.3, this view is very slightly different — a small search settings icon is introduced on the right hand top portion of the expanded search categories section.

Figure 23–3. *Global QSB with various application search contexts*

This is the default set of search applications (or contexts or search types or suggestion providers) that come with the emulator as of release 2.2 and 2.3. This list may vary with subsequent releases. The search context `All` behaves much like the global search of prior releases.

You can also create your own search context by coding search suggestion providers and local search activities. We will cover this as we work through the samples in this chapter.

Let's focus on the search context that is indicated by "`all`" (represented by the magnifying glass icon). You give focus to QSB (Figure 23–1) either by directly clicking on the QSB or by clicking on the search key. Do not type anything in the QSB yet. At this point, Android will display a screen that may look like Figure 23–2.

Depending on your usage of the device in the past, the image shown in Figure 23–2 may vary, since Android guesses what you are searching for based on past actions. This search mode, when there is no text entered in the QSB, is called *zero suggestions mode*.

Depending on the search text that is entered, Android will provide a number of suggestions to the user. These suggestions show up below the QSB as a list. These are often called *search suggestions*. As you type each letter, Android will dynamically replace the search suggestions. When there is no search text, Android will display what are called *zero suggestions*. In Figure 23–2, Android has determined that Settings is an application the user has used before and that it is a suitable suggestion to present even though no search text has been entered. Although we haven't typed anything in the QSB, Android also shows the "soft keyboard" in anticipation of an entry. This soft keyboard is also shown in Figure 23–2.

When we type **a** in the QSB, Android looks for suggestions that start with "a" or related to "a". You will see that Android has already searched for local installed applications that start with "a" and a number of other search suggestions.

Now we'll use the down arrow button to highlight the first suggestion. Figure 23–4 shows the view.

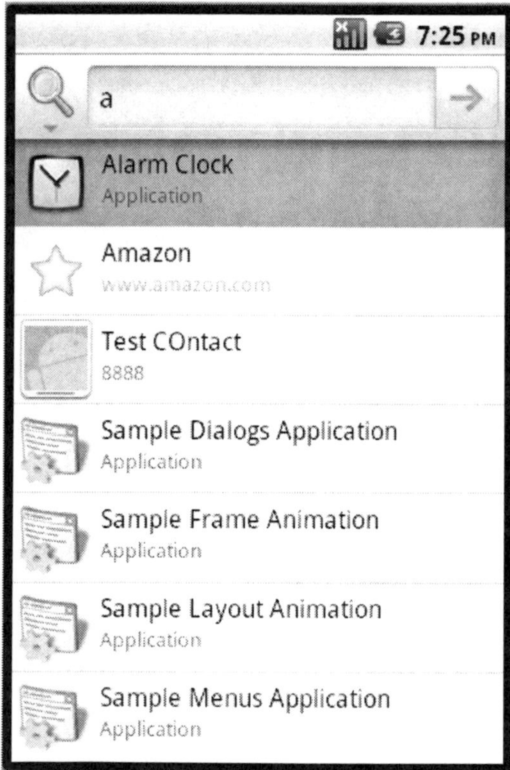

Figure 23–4. *Search suggestions*

Notice that the first suggestion is highlighted and the focus has shifted from QSB to the first highlighted suggestion. Click the arrow on the right side of the QSB to proceed with the search. Android also expanded the screen to full screen by removing the soft keyboard, because you will not be typing when you navigate. The expanded screen size shows you more suggestions as well.

But let's look at suggestions one more time. Android takes the search text that has been typed so far and looks for what are called *suggestion providers*. Android calls each suggestion provider asynchronously to retrieve a set of matching suggestions as a set of rows. Android expects that these rows (called *search suggestions*) conform to a set of predefined columns (*suggestion columns*). By exploring these well-known columns, Android will paint the suggestion list. When the search text changes, Android repeats the process all over again. This interaction of calling all suggestion providers for search suggestions is true for the "search all" context. However, if you were to choose a specific search application context from Figure 23–3 only the suggestion provider that is defined for that application will be invoked to retrieve search suggestions.

> **NOTE:** The set of search suggestions is also called the *suggestions cursor*. This is because the content provider representing the suggestion provider returns a `cursor` object.

At this point, if you were to navigate back to the QSB, Android would bring back the soft keyboard. Another thing to notice in Figure 23–4 is the relationship between the highlighted suggestion and the search text in the QSB. The search text remains "a" even though the highlighted suggestion is pointing to a specific item such as the Alarm Clock application. This is not always the case, however, as you can see in Figure 23–5, where we have navigated to a suggestion entry pointing Amazon.

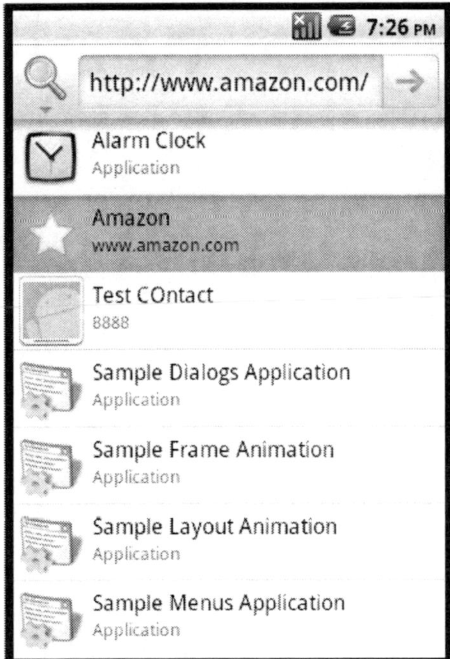

Figure 23–5. *Suggestion rewriting*

Notice how the search text "a" is replaced by a whole URL representing Amazon. Now you can either click on the arrow (which we'll call the Go Arrow) to go to Amazon, or simply click on the highlighted suggestion. Both have the same result.

> **NOTE:** This process of modifying the search text based on the highlighted suggestion is called *suggestion rewriting.*

We will talk about suggestion rewriting in greater detail a bit later, but briefly, Android uses one of the columns in the suggestion cursor to look for this text. If that column exists, it will rewrite the search text; otherwise it will leave the entered search text as it is.

When a suggestion is not rewritten, there are two possibilities. If you click the Go Arrow icon in the QSB it will search Google for that search text irrespective of what is highlighted. If you click the suggestion item directly it will call an activity called a *search activity* in the application that put up the suggestion to begin with. This search activity is then responsible for displaying the results of the search.

Figure 23–6 is an example of directly invoking a suggestion. In this example, the suggestion is an application called `Alarm Clock`. When you click it, Android will invoke that application directly. How this actually happens is a bit involved, and we will go through later in this chapter (see the section "Implementing a Custom Suggestions Provider").

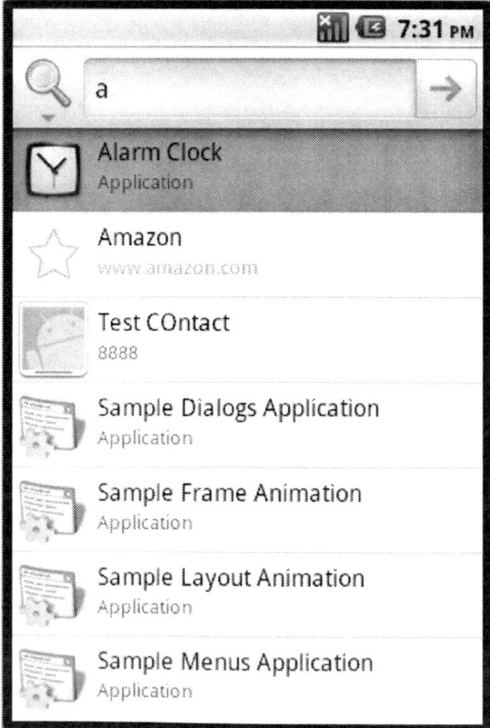

Figure 23–6. *Invoking an application through Search*

Figure 23–7 shows what happens if you click the Go Arrow when your search text is "a."

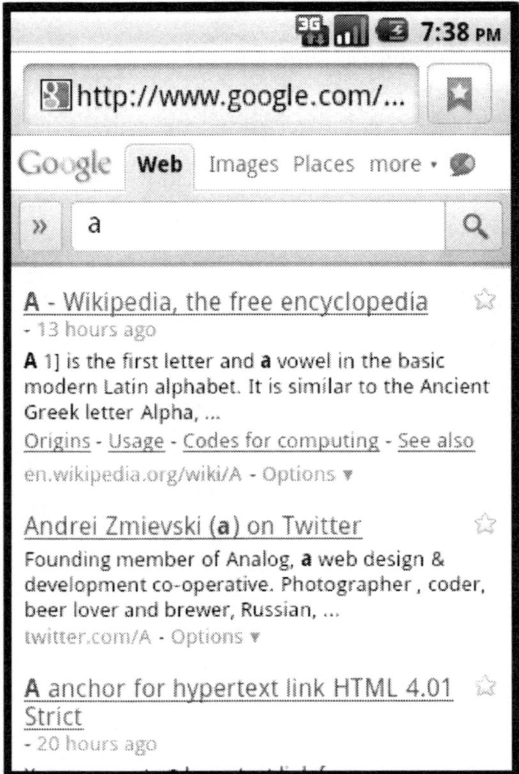

Figure 23–7. *Searching the Web*

Now that you are familiar with using the QSB for your searching needs, in the next part of our tour we will explain how to enable or disable specific applications from participating in global search.

Enabling Suggestion Providers for Global Search

As we have already pointed out, applications use suggestion providers to respond to searches. Just because your application has the infrastructure necessary to respond to searches doesn't mean your suggestions will show up in the QSB automatically. A user will need to explicitly allow your suggestion provider to participate. We will now walk you through the process of enabling or disabling available suggestion providers. The way you get to the settings that follow is slightly different between Android releases 2.2 and 2.3. We will cover 2.2 first.

Working with Search Settings in Android Release 2.2

Let's start with the screen that will take us to the Android settings (Figure 23–8).

Figure 23–8. *Locating the settings application*

You can reach this view by clicking on the List of Applications icon at the bottom of the device screen (see Figure 23–1 for the home screen). Use your arrow down key to navigate to the application that is named `Settings`, as shown in Figure 23–8. This will take you to the Android settings page, which looks like Figure 23–9.

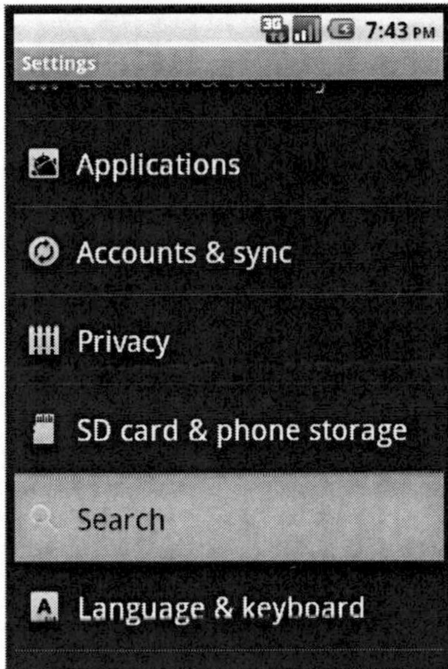

Figure 23–9. *Getting to the settings of the Searc" application*

Among the many Android settings, choose the Search (Manage search settings and history) option. This will bring you to the Search settings application shown in Figure 23–10.

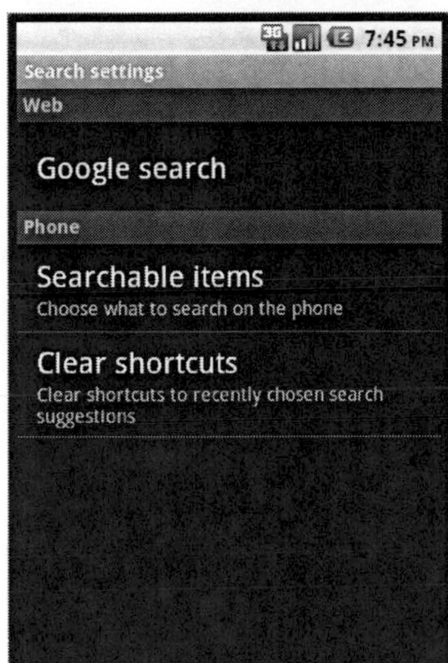

Figure 23–10. *Search settings application*

In this activity, look for the tab called Quick Search Box and choose Searchable items (Choose what to search on the phone). This will show a list of available suggestion providers (sometimes also referred as search applications), as shown in Figure 23–11. Again this list may vary from release to release.

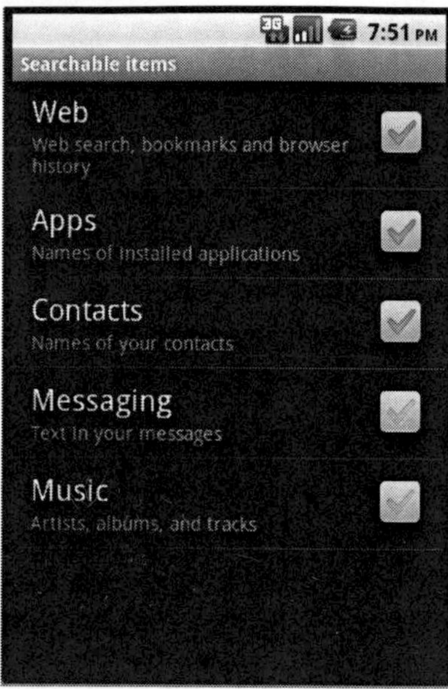

Figure 23–11. *Enabled/disabled search applications*

Suggestion providers (or the applications of which they are a part) that are included in global search are selected in Figure 23–11. By default, a new suggestion provider or search application is not selected. You can click on a suggestion provider to enable it for search. When it is enabled this suggestion provider will offer suggestions to the global search. The enabled suggestion provider will also show up in the list of searchable applications in Figure 23–3.

Working with Search Settings in Android Release 2.3

When you are looking to discover suggestion provider settings the difference between Android releases 2.2 and 2.3 (and hopefully future a future phone SDK release) is how you get to the search settings screen of Figure 23–10 or 23–11.

In Android release 2.3 you can directly reach figure 23–11 from the expanded search categories screen of Figure 23–2. In Android release 2.3 this figure 23–2 has a small settings icon on it. If you click this icon you will be directly taken to Figure 23–11 where you will see your custom search activities.

To get to the general search settings screen of Figure 23–10 you will need to revisit screen of Figure 23–2 or 23–3 or 23–4. Essentially you clicked on QSB. While the focus is with the QSB if you click the Menu button you will see a menu item called "Search Settings." If you click this menu item you will be taken to the general search settings of Figure 23–10. Once you are at this screen the instructions to work with the settings are same as those for Android release 2.2.

So far, we've given you a high-level view of how search works in Android. Next we will explore these ideas further and show you how all this works through examples. We'll start by exploring how simple activities interact with search.

Activities and Search Key Interaction

What happens when a user clicks on the search key when an activity is in focus? The answer depends on the type of activity that is in focus. We will explore behavior for the following types of activities:

- A regular activity that is unaware of search
- An activity that explicitly disables search
- An activity that invokes global search explicitly
- An activity that specifies a local search

We will explore these options by a working sample containing the following files (after going through each of them we will show you the screens from this application to demonstrate the concepts).

The primary Java files are

- `RegularActivity.java (Listing 23-1)`
- `NoSearchActivity.java (Listing 23-6)`
- `SearchInvokerActivity.java (Listing 23-8)`
- `LocalSearchEnabledActivity.java (Listing 23-13)`
- `SearchActivity.java (Listing 23-11)`

Each of these files, except the last one (`SearchActivity.java`), represents each type of activity that we want to examine as mentioned above. The last file, `SearchActivity.java`, is needed by the `LocalSearchEnabledActivity`. Each of these activities, including the `SearchActivity` has a simple layout with a text view in it. Each is supported by the following layout files:

- `res/layout/main.xml` (for the RegularActivity) (Listing 23–3)
- `res/layout/no_search_activity.xml Listing 23-7)`
- `res/layout/search_invoker_activity.xml (Listing 23-9)`
- `res/layout/local_search_enabled_activity.xml (Listing 23-14)`
- `res/layout/search_activity.xml (part of listing 23-11)`

The following two files define these activities to Android and also search metadata for the one local search activity:

- `AndroidManifest.xml (Listing 23-2)`
- `xml/searchable.xml (Listing 23-12)`

The following file contains the text commentary for each of the layouts:

- res/values/strings.xml (Listing 23-4)

The following two menu files provide menus needed to invoke the activities and also global search where needed:

- res/menu/main_menu.xml (Listing 23-5)
- res/menu/search_invoker_menu.xml (Listing 23-10)

We will now explore the interaction between activities and the search key by methodically walking through the source code of these files by each activity type.

> **NOTE:** If you would like to compile and test these files, we recommend you to download the importable Eclipse projects for this chapter from the URL provided at the end of this chapter.

Let us start to explore the behavior of search key in the presence of a regular Android activity.

Behavior of Search Key on a Regular Activity

To test what happens when an activity that is unaware of search is in focus we'll show you an example of a regular activity. Listing 23–1 shows the java source code representing this RegularActivity.

Listing 23–1. *Regular Activity Source Code*

```
//filename: RegularActivity.java
public class RegularActivity extends Activity
{
    private final String tag = "RegularActivity";

    @Override
     public void onCreate(Bundle savedInstanceState) {
       super.onCreate(savedInstanceState);
       setContentView(R.layout.main);
    }

    @Override
    public boolean onCreateOptionsMenu(Menu menu)
    {
       //call the parent to attach any system level menus
       super.onCreateOptionsMenu(menu);
       MenuInflater inflater = getMenuInflater();
       //getMenuInflater() is from base activity

       inflater.inflate(R.menu.main_menu, menu);
       return true;
    }

    @Override
    public boolean onOptionsItemSelected(MenuItem item)
    {
```

```
    appendMenuItemText(item);
    if (item.getItemId() == R.id.menu_clear) {
        this.emptyText();
        return true;
    }

    if (item.getItemId() == R.id.mid_no_search) {
        this.invokeNoSearchActivity();
        return true;
    }
    if (item.getItemId() == R.id.mid_local_search) {
        this.invokeLocalSearchActivity();
        return true;
    }
    if (item.getItemId() == R.id.mid_invoke_search) {
        this.invokeSearchInvokerActivity();
            return true;
    }
    return true;
}

private TextView getTextView()
{
    return (TextView)this.findViewById(R.id.text1);
}

private void appendMenuItemText(MenuItem menuItem)
{
    String title = menuItem.getTitle().toString();
    TextView tv = getTextView();
    tv.setText(tv.getText() + "\n" + title);
}
private void emptyText()
{
    TextView tv = getTextView();
    tv.setText("");
}
private void invokeNoSearchActivity()
{
    //Uncomment the following two lines when you
    //you add this activity to your project

    //Intent intent =
    //    new Intent(this,NoSearchActivity.class);
    //startActivity(intent);
}
private void invokeSearchInvokerActivity()
{
    //Uncomment the following two lines when you
    //you add this activity to your project

    //Intent intent =
    //    new Intent(this,SearchInvokerActivity.class);
    //startActivity(intent);
}
private void invokeLocalSearchActivity()
{
```

```
        //Uncomment the following two lines when you
        //you add this activity to your project

        //Intent intent =
        //  new Intent(this,LocalSearchEnabledActivity.class);
        //startActivity(intent);
    }
}
```

The goal of this activity is to play the role of a simple activity that is unaware of search. In this example, however, this activity also works as the driver to invoke other activity types that we would like to test. This is why you see some menu items being introduced to represent these additional activities. Each function that starts with `invoke...` has code to start the other type of activities that we want to test.

We will present the necessary files to compile this code in quick order. However, you may want to comment out the "invoke..." functions or include listings for those classes as well at this time. For your benefit we have already commented out these lines.

Let us take a look at the manifest file to see how this activity is defined (see Listing 23–2). You can also see the definition of other activities here, although they will not be explained until later. Again we have commented out those additional activities until a later time when they are needed.

Listing 23–2. ***Activity/Search Key Interaction: Manifest file***

```
//filename: AndroidManifest.xml
<manifest
   xmlns:android="http://schemas.android.com/apk/res/android"
   package="com.androidbook.search.nosearch">
<application android:icon="@drawable/icon"
      android:label="Test Activity QSB Interaction">
      <activity android:name=".RegularActivity"
        android:label="Activity/QSB Interaction:Regular Activity">
          <intent-filter>
            <action android:name="android.intent.action.MAIN" />
            <category android:name="android.intent.category.LAUNCHER" />
          </intent-filter>
      </activity>

<!-- Uncomment the following activities as you create them.
    We will indicate when you need to uncomment each activity

      <activity android:name=".NoSearchActivity"
         android:label="Activity/QSB Interaction::Disabled Search">
      </activity>

       <activity android:name=".SearchInvokerActivity"
          android:label="Activity/QSB Interaction::Search Invoker">
      </activity>

      <activity android:name=".LocalSearchEnabledActivity"
         android:label="Activity/QSB Interaction::Local Search">
           <meta-data android:name="android.app.default_searchable"
              android:value=".SearchActivity" />
      </activity>
```

```
        <activity android:name=".SearchActivity"
            android:label="Activity/QSB Interaction::Search Results">
            <intent-filter>
              <action android:name="android.intent.action.SEARCH"/>
              <category android:name="android.intent.category.DEFAULT"/>
            </intent-filter>
            <meta-data android:name="android.app.searchable"
                android:resource="@xml/searchable" />
        </activity>
-->
</application>
<uses-sdk android:minSdkVersion="4" />
</manifest>
```

Notice that the RegularActivity is defined as the main activity for this project and has no other characteristics related to search.

The layout file for this activity is shown in Listing 23–3.

Listing 23–3. *Regular Activity Layout File*

```
//filename: layout/main.xml
<?xml version="1.0" encoding="utf-8"?>
<LinearLayout
    xmlns:android="http://schemas.android.com/apk/res/android"
    android:orientation="vertical"
    android:layout_width="fill_parent"
    android:layout_height="fill_parent"
    >
<TextView
    android:id="@+id/text1"
    android:layout_width="fill_parent"
    android:layout_height="wrap_content"
    android:text="@string/regular_activity_prompt"
    />
</LinearLayout>
```

Now we'll show you the string resources used by this project. Listing 23–4 contains string resources for other activities of this project as well. However, these additional string resources should not interfere with compilation of the current activity, even if you haven't introduced the other activities.

With that, Listing 23–4 shows the strings.xml that is responsible for the text you will see on this activity's display. The individual string resources related to each activity are highlighted and commented.

Listing 23–4. *Activity/Search Key Interaction: strings.xml*

```
//filename: /res/values/strings.xml
<?xml version="1.0" encoding="utf-8"?>
<resources>
<!--
*************************************************
* regular_activity_prompt
*************************************************
-->
    <string name="regular_activity_prompt">
```

```
    This is a sample application to test how QSB and Search Key
    interacts with activities. This application has 4 activities
    including this one. The activity you are looking at is
    called a Regular Activity and is one of 4. The other three
    you can access through the menu.
    \n\n
    This activity is a regular activity that is unaware of
    any search capabilities. If you click search key now
    it will NOT invoke the global search.
    \n
    \nThe other activities demonstrate:`
    \n\n1) No search Activity: An activity that disables search
    \n2) Invoke search: programatically invoke global search
    \n3) Local Search Activity: Invoke Local Search
    \n
    \nYour debug will appear here
    </string>

<!--
**************************************************
* no_search_activity_prompt
**************************************************
-->
    <string name="no_search_activity_prompt">
    In this activity the onSearchRequested
    returns a false. The search button
    should be ignored now.
    \n
    \nYou can click back now to access the
    previous activity and use the menus again
    to choose other activities.
    </string>
<!--
**************************************************
* search_activity_prompt
**************************************************
-->
<string name="search_activity_prompt">
This is called a search activity or search results activity.
This activity is invoked by clicking on the search key when
some other activity uses this activity as its
search results activity.
\n\n
Typically you can retrieve the query string
from the intent to see what the query is.
</string>
<!--
**************************************************
* search_invoker_activity_prompt
**************************************************
-->
<string name="search_invoker_activity_prompt">
In this activity a search menu item is used
to invoke the default search. In this case
as there is no local search for this activity
specified global search is invoked. Use the
menu button to see the "search" menu. when you
```

```
click on that search menu you will see the
global search.
</string>
<!--
*************************************************
* local_search_enabled_activity_prompt
*************************************************
-->
<string name="local_search_enabled_activity_prompt">
This is a very simple activity that has indicated through
the manifest file that there is a an associated search
activity. With this association when the search key is
pressed the local search is presented instead of global.
\n\n
You can see the local nature of it by looking at the
label of the QSB and also the hint in the QSB. Both
came from the search metadata.
\n\n
Once you click on the query icon, it will transfer
you to the local search activity.
</string>
<!--
*************************************************
* Other values
*************************************************
-->
   <string name="search_label">Local Search Demo</string>
   <string name="search_hint">Local Search Demo Hint</string>
</resources>
```

Like the Android manifest, this single `strings.xml` is serving all of the activities in this project. You can see that the string constant named `regular_activity` in the `strings.xml` is pointing to the text you will see on the regular activity.

To assist the compilation of the regular activity let us present now the menu resource file in Listing 23–5. Although this menu file contains menu items for other activities yet to be introduced, it won't interfere with compiles and assists in having the regular activity of Listing 23–1 compiled.

Listing 23–5. *Regular Activity Menu File*

```
<menu xmlns:android="http://schemas.android.com/apk/res/android">
<!-- filename: /res/menu/main_menu.xml →
    <!-- This group uses the default category. -->
    <group android:id="@+id/menuGroup_Main">
        <item android:id="@+id/mid_no_search"
            android:title="No Search Activity" />

        <item android:id="@+id/mid_local_search"
            android:title="Local Search Activity" />

        <item android:id="@+id/mid_invoke_search"
            android:title="Search Invoker Activity" />

        <item android:id="@+id/menu_clear"
            android:title="clear" />
    </group>
```

```
</menu>
```

With these files in place, you should be able to compile and test this activity (or you can wait until we have looked at all the activities for this project). If you would like to compile now, you will need to keep the rest of activities commented out in listings 23-1 and 23-2. Or you can use the listings identified at the beginning of this sample to compile the entire application first and then follow along.

When you finish compiling the application and run the main regular activity we introduced, the layout should look like Figure 23–12.

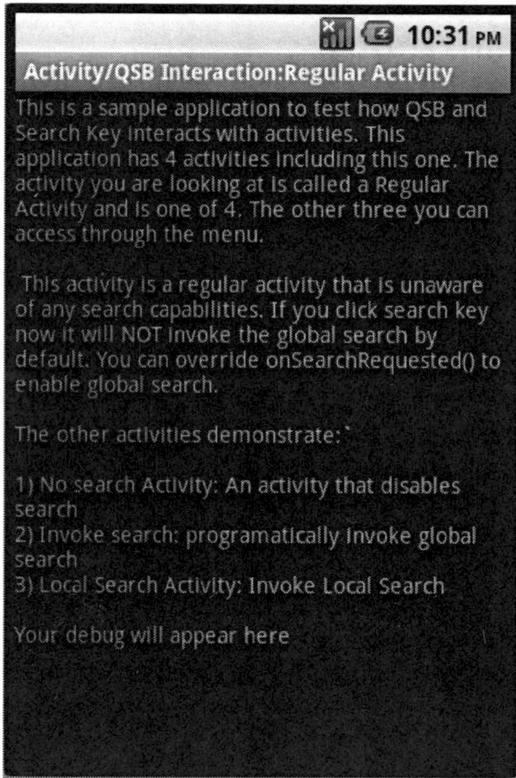

Figure 23–12. *Regular activity/search interaction*

Listing 23–5 shows the menu XML file that is used for the regular activity. You can see this menu in action in Figure 23–13.

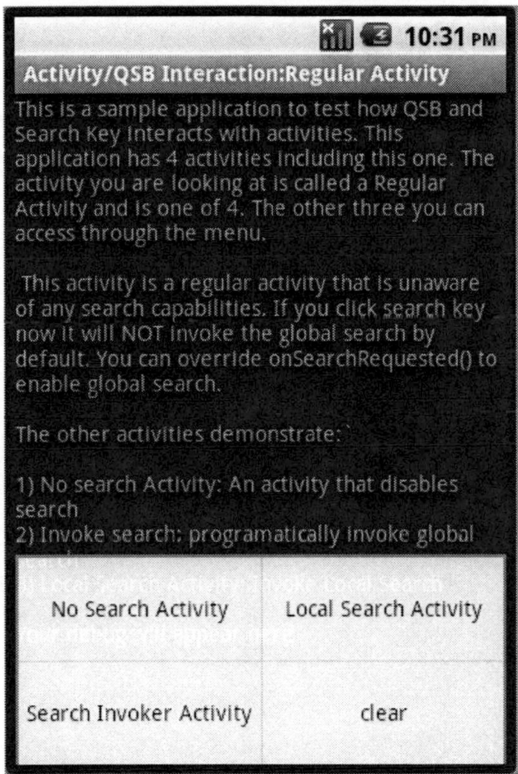

Figure 23–13. *Accessing other test activities*

Now, when you have this activity running (as in Figure 23–12) click the search key (see Figure 23–1 to locate the search key). The documentation indicates that this should invoke the global search dialog.

In releases prior to 2.0 the search key was bringing the global search in response. In releases 2.2 and 2.3 pressing the search key does not bring up the global search.

If you want to force this regular activity to allow global search instead it needs to override the onSearchRequested() and do the following:

```
@Override
public boolean onSearchRequested()
{
  Log.d(tag,"onsearch request called");
  this.startSearch("test",true,null,true);
  return true;
}
```

With this code in place in the `ReqularActivity.java`, you can press the search key and it will invoke the global search. The method “startSearch()” and its arguments are covered later in the chapter. This global search will look just like the global search in Figure 23-2.

Behavior of an Activity that Disables Search

An activity has the option to entirely disable the search (both global and local) by returning false from the onSearchRequested() callback method of the activity class. Listing 23–6 shows the source code for such an activity, which we named "NoSearchActivity".

Listing 23–6. *Activity-disabling Search*

```
//filename: NoSearchActivity.java
public class NoSearchActivity extends Activity
{
    @Override
    protected void onCreate(Bundle savedInstanceState) {
        super.onCreate(savedInstanceState);
        setContentView(R.layout.no_search_activity);
        return;
    }
   @Override
    public boolean onSearchRequested()
    {
       return false;
    }
}
```

Listing 23–7 shows the corresponding layout file for this activity.

Listing 23–7. *NoSearchActivity XML File*

```
//filename: layout/no_search_activity.xml
<?xml version="1.0" encoding="utf-8"?>
<LinearLayout
    xmlns:android="http://schemas.android.com/apk/res/android"
    android:orientation="vertical"
    android:layout_width="fill_parent"
    android:layout_height="fill_parent"
    >
<TextView
    android:id="@+id/text1"
    android:layout_width="fill_parent"
    android:layout_height="wrap_content"
    android:text="@string/no_search_activity_prompt"
    />
</LinearLayout>
```

With these two files in place (Listing 23–6 and 23–7), you need to uncomment a couple sections in the following two files:

```
RegularActivity.java (Listing 23-1)
AndroidManifest.xml (Listing 23-2)
```

In the RegularActivity.java file (Listing 23–1), uncomment the java code in the body of the function "invokeNoSearchActivity()".

In the AndroidManifest.xml (Listing 23–2) uncomment the activity definition for NoSearchActivity. Notice that this is an XML file. How you comment and uncomment an XML file differs from uncommenting Java code.

Once you complete these two uncommenting tasks you will be able to compile the project again. Now you can invoke this `NoSearchActivity` by clicking the menu item No Search Activity in Figure 23–13.

When displayed, this activity will look like that shown in Figure 23–14. Now if you press the search key, it will not have any impact; you will not see anything happen.

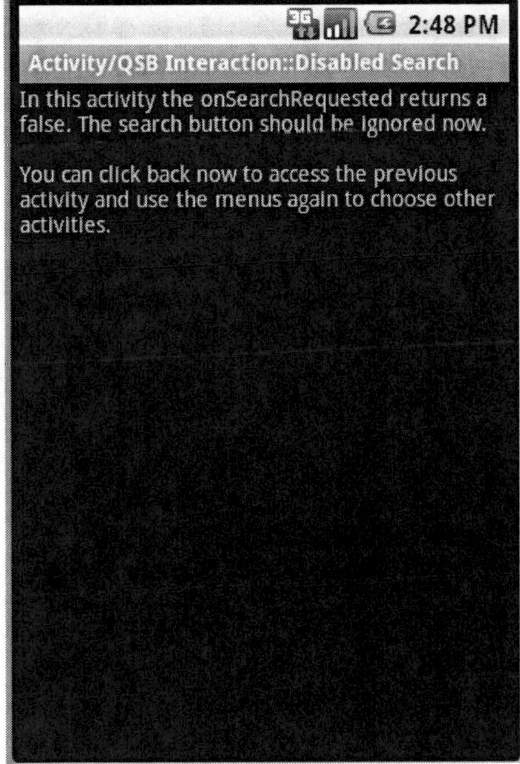

Figure 23–14. *Disabled search activity*

> **TIP:** When there is an activity that disables search, clicking the search key does not result in the invocation of search both local and global.

Explicitly Invoking Search Through a Menu

In addition to being able to respond to the search key, an activity can also choose to explicitly invoke search through a search menu item. Listing 23–8 shows the source code for an example activity (`SearchInvokerActivity`) that does this.

Listing 23–8. *SearchInvokerActivity*

```
//filename: SearchInvokerActivity.java
public class SearchInvokerActivity extends Activity
```

```
{
    @Override
    public void onCreate(Bundle savedInstanceState) {
        super.onCreate(savedInstanceState);
        setContentView(R.layout.search_invoker_activity);
    }

    @Override
    public boolean onCreateOptionsMenu(Menu menu)
    {
       super.onCreateOptionsMenu(menu);
       MenuInflater inflater = getMenuInflater();
       inflater.inflate(R.menu.search_invoker_menu, menu);
       return true;
    }

    @Override
    public boolean onOptionsItemSelected(MenuItem item)
    {
       appendMenuItemText(item);
       if (item.getItemId() == R.id.mid_si_clear)
       {
          this.emptyText();
          return true;
       }
       if (item.getItemId() == R.id.mid_si_search)
       {
          this.invokeSearch();
          return true;
       }
       return true;
    }

    private TextView getTextView()
    {
        return (TextView)this.findViewById(R.id.text1);
    }

    private void appendMenuItemText(MenuItem menuItem)
    {
       String title = menuItem.getTitle().toString();
       TextView tv = getTextView();
       tv.setText(tv.getText() + "\n" + title);
    }
    private void emptyText()
    {
          TextView tv = getTextView();
          tv.setText("");
    }
    private void invokeSearch()
    {
       this.onSearchRequested();
    }
    @Override
    public boolean onSearchRequested()
    {
        this.startSearch("test",true,null,true);
```

```
        return true;
    }
}
```

Key portions of source code are highlighted in bold. Notice how a menu ID (R.id.mid_si_search) is calling the function invokeSearch, which will in turn call the onSearchRequested(). This method, onSearchRequested(), invokes the search.

The base method "startSearch" has the following arguments

initialQuery: Text to search for.

selectInitialQuery: A boolean indicating whether to highlight the search text or not. In this case we used "true" to hightlight the text so that it can deleted in favor of a new text if desired.

appSearchData: A bundle object to pass to the search activity. In our case, we are not targeting any particular search activity we passed null.

globalSearch: If it is true, the global search is invoked. If it is false, a local search is invoked if available; otherwise a global search is invoked.

SDK documentation recommends to call the base onSearchRequested() unlike what we have shown in Listing 23–8. However, the default onSearchRequested() is using false for the last argument of startSearch(). According to the documentation this should invoke the global search if no local search is available. However, in this release (both 2.2 and 2.3) the global search is not being invoked. This could either be a bug or designed that way and requiring a documentation update.

In this example we have forced a global search by passing true to this last argument of startSearch().

Listing 23–9 shows the layout for this activity.

Listing 23–9. ***SearchInvokerActivity XML***

```
//filename: layout/search_invoker_activity.xml
<?xml version="1.0" encoding="utf-8"?>
<LinearLayout
    xmlns:android="http://schemas.android.com/apk/res/android"
    android:orientation="vertical"
    android:layout_width="fill_parent"
    android:layout_height="fill_parent"
    >
<TextView
   android:id="@+id/text1"
    android:layout_width="fill_parent"
    android:layout_height="wrap_content"
    android:text="@string/search_invoker_activity_prompt"
    />
</LinearLayout>
```

Listing 23–10 shows the corresponding menu XML for this activity.

Listing 23–10. *SearchInvokerActivity Menu XML*

```
//filename:menu/search_invoker_menu.xml
<menu xmlns:android="http://schemas.android.com/apk/res/android">
    <!-- This group uses the default category. -->
    <group android:id="@+id/menuGroup_Main">
        <item android:id="@+id/mid_si_search"
            android:title="Search" />

        <item android:id="@+id/mid_si_clear"
            android:title="clear" />
    </group>
</menu>
```

With these three files in place (Listing 23–8, 23–9, 23–10) you need to uncomment a couple sections in the following two files:

```
RegularActivity.java (Listing 23-1)
AndroidManifest.xml (Listing 23-2)
```

In the `RegularActivity.java` file (Listing 23–1) uncomment the java code in the body of the function “`invokeSearchInvokerActivity()`.”

In the `AndroidManifest.xml` (Listing 23–2) uncomment the activity definition for `SearchInvokerActivity`. Once you complete these two uncommenting tasks you will be able to compile the project again.

With the layout and menu in place, Figure 23–15 shows how this activity looks when invoked from the main menu on the `RegularActivity` (see Figure 23–13 for the menu item `Search Invoker Activity` that invokes this).

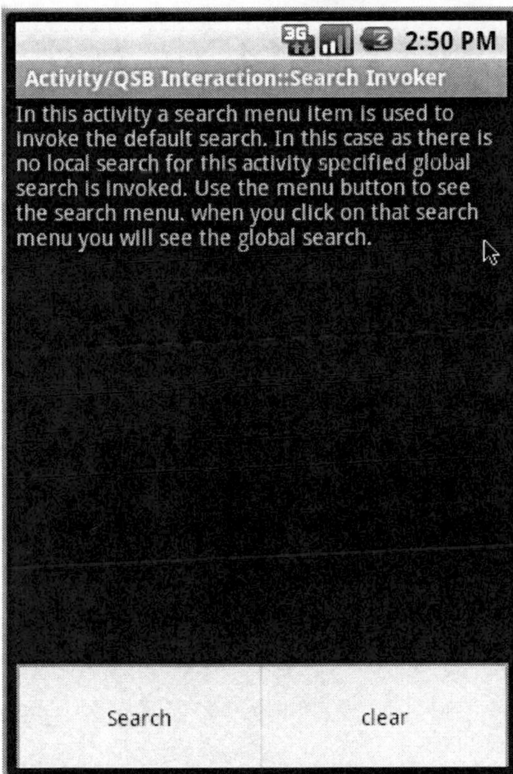

Figure 23–15. *Search invoker activity*

From this activity, if you click the Search menu option it will invoke the familiar global search QSB, as shown in Figure 23–2. As we have also overridden the "onSearchRequested()" from the base activity, the device Search Key will bring up the global QSB as well.

Understanding Local Search and Related Activities

Now let's look at the circumstances under which the search key will *not* invoke a global search, but instead invoke a local search. But first, we have to explain local search a bit further.

A local search has three components. The first component is a search box that is very similar, if not the same, as the global search QSB. This QSB, whether local or global, provides text control to enter text and a search icon to click. A local QSB is typically invoked instead of the global one when an activity declares in the manifest file that it wants a local search. You can distinguish the invoked local QSB from the global one by looking at the heading of the QSB (see the title of a future Figure 23–18) and the hint (the text inside the search box) in the QSB. These two values, as you will see, come from a search metadata XML file.

The second component of local search is an activity that can receive the search string from the local QSB and show a set of results or any output that is related to the search text. Often this activity is called the search activity or search results activity.

The optional third component of local search is an activity that is allowed to invoke the search results activity just described (the second component). This invoking activity is often called search invoker or search invoking activity. This search invoker activity is optional because it is possible to have the global search directly invoke the local search activity (the second component) through a suggestion.

You can see these three components and how they interact with each other in context in Figure 23–16.

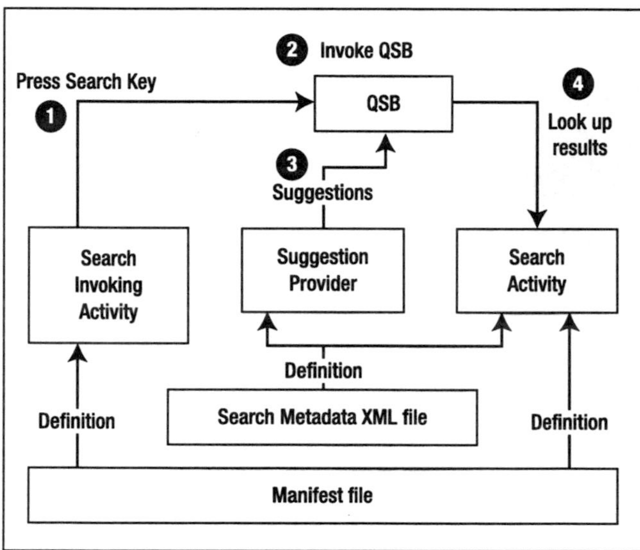

Figure 23–16. *Local search activity interaction*

In Figure 23–16 important interactions are shown as annotated (circled numbers) arrows. Here's a more detailed explanation:

- A `SearchActivity` needs to be defined in the manifest file as an activity that is capable of receiving search requests. `SearchActivity` also uses a mandatory XML file to declare how the local QSB should be presented (such as with a title, hint, and so on) and if there is an associated suggestion provider. (See Listing 23–12). In Figure 23–16 you can see this as a couple of "Definition" lines that go between the `SearchActivity` and the two XML files (manifest file and the search metadata file).
- Once the `SearchActivity` is defined in the manifest file (see Listing 23–2), the `Search InvokingActivity` indicates in the manifest file that it is associated with the `SearchActivity` through a metadata definition `android.app.default_searchable`.

- With the definitions for both activities in place, when the SearchInvokingActivity is in focus, the press of the search key will invoke the local QSB. You can see this in Figure 23–16 – the circles numbered 1 and 2. You can tell that the invoked QSB is a local QSB by looking at the caption and hint of the QSB. These two values are set up in the mandatory search metadata XML definition. Once QSB is invoked through the search key, you will be able to type query text in the QSB. This local QSB, similar to the global QSB, is capable of suggestions. You can see this in Figure 23–16 (circle 3).
- Once the query text is entered and the search icon is clicked, the local QSB will transfer the search to the SearchActivity which is responsible for doing something with it, such as displaying a set of results. This is shown in Figure 23–16 (circle 4).

We will examine each of these interactions by looking at the source code. We will start with Listing 23–11, the source code for SearchActivity, (which, again, is responsible for receiving the query and displaying search results).

Listing 23–11. ***SearchActivity and Its Layout File***

```
//filename: SearchActivity.java
public class SearchActivity extends Activity
{
    @Override
    protected void onCreate(Bundle savedInstanceState) {
        super.onCreate(savedInstanceState);
        setContentView(R.layout.search_activity);
        return;
    }
}

//And the corresponding res/layout/search_activity.xml

<?xml version="1.0" encoding="utf-8"?>
<LinearLayout
   xmlns:android="http://schemas.android.com/apk/res/android"
    android:orientation="vertical"
    android:layout_width="fill_parent"
    android:layout_height="fill_parent"
    >
<TextView
    android:id="@+id/text1"
    android:layout_width="fill_parent"
    android:layout_height="wrap_content"
    android:text="@string/search_activity_prompt"
    />
</LinearLayout>
```

We took a simplest possible search activity. Later you'll see how queries are retrieved by this activity. For now we will show how this activity ends up being invoked by the QSB. Here is how it is defined as a search activity responsible for results in the manifest file (see Listing 23–2):

```
<activity android:name=".SearchActivity"
```

```
    android:label="Activity/QSB Interaction::Search Results">
      <intent-filter>
         <action android:name="android.intent.action.SEARCH"/>
         <category android:name="android.intent.category.DEFAULT"/>
       </intent-filter>
      <meta-data android:name="android.app.searchable"
                        android:resource="@xml/searchable"/>
</activity>
```

> **NOTE:** There are two things that need to be specified for a search activity. The activity needs to indicate that it can respond to SEARCH actions. It also needs to specify an xml file that describes the metadata that is required to interact with this search activity.

Listing 23–12 shows the search metadata XML file for this `SearchActivity`.

Listing 23–12. ***Searchable.xml: Search Metadata***

```
<!-- /res/xml/searchable.xml -->
<searchable xmlns:android="http://schemas.android.com/apk/res/android"
    android:label="@string/search_label"
    android:hint="@string/search_hint"
    android:searchMode="showSearchLabelAsBadge"
/>
```

> **TIP:** The various options available in this XML are documented in the SDK at `http://developer.android.com/reference/android/app/SearchManager.html`.

We will cover more of these attributes later in the chapter. For now, the attribute `android:label` is used to label the search box. The attribute `android:hint` is used to place the text in the search box, similar to what's shown in Figure 23–18.

Now let's examine how an activity can specify this `SearchActivity` as its search. We will call this the `LocalSearchEnabledActivity`. Listing 23–13 shows the source code for this activity.

Listing 23–13. ***LocalSearchEnabledActivity***

```
//filename: LocalSearchEnabledActivity.java
public class LocalSearchEnabledActivity extends Activity
{
    @Override
    protected void onCreate(Bundle savedInstanceState) {
        super.onCreate(savedInstanceState);
        setContentView(R.layout.local_search_enabled_activity);
        return;
    }
}
```

Listing 23–14 shows the corresponding `layout xml` file for this activity.

Listing 23–14. ***LocalSearchEnabledActivity Layout File***

```
<?xml version="1.0" encoding="utf-8"?>
<!-- filename: layout/local_search_enabled_activity.xml -->
<LinearLayout
  xmlns:android="http://schemas.android.com/apk/res/android"
    android:orientation="vertical"
    android:layout_width="fill_parent"
    android:layout_height="fill_parent"
    >
<TextView
    android:id="@+id/text1"
    android:layout_width="fill_parent"
    android:layout_height="wrap_content"
    android:text="@string/local_search_enabled_activity_prompt"
    />
</LinearLayout>
```

Also notice how this `LocalSearchEnabledActivity` (Listing 23–13) is targeting the `SearchActivity` (Listing 23–11) as its target search activity. You can uncover this relationship by looking at the manifest file definition (Listing 23–2) for the `LocalSearchEnabledActivity`. Here is that definition replicated for quick browsing:

```
<activity android:name=".LocalSearchEnabledActivity"
   android:label="Activity/QSB Interaction::Local Search">
     <meta-data android:name="android.app.default_searchable"
         android:value=".SearchActivity" />
</activity>
```

It is time to review what new files we have presented so far so that you can test these two activities: `LocalSearchEnabledActivity` and the `SearchActivity`. These new files and their listing numbers are:

```
SearchActivity.java (Listing 23-11)
layoyut/search_activity.xml (presented as part of Listing 23-11)
res/xml/searchable.xml (Listing 23-12)
LocalSearchEnabledActivity.java (Listing 23-13)
local_search_enabled_activity (Listing 23-14)
```

With these files in place, you need to uncomment a couple sections in the following two files:

```
RegularActivity.java (Listing 23-1)
AndroidManifest.xml (Listing 23-2)
```

In the `RegularActivity.java` file (Listing 23–1) uncomment the java code in the body of the function "`invokeLocalSearchActivity()`."

In the `AndroidManifest.xml` (Listing 23–2) uncomment the activity definition for LocalSearchEanabledActivity and SearchActivity.

Once you complete these two uncommenting tasks, you will be able to compile the project again.

With these new activities and their layouts in place, you can invoke this `LocalSearchEnabledActivity` from the main `RegularActivity` by clicking the Local

Search Activity menu item (see Figure 23–13 to locate the menus). When invoked, this activity looks like Figure 23–17.

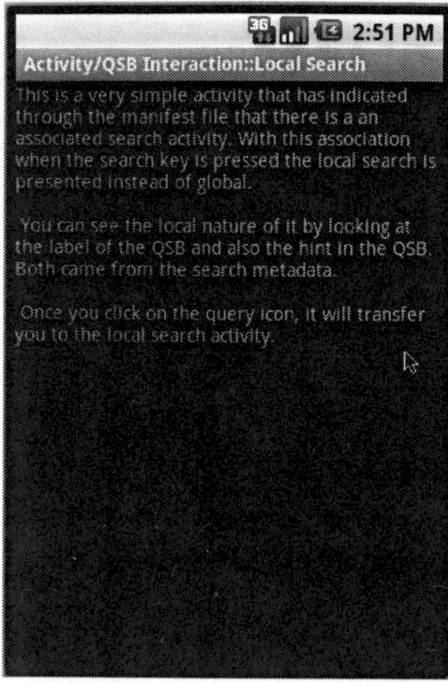

Figure 23–17. *Local search-enabled activity*

With this activity in focus, if you click on the device search it will invoke a local search box (local QSB), as shown in Figure 23–18.

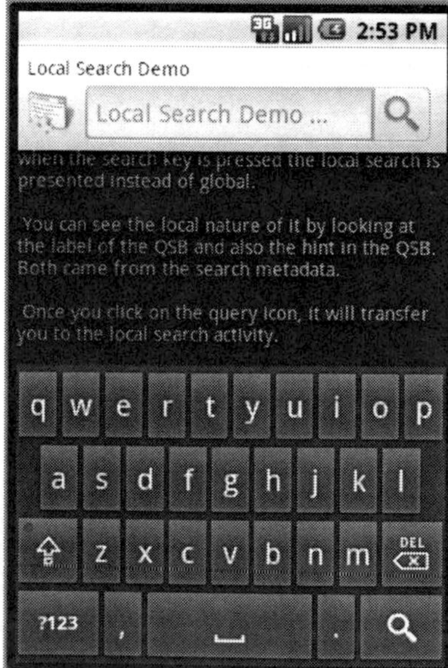

Figure 23–18. *Local Search QSB*

Notice the label of this search box and the hint of this search box. See how they differ from the global search (see Figure 23–2). The label and hint came from the search metadata (searchable.xml Listing 23–12) specified for the `SearchActivity.` Now if you type text in the QSB and click the search icon you will end up invoking the `SearchActivity` (see Listing 23–11). Here is what this `SearchActivity` looks like (Figure 23–19).

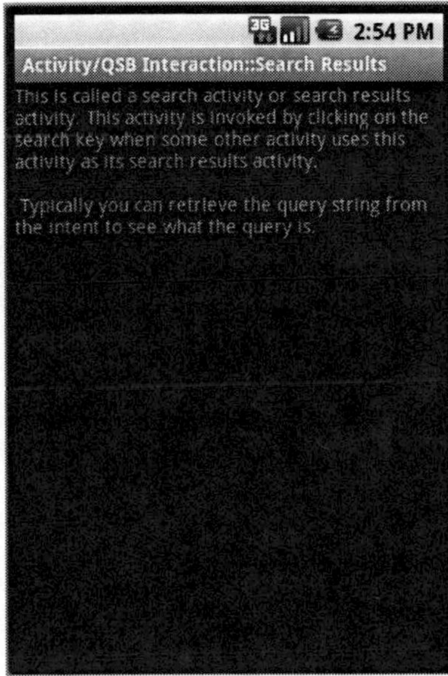

Figure 23–19. *Search results in response to the local search QSB*

Although this activity does not make use of any query search text to pull up results, it demonstrates how a search activity is defined and gets invoked. Later in the chapter we'll show how this `SearchActivity` makes use of search queries and various search-related actions to which it needs to respond.

Enabling Type-to-Search

So far we have explored a few ways of invoking search, both local and global. We have showed you how to search using QSB on the home page of the device. We have told you how to invoke global search from any activity as long as the activity doesn't prevent such a search. We have also showed you how an activity can specify local search. We will close this topic by showing one more way of invoking search called type-to-search.

When you are looking at an activity such as the `RegularActivity` shown in Figure 23–12 there is a way to invoke search by typing a random letter (such as "t," for example). This mode is called *type-to-search* because any key you type that is not handled by the activity will invoke search.

The intention of type-to-search is this. On any Android activity you can tell Android that any key press can invoke search—except for the keys that the activity explicitly handles.

For example, if an activity handles "x" and "y" but doesn't care about any other keys, the activity can choose to invoke the search for any other keys such as "z" or "a". This mode is useful for an activity that is already displaying search results. Such an activity can interpret a key press as a cue to start search again.

Here are a couple of lines of code you can use in `onCreate()` method of the activity to enable this behavior (the first line is used to invoke the global search and the second is used to invoke the local search):

```
this.setDefaultKeyMode(Activity.DEFAULT_KEYS_SEARCH_GLOBAL);
```

or

```
this.setDefaultKeyMode(Activity.DEFAULT_KEYS_SEARCH_LOCAL);
```

The invocation of the global search through this "type-to-search" mechanism doesn't seem to go through the `onSearchRequested()` route. These keys are directly invoking the global search. As a result, the `RegularActivity` we have in this example seem to invoke global search if we enable type to search. (If you recall, in our tests, the regular activity that doesn't explicitly enable or disable search failed to invoke global search if search key is pressed). You can test this type-to-search behavior by placing the following line at the end of the `onCreate()` method of the `RegularActivity` class (Listing 23–1)

```
this.setDefaultKeyMode(Activity.DEFAULT_KEYS_SEARCH_GLOBAL);
```

Then pressing a letter such as "t" in Figure 23–12 will invoke the global search.

This concludes our discussion of the various ways in which Android search interacts with activities and how to use search. We will now see how to participate in search and not just use it. We will implement a simple suggestion provider application that can provide search suggestions to a QSB, both local and global.

Implementing a Simple Suggestion Provider

This is a large chapter, so if you have been reading this chapter continuously thus far, take a break – as we are about to start another large body of text and will need your full attention.

We have indicated how suggestion providers are used to allow applications to participate in global search. We will now design and write a simple suggestion provider. You can create a simple suggestion provider using only a few lines by deriving from the prefabricated provider called `SearchRecentSuggestionsProvider`, which is available in the Android SDK.

We will start by explaining how a simple suggestion provider application is expected to work. We will give you the list of files that are used in the implementation. These files should give you a general idea of the application and what is involved in implementing it.

When you are writing a suggestion provider there are three main components. The first is a suggestion provider that is responsible for returning suggestions to Android search. The second is a search activity that takes a query or a suggestion and turns it into search results. The third is an XML file called search metadata, which is defined in the context of the search activity. We will describe the responsibilities of each of these components and show how they are implemented through source code.

But first, let us first plan our simple suggestions provider application.

Planning the Simple Suggestions Provider

Because we are planning on inheriting from the `SearchRecentSuggestionsProvider`, the functionality of the resulting suggestion provider is pretty fixed.

The `SearchRecentSuggestionsProvider` allows you to replay the queries as they are presented to the search activity from the QSB. Once these queries are saved by the search activity, they will be prompted back to the QSB through the suggestion provider as users type search letters or text in the QSB.

In the derived suggestion provider we initialize the base provider by indicating what portions of search text needs to be replayed. There is not much else we need to do there. We will also use a minimal search activity that is just a text view, to show that the search activity has been invoked. Inside the search activity we will show you the methods that are used to retrieve and save the queries so that they are available to the search provider.

Once the application is complete, our goal is to see the previous queries prompted as suggestions in the local and global QSB.

Now we'll show you the list of files that are used in the implementation of this project. You can also download importable projects for this chapter using the download URL at the end of this chapter.

Simple Suggestions Provider Implementation Files

The primary files that take part in the implementation of a suggestion provider application are `SearchActivity.java` , `SimpleSuggestionProvider.java`, and `searchable.xml` (search metadata). However, you will need a number of supporting files to complete the project. We will list all of these files first and briefly mention what each one does. We include the source code for all of the files as we explain the solution.

Let's start with java files first:

- `SimpleSuggestionProvider.java`: Implements the suggestion provider that we are talking about by inheriting from a base SDK provided suggestion provider. (Listing 23–15)
- `SearchActivity.java`: A mandatory file to work with the suggestion provider that receives search text to search and show search results. It is also responsible for saving the queries for the suggestion provider. (Listing 23–17)
- `SimpleMainActivity.java`: An activity to invoke local search and demonstrate local suggestions. (Listing 23–19)

Here are the corresponding layout files:

- `main.xml`: A layout file for the SimpleMainActivity (Part of Listing 23–19)
- `/res/layout/layout_search_activity.xml`: A layout file for the SearchActivity (Part of Listing 23–17)
- `/res/values/strings.xml`: The layout files use common string definitions from here (Part of Listing 23–19)

Here is the search metadata file.

- `/xml/searchable.xml`: This file is where the search activity is connected to the suggestion provider. (Listing 23–18)

Of course we need the manifest file as well:

- `AndroidManifest.xml`: This is where all application components are defined to Android. (Listing 23–16)

If you are planning on compiling this project from the source code presented in the book directly by copy/paste, we advise that you do so now with the files just mentioned by going to their listing numbers. Another method is to download the projects for this chapter using the link provided in the references at the end of this chapter.

Let us explore these files starting with the implementation of the `SimpleSuggestionProvider` class.

Implementing the SimpleSuggestionProvider class

In this simple suggestion provider project, the `SimpleSuggestionProvider` class acts as a suggestion provider by inheriting from the `SearchRecentSuggestionsProvider`. First let's look at the responsibilities of this simple suggestion provider.

Responsibilities of a Simple Suggestion Provider

Because the simple suggestion provider is derived from the `SearchRecentSuggestionsProvider` most of the responsibilities are handled by the base class. To give hints to the base provider the derived suggestion provider needs to initialize the base class with an authority that is unique. This is because Android search invokes a suggestion provider based on a unique content provider URI. And content providers in Android are invoked through their domain like string called authority (Refer to chapter 4 on content providers for fully understanding content provider authority strings)

Once the suggestion provider is implemented using this simple call to the base class, it needs to be configured in the manifest file as a regular content provider with an authority. It then needs to be tied (indirectly via the searchable metadata xml file) to a search activity. The search activity definition refers to the searchable.xml file which in turn points to the suggestion provider.

Let's examine the source code of this provider and see how some of these responsibilities are met.

Complete Source Code of SimpleSuggestionProvider

Because we are inheriting from the `SearchRecentSuggestionsProvider`, the source code for the simple suggestions provider is going to be quite simple, as shown in Listing 23–15.

Listing 23–15. *SimpleSuggestionProvider.java*

```
//SimpleSuggestionProvider.java
public class SimpleSuggestionProvider
extends SearchRecentSuggestionsProvider {

final static String AUTHORITY =
  "com.androidbook.search.simplesp.SimpleSuggestionProvider";

    final static int MODE =
         DATABASE_MODE_QUERIES | DATABASE_MODE_2LINES;

    public SimpleSuggestionProvider() {
        super();
        setupSuggestions(AUTHORITY, MODE);
    }
}
```

There are a couple of things noteworthy in Listing 23–15.

1. Initialize the parent class
2. Setup the base provider with an authority and mode (indicating what portions of a search text that needs to be remembered)

The authority string needs to be unique. The authority string needs to match its content provider definition in the manifest file. (See the future android manifest file for this project in Listing 23–16.)

Let us talk about the database mode, the second argument of `setupSuggestions()` method.

Understanding SearchRecentSuggestionsProvider Database Modes

Key functionality of Android-supplied `SearchRecentSuggestionsProvider` facility is to store/replay queries from the database so that they are available as future suggestions. A suggestion has two text strings with it (see Figure 23–2). Only the first string is mandatory. As you use `SearchRecentSuggestionsProvider` to replay these strings you need to tell it whether you want to use one string or two strings.

To accommodate this, there are two modes (mode bits) supported by the base suggestion provider. Both modes use the following prefix:

```
DATABASE_MODE_...
```

Here are these two modes:

- DATABASE_MODE_QUERIES (value of binary 1)
- DATABASE_MODE_2LINES (value of binary 2)

The first mode indicates that just a single query string needs is stored and replayed when needed. The second mode indicates that there are two strings that the suggestion provider can replay. One string is the query and the other is the description line that shows up in the suggestion display item.

The SearchActivity is responsible for saving these when it is called to respond to queries. The SearchActivity would call the following method to store these items (we will cover this in greater detail when we discuss the search activity):

```
pulbic class SearchRecentSuggestions
{
   ...
   public void saveRecentQuery (String queryString, String line2);
   ...
}
```

> **NOTE:** The class SearchRecentSuggestions is an SDK class and we will cover more of this when we cover the search activity code in Listing 23–17.

The queryString is the string as typed by the user. This string will be displayed as the suggestion, and if the user clicks on the suggestion, this string will be sent to your searchable activity (as a new search query).

Here is what the Android docs say about the line2 argument:

If you have configured your recent suggestions provider with DATABASE_MODE_2LINES, you can pass a second line of text here. It will be shown in a smaller font, below the primary suggestion. When typing, matches in either line of text will be displayed in the list. If you did not configure two-line mode, or if a given suggestion does not have any additional text to display, you can pass null here.

In our example we would like to save both the query and also the helpful text that shows along with the query in a suggestion. Or at least we want to show helpful text such as SSSP (Search Simple Suggestion Provider) at the bottom of the suggestion, so when suggestions from this provider are shown in the global search we can see what application is responsible for searching the text in the suggestion.

The way you specify this mode so you can save the suggestion and the helpful text is to set the two mode bits as indicated in Listing 23–15. If you just set the mode bit to saving two lines you will get an invalid argument exception. The mode bits must include at least the DATABASE_MODE_QUERIES bit. Essentially you need to do a bitwise OR. So the modes are complimentary in nature and not exclusive.

TIP: You can learn more about this prefabricated suggestions provider at http://developer.android.com/reference/android/provider/SearchRecentSuggestions.html.

Now that we have the source code for our simple suggestions provider, let's see how we register this provider in the manifest file.

Declaring the Suggestion Provider in the Manifest File

Because our SimpleSuggestionProvider is essentially a content provider, it is registered in the manifest file like any other content provider. Listing 23–16 shows the manifest file for this project. Note that key sections of this manifest file are highlighted.

Listing 23–16. *SimpleSuggestionProvider Manifest File*

```
//filename: AndroidManifest.xml
<?xml version="1.0" encoding="utf-8"?>
<manifest xmlns:android="http://schemas.android.com/apk/res/android"
      package="com.androidbook.search.simplesp"
      android:versionCode="1"
      android:versionName="1.0.0">
    <application android:icon="@drawable/icon"
       android:label="Simple Search Suggestion Provider:SSSP">
        <activity android:name=".SimpleMainActivity"
           android:label="SSSP:Simple Main Activity">
            <intent-filter>
               <action
                android:name="android.intent.action.MAIN" />
               <category
                android:name="android.intent.category.LAUNCHER" />
            </intent-filter>
        </activity>

<!--
**************************************************************
* Search related code: search activity
**************************************************************
 -->
   <activity android:name=".SearchActivity"
      android:label="SSSP: Search Activity"
      android:launchMode="singleTop">
     <intent-filter>
        <action android:name="android.intent.action.SEARCH" />
        <category android:name="android.intent.category.DEFAULT" />
      </intent-filter>
     <meta-data android:name="android.app.searchable"
                    android:resource="@xml/searchable" />
   </activity>
```

```
    <meta-data android:name="android.app.default_searchable"
                    android:value=".SearchActivity" />

    <provider android:name=".SimpleSuggestionProvider"
         android:authorities
           ="com.androidbook.search.simplesp.SimpleSuggestionProvider" />
</application>
    <uses-sdk android:minSdkVersion="4" />
</manifest>
```

Notice how the authority of the simple suggestions provider matches in the source code (Listing 23–15) and the manifest files (Listing 23–16). In both cases the value of this authority is

```
com.androidbook.search.simplesp.SimpleSuggestionProvider
```

We will talk about the other sections of this manifest file when we cover other aspects of this Simple Suggestions Provider. As you can see from this manifest file, a search activity plays a key role. So let's talk about that search activity now. We will cover the other activity SimpleMainActivity in this manifest file toward the end of this section, as it is just a driver activity to start things off.

Understanding Simple Suggestions Provider Search Activity

A search activity is invoked by Android search (QSB) with a query string. A search activity in turn needs to read this query string from the intent and do what is necessary and perhaps show results.

Because a search activity is an activity, it is possible that it can be invoked by other intents and other actions. For this reason, it is a good practice to check the intent action that invoked it. In our case, when the Android search invokes this activity this action is ACTION_SEARCH.

Under some circumstances a search activity can invoke itself. When this is likely to happen, you should define the search activity launch mode as a `singleTop`. The activity will also need to deal with firing of `onNewIntent()`. We will cover this as well in the section "Understanding onCreate and onNewIntent."

When it comes to doing something with the query string, we will just log it. Once the query is logged we will need to save it in the `SearchRecentSuggestionsProvider` so that it is available as a suggestion for future searches.

Now let's look at the source code of the search activity class.

Complete Source Code of a Search Activity

Listing 23–17 shows the source code for this SearchActivity class.

Listing 23–17. *SimpleSuggestionProvider Search Activity*

```
//filename: SearchActivity.java
public class SearchActivity extends Activity
{
    private final static String tag ="SearchActivity";
    @Override
    protected void onCreate(Bundle savedInstanceState) {
        super.onCreate(savedInstanceState);

        Log.d(tag,"I am being created");
        //otherwise do this
        setContentView(R.layout.layout_search_activity);
       //this.setDefaultKeyMode(Activity.DEFAULT_KEYS_SEARCH_GLOBAL);
        this.setDefaultKeyMode(Activity.DEFAULT_KEYS_SEARCH_LOCAL);

        // get and process search query here
        final Intent queryIntent = getIntent();
        final String queryAction = queryIntent.getAction();
        if (Intent.ACTION_SEARCH.equals(queryAction))
        {
           Log.d(tag,"new intent for search");
           this.doSearchQuery(queryIntent);
        }
        else {
           Log.d(tag,"new intent NOT for search");
        }
        return;
    }

    @Override
    public void onNewIntent(final Intent newIntent)
    {
        super.onNewIntent(newIntent);
        Log.d(tag,"new intent calling me");

        // get and process search query here
        final Intent queryIntent = getIntent();
        final String queryAction = queryIntent.getAction();
        if (Intent.ACTION_SEARCH.equals(queryAction))
        {
           this.doSearchQuery(queryIntent);
           Log.d(tag,"new intent for search");
        }
        else {
           Log.d(tag,"new intent NOT for search");
        }
    }
    private void doSearchQuery(final Intent queryIntent)
    {
        final String queryString =
           queryIntent.getStringExtra(SearchManager.QUERY);
```

```
            // Record the query string in the recent
            // queries suggestions provider.
            SearchRecentSuggestions suggestions =
               new SearchRecentSuggestions(this,
                  SimpleSuggestionProvider.AUTHORITY,
                  SimpleSuggestionProvider.MODE);
            suggestions.saveRecentQuery(queryString, "SSSP");
        }
    }

//Here is the corresponding Layout file presented in the same
//listing. Cut the following code and create a separate
//layoutfile. See the embedded file location

<?xml version="1.0" encoding="utf-8"?>
<!-- /res/layout/layout_search_activity.xml -->
<LinearLayout
  xmlns:android="http://schemas.android.com/apk/res/android"
    android:orientation="vertical"
    android:layout_width="fill_parent"
    android:layout_height="fill_parent"
    >
<TextView
    android:id="@+id/text1"
    android:layout_width="fill_parent"
    android:layout_height="wrap_content"
    android:text="Test Search Activity view"
    />
</LinearLayout>
```

Given code in Listing 23–17, let us see how the search activity checks the action and retrieves the query string.

Checking the Action and Retrieving the Query

The search activity code checks for the invoking action by looking at the invoking intent and comparing it to the constant intent.ACTION_SEARCH. If the action matches then it invokes the doSearchQuery() function.

In the doSearchQuery() function, search activity retrieves the query string using an intent extra. Here is the code:

```
final String queryString =
   queryIntent.getStringExtra(SearchManager.QUERY);
```

Notice that intent extra is defined as SearchManager.QUERY. As you work through this chapter, you will see a number of these extras defined in the SearchManager API reference. (Its URL is included in the “Resources” section at the end of this chapter.)

Understanding onCreate() and onNewIntent()

A search activity is kicked off by Android when a user enters text into a search box and clicks either a suggestion or the Go Arrow. This results in creating the search activity and calling its onCreate() method. The intent that is passed to this onCreate() will have the action set to ACTION_SEARCH.

There are times when the activity is not created, but instead passed the new search criteria through the onNewIntent() method. How does this happen? The callback onNewIntent() is closely related to the launching mode of an activity. If you look at Listing 23–16 you will notice that the search activity is set up as a singleTop in the manifest file.

When an activity is set up as a singleTop, it instructs Android not to create a new activity when that activity is already on top of the stack. In that case Android calls onNewIntent() instead of onCreate(). This is why in the activity source in Listing 23–17 we have two places where we examine the intent.

Testing for onNewIntent()

Once you have onNewIntent() implemented, you will start noticing that it doesn't get invoked in the normal flow of things. This begs the question: when will the search activity be on top of the stack? This usually doesn't happen.

Here;s why: say a search invoker Activity A invokes search and that causes a search Activity B to come up. Activity B then displays the results and the user uses a back button to go back, at which time the Activity B, which is our search activity, is no longer on top of the stack, Activity A is. Or the user may click home key and use the global search on the home screen in which case home activity is the activity on top.

One way the search activity can be on top is this: say Activity A results in Activity B due to search. If Activity B defines a type-to-search then when you are focused on Activity B a search will invoke Activity B again with the new criteria. Listing 23–17 shows how we have set up the type-to-search to demonstrate. Here is the code again:

```
this.setDefaultKeyMode(Activity.DEFAULT_KEYS_SEARCH_LOCAL);
```

Saving the Query Using SearchRecentSuggestionsProvider

We have talked about how the search activity needs to save the queries that it has encountered so that they can be played back as suggestions through the suggestion provider. Here is the code segment that saves these queries:

```
final String queryString =
    queryIntent.getStringExtra(SearchManager.QUERY);

// Record the query string in the
// recent queries suggestions provider.
SearchRecentSuggestions suggestions =
     new SearchRecentSuggestions(this,
          SimpleSuggestionProvider.AUTHORITY,
          SimpleSuggestionProvider.MODE);
suggestions.saveRecentQuery(queryString, "SSSP");
```

From this code you see that Android passes the query information as an EXTRA (SearchManager.QUERY) through the intent.

Once you have the query available you can make use of the SDK utility class `SearchRecentSuggestions` to save the query and a hint ("SSSP") by instantiating a new suggestions object and asking it to save. Because we have chosen to use the 2line mode and the query mode, the second argument to the `saveRecentQuery` is SSSP (again, this stands for Simple Search Suggestions Provider). You will see this text appear at the bottom of the suggestions from this provider.

Now we'll look at the search metadata definition where we tie the search activity with the search suggestion provider.

Search Metadata

The definition of Search in Android starts with a search activity. You first define a search activity in the manifest file. As part of this definition you will tell Android where to find the search metadata XML file. See Listing 23–16 where our search activity is defined along with a path to the search metadata xml file (searchable.xml)

Listing 23–18 shows this corresponding search metadata xml file.

Listing 23–18. *SimpleSuggestionProvider Search Metadata*

```
<!-- filename: /res/xml/searchable.xml -->
<searchable
 xmlns:android="http://schemas.android.com/apk/res/android"
    android:label="@string/search_label"
    android:hint="@string/search_hint"
    android:searchMode="showSearchLabelAsBadge"
    android:queryAfterZeroResults="true"

    android:includeInGlobalSearch="true"
    android:searchSuggestAuthority=
           "com.androidbook.search.simplesp.SimpleSuggestionProvider"
    android:searchSuggestSelection=" ? "
/>
```

Let's work through some of the key attributes in Listing 23–18.

The attribute `includeInGlobalSearch` tells Android to use this suggestion provider as one of the sources in global QSB.

The attribute, `searchSuggestAuthority`, points to the authority of the suggestion provider as defined in the manifest file for that suggestion provider (see Listing 23–16).

The attribute `queryAfterZeroResults` indicates whether the QSB should send more letters to a suggestion provider if the current set of letters did not return any results. Because we are testing, we don't want to leave any stones unturned, and so we set this attribute to true so that we give every opportunity to the provider to respond.

When you are deriving from the recent search suggestions provider, the attribute, `searchSuggestSelection`, is always the character string represented by " ? " . This string is passed to the suggestion provider as the `selection` string (where clause) of the content provider `query` method. Typically, this would represent the where clause that goes into a select statement of any content provider.

Specific to suggestion providers, when there is a value specified for "searchSuggestSelection", (as a protocol) Android passes the search query string (entered in the QSB) as the first entry in the select arguments array of the content provider query method.

The code to respond to these nuances (how these strings are used internally by the provider) is hidden in the recent search suggestions provider, we won't be able to show you how these arguments are used in the query method of the content provider.

We will go into this in more detail in the next section, in which you will see the full picture of the string " ? ". In fact it is quite unlikely that this string is used at all to narrow the results because it doesn't qualify any field to query on such as "someid == ?". It is likely that it's shear presence prompts the Android to pass the QSB string as the first argument to the provider. And the SDK search suggestion provider merely relies on this protocol to receive the QSB string in a convenient array provided by the select argument list of the content provider query() method.

Now let us talk about a search invoker activity that we will use as the main entry point for this application. This main activity allows us to test local search.

Search Invoker Activity

This main activity will let us invoke the local search when it is in focus. Listing 23–19 shows the source code for this search invoker activity, its layout file, and the strings.xml belonging to this project.

Listing 23–19. *SimpleSuggestionProvider: Main Activity*

```
public class SimpleMainActivity extends Activity
{
    @Override
    public void onCreate(Bundle savedInstanceState) {
        super.onCreate(savedInstanceState);
        setContentView(R.layout.main);
    }
}

//filename: /res/layout/main.xml
//Copy the following xml file as main.xml

<?xml version="1.0" encoding="utf-8"?>
<LinearLayout
  xmlns:android="http://schemas.android.com/apk/res/android"
    android:orientation="vertical"
    android:layout_width="fill_parent"
    android:layout_height="fill_parent"
    >
<TextView
    android:id="@+id/text1"
    android:layout_width="fill_parent"
    android:layout_height="wrap_content"
    android:text="@string/main_activity_text"
    />
```

```
</LinearLayout>

//filename: /res/values/strings.xml
//Copy the following xml file as strings.xml

<?xml version="1.0" encoding="utf-8"?>
<resources>
    <string name="main_activity_text">
    This is a simple activity. Click on the search key
    to invoke the local search.
    \n\n
    The suggestion provider will also participate
    in the global search. when you come to this
    application through the global search you will
    not see this view but instead be directly
    taken to the searchactivity view.
    </string>

    <string name="search_activity_text">
    If you are seeing this activity you are directed
    here either through the global search or through
    the local search.
    \n\n
    This activit also enables type-to-search. It also
    demonstrates the singletop/new intent concepts.
    </string>

    <string name="app_name">Simple Suggestion Provider</string>
   <string name="search_label">Local Search Demo</string>
   <string name="search_hint">Local Search Hint</string>
</resources>
```

If you see the activity definition for this activity in the manifest file (Listing 23–16) you will notice that it doesn't explicitly say that it uses the SearchActivity as its default local search. This is because we have used that specification at the application level as opposed to at the activity level by introducing the following lines in the manifest file:

```
<meta-data android:name="android.app.default_searchable"
       android:value=".SearchActivity" />
```

Notice how these lines are outside any activity in the manifest file (Listing 23–16). This specification tells Android that all activities in this application use SearchActivity as their default search activity, including SearchActivity itself. You can take advantage of this later fact to invoke onNewIntent() by clicking on the search key when you are examining the results on the SearchActivity. This won't be the case if you were to define the default search only for the search invoker activity and not the whole application.

Simple Suggestion Provider User Experience

As you are getting ready to run this program, make sure that your suggestion provider authority matches in the following three fields:

- `AndroidManifest.xml`
- `searchable.xml`
- `SimpleSuggestionProvider.java`

If you run this application you will see a home screen that looks like the one shown in Figure 23–20 (this is our main search invoker activity).

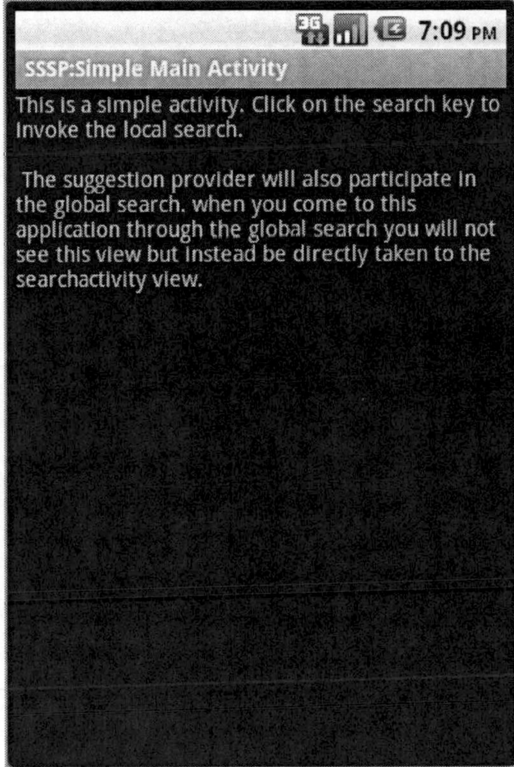

Figure 23–20. *Simple suggestion provider: main activity (enabled for local search)*

If you click the search key while this activity is in focus, you will see the local search invoked as in Figure 23–21.

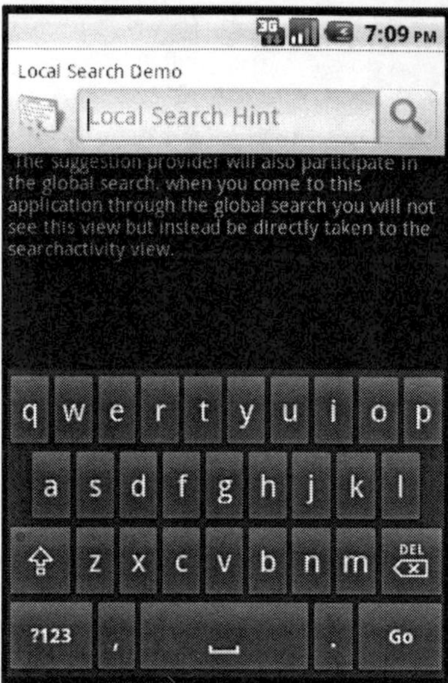

Figure 23–21. *Simple suggestion provider: local search QSB*

As you can see, there are no suggestions in Figure 23–21 because we haven't searched for any so far. You can also see that this is a local search; the label and hint of the search are as we specified in the search metadata XML file.

Let us go ahead and search for string `test1`. This will take you to the Search Activity screen as shown in Figure 23–22.

Figure 23–22. *Simple suggestion provider: local search results activity*

As you can see from the `SearchActivity` source in Listing 23–17, `SearchActivity` does nothing spectacular on the screen, but behind the scenes it is saving the query strings in the database. Now if you navigate back to the main screen (by pressing the back button) and invoke search again you will see the following screen (as shown in Figure 23–23) where the search suggestions are populated with the previous query text. You can also see in Figure 23–23 the bottom part of the suggestion "SSSP". This may seem extraneous here as this is a local search and clearly indicates that it comes from our application. However this string "SSSP" will distinguish the "test1" search string when it is displayed as part of the global search suggestions.

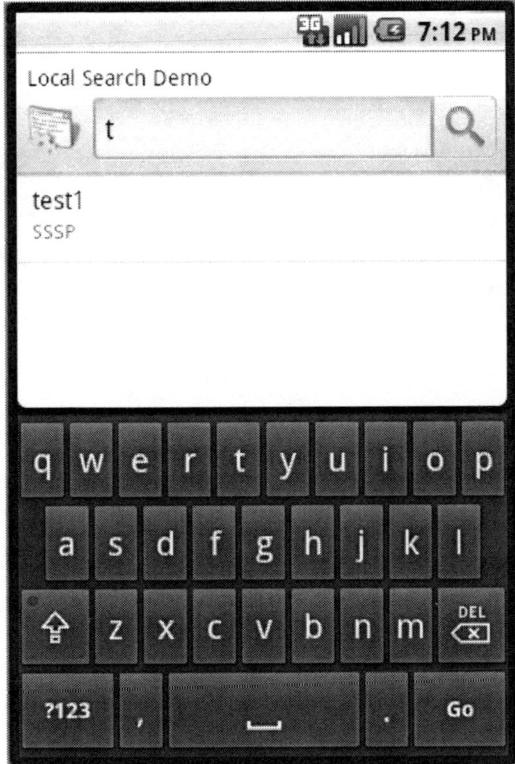

Figure 23–23. *Simple suggestion provider: retrieved local suggestion*

This is a good moment to see how we can invoke `onNewIntent()`. When you are on the search activity (Figure 23–22) you can type a letter like **t** and it will invoke the search again using type-to-search and you will see `onNewIntent()` called in the debug log.

Let us see what we need to see these suggestions show up in the global QSB. Because we have enabled `includeInGlobalSearch` in searchable.xml you should be able to see these suggestions in the global QSB as well. However, before you can do that you need to enable this application for global QSB suggestions as shown in Figure 23–24.

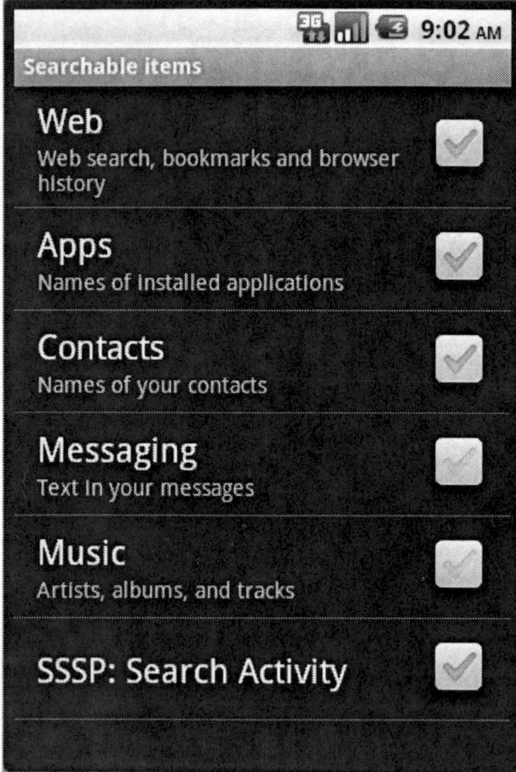

Figure 23–24. *Enable simple suggestion provider*

We showed you how to reach this screen at the beginning of the chapter. The simple custom suggestion provider we have coded is now available in the list of searchable applications as "SSSP:Search Activity". This text string comes from the activity name for the SearchActivity (see Listing 23–16).

With this selection in place you can see the global search shown in Figure 23–25 working with our suggestion provider.

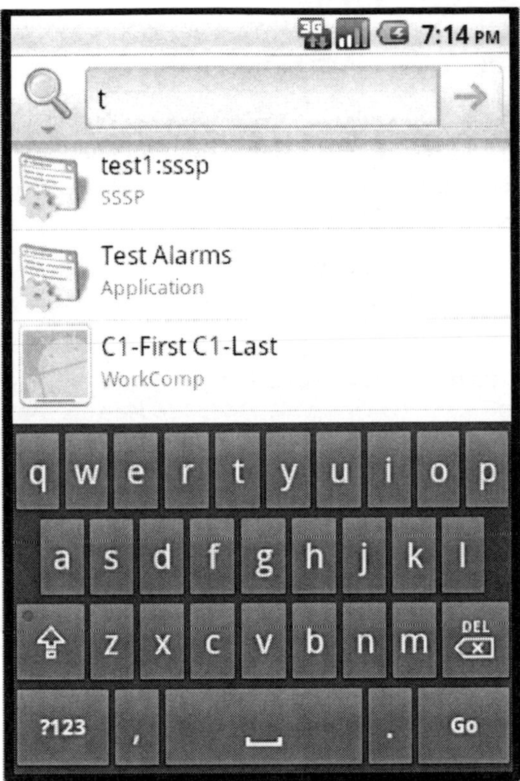

Figure 23–25. *Global Suggestions From Simple Suggestion provider*

In the global search, if you type a text like "t" it will bring up the suggestions from our suggestion provider of this section. When you navigate through the global search to the specific item you will see the local search activity as shown in Figure 23–22.

This concludes our discussion of the simple suggestion provider. You have learned about using the built-in `RecentSearchSuggestionProvider` to remember searches that are specific to your application. Using this approach, with minimal code you should be able to take local searches and make them available as suggestions even in a global context.

However, this simple exercise hasn't shown you how to write suggestion providers from scratch. More important, we haven't given you the slightest clue as to how a suggestion provider returns a set of suggestions and what columns are available in this suggestion set. To understand this and more, we need to implement a custom suggestions provider from scratch.

Implementing a Custom Suggestion Provider

Android search is too flexible not to customize. Because we used a pre-built suggestion provider in the last section, many features of a suggestion provider were hidden in the `SearchRecentSuggestionsProvider` and not discussed. We will explore these details next by implementing a custom suggestion provider called a `SuggestUrlProvider`.

We will start by explaining how this `SuggestUrlProvider` is expected work. We will then give you the file list in the implementation. These files should give you a general idea of how to build a custom suggestion provider.

Finally, we will show you how the completed application is used. Let's get started.

Planning the Custom Suggestion Provider

We are going to call our custom suggestion provider a `SuggestURLProvider`. The object of this provider is to monitor what is being typed in the QSB. If the search query has text that looks something like "great.m" (the suffix .m is chosen to represent meaning) the provider will interpret the first part of the query as a word and suggest an Internet-based URL that can be invoked to look up the meaning of the word.

For every word, this provider suggests two URLs. The first is a URL that allows the user to search for the word using `http://www.thefreedictionary.com` and a second URL using `http://www.google.com`. Choosing one of these suggestions takes the user to one of these sites directly. If the user clicks on the search icon of the QSB, then the search activity will simply log the query text on a simple layout of this activity. You will see this more clearly when we show you the screen images of this interaction.

Let's see the list of files that make up this project. You can also download the zip file for this project by following the URL at the end of this chapter.

SuggestURLProvider Project Implementation Files

The two primary files are `SearchActivity.java` and `SuggestUrlProvider.java`. However, you will need a number of supporting files to complete the project. Here is a list of these files and a brief description of what each one does. We have included the source code for all of the files with the solution.

- `SuggestUrlProvider.java`: This file implements the protocol of a custom suggestion provider. In this case the custom suggestion provider interprets query strings as words and returns a couple of suggestions using a suggestion cursor. (Listing 23–20)
- `SearchActivity.java`: This activity is responsible for receiving the queries or suggestions provided by the suggestion provider. `SearchActivity` definition is also responsible for tying up the suggestion provider with this activity. (Listing 23–23)

- `layout/layout_search_activity.xml`: This layout file is optionally used by the `SearchActivity`. In our example, we use this layout to log the query that is sent in. (Listing 23–24)
- `values/strings.xml`: Contains string definitions for the layout, local search title, local search hint, and the like. (Listing 23–25)
- `xml/searchable.xml`: Search metadata XML file that ties the `SearchActivity`, suggestion provider, and the QSB. (Listing 23–21)
- `AndroidManifest.xml`: application manifest file when the search activity and suggestion provider are defined. This is also where you declare that the `SearchActivity` is to be invoked as a local search for this application. (Listing 23–27)

We will start by exploring `SuggestUrlProvider`.

Implementing the SuggestUrlProvider Class

In our custom suggestion provider project, the `SuggestUrlProvider` class is the one that implements the protocol of the suggestion provider. We will explore the implementation of `SuggestUrlProvider` beginning with its responsibilities.

Responsibilities of a Suggestion Provider

At the core, a suggestion provider is a content provider. Much like a content provider a suggestion provider is invoked by Android search using a URI that identifies the provider and an additional argument representing the query.

Android search uses two types of URIs to invoke the provider. The first is called the *search URI.*, This URI is used to collect the set of suggestions. The response needs to be one or more rows, with each row containing a set of well-known columns.

The second URI is called a *suggest URI.* This URI is used to update a suggestion that is previously cached. The response needs to be a single row containing a set of well-known columns.

A suggestion provider also needs to specify in the search metadata XML file (searchable.xml) how it wants to receive the search query, including as it is getting typed. This can be done through the `select` argument of the `query` method of a provider or the last path segment of the URI itself (which is also passed as one of the arguments to the query method of the provider).

For a suggestion provider there are a number of columns that are available, each enabling a certain search behavior. A provider first needs to decide on this set of controlling columns it wants to return. Some of these controlling columns are:

- A column to enable/disable caching of suggestions that are returned to the Android search.

- Columns to control if you want the suggestions to rewrite the text in the query box.
- Columns to invoke an action directly instead of showing a set of search results when the user clicks on a suggestion.

Overall Source Code for SuggestUrlProvider

Listing 23–20 is the source code for the `SuggestUrlProvider class.` Sections of this code are also examined in greater detail later in the chapter as we explain each of the listed responsibilities in greater detail.

Listing 23–20. *CustomSuggestionProvider Source Code*

```
public class SuggestUrlProvider extends ContentProvider
{
    private static final String tag = "SuggestUrlProvider";
    public static String AUTHORITY =
        "com.androidbook.search.custom.suggesturlprovider";

    private static final int SEARCH_SUGGEST = 0;
    private static final int SHORTCUT_REFRESH = 1;
    private static final UriMatcher sURIMatcher =
                                buildUriMatcher();

    private static final String[] COLUMNS = {
            "_id",  // must include this column
            SearchManager.SUGGEST_COLUMN_TEXT_1,
            SearchManager.SUGGEST_COLUMN_TEXT_2,
            SearchManager.SUGGEST_COLUMN_INTENT_DATA,
            SearchManager.SUGGEST_COLUMN_INTENT_ACTION,
            SearchManager.SUGGEST_COLUMN_SHORTCUT_ID
            };

    private static UriMatcher buildUriMatcher()
   {
        UriMatcher matcher =
             new UriMatcher(UriMatcher.NO_MATCH);

        matcher.addURI(AUTHORITY,
              SearchManager.SUGGEST_URI_PATH_QUERY,
              SEARCH_SUGGEST);
        matcher.addURI(AUTHORITY,
              SearchManager.SUGGEST_URI_PATH_QUERY +
               "/*",
              SEARCH_SUGGEST);
        matcher.addURI(AUTHORITY,
              SearchManager.SUGGEST_URI_PATH_SHORTCUT,
            SHORTCUT_REFRESH);
        matcher.addURI(AUTHORITY,
              SearchManager.SUGGEST_URI_PATH_SHORTCUT +
            "/*",
            SHORTCUT_REFRESH);
        return matcher;
    }
```

```
@Override
public boolean onCreate() {
    //lets not do anything in particular
    Log.d(tag,"onCreate called");
    return true;
}

@Override
public Cursor query(Uri uri, String[] projection,
         String selection,
         String[] selectionArgs, String sortOrder)
{
   Log.d(tag,"query called with uri:" + uri);
   Log.d(tag,"selection:" + selection);

   String query = selectionArgs[0];
   Log.d(tag,"query:" + query);

    switch (sURIMatcher.match(uri)) {
        case SEARCH_SUGGEST:
           Log.d(tag,"search suggest called");
           return getSuggestions(query);
        case SHORTCUT_REFRESH:
           Log.d(tag,"shortcut refresh called");
           return null;
        default:
         throw
         new IllegalArgumentException("Unknown URL " + uri);
    }
}

private Cursor getSuggestions(String query)
{
   if (query == null) return null;
   String word = getWord(query);
   if (word == null)
      return null;

   Log.d(tag,"query is longer than 3 letters");

   MatrixCursor cursor = new MatrixCursor(COLUMNS);
   cursor.addRow(createRow1(word));
   cursor.addRow(createRow2(word));
   return cursor;
}
private Object[] createRow1(String query)
{
    return columnValuesOfQuery(query,
          "android.intent.action.VIEW",
          "http://www.thefreedictionary.com/" + query,
          "Look up in freedictionary.com for",
          query);
}

private Object[] createRow2(String query)
{
    return columnValuesOfQuery(query,
```

```
            "android.intent.action.VIEW",
"http://www.google.com/search?hl=en&source=hp&q=define%3A/"
         + query,
            "Look up in google.com for",
            query);
    }
    private Object[] columnValuesOfQuery(String query,
          String intentAction,
          String url,
          String text1,
          String text2)
    {
        return new String[] {
                query,     // _id
                text1,     // text1
                text2,     // text2
                url,
                // intent_data (included when clicking on item)
                intentAction, //action
                SearchManager.SUGGEST_NEVER_MAKE_SHORTCUT
        };
    }

    private Cursor refreshShortcut(String shortcutId,
                                String[] projection) {
        return null;
    }

    public String getType(Uri uri) {
        switch (sURIMatcher.match(uri)) {
            case SEARCH_SUGGEST:
                return SearchManager.SUGGEST_MIME_TYPE;
            case SHORTCUT_REFRESH:
                return SearchManager.SHORTCUT_MIME_TYPE;
            default:
             throw
             new IllegalArgumentException("Unknown URL " + uri);
        }
    }

    public Uri insert(Uri uri, ContentValues values) {
        throw new UnsupportedOperationException();
    }

    public int delete(Uri uri, String selection,
                            String[] selectionArgs) {
        throw new UnsupportedOperationException();
    }

    public int update(Uri uri, ContentValues values,
             String selection,
             String[] selectionArgs) {
        throw new UnsupportedOperationException();
    }

    private String getWord(String query)
    {
```

```
        int dotIndex = query.indexOf('.');
        if (dotIndex < 0)
           return null;
        return query.substring(0,dotIndex);
    }
}
```

Understanding Suggestion Provider URIs

Now that you have seen the complete source code of a custom suggestion provider, let's look at how portions of this source code that fulfills the URI responsibilities.

First let's look at the format of the URI that Android uses to invoke the suggestion provider. If our suggestion provider has an authority of

```
com.androidbook.search.custom.suggesturlprovider
```

then Android will send in two possible URIs. The first type of URI, a search URI, looks like one of the following:

```
content://com.androidbook.search.suggesturlprovider/search_suggest_query
```

or

```
content://com.androidbook.search.suggesturlprovider/search_suggest_query/<your-query>
```

This URI is issued when the user starts typing some text in the QSB. In one variation of this, the query is passed as an additional element at the end of the URI as a path segment. Whether or not to pass the query as a path segment is specified in the search metadata file `searchable.xml`. We will discuss that specification when we cover the search metadata in more detail.

The second type of URI that is targeted for a suggestion provider relates to Android search shortcuts. Android search shortcuts are suggestions (see Figure 23–3) that Android decides to cache, instead of calling the suggestion provider for fresh content. We will talk about Android search shortcuts more when we discuss the suggestion columns. For now, this second URI looks like the following:

```
content://com.androidbook.search.suggesturlprovider/search_suggest_shortcut
```

or this:

```
content://com.androidbook.search.suggesturlprovider/search_suggest_shortcut/<shortcut-
id>
```

This URI is issued by Android when it tries to determine if the shortcuts that it had cached are still valid. This type of URI is called the shortcut URI. If the provider returns a single row it will replace the current shortcut with the new one. If the provider sends a null then Android assumes this suggestion is no longer valid.

The `SearchManager` class in Android defines two constants to represent these URI segments that distinguish them (`search_suggest_search` and `search_suggest_shortcut`). They are, respectively:

```
SearchManager.SUGGEST_URI_PATH_QUERY
SearchManager.SUGGEST_URI_PATH_SHORTCUT
```

It is the responsibility of the provider to recognize these incoming URIs in its `query()` method. See Listing 23–20 to see how the `UriMatcher` is used to accomplish this. (You can refer to Chapter 5 on how to use `UriMatcher` in greater detail.)

Implementing getType() and Specifying MIME Types

Because a suggestion provider is ultimately a content provider it has the responsibility of implementing a content provider contract, which includes defining an implementation for the `getType()` method.

You can consult Listing 23–20 again to see how `getType()` is implemented in this case. That code is replicated here for a quick review.

```
public String getType(Uri uri) {
    switch (sURIMatcher.match(uri)) {
        case SEARCH_SUGGEST:
            return SearchManager.SUGGEST_MIME_TYPE;
        case SHORTCUT_REFRESH:
            return SearchManager.SHORTCUT_MIME_TYPE;
        default:
         throw
         new IllegalArgumentException("Unknown URL " + uri);
    }
}
```

Android search framework through its `SearchManager` class provides a couple of constants to help with these MIME types. These MIME types are

```
SearchManager.SUGGEST_MIME_TYPE
SearchManager.SHORTCUT_MIME_TYPE
```

These translate to

```
vnd.android.cursor.dir/vnd.android.search.suggest
vnd.android.cursor.item/vnd.android.search.suggest
```

Passing Query to the Suggestion Provider: The Selection Argument

When Android uses one of the URIs to call the provider, Android ends up calling the `query()` method of the suggestion provider to receive a suggestion cursor. If you see the implementation of the `query()` method in Listing 23–20 you will notice that we are using the `selection` argument and the `selectionArgs` argument in order to formulate and return the cursor. Here is that code replicated for quick review:

```
public Cursor query(Uri uri, String[] projection,
         String selection,
         String[] selectionArgs, String sortOrder)
{
    Log.d(tag,"query called with uri:" + uri);
    Log.d(tag,"selection:" + selection);

    String query = selectionArgs[0];
    Log.d(tag,"query:" + query);
```

```
        switch (sURIMatcher.match(uri)) {
              case SEARCH_SUGGEST:
               Log.d(tag,"search suggest called");
               return getSuggestions(query);
              case SHORTCUT_REFRESH:
               Log.d(tag,"shortcut refresh called");
               return null;
            default:
              throw
              new IllegalArgumentException("Unknown URL " + uri);
        }
    }
```

To understand what is passed to through the two arguments "selection" and "selectionArgs" you will need to see the `searchable.xml`, the search metadata file. Listing 23–21 shows the code for this search metadata XML file.

Listing 23–21. ***CustomSuggestionProvider Search Metadata***

```
//xml/searchable.xml
<searchable
  xmlns:android="http://schemas.android.com/apk/res/android"
    android:label="@string/search_label"
    android:hint="@string/search_hint"
    android:searchMode="showSearchLabelAsBadge"
    android:searchSettingsDescription="suggests urls"
    android:includeInGlobalSearch="true"
    android:queryAfterZeroResults="true"

    android:searchSuggestAuthority=
           "com.androidbook.search.custom.suggesturlprovider"

    android:searchSuggestIntentAction=
           "android.intent.action.VIEW"
    android:searchSuggestSelection=" ? "
/>
```

NOTE: Please note the searchSuggestAuthority string value. It should match the corresponding content provider URL definition in the Android manifest file.

Notice the `searchSuggestSelection` attribute in the previous search metadata definition file listing. It directly corresponds to the `selection` argument of the content provider's `query()` method. If you revisit Chapter4 you will know that this argument is used to pass the `where` clause with substitutable "?" symbols.

The array of substitutable values are then passed through the `selectionArgs` array argument. That indeed is the case here. When you specify `searchSuggestSelection` Android assumes that you don't want to receive the search text through the URI but instead through the `selection` argument of the `query()` method. In that case Android search will send the `" ? "` (notice the empty space before and after the "?" mark) as the value of the `selection` argument and passes the query text as the first element of the selection arguments array.

If you don't specify the searchSuggestSelection, then it will pass the search text as the last path segment of the URI. You can choose one or the other. In our example, we have chosen the selection approach and not the URI approach.

Exploring Search Metadata for Custom Suggestion Providers

While we are on this topic of search metadata attributes, let's explore what other attribute are available. We will cover those attributes that are often used or relevant to suggestion providers. For a complete list you can refer to the SearchManager API URL:

http://developer.android.com/guide/topics/search/searchable-config.html

The searchSuggestIntentAction attribute (Listing 23–21) is used to pass or specify the intent action when the SearchActivity is invoked through an intent. This allows the SearchActivity to do something other than the default search. Here is an example of how an intent action is used in the "onCreate()" of a responding search activity:

```
//Body of onCreate

// get and process search query here
final Intent queryIntent = getIntent();
//query action
final String queryAction = queryIntent.getAction();
if (Intent.ACTION_SEARCH.equals(queryAction))
{
   this.doSearchQuery(queryIntent);
}
else if (Intent.ACTION_VIEW.equals(queryAction))
{
   this.doView(queryIntent);
}
else {
   Log.d(tag,"Create intent NOT from search");
}
```

You will see this code in context in the future Listing 23–23 where the searchActivity is looking for either a VIEW action or the SEARCH action by examining the action value of the intent.

Another attribute that we are not using here, but available to suggestion providers, is called searchSuggestPath. If specified, this string value is appended to the URI (one that invokes the suggestion provider) after the SUGGEST_URI_PATH_QUERY. This allows a single custom suggestion provider to respond to two different search activities. Each SearchActivity will use a different URI suffix. The suggestion provider can use this path suffix to return different set of results to a targeted search activity.

Just as with the Intent action, you can also specify intent data using the searchSuggestIntentData attribute. This is a data URI that can be passed along the action to the search activity, as part of the intent, when invoked.

The attribute called searchSuggestThreshold indicates the number of characters that have to be typed in QSB before invoking this suggestion provider. The default threshold value is zero.

The attribute queryAfterZeroResults (true or false) indicates if the provider should be contacted if the current set of characters returned zero set of results for the next set of characters. In our particular url suggest provider it is important to turn this flag on so that we get a look at the whole query text every time.

Now that we have looked at the URIs, selection arguments, and search metadata, let's move on now to the most important aspect of a suggestion provider: the suggestion cursor.

Suggestion Cursor Columns

A suggestion cursor is, after all, a cursor. It is no different from the database cursors we discussed at length in Chapter 4. The suggestion cursor acts as the contract between the Android search facility and a suggestion provider. This means the names and types of the columns that the cursor returns are fixed and known to both parties.

To provide flexibility to search, Android search offers a large number of columns, most of which are optional. A suggestion provider does not need to return all these columns; it can ignore sending in the columns that are not relevant to this suggestion provider. In this section we will cover the meaning and significance of most of the columns (for the rest, you can refer to the SearchManager API URL, which we have mentioned a few times already).

First, we'll talk about the columns that are available for a suggestion provider to return, what each column means, and how it affects search.

Like all cursors, a suggestion cursor also has to have an _id column. This is a mandatory column. Every other column starts with a SUGGEST_COLUMN_ prefix. These constants are defined as part of the SearchManager API reference. We will talk about the most frequently used columns below. For the complete list use the API references indicated at the end of this chapter.

- text_1: This is the first line of text in your suggestion (see Figure 23–3).
- text_2: This is the second line of text in your suggestion (see Figure 23–3).
- icon_1: This is the icon on the left side in a suggestion and is typically a resource ID.
- icon_2: This is the icon on the right side in a suggestion and is typically a resource ID.
- intent_action: This is what is passed to the SearchActivity when it is invoked as the intent action. This will override the corresponding intent action when available in the search metadata (see Listing 23–21).
- intent_data: This is what is passed to the SearchActivity when it is invoked as the intent data. This will override the corresponding intent action when available in the search metadata (see Listing 23–21). This is a data URI.

- intent_data_id: This gets appended to the data URI. It is especially useful if you want to mention the root part of the data in the metadata one time and then change this for each suggestion. It is a bit more efficient that way.
- query: The query string to be used to send to the search activity.
- shortcut_id: As indicated earlier, Android search caches suggestions provided by a suggestion provider. These cached suggestions are called shortcuts. If this column is not present, Android will cache the suggestion and will never ask for an update. If this contains a value equivalent to SUGGEST_NEVER_MAKE_SHORTCUT, then Android will not cache this suggestion. If it contains any other value, this ID is passed as the last path segment of the shortcut URI. (See the section "Understanding Suggestion Provider URIs.")
- spinner_while_refreshing: This boolean value will tell Android if it should use a spinner when it is in the process of updating the shortcuts.

There is a variable set of additional columns for responding to action keys. We will cover that in the action keys section later. Let's see how our custom suggestion provider returns these columns.

Populating and Returning the List of Columns

Each custom suggestion provider is not required to return all these columns. For our suggestion provider we will return only a subset of the columns based on the functionality indicated in the "Planning the Custom Suggestion Provider" section.

By looking at Listing 23–20 you can see that out list of columns is as follows (extracted and reproduced in Listing 23–22).

Listing 23–22. *Defining Suggestion Cursor Columns*

```
private static final String[] COLUMNS = {
        "_id",  // must include this column
        SearchManager.SUGGEST_COLUMN_TEXT_1,
        SearchManager.SUGGEST_COLUMN_TEXT_2,
        SearchManager.SUGGEST_COLUMN_INTENT_DATA,
        SearchManager.SUGGEST_COLUMN_INTENT_ACTION,
        SearchManager.SUGGEST_COLUMN_SHORTCUT_ID
        };
```

These columns are chosen so that the following functionality is met:

The user enters a word with a hint like "great.m" in the QSB, our suggestion provider will not respond until there is a "." in the search text. Once it is recognized, the suggestion provider will extract the word from it (in this case, "great") and then provide two suggestions back.

The first suggestion is to invoke the thefreewebdictionary.com with this word and a second suggestion is to search Google with a pattern of define:great.

To accomplish this, the provider loads up the column `intent_action` as `intent.action.view` and the intent data containing the entire URI. The hope is that Android will launch the browser when it sees the data URI starting with `http://`.

We will populate the text1 column with `search some-website with:` and text2 with the word itself (again, `great`, in this case). We will also set the shortcut ID to SUGGEST_NEVER_MAKE_SHORTCUT to simplify things. This setting disables caching and also prevents the suggest shortcut URI being fired.

This completes our analysis of custom suggestion provider class source code. We have learned about URIs, suggestion cursors, and suggestion provider–specific search metadata. We also know how to populate suggestion columns.

Now let's look into implementing the search activity for our custom suggestion provider.

Implementing a Search Activity for a Custom Suggestion Provider

During the simple suggestion provider implementation we covered only some of the responsibilities of a search activity. Now let's look at the aspects we overlooked.

Android search invokes a search activity in order to respond to search actions from one of two ways. This can happen either when a search icon is clicked from the QSB or when the user directly clicks on a suggestion.

When invoked, a search activity needs to examine why it is invoked. This information is available in the intent action. The search activity needs to examine intent action to do the right thing. In many cases, this action is ACTION_SEARCH. However, a suggestion provider has the option of overriding it by specifying an explicit action either through search metadata or through a suggestion cursor column. This type of action can be anything. In our case, we are going to be using a VIEW action.

As we pointed out in our discussion of the simple suggestion provider, it is also possible to set up the launch mode of the search activity as a `singleTop`. In this case, the search activity has the added responsibility of responding to `onNewIntent()` in addition to `onCreate()`. We will cover both these cases and show how similar they are.

We will use both `onNewIntent()` and `onCreate()` to examine both ACTION_SEARCH and also ACTION_VIEW. In case of search action we will simply display the query text back to the user. In case of view action we will transfer control to a browser and finish the current activity so that the user has the impression of invoking the browser by directly clicking on the suggestion.

> **NOTE:** This `SearchActivity` does not need to be a launchable activity from the main applications menu of Android. Make sure you don't inadvertently set intent filters for this activity like other activities that need to be invoked from the device main applications screen.

With that, let's examine the source code of `SearchActivity.java`.

SearchActivity for a Custom Suggestion Provider

Now that we know the responsibilities of a search activity and, specifically, which ones are applicable for our example, we can show you the source code of this search activity (Listing 23–23).

Listing 23–23. *SearchActivity*

```
//file: SearchActivity.java
public class SearchActivity extends Activity
{
    private final static String tag ="SearchActivity";
    @Override
    protected void onCreate(Bundle savedInstanceState) {
        super.onCreate(savedInstanceState);

        Log.d(tag,"I am being created");
        setContentView(R.layout.layout_test_search_activity);

        // get and process search query here
        final Intent queryIntent = getIntent();

        //query action
        final String queryAction = queryIntent.getAction();
        Log.d(tag,"Create Intent action:"+queryAction);

        final String queryString =
           queryIntent.getStringExtra(SearchManager.QUERY);
        Log.d(tag,"Create Intent query:"+queryString);

        if (Intent.ACTION_SEARCH.equals(queryAction))
        {
           this.doSearchQuery(queryIntent);
        }
        else if (Intent.ACTION_VIEW.equals(queryAction))
        {
           this.doView(queryIntent);
        }
        else {
           Log.d(tag,"Create intent NOT from search");
        }
        return;
    }

    @Override
    public void onNewIntent(final Intent newIntent)
    {
        super.onNewIntent(newIntent);
        Log.d(tag,"new intent calling me");

        // get and process search query here
        final Intent queryIntent = newIntent;

        //query action
        final String queryAction = queryIntent.getAction();
        Log.d(tag,"New Intent action:"+queryAction);
```

```
        final String queryString =
           queryIntent.getStringExtra(SearchManager.QUERY);
        Log.d(tag,"New Intent query:"+queryString);

        if (Intent.ACTION_SEARCH.equals(queryAction))
        {
           this.doSearchQuery(queryIntent);
        }
        else if (Intent.ACTION_VIEW.equals(queryAction))
        {
           this.doView(queryIntent);
        }
        else {
           Log.d(tag,"New intent NOT from search");
        }
        return;
    }
    private void doSearchQuery(final Intent queryIntent)
    {
        final String queryString =
           queryIntent.getStringExtra(SearchManager.QUERY);
        appendText("You are searching for:" + queryString);
    }
    private void appendText(String msg)
    {
        TextView tv = (TextView)this.findViewById(R.id.text1);
        tv.setText(tv.getText() + "\n" + msg);
    }
    private void doView(final Intent queryIntent)
    {
        Uri uri = queryIntent.getData();
        String action = queryIntent.getAction();
        Intent i = new Intent(action);
        i.setData(uri);
        startActivity(i);
        this.finish();
    }
}
```

We'll start our analysis of this source code by examining first how this search activity is invoked.

Details of SearchActivity Invocation

Like all activities, we know that a search activity must have been invoked through an intent. However, it would be wrong to assume that it is always the `action` of the intent that is responsible for this. As it turns out, the search activity is invoked explicitly through its component name specification.

You might ask why this is important. Well, we know that in our suggestion provider we are explicitly specifying an intent `action` in the suggestion row. If this intent action is VIEW and the intent data is an HTTP URL, then an unsuspecting programmer would think that a browser will be launched in response, and not the search activity. That would certainly be desirable. But because the ultimate intent is also loaded with the component name of search activity in addition to the intent action and data, the component name will take precedence.

We are not sure why this restriction is there or how to overcome it. But the fact is, irrespective of the intent action that your suggestion provider specifies, search activity is the one that is going to be invoked. In our case, we will simply launch the browser from the search activity and close the search activity.

To demonstrate this, here is the intent that Android fires off to invoke our search activity when we click on a suggestion:

```
launching Intent {
act=android.intent.action.VIEW
dat=http://www.google.com
flg=0x10000000
cmp=com.androidbook.search.custom/.SearchActivity (has extras)
}
```

Notice the component spec of the intent. It is directly pointing to the search activity. So no matter what intent action you indicate, Android will always invoke search activity. As a result, it becomes the responsibility of the search activity to invoke the browser.

Now let's look at what we do with these intents in the search activity.

Responding to ACTION_SEARCH and ACTION_VIEW

We know that a search activity is explicitly invoked by name by Android search. However, the invoking intent also carries with it the action that is specified. When QSB invokes this activity through the search icon this action is ACTION_SEARCH.

This action could be different if it was invoked by a search suggestion. It depends on how the suggestion provider set up the suggestion. In our case, the suggestion provider set this up as an ACTION_VIEW.

As a result, a search activity needs to examine the type of action. Here is how we examine this code to see whether to call a search query method or the view method. (This code segment is extracted from Listing 23–23):

```
if (Intent.ACTION_SEARCH.equals(queryAction))
 {
    this.doSearchQuery(queryIntent);
 }
 else if (Intent.ACTION_VIEW.equals(queryAction))
 {
    this.doView(queryIntent);
 }
```

From the code you can see that we invoke doView() for a view action and doSearchQuery() in the case of a search action.

In the doView() function we will retrieve the action and the data URI and populate a new intent with them and then invoke the activity. This will invoke the browser. We will finish the activity so that the back button takes you back to whatever search invoked it.

In the doSearchQuery() we are just logging the search query text to the view. Let us take a look at the layout that is used to support doSearchQuery().

Search Activity Layout

Listing 23–24 is a simple layout that is used by a search activity in case of doSearchQuery().The only important element is highlighted in bold.

Listing 23–24. *SearchActivity Layout XML*

```
<?xml version="1.0" encoding="utf-8"?>
<!-- file: layout/layout_search_activity.xml -->
<LinearLayout xmlns:android="http://schemas.android.com/apk/res/android"
    android:orientation="vertical"
    android:layout_width="fill_parent"
    android:layout_height="fill_parent"
    >
<TextView
    android:id="@+id/text1"
    android:layout_width="fill_parent"
    android:layout_height="wrap_content"
    android:text="@string/search_activity_main_text"
    />
</LinearLayout>
```

It is appropriate at this point to show you the strings.xml that is responsible for some of the text needs of this application.

Corresponding strings.xml

This strings.xml as shown in Listing 23–25 defines text strings for the layout and also such things as the name of the application, some strings for configuring the local search, and the like.

Listing 23–25. *strings.xml*

```
<?xml version="1.0" encoding="utf-8"?>
<!-- file: values/strings.xml -->
<resources>
    <string name="search_activity_main_text">
    This is the search activity.
    \n\n
    This will be invoked if action_search
    is used as opposed to action_view.
    \n\n
    action_search happens if you press the search icon.
    \n\n
    action_view happens if you press on the suggestion
    </string>

    <string name="app_name">Custom Suggest Application
    </string>

    <string name="search_label">Custom Suggest Demo
```

```
    </string>

    <string name="search_hint">Custom Suggest Demo Hint
    </string>
</resources>
```

Responding to onCreate() and onNewIntent()

If you examine Listing 23–23, you will see that the code in `onCreate()` and `onNewIntent()` is almost identical. This is not an uncommon pattern.

When a search activity is invoked, depending on the launch mode of the search activity, either `onCreate()` or a `onNewIntent()` is called.

> **NOTE:** For a useful reference on launch modes and `onNewIntent()` see the "References" section at the end of this chapter.

Notes on Finishing a Search Activity

Earlier in this discussion we briefly mentioned how to respond to `doView()`. Listing 23–26 is the code for this function (excerpted from Listing 23–26).

Listing 23–26. *Finishing the Search Activity*

```
private void doView(final Intent queryIntent)
{
    Uri uri = queryIntent.getData();
    String action = queryIntent.getAction();
    Intent i = new Intent(action);
    i.setData(uri);
    startActivity(i);
    this.finish();
}
```

The goal of this function is to invoke the browser. If we were not doing the `finish()` at the end, the user would be taken back to the search activity from the browser after clicking the back button, instead of back to the search screen where they came from, as expected.

Ideally, to give the best user experience the control should never pass through the search activity. Finishing this activity solves that problem. Listing 23–26 also gives us an opportunity to examine how we transfer the intent action and intent data from the original intent (which are set by the suggestion provider) and then pass them on to a new browser intent.

We just covered a lot of ground. We have shown you a detailed suggestion provider implementation and a search activity implementation. In the process, we have also shown you the search metadata file and the `strings.xml`. We will conclude our examination of the files needed for implementing this chapter's project with a look at the application level manifest file.

Custom Suggestions Provider Manifest File

The manifest file is where you bring together many components of your application. For our custom suggestions provider application as in other examples, this is where you declare its components, such as the search activity and the suggestion provider. You also use the manifest file to declare that this application is enabled for local search by declaring the "search activity" as the default search. Also pay attention the intent filters defined for the search activity.

These details are highlighted bold in the manifest file code (Listing 23–27).

Listing 23–27. *Custom Suggestion Provider Manifest File*

```
//file:AndroidManifest.xml
<?xml version="1.0" encoding="utf-8"?>
<manifest xmlns:android="http://schemas.android.com/apk/res/android"
      package="com.androidbook.search.custom"
      android:versionCode="1"
      android:versionName="1.0.0">
    <application android:icon="@drawable/icon"
                    android:label="Custom Suggestions Provider">
<!--
****************************************************************
* Search related code: search activity
****************************************************************
 -->
   <activity android:name=".SearchActivity"
                 android:label="Search Activity Label"
                 android:launchMode="singleTop">
     <intent-filter>
        <action
        android:name="android.intent.action.SEARCH" />
        <category
        android:name="android.intent.category.DEFAULT" />
      </intent-filter>

     <meta-data android:name="android.app.searchable"
        android:resource="@xml/searchable" />
   </activity>

<!-- Declare default search -->
   <meta-data android:name="android.app.default_searchable"
       android:value=".SearchActivity" />

<!-- Declare Suggestion Provider -->
    <provider android:name="SuggestUrlProvider"
        android:authorities=
        "com.androidbook.search.custom.suggesturlprovider" />
</application>
    <uses-sdk android:minSdkVersion="4" />
</manifest>
```

As you can see, we have highlighted three things:

- Defining the search activity along with its search metadata XML file

- Defining the search activity as the default search for the application
- Defining the suggestion provider and its authority

With all of the source code in place, it is time to take a tour of the application and see how it looks in the emulator.

Custom Suggestion User Experience

Once you build and deploy this app through ADT you will not see any activity pop-up because there is no activity to start. Instead, you will see that the application is successfully installed in the Eclipse console.

This means that the suggestion provider is ready to respond to the global QSB. But before that can take place, you will need to enable this suggestion provider to participate in global search.

Earlier in this chapter we showed you how to reach the search settings application. Here is a shortcut which uses the very search facility we have learned so far.

Open the global QSB and type **sett** in the QSB. This will bring up the settings application as one of the suggestions to be invoked. See Figure 23–26.

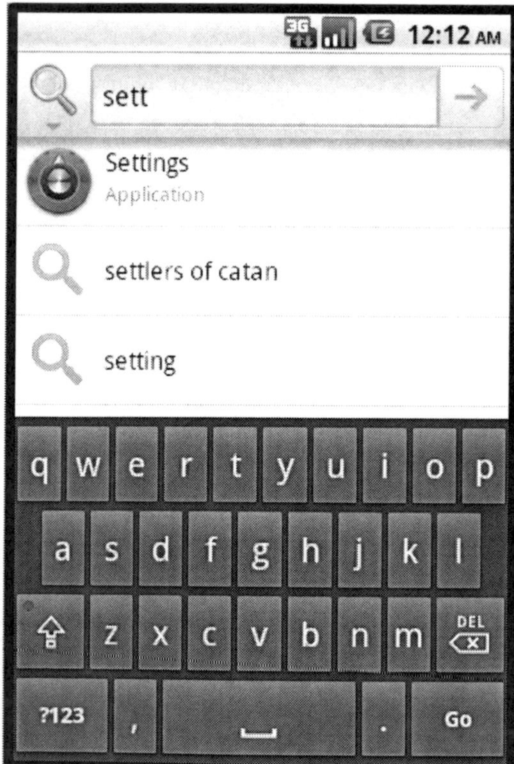

Figure 23–26. *Invoking settings through search*

Notice how we are using what we have learned about QSB to invoke the settings application. Follow the approach specified at the beginning of this chapter to enable this application for suggestions. Once this is done, type the text in the QSB shown in Figure 23–27.

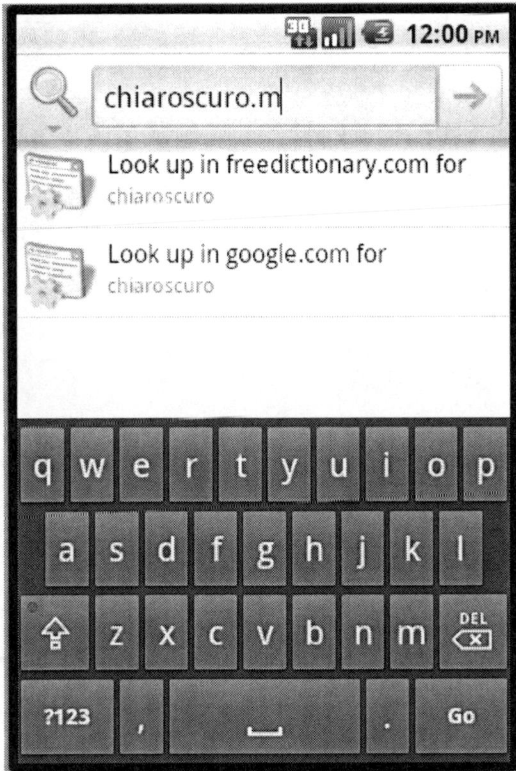

Figure 23–27. *More results from the custom suggestions provider*

Notice how search suggestions from the custom suggestions provider are presented. Now if you click on the search icon on the top left and change the search application to the "custom suggestion provider" application and navigate to one of the suggestions provided by our custom suggestions provider and click the QSB search icon, Android will take you to the search activity directly without invoking any browser, as shown in Figure 23–28. (This demonstrates the two types of intent actions we discussed: the search and the view.)

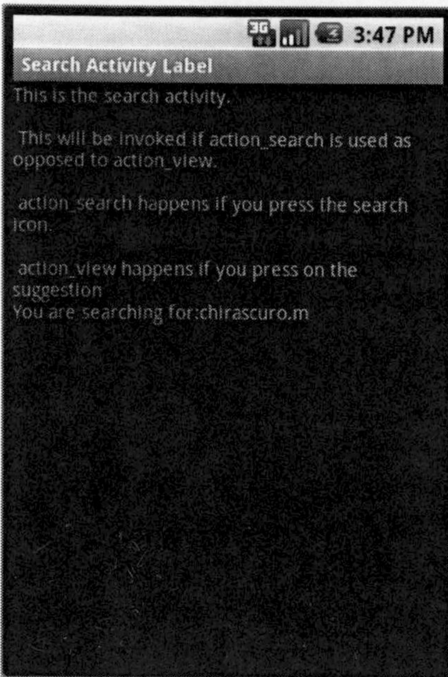

Figure 23–28. *Query search invoking search results*

So this example demonstrates the ACTION_SEARCH vs. the ACTION_VIEW.

Now if you click on the free dictionary suggestion in Figure 23–27, you will see the invoked browser as in Figure 23–29.

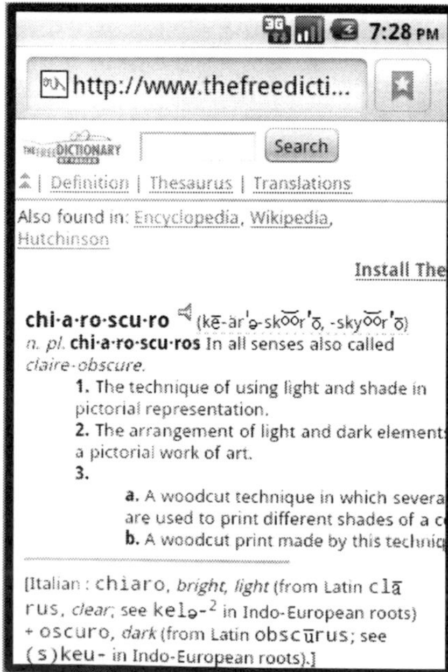

Figure 23–29. *Free dictionary*

If you click on the Google suggestion item in Figure 23–27, you will see the browser shown in Figure 23–30.

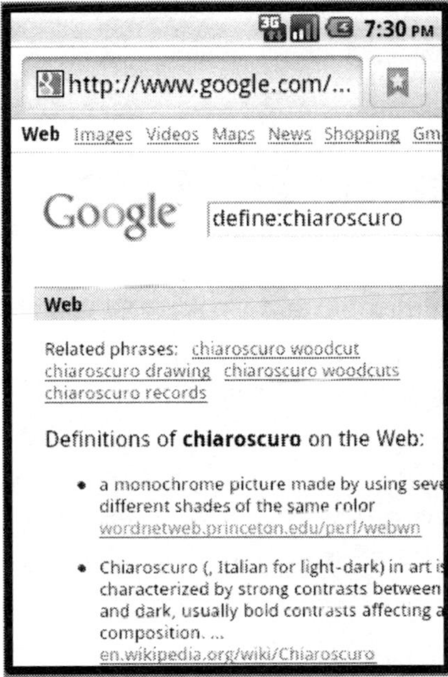

Figure 23–30. *Searching Google for a definition*

Figure 23–31 shows what happens if you don't type the suffix **.m** in the global search.

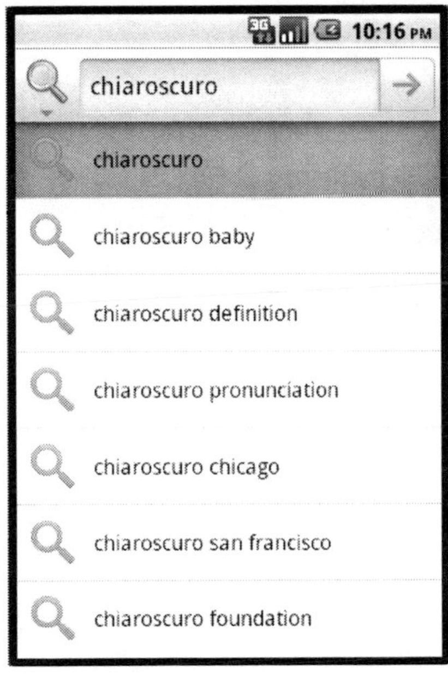

Figure 23–31. *Custom provider without a hint*

Notice how the suggestion provider hasn't provided anything back.

This concludes our discussion of building a functional custom suggestions provider from scratch. Although we've covered any aspects of search, there are still a couple of topics that we haven't talked about. These are action keys and Application-Specific search data. We will cover these next.

Using Action Keys and Application-Specific Search Data

Action keys and application-specific search data add further flexibility to Android search.

Action keys allow us to employ specialized device keys for search-related functionality. Application-specific search data allow an activity to pass additional data to the search activity.

> **NOTE:** Please note that the code listings in the rest of the chapter do not form a testable project. These code listings are there only to support the ideas presented in text.

Let's begin with action keys.

Using Action Keys in Android Search

So far we've shown a number of ways to invoke search:

- The search icon available in the QSB
- The search key that is part of a set of action keys (shown on the right side of Figure 23–1)
- An explicit icon or button that is displayed by an activity
- Any key press based on a type-to-search declaration

In this section we will look at invoking search through action keys. Action keys are a set of keys available on the device which are tied to specific actions. Some examples of these action keys are shown in Listing 23–28.

Listing 23–28. *List of Action Key Codes*

```
keycode_dpad_up
keycode_dpad_down
keycode_dpad_left
keycode_dpad_right
keycode_dpad_center
keycode_back
keycode_call
keycode_camera
keycode_clear
kecode_endcall
```

```
keycode_home
keycode_menu
keycode_mute
keycode_power
keycode_search
keycode_volume_up
keycode_volume_down
```

You can see these action keys defined in the API for KeyEvent, which is available at http://developer.android.com/reference/android/view/KeyEvent.html

NOTE: Not all of these action keys can be co-opted for search, but some can, such as keycode_call. You will have to try each and see which is suitable for your need.

Once you know which action key you want to use you can tell Android that you are interested in this key by dropping it in the metadata using the XML segment in Listing 23–29.

Listing 23–29. *Action Key Definition Example*

```
<searchable xmlns:android="http://schemas.android.com/apk/res/android"
    android:label="@string/search_label"
    android:hint="@string/search_hint"
    android:searchMode="showSearchLabelAsBadge"

    android:includeInGlobalSearch="true"
    android:searchSuggestAuthority=
       "com.androidbook.search.simplesp.SimpleSuggestionProvider"
    android:searchSuggestSelection=" ? "
>
   <actionkey
       android:keycode="KEYCODE_CALL"
       android:queryActionMsg="call"
       android:suggestActionMsg="call"
       android:suggestActionMsgColumn="call_column" />

   <actionkey
       android:keycode="KEYCODE_DPAD_CENTER"
       android:queryActionMsg="doquery"
       android:suggestActionMsg="dosuggest"
       android:suggestActionMsgColumn="my_column" />
   .....
</searchable>
```

You can also have multiple action keys for the same search context. Here is what each attribute of the actionKey element stands for and how it is used to respond to an action key press.

- *keycode*: This is the key code as defined in the `KeyEvent` API class that should be used to invoke the search activity. There are two times when this key identified by the keycode can be pressed. The first is when the user enters query text in the QSB but hasn't navigated to any suggestions. Typically the user, without an action key implementation, will have pressed the search icon of the QSB. With an action key specified in the metadata of the search, Android allows the user to click the action key instead of the QSB search Go icon. The second is when the user navigates to a specific suggestion and then clicks the action key. In both cases the search activity is invoked with an action of `ACTION_SEARCH`. To know that this action is invoked through an action key, look for an extra string called `SearchManager.ACTION_KEY`. If you see a value here, you know that you are being called in response to an action key press.
- *queryActionMsg*: Any text you enter in this element is passed to the search activity invoking intent as an extra string called `SearchManager.ACTION_MSG`. If you retrieve this message from the intent and it is the same as what you have specified in the metadata, then you know that you are being called directly from the QSB as a result of clicking on the action key. Without this test, you will not know if the `ACTION_SEARCH` is called due to an action key click on the suggestion directly.
- *suggestActionMsg*: Any text you enter in this element is passed to the search activity invoking intent as an extra string called `SearchManager.ACTION_MSG`. The extra keys for this and the `queryActionMsg` are the same. If you give the same value for both of these fields, such as `call`, then you will not know in what way user has invoked the action key. In many cases, this is irrelevant so you can just give the same value for both. But if you have a need to distinguish one from the other, you will need to specify a value that is different from the `queryActionMsg`.
- *suggestActionMsgColumn*: The values `queryActionMsg` and `suggestActionMsg` apply globally to this search activity and the suggestion provider. There isn't a way to alter the action meaning based on the suggestion. If you would like to do that then you will need to tell the metadata that there is an extra column in the suggestion cursor. This will allow Android to pick up the text from that extra column and send it to the activity as part of the invoking `ACTION_SEARCH` intent. Interestingly, the value of this additional column is sent through the same extra key in the intent, namely `SearchManager.ACTION_MSG`.

Among these attributes the key code is mandatory. In addition, there needs to be at least one of the additional three attributes present for the action key to fire.

If you were to use the suggestActionMsgColumn, you would need to populate this column in the suggestion provider class. In Listing 23–29 if you were to use both these keys then you would need to have two additional string columns defined in the suggest cursor (see Listing 23–22), namely call_column and my_column. In that case, your cursor column array would be as shown in Listing 23–30.

Listing 23–30. *Example of Action Key Columns in the Suggestion Cursor*

```
private static final String[] COLUMNS = {
        "_id",  // must include this column
        SearchManager.SUGGEST_COLUMN_TEXT_1,
        SearchManager.SUGGEST_COLUMN_TEXT_2,
        SearchManager.SUGGEST_COLUMN_INTENT_DATA,
        SearchManager.SUGGEST_COLUMN_INTENT_ACTION,
        SearchManager.SUGGEST_COLUMN_SHORTCUT_ID,
        "call_column",
        "my_column"
        };
```

Working with Application-Specific Search Context

Android search allows an activity to pass additional search data to the search activity when it is invoked. We will walk through the details of this now.

As we have shown, an activity in your application can override the onSearchRequested() method to disable search by returning false. Interestingly, the same method can be used instead to pass additional application-specific data to the search activity. Listing 23–31 is an example.

Listing 23–31. *Passing Additional Context*

```
public boolean onSearchRequested()
{
   Bundle applicationData = new Bundle();
   applicationData.putString("string_key","some string value");
   applicationData.putLong("long_key",290904);
   applicationData.putFloat("float_key",2.0f);

   startSearch(null,            // Initial Search search query string
      false,                    // don't "select initial query"
      applicationData,          // extra data
      false                     // don't force a global search
      );

   return true;
}
```

> **NOTE:** You can use the following Bundle API reference to see the various functions available on the bundle object:
> http://developer.android.com/reference/android/os/Bundle.html.

Once the search has started this way, the activity can use the extra called SearchManager.APP_DATA to retrieve the application data bundle. Listing 23–32 shows how you can retrieve each of the above fields.

Listing 23–32. *Retrieving Additional Context*

```
Bundle applicationData =
   queryIntent.getBundleExtra(SearchManager.APP_DATA);
if (applicationData != null)
{
   String s = applicationData.getString("string_key");
   long   l = applicationData.getLong("long_key");
   float  f = applicationData.getFloat("float_key");
}
```

We have introduced the startSearch() method earlier in the chapter briefly. You can find more about this method at the following URL as part of the Activity API:

http://developer.android.com/reference/android/app/Activity.html

Once again this method takes the following four arguments

- initialQuery // a string argument
- selectInitialQuery // boolean
- applicationDataBundle //Bundle
- globalSearchOnly //boolean

The first argument, if available, will populate the query text in the QSB.

The second boolean argument will highlight the text if true. Doing so will enable the user to replace all of the selected query text with what is typed over. If this is false, then the cursor will be at the end of the query text.

The third argument is, of course, the bundle that we are preparing.

The fourth argument, if true, will always invoke a global search. If it is false, then the local search is invoked first, if available; otherwise, it will use the global search.

Resources

As we come to the end of this chapter, we would like to give you a list of resources that we found valuable in writing it.

- www.google.com/googlephone/AndroidUsersGuide.pdf: This is a good Android 2.2.1 reference for understanding how to use Android Search from a user's perspective.
- www.google.com/help/hc/pdfs/mobile/AndroidUsersGuide-30-100.pdf: This is a users guide for Android 3.0 release. These URLs seem to change quickly every couple of months. You should be able to locate by searching google using the key words "Android User's Guide"

- http://developer.android.com/reference/android/app/SearchManager.html: You can use this URL to find the main documentation on Android search from Google. The same URL also works as the API reference for the main Android search facility, namely SearchManager
- http://developer.android.com/reference/android/app/Activity.html#onNewIntent(android.content.Intent): As you design your own search activities, it is sometimes advantageous to set them up as singleTop resulting in the generation of a onNewIntent(). You can find more about this method here.
- http://developer.android.com/guide/samples/SearchableDictionary/index.html: You can refer to this Google sample online to see how an example suggestion provider is implemented. This link points to the source code of the implementation.
- http://developer.android.com/reference/android/provider/SearchRecentSuggestions.html: At this URL you can read about the Search Recent Suggestions API.
- http://developer.android.com/guide/topics/fundamentals.html: This site will help you understand activities, tasks, and launch modes, especially the singleTop launch mode, which is used often as a search activity.
- http://developer.android.com/reference/android/os/Bundle.html:YYou can use this Bundle API reference to see the various functions available on the bundle object. This is useful for application-specific search data.
- http://www.androidbook.com/notes_on_search: At this URL you can find the authors' notes on Android search. We will continue to update the content even after this book goes to press.
- http://www.androidbook.com/projects: You can use this URL to download the test projects dedicated for this chapter. The name of the zip files for this chapter are: ProAndroid3_ch23_SearchRegularActivities.zip, ProAndroid3_ch23_SimpleSuggestionProvider.zip, ProAndroid3_ch23_CustomSuggestionProvider.zip.

Implications for Tablets

The underlying Search API remains unchanged in 3.0. However the QSB and search settings (essentially the user experience) are altered slightly to make use of more real estate. Other than that the ideas presented in this chapter are equally applicable for tablets.

Summary

In this chapter we presented, in a fair amount of detail, the internal workings of Android search. You have learned how activities and suggestion providers interact with Android search. We have showed you how to use the SearchRecentSuggestionsProvider.

We coded from scratch a custom suggestions provider and, in the process, demonstrated the suggestion cursor and its columns in detail. We explored the URIs that are responsible for getting data from suggestion providers. We have presented a lot of sample code that should make it easy to devise and implement your creative search strategies.

Based on the flexibility of the suggestion cursor alone, Android search transcends a simple search to a conduit of information at fingertips.

Chapter 24

Exploring Text to Speech

Android, versions 1.6 and later, features a multilingual speech synthesis engine called Pico. It allows any Android application to speak a string of text with an accent that matches the language. Text-to-speech software allows users to interact with applications without having to look at the screen. This can be extremely important for a mobile platform. How many people have accidentally walked into traffic when they were reading a text message? What if you could simply listen to your text messages instead? What if you could listen to a walking tour instead of reading while walking? There are countless applications where the inclusion of voice would improve an application's usefulness. In this chapter, we'll explore the `TextToSpeech` class of Android and learn what it takes to get our text spoken to us. We'll also learn how to manage the locales, languages, and voices available.

The Basics of Text-to-Speech Capabilities in Android

Before we begin to integrate text to speech (TTS) into an application, you should listen to it in action. In the emulator or device (Android SDK 1.6 or above), go to the main Settings screen and choose "Voice input & output" and then "Text-to-speech settings" (or from Settings choose Text-to-speech or "Speech synthesis", depending on which version of Android you're running). Click the "Listen to an example" option, and you should hear the words, "This is an example of speech synthesis in English with Pico." Notice the other options in this list (see Figure 24–1).

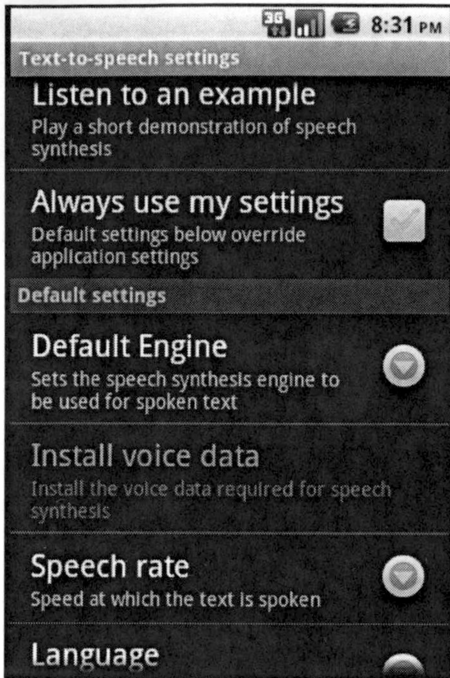

Figure 24–1. *Settings screen for Text to Speech*

You can change the language of the voice and the speech rate. The language option both translates the example words that are spoken and changes the accent of the voice doing the speaking, although the example is still "This is an example of speech synthesis" in whatever language you've set in the Language option. Be aware that the text-to-speech capability is really only the voice part. Translating text from one language to another is done via a separate component, such as Google Translate, which we covered in Chapter 11. Later, when we're actually implementing TTS in our application, we'll want to match the voice with the language, so the French text is spoken with a French voice. The speech rate value goes from "Very slow" to "Very fast".

Pay careful attention to the option "Always use my settings". If this is set by you or the user in system settings, your application may not behave as you expect, since the settings here could override what you want to do in your application.

With Android 2.2, we gained the ability to use TTS engines besides Pico (and thus, prior to Android 2.2, you would not see the Default Engine option in this Settings page). The choice provides flexibility, because Pico may not work well in all situations. Even with multiple TTS engines, there is only one TTS service on the device. The TTS service is shared across all activities on the device, so we must be aware that we may not be the only ones using TTS. Also, we cannot be sure when our text will be spoken or even if it will be spoken at all. However, the interface to the TTS service provides us with callbacks, so we have some idea of what is going on with the text we've sent to be spoken. The TTS service will keep track of which TTS engine we want and will use our desired TTS engine when doing things for us. The TTS service will use whatever TTS engine each calling activity wants, so other applications can use a different TTS engine than our application and we don't need to worry about it.

Let's explore what is happening when we play with these TTS settings. Behind the scenes, Android has fired up a text-to-speech service and Pico, a multilingual speech synthesis engine. The preferences activity we're in has initialized the engine for our current language and speech rate. When we click "Listen to an example", the preferences activity sends text to the service, and the engine speaks it to our audio output. Pico has broken down the text into pieces it knows how to say, and it has stitched those pieces of audio together in a way that sounds fairly natural. The logic inside the engine is actually much more complex than that, but for our purposes, we can pretend it's magic. Fortunately for us, this magic takes up very little room in terms of disk space and memory, so Pico is an ideal addition to a phone.

In this example, we're going to create an application that will read our typed text back to us. It is fairly simple, but it's designed to show you how easy it can be to set up text to speech. To begin, create a new Android Project using the artifacts from Listing 24–1.

> **NOTE:** We will give you a URL at the end of the chapter which you can use to download projects of this chapter. This will allow you to import these projects into your Eclipse directly.

Listing 24–1. ***XML and Java Code for Simple TTS Demo***

```
<?xml version="1.0" encoding="utf-8"?>
<!-- This file is /res/layout/main.xml -->
<LinearLayout xmlns:android="http://schemas.android.com/apk/res/android"
              android:orientation="vertical"
              android:layout_width="fill_parent"
              android:layout_height="fill_parent">

  <EditText android:id="@+id/wordsToSpeak"
    android:hint="Type words to speak here"
    android:layout_width="fill_parent"
    android:layout_height="wrap_content"/>

  <Button android:id="@+id/speak"
    android:text="Speak"
    android:layout_width="wrap_content"
    android:layout_height="wrap_content"
    android:onClick="doSpeak"
    android:enabled="false" />

</LinearLayout>


// This file is MainActivity.java
import android.app.Activity;
import android.content.Intent;
import android.os.Bundle;
import android.speech.tts.TextToSpeech;
import android.speech.tts.TextToSpeech.OnInitListener;
import android.util.Log;
import android.view.View;
```

```
import android.widget.Button;
import android.widget.EditText;

public class MainActivity extends Activity implements OnInitListener {
    private EditText words = null;
    private Button speakBtn = null;
    private static final int REQ_TTS_STATUS_CHECK = 0;
    private static final String TAG = "TTS Demo";
    private TextToSpeech mTts;

    /** Called when the activity is first created. */
    @Override
    public void onCreate(Bundle savedInstanceState) {
        super.onCreate(savedInstanceState);
        setContentView(R.layout.main);

        words = (EditText)findViewById(R.id.wordsToSpeak);
        speakBtn = (Button)findViewById(R.id.speak);

        // Check to be sure that TTS exists and is okay to use
        Intent checkIntent = new Intent();
        checkIntent.setAction(TextToSpeech.Engine.ACTION_CHECK_TTS_DATA);
        startActivityForResult(checkIntent, REQ_TTS_STATUS_CHECK);
    }

    public void doSpeak(View view) {
        mTts.speak(words.getText().toString(),
            TextToSpeech.QUEUE_ADD, null);
    }

    protected void onActivityResult(int requestCode, int resultCode,
            Intent data) {
        if (requestCode == REQ_TTS_STATUS_CHECK) {
            switch (resultCode) {
            case TextToSpeech.Engine.CHECK_VOICE_DATA_PASS:
                // TTS is up and running
                mTts = new TextToSpeech(this, this);
                Log.v(TAG, "Pico is installed okay");
                break;
            case TextToSpeech.Engine.CHECK_VOICE_DATA_BAD_DATA:
            case TextToSpeech.Engine.CHECK_VOICE_DATA_MISSING_DATA:
            case TextToSpeech.Engine.CHECK_VOICE_DATA_MISSING_VOLUME:
                // missing data, install it
                Log.v(TAG, "Need language stuff: " + resultCode);
                Intent installIntent = new Intent();
                installIntent.setAction(
                    TextToSpeech.Engine.ACTION_INSTALL_TTS_DATA);
                startActivity(installIntent);
                break;
            case TextToSpeech.Engine.CHECK_VOICE_DATA_FAIL:
            default:
                Log.e(TAG, "Got a failure. TTS not available");
            }
        }
        else {
            // Got something else
        }
```

```
    }

    public void onInit(int status) {
        // Now that the TTS engine is ready, we enable the button
        if( status == TextToSpeech.SUCCESS) {
            speakBtn.setEnabled(true);
        }
    }

    @Override
    public void onPause()
    {
        super.onPause();
        // if we're losing focus, stop talking
        if( mTts != null)
            mTts.stop();
    }

    @Override
    public void onDestroy()
    {
        super.onDestroy();
        mTts.shutdown();
    }
}
```

Our UI for this example is a simple EditText view to allow us to type in the words to be spoken, plus a button to initiate the speaking (see Figure 24–2). Our button has a doSpeak() method, which grabs the text string from the EditText view and queues it for the TTS service using speak() with QUEUE_ADD. Remember that the TTS service is being shared, so in this case, we queue up our text for speaking behind whatever else might be there (which is most likely nothing). The other option besides QUEUE_ADD is QUEUE_FLUSH, which will throw away the other text in the queue and immediately play ours instead. At the end of our onCreate() method, we initiate an Intent that requests the TTS engine to let us know if everything is OK for text to be spoken. Because we want the answer back, we use startActivityForResult() and pass a request code. We get the response in onActivityResult() where we look for CHECK_VOICE_DATA_PASS. Because the TTS service can return more than one type of resultCode meaning "OK," we cannot just look for RESULT_OK. See the other values we can get by reviewing the switch statement.

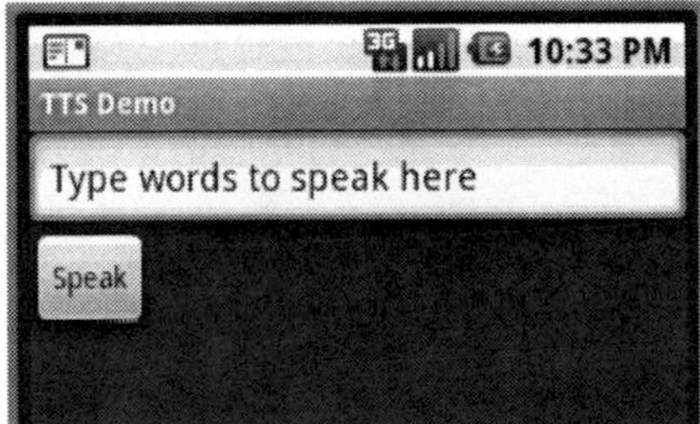

Figure 24–2. *User interface of TTS demonstration*

If we get CHECK_VOICE_DATA_PASS back, we instantiate a TextToSpeech object. Notice that our MainActivity implements OnInitListener. This allows us to receive a callback when the TTS service interface has been created and is available, which we receive with the onInit() method. If we get SUCCESS inside of onInit(), we know we're ready to speak text, and we enable our button in the UI. Two more things to note are the call to stop() in onPause(), and the call to shutdown() in onDestroy(). We call stop() because if something goes in front of our application, it's lost focus and should stop talking. We don't want to interrupt something audio-based in another activity that has jumped in front. We call shutdown() to notify Android that we're through with the TTS engine and that the resources, if not needed by anyone else, are eligible to be released.

Go ahead and experiment with this example. Try different sentences or phrases. Now, give it a large block of text so you can hear the speech go on and on. Consider what would happen if our application were interrupted while the large block of text was being read, perhaps if some other application made a call to the TTS service with QUEUE_FLUSH, or the application simply lost focus. To test out this idea, go ahead and press the Home button while a large block of text is being spoken. Because of our call to stop() in onPause(), the speaking stops, even though our application is still running in the background. If our application regains focus, how can we know where we were? It would be nice if we had some way to know where we left off so we could begin speaking again, at least close to where we left off. There is a way, but it takes a bit of work.

Using Utterances to Keep Track of Our Speech

The TTS engine can invoke a callback in your application when it has completed speaking a piece of text, called an *utterance* in the TTS world. We set the callback using the setOnUtteranceCompletedListener() method on the TTS instance, mTts in our example. When calling speak(), we can add a name/value pair to tell the TTS engine to let us know when that utterance is finished being played. By sending unique utterance IDs to the TTS engine, we can keep track of which utterances have been spoken and which have not. If the application regains focus after an interruption, we could resume speaking with the next utterance after the last completed utterance. Building on our previous example, change the code as shown in Listing 24–2, or see project TTSDemo2 in the source code from the book's web site.

Listing 24–2. *Changes to MainActivity to Illustrate Utterance Tracking*

```
// Add these imports
import java.util.HashMap;
import java.util.StringTokenizer;
import android.speech.tts.TextToSpeech.OnUtteranceCompletedListener;

// Change MainActivity
public class MainActivity extends Activity implements OnInitListener,
OnUtteranceCompletedListener {

    // Add these private fields
    private int uttCount = 0;
```

```
private int lastUtterance = -1;
private HashMap<String, String> params = new HashMap<String, String>();

// Modify onInit
public void onInit(int status) {
    // Now that the TTS engine is ready, we enable the button
    if( status == TextToSpeech.SUCCESS) {
        speakBtn.setEnabled(true);
        mTts.setOnUtteranceCompletedListener(this);
    }
}

// Add new method onUtteranceCompleted
public void onUtteranceCompleted(String uttId) {
    Log.v(TAG, "Got completed message for uttId: " + uttId);
    lastUtterance = Integer.parseInt(uttId);
}

// Modify doSpeak
public void doSpeak(View view) {
    StringTokenizer st = new StringTokenizer(words.getText().toString(),",.");
    while (st.hasMoreTokens()) {
        params.put(TextToSpeech.Engine.KEY_PARAM_UTTERANCE_ID,
                   String.valueOf(uttCount++));
        mTts.speak(st.nextToken(), TextToSpeech.QUEUE_ADD, params);
    }
}
```

The first thing we need to do is make sure our `MainActivity` also implements the `OnUtteranceCompletedListener` interface. This will allow us to get the callback from the TTS engine when the utterances finish being spoken. We also need to modify our button `doSpeak()` method to pass the extra information to associate an utterance ID to each piece of text we send. For this new version of our example, we're going to break up our text into utterances using the comma and period characters as separators. We then loop through our utterances passing each with `QUEUE_ADD` and not `QUEUE_FLUSH` (we don't want to interrupt ourselves!) and a unique utterance ID, which is a simple incrementing counter, converted to a `String`, of course. We can use any unique text for an utterance ID; since it's a `String`, we're not limited to numbers. In fact, we could use the string itself as the utterance ID, although if the strings get very long, we might not want to do that for performance reasons. We need to modify the `onInit()` method to register ourselves for receiving the utterance completed callbacks, and finally, we need to provide the callback method `onUtteranceCompleted()` for the TTS service to invoke when an utterance completes. For this example, we're simply going to log a message to `LogCat` for each completed utterance.

When you run this new example, type some text that contains commas and periods, and click the Speak button. Watch the `LogCat` window as you listen to the voice reading your text. You will notice that the text is queued up immediately, and as each utterance completes, our callback is invoked, and a message is logged for each utterance. If you interrupt this example, for instance, by clicking Home while the text is being read, you will see that the voice and the callbacks stop. We now know what the last utterance was, and we can pick up where we left off later when we regain control.

Using Audio Files for Your Voice

The TTS engine provides a way to properly pronounce words or utterances that, by default, come out wrong. For example, if you type in "Don Quixote" as the text to be spoken, you will hear a pronunciation of the name that is not correct. To be fair, the TTS engine is able to make a good guess at how words should sound and cannot be expected to know every exception to all the rules. So how can this be fixed? One way is to record a snippet of audio to be played back instead of the default audio. To get the same voice as everything else, we want to use the TTS engine to make the sound and record the result, and then we tell the TTS engine to use our recorded sound in place of what it would normally do. The trick is to provide text that sounds like what we want. Let's get started.

Create a new Android project in Eclipse. Use the XML from Listing 24–3 to create the main layout. We're going to make this simpler by putting text directly into our layout file instead of using references to strings. Normally, you would want to use string resource IDs in your layout file. The layout will look like Figure 24–3.

Listing 24–3. *A Layout XML file to Demonstrate Saved Audio for Text*

```
<?xml version="1.0" encoding="utf-8"?>
<!-- This file is /res/layout/main.xml -->
<LinearLayout xmlns:android="http://schemas.android.com/apk/res/android"
    android:orientation="vertical" android:layout_width="fill_parent"
    android:layout_height="fill_parent">

  <EditText android:id="@+id/wordsToSpeak"
    android:text="Dohn Keyhotay"
    android:layout_width="fill_parent"
    android:layout_height="wrap_content"/>

  <Button android:id="@+id/speakBtn"
    android:text="Speak"
    android:layout_width="wrap_content"
    android:layout_height="wrap_content"
    android:onClick="doButton"
    android:enabled="false" />

  <TextView android:id="@+id/filenameLabel"
    android:text="Filename:"
    android:layout_width="wrap_content"
    android:layout_height="wrap_content"/>

  <EditText android:id="@+id/filename"
    android:text="/sdcard/donquixote.wav"
    android:layout_width="fill_parent"
    android:layout_height="wrap_content"/>

  <Button android:id="@+id/recordBtn"
    android:text="Record"
```

```
    android:layout_width="wrap_content"
    android:layout_height="wrap_content"
    android:enabled="false"
    android:onClick="doButton"/>

  <Button android:id="@+id/playBtn"
    android:text="Play"
    android:layout_width="wrap_content"
    android:layout_height="wrap_content"
    android:onClick="doButton"
    android:enabled="false" />

  <TextView android:id="@+id/useWithLabel"
    android:text="Use with:"
    android:layout_width="wrap_content"
    android:layout_height="wrap_content"/>

  <EditText android:id="@+id/realText"
    android:text="Don Quixote"
    android:layout_width="fill_parent"
    android:layout_height="wrap_content"/>

  <Button android:id="@+id/assocBtn"
    android:text="Associate"
    android:layout_width="wrap_content"
    android:layout_height="wrap_content"
    android:onClick="doButton"
    android:enabled="false" />

</LinearLayout>
```

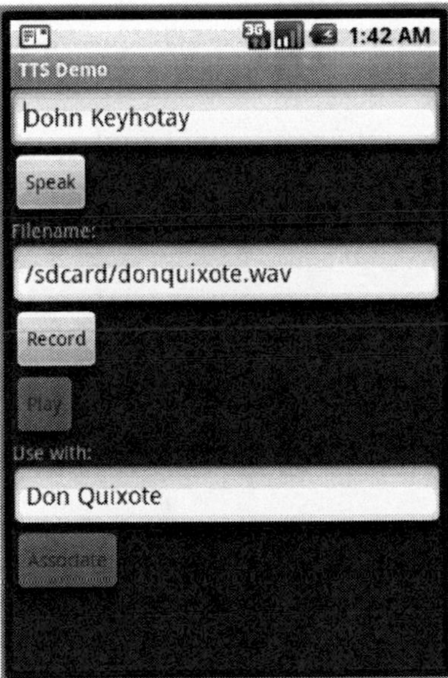

Figure 24–3. *User interface of TTS demonstration that associates a sound file with text*

We need a field to hold the special text that we'll record with the TTS engine into a sound file. We supply the file name in the layout as well. Finally, we need to associate our sound file to the actual string we want the sound file to play for.

Now, let's look at the Java code for our `MainActivity` (see Listing 24–4). In the `onCreate()` method, we set up button click handlers for the Speak, Play, Record, and Associate buttons, and then we initiate the TTS engine using an intent. The rest of the code consists of callbacks to handle the result from the intent that checks for a properly set up TTS engine and handles the initialization result from the TTS engine and the normal callbacks for pausing and shutting down our activity.

Listing 24–4. *Java Code to Demonstrate Saved Audio for Text*

```
import java.io.File;
import java.util.ArrayList;

import android.app.Activity;
import android.content.Intent;
import android.media.MediaPlayer;
import android.os.Bundle;
import android.speech.tts.TextToSpeech;
import android.speech.tts.TextToSpeech.OnInitListener;
import android.util.Log;
import android.view.View;
import android.view.View.OnClickListener;
import android.widget.Button;
import android.widget.EditText;
import android.widget.Toast;

public class MainActivity extends Activity implements OnInitListener {
    private EditText words = null;
    private Button speakBtn = null;
    private EditText filename = null;
    private Button recordBtn = null;
    private Button playBtn = null;
    private EditText useWith = null;
    private Button assocBtn = null;
    private String soundFilename = null;
    private File soundFile = null;
    private static final int REQ_TTS_STATUS_CHECK = 0;
    private static final String TAG = "TTS Demo";
    private TextToSpeech mTts = null;
    private MediaPlayer player = null;

    /** Called when the activity is first created. */
    @Override
    public void onCreate(Bundle savedInstanceState) {
        super.onCreate(savedInstanceState);
        setContentView(R.layout.main);

        words = (EditText)findViewById(R.id.wordsToSpeak);
        filename = (EditText)findViewById(R.id.filename);
        useWith = (EditText)findViewById(R.id.realText);

        speakBtn = (Button)findViewById(R.id.speakBtn);
        recordBtn = (Button)findViewById(R.id.recordBtn);
```

```
        playBtn = (Button)findViewById(R.id.playBtn);
        assocBtn = (Button)findViewById(R.id.assocBtn);

        // Check to be sure that TTS exists and is okay to use
        Intent checkIntent = new Intent();
        checkIntent.setAction(TextToSpeech.Engine.ACTION_CHECK_TTS_DATA);
        startActivityForResult(checkIntent, REQ_TTS_STATUS_CHECK);
    }

    public void doButton(View view) {
        switch(view.getId()) {
        case R.id.speakBtn:
            mTts.speak(words.getText().toString(),
                TextToSpeech.QUEUE_ADD, null);
            break;
        case R.id.recordBtn:
            soundFilename = filename.getText().toString();
            soundFile = new File(soundFilename);
            if (soundFile.exists())
                soundFile.delete();

            if(mTts.synthesizeToFile(words.getText().toString(),
                    null, soundFilename) == TextToSpeech.SUCCESS) {
                Toast.makeText(getBaseContext(),
                        "Sound file created",
                        Toast.LENGTH_SHORT).show();
                playBtn.setEnabled(true);
                assocBtn.setEnabled(true);
            }
            else {
                Toast.makeText(getBaseContext(),
                        "Oops! Sound file not created",
                        Toast.LENGTH_SHORT).show();
            }
            break;
        case R.id.playBtn:
            try {
                player = new MediaPlayer();
                player.setDataSource(soundFilename);
                player.prepare();
                player.start();
            }
            catch(Exception e) {
                Toast.makeText(getBaseContext(),
                        "Hmmmmm. Can't play file",
                        Toast.LENGTH_SHORT).show();
                e.printStackTrace();
            }
            break;
        case R.id.assocBtn:
            mTts.addSpeech(useWith.getText().toString(), soundFilename);
            Toast.makeText(getBaseContext(),
                  "Associated!",
                  Toast.LENGTH_SHORT).show();
            break;
        }
    }
```

```
protected void onActivityResult(int requestCode, int resultCode,
        Intent data) {
    if (requestCode == REQ_TTS_STATUS_CHECK) {
        switch (resultCode) {
        case TextToSpeech.Engine.CHECK_VOICE_DATA_PASS:
            // TTS is up and running
            mTts = new TextToSpeech(this, this);
            Log.v(TAG, "Pico is installed okay");
            ArrayList<String> available =
                    data.getStringArrayListExtra("availableVoices");
            break;
        case TextToSpeech.Engine.CHECK_VOICE_DATA_BAD_DATA:
        case TextToSpeech.Engine.CHECK_VOICE_DATA_MISSING_DATA:
        case TextToSpeech.Engine.CHECK_VOICE_DATA_MISSING_VOLUME:
            // missing data, install it
            Log.v(TAG, "Need language stuff: " + resultCode);
            Intent installIntent = new Intent();
            installIntent.setAction(
                TextToSpeech.Engine.ACTION_INSTALL_TTS_DATA);
            startActivity(installIntent);
            break;
        case TextToSpeech.Engine.CHECK_VOICE_DATA_FAIL:
        default:
            Log.e(TAG, "Got a failure. TTS not available");
        }
    }
    else {
        // Got something else
    }
}

public void onInit(int status) {
    // Now that the TTS engine is ready, we enable buttons
    if( status == TextToSpeech.SUCCESS) {
        speakBtn.setEnabled(true);
        recordBtn.setEnabled(true);
    }
}

@Override
public void onPause()
{
    super.onPause();
    // if we're losing focus, stop playing
    if(player != null) {
        player.stop();
    }
    // if we're losing focus, stop talking
    if( mTts != null)
        mTts.stop();
}

@Override
public void onDestroy()
{
    super.onDestroy();
```

```
        if(player != null) {
            player.release();
        }
        if( mTts != null) {
            mTts.shutdown();
        }
    }
}
```

For this example to work, we need to add a permission in our AndroidManifest.xml file for android.permission.WRITE_EXTERNAL_STORAGE. When you run this example, you should see the UI as displayed in Figure 24–3.

We're going to record some text that sounds like what we want "Don Quixote" to sound like, so we can't use the real words. We need to make up text to get the sounds we want. Click the Speak button to hear how the fake words sound. Not too bad! Next, click Record to write the audio to a WAV file. When the recording is successful, the Play and Associate buttons get enabled. Click the Play button to hear the WAV file directly using a media player. If you like how this sounds, click the Associate button. This invokes the addSpeech() method on the TTS engine, which then ties our new sound file to the string in the "Use with" field. If this is successful, go back up to the top EditText view; type **Don Quixote**, and click Speak. Now it sounds like it's supposed to.

Note that the synthesizeToFile() method only saves to the WAV file format, regardless of the file name extension, but you can associate other formatted sound files using addSpeech()—for example, MP3 files. The MP3 files will have to be created some way other than by using the synthesizeToFile() method of the TTS engine.

The uses of this method for speaking are very limited. In a scenario with unbounded words—that is, when you don't know in advance which words will be presented for speech—it is impossible to have at the ready all of the audio files you would need to fix the words that do not get pronounced correctly by Pico. In scenarios with a bounded domain of words—for example, reading the weather forecast—you could go through an exercise of testing all of the words in your application to find those that don't sound right and fixing them. Even in an unbounded situation, you could prepare some word sounds in advance so that critical words you expect will sound correct. You might, for instance, want to have a sound file at the ready for your company's name or your own name!

There's a dark side to the use of this method however: the text you pass to speak() must match exactly the text you used in the call to addSpeech(). Unfortunately, you cannot provide an audio file for a single word and then expect the TTS engine to use the audio file for that word when you pass that word as part of a sentence to speak(). To hear your audio file you must present the exact text that the audio file represents. Anything more or less causes Pico to kick in and do the best it can.

One way around this is to break up our text into words and pass each word separately to the TTS engine. While this could result in our audio file being played (of course, we'd need to record "Quixote" separately from "Don"), the overall result will be choppy speech, as if each word were its own sentence. In some applications, this might be acceptable. The ideal use case for audio files occurs when we need to speak predetermined canned words or phrases, where we know exactly in advance the text we'll need to have spoken.

So what are we to do when we know we'll get words in sentences that cannot be properly spoken by Pico? One method might be to scan our text for known "trouble" words and replace those words with "fake" words that we know Pico can speak properly. We don't need to show the text to the user that we give to the `speak()` method. So perhaps we could replace "Quixote" in our text with "Keyhotay" before we call `speak()`. The outcome is that it sounds right and the user is none the wiser. In terms of resource usage, storing the fake string is much more efficient than storing an audio file, even though we're still calling Pico. We had to call Pico for the rest of our text, so it's not much of a loss at all. However, we don't want to do too much second-guessing of Pico. That is, Pico has a lot of intelligence on how to pronounce things, and if we try to do Pico's job for it, we could run into trouble quickly.

In our last example, we recorded a sound file for a piece of text, so that when the TTS engine reads it back to us later, it accesses the sound file instead of generating the speech using Pico. As you might expect, playing a small sound file takes fewer device resources than running a TTS engine and interfacing with it. Therefore, if you have a manageable set of words or phrases to provide sound for, you might want to create sound files in advance, even if the Pico engine pronounces them correctly. This will help your application run faster. If you have a small number of sound files, you will probably use less overall memory too. If you take this approach, you will want to use the following method call:

```
TextToSpeech.addSpeech(String text, String packagename, int soundFileResourceId)
```

This is a very simple way of adding sound files to the TTS engine. The text argument is the string to play the sound file for; `packagename` is the application package name where the resource file is stored, and `soundFileResourceId` is the resource ID of the sound file. Store your sound files under your application's `/res/raw` directory. When your application starts up, add your prerecorded sound files to the TTS engine by referring to their resource ID (e.g., `R.raw.quixote`). Of course, you'll need some sort of database, or a predefined list, to know which text each sound file is for. If you are internationalizing your application, you can store the alternate sound files under the appropriate `/res/raw` directory; for example `/res/raw-fr` for French sound files.

Advanced Features of the TTS Engine

Now that you've, learned the basics of TTS, let's explore some advanced features of the Pico engine. We'll start with setting audio streams, which help you direct the spoken voice to the proper audio output channel. Next, we'll cover playing earcons (audible icons) and silence. Then, we'll cover setting language options and finish with a few miscellaneous method calls.

Setting Audio Streams

Earlier, we used a params HashMap to pass extra arguments to the TTS engine. One of the arguments we can pass (KEY_PARAM_STREAM) tells the TTS engine which audio stream to use for the text we want to hear spoken. See Table 24–1 for a list of the available audio streams.

Table 24–1. *Available Audio Streams*

Audio Stream	Description
STREAM_ALARM	The audio stream for alarms
STREAM_DTMF	The audio stream for DTMF tones (i.e., phone button tones)
STREAM_MUSIC	The audio stream for music playback
STREAM_NOTIFICATION	The audio stream for notifications
STREAM_RING	The audio stream for the phone ring
STREAM_SYSTEM	The audio stream for system sounds
STREAM_VOICE_CALL	The audio stream for phone calls

If the text we want spoken is related to an alarm, we want to tell the TTS engine to play the audio over the audio stream for alarms. Therefore, we'd want to make a call like this prior to calling the speak() method:

```
params.put(TextToSpeech.Engine.KEY_PARAM_STREAM,
                    String.valueOf(AudioManager.STREAM_ALARM));
```

Review Listing 24–2 to recall how we set up and passed a params HashMap to the speak() method call. You can put utterance IDs into the same params HashMap as the one you use to specify the audio stream.

Using Earcons

There is another type of sound that the TTS engine can play for us called an earcon. An earcon is like an audible icon. It's not supposed to represent text but rather provide an audible cue to some sort of event or to the presence of something in the text other than words. An earcon could be a sound to indicate that we're now reading bullet points from a presentation or that we've just flipped to the next page. Maybe your application is for a walking tour, and the earcon tells the listener to move on to the next location on the tour.

To set up an earcon for playback, you need to invoke the addEarcon() method, which takes two or three arguments, similar to addSpeech(). The first argument is the name of the earcon, similar to the text field of addSpeech(). Convention says that you should enclose your earcon name in square brackets (e.g., "[boing]"). In the two-argument case, the second argument is a file name string. In the three-argument case, the second argument is the package name, and the third argument is a resource ID that refers to an audio file most likely stored under /res/raw. To get an earcon played, use the playEarcon() method, which looks just like the speak() method with its three arguments. An example of using earcons is shown in Listing 24–5.

Listing 24–5: *Sample Code Using Earcons*

```
String turnPageEarcon = "[turnPage]";
mTts.addEarcon(turnPageEarcon, "com.androidbook.tts.demo",
    R.raw.turnpage);
mTts.playEarcon(turnPageEarcon, TextToSpeech.QUEUE_ADD, params);
```

We use earcons instead of simply playing audio files using a media player because of the queuing mechanism of the TTS engine. Instead of having to determine the opportune moment to play an audible cue and relying on callbacks to get the timing right, we can instead queue up our earcons among the text we send to the TTS engine. We then know that our earcons will be played at the appropriate time, and we can use the same pathway to get our sounds to the user, including the onUtteranceCompleted() callbacks to let us know where we are.

Playing Silence

The TTS engine has yet one more play method that we can use: playSilence(). This method also has three arguments like speak() and playEarcon(), where the second argument is the queue mode and the third is the optional params HashMap. The first argument to playSilence() is a long that represents the number of milliseconds to play silence for. You'd most likely use this method with the QUEUE_ADD mode to separate two different strings of text in time. That is, you could insert a period of silence between two strings of text without having to manage the wait time in your application. You'd simply call speak(), playSilence(), and speak() again to get the desired effect. Here is an example of using playSilence() to get a two-second delay:

```
mTts.playSilence(2000, TextToSpeech.QUEUE_ADD, params);
```

Choosing a Different Text-to-Speech Engine

To specify a particular TTS engine, the setEngineByPackageName() method can be used with an appropriate engine package name as the argument. For Pico, the package name is com.svox.pico. To get the user's default TTS engine package name, use the getDefaultEngine() method. These two methods must not be called before reaching the onInit() method, as they will not work otherwise. These two methods are also not available prior to Android 2.2.

Using Language Methods

We haven't yet addressed the question of language, so we'll turn to that now. The TTS capability reads text using a voice that corresponds to the language the voice was created for, that is, the Italian voice is expecting to see text in the Italian language. The voice recognizes features of the text to pronounce it correctly. For this reason, it doesn't make sense to use the wrong language voice with the text sent to the TTS engine. Speaking French text with an Italian voice is likely to cause problems; it is best to match up the locale of the text with the locale of the voice.

The TTS engine provides some methods for languages, to both find out what languages are available and set the language for speaking. The TTS engine has only a certain number of language packs available, although it will be able to reach out to the Android Market to get more if they are available. You saw some code for this in Listing 24–1 within the `onActivityResult()` callback, where an Intent was created to get a missing language. Of course, it is possible that the desired language pack has not been made available yet, but more and more will be available over time.

The `TextToSpeech` method to check on a language is `isLanguageAvailable(Locale locale)`. Since locales can represent a country and a language, and sometimes a variant too, the answer back is not a simple true or false. The answer could be one of the following: `TextToSpeech.LANG_COUNTRY_AVAILABLE`, which means that both country and language are supported; `TextToSpeech.LANG_AVAILABLE`, which means that the language is supported but not the country; and `TextToSpeech.LANG_NOT_SUPPORTED`, which means that nothing is supported. If you get back `TextToSpeech.LANG_MISSING_DATA`, the language is supported, but the data files were not found by the TTS engine. Your application should direct the user to the Android Market, or another suitable source, to find the missing data files. For example, the French language might be supported, but not Canadian French. If that were the case and `Locale.CANADA_FRENCH` was passed to the TTS engine, the response would be `TextToSpeech.LANG_AVAILABLE`, not `TextToSpeech.LANG_COUNTRY_AVAILABLE`. The other possible return value is a special case where the locale might include a variant, in which case the response could be `TextToSpeech.LANG_COUNTRY_VAR_AVAILABLE`, which means everything is supported.

Using `isLanguageAvailable()` is a tedious way to determine all of the languages supported by the TTS engine. Fortunately, we can ask the TTS engine to tell us which languages are ready to be used. If you look carefully at Listing 24–4, in the `onActivityResult()` callback contained in the section where we receive the response from the intent, you'll see that the data object contains a list of languages that are supported by the TTS engine. Look under the `CHECK_VOICE_DATA_PASS` case for the `ArrayList` variable called `available`. It has been set to an array of voice strings. The values will look something like `eng-USA` or `fra-FRA`. While locale strings are usually of the form `ll_cc` where `ll` is a two-character representation of a language and `cc` is a two-character representation of a country, these `lll-ccc` strings from the TTS engine can also be used to construct a locale object for use with the TTS engine. Unfortunately, we've received back an array of strings instead of locales, so we'll have to do some parsing or mapping to figure out what voices are truly available for your desired TTS engine.

The method to set a language is `setLanguage(Locale locale)`. This returns the same result codes as `isLanguageAvailable()`. If you wish to use this method, invoke it once the TTS engine has been initialized, that is, in the `onInit()` method or later. Otherwise, your language choice may not take effect. To get the current default locale of the device, use the `Locale.getDefault()` method, which will return a locale value such as `en_US` or the appropriate value for where you are. Use the `getLanguage()` method of the `TextToSpeech` class to find out the current locale of the TTS engine. As you did with `setLanguage()`, do not call `getLanguage()` before `onInit()`. Values from `getLanguage()` will look like eng_`USA`. Notice that now we've got an underscore instead of a hyphen between the language and the country. While Android appears to be forgiving when it comes to locale strings, it would be nice to see the API get more consistent in the future. It would have been quite acceptable for us to use something like this in our example to set the language for the TTS engine:

```
switch(mTts.setLanguage(Locale.getDefault())) {
case TextToSpeech.LANG_COUNTRY_AVAILABLE: …
```

At the beginning of this chapter, we pointed out the main text-to-speech setting of "Always use my settings", which overrides application settings for language. As of Android 2.2, the method `areDefaultsEnforced()` of the `TextToSpeech` class will tell you whether or not the user has selected this option by returning `true` or `false`. Within your application, you can tell if your language choice would be overridden and take appropriate action as necessary.

Finally, to wrap up this discussion of TTS, we'll cover a few other methods you can use. The `setPitch(float pitch)` method will change the voice to be higher or lower pitched, without changing the speed of the speaking. The normal value for pitch is 1.0. The lowest meaningful value appears to be 0.5 and the highest 2.0; you can set values lower and higher, but they don't appear to change the pitch any more after crossing these thresholds. The same thresholds appear to hold for the `setSpeechRate(float rate)` method. That is, you pass this method a float argument with a value between 0.5 and 2.0, where 1.0 would be a normal speech rate. A number higher than 1.0 yields faster speech, and one lower than 1.0 yields slower speech. Another method you might want to use is `isSpeaking()`, which returns `true` or `false` to indicate whether or not the TTS engine is currently speaking anything (including silence from `playSilence()`). If you need to be notified when the TTS engine has completed saying everything from its queue, you could implement a `BroadcastReceiver` for the `ACTION_TTS_QUEUE_PROCESSING_COMPLETED` broadcast.

References

Here are some helpful references to topics you may wish to explore further:

- http://www.androidbook.com/projects. Look here for a list of downloadable projects related to this book. For this chapter look for a zip file called ProAndroid3_Ch24_TextToSpeech.zip. This zip file contains all projects from this chapter, listed in separate root directories. There is also a README.TXT file that describes exactly how to import projects into Eclipse from one of these zip files.

- `http://groups.google.com/group/tts-for-android`: This URL is for the Google group for discussing the TextToSpeech API.
- `https://groups.google.com/group/eyes-free`: This URL is for the Eyes-Free Project Google Group, for discussing an open source project to provide accessibility capabilities for Android. Plus, there are links here to source code.

Summary

In this chapter, we've shown you how to get your Android application to talk to the user. Android has incorporated a very nice TTS engine to facilitate this functionality. For a developer, there's not much to figure out. The Pico engine takes care of most of the work for us. When Pico runs into trouble, there are ways to get to the desired effect, as we've demonstrated. The advanced features make life pretty easy too. The thing to keep in mind when working with text-to-speech engines is that you must be a good mobile citizen: conserve resources, share the TTS engine responsibly, and use your voice appropriately.

Chapter 25

Touch Screens

Many Android devices incorporate touch screens. When a device does not have a physical keyboard, much of the user input *must* come through the touch screen. Therefore your applications will often need to be able to deal with touch input from the user. You've most likely already seen the virtual keyboard that displays on the screen when text input is required from the user. We used touch with mapping applications in Chapter 17 to pan the maps sideways. The implementations of the touch screen interface have been hidden from you so far, but now we'll show you how to take advantage of the touch screen.

This chapter is made up of four major parts. The first section will deal with `MotionEvent` objects, which is how Android tells an application that the user is touching a touch screen. We'll also cover the `VelocityTracker` and drag and drop. The second section will deal with multitouch, where a user can have more than one finger at a time on the touch screen. The third section covers touches with maps, since there are some special classes and methods to help us with maps and touch screens. Finally, we will include a section on gestures, a specialized type of capability in which touch sequences can be interpreted as commands.

Understanding MotionEvents

In this section, we're going to cover how Android tells applications about touch events from the user. For now, we will only be concerned with touching the screen one finger at a time (we'll cover multi-touch in a later section).

At the hardware level, a touch screen is made up of special materials that can pick up pressure and convert that to screen coordinates. The information about the touch is turned into data, and that data is passed to the software to deal with it.

The MotionEvent Object

When a user touches the touch screen of an Android device, a `MotionEvent` object is created. The `MotionEvent` contains information about where and when the touch took place, as well as other details of the touch event. The `MotionEvent` object gets passed to an appropriate method in your application. This could be the `onTouchEvent()` method of a `View` object. Remember that the `View` class is the parent of quite a few classes in Android, including `Layouts`, `Buttons`, `Lists`, `Surfaces`, `Clocks`, and more. This means we can interact with all of these different types of `View` objects using touch events. When the method is called, it can inspect the `MotionEvent` object to decide what to do. For example, a `MapView` could use touch events to move the map sideways to allow the user to pan the map to other points of interest. Or a virtual keyboard object could receive touch events to activate the virtual keys to provide text input to some other part of the user interface (UI).

A `MotionEvent` object is one of a sequence of events related to a touch by the user. The sequence starts when the user first touches the touch screen, continues through any movements of the finger across the surface of the touch screen, and ends when the finger is lifted from the touch screen. The initial touch (an `ACTION_DOWN` action), the movements sideways (`ACTION_MOVE` actions) and the up event (an `ACTION_UP` action) of the finger all create `MotionEvent` objects. You could receive quite a few `ACTION_MOVE` events as the finger moves across the surface before you receive the final `ACTION_UP` event. Each `MotionEvent` object contains information about what action is being performed, where the touch is taking place, how much pressure was applied, how big the touch was, when the action occurred, and when the initial `ACTION_DOWN` occurred. There is a fourth possible action, which is `ACTION_CANCEL`. This action is used to indicate that a touch sequence is ending without actually doing anything. Finally, there is `ACTION_OUTSIDE`, which is set in a special case where a touch occurs outside of our window but we still get to find out about it.

There is another way to receive touch events, and that is to register a callback handler for touch events on a `View` object. The class to receive the events must implement the `View.OnTouchListener` interface, and the `View` object's `setOnTouchListener()` method must be called to set up the handler for that `View`. The implementing class of the `View.OnTouchListener` must implement the `onTouch()` method. Whereas the `onTouchEvent()` method takes just a `MotionEvent` object as a parameter, `onTouch()` takes both a `View` and a `MotionEvent` object as parameters. This is because the `OnTouchListener` could receive `MotionEvent` objects for multiple views. This will become clearer with our next example application.

If a `MotionEvent` handler (either through the `onTouchEvent()` or `onTouch()` method) consumes the event and no one else needs to know about it, the method should return `true`. This tells Android that the event does not need to be passed to any other views. If the `View` object is not interested in this event *or any future events related to this touch sequence*, it returns false. The `onTouchEvent()` method of the base class `View` doesn't do anything and returns `false`. Subclasses of `View` may or may not do the same. For example, a `Button` object will consume a touch event, since a touch is equivalent to a click, and therefore returns `true` from the `onTouchEvent()` method. Upon receiving an `ACTION_DOWN` event, the `Button` will change its color to indicate that it is in the process of being clicked. The `Button` also wants to receive the `ACTION_UP` event to know when the user has let go, so it can initiate the logic of clicking the button. If a `Button` object returned false from onTouchEvent(), it would not receive any more MotionEvent objects to tell it when the user lifted a finger from the touch screen.

When we want touch events to do something new with a particular View object, we can extend the class, override the onTouchEvent() method, and put our logic there. We can also implement the View.OnTouchListener interface and set up a callback handler on the View object. By setting up a callback handler with onTouch(), MotionEvents will be delivered there first before they go to the View's onTouchEvent() method. Only if the onTouch() method returned false would our View's onTouchEvent() method get called. Let's get to our example application where this should be easier to see.

> **NOTE:** We will give you a URL at the end of the chapter which you can use to download projects of this chapter. This will allow you to import these projects into your Eclipse directly.

Listing 25–1 shows the XML of a layout file. Create a new Android project in Eclipse starting with this layout.

Listing 25–1. *XML Layout File for TouchDemo1*

```
<?xml version="1.0" encoding="utf-8"?>
<!-- This file is res/layout/main.xml -->
<LinearLayout xmlns:android="http://schemas.android.com/apk/res/android"
    android:layout_width="fill_parent"
    android:layout_height="fill_parent"
    android:orientation="vertical" >

  <RelativeLayout  android:id="@+id/layout1"
    android:tag="trueLayoutTop"  android:orientation="vertical"
    android:layout_width="fill_parent"
    android:layout_height="wrap_content"
    android:layout_weight="1" >

    <com.androidbook.touch.demo1.TrueButton android:text="returns true"
    android:id="@+id/trueBtn1"  android:tag="trueBtnTop"
    android:layout_width="wrap_content"
    android:layout_height="wrap_content" />

    <com.androidbook.touch.demo1.FalseButton android:text="returns false"
    android:id="@+id/falseBtn1"  android:tag="falseBtnTop"
    android:layout_width="wrap_content"
    android:layout_height="wrap_content"
    android:layout_below="@id/trueBtn1" />

  </RelativeLayout>
  <RelativeLayout  android:id="@+id/layout2"
    android:tag="falseLayoutBottom"  android:orientation="vertical"
    android:layout_width="fill_parent"
    android:layout_height="wrap_content"
    android:layout_weight="1"  android:background="#FF00FF" >

    <com.androidbook.touch.demo1.TrueButton android:text="returns true"
    android:id="@+id/trueBtn2"  android:tag="trueBtnBottom"
    android:layout_width="wrap_content"
    android:layout_height="wrap_content" />
```

```
    <com.androidbook.touch.demo1.FalseButton android:text="returns false"
    android:id="@+id/falseBtn2"  android:tag="falseBtnBottom"
    android:layout_width="wrap_content"
    android:layout_height="wrap_content"
    android:layout_below="@id/trueBtn2" />

  </RelativeLayout>
</LinearLayout>
```

There are a couple of things to point out about this layout. We've incorporated tags on our UI objects, and we'll be able to refer to these tags in our code as events occur on them. We've also used `RelativeLayouts` to position our objects. Also notice how we've used custom objects (`TrueButton` and `FalseButton`). You'll see in the Java code that these are classes extended from the `Button` class. Since these are `Buttons`, we can use all of the same XML attributes we would use on other buttons. Figure 25–1 shows what this layout looks like, and Listing 25–2 shows our button Java code.

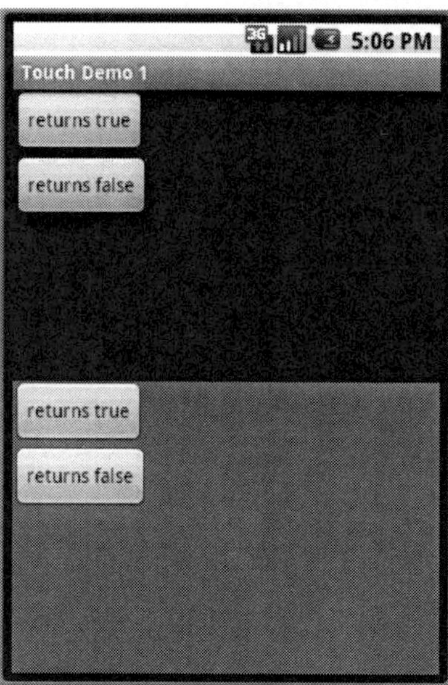

Figure 25–1. *The UI of our TouchDemo1 application*

Listing 25–2. *Java Code for the Button Classes for TouchDemo1*

```
// This file is BooleanButton.java
import android.content.Context;
import android.util.AttributeSet;
import android.util.Log;
import android.view.MotionEvent;
import android.widget.Button;

public abstract class BooleanButton extends Button {
    protected boolean myValue() {
        return false;
    }
```

```
    public BooleanButton(Context context, AttributeSet attrs) {
        super(context, attrs);
    }

    @Override
    public boolean onTouchEvent(MotionEvent event) {
        String myTag = this.getTag().toString();
        Log.v(myTag, "-----------------------------------");
        Log.v(myTag, MainActivity.describeEvent(this, event));
        Log.v(myTag, "super onTouchEvent() returns " +
                super.onTouchEvent(event));
        Log.v(myTag, "and I'm returning " + myValue());
        return(myValue());
    }
}


// This file is TrueButton.java
import android.content.Context;
import android.util.AttributeSet;

public class TrueButton extends BooleanButton {
    protected boolean myValue() {
        return true;
    }

    public TrueButton(Context context, AttributeSet attrs) {
        super(context, attrs);
    }
}


// This file is FalseButton.java
import android.content.Context;
import android.util.AttributeSet;

public class FalseButton extends BooleanButton {

    public FalseButton(Context context, AttributeSet attrs) {
        super(context, attrs);
    }
}
```

The BooleanButton class was built so we can reuse the onTouchEvent() method, which we've customized by adding the logging. Then, we created TrueButton and FalseButton, which will respond differently to the MotionEvents passed to them. This will be made clearer when you look at the main activity code, which is shown in Listing 25–3.

Listing 25–3. *Java Code for Our Main Activity*

```
// This file is MainActivity.java
import android.app.Activity;
import android.os.Bundle;
import android.util.Log;
import android.view.MotionEvent;
import android.view.View;
import android.view.View.OnTouchListener;
```

```
import android.widget.Button;
import android.widget.RelativeLayout;

public class MainActivity extends Activity implements OnTouchListener {
    /** Called when the activity is first created. */
    @Override
    public void onCreate(Bundle savedInstanceState) {
        super.onCreate(savedInstanceState);
        setContentView(R.layout.main);

        RelativeLayout layout1 =
                (RelativeLayout) findViewById(R.id.layout1);
        layout1.setOnTouchListener(this);
        Button trueBtn1 = (Button)findViewById(R.id.trueBtn1);
        trueBtn1.setOnTouchListener(this);
        Button falseBtn1 = (Button)findViewById(R.id.falseBtn1);
        falseBtn1.setOnTouchListener(this);

        RelativeLayout layout2 =
                (RelativeLayout) findViewById(R.id.layout2);
        layout2.setOnTouchListener(this);
        Button trueBtn2 = (Button)findViewById(R.id.trueBtn2);
        trueBtn2.setOnTouchListener(this);
        Button falseBtn2 = (Button)findViewById(R.id.falseBtn2);
        falseBtn2.setOnTouchListener(this);
    }

    @Override
    public boolean onTouch(View v, MotionEvent event) {
        String myTag = v.getTag().toString();
        Log.v(myTag, "-----------------------------");
        Log.v(myTag, "Got view " + myTag + " in onTouch");
        Log.v(myTag, describeEvent(v, event));
        if( "true".equals(myTag.substring(0, 4))) {
        /*  Log.v(myTag, "*** calling my onTouchEvent() method ***");
            v.onTouchEvent(event);
            Log.v(myTag, "*** back from onTouchEvent() method ***"); */
            Log.v(myTag, "and I'm returning true");
            return true;
        }
        else {
            Log.v(myTag, "and I'm returning false");
            return false;
        }
    }

    protected static String describeEvent(View view, MotionEvent event) {
        StringBuilder result = new StringBuilder(300);
        result.append("Action: ").append(event.getAction()).append("\n");
        result.append("Location: ").append(event.getX()).append(" x ")
                 .append(event.getY()).append("\n");
        if(    event.getX() < 0 || event.getX() > view.getWidth() ||
               event.getY() < 0 || event.getY() > view.getHeight()) {
            result.append(">>> Touch has left the view <<<\n");
        }
        result.append("Edge flags: ").append(event.getEdgeFlags());
        result.append("\n");
```

```
        result.append("Pressure: ").append(event.getPressure());
        result.append("    ").append("Size: ").append(event.getSize());
        result.append("\n").append("Down time: ");
        result.append(event.getDownTime()).append("ms\n");
        result.append("Event time: ").append(event.getEventTime());
        result.append("ms").append("  Elapsed: ");
        result.append(event.getEventTime()-event.getDownTime());
        result.append(" ms\n");
        return result.toString();
    }
}
```

Our main activity code sets up callbacks on our buttons and the layouts so we can process the touch events (i.e., the MotionEvent objects) for everything in our UI. We've added lots of logging, so you'll be able to tell exactly what's going on as touch events occur. When you compile and run this application, you should see a screen that looks like Figure 25–1.

To get the most out of this application, you need to open LogCat in Eclipse to watch the messages fly by as you touch the touch screen. This works in the emulator as well as on a real device. We also advise you to maximize the LogCat window, so you can more easily scroll up and down to see all of the generated events from this application. To maximize the window, just double-click the LogCat tab. Now, go to the application UI, and touch and release on the topmost button marked "returns true" (if you're using the emulator, use your mouse to click and release the button). You should see at least two events logged in LogCat. The messages are tagged as coming from trueBtnTop and were logged from the onTouch() method in MainActivity. See MainActivity.java for the onTouch() method's code. As you view the LogCat output, see which method calls are producing the values. For example, the value displayed after Action comes from the getAction() method. Listing 25–4 shows a sample of what you might see in LogCat from the emulator, and Listing 25–5 shows a sample of what you might see from a real device.

Listing 25–4. *Sample LogCat Messages from TouchDemo1 from the Emulator*

```
trueBtnTop        ----------------------------
trueBtnTop        Got view trueBtnTop in onTouch
trueBtnTop        Action: 0
trueBtnTop        Location: 52.0 x 20.0
trueBtnTop        Edge flags: 0
trueBtnTop        Pressure: 0.0   Size: 0.0
trueBtnTop        Down time: 163669ms
trueBtnTop        Event time: 163669ms  Elapsed: 0 ms
trueBtnTop        and I'm returning true
trueBtnTop        ----------------------------
trueBtnTop        Got view trueBtnTop in onTouch
trueBtnTop        Action: 1
trueBtnTop        Location: 52.0 x 20.0
trueBtnTop        Edge flags: 0
trueBtnTop        Pressure: 0.0   Size: 0.0
trueBtnTop        Down time: 163669ms
trueBtnTop        Event time: 163831ms  Elapsed: 162 ms
trueBtnTop        and I'm returning true
```

Listing 25–5. *Sample LogCat Messages from TouchDemo1 from a Real Device*

```
trueBtnTop        ----------------------------
trueBtnTop        Got view trueBtnTop in onTouch
trueBtnTop        Action: 0
trueBtnTop        Location: 42.8374 x 25.293747
trueBtnTop        Edge flags: 0
trueBtnTop        Pressure: 0.05490196   Size: 0.2
trueBtnTop        Down time: 24959412ms
trueBtnTop        Event time: 24959412ms  Elapsed: 0 ms
trueBtnTop        and I'm returning true
trueBtnTop        ----------------------------
trueBtnTop        Got view trueBtnTop in onTouch
trueBtnTop        Action: 2
trueBtnTop        Location: 42.8374 x 25.293747
trueBtnTop        Edge flags: 0
trueBtnTop        Pressure: 0.05490196   Size: 0.2
trueBtnTop        Down time: 24959412ms
trueBtnTop        Event time: 24959530ms  Elapsed: 118 ms
trueBtnTop        and I'm returning true
trueBtnTop        ----------------------------
trueBtnTop        Got view trueBtnTop in onTouch
trueBtnTop        Action: 1
trueBtnTop        Location: 42.8374 x 25.293747
trueBtnTop        Edge flags: 0
trueBtnTop        Pressure: 0.05490196   Size: 0.2
trueBtnTop        Down time: 24959412ms
trueBtnTop        Event time: 24959567ms  Elapsed: 155 ms
trueBtnTop        and I'm returning true
```

The first event has an action of 0, which is `ACTION_DOWN`. The last event has an action of 1, which is `ACTION_UP`. If you used a real device, you might see more than two events. Any events in between `ACTION_DOWN` and `ACTION_UP` will most likely have an action of 2, which is `ACTION_MOVE`. The other possibilities are an action of 3, which is `ACTION_CANCEL`, and 4, which is `ACTION_OUTSIDE`. When using real fingers on a real touch screen, you can't always touch and release without a slight movement on the surface, so some `ACTION_MOVE` events are not unexpected.

There are some other differences between the emulator and a real device. Notice that the precision of the location within the emulator is in whole numbers (52 by 20), whereas on a real device you see fractions (42.8374 by 25.293747). The location for a `MotionEvent` has an X and Y component, where X represents the distance from the left-hand side of the `View` object to the point touched and Y represents the distance from the top of the `View` object to the point touched.

You should also notice that the pressure in the emulator is 0, as is the size. For a real device, the pressure represents how hard the finger pressed down, and size represents how large the touch is. If you touch lightly with the tip of your pinky finger, the values for pressure and size will be small. If you press hard with your thumb, both pressure and size will be larger. The documentation says that the values of pressure and size will be between 0 and 1. However, due to differences in hardware, it may be very difficult to use any absolute numbers in your application for making decisions about pressure and size. It would be fine to compare pressure and size between `MotionEvents` as they occur in your application, but you may run into trouble if you decide that pressure must exceed a value such as 0.8 to be considered a hard press. On that particular device, you might never get a value above 0.8. You might not even get a value above 0.2.

The down time and event time values operate in the same way between the emulator and a real device, the only difference being that the real device has much larger values. The elapsed times work the same.

The edge flags are for detecting when a touch has reached the edge of the physical screen. The Android SDK documentation says that the flags are set to indicate that a touch has intersected with an edge of the display (top, bottom, left, or right). However, the `getEdgeFlags()` method may always return zero, depending on what device or emulator it is used on. With some hardware, it is too difficult to actually detect a touch at the edge of the display, so Android is supposed to pin the location to the edge and set the appropriate edge flag for you. This doesn't always happen, so you should not rely on the edge flags being set properly. The `MotionEvent` class provides a `setEdgeFlags()` method so you can set the flags yourself if you want to.

The last thing to notice is that our `onTouch()` method returns `true`, because our `TrueButton` is coded to return `true`. Returning `true` tells Android that the `MotionEvent` object has been consumed and there is no reason to give it to someone else. It also tells Android to keep sending touch events from this touch sequence to this method. That's why we got the `ACTION_UP` event, as well as the `ACTION_MOVE` event in the case of the real device.

Now touch the "returns false" button near the top of the screen. For the remainder of this section, we will show only sample LogCat output from a real device. The differences have been explained, so if you are working with the emulator, you should understand why you are seeing what you are seeing. Listing 25–6 shows a sample LogCat output for your "returns false" touch.

Listing 25–6. ***Sample LogCat from Touching the Top "returns false" Button***

```
falseBtnTop      -----------------------------
falseBtnTop      Got view falseBtnTop in onTouch
falseBtnTop      Action: 0
falseBtnTop      Location: 61.309372 x 44.281494
falseBtnTop      Edge flags: 0
falseBtnTop      Pressure: 0.0627451   Size: 0.26666668
falseBtnTop      Downtime: 28612178ms
falseBtnTop      Event time: 28612178ms  Elapsed: 0 ms
falseBtnTop      and I'm returning false
falseBtnTop      -----------------------------------
falseBtnTop      Action: 0
falseBtnTop      Location: 61.309372 x 44.281494
falseBtnTop      Edge flags: 0
falseBtnTop      Pressure: 0.0627451   Size: 0.26666668
falseBtnTop      Downtime: 28612178ms
falseBtnTop      Event time: 28612178ms  Elapsed: 0 ms
falseBtnTop      super onTouchEvent() returns true
falseBtnTop      and I'm returning false
trueLayoutTop      -----------------------------
trueLayoutTop      Got view trueLayoutTop in onTouch
trueLayoutTop      Action: 0
trueLayoutTop      Location: 61.309372 x 116.281494
```

```
trueLayoutTop        Edge flags: 0
trueLayoutTop        Pressure: 0.0627451   Size: 0.26666668
trueLayoutTop        Downtime: 28612178ms
trueLayoutTop        Event time: 28612178ms  Elapsed: 0 ms
trueLayoutTop        and I'm returning true
trueLayoutTop        ----------------------------
trueLayoutTop        Got view trueLayoutTop in onTouch
trueLayoutTop        Action: 2
trueLayoutTop        Location: 61.309372 x 111.90039
trueLayoutTop        Edge flags: 0
trueLayoutTop        Pressure: 0.0627451   Size: 0.26666668
trueLayoutTop        Downtime: 28612178ms
trueLayoutTop        Event time: 28612217ms  Elapsed: 39 ms
trueLayoutTop        and I'm returning true
trueLayoutTop        ----------------------------
trueLayoutTop        Got view trueLayoutTop in onTouch
trueLayoutTop        Action: 1
trueLayoutTop        Location: 55.08958 x 115.30792
trueLayoutTop        Edge flags: 0
trueLayoutTop        Pressure: 0.0627451   Size: 0.26666668
trueLayoutTop        Downtime: 28612178ms
trueLayoutTop        Event time: 28612361ms  Elapsed: 183 ms
trueLayoutTop        and I'm returning true
```

Now, you're seeing very different behavior, so we'll explain what happened. Android receives the `ACTION_DOWN` event in a `MotionEvent` object and passes it to our `onTouch()` method in the `MainActivity` class. Our `onTouch()` method records the information in LogCat and returns `false`. This tells Android that our `onTouch()` method did not consume the event, so Android looks to the next method to call, which in our case is the overridden `onTouchEvent()` method of our `FalseButton` class. Since `FalseButton` is an extension of the `BooleanButton` class, refer to the `onTouchEvent()` method in `BooleanButton.java` to see the code. In the `onTouchEvent()` method, we again write information to LogCat, we call the parent class's `onTouchEvent()` method, and then we also return `false`. Notice that the location information in LogCat is exactly the same as before. This should be expected because we're still in the same `View` object, the `FalseButton`. We see that our parent class wants to return `true` from `onTouchEvent()` and we can see why. If you look at the button in the UI it should be a different color from the "returns true" button. Our "returns false" button now looks like it's partway through being pressed. That is, it looks like a button looks when it has been pressed but has not been released. Our custom method returned `false` instead of `true`. Because we again told Android that we did not consume this event, by returning `false`, Android never sends the `ACTION_UP` event to our button so our button doesn't know that the finger ever lifted from the touch screen. Therefore, our button is still in the pressed state. If we had returned `true` like our parent wanted to, we would eventually have received the `ACTION_UP` event so we could change the color back to the normal button color. To recap, every time we return `false` from a UI object for a received `MotionEvent` object, Android stops sending `MotionEvent` objects to that UI object, and Android keeps looking for another UI object to consume our `MotionEvent` object.

You might have realized that when we touched our "returns true" button, we didn't get a color change in the button. Why is that? Well, our `onTouch()` method was called before any actual button methods got called, and `onTouch()` returned `true`, so Android never bothered to call the "returns true" button's onTouchEvent() method. If you add a v.onTouchEvent(event); line to the onTouch() method just before returning true, you will see the button change color. You will also see more log lines in LogCat, since our onTouchEvent() method is also writing information to LogCat.

Let's keep going through the LogCat output. Now that Android has tried twice to find a consumer for the ACTION_DOWN event and failed, it goes to the next View in the application that could possibly receive the event, which in our case is the layout underneath the button. We called our top layout trueLayoutTop, and we can see that it received the ACTION_DOWN event.

Notice that our onTouch() method got called again, although now with the layout view and not the button view. Everything about the MotionEvent object passed to onTouch() for trueLayoutTop is the same as before, including the times, except for the Y coordinate of the location. The Y coordinate changed from 44.281494 for the button to 116.281494 for the layout. This makes sense because the button is not in the upper left corner of the layout, it's below the "returns true" button. Therefore the Y coordinate of the touch relative to the layout is larger than the Y coordinate of the same touch relative to the button; the touch is further away from the top edge of the layout than it is from the top edge of the button. Because onTouch() for the trueLayoutTop returns true, Android sends the rest of the touch events to the layout and we see the log records corresponding to the ACTION_MOVE and the ACTION_UP events. Go ahead and touch the top "returns false" button again, and notice that the same set of log records occurs. That is, onTouch() is called for the falseBtnTop, onTouchEvent() is called for falseBtnTop, and then onTouch() is called for trueLayoutTop for the rest of the events. Android only stops sending the events to the button for one touch sequence at a time. For a new sequence of touch events, Android will send to the button unless it gets another return of false from the called method, which it still does in our sample application.

Now touch your finger on the top layout but not on either button, and then drag your finger around a bit and lift it off the touch screen (if you're using the emulator, just use your mouse to make a similar motion). Notice a stream of log messages in LogCat, where the first record has an action of ACTION_DOWN, and then many ACTION_MOVE events are followed by an ACTION_UP event.

Now, touch the top "returns true" button, and before lifting your finger from the button, drag your finger around the screen and then lift it off. Listing 25–7 shows some new information in LogCat.

Listing 25–7. *LogCat Records Showing a Touch Outside of Our View*

```
[ … log messages of an ACTION_DOWN event followed by some ACTION_MOVE events … ]

trueBtnTop          Got view trueBtnTop in onTouch
trueBtnTop          Action: 2
trueBtnTop          Location: 150.41768 x 22.628128
trueBtnTop          >>> Touch has left the view <<<
trueBtnTop          Edge flags: 0
trueBtnTop          Pressure: 0.047058824   Size: 0.13333334
trueBtnTop          Downtime: 31690859ms
```

```
trueBtnTop        Event time: 31691344ms  Elapsed: 485 ms
trueBtnTop        and I'm returning true

[ … more ACTION_MOVE events logged … ]

trueBtnTop        Got view trueBtnTop in onTouch
trueBtnTop        Action: 1
trueBtnTop        Location: 291.5864 x 223.43854
trueBtnTop        >>> Touch has left the view <<<
trueBtnTop        Edge flags: 0
trueBtnTop        Pressure: 0.047058824   Size: 0.13333334
trueBtnTop        Downtime: 31690859ms
trueBtnTop        Event time: 31692493ms  Elapsed: 1634 ms
trueBtnTop        and I'm returning true
```

Even after your finger drags itself off of the button, we continue to get notified of touch events related to the button. The first record in Listing 25–7 shows an event record where we're no longer on the button. In this case, the X coordinate of the touch event is to the right of the edge of our button object. However, we keep getting called with `MotionEvent` objects until we get an `ACTION_UP` event, because we continue to return `true` from the `onTouch()` method. Even when you finally lift your finger off of the touch screen, and even if your finger isn't on the button, our `onTouch()` method still gets called to give us the `ACTION_UP` event because we keep returning `true`. This is something to keep in mind when dealing with `MotionEvents`. When the finger has moved off of the view, we could decide to cancel whatever operation might have been performed and return `false` from the `onTouch()` method, so we don't get notified of further events. Or we could choose to continue to receive events (by returning `true` from the `onTouch()` method) and only perform the logic if the finger returns to our view before lifting off.

The touch sequence of events got associated to our top "returns true" button when we returned `true` from `onTouch()`. This told Android that it could stop looking for an object to receive the `MotionEvent` objects and just send all future `MotionEvent` objects for this touch sequence to us. Even if we encounter another view when dragging our finger, we're still tied to the original view for this sequence.

Let's see what happens with the lower half of our application. Go ahead and touch the "returns true" button in the bottom half. We see the same thing as happened with the top "returns true" button. Because `onTouch()` returns `true`, Android sends us the rest of the events in the touch sequence until the finger is lifted from the touch screen. Now, touch the bottom "returns false" button. Once again, the `onTouch()` method and `onTouchEvent()` methods return `false` (both associated with the `falseBtnBottom` view object). But this time, the next view to receive the `MotionEvent` object is the `falseLayoutBottom` object, and it also returns `false`. Now, we're finished.

Because the `onTouchEvent()` method called the super's `onTouchEvent()` method, the button has changed color to indicate it's halfway through being pressed. Again, the button will stay this way, because we never get the `ACTION_UP` event in this touch sequence, since our methods return `false` all the time. Unlike before, even the layout is not interested in this event. If you were to touch the bottom "returns false" button and hold it down and then drag your finger around the display, you would not see any extra records in LogCat, because no more `MotionEvent` objects are sent to us. We always returned false, so Android won't bother us with any more events for this touch sequence. Again, if we start a new touch sequence, we can see new LogCat records showing up. If you initiate a touch sequence in the bottom layout and not on a button, you will see a single event in LogCat for falseLayoutBottom that returns false and then nothing after that (until you start a new touch sequence).

So far, we've used buttons to show you the effects of MotionEvent events from touch screens. It's worth pointing out that, normally, you would implement logic on buttons using the onClick() method. We used buttons for this sample application, because they're easy to create and they are subclasses of View that can therefore receive touch events just like any other view. Remember that these techniques apply to any View object in your application, be it a standard or customized view class.

Recycling MotionEvents

You may have noticed the recycle() method of the MotionEvent class in the Android reference documentation. It is tempting to want to recycle the MotionEvents that you receive in onTouch() or onTouchEvent(), but don't do it. If your callback method is not consuming the MotionEvent object and you're returning false, the MotionEvent object is likely to be handed to some other method or view or our activity, so you don't want Android recycling it yet. Even if you consumed the event and returned true, the event object doesn't belong to you, so you should not recycle it.

If you look at MotionEvent, you will see a few variations of a method called obtain(). This is either creating a copy of a MotionEvent or a brand new MotionEvent. Your copy, or your brand new event object, is the event object that you should recycle when you are done with it. For example, if you want to hang onto an event object that is passed to you via a callback, you should use obtain() to make a copy, because once you return from the callback, that event object will be recycled by Android, and you may get strange results if you continue to use it. When you are finished using *your copy*, you invoke recycle() on it.

Using VelocityTracker

Android provides a class to help handle touch screen sequences, and that class is VelocityTracker. When a finger is in motion on a touch screen, it might be nice to know how fast it is moving across the surface. For example, if the user is dragging a finger quickly across the screen, this could indicate a flinging motion, for which your application may wish to perform flinging logic. Android provides VelocityTracker to help with the math involved.

To use VelocityTracker, you first get an instance of a VelocityTracker by calling the static method VelocityTracker.obtain(). You can then add MotionEvent objects to it with the addMovement(MotionEvent ev) method. You would call this method in your handler that receives MotionEvent objects, from a handler method such as onTouch(), or from a view's onTouchEvent(). The VelocityTracker uses the MotionEvent objects to figure out what is going on with the user's touch sequence. Once VelocityTracker has at least two MotionEvent objects in it, we can use the other methods to find out what's happening.

The two VelocityTracker methods—getXVelocity() and getYVelocity()—return the corresponding velocity of the finger in the X and Y directions respectively. The value returned from these two methods will represent pixels per time period. This could be pixels per millisecond or per second or really anything you want. To tell the VelocityTracker what time period to use, and before you can call these two getter methods, you need to invoke the VelocityTracker's computeCurrentVelocity(int units) method. The value of units represents how many milliseconds are in the time period for measuring the velocity. If you want pixels per millisecond, use a units value of 1; if you want pixels per second, use a units value of 1000. The value returned by the getXVelocity() and getYVelocity() methods will be positive if the velocity is toward the right (for X) or down (for Y). The value returned will be negative if the velocity is toward the left (for X) or up (for Y).

When you are finished with the VelocityTracker object you got with the obtain() method, call the VelocityTracker object's recycle() method. Listing 25–8 shows a sample onTouchEvent() handler for an activity. It turns out that an activity has an onTouchEvent() callback, which is called whenever no views have handled the touch event. Since we're using a stock, empty layout, we have no views consuming our touch events.

Listing 25–8. *Sample Activity That Uses VelocityTracker*

```
import android.app.Activity;
import android.os.Bundle;
import android.util.Log;
import android.view.MotionEvent;
import android.view.VelocityTracker;

public class MainActivity extends Activity {
    private static final String TAG = "VelocityTracker";

    /** Called when the activity is first created. */
    @Override
    public void onCreate(Bundle savedInstanceState) {
        super.onCreate(savedInstanceState);
        setContentView(R.layout.main);
    }

    private VelocityTracker vTracker = null;

    public boolean onTouchEvent(MotionEvent event) {
        int action = event.getAction();
        switch(action) {
            case MotionEvent.ACTION_DOWN:
                if(vTracker == null) {
                    vTracker = VelocityTracker.obtain();
                }
                else {
                    vTracker.clear();
                }
                vTracker.addMovement(event);
```

```
                break;
            case MotionEvent.ACTION_MOVE:
                vTracker.addMovement(event);
                vTracker.computeCurrentVelocity(1000);
                Log.v(TAG, "X velocity is " + vTracker.getXVelocity() +
                        " pixels per second");
                Log.v(TAG, "Y velocity is " + vTracker.getYVelocity() +
                        " pixels per second");
                break;
            case MotionEvent.ACTION_UP:
            case MotionEvent.ACTION_CANCEL:
                vTracker.recycle();
                break;
        }
        return true;
    }
}
```

There are a few key things to note about VelocityTracker. Obviously, when you've only added one MotionEvent to a VelocityTracker (i.e., the ACTION_DOWN event), the velocities cannot be computed as anything other than zero. But we need to add the starting point so that the subsequent ACTION_MOVE events can calculate velocities then. It turns out that the velocities reported after ACTION_UP is added to our VelocityTracker are also zero. Therefore, do not read the X and Y velocities after adding ACTION_UP expecting to get motion. For example, if you're writing a gaming application in which the user is throwing an object on the screen, use the velocities after adding the last ACTION_MOVE event to calculate the object's trajectory across the game view.

VelocityTracker is somewhat costly in terms of performance, so use it sparingly. Also, make sure that you recycle it as soon as you are done with it in case someone else wants to use one. There can be more than one VelocityTracker in use in Android, but they can take up a lot of memory, so give yours back if you're not going to continue to use it. In Listing 25–8, we also use the clear() method if we're starting a new touch sequence (i.e., if we get an ACTION_DOWN event and our VelocityTracker object already exists) instead of recycling this one and obtaining a new one.

Exploring Drag and Drop

Now that you've seen how to receive MotionEvent objects in code, let's do something interesting with them. We're going to explain how to implement drag and drop. To start, let's do some dragging. In this next sample application, we're going to take a white dot and drag it to a new location in our layout. Using Listing 25–9, create a new Android project, set up the layout XML file as indicated, and add a new class called Dot using the Java code. Note that the package name in the layout XML file for the Dot element must match the package name you use for your application. Also note that we can leave the main Activity class alone, since it is fine as-is. The UI for this application is shown in Figure 25–2.

Listing 25–9. ***Sample Layout XML and Java Code for Our Drag Example***

```
<?xml version="1.0" encoding="utf-8"?>
<!-- This file is res/layout/main.xml -->
```

```
<LinearLayout xmlns:android="http://schemas.android.com/apk/res/android"
    android:orientation="vertical"
    android:layout_width="fill_parent"
    android:layout_height="fill_parent" >

  <com.androidbook.touch.dragdemo1.Dot
    android:id="@+id/dot"  android:tag="trueDot"
    android:layout_width="wrap_content"
    android:layout_height="wrap_content" />

</LinearLayout>
```

```
import android.content.Context;
import android.graphics.Canvas;
import android.graphics.Color;
import android.graphics.Paint;
import android.util.AttributeSet;
import android.view.MotionEvent;
import android.view.View;

public class Dot extends View {
    private static final float RADIUS = 20;
    private float x = 30;
    private float y = 30;
    private float initialX;
    private float initialY;
    private float offsetX;
    private float offsetY;
    private Paint backgroundPaint;
    private Paint myPaint;

    public Dot(Context context, AttributeSet attrs) {
        super(context, attrs);

        backgroundPaint = new Paint();
        backgroundPaint.setColor(Color.BLUE);

        myPaint = new Paint();
        myPaint.setColor(Color.WHITE);
        myPaint.setAntiAlias(true);
    }

    @Override
    public boolean onTouchEvent(MotionEvent event) {
        int action = event.getAction();
        switch(action) {
        case MotionEvent.ACTION_DOWN:
            // Need to remember where the initial starting point
            // center is of our Dot and where our touch starts from
            initialX = x;
            initialY = y;
            offsetX = event.getX();
            offsetY = event.getY();
            break;
        case MotionEvent.ACTION_MOVE:
        case MotionEvent.ACTION_UP:
```

```
            case MotionEvent.ACTION_CANCEL:
                x = initialX + event.getX() - offsetX;
                y = initialY + event.getY() - offsetY;
                break;
            }
            return(true);
        }

        @Override
        public void draw(Canvas canvas) {
            int width = canvas.getWidth();
            int height = canvas.getHeight();
            canvas.drawRect(0, 0, width, height, backgroundPaint);

            canvas.drawCircle(x, y, RADIUS, myPaint);
            invalidate();
        }
    }
```

Figure 25–2. *User interface for our Drag Demo application*

When you run this application, you will see a white dot on a blue background. You can touch the dot and drag it around the screen. When you lift your finger, the dot stays where it is until you touch it again and drag it somewhere else. We've really simplified this to show you just the basics of how to move an object on the screen. The `draw()` method puts the dot at its current location of X and Y. By receiving `MotionEvent` objects in the `onTouchEvent()` method, we can modify the X and Y values by the movement of our touch. We record the starting position of the dot when we get the `ACTION_DOWN` action, as well as the starting touch location. Because the user won't always touch the exact center of the object, the touch coordinates will not be the same as the location coordinates of the object. Also, if our object's reference point is not the center but the upper-left corner, we must be sure we take that into account as well.

When your finger starts moving across the screen, we adjust the location of the object by the deltas in x and y based on the `MotionEvents` that we get. When you stop moving (i.e., `ACTION_UP`), we finalize our location using the last coordinates of your touch. We're doing a little cheating here because our `Dot` view is positioned on the screen relative to (0,0). That means that we can simply draw the circle relative to (0,0) as opposed to some other reference point. If our object is not positioned relative to (0,0), we might need to provide additional offsets for the location of our object. We also don't have to worry about scrollbars in this example, which could complicate the calculation of the position of our object on the screen. But the basic principle is still the same. By knowing the starting location of the object to be moved, and keeping track of the delta values of a touch from `ACTION_DOWN` through to `ACTION_UP`, we can adjust the location of the object on the screen.

Dropping an object onto another object on the screen has much less to do with touch than it does with knowing where things are on the screen. We're not going to provide an example here of dropping, but we will explain the principles. As you saw earlier, as we drag an object around the screen, we are aware of its position relative to one or more reference points. We can also interrogate objects on the screen for their locations and sizes. We can then determine if our dragged object is "over" another object. The typical process of figuring out a drop target for a dragged object is to iterate through the available objects that can be dropped on and determine if our current position overlaps with that object. Each object's size and position (and sometimes shape) can be used to make this determination. If we get an `ACTION_UP` event, meaning that the user has let go of our dragged object, and the object is over something we can drop onto, we can fire the logic to process the drop action. This might be the action of dragging something to the trash can, where the object being dragged should be deleted, or it could be dragging a file to a folder for the purposes of moving or copying it.

> **NOTE:** With Honeycomb (i.e., Android 3.0), Android provides direct support for drag and drop. We'll revisit drag and drop in Chapter 31.

Multitouch

Now that you've seen single touches in action, let's move on to multitouch. Multitouch has gained a lot of interest ever since the TED conference in 2006 at which Jeff Han demonstrated a multitouch surface for a computer user interface. Using multiple fingers on a screen opens up a lot of possibilities for manipulating what's on the screen. For example, putting two fingers on an image and moving them apart could zoom in on the image. By placing multiple fingers on an image and turning clockwise, you could rotate the image on the screen. Android introduced support for multitouch with Android SDK 2.0. In that release you were able to (technically) use up to three fingers on a screen at the same time to perform actions such as zoom, rotate, or whatever else you could imagine doing with multiple touches (we say "technically" because the first Android *devices* to support multitouch only supported two fingers). If you think about it, though, there is no magic to this. If the screen hardware can detect multiple touches as they initiate on the screen, notify your application as those touches move in time across the surface of the screen, and notify you when those touches lift off of the screen, your application can figure out what the user is trying to do with those touches. While it's not magic, it isn't easy either. We're going to help you understand multitouch in this section.

> **NOTE:** With Android 2.2, the `MotionEvent` class underwent some changes that make mutlitouch even more difficult to keep straight, including deprecating a couple of the constants we're going to talk about in this section (`ACTION_POINTER_ID_MASK` and `ACTION_POINTER_ID_SHIFT`). This means that for older devices, you will use what we'll talk about next. For devices at 2.2 or later, you can make some modifications, which we'll cover after this section.

Multitouch Before Android 2.2

The basics of multitouch are exactly the same as for single touches. `MotionEvent` objects get created for touches, and these `MotionEvent` objects are passed to your methods just like before. Your code can read the data about the touches and decide what to do. At a basic level, the methods of `MotionEvent` are the same; that is, we call `getAction()`, `getDownTime()`, `getX()`, and so on. However, when more than one finger is touching the screen, the `MotionEvent` object must include information from all fingers, with some caveats. The action value from `getAction()` is for one finger, not all. The down time value is for the very first finger down and measures the time as long as at least one finger is down. The location values `getX()` and `getY()`, as well as `getPressure()` and `getSize()`, can take an argument for the finger; therefore, you need to use a pointer index value to request the information for the finger you're interested in. There are method calls that we used previously that did not take any argument to specify a finger (e.g., `getX()`, `getY()`), so which finger would the values be for if we used those methods? You can figure it out, but it takes some work. Therefore, if you don't take into account multiple fingers all of the time, you might end up with some strange results. Let's dig into this to figure out what to do.

The first method of `MotionEvent` you need to know about for multitouch is `getPointerCount()`. This tells you how many fingers are represented in the `MotionEvent` object but doesn't necessarily tell you how many fingers are actually touching the screen; that depends on the hardware and on the implementation of Android on that hardware. You may find that, on certain devices, `getPointerCount()` does not report all fingers that are touching, just some. But let's press on. As soon as you've got more than one finger being reported in `MotionEvent` objects, you need to start dealing with the pointer indexes and the pointer IDs.

The MotionEvent object contains information for pointers starting at index 0 and going up to the number of fingers being reported in that object. The pointer index always starts at 0; if three fingers are being reported, pointer indexes will be 0, 1, and 2. Calls to methods such as getX() must include the pointer index for the finger you want information about. Pointer IDs are integer values representing which finger is being tracked. Pointer IDs start at 0 for the first finger down, but don't always start at 0 once fingers are coming and going on the screen. Think of a pointer ID as the name of that finger while it is being tracked by Android. For example, imagine a pair of touch sequences for two fingers, starting with finger 1 down, and followed by finger 2 down, finger 1 up, and finger 2 up. The first finger down will get pointer ID 0. The second finger down will get pointer ID 1. Once the first finger goes up, the second finger will still be associated with pointer ID 1. At that point, the pointer index for the second finger becomes 0, because the pointer index always starts at 0. In this example, the second finger (pointer ID 1) starts as pointer index 1 when it first touches down and then shifts to pointer index 0 once the first finger leaves the screen. But even when the second finger is the only finger on the screen, it remains as pointer ID 1. Your applications will use pointer IDs to link together the events associated to a particular finger even as other fingers are involved. Let's look at an example.

Listing 25–10 shows our new XML layout plus our Java code for a multitouch application. Create a new application using Listing 25–10, and run it. Figure 25–3 shows what it should look like.

Listing 25–10. ***XML Layout and Java for a Multitouch Demonstration***

```
<?xml version="1.0" encoding="utf-8"?>
<!-- This file is /res/layout/main.xml -->
<RelativeLayout  xmlns:android="http://schemas.android.com/apk/res/android"
    android:id="@+id/layout1"
    android:tag="trueLayout"  android:orientation="vertical"
    android:layout_width="fill_parent"
    android:layout_height="wrap_content"
    android:layout_weight="1"
    >

    <TextView android:text="Touch fingers on the screen and look at LogCat"
    android:id="@+id/message"
    android:tag="trueText"
    android:layout_width="wrap_content"
    android:layout_height="wrap_content"
    android:layout_alignParentBottom="true" />

</RelativeLayout>


// This file is MainActivity.java
import android.app.Activity;
import android.os.Bundle;
import android.util.Log;
import android.view.MotionEvent;
import android.view.View;
import android.view.View.OnTouchListener;
import android.widget.RelativeLayout;
```

```
public class MainActivity extends Activity implements OnTouchListener {
    /** Called when the activity is first created. */
    @Override
    public void onCreate(Bundle savedInstanceState) {
        super.onCreate(savedInstanceState);
        setContentView(R.layout.main);

        RelativeLayout layout1 =
                (RelativeLayout) findViewById(R.id.layout1);
        layout1.setOnTouchListener(this);
    }

    public boolean onTouch(View v, MotionEvent event) {
        String myTag = v.getTag().toString();
        Log.v(myTag, "-----------------------------");
        Log.v(myTag, "Got view " + myTag + " in onTouch");
        Log.v(myTag, describeEvent(event));
        logAction(event);
        if( "true".equals(myTag.substring(0, 4))) {
            return true;
        }
        else {
            return false;
        }
    }

    protected static String describeEvent(MotionEvent event) {
        StringBuilder result = new StringBuilder(500);
        result.append("Action: ").append(event.getAction()).append("\n");
        int numPointers = event.getPointerCount();
        result.append("Number of pointers: ");
        result.append(numPointers).append("\n");
        int ptrIdx = 0;
        while (ptrIdx < numPointers) {
            int ptrId = event.getPointerId(ptrIdx);
            result.append("Pointer Index: ").append(ptrIdx);
            result.append(", Pointer Id: ").append(ptrId).append("\n");
            result.append("   Location: ").append(event.getX(ptrIdx));
            result.append(" x ").append(event.getY(ptrIdx)).append("\n");
            result.append("   Pressure: ");
            result.append(event.getPressure(ptrIdx));
            result.append("   Size: ").append(event.getSize(ptrIdx));
            result.append("\n");

            ptrIdx++;
        }
        result.append("Downtime: ").append(event.getDownTime());
        result.append("ms\n").append("Event time: ");
        result.append(event.getEventTime()).append("ms");
        result.append("  Elapsed: ");
        result.append(event.getEventTime()-event.getDownTime());
        result.append(" ms\n");
        return result.toString();
    }

    private void logAction(MotionEvent event) {
        int action = event.getAction();
```

```
        int ptrIndex = (action & MotionEvent.ACTION_POINTER_ID_MASK) >>>
                                MotionEvent.ACTION_POINTER_ID_SHIFT;
        action = action & MotionEvent.ACTION_MASK;
        if(action == 5 || action == 6)
            action = action - 5;
        int ptrId = event.getPointerId(ptrIndex);

        Log.v("Action", "Pointer index: " + ptrIndex);
        Log.v("Action", "Pointer Id: " + ptrId);
        Log.v("Action", "True action value: " + action);
    }
}
```

Figure 25–3. *Our multitouch demonstration application*

If you only have the emulator, this application will still work, but you won't be able to get multiple fingers simultaneously on the screen. You'll see output similar to what we saw in the previous application. Listing 25–11 shows sample LogCat messages for a touch sequence like we described earlier. That is, the first finger presses on the screen, and then the second finger presses, the first finger leaves the screen, and the second finger leaves the screen.

Listing 25–11. *Sample LogCat Output for a Multitouch Application*

```
trueLayout       -----------------------------
trueLayout       Got view trueLayout in onTouch
trueLayout       Action: 0
trueLayout       Number of pointers: 1
trueLayout       Pointer Index: 0, Pointer Id: 0
trueLayout          Location: 114.88211 x 499.77502
```

```
trueLayout           Pressure: 0.047058824   Size: 0.13333334
trueLayout        Downtime: 33733650ms
trueLayout        Event time: 33733650ms  Elapsed: 0 ms
Action            Pointer index: 0
Action            Pointer Id: 0
Action            True Action value: 0
trueLayout        ----------------------------
trueLayout        Got view trueLayout in onTouch
trueLayout        Action: 2
trueLayout        Number of pointers: 1
trueLayout        Pointer Index: 0, Pointer Id: 0
trueLayout           Location: 114.88211 x 499.77502
trueLayout           Pressure: 0.05882353   Size: 0.13333334
trueLayout        Downtime: 33733650ms
trueLayout        Event time: 33733740ms  Elapsed: 90 ms
Action            Pointer index: 0
Action            Pointer Id: 0
Action            True Action value: 2
trueLayout        ----------------------------
trueLayout        Got view trueLayout in onTouch
trueLayout        Action: 261
trueLayout        Number of pointers: 2
trueLayout        Pointer Index: 0, Pointer Id: 0
trueLayout           Location: 114.88211 x 499.77502
trueLayout           Pressure: 0.05882353   Size: 0.13333334
trueLayout        Pointer Index: 1, Pointer Id: 1
trueLayout           Location: 320.30692 x 189.67395
trueLayout           Pressure: 0.050980393   Size: 0.13333334
trueLayout        Downtime: 33733650ms
trueLayout        Event time: 33733962ms  Elapsed: 312 ms
Action            Pointer index: 1
Action            Pointer Id: 1
Action            True Action value: 0
trueLayout        ----------------------------
trueLayout        Got view trueLayout in onTouch
trueLayout        Action: 2
trueLayout        Number of pointers: 2
trueLayout        Pointer Index: 0, Pointer Id: 0
trueLayout           Location: 111.474594 x 499.77502
trueLayout           Pressure: 0.05882353   Size: 0.13333334
trueLayout        Pointer Index: 1, Pointer Id: 1
trueLayout           Location: 320.30692 x 189.67395
trueLayout           Pressure: 0.050980393   Size: 0.13333334
trueLayout        Downtime: 33733650ms
trueLayout        Event time: 33734189ms  Elapsed: 539 ms
Action            Pointer index: 0
Action            Pointer Id: 0
Action            True Action value: 2
trueLayout        ----------------------------
trueLayout        Got view trueLayout in onTouch
trueLayout        Action: 6
trueLayout        Number of pointers: 2
trueLayout        Pointer Index: 0, Pointer Id: 0
trueLayout           Location: 111.474594 x 499.77502
trueLayout           Pressure: 0.05882353   Size: 0.13333334
trueLayout        Pointer Index: 1, Pointer Id: 1
trueLayout           Location: 320.30692 x 189.67395
```

```
trueLayout        Pressure: 0.050980393   Size: 0.13333334
trueLayout     Downtime: 33733650ms
trueLayout     Event time: 33734228ms  Elapsed: 578 ms
Action         Pointer index: 0
Action         Pointer Id: 0
Action         True Action value: 1
trueLayout     -----------------------------
trueLayout     Got view trueLayout in onTouch
trueLayout     Action: 2
trueLayout     Number of pointers: 1
trueLayout     Pointer Index: 0, Pointer Id: 1
trueLayout        Location: 318.84656 x 191.45105
trueLayout        Pressure: 0.050980393   Size: 0.13333334
trueLayout     Downtime: 33733650ms
trueLayout     Event time: 33734240ms  Elapsed: 590 ms
Action         Pointer index: 0
Action         Pointer Id: 1
Action         True Action value: 2
trueLayout     -----------------------------
trueLayout     Got view trueLayout in onTouch
trueLayout     Action: 1
trueLayout     Number of pointers: 1
trueLayout     Pointer Index: 0, Pointer Id: 1
trueLayout        Location: 314.95224 x 190.5625
trueLayout        Pressure: 0.050980393   Size: 0.13333334
trueLayout     Downtime: 33733650ms
trueLayout     Event time: 33734549ms  Elapsed: 899 ms
Action         Pointer index: 0
Action         Pointer Id: 1
Action         True Action value: 1
```

We'll now discuss what is going on with this application. The first event we see is the ACTION_DOWN (action value of 0) of the first finger. We learn about this using the getAction() method. Please refer to the describeEvent() method in MainActivity.java to follow along with which methods produce which output. We get one pointer with index 0 and pointer ID 0. After that, you'll probably see several ACTION_MOVE events (action value of 2) for this first finger, even though we're only showing one of these in Listing 25–11. We still only have one pointer and the index and ID are still both 0.

A little later we get the second finger touching the screen. The action is now a decimal value of 261. What does this mean? The action value is actually made up of two parts: an indicator of which pointer the action is for and what action that pointer is doing. Converting decimal 261 to hexadecimal, we get 0x00000105. The action is the smallest byte (5 in this case), and the pointer index is the next byte over (1 in this case). Note that this tells us the pointer index but not the pointer ID. If you pressed a third finger onto the screen, the action would be 0x00000205 (or decimal 517). A fourth finger would be 0x00000305 (or decimal 773) and so on. You haven't seen an action value of 5 yet, but it's known as ACTION_POINTER_DOWN. It's just like ACTION_DOWN except that it's used in multitouch situations.

Now, look at the next pair of records from LogCat in Listing 25–11. The first record is for an ACTION_MOVE event (action value of 2). Remember that it is difficult to keep fingers from moving on a real screen. We're only showing one ACTION_MOVE event but you might see several. When the first finger is lifted off of the screen, we get an action value of

0x00000006 (or decimal 6). Like before, we have pointer index 0 and an action value that is ACTION_POINTER_UP (similar to ACTION_UP but for multitouch situations). If the second finger was lifted in a multitouch situation, we would get an action value of 0x00000106 (or decimal 262). Notice how we still have information for two fingers when we get the ACTION_UP for one of them.

The last pair of records in Listing 25–11 shows one more ACTION_MOVE event for the second finger, followed by an ACTION_UP for the second finger. This time, we see an action value of 1 (ACTION_UP). We didn't get an action value of 262, but we'll explain that next. Also, notice that once the first finger left the screen, the pointer index for the second finger has changed from 1 to 0, but the pointer ID has remained as 1.

ACTION_MOVE events do not tell you which finger moved. You will always get an action value of 2 for a move regardless of how many fingers are down or which finger is doing the moving. All down finger positions are available within the MotionEvent object, so you need to read the positions and then figure things out. If there's only one finger left on the screen, the pointer ID will tell you which finger it is that's still moving since it's the only finger left. In Listing 25–11, when the second finger was the only one left on the screen, the ACTION_MOVE event had a pointer index of 0 and a pointer ID of 1, so we knew it was the second finger that was moving.

Going back to the beginning of Listing 25–11, the first finger down is pointer index 0 and pointer ID 0, so why don't we get 0x00000005 (or decimal 5) for the action value when the first finger is pressed to the screen before any other fingers? Unfortunately, this question doesn't have a happy answer. We can get an action value of 5 in the following scenario: Press the first finger to the screen and then the second finger, resulting in action values of 0 and 261 (ignoring the ACTION_MOVE events for the moment). Now, lift the first finger (action value of 6), and press it back down on the screen. The pointer ID of the second finger remained as 1. For the moment when the first finger was in the air, our application knew about pointer ID 1 only. Once the first finger touched the screen again, Android re-assigned pointer ID 0 to the first finger. Since now we know there are multiple fingers involved, we get an action value of 5 (pointer index of 0 and the action value of 5). The answer to the question, therefore, is backward compatibility, but it is not a happy answer. The action values of 0 and 1 are pre-multitouch, and applications written before multitouch will still work as long as only one finger is used. In a scenario with two fingers, if the first finger touches the screen in one location followed by a second finger in a different location on the screen, the up action of the first finger would not be recognized by an application not expecting multitouch events. This is because the lifting of the first finger first would give an action value of 6, not 1. It's when the second finger is lifted that the application will receive an action value of 1. This application would think that the first finger magically moved across the screen to where the second finger was.

When only one finger remains on the screen, Android treats it like a single-touch case. So we get the old ACTION_UP value of 1 instead of a multitouch ACTION_UP value of 6. Our code will need to consider these cases carefully. A pointer index of 0 could result in an ACTION_DOWN value of 0 or 5, depending on which pointers are in play. The last finger up will get an ACTION_UP value of 1 no matter which pointer ID it has.

The MotionEvent class used to come with some helper constants to figure out what is going on, for example, MotionEvent.ACTION_POINTER_3_DOWN is 0x00000205 (or decimal 517), which we described earlier as the third finger down. These values were not all that useful, however, since you'd be better off looking at the pointer index in the second byte and the action in the first byte. In fact, it would be even better to use some other constants from the MotionEvent class to read the value returned by getAction(). Those constants are MotionEvent.ACTION_POINTER_ID_MASK, MotionEvent.ACTION_MASK, and MotionEvent.ACTION_POINTER_ID_SHIFT. By combining the action value with each of these masks using "and," and shifting the result for the pointer index, you'd be able to reliably figure out what is going on, no matter how many fingers the device can support. The Android team must have also realized this because the constants like ACTION_POINTER_3_DOWN have been deprecated.

But wait; these index constants use ID and not INDEX in their names, and we told you the second byte is the pointer index. Sadly, before version 2.2, Android is confused with regard to what is in that byte. With Android 2.2, these constants have been renamed ACTION_POINTER_INDEX_MASK and ACTION_POINTER_INDEX_SHIFT while keeping the same values as before. The second byte has always been the pointer index, but prior to Android 2.2, the names of the constants were just plain wrong. The constants' names have been replaced since Android 2.2, and the constant names with ID in them have been deprecated. Feel free to create your own constants that you can use across all versions of Android.

We used a logAction() method in the previous example, which used these constants to decode our action value. We provide the relevant code again in Listing 25–12.

Listing 25–12. *Sample Code for Figuring Out the Result from MotionEvent.getAction()*

```
int action = event.getAction();
int ptrIndex = (action & MotionEvent.ACTION_POINTER_ID_MASK) >>>
                                MotionEvent.ACTION_POINTER_ID_SHIFT;
action = action & MotionEvent.ACTION_MASK;
if(action == 5 || action == 6)
    action = action - 5;
int ptrId = event.getPointerId(ptrIndex);
```

After these statements in Listing 25–12 have executed, ptrId will hold the pointer ID associated to the action; action will have a value between 0 and 4, and ptrIndex will have the pointer index value for use with getX() and similar methods of MotionEvent. One way to look at the values returned from getAction() is to realize that any value greater than 4 represents a value that relates to a pointer ID. Any value less than or equal to 4 represents a value that relates to the only finger we know about, regardless of what its pointer ID is. In some cases, you may want to subtract 5 from the action to get ACTION_DOWN and ACTION_UP even in multitouch situations. At other times, it's useful to not do so. The choice is yours.

Multitouch Since Android 2.2

Android 2.2 introduced a few changes to how multitouch works. We mentioned the deprecation of some of the constants and the addition of new ones in the previous section. With version 2.2, we also get a couple of new methods—getActionMasked() and getActionIndex()— to make it easier to figure out which pointer and which index are involved in the action. With these new methods, we can replace the code from Listing 25–12 with the code in Listing 25–13.

Listing 25–13. *Sample Code for Figuring Out Our Action*

```
int action = event.getActionMasked();
int ptrIndex = event.getActionIndex();
int ptrId = event.getPointerId(ptrIndex);
```

This is a lot simpler than the code in Listing 25–12. However, note that our action variable is going to be ACTION_DOWN, ACTION_UP, ACTION_MOVE, ACTION_CANCEL, ACTION_OUTSIDE, ACTION_POINTER_DOWN, or ACTION_POINTER_UP (these are the values 0 through 6 respectively). If you wanted to make it just like before, you could subtract the value 5 if getActionMasked() returns a value above 4. Or you could simply deal with the extra two values.

As mentioned before, if you choose to do your own masking, as in Listing 25–12, in Android 2.2 or later, the constants ACTION_POINTER_ID_MASK and ACTION_POINTER_ID_SHIFT have been deprecated, and new constants were created with the names ACTION_POINTER_INDEX_MASK and ACTION_POINTER_INDEX_SHIFT to represent the exact same values. Because the new constants are not known in earlier versions of Android, you'd be better off creating your own constants with the values 0x0000ff00 and 0x00000008 respectively, since those constants will be valid in any version of Android.

Touches with Maps

Maps can receive touch events as well. You have already seen how touching a map can bring up a zoom control or allow us to pan the map sideways. These are built-in functions of maps. But what if we want to do something different? We're going to show you how to implement some interesting functionality with maps, including the ability to click a location and get its latitude and longitude. From there, we can do lots of very useful things.

One of the main classes for maps is MapView. This class has an onTouchEvent() method just like the Views we covered earlier and takes a MotionEvent object as its only argument. We can also use the setOnTouchListener() method to set up a callback handler for touch events on a MapView. Other main types of objects for maps are the set of Overlays, including ItemizedOverlay and MyLocationOverlay. These were all introduced in Chapter 17. These Overlay classes also have an onTouchEvent() method, although the signature is slightly different from the onTouchEvent() method on a regular View. For an Overlay, the method signature is

```
onTouchEvent(android.view.MotionEvent e, MapView mapView)
```

We can override this onTouchEvent() method if we want to do different things with maps. It is more common to override methods in an Overlay class than in MapView, so we will focus our attention there in this section. As before, the onTouchEvent() method for Overlays deals with MotionEvent objects. Even with maps, the MotionEvent object gives us X and Y coordinates of where the user has touched the touch screen. This is only marginally useful when dealing with maps, since we often want to know the actual location on the map where the user touched. Fortunately, there are ways to figure this out.

MapView provides an interface called Projection, and Projection has methods to convert from a pixel to a GeoPoint or from a GeoPoint to a pixel. To get a Projection, call the MapView.getProjection() method. Once you have the Projection, the methods fromPixels() and toPixels() can be used for the conversions. Keep in mind that the Projection is only good while the map doesn't change in the view. Within your onTouchEvent() method, you can convert the X and Y location values to a GeoPoint using fromPixels().

An interesting and very useful method of Overlay is the onTap() method, which is similar to the onTouch() method you saw earlier in this chapter but different in a key way. Map Overlays do not have an onTouch() method. The signature of the onTap() method is

```
public boolean onTap(GeoPoint p, MapView mapView)
```

This means that when a user touches on our Overlay, our onTap() method gets called with the GeoPoint of where the user touched. This will save us a lot of time trying to figure out where on the map the user is touching. We no longer need to worry about converting from an X and Y coordinate location to a latitude and longitude coordinate; Android takes care of this for us.

We're now going to revisit the example from Chapter 17 in which we displayed a map with buttons for the different modes (Satellite, Street, Traffic, and Normal). We're going to add the ability to launch StreetView on a location from the map. To do this we need to add an Overlay object to our MapView, and when the Overlay object receives a touch event, we'll convert that touch event to a location on the map. With the converted location, we'll launch an intent to invoke StreetView on that location. We'll start by making a copy in Eclipse of our MapViewDemo from Chapter 17 (see Listings 17-2 and 17-3). Then, we'll use Listing 25–14 to modify the onCreate() method of the main Activity, plus add a new class with the file ClickReceiver.java, also provided in this listing. The changes to the onCreate() method are shown in bold. The UI will still look just like it did in Figure 17-3.

Listing 25–14. ***Adding Touch to Our Maps Demonstration***

```
@Override
protected void onCreate(Bundle savedInstanceState) {
    super.onCreate(savedInstanceState);
    setContentView(R.layout.mapview);

    mapView = (MapView)findViewById(R.id.mapview);

    ClickReceiver clickRecvr = new ClickReceiver(this);
    mapView.getOverlays().add(clickRecvr);
    mapView.invalidate();
```

```
    }

// This file is ClickReceiver.java
import android.content.Context;
import android.content.Intent;
import android.net.Uri;
import android.util.Log;
import com.google.android.maps.GeoPoint;
import com.google.android.maps.MapView;
import com.google.android.maps.Overlay;

public class ClickReceiver extends Overlay{
    private static final String TAG = "ClickReceiver";
    private Context mContext;

    public ClickReceiver(Context context) {
        mContext = context;
    }

    @Override
    public boolean onTap(GeoPoint p, MapView mapView) {
        Log.v(TAG, "Received a click at this point: " + p);

        if(mapView.isStreetView()) {
            Intent myIntent = new Intent(Intent.ACTION_VIEW, Uri.parse
                ("google.streetview:cbll=" +
                (float)p.getLatitudeE6() / 1000000f +
                "," + (float)p.getLongitudeE6() / 1000000f
                +"&cbp=1,180,,0,1.0"
                ));
            mContext.startActivity(myIntent);
             return true;
        }
        return false;
    }
}
```

That's all we need to do for this new example to work—unless of course you don't have `StreetView` available in your emulator or device. `StreetView` was included in the emulators for CupCake (1.5) and Donut (1.6) but was not in the Éclair (2.0) emulator. If you're missing `StreetView` in your emulator, one workaround is to get a real device, which should have it installed, and test there. If all you have is an emulator, you could try the following simple procedure:

1. Set up an AVD that is based on Google APIs version 1.6 or 1.5.
2. Start the emulator with the AVD from step 1.
3. Use `adb pull /system/app/StreetView.apk StreetView.apk` to copy this application from your emulator to your workstation's hard drive.
4. Set up an AVD that is based on Google APIs for the version you want to run on.
5. Stop the emulator from step 2 and start the emulator from step 4.

6. Use adb install StreetView.apk for the .apk file you copied in step 3.

This should install the StreetView application into your emulator and allow our example above to work. In later versions of Android, the .apk file is called Street.apk, so you may be able to find something newer than 1.6 and use that.

When you run your newly modified Maps Demo application, zoom in on a city so you can see the streets. Click the Street button to get the blue outlines on streets that support StreetView (i.e., the streets have pictures in the Google database). Now, you can touch a street and the onTap() method of our ClickReceiver will be called, which in turn will contact the StreetView activity with the location from our touch event using an intent. If you touch an area of the map where StreetView does not have pictures, you will see an empty StreetView screen with an indication such as "Invalid panorama." This means Google can't find any images near enough to that location. Click the back button to return to our Maps application and try another location. If you look in LogCat you will see that we've logged the latitude and longitude of the map location that was touched. Notice that the GeoPoint object uses ints for the lat and long, while the StreetView Uri requires floats.

For this sample application, we've chosen to send an intent with the lat/long of our touched location to the StreetView activity. But you can imagine the other possibilities open to you. With the lat/long of a location, we could use the Geocoder to find out what's around that location. We could use the location to navigate to it using turn-by-turn directions. We could measure how far away the location is from where we are. We can even store the location for later use.

Gestures

Gestures are a special type of a touch screen event. The term "gesture" is used for a variety of things in Android, from a simple touch sequence like a fling or a pinch to the formal Gesture class that we're going to talk about later in this section. Flings, pinches, long presses, and scrolls have expected behaviors with expected triggers. That is, it is pretty clear to most people that a fling is a gesture where a finger touches the screen, drags somewhat quickly off in a single direction, and then lifts up. For example, when someone use a fling in the Gallery application (the one that shows images in a left-to-right chain), the images will move sideways to show new images to the user.

In this section, we're going to take what you've learned about MotionEvents and expand on that to show how to use the pinch gesture. It's not as hard as you might think. The pinch gesture is not explicitly supported in Android prior to version 2.2, so to implement the pinch gesture in prior versions, you have to create code yourself to read event objects and take appropriate action, which is what we will do here. From version 2.2 onward, we have some helpful new features to use with gestures such as the pinch; you'll see these later in the section.

Next, we're going to introduce some helpful classes for other gestures, such as flings and long presses. From there, we'll cover custom gestures, that is, gestures that you can prerecord to allow the user to initiate action in your application by dragging a finger in custom patterns. But first, let's get pinching!

The Pinch Gesture

One of the cool applications of multitouch is the pinch gesture, which is used for zooming. The idea is that if you place two fingers on the screen and spread them apart, the application should respond by zooming in. If your fingers come together, the application should zoom out. The application is usually showing images, which could be maps.

To demonstrate one way to implement pinches, we're going to modify the previous application to include a pinch capability for zooming. Listing 25–15 shows a replacement for the `ClickReceiver` class of that example; everything else stays the same. Note that this example will work fine on a device running Android 2.2 or later, which we'll explain after the code listing.

Listing 25–15. *Java Code for the Pinch Gesture*

```
// This file is ClickReceiver.java
import android.content.Context;
import android.content.Intent;
import android.net.Uri;
import android.util.FloatMath;
import android.util.Log;
import android.view.MotionEvent;
import com.google.android.maps.GeoPoint;
import com.google.android.maps.MapView;
import com.google.android.maps.Overlay;

public class ClickReceiver extends Overlay {
    private static final String TAG = "ClickReceiver";
    private static final float ZOOMJUMP = 75f;
    private Context mContext;
    private boolean inZoomMode = false;
    private boolean ignoreLastFinger = false;
    private float mOrigSeparation;

    public ClickReceiver(Context context) {
        mContext = context;
    }

    @Override
    public boolean onTap(GeoPoint p, MapView mapView) {
        Log.v(TAG, "Received a click at this point: " + p);

        if(mapView.isStreetView()) {
            Intent myIntent = new Intent(Intent.ACTION_VIEW, Uri.parse
                ("google.streetview:cbll=" +
                (float)p.getLatitudeE6() / 1000000f +
                "," + (float)p.getLongitudeE6() / 1000000f
                +"&cbp=1,180,,0,1.0"
                ));
            mContext.startActivity(myIntent);
```

```
            return true;
        }
        return false;
    }

    public boolean onTouchEvent(MotionEvent e, MapView mapView) {
        Log.v(TAG, "in onTouchEvent, action is " + e.getAction());
        int action = e.getAction() & MotionEvent.ACTION_MASK;

        if(e.getPointerCount() == 2) {
            inZoomMode = true;
        }
        else {
            inZoomMode = false;
        }

        if(inZoomMode) {
            switch(action) {
            case MotionEvent.ACTION_POINTER_DOWN:
                // We may be starting a new pinch so get ready
                mOrigSeparation = calculateSeparation(e);
                break;
            case MotionEvent.ACTION_POINTER_UP:
                // We're ending a pinch so prepare to
                // ignore the last finger while it's the
                // only one still down.
                ignoreLastFinger  = true;
                break;
            case MotionEvent.ACTION_MOVE:
                // We're in a pinch so decide if we need to change
                // the zoom level.
                float newSeparation = calculateSeparation(e);
                if(newSeparation - mOrigSeparation > ZOOMJUMP) {
                    // we got wider, zoom in
                    mapView.getController().zoomIn();
                    mOrigSeparation = newSeparation;
                }
                else if (mOrigSeparation - newSeparation > ZOOMJUMP) {
                    // we got narrower, zoom out
                    mapView.getController().zoomOut();
                    mOrigSeparation = newSeparation;
                }
                break;
            }
            // Don't pass these events to Android because we're
            // taking care of them.
            return true;
        }
        else {
            // cleanup if necessary from zooming logic
        }

        // Throw away events if we're on the last finger
        // until the last finger goes up.
        if(ignoreLastFinger) {
            if(action == MotionEvent.ACTION_UP)
                ignoreLastFinger = false;
```

```
            return true;
        }

        return super.onTouchEvent(e, mapView);
    }

    private float calculateSeparation(MotionEvent e) {
        float x = e.getX(0) - e.getX(1);
        float y = e.getY(0) - e.getY(1);
        return FloatMath.sqrt(x * x + y * y);
    }
}
```

We've added an onTouchEvent() callback to our ClickReceiver overlay. Within this callback, we're getting every single MotionEvent object from the touch screen that is directed to our MapView. For most of them, we simply want to pass them along. This will allow dragging to continue to work, as well as launching StreetView from a tap when in StreetView mode. When there are two fingers down on the touch screen though, we could be sensing a pinch, so we set zoom mode to true. If we're getting information on two fingers, we need to decide what's going on, hence the switch statement on the event action.

If we just got the ACTION_POINTER_DOWN action (remember that we only get this in multitouch situations, which this must be since we have two fingers reporting), we just went from one finger to two fingers. After this event, we could see a pinch from the user. To determine if the fingers move closer together or further apart, we must remember the separation distance of the fingers at the beginning of the gesture. The distance calculation is a square root of the sum of the squares of the coordinate differences between the two fingers—in other words, we use the Pythagorean theorem. We are confident that with two fingers down, the event object will have coordinates at indexes 0 and 1, and it doesn't really matter which finger is which.

If we just got the ACTION_POINTER_UP action, this is the last event we'll see with two fingers reported before the MotionEvent objects start coming to us with only one finger reported. We know that our pinch is over. If we simply start letting Android see event objects with one finger on the screen, we could get some weird behavior. For example, if Android were to get the ACTION_UP event from the last finger, Android could decide that it has seen a tap on a location and launch the StreetView application, which would not be desirable. We expect that the user will be lifting the last finger off of the screen to end the pinch gesture, so we decide to throw away any events until that happens. We do this by setting the ignoreLastFinger variable to true, which we'll check later when deciding what to do with events.

If we just got the ACTION_MOVE action, our fingers may have moved together or apart. By calculating the new separation distance between the two fingers and comparing to the old separation distance, we can decide if we want to zoom in, zoom out, or do no zooming at all. If we do some zooming, we need to reset the old separation distance for the next time. The user could leave the fingers on the screen and spread them apart and together, and our application should respond properly to those gestures. If we don't detect a significant change in the separation distance, we're simply going to continue to receive events until either we do get sufficient separation or the user ends the pinch gesture.

Regardless of what action comes in, if we're in zoom mode, we return `true` from `onTouchEvent()`. This tells Android we took care of the event and to keep sending new ones to us. At the end of our `onTouchEvent()` method, we need to decide whether or not to let Android have the event. Using the `ignoreLastFinger` variable, we decide not to give events to Android if we're after a pinch gesture and the last finger is still down. Once the last finger goes up, which we learn from the `ACTION_UP` event action, we can go back to passing events to Android. In this way, we let Android take care of the tap and the drag, but we take care of the pinch. Of course, if you wanted to, you could take care of the tap and drag features too in this callback.

When you try this application, you will see you can still drag the map sideways, and when in street mode, you can tap a location to launch the `StreetView` activity. But now, you can also pinch to zoom in and out on the map.

We've ignored for the moment the possibility that the user could get to two fingers by lifting one finger off from having three fingers down. Many devices only recognize up to two fingers down, but you should probably expect that some device will eventually allow more than two. If you want to use the pinch gesture on things other than maps, you will need to figure out how to do zooming for those things. For example, if you have an image on the screen and you want to zoom in and out using a pinch, you would need to manipulate the image to make it bigger or smaller triggered by the `ACTION_MOVE` events similarly to how we've done things here. We'll be getting to an example like that very soon in this chapter.

As mentioned before, the pinch gesture was not explicitly supported until Android 2.2, and while the preceding code will work for Android 2.2, you might want to take advantage of the newer features to get the pinch gesture into your application. It's worth noting here that the `MapView` class in Android versions 2.2 and above supports pinch zooming with nothing required from the developer at all; it just works, so we don't need to address the pinch gesture for maps from newer Android versions. Before we get to the pinch gesture's native support, we first need to cover a class that's been around from the beginning—`GestureDetector`.

GestureDetector and OnGestureListeners

The work we just did to implement the pinch gesture wasn't too bad, but it would be nice if Android could provide some help so gestures that are common could be figured out for us. Then, all we'd have to do is perform the appropriate application logic when that gesture occurred. Fortunately, Android has exactly that, although it took until Android 2.2 to get a class that deals explicitly with the pinch gesture.

The first class is `GestureDetector`, which has been around from the very beginning of Android, and its purpose in life is to receive `MotionEvent` objects and tell us when a sequence of events looks like a common gesture. We pass all of our event objects to the `GestureDetector` from our callback, and it calls other callbacks when it recognizes a gesture, such as a fling or long press. We need to register a listener for the callbacks from the GestureDetector, and this is where we put our logic that says what to do if the user has performed one of these common gestures. Unfortunately, this class does not tell us if a pinch gesture is taking place; for that, we need to use a new class, which we'll get to shortly.

There are a few ways to build the listener side. Your first option is to write a new class that implements the appropriate gesture listener interface, for example, the GestureDetector.OnGestureListener interface. There are several abstract methods that must be implemented for each of the possible callbacks.

Your second option is to pick one of the simple implementations of a listener and override the appropriate callback methods that you care about. For example, the GestureDetector.SimpleOnGestureListener class has implemented all of the abstract methods to do nothing and return false. All you have to do is extend that class and override the few methods you need to act on those few gestures you care about. The other methods have their default implementations. It's more future-proof to choose the second option even if you decide to override all of the callback methods, since if a future version of Android adds another abstract callback method to the interface, the simple implementation will provide a default callback method, so you're covered.

Android 2.2 introduced the ScaleGestureDetector class, and this is the one that figures out the pinch gesture for us. We're going to explore this, plus the corresponding listener class, to see how to use the pinch gesture to resize an image. In this example, we extend the simple implementation (ScaleGestureDetector.SimpleOnScaleGestureListener) for our listener. Listing 25–16 has the XML layout and the Java code for our MainActivity.

Listing 25–16. *Layout and Java Code for the Pinch Gesture Using ScaleGestureDetector*

```
<?xml version="1.0" encoding="utf-8"?>
<LinearLayout xmlns:android="http://schemas.android.com/apk/res/android"
    android:id="@+id/layout"  android:orientation="vertical"
    android:layout_width="fill_parent"  android:layout_height="fill_parent" >

  <TextView  android:text="Use the pinch gesture to change the image size"
    android:layout_width="fill_parent"  android:layout_height="wrap_content" />

  <ImageView android:id="@+id/image"  android:src="@drawable/icon"
    android:layout_width="match_parent"  android:layout_height="match_parent"
    android:scaleType="matrix" />

</LinearLayout>


// This file is MainActivity.java
import android.app.Activity;
import android.graphics.Matrix;
import android.os.Bundle;
import android.util.Log;
import android.view.MotionEvent;
import android.view.ScaleGestureDetector;
import android.widget.ImageView;
```

```
public class MainActivity extends Activity {
    private static final String TAG = "ScaleDetector";
    private ImageView image;
    private ScaleGestureDetector mScaleDetector;
    private float mScaleFactor = 1f;
    private Matrix mMatrix = new Matrix();
    @Override
    public void onCreate(Bundle savedInstanceState) {
        super.onCreate(savedInstanceState);
        setContentView(R.layout.main);

        image = (ImageView)findViewById(R.id.image);
        mScaleDetector = new ScaleGestureDetector(this,
                new ScaleListener());
    }

    @Override
    public boolean onTouchEvent(MotionEvent ev) {
        Log.v(TAG, "in onTouchEvent");
        // Give all events to ScaleGestureDetector
        mScaleDetector.onTouchEvent(ev);

        return true;
    }

    private class ScaleListener extends
ScaleGestureDetector.SimpleOnScaleGestureListener {
        @Override
        public boolean onScale(ScaleGestureDetector detector) {
            mScaleFactor *= detector.getScaleFactor();

            // Make sure we don't get too small or too big
            mScaleFactor = Math.max(0.1f, Math.min(mScaleFactor, 5.0f));

            Log.v(TAG, "in onScale, scale factor = " + mScaleFactor);
            mMatrix.setScale(mScaleFactor, mScaleFactor);

            image.setImageMatrix(mMatrix);
            image.invalidate();
            return true;
        }
    }
}
```

Our layout is straightforward. We have a simple `TextView` with our message to use the pinch gesture, and we have our `ImageView` with the standard Android icon. We're going to resize this icon image using a pinch gesture. Of course, feel free to substitute your own image file instead of the icon. Just copy your image file into a drawable folder, and be sure to change the `android:src` attribute in the layout file. Notice the `android:scaleType` attribute in the XML layout for our image. This tells Android that we'll be using a graphics matrix to do scaling operations on the image. While a graphics matrix can also do movement of our image within the layout, we're only going to focus on scaling for now. Also notice that we set the ImageView size to as big as possible. As we scale the image, we don't want it clipped by the boundaries of the `ImageView`.

The code is also straightforward. Within onCreate(), we get a reference to our image and create our ScaleGestureDetector. Within our onTouchEvent() callback, all we do is pass every event object we get to the ScaleGestureDetector's onTouchEvent() method and return true so we keep getting new events. This allows the ScaleGestureDetector to see all events and decide when to notify us of gestures.

The ScaleListener is where the zooming happens. There are actually three callbacks within the listener class, onScaleBegin(), onScale(), and onScaleEnd(). We don't need to do anything special with the begin and end methods, so we didn't implement them here.

Within onScale(), the detector passed in can be used to find out lots of information about the scaling operation. The scale factor is a value that hovers around 1. That is, as the fingers pinch closer together, this value is slightly below 1; as the fingers move apart, this value is slightly larger than 1. Our mScaleFactor member starts at 1, so it gets progressively smaller or larger than 1 as the fingers move together or apart. If mScaleFactor equals 1, our image will be normal size. Otherwise, our image will be smaller or larger than normal as mScaleFactor moves below or above 1. We set some bounds on mScaleFactor with the elegant min/max function combination. This prevents our image from getting too small or too large. We then use mScaleFactor to scale the graphics matrix, and we apply the newly scaled matrix to our image. The invalidate() call forces a redraw of the image on the screen.

As you can see, this is a lot less effort than in the previous example where we had to deal with the event objects ourselves. We can concern ourselves with performing the appropriate application logic when the common gesture has been performed. To work with the OnGestureListener interface, you'd do something very similar to what we've done here with our ScaleListener, except that the callbacks will be for different common gestures.

Common gestures are one thing, but what if you want to have custom gestures with your application? For example, what if you wanted the user to be able to draw a checkmark on the screen and have your application perform some function? For that, we need custom gestures, which is where we turn next.

Custom Gestures

In the final section of this chapter, we'll cover the formal Gesture classes of Android. Formally, a gesture is a prerecorded touch screen motion that your application can expect from the user. If the user performs the same gesture as the prerecorded gesture when using your application, your application can invoke specific logic according to what that gesture means to your application. Gestures require an overlay that can detect a gesture by the user to pass it to the underlying activity. Using gestures can simplify a user interface by eliminating buttons or other controls in favor of finger swipes or drawing motions. They can also make for interesting game interfaces. In this section, we will explore how to record custom gestures and how to use them in your application. Note that the gesture-related classes we used earlier are not used in this example at all; this section explores a different set of gesture classes.

The Gestures Builder Application

Before we get into gesture code, let's play with the Gestures Builder application that comes with the Android SDK, which will help you understand what a gesture is. Gestures Builder creates and manages a gestures file that contains a library of gestures. Launch an emulator from Eclipse; unlock the emulator device; go to your applications, and choose Gestures Builder. Figure 25–4 shows the application icon.

Figure 25–4. *The Gestures Builder icon*

If you don't see Gestures Builder within your emulator, you'll have to create a new project in Eclipse. Gestures Builder is provided as a sample application under your Android SDK directory, in `platforms/<version>/samples/GestureBuilder`, or in `samples` under the Android SDK directory. You can create a new Android project in Eclipse using the "Create project from existing sample" option. Select the desired Android version as a Build Target to enable the "Create project from existing sample" drop-down menu, then choose GestureBuilder from the drop-down menu. You can then deploy this application to your emulator.

The Gestures Builder application will open to a mostly blank screen. Click the Add gesture button. You will be prompted for a name; the name you give will be associated to the gesture you're about to record. This name will be used in your code to refer to the gesture and will serve as a sort of command name. When the user performs the gesture to your application, the name will be passed to your methods so your application can do what the user is expecting it to do. The name you give could be a noun like "spiral" or "checkmark," or it could be like a command such as "fetch" or "stop." For now, let's call our first gesture "checkmark," so type **checkmark** for the Name. Now, draw a check mark in the big blank space underneath, either with your mouse if using the emulator, or with your finger if using a device. If you don't like your first attempt, simply redraw a new check mark; the old one will be erased as soon as you start drawing a new one. When you're happy with your check mark, click Done. You should see a screen like the one shown in Figure 25–5.

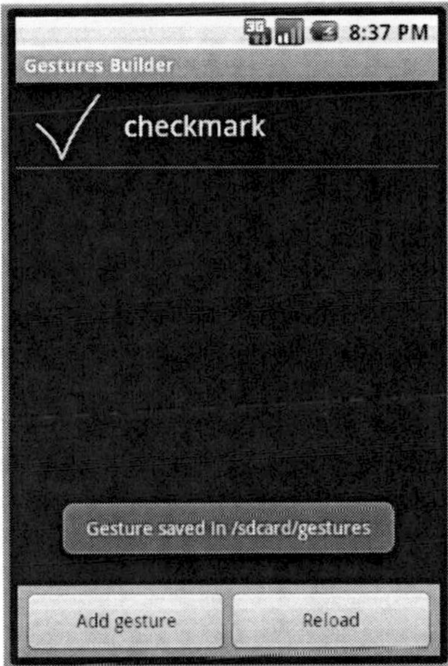

Figure 25–5. *Our check mark gesture saved to the /sdcard*

Note that you could record different types of check marks and give them all the same name of "checkmark." Record at least one more check mark–like gesture and name it `checkmark` too; it could be smaller or bigger or in some way different than your first check mark while still retaining the same basic shape. Add some different gestures with different names using the "Add gesture" button. Each time you click Done, you add another gesture to your library. You might try to use a multitouch gesture, for example, drawing two fingers across the screen at the same time to make an equals sign. This doesn't work and you get only one line. Maybe in the future, multitouch gestures—that is, gestures where two or more fingers are touching the screen at the same time—will be supported.

Each gesture has a name and is made up of strokes. A *gesture stroke* is a touch sequence starting from when a finger touches down on the screen to when that finger lifts from the screen. As you learned earlier, a touch sequence is made up of `MotionEvent` objects. Similarly, a gesture stroke is made up of gesture points. Gestures get collected into a *gesture store*. A *gesture library* contains one gesture store. In Android, these are all classes that you can use in your code. See Figure 25–6 for a diagram that shows the classes' relationships.

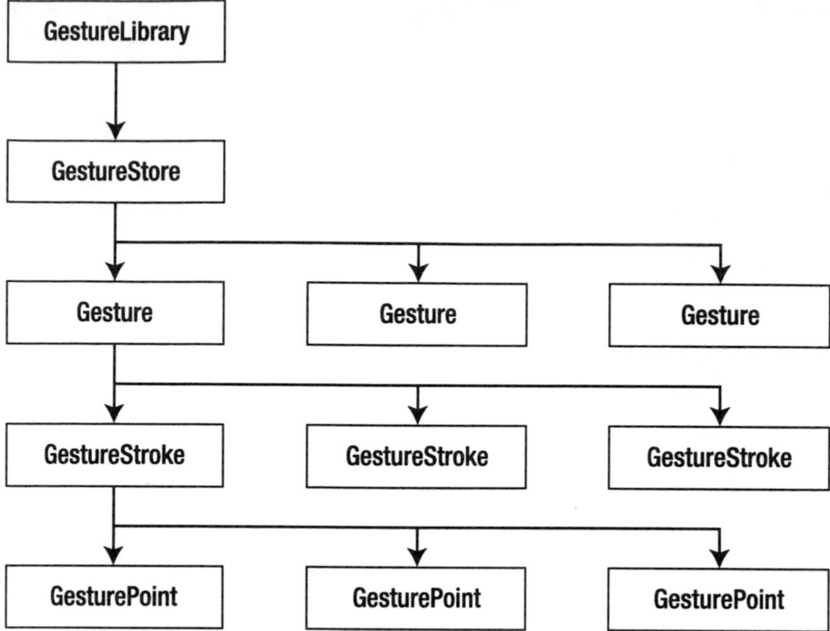

Figure 25–6. *The structure of gesture classes*

While we can't use multitouch to create a custom gesture, we can have multiple gesture strokes in a single gesture. For example, to create a letter "E" gesture, you would need at least two gesture strokes: one gesture stroke could trace the top, back, and bottom sides of the "E," and a second stroke could provide the center dash to complete the letter. You could also draw the back of the "E" with a vertical gesture stroke, followed by three separate horizontal gesture strokes to finish the letter. There are other ways you could draw an "E," and fortunately, the gesture library allows you to give all of them the name "E" while recording different gestures. Go ahead and record "E" a few different ways, since your users might draw the letter in any one of those ways and you want your application to recognize an "E" however the user decides to draw it. Figure 25–7 shows different ways of recording an E.

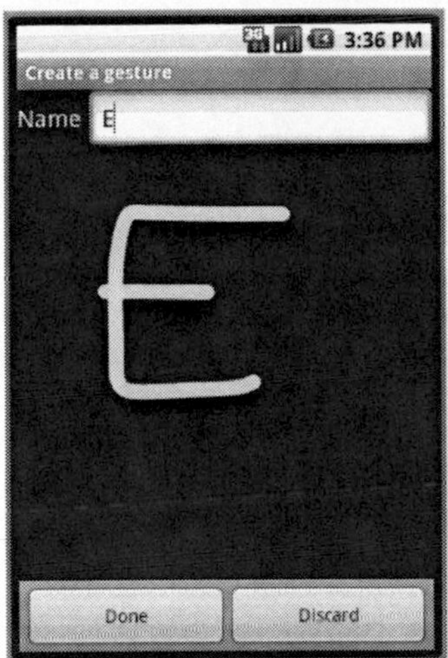

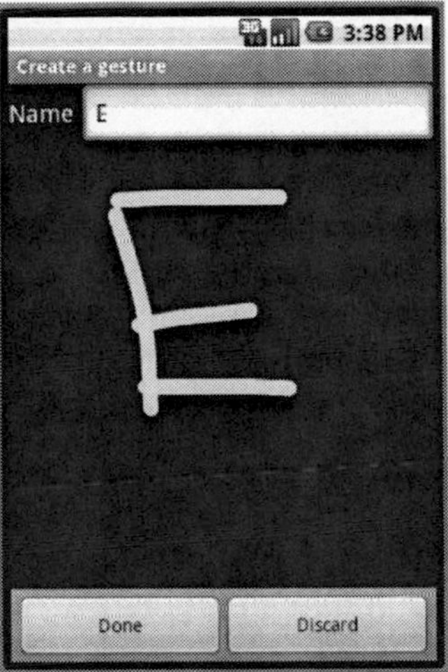

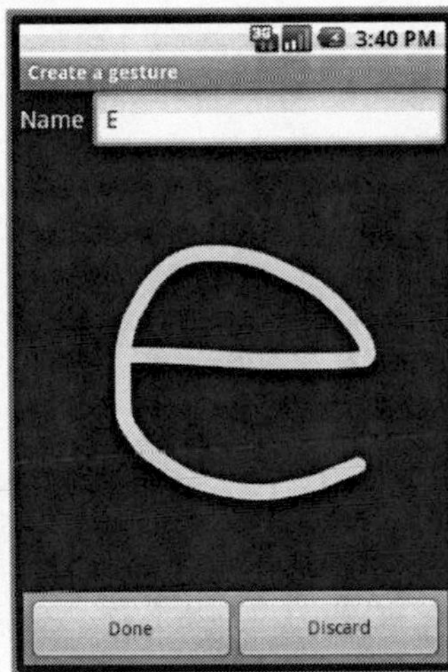

Figure 25–7. *Different ways to record an "E" gesture*

You may find it challenging to create a multistroke gesture in Gestures Builder in the emulator. As we noted earlier, you can simply redraw your gesture over the last one, and the preceding one will be erased. So how does Android know when you're starting over and when you're adding another gesture stroke to the current gesture? Android uses a value called the `FadeOffset`, which is a time value in milliseconds. If you wait longer than this time value to start the next gesture stroke, Android assumes you're starting over or starting a new gesture. By default, the time value is 420 milliseconds. This means that if you are drawing a gesture on the screen, and you lift your finger for longer than 420 milliseconds before drawing the next gesture stroke in your gesture, Android will assume you've already finished and will use what you've just drawn so far as the entirety of your gesture. On a real device, the default value might be long enough to start the next stroke of a gesture. On the emulator, though, it might not be. It depends on how fast your workstation is.

If you're having trouble getting Gestures Builder in the emulator to accept a multistroke gesture, you can create your own version of Gestures Builder and modify the default value of `FadeOffset`. We described earlier how to create a Gestures Builder project in Eclipse. Follow those instructions, and then go into the project's `/res/layout/create_gesture.xml` file to add the attribute `android:fadeOffset="1000"` to the `GestureOverlayView` element. This will extend `FadeOffset` to 1 second (1,000 milliseconds). You are free to choose a different value if you wish.

Let's investigate where these gestures went. The Toast message in Gestures Builder tells us the gestures are being saved to `/sdcard/gestures` (or `/mnt/sdcard/gestures` on Android 2.2 and later). Use File Explorer in Eclipse, or `adb`, to navigate to the `/sdcard` folder of the emulator. There, you will see a file called `gestures`. Notice that it is not very big. The `gestures` file is a binary file, so you will not be able to edit it by hand. To modify the contents, you will need to use the Gestures Builder application. When building your gesture-enabled application, you will need to copy the `gestures` file to your application's `/res/raw` directory. For this, you will need to use the File Copy feature of File Explorer, or use adb pull to get the gestures file onto your workstation so you can copy it into your project.

Besides adding new gestures in Gestures Builder, you can click and hold an existing gesture to bring up a menu. From the menu, you can change the gesture's name or delete it. You cannot record the gesture again, so if you don't like the gesture itself, you'll need to delete it and add it anew. As mentioned earlier, one thing you might want to do is record variations of gestures and give them the same name to account for user variation in inputting the gesture. The gesture name does not have to be unique, although gestures with the same name should be similar.

Now, we're going to create a sample application that uses our new gestures file. Using Eclipse, create a new Android Project. See Listing 25–17 for the XML of our layout file and for the code of our Activity class.

Listing 25–17. *Java Code for Our Gesture Revealer Application*

```
<?xml version="1.0" encoding="utf-8"?>
<!-- This file is /res/layout/main.xml -->
<LinearLayout xmlns:android="http://schemas.android.com/apk/res/android"
    android:orientation="vertical"
    android:layout_width="fill_parent"
    android:layout_height="fill_parent" >
  <TextView
    android:layout_width="fill_parent"
    android:layout_height="wrap_content"
    android:text="Draw gestures and I'll guess what they are" />

  <android.gesture.GestureOverlayView  android:id="@+id/gestureOverlay"
    android:layout_width="fill_parent"
    android:layout_height="fill_parent"
    android:gestureStrokeType="multiple"  android:fadeOffset="1000" />

</LinearLayout>


import java.util.ArrayList;
import android.app.Activity;
import android.gesture.Gesture;
import android.gesture.GestureLibraries;
import android.gesture.GestureLibrary;
import android.gesture.GestureOverlayView;
import android.gesture.Prediction;
import android.gesture.GestureOverlayView.OnGesturePerformedListener;
import android.os.Bundle;
import android.util.Log;
import android.widget.Toast;

public class MainActivity extends Activity implements OnGesturePerformedListener {
    private static final String TAG = "Gesture Revealer";
    GestureLibrary gestureLib = null;

    @Override
    public void onCreate(Bundle savedInstanceState) {
        super.onCreate(savedInstanceState);
        setContentView(R.layout.main);
```

```
//        gestureLib = GestureLibraries.fromRawResource(this,
//                             R.raw.gestures);
        gestureLib = GestureLibraries.fromFile("/sdcard/gestures");
        if (!gestureLib.load()) {
            Toast.makeText(this, "Could not load /sdcard/gestures",
                Toast.LENGTH_SHORT).show();
            finish();
        }

        // Let's take a look at the gesture library we have work with
        Log.v(TAG, "Library features:");
        Log.v(TAG, "  Orientation style: " +
                gestureLib.getOrientationStyle());
        Log.v(TAG, "  Sequence type: " + gestureLib.getSequenceType());
        for( String gestureName : gestureLib.getGestureEntries() ) {
            Log.v(TAG, "For gesture " + gestureName);
            int i = 1;
            for( Gesture gesture : gestureLib.getGestures(gestureName) )
            {
                Log.v(TAG, "    " + i + ": ID: " + gesture.getID());
                Log.v(TAG, "    " + i + ": Strokes count: " +
                        gesture.getStrokesCount());
                Log.v(TAG, "    " + i + ": Stroke length: " +
                        gesture.getLength());
                i++;
            }
        }

        GestureOverlayView gestureView =
            (GestureOverlayView) findViewById(R.id.gestureOverlay);
        gestureView.addOnGesturePerformedListener(this);
    }

    @Override
    public void onGesturePerformed(GestureOverlayView view,
                Gesture gesture)
    {
        ArrayList<Prediction> predictions =
                gestureLib.recognize(gesture);

        if (predictions.size() > 0) {
            Prediction prediction = (Prediction) predictions.get(0);
            if (prediction.score > 1.0) {
                Toast.makeText(this, prediction.name,
                        Toast.LENGTH_SHORT).show();
                for(int i=0;i<predictions.size();i++)
                    Log.v(TAG, "prediction " + predictions.get(i).name +
                            " - score = " + predictions.get(i).score);
            }
        }
    }
}
```

In this example, we're going to simply access the exact same file that the Gestures Builder application wrote to. In our `onCreate()` method, we use the `GestureLibraries.fromFile()` method to do this. But we also show in the comments how you would access a gestures file that is part of your application. If you were to use the `fromRawResource()` method, you'd use an argument like our regular resource IDs, and you'd put the gestures file into the `/res/raw` directory.

Our application doesn't do a whole lot, but running it will give you a better understanding of what is going on inside Android as it processes gestures. At startup, our application loads the gestures file and logs what it finds. It also logs the results of trying to match a sample gesture drawn into the input screen of our application. Go ahead and run the Gesture Revealer application, assuming, of course, that you've run Gestures Builder already and have some gestures in the `/sdcard/gestures` file. See how each gesture is logged with the ID, the number of strokes, and the length.

Use some gestures on the screen that you know exist in your gesture library. Then use some that you know do not exist. Watch the LogCat records to see what's happening. You may notice that sometimes what you draw is not recognized when you think it should be or that what Android recognized was not what you had in mind, but most of the time it correctly recognizes what you drew. You may also have noticed that when Android recognizes your input gesture, you get scores for all gestures in your library in predictions, but when Android doesn't recognize your input gesture, you don't get anything at all.

Also note what happens if you have a multistroke gesture, such as the letter E, and you take too long between strokes. The application will take what you've drawn so far and use that to compare to your gesture library, which is likely to result in an incorrect match or no match at all. This time delay is controlled by `FadeOffset`. Here is where it gets tricky. We want Android to begin matching gestures as soon as we're finished making our gesture, but we have no way to know if the user is finished unless we wait for some period of time and don't see the start of a new gesture stroke. Therefore, `FadeOffset` serves two purposes: one is to control how long to wait for a new gesture stroke as part of the current gesture, and the other is to control how long to wait to begin matching our gesture against the known gestures in our gesture library. Making `FadeOffset` very large means having to wait a long time before the matching process begins. Making `FadeOffset` too small means not being able to use a multistroke gesture because Android will think the gesture is finished before the user gets to the next gesture stroke. Whether 420 milliseconds is the right value to use is up to you. You might want to use a Preference value so users can adjust it for themselves.

While we're on the topic of multistroke gestures, note that the `GestureOverlayView` has a setting that controls whether or not multistroke gestures are expected. The attribute in XML is `android:gestureStrokeType`, and its value is either `single` (the default) or `multiple`. If you want to be able to draw multistroke gestures, this attribute must be set. You can also set it programmatically using `setGestureStrokeType(int type)`, using an argument of either GestureOverlayView.`GESTURE_STROKE_TYPE_SINGLE or GestureOverlayView.GESTURE_STROKE_TYPE_MULTIPLE`. `GestureOverlayView` also has XML attributes and methods for setting colors and line thicknesses.

To create your own gesture-aware application, you will need to decide what gestures your application will act on, create a library of those gestures, and implement the onGesturePerformedListener interface, probably in your Activity, to recognize the gestures and take appropriate action.

What if you want your users to be able to record their own gestures? For example, what about using a different gesture for an action in your application than the one that you provide? This is possible, but means that you need to have a gesture library file that can be written to, and the logical place to put this is the SD card. It's fairly simple to create a new gesture library file, read out the default gestures from the gesture library file that comes with your application, and overwrite gestures that the user wants to replace. You can use the implementation of the Gestures Builder application as mentioned previously to see how to create a gesture recorder. Or maybe someone will write a Gestures Builder application that responds to intents, so you could simply invoke that activity to add a new gesture. Alternatively, you could record just the user's gestures into a new writable gesture library file and load two gesture libraries into your application, the user's and your original. Within the onGesturePerformed() method, you could first try recognize() on the user's library and then on your own. You could compare the top scores from any predictions from each library to decide which action to take.

References

Here are some helpful references to topics you may wish to explore further.

- http://www.androidbook.com/projects. Look here for a list of downloadable projects related to this book. For this chapter look for a zip file called ProAndroid3_Ch25_Touchscreens.zip. This zip file contains all projects from this chapter, listed in separate root directories. There is also a README.TXT file that describes exactly how to import projects into Eclipse from one of these zip files.
- http://www.ted.com/talks/jeff_han_demos_his_breakthrough_touchscreen.html: Jeff Han demonstrates his multi-touch computer user interface at TED in 2006—very cool.
- http://android-developers.blogspot.com/2010/06/making-sense-of-multitouch.html: This Android blog post about multi-touch offers yet another way to implement a GestureDetector inside an extension of a view.

Summary

In this chapter, we showed you how to deal with touch screens, starting with single-touch applications and then moving on to multi-touch. We explained how touch works with maps and the helpful classes and methods Android provides for dealing with touches and maps. Finally, we explored the gesture mechanisms in Android that allow your applications to receive user input in a new, and perhaps simpler, way than using keyboards or other UI controls.

Chapter 26

Using Sensors

Android devices often come with hardware sensors built in, and Android provides a framework for working with those sensors. Working with sensors can be fun. Measuring the outside world and using that in software in a device is pretty cool. It is the kind of programming experience you just don't get on a regular computer that sits on a desk or in a server room. The possibilities for new applications that use sensors are huge, and we hope you are inspired to realize them.

In this chapter we'll explore the Android sensor framework. We'll explain what sensors are, how we get sensor data, and then discuss some specifics of the kinds of data we can get from sensors and what we can do with it. While Android has defined several sensor types already, there are no doubt more sensors in Android's future, and we expect that future sensors will get incorporated into the sensor framework.

What Is a Sensor?

In Android, a sensor is a piece of hardware that has been wired into the device to feed data from the physical world to applications. Applications in turn use the sensor data to inform the user about the physical world, to control game play, to do augmented reality, or to provide useful tools for working in the real world. Sensors operate in one direction only; they're read-only (with one exception, the NFC sensor, which we'll cover). That makes using them fairly straightforward. You set up a listener to receive sensor data, then you process the data as it comes in. GPS hardware is like the sensors we cover in this chapter. In Chapter 17 we set up listeners for GPS location updates, and we processed those location updates as they came in. But although GPS is similar to a sensor, it is not part of the sensor framework that is provided by Android.

Some of the sensor types that can appear in an Android device include:

- Light sensor
- Proximity sensor
- Temperature sensor
- Pressure sensor

- Gyroscope sensor
- Accelerometer
- Magnetic field sensor
- Orientation sensor
- Gravity sensor (as of Android 2.3)
- Linear acceleration sensor (as of Android 2.3)
- Rotation vector sensor (as of Android 2.3)
- Near Field Communication (NFC) sensor (as of Android 2.3)

The NFC sensor is not like the others in this list. We're going to cover the NFC sensor later on in this chapter, because it is accessed in a completely different way from the rest of these sensors.

Detecting Sensors

Please don't assume, however, that all Android devices have all of these sensors. In fact, many devices have just some of these sensors. The Android emulator, for example, has only an accelerometer. So how do you know which sensors are available on a device? There are two ways, one direct and one indirect.

The first way is that you ask the SensorManager for a list of the available sensors. It will respond with a list of sensor objects that you can then set up listeners for and get data from. We'll show you how a bit later in this chapter. This method assumes that the user has already installed your application onto a device, but what if the device doesn't have a sensor that your application needs?

That's where the second method comes in. Within the AndroidManifest.xml file, you can specify the features a device must have in order to properly support your application. If your application needs a proximity sensor, you specify that in your manifest file with a line such as the following:

```
<uses-feature android:name="android.hardware.sensor.proximity" />
```

Now your application will only be installed on a device that has a proximity sensor, so you know it's there when your application runs.

What Can We Know About a Sensor?

While using the `uses-feature` tags in the manifest file lets you know that a sensor your application requires exists on a device, it doesn't tell you everything you may want to know about the actual sensor. Let's build a simple application that queries the device for sensor information. Listing 26–1 shows the XML of our layout, and the Java code of our `MainActivity`.

NOTE: You can download this chapter's projects. We will give you the URL at the end of the chapter. This will allow you to import these projects into your Eclipse directly.

Listing 26–1. *XML and Java for a Sensor List app*

```
<?xml version="1.0" encoding="utf-8"?>
<!-- This file is /res/layout/main.xml -->
<LinearLayout xmlns:android="http://schemas.android.com/apk/res/android"
    android:orientation="vertical"
    android:layout_width="fill_parent"
    android:layout_height="fill_parent" >
  <ScrollView android:layout_width="fill_parent"
    android:layout_height="0dip"
    android:layout_weight="1" >
    <TextView  android:id="@+id/text"
      android:layout_width="fill_parent"
      android:layout_height="wrap_content" />
  </ScrollView>
</LinearLayout>


// This file is MainActivity.java
import java.util.HashMap;
import java.util.List;
import android.app.Activity;
import android.hardware.Sensor;
import android.hardware.SensorManager;
import android.os.Bundle;
import android.widget.TextView;

public class MainActivity extends Activity {
    @Override
    public void onCreate(Bundle savedInstanceState) {
        super.onCreate(savedInstanceState);
        setContentView(R.layout.main);

        TextView text = (TextView)findViewById(R.id.text);

        SensorManager mgr =
            (SensorManager) this.getSystemService(SENSOR_SERVICE);

        List<Sensor> sensors = mgr.getSensorList(Sensor.TYPE_ALL);

        StringBuilder message = new StringBuilder(2048);
        message.append("The sensors on this device are:\n");

        for(Sensor sensor : sensors) {
            message.append(sensor.getName() + "\n");
            message.append("  Type: " +
                    sensorTypes.get(sensor.getType()) + "\n");
            message.append("  Vendor: " +
                    sensor.getVendor() + "\n");
            message.append("  Version: " +
                    sensor.getVersion() + "\n");
            message.append("  Resolution: " +
```

```
                sensor.getResolution() + "\n");
        message.append("  Max Range: " +
                sensor.getMaximumRange() + "\n");
        message.append("  Power: " +
                sensor.getPower() + " mA\n");
      }
      text.setText(message);
    }

    private HashMap<Integer, String> sensorTypes =
                    new HashMap<Integer, String>();

    {
      sensorTypes.put(Sensor.TYPE_ACCELEROMETER, "TYPE_ACCELEROMETER");
      sensorTypes.put(Sensor.TYPE_GYROSCOPE, "TYPE_GYROSCOPE");
      sensorTypes.put(Sensor.TYPE_LIGHT, "TYPE_LIGHT");
      sensorTypes.put(Sensor.TYPE_MAGNETIC_FIELD, "TYPE_MAGNETIC_FIELD");
      sensorTypes.put(Sensor.TYPE_ORIENTATION, "TYPE_ORIENTATION");
      sensorTypes.put(Sensor.TYPE_PRESSURE, "TYPE_PRESSURE");
      sensorTypes.put(Sensor.TYPE_PROXIMITY, "TYPE_PROXIMITY");
      sensorTypes.put(Sensor.TYPE_TEMPERATURE, "TYPE_TEMPERATURE");
      sensorTypes.put(Sensor.TYPE_GRAVITY, "TYPE_GRAVITY");
      sensorTypes.put(Sensor.TYPE_LINEAR_ACCELERATION,
                          "TYPE_LINEAR_ACCELERATION");
      sensorTypes.put(Sensor.TYPE_ROTATION_VECTOR,
                          "TYPE_ROTATION_VECTOR");
    }
}
```

Notice that we've used a ScrollView in this example, since we could easily get more rows than our screen can display at one time. Within our onCreate() method, we start by getting a reference to the SensorManager. There can only be one of these, so we retrieve it as a system service. We then call its getSensorList() method to get a list of sensors. For each sensor, we write out information about it. The output will look something like Figure 26–1.

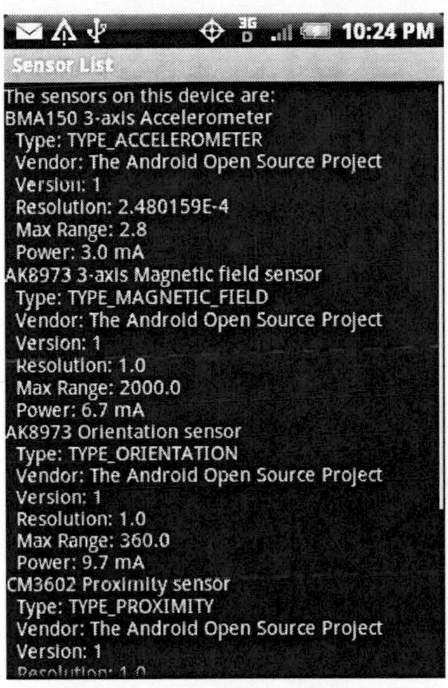

Figure 26–1. *Output from our Sensor List app*

There are a few things to know about this sensor information. The type value tells you the basic type of the sensor without getting specific. A light sensor is a light sensor, but you could get variations in light sensors from one device to another. For example, the resolution of a light sensor on one device could be different than on another device. When you specify that your app needs a light sensor in a `<uses-feature>` tag, you don't know in advance exactly what type of light sensor you're going to get. So you'll need to query the device to find out, and adjust your code accordingly.

The values you get for resolution and maximum range will be in the appropriate units for that sensor. The power measurement is in milliamperes (mA) and represents the electrical current that the sensor draws from the device's battery; smaller is better.

Now that we know what sensors we have available to us, how do we go about getting data from them? As we explained earlier, we set up a listener in order to get sensor data sent to us. Let's explore that now.

Getting Sensor Events

Sensors provide data to our application once we register a listener to receive the data. When our listener is not listening, the sensor can be turned off, conserving battery life, so make sure you only listen when you really need to. Setting up a sensor listener is easy to do. Let's say that we want to measure the light levels from the light sensor. Listing 26–2 shows the Java code for a sample app that does this. We'll use the same XML layout as in Listing 26–1 for this example.

Listing 26–2. *Java Code for a Light Sensor Monitor app*

```
// This file is MainActivity.java
import android.app.Activity;
import android.hardware.Sensor;
import android.hardware.SensorEvent;
import android.hardware.SensorEventListener;
import android.hardware.SensorManager;
import android.os.Bundle;
import android.widget.TextView;

public class MainActivity extends Activity implements SensorEventListener {
    private SensorManager mgr;
    private Sensor light;
    private TextView text;
    private StringBuilder msg = new StringBuilder(2048);

    @Override
    public void onCreate(Bundle savedInstanceState) {
        super.onCreate(savedInstanceState);
        setContentView(R.layout.main);

        mgr = (SensorManager) this.getSystemService(SENSOR_SERVICE);

        light = mgr.getDefaultSensor(Sensor.TYPE_LIGHT);

        text = (TextView) findViewById(R.id.text);
    }

    @Override
    protected void onResume() {
        mgr.registerListener(this, light,
                SensorManager.SENSOR_DELAY_NORMAL);
        super.onResume();
    }

    @Override
    protected void onPause() {
        mgr.unregisterListener(this, light);
        super.onPause();
    }

    public void onAccuracyChanged(Sensor sensor, int accuracy) {
        msg.insert(0, sensor.getName() + " accuracy changed: " +
            accuracy + (accuracy==1?" (LOW)":(accuracy==2?" (MED)":
            " (HIGH)")) + "\n");
        text.setText(msg);
        text.invalidate();
    }

    public void onSensorChanged(SensorEvent event) {
        msg.insert(0, "Got a sensor event: " + event.values[0] +
            " SI lux units\n");
        text.setText(msg);
        text.invalidate();
    }
}
```

In this sample app, we again get a reference to the SensorManager, but instead of getting a list of sensors, we query specifically for the light sensor. We then set up a listener in the onResume() method of our activity, and we unregister the listener in the onPause() method. We don't want to be worrying about the light levels when our application is not in the foreground.

For the registerListener() method, we pass in a value representing how often we want to be notified of sensor value changes. This parameter could be

- SENSOR_DELAY_NORMAL
- SENSOR_DELAY_UI
- SENSOR_DELAY_GAME
- SENSOR_DELAY_FASTEST

It is important to select an appropriate value for this parameter. Some sensors are very sensitive and will generate a lot of events in a short amount of time. If you choose SENSOR_DELAY_FASTEST you might even overrun your application's ability to keep up. Depending on what your application does with each sensor event, it is possible that you will be creating and destroying so many objects in memory that garbage collection will cause noticeable slowdowns and hiccups on the device. On the other hand, certain sensors pretty much demand to be read as often as possible; this is true of the rotation vector sensor in particular.

Because our Activity implements the SensorEventListener interface, we have two callbacks for sensor events: onAccuracyChanged() and onSensorChanged(). The first method will let us know if the accuracy changes on our sensor (or sensors, since it could be called for more than one). The value of the accuracy parameter will be 0, 1, 2 or 3 for unreliable, low, medium, or high accuracy, respectively. Unreliable accuracy does not mean that the device is broken; it normally means that the sensor needs to be calibrated. The second callback method tells us when the light level has changed, and we get a sensor event object to tell us the details of the new value or values from the sensor.

A SensorEvent object has several members, one of them being an array of float values. For a light sensor event, only the first float value has meaning, which is the SI lux value of the light that was detected by the sensor. For our sample app, we build up a message string by inserting the new messages on top of the older messages, and then display the batch of messages in a TextView. Our newest sensor values will always be displayed at the top of the screen.

When you run this application (on a real device, of course, since the emulator does not have a light sensor), you may notice that nothing is displayed at first. Just change the light that is shining on the upper left corner of your device. This is most likely where your light sensor is. If you look very carefully, you might see the dot behind the screen that is the light sensor. If you cover this dot with your finger, the light level will probably change to a very small value (although may not reach zero). The messages should display on the screen telling you about the changing light levels.

NOTE: You might also notice that, by covering up the light sensor, your buttons light up (if you have a device with lighted buttons). This is because Android has detected the darkness and lights up the buttons to make the device easier to use.

Issues with Getting Sensor Data

The Android sensor framework has problems that you need to be aware of. This is the part that's not fun. In some cases, we have ways of working around the problem, in others we don't, or it's very difficult.

onAccuracyChanged() Always Says the Same Thing

Up until Android 2.2, the `onAccuracyChanged()` callback would get called every time there was a new sensor reading, and the accuracy parameter would always be 3 (for high). It's a good idea to accommodate changing accuracies of sensor data, but don't be surprised if this method gets called all the time even though the accuracy has not changed.

No Direct Access to Sensor Values

You may have noticed that there is no direct way to query the sensor's current value. The only way to get data from a sensor is through a listener. This means that, even once we've setup the listener, there are no guarantees that we'll get a new datum within a set period of time. At least the callback is asynchronous so we won't block the UI thread waiting for a piece of data from a sensor. However, your application has to accommodate the fact that sensor data may not be available at the exact moment that you want it.

It is possible to directly access sensors using native code and the JNI feature of Android. You'll need to know the low-level native API calls for the sensor driver you're interested in, plus be able to setup the interface back to Android. So it can be done, but it's not easy.

Sensor Values not Sent Fast Enough

Even at `SENSOR_DELAY_FASTEST`, we might not get new values more often than every 20 ms (it depends on the device). If you need more rapid sensor data than you can get with a rate setting of `SENSOR_DELAY_FASTEST`, it is possible to use native code and JNI to get to the sensor data faster, but similar to the previous situation, it is not easy.

Sensors Turn Off with Screen in Android 2.1

There have been problems in Android 2.1 with sensor updates that get turned off when the screen is turned off. Apparently someone thought it was a good idea to not send sensor updates if the screen is off, even if your application (most likely using a service) has a wake lock. Basically your listener gets unregistered when the screen turns off. There are several workarounds to this problem. The first is that you can set the screen timeout so it doesn't turn off while you want to continue receiving sensor updates. This has the major disadvantage of using up the battery. In order to change the screen off timeout, you'll need to do something like the following where myDelay is a time period in milliseconds:

```
Settings.System.putInt(getContentResolver(),
                    Settings.System.SCREEN_OFF_TIMEOUT, myDelay);
```

You can use a value of -1 so the screen will never turn off. Your application also needs to have the proper permission (android.permission.WRITE_SETTINGS) in the AndroidManifest.xml file in order to do this. The other drawback to this approach is that the screen-off timeout is a global value. When your application changes it, it's changed for everyone. Your application should really remember the previous setting and restore it when your application ends. Even this can be problematic because, in theory, the user could start your application, wonder why the screen doesn't turn off anymore, go into Settings, and change it to something else entirely, then return to your application later and end it. Not to mention that if the user changes the setting after your application has started, the screen could then turn off and your application would stop getting sensor updates.

The Unregister/Register Technique for Continual Sensor Updates

One method to keep sensor updates coming is to register to receive a broadcast notification when the screen turns off, then unregister your sensor event listener, and re-register your sensor event listener in the onReceive() method of your BroadcastReceiver. This has been shown to work on some 2.1 phones, but not all.

Because your application would normally be paused when the screen goes dark, first you need to acquire a partial wake lock to keep your application running even when the screen is off. Our example uses an Activity but in a real application you'd most likely put your sensor listening code into a service. Listing 26–3 shows what this might look like as an Activity.

Listing 26–3. *Working Around Issues with SensorListeners Turning Off*

```
package com.androidbook.sensor.accel;

// This file is MainActivity.java
import java.io.BufferedWriter;
import java.io.FileWriter;
import java.io.IOException;
import java.text.SimpleDateFormat;
import java.util.Date;
import android.app.Activity;
```

```
import android.content.BroadcastReceiver;
import android.content.Context;
import android.content.Intent;
import android.content.IntentFilter;
import android.hardware.Sensor;
import android.hardware.SensorEvent;
import android.hardware.SensorEventListener;
import android.hardware.SensorManager;
import android.os.Bundle;
import android.os.Environment;
import android.os.PowerManager;
import android.os.PowerManager.WakeLock;
import android.provider.Settings;
import android.util.Log;

public class MainActivity extends Activity implements SensorEventListener {
    private static final String TAG = "AccelerometerRecordToFile";
    private WakeLock mWakelock = null;
    private SensorManager mMgr;
    private Sensor mAccel;
    private BufferedWriter mLog;
    final private SimpleDateFormat mTimeFormat =
                new SimpleDateFormat("HH:mm:ss - ");
    private int mSavedTimeout;

    @Override
    public void onCreate(Bundle savedInstanceState) {
        super.onCreate(savedInstanceState);
        setContentView(R.layout.main);

        mMgr = (SensorManager) this.getSystemService(SENSOR_SERVICE);

        mAccel = mMgr.getDefaultSensor(Sensor.TYPE_ACCELEROMETER);

        // Setup the log file to write to. We will append it just
        // in case this activity restarts in the middle of our
        // experiment.
        try {
            String filename =
    Environment.getExternalStorageDirectory().getAbsolutePath() +
                "/accel.log";
            mLog = new BufferedWriter(new FileWriter(filename, true));
        }
        catch(Exception e) {
            Log.e(TAG, "Unable to initialize the logfile");
            e.printStackTrace();
            finish();
        }

        PowerManager pwrMgr =
                (PowerManager) this.getSystemService(POWER_SERVICE);
        mWakelock = pwrMgr.newWakeLock(PowerManager.PARTIAL_WAKE_LOCK,
                                "Accel");
        mWakelock.acquire();

        // Save the current value of the screen timeout, then set it
        // to a small value
```

```
        try {
            mSavedTimeout = Settings.System.getInt(getContentResolver(),
                Settings.System.SCREEN_OFF_TIMEOUT);
        }
        catch(Exception e) {
            mSavedTimeout = 120000;  // default to 2 minutes if we
                                     // can't read the current value
        }
        Settings.System.putInt(getContentResolver(),
            Settings.System.SCREEN_OFF_TIMEOUT, 5000);  // 5 seconds
    }

    public BroadcastReceiver mReceiver = new BroadcastReceiver() {
        public void onReceive(Context context, Intent intent) {
            if (Intent.ACTION_SCREEN_OFF.equals(intent.getAction())) {
                writeLog("The screen has turned off");
                // Unregisters the listener and registers it again.
                // Should only need to do this in Android 2.1 although
                // it doesn't hurt to do this in any version.

                mMgr.unregisterListener(MainActivity.this);
                mMgr.registerListener(MainActivity.this, mAccel,
                    SensorManager.SENSOR_DELAY_NORMAL);

            }
        }
    };

    @Override
    protected void onStart() {
        writeLog("starting...");
        mMgr.registerListener(this, mAccel,
                        SensorManager.SENSOR_DELAY_NORMAL);

        IntentFilter filter = new IntentFilter(Intent.ACTION_SCREEN_OFF);
        registerReceiver(mReceiver, filter);

        super.onStart();
    }

    @Override
    protected void onStop() {
        writeLog("stopping...");
        mMgr.unregisterListener(this, mAccel);
        unregisterReceiver(mReceiver);
        try {
            mLog.flush();
        } catch (IOException e) {
            // ignore any errors with the logfile
        }
        super.onStop();
    }

    @Override
    protected void onDestroy() {
        writeLog("shutting down...");
        try {
```

```
            mLog.flush();
            mLog.close();
        }
        catch(Exception e) {
            // ignore any errors with the logfile
        }

        // Restore the screen off timeout to the previous value
        Settings.System.putInt(getContentResolver(),
                Settings.System.SCREEN_OFF_TIMEOUT, mSavedTimeout);

        mWakelock.release();

        super.onDestroy();
    }

    public void onAccuracyChanged(Sensor sensor, int accuracy) {
        // ignore
    }

    public void onSensorChanged(SensorEvent event) {
        writeLog("Got a sensor event: " + event.values[0] + ", " +
                event.values[1] + ", " + event.values[2]);
    }

    private void writeLog(String str) {
        try {
            Date now = new Date();
            mLog.write(mTimeFormat.format(now));
            mLog.write(str);
            mLog.write("\n");
        }
        catch(IOException ioe) {
            ioe.printStackTrace();
        }
    }
}
```

We don't need to worry about an XML layout with this example since we're not displaying anything other than our application title. We do need to worry about permissions though, so Listing 26–4 shows our AndroidManifest.xml file for this application.

Listing 26–4. *AndroidManifest.xml for our Accelerometer Monitor app*

```
<?xml version="1.0" encoding="utf-8"?>
<manifest xmlns:android="http://schemas.android.com/apk/res/android"
      android:versionCode="1"
      android:versionName="1.0" package="com.androidbook.sensor.accel">
    <application android:icon="@drawable/icon"
          android:label="@string/app_name">
        <activity android:name=".MainActivity"
                  android:label="@string/app_name">
          <intent-filter>
            <action android:name="android.intent.action.MAIN" />
            <category android:name="android.intent.category.LAUNCHER" />
          </intent-filter>
        </activity>
```

```
    </application>
    <uses-sdk android:minSdkVersion="3" />

<uses-permission android:name="android.permission.WRITE_EXTERNAL_STORAGE" />
<uses-permission android:name="android.permission.WRITE_SETTINGS" />
<uses-permission android:name="android.permission.WAKE_LOCK" />
</manifest>
```

In this example, the main objective is writing accelerometer events to a log file. In the onCreate() method, we need to acquire a partial wake lock so our application will not be put to sleep when the screen is turned off (we covered wake locks in Chapter 14). We also set the screen off timeout to a value of five seconds so it will turn off fairly quickly, but the previous value of the timeout is saved so it can be restored in the onDestroy() method later.

> **NOTE:** We're modifying the screen off timeout so you can see what happens to our sensor event listener when the screen turns off. We wouldn't want to do this in a real application.

We also set up a BroadcastReceiver that is notified when the screen is turned off. We log that fact in onReceive() and then do the Android 2.1 workaround for continuing to receive sensor events. The onStart() method is where the sensor event listener is registered, and also where the BroadcastReceiver is registered. Both of these listeners are unregistered in onStop(). We use onStart() and onStop() instead of onResume() and onPause() because we want to keep listening to sensors even if the user goes to another Activity while we're running.

The onDestroy() method does the cleanup, flushing and closing the log file, restoring the screen off timeout, and releasing the wake lock. Unlike the previous example, the onAccuracyChanged() callback does nothing. The onSensorChanged() method is where the event data is written to the log file.

This pattern of working with a sensor event listener is what you would do as well in a real application. Unlike in our previous example that did not concern itself with the device going to sleep, you most likely need to acquire a wake lock to ensure that your application is capturing events as they happen even if the screen goes dark. Note that if you are targetting Android 2.2 and later, you shouldn't need to worry about the unregistering and re-registering of the sensor event listener in a BroadcastReceiver. And with versions of Android prior to 2.0, you should be fine as well.

This is an interesting application to run. One thing you may want to do is

1. Install the app, then disconnect your device from your workstation so it is not tethered with a USB cable (this sometimes causes the screen to stay on regardless of the display setting).

   The application will appear, then you move the device around and in approximately five seconds the screen will go dark.

2. Continue to move the device around to trigger accelerometer events, then after several seconds, unlock the device and use the Back key to end the application.

   You will find a log file called access.log in the main directory of the SD card of the device.

3. Plug the device back into the USB cable for your workstation, then copy the access.log file to your workstation and take a look.

   You should see a start message, many event messages, and then a message that says "The screen has turned off." Depending on your device and the version of Android it is running, you will either see additional events occurring immediately after this message, or you will see a gap in events until the time you unlocked the device and ended the application.

The Keep-the-Screen-On Technique for Continual Sensor Updates

There is another possible workaround for Android 2.1. The basic symptom is that the sensors on some Android 2.1 devices are simply off anytime the screen is off. So the workaround is to make sure the screen stays on. Listing 26–5 shows an alternate version of our `BroadcastReceiver` from the previous example application, only this time we turn the screen back on (albeit in dimmed mode) as soon as it goes off, plus some small modifications to other parts of the code. Since the screen is technically on even when dimmed, the sensor data continues to flow to our Android 2.1 application. If you're importing projects from our website, this project is called `AccelerometerRecordToFileAlwaysOn`.

Listing 26–5. *Keeping the Screen on Even When the User Turns It Off*

```
// Add these objects to our Activity
    private PowerManager mPwrMgr;
    private WakeLock mTurnBackOn = null;
    private Handler handler = new Handler();

// Add these 3 lines to our onCreate() method
        mPwrMgr = (PowerManager) this.getSystemService(POWER_SERVICE);
        mWakelock = mPwrMgr.newWakeLock(PowerManager.PARTIAL_WAKE_LOCK, "Accel");
        mWakelock.acquire();

// This code replaces BroadcastReceiver in MainActivity.java
    public BroadcastReceiver mReceiver = new BroadcastReceiver() {
        public void onReceive(Context context, Intent intent) {
            if (Intent.ACTION_SCREEN_OFF.equals(intent.getAction())) {
                writeLog("The screen has turned off");
                // Turn the screen back on again, from the main thread
                handler.post(new Runnable() {
                    public void run() {
                        if(mTurnBackOn != null)
                            mTurnBackOn.release();

                        mTurnBackOn = mPwrMgr.newWakeLock(
```

```
                                PowerManager.SCREEN_DIM_WAKE_LOCK |
                                    PowerManager.ACQUIRE_CAUSES_WAKEUP,
                                "AccelOn");
                        mTurnBackOn.acquire();
                    }});
            }
        }
    };

// Don't forget to add this to onDestroy()
    if(mTurnBackOn != null)
        mTurnBackOn.release();
```

Now when you run this application, even if the user presses the Power key to turn off the screen, this application catches the event, and using a wake lock, turns the screen back on in dimmed mode. There may be a very short gap in sensor events while this is happening, but it's better than a big gap with the screen off. Notice how we used a Handler to post a `Runnable` from the `BroadcastReceiver`. This ensures that our code runs on the main thread, which is important for when we want to release the wake lock in `onDestroy()`. The acquire and release must be from the same thread.

Also notice that we release the wake lock in the `onReceive()` method of our `BroadcastReceiver` before getting one. This is done in case the user presses the Power key more than once while we're recording sensor events. We need to match wake lock releases with acquires so if we had one coming in, we release that one before getting a new one.

Now that you know how to get data from sensors, what can you do with the data? As we said earlier, depending on which sensor you're getting data from, the values returned in the values array mean different things. The next section will explore each of the sensor types and what their values mean.

Interpreting Sensor Data

Now that we understand how to get data from a sensor, we must do something meaningful with the data. The data we get, however, will depend on which sensor we're getting the data from. Some sensors are simpler than others. In the sections that follow, we will describe the data that you'll get from the sensors we currently know about. As new devices come into being, new sensors will undoubtedly be introduced as well. The sensor framework is very likely to remain the same, so the techniques we show here should apply equally well to the new sensors.

Light Sensors

The light sensor is one of the simplest sensors on a device, and one we've used in our first sample applications of this chapter. The sensor gives a reading of the light level detected by the light sensor of the device. As the light level changes, the sensor readings change. The units of the data are in SI lux units. To learn more about what this means, please see the References section at the end of this chapter for links to more information.

For the values array in the SensorEvent object, a light sensor uses just the first element, values[0]. This value is a float, and ranges technically from zero to the maximum value for the particular sensor. We say technically because the sensor may only send very small values when there's no light, and never actually send a value of 0.

Remember also that the sensor can tell us the maximum value that it can return and that different sensors can have different maximums. For this reason, it may not be useful to consider the light-related constants in the SensorManager class. For example, SensorManager has a constant called LIGHT_SUNLIGHT_MAX, which is a float value of 120,000; however, when we queried our device earlier, the maximum value returned was 10,240, clearly much less than this constant value. There's another one called LIGHT_SHADE at 20,000 which is also above the maximum of the device we tested. So keep this in mind when writing code that uses light sensor data.

Proximity Sensors

The proximity sensor measures either the distance that some object is from the device (in centimeters), or represents a flag to say whether an object is close or far. Some proximity sensors will give a value ranging from 0.0 to the maximum in increments, while others return either 0.0 or the maximum value only. If the maximum range of the proximity sensor is equal to the sensor's resolution, then you know it's one of those that only returns 0.0, or the maximum. There are devices with a maximum of 1.0; others where it's 6.0. Unfortunately, there's no way to tell before the application is installed and run which proximity sensor you're going to get. Even if you put a <uses-feature> tag in your AndroidManifest.xml file for the proximity sensor, you could get either kind. Unless you absolutely need to have the more granular proximity sensor, your application should accommodate both types gracefully.

Here's an interesting fact about proximity sensors: the proximity sensor is sometimes the same hardware as the light sensor. Android still treats them as logically separate sensors though, so if you need data from both you will need to set up a listener for each one. Here's another interesting fact: the proximity sensor is often used in the phone application to detect the presence of a person's head next to the device. If the head is that close to the touchscreen, the touchscreen is disabled so no keys will be accidently pressed by the ear or cheek while the person is talking on the phone.

The source code projects for this chapter include a simple proximity sensor monitor application, which is basically the light sensor monitor application modified to use the proximity sensor instead of the light sensor. We won't include the code text here in this chapter, but feel free to experiment with it on your own.

Temperature Sensors

The temperature sensor provides a temperature reading, and also returns just a single value in `values[0]`. The value represents the temperature in degrees Celsius. You can get to Fahrenheit degrees from Celsius by multiplying by 9/5 and adding 32. For example, 0 degrees Celsius is 32 Fahrenheit (temperature at which water freezes) and 100 degrees Celsius is 212 degrees Fahrenheit (temperature at which water boils).

The placement of the temperature sensor is device-dependent, and it is possible that the temperature readings could be impacted by the heat generated by the device itself. For example, on some devices, the temperature sensor is reading the temperature of the device's battery. Keep this in mind when writing applications that use the temperature sensor, and don't expect that the readings from the temperature sensor are the air temperature around the device.

The projects for this chapter include one for the temperature sensor called `TemperatureSensor`.

Pressure Sensors

Interestingly, these sensors haven't been seen in any devices as of this writing. The idea is that future devices could have a barometric pressure sensor, which could detect altitude for example. This sensor should not be confused with the ability of a touchscreen to generate a `MotionEvent` with a pressure value (the pressure of the touch). We covered this touch type of pressure sensing in Chapter 25. Touchscreen pressure sensing doesn't use the Android sensor framework.

While it would be easy to copy and modify the sensor monitor applications used so far to accommodate a pressure sensor, we have no way yet to know what the unit of measurement is going to be, so it won't do us much good. Obviously the folks at Google are thinking ahead.

Gyroscope Sensors

Gyroscopes are very cool components that can measure the twist of a device about a reference frame. Said another way, gyroscopes measure the rate of rotation about an axis. When the device is not rotating, the sensor values will be zeroes. When there is rotation in any direction, you'll get non-zero values from the gyroscope. By itself, a gyroscope can't tell you everything you need to know. And unfortunately, errors creep in over time with gyroscopes. But coupled with accelerometers, you can determine the path of movement of the device. Kalman filters can be used to link data from the two sensors together. Accelerometers are not terribly accurate in the short-term, and gyroscopes are not very accurate in the long-term, so combined they can be reasonably accurate all the time. While Kalman filters are very complex, there is an alternative called Complementary filters which are easier to implement in code, and produce results that are pretty good. These concepts are beyond the scope of this book.

The Gyroscope sensor returns three values in the values array for the *x*, *y*, and *z* axes. The units are radians per second and represent the rate of rotation around each of those axes. One way to work with these values is to integrate them over time to calculate an angle change. This is a similar calculation to integrating linear speed over time to calculate distance.

Accelerometers

Accelerometers are probably the most interesting of the sensors on a device. Using these sensors our application can determine the physical orientation of the device in space relative to gravity's pull straight down, plus be aware of forces pushing on the device. Providing this information allows an application to do all sorts of interesting things, from game play to augmented reality. And of course, the accelerometers tell Android when to switch the orientation of the user interface from portrait to landscape and back again.

The accelerometer coordinate system works like this: the accelerometer's *x* axis originates in the bottom left corner of the device and goes across the bottom to the right. The *y* axis also originates in the bottom left corner and goes up along the left of the display. The *z* axis originates in the bottom left corner and goes up in space away from the device. Figure 26–2 shows what this means.

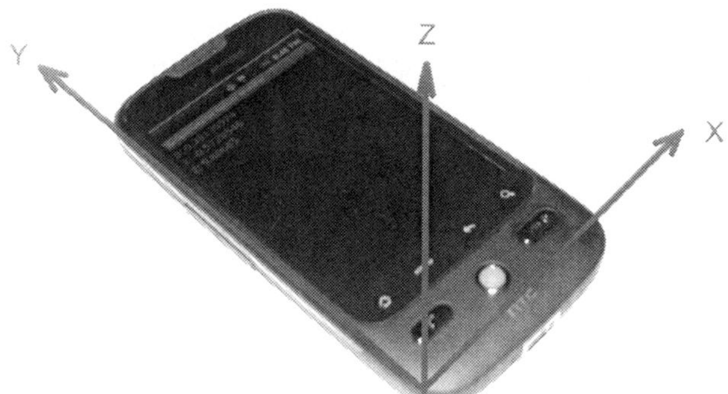

Figure 26–2. *Accelerometer coordinate system*

This coordinate system is different than the one used in layouts and 2D graphics. In that coordinate system, the origin (0, 0) is at the top left corner and Y is positive in the direction down the screen from there. It is easy to get confused when dealing with coordinate systems in different frames of reference so be careful.

We haven't yet said what the accelerometer values mean, so what *do* they mean? Acceleration is measured in meters per second squared (m/s^2). Normal earth gravity is 9.81 m/s^2 pulling down toward the center of the earth. From the accelerometer's point of view, the measurement of gravity is -9.81. If your device is completely at rest (not moving), and is on a perfectly flat surface, the *x* and *y* readings will be 0 and the *z* reading will be +9.81. Actually, the values won't be exactly these because of the sensitivity and accuracy of the accelerometer, but they will be close. Gravity is the only force acting on the device when the device is at rest, and because gravity pulls straight down, and if our device is perfectly flat, its effect on the *x* and *y* axes is zero. On the *z* axis, the accelerometer is measuring the force on the device minus gravity. Therefore, 0 minus -9.81 is +9.81 and that's what the *z* value will be (a.k.a. `values[2]` in the `SensorEvent` object).

The values sent to our application by the accelerometer always represent the sum of the forces on the device minus gravity. If we were to take our perfectly flat device and lift it straight up, the *z* value would increase at first, because we increased the force in the up (*z*) direction. As soon as our lifting force stops, the overall force will return to being just gravity. If the device were to be dropped (hypothetically – please don't do this) it would be accelerating toward the ground, which zeroes out gravity so the accelerometer would read 0 force.

Let's take the device from Figure 26–2 and rotate it up so it is in portrait mode and vertical. The *x* axis is the same, pointing left to right. Our *y* axis is now straight up and down, and the *z* axis is pointing out of the screen straight at us. The *y* value will be +9.81 and both *x* and *z* will be zero.

What happens when we rotate the device to landscape mode and continue to hold it vertically, i.e. so the screen is right in front of our face? If you guessed that *y* and *z* are now zero and *x* is +9.81 you'd be correct. Figure 26–3 shows what it might look like.

Figure 26–3. *Accelerometer values in landscape vertical*

When the device is not moving, or is moving with a constant velocity, the accelerometers are only measuring gravity. And in each axis, the value from the accelerometer is gravity's component in that axis. Therefore, using some trigonometry, you could figure out the angles and know how the device is oriented relative to gravity's pull. That is, you could tell if the device were in portrait mode or in landscape mode or in some tilted mode. In fact, this is exactly what Android does to figure out which display mode to use (portrait or landscape). Note, however, that the accelerometers do not say how the device is oriented with respect to magnetic north. That's where the magnetic field sensor will come in, which we will cover in the next section.

Accelerometers and Display Orientation

Accelerometers in a device are hardware and they're firmly attached, and as such have a specific orientation relative to the device that does not change as the device is turned this way or that. The values that the accelerometers send into Android will change of course as a device is moved, but the coordinate system of the accelerometers will stay the same relative to the physical device. The coordinate system of the display, however, changes as the user goes from portrait to landscape and back again. In fact depending on which way the screen is turned, portrait could be right-side up, or 180 degrees upside down. Similarly, landscape could be in one of two different rotations 180 degrees apart.

When our application is reading accelerometer data and wanting to affect the user interface correctly, our application must know how much rotation of the display has occurred to properly compensate. As our screen is re-oriented from portrait to landscape, the screen's coordinate system has rotated with respect to the coordinate system of the accelerometers. To handle this, our application must use the method `Display.getRotation()`, which was introduced in Android 2.2. The return value is a simple integer but not the actual number of degrees of rotation. The value will be one of `Surface.ROTATION_0`, `Surface.ROTATION_90`, `Surface.ROTATION_180`, or `Surface.ROTATION_270`. These are constants with values of 0, 1, 2, and 3 respectively. This return value tells us how much the display has rotated from the "normal" orientation of the device. Because not all Android devices are normally in portrait mode, we cannot assume that portrait is at `ROTATION_0`.

Not all devices will give you all four return values. On the HTC Droid Eris running Android 2.1, `Display.getOrientation()` (the precursor to `Display.getRotation()` and now deprecated) will return 0 or 1 and that's it. In normal portrait mode, the value returned is 0. If you turn the device 90 degrees counter-clockwise, the screen will rotate and `Display.getOrientation()` will return 1. If you turn the device clockwise 90 degrees from portrait mode, the screen stays in portrait mode, and you still get a return value of 0 `from Display.getOrientation()`.

On the Motorola Droid running Android 2.2, `Display.getRotation()` returns 0, 1, or 3. It does not return a 2 and will not show portrait upside down. Here is a disappointing result though: if you rotate the device 270 degrees in the counter-clockwise direction from straight-up portrait, `Display.getRotation()` returns a 1 at 90 degrees and the display switches to landscape mode, at 180 degrees you still get a 1 and the display does not change, at 270 degrees the display flips to the other landscape mode, but `Display.getRotation()` still returns 1. If you rotate the device 90 degrees in the clockwise direction from normal portrait mode, then you'll get a 3 from `Display.getRotation()`. This last position looks exactly the same as 270 degrees counter-clockwise, but you get a different return value from `Display.getRotation()` depending on how you got there.

Accelerometers and Gravity

So far we've only briefly touched on what happens to the accelerometer values when the device is moved. Let's explore that further. All forces acting on the device will be detected by the accelerometers. If we lift the device, the initial lifting force is positive in the *z* direction, and we get a *z* value greater than +9.81. If we push the device on its left side, we'll get an initial negative reading in the *x* direction.

What we'd like to be able to do is separate out the force of gravity from the other forces acting on the device. There's a fairly easy way to do this, and it's called a low-pass filter. Forces other than gravity acting on the device will do so in a way that is typically not gradual. In other words, if the user is shaking the device, the shaking forces are reflected in the accelerometer values quickly. A low-pass filter will in effect strip out the shaking forces and leave only the steady force which for us is gravity. Let's use a sample application to illustrate this concept. It's called `GravityDemo`. Listing 26–6 shows the layout XML and the Java code.

Listing 26–6. ***Measuring gravity From the accelerometers***

```
<?xml version="1.0" encoding="utf-8"?>
<!-- This file is /res/layout/main.xml -->
<LinearLayout xmlns:android="http://schemas.android.com/apk/res/android"
    android:orientation="vertical"
    android:layout_width="fill_parent"
    android:layout_height="fill_parent" >
  <TextView  android:id="@+id/text"  android:textSize="20sp"
      android:layout_width="fill_parent"
      android:layout_height="wrap_content" />
</LinearLayout>


// This file is MainActivity.java
import android.app.Activity;
import android.hardware.Sensor;
import android.hardware.SensorEvent;
import android.hardware.SensorEventListener;
import android.hardware.SensorManager;
import android.os.Bundle;
import android.widget.TextView;

public class MainActivity extends Activity implements SensorEventListener {
    private SensorManager mgr;
    private Sensor accelerometer;
    private TextView text;
    private float[] gravity = new float[3];
    private float[] motion = new float[3];
    private double ratio;
    private double mAngle;
    private int counter = 0;

    @Override
    public void onCreate(Bundle savedInstanceState) {
        super.onCreate(savedInstanceState);
        setContentView(R.layout.main);

        mgr = (SensorManager) this.getSystemService(SENSOR_SERVICE);

        accelerometer = mgr.getDefaultSensor(Sensor.TYPE_ACCELEROMETER);

        text = (TextView) findViewById(R.id.text);
```

```
    }

    @Override
    protected void onResume() {
        mgr.registerListener(this, accelerometer,
                    SensorManager.SENSOR_DELAY_UI);
        super.onResume();
    }

    @Override
    protected void onPause() {
        mgr.unregisterListener(this, accelerometer);
        super.onPause();
    }

    public void onAccuracyChanged(Sensor sensor, int accuracy) {
        // ignore
    }

    public void onSensorChanged(SensorEvent event) {
        // Use a low-pass filter to get gravity.
        // Motion is what's left over
        for(int i=0; i<3; i++) {
            gravity [i] = (float) (0.1 * event.values[i] +
                                   0.9 * gravity[i]);
            motion[i] = event.values[i] - gravity[i];
        }

        // ratio is gravity on the Y axis compared to full gravity
        // should be no more than 1, no less than -1
        ratio = gravity[1]/SensorManager.GRAVITY_EARTH;
        if(ratio > 1.0) ratio = 1.0;
        if(ratio < -1.0) ratio = -1.0;

        // convert radians to degrees, make negative if facing up
        mAngle = Math.toDegrees(Math.acos(ratio));
        if(gravity[2] < 0) {
            mAngle = -mAngle;
        }

        // Display every 10th value
        if(counter++ % 10 == 0) {
            String msg = String.format(
                "Raw values\nX: %8.4f\nY: %8.4f\nZ: %8.4f\n" +
                "Gravity\nX: %8.4f\nY: %8.4f\nZ: %8.4f\n" +
                "Motion\nX: %8.4f\nY: %8.4f\nZ: %8.4f\nAngle: %8.1f",
                event.values[0], event.values[1], event.values[2],
                gravity[0], gravity[1], gravity[2],
                motion[0], motion[1], motion[2],
                mAngle);
            text.setText(msg);
            text.invalidate();
            counter=1;
        }
    }
}
```

The result of running this application is a display that looks like Figure 26–4. This screenshot was taken as the device lay flat on a table.

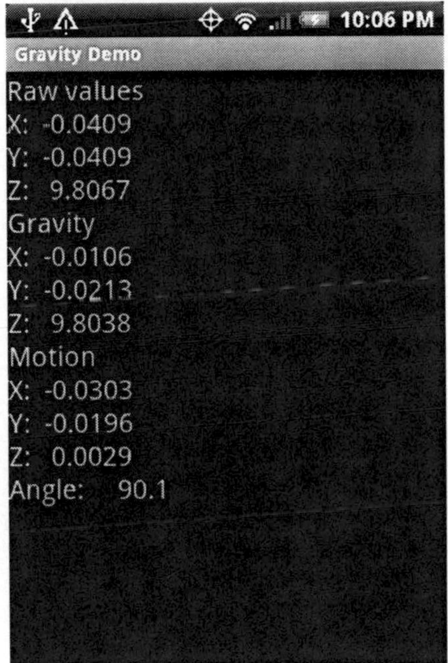

Figure 26–4. *Gravity, motion, and angle values*

Most of this sample application is the same as our Accel Sensor application from before. The differences are in the `onSensorChanged()` method. Instead of simply displaying the values from the event array, we attempt to keep track of gravity and motion. We get gravity by using only a small portion of the new value from the event array, and we use a large portion of the previous value of the gravity array. The two portions used must add up to 1.0. We used 0.9 and 0.1. You could try other values, too, such as 0.8 and 0.2. Our gravity array cannot possibly change as fast as the actual sensor values are changing. But this is closer to reality. And this is what a low-pass filter does. The event array values would only be changing if forces were causing the device to move, and we don't want to measure those forces as part of gravity. We only want to record into our gravity array the force of gravity itself. The math here does not mean we're magically recording only gravity, but the values we're calculating are going to be a lot closer than the raw values from the event array.

Notice also the motion array in the code. By tracking the difference between the raw event array values and the calculated gravity values, we are basically measuring the active, non-gravity, forces on the device in the motion array. If the values in the motion array are zero or very close to zero, it means the device is probably not moving. This is useful information. Technically, a device moving in a constant speed would also have values in the motion array close to zero, but the reality is that if a user is moving the device, the motion values will be somewhat larger than zero.

Using Accelerometers to Measure the Device's Angle

We wanted to show you one more thing about the accelerometers before we move on. If we go back to our trigonometry lessons, we remember that the cosine of an angle is the ratio of the near side and the hypotenuse. If we consider the angle between the Y axis and gravity itself, we could measure the force of gravity on the Y axis, and take the arccosine to determine the angle. We've done that in this code as well. Although here we have to deal yet again with some of the messiness of sensors in Android. There are constants in `SensorManager` for different gravity constants, including Earth's. But our actual measured values could possibly exceed the defined constants. We will explain what we mean by this next.

In theory, our device at rest would measure a value for gravity equal to the constant value, but this is rarely the case. At rest, the accelerometer sensor is very likely to give us a value for gravity that is larger or smaller than the constant. Therefore, our ratio could end up greater than one, or less than negative one. This would make the acos() method complain so we fix the ratio value to be no more than 1 and no less than -1. The corresponding angles in degrees range from 0 to 180. That's fine except that we don't get negative angles from 0 to -180 this way. To get the negative angles, we use another value from our gravity array, which is the *z* value. If the *Z* value of gravity is negative, it means the device's face is oriented downward. For all those values where the device face is pointed down, we make our angle negative as well, with the result being that our angle goes from -180 to +180, just as we would expect.

Go ahead and experiment with this sample application. Notice that the value of the angle is 90 when the device is laid flat, and it's zero (or close to it) when the device is held straight up and down in front of us. If we keep rotating down past flat we will see the value of the angle exceed 90. If we tilt the device up more from the 0 position, the value of angle goes negative until we're holding the device above our heads and the value of the angle is -90. Finally, you may have noticed our counter that controls how often the display is updated. Because the sensor events can come rather frequently, we decided to only display every tenth time we get values.

Magnetic Field Sensors

The magnetic field sensor measures the ambient magnetic field in the *x*, *y*, and z axes. This coordinate system is aligned just like the accelerometers, so *x*, *y*, and z are as shown in Figure 26–2. The units of the magnetic field sensor are micro-Teslas (uT). This sensor can detect the earth's magnetic field and therefore tell us where north is. This sensor is also referred to as the compass, and in fact the `<uses-feature>` tag uses `android.hardware.sensor.compass` as the name of this sensor. Because this sensor is so tiny and sensitive, it can be affected by magnetic fields generated by things near the device, and even to some extent to components within the device. Therefore the accuracy of the magnetic field sensor may at times be suspect.

We've included a simple `CompassSensor` application in the download section of the web site, so feel free to import that and play with it. If you bring metal objects close to the device while this application is running, you might notice the values changing in response. Certainly if you bring a magnet close to the device you will see the values change but we don't recommend that you mix Android devices and magnets.

You might be asking, can I use the compass sensor as a compass to detect where north is? And the answer is: not by itself. While the compass sensor can detect magnetic fields around the device, if the device is not being held perfectly flat in relation to the earth's surface, you'd have no way of correctly interpreting the compass sensor values. But we have accelerometers that can tell us the orientation of the device relative to the earth's surface! Therefore, we can create a compass from the compass sensor, but we need help from the accelerometers too. So let's see how to do that.

Using Accelerometers and Magnetic Field Sensors Together

The `SensorManager` provides some methods that allow us to combine the compass sensor and the accelerometers to figure out orientation. As we just discussed, you can't use just the compass sensor alone to do the job. So `SensorManager` provides a method called `getRotationMatrix()`, which takes the values from the accelerometers and from the compass and returns a matrix that can be used to determine orientation.

Another `SensorManager` method, `getOrientation()`, takes the rotation matrix from the previous step and gives an orientation matrix. The values from the orientation matrix tell us our device's rotation relative to the earth's magnetic north, as well as the device's pitch and roll relative to the ground. This would be terrific if it did the job for us. Unfortunately, at least until Android 2.2, using this mechanism has some big challenges, not the least of which is the discontinuity when the device is in front of us and it goes from facing us, to where we've tilted it up a bit as if we're looking up at the screen. This discontinuity is basically saying that as soon as we tip up past the 0 degree mark (where it seems we're still facing forward), our orientation is now pointing behind us. This is not intuitive at all. Fortunately, Android 2.3 came along and provided additional methods to clear this all up for us (see Rotation Vector Sensors). But in the meantime, as long as you deploy applications to pre-Android 2.3 devices, you'll need to worry about what values to use with your sensors.

Orientation Sensors

We've avoided the orientation sensors until now, but it's time we introduced them. We've just explained how the magnetic field and the accelerometer sensors can be combined and made to work together to produce orientation values to tell you in which direction the phone is facing. There is another sensor that does the same thing: the orientation sensor. The orientation sensor is actually a combination of the magnetic field and accelerometer sensors at the driver level of Android. In other words, there is no extra hardware for the orientation sensor, but within the Android OS, there is code to expose these two sensors as if they were another sensor for orientation.

> **NOTE:** We avoided talking about orientation sensors until now because they were deprecated as of Android 2.2 and you're not supposed to use them anymore. However, this sensor is very useful and much easier to use than the preferred method, as you'll soon see.

We just discussed how using the preferred method of calculating orientation is challenging. In our next sample application, we'll expose the orientation values from the preferred method as well as the orientation sensor so you can see for yourself the differences between them.

We're going to have a little fun with this application. While we can easily show the values returned from the sensors, we're also going to do something interesting with them. Imagine you're standing in a street in Jacksonville, FL. Our application is going to show you pictures from Streetview as if you were there, using the orientation of your phone to select which way you're facing. As you change the orientation of your phone, the view in Streetview will change accordingly. Listing 26–7 shows the XML layout and the Java code for our sample application which we call VirtualJax.

Listing 26–7. *Getting orientation from sensors*

```
<?xml version="1.0" encoding="utf-8"?>
<!-- This file is res/layout/main.xml -->
<RelativeLayout
    xmlns:android="http://schemas.android.com/apk/res/android"
    android:layout_width="fill_parent"
    android:layout_height="fill_parent" >
  <Button  android:id="@+id/update"  android:text="Update Values"
    android:layout_width="wrap_content"
    android:layout_height="wrap_content"
    android:onClick="doUpdate" />
  <Button  android:id="@+id/show"  android:text="Show Me!"
    android:layout_width="wrap_content"
    android:layout_height="wrap_content"
    android:onClick="doShow" android:layout_toRightOf="@id/update" />
  <TextView  android:id="@+id/preferred" android:textSize="20sp"
    android:layout_width="wrap_content"
    android:layout_height="wrap_content"
    android:layout_below="@id/update" />
  <TextView  android:id="@+id/orientation" android:textSize="20sp"
    android:layout_width="wrap_content"
    android:layout_height="wrap_content"
    android:layout_below="@id/preferred" />
</RelativeLayout>


// This file is MainActivity.java
import android.app.Activity;
import android.content.Intent;
import android.hardware.Sensor;
import android.hardware.SensorEvent;
import android.hardware.SensorEventListener;
import android.hardware.SensorManager;
import android.net.Uri;
import android.os.Build;
```

```
import android.os.Bundle;
import android.view.View;
import android.view.WindowManager;
import android.widget.TextView;

public class MainActivity extends Activity implements SensorEventListener {
    private static final String TAG = "VirtualJax";
    private SensorManager mgr;
    private Sensor accel;
    private Sensor compass;
    private Sensor orient;
    private TextView preferred;
    private TextView orientation;
    private boolean ready = false;
    private float[] accelValues = new float[3];
    private float[] compassValues = new float[3];
    private float[] inR = new float[9];
    private float[] inclineMatrix = new float[9];
    private float[] orientationValues = new float[3];
    private float[] prefValues = new float[3];
    private float mAzimuth;
    private double mInclination;
    private int counter;
    private int mRotation;

    @Override
    public void onCreate(Bundle savedInstanceState) {
        super.onCreate(savedInstanceState);
        setContentView(R.layout.main);

        preferred = (TextView)findViewById(R.id.preferred);
        orientation = (TextView)findViewById(R.id.orientation);

        mgr = (SensorManager) this.getSystemService(SENSOR_SERVICE);

        accel = mgr.getDefaultSensor(Sensor.TYPE_ACCELEROMETER);
        compass = mgr.getDefaultSensor(Sensor.TYPE_MAGNETIC_FIELD);
        orient = mgr.getDefaultSensor(Sensor.TYPE_ORIENTATION);

        WindowManager window = (WindowManager)
                this.getSystemService(WINDOW_SERVICE);
        int apiLevel = Integer.parseInt(Build.VERSION.SDK);
        if(apiLevel < 8) {
            mRotation = window.getDefaultDisplay().getOrientation();
        }
        else {
            mRotation = window.getDefaultDisplay().getRotation();
        }
    }

    @Override
    protected void onResume() {
        mgr.registerListener(this, accel,
                SensorManager.SENSOR_DELAY_GAME);
        mgr.registerListener(this, compass,
                SensorManager.SENSOR_DELAY_GAME);
        mgr.registerListener(this, orient,
```

```
                SensorManager.SENSOR_DELAY_GAME);
        super.onResume();
    }

    @Override
    protected void onPause() {
        mgr.unregisterListener(this, accel);
        mgr.unregisterListener(this, compass);
        mgr.unregisterListener(this, orient);
        super.onPause();
    }

    public void onAccuracyChanged(Sensor sensor, int accuracy) {
        // ignore
    }

    public void onSensorChanged(SensorEvent event) {
        // Need to get both accelerometer and compass
        // before we can determine our orientationValues
        switch(event.sensor.getType()) {
        case Sensor.TYPE_ACCELEROMETER:
            for(int i=0; i<3; i++) {
                accelValues[i] = event.values[i];
            }
            if(compassValues[0] != 0)
                ready = true;
            break;
        case Sensor.TYPE_MAGNETIC_FIELD:
            for(int i=0; i<3; i++) {
                compassValues[i] = event.values[i];
            }
            if(accelValues[2] != 0)
                ready = true;
            break;
        case Sensor.TYPE_ORIENTATION:
            for(int i=0; i<3; i++) {
                orientationValues[i] = event.values[i];
            }
            break;
        }

        if(!ready)
            return;

        if(SensorManager.getRotationMatrix(
                inR, inclineMatrix, accelValues, compassValues)) {
            // got a good rotation matrix

            SensorManager.getOrientation(inR, prefValues);

            mInclination = SensorManager.getInclination(inclineMatrix);

            // Display every 10th value
            if(counter++ % 10 == 0) {
                doUpdate(null);
                counter = 1;
            }
```

```
        }
    }

    public void doUpdate(View view) {
        if(!ready)
            return;

        mAzimuth = (float) Math.toDegrees(prefValues[0]);
        if(mAzimuth < 0) {
            mAzimuth += 360.0f;
        }

        String msg = String.format(
                "Preferred:\nazimuth (Z): %7.3f \npitch (X): %7.3f\nroll (Y): %7.3f",
                mAzimuth, Math.toDegrees(prefValues[1]),
                Math.toDegrees(prefValues[2]));
        preferred.setText(msg);

        msg = String.format(
           "Orientation Sensor:\nazimuth (Z): %7.3f\npitch (X): %7.3f\nroll (Y): %7.3f",
           orientationValues[0],
           orientationValues[1],
           orientationValues[2]);
        orientation.setText(msg);

        preferred.invalidate();
        orientation.invalidate();
    }

    public void doShow(View view) {
        // google.streetview:cbll=30.32454,-81.6584&cbp=1,yaw,,pitch,1.0
        // yaw = degrees clockwise from North
        // For yaw we can use either mAzimuth or orientationValues[0].
        //
        // pitch = degrees up or down. -90 is looking straight up,
        // +90 is looking straight down
        // except that pitch doesn't work properly
        Intent intent=new Intent(Intent.ACTION_VIEW, Uri.parse(
            "google.streetview:cbll=30.32454,-81.6584&cbp=1," +
            Math.round(orientationValues[0]) + ",,0,1.0"
            ));
        startActivity(intent);
        return;
    }
}
```

The user interface is two buttons and a pair of sensor value listings, one for the preferred method and one for the orientation sensor output. When you run this, you should see something like Figure 26–5.

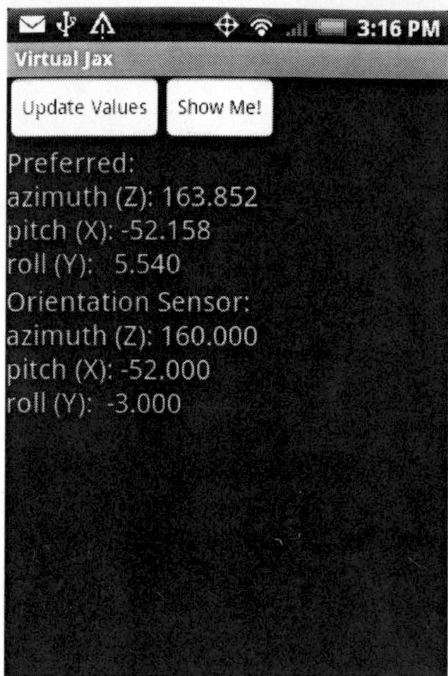

Figure 26–5. *Orientation done two ways*

Before we look at the results, let's explain what this application is doing. In the `onCreate()` method, we're doing the same sorts of things we did before: we're getting references to our text views, a `SensorManager` and the three sensors we want to use here: accelerometers, compass, and the orientation sensor. We're also defining a variable to hold a rotation value. We'll get to that in a minute.

In `onResume()` we activate the sensors and in `onPause()` we disable them.

When we get a sensor value update, we switch on which type it is and record the values into local members: `accelValues`, `compassValues`, or `orientationValues`. Note that we could have cloned the event array to keep local copies of the values; however, that would mean instantiating objects constantly, which we don't really want to do. The cost of creating new objects, and garbage cleaning up after them, could really hurt performance so we simply update our existing arrays.

Notice how we make sure we have values for both the `accelValues` and `compassValues`, using the boolean ready, before we proceed into the next section of code. Now we see the `getRotationMatrix()` method call, followed by the `getOrientation()` method call. We also included the `getInclination()` method call. We're not going to use that here, but know that it represents the angle of the magnetic waves relative to the earth's surface. The closer you are to the earth's poles, the larger an angle this returns. Next we check a counter, like before, to only update the display every tenth update. Again, this is to prevent too much UI activity which might cause our application to behave very poorly.

Within our `doUpdate()` method, which can also be called via the button in the UI, we're doing a few calculations and displaying the results. Using the preferred method, the first value, the azimuth, has a value in radians from negative pi to positive pi, representing −180 degrees to +180 degrees. The orientation sensor provides a value from 0 (north) to 360 degrees. To make these values comparable, we took the first value from the prefValues array, converted from radians to degrees, and added 360 if the value was negative. Now we're comparable to the orientation sensor. The rest of this method simply displays the sensor values in the UI.

Our last method in this sample application is `doShow()`. This is the fun one. In Chapter 25, we showed you how to invoke the Streetview application using an intent. In that chapter, we skipped over the part about setting the yaw value to indicate which way we want to be facing when displaying the image. Now we can show you how to pass in the yaw value as well as the pitch value.

For the latitude and longitude, we've preselected a location in Jacksonville, FL. You're free of course to substitute your own value. For yaw, we need to pass the number of degrees from north (0 - 360) so we use the value from either mAzimuth or orientationValues[0], converted to an integer. For pitch, in theory we could use the second value from either array, after adding 90 to it. However, the Streetview application doesn't seem to like pitch values other than 0, at least in this location. So we chose to set it to 0 for now. If you click on the **Show Me!** button, you will get Streetview and the image will be as if you were facing in the same direction as you are now, but in that location. If you click on the Back button, rotate yourself, and click **Show Me!** again, you'll see the image from your new perspective. Now let's look more closely at the actual values from the sensors.

The values between the preferred method and the orientation sensor seem to be the same or very close to it. The values from the orientation sensor appear to be more stable. They also appear to be integer values. Looks pretty good right? But not so fast. When you start moving the device around, you'll find that if you tilt it such that you're looking up at it, the values get quite different. Now rotate the device so it's in landscape mode. You might see something that looks like Figure 26–6.

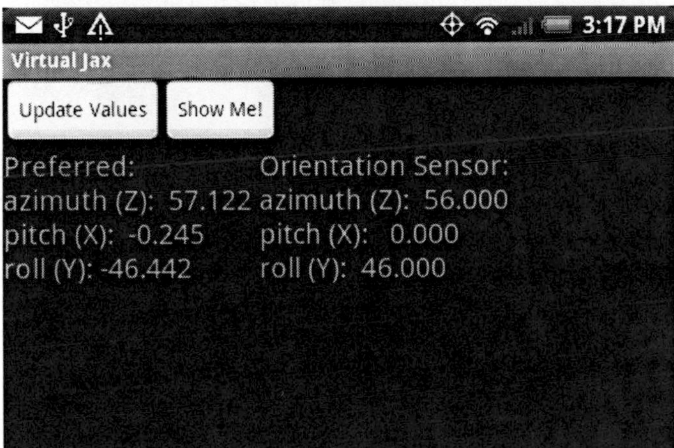

Figure 26–6. *Orientation done two ways in landscape mode*

What happened? Our roll value is opposite between the preferred method and the orientation sensor. What's going on is that the frames of reference are different between the two.

We haven't discussed yet what happens if we're not in portrait mode but rather in landscape mode. If the device is right in front of us in landscape mode, the accelerometers are still fixed in position, so instead of *y* going up, it's really *x*. We could do some math gymnastics to make everything work out for us, but fortunately, the `SensorManager` class has yet another method to help us out. This time the method is called `remapCoordinateSystem()`. It would be called in between getting the rotation matrix and calling `getOrientation()`. The basic function of `remapCoordinateSystem()` is to modify the rotation matrix by swapping axes around. The method signature looks like this:

```
public static boolean remapCoordinateSystem (float[] inR, int X, int Y, float[] outR)
```

We pass in our rotation matrix, plus values to indicate how to swap our *x* and *y* axes, and we get back a new rotation matrix (`outR`) plus a boolean return value that indicates if the remapping was successful. The values for *x* and *y* are constants from `SensorManager`, such as `AXIS_Z` or `AXIS_MINUS_Y`.

We've included a new sample application called `VirtualJaxWithRemap` with the downloads on the web site so you can see what this looks like.

Magnetic Declination and GeomagneticField

There's another topic we want to cover with regard to orientation and devices. The compass sensor will tell you where magnetic north is, but it won't tell you where true north is (a.k.a., geographic north). Imagine you are standing at the midpoint between the magnetic north pole and the geographic north pole. They'd be 180 degrees apart. The further away you get from the two north poles, the smaller this angle difference becomes. The angle difference between magnetic north and true north is called magnetic declination. And the value can only be computed relative to a point on the planet's surface. That is, you have to know where you're standing to know where geographic north is in relation to magnetic north. Fortunately, Android has a way to help us out, and it's the `GeomagneticField` class.

In order to instantiate an object of the `GeomagneticField` class, you need to pass in a latitude and longitude. Therefore, in order to get a magnetic declination angle, we need to know where the point of reference is. You also need to know the time at which you want the value. Magnetic north drifts over time. Once instantiated, you simply call this method to get the declination angle (in degrees):

```
float declinationAngle = geoMagField.getDeclination();
```

The value of `declinationAngle` will be positive if magnetic north is to the east of geographic north.

Gravity Sensors

Android 2.3 introduced the gravity sensor. This isn't really a separate piece of hardware. It's a virtual sensor based on the accelerometers. In fact, this sensor uses logic similar to what we described earlier for accelerometers to produce the gravity component of the forces acting on a device. We cannot access this logic however, so whatever factors and logic is used inside of the gravity sensor class are what we must accept. It's possible, though, that the virtual sensor will take advantage of other hardware such as a gyroscope to help it calculate gravity more accurately. The values array for this sensor reports gravity just like the accelerometer sensor reports its values.

Linear Acceleration Sensors

Similar to the gravity sensor, the linear acceleration sensor is a virtual sensor that represents the accelerometer forces minus gravity. Again, we did our own calculations earlier on the accelerometer sensor values to strip out gravity to get just these linear acceleration force values. This sensor makes that more convenient for us. And it could take advantage of other hardware, such as a gyroscope, to help it calculate linear acceleration more accurately. The values array reports linear acceleration just like the accelerometer sensor reports its values.

Rotation Vector Sensors

The rotation vector sensor is like the deprecated orientation sensor in that it represents the orientation of the device in space, with angles relative to the frame of reference of the hardware accelerometer (see Figure 26–2). As of this writing, information about this sensor is not readily available. Please check our website (`www.androidbook.com`) for updates on this particular sensor.

Near Field Communication Sensors

With the introduction of Android 2.3, we now have the ability to work with special tags using Near Field Communications (NFC). NFC tags are similar to Radio Frequency ID tags (RFID) except that the range for NFC is less than four inches. This means the sensor in the Android device must come very close to the tag to be scanned. NFC tags can be programmed to give out text information, URIs and metadata, such as the language of the information.

Note that NFC is not a new technology, and has been used in other parts of the world for years. In fact, in several countries, point of sale terminals that read NFC tags are quite common. When these terminals detect an NFC tag, the shopper can complete the financial transaction using an account linked to their NFC tag ID. There are many demonstration videos on the Internet that show how a user can tap an object carrying an NFC tag next to one of these terminals to begin the payment process. Google talks about a promise of one day being able to use the phone in place of your wallet. This is a promising concept indeed. Android supports being able to let the device act like a tag to another reader, or to be a reader to detect and scan NFC tags.

There are actually three modes of NFC operation. The first mode of NFC is the reading and writing of contactless tags. The second mode is card emulation mode. This allows an Android device to act like a tag itself. The obvious benefit of this is that your device could act like one tag, then act like a different tag at the touch of a button. This is how an Android device could replace your wallet. Whatever credit card you own, or bus pass, or ticket, your Android device could impersonate (securely of course) that item, so the reader on the other side of the transaction thinks it is working with your credit card when in fact it's dealing with your Android device. The third mode of NFC is peer-to-peer communication. In this last mode, each side recognizes that it is talking to another device and not just a tag.

With the release of Android 2.3.3, you can read tags with an Android device, similar to what a point of sale terminal would do in the example above, and you can also write to writable NFC tags. If the user's device has been setup properly, it can transmit data via NFC to another NFC device, using a peer-to-peer protocol defined by Google. What is not yet available, as of this writing, is the ability to emulate a card, or more precisely, an NFC tag. This is actually very difficult to do, in part due to the very different ways that NFC can be done in hardware. There is no published date when NFC card emulation might be supported in the SDK, but we expect that it will be someday. In the meantime, it is possible to do some amount of card emulation at the driver level, using the Android Native Development Kit (NDK). But we won't be covering that here.

Beyond using NFC to conduct financial transactions, NFC tags could be used in many other scenarios. For example, a museum could place an NFC tag next to items in its collection, allowing visitors to wave their phone close to the tag in order to access a web page that could provide multi-media information about that item. Bus stops could display an NFC tag allowing people to find out when the next bus is coming and where it is going. Businesses could display an NFC tag allowing easy check-in for location-aware services as a person walks in. Perhaps hotel room keys will be irrelevant when you can use your phone to unlock an NFC-equipped door. Even products on store shelves could come with NFC tags to allow shoppers to get more information on that product, such as nutritional information, or perhaps technical specifications and promotional videos.

Enabling The NFC Sensor

The support in Android for NFC is not like the other sensor types. Instead of working with the SensorManager, you work with the NfcAdapter. There is typically only one adapter on a device, and its job is to manage the reading and writing of tags, and the distribution of tags to activities on the device. The adapter can be either on or off, and there are controls under Settings to enable or disable the NFC adapter. The NFC adapter setting is with the Wireless settings. If the adapter is on, and an NFC tag is detected, a somewhat complicated process is followed to determine which activity, if any, should receive an intent informing the activity about the detected NFC tag. Everything hinges around what sort of data is in the NFC tag, and what intent filters exist for the installed applications on the device. And there is one other bit of information that is considered, and that is whether or not the activity currently in the foreground on the device has expressed a specific desire to receive NFC tags. We'll explore this more fully very soon.

To access the adapter, you first acquire an NfcManager instance using getSystemService(). Then you call the `getDefaultAdapter()` method on that, like so:

```
NfcManager manager = (NfcManager)
    context.getSystemService(Context.NFC_SERVICE);
NfcAdapter adapter = manager.getDefaultAdapter();
```

This returns the singleton object that is the NfcAdapter. To determine if the NfcAdapter is currently enabled, use the `isEnabled()` method, which returns a boolean answer telling you whether the NFC adapter is enabled in Settings. There is no documented way to programmatically turn on (or off) the NFC adapter. If the NFC adapter is off and you want it turned on, you'll need to notify the user to ask them to enable the NFC adapter under Settings. To launch the appropriate Settings screen for the user from your application, you could use code like the following:

```
startActivityForResult(new Intent(
     android.provider.Settings.ACTION_WIRELESS_SETTINGS), 0);
```

When this runs, the appropriate Settings screen will be displayed and the user can choose to enable NFC, or not. Your activity's `onActivityResult()` callback will be called when the user is finished with the wireless settings screen. Keep in mind that the user may choose *not* to enable NFC even though you asked them to. Your application should take appropriate action if the NFC adapter stays disabled.

Routing NFC Tags

This seems like a good time to discuss the different types of NFC tags and technologies. NFC is not one single standard. In fact there are several types of NFC tags that a user could come across. There is variation among the tag types, which means that Android must support them with different classes related to each tag type. If you look inside the android.nfc.tech package, you will find several different tag technology classes, from MifareClassic to NfcV to ISO-DEP. The internal structures of each tag type can be different, and there are different methods for accessing and manipulating data in these tag types. Fortunately, Android provides a Tag class to help manage NFC communications, and each specific type of tag can be created from a Tag object. Once you have an instance of a specific NFC tag, you can perform operations on it that are specific to that tag type. This also means that to choose which activity to send a tag to, several factors must be considered. We'll first describe how an NFC tag intent is created, then you can understand how to create an appropriate intent filter.

When an intent is being sent with tag data, a Tag object is always parceled into the intent's extras bundle, with a key of EXTRA_TAG. If the tag contains NDEF data, another extras value is set with a key of EXTRA_NDEF_MESSAGES. Lastly, the intent could have an extras value of the tag's Id with a key of EXTRA_ID. These last two extras values are optional and depend on the existence of the data on the tag. All NFC intents are sent using `startActivity()`. Note that you never need to actually access the NFC adapter to receive NFC messages. The intent messages will come into your application just like other intents that are sent from other sources, as long as they match your intent filter(s).

> **NOTE:** It is important to note that there is an NFC ecosystem in an Android device that supports NFC. The logic to create these NFC intents uses capabilities that are not exposed in the Android SDK. That means you cannot easily create a fake sender activity yourself. What we're about to explain is what happens in the NFC ecosystem, and it is not something you can write your own code for. This also means that if you really want to test an NFC application, you will need to use a real device, with real NFC tags. Unless Google someday provides some support in the emulator or in DDMS or both.

The action value of the tag intent depends on what information was discovered about the detected tag. There are three possible action values for the intent:

1. ACTION_NDEF_DISCOVERED is the action if an NDEF payload is found in the tag. If this is the case, Android then looks for the existence of a NdefRecord in the first NdefMessage. If that NdefRecord is a URI or SmartPoster record, the intent will get the URI in its data field. If a MIME record is found, the intent's type field will be set to the MIME type of the tag. Android then looks for a suitable activity to start using this intent and the intent matching algorithm. If no activity can be found, this intent is abandoned and Android tries to create the next type of NFC intent.

2. ACTION_TECH_DISCOVERED is the action if NDEF is not detected, or no NDEF activity could be found, but a tag technology exists. In this scenario, Android adds meta-data to the intent indicating which tag technologies were detected. An NFC tag can implement more than one technology, especially since Ndef is more like a virtual technology. Android looks for an activity that will match this intent and if found, sends it on. If not, Android throws this intent away and tries the third type of NFC intent.

3. ACTION_TAG_DISCOVERED is the final action choice for an NFC tag. This is the action when all others failed to match an activity. This intent also does not carry data or a MIME type. If this intent does not match an activity on the device, then the NFC ecosystem gives up, and the tag information is thrown away.

Receiving NFC Tags

Whether you decide to create your intent filters in code or in the AndroidManifest.xml file, you will need to know what you are looking for and prepare your intent filters carefully. For example, if you specify too rigidly, you won't get notified of tags. If you specify too loosely, you'll get called for tags that you don't want to handle. And if your app is sent an NFC tag that you don't want to handle, that means another app might possibly exist on the device that could handle it, but didn't get it. This could happen if the intent matching logic found more than one app and asked the user which one to run, and the user chose yours. That's yet another reason you want to be careful when defining your intent filters for NFC tags; if the user is prompted for which app to run, they very likely need to move the device away from the NFC tag to make the choice, and now the tag is out of range. If you have choice in what data the tags are going to have on them, you could make that data very specific to your needs, using a custom URI scheme or a custom MIME type for example.

Your choice of intent filter depends on which action was put into the NFC tag intent (see above). Listing 26–8 shows a sample intent filter for an NDEF tag that would go into your AndroidManifest.xml file.

Listing 26–8. *Intent filter for an NDEF tag with a MIME type*

```
<intent-filter>
  <action android:name="android.nfc.action.NDEF_DISCOVERED"/>
  <data android:mimeType="type/subtype" />
</intent-filter>
```

Instead of "type/subtype" you would of course put the specific MIME type that you are looking for, or use wildcards if you will accept any type or subtype. For example you could set mimeType to "text/*" to match all text types. But you don't need to specify a MIME type for an NDEF tag. If the tag has a URI instead of a MIME type, you would want to use an intent filter like in Listing 26–9.

Listing 26–9. *Intent filter for an NDEF tag with a URI*

```
<intent-filter>
  <action android:name="android.nfc.action.NDEF_DISCOVERED"/>
  <data android:scheme="geo" />
</intent-filter>
```

In this example we use the geo scheme so our activity would be launched if a tag with a geo: URI was detected. You could use any of the other attributes of the <data> tag to specify what NFC data your activity is looking for.

If your activity is looking for NFC tags that have a particular technology, you would use an intent filter as in Listing 26–10. It is also possible that a tag with NDEF was detected, but no activity could be found to process the NDEF_DISCOVERED intent. That could also result in your activity receiving the intent, as long as it matches your intent filter. In other words, if an NDEF_DISCOVERED tag intent could not be delivered to an activity looking for NDEF tags, an activity looking for a particular technology could end up receiving a technology intent for that tag.

Listing 26–10. *Intent filter for an NFC tag with technology*

```
<intent-filter>
  <action android:name="android.nfc.action.TECH_DISCOVERED"/>
</intent-filter>
<meta-data android:name="android.nfc.action.TECH_DISCOVERED"
                android:resource="@xml/nfc_tech_filter" />
```

Notice that we have a different action now to match technology, and instead of a <data> tag, we have a <meta-data> tag, and it's outside of the <intent-filter> tag. The attributes of the <meta-data> tag are different too, and refer to another file that we must create under the /res/xml directory of our application's project. Listing 26–11 shows a sample nfc_tech_filter.xml file.

Listing 26–11. *A sample NFC tech filter XML file*

```
<resources xmlns:xliff="urn:oasis:names:tc:xliff:document:1.2">
    <tech-list>
        <tech>android.nfc.tech.NfcA</tech>
        <tech>android.nfc.tech.MifareUltralight</tech>
    </tech-list>
</resources>

<resources xmlns:xliff="urn:oasis:names:tc:xliff:document:1.2">
    <tech-list>
        <tech>android.nfc.tech.NfcB</tech>
        <tech>android.nfc.tech.Ndef</tech>
    </tech-list>
</resources>
```

What this filter file does is specify two types of tags that our activity wants to see. An NFC tag usually has its list of technologies that it enumerates. If any one of the tech-lists in Listing 26–11 is a subset of our Tag's tech-list, then this is a match and our activity will get that NFC tag intent.

In Listing 26–11, the first type of tag has NfcA and MifareUltralight technologies, and the second type of tag has NfcB and Ndef technologies. We could add additional <resources> to this file to specify additional tags that our activity could want to see. The list of available technologies to put into this file are the tag class names that are available in the android.nfc.tech package, but only put in what you want your activity to receive. The child tags of a <tech-list> specify all of the technologies that a tag must report for its intent to match our activity. All of the technologies in a specific tech-list must exist in the list of technologies enumerated by the tag. Therefore, the tech-list in the intent-filter could have fewer technologies than the tag specifies, but could not have more and still match. For the example above in Listing 26–11, if a tag presented just the Ndef technology it would not match either specification and your activity would not receive the intent. None of the intent-filter tech-lists is a sub-set of the tag's list. If a tag had NfcA, NfcB and Ndef technologies it would match the second specification and your activity would receive the intent. The second tech-list is a sub-set of the tag's tech list. We would match even though the tag enumerates one more technology than is in the intent filter's tech-list.

The final intent filter that you might use is shown in Listing 26–12, and represents the catch-all intent filter. That is, if a tag was received and no NDEF or tech activity could be found to process the intent, or if the tag is an unknown type, an intent will be created with the ACTION_TAG_DISCOVERED action.

Listing 26–12. *Intent filter for an unknown or unprocessed NFC tag*

```
<intent-filter>
  <action android:name="android.nfc.action.TAG_DISCOVERED"/>
</intent-filter>
```

Notice that there is no <data> and no <meta-data> tags for this intent filter, because there will not be any data in an intent that has an action of ACTION_TAG_DISCOVERED. Which would normally mean that we must have a <category> tag. However, this is not the case with NFC tag intents. NFC tag intents are special, so no <category> tags are required in intent-filters for NFC tag intent matching. Getting back to our tag matching flow, when we're getting an ACTION_TAG_DISCOVERED intent, Android has almost given up trying to find an activity for the detected NFC tag. At this point, any activity that will take an ACTION_TAG_DISCOVERED action will receive these tag intents. In most normal operations, you won't ever see an ACTION_TAG_DISCOVERED tag intent, because almost all NFC tags that you'll come across will match on NDEF or on TECH.

There is one other way that your activity could receive an NFC tag intent, and that is by using the foreground dispatch system. If your activity is in the foreground (which means onResume() is firing or has fired and the user can interact with your activity), you can make a pending intent, an array of intent filters, an array of techlists lists, and then you make a call like the following:

```
mAdapter.enableForegroundDispatch(this, pendingIntent,
                        intentFiltersArray, techListsArray);
```

where `mAdapter` is the NFC adapter, and `this` is a reference to your activity. By making this call, you effectively insert your activity in front of all others, and if any of this activity's intent filters match a detected tag, your activity will get to process it. If your activity does not get the NFC tag intent because it doesn't match the setup of this call, the NFC tag intent will be tried with other activities using the logic above. You must call this method from the UI thread, and the best place to call this is from the onResume() method of your activity. You would also need to call:

```
mAdapter.disableForegroundDispatch(this);
```

from the onPause() callback of your activity, so that your activity won't get an intent it can't process. When your activity does get an intent in this way, the onNewIntent() callback will be used to receive it into your activity.

The pending intent is a standard one. The intentFiltersArray would be the collection of IntentFilter objects that you desire, each one specifying an appropriate action and any data or MIME types as needed. For example, Listing 26–13 shows some code to create an intent filter for Ndef and then add it to an array.

Listing 26–13. ***Code for an intent filter for Ndef***

```
IntentFilter ndef = new IntentFilter(NfcAdapter.ACTION_NDEF_DISCOVERED);
try {
    ndef.addDataType("text/*");
}
catch (MalformedMimeTypeException e) {
    throw new RuntimeException("fail", e);
}
intentFiltersArray = new IntentFilter[] {
        ndef,
};
```

Keep in mind that the intent filter array can contain multiple instances of IntentFilter, each set with the same or different action, and with or without data and/or type field values.

The techListsArray is an array of arrays, where each inside array is the list of class names that a tag would enumerate, and you can have multiple lists of class names to match against. Listing 26–14 shows a sample of this, which is equivalent to the tech-list resource file shown in Listing 26–11.

Listing 26–14. *Code for a tech-list array*

```
techListsArray = new String[][] {
    new String[] { NfcA.class.getName(),
                   MifareUltralight.class.getName() },
    new String[] { NfcB.class.getName(),
                   Ndef.class.getName() }
    };
```

When all of this setup has been done, if this activity does receive an NFC tag intent, it will be the onNewIntent() callback that will be triggered to receive it. From there, you would access the extras bundle to read the tag, which we'll cover next. This is a lot of setup to do a dynamic claim for an NFC tag intent, but on the flip side, if you only want this activity to receive tags if it has already been started by the user, this is the way to do it. Note that it probably doesn't make sense to use this method and to also have intent filters in the manifest to receive NFC tag intents, but technically it is possible.

Reading NFC Tags

As alluded to earlier, the reading of NFC tags is somewhat complicated. Or rather, the process by which a tag gets delivered to your application can be complicated. At the most basic level, when an NFC tag is detected, the system will determine an activity to send the tag to, and then send it. Unlike with the sensors covered earlier in this chapter, the activity interested in NFC tags may not be running at the time of tag detection, and certainly won't receive the tag information through a sensor listener. A notified activity will receive an intent, and this may mean launching the activity in order for it to process the NFC tag intent.

One of your first considerations when designing an application that receives and processes NFC tag information is that you are dealing with a physical tag in the environment of the device through a hardware interface. The NFC API has blocking calls, which means they might not return as quickly as you'd like, which means you need to run the tag methods on a separate thread from the main UI thread.

The NFC tag data will be in the extras bundle of the received intent. Upon receiving the intent, you would access the NFC data using something like this:

```
Tag tag = intent.getParcelableExtra(NfcAdapter.EXTRA_TAG);
String[] techlists = tag.getTechLists();
```

If your intent filter was very precise, you already know what type of tag you have. But if there is a selection of tag technologies that could be present, you can now interrogate techlists to find out what technologies are in the tag. Each string is the class name of the tag technology that is enumerated by the detected tag.

If you find out that `android.nfc.tech.Ndef` is supported in this tag, you could do the following to get to the NDEF data more directly:

```
NdefMessage[] ndefMsgs = intent.getParcelableArrayExtra(NfcAdapter.EXTRA_NDEF_MESSAGES);
```

In theory you could get a null value if no NDEF messages were in the intent. Otherwise, you should now be able to parse the NDEF messages sent to you. You could read the NdefMessages from the intent, count them, and for each one, retrieve the NdefRecords contained within.

The NdefRecords are where things get interesting. You would be well-served to refer to the NFC specifications, located here: http://`www.nfc-forum.org/specs/`. To access these specifications, you will need to accept a licensing agreement with the NFC Forum. It is free but you will need to provide your name, address, telephone number and email address. Your other option is to look at the NfcDemo application that Google provides. That sample is included with the Android 2.3.3 SDK package under the samples folder. You can also view the source of that application here: http://developer.android.com/resources/samples/NFCDemo/index.html. This sample application receives NFC intents and displays the contents of the NdefRecords in a ListView. The reason this gets complicated is that there are several types of NdefRecords that you could receive in each NdefMessage. Each type serves a different purpose. For example, the Text type contains text in a specified language. The Uri type contains a Uri. Of the known NDEF record types, the NfcDemo sample application uses just three, the two just described and SmartPoster, which we'll describe shortly.

The format of an NdefRecord includes a 3-bit Type Name Format (TNF) field, a variable length type field, a variable length ID field, and a variable length payload field. Yes there are two type fields. The TNF field is the top-level type of this record, and tells you what the rest of the record is. For example, it could be an absolute URI record (TNF_ABSOLUTE_URI), or an official RTD record (TNF_WELL_KNOWN). The next type field gets more specific about what this record is, based on the value of TNF. If the TNF value is TNF_WELL_KNOWN, this next type field will be one of the RTD_* constants of the NdefRecord class, such as RTD_SMART_POSTER. If the TNF value is TNF_ABSOLUTE_URI, the next type field will follow the absolute-URI BNF construct defined by RFC 3986.

> **NOTE:** The TNF_UNCHANGED record type is used when the message payload spans multiple NdefRecords because of its size. Google has taken care of handling chunked NdefRecords for you, so you should never see a type value of TNF_UNCHANGED. The android.nfc package combines the pieces of the payload into one big, single NdefRecord.

The next field in an NdefRecord is an identifier for this NdefRecord. The NdefRecord you're reading may or may not have an identifier.

Finally, there is the payload. This can be a rather large byte array, but it has some internal structure to it that you must be aware of, depending on which type of NdefRecord this is. For an RTD URI record type, the first byte of the payload byte array represents the beginning of the URI. For example, the byte value of 1 represents "http://www." and this would precede the rest of the URI in the rest of the payload. For a Text record type, the first byte of the payload byte array represents the "status byte encodings" value, which identifies the text encoding value (UTF-8 or UTF-16), as well as the length of the language byte array which immediately follows this status field. After the language field is the text. For SmartPoster, things get more complicated, with the NdefRecord containing an NdefMessage which in turn contains more NdefRecords. The bottom NdefRecords can include Title records (just like a Text record), a URI record (just like before), a recommended action record, a size record, an icon record and a type record. The recommended action value indicates what your application might want to do with the SmartPoster data. Note that these values are not provided as part of Android's NdefRecord class documentation. And they are:

```
-1    UNKNOWN
0     DO_ACTION
1     SAVE_FOR_LATER
2     OPEN_FOR_EDITING
```

What you do with them is up to you, although obviously you probably want to attempt to perform the recommended action for the tag being read. For example, if TNF is TNF_WELL_KNOWN, the type is RTD_SMART_POSTER and the recommended action is 0 (DO_ACTION) combined with a web page URL, you might want to launch the browser with that URL. The size record allows the tag to say how big the thing is at the other end of that URL. If the tag is referring to a downloadable executable, the size record could say how big the download file is. The icon record holds an icon image that can be used by a device to display an image along with the title and the URI.

The type record is yet another type value, different from the TNF and the NdefRecord's type. The type record is for SmartPoster tags, and in this case, the type represents the MIME type of the thing at the other end of the URI. A device could decide it can't support that object type, so avoid downloading it in the first place.

The only mandatory sub-record for a SmartPoster tag is the URI record, and there can be only one per SmartPoster. You can have multiple Title records, as long as each record is for a different language. You can also have multiple icon records as long as each has a different MIME type for its format.

For all types of NFC tags, including the NDEF tags, you can use something like the following to get an instance of that particular tag type:

```
NfcA nfca = NfcA.get(tag);
```

From this new object, we can access the specific methods that are appropriate for that tag type. For Ndef and NdefFormatable tags, the NdefMessage and NdefRecord classes are very helpful to deal with the tag data. The other tag classes have appropriate methods to help deal with those tags and their data. There are methods for reading and for writing data to a tag. Note that writing to a tag is not the same as the device doing card emulation. Writing a tag means that the device is close enough to some other tag to be able to write to it (with proper permissions of course). Card emulation is different.

NFC Card Emulation

Card emulation means that the device will appear to another NFC reader as if the device is an NFC tag. This means our local device has a place in the hardware to store some data, and if an NFC reader gets within range of our device, and asks for the data, our device will send that data to the reader. This feature was not available at the time of this writing, although we expect it will be available eventually. If you really want to do card emulation, check out online resources that describe how to do this at the lowest level of the device, that is, in the Native Development Kit (NDK) level.

NFC Peer-to-Peer (P2P)

The Android SDK provides some limited support for peer-to-peer (P2P) communication over NFC between two devices.

There are some caveats to this feature, namely that P2P only works when your application is running and in the foreground, and also that your application must format with NDEF. Other tag technologies may be supported in P2P in the future, but for now it's just NDEF. This also means that your phone must be turned on and running your application for it to be able to talk NFC with another device.

To implement the P2P feature, you will use the NfcAdapter method called enableForegroundNdefPush(). This takes two parameters, the activity and the NdefMessage to be sent when an NFC device asks for our data. Similar to the foreground dispatch system described above, this method should be called in onResume(), and disabled in onPause(). Your NdefMessage can be whatever you want it to be, but your activity should be in the foreground when the reader attempts to get our data. Google has said that for the other device to be able to pick up our information, it will have to implement the com.android.npp NDEF push protocol, but there is no information on that at the time of this writing. Check our website for updates.

Earlier we covered the use of the `uses-feature` tag and sensors, so you can make sure that a device has the appropriate sensor in order to see your application. The NFC sensor is no exception. You should use the following in your AndroidManifest.xml to ensure that the device for your application has the necessary NFC hardware:

```
<uses-feature android:name="android.hardware.nfc" />
```

You should also ensure that your AndroidManifest.xml file contains an appropriate permission to allow your application to access the NFC hardware:

```
<uses-permission android:name="android.permission.NFC" />
```

Testing NFC with NFCDemo

We've covered much of the NFC API for Android, but the question now is, how do you test your application? For NFC tags, maybe you could find some objects that already have NFC tags in them. In countries that have been using NFC for a while, this might not be too difficult. In the US it's likely much harder. You could buy your own NFC tags; several vendors around the world sell tags as well as developer kits so you could write what you want onto your tags. Unfortunately, DDMS does not yet come with support for sending tag discovery intents to the emulator. The NfcDemo sample application that is available in the Android SDK was first released with Android 2.3, back when there was only ACTION_TAG_DISCOVERED for the intents. Android advanced a lot with the release of 2.3.3, and unfortunately the NfcDemo couldn't keep up. There is some useful information in there about NFC tag layouts, and what the bytes mean for NDEF tags. Hopefully this will get an update soon and will work with real tags and the new NFC ecosystem.

If you do decide to load the NfcDemo sample application, you will need to add an external library to your project. The download file for this library is located here: `http://code.google.com/p/guava-libraries/`. When you open the zip file you will find jar files. Save the guava jar file, the one without gwt, onto your workstation. You need to refer to the guava jar file from your Eclipse project by right-clicking on the project, choosing Build Path, then Configure Build Path and the Libraries tab. Next click on Add External JARs, navigate to the guava jar file, select it and click Open. Now rebuild the NfcDemo project by right-clicking on the project and choosing Build Project.

References

Here are some helpful references to topics you may wish to explore further.

- `www.androidbook.com/projects`. Look here for a list of downloadable projects related to this book. For this chapter look for a zip file called ProAndroid3_Ch26_Sensors.zip. This zip file contains all projects from this chapter, listed in separate root directories. There is also a README.TXT file that describes exactly how to import projects into Eclipse from one of these zip files.
- `http://en.wikipedia.org/wiki/Lux`. This is the Wikipedia entry for lux, the unit of light measurement.
- `http://android-developers.blogspot.com/2010/09/one-screen-turn-deserves-another.html`. This is an Android blog post on dealing with screen rotation and updating the display properly.
- `www.ngdc.noaa.gov/geomag/faqgeom.shtml`. Here you'll find information on geomagnetism from NOAA.
- `www.youtube.com/watch?v=C7JQ7Rpwn2k`. This is a Google TechTalk from David Sachs on accelerometers, gyroscopes, compasses and Android development.

- `http://stackoverflow.com/questions/1586658/combine-gyroscope-and-accelerometer-data`. A nice posting on stackoverflow.com that talks about combining gyroscope and accelerometer sensor data for use in applications.
- `www.nfc-forum.org/specs`. The official site for the NFC specifications.
- `www.slideshare.net/tdelazzari/architecture-and-development-of-nfc-applications`. A very thorough Slideshare presentation by Thomas de Lazzari on NFC.

Summary

In this chapter, we covered the main Sensor framework, as well as Near Field Communications capabilities in Android. We showed how your applications can read sensor values and act on them. This should help you develop some really cool applications that can respond to the real world.

Chapter 27

Exploring the Contacts API

In Chapter 4, which covered content providers, we listed the benefits of exposing data through content provider abstraction and showed that such abstracted data is exposed as a series of URLs that can be used to read, query, update, insert, and delete. These URLs and their corresponding cursors become the API for that content provider.

The Contact API is one such content provider API for working with the contact data. Contacts in Android are maintained in a database and exposed through a content provider whose authority is rooted at

```
content://com.android.contacts
```

The Android SDK documents the various contracts offered by this contact content provider using a set of java interfaces and classes that are rooted at the Java package

```
android.provider.ContactsContract
```

You will see numerous classes whose parent context is `ContactsContract` that are useful in querying, reading, updating, and inserting contacts into and from the content database. The primary documentation for using the contacts API is available on the Android site at

```
http://developer.android.com/resources/articles/contacts.html
```

The primary API entry point `ContactsContract` is appropriately named because this class defines the contract between the clients of the contacts and the provider and protector of the contacts database.

This chapter explores this contract in a fair amount of detail but does not cover every nuance. The contacts API is large and its tentacles far-reaching. However, when you approach the contact API it will take a few weeks of research to realize that it is simple in its underlying structure. This is where we would like to contribute the most and explain these basics in the time it takes to read this chapter.

Understanding Accounts

All contacts in Android work in the context of an account. What is an account? Well, for example, f you have your e-mail through Google, you are said to have an account with Google. If you set up yourself as a user of Facebook, you are said to have an account with Facebook.

Even though you use only the e-mail service with Google, the same login and password could be used to access other Google services, meaning that e-mail account of yours with Google is not limited to just e-mail. However, some be accounts are restricted to just one type of service such as a POP (Post Office Protocol) e-mail account. On your mobile device, you may be able to register to a variety of these account-based services.

You will be able to set up some of these accounts such as Google or Facebook or a corporate Microsoft Exchange account through the "Accounts & sync" Settings option on the device. See the *Android User's Guide* to get more details around accounts. We have included a URL for the *Android User's Guide* in the References section at the end of this chapter.

A Quick Tour of Account Screens

To solidify the nature of accounts, let's show you a few account related screens from the emulator. To start off, Figure 27–1 shows the account Settings options screen.

Figure 27–1. *Invoking "Accounts & sync" application settings*

When you choose the "Accounts & sync" menu item, you will see the "Accounts & sync settings" screen shown in Figure 27–2. This screen displays, along with some account-based options, a list of available accounts.

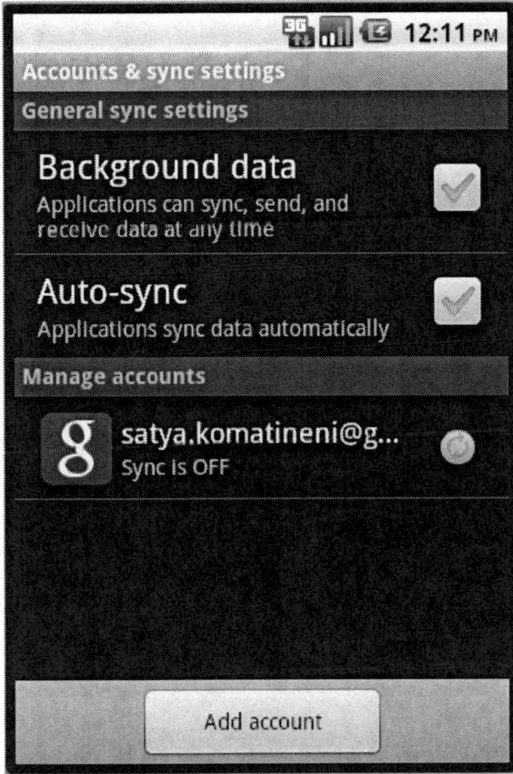

Figure 27–2. *Accounts & sync settings*

In Figure 27–2, we are mainly interested in the list of available accounts. To practice adding a new account, click the "Add account" button, and you will see the screen in Figure 27–3 with a list of possible accounts that can be set up or added.

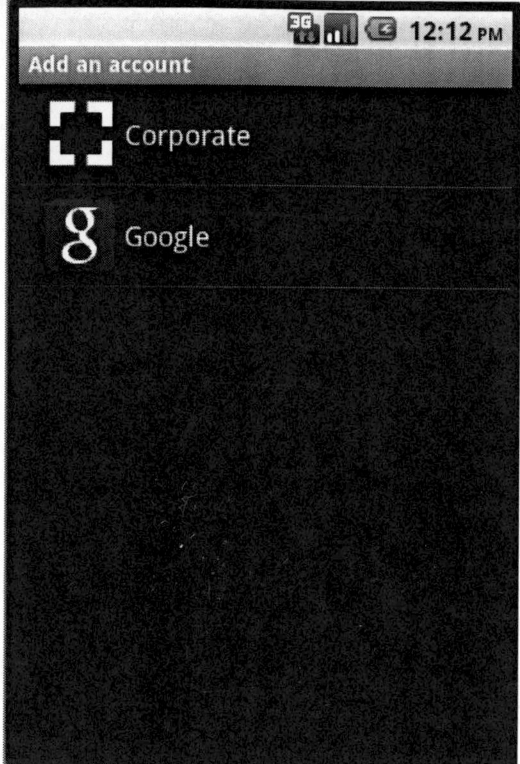

Figure 27–3. *List of accounts that can be set up*

This list of possible accounts to add will vary based on the type of device and what is available. The list in Figure 27–3 shows what is available in the Android 2.3 emulator when it is set up with Google API 9 as the target. If you have only downloaded the core SDK, you will not see the option to choose the Google API as the target for that emulator, so you won't see the option for setting up the Google account in Figure 27–3. This also means that this picture of available accounts could change with each Andriod release, device maker, and carrier or service provider.

Also the fields needing to be set up for each account vary by account provider. For example, if you click to add a Google account in our emulator example, you will be presented with an option to create or sign in to a Google account (see Figure 27–4).

Figure 27–4. *Adding a Google account*

If you click the Create button, the fields to create a Google account appear, as shown in Figure 27–5.

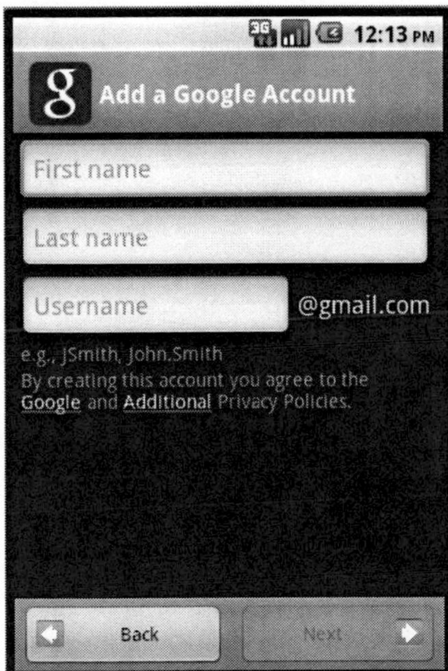

Figure 27–5. *Creating a Google account*

Figure 27–5 illustrates the fields required to set up a Google account if you don't have one already. As stated, these fields could clearly vary from account type to account type. For example, we'll show you the account settings if you already have a Google account. In this case, the account setup merely involves signing into the account, as shown in Figure 27–6.

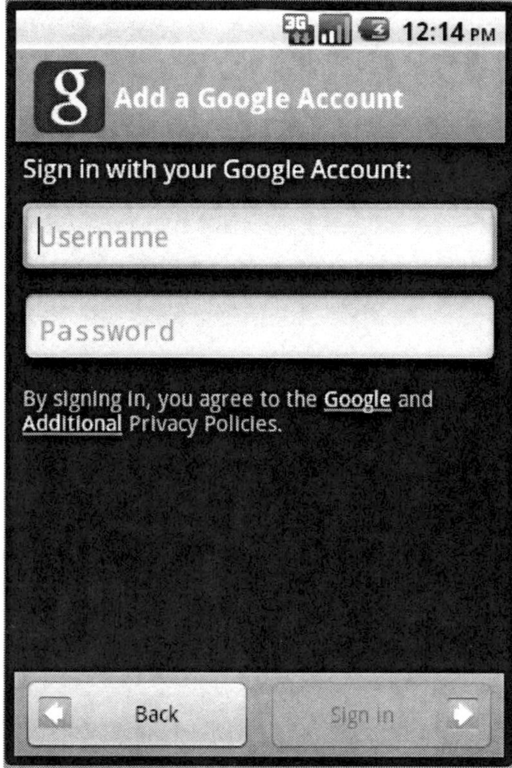

Figure 27–6. *Signing into an existing Google account*

Now that we have demonstrated the basics of an account and how it might end up on a device, the next section goes into how accounts become relevant to contacts.

Relevance of Accounts to Contacts

The contacts you manage are tied to a specific account. In other words, each account you have registered on the device can hold a number of contacts that are specific to that account. An account owns its set of contacts—or an account is said to be the parent of a contact. Also, an account may have zero or more contacts.

An account is identified by two strings: the account name and the account type. In the case of Google, your account name is your e-mail user name at Gmail and your account type is `com.google`. Clearly, the account type must be unique across the device. Your account name is unique with in that account type. Together an account type and an account name form an account, and only once the account is formed can a set of contacts be inserted using it.

Enumerating Accounts

The contact API primarily deals with contacts that exist in various accounts. The mechanism of creating accounts is outside of the contact API, so explaining the ability to write your own account providers and how to sync the contacts with in those accounts is outside the scope of this chapter. For this chapter, how accounts get set up is not very relevant. However, when you want to add a contact or a list of contacts, you do need to know what accounts exist on the device. You can use the code in Listing 27–1 to enumerate the accounts and their necessary properties (the account name and type). The code in Listing 27–1 lists the account name and types given a context variable.

Listing 27–1. *Code to Display a List of Accounts*

```
public void listAccounts(Context ctx)
{
    AccountManager am = AccountManager.get(ctx);
    Account[] accounts = am.getAccounts();
    for(Account ac: accounts)
    {
        String acname=ac.name;
        String actype = ac.type;
        Log.d("accountInfo", acname + ":" + actype);
    }
}
```

Of course, to run the code in Listing 27–1 , the manifest file needs to ask for permission using the line in Listing 27–2.

Listing 27–2. *Permission to Read Accounts*

```
<uses-permission android:name="android.permission.GET_ACCOUNTS"/>
```

The code from Listing 27–1 will print something like the following:

```
Your-email-at-gmail:com.google
```

This assumes that you have only one account (Google) configured. If you have more than one account, all of those accounts will be listed in a similar manner.

Before diving more deeply into the contact details, let's consider how end users create contacts using the contacts application that comes with the Android platform.

Understanding Contacts Application

In case your device maker, like Motorola, or carrier, such as Verizon, does not provide its own contacts application, the Android platform comes with a default contacts application. You can easily find this application in the roster of applications on the device and see it's documentation in the *Android User's Guide*.

Show Contacts

When you choose the contacts application, the first screen you see is a list of contacts (see Figure 27–7). A contact is essentially a person that you know in the context of an account such as your Gmail account. If you have more than one account, the screen in Figure 27–7 will list all contacts from all accounts. By looking at this screen, you will not know what contact came from what account. Unless explicitly prevented, Android tries not to repeat contacts if they appear similar between two different accounts. We will cover this "appear similar" heuristic in the next main section.

Figure 27–7. *Displaying aggregated contacts*

Figure 27–7 assumes you have a couple of contacts available, and the listed contacts are grouped alphabetically.

Show Contact Detail

If you click one of the contacts in Figure 27–7, the contacts application will show the details of that contact, as in Figure 27–8.

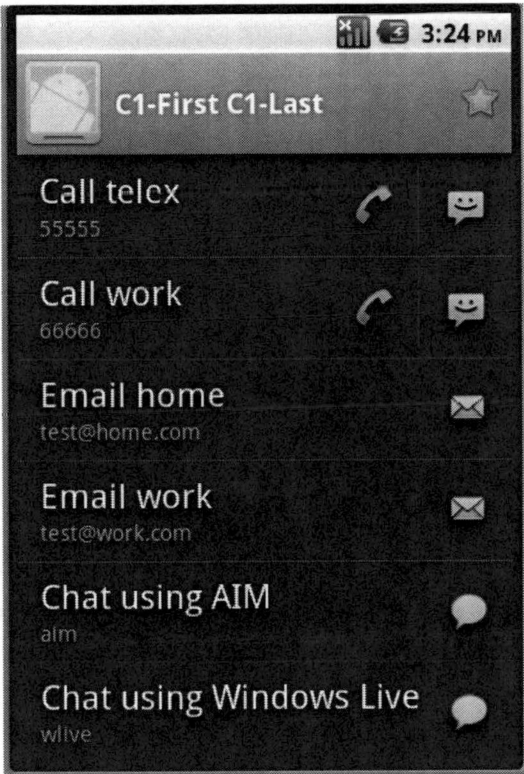

Figure 27–8. *A contact's details*

Figure 27–8 illustrates the various sets of information a contact can carry. The figure also shows the number of actions the contact application can directly provide for each contact based on information in that row. For some rows, the contacts application enabled calling and texting, and for others, e-mail or chat.

Edit Contact Details

Let's now look at how a contact, like the one in Figure 27–8, can be edited (or a new one created). You can do this by clicking the menu and choosing Edit or New contact. This will bring up the screen shown in Figure 27–9.

Figure 27–9. *Editing a contact*

In Figure 27–9, at the top of the "Edit contact" screen, you see the account under which this contact is being edited or created. For this contact, the account is shown as phone only, which implies there is no sever side account (like Google) available on the phone but just a local default one. In fact, in the database of contacts, both the account name and type null values.

Google strongly suggests that you create at least one Google account before proceeding to activate an Android device, be it a phone or a tablet.

However, as you can see, it does allow a contact to be created without a particular associated account, and in such cases, what you see when you create a contact is shown in Figure 27–9.

Following the account indicator (e.g., "Phone-Only...") in Figure 27–9 is the photo for the contact and then a series of fields. Figure 27–10 shows more fields belonging to that contact that appear as you scroll down.

Figure 27–10. *Further contact editing fields*

As Figure 27–10 illustrates, it is possible to have different types of phone numbers and e-mail addresses. You may also be wondering if the contacts allow an arbitrary set of rows containing arbitrary data. (For example in Figure 27–10 phone and email are well known predefined data types. What if you want store some data that is not anticipated. This is what we mean by arbitrary). Contact API does allow this arbitrary set of set of data, as shown in Figure 27–11 where address information is added to a contact.

Figure 27–11. *Editing arbitrary contact data*

Setting a Contact's Photo

You can also set up the photo for a contact. Figure 27–12 shows the photo setting screen that opens when you click the photo icon shown in Figure 27–9 (the first page of the contact details).

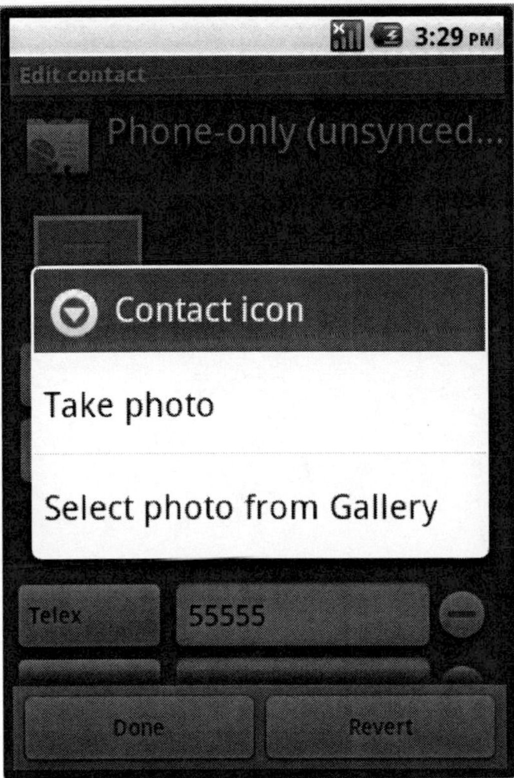

Figure 27–12. *Editing a contact's photo*

Exporting Contacts

Let's conclude this tour of the contacts application by showing how you can export contacts to an SD card. Among other things, this sdcard export facility allows you to see what kind of information is captured for a contact and how it is exposed as text.

Figure 27–13. *Exporting contacts*

Once you export the contacts to an SD card, you can explore the SD card files using the Eclipse ADT. See Figure 27–14, where one of the exported `.vcf` files is visible in the Eclipse File Explorer.

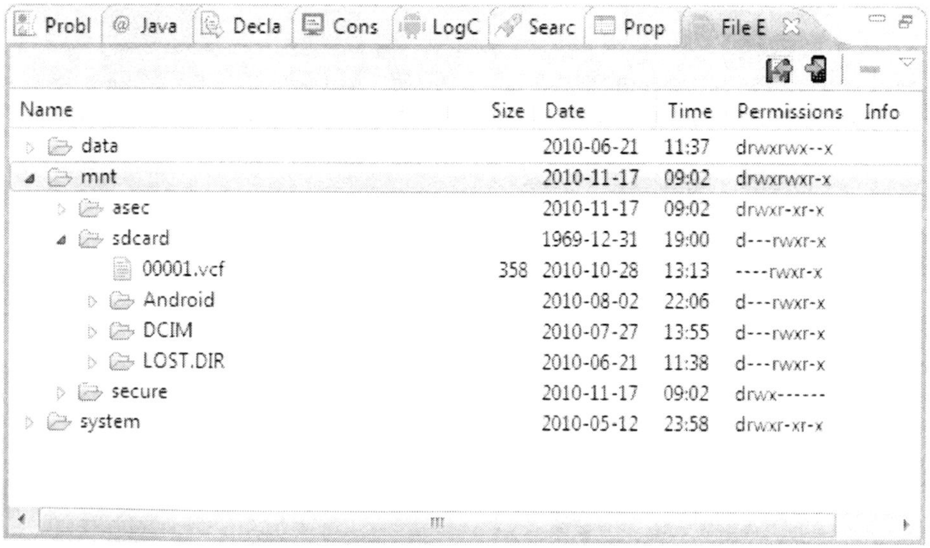

Probl | Java | Decla | Cons | LogC | Searc | Prop | File E

Name	Size	Date	Time	Permissions	Info
data		2010-06-21	11:37	drwxrwx--x	
mnt		2010-11-17	09:02	drwxrwxr-x	
asec		2010-11-17	09:02	drwxr-xr-x	
sdcard		1969-12-31	19:00	d---rwxr-x	
00001.vcf	358	2010-10-28	13:13	----rwxr-x	
Android		2010-08-02	22:06	d---rwxr-x	
DCIM		2010-07-27	13:55	d---rwxr-x	
LOST.DIR		2010-06-21	11:38	d---rwxr-x	
secure		2010-11-17	09:02	drwx------	
system		2010-05-12	23:58	drwxr-xr-x	

Figure 27–14. *Contact information on an SD Card*

You can copy the .vcf file in Figure 27–14 from the device to a local file using the icons at the top-right corner of the File Explorer tab. For the two contacts shown in Figure 27–8, the contents of the .vcf file are displayed in Listing 27–3.

Listing 27–3. *Exported Contacts in VCF Format*

```
BEGIN:VCARD
VERSION:2.1
N:C1-Last;C1-First;;;
FN:C1-First C1-Last
TEL;TLX:55555
TEL;WORK:66666
EMAIL;HOME:tcst@home.com
EMAIL;WORK:test@work.com
ORG:WorkComp
TITLE:President
ORG:Work Other
TITLE:President
URL:www.com
NOTE:Note1
X-AIM:aim
X-MSN:wlive
END:VCARD

BEGIN:VCARD
VERSION:2.1
N:C2-Last;C2-first;;;
FN:C2-first C2-Last
END:VCARD
```

Various Contact Data Types

In the figures so far, you have seen how to add distinct sets of information for a contact. Listing 27–4 shows a list of these data types as defined in the API (this list could grow with new releases and is current as of version 2.3).

Listing 27–4. *Standard Contact Data Types*

```
email
event
groupmemebership
im
nickname
note
organization
phone
photo
relation
SipAddress
structuredname
structuredpostal
website
```

Each data type, such as `email` or `structuredpostal` (indicating a postal address), has its own set of fields. So how do you know what these fields are? They are defined in the helper classes available in

```
android.provider.ContactsContract.CommonDataKinds
```

The URL for this class is
`http://developer.android.com/reference/android/provider/ContactsContract.CommonDataKinds.html`.

For example the class `CommonDataKinds.Email` defines the fields shown in Listing 27–5.

Listing 27–5. ***Specific Fields of an Email Contact***

```
Email address
Type of email: type_home, type_work, type_other, type_mobile
Label: to support type_other
```

Now that you have the background and tools necessary to work with accounts and contacts, let's get into the real details of the contacts API.

Understanding Contacts

As we have stated contacts are owned by an account. Each account has its own set of contacts. Each contact then has its own set of data elements (for example, e-mail address, phone number, name, and postal address). Furthermore, Android presents an aggregated view of raw contacts by listing only once any contacts that seem to match. These aggregated contacts form the set of contacts you see when you open the contact application (see Figure 27–8).

We will now examine how contact-related data is stored in various tables. Understanding these contact tables and their associated views is key to understanding the contacts API.

Examining the Contents SQLite Database

One way to understand and examine the content database tables is to download the content database from the device or the emulator and open it using one of the SQLite explorer tools.

To download the contacts database, use the File Explorer shown in Figure 27–14, and navigate to the following directory on your emulator:

```
/data/data/com.android.providers.contacts/databases
```

Depending on the release, the database file name may differ slightly, but it should be called `contacts.db` or `contacts2.db` or something similar.

In theory, all you have to do is open it with a SQLite tool. However, we found a problem opening this database. Most tools we tried barfed (figuratively speaking). The problem is to do with the custom collation sequences defined by Android for such things as comparing phone numbers.

Apparently, for SQLite, the custom collation sequences are compiled as part of the SQLite distribution. If you don't have the DLL files that were compiled with the Android distribution, the general-purpose explorer tools won't be able to read the database accurately. Because the tools are using the Windows SQLite DLL files to open the database that was created with Linux distribution of Android, they are not successful. And the Windows distribution of SQLite does not have the collations sequences that are defined as required by the contacts database.

However, we are lucky enough that a program called SQLite Explorer has a glitch that allowed us to browse the tables even though it refused to publish the schema for the database. You may have better luck with other pricier tools. If you would like to explore further options, here is a link to see a list of available tools for SQLite:

`http://www.sqlite.org/cvstrac/wiki?p=ManagementTools`

Should you be really inquisitive, you can read more about the collation sequences from our research article "Exploring Contacts db" available at `http://www.androidbook.com/item/3582`.

If you do have difficulties exploring the database, all is not lost, because we have listed all the important tables in this chapter. With that, we will start with exploring what are called raw contacts first.

Raw Contacts

Again, the contacts we have seen when opening up the contacts application are called aggregated contacts. Underneath each aggregated contact lies a set of contacts called raw contacts. An aggregated contact is merely a view on a set of similar raw contacts. To understand the aggregated contacts, one has to understand the raw contacts and the data that belongs to a raw contact. So we will talk about the raw contacts first.

The set of contacts belonging to an account are really called raw contacts. Each raw contact points to the detail of one person that you know in the context of that account. This is in contrast to an aggregated contact, which crosses account boundaries and ends up belonging to the device as a whole.

This relationship between an account and its set of raw contacts is maintained in the raw contacts table. Listing 27–6 shows the structure of the raw contacts table in the contacts database.

Listing 27–6. *Raw Contact Table Definition*

```
CREATE TABLE raw_contacts
(_id INTEGER PRIMARY KEY AUTOINCREMENT,
is_restricted INTEGER DEFAULT 0,
account_name STRING DEFAULT NULL,
account_type STRING DEFAULT NULL,
sourceid TEXT,
version INTEGER NOT NULL DEFAULT 1,
dirty INTEGER NOT NULL DEFAULT 0,
deleted INTEGER NOT NULL DEFAULT 0,
contact_id INTEGER REFERENCES contacts(_id),
aggregation_mode INTEGER NOT NULL DEFAULT 0,
aggregation_needed INTEGER NOT NULL DEFAULT 1,
custom_ringtone TEXT
send_to_voicemail INTEGER NOT NULL DEFAULT 0,
```

```
times_contacted INTEGER NOT NULL DEFAULT 0,
last_time_contacted INTEGER,
starred INTEGER NOT NULL DEFAULT 0,
display_name TEXT,
display_name_alt TEXT,
display_name_source INTEGER NOT NULL DEFAULT 0,
phonetic_name TEXT,
phonetic_name_style TEXT,
sort_key TEXT COLLATE PHONEBOOK,
sort_key_alt TEXT COLLATE PHONEBOOK,
name_verified INTEGER NOT NULL DEFAULT 0,
contact_in_visible_group INTEGER NOT NULL DEFAULT 0,
sync1 TEXT, sync2 TEXT, sync3 TEXT, sync4 TEXT )
```

The important fields are highlighted. As with every other Android table, the raw contacts table has the _ID column that uniquely identifies a raw contact. Together, the fields account_name and account_type identify the account this contact (specifically, the raw contact) belongs to. The sourceid field indicates how this raw contact is uniquely identified in the account identified by the account name and account type fields. For example, assume you need to know how a raw contact id is identified in the Google e-mail account. Typically, in that case, this field would have carried the user's e-mail ID.

The field contact_id refers to the aggregated contact that this raw contact is one of. An aggregated contact points to one or more similar contacts that are essentially the same person set up among multiple accounts.

The field display_name points to the display name of the contact. This is primarily a read-only field. It is set by triggers based on the data rows added in the data table (which is covered in the next subsection) for this raw contact.

The sync fields are used by the account to sync contacts between the device and the server-side account such as Google mail.

Although we have used SQLite tools to explore these fields, there is more than one way to discover these fields. The recommended way is to follow the class definitions as declared in the ContactsContract API. To explore the columns belonging to a raw contact, you can look at the class documentation for ContactsContract.RawContact.

There are advantages and disadvantages to this approach. A significant advantage is that you get to know the published and acknowledged fields by the Android SDK. The database columns may get added or dropped with out changing the public interface. So if you were to use the database columns directly, they may or may not be there. Instead, if you use the public definitions for these columns, you are safe between releases.

One disadvantage, however, is that the class documentation has many other constants interspersed with column names, even we kind of got lost in figuring out what was what. These numerous class definitions give the impression that the API is complex when, in reality, 80 percent of the class documentation for the contact API is to define constants for these columns and the URIs to access these rows.

When we practice using the contacts API in later sections, we will use the class-documentation–based constants instead of direct column names. However, we felt the direct exploration of the tables is the quickest way to help you understand the contacts API.

Let's talk next about how the data relating to a contact such as e-mail and phone number are stored.

Data Table

As indicated from the raw contact table definition, the raw contact (in an anticlimactic sense) is just an ID indicating what account it belongs to. Most of the data pertaining to the contact is not in the raw contact table but saved in the data table. Each data element, such as e-mail and phone number, are stored as separate rows in the data table. All of these related data rows are tied to a raw contact through the raw contact ID, which is one of the columns of the data table and also the primary ID of the raw contact table.

This data table contains 16 generic columns that can store any 16 different data points for any given data element, such as e-mail. Listing 27–7 describes how the data table is organized.

Listing 27–7. *Contact Data Table Defintion*

```
CREATE TABLE data
(_id INTEGER PRIMARY KEY AUTOINCREMENT,
package_id INTEGER REFERENCES package(_id),
mimetype_id INTEGER REFERENCES mimetype(_id) NOT NULL,
raw_contact_id INTEGER REFERENCES raw_contacts(_id) NOT NULL,
is_primary INTEGER NOT NULL DEFAULT 0,
is_super_primary INTEGER NOT NULL DEFAULT 0,
data_version INTEGER NOT NULL DEFAULT 0,
data1 TEXT,data2 TEXT,data3 TEXT,data4 TEXT,data5 TEXT,
data6 TEXT,data7 TEXT,data8 TEXT,data9 TEXT,data10 TEXT,
data11 TEXT,data12 TEXT,data13 TEXT,data14 TEXT,data15 TEXT,
data_sync1 TEXT, data_sync2 TEXT, data_sync3 TEXT, data_sync4 TEXT )
```

Critical columns in the data table shown in Listing 27–7 are bolded. As you might have anticipated, the `raw_contact_id` points to the raw contact to which this data row belongs.

The `mimetype_id` points to the MIME type entry indicating one of the types identified in the contact data types in Listing 27–4. The columns `data1` through `data15` are generic string-based tables that can store anything that is necessary based on the MIME type. Again, the sync fields are there to support contact syncing. The table that resolves the MIME type IDs is in Listing 27–8.

Listing 27–8. *MIME Type Lookup Table Definition*

```
CREATE TABLE mimetypes
(_id INTEGER PRIMARY KEY AUTOINCREMENT,
mimetype TEXT NOT NULL)
```

As with the raw contacts table, you can discover the data table columns through the helper class documentation for `ContactsContract.Data`.

Although you can figure out the columns from this class definition, you will not know what is stored in each of the generic columns from data1 through data15. To know this, you will need to see the class definitions for a number of classes under the namespace ContactsContract.CommonDataKinds.

Some examples of these classes follow:

- ContactsContract.CommonDataKinds.Email
- ContactsContract.CommonDataKinds.Phone

In fact, you will see one class for each of the listed common data types in Listing 27–4. Ultimately, all the CommonDataKinds classes do is indicate which generic data fields (data1 through data15) are in use and what for.

Aggregated Contacts

Ultimately, a contact and its related data are unambiguously stored in the raw contacts table and the data table. An aggregated contact on the other hand is more of heuristic in nature and could be a bit ambiguous.

When there is a contact that is the same between multiple accounts, you may want to see one name instead of seeing the same or similar name repeated once for every account. Android addresses this by aggregating contacts into a read-only view. Android stores these aggregated contacts in a table called contacts. Android uses a number of triggers on the raw contact table and the data table to populate or change this aggregated contact table.

Before going into explaining the logic behind aggregation, let us show you the contact table definition (see Listing 27–9).

Listing 27–9. *Aggregated Contact Table Definition*

```
CREATE TABLE contacts
(_id INTEGER PRIMARY KEY AUTOINCREMENT,
name_raw_contact_id INTEGER REFERENCES raw_contacts(_id),
photo_id INTEGER REFERENCES data(_id),
custom_ringtone TEXT,
send_to_voicemail INTEGER NOT NULL DEFAULT 0,
times_contacted INTEGER NOT NULL DEFAULT 0,
last_time_contacted INTEGER,
starred INTEGER NOT NULL DEFAULT 0,
in_visible_group INTEGER NOT NULL DEFAULT 1,
has_phone_number INTEGER NOT NULL DEFAULT 0,
lookup TEXT,
status_update_id INTEGER REFERENCES data(_id),
single_is_restricted INTEGER NOT NULL DEFAULT 0)
```

The important columns are highlighted. No client directly updates this table. When a raw contact is added with its concomitant detail, Android searches other raw contacts to see if there are similar raw contacts. If there is one, it will use the aggregated contact ID of that raw contact as the aggregated contact ID of the new raw contact as well. No entry is made into the aggregated contact table. If none is found it will create an aggregated contact and uses that aggregated contact as the contact id for that raw contact.

Android uses the following algorithm to determine which raw contacts are similar:

1. The two raw contacts have matching names.
2. The words in the name are the same but vary in order: "first last" or "first, last" or "last, first."
3. The shorter versions of the names match, such as "Bob" for "Robert."
4. If one of the raw contacts has just a first or last name, this will trigger a search for other attributes, such as phone number or e-mail, and if the other attributes match, the contact will be aggregated.
5. If one of the raw contacts is missing the name altogether, this will also trigger a search for other attributes as in step 4.

Because these rules are heuristic, some contacts may be aggregated unintentionally. The client applications need to provide a mechanism to separate the contacts in such a case. If you refer to the *Android User's Guide*, you will see that the default contacts application allows you to separate contacts that are unintentionally merged.

You can also prevent the aggregation by setting the aggregation mode when you insert the raw contact. The available aggregation modes are shown in Listing 27–10.

Listing 27–10. *Aggregation Mode Constants*

```
AGGREGATION_MODE_DEFAULT
AGGREGATION_MODE_DISABLED
AGGREGATION_MODE_SUSPENDED
```

The first options is obvious; it is how aggregation works.

The second option (`disabled`) indicates that keep this raw contact out of aggregation. Even if it is aggregated already, Android will pull it out of aggregation and allocate a new aggregated contact ID dedicated to this raw contact.

The third option `suspended` indicates that even though the properties of the contact may change, which will make it invalid for the aggregation into that batch of contacts keep it tied to that aggregated contact.

The last point brings out the volatile dimension of the aggregated contact. Say you have a unique raw contact with a first name and a last name. Right now, it doesn't match any other raw contact, so this unique raw contact gets its own allocation of an aggregated contact. The aggregated contact ID will be stored in the raw contact table against that raw contact row.

However, you go and change the last name of this raw contact, which makes it a match to another set of contacts that are aggregated. In that case, it will remove the raw contact from this aggregated contact and move it to the other one abandoning this single aggregated contact by itself. In this case, the ID of the aggregated contact becomes entirely abandoned, as it will not match anything in the future because it is just an ID without an underlying raw contact.

So an aggregated contact is volatile. There is not a significant value to hold on to this aggregated contact ID over time.

Android offers some respite from this predicament by providing a field called `lookup` in the aggregated contacts tables.

This lookup field is an aggregation (concatenation) of the account and the unique ID of this contact in that account for each raw contact. This information is further codified so that it can be passed as a URL parameter to retrieve the latest aggregated contact ID. Android looks at the lookup key and sees which underlying raw contact IDs are there for this lookup key. It then uses a best-fit algorithm to return a suitable (or perhaps new) aggregated contact ID.

While we are explicitly examining the contacts database, let's consider a couple of contact-related database views that are useful.

view_contacts

The first of these views is the `view_contacts`. Although there is a table that holds the aggregated contacts (contacts table) the API doesn't expose the contacts table directly. Instead, it uses `view_contacts` as the target for reading the aggregated contacts. When you query based on the URI `ContactsContract.Contacts.CONTENT_URI`. The columns returned are based on this view `view_contacts`. The definition of this view is shown in Listing 27–11.

Listing 27–11. *A View to Read Aggregated Contacts*

```
CREATE VIEW view_contacts AS

SELECT contacts._id AS _id,
contacts.custom_ringtone AS custom_ringtone,
name_raw_contact.display_name_source AS display_name_source,
name_raw_contact.display_name AS display_name,
name_raw_contact.display_name_alt AS display_name_alt,
name_raw_contact.phonetic_name AS phonetic_name,
name_raw_contact.phonetic_name_style AS phonetic_name_style,
name_raw_contact.sort_key AS sort_key,
name_raw_contact.sort_key_alt AS sort_key_alt,
name_raw_contact.contact_in_visible_group AS in_visible_group,
has_phone_number,
lookup,
photo_id,
contacts.last_time_contacted AS last_time_contacted,
contacts.send_to_voicemail AS send_to_voicemail,
contacts.starred AS starred,
contacts.times_contacted AS times_contacted, status_update_id

FROM contacts JOIN raw_contacts AS name_raw_contact
ON(name_raw_contact_id=name_raw_contact._id)
```

Notice that this view combines the contacts table with the raw contact table based on the aggregated contact id.

contact_entities_view

Another useful view is the view that combines raw contacts table with the data table. This view allows retrieving all the data elements of a given raw contact one time. Or even the data elements of multiple raw contacts belonging to the same aggregated contact. Listing 27–12 presents the definition of the entities view.

Listing 27–12. *Contact Entities View*

```
CREATE VIEW contact_entities_view AS

SELECT raw_contacts.account_name AS account_name,
raw_contacts.account_type AS account_type,
raw_contacts.sourceid AS sourceid,
raw_contacts.version AS version,
raw_contacts.dirty AS dirty,
raw_contacts.deleted AS deleted,
raw_contacts.name_verified AS name_verified,
package AS res_package,
contact_id,
raw_contacts.sync1 AS sync1,
raw_contacts.sync2 AS sync2,
raw_contacts.sync3 AS sync3,
raw_contacts.sync4 AS sync4,
mimetype, data1, data2, data3, data4, data5, data6, data7, data8,
data9, data10, data11, data12, data13, data14, data15,
data_sync1, data_sync2, data_sync3, data_sync4,

raw_contacts._id AS _id,

is_primary, is_super_primary,
data_version,
data._id AS data_id,
raw_contacts.starred AS starred,
raw_contacts.is_restricted AS is_restricted,
groups.sourceid AS group_sourceid

FROM raw_contacts LEFT OUTER JOIN data
   ON (data.raw_contact_id=raw_contacts._id)
LEFT OUTER JOIN packages
  ON (data.package_id=packages._id)
LEFT OUTER JOIN mimetypes
  ON (data.mimetype_id=mimetypes._id)
LEFT OUTER JOIN groups
  ON (mimetypes.mimetype='vnd.android.cursor.item/group_membership'
    AND groups._id-data.data1)
```

The URIs needed to access this view are available in the class `ContactsContract.RawContacts.RawContactsEntity`.

Working with the Contacts API

So far, we have explored the basic idea behind the contacts API by exploring its tables and views. We will now develop a few sample programs exercising what we learned. Although you can use the listings in this chapter to make your Eclipse projects, we have also included a URL for the downloadable project files at the end of this chapter.

Exploring Accounts

We will start out our exercise by writing a program that can print out the list of accounts.

To do this, we have prepared the following files

- `TestContactsDriverActivity.java`: The main driver activity for this chapter with a set of menu items to invoke various samples.
- `DebugActivity.java`: Base class of the driver activity to hide a few implementation details that don't directly contribute to the understanding of the contacts API.
- `debug_activity_layout.xml`: Layout file required by the debug activity and resides in the `/res/layout` filesubdirectory.
- `AccountFunctionTester.java`: Java class that will respond to the menu item to print available accounts on the emulator or the device through the driver activity.
- `BaseTester.java`: A base class for the `AccountFunctionTester` that hides the details of coordination between the main driver activity and each of the individual function testers (Each exercise we demonstrate is implemented as one of these function testers so that each concept can be presented in a file that is meaningful to that function.)
- `IReportBack.java`: An interface implemented by the `DebugActivity` and passed to the BaseTester, which allows the inherited function testers to report text to be displayed or debug messages to be logged and printed to the screen using `DebugActivity`
- `main_menu.xml`: Menu file to support each of the functions that we are going to demonstrate
- `AndroidManifest.xml`: The mandatory manifest file

We will now present these files one by one. We will start with the menu file

The Menu file

The menu file in Listing 27–13 needs to be named main_menu.xml and made available in the /res/menu subdirectory of your project.

Listing 27–13. *Main Menu File for the Project*

```
<menu xmlns:android="http://schemas.android.com/apk/res/android">
    <!-- This group uses the default category. -->
    <group android:id="@+id/menuGroup_Main">
        <item android:id="@+id/menu_show_accounts"
            android:title="Accounts" />

        <item android:id="@+id/menu_da_clear"
         android:title="clear" />
    </group>
</menu>
```

At this point in the exercise, we have listed only two menu items. As we go through the other exercises later in this chapter, you will be adding to those menu items. The first menu item is intended to list the accounts available, and the second is a general-purpose helpful menu item to clear the debug/informational messages from the test driver activity.

Account Function Tester-Related files

With the menu file in place, let's look at the files that are related to implementing code that will be called in response to the menu item Accounts from Listing 27–13.

IReportBack.java

The first of these files is IReportBack.java, shown in Listing 27–14.

Listing 27–14. *IReportBack.java*

```
//IReportBack.java
public interface IReportBack
{
    public void reportBack(String tag, String message);
    public void reportTransient(String tag, String message);
}
```

This interface is a contract to its inherited clients that they will be able to send informational and debug messages not worrying about where those messages to be displayed and how.

BaseTester.java

All function testers will have access to the IReportBack interface so that they can report messages as they perform the function of a menu item. This is done through a base class for all function testers called BaseTester. The source code for the BaseTester class is given in Listing 27–15.

Listing 27–15. *BaseTester Source Code*

```
public class BaseTester
{
    protected IReportBack mReportTo;
    protected Context mContext;
    public BaseTester(Context ctx, IReportBack target)
    {
        mReportTo = target;
        mContext = ctx;
    }
}
```

BaseTester class keeps an interface for IReportBack and a reference to the Context (usually the parent driver activity). These two variables are utilized by the derived function testers.

AccountsFunctionTester.java

We will show now the first of these function testers the AccountFunctionTester in Listing 27–16.

Listing 27–16. *AccountsFunctionTester*

```
public class AccountsFunctionTester extends BaseTester
{
    private static String tag = "tc>";
    public AccountsFunctionTester(Context ctx, IReportBack target)
    {
        super(ctx, target);
    }
    public void testAccounts()
    {
        AccountManager am = AccountManager.get(this.mContext);
        Account[] accounts = am.getAccounts();
        for(Account ac: accounts)
        {
            String acname=ac.name;
            String actype = ac.type;
            this.mReportTo.reportBack(tag,acname + ":" + actype);
        }
    }
}
```

The code in Listing 27–16 is quite simple. We have already covered the topic of accounts and how we go about getting a list of accounts in the beginning of this chapter. The code in Listing 27–16 is merely getting the account name and type for each account and then calling the report back interface to log it. As long as there is a driver activity that can call the method testAccounts(), this code can report back the account name and type. Let's now examine the driver-activity—related classes.

Driver Activity Classes

We will start with the base class of the driver activity class. This base class activity has the following responsibilities:

- Provide a text view to report messages. It uses a layout resource called `debug_activity_layout`.
- Provide a menu so that individual function testers can be invoked. It takes in the menu resource ID from the derived classes through its constructor. It then assumes that there is a predefined menu item called `menu_da_clear` to clear the text view as defined in the debug layout. This base class also writes out the menu item that is selected to the debug text view in the debug layout.

With that here is the source code for `DebugActvity.java` in Listing 27–17

DebugActivity.java

Listing 27–17. *DebugActivity Class Definition*

```
public abstract class DebugActivity extends Activity
implements IReportBack
{
    //Derived classes needs first
    protected abstract boolean onMenuItemSelected(MenuItem item);

    //private variables set by constructor
    private static String tag=null;
    private int menuId = 0;

    public DebugActivity(int inMenuId, String inTag)
    {
        tag = inTag;
        menuId = inMenuId;

    }

    @Override
    public void onCreate(Bundle savedInstanceState) {
        super.onCreate(savedInstanceState);
        setContentView(R.layout.debug_activity_layout);
    }
    @Override
    public boolean onCreateOptionsMenu(Menu menu){
        super.onCreateOptionsMenu(menu);
            MenuInflater inflater = getMenuInflater();
            inflater.inflate(menuId, menu);
        return true;
    }
    @Override
    public boolean onOptionsItemSelected(MenuItem item){
        appendMenuItemText(item);
        if (item.getItemId() == R.id.menu_da_clear){
            this.emptyText();
```

```
            return true;
        }
        return onMenuItemSelected(item);
    }
    private TextView getTextView(){
        return (TextView)this.findViewById(R.id.text1);
    }
    protected void appendMenuItemText(MenuItem menuItem){
       String title = menuItem.getTitle().toString();
       TextView tv = getTextView();
       tv.setText(tv.getText() + "\n" + title);
    }
    protected void emptyText(){
       TextView tv = getTextView();
       tv.setText("");
    }
    private void appendText(String s){
       TextView tv = getTextView();
       tv.setText(tv.getText() + "\n" + s);
       Log.d(tag,s);
    }
    public void reportBack(String tag, String message)
    {
        this.appendText(tag + ":" + message);
        Log.d(tag,message);
    }
    public void reportTransient(String tag, String message)
    {
        String s = tag + ":" + message;
        Toast mToast = Toast.makeText(this, s, Toast.LENGTH_SHORT);
        mToast.show();
        reportBack(tag,message);
        Log.d(tag,message);
    }
}
```

In addition to the methods available to report back debug and informational messages on the debug text view, the method `reportTransient()` from the `IReportBack` is available to present text through the `Toast` interface of Android.

debug_layout_activity.java

This file debug_layout_activity.xml, shown in Listing 27–18, needs to be in the /res/layout subdirectory.

Listing 27–18. *Debug Layout File: debug_activity_layout.xml*

```
<?xml version="1.0" encoding="utf-8"?>
<LinearLayout xmlns:android="http://schemas.android.com/apk/res/android"
    android:orientation="vertical"
    android:layout_width="fill_parent"
    android:layout_height="fill_parent"
    >
<TextView
    android:id="@+id/text1"
    android:layout_width="fill_parent"
```

```
    android:layout_height="wrap_content"
    android:text="Debut Text Appears here"
    />
</LinearLayout>
```

TestContactsDriverActivity.java

Listing 27–19 is the main driver activity that coordinates the menu items and calling the respective methods from the corresponding function testers.

Listing 27–19. *Main Driver Activity*

```
public class TestContactsDriverActivity
extends DebugActivity
implements IReportBack
{
    public static final String tag="Test Contacts";
    AccountsFunctionTester accountsFunctionTester = null;

    public TestContactsDriverActivity()
    {
        super(R.menu.main_menu,tag);
        accountsFunctionTester = new AccountsFunctionTester(this,this);
    }
    protected boolean onMenuItemSelected(MenuItem item)
    {
        Log.d(tag,item.getTitle().toString());
        if (item.getItemId() == R.id.menu_show_accounts)
        {
            accountsFunctionTester.testAccounts();
            return true;
        }
        return true;
    }
}
```

Because we pushed most of the functionality of the driver to the base class, the driver activity is clean and direct.

First thing to notice in Listing 27–19 is how the driver activity passes the menu resource as defined in Listing 27–13 (`main_menu.xml`) to the base debug activity. The debug activity then attaches this menu.

Second thing to notice is how this driver activity uses function testers. In the code in Listing 27–19, we have shown only the accounts function tester. We will be adding more function testers as we go along. The pattern to use those additional function testers is identical.

Manifest File

Listing 27–20 shows the manifest file to round off all the files necessary.

Listing 27–20. *Manifest File for the Program*

```
<?xml version="1.0" encoding="utf-8"?>
<manifest xmlns:android="http://schemas.android.com/apk/res/android"
      package="com.androidbook.contacts"
      android:versionCode="1"
      android:versionName="1.0.0">
    <application android:icon="@drawable/icon"
        android:label="Test Contacts">
        <activity android:name=".TestContactsDriverActivity"
                  android:label="Test Contacts">
            <intent-filter>
                <action android:name="android.intent.action.MAIN" />
                <category android:name="android.intent.category.LAUNCHER" />
            </intent-filter>
        </activity>
</application>
    <uses-sdk android:minSdkVersion="5" />
    <uses-permission android:name="android.permission.GET_ACCOUNTS"/>
</manifest>
```

Running the Program

Listing 27–21 contains the files you will need to compile and run this simple test

Listing 27–21. *Complete List of Files for the First Sample*

```
IReportBack.java
BaseTester.java
AccountsFunctionTester.java
DebugActivity.java
TestContactsDriverActivity.java
/res/menu/main_menu.xml
/res/layout/debug_layout_activity.xml
Manifest.xml
```

When you compile and run this file and click the menu item while looking at the main driver activity, you will see the screen shown in Figure 27–15.

Figure 27–15. *Main driver activity with the menu*

Figure 27–15 has two menu options. The "clear" option is a generic menu provided by the base class debug activity, which will clear any text in the debug text view. "Acccounts" will list the set of accounts available. Go ahead and click that menu item if you are playing along. This will bring up the screen shown in Figure 27–16.

Figure 27–16. *Main driver activity showing a list of accounts*

The emulator we tested on has only one account setup, which is a Google account. So our sample has shown that one account.

Exploring Aggregated Contacts

In the next sample, let's see how we can explore aggregated contacts. We will demonstrate three things in this exercise around aggregated contacts:

- Discover all the fields returned by firing off a URI that knows how to read aggregated contacts.
- List all aggregated contacts.
- Discover all the fields returned by a cursor based on a lookup URI.

To read contacts, you need to request the following permission in the manifest file (Listing 27–20):

```
android.permission.READ_CONTACTS
```

You will also need the following new files (in addition to the ones from the previous sample) to test this sample:

- `Utils.java`
- `URIFunctionTester.java`

- AggregatedContactFunctionTester.java
- AggregatedContact.java

These files will be presented as we cover the details of this sample in this section.

You will also need to update the following files from the previous example:

- main_menu.xml
- TestContactsDriverActivity.java

The changes you need to make to these files are also covered in this section.

As the functionality we are testing deals with content providers, URIs, and cursors, we have coded a couple of utility functions in the file Utils.java shown in Listing 27–22.

Listing 27–22. *Utility Functions for Working with Cursors*

```
public class Utils
{
    public static String getColumnValue(Cursor cc, String cname)
    {
        int i = cc.getColumnIndex(cname);
        return cc.getString(i);
    }

    protected static String getCursorColumnNames(Cursor c)
    {
        int count = c.getColumnCount();
        StringBuffer cnamesBuffer = new StringBuffer();
        for (int i=0;i<count;i++)
        {
            String cname = c.getColumnName(i);
            cnamesBuffer.append(cname).append(';');
        }
        return cnamesBuffer.toString();
    }
}
```

The first function getColumnValue() returns the value of a column given its name from the current row of the cursor. It returns the value of the column as a string irrespective of its fundamental type.

The second function is quite useful. It takes any cursor and returns a separated list of all its available columns. This is handy when we explore new URIs to discover the type of fields those URIs return. Although one is supposed to document such columns in the Java code, this method of discovering them at run time could come handy.

As this example and the upcoming examples in this chapter use the idea of submitting a URI and getting the cursor back through an activity, we have abstracted out those utility functions into a base class called URIFunctionTester. Listing 27–23 shows the source code followed by an explanation of each method of this base class

Listing 27–23. *A Base Class to Explore URI-Related Functions*

```
public class URIFunctionTester extends BaseTester
{
    protected static String tag = "tc>";
    public URIFunctionTester(Context ctx, IReportBack target)
    {
        super(ctx, target);
    }
    protected Cursor getACursor(String uri,String clause)
    {
        // Run query
        Activity a = (Activity)this.mContext;
        return a.managedQuery(Uri.parse(uri), null, clause, null, null);
    }

    protected Cursor getACursor(Uri uri,String clause)
    {
        // Run query
        Activity a = (Activity)this.mContext;
        return a.managedQuery(uri, null, clause, null, null);
    }
    protected void printCursorColumnNames(Cursor c)
    {
        this.mReportTo.reportBack(tag,Utils.getCursorColumnNames(c));
    }
}
```

The function `getACursor()` takes a URI either as a string or a URI object and a string-based where clause and returns a cursor. Throughout the examples, as we often print out the column names of a cursor returned, we have created a method called `printCursorColumnNames()`, which, in turn, uses the `Utils` class to explore the cursor and get the column names.

Each row returned by the contact cursor will have a number of fields. For our example, we are not interested in all the fields but a few. We have abstracted this out into another class called an `AggregatedContact`. Listing 27–24 defines this class

Listing 27–24. *A Few Fields from an Aggregated Contact*

```
public class AggregatedContact
{
    public String id;
    public String lookupUri;
    public String lookupKey;
    public String displayName;

    public void fillinFrom(Cursor c)
    {
        id = Utils.getColumnValue(c,"_ID");
        lookupKey = Utils.getColumnValue(c,ContactsContract.Contacts.LOOKUP_KEY);
        lookupUri = ContactsContract.Contacts.CONTENT_LOOKUP_URI + "/" + lookupKey;
        displayName = Utils.getColumnValue(c,ContactsContract.Contacts.DISPLAY_NAME);
    }
}
```

Listing 27–24 is nothing too complex. In this code, we used the cursor to load up the fields that we are interested in. We'll now present you with the `AggregatedFunctionTester`, which will help us with the goals set at the beginning of this example.

Listing 27–25. *Code Testing Aggregated Contacts*

```
public class AggregatedContactFunctionTester extends URIFunctionTester
{
    public AggregatedContactFunctionTester(Context ctx, IReportBack target)
    {
        super(ctx, target);
    }
    /*
     * Get a cursor of all contacts
     * No where clause
     * Don't use it on a large set
     */
    private Cursor getContacts()
    {
        // Run query
        Uri uri = ContactsContract.Contacts.CONTENT_URI;
        String sortOrder = ContactsContract.Contacts.DISPLAY_NAME
                              + " COLLATE LOCALIZED ASC";
        Activity a = (Activity)this.mContext;
        return a.managedQuery(uri, null, null, null, sortOrder);
    }

    /*
     * Use the getContacts above
     * to list the set of columns in the cursor
     */
    public void listContactCursorFields()
    {
        Cursor c = null;
        try
        {
            c = getContacts();
            int i = c.getColumnCount();
            this.mReportTo.reportBack(tag, "Number of columns:" + i);
            this.printCursorColumnNames(c);
        }
        finally
        {
            if (c!= null) c.close();
        }
    }

    /*
     * Given a cursor worth of contacts
     * Print the contact names followed by
     * their look up keys
     */
    private void printLookupKeys(Cursor c)
    {
        for(c.moveToFirst();!c.isAfterLast();c.moveToNext())
        {
```

```
            String name=this.getContactName(c);
            String lookupKey = this.getLookupKey(c);
            String luri = this.getLookupUri(lookupKey);
            this.mReportTo.reportBack(tag, name + ":" + lookupKey);
            this.mReportTo.reportBack(tag, name + ":" + luri);
        }
    }

    /*
     * Use the getContacts() function
     * to get a cursor and print all
     * the contact names followed by look up keys
     * uses the printLookyupKeus() function
     */
    public void listContacts()
    {
        Cursor c = null;
        try
        {
            c = getContacts();
            int i = c.getColumnCount();
            this.mReportTo.reportBack(tag, "Number of columns:" + i);
            this.printLookupKeys(c);
        }
        finally
        {
            if (c!= null) c.close();
        }
    }

    /*
     * A utility function to retrieve the
     * look up key from a contact cursor
     */
    private String getLookupKey(Cursor cc)
    {
        int lookupkeyIndex = cc.getColumnIndex(ContactsContract.Contacts.LOOKUP_KEY);
        return cc.getString(lookupkeyIndex);
    }

    /*
     * A utility function to retrieve the
     * display name from a contact cursor
     */
    private String getContactName(Cursor cc)
    {
        return Utils.getColumnValue(cc,ContactsContract.Contacts.DISPLAY_NAME);
    }

    /**
     * Construct a look up URI based on the
     * Contacts URI and a lookup key
     */
    private String getLookupUri(String lookupkey)
    {
        String luri = ContactsContract.Contacts.CONTENT_LOOKUP_URI + "/" + lookupkey;
        return luri;
```

```
}

/**
 * Use the lookup uri
 * to retrieve a single aggregated contact
 */
private Cursor getASingleContact(String lookupUri)
{
    // Run query
    Activity a = (Activity)this.mContext;
    return a.managedQuery(Uri.parse(lookupUri), null, null, null, null);
}

/*
 * A function to see if the URI constructed by the lookup
 * uri returns a cursor that has a different set of columns.
 * It returns a similar cursor with similar columns
 * as one would expect.
 */
public void listLookupUriColumns()
{
    Cursor c = null;
    try
    {
        c = getContacts();
        String firstContactLookupUri = getFirstLookupUri(c);
        printLookupUriColumns(firstContactLookupUri);
    }
    finally
    {
        if (c!= null) c.close();
    }
}

public void printLookupUriColumns(String lookupuri)
{
    Cursor c = null;
    try
    {
        c = getASingleContact(lookupuri);
        int i = c.getColumnCount();
        this.mReportTo.reportBack(tag, "Number of columns:" + i);
        int j = c.getCount();
        this.mReportTo.reportBack(tag, "Number of rows:" + j);
        this.printCursorColumnNames(c);
    }
    finally
    {
        if (c!=null)c.close();
    }
}

/*
 * Take a list of contacts
 * look up the first contact
 * return null if there are no contacts
 */
```

```
    private String getFirstLookupUri(Cursor c)
    {
        c.moveToFirst();
        if (c.isAfterLast())
        {
            Log.d(tag,"No rows to get the first contact");
            return null;
        }
        //There is a row
        String lookupKey = this.getLookupKey(c);
        String luri = this.getLookupUri(lookupKey);
        return luri;
    }

    /*
     * Take a list of contacts
     * look up the first contact and return it
     * as an object AggregatedContact.
     */
    protected AggregatedContact getFirstContact()
    {
        Cursor c=null;
        try
        {
            c = getContacts();
            c.moveToFirst();
            if (c.isAfterLast())
            {
                Log.d(tag,"No contacts");
                return null;
            }
            //contact is there
            AggregatedContact firstcontact = new AggregatedContact();
            firstcontact.fillinFrom(c);
            return firstcontact;
        }
        finally
        {
            if (c!=null) c.close();
        }
    }
}
```

The key public functions are highlighted. The comments section for each of the functions explains what each function does. Once you have this function tester available, add the menu items in Listing 27–26 to the menu XML (`/res/menu/main_menu.xml`).

Listing 27–26. ***Testing Aggregated Contacts Menu Items***

```
        <item android:id="@+id/menu_show_contact_cursor"
            android:title="Contacts Cursor" />

        <item android:id="@+id/menu_show_contacts"
            android:title="Contacts" />

        <item android:id="@+id/menu_show_single_contact_cursor"
            android:title="Single Contact Cursor" />
```

You can add them anywhere in the main_menu.xml, but we suggest you add them from top to bottom so that newer menu items show first in the menu list. Once you have added the menus, change the main driver activity so that it looks like Listing 27–27.

Listing 27–27. *Main Driver Activity Updated for Testing Aggregated Contacts*

```
public class TestContactsDriverActivity extends DebugActivity
implements IReportBack
{
    public static final String tag="TestContactsDriverActivity ";
    AccountsFunctionTester accountsFunctionTester = null;
    AggregatedContactFunctionTester aggregatedContactFunctionTester = null;

    public TestContactsDriverActivity()
    {
        super(R.menu.main_menu,tag);
        accountsFunctionTester = new AccountsFunctionTester(this,this);
        aggregatedContactFunctionTester =
           new AggregatedContactFunctionTester(this,this);
    }
    protected boolean onMenuItemSelected(MenuItem item)
    {
        Log.d(tag,item.getTitle().toString());
        if (item.getItemId() == R.id.menu_show_accounts)
        {
            accountsFunctionTester.testAccounts();
            return true;
        }
        if (item.getItemId() == R.id.menu_show_contact_cursor)
        {
            aggregatedContactFunctionTester.listContactCursorFields();
            return true;
        }
        if (item.getItemId() == R.id.menu_show_contacts)
        {
            aggregatedContactFunctionTester.listContacts();
            return true;
        }
        if (item.getItemId() == R.id.menu_show_single_contact_cursor)
        {
            aggregatedContactFunctionTester.listLookupUriColumns();
            return true;
        }
        return true;
    }
}
```

Notice the three public functions that we end up calling for each of the menu options:

- listContactCursorFields()
- listContacts()
- listLookupUriColumns()

Let's talk about what each of these functions does based on the code in Listing 27–26. The listContactCursorFields function reads the entire list of contacts and prints out the column names in the cursor. The URI used to read all the contacts is ContactsContract.Contacts.CONTENT_URI.

You can pass this URI to the managedQuery() function to retrieve a cursor. You can pass null as the column projection to receive all columns. Although this is not recommended in practice, in our case, it makes sense because we want to know about all the columns it returns. Listing 27–28 contains list of columns returned by this URI.

Listing 27–28. *Contacts Content URI Cursor Columns*

```
times_contacted;
contact_status;
custom_ringtone;
has_phone_number;
phonetic_name;
phonetic_name_style;
contact_status_label;
lookup;
contact_status_icon;
last_time_contacted;
display_name;
sort_key_alt;
in_visible_group;
_id;
starred;
sort_key;
display_name_alt;
contact_presence;
display_name_source;
contact_status_res_package;
contact_status_ts;
photo_id;
send_to_voicemail;
```

The sample program will print these columns both to the screen and LogCat. We copied these fields from LogCat and formatted them as shown in Listing 27–28.

> **NOTE:** When working with content providers, the technique of going after the URIs and printing the columns they return can be very useful.

Now that we've explored the columns available with the contacts content URI, let's pick a few columns and see what contact rows are available. To do this, click the menu item "contacts". This will invoke the function listContacts(). listContacts() method uses the same contacts content URI but now prints the following columns for each contact:

- display name
- lookup key
- lookup uri

We are considering these fields because we wanted to see what the lookup key and lookup key URI look like based on what is covered in the theory part of this chapter. Specifically, we are interested in firing off the lookup URI and see what type of a cursor it would return. To see this, click the menu item Single Contact Cursor. This will invoke the function `listLookupUriColumns()`. This function will take the first contact from the list of all contacts and then formulate a look up URI for that contact and fire off the URI to see what it returns.

As it turns out, it just returns a cursor that is identical in the columns in Listing 27–28, except that it has only one row pointing to the contact for which this is the lookup key. Also notice that we have used the following lookup URI definition

```
ContactsContract.Contacts.CONTENT_LOOKUP_URI
```

You know from the discussion of the contact lookup URIs that each lookup URI represents a collection of raw contact identities that have been concatenated. That being the case, you might have expected the lookup URI to return a series of matching raw contacts. However, the test above (Listing 27–28) is showing that it is not returning a cursor of raw contacts but instead a cursor of contacts.

> **NOTE:** A lookup based on the contact lookup Uri returns an aggregated contact and not a raw contact.

Another important tidbit is that the lookup process for the aggregated contact based on the lookup URI is not linear or exact. Meaning, Android will not look for an exact match of the lookup key. Instead, Android parses the lookup key into its constituent raw contacts. Then find the aggregated contact ID that matches the most of the raw contact records and return that aggregated contact record back.

One consequence of this is that there is no public mechanism available to go from the look up key to its constituent raw contacts. Instead, you have to find the contact id for that lookup key and then fire off a raw contact URI for that contact ID to retrieve the corresponding raw contacts.

Exploring Raw Contacts

In the next sample, let's see how we can explore the raw contacts. We will try to do three things in this exercise around raw contacts:

- Discover all the fields returned by firing off a URI that knows how to read raw contacts.
- Show all raw contacts.
- List all raw contacts for a set of aggregated contacts.

You will need the following new files to test this sample:

- `RawContact.java`
- `RawContactFunctionTester.java`

These files will be presented as we cover the details of this sample in this section. You will also need to update the following files from the previous example:

- main_menu.xml
- TestContactsDriverActivity.java

The changes you need to make these files are also covered in this section.

The file in Listing 27–29, RawContact.java, is there to capture a few important fields from the raw contacts table.

Listing 27–29. *Raw Contact*

```
public class RawContact
{
    public String rawContactId;
    public String aggregatedContactId;
    public String accountName;
    public String accountType;
    public String displayName;

    public void fillinFrom(Cursor c)
    {
        rawContactId = Utils.getColumnValue(c,"_ID");
        accountName = Utils.getColumnValue(c,ContactsContract.RawContacts.ACCOUNT_NAME);
        accountType = Utils.getColumnValue(c,ContactsContract.RawContacts.ACCOUNT_TYPE);
        aggregatedContactId = Utils.getColumnValue(c,
                                        ContactsContract.RawContacts.CONTACT_ID);
        displayName = Utils.getColumnValue(c,"display_name");
    }
    public String toString()
    {
        return displayName
            + "/" + accountName + ":" + accountType
            + "/" + rawContactId
            + "/" + aggregatedContactId;
    }
}
```

To test the functionality of this sample, you will need to add the menu items in Listing 27–30 to the main_menu.xml.

Listing 27–30. *Menu Items to Test Raw Contacts*

```
        <item android:id="@+id/menu_show_rc_all"
            android:title="all raw contacts" />

        <item android:id="@+id/menu_show_rc"
            android:title="raw contacts" />

        <item android:id="@+id/menu_show_rc_cursor"
            android:title="raw contacts cursor" />
```

Each of these menu options ends up calling three public functions from the RawContactFunctionTester.java. The code for this file is in Listing 27–31.

Listing 27–31. *Testing Raw Contacts*

```
public class RawContactsFunctionTester
extends AggregatedContactFunctionTester
{
    public RawContactsFunctionTester(Context ctx, IReportBack target)
    {
        super(ctx, target);
    }
    public void showAllRawContacts()
    {
        Cursor c = null;
        try
        {
            c = this.getACursor(getRawContactsUri(), null);
            this.printRawContacts(c);
        }
        finally
        {
            if (c!=null) c.close();
        }
    }
    public void showRawContactsForFirstAggregatedContact()
    {
        AggregatedContact ac = getFirstContact();
        this.mReportTo.reportBack(tag, ac.displayName + ":" + ac.id);

        Cursor c = null;

        try
        {
            c = this.getACursor(getRawContactsUri(), getClause(ac.id));
            this.printRawContacts(c);
        }
        finally
        {
            if (c!=null) c.close();
        }
    }
    private void printRawContacts(Cursor c)
    {
        for(c.moveToFirst();!c.isAfterLast();c.moveToNext())
        {
            RawContact rc = new RawContact();
            rc.fillinFrom(c);
            this.mReportTo.reportBack(tag, rc.toString());
        }
    }
    public void showRawContactsCursor()
    {
        AggregatedContact ac = getFirstContact();
        this.mReportTo.reportBack(tag, ac.displayName + ":" + ac.id);

        Cursor c = null;

        try
        {
            c = this.getACursor(getRawContactsUri(),null);
```

```
            this.printCursorColumnNames(c);
        }
        finally
        {
            if (c!=null) c.close();
        }
    }
    private Uri getRawContactsUri()
    {
        return ContactsContract.RawContacts.CONTENT_URI;
    }
    private String getClause(String contactId)
    {
        return "contact_id = " + contactId;
    }
}
```

Listing 27–32 presents the updated driver file that facilitates the menu items from calling the public functions of the raw contacts function tester.

Listing 27–32. *Updated Driver Activity to Test Raw Contacts*

```
public class TestContactsDriverActivity extends DebugActivity
implements IReportBack
{
    //........continuation
    RawContactsFunctionTester rawContactFunctionTester = null;

    public TestContactsDriverActivity()
    {
        //........continuation
        rawContactFunctionTester = new RawContactsFunctionTester(this,this);
    }
    protected boolean onMenuItemSelected(MenuItem item)
    {
        //........continuation
        if (item.getItemId() == R.id.menu_show_single_contact_cursor)
        {
            aggregatedContactFunctionTester.listLookupUriColumns();
            return true;
        }
        //new entries start
        if (item.getItemId() == R.id.menu_show_rc_cursor)
        {
            rawContactFunctionTester.showRawContactsCursor();
            return true;
        }
        if (item.getItemId() == R.id.menu_show_rc_all)
        {
            rawContactFunctionTester.showAllRawContacts();
            return true;
        }
        if (item.getItemId() == R.id.menu_show_rc)
        {
            rawContactFunctionTester.showRawContactsForFirstAggregatedContact();
            return true;
        }
        //new entries end
```

```
        return true;
    }
}
```

We have only indicated the new lines you need to add to this driver file, because this is an update file.

As with the aggregated contact URIs, let's first examine the nature of the raw contact URI and what it returns. The signature for the raw contact uri is defined as follows:

```
ContactsContract.RawContacts.CONTENT_URI;
```

If you follow the code path for the function `showRawContactsCursor()`, you will notice that it is using the preceding raw contacts contact URI and is printing out the cursor fields. Go ahead and click the "raw contacts cursor" menu item. This will show that the raw contact cursor has the fields shown in Listing 27–33.

Listing 27–33. *Raw Contacts Cursor Fields*

```
times_contacted;
phonetic_name;
phonetic_name_style;
contact_id;version;
last_time_contacted;
aggregation_mode;
_id;
name_verified;
display_name_source;
dirty;
send_to_voicemail;
account_type;
custom_ringtone;
sync4;sync3;sync2;sync1;
deleted;
account_name;
display_name;
sort_key_alt;
starred;
sort_key;
display_name_alt;
sourceid;
```

Once you know the columns of a raw contact cursor, you may be curious as to see the rows of this table. Go ahead and click "all raw contacts". This will call the method `showAllRawContacts()`. This method will walk the cursor with no `WHERE` clause (so that it can get all the rows) and creates a `RawContact` object for each row and prints it out. You can see these raw contacts both on the screen and LogCat.

Using the columns of the cursor in Listing 27–34, let's see if we can refine our query to retrieve the contacts for a given aggregated contact ID. You can test this by clicking the "raw contacts" menu item. This will look up the first aggregated contact and then issue a raw contact URI with a where clause specifying a value for the `contact_id` column. You can see the results of this both in the UI and also in LogCat.

Although we have explored aggregated contacts and raw contacts, we haven't really retrieved the important parts of a contact, such as the e-mail address and phone number. You'll see how to do this in the next section.

Exploring Raw Contact Data

In the this example, you'll see how we can explore the data values corresponding to raw contacts. We will try to do two things in this exercise around raw contact data:

- Discover all the fields returned by firing off a URI that knows how to read raw contact data.
- Retrieve the data elements for a set of aggregated contacts.

You will need the following new files to test this sample:

- ContactData.java
- ContactDataFunctionTester.java

These files will be presented as we cover the details of this sample in this section. You will also need to update the following files from the previous sample:

- main_menu.xml
- TestContactsDriverActivity.java

The changes you need to make to these files are also covered in this section. The file ContactData.java is there to capture a representative set of a contact data. The source code for this file is given in Listing 27–34.

Listing 27–34. *Contact Data*

```
public class ContactData
{
    public String rawContactId;
    public String aggregatedContactId;
    public String dataId;
    public String accountName;
    public String accountType;
    public String mimetype;
    public String data1;

    public void fillinFrom(Cursor c)
    {
        rawContactId = Utils.getColumnValue(c,"_ID");
        accountName = Utils.getColumnValue(c,ContactsContract.RawContacts.ACCOUNT_NAME);
        accountType = Utils.getColumnValue(c,ContactsContract.RawContacts.ACCOUNT_TYPE);
        aggregatedContactId =
                Utils.getColumnValue(c,ContactsContract.RawContacts.CONTACT_ID);
        mimetype = Utils.getColumnValue(c,ContactsContract.RawContactsEntity.MIMETYPE);
        data1 = Utils.getColumnValue(c,ContactsContract.RawContactsEntity.DATA1);
        dataId = Utils.getColumnValue(c,ContactsContract.RawContactsEntity.DATA_ID);
    }
    public String toString()
    {
```

```
        return data1 + "/" + mimetype
            + "/" + accountName + ":" + accountType
            + "/" + dataId
            + "/" + rawContactId
            + "/" + aggregatedContactId;
    }
}
```

The functionality for this sample is defined in the file `ContactFunctionTester.java`. The code for this file is in Listing 27–35.

Listing 27–35. ***Testing Contact Data***

```
public class ContactDataFunctionTester extends RawContactFunctionTester
{
    public ContactDataFunctionTester(Context ctx, IReportBack target)
    {
        super(ctx, target);
    }
    public void showRawContactsEntityCursor()
    {
        Cursor c = null;
        try
        {
            Uri uri = ContactsContract.RawContactsEntity.CONTENT_URI;
            c = this.getACursor(uri,null);
            this.printCursorColumnNames(c);
        }
        finally
        {
            if (c!=null) c.close();
        }
    }
    public void showRawContactsData()
    {
        Cursor c = null;
        try
        {
            Uri uri = ContactsContract.RawContactsEntity.CONTENT_URI;
            c = this.getACursor(uri,"contact_id in (3,4,5)");
            this.printRawContactsData(c);
        }
        finally
        {
            if (c!=null) c.close();
        }
    }
    protected void printRawContactsData(Cursor c)
    {
        for(c.moveToFirst();!c.isAfterLast();c.moveToNext())
        {
            ContactData dataRecord = new ContactData();
            dataRecord.fillinFrom(c);
            this.mReportTo.reportBack(tag, dataRecord.toString());
        }
    }
}
```

To invoke the public functions from this class, we will need the menu items in Listing 27–36 added to the `main_menu.xml`.

Listing 27–36. *Menu Items to Test Contact Data*

```
<item android:id="@+id/menu_show_rce_data"
    android:title="contact data" />
<item android:id="@+id/menu_show_rce_cursor"
    android:title="contact entity cursor" />
```

The driver activity needs to be changed as shown in listing 27–37 to respond to these menu items and call the public functions of the `ContactDataFunctionTester`.

Listing 27–37. *Updated main activity for testing contact data*

```
public class TestContactsDriverActivity extends DebugActivity
implements IReportBack
{
    public static final String tag="TestContacts";
    ...other testers
    ...add this at the end of these testers
    ContactDataFunctionTester contactDataFunctionTester = null;

    public TestContactsDriverActivity()
    {
        ...add this line at the end of this function
        contactDataFunctionTester = new ContactDataFunctionTester(this,this);
    }
    protected boolean onMenuItemSelected(MenuItem item)
    {
        ....respond to other menu items
        ....Add the following lines
        if (item.getItemId() == R.id.menu_show_rce_cursor)
        {
            contactDataFunctionTester.showRawContactsEntityCursor();
            return true;
        }
        if (item.getItemId() == R.id.menu_show_rce_data)
        {
            contactDataFunctionTester.showRawContactsData();
            return true;
        }
        ...end of new lines
        return true;
    }
}
```

Let's analyze this code and sample now. Android presents a special view called a `RawContactEntity` view to retrieve data from a raw contact table and the corresponding data tables as indicated in section `Contact_entities_view` of this chapter. The URI to access this view is defined in a java helper class. The full Java path for this URI constant is in Listing 27–38.

Listing 27–38. *Raw Entities Content URI*

```
ContactsContract.RawContactsEntity.CONTENT_URI
```

This sample uses this URI to get an idea of the fields that are returned. You can see this set of fields by clicking "contact entity cursor." Listing 27–39 shows what this menu item prints out as the list of columns returned by this cursor.

Listing 27–39. *Contact Entities Cursor Columns*

```
data_version;
contact_id;
version;
data12;data11;data10;
mimetype;
res_package;
_id;
data15;data14;data13;
name_verified;
is_restricted;
is_super_primary;
data_sync1;dirty;data_sync3;data_sync2;
data_sync4;account_type;data1;sync4;sync3;
data4;sync2;data5;sync1;
data2;data3;data8;data9;
deleted;
group_sourceid;
data6;data7;
account_name;
data_id;
starred;
sourceid;
is_primary;
```

Once you know this set of columns, you can narrow down the result set of this cursor by formulating a proper where clause. For example, in the next menu item of this example, we will retrieve the data elements pertaining to the contact IDs 3, 4, and 5. To do this, all you have to do in code is add a `WHERE` clause such as

```
"contact_id in (3,4,5)"
```

and send it along with the cursor. This is exactly what we did in the "contact data" menu item. If you click this item, you will such things as name and e-mail address printed out (you can identify the data element by looking at the MIME type).

Adding a Contact and Its Details

So far, we have only read the contacts. Let's see through an example what it takes to add a contact with a name, e-mail, and phone number.

To write to contacts, you need to request the following permission in the manifest file (see Listing 27–20):

```
android.permission.WRITE_CONTACTS
```

You will need the following new file to test this sample:

- AddContactFunctionTester.java

You will also need to update the following files from the previous sample:

- main_menu.xml
- TestContactsDriverActivity.java

The file AddContactFunctionTester.java is responsible for adding a contact with its details. Listing 27–40 shows the source code for it.

Listing 27–40. *Adding Contacts with Details*

```
Import android.provider.ContactsContract.Data;
//..other imports that you can use eclipse to resolve

public class AddContactFunctionTester extends ContactDataFunctionTester
{
    public AddContactFunctionTester(Context ctx, IReportBack target)
    {
        super(ctx, target);
    }
    public void addContact()
    {
        long rawContactId = insertRawContact();
        this.mReportTo.reportBack(tag, "RawcontactId:" + rawContactId);
        insertName(rawContactId);
        insertPhoneNumber(rawContactId);
        showRawContactsDataForRawContact(rawContactId);
    }
    private void insertName(long rawContactId)
    {
        ContentValues cv = new ContentValues();
        cv.put(Data.RAW_CONTACT_ID, rawContactId);
        cv.put(Data.MIMETYPE, StructuredName.CONTENT_ITEM_TYPE);
        cv.put(StructuredName.DISPLAY_NAME,"John Doe_" + rawContactId);
        this.mContext.getContentResolver().insert(Data.CONTENT_URI, cv);
    }
    private void insertPhoneNumber(long rawContactId)
    {
        ContentValues cv = new ContentValues();
        cv.put(Data.RAW_CONTACT_ID, rawContactId);
        cv.put(Data.MIMETYPE, Phone.CONTENT_ITEM_TYPE);
        cv.put(Phone.NUMBER,"123 123 " + rawContactId);
        cv.put(Phone.TYPE,Phone.TYPE_HOME);
        this.mContext.getContentResolver().insert(Data.CONTENT_URI, cv);
    }
    private long insertRawContact()
    {
        ContentValues cv = new ContentValues();
        cv.put(RawContacts.ACCOUNT_TYPE, "com.google");
        cv.put(RawContacts.ACCOUNT_NAME, "satya.komatineni@gmail.com");
        Uri rawContactUri =
            this.mContext.getContentResolver()
                 .insert(RawContacts.CONTENT_URI, cv);
        long rawContactId = ContentUris.parseId(rawContactUri);
        return rawContactId;
```

```
    }
    private void showRawContactsDataForRawContact(long rawContactId)
    {
        Cursor c = null;
        try
        {
            Uri uri = ContactsContract.RawContactsEntity.CONTENT_URI;
            c = this.getACursor(uri,"_id = " + rawContactId);
            this.printRawContactsData(c);
        }
        finally
        {
            if (c!=null) c.close();
        }
    }
}
```

The only public function is the addContact(). You will need to add the menu indicated in Listing 27–41 to invoke this function.

Listing 27–41. *Menu Item for Adding a Contact*

```
<item android:id="@+id/menu_add_contact"
    android:title="Add Contact" />
```

You will be adding these lines to the main_menu.xml. You will also need to change the driver activity to translate this menu item to the method call of addContact(). Listing 27–42 shows the source code for the driver activity (note this is not a new file but an update to the corresponding file).

Listing 27–42. *Updated Driver Activity to Test Adding a Contact*

```
public class TestContactsDriverActivity extends DebugActivity
implements IReportBack
{
    ...other stuff
    AddContactFunctionTester addContactFunctionTester = null;

    public TestContactsDriverActivity()
    {
        ...other stuff
        addContactFunctionTester = new AddContactFunctionTester(this,this);
    }
    protected boolean onMenuItemSelected(MenuItem item)
    {
        .....other stuff
        if (item.getItemId() == R.id.menu_add_contact)
        {
            addContactFunctionTester.addContact();
            return true;
        }
        return true;
    }
}
```

Now if you click the Add Contact menu item, the code in listing 27–40 (add contact function tester) will do the following:

1. First add a new raw contact for a predefined account using its name and type, represented by the method insertRawContact().

2. Take the raw contact ID, and insert a name record—the insertName() method—in the data table.

3. Take the raw contact ID, and insert a phone number record—the insertPhone() method—in the data table.

Listing 27–40 shows the column aliases used by these methods as they insert records. These columns aliases are repeated here in Listing 27–43 for quick review.

Listing 27–43. *Using Column Aliases for Standard Contact Data Structures*

```
cv.put(Data.RAW_CONTACT_ID, rawContactId);
cv.put(Data.MIMETYPE, StructuredName.CONTENT_ITEM_TYPE);
cv.put(StructuredName.DISPLAY_NAME,"John Doe_" + rawContactId);

cv.put(Data.RAW_CONTACT_ID, rawContactId);
cv.put(Data.MIMETYPE, Phone.CONTENT_ITEM_TYPE);
cv.put(Phone.NUMBER,"123 123 " + rawContactId);
cv.put(Phone.TYPE,Phone.TYPE_HOME);

cv.put(RawContacts.ACCOUNT_TYPE, "com.google");
cv.put(RawContacts.ACCOUNT_NAME, "satya.komatineni@gmail.com");
```

Especially important to know is that constants like Phone.TYPE and Phone.NUMBER actually point to generic data table column names data1 and data2.

Finally, to see a record added, go ahead and click the "add contact" menu option. This will add the record and show you the details of that record by reading it back through the function showRawContactsDataForRawContact(). You will see each of the data fields displayed through the ContactData structure.

Controlling Aggregation

It should be clear by now that clients that update or insert contacts do not explicitly change the contact table. The contact table is updated by triggers that look into the raw contact table and raw contact data table.

Raw contacts that get added or changed, in turn, affect the aggregated contacts in the contacts table. However, you may not want to allow two contacts to be aggregated.

You can control the aggregation behavior of a raw contact by setting the aggregation mode when that contract is created. As you can see from raw contact table columns in Listing 27–33, the raw contact table contains a field called aggregation_mode. The values for these aggregation modes are shown in Listing 27–2 and explained in section titled "Aggregated Contacts."

You can also keep two contacts always apart by inserting rows into a table called agg_exceptions. The URIs needed to insert into this table are defined in the Java class

ContactsContract.AggregationExceptions. The table structure of agg_exceptions is shown in Listing 27–44.

Listing 27–44. *Aggregate Exceptions Table Definition*

```
CREATE TABLE agg_exceptions
(_id INTEGER PRIMARY KEY AUTOINCREMENT,
type INTEGER NOT NULL,
raw_contact_id1 INTEGER REFERENCES raw_contacts(_id),
raw_contact_id2 INTEGER REFERENCES raw_contacts(_id))
```

The type column can hold one of the constants in Listing 27–45.

Listing 27–45. *Aggregation Types in Aggregation Exception Table*

```
TYPE_KEEP_TOGETHER
TYPE_KEEP_SEPARATE
TYPE_AUTOMATIC
```

The type definition and what they indicate is fairly clear. The TYPE_KEEP_TOGETHER says the two raw contacts should never be broken apart. The TYPE_KEEP_SEPARATE says that these raw contacts should never be joined. The TYPE_AUTOMATIC indicates that use the default algorithm to aggregate contacts.

They URI you will use insert, read, and update this table is defined as

```
ContactsContract.AggregationExceptions.CONTENT_URI
```

Constants for the field definitions to work with this table are also available in the Java class ContactsContract.AggregationExceptions.

Impacts of Syncing

So far, we have mainly talked about manipulating the contacts on the device. However, accounts and their contacts typically work hand in hand with syncing. For example, if you have created a Google account on your Android phone, the account will pull all your Gmail contacts and make them available to you on your device.

Every time you add a new contact on the device or a new server account, those contacts will be synced and reflected in both places.

However, we have not covered the syncing API and how it works in this edition of the book. Like contacts, it is a large topic. Knowing how contacts work significantly helps to understand the sync API. Please check our updates at www.androidbook.com.

The nature of a sync also has impacts to deleting contacts on the device. When you delete a contact using the aggregated contact URI, it will delete all its corresponding raw contacts and the data elements of each of those raw contacts. However, Android will only mark them as deleted on the device and expects the background sync to actually sync with the server and then delete the contacts permanently from the device. This cascading of deletes also happens at the raw contact level where the corresponding data elements of that raw contact are deleted.

References

The following annotated references are useful for supporting and enhancing material of this chapter. The last reference URL of this section allows you to download projects developed for this chapter.

- `http://www.google.com/googlephone/AndroidUsersGuide.pdf`: This URL points to the 2.2.1 version of the *Android User's Guide*. You can use this guide to read about the contacts application that allows you manage your contacts. Although we have covered the basic information here on how to use the contacts application, this user's guide is the authority, and you may pick up things that we might have overlooked.
- `http://www.google.com/help/hc/pdfs/mobile/AndroidUsersGuide-30-100.pdf`: You will find Android 3.0 users guide here.
- `http://developer.android.com/resources/articles/contacts.html`: This URL points to an article on the Android site that documents how to use the contacts API. This is the primary documentation on the contacts API from Google.
- `http://www.androidbook.com/item/3585`: Understanding the contacts API is about understanding its table structure. The `ContactsContract` is just a thin wrapper around this basic table structure. The authors have published the various table structures at this URL. You will be able to see the field names, their types, aggregated views, and so on.
- `http://developer.android.com/reference/android/provider/ContactsContract.html`: This URL points to the Javadoc of the entry class for the published contacts contract. You will need this URL often as you code to the contacts API.
- `http://www.netmite.com/android/mydroid/2.0/packages/providers/ContactsProvider/`: Because of the paucity of information on how contacts are treated, you may want to see the source code of the contacts content provider. This URL from Netmite provides access to all the source files of the content provider.
- `http://www.netmite.com/android/mydroid/2.0/packages/apps/Contacts/src/com/android/contacts`: Similarly, this URL points to the source code of the contacts application. If you want to know how the aggregated contact is painted or updated, this is your ticket to research.
- `http://www.androidbook.com/item/3537`: If you were to go through the source code of the preceding two URLs, you will see that Java generics will generously befuddle you. This URL contains the summarization of Java generics that could be of some help.
- `http://www.androidbook.com/projects`: You can use this URL to download the test project dedicated for this chapter. The name of the ZIP file is `ProAndroid3_ch20_TestContacts.zip`.

Summary

In this chapter, we unraveled the structure of contacts on the Android platform. You can use this information to read or update contacts through the public contact API.

Although we have covered the contacts API extensively in this chapter, we haven't covered the mode of working with content provides in a batch mode to add or update contacts in a batch mode. Android SDK uses a class called `ContentProviderOperation` to batch up database inserts, updates, and deletes as an optimization for individual updates.

The batch mode is much more important for sync providers as a large number of contacts get added and updated. For queries and occasional updates, what we have covered in this chapter is sufficient. However, do check with `www.androidbook.com` for updates on this topic.

Chapter 28

Deploying Your Application: Android Market and Beyond

Creating a great application that people will love is one thing, but you also need an easy way for people to find and download it. Google created Android Market for this purpose. From an icon right on the device, users can click straight into the Market to browse, search, review, and download applications. Users can also access Android Market over the Internet to do those same things, although the downloading is not to the computer but rather is sent to the user's device. Many applications are free; for those that are not, the Market provides payment mechanisms for easy purchasing.

The Market is even accessible from intents inside of applications, making it easy for applications to reach out to the Market to guide the user into getting what they need for your application to be successful. For example, when a new version of your application becomes available, you can make it easy for the user to go straight to that Market page to get or buy the new version. Android Market is not the only way to get applications to devices, however; other channels are popping up on the Internet.

The Android Market application is not available from within the emulator (although hacks exist to make it available). This makes things a little more difficult for a developer. Ideally you will have a device of your own that you can use with Android Market. Android Market is available on the Android Developer Phone, but will not show or download any paid applications. This is one of Google's ways to attempt to keep paid apps from being pirated.

In this chapter, we'll explore how to get you set up for publishing applications to the Market, how to prepare your application for sale through the Market, how you can protect yourself from piracy, how users will find, download, and use your applications, and finally, alternative ways to make your applications available.

Becoming a Publisher

Before you can upload an application to Android Market, you need to become a publisher. To do so, you must create a Developer Account. Once that's done, you will be able to upload your applications to the Market so they can be found and downloaded by users. Google has made the process to get a Developer Account relatively painless, and reasonably priced.

To publish anything, you first need to have a Google account—for example, a `gmail.com` e-mail account. Next, you establish an identity with the Android Market. You do this by going to `http://market.android.com/publish/signup`. You will need to provide a developer name, an e-mail address, a web site address, and a phone number where you can be contacted. You will be able to change these values later, once your account is set up. You will also need to pay the registration fee. This is done via Google Checkout. In order to continue with the transaction, you will be required to log in with a Google account.

One of the options presented to you during the payment process is "Keep my email address confidential." This refers to the current transaction between you and Google Android Market to "purchase" publisher access. If you choose yes, you'll keep your e-mail address secret from Google Android Market. This has nothing to do with keeping your e-mail address secret from buyers of your application. Buyers' ability to see your e-mail address has nothing to do with this option. More on that later.

Next up is the Android Market Developer Distribution Agreement. This is the legal contract between Google and you. It spells out the rules for distributing apps, collecting payments, granting refunds, feedback, ratings, user rights, developer rights, and so on. There's more on these in the "Following the Rules" section of this chapter.

Upon accepting the Agreement, you will be taken to a page commonly called the Developer Console at `http://market.android.com/publish/Home`.

Following the Rules

The Android Market Developer Distribution Agreement (AMDDA) spells out a lot of rules. You might want legal counsel to review the contract before agreeing to it, depending on how seriously you plan to operate within Android Market. This section describes some highlights you might be interested in.

- You have to be a developer in good standing to use the Android Market. This means you must go through the process as described to get registered, you must accept the Agreement, and you must abide by the rules in the Agreement. Breaking the rules could get you barred and your products removed from the Market.

- You can distribute products for free or for a price. The Agreement applies either way. If selling products, you must have a payment processor such as Google Checkout. When Android 2.0 was introduced, Google Checkout was the only way to collect money through the Android Market. It is becoming possible for users to simply charge to their phone bill for downloading applications from Android Market, as announced by T-Mobile in 2009 and AT&T in 2010. PayPal announced integration with the Android Market in October of 2010, but five months later it still isn't an option. This may change in a future release, however.
- Paid apps will incur a transaction fee, and possibly a fee from the device carrier, to be deducted from the sale price. As of January 2011, the transaction fee is 30 percent, so if the sale price is $10, Google collects $3 and you get $7 (assuming no carrier fees).
- It is your responsibility to remit appropriate taxes to your taxing authorities. When you set up your merchant account, you specify the appropriate tax rates to apply to purchases from people in other locations. Google Checkout will collect the appropriate taxes based on how you set up Google Checkout. This money will be provided to you, and you must remit it appropriately. For additional information on sales taxes in the U.S., try `http://biztaxlaw.about.com/od/businesstaxes/f/onlinesalestax.htm` and `www.thestc.com`.
- You are allowed to distribute a free demo version of your application, with an option to pay to unlock the application's full set of features; however, you must collect the payment via an authorized Android Market Payment Processor. You are not allowed to redirect users of your free application to some other payment processor to collect upgrade fees. You are also not allowed to charge a subscription fee for applications distributed through Android Market. Service fees are actually a good way to go if you can, since they help prevent piracy of your application and can improve your overall cash flow. However, applying service fees means you can't sell that version of your application from within Android Market. This feature may be provided in Android Market in the future. You could think of it this way: if you're making money via the Android Market, Google wants its share.
- In February 2011, Google announced in-app billing. This is an add-on SDK that allows an application to charge for digital goods or assets used within the application. A digital asset could be something like a virtual weapon or new levels for a game, or a music or graphics file. The checkout process is the same as for purchasing applications, which means users could pay from their phone bill for these digital assets.

- If your application requires a user to have a login on a web server somewhere, and that web server charges the user a subscription fee, that web server could collect the subscription fee any way it wants to. In this way you have disconnected the subscription fee from the application and it's okay by Google to make the application available in Android Market—as long as your free application is not directing users to the web site. But really, why not just distribute your free Android app from the same web server as the service?
- It seems that you can use alternate payment processors to accept donations from users of your free app, but you cannot create incentives within your app to encourage those donations.
- Refunds are a nasty subject with Android Market. Originally, users had 24 hours to request a refund of the purchase price. Then it was changed to 48 hours. In December 2010 it was changed to 15 minutes! And that's 15 minutes from when the purchase is made, not from when the download has successfully completed. There have been cases where a user hasn't even been able to finish downloading the application and the refund window has passed. Strangely, the AMDDA was not updated in December 2010 to reflect 15 minutes and still said 48 hours. Refunds are not given to users who can preview the product prior to download. This includes ringtones and wallpapers. Google Checkout however, does allow the developer to issue a refund even if the refund window has passed, so users do have a way to get a refund no matter what. But developers don't want to be issuing refunds manually.
- You are required to provide adequate support for your product. If adequate support is not provided, users can request refunds and these will be charged back to you, possibly including handling fees.
- Users get unlimited reinstalls of applications downloaded from the Android Market. If a user does a factory reset of their device, this feature allows them to get all their apps back without having to repurchase.
- Developers agree to protect the privacy and legal rights of users. This includes protecting (securing) any data that might be collected in the process of using the application. It is possible to change the rules regarding users' data protection, but only by displaying and having the user accept a separate agreement between you and that user.

- Your application must not compete with Android Market. Google does not want an application from within Android Market to sell Android products from outside of Android Market, thus bypassing its payment processor. This does not mean that you can't also sell your application through other channels: but your application on Android Market cannot itself be doing the selling of Android products outside of the Android Market.
- Google will assign product ratings to your products. The ratings could be based on user feedback, install rates, uninstall rates, refund rates, and/or a Developer Composite Score. The Developer Composite Score may be calculated by Google using past history across applications, and this could influence the rating of new applications. For this reason, it is important to release good quality applications associated to you, even the free ones. It's not clear that the Developer Composite Score even exists, but if it does there's no way to see yours.
- By selling your application through Android Market, you are granting the user a "non-exclusive, worldwide, perpetual license to perform, display and use the Product on the device." However, it is quite all right for you to write a separate End User License Agreement (EULA) that supersedes this statement. Make this EULA available on your web site, or provide another way for shoppers and users to be able to read it.
- Google requires that you abide by the branding rules for Android. These include restrictions on the use of the word Android, as well as use of the robot graphic, logo, and custom typeface. For more details, go to `www.android.com/branding.html`.

Developer Console

The Developer Console is your landing page for controlling your applications in Android Market. From the Developer Console you can buy an Android development phone, set up a merchant account in Google Checkout (so you can charge for your applications), upload applications, and get information about your uploaded applications. You can also edit your account details including developer name, e-mail address, web address, and phone number. Figure 28–1 shows the Developer Console.

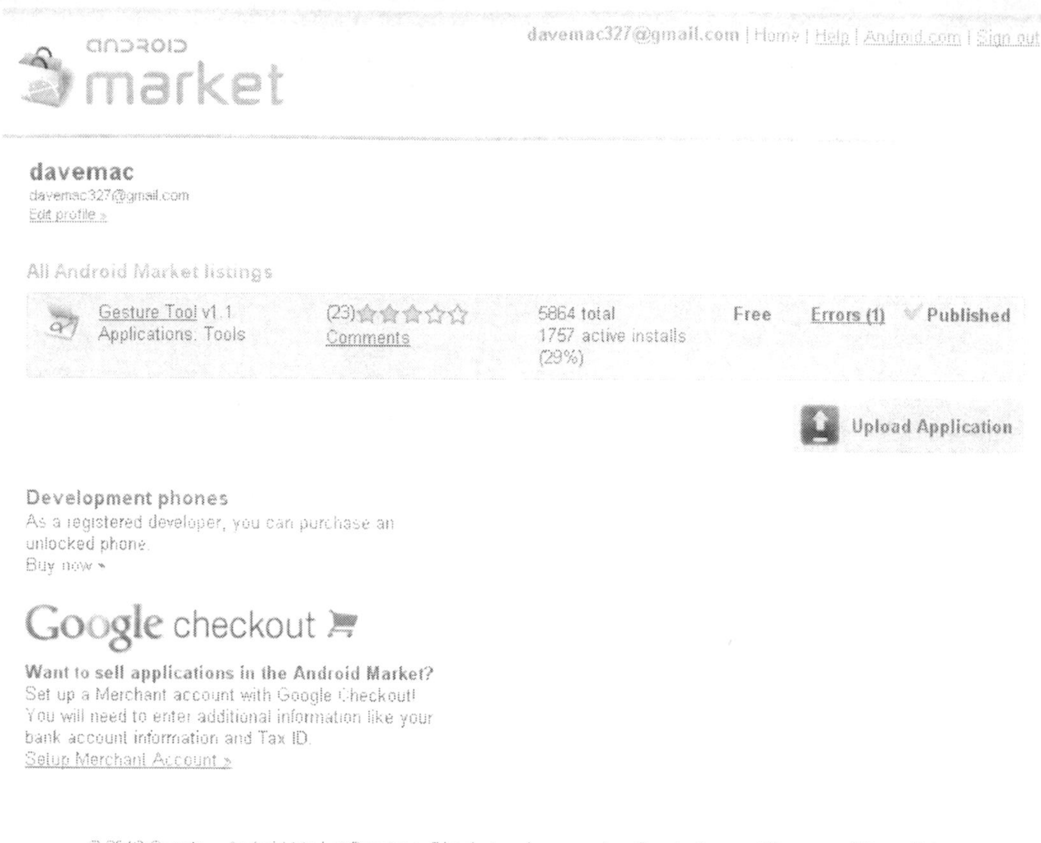

Figure 28–1. *The Android Market Developer Console*

There are now three Android development phones: the Android Developer Phone, the Google Nexus One, and the Google Nexus S. The Android Developer Phone (ADP) was the one-and-only original development phone for Android developers. The ADP is a special device created specifically for Android developers. It is a full-featured device that is unlocked and not tied to any particular carrier. It will accept all SIM cards and comes with a 1GB SD card, a camera, a slider keyboard, and GPS. *Unlocked* means that you can do just about anything to it, including load a new version of the firmware and the Android platform, not just applications. While you can load new versions of firmware on the ADP, it ships with Android 1.6.

You may remember when Google introduced its first phone, called the Nexus One. Built in collaboration with HTC, Google discontinued the Nexus One due to lackluster sales, and then offered it to developers as the second developer phone to clear their inventory. It became very popular, so Google ordered more. The specs of the Nexus One are very good. In the sensor category, it comes with a proximity sensor, light sensor, G-sensor (accelerometers), and a compass. It easily runs Android 2.2 and will most likely support the latest versions of Android for some time. The specification page can be found at www.htc.com/www/product/nexusone/specification.html. On the negative side, the Nexus One does not work with all carriers' 3G signals, so it uses other wireless network types (AT&T and 2G or EDGE).

In December 2010, Google released the Nexus S, but this phone is not available through the Developer Console. It was first released through Best Buy in the U.S., and The Carphone Warehouse in the UK, and could be purchased with or without a carrier contract. Even more advanced and faster than the Nexus One, this phone adds support for a gyroscope sensor, a Near Field Communication (NFC) sensor, and a front-facing camera. It also ships with Android 2.3 (a.k.a. Gingerbread). The specs, complete with videos, can be found at `www.google.com/nexus/#`.

If you want to test out new versions of Android firmware, or the Android platform itself, then you'll need to get a developer phone. Of the three developer phones, your best bet is the Nexus S. One of the nice aspects of the Nexus phones is that they are usually one of the first devices to get Android updates. This is another reason you might choose to go with a Nexus over a commercial phone tied to a carrier. If all you want to do is develop applications and not mess with the Android OS itself, the commercial phones can do the job for you. Any Android device can be connected to your workstation to do development and testing work. You'll want to pay attention to the hardware specs though. Not all phones get upgraded to the latest version of Android, especially the less powerful ones.

If you do not set up a merchant account using Google Checkout, you will be unable to charge for your products in the Android Market. Setting up a merchant account is not difficult. Click the link from the Developer Console, fill out the application, agree to the Terms of Service, and you're all set. You will need to provide a US Federal tax ID (EIN), a credit card number plus a US Social Security Number (SSN), or just a credit card number. The tax information is used to verify your credit status to ensure timely deposits. The credit card information is used to handle chargebacks due to buyer disputes when there are insufficient funds in your Google Checkout account. You can also supply bank account information to enable electronic funds transfers from the proceeds of your sales. Note that Google Checkout is a service for more than just Android Market. Therefore, do not get confused by the transaction fee information for Google Checkout for non-Android Market sales. The 30 percent mentioned previously is the transaction fee rate for Android Market. There is also additional Google Checkout transaction fee information for non-Android Market sales and those do not apply to Android Market.

Uploading and monitoring your applications are probably the main functions of the Developer Console that you will use. We'll discuss uploading applications later in this chapter. For monitoring, the Market provides tools to see how your application is doing in terms of total downloads, and how many users still have it installed. You can see the overall rating of your apps in terms of 0 to 5 stars, and how many people have submitted a rating. The Developer Console allows you to republish your application—for upgrades, for example—or to unpublish the application. Unpublishing does not remove it from devices, nor does it even necessarily remove it from the Google servers, especially if it's a paid app. A user who has paid for your application and who has uninstalled it, but not requested a refund, is allowed to reinstall it later even if you've unpublished it. The only way it is truly unavailable to users is if Google pulls it due to violation of the rules. In March 2011, Google added charts and graphs to the Developer Console so you can see how your application is doing in different versions of Android, on different devices, in different countries and in different languages.

Users can submit comments in addition to rating your application. It is in your best interest to read the comments in order to address any problems quickly. Included with a comment is the user's rating of your app, a name of the user as typed by them, and the date of the comment. Unfortunately, there is no way to reply to commenters directly, or even comment on the comment. In an extreme case, where a comment is particularly harmful or inappropriate, you can contact Google support by starting here: http://market.android.com/support/

You can also look at errors that were generated by your application and see application freezes and crashes. Figure 28–2 shows the Application Error Reports screen.

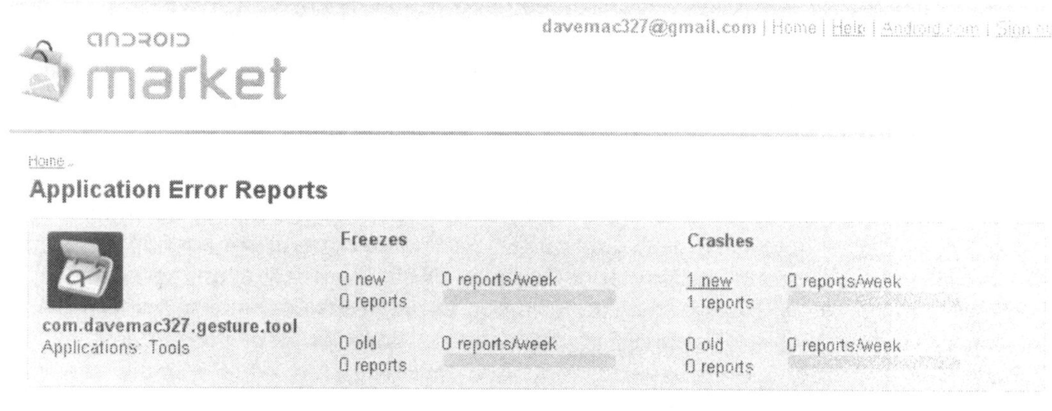

Figure 28–2. *The Application Error Reports screen*

Drilling into the details of a crash report, you can see the stack trace of the crash, as well as which type of device was running the application and the time of the crash. But as with the user comments, you cannot communicate back to the user who experienced the problem to get additional details, or to help them get the issue resolved. You have to hope that the affected users will get in touch with you through e-mail or your web site. Otherwise, you'll just have to figure out from the crash report what went wrong and try to fix it.

There's one more feature of the Developer Console you may need to use: the Help portion of the web site. The Help button is in the upper right corner. Clicking it takes you to a Help web site that has a lot of decent documentation on how to use Android

Market, and it also has a forum where you can search for questions and answers, and post your own. For example, the forum is where you can read up on the latest refund policies, issues, and complaints. If the forum is not helpful, there is a Contacting Support link that will take you to a page where you can send a message specifically to Google for help.

We've now introduced you to some of the nice features of the Developer Console, but you probably want to get into the most useful part, which is getting your applications into the Android Market so users can find them and download them. But before we do that, let's go over how to prepare your application for upload and sale.

Preparing Your Application for Sale

There are quite a few things to think about and do to take an application from code complete to Android Market. This section will help you through those items.

Testing for Different Devices

With more and more Android devices becoming available, and each one potentially having some new hardware configuration, it is very important that you test for those devices you want to support. The ideal case would be to get access to one of each type of device to test your application on. That's an expensive proposition. The next best choice is to configure Android Virtual Devices (AVDs) for each type of device, specifying the appropriate hardware configuration, then testing with the emulator and each AVD. Some device manufacturers make Android packages available that are specific to their devices, so check out their web sites for download options. The Android SDK provides the `Instrumentation` class to assist with testing, as well as the UI/Application Exerciser Monkey. These tools will help you do automated testing so you don't spend forever testing your application. Before you begin testing, you probably want to remove any testing artifacts that you no longer need from your code and from `/res`. You want your application to be as small as possible and to run as quickly as possible with the least amount of memory.

Supporting Different Screen Sizes

When Android SDK 1.6 came out, developers had to contend with new screen sizes. In order to run on the new smaller size, you must set a specific `<supports-screens>` element as a child element of `<manifest>` within the `AndroidManifest.xml` file. Without this new tag specifying that your application supports the small screen size, your application will not be visible in Market to devices that have a small screen. Of course this means that your application needs to be compiled against Android SDK 1.6 or newer. If you want your application to run on devices still using Android SDK 1.5, you'll need to be sure you don't take advantage of any new APIs that were introduced with Android SDK 1.6 or later. Then test against AVDs for older devices as well as newer devices. To support different screen sizes, you may need to create alternate resource files under /res. For example, for files in /res/layout, you may need to create corresponding files in /res/layout-small to support small screens. This does not mean you must also create corresponding files in /res/layout-large and /res/layout-normal, since Android will look in /res/layout if it can't find what it needs in a more specific resource directory such as /res/layout-large. Remember, too, that you can have combinations of qualifiers for these resource files; for example, /res/layout-small-land would contain layouts for small screens in landscape mode. We talked about this in Chapter 6. Supporting small screens probably means creating alternate versions of drawables such as icons, too. For drawables, you may need to create alternate resource directories, taking into account screen resolution as well as screen size.

Tablets of course go in the opposite direction in terms of screen size, using the label "xlarge". The same <supports-screen> tag as before is used to specify if your application will run on extra large screens, and the attribute to use inside of this tag is android:xlargeScreens. In some cases, you may have a tablet-only application, in which case you would specifically indicate that for the other sizes, their attribute value is "false".

Preparing AndroidManifest.xml for Uploading

Your AndroidManifest.xml file may need to be tweaked a little bit before you can upload it to Android Market. ADT normally puts the android:icon attribute in the <application> tag, and not in <activity> tags. If you have more than one activity that can be launched, you'll want to specify separate icons for each activity so the user can more easily tell them apart. But you'll still need an icon specified in <application>, which also serves as the default activity icon for any activities that don't specify their own icon. Your application will work fine on devices and in the emulator with the android:icon only specified in the <activity> tags, but when Android Market inspects your application's .apk file when uploading, it looks for icon information in the <application> tag. Android Market also prevents uploading your application if the package name you've used starts with com.google, com.android, android, or com.example, but hopefully you didn't use one of those in your application.

There are many other compatibilities to consider as you test your application against device configurations. Some devices have cameras, some don't have physical keyboards, and some have trackballs instead of directional pads. Use <uses-configuration> and <uses-feature> tags in your AndroidManifest.xml file as needed to define what hardware/platform requirements your application has. Android Market will enforce this and not let your application be shown to a user on a device that won't support your application. Note that these tags are different and separate from the <uses-permission> tags of the AndroidManifest.xml file. While the user's device may come equipped with a camera, that doesn't mean the user wants to grant your application permission to use it. At the same time, declaring that your application needs permission to use the camera does not tell Android Market that your application requires a camera on the device. In most cases, you would end up with both tags in your AndroidManifest.xml file, for specifying that a camera is required, and for specifying that permission to use the camera is required. But not all features require permission, so it is in your best interest to specify the features you need.

There is another big difference between `<uses-permissions>` and `<uses-feature>`: the `<uses-feature>` tag can say that your application requires that feature, or that your application can function without it. That is, there is an attribute called `android:required` that can be set to either `true` or `false` and by default it's `true`. For example, your application may take advantage of Bluetooth if it's available, but will work just fine if it is not. Therefore, in the manifest file, you'd have something like this:

```
<uses-feature android:name="android.hardware.bluetooth" android:required="false" />
```

Within your application's code, you should make a call to the `PackageManager` to find out if Bluetooth is available or not, which you could do with the following:

```
boolean hasBluetooth = getPackageManager().hasSystemFeature(
                PackageManager.FEATURE_BLUETOOTH);
```

Then take appropriate action in your application if Bluetooth is not there. The Android documentation can be confusing in this area. If you look at the Developer Guide page for `<uses-feature>`, you will not see as many features as are described on the `PackageManager` reference page, which defines a `FEATURE_*` constant for each available feature.

The `<uses-configuration>` tag is a little different. It specifies what sort of keyboard, touchscreen, and/or navigational controls the device must have. But instead of being independent choices such as `<uses-feature>`, you would put the combinations of configuration choices together into what your application requires. For example, if your application requires a five-way navigation control (i.e., a D-pad or a trackball) and a touchscreen (using either a stylus or a finger), you would specify two tags as follows:

```
<uses-configuration android:reqFiveWayNav="true" android:reqTouchScreen="stylus" />
<uses-configuration android:reqFiveWayNav="true" android:reqTouchScreen="finger" />
```

Localizing Your Application

If your application will be used in other countries, you might want to consider localizing it. This is relatively easy to do technically. Finding someone to do the localizing is another matter. From the technical point of view, you simply create another folder under `/res`—for example, `/res/values-fr` to hold a French version of `strings.xml`. Take your existing `strings.xml` file, translate the string values to the new language, and save the new translated file under the new resource folder using the same file name as the original file. The same technique works for the other types of resource files—for example, drawables and menus. Images and colors may work better for your users if they are different for different countries or cultures. For this reason, it is a good idea to not use true color names for your resource names for colors. In the online documentation for colors, it is common to see something like this:

```
<color name="solid_red">#f00</color>
```

This means that in your code or other resource files, you're referring to the color by the actual name of the color, in this case, solid_red. In order to localize the color to something more appropriate for the other country or culture, it would be better to use a color name such as accent_color1 or alert_color. In English, red might be the appropriate color value to use while in Spanish it might be better to use a shade of yellow. Because a color name like alert_color does not reveal the actual color that you're using, it is less confusing when you want to change the actual color value to something else. At the same time, you can design a pleasing color scheme, with base colors and accent colors, and be more confident that you're using the correct colors in the correct places.

Menu choices might need to be changed in different countries, using fewer or more menu items, or be organized differently, depending on where the application is being used. Menus are typically stored under `/res/menu`. If you are faced with this situation, you are probably better off putting all your string text into `strings.xml`, or other files located under the `/res/values` directory, and using string IDs in the appropriate resource files everywhere else. This makes it far less likely that you will miss translating a string value in some obscure resource file. Your language translation work is then limited to the files under `/res/values`.

Preparing Your Application Icon

Shoppers and your users will see your application's icon and label prominently in both Android Market and on their device once they've downloaded it. Please take special care to create good icons and good labels for your application and its activities. Localize them as necessary or desired. And remember that for different screen sizes, your icons may need to be tweaked to look good. Check out what other developers have done with their icons, especially those applications in the same category as your application. You want your application to get noticed, so it's better not to blend in with all the others. At the same time, you want your icon and label to work well on a device when surrounded by lots of other application icons that do other things. You don't want a user to be confused about what your application does, so make the icon representative of the functionality of your application.

When creating any image for your application, but especially your icon, you need to consider the screen density of the target device. Density means the number of pixels per inch. A small screen usually has low density, meaning fewer pixels per unit of distance, whereas a large screen is often higher density. For a low-density screen, making an icon appear to be the right size means making the icon with fewer pixels, typically 36x36. For a high-density screen, you will probably choose an icon with 72x72 pixels. The medium-density icon will usually be of size 48x48 pixels. And for extra-high-density it's 96x96 pixels.

Considerations for Making Money From Apps

If you are selling your application for a price, you have some other considerations to think about. Do you offer separate free and paid applications, requiring you to build and manage two applications? Or do you keep one code base and use some sort of technique to tell if this application was paid for or not? No matter which approach you take, how do you protect your application from being copied and installed on other devices for other people? Due to security vulnerabilities in phones, and due to the ability of certain people to get inside devices, foolproof guarantees of copy protection are extremely difficult to manage.

One technique for maintaining a single code base, but allowing for separate free and paid modes, is to take advantage of the `PackageManager`:

```
this.getPackageManager().checkSignatures(mainAppPkg, keyPkg)
```

This method compares the signatures of the two named packages and returns `PackageManager.SIGNATURE_MATCH` if they both exist and are the same. The package names must be different for each app to coexist in Android Market, but that's fine. In your code, when you need to decide whether or not to allow functionality, you can call this method and provide the package name of your main application as well as the package name of your unlocking application. You then make the unlocking application a paid app in Android Market. If the user buys the unlocking application and downloads it to their device, the main application will then get a signature match and unlock the extra functionality. A less clean way to deal with a single code base is to use source code versioning systems to configure appropriate sharing of common elements, and build scripts to handle creating the free and paid versions of your application.

Another way that you can make money from Android apps is with in-app advertising. There are many opportunities for embedding ads in your app. A couple of common examples are AdMob and AdSense. The process is basically to incorporate their SDK into your application, figure out where and when to display ads in your app, add the `INTERNET` permission to your app (so the ad SDK can get to the ads to display), and you get paid as users click on the ads. Your app can be free, so it's easier to get it into Android Market, plus you don't need to worry as much about piracy. Many developers report making some decent money from ads.

Another new feature introduced in February 2011 is Buyer's Currency. Prior to this time, buyers had to pay in the currency of the seller, which could easily get confusing for buyers who had a hard time converting from the seller's currency amount to their own. It also meant that a seller could only really have one price for the world. Now that the seller can specify a price for a country, not only can the selling price be higher or lower in other countries, but the buyers' experience is much nicer and more convenient.

Directing Users Back to the Market

Android has introduced a new URI scheme to help facilitate finding applications in Android Market: `market://`. For example, if you want to direct your users to the Market to locate a needed component, or to upsell to an additional app that unlocks features in your application, you would do something shown here, where `MY_PACKAGE_NAME` would be replaced by your real package name:

```
Intent intent = new Intent(Intent.ACTION_VIEW,
        Uri.parse("market://search?q=pname:MY_PACKAGE_NAME"));
startActivity(intent);
```

This will launch the Market app on the device and take the user to that package name. The user can then choose to download or buy the application. Note that this scheme does not work in a normal web browser. In addition to searching using package name (pname), you can search by developer name using `market://search?q=pub:\"Fname Lname\"` or against any of the public fields (application title, developer name, and application description) in Android Market using `market://search?q=<querystring>`.

If we combine what we've just learned with the technique in the previous section, our code could look for the unlocking package on the device. If we don't find it, we could prompt the user to see if they want to go get the unlocking app. If they answer yes, we invoke an intent, which opens the Market app and takes the user straight to our unlocking app to be purchased and downloaded.

The Android Licensing Service

The way that Android apps are constructed unfortunately makes them targets for piracy. It is possible to make copies of Android apps that can then be distributed to other devices. So how can you ensure that users who have not purchased your application cannot run it? The Android team has created something called the License Verification Library (LVL) to meet this need. Here's how it works.

If your application was downloaded via Android Market, then there must be a copy of the Android Market app on the device. In addition, the Android Market app has elevated permissions to be able to read values from the device such as the user's Google account name, the IMSI, and other information. The Android Market app has been modified, going back to Android version 1.5, to respond to a license verification request from an application. You make calls into the LVL from your application, LVL communicates with the Android Market app, the Android Market app communicates with Google servers, and your application gets an answer back indicating whether or not this user on this device is licensed to use your application. There are settings under your control to decide what to do if the network is unavailable. A full description of the process of implementing LVL can be found at http://developer.android.com/guide/publishing/licensing.html.

One thing to be aware of though is that the LVL mechanism is subject to hacking. If someone can get to your application's apk file, they can disassemble the app and then patch it if they know where to look for the return value from the LVL call. If you use the obvious pattern of a `switch` statement after getting the response from LVL, to branch to the appropriate logic based on the return code, a hacker can simply force a successful return code value and they own your app. For this reason, the Android team highly recommends that you implement obfuscation of your app to hide the part of your application where you check the return code from LVL. This gets fairly complicated as you can imagine.

With Android 2.3, Google has provided some support for obfuscation in the form of the ProGuard feature. When you set the target build of your application to 2.3 or later, your application will automatically get a proguard.cfg file. By configuring ProGuard using this file, you can tell ADT to obfuscate your code when building a production version of your apk file. You can also configure ant to obfuscate using ProGuard if you use ant to do your builds. To turn on obfuscation, you need to set the `proguard.config` property in the application's default.properties file to the location of the proguard.cfg file. When ProGuard does its thing, you'll get a file called `mapping.txt` along with your apk file. Hang onto this file because you will need it to de-obfuscate a stack trace from your application.

Preparing Your .apk File for Uploading

To get your tested application ready for uploading—that is, to create the .apk file to upload— you need to do the following things (all covered in Chapter 10):

1. Create (if you haven't already) a production certificate with which to sign your application.
2. If you're using maps, replace the MAP API key in `AndroidManifest.xml` with your production MAP API key. If you forget to do this, none of your users will be able to see maps.
3. Export your application by right-clicking on your project in Eclipse, choosing Android Tools ➤ Export Unsigned Application Package, and choosing an appropriate file name. It is convenient to give this file a temporary name, because when you run zipalign in step 5, you need to provide an output file name and that should be your production .apk file name.
4. Run `jarsigner` on your new .apk file to sign it with the production certificate from step 1.
5. Run `zipalign` on your new .apk file to adjust any uncompressed data to the appropriate memory boundaries for better performance at runtime. This is where you will provide the final filename for your application's .apk file.
6. Android now provides an Export Signed Application Package option in Eclipse, which uses a wizard to do steps 3, 4 and 5.

Uploading Your Application

Uploading is easy to do, but takes some preparation. Before you begin an upload, there are some things you will need to have ready and decisions you have to make. This section covers that preparation and those decisions. Then when you've got everything you need, go to the Developer Console and choose Upload Application. You'll be prompted to supply lots of information about your application, the Market will run some processing of your application and the information, and then your application will be ready to publish to the Market.

The previous section covered preparing your application .apk file for uploading. Making your application attractive to shoppers requires some marketing on your part. You need good descriptions of what it is and does, and you need good images so shoppers understand what they might download.

One of the first items you'll be asked for when uploading an application is screenshots. The easiest way to capture screenshots of your application is to use DDMS. Fire up Eclipse, launch your application in the emulator or on a real device, and then switch Eclipse perspectives to DDMS and the Device view. From within the Device view, select the device where your application is running, and then click on the Screen Capture button (it looks like a little painting in the upper-right corner) or choose it from the View menu. If you have a choice when saving, choose 24-bit color. Android Market will convert your screenshots to compressed JPEG; starting with 24-bit will produce better results than starting with 8-bit color. Choose screenshots that will make your application stand out from the rest, but that also show the important functionality. You must supply at least two screenshots, and you can provide up to eight.

Next up is a high-res application icon. This could be the exact same design as your application icon, but Android Market wants a 512x512 icon image. This is required.

You can provide a promotional graphic as well, but its size is smaller than a screenshot. Although this graphic is optional, it is a good idea to include it. You never know when the graphic could be displayed; without one, you don't know what will be displayed in its place, if anything. One place the Promo Graphic appears is at the top of your application's Details page in Android Market.

The feature graphic is another optional field and is a large 1024x500 in size. This graphic is used in the Featured section of Android Market so you want this to look really good.

The last bit of graphics related to your application is an optional video that you can put out on YouTube and link to from your Android Market page.

Android Market asks for textual information about your application to display to shoppers, including the title, descriptive text, and promotional text. Promotional text can only be provided if you already provided a promotional graphic. Text can be provided in multiple languages, since you can choose to distribute your application to countries all over the world. The graphics mentioned can only be supplied to Android Market once, so if your screenshots look different in different locales, you'll need to consider other ways to make those available to shoppers, perhaps on your own web site. This may change in the future.

If you have written a separate EULA for your users, provide a link to it in your descriptive text so shoppers can view it prior to downloading your application. Consider that shoppers will likely use search to locate applications, so be sure to put appropriate words into your text to maximize your hit rate on searches related to your application's functionality. Finally, it's worthwhile to put a short comment in the text that says to e-mail you if the user runs into problems. Without this simple prompt, people are more likely to leave a negative comment, and a negative comment really limits your ability to troubleshoot and solve the problem, as compared to an e-mail exchange with the affected user.

One drawback to the user comments mechanism described earlier is that it does not distinguish the version of your application. If negative reviews are received against version 1 and you release version 2 with everything fixed, the reviews from version 1 are still there and shoppers may not realize that those comments don't apply to the new version. When releasing a new version of an application, the application rating (number of stars) does not get reset, either. Partly for this reason, Google started providing a Recent Changes text field where you can describe what's new in this release. This is where you could indicate that a certain problem has been fixed, or tell what the new features are.

There's also a separate Promo Text field which only has 80 characters. When your app is shown at the top of a list in Android Market, it's the Promo Graphic and the Promo Text that get displayed here. It's definitely a good idea to supply these.

One of your responsibilities when writing the text for your application is to disclose the permissions that are required. These are the same permissions as set in the `<uses-permission>` tags of your `AndroidManifest.xml` file within your application. When the user downloads your application to their device, Android will check the `AndroidManifest.xml` file and ask the user about all of the uses-permission requirements before completing the install. So you might as well disclose this upfront. Otherwise you risk negative reviews from users surprised that an application requires some permission that they are not prepared to grant. Not to mention the refunds, which also count against your Developer Composite Score. Similar to permissions, if your application requires a certain type of screen, a camera, or other device feature, this should be disclosed in your text descriptions of your application. As a best practice, you should not only disclose what permissions and features your application needs, but what your application will do with them. You should answer the user's question in advance: why does this app require X?

When uploading your application, you will need to choose an application type and a category. As these values change with time we won't list them here, but it's easy to go to the Upload Application screen to see what they are.

Next you set the price of your application. By default the price is "Free," and you must have previously set up a Merchant Account in Google Checkout if you want to charge for your application. Setting the right price for an application is tricky, unless you've got some sophisticated market research capabilities, and even then it's still tricky. Prices set too high could turn people off, and you risk the effects of refunds if people don't feel the price was worth it. Prices set too low could also turn people off because they might think it's a cheap application.

Android Market provides an option to set copy protection on applications when you are uploading them. The Market takes care of applying this copy protection for you, but note that the copy protection will make your application use more device memory. It is also not fool-proof, and there are no guarantees that your application cannot be copied off of a device. Since the copy protection method is being deprecated, you probably want to consider additional or alternative ways to prevent pirating of your application, such as the Android Licensing Service described earlier.

In late 2010, Google introduced an application rating scheme. The idea is to give consumers an idea of the appropriateness of an application for certain age groups. Unfortunately, half of the age groups have the word "teen" in them. The ratings are All, Pre-teen, Teen, and Mature. Choosing the right level depends on the content in your application and how much of that content there is. Google has rules about location-awareness and posting or publishing locations. It's best to read the rules for yourself here: www.google.com/support/androidmarket/bin/answer.py?hl=en&answer=188189.

One of the last decisions to make before uploading your application is to choose the locations and carriers for your application to be visible to. By choosing All, your application will be available everywhere. However, you may want to restrict distribution geographically or by carrier. Depending on what functionality is in your application, you may need to restrict by location in order to comply with US export law. You may choose to restrict your application by carrier if your application has compatibility issues with certain carrier's devices or policies. To see carriers, click on a country link and the available carriers for that country will be displayed, allowing you to choose the ones you want. Choosing All also means that any new locations or carriers that Google adds will automatically see your application with no intervention from you.

Even though your developer profile contains your contact information, you can set different information when uploading each application. The Market asks for the web site, e-mail address, and phone number as contact information related to this application. You must supply at least one of these so buyers can get support, but you don't need to supply all three. It is a good idea to not use your personal e-mail address here, just as you probably wouldn't really want to give your personal phone number out. When you've made millions of dollars from selling your application, you'll want to let someone else receive and deal with the e-mails from users. By setting up an application-support type of e-mail address in advance, you can easily separate the support e-mails from your personal e-mails.

With all these decisions made, you must then attest that your application abides by Android's Content Guidelines (basically no nasty stuff), and make a second attestation that the software is okay for export from the United States. US export laws apply because Google's servers are located inside the US, even if you are outside of the US, and even if both you and your customer are outside of the US. Remember that you can always choose to distribute your application through other channels. When all your information is in and your graphics uploaded, go ahead and press the Save button. This will prepare everything for your application to be ready to "go live."

You can then publish your application by clicking on the Publish button. Android Market will perform some checks on your application, for instance checking your application's certificate for the expiration date. If all goes well, your application will now be available for download. Congratulations!

User Experience on Android Market

Android Market has been available on devices for some time now, and as of February 2011 is available over the Internet. Developers don't have any control over how Android Market works, other than to provide good text and graphics for their application's listing in the Market. Therefore, the user experience is pretty much up to Google. From a device, a user can search by keyword, look at top downloaded applications (both free and paid), featured applications, or new applications, or browse by categories. Once they find an application they want they simply select it, which pops up an item details screen allowing them to install it or buy it. Buying will take the user to Google Checkout to conduct the financial part of the transaction. Once downloaded, the new application shows up with all the other applications.

From the Internet web site for Android Market (http://market.android.com), the user interface looks about the same, albeit much larger than most device screens. One difference is that the web-based Android Market expects the user to login to their Google account to use the Market. This allows Google to connect your web experience on Android Market to your actual device. This means two things: when using the web site, Android Market knows what applications are already installed on your device, and when you make a purchase on the Android Market web site, the download can be sent to your device and not to whatever computer you happen to be browsing on.

Android Market has an option to view downloaded applications in My Downloads. This area contains all installed apps, and any apps that you've purchased, even if you've removed them (perhaps you removed them just to make room for other applications). This means you could delete a paid app from your phone, then reinstall it later without having to repurchase it. Of course, if you opted for a refund, the app will not show up in My Downloads. Also, free apps that you remove from your device will also not show up in My Downloads. The list of apps in My Downloads is tied to your Google Account used for the device. This means you could switch to a new physical device and still have access to all the apps you've paid for. But beware. Since you might have multiple identities with Google, you must use the exact same identity as before to get your apps on a new device. When viewing apps in My Downloads, any that have upgrades available will indicate this and allow you to get the upgrade.

Android Market filters applications available to users. It does this in a number of ways. Users in some countries can only see free applications because of the commerce legalities involved for Google in that country. Google is trying hard to overcome commerce hurdles so all paid apps will be available everywhere. Until that time comes, users in some countries will be unable to access paid apps. Users with devices running older versions of Android will not be able to see applications that require a newer version of the Android SDK. Users with device configurations that are not compatible with the requirements of the application (expressed via <uses-feature> tags in the `AndroidManifest.xml` file) will not be able to see those applications. For example, applications not specifically supporting small screens cannot be seen in Android Market by users on devices with small screens. This filtering is mostly intended to protect users from downloading applications that will not work on their device.

If you are purchasing apps in Android Market from other countries, your transaction may be subject to currency conversion, which can also carry an additional fee. Unless of course the seller has specified pricing in your local currency. You're really purchasing using the Google Checkout from the seller's country. Android Market will display an approximate amount but the actual charges could vary, depending on when the transaction is placed, and with which payment processor. Buyers may notice a pending transaction against their account for a small amount (for example US$1). This is done by

Google to ensure that the payment information provided is correct, and this pending charge will not actually go through.

A few web sites are available that mirror Android Market. Shoppers can search, browse categories, and find out about Android Market applications over the Internet without having a device. This gets around the filtering that Android Market does based on your device configuration and location. However, this does not get apps onto your device. Examples of these mirror sites are `www.cyrket.com`, `www.androlib.com`, and `www.androidzoom.com`.

Beyond Android Market

Android Market is not the only game in town. You are not forced into using the Android Market at all. You should consider utilizing other channels of distribution, not only to make your app available to more people in more countries, but also to take advantage of other payment processors and opportunities to make money.

There are Android app stores completely separate from Android Market. Examples of these are `www.andappstore.com`, `http://slideme.org`, `www.getjar.com`, and `www.androidgear.com`. Amazon is launching an Android App Store. From these sites you can search, browse, find out about apps, and also download apps, either from a device or via a web browser. These sites don't have to abide by Google's rules, including the transaction fees for paid apps and methods of payment. PayPal and other payment processors can be used to purchase apps on these separate sites. These sites also don't restrict by location or device configuration. Some of them provide an Android client that can be installed, or in some cases may come pre-installed on a device. Users can simply launch a browser on their device and find the app they want to download via the web site; when the file is saved to the device, Android knows what to do with it. That is to say, a downloaded .apk file is treated as an Android application. If you click on it in the Download history of the browser (not to be confused with My Downloads, covered earlier) you will be prompted to see if you want to install it or not. This freedom means you can set up your own methods of downloading Android applications to users, even from your own web site and with your own payment methods. You must still deal though with collecting any necessary sales tax and remitting those to the appropriate authorities.

While not restricted by Google's rules, these alternate methods of app distribution may not offer the same sort of buyer protections that are found in Android Market. It may be possible to purchase an application through an alternate market that will not work on the buyer's device. The buyer may also be responsible for creating backups, in case they lose the application from their device, or for transferring applications if they switch to a new device.

These other markets allow you to make money on the sale of each app, which is very similar to what you get from Android Market. You've also got the ability within these other markets to implement alternate payment mechanisms. You can of course implement ads as we described above and make money that way. You can also embed other payment mechanisms right into your application. For example, PayPal introduced a payment library for Android apps (see http://www.x.com). With it you could allow users to purchase add-ons, content or upgrades from right inside your app. They could make donations too. You could implement a mobile store using PayPal for checkout.

Remember that Google does not restrict developers from selling their applications in multiple markets at the same time as they sell through Android Market. So consider all your options to make the most of your efforts.

References

Here are some helpful references to topics you may wish to explore further.

- `http://developer.android.com/guide/topics/manifest/manifest-intro.html`. This is the Developer Guide page to the AndroidManifest.xml file, with descriptions of how to use the supports-screen, uses-configuration and uses-feature tags.
- `http://developer.android.com/guide/practices/screens_support.html`. This is the Developer Guide page called Supporting Multiple Screens and contains lots of good information on dealing with different sizes and densities of screens.
- `http://developer.android.com/guide/practices/ui_guidelines/icon_design.html`. This is the Developer Guide page called Icon Design Guidelines and contains lots of good information on designing effective icons for your application.
- `http://android-developers.blogspot.com/2010/09/securing-android-lvl-applications.html` and `http://android-developers.blogspot.com/2010/09/proguard-android-and-licensing-server.html`. A couple of blog posts on how to use the License Verification Library (LVL) in ways that prevent piracy.
- `http://developer.android.com/guide/market/billing/index.html`. This is the documentation for the in-app billing module.

Summary

You are now equipped to take on the world with your Android applications! We've shown you how to get yourself ready, how to get your application ready, how to publish, and how users will find, download and use your application.

Chapter 29

Fragments for Tablets and More

Up until this chapter, we've covered topics that are common to all versions of Android. It's amazing to think that Android had only been seen on commercial devices for about two years before the dawn of a new era of Android device: the Android tablet. The Android 3.0 UI is described as being designed from the ground up for tablets. Thankfully, this does not mean you must throw away everything you've learned so far and start over. In fact, *everything* you've learned will help you write Android applications for tablets. What Android 3.0 brings is a set of new concepts and features that you must master to write applications that take advantage of the extra large (xlarge) screen sizes of Android tablets. While most applications written prior to Android 3.0 will work on an Android 3.0 tablet, they won't be optimized for tablets. This chapter starts your learning on these new concepts and features.

One of the new core classes in Android 3.0 is the `Fragment` class, which has several offspring. This chapter will introduce you to the fragment, what it is, how it fits into an application's architecture, and how to use it. Fragments make a lot of interesting things possible that were difficult before. Also interesting is that you can use fragments with older versions of Android because Google released a fragment SDK that works on old Androids. So even if you're not interested in writing applications for tablets, you may find that fragments will make your life easier on non-tablet devices as well.

Let's get started with Android fragments.

What is a Fragment?

This first section will explain what a fragment is and what it does. But first, let's set the stage to see why we need fragments at all. As you learned earlier, an Android application on small screen devices uses activities to show data and functionality to a user, and each activity has a fairly simple, well-defined purpose. For example, an activity might show the user a list of contacts from their address book. Another activity might allow the user to type an e-mail. The Android application is the series of these activities grouped together to achieve a larger purpose, such as managing an e-mail account via the reading and sending of messages. This is fine for a small screen device, but when the user's screen is very large (10 inches or larger), there's room on the screen to do more than just one simple thing. An application might want to let the user view the list of e-mails in their inbox and at the same time show the currently selected e-mail text in another window. Or an application might want to show a list of contacts and at the same time show the currently selected contact in a detail view.

As an Android developer, you know that this functionality could be accomplished by defining yet another layout for the xlarge screen with ListViews and layouts and all sorts of other views. And by "yet another layout" we mean layouts in addition to those you've probably already defined for the smaller screens. Of course you'll want to have separate layouts for the portrait case as well as the landscape case. And with the size of an xlarge screen, this could mean quite a few views for all of the labels and fields and images and so on that you'll need to lay out and then provide code for. If only there were a way to group these view objects together and consolidate the logic for them, so that chunks of an application could be reused across screen sizes and devices, minimizing how much work a developer has to do to maintain their application. And that is why we have fragments.

One way to think of a fragment is as a sub-activity. And in fact, the semantics of a fragment are a lot like an activity. A fragment can have a view hierarchy associated with it, and it has a lifecycle much like an activity's lifecycle. Fragments can even respond to the Back button like activities do. If you were thinking, if only I could put multiple activities together on a tablet's screen at the same time, then you're on the right track. But because it would be too messy to have more than one activity of an application active at the same time on a tablet screen, fragments were created to implement basically that thought. This means that fragments are contained within an activity. Fragments can only exist within the context of an activity; you can't use a fragment without an activity. Fragments can co-exist with other elements of an activity, which means you do *not* need to convert the entire user interface of your activity to use fragments. You can create an activity's layout as before and only use a fragment for one piece of the user interface.

Fragments are not like activities, however, when it comes to saving state and restoring it later. The fragments framework provides several features to make saving and restoring fragments much simpler than the work you need to do on activities.

How you decide when to use a fragment depends on a few considerations, which are discussed next.

When to Use Fragments

One of the primary reasons to use a fragment is so you can reuse a chunk of user interface and functionality across devices and screen sizes. This is especially true with tablets. Think of how much can happen when the screen is as large as a tablet's. It's more like a desktop than a phone, and many of your desktop applications have a multi-pane user interface. As described earlier, you can have a list and a detail view of the selected item on screen at the same time. This is easy to picture in a landscape orientation with the list on the left and the details on the right. But what if the user rotates the device to portrait mode so that now the screen is taller than it is wide? Perhaps you now want the list to be in the top portion of the screen and the details in the bottom portion. But what if this application is running on a small screen and there's just no room for the two portions to be on the screen at the same time? Wouldn't you want the separate activities for the list and for the details to be able to share the logic that you've built into these portions for a large screen? We hope you answered yes. Fragments can help with that.

Let's go back to the rotating orientation example. If you've had to code for orientation changes of an activity, you know that it can be a real pain to save the current state of the activity and to restore the state once the activity has been recreated. Wouldn't it be nice if your activity had chunks that could be easily retained across orientation changes, so you could avoid all the tearing down and recreating every time the orientation changes? Of course it would. Fragments can help with that.

Now imagine that a user is in your activity and they've been doing some work. And imagine that the user interface has changed within the same activity, and now the user wants to go back a step, or two, or three. In an old-style activity, pressing the Back button will take the user out of the activity entirely. With fragments, the Back button can step backwards through a stack of fragments while staying inside the current activity.

Next, think about an activity's user interface where a big chunk of content changes; you'd like to make the transition look smooth, like a polished application. Fragments can do that, too.

Now that you have some idea of what a fragment is and why you'd want to use one, let's dig a little deeper into the structure of a fragment.

The Structure of a Fragment

As mentioned, a fragment is like a sub-activity: it has a fairly specific purpose and almost always displays a user interface. But where an activity is subclassed below `Context`, a fragment is extended from `Object` in package `android.app`. A fragment is *not* an extension of activity. Like Activities however, you will always extend `Fragment` (or one of its subclasses) so you can override its behavior.

A fragment can have a view hierarchy to engage with a user. This view hierarchy is like any other view hierarchy in that it can be created (inflated) from an XML layout specification or created in code. The view hierarchy needs to be attached to the view hierarchy of the surrounding activity if it is to be seen by the user, which you'll get to shortly. The view objects that make up a fragment's view hierarchy are the same sorts of views that are used elsewhere in Android. So everything you know about views applies to fragments as well.

Besides the view hierarchy, a fragment has a bundle that serves as its initialization arguments. Similar to an activity, a fragment can be saved and later restored automatically by the system. When the system restores a fragment, it calls the default constructor (i.e., with no arguments), then restores this bundle of arguments to the newly created fragment. Subsequent callbacks on the fragment have access to these arguments and can use them to get the fragment back to its previous state. For this reason, it is imperative that you

- Ensure there's a default constructor for your fragment class .
- Add a bundle of arguments as soon as you create a new fragment so these subsequent methods can properly setup your fragment, and so the system can restore your fragment properly if necessary.

An activity can have multiple fragments in play at one time, and if a fragment has been switched out with another fragment, the fragment-switching transaction can be saved on a back stack. The back stack is managed by the fragment manager tied to the activity. The back stack is how the Back button behavior is managed. The fragment manager is discussed later in this chapter. What you need to know here is that a fragment knows which activity it is tied to, and from there it can get to its fragment manager. A fragment can also get to the activity's resources through its activity.

Because a fragment can be managed, it has some identifying information about itself, including a tag and an ID. These identifiers can be used to find this fragment later, which helps with reuse.

Also similar to an activity, a fragment can save state into a bundle object when the fragment is being recreated, and this bundle object gets given back to the fragment's `onCreate()` callback. This saved bundle is also passed to `onInflate()`, `onCreateView()`, and `onActivityCreated()`. Note that this is not the same bundle as the one attached as initialization arguments. This bundle is one in which you are likely to store the current state of the fragment, not the values that should be used to initialize it.

A Fragment's Lifecycle

Before you start using fragments in sample applications, you really need understand the lifecycle of a fragment. Why? A fragment's lifecycle is more complicated than an activity's lifecycle, and it's very important to understand *when* you can do things with fragments. Figure 29–1 shows the lifecycle of a fragment.

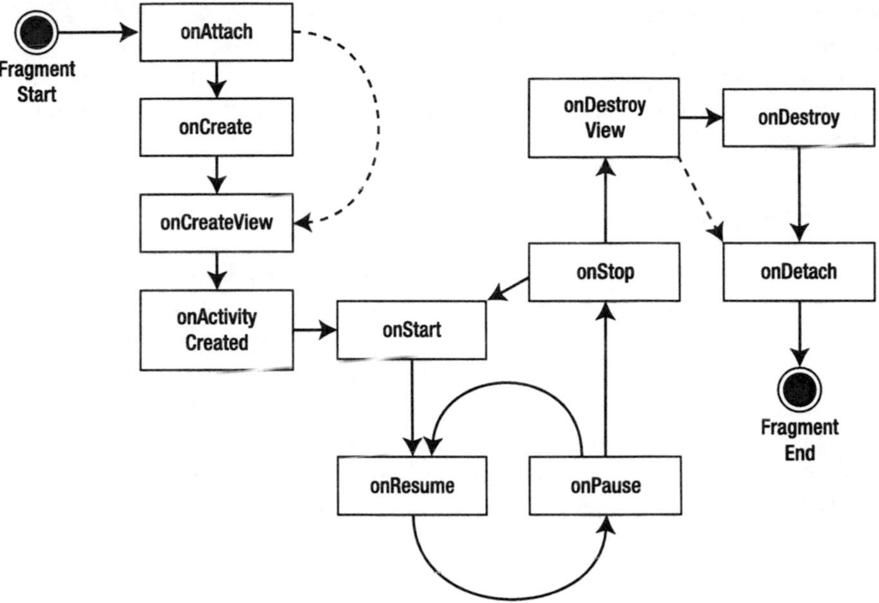

Figure 29–1. *Lifecycle of a fragment*

If you compare this to Figure 2-15 (the lifecycle for an activity), you'll notice several differences, due mostly to the interaction required between an activity and a fragment. A fragment is very dependent on the activity in which it lives and can go through multiple steps while its activity goes through one.

At the very beginning, a fragment is instantiated. It now exists as an object in memory. The first thing that is likely to happen is that initialization arguments will be added to your fragment object. This is definitely true in the situation where the system is recreating your fragment from a saved state. When the system is restoring a fragment from saved state, the default constructor is invoked, followed by the attachment of the initialization arguments bundle. If you are doing the creation of the fragment, a nice pattern to use is that of Listing 29–1, which shows a factory type of instantiator within the `MyFragment` class definition.

Listing 29–1. *Instantiating a Fragment Using a Static Factory Method*

```
public static MyFragment newInstance(int index) {
    MyFragment f = new MyFragment();
    Bundle args = new Bundle();
    args.putInt("index", index);
    f.setArguments(args);
    return f;
}
```

From the client's point of view, they get a new instance by calling the static `newInstance()` method with a single argument. They get the instantiated object back, and the initialization argument has been set on this fragment in the arguments bundle. If this fragment gets saved and reconstructed later, the system will go through a very similar process of calling the default constructor, then reattaching the initialization arguments. For your particular case, you would define the signature of your newInstance() method (or methods) to take the appropriate number and type of arguments, and then build the arguments bundle appropriately. This is all you want your newInstance() method to do. The callbacks that follow will take care of the rest of the setup of your fragment.

The onInflate() Callback

The next thing that *could* happen is layout view inflation. If your fragment is defined by a <fragment> tag in a layout that is being inflated (typically when an activity has called setContentView() for its main layout), your fragment would have its onInflate() callback called. This passes in an AttributeSet, with the attributes from the <fragment> tag, and a saved bundle. If the fragment is being recreated and if some state was saved previously in onSaveInstanceState(), this bundle is the one with the saved state values in it. The expectation of onInflate() is that you'll read attribute values and save them for later use. At this stage in the fragment's life, it's too early to actually do anything with the user interface. The fragment is not even associated to its activity yet. But that's the next event to occur to your fragment.

> **NOTE:** Defect #14796 was filed because of a discrepancy between the documentation for onInflate() and reality in Honeycomb. The documentation says that onInflate() will always be called before onAttach(). In reality, after an activity restart, onInflate() could be called after onCreateView(). This is too late for setting values into a bundle and calling setArguments(). See http://code.google.com/p/android/issues/detail?id=14796. This is also why onInflate() does not appear in the state diagram in Figure 29–1; it's too difficult to predict when this callback will be called.

The onAttach() Callback

The onAttach() callback gets invoked after your fragment is associated with its activity. The activity reference is passed to you if you want to use it. You can at least use the activity to interrogate information about your enclosing activity. You can also use the activity as a context to do other operations. One thing to note is that the Fragment class has a getActivity() method that will always return the attached activity for your fragment should you need it. Keep in mind that all along this lifecycle, the initialization arguments bundle is available to you from the getArguments() method of fragment. However, once the fragment is attached to its activity, you can't call setArguments() again. So you can't add to the initialization arguments except in the very beginning.

The onCreate() Callback

Next up is the onCreate() callback. While this is similar to the activity's onCreate(), the difference is that you should not put code in here that relies on the existence of the activity's view hierarchy. While your fragment may be associated to its activity by now, you haven't yet been notified that the activity's onCreate() has finished. That's coming up. This callback gets the saved state bundle passed in if there is one. This callback is about as early as possible to create a background thread to go get data that this fragment will need. Your fragment code is running on the UI thread, and you don't want to do disk I/O or network accesses on the UI thread. In fact, it makes a lot of sense to fire off a background thread to get things ready. Your background thread is where blocking calls should be. You'll need to hook up with the data later, but there are ways to do that.

> **NOTE:** One of the ways to load data in a background thread is to use the Loader class. We didn't have room in the book to cover this, but check our website for more information.

The onCreateView() Callback

The next callback is onCreateView(). The expectation here is that you will return a view hierarchy for this fragment. The arguments passed in to this callback include a LayoutInflater (which you can use to inflate a layout for this fragment), a ViewGroup parent (called *container* in Listing 29–2), and the saved bundle if one exists. It is very important to note here that you should not attach the view hierarchy to the ViewGroup parent passed in. That association will happen automatically later. The parent is provided so you can use it with the inflate() method of the LayoutInflater, although you could also interrogate the parent yourself if necessary. But you will very likely get exceptions if you attach the fragment's view hierarchy to the parent in this callback. Listing 29–2 shows a sample of what you might want to do in this method.

Listing 29–2. *Creating a Fragment View Hierarchy in onCreateView()*

```
@Override
public View onCreateView(LayoutInflater inflater,
                               ViewGroup container, Bundle savedInstanceState) {
        View v = inflater.inflate(R.layout.details, container, false);
        TextView text1 = (TextView) v.findViewById(R.id.text1);
        text1.setText(myDataSet[ getPosition() ] );
        return v;
}
```

Here you see how you can access a layout XML file that is just for this fragment and inflate it to a view that you return to the caller. There are several advantages to this approach. You could always construct the view hierarchy in code, but by inflating a layout XML file, you're taking advantage of the resource-finding logic of the system. Depending on which configuration the device is in, or for that matter which device you're on, the appropriate layout XML file will be chosen. You can then access a particular view within the layout; in your case, the text1 TextView field, to do what you want with it. To repeat a very important point: do not attach the fragment's view to the container parent in this callback. You can see in Listing 29–2 that you use container in the call to inflate(), but you also pass false for the attachToRoot parameter.

The onActivityCreated() Callback

You're now getting close to the point where the user can interact with your fragment. The next callback is `onActivityCreated()`. This is called after the activity has completed its `onCreate()` callback. You can now trust that the activity's view hierarchy, including your own view hierarchy if you returned one earlier, is ready and available. This is where you can do final tweaks to the user interface before the user sees it. This could be especially important if this activity and its fragments are being recreated from a saved state. It's also where you can be sure that any other fragment for this activity has been attached to your activity.

The onStart() Callback

The next callback in your fragment lifecycle is `onStart()`. Now your fragment is visible to the user. But you haven't started interacting with the user just yet. This callback is tied to the activity's `onStart()`. As such, where previously you may have put your logic into the activity's `onStart()`, now you're more likely to put your logic into the fragment's `onStart()`, since that is also where the user interface components are.

The onResume() Callback

The last callback before the user can interact with your fragment is `onResume()`. This callback is tied to the activity's `onResume()`. When this callback returns, the user is free to interact with this fragment. For example, if you have a Camera preview in your fragment, you would probably enable it in the fragment's `onResume()`.

So now you've reached the point where the app is happily making the user happy. And then the user decides to get out of your app, either by Back'ing out, or pressing the Home button, or by launching some other application. The next sequence, similar to what happens with an activity, goes in the opposite direction of setting up the fragment for interaction.

The onPause() Callback

The first undo callback on a fragment is `onPause()`. This callback is tied to the activity's `onPause()`; just like with an activity, if you have a media player in your fragment or some other shared object, you could pause it, stop it, or give it back via your `onPause()` method. The same "good citizen" rules apply here: you don't want to be playing audio if the user is taking a phone call. It is possible that a fragment could go from `onPause()` back to `onResume()`.

The onStop() Callback

The next undo callback is `onStop()`. This one is tied to the activity's `onStop()` and serves a similar purpose as an activity's `onStop()`. A fragment that has been stopped could go straight back to the `onStart()` callback, which then leads to `onResume()`.

The onDestroyView() Callback

If your fragment is on its way to being killed off or saved, the next callback in the undo direction is `onDestroyView()`. This will be called after the view hierarchy you created on your `onCreateView()` callback earlier has been detached from your fragment.

The onDestroy() Callback

Next up is `onDestroy()`. This is called when the fragment is no longer in use. Note that it is still attached to the activity and is still "findable," but it can't do much.

The onDetach() Callback

The final callback in a fragment's lifecycle is `onDetach()`. Once this is invoked, the fragment is not tied to its activity, it does not have a view hierarchy anymore, and all its resources should have been released.

Using setRetainInstance()

You may have noticed the dotted lines in the diagram in Figure 29–1. One of the cool features of a fragment is that you can specify that you don't want the fragment completely destroyed if the activity is being recreated and therefore your fragments will be coming back also. Therefore, fragment comes with a method called `setRetainInstance()`, which takes a boolean parameter to tell it "Yes; I want you to hang around when my activity restarts" or "No; go away and I'll create a new fragment from scratch." The best place to call `setRetainInstance()` is in the `onCreate()` callback of a fragment.

If the parameter is `true`, that means you want to keep your fragment object in memory and not start over completely from scratch. However, if your activity is going away and being recreated, you'll have to detach your fragment from this activity and attach it to the new one. The bottom line is that if the retain instance value is `true`, you won't actually destroy your fragment instance, and therefore you won't need to create a new one on the other side. All other callbacks will be invoked, however. The dotted lines on the diagram mean that you would skip the `onDestroy()` callback on the way out, and you'd skip the `onCreate()` callback when your fragment is being re-attached to your new activity. Since an activity will get recreated most likely for configuration changes, your fragment callbacks should probably assume that the configuration has changed and therefore should take appropriate action. This would include inflating the layout to create a new view hierarchy in `onCreateView()`, for example. The code provided in Listing 29–2 would take care of that as it is written. If you choose to use the retain instance feature, you may decide not to put some of your initialization logic in `onCreate()` since it won't always get called the way the other callbacks will.

Sample Fragment App Showing the Lifecycle

There's nothing like seeing a real example to get an appreciation for a concept. You'll create a sample application that has been instrumented so you can see all these callbacks in action. You're going to work with a sample application that uses a list of Shakespeare titles in one fragment; when the user clicks on one of the titles, some text from that play will appear in a separate fragment. This sample application will work in both landscape and portrait modes on a tablet. Then you'll configure it to run as if on a smaller screen so you can see how to separate the text fragment into an activity. You'll start with the XML layout of your activity in landscape mode in Listing 29–3, which will look like Figure 29–2 when it runs.

> **NOTE:** At the end of the chapter is the URL that you can use to download the projects in this chapter. This will allow you to import these projects into your Eclipse directly.

Listing 29–3. *Your Activity's Layout XML for Landscape Mode*

```
<?xml version="1.0" encoding="utf-8"?>
<!-- This file is res/layout-land/main.xml -->
<LinearLayout xmlns:android="http://schemas.android.com/apk/res/android"
        android:orientation="horizontal"
        android:layout_width="match_parent"
        android:layout_height="match_parent">

    <fragment class="com.androidbook.fragments.bard.TitlesFragment"
            android:id="@+id/titles" android:layout_weight="1"
            android:layout_width="0px"
            android:layout_height="match_parent" />

    <FrameLayout
            android:id="@+id/details" android:layout_weight="2"
            android:layout_width="0px"
            android:layout_height="match_parent" />

</LinearLayout>
```

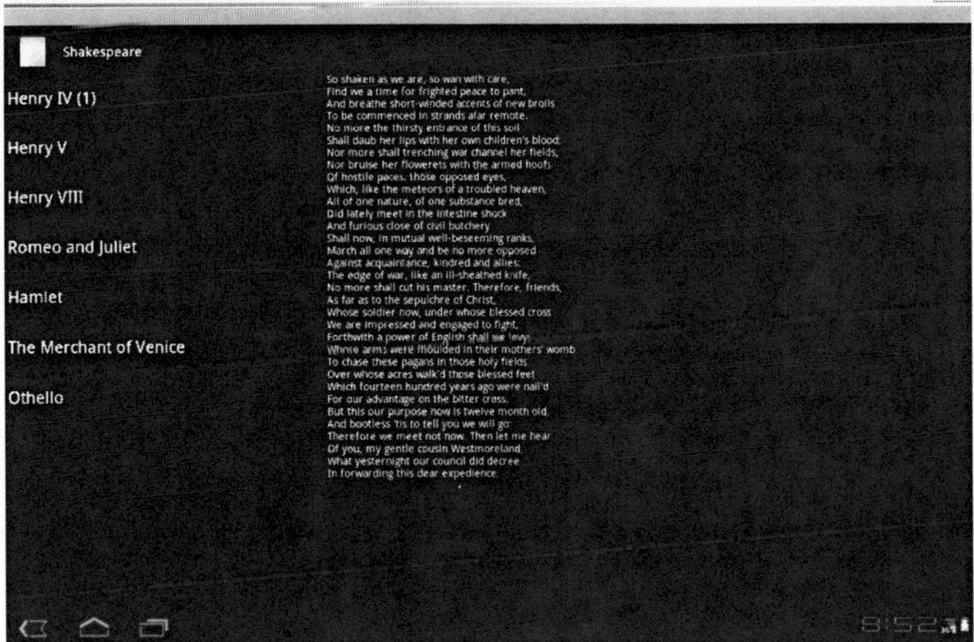

Figure 29–2. *The user interface of your sample fragment application*

This layout looks like a lot of other layouts you've seen throughout the book, horizontally left to right with two main objects. Three's a special new tag, though, called `<fragment>` and this tag has a new attribute called `class`. Keep in mind that a fragment is not a view, so the layout XML is a little different for a fragment than it is for everything else. The other thing to keep in mind is that the `<fragment>` tag is just a placeholder in this layout. You should not put child tags under `<fragment>` in a layout XML file.

The other attributes for a fragment look familiar and serve a similar purpose as they do for a view. The fragment tag's `class` attribute specifies your extended class for the titles of your application. That is, you must extend one of the Android `Fragment` classes to implement your logic, and the `<fragment>` tag must know the name of your extended class. A fragment has its own view hierarchy that will be created later by the fragment itself. The next tag is a `FrameLayout`—not another `<fragment>` tag. Why is that? We'll explain in more detail later but for now, you should be aware that you're going to be doing some transitions on the text, swapping out one fragment with another. You use the `FrameLayout` as the view container to hold the current text fragment. With your titles fragment, you have one—and only one—fragment to worry about; no swapping and no transitions. For the area that displays the Shakespearean text, you'll have several fragments.

Your `MainActivity` Java code is in Listing 29–4.

Listing 29–4. *Your MainActivity Source Code*

```
// This file is MainActivity.java
import android.app.Activity;
import android.app.Fragment;
```

```
import android.app.FragmentManager;
import android.app.FragmentTransaction;
import android.content.Intent;
import android.content.res.Configuration;
import android.os.Bundle;
import android.os.Environment;
import android.util.Log;

public class MainActivity extends Activity {
    public static final String TAG = "Shakespeare";

    @Override
    public void onCreate(Bundle savedInstanceState) {
        Log.v(TAG, "in MainActivity onCreate");
        super.onCreate(savedInstanceState);
        FragmentManager.enableDebugLogging(true);
        setContentView(R.layout.main);
    }

    @Override
    public void onAttachFragment(Fragment fragment) {
        Log.v(TAG, "in MainActivity onAttachFragment. fragment id = "
                + fragment.getId());
        super.onAttachFragment(fragment);
    }

    @Override
    public void onStart() {
        Log.v(TAG, "in MainActivity onStart");
        super.onStart();
    }

    @Override
    public void onResume() {
        Log.v(TAG, "in MainActivity onResume");
        super.onResume();
    }

    @Override
    public void onPause() {
        Log.v(TAG, "in MainActivity onPause");
        super.onPause();
    }

    @Override
    public void onStop() {
        Log.v(TAG, "in MainActivity onStop");
        super.onStop();
    }

    @Override
    public void onSaveInstanceState(Bundle outState) {
        Log.v(MainActivity.TAG, "in MainActivity onSaveInstanceState");
        super.onSaveInstanceState(outState);
    }

    @Override
```

```
    public void onDestroy() {
        Log.v(TAG, "in MainActivity onDestroy");
        super.onDestroy();
    }

    public boolean isMultiPane() {
        return getResources().getConfiguration().orientation
                == Configuration.ORIENTATION_LANDSCAPE;
    }

    /**
     * Helper function to show the details of a selected item, either by
     * displaying a fragment in-place in the current UI, or starting a
     * whole new activity in which it is displayed.
     */
    public void showDetails(int index) {
        Log.v(TAG, "in MainActivity showDetails(" + index + ")");

        if (isMultiPane()) {
            // Check what fragment is shown, replace if needed.
            DetailsFragment details = (DetailsFragment)
                    getFragmentManager().findFragmentById(R.id.details);
            if (details == null || details.getShownIndex() != index) {
                // Make new fragment to show this selection.
                details = DetailsFragment.newInstance(index);

                // Execute a transaction, replacing any existing
                // fragment with this one inside the frame.
                Log.v(TAG, "about to run FragmentTransaction...");
                FragmentTransaction ft
                        = getFragmentManager().beginTransaction();
                ft.setTransition(
                        FragmentTransaction.TRANSIT_FRAGMENT_FADE);
                //ft.addToBackStack("details");
                ft.replace(R.id.details, details);
                ft.commit();
            }

        } else {
            // Otherwise you need to launch a new activity to display
            // the dialog fragment with selected text.
            Intent intent = new Intent();
            intent.setClass(this, DetailsActivity.class);
            intent.putExtra("index", index);
            startActivity(intent);
        }
    }
}
```

This is a very simple activity to write. The only reason most callbacks are in the source code is to include a logging message. Otherwise, you'd only need `onCreate()` and the helper methods `isMultiPane()` and `showDetails()`. And you can't get much simpler than your `onCreate()`. All it does is turn on fragment manager debugging and set the content view to the layout from Listing 29–3. To determine multi-pane mode (i.e., if you need to use fragments side by side), you just use the orientation of the device. If you're in landscape mode, you're multi-pane; if you're in portrait mode, you're not. Lastly, the helper method showDetails() is there to figure out how to show the text when a title is selected. The index is just the position of the title in the title list. If you're in multi-pane mode, you're going to use a fragment to show the text. You're calling this fragment a DetailsFragment, and you use a factory-type method to create one with the index. The code for the DetailsFragment class is shown in Listing 29–5. You'll come back to your showDetails() method later.

Listing 29–5. *Source Code for DetailsFragment*

```
import android.app.Activity;
import android.app.Fragment;
import android.os.Bundle;
import android.util.AttributeSet;
import android.util.Log;
import android.view.LayoutInflater;
import android.view.View;
import android.view.ViewGroup;
import android.widget.TextView;

public class DetailsFragment extends Fragment {

    private int mIndex = 0;

    public static DetailsFragment newInstance(int index) {
        Log.v(MainActivity.TAG, "in DetailsFragment newInstance(" +
                                 index + ")");

        DetailsFragment df = new DetailsFragment();

        // Supply index input as an argument.
        Bundle args = new Bundle();
        args.putInt("index", index);
        df.setArguments(args);
        return df;
    }

    public static DetailsFragment newInstance(Bundle bundle) {
        int index = bundle.getInt("index", 0);
        return newInstance(index);
    }

    @Override
    public void onInflate(AttributeSet attrs, Bundle savedInstanceState)
    {
        Log.v(MainActivity.TAG,
                "in DetailsFragment onInflate. AttributeSet contains:");
        for(int i=0; i<attrs.getAttributeCount(); i++)
            Log.v(MainActivity.TAG, "    " + attrs.getAttributeName(i) +
                    " = " + attrs.getAttributeValue(i));
        super.onInflate(attrs, savedInstanceState);
    }

    @Override
    public void onAttach(Activity myActivity) {
        Log.v(MainActivity.TAG,
                "in DetailsFragment onAttach; activity is: " +
                myActivity);
```

```
        super.onAttach(myActivity);
    }

    @Override
    public void onCreate(Bundle myBundle) {
        Log.v(MainActivity.TAG,
                "in DetailsFragment onCreate. Bundle contains:");
        if(myBundle != null) {
            for(String key : myBundle.keySet()) {
                Log.v(MainActivity.TAG, "    " + key);
            }
        }
        else {
            Log.v(MainActivity.TAG, "    myBundle is null");
        }
        super.onCreate(myBundle);

        mIndex = getArguments().getInt("index", 0);
    }

    public int getShownIndex() {
        return mIndex;
    }

    @Override
    public View onCreateView(LayoutInflater inflater,
            ViewGroup container, Bundle savedInstanceState) {
        Log.v(MainActivity.TAG,
                "in DetailsFragment onCreateView. container = " +
                container);

        // Don't tie this fragment to anything through the inflater.
        // Android takes care of attaching fragments for us. The
        // container is only passed in so you can know about the
        // container where this View hierarchy is going to go.
        View v = inflater.inflate(R.layout.details, container, false);
        TextView text1 = (TextView) v.findViewById(R.id.text1);
        text1.setText(Shakespeare.DIALOGUE[ mIndex ] );
        return v;
    }

    @Override
    public void onActivityCreated(Bundle savedState) {
        Log.v(MainActivity.TAG,
           "in DetailsFragment onActivityCreated. savedState contains:");
        if(savedState != null) {
            for(String key : savedState.keySet()) {
                Log.v(MainActivity.TAG, "    " + key);
            }
        }
        else {
            Log.v(MainActivity.TAG, "    savedState is null");
        }
        super.onActivityCreated(savedState);
    }

    @Override
```

```
    public void onStart() {
        Log.v(MainActivity.TAG, "in DetailsFragment onStart");
        super.onStart();
    }

    @Override
    public void onResume() {
        Log.v(MainActivity.TAG, "in DetailsFragment onResume");
        super.onResume();
    }

    @Override
    public void onPause() {
        Log.v(MainActivity.TAG, "in DetailsFragment onPause");
        super.onPause();
    }

    @Override
    public void onSaveInstanceState(Bundle outState) {
        Log.v(MainActivity.TAG,
                "in DetailsFragment onSaveInstanceState");
        super.onSaveInstanceState(outState);
    }

    @Override
    public void onStop() {
        Log.v(MainActivity.TAG, "in DetailsFragment onStop");
        super.onStop();
    }

    @Override
    public void onDestroyView() {
        Log.v(MainActivity.TAG,
                "in DetailsFragment onDestroyView, view = " +
                getView());
        super.onDestroyView();
    }

    @Override
    public void onDestroy() {
        Log.v(MainActivity.TAG, "in DetailsFragment onDestroy");
        super.onDestroy();
    }

    @Override
    public void onDetach() {
        Log.v(MainActivity.TAG, "in DetailsFragment onDetach");
        super.onDetach();
    }
}
```

The `DetailsFragment` class is actually fairly simple as well. The only reason the source code is so long is because you added all the logging statements. If you didn't need to show the logging statements, you'd only need the `newInstance()` methods, `getShownIndex()`, `onCreate()`, and `onCreateView()`. Now you can see how to instantiate this fragment. It's important to point out that you're instantiating this fragment in code because your layout defines the ViewGroup container (a FrameLayout) that your details fragment is going to go into. Since the fragment is not itself defined in the layout XML for the activity, as your titles fragment was, you need to instantiate your details fragments in code.

To create a new details fragment , you use your newInstance() method. As discussed earlier, this factory method invokes the default constructor and then sets the arguments bundle with the value of index. Once newInstance() has run, your details fragment can retrieve the value of index in any of its callbacks by referring to the arguments bundle via getArguments(). For your convenience, in onCreate() you can save the index value from the arguments bundle to a member field in your DetailsFragment class.

You might wonder why you didn't simply set the mIndex value in newInstance(). The reason is because Android will, behind the scenes, recreate your fragment using the default constructor. Then it sets the arguments bundle to what it was before. Android won't use your newInstance() method, so the only reliable way to ensure mIndex is set is to read the value from the arguments bundle and set it in onCreate(). The convenience method getShownIndex() retrieves the value of that index. Now the only method left to describe in the details fragment is onCreateView(). And this is very simple, too.

The purpose of onCreateView() is to return the view hierarchy for your fragment. Remember that based on your configuration, you could want all kinds of different layouts for this fragment. Therefore, the most common thing to do is utilize a layout XML file for your fragment. In your sample application, you specify the layout for the fragment to be details.xml using the resource R.layout.details. The XML for details.xml is in Listing 29–6.

Listing 29–6. *The details.xml Layout File for the Details Fragment*

```
<?xml version="1.0" encoding="utf-8"?>
<!-- This file is res/layout/details.xml -->
<LinearLayout
  xmlns:android="http://schemas.android.com/apk/res/android"
  android:layout_width="match_parent"
  android:layout_height="match_parent">
  <ScrollView android:id="@+id/scroller"
      android:layout_width="match_parent"
      android:layout_height="match_parent">
    <TextView android:id="@+id/text1"
        android:layout_width="match_parent"
        android:layout_height="match_parent" />
  </ScrollView>
</LinearLayout>
```

For your sample application, you can use the exact same layout file for details whether you're in landscape mode or in portrait mode. This layout is not for the activity, it's just for your fragment to display the text. Because it could be considered the default layout, you can store it in the /res/layout directory and it will be found and used even if you're in landscape mode. When Android goes looking for the details XML file, it tries the specific directories that closely match the device's configuration, but it will end up in the /res/layout directory if it can't find the details.xml file in any of the other places. Of course, if you want to have a different layout for your fragment in landscape mode, you could define a separate details.xml layout file and store it under /res/layout-land. Feel free to experiment with different details.xml files.

When your details fragment's onCreateView() is called, you will simply grab the appropriate details.xml layout file, inflate it, and set the text to the text from the Shakespeare class. I won't include the entire Java code for Shakespeare here, but a portion is in Listing 29–7 so you understand how it was done. For the complete source, please access the projects download files, as described in the References section at the end of this chapter.

Listing 29–7. *Source Code for Shakespeare*

```
public class Shakespeare {
    public static String TITLES[] = {
            "Henry IV (1)",
            "Henry V",
            "Henry VIII",
            "Romeo and Juliet",
            "Hamlet",
            "The Merchant of Venice",
            "Othello"
    };
    public static String DIALOGUE[] = {
        "So shaken as we are, so wan with care,\n...
... and so on ...
```

So now your details fragment view hierarchy contains the text from the selected title. Your details fragment is ready to go. And now you can return to the showDetails() method to talk about FragmentTransactions.

FragmentTransactions and the Fragment Back Stack

The code in showDetails() that pulls in your new details fragment (shown again in Listing 29–8) looks rather simple, but there's a lot going on here. It's worth spending some time to explain what is happening and why. If your activity is in multi-pane mode, you want to show the details in a fragment next to the title list. You may already be showing details, which means you may have a details fragment visible to the user. Either way, the resource ID R.id.details is for the FrameLayout for your activity, as listed in Listing 29–3. If you have a details fragment sitting in the layout, because you didn't assign any other ID to it, it will have this ID. Therefore, to find out if there's a details fragment in the layout, you can ask the fragment manager using findFragmentById(). This will return null if the frame layout is empty or will give you the current details fragment. You can then decide if you need to place a new details fragment in the layout, either because the layout is empty, or there's a details fragment there for some other title. Once you make the determination to create and use a new details fragment, you invoke the factory method to create a new instance of a details fragment. Now you can put this new fragment into place for the user to see it.

Listing 29–8. *Fragment Transaction Example*

```
public void showDetails(int index) {
    Log.v(TAG, "in MainActivity showDetails(" + index + ")");

    if (isMultiPane()) {
        // Check what fragment is shown, replace if needed.
        DetailsFragment details = (DetailsFragment)
                getFragmentManager().findFragmentById(R.id.details);
        if (details == null || details.getShownIndex() != index) {
            // Make new fragment to show this selection.
            details = DetailsFragment.newInstance(index);

            // Execute a transaction, replacing any existing
            // fragment with this one inside the frame.
            Log.v(TAG, "about to run FragmentTransaction...");
            FragmentTransaction ft
                    = getFragmentManager().beginTransaction();
            ft.setTransition(
                    FragmentTransaction.TRANSIT_FRAGMENT_FADE);
            //ft.addToBackStack("details");
            ft.replace(R.id.details, details);
            ft.commit();
        }
            // The rest was left out to save space.
}
```

A key concept to understand is that a fragment must live inside of a view container, also known as a view group. This is partly because a fragment is not a view itself. The `ViewGroup` class includes such things as layouts and their derived classes. This is why you chose the `FrameLayout` for the `main.xml` layout file of your activity. The `FrameLayout` is where your details fragment is going to go. If you had instead specified another `<fragment>` tag in the activity's layout file, you would not be able to do the swapping that you want to do. The FragmentTransaction is what you use to do your swapping. You tell the fragment transaction that you want to replace whatever is in your frame layout with your new details fragment. You could have avoided all this by locating the resource ID of the details TextView and just setting the text of it to the new text for the new Shakespeare title. But there's another side to fragments that explains why you use `FragmentTransactions`.

As you know, activities are arranged in a stack, and as you get deeper and deeper into an application, it's not uncommon to have a stack of several activities going at once. When you press the Back button, the top-most activity goes away and you are returned to the activity below, which resumes for you. This can continue all the way down until you're at the home screen again.

This was fine when an activity was just single-purpose, but now that an activity can have several fragments going at once, and because you can go deeper into your application without leaving the top-most activity, Android really needed to extend the Back button stack concept to include fragments as well. In fact, fragments demand this even more. When there are several fragments interacting with each other at the same time in an activity, and there's a transition to new content across several fragments at once, pressing the Back button should cause each of the fragments to roll back one step *together*. To ensure that each fragment properly participates in the rollback, a FragmentTransaction is created and managed to perform that coordination.

Be aware that a back stack for fragments is not required within an activity. You can code your application to let the Back button work at the activity level and not at the fragment level at all. If there's no back stack for your fragments, pressing the Back button will pop the current activity off the stack and return the user to whatever was underneath. If you choose to take advantage of the back stack for fragments, you will want to uncomment in Listing 29–8 the line that says ft.addToBackStack("details"). For this particular case, you've hardcoded the tag parameter to be the string "details". This tag should be an appropriate string name that represents the state of the fragments at the time of the transaction. You will be able to interrogate the back stack in code using the tag value to delete entries, as well as pop entries off. You will want meaningful tags on these transactions to be able to find the appropriate ones later.

Fragment Transaction Transitions and Animations

One of the very nice things about fragment transactions is that you can perform transitions from an old fragment to a new fragment using transitions and animations. These are not like the animations in Chapters 16 and 20. These are much simpler and do not require in-depth graphics knowledge. Let's use a fragment transaction transition to add special effects when you swap out the old details fragment with a new details fragment. This can add polish to your application, making the switch from the old to the new fragment look smooth. One method to accomplish this is setTransition(), as shown in Listing 29–8. However, there are a few different transitions available. You used a fade in your example, but you can also use the setCustomAnimations() method to describe other special effects, such as sliding one fragment out to the right as another slides in from the left. The custom animations use the new object animation definitions, not the old ones. The old anim XML files use tags such as <translate>, while the new XML files use <objectAnimator>. The old standard XML files are located in the /data/res/anim directory under the appropriate Android SDK platforms directory (such as platforms/android-11 for Honeycomb). There are some new XML files located in the /data/res/animator directory here, too. Your code could be something like

```
ft.setCustomAnimations(android.R.animator.fade_in, android.R.animator.fade_out);
```

which will cause the new fragment to fade in as the old fragment fades out. The first parameter applies to the fragment entering and the second parameter applies to the fragment exiting. Feel free to explore the Android animator directory for more stock animations. If you'd like to create your own, there's section on the object animator later in this chapter to help you out. The other very important bit of knowledge you need is that the transition calls need to come before the replace() call, otherwise they will have no effect.

Using object animator for special effects on fragments can be a fun way to do transitions. There are two other methods on FragmentTransaction you should know about: hide() and show(). Both of these methods take a fragment as a parameter, and they do exactly what you'd expect. For a fragment in the fragment manager associated to a view container, the methods simply hide or show the fragment in the user interface. The fragment does not get removed from the fragment manager in the process, but it certainly must be tied into a view container in order to affect its visibility. If a fragment does not have a view hierarchy, or if its view hierarchy is not tied into the displayed view hierarchy, then these methods won't do anything.

Once you've specified the special effects for your fragment transaction, you have to tell it the main work that you want done. In your case, you're replacing whatever is in the frame layout with your new details fragment. That's where the `replace()` method comes in. This is equivalent to calling `remove()` for any fragments that are already in the frame layout and then `add()` for your new details fragment, which means you could just call `remove()` or `add()` as needed instead.

The final action you must take when working with a fragment transaction is to commit it. The `commit()` method does not cause things to happen immediately but rather schedules the work for when the UI thread is ready to do it.

Now you should understand why you need to go to so much trouble to change the content in a simple fragment. It's not just that you want to change the text; you might want a special graphics effect during the transition. You may also want to save the transition details in a fragment transaction that you can reverse later. That last point may be confusing so we'll clarify.

This is not a transaction in the truest sense of the word. When you pop fragment transactions off of the back stack, you are not undoing the data changes that may have taken place. If data changed within your activity, for example, as you created fragment transactions on the back stack, pressing the back button does not cause the activity data changes to revert back to their previous values. You are merely stepping back through the user interface views the way you came in, just like you do with activities, but in this case it's for fragments. Because of the way that fragments are saved and restored, the inner state of a fragment that has been restored from a saved state will depend on what values you saved with the fragment and how you manage to restore them. So your fragments may look the same as they did previously but your activity will not, unless you take steps to restore activity state when you restore fragments.

In your example, you're only working with one view container and bringing in one details fragment. If your user interface were more complicated, you could manipulate other fragments within the fragment transaction. What you are actually doing is beginning the transaction, replacing any existing fragment in your details frame layout with your new details fragment, specifying a fade-in animation, and committing the transaction. You commented out the part where this transaction is added to the back stack, but you could certainly uncomment that to take part in the back stack.

The FragmentManager

The `FragmentManager` is a component that takes care of the fragments belonging to an activity. This includes fragments on the back stack and fragments that may just be hanging around. We'll explain. Fragments should only be created within the context of an activity. This occurs either through the inflation of an activity's layout XML or through direct instantiation using code like that in Listing 29–1. When instantiated through code, a fragment usually gets attached to the activity using a fragment transaction. In either case, the FragmentManager class is used to access and manage these fragments for an activity.

You use the getFragmentManager() method on either an activity or an attached fragment to retrieve a fragment manager. You saw in Listing 29–8 that a fragment manager is where you get a fragment transaction from. Besides getting a fragment transaction, you can also get a fragment using the fragment's ID, tag, or a combination of bundle and key.

For this, the getter methods include findFragmentById(), findFragmentByTag(), and getFragment(). The latter method would be used in conjunction with putFragment() which also takes a bundle, a key, and the fragment to be put. The bundle is most likely going to be the savedState bundle and the putFragment() will be used in the onSaveInstanceState() callback to save the state of the current activity (or another fragment). The getFragment() method would probably be called in onCreate() to correspond to the putFragment(), although for a fragment, the bundle is available to the other callback methods, as described earlier.

Obviously you can't use the getFragmentManager() method on a fragment that has not been attached to an activity yet. But it's also true that you can attach a fragment to an activity without making it visible to the user yet. If you do this, you really should associate a String tag to the fragment so that you can get to it in the future. You'd most likely use this method of FragmentTransaction to do this:

```
public FragmentTransaction add (Fragment fragment, String tag)
```

In fact, you can have a fragment that does not exhibit a view hierarchy. This might be done to encapsulate certain logic together such that it could be attached to an activity, yet still retain some autonomy from the activity's lifecycle and from other fragments. When an activity goes through a recreate cycle due to a device configuration change, this non-UI fragment could remain largely intact while the activity goes away and comes back again. This would be a good candidate for the setRetainInstance() option.

The fragment back stack is also the domain of the fragment manager. While a fragment transaction is used to put fragments onto the back stack, the fragment manager can take fragments off the back stack. This is usually done using the fragment's ID or tag, but it can be done based on position in the back stack or just to pop the top-most fragment.

Finally, the fragment manager has methods for some debugging features, such as turning on debugging messages to LogCat using enableDebugLogging() or dumping the current state of the fragment manager to a stream using dump(). Note that you turned on fragment manager debugging in the onCreate() method of your activity in Listing 29–4.

Caution When Referencing Fragments

It's time to revisit the earlier discussion of the fragment's lifecycle and the arguments and saved-state bundles. Android could save off one of your fragments at many different times. This means that at the moment your application wants to retrieve that fragment, it's possible that it is not in memory. For this reason, I caution you *not* to think that a variable reference to a fragment is going to remain valid for a long time. If fragments are being replaced in a container view using fragment transactions, any reference to the old fragment is now pointing to a fragment that is possibly on the back stack. Or a fragment may get detached from the activity's view hierarchy during an application configuration change such as a screen rotation. Be careful.

If you're going to hold onto a reference to a fragment, be aware of when it could get saved away; when you need to find it again, use one of the getter methods of the fragment manager. If you want to hang onto a fragment reference, such as when an activity is going through a configuration change, you can use the `putFragment()` method with the appropriate bundle. In the case of both activities and fragments, the appropriate bundle is the `savedState` bundle that is used in `onSaveInstanceState()` and that reappears in `onCreate()` (or in the case of fragments, the other early callbacks of the fragment's lifecycle). You will probably never store a direct fragment reference into the arguments bundle of a fragment; if you're tempted to do so, please think very carefully about it first.

The other way you can get to a specific fragment is by querying for it using a known tag or known ID. The getter methods described previously will allow retrieval of fragments from the fragment manager this way, which means you have the option of just remembering the tag or ID of a fragment so that you can retrieve it from the fragment manager using one of those values, as opposed to using `putFragment()` and `getFragment()`.

ListFragments and <fragment>

There are still a few more things to cover to make your sample application complete. The first is the `TitlesFragment` class. This is the one that is created via the `layout.xml` file of your main activity. The `<fragment>` tag serves as your placeholder for where this fragment will go and does not define what the view hierarchy will look like for this fragment. The code for your `TitlesFragment` is in Listing 29–9. `TitlesFragment` displays the list of titles for your application.

Listing 29–9. *TitlesFragment Java Code*

```
import android.app.Activity;
import android.app.ListFragment;
import android.os.Bundle;
import android.util.AttributeSet;
import android.util.Log;
import android.view.LayoutInflater;
import android.view.View;
import android.view.ViewGroup;
import android.widget.ArrayAdapter;
```

```
import android.widget.ListView;

public class TitlesFragment extends ListFragment {
    private MainActivity myActivity = null;
    int mCurCheckPosition = 0;

    @Override
    public void onInflate(AttributeSet attrs, Bundle savedInstanceState) {
        Log.v(MainActivity.TAG,
                "in TitlesFragment onInflate. AttributeSet contains:");
        for(int i=0; i<attrs.getAttributeCount(); i++) {
            Log.v(MainActivity.TAG, "    " + attrs.getAttributeName(i) +
                 " = " + ("id".equals(attrs.getAttributeName(i))?
                 Integer.toHexString(attrs.getAttributeIntValue(i, -1)):
                 attrs.getAttributeValue(i)));
        }
        super.onInflate(attrs, savedInstanceState);
    }

    @Override
    public void onAttach(Activity myActivity) {
        Log.v(MainActivity.TAG,
            "in TitlesFragment onAttach; activity is: " + myActivity);
        super.onAttach(myActivity);
        this.myActivity = (MainActivity)myActivity;
    }

    @Override
    public void onCreate(Bundle myBundle) {
        Log.v(MainActivity.TAG,
            "in TitlesFragment onCreate. Bundle contains:");
        if(myBundle != null) {
            for(String key : myBundle.keySet()) {
                Log.v(MainActivity.TAG, "    " + key);
            }
        }
        else {
            Log.v(MainActivity.TAG, "    myBundle is null");
        }
        super.onCreate(myBundle);
    }

    @Override
    public View onCreateView(LayoutInflater myInflater,
                ViewGroup container, Bundle myBundle) {
        Log.v(MainActivity.TAG,
            "in TitlesFragment onCreateView. container is "
            + container);
        return super.onCreateView(myInflater, container, myBundle);
    }

    @Override
    public void onActivityCreated(Bundle savedState) {
        Log.v(MainActivity.TAG,
            "in TitlesFragment onActivityCreated. savedState contains:");
        if(savedState != null) {
            for(String key : savedState.keySet()) {
```

```
                Log.v(MainActivity.TAG, "    " + key);
            }
        }
        else {
            Log.v(MainActivity.TAG, "    savedState is null");
        }
        super.onActivityCreated(savedState);

        // Populate list with your static array of titles.
        setListAdapter(new ArrayAdapter<String>(getActivity(),
                android.R.layout.simple_list_item_1,
                Shakespeare.TITLES));

        if (savedState != null) {
            // Restore last state for checked position.
            mCurCheckPosition = savedState.getInt("curChoice", 0);
        }

        // Get your ListFragment's ListView and update it
        ListView lv = getListView();
        lv.setChoiceMode(ListView.CHOICE_MODE_SINGLE);
        lv.setSelection(mCurCheckPosition);

        // Activity is created, fragments are available
        // Go ahead and populate the details fragment
        myActivity.showDetails(mCurCheckPosition);
    }

    @Override
    public void onStart() {
        Log.v(MainActivity.TAG, "in TitlesFragment onStart");
        super.onStart();
    }

    @Override
    public void onResume() {
        Log.v(MainActivity.TAG, "in TitlesFragment onResume");
        super.onResume();
    }

    @Override
    public void onPause() {
        Log.v(MainActivity.TAG, "in TitlesFragment onPause");
        super.onPause();
    }

    @Override
    public void onSaveInstanceState(Bundle outState) {
        Log.v(MainActivity.TAG, "in TitlesFragment onSaveInstanceState");
        super.onSaveInstanceState(outState);
        outState.putInt("curChoice", mCurCheckPosition);
    }

    @Override
    public void onListItemClick(ListView l, View v, int pos, long id) {
        Log.v(MainActivity.TAG,
            "in TitlesFragment onListItemClick. pos = "
```

```
                + pos);
        myActivity.showDetails(pos);
        mCurCheckPosition = pos;
    }

    @Override
    public void onStop() {
        Log.v(MainActivity.TAG, "in TitlesFragment onStop");
        super.onStop();
    }

    @Override
    public void onDestroyView() {
        Log.v(MainActivity.TAG, "in TitlesFragment onDestroyView");
        super.onDestroyView();
    }

    @Override
    public void onDestroy() {
        Log.v(MainActivity.TAG, "in TitlesFragment onDestroy");
        super.onDestroy();
    }

    @Override
    public void onDetach() {
        Log.v(MainActivity.TAG, "in TitlesFragment onDetach");
        super.onDetach();
        myActivity = null;
    }
}
```

Similar to before, most of this code doesn't need to be here except that you've added logging statements so you'll be able to see when things fire. Unlike the `DetailsFragment`, for this fragment you don't do anything in the `onCreateView()` callback. This is because you're extending the `ListFragment` class, which contains a `ListView` already. The default `onCreateView()` for a `ListFragment` creates this `ListView` for you and returns it. It's not until `onActivityCreated()` that you do any real application logic. By this time in your application, you can be sure that the activity's view hierarchy, plus this fragment's, has been created. The resource ID for that `ListView` is `android.R.id.list1` but you can always call `getListView()` if you need to get a reference to it, which you do in `onActivityCreated()`. However, because a `ListFragment` is not the same as a `ListView`, do not attach the adapter to the `ListView` directly. You must use the `ListFragment`'s `setListAdapter()` method instead. Because the activity's view hierarchy is set up, you're safe going back into the activity to do the `showDetails()` call.

At this point in your sample activity's life, you've added a list adapter to your list view, you've restored the current position (if you came back from a restore, due perhaps to a configuration change), and you've asked the activity (in `showDetails()`) to set the text to correspond to the selected Shakespearean title.

Your `TitlesFragment` class also has a listener on the list so when the user clicks on another title, the `onListItemClick()` callback is called, and you switch the text to correspond to that title, again using the `showDetails()` method.

Another difference between this fragment and the earlier details fragment is that when this fragment is being destroyed and recreated, you save state in a bundle (the value of the current position in the list) and you read it back in `onCreate()`. Unlike the details fragments that get swapped in and out of the `FrameLayout` on your activity's layout, there is just one titles fragment to think about. So when there is a configuration change and your titles fragment is going through a save-and-restore operation, you want to remember where you were. With the details fragments, you can recreate them without having to remember the previous state.

Invoking a Separate Activity When Needed

There's a piece of code I haven't talked about yet, and that is in `showDetails()` when you're in portrait mode and the details fragment won't fit properly on the same page as the titles fragment. You're going to pretend that's the case even though it really isn't on a tablet screen. As fragments get made available for the older Android releases, you will be able to use fragments on phones as well as tablets, which means the scenario described here could be quite common. If the screen real estate won't permit feasible viewing of a fragment that would otherwise be shown alongside the other fragments, you will need to launch a separate activity to show the user interface of that fragment. For your sample application, you chose to implement a details activity; the code is in Listing 29–10.

Listing 29–10. ***Showing a New Activity When a Fragment Won't Fit***

```
// This file is DetailsActivity.java
import android.app.Activity;
import android.content.res.Configuration;
import android.os.Bundle;
import android.util.Log;

public class DetailsActivity extends Activity {

    @Override
    public void onCreate(Bundle savedInstanceState) {
        Log.v(MainActivity.TAG, "in DetailsActivity onCreate");
        super.onCreate(savedInstanceState);

        if (getResources().getConfiguration().orientation
                == Configuration.ORIENTATION_LANDSCAPE) {
            // If the screen is now in landscape mode, it means
            // that your MainActivity is being shown with both
            // the titles and the text, so this activity is
            // no longer needed. Bail out and let the MainActivity
            // do all the work.
            finish();
            return;
        }

        if(getIntent() != null) {
            // This is another way to instantiate a details
            // fragment.
            DetailsFragment details =
                DetailsFragment.newInstance(getIntent().getExtras());
```

```
                getFragmentManager().beginTransaction()
                    .add(android.R.id.content, details)
                    .commit();
            }
        }
    }
```

There are several interesting aspects to this code. For one thing, it is really simple to implement. You make a simple determination of the device's orientation, and as long as you're in portrait mode, you set up a new details fragment within this details activity. If you're in landscape mode, your `MainActivity` is able to display both the titles fragment and the details fragment, so there is no reason to be displaying this activity at all. You may wonder why you would ever launch this activity if you're in landscape mode, and the answer is, you wouldn't. However, once this activity has been started in portrait mode, if the user rotates the device to landscape mode, this details activity will get restarted due to the configuration change. So now the activity is starting up and it's in landscape mode. At that moment, it makes sense to just finish this activity and let the `MainActivity` take over and do all the work.

Another interesting aspect about this details activity is that you never set the root content view using `setContentView()`. So how does the user interface get created? If you look carefully at the `add()` method call on the fragment transaction, you will see that the view container that you add the fragment to is specified as the resource `android.R.id.content`. This is the top-level view container for an Activity, and therefore when you attach your fragment view hierarchy to this container, it means your fragment view hierarchy becomes the only view hierarchy for the activity. You used the very same `DetailsFragment` class as before with the other `newInstance()` method to create the fragment (i.e., the one that takes a bundle as a parameter), then you simply attached it to the top of the activity's view hierarchy. This causes the fragment to be displayed within this new activity.

From the user's point of view, they are now looking at just the details fragment view, which is the text from the Shakespeare play. If the user wants to select a different title, they would press the Back button, which would pop this activity to reveal your main activity below (with the titles fragment only). The other choice for the user is to rotate the device to get back to landscape mode. Then your details activity will call `finish()` and go away, revealing the also-rotated main activity underneath.

When the device is in portrait mode, if you're not showing the details fragment in your main activity, you should have a separate `main.xml` layout file for portrait mode like the one in Listing 29–11.

Listing 29–11. *The Layout for a Portrait Main Activity*

```
<?xml version="1.0" encoding="utf-8"?>
<!-- This file is res/layout/main.xml -->
<LinearLayout xmlns:android="http://schemas.android.com/apk/res/android"
        android:orientation="vertical"
        android:layout_width="match_parent"
        android:layout_height="match_parent">
```

```
    <fragment class="com.androidbook.fragments.bard.TitlesFragment"
            android:id="@+id/titles"
            android:layout_width="match_parent"
            android:layout_height="match_parent" />

</LinearLayout>
```

Of course, you could make this layout whatever you want it to be. For your purposes here, you simply make it show the titles fragment by itself. It's very nice that your titles fragment class doesn't need to include much code to deal with the device reconfiguration.

The final piece that you'd like to include in this section is the AndroidManifest.xml file, as shown in Listing 29–12.

Listing 29–12. *The AndroidManifest.xml File*

```
<?xml version="1.0" encoding="utf-8"?>
<manifest xmlns:android="http://schemas.android.com/apk/res/android"
      android:versionCode="1"
      android:versionName="1.0" package="com.androidbook.fragments.bard">
    <uses-sdk android:minSdkVersion="11" />

    <application android:icon="@drawable/icon"
                 android:label="Shakespeare">

        <activity
              android:name="com.androidbook.fragments.bard.MainActivity"
              android:label="Shakespeare">
          <intent-filter>
             <action android:name="android.intent.action.MAIN" />
             <category android:name="android.intent.category.LAUNCHER" />
          </intent-filter>
        </activity>

        <activity
           android:name="com.androidbook.fragments.bard.DetailsActivity"
           android:label="ShakespeareD">

            <intent-filter>
              <action android:name="android.intent.action.VIEW" />
              <category android:name="android.intent.category.DEFAULT" />
            </intent-filter>
        </activity>

    </application>
</manifest>
```

This is a pretty standard manifest file. You have the main activity with a category of LAUNCHER so that it will show up in the device's list of Apps. Then you have the separate DetailsActivity with a category of DEFAULT. This allows you to start the details activity from code but will not show the details activity as an App in the App list.

Persistence of Fragments

When you play with this sample application, make sure you rotate the device (pressing the Ctrl-F11 keys rotates the device in the emulator). You will see that the device rotates, and that the fragments rotate right along with it. If you watch the LogCat messages, you will see a lot of them for this application. In particular, during a device rotation, pay careful attention to the messages about fragments; not only does the activity get destroyed and recreated, but the fragments do also.

So far, you only wrote a tiny bit of code on the titles fragment to remember the current position in the titles list across restarts. You didn't do anything in the details fragment code to handle reconfigurations, and that's because you didn't need to. Android will take care of hanging onto the fragments that are in the fragment manager, saving them away, then restoring them when the activity is being recreated. You should realize that the fragments you get back after the reconfiguration is complete are very likely not the same fragments in memory that you had before. These fragments have been reconstructed for you. Android saved away the arguments bundle and the knowledge of which type of fragment it was, and it saved the icicle bundles for each fragment that contain saved state information about the fragment to use to restore it on the other side.

The LogCat messages show you the fragments going through their lifecycles in sync with the activity. You will see that your details fragment gets recreated but your `newInstance()` method does not get called again. Instead, Android simply uses the default constructor, then attaches the arguments bundle to it, then starts calling the callbacks on the fragment. This is why it is so important not to do anything fancy in the `newInstance()` method, since when the fragment gets recreated, it won't do it through `newInstance()`.

You should also appreciate by now that you've been able to reuse your fragments in a few different places. The titles fragment was used in two different layouts, but if you look at the titles fragment code, it doesn't worry about the attributes of each layout. You could make the layouts rather different from each other and the titles fragment code would look the same. The same can be said of the details fragment. It was used in your main landscape layout and within the details activity all by itself. Again, the layout for the details fragment could have been very different between the two and the code of the details fragment would be the same. The code of the details activity was very simple, also.

So far, you've explored two of the fragment types: the base `Fragment` class and the `ListFragment` subclass. Now you'll move on to one of the other subclasses of `Fragment`, namely the `DialogFragment`.

Understanding Dialog Fragments

In Chapter 8, you learned how to approach Android dialogs for SDKs prior to Android 3.0. Android SDK 3.0 has provided another mechanism to work with dialogs that is based on fragments. The fragment-based approach to dialogs is expected to supercede the Android managed dialog protocol that was presented in Chapter 8.

In this section, you'll learn how to use dialog fragments to present a simple alert dialog and a custom dialog that is used to collect prompt text.

DialogFragment Basics

Before we show you working examples of prompt dialog and alert dialog, we would like to cover the high level idea of dialog fragments first. Dialog-related functionality in release 3.0 is focused in a class called `DialogFragment`. A `DialogFragment` is derived from the class `Fragment` and behaves much like a fragment. You will then use the `DialogFragment` as your base class for your dialogs. Once you have a derived dialog from this class such as

```
public class MyDialogFragment extends DialogFragment { ... }
```

you can then show this dialog fragment `MyDialogFragment` as a dialog using a fragment transaction. Listing 29–13 shows the pseudo code to do this.

Listing 29–13. *Showing a Dialog Fragment*

```
SomeActivity
{
    //....other activity functions
    public void showDialog()
    {
        //construct MyDialogFragment
        MyDialogFragment mdf = MyDialogFragment.newInstance(arg1,arg2);
        FragmentManager fm = getFragmentManager();
        FragmentTransaction ft = fm.beginTransaction();
        mdf.show(ft,"my-dialog-tag");
    }
    //....other activity functions
}
```

From Listing 29–13 the steps to show a dialog fragment are

1. Create a dialog fragment.
2. Get a fragment transaction.
3. Show the dialog using the fragment transaction from step 2.

Let's talk about each of these steps.

Constructing a Dialog Fragment

A dialog fragment being a fragment, the same rules and regulations apply when constructing a dialog fragment. The recommended pattern is to use a factory method such as `newInstance()` as you did before. Inside that `newInstance()` method, you would use the default constructor for your dialog fragment, then you would add an arguments bundle that contains your passed-in parameters. You don't want to do other work inside this method because you must make sure that what you do here will be the same as what Android will do when it restores your dialog fragment from a saved state. And all that Android will do is call the default constructor and recreate the arguments bundle on it.

Overriding onCreateView

When you inherit from a dialog fragment, you need to override one of two methods to provide the view hierarchy for your dialog. The first option is to override onCreateView() and return a view. The second option is to override onCreateDialog() and return a Dialog (like the one constructed by an AlertDialog.Builder).

Listing 29–14 shows an example of overriding the onCreateView().

Listing 29–14. *Overriding onCreateView() of a DialogFragment*

```
MyDialogFragment
{
    .....other functions
    public View onCreateView(LayoutInflater inflater,
            ViewGroup container, Bundle savedInstanceState)
    {
        //Create a view by inflating desired layout
        View v =
            inflater.inflate(R.layout.prompt_dialog,container,false);

        //you can locate a view and set values
        TextView tv = (TextView)v.findViewById(R.id.promptmessage);
        tv.setText(this.getPrompt());

        //You can set callbacks on buttons
        Button dismissBtn = (Button)v.findViewById(R.id.btn_dismiss);
        dismissBtn.setOnClickListener(this);

        Button saveBtn = (Button)v.findViewById(
                                    R.id.btn_save);
        saveBtn.setOnClickListener(this);
        return v;
    }
    .....other functions
}
```

In Listing 29–14 you are loading a view identified by a layout. Then you look for two buttons and set up callbacks on them. This is very similar to how you created your details fragment earlier. However, unlike the earlier fragments, a dialog fragment has another way to create the view hierarchy.

Overriding onCreateDialog

As an alternate to supplying a view in onCreateView(), you can override onCreateDialog() and supply a dialog instance. Listing 29–15 supplies sample code for this approach.

Listing 29–15. *Overriding onCreateDialog of a DialogFragment*

```
MyDialogFragment
{
    .....other functions
    @Override
    public Dialog onCreateDialog(Bundle icicle)
    {
```

```
        AlertDialog.Builder b = new AlertDialog.Builder(getActivity());
        b.setTitle("My Dialog Title");
        b.setPositiveButton("Ok", this);
        b.setNegativeButton("Cancel", this);
        b.setMessage(this.getMessage());
        return b.create();
    }
    .....other functions
}
```

In this example, you use the alert dialog builder to create a dialog object to return. This will work well for simple dialogs. The first option of overriding onCreateView() is equally easy and provides much more flexibility.

Displaying a Dialog Fragment

Once you have a dialog fragment constructed, you will need a fragment transaction to show it. Like all other fragments, operations on dialog fragments are conducted through fragment transactions.

The show() method on a dialog fragment takes a fragment transaction as an input. You can see this in Listing 29–13. The show() method uses the fragment transaction to add this dialog to the activity and then commits the fragment transaction. However, the show() method does not add the transaction to the back stack. If you want to do this, you need to add this transaction to the back stack first and then pass it to the show() method. The show() method of a dialog fragment has the following signatures:

```
public int show(FragmentTransaction transaction, String tag)
public int show(FragmentManager manager, String tag)
```

The first show() method displays the dialog by adding this fragment to the passed-in transaction with the specified tag. This method then returns the identifier of the committed transaction.

The second show() method automates getting a transaction from the transaction manager. This is a shortcut method. However, when you use this second method, you don't have an option to add the transaction to the back stack. If you want that control, you will need to use the first method. The second method could be used if you wanted to simply display the dialog and you had no other reason to work with a fragment transaction at that time.

A nice thing about a dialog being a fragment is that the underlying fragment manager does the basic state management. For example, even if the device rotates when a dialog is being displayed, the dialog is reproduced without you performing any state management.

The dialog fragment also offers methods to control the frame in which the dialog's view is displayed such as the title and the appearance of the frame. Refer to the DialogFragment class documentation to see more of these options; this URL is provided at the end of this chapter.

Dismissing a Dialog Fragment

There are two ways you can dismiss a dialog fragment. The first one is to explicitly call the dismiss() method on the dialog fragment in response to a button or some action on the dialog view, as shown in Listing 29–16.

Listing 29–16. *Calling dismiss()*

```
if (someview.getId() == R.id.btn_dismiss)
{
    //use some callbacks to advise clients
    //of this dialog that it is being dismissed
    //and call dismiss
    dismiss();
    return;
}
```

The dialog fragment's dismiss() method will remove the fragment from the fragment manager and then commit that transaction. If there is a back stack for this dialog fragment, then the dismiss() will just pop the current dialog out of the transaction stack and present the previous fragment transaction state. Whether there is a back stack or not, calling dismiss() will result in calling the standard dialog fragment destroy callbacks including onDismiss().

One thing to note is that you can't rely on onDismiss() to conclude that a dismiss() has been called by your code. This is because onDismiss() is also called when a device configuration changes and hence is not a good indicator of what the user did to the dialog itself. If the dialog is being displayed when the user rotates the device, the dialog fragment will see onDismiss() called even though the user did not press a button inside of the dialog. Instead, you should probably always rely on explicit button clicks on the dialog view.

If the user presses the Back button while the dialog fragment is displayed, this will cause the onCancel() callback to fire on the dialog fragment. By default, Android will make the dialog fragment go away, so you won't need to call dismiss() on the fragment yourself. But if you want the calling activity to be notified that the dialog has been cancelled, you will need to invoke logic from within onCancel() to make that happen. This is a difference between onCancel() and onDismiss() with dialog fragments. With onDismiss(), you still can't be sure exactly what happened that caused the onDismiss() callback to fire. You might also have noticed that a dialog fragment does not have a cancel() method, just dismiss(), but as we said, when a dialog fragment is being cancelled by pressing the Back button, Android takes care of cancelling/dismissing it for you.

The other way to dismiss a dialog fragment is to present another dialog fragment. The way you dismiss the current dialog and present the new one is slightly different than just dismissing the current dialog. Listing 29–17 shows an example.

Listing 29–17. *Setting Up a Dialog for Back Stack*

```
if (someview.getId() == R.id.btn_invoke_another_dialog)
{
    Activity act = getActivity();
```

```
    FragmentManager fm = act.getFragmentManager();
    FragmentTransaction ft = fm.beginTransaction();
    ft.remove(this);

    ft.addToBackStack(null);
    //null represents no name for the back stack transaction

    HelpDialogFragment hdf =
        HelpDialogFragment.newInstance(R.string.helptext);
    hdf.show(ft, "HELP");
    return;
}
```

Within a single transaction you're removing the current dialog fragment and you're adding the new dialog fragment. This has the effect of making the current dialog disappear visually and making the new dialog appear. If the user presses the Back button, because you've saved this transaction on the back stack, the new dialog would be dismissed and the previous dialog would be displayed. This is a handy way of displaying a help dialog, for example.

Implications of a Dialog Dismiss

When you add any fragment to a fragment manager, the fragment manager will do the state management for that fragment. This means when a device configuration changes (for example, the device rotates), the activity will be restarted and the fragments are also restarted. You saw this earlier when you rotated the device while running the Shakespeare sample application.

A device configuration change doesn't affect dialogs because they are also managed by the fragment manager. But the implicit behavior of `show()` and `dismiss()` means that you can easily lose track of a dialog fragment if you're not careful. The `show()` method automatically adds the fragment to the fragment manager; the `dismiss()` method automatically removes the fragment from the fragment manager. You may have a direct pointer to a dialog fragment before you start showing the fragment. But you can't add this fragment to the fragment manager and later call `show()`, since a fragment can only be added once to the fragment manager. You may plan to retrieve this pointer through restore of the activity. However, if you were to show and dismiss this dialog, this fragment is implicitly removed from fragment manager, thereby denying the ability for that fragment to be restored and repointed (because the fragment manager doesn't know this fragment exists after it gets removed).

If you want to keep the state of a dialog after it was dismissed you will need to maintain the state outside of the dialog either in the parent activity or a non-dialog fragment that hangs around for a longer time.

DialogFragment Sample Application

You'll now create a sample application that demonstrates these concepts of a dialog fragment. You're also going to introduce a concept of communication between a fragment and the activity that contains it. To make it all happen, you need five Java files.

- `MainActivity.java` is the main activity of your application. This will display a simple view with help text in it and a menu from which dialogs can be started.
- `PromptDialogFragment.java` is an example of a dialog fragment that defines its own layout in XML and allows input from the user. It has three buttons on the dialog: Save, Dismiss (i.e., cancel), Help.
- `AlertDialogFragment.java` is an example of a dialog fragment that uses the `AlertBuilder` class to create a dialog within this fragment. This is the old-school way of creating a dialog; it allows you to reuse what you already know about dialogs within a fragment.
- `HelpDialogFragment.java` is a very simple fragment that displays a help message from the applications resources. The specific help message is identified when a help dialog object is created. This help fragment can be shown from both the main activity and from the prompt dialog fragment.
- `OnDialogDoneListener.java` is an interface that you'll require your activity to implement in order to get messages back from the fragments. Using an interface means that your fragments don't need to know too much about the calling activity, except that it must have implemented this interface. This helps encapsulate functionality where it belongs. From the activity's point of view, it has a common way to receive information back from fragments without having to know too much about them.

There are three layouts for this application: for your main activity, for the prompt dialog fragment, and for the help dialog fragment. Note that you don't need a layout for the alert dialog fragment because the `AlertBuilder` will take care of that layout for you internally. When you're done, your application will look like Figure 29–3.

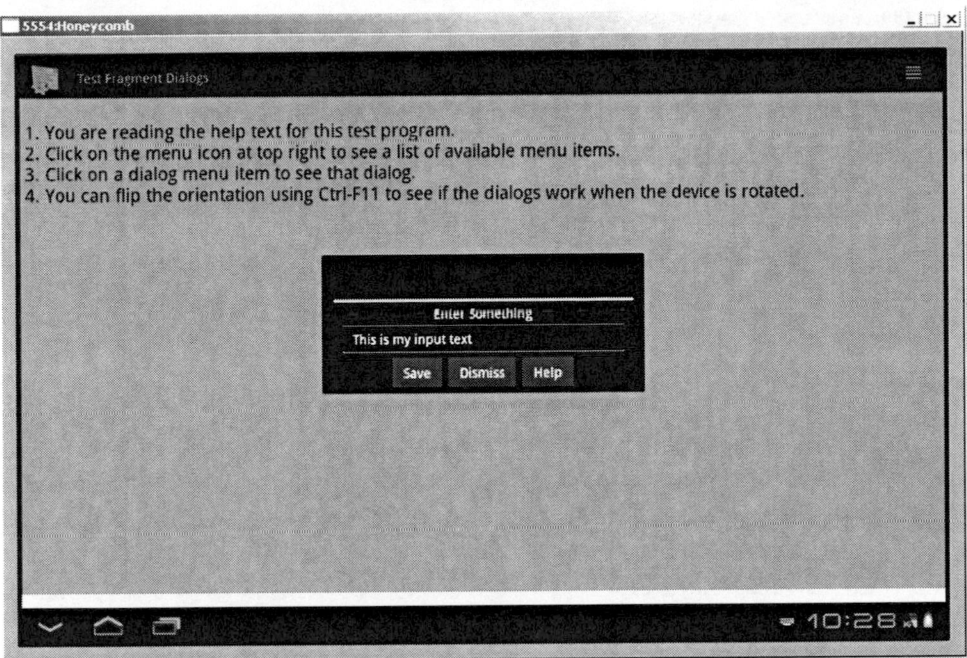

Figure 29–3. *The user interface for the dialog fragment sample application*

Dialog Sample: MainActivity

Let's get to the source code. Listing 29–18 shows your main activity.

Listing 29–18. *The Main Activity for Dialog Fragments*

```
// This file is MainActivity.java
import android.app.Activity;
import android.app.FragmentManager;
import android.app.FragmentTransaction;
import android.os.Bundle;
import android.util.Log;
import android.view.Menu;
import android.view.MenuInflater;
import android.view.MenuItem;
import android.widget.Toast;

public class MainActivity extends Activity
implements OnDialogDoneListener
{
    public static final String LOGTAG = "DialogFragmentDemo";
    public static final String ALERT_DIALOG_TAG = "ALERT_DIALOG_TAG";
    public static final String HELP_DIALOG_TAG = "HELP_DIALOG_TAG";
    public static final String PROMPT_DIALOG_TAG = "PROMPT_DIALOG_TAG";

    @Override
    public void onCreate(Bundle savedInstanceState)
    {
        super.onCreate(savedInstanceState);
```

```
        setContentView(R.layout.main);
        FragmentManager.enableDebugLogging(true);
    }

    @Override
    public boolean onCreateOptionsMenu(Menu menu){
        super.onCreateOptionsMenu(menu);
        MenuInflater inflater = getMenuInflater();
        inflater.inflate(R.menu.menu, menu);
        return true;
    }

    @Override
    public boolean onOptionsItemSelected(MenuItem item)
    {
        if (item.getItemId() == R.id.menu_show_alert_dialog)
        {
            this.testAlertDialog();
            return true;
        }
        if (item.getItemId() == R.id.menu_show_prompt_dialog)
        {
            this.testPromptDialog();
            return true;
        }
        if (item.getItemId() == R.id.menu_help)
        {
            this.testHelpDialog();
            return true;
        }
        return true;
    }

    private void testPromptDialog()
    {
        FragmentTransaction ft = getFragmentManager().beginTransaction();

        PromptDialogFragment pdf =
            PromptDialogFragment.newInstance("Enter Something");

        pdf.show(ft, PROMPT_DIALOG_TAG);
    }

    private void testAlertDialog()
    {
        FragmentTransaction ft = getFragmentManager().beginTransaction();

        AlertDialogFragment adf =
            AlertDialogFragment.newInstance("Alert Message");

        adf.show(ft, ALERT_DIALOG_TAG);
    }

    private void testHelpDialog()
    {
        FragmentTransaction ft = getFragmentManager().beginTransaction();
```

```
        HelpDialogFragment hdf =
            HelpDialogFragment.newInstance(R.string.help_text);

        hdf.show(ft, HELP_DIALOG_TAG);
    }

    public void onDialogDone(String tag, boolean cancelled,
                             CharSequence message) {
        String s = tag + " responds with: " + message;
        if(cancelled)
            s = tag + " was cancelled by the user";
        Toast.makeText(this, s, Toast.LENGTH_LONG).show();
        Log.v(LOGTAG, s);
    }
}
```

The code for your main activity is very straightforward. In `onCreate()`, you set the content view and you turn on fragment manager debugging. You then have a couple of methods related to setting up your options menu. For each menu option chosen, you call a simple method. Each method does basically the same thing: gets a fragment transaction, creates a new fragment, and shows the fragment. Note that each fragment has a unique tag supplied to the `show()` method. This tag becomes associated to the fragment in the fragment manager, so you can locate these fragments later by tag name. The fragment can also determine its own tag value with the `getTag()` method on `Fragment`.

The last method definition in your main activity is `onDialogDone()`, which is a callback that is part of the `OnDialogDoneListener` interface that your activity is implementing. As you can see, the callback supplies a tag of the fragment that is calling you, a boolean value indicating whether or not the dialog fragment was cancelled, and a message. For your purposes, you merely want to log the information to LogCat; you also show it to the user using Toast.

Dialog Sample: OnDialogDoneListener

So that you can know when a dialog has gone away, create a listener interface that your dialog callers will implement. The code of the interface is in Listing 29–19.

Listing 29–19. *The Listener Interface*

```
// This file is OnDialogDoneListener.java
/*
 * An interface implemented typically by an activity
 * so that a dialog can report back
 * on what happened.
 */
public interface OnDialogDoneListener {
  public void onDialogDone(String tag, boolean cancelled, CharSequence message);
}
```

This is a very simple interface, as you can see. You've only chosen one callback for this interface, which the activity will have to implement. Your fragments won't need to know the specifics of the calling activity, only that the calling activity must implement the

OnDialogDoneListener interface; therefore the fragments can call this callback to communicate with the calling activity. Depending on what the fragment is doing, there could be multiple callbacks in the interface. For this sample application, you're showing the interface separately from the fragment class definitions. For easier management of code, you could embed the fragment listener interface inside of the fragment class definition itself, thus making it easier to keep the listener and the fragment in sync with each other.

Dialog Sample: PromptDialogFragment

Now let's take a look at your first fragment, the PromptDialogFragment, whose layout and Java code is shown in Listing 29–20.

Listing 29–20. *The PromptDialogFragment Layout and Java Code*

```
<?xml version="1.0" encoding="utf-8"?>
<!-- This file is /res/layout/prompt_dialog.xml -->
<LinearLayout xmlns:android="http://schemas.android.com/apk/res/android"
    android:orientation="vertical" android:padding="4dip"
    android:gravity="center_horizontal"
    android:layout_width="match_parent"
    android:layout_height="match_parent">

    <TextView
        android:id="@+id/promptmessage"
        android:layout_height="wrap_content"
        android:layout_width="wrap_content"
        android:layout_marginLeft="20dip"
        android:layout_marginRight="20dip"
        android:text="Enter Text"
        android:layout_weight="1"
        android:layout_gravity="center_vertical|center_horizontal"
        android:textAppearance="?android:attr/textAppearanceMedium"
        android:gravity="top|center_horizontal" />

    <EditText
        android:id="@+id/inputtext"
        android:layout_height="wrap_content"
        android:layout_width="400dip"
        android:layout_marginLeft="20dip"
        android:layout_marginRight="20dip"
        android:scrollHorizontally="true"
        android:autoText="false"
        android:capitalize="none"
        android:gravity="fill_horizontal"
        android:textAppearance="?android:attr/textAppearanceMedium" />

    <LinearLayout
        android:orientation="horizontal"
        android:layout_width="wrap_content"
        android:layout_height="wrap_content">

      <Button android:id="@+id/btn_save"
        android:layout_width="wrap_content"
        android:layout_height="wrap_content"
```

```
        android:layout_weight="0"
        android:text="Save">
      </Button>

      <Button android:id="@+id/btn_dismiss"
        android:layout_width="wrap_content"
        android:layout_height="wrap_content"
        android:layout_weight="0"
        android:text="Dismiss">
      </Button>

      <Button android:id="@+id/btn_help"
        android:layout_width="wrap_content"
        android:layout_height="wrap_content"
        android:layout_weight="0"
        android:text="Help">
      </Button>

    </LinearLayout>
</LinearLayout>
```

```
// This file is PromptDialogFragment.java
import android.app.Activity;
import android.app.DialogFragment;
import android.app.FragmentTransaction;
import android.content.DialogInterface;
import android.os.Bundle;
import android.util.Log;
import android.view.LayoutInflater;
import android.view.View;
import android.view.ViewGroup;
import android.widget.Button;
import android.widget.EditText;
import android.widget.TextView;

public class PromptDialogFragment
extends DialogFragment
implements View.OnClickListener
{
    private EditText et;

    public static PromptDialogFragment
    newInstance(String prompt)
    {
        PromptDialogFragment pdf = new PromptDialogFragment();
        Bundle bundle = new Bundle();
        bundle.putString("prompt",prompt);
        pdf.setArguments(bundle);

        return pdf;
    }

    @Override
    public void onAttach(Activity act) {
        // If the activity you're being attached to has
        // not implemented the OnDialogDoneListener
```

```
        // interface, the following line will throw a
        // ClassCastException. This is the earliest you
        // can test if you have a well-behaved activity.
        OnDialogDoneListener test = (OnDialogDoneListener)act;
        super.onAttach(act);
    }

    @Override
    public void onCreate(Bundle icicle)
    {
        super.onCreate(icicle);
        this.setCancelable(true);
        int style = DialogFragment.STYLE_NORMAL, theme = 0;
        setStyle(style,theme);
    }

    public View onCreateView(LayoutInflater inflater,
            ViewGroup container, Bundle icicle)
    {
        View v = inflater.inflate(R.layout.prompt_dialog, container,
                                  false);

        TextView tv = (TextView)v.findViewById(R.id.promptmessage);
        tv.setText(getArguments().getString("prompt"));

        Button dismissBtn = (Button)v.findViewById(R.id.btn_dismiss);
        dismissBtn.setOnClickListener(this);

        Button saveBtn = (Button)v.findViewById(R.id.btn_save);
        saveBtn.setOnClickListener(this);

        Button helpBtn = (Button)v.findViewById(R.id.btn_help);
        helpBtn.setOnClickListener(this);

        et = (EditText)v.findViewById(R.id.inputtext);
        if(icicle != null)
            et.setText(icicle.getCharSequence("input"));
        return v;
    }

    @Override
    public void onSaveInstanceState(Bundle icicle) {
        icicle.putCharSequence("input", et.getText());
        super.onPause();
    }

    @Override
    public void onCancel(DialogInterface di) {
        Log.v(MainActivity.LOGTAG, "in onCancel () of PDF");
        super.onCancel (di);
    }

    @Override
    public void onDismiss(DialogInterface di) {
        Log.v(MainActivity.LOGTAG, "in onDismiss() of PDF");
        super.onDismiss(di);
    }
```

```
    public void onClick(View v)
    {
        OnDialogDoneListener act = (OnDialogDoneListener)getActivity();
        if (v.getId() == R.id.btn_save)
        {
            TextView tv =
                (TextView)getView().findViewById(R.id.inputtext);
            act.onDialogDone(this.getTag(), false, tv.getText());
            dismiss();
            return;
        }
        if (v.getId() == R.id.btn_dismiss)
        {
            act.onDialogDone(this.getTag(), true, null);
            dismiss();
            return;
        }
        if (v.getId() == R.id.btn_help)
        {
            FragmentTransaction ft =
                getFragmentManager().beginTransaction();
            ft.remove(this);

            // in this case, you want to show the help text, but
            // come back to the previous dialog when you're done
            ft.addToBackStack(null);
            //null represents no name for the back stack transaction

            HelpDialogFragment hdf =
                    HelpDialogFragment.newInstance(R.string.help1);
            hdf.show(ft, MainActivity.HELP_DIALOG_TAG);
            return;
        }
    }
}
```

Your prompt dialog layout looks like many you've seen previously. There is a TextView to serve as the prompt; an EditText to take the user's input; and three buttons for saving the input, dismissing (i.e., cancelling) the dialog fragment, and popping a help dialog.

Your PromptDialogFragment Java code starts out looking just like your earlier fragments. You have a newInstance() static method to create new objects, and within this method you call the default constructor, build an arguments bundle, and attach it to your new object. Next, you have something new within the onAttach() callback. You want to make sure that the activity you just got attached to has implemented the OnDialogDoneListener interface. In order to test that, you cast the activity passed in to the OnDialogDoneListener interface. If the activity does not implement this interface, you'll get a ClassCastException thrown. You could have handled this exception and dealt with it more gracefully, but you're trying to keep the code as simple as possible for now.

Next up is the onCreate() callback. As is common with fragments, you don't build your user interface here, but you can set the dialog style. This is unique to dialog fragments.

You can set both the style and the theme yourself, or you can set just style and use a theme value of zero (0) to let the system choose an appropriate theme for you.

In onCreateView() you create the view hierarchy for your dialog fragment. Just like other fragments, you do not attach your view hierarchy to the view container passed in (i.e., by setting the attachToRoot parameter to false). You then proceed to set up the button callbacks and you set the dialog prompt text to the prompt that was passed originally to newInstance(). Finally, you check to see if there are any values being passed in through the icicle bundle. This would indicate that your fragment is being recreated, most likely due to a configuration change, and it's possible that the user had already typed some text. If so, you need to populate the EditText with what the user had done so far. Remember that because your configuration has changed, the actual view object in memory is not the same as before, so you must locate it and set the text accordingly. The very next callback is onSaveInstanceState(); it's where you save any current text typed in by the user into the icicle bundle.

Your onCancel() and onDismiss() callbacks are only shown because of the logging, so you'll be able to see when these callbacks fire during the lifecycle of your fragment.

The final callback in your prompt dialog fragment is for the buttons. Once again, you grab a reference to your enclosing activity and you cast it to the interface you expect the activity to have implemented. If the user pressed the Save button, you grab the text as entered and you call the interface's callback onDialogDone(). As shown earlier, this callback takes the tag name of this fragment, a boolean indicating whether or not this dialog fragment was cancelled, and a message, which in this case is the text as typed by the user.

You then call dismiss() to get rid of the dialog fragment. Remember that dismiss() not only makes the fragment go away visually, but it pops the fragment out of the fragment manager so it is no longer available to you. If the button pressed is Dismiss, you again call the interface callback, this time with no message, and then you call dismiss(). And finally, if the user pressed the Help button, you don't actually want to lose the prompt dialog fragment, so you do something a little different. We described this earlier. In order to remember your prompt dialog fragment so you can come back to it later, you need to create a fragment transaction to remove the prompt dialog fragment and to add the help dialog fragment with the show() method; this needs to go onto the back stack. Notice, too, how the help dialog fragment is created with a reference to a resource ID. This means your help dialog fragment can be used with any help text available to your application.

Dialog Sample: HelpDialogFragment

We'll show the code for the help dialog fragment shortly, but we'll describe the operation now. You created a fragment transaction to go from the prompt dialog fragment to the help dialog fragment, and you placed that fragment transaction on the back stack. This has the effect of making the prompt dialog fragment disappear from view, but it's still accessible through the fragment manager and the back stack. The new help dialog fragment appears in its place and allows the user to read the help text. When the user dismisses the help dialog fragment, the fragment back stack entry will be popped, with the effect of the help dialog fragment being dismissed (both visually and from the fragment manager) and the prompt dialog fragment restored to view. This is actually a pretty easy way to make all this happen. The code in Listing 29–21 is very simple yet very powerful; it even works if the user rotates the device while these dialogs are being displayed.

Listing 29–21. *The HelpDialogFragment Layout and Java Code*

```
<?xml version="1.0" encoding="utf-8"?>
<!-- this file is /res/layout/help_dialog.xml -->
<LinearLayout xmlns:android="http://schemas.android.com/apk/res/android"
    android:orientation="vertical" android:padding="4dip"
    android:layout_width="match_parent"
    android:layout_height="match_parent">

    <TextView
        android:id="@+id/helpmessage"
        android:layout_height="wrap_content"
        android:layout_width="wrap_content"
        android:layout_marginLeft="20dip"
        android:layout_marginRight="20dip"
        android:text="Help Text"
        android:layout_weight="1"
        android:layout_gravity="center_vertical|center_horizontal"
        android:textAppearance="?android:attr/textAppearanceMedium"
        android:gravity="top|center_horizontal" />

      <Button android:id="@+id/btn_close"
        android:layout_width="wrap_content"
        android:layout_height="wrap_content"
        android:layout_weight="0"
        android:text="Close">
      </Button>

</LinearLayout>


// This file is HelpDialogFragment.java
import android.app.DialogFragment;
import android.os.Bundle;
import android.view.LayoutInflater;
import android.view.View;
import android.view.ViewGroup;
import android.widget.Button;
import android.widget.TextView;

public class HelpDialogFragment
extends DialogFragment
implements View.OnClickListener
{
    public static HelpDialogFragment
    newInstance(int helpResId)
    {
        HelpDialogFragment hdf = new HelpDialogFragment();
        Bundle bundle = new Bundle();
        bundle.putInt("help_resource", helpResId);
```

```
        hdf.setArguments(bundle);

        return hdf;
    }

    @Override
    public void onCreate(Bundle icicle)
    {
        super.onCreate(icicle);
        this.setCancelable(true);
        int style = DialogFragment.STYLE_NORMAL, theme = 0;
        setStyle(style,theme);
    }

    public View onCreateView(LayoutInflater inflater,
            ViewGroup container,
            Bundle icicle)
    {
        View v = inflater.inflate(R.layout.help_dialog, container,
                                  false);

        TextView tv = (TextView)v.findViewById(R.id.helpmessage);
        tv.setText(getActivity().getResources()
                .getText(getArguments().getInt("help_resource")));

        Button closeBtn = (Button)v.findViewById(R.id.btn_close);
        closeBtn.setOnClickListener(this);
        return v;
    }

    public void onClick(View v)
    {
        dismiss();
    }
}
```

Here is another dialog fragment, and it's even simpler than the last one. The point of this dialog fragment is to display some help text. The layout is a `TextView` and a Close button. The Java code should be starting to look familiar to you now. There's a `newInstance()` method to create a new help dialog fragment, an `onCreate()` to set the style and theme, and an `onCreateView()` to build the view hierarchy. In this particular case, you want to locate a string resource to populate the `TextView`, so you access the resources through the activity, and choose the resource ID as was passed in to `newInstance()`. Finally, `onCreateView()` sets up a button click handler to capture the clicks on the Close button. In this case, you don't need to do anything interesting at the time of dismissal.

There are two ways this fragment is being called: from the activity and from the prompt dialog fragment. When this help dialog fragment is shown from the main activity, dismissing it will simply pop the fragment off the top and reveal the main activity underneath. When this help dialog fragment is shown from the prompt dialog fragment, because this fragment was part of a fragment transaction on the back stack, dismissing it will cause the fragment transaction to be rolled back, which will pop the help dialog fragment, but will restore the prompt dialog fragment. The user will see the prompt dialog fragment reappear.

Dialog Sample: AlertDialogFragment

We have one last dialog fragment to show you in this sample application, and that is the alert dialog fragment. While you could always create an alert dialog fragment in a way similar to the help dialog fragment, you can also create a dialog fragment using the old `AlertBuilder` framework that has worked for many releases of Android. Listing 29–22 shows the source code of the alert dialog fragment.

Listing 29–22. *The AlertDialogFragment Java Code*

```
import android.app.AlertDialog;
import android.app.Dialog;
import android.app.DialogFragment;
import android.content.DialogInterface;
import android.os.Bundle;

public class AlertDialogFragment
extends DialogFragment
implements DialogInterface.OnClickListener
{
    public static AlertDialogFragment
    newInstance(String message)
    {
        AlertDialogFragment adf = new AlertDialogFragment();
        Bundle bundle = new Bundle();
        bundle.putString("alert-message",message);
        adf.setArguments(bundle);

        return adf;
    }

    @Override
    public void onCreate(Bundle savedInstanceState)
    {
        super.onCreate(savedInstanceState);
        this.setCancelable(true);
        int style = DialogFragment.STYLE_NORMAL, theme = 0;
        setStyle(style,theme);
    }

    @Override
    public Dialog onCreateDialog(Bundle savedInstanceState)
    {
        AlertDialog.Builder b =
            new AlertDialog.Builder(getActivity());
        b.setTitle("Alert!!");
        b.setPositiveButton("Ok", this);
        b.setNegativeButton("Cancel", this);
        b.setMessage(this.getArguments().getString("alert-message"));
        return b.create();
    }
```

```
    public void onClick(DialogInterface dialog, int which)
    {
        OnDialogDoneListener act = (OnDialogDoneListener) getActivity();
        boolean cancelled = false;
        if (which == AlertDialog.BUTTON_NEGATIVE)
        {
            cancelled = true;
        }
        act.onDialogDone(getTag(), cancelled, "Alert dismissed");
    }
}
```

You don't need a layout for this one because the AlertBuilder takes care of that for you. You'll note that this dialog fragment starts out like any other, but instead of an onCreateView() callback, you now have a onCreateDialog() callback instead. You either implement onCreateView() or onCreateDialog() but not both. The return from onCreateDialog() is not a view; it's a Dialog. Now you can reuse what you learned in Chapter 8 to build a dialog the old-fashioned way. What's different is that to get parameters for your dialog, you should be accessing your arguments bundle. In this example application, you only do this for the alert-message, but you could access other parameters through the arguments bundle as well.

Notice also that with this type of dialog fragment, you need your fragment class to implement the DialogInterface.OnClickListener, which means your dialog fragment must implement the onClick() callback. This callback will be fired when the user acts on the embedded dialog. Once again, you get a reference to the dialog that fired and an indication of which button was pressed. As before, you should be careful not to depend on an onDismiss() because this could fire when there is a device configuration change.

Dialog Sample: Main Layout main.xml

For completeness, Listing 29–23 shows the layout for your main activity.

Listing 29–23. *The Main Layout*

```
<?xml version="1.0" encoding="utf-8"?>
<!-- /res/layout/main.xml -->
<LinearLayout
    xmlns:android="http://schemas.android.com/apk/res/android"
    android:orientation="vertical"
    android:layout_width="match_parent"
    android:layout_height=" match_parent"
    android:gravity="fill"
    >
<TextView android:id="@+id/textViewId"
    android:layout_width=" match_parent"
    android:layout_height="match_parent"
    android:background="@android:color/white"
    android:text="@string/help_text"
    android:textColor="@android:color/black"
    android:textSize="25sp"
    android:scrollbars="vertical"
    android:scrollbarStyle="insideOverlay"
    android:scrollbarSize="25dip"
```

```
    android:scrollbarFadeDuration="0"
    />
</LinearLayout>
```

When you run this sample application, make sure you try all the menu options in different orientations of the device. Try to rotate the device while the dialog fragments are displayed. You should be pleased to see that the dialogs go with the rotations and you do not need to worry about a lot of code to manage the saving and restoring of fragments due to configuration changes.

The other thing we hope you appreciate is the ease with which you can communicate between the fragments and the activity. Of course, the activity has references, or can get references, to all of the available fragments, so it can access methods exposed by the fragments themselves. This isn't the only way to communicate between fragments and with the activity. You can always use the getter methods on the fragment manager to retrieve an instance of a managed fragment, then cast that reference appropriately and call a method on that fragment directly. You can even do this from within another fragment. The degree to which you isolate your fragments from each other with interfaces and through activities, or build in dependencies with fragment-to-fragment communication, is based on how complex your application is and how much reuse you want to get.

More Communications with Fragments

We've covered a clean way to do communication between fragments, that is, to define and use an interface to implement callbacks from fragments back to the calling activity. But this is not the only way to do communication between fragments. Since the fragment manager knows about all fragments attached to the current activity, the activity or any fragment in that activity can ask for any other fragment using the getter methods described earlier.

Once the fragment reference has been obtained, the activity or fragment could cast the reference appropriately and then call methods directly on that activity or fragment. This would cause your fragments to have more knowledge about the other fragments than might normally be desired, but don't forget that you're running this application on a mobile device, so cutting corners can sometimes be justified. A code snippet is provided in Listing 29–24 to show how one fragment might communicate directly with another fragment.

Listing 29–24. *Direct Fragment-to-Fragment Communication*

```
FragmentOther fragOther =
        (FragmentOther)getFragmentManager().findFragmentByTag("other");
fragOther.callCustomMethod( arg1, arg2 );
```

In Listing 29–24, there is no interface involved. The current fragment has direct knowledge of the class of the other fragment and also which methods exist on that class. This may be okay since these fragments are part of one application, and it can be easier to simply accept the fact that some fragments will know about other fragments.

Using startActivity() and setTargetFragment()

A feature of fragments that is very much like activities is the ability of a fragment to start an activity. Fragment has a `startActivity()` method and `startActivityForResult()` method. These work just like the ones for activities do; when a result is passed back, it will cause the `onActivityResult()` callback to fire on the fragment that started the activity.

There's another communication mechanism you should know about. When one fragment wants to start another fragment, there is a feature that lets the calling fragment set its identity with the called fragment. Listing 29–25 shows an example of what it might look like.

Listing 29–25. *Fragment-to-Target-Fragment Setup*

```
mCalledFragment = new CalledFragment();
mCalledFragment.setTargetFragment(this, 0);
fm.beginTransaction().add(mCalledFragment, "work").commit();
```

With these few lines, you've created a new `CalledFragment` object, set the target fragment on the called fragment to the current fragment, and added the called fragment to the fragment manager and activity using a fragment transaction. When the called fragment starts to run, it will be able to call `getTargetFragment()`, which will return a reference to the calling fragment. With this reference, the called fragment could invoke methods on the calling fragment or even access view components directly. For example, in Listing 29–26, the called fragment could set text in the UI of the calling fragment directly.

Listing 29–26. *Target Fragment-to-Fragment Communication*

```
TextView tv = (TextView)
    getTargetFragment().getView().findViewById(R.id.text1);
tv.setText("Set from the called fragment");
```

Custom Animations with ObjectAnimator

Earlier we exposed you to a little custom animations on fragments. You used a custom animation to fade out the current details fragment while you faded in the new details fragment. We also told you that the stock animations under the Android SDK were few and some don't even work. This section will help you understand how to create your own custom animations so you can do interesting transitions between old fragments and new fragments.

The mechanism for implementing custom animations on fragments is the `ObjectAnimator` class. This is actually a generic feature in Android that can be applied to View objects and not just fragments. You're only going to worry about fragments in this section, but the principles here can apply to other objects as well. An object animator is a device that takes an object and animates it from a "from" state to a "to" state over a period of time. The period of time is defined in the animator in milliseconds. There is a routine that defines how the animation behaves over that period of time; these routines are called interpolators.

If you imagine the transition from the "from" state to the "to" state as a straight line, the interpolator defines where along that straight line the transition will be at any point during the time period. One of the simplest interpolators is the linear interpolator; it divides the straight line into equal chunks and steps evenly through those chunks for the duration of the time period. The effect is that the object moves at a constant speed from the "from" to the "to" with no acceleration at the beginning and no deceleration at the end.

The default interpolator is `accelerate_decelerate` which adds a smooth accelerated beginning and a smooth decelerated end. What's really interesting is that the interpolator could go past the "to" point on that line and then come back. This is what the overshoot interpolator does. There's another interpolator called bounce that goes from "from" to "to," but when it first gets to the "to" point, it bounces back towards "from" a few times before finally settling to rest on the "to" point.

An interpolator acts on a dimension of the object. For the `fade_in` and `fade_out` animators you used earlier, the dimension was the fragment's alpha (that is, the amount of transparency of the object). The `fade_in` animator took the alpha dimension from zero (0) to one (1). The `fade_out` animator took the alpha dimension of the other fragment from one (1) to zero (0). One fragment went from invisible to completely visible, while the other went from completely visible to invisible.

Behind the scenes, the object animator is finding the root view of the fragment and applying repeated calls to the `setAlpha()` method, changing the parameter value over the time period a little bit in each call. The frequency of the repeated calls depends on the interpolator. The linear interpolator makes regular calls at regular intervals in time. The `accelerate_decelerate` interpolator starts out setting the parameter values smaller at first per unit of time, then makes the parameter values larger, creating the effect of an acceleration. It then does the opposite at the other end making the object appear to decelerate on its dimension.

Dimensions can be many of the values that are settable and gettable on a View. In fact, reflection is used by the object animator to work on the view being manipulated. If you specify that you want to animate rotation, the object animator will call the `setRotation()` method on the object (or object's view). The animator takes a "from" and a "to" value, and uses them to animate the object from "from" to "to". If the "from" value is not specified, a getter method will be determined and used to get the current value from the object. Let's see how this applies to your fragments.

The only method in the `FragmentTransaction` class that specifies a custom animation is the `setCustomAnimations()` method, which takes two resource ID parameters.

- The first parameter specifies an animator resource for the fragment entering the view container.
- The second specifies an animator resource for the fragment exiting the view container.

These two animators do not need to even be related, but it's probably best visually to pair them. In other words, if you're fading one fragment out, fade the other fragment in. Or if you're sliding one fragment out to the right, slide the other fragment in from the left.

Animator resources can be found in the Android SDK folder, under the appropriate platform, then under `/data/res/animator`. This is where you will find `fade_in.xml` and `fade_out.xml` that you used earlier. Or you could create your own. If you decide to create your own, it would be best to use your project's `/res/animator` directory, creating it manually if you need to. For an example of a simple local animator XML file (`slide_in_left.xml`), refer to Listing 29–27.

Listing 29–27. *A Custom Animator to Slide in From the Left*

```
<?xml version="1.0" encoding="utf-8" ?>
<objectAnimator xmlns:android="http://schemas.android.com/apk/res/android"
    android:interpolator="@android:interpolator/accelerate_decelerate"
    android:valueFrom="-1280"
    android:valueTo="0"
    android:valueType="floatType"
    android:propertyName="x"
    android:duration="2000" />
```

This resource file uses the new (in Android 3.0) `objectAnimator` tag. The basic structure of this file should look familiar to you. It is a bunch of android: attributes to indicate what you want to do. For object animator, there are several things that you need to specify. The first one is the interpolator. The types that are available to you are listed in `android.R.interpolator`. Using your knowledge of resource names, the interpolator attribute resolves to a file in the Android SDK, under the appropriate platform, in `/data/res/interpolator`, with a filename of `accelerate_decelerate.xml`.

The `android:propertyName` attribute specifies the dimension that you want to animate on. In this case, you want to animate on the X dimension. If you investigate the `setX()` method on a View, you will find that it takes a float value as a parameter, and that is why the `android:valueType` attribute is set to `floatType`. The `android:duration` value is set to 2000, which means 2 seconds. This is probably too slow for a real production app, but it helps you to see what's happening as it happens. Finally, the `android:valueFrom` and `android:valueTo` attributes have values of -1280 and 0 respectively. These are chosen because you want the fragment to be at 0 when the animation is done. That is, you want the fragment to be visible to the user with its left edge on the left edge of the view container when the animation stops. Because you want to have the effect of the fragment sliding in from the left, you want it to start from off to the left, and -1280 seems like a big enough number to make that happen. As you might expect, an animator resource file that slides out to the right would look very similar to the one in Listing 29–27, except that the `valueFrom` would be 0 and the `valueTo` would be some large positive number, such as 1280.

Most of the time, you will find that the dimension you're interested in animating is a `floatType`, although there may be times when you pick an `intType`. Just look at the type of the parameter that the setter requires. This is where the object animator gets really powerful. In fact, it does not care where the setter method came from. That means you could add your own dimension to an object, and the object animator can animate it for you. All you need to do is supply the setter method, then set the attributes in a resource file; the object animator will do the rest. One caveat here is that if you do not specify a `valueFrom` attribute in your XML, the object animator will use a getter method to determine the starting value for the object. The getter method must return the appropriate type for the dimension in question.

You might also be interested in animating more than one dimension at a time. For this, you can use the `<set>` tag to enclose more than one `<objectAnimator>` tag. Listing 29–28 shows an animator resource file (`slide_out_down.xml`) that animates along Y at the same time that it animates on alpha.

Listing 29–28. *A Custom Animator that Animates on Y and Alpha*

```
<?xml version="1.0" encoding="utf-8" ?>
<set xmlns:android="http://schemas.android.com/apk/res/android">
<objectAnimator
    android:interpolator="@android:interpolator/accelerate_cubic"
    android:valueFrom="0"
    android:valueTo="1280"
    android:valueType="floatType"
    android:propertyName="y"
    android:duration="2000" />
<objectAnimator
    android:interpolator="@android:interpolator/accelerate_cubic"
    android:valueFrom="1"
    android:valueTo="0"
    android:valueType="floatType"
    android:propertyName="alpha"
    android:duration="2000" />
</set>
```

The `<set>` tag corresponds to the `AnimatorSet` class in Android; however in XML, `<set>` only has one attribute and that is `android:ordering`. The allowed attribute values are `together`, the default, which causes the enclosed object animators to run in parallel, and `sequential`, which causes the object animators to run one after the other in the order in which they are declared in the XML file.

References

Here are some helpful references to topics you may wish to explore further:

- `www.androidbook.com/projects`. This is a list of downloadable projects related to this book. The file called `ProAndroid3_Ch29_Fragments.zip` contains all projects from this chapter, listed in separate root directories. There is also a `README.TXT` file that describes exactly how to import projects into Eclipse from one of these zip files. It includes some projects that utilize the Fragment Compatibility SDK for older Androids as well.
- ApiDemos. Within the Android SDK samples, there is a project called ApiDemos. This project includes several example applications that use fragments and should help you to understand how to use them.
- `http://developer.android.com/guide/topics/fundamentals/fragments.html`. This is the Android Developer's Guide page to fragments.

- `http://android-developers.blogspot.com/2011/02/android-30-fragments-api.html`. The Android blog post that introduced fragments.
- `http://android-developers.blogspot.com/2011/02/animation-in-honeycomb.html`. The Android blog post that introduced the new animations framework and object animators.

Summary

This chapter introduced a core new class in Android 3.0, the Fragment class, and its related classes for the manager, transactions, and subclasses. Fragments are a powerful new way to organize functionality and the corresponding user interfaces. While they were developed with tablet screens in mind, fragments will also be available on small screen devices to help encapsulate behavior into nice, neat chunks that can be reused, moved around, and managed in ways that you couldn't do before. You learned about one of the cool new features in Android, the object animator, which can very easily make fragment transitions very interesting.

The next chapter will cover another significant new aspect of Android tablet applications, namely the ActionBar.

Chapter 30

Exploring ActionBar

ActionBar is a new API in Android 3.0 SDK. It allows you to customize the title bar of an activity. Prior to the 3.0 SDK release, the title bar of an activity merely contained the title of an activity.

As the Android SDK matures with each new release, it is taking on more and more desktop UI patterns. In a desktop application, you see a menu bar and a number of action icons. It is this desktop title/menu bar pattern that is emulated in the ActionBar implementation.

Android ActionBar is particularly modeled after the menu/title bar of a web browser. The ActionBar is designed in such a way that you can apply the familiar browser-like navigation patterns to your applications.

> **NOTE:** In this chapter we refer to both ActionBar and "action bar." When we say ActionBar we are referring to the actual class, and when we want to talk about the concept we refer to it as "action bar."

A key goal of the action bar design is to make the frequently used actions easily available to the user without searching through option menus or context menus.

> **NOTE:** In the current computer technology literature, the convenient access to actions is fashionably called "Affordance," which refers to the ability to conveniently discover/invoke actions. We have included a few reference URLs on Affordance at the end of the chapter.

As you go through this chapter we are going to demonstrate the following about an action bar:

- An action bar is owned by an Activity and follows its lifecycle.
- An action bar can take one of three forms: tabbed action bar, list action bar and a standard action bar. We will show how these various action bars look and behave in each of the modes.

- We will talk about how tabbed listeners allow us to interact with a tabbed action bar.
- We will talk about how spinner adapters and list listeners are used to interact with the list action bar.
- We will show you how the Home icon of an action bar interacts with the menu infrastructure.
- We will show you how icon menu items can be shown and reacted to on the action bar real estate.

We will demonstrate these concepts by planning three different activities. Each activity will sport an action bar in a different mode. This will give us an opportunity to examine the behavior of the action bar in each mode. But first, let's take a quick look at visual aspects of an action bar.

Anatomy of an ActionBar

Figure 30–1 shows a typical action bar in tabbed navigation mode.

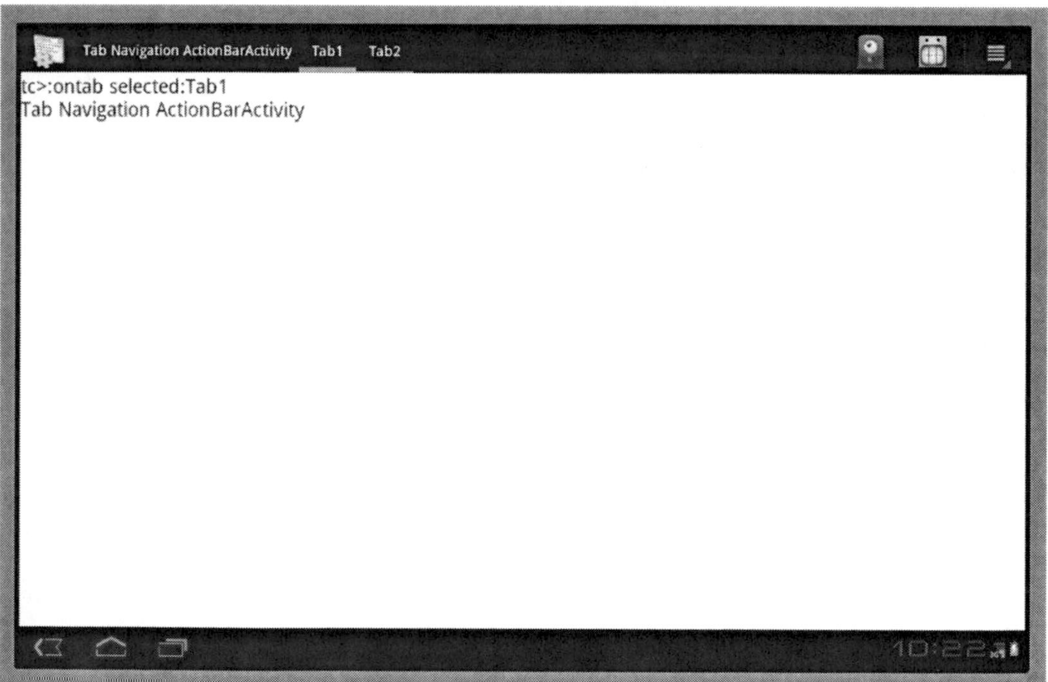

Figure 30–1. *An Activity with a Tabbed ActionBar*

This screenshot is taken from the actual working example that is presented later in the chapter. This action bar in Figure 30–1 has five parts in it. These parts are (from left to right):

Home Icon area: The icon on the top left-hand side of the action bar is sometimes called the “Home” icon. This is similar to a web site navigation context, where clicking on the Home icon will take you to a starting point. You will see later that clicking on this Home icon will send a callback to the option menu call back with menu id: `android.R.id.home.`

Title area: The Title area displays the title for the action bar.

Tabs area: The Tabs area is where the action bar paints the list of tabs specified. The content of this area is variable. If the action bar navigation mode is Tabs, then tabs are shown here. If the mode is list navigation mode then a navigable list of drop-down items are shown. In standard mode this area is ignored and left empty.

Action Icon area: Following the Tabs area, the Action Icon area shows some of the option menu items as icons. We will show you how to choose which option menus are displayed as action icons in our example later.

Menu Icon area: The last area is the Menu area. It is a single standard menu icon. When you click on this menu icon you will see the expanded menu. This expanded menu will look differently or show up in a different location depending on the size of the Android device.

In addition to the action bar, the activity in Figure 30–1 is showing a debug text view where a number of actions are logged to. These actions may be a result of clicking the tabs or the home icon or the action menus or the actual option menus.

Let’s look at how to implement the three types of action bar activities we talked about earlier: the tabbed action bar, the list action bar, and the standard action bar. As we have introduced the tabbed action bar as the visual example of an action bar, we will start with the implementation of a Tabbed Action bar first.

Tabbed Navigation Action Bar Activity

Although we are planning three different activities, each with its own type of action bar, there is a lot of common functionality we would like to see in all these activities.

All of these activities have the same debug text view so that we can monitor the actions as they get invoked.

All of these activities have the same Home icon.

All of these activities have a title.

All of these activities have the same Action icons.

All of these activities have the same Options menu.

The primary difference with these activities is that each configures the action bar differently. In our example we will encapsulate the common behavior in a base class and allow each of the derived activities, including this tabbed action bar activity, to configure the action bar.

It is difficult to explain these common files with out the context of at least one action bar activity. So we will present these common files and how the tabbed action bar activity uses these common files in one section first. Then the other two status bar activities can be added to this project with fewer files.

Below is a list of files that are needed for this tabbed action bar exercise. These files include both the common files and the files specific to the tabbed action bar. The list seems numerous because we are encapsulating the common behavior into base classes. This will reduce the number of files for later examples. We have also indicated the listing numbers for each of the files.

DebugActivity.java: Base class activity that allows for a debug text view as shown in Figure 30–1 (Listing 30–2).

BaseActionBarActivity.java: Derived from `DebugActivity` and allows for common navigation (such as responding to common actions including switching between the three activities) (Listing 30–3).

IReportBack.java: An interface that works as a communication vehicle between the debug activity and the various listeners of the action bar (Listing 30–1).

BaseListener.java: Base listener class that works with the `DebugActivity` and the various actions that gets invoked from the action bar. Acts as a base class for both tab listeners and list navigation listeners (Listing 30–4).

TabNavigationActionBarActivity.java: inherits from `BaseActionBarActivity`.java and configures the action bar as a tabbed action bar. Most of the code pertaining to the tabbed action bar is in this class (Listing 30–6).

TabListener.java: Required to add a tab to the tabbed action bar. This where you respond to tab clicks. In our case this simply logs a message to the debugview through the `BaseListener` (Listing 30–5).

AndroidManifest.xml: where activities are defined to be invoked (Listing 30–13).

Layout/main.xml: Layout file for the `DebugActivity`. As all the three status bar activities inherit this base `DebugActivity` they all share the this layout file (Listing 30–7).

menu/menu.xml: A set of menu items to test the menu interaction with the action bar. The menu file is also shared across all the derived status bar activities (Listing 30–9).

Implementing Base Activity Classes

A number of the base classes use IReportBack interface. This interface was introduced in previous chapters. It serves the same purpose here. It is reintroduced in Listing 30–1 so that you don't have to refer back to previous chapters.

Listing 30–1. *IReportBack.java*

```
//IReportBack.java
package com.androidbook.actionbar;

public interface IReportBack
{
   public void reportBack(String tag, String message);
   public void reportTransient(String tag, String message);
}
```

A class that implements this interface takes a message and report it on a screen, like a debug message. This is done through the reportBack() method. The method reportTransient does the same except it uses a Toast to report that message to the user.

In our example the class that implements IReportBack is DebugActivity. The source code for DebugActivity is presented in listing 30–2.

Listing 30–2. *DebugActivity with a Debug Text View*

```
//DebugActivity.java
package com.androidbook.actionbar;
//
//Use CTRL-SHIFT-O to import dependencies
//
public abstract class DebugActivity
extends Activity
implements IReportBack
{
   //Derived classes needs first
   protected abstract boolean
   onMenuItemSelected(MenuItem item);

   //private variables set by constructor
   private static String tag=null;
   private int menuId = 0;
   private int layoutid = 0;
   private int debugTextViewId = 0;

   public DebugActivity(int inMenuId,
         int inLayoutId,
         int inDebugTextViewId,
         String inTag)
   {
      tag = inTag;
      menuId = inMenuId;
      layoutid = inLayoutId;
      debugTextViewId = inDebugTextViewId;

   }
```

```
@Override
protected void onCreate(Bundle savedInstanceState) {
    super.onCreate(savedInstanceState);
    setContentView(this.layoutid);

    //You need the following to be able to scroll
    //the text view.
    TextView tv = this.getTextView();
    tv.setMovementMethod(
      ScrollingMovementMethod.getInstance());
}
@Override
public boolean onCreateOptionsMenu(Menu menu){
   super.onCreateOptionsMenu(menu);
      MenuInflater inflater = getMenuInflater();
      inflater.inflate(menuId, menu);
   return true;
}
@Override
public boolean onOptionsItemSelected(MenuItem item){
   appendMenuItemText(item);
   if (item.getItemId() == R.id.menu_da_clear){
      this.emptyText();
      return true;
   }
   boolean b = onMenuItemSelected(item);
   if (b == true)
   {
      return true;
   }
   return super.onOptionsItemSelected(item);
}
protected TextView getTextView(){
    return
    (TextView)this.findViewById(this.debugTextViewId);
}
protected void appendMenuItemText(MenuItem menuItem){
   String title = menuItem.getTitle().toString();
   appendText("MenuItem:" + title);
}
protected void emptyText(){
   TextView tv = getTextView();
   tv.setText("");
}
protected void appendText(String s){
   TextView tv = getTextView();
   tv.setText(s + "\n" + tv.getText());
   Log.d(tag,s);
}
public void reportBack(String tag, String message)
{
   this.appendText(tag + ":" + message);
   Log.d(tag,message);
}
public void reportTransient(String tag, String message)
{
   String s = tag + ":" + message;
```

```
            Toast mToast =
              Toast.makeText(this, s, Toast.LENGTH_SHORT);
            mToast.show();
            reportBack(tag,message);
            Log.d(tag,message);
        }
}//eof-class
```

The primary goal of this base activity class is to present an activity with a debug text view in it. This text view is used to log messages coming from the reportBack() method. We will use this activity as the base activity for the action bar activities.

Assigning Uniform Behavior for the ActionBar

We have more opportunities to refactor the code from the derived activities into another level of a base class called BaseActionBarActivity.

The primary goal of this refactoring class is to provide a common behavior in response to the menu items. These menu items are there to switch between the three activities that represent three different action bar modes. Once switched you can test that particular action bar activity.

This activity is presented in Listing 30–3.

Listing 30–3. *A Common Base Class for Action Bar Enabled Activities*

```
// BaseActionBarActivity.java
package com.androidbook.actionbar;
//
//Use CTRL-SHIFT-O to import dependencies
//
public abstract class BaseActionBarActivity
extends DebugActivity
{
    private String tag=null;
    public BaseActionBarActivity(String inTag)
    {
        super(R.menu.menu,
            R.layout.main,
            R.id.textViewId,
        inTag);
        tag = inTag;
    }
    @Override
    public void onCreate(Bundle savedInstanceState)
    {
        super.onCreate(savedInstanceState);
        TextView tv = this.getTextView();
        tv.setText(tag);
    }
    protected boolean onMenuItemSelected(MenuItem item)
    {
        //Responding to Home Icon
        if (item.getItemId() == android.R.id.home) {
            this.reportBack(tag,"Home Pressed");
```

```
            return true;
        }

        //Common behavior to invoke sibling activities
        if (item.getItemId() == R.id.menu_invoke_tabnav){
            if (getNavMode() ==
              ActionBar.NAVIGATION_MODE_TABS)
            {
                this.reportBack(tag,
                  "You are already in tab nav");
            }
            else {
                this.invokeTabNav();
            }
            return true;
        }
        if (item.getItemId() == R.id.menu_invoke_listnav){
            if (getNavMode() ==
            ActionBar.NAVIGATION_MODE_LIST)
            {
                this.reportBack(tag,
                "You are already in list nav");
            }
            else{
                this.invokeListNav();
            }
            return true;
        }
        if (item.getItemId() == R.id.menu_invoke_standardnav){
            if (getNavMode() ==
            ActionBar.NAVIGATION_MODE_STANDARD)
            {
                this.reportBack(tag,
                "You are already in standard nav");
            }
            else{
                this.invokeStandardNav();
            }
            return true;
        }
        return false;
    }
    private int getNavMode(){
        ActionBar bar = this.getActionBar();
        return bar.getNavigationMode();
    }
    private void invokeTabNav(){
        Intent i = new Intent(this,
          TabNavigationActionBarActivity.class);
        startActivity(i);
    }

    //Uncomment the following method bodies
    //as you implement these additional activities

    private void invokeListNav(){
        //Intent i = new Intent(this,
```

```
        //  ListNavigationActionBarActivity.class);
        //startActivity(i);
    }
    private void invokeStandardNav(){
        //Intent i = new Intent(this,
        //  StandardNavigationActionBarActivity.class);
        //startActivity(i);
    }
}//eof-class
```

If you notice the code responding to menu items in Listing 30–3, you see that we are checking if the current activity is also the one that is being asked to switch to. If it is, we log a message and don't switch the current activity.

This base action bar activity also simplifies the derived action bar navigation activities including the tabbed navigation action bar activity.

Implementing the Tabbed Listener

Before we are able to work with a tabbed action bar we need a tabbed listener. A tabbed listener allows us to respond to the click events on the tabs. We will derive our tabbed listener from a base listener that will allow us to log tab actions. Listing 30–4 shows the base listener that uses the IReportBack for logging.

Listing 30–4. *A Common Listener for Action Bar Enabled Activities*

```
//BaseListener.java
package com.androidbook.actionbar;
//
//Use CTRL-SHIFT-O to import dependencies
//
public class BaseListener
{
   protected IReportBack mReportTo;
   protected Context mContext;
   public BaseListener(Context ctx, IReportBack target)
   {
      mReportTo = target;
      mContext = ctx;
   }
}
```

This base class holds a reference to an implementation of IReportBack and also the activity that can be used as a context. In our case, the DebugActivity of Listing 30–2 is the implementer of IReportBack and also plays the role of the context.

Now that we have a base listener, Listing 30–5 shows the tabbed listener.

Listing 30–5. *Tab Listener to Respond to Tab Actions*

```
// TabListener.java
package com.androidbook.actionbar;
//
//Use CTRL-SHIFT-O to import dependencies
//
public class TabListener extends BaseListener
```

```
implements ActionBar.TabListener
{
    private static String tag = "tc>";
    public TabListener(Context ctx,
                IReportBack target)
    {
        super(ctx, target);
    }
    public void onTabReselected(Tab tab,
                  FragmentTransaction ft)
    {
        this.mReportTo.reportBack(tag,
          "ontab re selected:" + tab.getText());
    }
    public void onTabSelected(Tab tab,
               FragmentTransaction ft)
    {
        this.mReportTo.reportBack(tag,
          "ontab selected:" + tab.getText());
    }
    public void onTabUnselected(Tab tab,
                 FragmentTransaction ft)
    {
        this.mReportTo.reportBack(tag,
          "ontab un selected:" + tab.getText());
    }
}
```

This tabbed listener merely documents the call backs from the action bar tabs to the debug text view of Figure 30–1.

Implementing the Tabbed Action Bar Activity

With the tabbed listener in place, we can finally construct the tabbed navigation activity. This is presented in Listing 30–6.

Listing 30–6. *Tab-navigation Enabled Action Bar Activity*

```
// TabNavigationActionBarActivity.java
package com.androidbook.actionbar;
//
//Use CTRL-SHIFT-O to import dependencies
//
public class TabNavigationActionBarActivity
extends BaseActionBarActivity
{
    private static String tag =
      "Tab Navigation ActionBarActivity";
    public TabNavigationActionBarActivity()
    {
        super(tag);
    }
    @Override
    public void onCreate(Bundle savedInstanceState)
    {
        super.onCreate(savedInstanceState);
```

```
        workwithTabbedActionBar();
    }

    public void workwithTabbedActionBar()
    {
        ActionBar bar = this.getActionBar();
        bar.setTitle(tag);
        bar.setNavigationMode(
          ActionBar.NAVIGATION_MODE_TABS);

        TabListener tl = new TabListener(this,this);

        Tab tab1 = bar.newTab();
        tab1.setText("Tab1");
        tab1.setTabListener(tl);
        bar.addTab(tab1);

        Tab tab2 = bar.newTab();
        tab2.setText("Tab2");
        tab2.setTabListener(tl);
        bar.addTab(tab2);
    }
}//eof-class
```

We will now discuss this code of tabbed action bar activity (Listing 30–6) in multiple sub sections as we draw attention to each aspect of working with a tabbed action bar. We will start with getting access to the action bar belonging to an activity.

Obtaining an Action Bar Instance

In Listing 30–6, notice that the code that controls the action bar is pretty simple. You get access to the action bar of an activity by calling `getActionbar()` on the activity. Here is that line of code again:

```
ActionBar bar = this.getActionBar();
```

As this snippet of code shows, action bar is a property of the activity, and does not cross activity boundaries. In other words, one cannot use an action bar to control or influence multiple activities.

Action Bar Navigation Modes

In Listing 30–6, once we obtain the action bar for an activity we set its navigation mode to `ActionBar.NAVIGTION_MODE_TABS`: Here is that line of code again:

```
bar.setNavigationMode(
  ActionBar.NAVIGATION_MODE_TABS);
```

The other two possible action bar navigation modes are

```
ActionBar.NAVIGTION_MODE_LIST

ActionBar.NAVIGTION_MODE_STANDARD
```

Once we set the tabbed navigation mode we have a number of tab related methods in the API of ActionBar class to work with. In Listing 30–6 we have used these tab related APIs to add two tabs to the action bar. We have also used the tabbed listener of listing 30–5 to initialize the tabs.

Here is a quick code snippet borrowed from Listing 30–6 that shows how a tab is added to the action bar:

```
Tab tab1 = bar.newTab();
tab1.setText("Tab1");
tab1.setTabListener(tl);
bar.addTab(tab1);
```

If you were to forget to call the setTabListener() on a tab that is added to the action bar, you will get a runtime error indicating that a listener is needed.

Scrollable Debug Text View Layout

As the tabs of the action bar are clicked on, the tab listeners are set up in such a way that debug messages are sent to the debug text view. Listing 30–7 shows the layout file for the DebugActivity, which in turn contains the debug text view.

Listing 30–7. ***Debug Activity Text View Layout File***

```
<?xml version="1.0" encoding="utf-8"?>
<!-- /res/layout/main.xml -->
<LinearLayout
xmlns:android="http://schemas.android.com/apk/res/android"
    android:orientation="vertical"
    android:layout_width="fill_parent"
    android:layout_height="fill_parent"
    android:gravity="fill"
    >
<TextView android:id="@+id/textViewId"
    android:layout_width="fill_parent"
    android:layout_height="fill_parent"
    android:background="@android:color/white"
    android:text="Initial Text Message"
    android:textColor="@android:color/black"
    android:textSize="25sp"
    android:scrollbars="vertical"
    android:scrollbarStyle="insideOverlay"
    android:scrollbarSize="25dip"
    android:scrollbarFadeDuration="0"
    />
</LinearLayout>
```

There are a few things worth noting about this layout. We set the background color of the text view to white. This will let us capture screens in brighter light. The text size is also set to large font to aid screen capture.

We have also set up the text view so that it is enabled for scrolling. Although typically layouts use ScrollView, a text view is already enabled for scrolling by itself. In addition to enabling the scrolling properties in the XML file for the text view you will need to call the setMovementMethod() on the text view as shown in Listing 30–8.

Listing 30–8. *Enabling Text View for Scrolling*

```
TextView tv = this.getTextView();
tv.setMovementMethod(
     ScrollingMovementMethod.getInstance());
```

This code is extracted from the DebugActivity (Listing 30–2).

Also as the text view is scrolled you notice that the scroll bar appears and then fades away. This is not a good indicator if there is text beyond visible range. You can tell the scrollbar to stay by setting the fade duration to 0. See listing 30–7 for how to set this parameter.

Action Bar and Menu Interaction

We also want to demonstrate in this example how menus interact with action bar. So we will need to set up a menu file. This file is presented in Listing 30–9.

Listing 30–9. *Menu XML File for This Project*

```
<!-- /res/menu/menu.xml -->
<menu
xmlns:android="http://schemas.android.com/apk/res/android">
    <!-- This group uses the default category. -->
    <group android:id="@+id/menuGroup_Main">

        <item android:id="@+id/menu_action_icon1"
            android:title="Action Icon1"
            android:icon="@drawable/creep001"
            android:showAsAction="ifRoom"/>

        <item android:id="@+id/menu_action_icon2"
            android:title="Action Icon2"
            android:icon="@drawable/creep002"
            android:showAsAction="ifRoom"/>

        <item android:id="@+id/menu_icon_test"
            android:title="Icon Test"
            android:icon="@drawable/creep003"/>

        <item android:id="@+id/menu_invoke_listnav"
            android:title="Invoke List Nav"
            />
        <item android:id="@+id/menu_invoke_standardnav"
            android:title="Invoke Standard Nav"
            />
        <item android:id="@+id/menu_invoke_tabnav"
            android:title="Invoke Tab Nav"
            />
        <item android:id="@+id/menu_da_clear"
            android:title="clear" />
    </group>
</menu>
```

NOTE: This menu XML file in listing 30–9 uses 3 icons (creep001, 002, and 003) from www.androidicons.com. As per the web site, these icons are under Creative Commons License 3.0.

The following section talks about this menu in a bit more detail.

Displaying the Menu

In releases 2.3 and earlier, devices often had an explicit menu button. In 3.0 the emulator doesn't show physical Home, Back, or Menu buttons. These may still be available on some devices.

As seen in Figure 30–2, the Back and Home buttons are now soft buttons available at the bottom of the screen. However, the Menu button is shown in the context of an application, specifically as part of the action bar to the top right-hand corner.

Figure 30–2 shows what the menu looks when it is expanded.

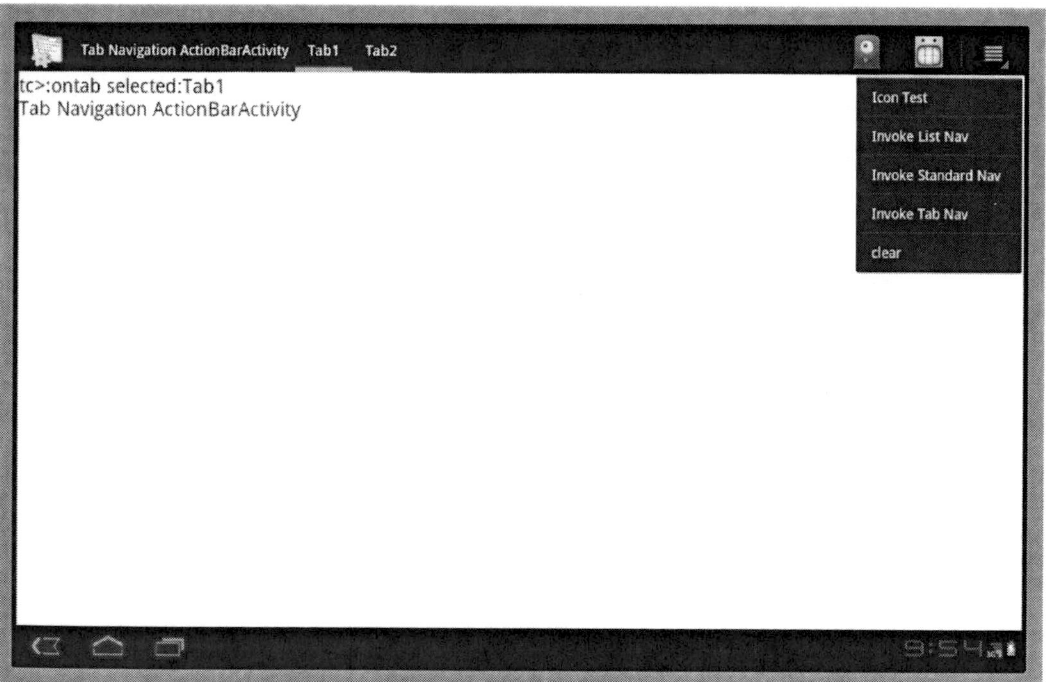

Figure 30–2. *An activity with a tabbed action bar and expanded menu*

One thing of note is that a menu bar may not show the icons for menu items. One should not rely on icons for menu items being shown in all cases.

Menu Items as Actions

As indicated at the beginning of the chapter, you can assign some of the menu items to show up directly on the action bar. These menu items are indicated with the tag `showAsAction`. You can see this tag in Listing 30–9 of the menu XML file. This tag line is extracted and shown again listing 30–10.

Listing 30–10. *Menu Item Attribute for showAsAction*

```
android:showAsAction="ifRoom"
```

The other possible values for this Xml tag are:

```
always
never
withText
```

You can also accomplish the same affect with a Java API available on the `MenuItem` class.

```
menuItem.setShowAsAction(int actionEnum)
```

The values for the `actionEnum` are:

```
SHOW_AS_ACTION_ALWAYS
SHOW_AS_ACTION_IF_ROOM
SHOW_AS_ACTION_NEVER
SHOW_AS_ACTION_WITH_TEXT
```

Because these actions are merely menu items they behave as such and call the `onOptionsItemSelected()` callback method of the activity class.

Finally the example uses a number of icons. You can replace these icons with some of your own or you can download the project for this chapter using the URL at the end of this chapter.

Android Manifest File

Listing 30–11 shows the manifest file for this project so far.

Listing 30–11. *AndroidManifest.xml*

```
<?xml version="1.0" encoding="utf-8"?>
<manifest xmlns:android="http://schemas.android.com/apk/res/android"
      package="com.androidbook.actionbar"
      android:versionCode="1"
      android:versionName="1.0.0">
    <application android:icon="@drawable/icon"
        android:label="ActionBars Demo App">
        <activity android:name=".TabNavigationActionBarActivity"
                  android:label="Action Bar Demonstration: TabNav">
            <intent-filter>
                <action android:name="android.intent.action.MAIN" />
```

```
                <category android:name="android.intent.category.LAUNCHER" />
            </intent-filter>
        </activity>
    </application>
    <uses-sdk android:minSdkVersion="11" />
</manifest>
```

The minSDKVersion need to point to 11, the API number for release 3.0.

Examining the Tabbed Action Bar Activity

Once you compile these files and run you will see the tabbed action bar, as seen Figure 30–1. Then if you click on the menu icon to the right you will see the menu of the application, as expanded in Figure 30–2.

The application is designed such a way that any action on the action bar is logged to the debug text view. While you are running this application you can test the following:

- If you click the Home icon you will see a message logged to the debug screen indicating that the Home button is pressed.
- If you click on tab1, you will see a message that the "tab1" is reselected.
- If you click on tab2, you will see two messages. The first one indicates that tab1 is losing focus and that tab2 is clicked. These messages are provisioned through the tab listener in Listing 30–5.
- If you click on the action buttons on the right-hand side, you will see that their corresponding menu items are invoked and debug messages logged to the debug view.
- If you expand the menu, you will see that there are menu items to invoke other activities, which will demonstrate the rest of the action bar modes. However, you will need to wait until the other activities are developed later in the chapter. Until then you will just notice that those items are invoked and debug messages logged.

This concludes our implementation of not only the tabbed action bar activity but also the setting up of the base framework so that coding the rest of the two activities is much simpler. Let's move onto the list navigation mode action bar.

List Navigation Action Bar Activity

As our base classes are carrying the most of the work, it is fairly easy to implement and test the list action bar navigation activity. You will need the following additional files to implement this activity:

- **SimpleSpinnerArrayAdapter**.java: This class is needed to setup the list navigation bar along with the listener. This class provides the rows required by a drop-down navigation list (Listing 30–12).

ListListener.java: This class acts as a listener to the list navigation activity. This class needs to be passed to the action bar when setting it up as a list action bar (Listing 30–13).

ListNavigationActionBarActivity.java: This is where we implement the list navigation action bar activity (Listing 30–14).

Once you have these three new files you will need to update the following two files:

BaseActionBarActivity.java: You will need to uncomment the invocation of list action bar activity (Listing 30–3).

AndroidManifest.xml: You will need to define the new list navigation action bar activity in the manifest file (Listing 30–11).

Creating a SpinnerAdapter

To be able to initialize the action bar with list navigation mode we need the following two things:

A spinner adapter that can tell the list navigation what the list of navigation text is.

To supply a list navigation listener so that when one of the list items is picked we can get a call back.

Listing 30–12 presents the `SimpleSpinnerArrayAdapter` that implements the `SpinnerAdapter` interface. As stated earlier the goal of this class is to give a list of items to show.

Listing 30–12. ***Creating a Spinner Adapter for List Navigation***

```
//SimpleSpinnerArrayAdapter.java
package com.androidbook.actionbar;
//
//Use CTRL-SHIFT-O to import dependencies
//
public class SimpleSpinnerArrayAdapter
extends ArrayAdapter<String>
implements SpinnerAdapter
{
    public SimpleSpinnerArrayAdapter(Context ctx)
    {
        super(ctx,
          android.R.layout.simple_spinner_item,
          new String[]{"one","two"});

        this.setDropDownViewResource(
          android.R.layout.simple_spinner_dropdown_item);
    }
    public View getDropDownView(
      int position, View convertView, ViewGroup parent)
    {
        return super.getDropDownView(
          position, convertView, parent);
    }
}
```

There is no SDK class that directly implements the SpinnerAdapter interface required by list navigation. So we have derived this class from an ArrayAdapter and provided a simple implementation for the SpinnerAdapter. We have also provided a reference URL on spinner adapters for further reading. Let's move on now to the list navigation listener.

Creating a List Listener

This is a simple class implementing the ActionBar.OnNavigationListener. Listing 30–13 shows the code for this class.

Listing 30–13. *Creating a List Listener for List Navigation*

```
//ListListener.java
package com.androidbook.actionbar;
//
//Use CTRL-SHIFT-O to import dependencies
//
public class ListListener
extends BaseListener
implements ActionBar.OnNavigationListener
{
    public ListListener(
    Context ctx, IReportBack target)
    {
        super(ctx, target);
    }
    public boolean onNavigationItemSelected(
    int itemPosition, long itemId)
    {
        this.mReportTo.reportBack(
          "list listener","ItemPostion:" + itemPosition);
        return true;
    }
}
```

Like the tabbed listener of Listing 30–5, we have inherited from our BaseListener so that we can log events to the debug text view through the IReportBack interface.

Setting Up a List Action Bar

We now have what we require to set up a list navigation action bar. Let us show you the source code for the list navigation action bar activity in Listing 30–14. This class is very similar to the tabbed activity we have coded earlier.

Listing 30–14. *List Navigation Action Bar Activity*

```
// ListNavigationActionBarActivity.java
package com.androidbook.actionbar;
//
//Use CTRL-SHIFT-O to import dependencies
//
public class ListNavigationActionBarActivity
extends BaseActionBarActivity
{
```

```
    private static String tag=
      "List Navigation ActionBarActivity";

    public ListNavigationActionBarActivity()
    {
        super(tag);
    }
    @Override
    public void onCreate(Bundle savedInstanceState)
    {
        super.onCreate(savedInstanceState);
        workwithListActionBar();
    }
    public void workwithListActionBar()
    {
        ActionBar bar = this.getActionBar();
        bar.setTitle(tag);
        bar.setNavigationMode(ActionBar.NAVIGATION_MODE_LIST);
        bar.setListNavigationCallbacks(
           new SimpleSpinnerArrayAdapter(this),
           new ListListener(this,this));
    }
}//eof-class
```

The important code is highlighted in Listing 30–14. The code is quite simple. We take a spinner adapter and a list listener and set them as list navigation callbacks on the action bar.

Making Changes to BaseActionBarActivity

Once this list navigation action bar activity (listing 30–14) is available we can go back and change the `BaseActionBarActivity` so that the menu item intended for `ListNavigationActionBarActivity` will invoke this activity. When uncommented, the corresponding function in Listing 30-3 will look like the extracted and uncommented code in Listing 30–15.

Listing 30–15. ***Code to Uncomment for Invoking List Navigation Action Bar Activity***

```
private void invokeListNav(){
     Intent i = new Intent(this,
        ListNavigationActionBarActivity.class);
     startActivity(i);
}
```

Once you uncomment this, the menu item and the code are already wired to invoke this list navigation action bar activity.

Making Changes to AndroidManifest.xml

Before you will be able to invoke the activity, you will need to register this activity in the Android Manifest file. You will need to add the code in Listing 30–16 to the Android Manifest file of Listing 30–11 to complete the activity registration.

Listing 30–16. *Registering List Navigation Action Bar Activity*

```
<activity android:name=".ListNavigationActionBarActivity"
        android:label="Action Bar Demonstration: ListNav">
</activity>
```

Examining the List Action Bar Activity

Once you compile these files covered so far (the new and changed files mentioned at the beginning of this section on list navigation action bar) and run the application you will see the list action bar as shown in Figure 30–3.

Figure 30–3. *An activity with list navigation action bar*

In Figure 30–3 you can see the unexpanded list right next to the title of the activity. This is the same place the SDK puts the tabs when the action bar mode is tab navigation. Now if you click on the item that said “one,” you will see the list expand allowing you to choose. This is shown in Figure 30–4.

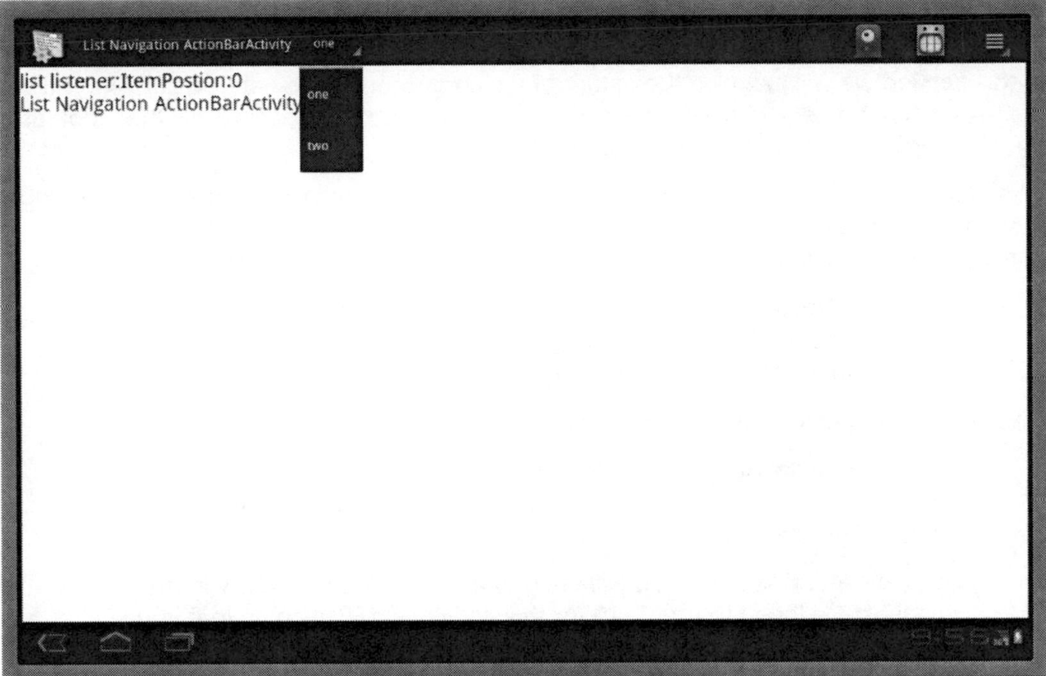

Figure 30–4. *An activity with opened navigation list*

When you compare this activity to the activity in figures 30–1 and 30–2, you realize that these activities look very similar, except that in one case you have tabs and in the other case you have a list to navigate. The motif of these two activities is illustrating an important parallel to the way web sites are designed.

In a web site, there might be a number of web pages, but each page will display a uniform look and feel through master pages. In our simpler case we have used the base class to accomplish this effect.

Although we have used multiple activities to showcase action bars, the action bars in 3.0 seem to be more applicable to orchestrate fragments on a single activity. However, should you need to work with multiple activities, you can use this pattern of base class to provide that master page design pattern.

The behavior of this list navigation activity is very much like the one for the tabbed activity of the previous section. The difference here is what happens when you click the list items. Each time you choose a list item you will see a call back to the list listener and the list listener will send a message to the debug text view.

Now that we have two activities available, the menu items will allow you to switch between tabbed activity and the list activity.

Let's now move on to the simpler standard action bar activity

Standard Navigation Action Bar Activity

In this section we will examine the nature of a standard navigation action bar. We will set up an activity and sets its action bar navigation mode as standard. We will then look at the standard navigation looks like and its behavior.

Like in the case of `ListNavigationActionBarActivity`, as our base classes are carrying most of the work, it is easy to implement and test the standard action bar navigation activity. You will need the following additional file to implement this activity:

> **StandardNavigationActionBarActivity**.java: This is the implementation file for configuring the action bar as a standard navigation mode action bar (Listing 30–17).

Once you have this new file you will need to update the following two files:

> **BaseActionBarActivity**.java: You will need to uncomment the invocation of standard action bar activity in response to a menu item (see Listing 30–18 for changes and Listing 30–3 for the original file).
>
> **AndroidManifest**.xml: You will need to define this new activity in the manifest file (see Listing 30–19 for this activity's definition so that you can add this to the main AndroidManifest file Listing 30–11).

We will explore each of these files now.

Standard Navigation Action Bar Activity

We have used tabbed listeners while setting up the tabbed action bar and we have used list listeners for setting up the list navigation action bar. For a standard action bar there are no listeners other than of course the menu call backs. The menu callbacks don't need to be specially set up as they are already hooked up automatically by the SDK. As a result it is quite easy to set up the action bar in the standard navigation mode.

Listing 30–17 presents the source code for the standard navigation action bar activity

Listing 30–17. *Standard Navigation Action Bar Activity*

```
//StandardNavigationActionBarActivity.java
package com.androidbook.actionbar;
//
//Use CTRL-SHIFT-O to import dependencies
//
public class StandardNavigationActionBarActivity
extends BaseActionBarActivity
{
    private static String tag=
      "Standard Navigation ActionBarActivity";
    public StandardNavigationActionBarActivity()
    {
        super(tag);
    }
    @Override
```

```
    public void onCreate(Bundle savedInstanceState)
    {
        super.onCreate(savedInstanceState);
        workwithStandardActionBar();
    }

    public void workwithStandardActionBar()
    {
        ActionBar bar = this.getActionBar();
        bar.setTitle(tag);
        bar.setNavigationMode(ActionBar.NAVIGATION_MODE_STANDARD);
        //test to see what happens if you were to attach tabs
        attachTabs(bar);
    }
    public void attachTabs(ActionBar bar)
    {
        TabListener tl = new TabListener(this,this);

        Tab tab1 = bar.newTab();
        tab1.setText("Tab1");
        tab1.setTabListener(tl);
        bar.addTab(tab1);

        Tab tab2 = bar.newTab();
        tab2.setText("Tab2");
        tab2.setTabListener(tl);
        bar.addTab(tab2);
    }
}//eof-class
```

The only thing necessary to set up an action bar as a standard navigation action bar is to set its navigation mode as such. In Listing 30–17 we have done this and highlighted that portion of the code.

> **NOTE:** In listing 30–17 we have also included code to see what would happen if we were to add tabs while the mode is standard navigation. Our testing shows that these tabs do not cause any run time error but will be ignored by the framework.

Before seeing how the standard action bar looks like you will need to make a couple of changes to existing files.

Making Changes to BaseActionBarActivity

Once the standard navigation action bar activity (Listing 30–17) is available we can go back and change the `BaseActionBarActivity` (listing 30–3) so that the menu item intended for `StandardNavigationActionBarActivity` will invoke this activity. When uncommented, the corresponding function in Listing 30–3 will look like the code in listing 30–18.

Listing 30–18. *Section to Uncomment to Invoke Standard Navigation Action Bar Activity*

```
private void invokeStandardNav(){
    Intent i = new Intent(this,
      StandardNavigationActionBarActivity.class);
    startActivity(i);
}
```

Once you uncomment this, the menu item and the code are already wired to invoke the `StandardNavigationActionBarActivity`.

Making Changes to AndroidManifest.xml

However before you will be able to invoke this activity you will need to register this activity in the android manifest file. You will need to add the following lines to the Android Manifest file in Listing 30–11 to complete the activity registration.

Listing 30–19. *Registering Standard Navigation Action Bar Activity*

```
<activity android:name=".StandardNavigationActionBarActivity "
        android:label="Action Bar Demonstration: Standard Nav">
</activity>
```

Examining the Standard Action Bar activity

Once you compile these files covered so far (and listed in section "Standard Navigation Action Bar Activity") and run the application you will see the application opened up with the tabbed activity as the first activity (Figure 30–1). Now if you click on the menu item you will see the figure 30–2. From this menu if you choose the menu item "Invoke Standard Nav" you will see the standard navigation action bar activity as in the following figure 30–5

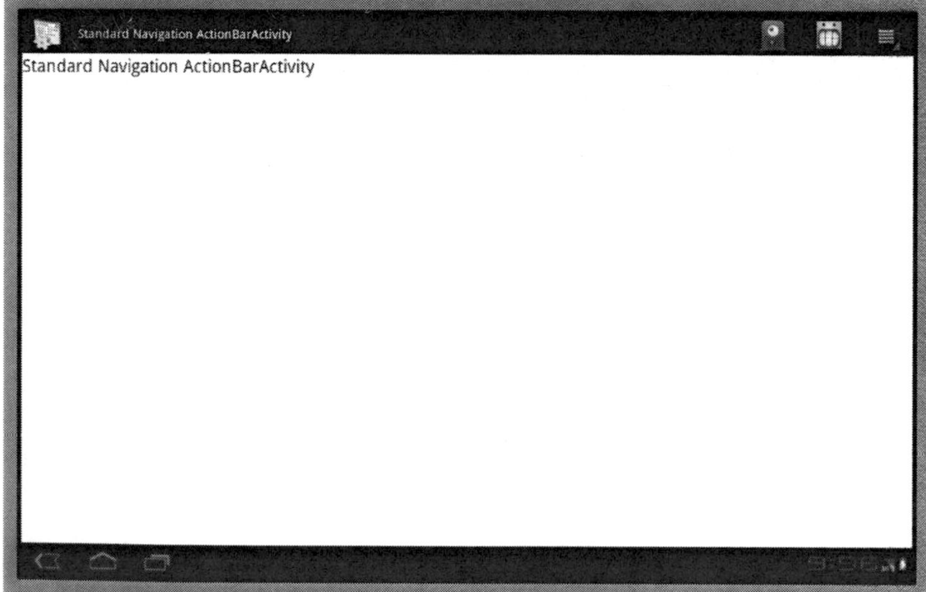

Figure 30–5. *An activity with a standard navigation action bar*

The first thing you notice in Figure 30–5 is that this action bar is missing the area that was previously dedicated to either a tab or a list navigation. Now if you go ahead and click the action buttons on the right, they will write their invocation to the debug text view. Now go ahead and click the Home button. This will also write its invocation signature to the debug text view. At the end of these three clicks the debug text view looks like Figure 30–6.

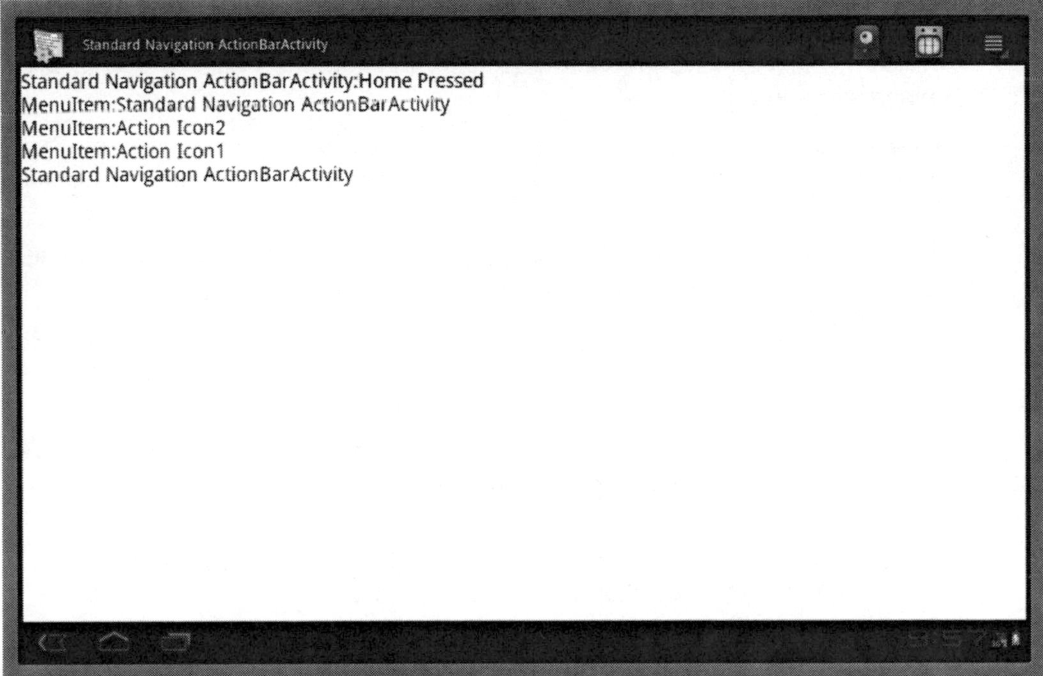

Figure 30–6. *Responding to events from an action bar*

References

The following URLs have been very helpful to us as we researched material for this chapter. The URLs also include further reading material. In addition the final URL allows you to download a zip file of the project of this chapter.

> *The Design of Everyday Things*, **Donald A Norman**. This book appropriated a previous idea in "visual perception" called "Affordance" for HCI (Human Computer Interaction). This term is being increasingly used in Android UI literature. The action bar of this chapter is touted as one of the key UI affordances.
>
> http://en.wikipedia.org/wiki/Affordance: WikiPedia Reference for understanding UI Affordances.

www.androidbook.com/item/3624: This points to our research on Android action bar. You will see here a list of further references, sample code, links to sample examples, and UI figures representing various action bar modes.

http://developer.android.com/reference/android/app/ActionBar.html: This is the API URL for the ActionBar class.

Using Spinner Adapter (www.androidbook.com/item/3627): To set up the list navigation mode you need to understand how dropdown lists and spinners work. This brief article shows a few samples and reference links on how to use spinners in Android.

www.androidicons.com: A couple of the icons we have used in this chapter are borrowed from this web site. These icons are under Creative Commons License 3.0.

Pleasing Android Layouts (www.androidbook.com/item/3302): We have at this URL few quick notes and sample source code for simple layouts.

http://developer.android.com/reference/android/view/MenuItem.html: This URL points to the API for the `MenuItem` class. You will find here documentation for attaching menu items as action icons on the action bar.

http://developer.android.com/guide/topics/resources/menu-resource.html: This URL documents the XML elements available for defining menu items as action bar icons.

www.androidbook.com/projects: You can use this URL to download the test project dedicated for this chapter. The name of the zip file is ProAndroid3_ch30_TestActionbar.zip

Summary

As you can see, an action bar is not mysterious. It is a known paradigm that is used in desktop programming. What makes it a bit hard to the beginner is that a single class is behaving in three different ways based on a mode bit. One would always wonder if a set of derived classes could have done the trick. But again the difference between the modes is so small it may be better off as a single class as it is now.

The motivation for the action bar design seems to swerve towards a browser based web navigation model.

The Android designers also seem to indicate to use action bar in association with fragments to get the desired UI uniformity. When you have a need to switch between activities, the designers are asking us to take a look to see if same thing can be accomplished through fragments rather than new activities. Fragments bring lot of advantages especially their state management as device is flipped around causing configuration changes. An activity with fragments maintains state between configuration changes Fragments are covered in greater detail in the previous Chapter 29.

This chapter has also presented one possible way to get the design uniformity using a base level navigation activity. This can potentially be achieved also through delegation as opposed to inheritance. One could also borrow from well-known patterns that are used to create master pages on web sites and see how best to orchestrate Android SDK classes to that effect.

Action bar facilities are available only in SDKs starting at 3.0. As of now there is no indication that these facilities are available as libraries for older releases.

There is also a bit of discrepancy between documentation and the Java API. The documentation indicates there are only three action bar modes. However there is an additional mode in Java API called dropdown navigation mode. When we tested this it behaved just a list navigation mode except that it removed the title.

Also you can control what is displayed on the action bar through display flags. Refer to the API documentation as this is pretty straightforward.

Chapter 31

Additional Topics in 3.0

After 30 chapters, there are still a few topics in Android 3.0 that we haven't had a chance to cover! In this final chapter we're going to discuss the enhancements to home screen widgets and the new Drag and Drop API.

There are significant enhancements to widget capabilities in 3.0. With these enhancements, you now can add list-based widgets to the home screen. The Drag and Drop API is entirely new in 3.0. With the Drag and Drop API, you can build rich user interfaces similar to those so common on desktops. We will address both topics in great detail.

List-Based Home Screen Widgets

In Chapter 22, we covered how widgets work in Android releases 2.3 and prior releases. There are robust enhancements to home screen Widgets in Android release 3.0; it's very likely that these changes will be incorporated into the next optimized version of Android for phones as well.

As a pre-requisite to reading this topic, we urge you to brush up on Chapter 22 to appreciate the new coverage on widgets. However, this chapter will present a comprehensive view of widgets that you can follow even if you haven't delved into the nuances of Chapter 22.

As you learned in Chapter 22, remote views form the core of home screen widgets. A home screen widget is essentially a remote view that is painted on the home screen. A remote view is a view that is entirely disconnected from the underlying data, much like a web page is disconnected from its server.

Chapter 22 featured a list of layouts and widgets that are capable of being part of a remote view. Collection views such as lists and grids were not part of allowed widgets in the 2.3 release. In release 3.0 they are, allowing for a richer experience on the home screen. Release 3.0 also offers a mini-framework around these collection-based widgets to load and present data asynchronously. There are new classes and methods in 3.0 to support these aspects.

We will first cover these enhancements conceptually and then present a working sample to solidify that understanding. Let's start with the new remote views in 3.0

New Remote Views in 3.0

In Android 2.3, there are 13 possible layouts and UI widgets that can be part of remote views.

- AbsoluteLayout
- FrameLayout
- LinearLayout
- RelativeLayout
- AnalogClock
- Button
- Chronometer
- ImageButton
- ProgressBar
- ViewFlipper
- DateTimeView
- ImageView
- TextView

Some of these layouts and views may be deprecated such as the AbsoluteLayout. Do check these classes before using them in your code. You may ask why this remote view list is important. Do you use these view/layout classes directly to construct your remote views?

As it turns out, the class RemoteViews can't be constructed by passing explicit objects of any of the types listed above. Nor can these types of objects be added to a RemoteViews directly. Instead, a RemoteViews object is constructed by passing a layout file to its constructor. The importance of this list is that you can have only these xml nodes in the layout files that can become remote views.

The following is the enhanced list of 16 allowed layouts, UI widgets, and views in Android release 3.0:

- FrameLayout
- LinearLayout
- RelativeLayout
- AnalogClock
- Button
- Chronometer

- ImageButton
- ProgressBar
- ListView
- GridView
- StackView
- TextView
- DateTimeView
- ImageView
- AdapterViewFlipper
- ViewFlipper

More remote views may be added in future releases. The key to finding out which of the current UI objects are enabled for RemoteViews is the fact these classes are annotated with an interface called RemoteViews.RemoteView.

Armed with this information, you can use Eclipse to figure out which classes in a project use this annotation. Here's how you do it:

1. In your source code, put an import statement for the RemoteView interface.
2. Highlight that interface name.
3. Right click and go to References tab.
4. Choose to look for references of this interface in this project.

This will present a list of classes that are annotated with the RemoteView interface.

Working with Lists in Remote Views

In Chapter 22 we covered the existing set of classes in the SDK that support home screen widgets. The primary ones are the AppWidgetProvider, the AppWidgetManager, the RemoteViews, and an activity that can be used to configure an AppWidgetProvider with initialization parameters.

Briefly, here is the core idea of how home screen widgets work (knowing this should make the rest of this section a bit easier to follow). An AppWidgetProvider is a broadcast receiver that gets invoked every once in a while based on a timer interval that you specify in a configuration file. This AppWidgetProvider then loads a RemoteViews instance based on a layout file. This RemoteViews object is then passed to the AppWidgetManager to be displayed on the home screen.

Optionally, you can tell Android that you have an activity that needs to be invoked before placing the widget for the first time on the home screen. This allows the configuration activity to set initialization parameters for the widget.

You also can set up onClick events on the remote views of the widget so that intents can get fired based on those events. These intents then can invoke whatever components necessary, including sending messages to the AppWidgetProvider broadcast receiver.

At a high level, this is all there is to home screen widgets. The rest is the mechanics and variations on each of these basic ideas.

However, Android 2.3 and earlier didn't allow list-based remote views and didn't provide a mechanism to efficiently populate the list-based remote views. To support list-based remote views, Android 3.0 has added the following new classes:

- RemoteViewsFactory: This class allows you to populate a list remote view much like list adapters populate regular list views. This class is a thin wrapper around a list view adapter to supply individual remote views to the list remote view in an asynchronous manner.
- RemoteViewsService: This class is a service that is responsible for returning a RemoteViewsFactory to the list RemoteViews object. It is the responsibility of the AppWidgetProvider to tie one of these remote views services' to a list remote view. This is done by attaching an intent that knows how to invoke this service to the list remote view. This service allows you to extend the life of the process containing the AppWidgetProvider. Otherwise, when the broadcast receiver returns, the process can be reclaimed. Chapter 14 explains the symbiotic relationship between broadcast receivers and long-running services.

The following new API methods have been added to support list-based remote views:

- RemoteViews.setPendingIntentTemplate(): This method allows you to set a pending intent template on the list remote view in order to respond to click events on the list items. We will talk about the idea of "template" when we cover the details later.
- RemoteViews.setOnClickFillIntent(): This is set on the individual list items of the list remote view and works closely with the previous method.

These additional two methods in concert will let you respond to clicks on list-based remote views. These two methods are designed so that as few pending intents are set as possible.

We will cover these classes and methods in detail as we go through this chapter. Given these new features, here are the general steps to work with a list view on a home screen widget. Do re-read the brief overview of home screen widgets (from earlier in this section) as you grasp these steps.

1. **Prepare a remote layout**: Create a suitable remote layout with a list view in it. A remote layout is a regular layout with only allowed remotable views. This is no different than what you have to do for any home screen widget (and is clearly shown in Chapter 22).

2. **Load remote layout**: In the onUpdate() method of the widget provider, load this compound remote layout view from the previous step as a remote view. Here, also, there is no difference. Then hook up the list remote view with a remote view service so that the list view can get populated through the remote view factory returned by the remote view service.

3. **Set up** RemoteViewService: Locate the list remote view by its ID and set an intent on that list remote view so that the intent invokes the list remote view service. RemoteViewService then passes the RemoteViewFactory to the list view so that the remote list view can get populated.

4. **Set up** RemoteViewFactory**:** The list remote view service will need to return a list RemoteViewFactory that knows how to populate the list remote view

5. **Set up click events**: As part of setting up the list remote view in the AppWidgetProvider, also set the onClick pending intent template so that you can respond to that intent. However, you will also need to correspondingly set up the individual clicks using the RemoteViewFactory for each view in the list. This is because the items in the remote list view are populated from the list view factory.

6. **Respond to click events:** Someone needs to respond to the onClick events set on the remote list views. You can choose your AppWidgetProvider to be the receiver for these events. You need to prepare the broadcast receiver to receive and respond to onClick events from remote views.

Let's look at each of these steps with annotated sample code.

Preparing a Remote Layout

As described in the previous section, the layout for a remote view that can be displayed as a home widget can now include a list view. Listing 31–1 shows an example remotable layout with a list view in it.

Listing 31–1. ***A Remote Layout File with a List View***

```
<?xml version="1.0" encoding="utf-8"?>
<!-- /res/layout/test_list_widget_layout.xml -->
<LinearLayout xmlns:android="http://schemas.android.com/apk/res/android"
    android:orientation="vertical"
    android:layout_width="150dp"
    android:layout_height="match_parent"
    android:background="@drawable/box1">
<TextView
    android:id="@+id/listwidget_header_textview_id"
```

```
    android:layout_width="fill_parent"
    android:layout_height="30dp"
    android:text="Header View"
    android:background="@drawable/box1"
    android:gravity="center"
    android:layout_weight="0"/>
<FrameLayout
    android:layout_width="match_parent"
    android:layout_height="match_parent"
    android:layout_weight="1"
    android:layout_gravity="center">
        <ListView android:id="@+id/listwidget_list_view_id"
           android:layout_width="match_parent"
           android:layout_height="match_parent"/>
        <TextView
        android:id="@+id/listwidget_empty_view_id"
        android:layout_width="match_parent"
        android:layout_height="match_parent"
        android:gravity="center"
        android:visibility="gone"
        android:textColor="#ffffff"
        android:text="Empty Records View"
        android:textSize="20sp" />
</FrameLayout>
<TextView
    android:id="@+id/listwidget_footer_textview_id"
    android:layout_width="fill_parent"
    android:layout_height="30dp"
    android:text="Footer View"
    android:background="@drawable/box1"
    android:gravity="center"
    android:layout_weight="0"/>
</LinearLayout>
```

In Listing 31–1, every XML node represents a valid remote view. This layout is presented in such a way that when shown as a home screen widget, the layout would look like that in Figure 31–1.

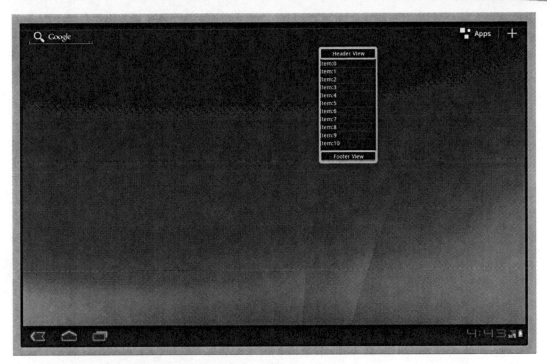

Figure 31–1. *Home screen populated with a list view widget*

The layout pattern in Listing 31–1 follows a simple header, body, footer format. The header and footer are both set at a fixed height; in this example, these heights are set to 30dp. However, you want the body height to be stretchable to take the rest of the vertical height. The way to accomplish this is to set the `android:layout_weight` to zero on the header and footer. On the body you set the `android:layout_weight` to 1 and the `android:layout_height` to `match_parent`.

The framelayout that is taking the position of the body of this widget needs a bit of explanation. A framelayout chooses one of its children as the view exclusively. In this case, when you have data in the list, you will use the listview. When the list is empty, you will use the empty text view. You can set this up using the `RemoteViewFactory`.

Also in this layout file is a custom drawable identified by `@drawable/box1` to make the corners round. Listing 31–2 is the `box1.xml` file that needs to be placed in the `/res/drawable` sub directory.

Listing 31–2. *res/drawable/box1.xml*

```
<shape xmlns:android="http://schemas.android.com/apk/res/android">
    <stroke android:width="4dp" android:color="#888888" />
    <padding android:left="2dp" android:top="2dp"
            android:right="2dp" android:bottom="2dp" />
    <corners android:radius="4dp" />
</shape>
```

Now that you have a sample layout for a home screen widget, let's discuss how you would go about loading this layout into a remote view.

Loading a Remote Layout

For a home screen widget, a remote view is loaded and displayed in the `onUpdate()` callback of the `AppWidgetProvider`. Listing 31–3 shows an example of how this is done.

Listing 31–3. *Loading a Remote Layout in onUpdate()*

```
public void onUpdate(Context context,
                     AppWidgetManager appWidgetManager,
                     int[] appWidgetIds)
{
    int N = appWidgetIds.length;
    for (int i=0; i<N; i++)
    {
        int appWidgetId = appWidgetIds[i];

        RemoteViews rv =
        new RemoteViews(context.getPackageName(),
                R.layout.test_list_widget_layout);

        rv.setEmptyView(R.id.listwidget_list_view_id,
                       R.id.listwidget_empty_view_id);

        //update this instance of the app widget
        appWidgetManager.updateAppWidget(appWidgetId, rv);
    }
    super.onUpdate(context,appWidgetManager, appWidgetIds);
}
```

Notice that a `RemoteViews` object is constructed using the ID of the layout file describing the entire widget. This layout file is the same one that is in Listing 31–1. You then take the resulting `RemoteViews` object and set an empty view for the specific list view resource (located by its ID) inside that layout file.

In the example in Listing 31–3, the layout file is identified by

```
R.layout.test_list_widget_layout
```

The list view resource within this file is identified by

```
R.id.listwidget_list_view_id
```

The empty view for this list view resource is identified by

```
R.id.listwidget_empty_view_id
```

With these IDs, the code in Listing 31–4 demonstrates how to construct a remote view and set an empty view for one of its list views.

Listing 31–4. *Loading Remote Views*

```
RemoteViews rv =
new RemoteViews(context.getPackageName(),
   R.layout.test_list_widget_layout);
```

```
rv.setEmptyView(R.id.bdw_list_view_id,
   R.id.empty_view_id);
```

Setting up RemoteViewsService

So far you have successfully loaded the remote views in the onUpdate() method of the AppWidgetProvider. Now you need to hook up the list remote view with a remote view service so that the remote view service can return the remote view adapter that can populate the list remote view.

Why a service? Why not directly hook up the remote view factory to the remote list view view?

Because an AppWidgetProvider is a broadcast receiver, the onUpdate() method of the widget provider runs under the time constraints of a broadcast receiver. To avoid the time criticality, Android 3.0 delegated the job of populating the list view to a separate service that is inherited from android.widget.RemoteViewsService. This RemoteViewsService is then responsible for returning a list adapter that can populate the list. This adapter needs to be of type RemoteViewsService.RemoteViewsFactory. In a way, this is a rote procedure of ultimately getting the remote list view with the remote list view factory.

Listing 31–5 shows an example of how a remote view service is coded and how it returns the remote view factory.

Listing 31–5. *RemoteViewService Example*

```
public class TestRemoteViewsService
extends android.widget.RemoteViewsService
{
    @Override
    public RemoteViewsFactory onGetViewFactory(Intent intent)
    {
        return new TestRemoteViewsFactory(
                this.getApplicationContext(), intent);
    }
}
```

Notice the following in Listing 31–5:

- You will need to inherit from the RemoteViewsService.
- You will need to specialize a RemoteViewsFactory and return that factory. We will cover this factory soon.

Being a service, the inherited RemoteViewsService (TestRemoteViewsService, in this case) needs to be declared in the manifest file as well. Listing 31–6 shows an example.

Listing 31–6. *Declaring RemoteViewsService in the Manifest File*

```
<!-- The service serving the RemoteViews to the collection widget -->
<service android:name=".TestRemoteViewsService"
  android:permission="android.permission.BIND_REMOTEVIEWS"
  android:exported="false" />
```

Once you have this remote views service coded, you can attach this service to the list remote view object using the code in Listing 31–7. (Recall that this code runs in the onUpdate() method of the AppWidgetProvider.)

Listing 31–7. *Associating RemoteViewsService with a RemoteViewList*

```
final Intent intent =
    new Intent(context, TestRemoteViewsService.class);
intent.putExtra(AppWidgetManager.EXTRA_APPWIDGET_ID,
                                   appWidgetId);
intent.setData(
        Uri.parse(
                intent.toUri(Intent.URI_INTENT_SCHEME)));

rv.setRemoteAdapter(appWidgetId,
        R.id.listwidget_list_view_id, intent);
```

In Listing 31–7, you first create an explicit intent by identifying the RemoteViewService class to this intent. Then you put an extra in the intent identifying the app widget ID for which you are calling the service. Then you do this weird self-referential act where by you load the data portion of this intent with a string representation of the intent itself. This approach makes the intent unique because the extras are now part of the data portion of the intent. Without this, intents are not unique just because of their extras. Once the uniqueness of the intent is taken care of, you can attach this intent to the remote list view by calling setRemoteAdapter() and passing the list view ID.

Setting up RemoteViewsFactory

Although you have specified a RemoteViewService to delegate the list population, ultimately a RemoteViewsFactory is responsible for populating the list view. To populate a list view, you will start by implementing this adapter-like interface RemoteViewsFactory. (See Chapter 6 to understand list controls and list adapters.)

Listing 31–8 shows the method signatures of a class that implements this factory interface.

Listing 31–8. *A RemoteViewsFactory Contract*

```
class TestRemoteViewsFactory
implements RemoteViewsService.RemoteViewsFactory
{
    public TestRemoteViewsFactory(Context context, Intent intent);
    public void onCreate();
    public void onDestroy();
    public int getCount();
    public RemoteViews getViewAt(int position);
    private void loadItemOnClickExtras(RemoteViews rv, int position);
    public RemoteViews getLoadingView();
    public int getViewTypeCount();
    public long getItemId(int position);
    public boolean hasStableIds();
    public void onDataSetChanged();
}
```

Let's talk about each of these methods and what needs to be done in each of the methods, starting with the constructor.

RemoteViewsFactory Constructor

The constructor here takes two arguments. (You can have a different factory that takes different arguments.) In case of widgets, this factory is constructed by a RemoteViewsService (as shown in Listing 31–5), so the context is the context of the widget provider which in itself is a broadcast receiver.

The second argument to the constructor is an intent. This intent is the same intent that is used to invoke the remote views service. When this intent is created (see Listing 31–7) and attached to the remote view, one typically drops an extra value representing the widget ID.

In the constructor, both these values (the context and the intent) could be maintained as local variables so that subsequent methods could make use of these variables. It is especially convenient to extract the widget ID from the intent and save it as a local variable.

onCreate() Callback

The signature of onCreate() is

```
Public void onCreate()
```

Following the pattern of a number of components in Android, a RemoteViewsFactory provides onCreate() and onDestroy() methods. The documentation suggests that the onCreate() method is called by a client remote view when this class is first created. The documentation further says that this factory can be shared across multiple remote view adapters depending on the intent passed.

However, this pattern is not particularly clear in the case of RemoteViewsFactory because, unlike an activity component or a service component, the creation of the RemoteViewFactory is in the explicit control of the programmer. The programmer could have done the initialization in the constructor itself. It is not clear from the documentation if this factory object is cached by the framework based on the intent passed to invoke the remote view service. The log messages indicate that the onCreate() is definitely called. So you have an opportunity to initialize in this method as well instead of the constructor.

onDestroy() Callback

The signature of onDestroy() is

```
Public void
 onDestroy()
```

This is the complement of onCreate() method. Documentation suggests that this method is called when the last remote views adapter that is associated with this object (or factory) is unbound. However, it's not very clear when this method is called; we have not noticed this method being called either after a single widget is removed from the home page or the last widget is removed from the home screen.

getCount() Callback

The signature of `getCount()` method is

```
public int getCount()
```

You will need to return the total number of items in this list view. This method is very much like the corresponding method in the list adapters in Chapter 6 on controls.

getViewAt() Callback

The signature of `getViewAt()` method is

```
public RemoteViews getViewAt(int position)
```

The responsibility of this method is to return a remote view appropriate for this position in the list view. Typically in this method you will load a layout that is specific to this type of remote view at this position and then set the values in that remote view using the position as an indicator to load the corresponding data. Listing 31–9 is an example of loading an individual layout for a list view item.

Listing 31–9. *Loading an Individual List View Item Layout*

```
RemoteViews rv =
    new RemoteViews(
        this.mContext.getPackageName(),
        R.layout.list_item_layout);
```

The layout that is referred to in Listing 31–9 could look like the layout in Listing 31–10.

Listing 31–10. *An Individual List View Item Layout*

```
<?xml version="1.0" encoding="utf-8"?>
<TextView  xmlns:android="http://schemas.android.com/apk/res/android"
    android:id="@+id/textview_widget_list_item_id"
    android:layout_width="fill_parent"
    android:layout_height="wrap_content"
    android:text="Temporary text"
/>
```

Once you load the remote view (Listing 31–9), you can return that remote view to the calling list remote view to be painted. This is also the place where you can set onClick behavior for this particular list view.

getLoadingView() Callback

The signature of `getLoadingView()` method is

```
public RemoteViews getLoadingView()
```

This method returns a custom loading view that appears between the time `getViewAt(position)` is called and returns. You can return null if you want to use the default loading view.

getViewTypeCount() Callback

The signature of `getViewTypeCount()` method is

```
public int getViewTypeCount()
```

If the remote list view contains only one type of view as a child, this method will return 1. If there is more than one type of view, this method will need to return as many various types of child views as are present.

getItemId() Callback

The signature of `getItemId()` method is

```
public long getItemId(int position)
```

This method returns the appropriate ID of the underlying item for this position in the list view. This method is very much like the corresponding method in the list adapters documented in Chapter 6 on controls.

hasStableIds() Callback

The signature of `hasStableIds()` method is

```
public boolean hasStableIds()
```

This method should return true if the same item ID from `getItemId()` points to the same object. This method is very much like the corresponding method in the list adapters in Chapter 6 on controls.

onDataSetChanged() Callback

The signature of `onDataSetChanged()` is

```
public void onDataSetChanged()
```

This method is called when someone tells the `AppWidgetManager` that the widget containing this remote list view has changed. This call to the widget manager will eventually trickle down to the remote view factory as an `onDataSetChanged()`. In response, you will need to set up the underlying data so that other callbacks such as `getViewAt()`and `getCount()` can respond with new data. The documentation assures that long-running operations are permitted in this method to set up the data.

This completes the discussion of how to make a remote list view visible in a widget. Let's now tackle how to attach click events to a list view and even to its child views.

Setting up onClick Events

Setting up click events for a list remote view is a two step process. First, you register an `onClick` on the list view in the `onUpdate()` method of the widget provider. Then you register onclick events for each of the individual child views of that list view in the remote view factory's `getViewAt()` method.

First you'll learn how to register for click events on the main list view. When you set up a click event on a remote view, you need an intent to fire when that list remote view is clicked on. Because an appwidget provider is a broadcast receiver, you can set up this underlying app widget provider as a target for this intent. You then need to make provisions in the app widget provider to specialize the `onReceive()` callback so that you can handle this intent.

The code snippet in Listing 31–11 shows how you can set up an onClick intent with a widget provider as its target.

Listing 31–11. *Creating an Intent to Self-Invoke the Appwidget Provider*

```
Intent onListClickIntent =
    new Intent(context,TestListWidgetProvider.class);
```

Notice how you set up the class name of a widget provider as the target component for this intent. This intent will be delivered to the widget provider. However, a widget provider is already responding to intents coming in with other widget-related actions. To distinguish this intent from other intents, you need to set up an explicit action for it. Listing 31–12 shows an example.

Listing 31–12. *Defining a Unique Action for an onclick in the Widget Provider*

```
onListClickIntent.setAction(
        TestListWidgetProvider.ACTION_LIST_CLICK);
```

Of course, the action `TestListWidgetProvider.ACTION_LIST_CLICK` is custom and is best defined as part of the widget provider `TestListWidgetProvider`.

Because the clicks could happen on multiple instances of this widget, you need to load the widget ID as an extra on the invoking intent. Listing 31–13 shows how to do this.

Listing 31–13. *Loading Widget ID into the onclick Intent*

```
onListClickIntent.putExtra(
        AppWidgetManager.EXTRA_APPWIDGET_ID, appWidgetId);
```

Now this intent is almost ready to be set on the remote list view as an onClick intent. You need to do one more thing to this intent. When intents are set to invoke at a later point of time, they are set as pending intents. See Chapter 5 on intents and Chapter 15 on alarm managers for more detail on pending intents.

A pending intent does not take into account any subsequent extras you set on the underlying intent unless that intent is unique after taking into account the extras. However, intents don't take into account their extras when considering if they are unique. To circumvent this issue you need to use a method called `toUri()` on an intent.

This toUri() method takes all the extras of an intent and then makes a long string representing this intent with extras at the end. When you take this long string and set it as the data portion of the same intent, you essentially made this intent unique. This is because an intent will take its data portion under consideration for uniqueness. Listing 31–14 is an example of making an intent unique by using its toUri() method.

Listing 31–14. *Use of toUri() Method*

```
onListClickIntent.setData(
    Uri.parse(
        onListClickIntent.toUri(Intent.URI_INTENT_SCHEME)));
```

Once you made the intent unique, you can get the necessary broadcast pending intent, as shown in Listing 31–15.

Listing 31–15. *Getting a Broadcast Pending Intent from Intent*

```
PendingIntent onListClickPendingIntent =
    PendingIntent.getBroadcast(context, 0,
        onListClickIntent,
        PendingIntent.FLAG_UPDATE_CURRENT);
```

In Listing 31–15, the FLAG_UPDATE_CURRENT flag means that if you find a similar underlying intent, just update its extras. You'll understand why this may be necessary when we discuss how this pending intent is utilized by the remote views.

Once you have the necessary pending intent, such as the one from Listing 31–15, you can set the click behavior for the list view. Use a method called setPendingIntentTemplate() to do this association between a pending intent and a list view. Listing 31–16 shows an example of how to use setPendingIntentTemplate() method.

Listing 31–16. *Using setPendingIntentTemplate*

```
RemoteViews rv;
rv.setPendingIntentTemplate(R.id.listwidget_list_view_id,
        onListClickPendingIntent);
```

In Listing 31–16, the first argument is the list view ID for the list view in the main layout (see Listing 31–1). The second argument is the pending intent you have created and prepared in Listings 31–11 through 31–14. Note in Listing 31–16 that you are calling the pending intent a *pending intent template*. What's up with the word "template"?

As per SDK docs, the Android team doesn't want to create a pending intent for each of the rows in a list. They want to create one pending intent for the whole list and then just override its extras as users click on the individual items of that list. The way they have facilitated this is to create one pending intent at the list level and then reissue that intent with different extras. This is why the pending intent in Listing 31–15 is set with a flag of update for its extras.

Let's now see how the extras are supplied from the individual list item remoteviews. As you might expect, this is done in the same place where the list remote view items are constructed. This is in the getViewAt() method of remote view factory (see Listing 31–9). Listing 31–17 shows how to attach intents with extras to a list view item when it is clicked on.

Listing 31–17. *Attaching Intents with Extras to a List Item View when Clicked*

```
//Load your list item remote view
RemoteViews listItemRv;

//Get a fresh new intent
Intent ei = new Intent();

//Load it with whatever extra you want
ei.putExtra("com.androidbook.widgets.some_unique_extra_string_key",
       "Position of the item Clicked:" + position);

//Set it on the list remote view
listItemRv.setOnClickFillInIntent(R.id.textview_widget_list_item_id, ei);
```

In Listing 31–17 the key method is `setOnClickFillIntent()`. This method allows you to supply a fresh intent loaded with whatever extras what you want to load. Internally, the framework will take these extras and superimpose them on the pending intent template that you set up as part of the view onClick.

In Listing 31–17 you just took the text from the current row and embellished it a little and then set it as the extra. With this code in Listing 31–17, if one were to click on the list item on the widget, it would raise an intent that is sent to the broadcast receiver with the extras. Let's see, then, how to prepare the broadcast receiver and retrieve this extra that is specific for each list view item.

Responding to onClick Events

In the list view pending intent template (Listing 31–16) you see the following two things:

- The component to invoke is the widget provider itself.
- The action is set to a specific action that is unique to this widget provider.

In response, the widget provider needs to do the following:

1. Declare a string action that it can recognize.
2. Override the `onReceive()` method and deal with the action in step 1.

Listing 31–18 shows how to define the unique action in the provider as a string constant.

Listing 31–18. *Custom Action Definition*

```
public static final String ACTION_LIST_CLICK =
    "com.androidbook.homewidgets.listclick";
```

Listing 31–19 shows how to override the `onReceive()`. It shows how to test for the action of the intent and call the `dealWithThisAction()` method. At the end of this method, you must call the base class's `onReceive()` for all other actions. If you don't do so, the widget itself will not receive widget-based actions.

Listing 31–19. *Overriding onReceive*

```
@Override
public void onReceive(Context context, Intent intent)
{
    if (intent.getAction()
            .equals(TestListWidgetProvider.ACTION_LIST_CLICK))
    {
        //this action is not one widget actions
        //this is a specific action that is directed here
        dealwithListAction(context,intent);
        return;
    }

    //make sure you call this
    super.onReceive(context, intent);
}
```

Listing 31–20 shows the dealWithThisAction() method where you retrieve the extra that you have loaded the intent with in Listing 31–17.

Listing 31–20. *Responding to List View Item onClick*

```
public void dealwithListAction(Context context, Intent  intent)
{
    String clickedItemText =
        intent.getStringExtra(
                TestListWidgetProvider.EXTRA_LIST_ITEM_TEXT);
    if (clickedItemText == null)
    {
        clickedItemText = "Error";
    }
    clickedItemText =
        clickedItemText
        + "You have clicked on item:"
        + clickedItemText;

    Toast t =
        Toast.makeText(context,clickedItemText,Toast.LENGTH_LONG);
    t.show();
}
```

In Listing 31–20 you retrieved the extra through a predefined constant and provided a toast. This method runs on the main thread so you need to make sure you don't run long-running operations on it. (See Chapter 14 on long running services to understand this aspect in greater depth.)

This completes the conceptual understanding of all the new features provided around list widgets. Let's now look at a working example to test and demonstrate these features in action. Much of the code presented so far has been taken from this working sample, so the working sample should be easy to follow.

Working Sample: Test Home Screen List Widget

This home screen list widget sample will demonstrate the ideas covered thus far about list-based home screen widgets. At the end of this sample you will see a list-based widget that you can drag on to the home screen. When you drag it, you will see a widget displaying 20 rows of list items filled with sample text. When you click on one of these list item rows, you will see a toast on the home screen containing text from that specific row of the list.

Here is the list of files you will need:

- `TestListWidgetProvider.java` is the primary class; it's the test widget provider that implements a widget with a list view as one of its views (Listing 31–21).
- `TestRemoteViewsFactory.java` is the class that provides a list items to show for the list view loaded by the widget provider (Listing 31–22).
- `TestRemoteViewsService.java` is the remote views service that instantiates the `TestRemoteViewsFactory` (Listing 31–23).
- `layout\test_list_widget_layout.xml` is the primary layout for the whole widget loaded by the widget provider (Listing 31–1).
- `layout\list_item_layout.xml` is the layout file for the individual list item view. This layout is loaded by the remote view factory (Listing 31–10).
- `drawable\box1.xml` is a simple layout helper class to provide rounded corners to the main widget layout (Listing 31–2).
- `xml\test_list_appwidget_provider.xml` is the metadata file for defining the widget to Android (Listing 31–24).
- `AndroidManifest.xml` is the configurations file for the application where you define the widget provider and the remote view service (Listing 31–25).

Creating the Test Widget Provider

The process of creating a home screen widget starts with creating a widget provider inheriting from `AppWidgetProvider` and overloading its `onUpdate()` method to provide a view for the widget. This process is explained in great detail in Chapter 22. In this example, you call your example provider `TestListWidgetProvider`. Listing 31–21 provides the source code with comments for this class.

Listing 31–21. *TestWidgetProvider.java*

```
package com.androidbook.homewidgets.listwidget;

/*
 * Use CTRL-SHIFT-O in Eclipse to fill in imports
 */
```

```
public class TestListWidgetProvider extends AppWidgetProvider
{
    private static final String tag = "TestListWidgetProvider";

    public static final String ACTION_LIST_CLICK =
        "com.androidbook.homewidgets.listclick";

    public static final String EXTRA_LIST_ITEM_TEXT =
        "com.androidbook.homewidgets.list_item_text";

    public void onUpdate(Context context,
                        AppWidgetManager appWidgetManager,
                        int[] appWidgetIds)
   {
        Log.d(tag, "onUpdate called");
        final int N = appWidgetIds.length;
        Log.d(tag, "Number of widgets:" + N);
        for (int i=0; i<N; i++)
        {
            int appWidgetId = appWidgetIds[i];
            updateAppWidget(context, appWidgetManager, appWidgetId);
        }
        super.onUpdate(context,appWidgetManager, appWidgetIds);
    }

    public void onDeleted(Context context, int[] appWidgetIds)
    {
        Log.d(tag, "onDelete called");
        super.onDeleted(context,appWidgetIds);
    }

    public void onEnabled(Context context)
    {
        Log.d(tag, "onEnabled called");
        super.onEnabled(context);
    }

    public void onDisabled(Context context)
    {
        Log.d(tag, "onDisabled called");
        super.onEnabled(context);
    }

    private void updateAppWidget(Context context,
                          AppWidgetManager appWidgetManager,
                           int appWidgetId)
   {
        Log.d(tag, "onUpdate called for widget:" + appWidgetId);

        final RemoteViews rv =
        new RemoteViews(context.getPackageName(),
                R.layout.test_list_widget_layout);

        rv.setEmptyView(R.id.listwidget_list_view_id,
                R.id.listwidget_empty_view_id);

        // Specify the service to provide data for the
```

```
// collection widget. Note that you need to
// embed the appWidgetId via the data otherwise
// it will be ignored.
final Intent intent =
    new Intent(context, TestRemoteViewsService.class);
intent.putExtra(AppWidgetManager.EXTRA_APPWIDGET_ID,
                                   appWidgetId);

intent.setData(
        Uri.parse(
                intent.toUri(Intent.URI_INTENT_SCHEME)));

rv.setRemoteAdapter(appWidgetId,
        R.id.listwidget_list_view_id, intent);

//setup a list view call back.
//you need a pending intent that is unique
//for this widget id. Send a message to
//ourselves which you will catch in OnReceive.
Intent onListClickIntent =
    new Intent(context,TestListWidgetProvider.class);

//set an action so that this receiver can distinguish it
//from other widget related actions
onListClickIntent.setAction(
        TestListWidgetProvider.ACTION_LIST_CLICK);

//because this receiver serves all instances
//of this app widget. You need to know which
//specific instance this message is targeted for.
onListClickIntent.putExtra(
        AppWidgetManager.EXTRA_APPWIDGET_ID, appWidgetId);

//Make this intent unique as you are getting ready
//to create a pending intent with it.
//The toUri method loads the extras as
//part of the uri string.
//The data of this intent is not used at all except
//to establish this intent as a unique pending intent.
//See intent.filterEquals() method to see
//how intents are compared to see if they are unique.
onListClickIntent.setData(
    Uri.parse(
        onListClickIntent.toUri(Intent.URI_INTENT_SCHEME)));

//you need to deliver this intent later when
//the remote view is clicked as a broadcast intent
//to this same receiver.
final PendingIntent onListClickPendingIntent =
    PendingIntent.getBroadcast(context, 0,
        onListClickIntent,
        PendingIntent.FLAG_UPDATE_CURRENT);

//Set this pending intent as a template for
//the list item view.
//Each view in the list will then need to specify
//a set of additional extras to be appended
```

```
            //to this template and then broadcast the
            //final template.
            //See how the remoteviewsfactory() sets up
            //the each item in the list remoteview.
            //See also docs for RemoteViews.setFillIntent()
            rv.setPendingIntentTemplate(R.id.listwidget_list_view_id,
                    onListClickPendingIntent);

            //update the widget
            appWidgetManager.updateAppWidget(appWidgetId, rv);
        }

    @Override
    public void onReceive(Context context, Intent intent)
    {
        if (intent.getAction()
                .equals(TestListWidgetProvider.ACTION_LIST_CLICK))
        {
            //this action is not one widget actions
            //this is a specific action that is directed here
            dealwithListAction(context,intent);
            return;
        }

        //make sure you call this
        super.onReceive(context, intent);
    }
    public void dealwithListAction(Context context, Intent  intent)
    {
        String clickedItemText =
            intent.getStringExtra(
                    TestListWidgetProvider.EXTRA_LIST_ITEM_TEXT);
        if (clickedItemText == null)
        {
            clickedItemText = "Error";
        }
        clickedItemText =
            clickedItemText
            + "You have clicked on item:"
            + clickedItemText;

        Toast t =
            Toast.makeText(context,clickedItemText,Toast.LENGTH_LONG);
        t.show();
    }
}//eof-class
```

With the background information provided, much of what this class needs to do is already explained. The source code is also amply peppered with comments to restate much that was discussed; however, here's a quick overview of the functionality:

1. In `onUpdate()`, load the remote view.
2. Locate the list remote view and hook it up with a remote view factory via a remote view service.

3. Set the remote view with a pending intent template for onClick behavior.
4. Override onReceive() method and deal with the specialized onClick action.

Wait until you load all files into Eclipse before compiling this file as there are other files referenced by this file.

Creating the Remote Views Factory

Listing 31–22 provides the source code for the remote view factory that is responsible for populating the list view.

Listing 31–22. *TestRemoteViewFactory.java*

```
package com.androidbook.homewidgets.listwidget;
/*
 * Use CTRL-SHIFT-O in Eclipse to fill in imports
 */
class TestRemoteViewsFactory
implements RemoteViewsService.RemoteViewsFactory
{
    private Context mContext;
    private int mAppWidgetId;
    private static String tag="TRVF";
    public TestRemoteViewsFactory(Context context, Intent intent)
    {
        mContext = context;
        mAppWidgetId =
            intent.getIntExtra(
                AppWidgetManager.EXTRA_APPWIDGET_ID,
                AppWidgetManager.INVALID_APPWIDGET_ID);

        Log.d(tag,"factory created");
    }

    //Called when your factory is first constructed.
    //The same factory may be shared across multiple
    //RemoteViewAdapters depending on the intent passed.
    public void onCreate()
    {
        Log.d(tag,"onCreate called for widget id:" + mAppWidgetId);
    }

    //Called when the last RemoteViewsAdapter that is
    //associated with this factory is unbound.
    public void onDestroy()
    {
        Log.d(tag,"destroy called for widget id:" + mAppWidgetId);
    }

    //The total number of items
    //in this list
    public int getCount()
    {
       return 20;
    }
```

```
public RemoteViews getViewAt(int position)
{
     Log.d(tag,"getview called:" + position);
     RemoteViews rv =
         new RemoteViews(
             this.mContext.getPackageName(),
             R.layout.list_item_layout);
     String itemText  = "Item:" + position;
     rv.setTextViewText(
         R.id.textview_widget_list_item_id, itemText);

     this.loadItemOnClickExtras(rv, position);
     return rv;
}
private void loadItemOnClickExtras(RemoteViews rv, int position)
{
    Intent ei = new Intent();
    ei.putExtra(TestListWidgetProvider.EXTRA_LIST_ITEM_TEXT,
            "Position of the item Clicked:" + position);
    rv.setOnClickFillInIntent(R.id.textview_widget_list_item_id, ei);
    return;
}

//This allows for the use of a custom loading view
//which appears between the time that getViewAt(int)
//is called and returns. If null is returned,
//a default loading view will be used.
public RemoteViews getLoadingView()
{
    return null;
}

//How many different types of views
//are there in this list.
public int getViewTypeCount()
{
    return 1;
}

//The internal id of the item
//at this position
public long getItemId(int position)
{
    return position;
}

//True if the same id
//always refers to the same object.
public boolean hasStableIds()
{
    return true;
}

//Called when notifyDataSetChanged() is triggered
//on the remote adapter. This allows a RemoteViewsFactory
```

```
    //to respond to data changes by updating
    //any internal references.
    //Note: expensive tasks can be safely performed
    //synchronously within this method.
    //In the interim, the old data will be displayed
    //within the widget.
    public void onDataSetChanged()
    {
        Log.d(tag,"onDataSetChanged");
    }
}
```

Much of this code has been explained already. At a high level, this class assumes there are 20 rows. Each row's layout is loaded from a layout file and its text set to the corresponding position. It then loads the text from each position into the onClick intent. This is the text that you would see as toast.

Coding Remote Views Service

Listing 31–23 shows the source code for the class that returns the remote view factory.

Listing 31–23. *TestRemoteViewsService.java*

```
package com.androidbook.homewidgets.listwidget;
import android.content.Intent;

public class TestRemoteViewsService
extends android.widget.RemoteViewsService
{
    @Override
    public RemoteViewsFactory onGetViewFactory(Intent intent)
    {
        return new TestRemoteViewsFactory(
                this.getApplicationContext(), intent);
    }
}
```

Main Widget Layout file

The main layout file that corresponds to how the widget looks on the home page needs to be at `\res\layout\test_list_widget_layout.xml` (note that this layout file was presented in Listing 31–1). This main layout file also requires rounded corners, which are provided a box drawable located at `\res\drawable\box1.xml`, which was presented in Listing 31–2.

Layout for the Individual List Items

This layout file corresponds to the layout of the individual list item inside the list. This layout file needs to be at `layout\list_item_layout.xml`. This layout file was presented in Listing 31–10.

Widget Provider Metadata

A widget provider needs to specify a metadata XML file when that widget provider is declared in the android manifest file. This file needs to be at \res\xml\test_list_appwidget_provider.xml. Listing 31–24 shows this widget metadata information file.

Listing 31–24. *Widget Information File*

```
<!-- xml/test_list_widget_layout.xml -->
<appwidget-provider xmlns:android="http://schemas.android.com/apk/res/android"
    android:minWidth="222dp"
    android:minHeight="222dp"
    android:updatePeriodMillis="1000000"
    android:initialLayout="@layout/test_list_widget_layout"
    android:label="Test List Widget"
    >
</appwidget-provider>
```

This provider metadata file specifies the size for the widget and how often to fire the onUpdate callback on the widget, specified in milliseconds. Note that this file is discussed in greater detail in Chapter 22.

AndroidManifest.xml

Listing 31–25 shows the configuration file for the application. The widget provider definition and the remote view service definition are highlighted.

Listing 31–25. *AndroidManifest File*

```
<?xml version="1.0" encoding="utf-8"?>
<manifest xmlns:android="http://schemas.android.com/apk/res/android"
      package="com.androidbook.homewidgets.listwidget"
      android:versionCode="1"
      android:versionName="1.0.0">
    <application android:icon="@drawable/icon"
       android:label="Test List Widget Application">
<!--
**********************************************************************
*  Test List Widget Provider
**********************************************************************
 -->
    <receiver android:name=".TestListWidgetProvider">
       <meta-data android:name="android.appwidget.provider"
         android:resource="@xml/test_list_appwidget_provider" />
       <intent-filter>
         <action
           android:name="android.appwidget.action.APPWIDGET_UPDATE" />
       </intent-filter>
    </receiver>

   <!-- The service serving the RemoteViews to the collection widget -->
   <service android:name=".TestRemoteViewsService"
     android:permission="android.permission.BIND_REMOTEVIEWS"
     android:exported="false" />
```

```
    </application>
    <uses-sdk android:minSdkVersion="11" />
</manifest>
```

Testing the Test List Widget

Once you build and deploy this project, you will see in Eclipse that the project is successfully deployed. Because this project doesn't contain an activity that is identified to run at startup, you won't see anything on the emulator by default.

To install the widget created in this sample, you need to see a list of available widgets first. Clicking on the home screen will bring up a list of available widgets screen, as shown in Figure 31–2.

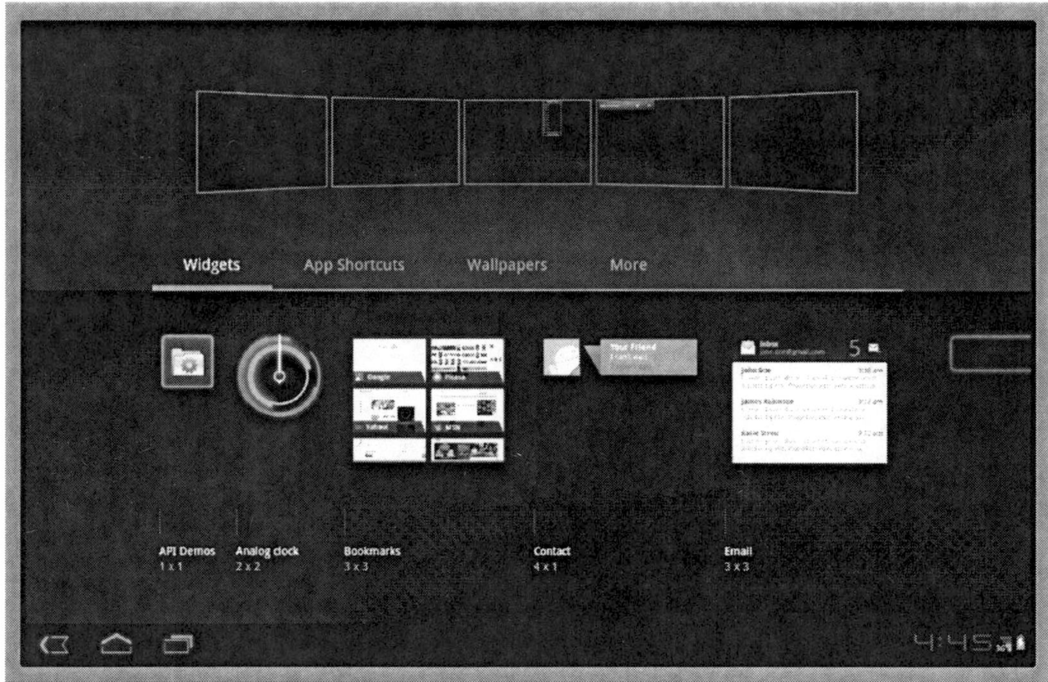

Figure 31–2. *List of widgets*

The name of your widget is "Test List Widget Application," so it may be to the farthest on the right and you may have to scroll to the right side screen to see it, as shown in Figure 31–3.

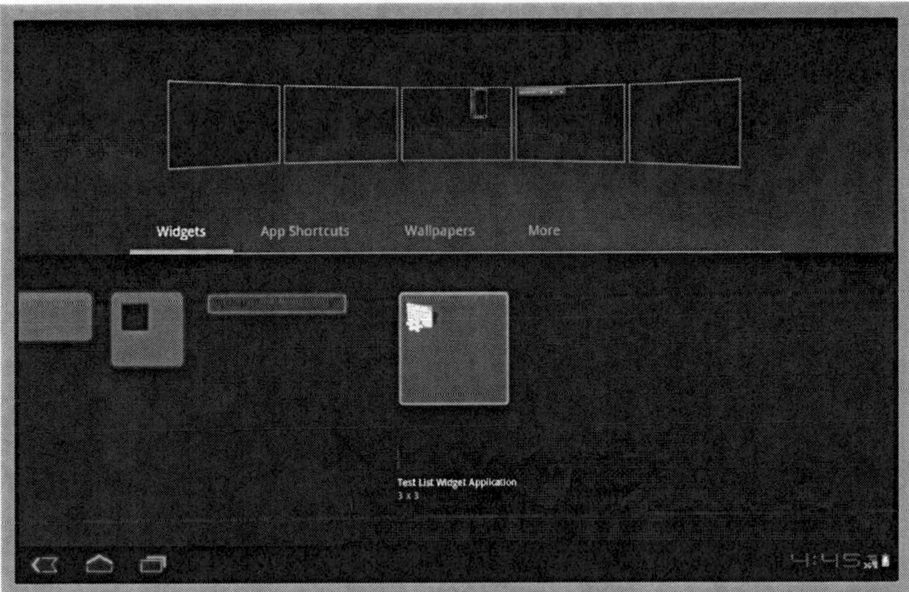

Figure 31–3. *Scrolling to the right to find the Test List Widget Application*

Now you can drag the Test List Widget Application to the home screen of your choice. Once your drag is recognized, you can select the Home button at the bottom to go to the home screen. At that time you will see the widget in its main form, as shown previously in Figure 31–1. If you click on one of the list items, a toast message appropriate to the line item you have clicked on will appear (see Figure 31–4).

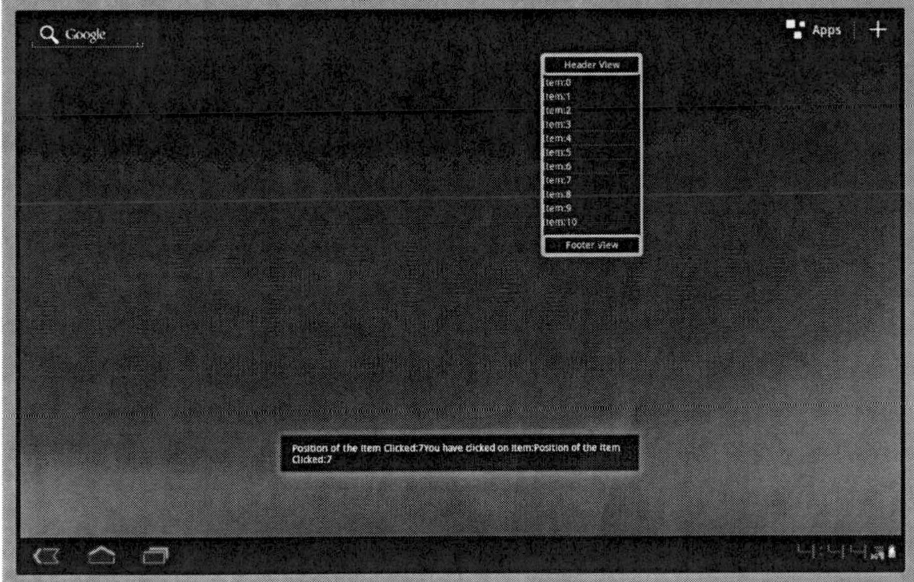

Figure 31–4. *Toast in response to a list view item click*

This concludes the discussion of enhancements to widgets in the 3.0 release. Now let's discuss the new Drag and Drop API.

Drag and Drop

Prior to Android 3.0, there was no direct support for drag and drop. You learned in Chapter 25 how to drag a View around the screen; you also learned that it was possible to use the current location of the dragged object to determine if there was a drop target underneath. When the `MotionEvent` for the finger up event was received, your code could figure out if that meant a drop had occurred. While this was doable, it certainly wasn't as easy as having direct support in Android for the drag-and-drop operation. You now have that direct support in 3.0.

Basics of Drag and Drop in 3.0

At its most basic, the drag-and-drop operation starts with a view declaring that a drag has started, then all interested parties watch the drag take place until the drop event is fired. If a view catches the drop event and wants to receive it, then a drag and drop has just occurred. If there is no view to receive the drop, or if the view that receives it doesn't want it, then no drop takes place. Dragging is communicated through the use of a `DragEvent` object, which is passed to all of the drag listeners available.

Within the `DragEvent` object are descriptors for lots of information, depending on the initiator of the drag sequence. For example, the DragEvent can contain object references to the initiator itself, state information, textual data, Uris, or pretty much whatever you want to pass through the drag sequence.

Information could be passed that results in view-to-view dynamic communication; however, the originator data in a `DragEvent` object is set when the `DragEvent` is created and it stays the same thereafter. In addition to this data, the `DragEvent` has an action value, indicating what is going on with the drag sequence, and location information indicating where the drag is on the screen.

A `DragEvent` has six possible actions:

- `ACTION_DRAG_STARTED` indicates that a new drag sequence has begun.
- `ACTION_DRAG_ENTERED` indicates that the dragged object has been dragged into the boundaries of a specific view.
- `ACTION_DRAG_LOCATION` indicates that the dragged object has been dragged on the screen to a new location.
- `ACTION_DRAG_EXITED` indicates that the dragged object has been dragged outside the boundaries of a specific view.
- `ACTION_DROP` indicates that the user has let go of the dragged object. It is up to the receiver of this event to determine if this truly means a drop has occurred.

- ACTION_DRAG_ENDED tells all drag listeners that the previous drag sequence has ended. The DragEvent.getResult() method indicates a successful drop or failure.

You might think that you need to set up a drag listener on each view in the system that could participate in a drag sequence, but, in fact, you can define a drag listener on just about anything in your application and it will receive all of the drag events for all views in the system. This can make things a little confusing since the drag listener does not need to be associated with either the object being dragged or the drop target. The listener can manage all of the coordination of the drag and drop.

In fact, if you inspect the drag-and-drop sample project that comes with the Android SDK, you will see that they set up a listener on a TextView that has nothing to do with the actual dragging and dropping. The upcoming sample project uses drag listeners that are tied to specific views. These drag listeners each receive a DragEvent object for the drag events that occur in the drag sequence. This means a view could receive a DragEvent object that can be ignored because it is really about a different view. This also means that the drag listener must make that determination in code and that there must be enough information within the DragEvent object for the drag listener to figure out what to do.

If a drag listener got a DragEvent object that merely said there's an unknown object being dragged and it's at coordinates (15, 57), there isn't much the drag listener can do with it. It is much more helpful to get a DragEvent object that says a particular object is being dragged, it's at coordinates (15, 57), it's a copy operation, and the data is a specific URI. When that drops, there's enough information to be able to initiate a copy operation.

Drag and Drop Sample Application

For your sample application, you're going to employ a staple of 3.0, the fragments. This, among other things, will prove that drags can cross fragment boundaries. You'll create a palette of dots on the left and a square target on the right. When a dot is grabbed using a long click, you'll change the color of that dot in the palette and Android will show a shadow of the dot as you drag. When the dragged dot reaches the square target, the target will begin to glow. If you drop the dot on the square target, a message will indicate that you've just added one more drop to the drop count, the glowing will stop, and the original dot will go back to its original color.

List of Files

This application will rely on the following files:

- main.xml is the main layout that lays out the 2 fragments (Listing 31–26).
- palette.xml is the fragment layout for the dots on the left-hand side (Listing 31–27).

- dropzone.xml is the fragment layout for the square target on the right-hand side, plus the drop count message (Listing 31–28).
- MainActivity.java is about as simple an activity as you can get. It only sets the root content view, then leaves all the work to the fragments (Listing 31–29).
- Palette.java is the code for the palette, which is also very simple. It merely inflates the palette fragment layout file (Listing 31–30).
- DropZone.java is a little more complex because you implement the drop behavior in this file. This one inflates the dropzone.xml fragment layout file, then implements the drag listener for the drop target (Listing 31–31).
- Dot.java is your custom view class for the objects you're going to drag. It handles beginning the drag sequence, watching drag events, and drawing the dots (Listing 31–32).
- attrs.xml defines a couple of XML attributes used in the palette.xml layout file to describe attributes of your dots (Listing 31–33).
- AndroidManifest.xml is the main manifest file for this application (Listing 31–34).
- strings.xml contains the strings used by the AndroidManifest for this application (Listing 31–35).

Laying out the Sample Drag and Drop Application

Before we get into the code, Figure 31–5 shows what the application will look like.

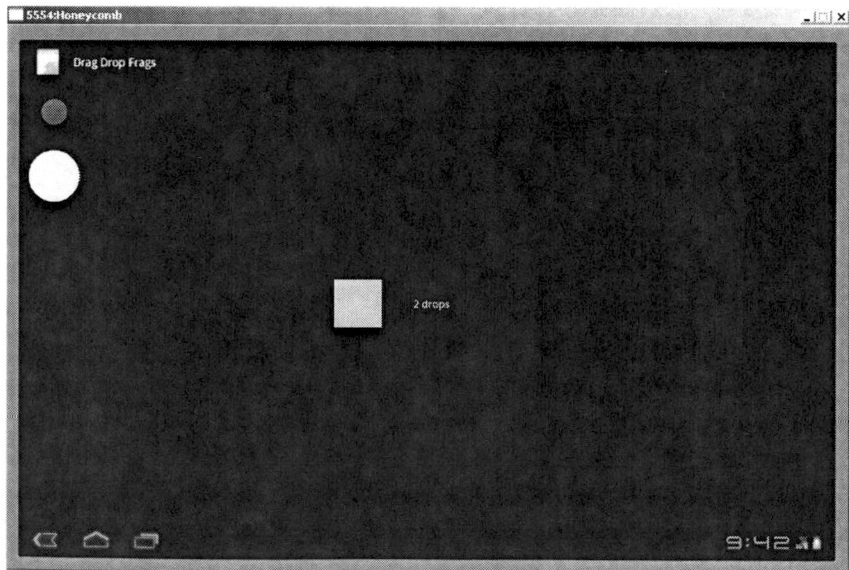

Figure 31–5. *Drag Drop Frags demo application user interface*

Listing 31–26 shows the main layout file to support Figure 31–5. Similar to what you saw in Chapter 29, this layout file has a simple horizontal linear layout and two fragment specifications. The first fragment will be for the palette of dots and the second will be for the dropzone.

Listing 31–26. *The Main Layout File*

```
<?xml version="1.0" encoding="utf-8"?>
<!-- This file is res/layout/main.xml -->
<LinearLayout xmlns:android="http://schemas.android.com/apk/res/android"
    android:orientation="horizontal"
    android:layout_width="match_parent"
    android:layout_height="match_parent" >

  <fragment class="com.androidbook.drag.drop.demo.Palette"
      android:id="@+id/palette"
      android:layout_width="wrap_content"
      android:layout_height="match_parent" />

  <fragment class="com.androidbook.drag.drop.demo.DropZone"
      android:id="@+id/dropzone"
      android:layout_width="0px"
      android:layout_height="match_parent"
      android:layout_weight="1" />

</LinearLayout>
```

The palette fragment layout file (Listing 31–27) gets a bit more interesting. While this layout represents a fragment, you don't need to include a fragment tag within this layout. This layout will be inflated to become the view hierarchy for your palette fragment. The dots are specified as your custom dots, and there are two of them arranged vertically. Notice that there are a couple of custom XML attributes in the definition of your dots (`dot:color` and `dot:radius`). As you can see, these attributes specify the color and the radius of your dots. These will be explained later when the `attrs.xml` file is discussed. The other XML attributes are standard view attributes.

Listing 31–27. *The palette.xml Layout File for the Dots*

```
<?xml version="1.0" encoding="utf-8"?>
<!-- This file is res/layout/palette.xml -->
<LinearLayout
  xmlns:android="http://schemas.android.com/apk/res/android"
  xmlns:dot="http://schemas.android.com/apk/res/com.androidbook.drag.drop.demo"
  android:layout_width="match_parent"
  android:layout_height="match_parent"
  android:orientation="vertical">
  <com.androidbook.drag.drop.demo.Dot android:id="@+id/dot1"
    android:layout_width="wrap_content"
    android:layout_height="wrap_content"
    android:padding="30dp"
    android:tag="Blue dot"
    dot:color="#ff1111ff"
    dot:radius="20dp"
  />
  <com.androidbook.drag.drop.demo.Dot android:id="@+id/dot2"
    android:layout_width="wrap_content"
```

```
    android:layout_height="wrap_content"
    android:padding="10dp"
    android:tag="White dot"
    dot:color="#ffffffff"
    dot:radius="40dp"
  />

</LinearLayout>
```

The dropzone fragmentlayout file in Listing 31–28 is also easy to understand. There's a green square and a text message arranged horizontally. This will be the drop zone for the dots you'll be dragging. The text message will be used to display a running count of the drops.

Listing 31–28. *The dropzone.xml Layout File*

```
<?xml version="1.0" encoding="utf-8"?>
<!-- This file is res/layout/dropzone.xml -->
<LinearLayout
  xmlns:android="http://schemas.android.com/apk/res/android"
  android:layout_width="match_parent"
  android:layout_height="match_parent"
  android:orientation="horizontal" >

  <View android:id="@+id/droptarget"
    android:layout_width="75dp"
    android:layout_height="75dp"
    android:layout_gravity="center_vertical"
    android:background="#00ff00" />

  <TextView android:id="@+id/dropmessage"
    android:text="0 drops"
    android:layout_width="wrap_content"
    android:layout_height="wrap_content"
    android:layout_gravity="center_vertical"
    android:paddingLeft="50dp"
    android:textSize="17sp" />

</LinearLayout>
```

As you can see in Listing 31–29, activity files don't get much simpler. All this does is set the root content view of the activity to the layout file, the one that contains the two fragments. The interesting logic is contained in other files.

Listing 31–29. *The MainActivity*

```
package com.androidbook.drag.drop.demo;

// This file is MainActivity.java
import android.app.Activity;
import android.os.Bundle;

public class MainActivity extends Activity {

    @Override
    public void onCreate(Bundle savedInstanceState) {
        super.onCreate(savedInstanceState);
        setContentView(R.layout.main);
    }
}
```

The file in Listing 31–30 is also very simple to understand. It is the code for a fragment, so it overrides the onCreateView() method with one that inflates the layout file into a view, and returns that.

Listing 31–30. *The Palette.java File*

```
package com.androidbook.drag.drop.demo;

// This file is Palette.java
import android.app.Fragment;
import android.os.Bundle;
import android.view.LayoutInflater;
import android.view.View;
import android.view.ViewGroup;

public class Palette extends Fragment {

    @Override
    public View onCreateView(LayoutInflater inflater,
            ViewGroup containcr, Bundlc icicle) {
        View v = inflater.inflate(R.layout.palette, container, false);
        return v;
    }
}
```

Responding to onDrag in the Drop Zone

Now that you have the main application layout set, let's see how the drop target needs to be organized by examining Listing 31–31.

Listing 31–31. *The DropZone.java File*

```
package com.androidbook.drag.drop.demo;

// This file is DropZone.java
import android.animation.ObjectAnimator;
import android.app.Fragment;
import android.content.ClipData;
import android.os.Bundle;
import android.util.Log;
import android.view.DragEvent;
import android.view.LayoutInflater;
import android.view.View;
import android.view.ViewGroup;
import android.view.animation.CycleInterpolator;
import android.widget.TextView;

public class DropZone extends Fragment {

    private View dropTarget;
    private TextView dropMessage;

    @Override
    public View onCreateView(LayoutInflater inflater,
            ViewGroup container, Bundle icicle)
    {
        View v = inflater.inflate(R.layout.dropzone, container, false);
```

```
dropMessage = (TextView)v.findViewById(R.id.dropmessage);

dropTarget = (View)v.findViewById(R.id.droptarget);
dropTarget.setOnDragListener(new View.OnDragListener() {
    private static final String DROPTAG = "DropTarget";
    private int dropCount = 0;
    private ObjectAnimator anim;

    public boolean onDrag(View v, DragEvent event) {
        int action = event.getAction();
        boolean result = true;
        switch(action) {
        case DragEvent.ACTION_DRAG_STARTED:
            Log.v(DROPTAG, "drag started in dropTarget");
            break;
        case DragEvent.ACTION_DRAG_ENTERED:
            Log.v(DROPTAG, "drag entered dropTarget");
            anim = ObjectAnimator.ofFloat((Object)v, "alpha", 1f, 0.5f);
            anim.setInterpolator(new CycleInterpolator(40));
            anim.setDuration(30*1000); // 30 seconds
            anim.start();
            break;
        case DragEvent.ACTION_DRAG_EXITED:
            Log.v(DROPTAG, "drag exited dropTarget");
            if(anim != null) {
                anim.end();
                anim = null;
            }
            break;
        case DragEvent.ACTION_DRAG_LOCATION:
            Log.v(DROPTAG, "drag proceeding in dropTarget: " +
                    event.getX() + ", " + event.getY());
            break;
        case DragEvent.ACTION_DROP:
            Log.v(DROPTAG, "drag drop in dropTarget");
            if(anim != null) {
                anim.end();
                anim = null;
            }

            ClipData data = event.getClipData();
            Log.v(DROPTAG, "Item data is " + data.getItemAt(0).getText());

            dropCount++;
            String message = dropCount + " drop";
            if(dropCount > 1)
                message += "s";
            dropMessage.setText(message);
            break;
        case DragEvent.ACTION_DRAG_ENDED:
            Log.v(DROPTAG, "drag ended in dropTarget");
            if(anim != null) {
                anim.end();
                anim = null;
            }
            break;
```

```
                default:
                    Log.v(DROPTAG, "other action in dropzone: " + action);
                    result = false;
                }
                return result;
            }
        });
        return v;
    }
}
```

Now you're starting to get into interesting code. For the drop zone, you need to create the target upon which you want to drag the dots. As you saw earlier, the layout specifies a green square on the screen with a text message next to it. Because the drop zone is also a fragment, you're overriding the onCreateView() method of DropZone. The first thing to do is inflate the drop zone layout, then extract out the view reference for the square target (dropTarget) and for the text message (dropMessage). Then you need to set up a drag listener on the target so it will know when a drag is underway.

The drop target drag listener has a single callback method in it: onDrag(). This callback will receive a view reference as well as a DragEvent object. The view reference relates to the view that the DragEvent is related to. As mentioned, the drag listener is not necessarily connected to the view that will be interacting with the drag event, so this callback must identify the view for which the drag event is taking place.

One of the first things you likely want to do in any onDrag() callback is read the action from the DragEvent object. This will tell you what's going on. For the most part, the only thing you want to do in this callback is log the fact that a drag event is taking place. You don't need to actually do anything for ACTION_DRAG_LOCATION, for example. But you do want to have some special logic for when the object is dragged within your boundaries (ACTION_DRAG_ENTERED) that will be turned off when the object is either dragged outside of your boundaries (ACTION_DRAG_EXITED) or when the object is dropped (ACTION_DROP).

You're using the ObjectAnimator class that was introduced in Chapter 29, only here you're using it in code to specify a cyclic interpolator that modifies the target's alpha. This will have the effect of pulsing the transparency of the green target square, which will be the visual indication that the target is willing to accept a drop of the object onto it. Since you turn on the animation, you must make sure to also turn it off when the object leaves, is dropped, or the drag and drop is ended. In theory, you shouldn't need to stop the animation on ACTION_DRAG_ENDED but it's wise to do it anyway.

For this particular drag listener, you're only going to get ACTION_DRAG_ENTERED and ACTION_DRAG_EXITED if the dragged object interacts with the view with which you're associated. And as you'll see, the ACTION_DRAG_LOCATION events only happen if the dragged object is inside your target view.

The only other interesting condition is the ACTION_DROP itself (notice that DRAG_ is not part of the name of this action). If a drop has occurred on your view, it means the user has let go of the dot over top of the green square. Because you're expecting this object to be dropped on the green square, you can just go ahead and read the data from the first item, then log it to LogCat. In a production application, you might pay closer attention to the ClipData object that is contained in the drag event itself. By inspecting its properties, you could decide if you even want to accept the drop or not.

This is a good time to point out the result boolean in this onDrag() callback method. Depending on how things go, you either want to let Android know you took care of the drag event (by returning true) or that you didn't (by returning false). If you don't see what you want to see inside of the drag event object, you could certainly return false from this callback, which would tell Android that this drop was not handled.

Once you log the information from the drag event in LogCat, you increment the count of the drops received; this is updated in the user interface, and that's about it for DropZone.

If you look this class over, it's really rather simple. You don't actually have any code in here that deals with MotionEvents, nor do you even need to make your own determination on whether or not there is a drag going on. You just get appropriate callback calls as a drag sequence unfolds.

Setting up the Drag Source Views

Let's now consider how views corresponding to a drag source are organized, starting by looking at Listing 31–32.

Listing 31–32. *The Java for the Custom View: Dot*

```
package com.androidbook.drag.drop.demo;

// This file is Dot.java
import android.content.ClipData;
import android.content.Context;
import android.content.res.TypedArray;
import android.graphics.Canvas;
import android.graphics.Color;
import android.graphics.Paint;
import android.util.AttributeSet;
import android.util.Log;
import android.view.DragEvent;
import android.view.View;

public class Dot extends View
    implements View.OnDragListener
{
    private static final int DEFAULT_RADIUS = 20;
    private static final int DEFAULT_COLOR = Color.WHITE;
    private static final int SELECTED_COLOR = Color.MAGENTA;
    protected static final String DOTTAG = "DragDot";
    private Paint mNormalPaint;
    private Paint mDraggingPaint;
    private int mColor = DEFAULT_COLOR;
    private int mRadius = DEFAULT_RADIUS;
    private boolean inDrag;

    public Dot(Context context, AttributeSet attrs) {
        super(context, attrs);

        // Apply attribute settings from the layout file.
```

```
        // Note: these could change on a reconfiguration
        // such as a screen rotation.
        TypedArray myAttrs = context.obtainStyledAttributes(attrs,
                R.styleable.Dot);

        final int numAttrs = myAttrs.getIndexCount();
        for (int i = 0; i < numAttrs; i++) {
            int attr = myAttrs.getIndex(i);
            switch (attr) {
            case R.styleable.Dot_radius:
                mRadius = myAttrs.getDimensionPixelSize(attr, DEFAULT_RADIUS);
                break;
            case R.styleable.Dot_color:
                mColor = myAttrs.getColor(attr, DEFAULT_COLOR);
                break;
            }
        }
        myAttrs.recycle();

        // Setup paint colors
        mNormalPaint = new Paint();
        mNormalPaint.setColor(mColor);
        mNormalPaint.setAntiAlias(true);

        mDraggingPaint = new Paint();
        mDraggingPaint.setColor(SELECTED_COLOR);
        mDraggingPaint.setAntiAlias(true);

        // Start a drag on a long click on the dot
        setOnLongClickListener(lcListener);
        setOnDragListener(this);
    }

    private static View.OnLongClickListener lcListener =
        new View.OnLongClickListener() {
        private boolean mDragInProgress;

        public boolean onLongClick(View v) {
            ClipData data =
            ClipData.newPlainText("DragData", (String)v.getTag());

            mDragInProgress =
            v.startDrag(data, new View.DragShadowBuilder(v),
                    (Object)v, 0);

            Log.v((String) v.getTag(),
              "starting drag? " + mDragInProgress);

            return true;
        }
    };

    @Override
    protected void onMeasure(int widthSpec, int heightSpec) {
        int size = 2*mRadius + getPaddingLeft() + getPaddingRight();
        setMeasuredDimension(size, size);
    }
```

```
// The dragging functionality
public boolean onDrag(View v, DragEvent event) {
    String dotTAG = (String) getTag();
    // Only worry about drag events if this is us being dragged
    if(event.getLocalState() != this) {
        Log.v(dotTAG, "This drag event is not for us");
        return false;
    }
    boolean result = true;

    // get event values to work with
    int action = event.getAction();
    float x = event.getX();
    float y = event.getY();

    switch(action) {
    case DragEvent.ACTION_DRAG_STARTED:
        Log.v(dotTAG, "drag started. X: " + x + ", Y: " + y);
        inDrag = true; // used in draw() below to change color
        break;
    case DragEvent.ACTION_DRAG_LOCATION:
        Log.v(dotTAG, "drag proceeding... At: " + x + ", " + y);
        break;
    case DragEvent.ACTION_DRAG_ENTERED:
        Log.v(dotTAG, "drag entered. At: " + x + ", " + y);
        break;
    case DragEvent.ACTION_DRAG_EXITED:
        Log.v(dotTAG, "drag exited. At: " + x + ", " + y);
        break;
    case DragEvent.ACTION_DROP:
        Log.v(dotTAG, "drag dropped. At: " + x + ", " + y);
        // Return false because we don't accept the drop in Dot.
        result = false;
        break;
    case DragEvent.ACTION_DRAG_ENDED:
        Log.v(dotTAG, "drag ended. Success? " + event.getResult());
        inDrag = false; // change color of original dot back
        break;
    default:
        Log.v(dotTAG, "some other drag action: " + action);
        result = false;
        break;
    }
    return result;
}

// Here is where you draw our dot, and where you change the color if
// you're in the process of being dragged. Note: the color change affects
// the original dot only, not the shadow.
public void draw(Canvas canvas) {
    float cx = this.getWidth()/2 + getLeftPaddingOffset();
    float cy = this.getHeight()/2 + getTopPaddingOffset();
    Paint paint = mNormalPaint;
    if(inDrag)
        paint = mDraggingPaint;
    canvas.drawCircle(cx, cy, mRadius, paint);
```

```
            invalidate();
        }
    }
```

The Dot code looks somewhat similar to the code for DropZone. This is in part because you're also receiving drag events in this class. The constructor for a Dot figures out the attributes in order to set the correct radius and color, and then it sets up the two listeners, one for long clicks and another for the drag events.

The part where the constructor figures out the attributes is interesting. What you want is to be able to specify properties of your dot in the XML layout file, but custom XML attributes require some setup somewhere. In your case, this setup occurs in the attrs.xml file located under /res/values. The attrs.xml file specifies a styleable called Dot as well as a couple of attributes color and radius. Listing 31–33 shows the contents of the attrs.xml file.

Listing 31–33. *The attrs.xml File Used to Define New XML Attributes for the Dot*

```
<?xml version="1.0" encoding="utf-8"?>
<!-- This file is res/values/attrs.xml -->
<resources>
    <declare-styleable name="Dot">
        <attr name="color" format="color" />
        <attr name="radius" format="dimension" />
    </declare-styleable>
</resources>
```

As you can see, you get the name from the tag, and the attribute names (and types) are underneath. By specifying the XML attributes in the attrs.xml file, you can then use those attributes in your layout XML file and you can use them in code to locate specific attributes. In code, you loop through the known attributes, and when you find either a radius or a color, you grab the value and assign it to this dot. This is a pretty nice way to be able to specify in XML what your objects are going to look like.

The two paints are going to be used to draw your circle. You use the normal paint when the dot is just sitting there. But when the dot is being dragged, you want to indicate that by changing the color of the original to magenta.

The long click listener is where you initiate a drag sequence. The only way you let the user start dragging a dot is if the user clicks and holds on a dot. When the long click listener is firing, you create a new ClipData object using a string and the dot's tag. You happen to know that the tag is the name of the dot as specified in the XML layout file. There are several other ways to specify data into a ClipData object, so feel free to read the reference documentation on other ways to store data in a ClipData object.

The next statement is the critical one: startDrag(). This is where Android will take over and start the process of dragging. Note that the first argument is the ClipData object from before, then it's the drag shadow object, then a "local state" object, and finally the number zero.

The drag shadow object is the image that will be displayed as the dragging is taking place. In your case, this does not replace the original dot image on the screen but shows a shadow of a dot as the dragging is taking place, in addition to the original dot on the screen. The default DragShadowBuilder behavior is to create a shadow that looks very much like the original, so for your purposes, you merely call it and pass in your view. You can get fancy here and create whatever sort of shadow view you want, but if you do override this class, you'll need to implement a few methods to make it work.

The onMeasure() method is here to supply dimension information to Android for the custom view you're using here. You have to tell Android how big your view is so it knows how to lay it out with everything else.

Finally there's the onDrag() callback. As mentioned, each drag listener can receive drag events. They all get ACTION_DRAG_STARTED and ACTION_DRAG_ENDED, for example. So when events happen, you must be careful what you do with the information. Since there are two dots in play in this sample application, whenever you do something with the dots, you must be careful that you're affecting the correct one.

When both dots receive the ACTION_DRAG_STARTED action, only one should set the color of the dot to magenta. To figure out which one is correct, compare the local state object passed in with yourself. If you look back where you set the local state object, you passed the current view in. So now when you've received the local state object out, you compare it to yourself to see if you're the view that initiated the drag sequence.

If you aren't the same view, you write a log message to LogCat saying this is not for you, and you return false to say you're not handling this message.

If you are the view that should be receiving this drag event, you collect some values from the drag event, then you mostly just log the event to LogCat. The first exception to this is ACTION_DRAG_STARTED. If you got this action and it's for you, you then know that your dot has begun a drag sequence. Therefore, you set the inDrag boolean so the draw() method later on will do the right thing and display a different colored dot. This different color only lasts until ACTION_DRAG_ENDED is received, at which time you restore the original color of the dot.

If a dot gets the ACTION_DROP action, this means the user tried to drop a dot on a dot, maybe even the original dot. This shouldn't do anything, so you just return false from this callback in this case.

Finally, the draw() method of your custom view figures out the location of the center point of your circle (i.e. dot), then draws it with the appropriate paint. The invalidate() method is there to tell Android that you've modified the view and that Android should re-draw the user interface. By calling invalidate(), you ensure that the user interface will be updated very shortly with whatever is new.

Listing 31–34 shows the manifest file for this application.

Listing 31–34. *The AndroidManifest.xml file*

```
<?xml version="1.0" encoding="utf-8"?>
<!-- This file is AndroidManifest.xml -->
<manifest xmlns:android="http://schemas.android.com/apk/res/android"
      package="com.androidbook.drag.drop.demo"
      android:versionCode="1"
      android:versionName="1.0">
    <uses-sdk android:minSdkVersion="11" />
```

```
    <application android:icon="@drawable/icon"
                 android:label="@string/app_name">
        <activity android:name=".MainActivity"
                  android:label="@string/app_name">
            <intent-filter>
                <action android:name="android.intent.action.MAIN" />
                <category android:name="android.intent.category.LAUNCHER" />
            </intent-filter>
        </activity>

    </application>
</manifest>
```

Listing 31–35 shows the `strings.xml` containing string values used by the manifest file.

Listing 31–35. *The strings.xml*

```
<?xml version="1.0" encoding="utf-8"?>
<!-- This file is res/values/strings.xml -->
<resources>
    <string name="app_name">Drag Drop Frags</string>
</resources>
```

You now have all the files and the background necessary to compile and deploy this sample drag-and-drop application.

Testing the Sample Drag-and-Drop Application

Below is some sample output from LogCat when we ran this sample application. Notice how the log message used "Blue dot" to indicate messages from the blue dot, "White dot" for messages from the white dot, and "DropTarget" for the view where the drops are allowed to go.

```
White dot:  starting drag? true
Blue dot:   This drag event is not for us
White dot:  drag started. X: 53.0, Y: 206.0
DropTarget: drag started in dropTarget
DropTarget: drag entered dropTarget
DropTarget: drag proceeding in dropTarget: 29.0, 36.0
DropTarget: drag proceeding in dropTarget: 48.0, 39.0
DropTarget: drag proceeding in dropTarget: 45.0, 39.0
DropTarget: drag proceeding in dropTarget: 41.0, 39.0
DropTarget: drag proceeding in dropTarget: 40.0, 39.0
DropTarget: drag drop in dropTarget
DropTarget: Item data is White dot
ViewRoot:   Reporting drop result: true
White dot:  drag ended. Success? true
Blue dot:   This drag event is not for us
DropTarget: drag ended in dropTarget
```

In this particular case, the drag was started with the white dot. Once the long click has triggered the beginning of the drag sequence, we get the "starting drag?" message.

Notice how the next three lines all indicate that an `ACTION_DRAG_STARTED` action was received. Blue dot determined that the callback was not for him. It was also not for dropTarget.

Next, notice how the drag proceeding messages show the drag happening through `DropTarget`, beginning with the `ACTION_DRAG_ENTERED` action. This means that the dot was being dragged on top of the green square. The X and Y coordinates reported in the drag event object are the coordinates of the drag point relative to the upper left corner of the view. So in the sample app, the first record of the drag in the drop target is at (x, y) = (29, 36) and the drop occurred at (40, 39). See how the drop target was able to extract out the tag name of the white dot to write it to LogCat.

Also see how once again, all drag listeners received the `ACTION_DRAG_ENDED` action. Only White dot determined that it's okay to display the results using `getResult()`.

Feel free to experiment with this sample application. Drag a dot to the other dot, or even to itself. Go ahead and add another dot to `palette.xml`. Notice how when the dragged dot leaves the green square, there's a message saying that the drag exited. Note also that if you drop a dot somewhere other than the green square, the drop is considered failed.

References

- `http://developer.android.com/sdk/android-3.0-highlights.html`: New features of Android in release 3.0 are listed here and there's a section on what's new with home screen widgets.
- `www.androidbook.com/item/3624`: Our work notes for preparing the material for home screen widgets topic of this chapter for release 3.0. You'll find links to APIs, code snippets, open questions, and more research.
- `www.androidbook.com/item/3299`: Our work notes for preparing the material for home screen widgets topic for release 2.2. You'll find links to APIs, code snippets, open questions, and previous research.
- `www.androidbook.com/item/3637`: Our notes on RemoteViews, updated with 3.0 material including code samples, pondered questions, and internal and external references.
- `http://developer.android.com/guide/topics/appwidgets/index.html`: The main document on app widgets from the previous releases. Note that this document is not updated for 3.0 enhancements but you can get the basics.
- `http://developer.android.com/reference/android/appwidget/AppWidgetManager.html`: The reference page for the important AppWidgetManager API.
- `http://developer.android.com/reference/android/widget/RemoteViewsService.RemoteViewsFactory.html`: RemoteViewFactory API reference URL.
- `http://developer.android.com/reference/android/widget/RemoteViews.html`: RemoteViews API reference URL.

- http://developer.android.com/reference/android/widget/RemoteViewsService.html: RemoteViewsService API reference URL.
- www.androidbook.com/projects: The URL to download the test projects for this chapter. The names of the zip files for this chapter are ProAndroid3_ch31_TestListWidgets.zip and ProAndroid3_ch31_TestDragAndDrop.zip.

Summary

This chapter covered two important enhancements in Android 3.0: list-based home screen widgets and the Drag and Drop API.

First, we thoroughly examined the list-based home screen widget enhancements. You learned how to load and populate list-based remote views through remote views service and a remote views factory. You also learned how to set up onClick events and how to rig the AppWidgetProvider itself to receive the onClick events and respond to them. This material will allow you to implement rich useful widgets on your home screen.

In the Drap and Drop section, we covered all of the API nuances available to make use of drag and drop operations for a rich user experience that's on par with that of a desktop. You have learned about drag sources, drag events, and drag targets in depth.

It's now up to your imagination how best to put these facilities to use.

Index

Special Characters & Numbers

sign, 93
$JAVA_HOME/bin directory, 25
* (asterisk) symbol, 138
*.db files, 94
(/res/xml/bday_appwidget_provider.xml) file, 725
3D graphics, 12
3GPP (3rd Generation Partnership Project), 600
100ANDRO directory, 579

A

A command, 38
AAPT (Android Asset Packaging Tool), 42, 70
AbsoluteLayout layout manager, 198
Abstract Window Toolkit (AWT), Java SE, 2
abstracting common texture handling, 669–672
AbstractRenderer class, 639, 648–649, 665
AbstractRenderer.java file, 647
accelerate_decelerate interpolator, 1065
accelerate_decelerate.xml file, 1066
accelerateInterpolator tag, 506
AccelerometerRecordToFileAlwaysOn project, 904
accelerometers, interpreting data from, 908–914
  and display orientation, 910
  and gravity, 910–913
  and magnetic field sensors together, 915
  using to measure device angle, 914
ACCESS_ALL_DOWNLOADS permission, 334, 337
access.log file, 904
AccountFunctionTester.java file, 960
account_name field, 954
accounts
  contacts API, 938–943, 960–968
    driver activity classes, 963–966
    enumerating, 943
    function tester-related files, 961–962
    menu file, 961
    relevance to contacts, 942–943
    running program, 966–968
    screens, 938–942
  Google, 994
"Accounts & sync settings" screen, 939
AccountsFunctionTester.java file, 962
account_type field, 954
acos( ) method, 914
Action Icon area, 1071
Action icons, 1071
action keys, in Android search, 818–821
<action> tag, 351, 361
ACTION_ANSWER, 570
ActionBar API, 1069–1095
  anatomy, 1070–1071
  list navigation, 1084–1089
    AndroidManifest.xml file, 1087
    BaseActionBarActivity class, 1087
    examining, 1088–1089
    list listener, 1086
    setting up, 1086–1087
    SpinnerAdapter interface, 1085–1086
  standard navigation, 1090–1095
    AndroidManifest.xml file, 1092
    BaseActionBarActivity class, 1091–1092
    examining, 1092–1095
    source code, 1090–1091
  tabbed navigation, 1071–1084
    action bar and menu interaction, 1081–1083
    assigning uniform behavior, 1075–1077
    base classes, 1073–1075
    examining, 1084
    manifest file, 1083–1084
    navigation modes, 1079–1080
    obtaining action bar instance, 1079
    scrollable debug text view layout, 1080–1081
    tabbed listener, 1077–1078
ActionBar.OnNavigationListener, 1086
ACTION_CALL activity, 129
ACTION_CANCEL action, 846, 852
ACTION_DIAL activity, 129
ACTION_DOWN action, 846, 852
ACTION_DOWN event, 846, 854–855, 859, 862, 868–870
ACTION_DOWN method, 861
ACTION_DRAG_ENDED action, 1125, 1131, 1136, 1138
ACTION_DRAG_ENTERED action, 1124, 1131, 1138
ACTION_DRAG_EXITED action, 1124, 1131
ACTION_DRAG_LOCATION action, 1124, 1131
ACTION_DRAG_STARTED action, 1124, 1136, 1138
ACTION_DROP action, 1124, 1131, 1136
actionEnum, 1083
ACTION_GET_CONTENT intent, 141–142
actionKey element, 819
ACTION_KEY, SearchManager class, 820
ACTION_MASK constant, MotionEvent class, 870

ACTION_MOVE action, 846, 852, 877
ACTION_MOVE events, 852–853, 855, 859, 868–869, 878
ACTION_MSG string, SearchManager class, 820
ACTION_OUTSIDE action, 846, 852
ACTION_PICK action, 139–141
ACTION_PICK code, 142
ACTION_PICK intent, 140–141
ACTION_POINTER_3_DOWN constant, MotionEvent class, 870
ACTION_POINTER_DOWN action, 877
ACTION_POINTER_DOWN event, 868
ACTION_POINTER_ID_MASK constant, MotionEvent class, 870
ACTION_POINTER_ID_SHIFT constant, MotionEvent class, 870
ACTION_POINTER_INDEX_MASK constants, 871
ACTION_POINTER_INDEX_SHIFT constants, 871
ACTION_POINTER_UP action, 877
ACTION_POINTER_UP event, 869
ACTION_SEARCH action, 784, 787, 807, 810–811, 816, 820
ACTION_SEND, 567
ACTION_TTS_QUEUE_PROCESSING_COMPLETED broadcast, 842
ACTION_UP action, 846, 852
ACTION_UP event, 846, 853–855, 859, 862, 869–870, 877–878
ACTION_VIEW, 807, 810–811, 816
activities, 9, 29, 400
  code for layout animation, 501
  directly invoking with components, 133
  files for, 414, 416
  invoking separate, 1041–1043
  life cycles of, 52, 418–419
  regular, 758–765
  related to local search, 771–777
  simple suggestion provider search, 784–789
  widget configuration, 738–742
Activity class, 67, 141, 191, 224, 228, 234, 240, 266, 392, 872
activity node, 725
activity object, 77
<activity> tags, 345, 606, 1002
activity windows, management of, 9
activity.onCreateContextMenu( ) method, 232
activity.registerForContextMenu( ) method, 232
AdapterContextMenuInfo class, 234
adapters
  ArrayAdapter, 172–174
  creating, 188–193, 213
  overview, 170
  SimpleCursorAdapter, 171–172
  using with AdapterViews
    ListView control, 175–183
    overview, 174
AdapterView class, 171
Adaptive Multi-Rate (AMR), 600
adb (Android Debug Bridge) command, 55, 576
(adb) Android Debug Bridge tool, 91
adb pull, 886
adb shell, 94
adb tool, 294, 578
Add gesture button, 882–883
add( ) method, 174, 1035, 1042
addContact( ) function, 987
AddContactFunctionTester.java file, 986
addEarcon( ) method, 839
addFrame( ) method, 496
addIntentOptions method
  Menu class, 236
  MenuBuilder class, 237
addMovement method, 857
addPart( ) method, 312
addPreferencesFromResource( ) method, 267, 276
addRegularMenuItems function, 225
Address class, 15
addressContainer, 149
addSpeech( ) method, 837, 839
addSubMenu method, 231
ADP (Android Developer Phone), 997–998
ADT (Android Development Tools)
  Eclipse plug-in, 8, 92
  setting up environments, 26–29
ADT plug-in, Eclipse, 8
Advanced RISC Machine (ARM), 9
advanced UI (User Interface) concepts, 11–13
AGC (Auto Gain Control), 600
agg_exceptions table, 988–989
aggregated contacts, 968–977
AggregatedContact class, 970
AggregatedFunctionTester, 971
aggregation, controlling, 988–989
AIDL (Android Interface Definition Language)
  defining service interface in, 347–349
  implementing interface in, 349–351
  services, 346
AIDL-supporting service. *See* remote services
Alarm Clock application, 751–752
alarm manager, 465–489
  cancelling alarm, 479–480
  intent primacy in setting off alarms, 484–487
  multiple alarms, 480–484
  persistence of alarms, 487
  predicates, 487–489
  repeating alarm, 476–479
  simple alarm, 465–476
    obtaining alarm manager, 466
    PendingIntent class suitable for alarm, 467–468
    receiver for alarm, 467
    setting alarm, 468
    test project, 468–476
    time for alarm, 466–467
Alarm Manager class, 726
alarm value, 280
AlarmClock application, 18
AlarmManager class, 721
alert-dialog builder, setting up with user view, 248
alert dialogs, 244–246
alert function, 244
AlertBuilder class, 1050
AlertBuilder framework, 1061
AlertDialog builder class, 264
AlertDialogFragment dialog fragment, 1061–1062

AlertDialogFragment.java file, 1050
Alerts.showPrompt( ) method, 252
alias argument, 289–290
All option, 1010
all value, 280
AllContactsLiveFolderCreatorActivity.java file, 700–703
ALongRunningNonStickyBroadcastService class, 445–446, 460
ALongRunningNonStickyBroadcastService.java file, 462
ALongRunningReceiver class, 448
ALongRunningReceiver.java file, 460, 462
alpha animation, 498
AlphaAnimation class, 17
alphabeticShortcut tag, 242
ALTERNATIVE activity, 135
alternative menus, 234–238
Always use my settings option, 826
AMR (Adaptive Multi-Rate), 600
AnalogClock control, 169
AnalogClock view, 718
AnalogClock widget, 17
Android 2.0, 5
Android 2.3, 5
Android 3.0, 5
Android Asset Packaging Tool (AAPT), 42, 70
.android\AVD folder, 38
android/AVD folder, 39
Android computing platform, overview, 1–3
Android Content Guidelines, 1010
android create avd command, 39
Android cursors, 100, 694
Android DDMS node, 27
Android Debug Bridge (adb) command, 55, 576
Android Developer Phone (ADP), 997–998
Android Development Tools. *See* ADT
Android emulator, 8–9
android file, 37–38
Android for tablets, 5
Android foundational components, 10–11
Android home page, 695, 1070, 1082, 1088–1089, 1092, 1103, 1122–1123
Android Inc., 4
Android Interface Definition Language. *See* AIDL
Android Java API's main libraries, 8
Android Java packages, 14–18
android\:launchMode, 345
android list target command, 39
Android LiveFolder framework, 707
Android manifest editor tool, Eclipse, 297
Android Market
  becoming publisher, 994–1001
  Developer Distribution Agreement, 994
  directing users back to, 1005–1006
  mirror sites of, 1012
  Payment Processor, 995
  preparing applications for sale, 1001
  uploading applications, 1007–1010
  user experience, 1010–1012
Android media and telephony components, 13–14
android\:onClick attribute, 343
Android OS version 1.6, 5
android\:path attribute, 304
android/:pathPrefix, 304
android\:permission attribute, 305
Android platform, 3
Android Project option, 42, 422
android\:readPermission attribute, 305
Android SDK
  advanced UI concepts, 11–13
  Android emulator, 8–9
  Android foundational components, 10–11
  Android Java packages, 14–18
  Android media and telephony components, 13–14
  Android service components, 13
  Android UI, 9
  Release Candidate 1.0, 5
  setting up environments, 23–26
  for smartphones, 5
  updating PATH environment variable, 25–26
Android SDK/platforms/<android-version>/data/res/values/ folder, 197
Android service components, 13
Android settings page, 754
Android SmsMessage object, 565
android\:src property, 159
android\:text attribute, 151
Android UI (User Interface), 9
Android URIs (Uniform Resource Identifiers), 14
Android User's Guide, 944
Android views, 694
Android Virtual Device (AVD), 30–39, 92, 576, 1001
android\:writePermission attribute, 305
android:apiKey attribute, MapView control, 524
android:apiKey property, 522
android.app package, 14, 1017
android.app.Activity class, 298, 522, 541
android.app.AlertDialog.Builder class, 244
android.app.Application class, 53, 318
android.app.ListActivity, 175
android.app.Service, 338
android.appwidget.provider, 725
android.bat program, 39
android.bluetooth package, 14
android:bottomPadding property, 205
android:clickable="true"attribute, 526
android:collapseColumns property, 204
android.content package, 14
android.content.BroadcastReceiver, 563
android.content.ContentProvider interface, 16, 108
android.content.ContentResolver, 106
android.content.ContentValues class, 106
android.content.pm package, 14
android.content.res package, 14
android.database package, 14–15
android.database.sqlite package, 15, 105
android:defaultValue attribute, 268
android:description attribute, 300
android:dialogTitle attribute, 268
android:drawable tag, 496
android:entries attribute, 268
android:entryValues attribute, 268
android.gesture package, 15

android:gestureStrokeType, 888
android.graphics package, 15
android.graphics.drawable package, 15
android.graphics.drawable.shapes package, 15
android:gravity attribute, 200–201
android:gravity versus android:layout_gravity, 201–202
android.hardware package, 15
android:hint attribute, 774
AndroidHttpClient class, 319–320
android:icon attribute, 300, 1002
android.intent.action.CREATE_LIVE_FOLDER intent, 701
android.intent.action.MAIN action, 44
android.intent.category.DEFAULT, 139
android.intent.extra.EMAIL, 132
android.intent.extra.SUBJECT, 132
android.jar file, 18–19
android.jar source files, 19
android:key attribute, 268
android:label attribute, 300, 774
android:layout_alignParentBottom property, 207
android:layout_alignParentTop property, 207
android:layoutAnimation tag, 504
android:layout_below property, 207
android:layout_gravity attribute, 201
android:layout_gravity versus android:gravity, 201–202
android:layout_height attribute, 204
android:layout_margin property, 205
android:layout_weight attribute, 200
android:leftPadding property, 205
android.location package, 15, 533, 541
android.location.Geocoder class, 534
AndroidManfiest.xml file
  Android 3.0, 1121–1122
  exploring ActionBar, 1072, 1085
  list navigation, 1087
  and live folders, 700–702
  NotesList activity, 45
  preparing for uploading, 1002–1003
  standard navigation, 1090, 1092
  tweaking, 228–229
  vs. web.xml file, 30
android.media package, 15, 575
android.media.MediaPlayer class, 575
android.media.MediaRecorder class, 596
android:name attribute, 300
android.net package, 15
android.net.wifi package, 16
android.nfc package, 931
android.opengl package, 16, 638, 690
android:ordering attribute, 1067
android.os package, 16
android.os.Bundle class, 131
android.os.Debug class, 55
android.os.Handler class, 540
android.os.Parcelable interface, 131, 355
android.os.Parcelable.Creator<T> interface, 357
android:padding property, 204–205
android:permission attribute, 299, 305
android.permission.ACCESS_COARSE_LOCATION, 296
android.permission.ACCESS_COARSE_LOCATION permission, 542
android.permission.ACCESS_FINE_LOCATION, 296
android.permission.BATTERY_STATS, 296
android.permission.BLUETOOTH, 296
android.permission.CALL_PHONE permission, 571
android.permission.CAMERA permission, 296, 613
android:permissionGroup attribute, 300
android.permission.INTERNET permission, 296, 574, 584, 594
android.permission.READ_CALENDAR, 296
android.permission.READ_CONTACTS, 296
android.permission.READ_PHONE_STATE permission, 570
android.permission.READ_SMS permission, 565
android.permission.RECEIVE_SMS permission, 563
android.permission.RECORD_AUDIO permission, 296, 600, 613
android.permission.USE_SIP, 574
android.permission.WRITE_CALENDAR, 296
android.permission.WRITE_CONTACTS, 296
android.permission.WRITE_EXTERNAL_STORAGE, 837
android.permission.WRITE_EXTERNAL_STORAGE, permission, 613
android.preference package, 16
android.preference.PreferenceActivity class, 267
android:propertyName attribute, 1066
android:protectionLevel attribute, 300
android.provider package, 16
android.provider.Contacts.PeopleColumns class, 102
android.provider.LiveFolders class, 702
android.providers.Contacts package, 102
android.provider.Telephony.SMS_RECEIVED action, 563
android.R.color namespace, 76
android:required attribute, 1003
android:resource node, 725
android.R.id.home, 1071
android:rightPadding property, 205
android.sax package, 16
android:scaleType attribute, 880
android:screenOrientation="landscape" attribute, 606
android:shrinkColumns property, 204
android.speech package, 16
android.speech.tts package, 16
android:src attribute, 880
android:src property, 159
android:stretchColumns property, 204
android:summary attribute, 268
android.telephony package, 16
android.telephony.cdma package, 17
android.telephony.gsm package, 17
android.telephony.SmsManager class, 559
android.telephony.TelephonyManager manager, 568
android:text attribute, 160
android.text package, 17
android.text.method package, 17
android:textOff property, 160
android:textOn property, 160

android.text.style package, 17
android.text.util.Linkify class, 154
android:title attribute, 268
android:topPadding property, 205
android.util.Log class, 54
android.utils package, 17
android:valueFrom attribute, 1066
android:valueTo attribute, 1066
android:valueType attribute, 1066
android.view package, 17
android.view.animation package, 17, 499
android.view.animation.Animation class, 511
android.view.inputmethod package, 17
android.view.LayoutInflater class, 248
android.view.Menu class, 217, 220
android.view.MenuInflater class, 239
android.view.MenuItem, 217
android.view.SubMenu, 217
android.view.View class, 145, 233
android.view.ViewGroup class, 145
android.webkit package, 17
android.widget package, 17
android.widget.AdapterView, 170
android.widget.Button class, 157
android.widget.CheckBox, 160
android.widget.ListAdapter, 183
android.widget.RadioButton, 162
android.widget.RadioGroup, 162
android.widget.VideoView control, 593
android.widget.View, 203
android.widget.ViewGroup, 171, 199
anim/accelerate_interpolator, 506
anim directory, 41, 70
animate( ) method, 497
AnimatedSimpleTriangleRenderer class, 652–653
animateListView( ) method, 510
animateListView method, 516
Animation class, 17, 515
animation-list tag, 496
AnimationDrawable class, 494–496
AnimationListener class, 515–516
animations
  2D frame-by-frame, 492–497
    adding to activity, 494–497
    creating activity, 493–494
    planning for, 492–493
  2D layout, 498–507
    animating ListView, 502–505
    creating activity and ListView, 500–502
    interpolators, 506–507
    planning test harness, 499
    types of, 498–499
  2D view, 507–516
    adding animation to ListView, 511–514
    AnimationListener class, 515–516
    overview, 507–510
    providing depth perception with camera, 514–515
    transformation matrices, 516
  custom, with ObjectAnimator class, 1064–1067
  FragmentTransaction objects, 1034–1035
  frame-by-frame, 11
  tweening, 11, 17
AnimatorSet class, 1067
ANR (Application Not Responding), 399, 425
apache-http libraries, 18
Apache HttpClient, 307–309
Apache License, Version 2.0, 4
apk files, 292, 575, 585–586, 722, 874, 1002, 1007, 1012
aPosition variable, 683
appendText( ) method, 412
Application class, 14, 58, 318
application element, 128
Application model, 14
application node, 725
Application Not Responding (ANR), 399, 425
application preferences, 265
application-specific search context, 821–822
<application> tag, 55, 59, 1002
applicationDataBundle argument, 822
ApplicationInfo object, 59
applications
  demo versions of, 995
  distributing, via other methods, 1012–1013
  distribution of, 1010
  labels for, 1004
  licensing service for, 1006–1007
  localizing, 1003–1004
  paid, considerations for, 1004–1005
  preparing for sale, 1001
  preparing icons for, 1004
  reinstalls of, 996
  screenshots for, 1008
  selling through Android Market, 997
  textual information for, 1008
  updating and signing, 294
  uploading, 1007–1010
  viewing, 1011
applyTransformation method, 511
appSearchData argument, 769
APPWIDGET_CONFIGURE action, 725
AppWidgetManager class, 719, 721–722, 740
AppWidgetProvider class, 717, 719–721, 723
AppWidgetProviderInfo class, 718
APrefWidgetModel class, 732
APrefWidgetModel file, 723
arbitrary XML resource files, 80–81
architecture of content providers, 96–108
ArcShape, 15
areDefaultsEnforced( ) method, 842
arguments, for earcon, 839
ARM (Advanced RISC Machine), 9
array index values, 271
ArrayAdapter, 172–174, 1086
ArrayAdapter.createFromResource( ) method, 187
ArrayAdapter<T> adapter, 174
ArrayList variable, 841
arrays, string, 73
AssetFileDescriptor, 586
AssetManager class, 14, 82
assets folder, 40–41, 82, 575
Associate button, 834, 837
asterisk (*) symbol, 138

AsyncPlayer, 591–592
AsyncTask class
  and configuration changes, 327–331
  overview, 320–326
attachToRoot parameter, 1021, 1058
attrs.xml file, 1126, 1135
audible icon. *See* earcons
audio
  files for TTS APIs, 832–838
  playing content, 581–585
  recording
    with AudioRecord, 600–604
    overview, 596
    required permission for, 296
    using intent, 615–618
  setting streams with TTS APIs, 839
audioBufferSampleSize, 603
audioBufferSize, 603
AudioManager class, 15
AudioManager.STREAM_MUSIC value, 590
AUDIO_PATH variable, 586, 595
AudioRecord class, 592
AudioTrack class, 592
authority, 96
Auto Gain Control (AGC), 600
AutoCompleteTextView control, 155–156
autoPause( ) method, 590–591
autoResume( ) method, 590
autoText property, 154
AVD (Android Virtual Device), 30–39, 92, 576, 1001
AWT (Abstract Window Toolkit), Java SE, 2
awt.font package, 18

B

Back button, 700, 1016, 1082
back stacks, fragment, 1032–1035
background threads, geocoding with, 538–540
BackgroundService, 339, 346
base classes, tabbed navigation, 1073–1075
BaseActionBarActivity class
  list navigation, 1087
  standard navigation, 1091–1092
BaseActionBarActivity java file, 1072–1085, 1090
BaseAdapter class, 188
BaseColumns class, 110
BaseListener java file, 1072–1086
BaseTester.java file, 960–962
BasicResponseHandler object, 317–318
BasicViewActivity class, 126, 133
battery information, required permission for, 296
BatteryManager class, 16
BCRs (broadcast receivers)
  accommodating multiple, 431–433
  coding simple, sample code, 426–427
  compiling code, 461–463
  extending IntentService implementation for, 445–455
    abstracting wake locks with LightedGreenRoom abstraction, 449–455
    broadcast service abstractions, 445–447
    long-running receivers, 447–449
  notifications from, 434–440
    monitoring through notification manager, 435–437
    sending, 437–440
  out-of-process, project for, 433–434
  protocol, 441–442
  references, 464
  registering in manifest file, 427–428
  sending broadcasts, 426–431
bday field, 735
BDayAppWidgetProvider, 724
BDayWidgetModel class, 729–730, 738
BDayWidgetModel file, 723
BDayWidgetProvider class, 717, 731
BDayWidgetProvider file, 723
Begin Recording button, 610
beginRecording( ) method, 599, 612
Bellard, Fabrice, 8
Berkeley Software Distribution (BSD), 7
BetterCursorWrapper class, 708–709
BetterCursorWrapper.java file, 700, 708–709
bind( ) method, 346
Binder class, 16
bindService( ) method, 30, 352, 354
birthday widget, 714–716
Bitmap class, 15, 323
BitmapDrawable class, 80
Bluetooth, required permission for, 296
BluetoothAdapter class, 14
BluetoothClass class, 14
BluetoothDevice class, 14
BluetoothServerSocket class, 14
BluetoothSocket class, 14
BookProvider content provider, 118–119
BookProviderMetaData class, 109–110
BookTableMetaData class, 110, 116
BooleanButton class, 849, 854
Bornstein, Dan, 6
BounceInterpolator, 507
boundCenter( ) method, 532
boundCenterBottom( ) method, 532
bounding box, 629
bounding volume, 629
box1.xml file, 727, 1103
broadcast menu item, 431, 434
broadcast receivers. *See* BCRs
BroadcastReceiver class, 427, 562–565, 842
BROWSABLE activity, 135
Browser application, 16, 18
BSD (Berkeley Software Distribution), 7
build( ) method, 58
Builder class, 58, 244, 247
built-in content providers, 90–95
Bundle API reference, 821
bundle object, 823
Button class, 158, 846, 848
Button controls, 157–165
  Button, 157–158
  CheckBox, 160–162
  ImageButton, 158–159
  RadioButton, 162–165
  ToggleButton, 159–160

Button tag, 343
Button view, 718, 855
Button widget, 17
buttons, setting up for prompt dialog, 248

C

C\:\android directory, 23
c\:\android\release\myappraw.apk file, 292
c\:\avd\ folder, 38
c command, 38
C\:\eclipse folder, 23
C runtime library (libc), 7
CacheManager class, 17
calcArrays method, 664, 669
calcTextureArrays method, 669
Calculator application, 18
Calendar application, 18
CalendarProvider project, 19
CALL action, 129
call value, 820
callbacks, handleMessage method, 408
call_column, 821
callService( ) method, 364
CALL_STATE_RINGING state, 570
CAMCORDER audio source, 599
camcorder profiles, 613–614
Camera application, 18
Camera class, 12, 15, 515, 624
Camera directory, 579
Camera.getCameraInfo( ) method, 614
camera.getMatrix( ) method, 515
Camera.getNumberOfCameras( ) method, 614
camera.rotateY method, 515
cameras
  and Coordinates
    glFrustum and viewing volume, 636–637
    gluLookAt and camera symbolism, 634–635
    glViewport and screen size, 637
  providing depth perception for 2D view animation, 514–515
  required permission for, 296
cancel( ) method, 246, 1048
cancelAll( ) method, 342
Canvas class, 15
captureImage( ) method, 618
CATEGORY_ALTERNATIVE category, 135, 235
CATEGORY_BROWSABLE category, 135
CATEGORY_DEFAULT category, 135
CATEGORY_EMBED category, 135
CATEGORY_GADGET category, 134–135
CATEGORY_HOME category, 134–135
CATEGORY_LAUNCHER category, 134–136
CATEGORY_PREFERENCE category, 135
CATEGORY_SAMPLE_CODE category, 135
CATEGORY_SELECTED_ALTERNATIVE category, 135
CATEGORY_TAB category, 135
CATEGORY_TEST category, 135
CellLocation class, 16
certificates, self-signed, 288–291
CHANNEL* values, 603
check-box widget, 275
Check for Updates option, Eclipse, 27
checkable behavior tags, 241
CheckBox control, 160–162
Checkbox widget, 17
CheckBoxPreference class, 16, 275–277
CheckBoxPreference view, 275
checked tag, 241
Checkout, Google, 994–995, 999, 1009, 1011
CHECK_VOICE_DATA_PASS intent, 829–830
chkbox.xml file, 276
CHOICE_MODE_MULTIPLE mode, 181
Choose Flight Options view, 267
chown command, 383
Chronometer control, 194
Chronometer view, 718
Chronometer widget, 17
ClassCastException, 1057
ClassNotFoundException, 59
Clean option, Eclipse, 43
clear( ) method, 859
clearAllData( ) method, 730
clearAllPreferences( ) method, 729–730
clearCheck( ) method, 164
ClickReceiver class, 874–875
ClickReceiver overlay, 877
ClickReceiver.java file, 872
client applications, calling services from, 351–355
Client Manifest File, 302
ClientConnectionManager, 317
ClientCustPermMainActivity class, 302
client.execute( ) method, 309
Close button, 1060
Closeable object, 58
cloud-computing model, 5
Cochran, Wayne O., 690
Color class, 15
Color Drawables resources, 72, 79–80
color resources, 76
colored-ballN pattern, 493
colors, localizing, 1003
Colors resource, 71
Columns interface, 102
com.androidbook.bcr package, 462
com.androidbook.handlers package, 422
com.androidbook.hello package name, 32
com.androidbook.intents.testbc action, 427
com.androidbook.provider.BookProvider, 110
com.androidbook.salbcr package, 463
com.androidbook.samplepackage1 package, 384
com.androidbook.stockquoteclient, 351
com.android.browser package, 379
com.cust.perm package, 302
com.cust.perm.PrivActivity, 302
com.google.android.maps package, 17, 519
comma character, 831
command-line tools, 8
CommaTokenizer, 156
commit( ) method, 285, 734, 1035
CommonDataKinds classes, 956
CommonDataKinds.Email class, 952
Commons IO web site, 311

commons-lang JAR file, 375
communications, between fragments, 1063–1064
CompassSensor application, 914
compiled resources, 70
compiling code, instructions for, 421–422
complex types, passing to services, 355–366
components
  Android, 10–11, 13–14
  directly invoking activities with, 133
  lifetimes of, 418–421
    activities, 418–419
    providers, 421
    receivers, 420–421
    services, 420
  rules for resolving intents to, 137–139
  and threading, 399–403
    content providers, 401
    external service components, 401
    main thread, 400–401
    thread pools, 401
    thread utilities, 401, 403
computeCurrentVelocity method, 858
computing platform, Android, 1–3
com.syh package, 357
configuration activity class, 726
configuration qualifiers, 84
configure attribute, 726
ConfigureBDayWidgetActivity activity, 719, 724
ConfigureBDayWidgetActivity class, 738
ConfigureBDayWidgetActivity.java file, 724
ConnectivityManager class, 15
consoles, Eclipse, 814
constant intent.ACTION_SEARCH, 786
constructors, RemoteViewsFactory interface, 1107
contact table field, 988
ContactData structure, 988
ContactDataFunctionTester, 982, 984
ContactData.java file, 982
Contact_entities_view, 984
ContactFunctionTester.java file, 983
contact_id column, 981
contact_id field, 954
contacts
  aggregated contacts, 956–958
  contact_entities_view view, 959
  data tables, 955–956
  editing, 699
  live-folder, 698
  raw contacts, 953–955
  view_contacts view, 958–959
contacts API, 937–991
  accounts, 938–943, 960–968
    driver activity classes, 963–966
    enumerating, 943
    function tester-related files, 961–962
    menu file, 961
    relevance to contacts, 942–943
    running program, 966–968
    screens, 938–942
  contacts, 952–959
    adding with details, 985–988
    aggregated, 956–958, 968–977
    contact_entities_view view, 959
    data table, 955–956
    examining contents SQLite database, 952–953
    raw, 953–955, 977–982
    view_contacts view, 958–959
  contacts application, 944–952
    contact data types, 951–952
    edit contact screen, 946–948
    exporting contacts, 949–951
    photo setting screen, 948–949
    show contact detail screen, 945
    show contacts screen, 944
  controlling aggregation, 988–989
  impacts of syncing, 989–991
Contacts application, 18
Contacts content provider, 693, 707
Contacts LF folder, 698, 700
Contacts LF icon, 698, 709
Contacts provider, 100
contacts2.db, 952
ContactsContract.AggregationExceptions class, 989
ContactsContract.CommonDataKinds, 956
ContactsContract.Contacts.CONTENT_URI, 976
ContactsContract.Data, 955
ContactsContract.RawContact class, 954
ContactsContract.RawContacts.RawContactsEntity class, 959
contacts.db database, 102
contacts.db file, 94, 952
Contacts.People.CONTENT_URI, 101
ContactsProvider project, 19
containers, description of, 146
Content Guidelines, Android, 1010
content providers
  adding files to, 107
  architecture of, 96–108
  built-in, 90–95
  concept of, 10, 694
  cursor, 102–104
  databases on emulator and available devices, 91–95
  deletes from, 108
  extending ContentProvider, 110–111
  fulfilling MIME-Type contracts, 116
  implementing delete method, 117
  implementing insert method, 116–117
  implementing query method, 116
  implementing update method, 117
  inserting records in, 106–107
  planning database, 109–110
  reading data with URIs, 100–102
  registering, 119–123
  setting up development environment, 30
  SQLite primer, 95
  structure of MIME types, 98–100
  structure of URIs, 97–98
  updates of, 108
  using projection maps, 119
  using UriMatcher to figure out URIs, 117–118
  where clauses, 104–106
    explicit, 105–106
    passing through URIs, 104–105

(content\://sms/inbox), 566
content\://sms/sent, 567
ContentProvider class, 49–50, 108, 110–111
ContentResolver object, 106–108, 707, 710
contents SQLite database, 952–953
CONTENT_URI, 46
ContentValues argument, 108
ContentValues class, 106, 618
ContentValues dictionary, 106
Context class, 425, 586
context menus, 231–233
  populating, 233–234
  registering view for, 233
  responding to items on, 234
context.getSharedPreferences( ) method, 734
CONTEXT_IGNORE_SECURITY flag, 384
CONTEXT_INCLUDE_CODE flag, 384
ContextMenu class, 231–233
ContextMenuInfo class, 233–234
Context.NOTIFICATION_SERVICE service, 438
CONTEXT_RESTRICTED flag, 384
Context.startService( ) method, 338–339, 346
context.startService(new Intent(MyService.class)) method, 443
Context.stopService( ) method, 339
controls, 152–198
  buttons, 157–165
    Button, 157–158
    CheckBox, 160–162
    ImageButton, 158–159
    RadioButton, 162–165
    ToggleButton, 159–160
  date and time
    AnalogClock, 169
    DatePicker, 167–168
    DigitalClock, 169
    TimePicker, 167–168
  description of, 146
  Gallery, 187–188
  GridView control, 183–185
  ImageView control, 165–166
  MapView, 169–170
  Spinner, 185–187
  text, 152–157
    AutoCompleteTextView, 155–156
    EditText, 154–155
    MultiAutoCompleteTextView, 156–157
    TextView, 153–154
convertView value, 193
CookieManager class, 17
Copy projects into work space option, Eclipse, 421, 461
CountDownTimer class, 194
create avd command, 38
create( ) method, 585
Create new project in work space option, 422
Create project from existing sample option, Eclipse, 882
create statement, 95
createAlertDialog( ) method, 254
createFromResource( ) method, 173
createHttpClient( ) method, ApplicationEx, 317
createItem method, 531
CREATE_LIVE_FOLDER intent, 701
createLiveFolder method, 703
createPackageContext( ) API, 383
createScaledBitmap( ) method, 193
Criteria object, 543
CrossProcessCursor, 708
crypto package, 18
crypto.spec package, 18
CupcakeMaps.ini file, 39
Cursor interface, 14
cursor object, 97, 337, 751
CursorAdapter adapter, 174
cursors, 100, 102–104, 693–694, 700, 707
cursor.setNotificationUri, 707
CursorWrapper class, 181, 708
custom gestures, 881
custom method, 854
custom suggestion providers, 796–818
  manifest file, 813–814
  planning, 796
  search metadata, 804–805
  SuggestURLProvider class, 797–807
  SuggestURLProvider project implementation files, 796–797
  user experience, 814–818
CustomHttpClient class, 317, 323
CustPermMainActivity, 298

D

Dalvik Debug Monitor Service (DDMS), 577, 1008
Dalvik Executable (.dex) file, 6
Dalvik VM (Virtual Machine), 6–8
_data column, 107
/data directory, 271, 586
data element, 130
_data field, 107
data portion, of intents, 129
/data/res/anim directory, 1034
/data/res/animator directory, 1034, 1066
/data/res/interpolator directory, 1066
database modes for SearchRecentSuggestionsProvider, 781–783
DatabaseHelper class, 50
DATABASE_MODE_2LINES, 782
DATABASE_MODE_QUERIES, 782–783
databases, planning, 109–110
data.getData( ) method, 616
date and time controls
  AnalogClock, 169
  DatePicker, 167–168
  DigitalClock, 169
  TimePicker, 167–168
date-related utilities, 737–738
DatePicker control, 167–168
DatePicker widget, 17
DatePickerDialog, 264
DCIM directory, 579
DDMS (Dalvik Debug Monitor Service), 577, 1008
DDMS node, Android, 27
dealWithThisAction( ) method, 1112–1113

Debug Bridge (adb) command, Android, 55, 576
debug log, 793
debug text view layout, scrollable, 1080–1081
DebugActivity java file, 960, 963–964, 1072–1073, 1077–1081
debug_activity_layout.xml file, 960, 963
DebugActvity.java file, 963
debugging
  applications, 54–62
  using Toast objects, 263
debug_layout_activity.java file, 964
Debug.startMethodTracing( ) method, 55
DebugUtils class, 17
declaring menus, 11
DEFAULT activity, 135
DEFAULT category, 139, 1043
DefaultHttpClient( ) method, 315, 317
defaultValue attribute, 267
DeferWorkHandler class, 408, 412–413, 417
DeferWorkHandler handler, 405, 407–408
delete method, 108, 110, 117
deleting
  from content providers, 108
  widget instances, 722
demo versions, distributing, 995
density-independent pixels, 206
describeEvent( ) method, 868
DESCRIPTION field, 706
DESCRIPTION value, 618
designing widgets, 743
DetailsFragment class, 1028, 1030–1031, 1042
details.xml file, 1031–1032
detectAll( ) method, 58, 60
detectDiskReads( ) method, 60
detecting sensors, 892
(detectOpenGLES20) function, 679
Developer Account, 994
Developer Composite Score, 997, 1009
Developer Console, 994, 997–1001, 1007
developer name, 1006
Development Tools node, Android, 27
Device view, 1008
Devices screen, Hierarchy Viewer, 214
devices, testing, 1001
.dex (Dalvik Executable) file, 6
dialog fragments, 1044–1063
  DialogFragment class, 1045–1049
    constructing, 1045–1047
    dismissing, 1048–1049
    displaying, 1047
  sample application
    AlertDialogFragment dialog fragment, 1061–1062
    HelpDialogFragment dialog fragment, 1058–1061
    Main Layout main.xml application, 1062–1063
    MainActivity class, 1051–1053
    OnDialogDoneListener interface, 1053–1054
    PromptDialogFragment dialog fragment, 1054–1058
Dialog object, 264
dialog1.getValue1( ) method, 255
dialog1.show( ) method, 255
dialogFinished( ) method, 255, 259, 262
DialogFragment class, 1045–1049
  constructing, 1045–1047
    overriding onCreateDialog method, 1046–1047
    overriding onCreateView method, 1046
  dismissing, 1048–1049
  displaying, 1047
DialogInterface, 246
DialogRegistry class, 259
dialogs, 243
  alert, 244–246
  nature of in Android, 251–252
  prompt, 246–251
    creating and showing, 249
    PromptListener class, 249
    rearchitecting, 252
    setting up alert-dialog builder with user view, 248
    setting up buttons and listeners, 248
    XML layout file for, 247
  recasting as managed dialogs, 253–255
dialog.show( ) method, 244
dialogTitle attribute, 267
dictionary, free, 816
Digital Camera Images directory, 579
digital certificates, 288
DigitalClock control, 169
DigitalClock widget, 17
Dimensions resource, 71, 77
DIRECTORY_ALARMS directory, 579
DIRECTORY_DCIM directory, 579
DIRECTORY_DOWNLOADS directory, 579
DIRECTORY_MOVIES directory, 579
DIRECTORY_MUSIC directory, 580
DIRECTORY_NOTIFICATIONS directory, 580
DIRECTORY_PICTURES directory, 580
DIRECTORY_PODCASTS directory, 580
DIRECTORY_RINGTONES directory, 580
disabled option, 957
disabling search activity, 766–767
Dismiss button, 1058
dismiss( ) method, 246, 1048–1049, 1058
display orientation, and accelerometers, 910
Display.getOrientation( ) method, 910
Display.getRotation( ) method, 910
display_name field, 954
displayNotificationMessage( ) method, 341
distanceBetween( ) method, 543
distanceTo( ) method, 543
divideMessage( ) method, 563
doClick( ) method, 325, 334, 344, 540, 599
doDeferredWork( ) method, 405
doInBackground( ) method, 323–324, 326
Done option, 882
doSearchQuery( ) method, 786, 810–811
doShow( ) method, 921
doSpeak( ) method, 831
Dot class, 859
Dot element, 859
Dot view, 862
Dot.java file, 1126
doUpdate( ) method, 920
doView( ) function, 810
doView( ) method, 810, 812

downloadImage( ) method, 323, 331
DownloadImageTask class, 323, 326, 328
DownloadManager class, 331–337
DownloadManager.Query object, 337
DownloadManager.Request object, 334, 336
DownloadProvider project, 19
DOWNLOAD_SERVICE service, 334
drag and drop, 859–862
Drag and Drop API, sample application, 1124–1137
  drag source views, 1132–1137
  laying out, 1126–1129
  list of files, 1125–1126
  overview, 1124–1125
  responding to onDrag( ) callback method in drop zone, 1129–1132
  testing, 1137–1139
drag source views, 1132–1137
DragShadowBuilder behavior, 1136
Draw 9-patch tool, 79
draw( ) method, 532, 624, 639–640, 665, 674, 676, 861, 1136
drawable\box1.xml file, 1114
Drawable class, 166, 494–496, 532
drawable directory, 41, 70
<drawable> value, 72
drawing
  with OpenGL ES, 628–633
  with textures, 672–673
driver activity classes, 963–966
  DebugActivity.java, 963–964
  debug_layout_activity.java file, 964
  manifest file, 966
  TestContactsDriverActivity.java, 965
driver classes, examples, 413–418
  activity file, 414, 416
  layout file, 417
  manifest file, 417–418
  menu file, 417
DrmProvider project, 19
drop zone, responding to onDrag( ) call back method in, 1129–1132
DropZone class, 1132
DropZone.java file, 1126
dropzone.xml file, 1126
dump( ) method, 1036
dynamic menus, 238

E

e-mail, SMS (Short Message Service), 567–568
earcons, 839–840
Éclair, 873
Eclipse 3.5, setting up environments, 23
Eclipse ADT plug-in, 8
Eclipse console, 814
Eclipse File Explorer tool, 577, 950
edge flags, 853
edit contact screen, contacts API, 946–948
editing contacts, 699
EditText control, 154–155, 205
EditText field, 156, 537, 561
EditText view, 829, 837
EditText widget, 17
EditTextPreference view, 275, 277–278
EGL Native Platform Graphics Interface, 625
Element class, 16
ElementListener interface, 16
Email application, 18
emo_im_happy.png image file, 360
emo_im_winking drawable, 342
EmptyOnClickListener, 254
emulator, 8–9, 36–37, 43
enableDebugLogging( ) method, 1036
enableDefaults( ) method, 59–60
enabling NFC (Near Field Communication) sensors, 925
End User License Agreement (EULA), 997, 1008
enqueue( ) method, 334
entries attribute, 267
entryValues attribute, 267
enumerating accounts, contacts API, 943
Environment method, 579
Environment Variables window, 23, 25
Environment.getExternalStorageDirectory( ) method, 579
Environment.getExternalStoragePublicDirectory(String type), 580
environments, setting up
  ADT, 26–29
  Android SDK, 23–26
  Eclipse 3.5, 23
  JDK 6, 22–23
ErrorText style, 196
ErrorText.Danger style, 197
ES20SimpleTriangleRenderer class, 679
EULA (End User License Agreement), 997, 1008
exceptions, consuming HTTP services, 313–315
execute( ) method, 310, 314, 318, 325–326
executeHttpGet( ) method, 315
executeHttpGetWithRetry( ) method, 315
Existing Projects into Workspace option, Eclipse, 421
ExpandableContextMenuInfo class, 234
expanded menus, 229
explicit class name, 129
explicit intent, 129, 137
explicit where clauses, 105–106
exporting contacts, contacts API, 949–951
extending ContentProvider, 110–111
Extensible Markup Language. *See* XML
extensions for widgets, 742–743
external service components, 401
EXTRA_BCC, 568
EXTRA_CC, 568
EXTRA_EMAIL key, 132
extras attribute, 131
EXTRA_SUBJECT key, 132
eye point, 634

F

f data type, 628
FaceDetector class, 15
fade_in animator, 1065
fade_in.xml file, 1066

FadeOffset value, 885, 888
fade_out animator, 1065
fade_out.xml file, 1066
fake words, 838
falseBtnBottom object, 856
falseBtnTop, 855
FalseButton class, 848–849, 854
falseLayoutBottom object, 856–857
far point, 636
File Copy feature, 885
File Explorer tab, 577
File Explorer tool, Eclipse, 577, 950
File/Import menu, Eclipse, 461
File object, 579–580
FileDescriptor, 585–586
FileObserver class, 16
files
  .apk, 1007
  adding to content providers, 107
  custom suggestion provider manifest, 813–814
  widget background shape, 727–728
  widget layout, 726–727
  widget layout-related, 726–728
FILL_PARENT constant, vs. MATCH_PARENT constant, 152
fillWindow method, 709
find command, 94
findFragmentById( ) method, 1032, 1036
findFragmentByTag( ) method, 1036
findLocation( ) method, 540
findPreference( ) method, 283
findViewById( ) method, 67, 151, 284
finish( ) method, 812, 1042
flag_update_current flag, 1111
flight-options preference, 266–267
flightoptions.xml file, 274
FlightPreferenceActivity class, 267, 273
flight_sort_option_default_value string, 272
flight_sort_options, 274
floats, 874
Folders option, 696
folders, SMS (Short Message Service), 565–567
for loop, navigating through cursors using, 103
foundational components of Android, 10–11
Fragment class, 1015, 1020, 1025, 1044–1045
<fragment> tag, 1020, 1025, 1033, 1037–1041
FragmentManager class, 1035–1044
  invoking separate activities, 1041–1043
  ListFragment class and <fragment> tag, 1037–1041
  persistence of fragments, 1044
  referencing fragments, 1037
fragments for tablets, 1015–1068
  communications between, 1063–1064
  custom animations with ObjectAnimator class, 1064–1067
  dialog, 1044–1063
    DialogFragment class, 1045–1049
    sample application, 1050–1063
  fragment back stacks, 1032–1035
  FragmentManager class, 1035–1044
    invoking separate activities, 1041–1043
    ListFragment class and <fragment> tag, 1037–1041
    persistence of fragments, 1044
    referencing fragments, 1037
  FragmentTransaction objects, 1032–1035
  lifecycle, 1018–1023
    onActivityCreated( ) callback, 1022
    onAttach( ) callback, 1020
    onCreate( ) callback, 1020–1021
    onCreateView( ) callback, 1021
    onDestroy( ) callback, 1023
    onDestroyView( ) callback, 1023
    onDetach( ) callback, 1023
    onInflate( ) callback, 1020
    onPause( ) callback, 1022
    onResume( ) callback, 1022
    onStart( ) callback, 1022
    onStop( ) callback, 1022
    sample fragment app showing, 1024–1032
    setRetainInstance( ) method, 1023
  references, 1067–1068
  structure of, 1017–1018
  when to use, 1016–1017
FragmentTransaction class, 1032–1035, 1065
frame-by-frame animation, 2D, 492–497
  adding animation to activity, 494–497
  creating activity, 493–494
  planning for, 492–493
frame_animation.xml file, 496
FrameLayout, 208–209
FrameLayout layout manager, 198
FrameLayout view, 718
FrameLayout widget, 17
frameworks/base directory, 18–19
free dictionary, 816
FreeType library, 7
from parameter, 172
fromPixels( ) method, 872
fromRawResource( ) method, 888
frustum, 625, 629, 636
function tester-related files, 961–962
  AccountsFunctionTester.java, 962
  BaseTester.java, 961–962
  IReportBack.java, 961
fundamental components, 29–30
  activities, 29
  Android Virtual Devices, 30
  AndroidManifest.xml, 30
  content providers, 30
  intents, 29–30
  services, 30
  views, 29

G

GADGET category, 135
Gallery control, 187–188
geGeocoder class, 537
General/Existing Projects into Workspace menu item, Eclipse, 461
generic actions, 130–131
GenericManagedAlertDialog class, 257, 261

GenericPromptDialog class, 257, 262
genkey argument, 289
geo fix command, 558
GeoCoder class, 15, 520, 533, 540, 874
geocode.xml file, 538
geocoding
with Android, 534–537
with background threads, 538–540
GeomagneticField class, 922
GeoPoint class, 533, 872, 874
Gesture class, 15
gesture library, 883–884
gesture points, 883
gesture store, 883
gesture strokes, 883–884
GestureDetector class, 878–881
GestureLibraries.fromFile( ) method, 887
GestureLibrary class, 15
GestureOverlayView class, 15, 888
GesturePoint class, 15
gestures, 874–889
custom, 881
GestureDetector class, 878–881
and Gestures Builder app, 882–889
multi-touch, 883
pinch gesture, 875–878
Gestures Builder app, 882–889
Gestures Builder icon, 882
gestures file, 885
GestureStore class, 15
GestureStroke class, 15
getAccuracy( ) method, 543
getAction( ) method, 851, 863, 868, 870
getActionbar( ) method, 1079
getActionIndex( ) method, 871
getActionMasked( ) method, 871
getACursor( ) method, 970
getAllProviders( ) method, 542
getAngleArrays method, 663
getArguments( ) method, 1031
getBoolean( ) method, 277
getBroadcast( ) method, 556
getCacheDir( ) method, 586
getCenter( ) method, 533
getCenterPt( ) method, 533
getCheckedItemIds( ) method, 182–183
getCheckedItemPositions( ) method, 181
getColumnValue( ) method, 969
getComponentName( ) method, 236
GET_CONTENT action, 141–142
getContextViewInfo( ) method, 233
getCount( ) method, 104, 120, 192, 1108–1109
getCurrentPosition( ) method, 584, 592
getDefaultAdapter( ) method, 925
getDefaultEngine( ) method, 840
getDownTime( ) method, 863
getDrawable( ) method, 531
getDuration( ) method, 592
getEdgeFlags( ) method, 853
getEditText( ) method, 278
getEventsFromAnXMLFile function, 81
getExternalStorageDirectory( ) method, 581
getExternalStoragePublicDirectory( ) method, 581
getExtras, 131
getFilesDir( ) method, 586
getFragment( ) method, 1036–1037
getFragmentManager( ) method, 1036
getFromLocationName( ) method, 534, 537
getHttpClient( ) method, 318
getInclination( ) method, 920
getIndexBuffer method, 664
getIntent( ) method, Activity class, 235
getInterpolation method, 506
getIntrinsicHeight( ) method, 532
getIntrinsicWidth( ) method, 532
getItemAtPosition( ) method, 181
getItemId( ) method, 193, 221, 227, 1109
getItemViewType( ) method, 192
getLanguage( ) method, 842
getLastKnownLocation( ) method, 542
getLastNonConfigurationInstance( ) method, 327–328
getLatSpanE6( ) method, 533
getListView( ) method, 1040
getLoadingView( ) method, 1108–1109
getLonSpanE6( ) method, 533
getLRSClass( ) method, 448–449
getMinBufferSize( ) method, 603
getOrientation( ) method, 915, 920, 922
getPathSegments( ) method, 116
getPointerCount( ) method, 863
getPreferences(int mode) method, 284
getPrefname( ) method, 731
getPrefsToSave( ) method, 731
getPressure( ) method, 863
getProjection( ) method, 872
getPromptReply( ) method, 251
getProvider( ) method, 542
getProviders(boolean enabledOnly) method, 542
getProviders(Criteria criteria, boolean enabledOnly) method, 542
getQuote( ) method, 352, 358
getResources( ) method, 77, 586
getResult( ) method, 1138
getRotationMatrix( ) method, 915, 920
getSamples( ) method, 603
getSensorList( ) method, 894
getShownIndex( ) method, 1030–1031
getSize( ) method, 863
getString( ) method, 273, 275
getSystemService( ) method, 541
getTag( ) method, 1053
getTargetFragment( ) method, 1064
getText( ) method, 178, 278
getType( ) method, 50, 108, 110, 116, 802
getVertexBuffer method, 664
getView( ) method, 172–173, 192–193
getViewAt( ) method, 1108–1111
getViewAt(position) method, 1109
getViewTypeCount( ) method, 192, 1109
getX( ) method, 863–864, 870
getXMultiplierArray method, 663
getXVelocity( ) method, 858
getY( ) method, 863
getYMultiplierArray method, 663

getYVelocity( ) method, 858
Git system, 18–19
glActiveTexture method, 672
glBindTexture method, 671
GL_CLAMP option, 672
glClear method, 632–633
glColor method, 632–633
glColor4f method, 633
GL_COLOR_BUFFER_BIT, GL_DEPTH_BUFFER_BIT, 632
glDraw method, 674
glDrawElements( ) method, 628, 630–632, 676
gl_FragColor variable, 684
glFrustum method, 633, 636, 648
glGenTextures method, 671
GL_LINE_LOOP, 631
GL_LINES, 631
GL_LINE_STRIP, 631
global search
  enabling suggestion providers for
    in Android 2.2, 754–756
    in Android 2.3, 756–757
    overview, 753
  overview, 746
  QSB, 771, 793, 814
globalSearch argument, 769
globalSearchOnly argument, 822
GL_POINTS, 631
GL_REPEAT option, 672
GL_STENCIL_BUFFER_BIT, 632
GLSurfaceView class, 638, 651, 679
GLSurfaceView.Renderer interface, 638
GLSurfaceView.setEGLContextClientVersion function, 679
glTexCoordpointer method, 672
glTexEnv method, 672
glTexParameter method, 672
GL_TRIANGLE_FAN, 631
GL_TRIANGLES, 631, 655
GL_TRIANGLE_STRIP, 631
gluLookAt method, 633, 635
GLUtils.texImage2D method, 672
glVertexPointer method, and specifying drawing vertices, 628–630
glViewport method, 634, 637
Google
  obtaining map-api key from, 520–522
  searching with, 817
Google account, 994
Google Checkout, 994–995, 999, 1009, 1011
Google Translate example, using services, 366–375
GoogleContactsProvider project, 19
GoogleSearch application, 18
GoogleSubscribedFeedsProvider project, 19
GPS location information, required permission for, 296
GPS_PROVIDER, 552
GPX files, 547
GradientDrawable, 80
<grant-uri-permission> tag, 304
graphics library, 12
gravity
  and accelerometers, 910–913
  android:gravity versus android:layout_gravity, 201–202
  in LinearLayout, 199–201
  sensors, interpreting data from, 923
GravityDemo application, 911
grep, 19
GridView control, 183–185, 191, 498, 693–694
GridView widget, 17
gridviewcustom.xml file, 191
GridViews, 694
group tags, 239, 241
guava jar file, 934
gyroscope sensors, interpreting data from, 907–908

H

Han, Jeff, 862
handleBroadcastIntent( ) method, 460
handleMessage( ) method, 403, 405, 408, 412, 422
Handler class, 16, 407
handlers, 399–423
  compiling code for, 421–422
  and components, 401
  constructing message objects, 407
  example driver classes, 413–418
    activity file, 414–416
    layout file, 417
    manifest file, 417–418
    menu file, 417
  example that defers work, 405–406
  and holding main thread, 404
  and lifetimes, 418–421
    of activities, 418–419
    of providers, 421
    of receivers, 420–421
    of services, 420
  references, 422–423
  responding to handleMessage method callback, 408
  sending message objects to queue, 407–408
  and threading
    main thread, 400–401
    thread pools, 401
    thread utilities, 401–403
  using to defer work on main thread, 405
  and worker threads, 408–413
    communicating between main threads and, 410–412
    invoking from menu, 409–410
    thread behavior, 412–413
hasAccuracy( ) method, 543
_has_set_default_values.xml file, 274
hasStableIds( ) method, 183, 1109
Hello Android application name, 32
Hello World! application, 31–37
HelloActivity Create Activity name, 32
HelloActivity.java file, 33
HelloAndroid project, 32–33
helloworld message, 431–432

Help button, 1058
Help menu, Eclipse, 27
HelpDialogFragment dialog fragment, 1058–1061
HelpDialogFragment.java file, 1050
hide( ) method, 1034
Hierarchy Viewer, debugging and optimizing layouts with, 213–216
hierarchyviewer.bat file, 214
history, of Android, 3–5
Home button, 1082
HOME category, 136
Home icon, 1071–1084
HOME key, 748
home page, Android, 695, 1070, 1082, 1088–1089, 1092, 1103, 1122–1123
home screen context menu, 713
home screen widgets
  definition of, 712
  lifecycle of widget, 716–722
    definition phase, 717–719
    deleting widget instance, 722
    instance creation phase, 719–720
    onUpdate phase, 720–721
    uninstalling widget packages, 722
    widget view mouse click event callbacks phase, 722
  list-based, 1097–1124
    remote views, 1098–1113
    sample list widget, 1114–1122
  sample widget application, 722–742
    abstract implementation of widget model, 732–734
    date-related utilities, 737–738
    defining widget provider, 724–725
    defining widget size, 725–726
    implementation of widget model for birthday widget, 735–737
    implementing widget configuration activity, 738–742
    implementing widget provider, 728–730
    interface for widget model, 731–732
    widget layout-related files, 726–728
  user experience, 713–716
  widget limitations and extensions, 742–743
howManyDays attribute, 735
hreadSafeClientConnManager, 315
HTML Viewer application, 18
HTTP GET requests, HttpClient, 308–310
HTTP POST requests, HttpClient, 310–312
HTTP services, consuming
  exceptions, 313–315
  multithreading issues, 315
  overview, 307–308
  timeouts for, 318–319
  using AndroidHttpClient, 319–320
  using AsyncTask, 320–331
  using DownloadManager, 331–337
  using HttpClient for HTTP GET requests, 308–310
  using HttpClient for HTTP POST requests, 310–312
  using HttpURLConnection, 319
HttpClient
  HTTP GET requests, 308–310
  HTTP POST requests, 310–312
HttpGet object, 318–319
HttpMime web site, 311
HttpParams object, 318
HttpPost object, 318–319
HttpURLConnection class, 319

I

IANA (Internet Assigned Numbers Authority) web site, 99
ICON field, 706
icon menus, 229–230
icon_1, 805
icon_2, 805
id attribute, 67
_ID column, 47, 50, 102, 805
id field, 110, 732
IDE (Integrated Development Environment) tool, 8
identity matrix, 508
IDialogFinishedCallBack interface, 260
IDialogProtocol interface, 256, 258–259
IDs, for resources, 69
ifconfig command, 26
ignoreLastFinger variable, 877–878
IllegalArgumentException, 603
IM application, 18
image resources, 78–79
ImageButton control, 158–159
ImageButton view, 718
ImageButton widget, 17
Images resource, 72
images, stretchable, 78
ImageView control, 165–166, 331, 880
ImageView objects, 209
ImageView view, 718
implicit intents, 129, 139
Import menu option, Eclipse, 421
import statement, 355, 1099
ImProvider project, 19
inches, 205
includeInGlobalSearch attribute, 788, 793
inflate( ) method, 1021
init( ) method, 731
initCamera( ) method, 609
initialize method, 511
Initialize Recorder button, 609
initialized, 285
initialQuery argument, 769, 822
initRecorder( ) method, 611, 613
InputStream method, 166
insert( ) method, 50–51, 108, 110, 116–117, 174
insertName( ) method, 988
insertPhone( ) method, 988
insertRawContact( ) method, 988
install command, 294
Install New Software feature, Eclipse, 27
Install New Software...option, Eclipse, 26
Instrumentation class, 1001
int constant, 68
Integrated Android Search, 12
Integrated Development Environment (IDE) tool, 8

Intent action, 804
Intent class, 10, 131–133, 135, 273, 829
INTENT field, 706
intent filter, 137–138
<intent-filter> tag, 351
INTENT item, 706
Intent object, 236
Intent parameter, 140
intent primacy, in setting off alarms, 484–487
intent_action, 805, 807
Intent.ACTION_CALL action, 130
Intent.ACTION_DIAL action, 130
Intent.ACTION_VIEW action, 303, 571
intent_data, 805–806
Intent.FLAG_GRANT_READ_URI_PERMISSION flag, 304
intent.getExtras( ) method, 565
intents, 29–30
  ACTION_PICK action, 139–141
  available in Android, 127–128
  categories of, 134–136
  data portion of, 129
  directly invoking activities with components, 133
  extra information, 131–132
  generic actions, 130–131
  GET_CONTENT action, 141–142
  overview, 125–126
  pending, 142–144
  recording audio using, 615–618
  relationship to data Uniform Resource Identifiers (URIs), 129
  responding to menu items with, 222
  rules for resolving to components, 137–139
IntentService class, 423, 442, 457
IntentService implementation
  extending for broadcast receivers, 445–455
    abstracting wake locks with LightedGreenRoom abstraction, 449–455
    broadcast service abstractions, 445–447
    long-running, 447–449
  overview, 442–443
  source code, 443–444
IntentService.java file, 423
IntentUtils code, 130
internalCursor variable, 709
internal.db database, 620
Internet Assigned Numbers Authority (IANA) web site, 99
Internet, required permission for, 296
interpolatedTime method, 511, 515
interpolators, 506–507
interprocess communication
  calling services from client applications, 351–355
  passing complex types to services, 355–366
interrupt( ) method, 342
ints, 874
Invalid panorama indication, 874
invalidate( ) method, 881, 1136
invokeLocalSearchActivity( ) function, 775
invokeSearch function, 769
invokeSearchInvokerActivity( ) function, 770
invoking activities directly with components, 133
io package, 18
IP address, 26
ipconfig command, 26
IReportBack interface, 961–962, 964, 1073–1077, 1086
IReportBack.java file, 960–961, 1072
Is Library check box, 389
Is Library flag, 385
isAlive( ) method, 413
isCancelled( ) method, 326
isChecked( ) method, 161
isEnabled( ) method, 925
isLanguageAvailable( ) method, 841
isLocationDisplayed( ) method, 526, 551
isMultiPane( ) method, 1027
isPlaying( ) method, 592
isProviderEnabled(String providerName) method, 542
isRouteDisplayed( ) method, 526
isSpeaking( ) method, 842
IStockQuoteService interface, 347, 349–350, 354, 358
IStockQuoteService service, 352
IStockQuoteService.aidl file, 352, 361
IStockQuoteService.java file, 365
item node, 74
item tag, 69, 196
ItemizedOverlay class, 528, 531–532, 871
IWidgetModelSaveContract file, 723

J

J2EE (Java 2 Platform, Enterprise Edition), 29
jarsigner command, 381, 1007
Jarsigner tool, 288, 292
Java 2 Platform, Enterprise Edition (J2EE), 29
Java API's main libraries, Android, 8
Java Binding for the OpenGL ES API (JSR 239), documentation for, 690
Java ME
  M3G, 626–627
  OpenGL ES, 626
Java packages, for Android, 14–18
Java SE (Java Platform, Standard Edition), 2
Java Specification Request (JSR) 239, 12
Java Virtual Machine (JVM), 2
JAVA_HOME environment variable, 23
java.nio classes, 629
java.nio package, 631
JavaScript Object Notation (JSON), support for, 313
JavaServer Pages (JPS), 29
javax.microedition.khronos.egl package, 16
javax.microedition.khronos.nio package, 16
javax.microedition.khronos.opengles package, 16
JDK 6, setting up environments, 22–23
JDK bin directory, 288, 292
JETCreator tool, 591
JetPlayer, 591
JIT (just-in-time) compiler, 6
JPS (JavaServer Pages), 29
JSON (JavaScript Object Notation), support for, 313
JSR 239 (Java Binding for the OpenGL ES API), documentation for, 690

JSR (Java Specification Request) 239, 12
just-in-time (JIT) compiler, 6
JVM (Java Virtual Machine), 2

K

kecode_endcall action key, 818
key attribute, 267, 277
key pair, 288
key property, 267
key/value pairs, 106
keyalg argument, 289
keycode attribute, 820
keycode_back action key, 818
keycode_call action key, 818–819
keycode_camera action key, 818
keycode_clear action key, 818
keycode_dpad_center action key, 818
keycode_dpad_down action key, 818
keycode_dpad_left action key, 818
keycode_dpad_right action key, 818
keycode_dpad_up action key, 818
keycode_home action key, 819
keycode_menu action key, 819
keycode_mute action key, 819
keycode_power action key, 819
keycode_search action key, 819
keycode_volume_down action key, 819
keycode_volume_up action key, 819
KeyEvent class, 819–820
KEY_PARAM_STREAM argument, 839
keypass argument, 289
keys, 734
keystore argument, 289
keytool command, 381
keytool utility, 288–291, 521
Khronos Group, 8, 624–625
Khronos Group OpenGL ES Reference Manual, 690
killMediaPlayer( ) method, 584
KMZ files, 547

L

labels, for applications, 1004
landscape mode, 1042
lang package, 18
lang.annotation package, 18
lang.ref package, 18
lang.reflect package, 18
language methods, 840–842
Language option, 826
Launch Options dialog, 56
Launcher application, 18
LAUNCHER category, 44, 139, 274, 1043
layout animation, 2D, 498–507
  animating ListView, 502–505
  creating activity and ListView, 500–502
  interpolators, 506–507
  planning test harness, 499
  types of, 498–499
layout attribute, 726
layout directory, 70
layout/edit_bday_widget.xml file, 724
layout-en directory, 85
layout files, 417
layout folder, 41, 44
layout/layout_search_activity.xml file, 797
layout/lib_main.xml file, 387
layout\list_item_layout.xml file, 1114, 1120
layout/main.xml file, 390, 414, 417, 428, 1072
layout managers
  customizing layouts for multiple devices, 210–212
  FrameLayout, 208–209
  LinearLayout, 199–202
    android:gravity versus android:layout_gravity, 201–202
    weight and gravity, 199–201
  overview, 198
  RelativeLayout, 206–208
  TableLayout, 202–206
layout resources, 66–67
layout\test_list_widget_layout.xml file, 1114
layout view, 855
layout xml file, 774, 832
layoutAnimation tag, 504–505
LayoutAnimationActivity, 502
LayoutInflater object, 248
layouts
  customizing for multiple devices, 210–212
  debugging and optimizing with Hierarchy Viewer, 213–216
  description of, 146
  Drag and Drop API, 1126–1129
  main widget layout file, 1120
  remote view
    loading, 1104–1105
    preparing, 1101–1104
layout.xml file, 1037
libc (C runtime library), 7
lib_main_menu menu, 397
library projects, 384–397
  adding as dependency to package, 390–397
  creating, 387–390
  defined, 384
  facts about, 385–387
License Verification Library (LVL), 1006
lifecycles
  of activities, 418–419
  of applications, 51–54
  fragments, 1018–1023
    onActivityCreated( ) callback, 1022
    onAttach( ) callback, 1020
    onCreate( ) callback, 1020–1021
    onCreateView( ) callback, 1021
    onDestroy( ) callback, 1023
    onDestroyView( ) callback, 1023
    onDetach( ) callback, 1023
    onInflate( ) callback, 1020
    onPause( ) callback, 1022
    onResume( ) callback, 1022
    onStart( ) callback, 1022
    onStop( ) callback, 1022
    sample fragment app showing, 1024–1032

setRetainInstance( ) method, 1023
methods of activities, 52
of providers, 421
of receivers, 420–421
of services, 420
light sensors, interpreting data from, 905–906
LightedGreenRoom abstraction, wake locks with, 449–455
LightedGreenRoom class, 449
LightedGreenRoom.java file, 460, 462
LightedGreenRoom.setup( ) method, 458
limitations of widgets, 742–743
linear acceleration sensors, interpreting data from, 923
LinearLayout class, 199–202
android:gravity versus android:layout_gravity, 201–202
weight and gravity, 199–201
LinearLayout containers, 150
LinearLayout controls, 148–149
LinearLayout layout manager, 198–199
LinearLayout node, 67, 727
LinearLayout objects, 148
LinearLayout view, 718
Linkify class, 154
Linux kernel, 7
list-based home screen widgets, 1097–1124
remote views, 1098–1113
layout, 1101–1105
onClick events, 1110–1113
RemoteViewsFactory interface, 1106–1109
RemoteViewsService class, 1105–1106
sample list widget, 1114–1122
AndroidManifest.xml file, 1121–1122
main widget layout file, 1120
remote views, 1118–1120
test widget provider, 1114–1118
testing, 1122–1124
widget provider metadata, 1121
list listener, 1086
list navigation, 1084–1089
AndroidManifest.xml file, 1087
BaseActionBarActivity class, 1087
examining, 1088–1089
list listener, 1086
setting up, 1086–1087
SpinnerAdapter interface, 1085–1086
List Navigation Action Bar Activity, 1088
list preference view, 267
ListActivity class, 46, 175, 501, 566
listContactCursorFields function, 975
listContacts( ) method, 976
listen( ) method, 570
Listen to an example option, 825
listeners
list, 1086
responding to menu items through, 221–222
setting up for prompt dialog, 248
tabbed, 1077–1078
LISTEN_MESSAGE_WAITING_INDICATOR, 570
ListFragment class, 1037–1041, 1044
listings, creating projects from, 422, 461–463
list_layout_controller.xml file, 503
list_layout.xml file, 500, 503–504
ListListener.java file, 1085
listLookupUriColumns( ) function, 977
ListNavigationActionBarActivity.java file, 1085, 1087
ListPreference class, 266–275, 284
ListPreference specification, 274
ListPreference view, 275
ListView control
adding 2D view animation to, 511–514
adding controls in, 179–182
animating, 502–505
clickable items in, 177–179
creating for 2D layout animation, 500–502
displaying values in, 175–176
overview, 175
reading user input from, 182–183
ListView widget, 17
list.xml file, 182
live-folder contacts, 698
live-folder icon, 693–694, 697
live folders
building
AllContactsLiveFolderCreatorActivity.java, 702–703
AndroidManifest.xml, 700–702
BetterCursorWrapper.java, 708–709
code for, 709–710
MyContactsProvider.java, 703–707
MyCursor.java, 708
overview, 700
overview, 693–694
testing, 709
user experience, 694–700
viewing, 697
LiveFolder framework, Android, 707
LiveFolders class, 710
llContactsLiveFolderCreatorActivity activity, 700
load( ) method, 590
loadNewData( ) function, 707
local QSB (Quick Search Box), 771, 773, 776, 791–792
local search, 748, 771–777
Local Search Activity option, 776
local search-enabled activity, 776
local services, 30, 337, 339–346
Locale.getDefault( ) method, 842
localizing
colors, 1003
menu choices, 1004
LocalSearchEnabledActivity, 757, 774–775
LocalServerSocket class, 15
LocalSocket class, 15
location-based services, 519–558
location package, 533–558
geocoding with Android, 534–537
geocoding with background threads, 538–540
LocationManager service, 541–549
MyLocationOverlay overlay, 549–553
using proximity alerts, 554–558
mapping package, 520–533
MapView and MapActivity, 522–528

obtaining map-api key from Google, 520–522
overlays, 528–533
Location class, 15, 542–543
location package, 533–558
geocoding with Android, 534–537
geocoding with background threads, 538–540
LocationManager service, 541–549
enabling providers for, 543
methods for, 543–544
sending location updates to emulator, 544–549
MyLocationOverlay overlay, 549–553
using proximity alerts, 554–558
LocationManager class, 15, 542
LocationManager service, 541–549
enabling providers for, 543
methods for, 543–544
sending location updates to emulator, 544–549
LocationProvider class, 15
Log class, 17
Log command, 54
logAction( ) method, 870
LogCat window, 831, 851, 853–857, 866, 868, 874
Log.d debug method, 81
logThreadSignature( ) method, 402, 443
long click, 231
long-running services. *See* LRS
look-at point, 635
lookup field, 958
Looper class, 16
LRS (long-running services)
abstractions, 445–447
broadcast receiver protocol, 441–442
compiling code, 461–463
implementation, 455–460
controlling wake lock from two places, 458
nonsticky services, 456–457
picking suitable stickiness, 457–458
specifying service flags in OnStartCommand method, 457
sticky services, 457
testing long-running services, 460
IntentService implementation
overview, 442–443
source code, 443–444
receivers, 447–449
references, 464
testing, 460
LVL (License Verification Library), 1006

M

m1.postTranslate( ) method, 517
m1.preTranslate( ) method, 516
M3G, 626–627
mA (milliamperes), 895
magnetic declination, and GeomagneticField class, 922
magnetic field sensors, interpreting data from, 914–915
MAIN action, 44
MAIN category, 139
Main Layout main.xml application, 1062–1063
Main method, equivalent of in Android, 44
main threads
activities, 400
broadcast receivers, 401
communicating between worker threads and, 410–412
ReportStatusHandler class implementation, 411–412
WorkerThreadRunnable class implementation, 410–411
content providers, 401
implications of holding, 404
implications of singular, 401
services, 401
using handlers to defer work on, 405
MainActivity class, 147, 584, 607, 830–831, 834, 854, 1051–1053
MainActivity.java file, 332, 339, 352, 361, 1050, 1126
MainActivity's stopService( ) method, 345
main_layout.xml file, 85
main_menu menu, 397
main_menu.xml file, 960, 975, 978, 982, 984, 986–987
main.xml file, 66, 149, 212, 301, 344, 549, 780, 1033, 1042, 1125
makeCall( ) method, 573
makeText( ) method, 263
managed dialogs, 253–262
managed-dialog protocol
DialogRegistry class, 259
GenericManagedAlertDialog class, 261
GenericPromptDialog class, 262
IDialogFinishedCallBack interface, 260
IDialogProtocol interface, 258
ManagedActivityDialog class, 258
ManagedDialogsActivity class, 259
overview, 253
simplifying, 255–257
recasting non-managed dialog as, 253–255
ManagedActivityDialog class, 257–258, 260, 262
ManagedDialogsActivity class, 257, 259
managedQuery( ) method, 46–48, 101, 104–105, 176, 976
manifest editor tool, Android, 297
<manifest> element, 45, 574, 1001
manifest file
Contacts API, 966
for custom suggestion provider, 813–814
registering broadcast receivers in, 427–428
tabbed navigation, 1083–1084
manifest.xml file, 387, 390, 414, 428, 433, 463, 701, 780, 797, 960
MAP API key, 1007
map-api key, obtaining from Google, 520–522
map object, 110
MapActivity class, 17, 170, 519, 522–528
MapController class, 17, 525
mapping package, 520–533
MapView and MapActivity, 522–528
obtaining map-api key from Google, 520–522
overlays, 528–533
mapping.txt file, 1007

maps, touches with, 871–874
MapView class, 17, 522–528, 871–872, 878
MapView control, 169–170, 526
MapView UI control, 519
mapView.getController( ) method, 525
mapView.postInvalidateDelayed(2000)statement, 526
Market, Android. *See* Android Market
Market app, 1005
market:// scheme, 1005
match method, 118
Matcher, 117–118
MATCH_PARENT constant, vs. FILL_PARENT constant, 152
math package, 18
Matrix class, 15, 512, 514, 516, 688
MatrixCursor class, 703, 707–708
maxResults parameter, 537
MD5 fingerprint, 520–521
media APIs
  adding media content to media store, 618–620
  AsyncPlayer, 591–592
  audio recording, 596
  AudioTrack, 592
  JetPlayer, 591
  MediaPlayer oddities, 592–593
  MediaStore class, 614–615
  overview, 575
  playing audio content, 581–585
  playing video content, 593–595
  Secure Digital (SD) cards, 576–580
  setDataSource method, 585–586
  SoundPool class, 587–591
  triggering MediaScanner for SD card, 621
  video recording, 605–614
media components, of Android, 13–14
media content, adding to media store, 618–620
media store, adding media content to, 618–620
MediaController widget, 17, 595
MediaPlayer class, 15, 575, 581, 584–585, 592–593
MediaPlayer(Context context,int resourceId) constructor, 585
MediaProvider project, 19
MediaRecorder class, 15, 595, 614–615
MediaRecorder interface, 607
MediaRecorder.AudioSource, 599, 603
MediaScanner, triggering for SD card, 621
MediaScannerConnection class, 618
MediaStore class, 16, 614–615
MediaStore provider, 100
MediaStore.ACTION_IMAGE_CAPTUR, 618
MediaStore.Images.ImageColumns, 618
Menu button, 271, 280, 699, 1082
menu callback, 273
menu choices, localizing, 1004
Menu class, 17, 226, 237
menu enabling/disabling tag, 242
menu file, contacts API, 961
menu folder, 41
Menu Icon area, 1071
menu icon tag, 241
Menu interface, 237
menu item shortcuts, 242
menu items, invoking worker threads from, 409–410
Menu key, Notepad application, 42
menu/lib_main_menu.xml file, 387
menu/main_menu.xml file, 390, 417, 428
menu/menu.xml, 1072
Menu object, 225, 230–231, 236
menu tag, 239
menu types
  alternative menus, 234–238
  context menus, 231–233
    populating, 233–234
    registering view for, 233
    responding to items on, 234
  dynamic menus, 238
  expanded menus, 229
  icon menus, 229–230
  submenus, 230–231
  system menus, 231
menu XML file, 764
menu.add method, 230
Menu.addSubMenu method, 230
MenuBuilder class, 237
Menu.CATEGORY_ALTERNATIVE constant, 218, 236
Menu.CATEGORY_CONTAINER constant, 218
Menu.CATEGORY_SECONDARY constant, 218, 226
Menu.CATEGORY_SYSTEM constant, 218–219
menu_da_clear menu item, 963
Menu.FLAG_APPEND_TO_GROUP flag, 236
MenuItem class, 221, 1083–1094
menus. *See also* menu types
  creating, 219–220
  creating test harness for, 222–224
    adding regular menu items, 225–226
    adding secondary menu items, 226
    creating activity, 224–225
    creating XML layout, 224
    responding to menu-item clicks, 227–228
    setting up menu, 225
    tweaking AndroidManifest.xml file, 228–229
  declaring, 11
  groups of, 220
  interaction with action bar, 1081–1083
    displaying menu, 1082
    menu items as actions, 1083
  invoking search through, 767–771
  overview, 217–219
  responding to items on
    with intents, 222
    through listeners, 221–222
    through onOptionsItemSelected method, 221
  XML based, 238–242
    checkable behavior tags, 241
    group category tag, 241
    inflating resource files, 239–240
    menu enabling/disabling tag, 242
    menu icon tag, 241
    menu item shortcuts, 242
    menu visibility, 242
    responding to items, 240–241
    structure of resource files, 239
    tags to simulate submenu, 241
merchant account, 999, 1009

message objects
  constructing, 407
  sending to queue, 407–408
metadata, searching, 788–789, 804–805
micro-Teslas (uT), 914
microedition.khronos.egl package, 18
microedition.khronos.opengles package, 18
MIDI (Musical Instrument Digital Interface), 591
"mid_opengl_current" menu id, 644
milliamperes (mA), 895
millimeters, 205
MIME (Multipurpose Internet Mail Extensions) types
  fulfilling contracts, 116
  specifying, 802
  structure of, 98–100
MIme4j web site, 311
mimeType attribute, 130
mimetype_id, 955
min/max function, 881
Miner, Rich, 4
minSdkVersion, 580
mirror sites, 1012
mksdcard utility, 576
mmap( ) method, 293
mMMatrix variable, 688
Mms application, 18
mMVPMatrix variable, 688
MODE_PRIVATE mode, 285
MODE_WORLD_READABLE flag, 382
MODE_WORLD_READABLE mode, 285
MODE_WORLD_WRITEABLE flag, 382
MODE_WORLD_WRITEABLE mode, 285
MotionEvent class, 853, 863, 870
MotionEvent events, 857
MotionEvent handler, 846
MotionEvent objects, 845–846, 851, 853, 856, 863–864, 869, 877–878
MotionEvent.ACTION_MASK constant, 870
MotionEvent.ACTION_POINTER_3_DOWN constant, 870
MotionEvent.ACTION_POINTER_ID_MASK constant, 870
MotionEvent.ACTION_POINTER_ID_SHIFT constant, 870
MotionEvents
  drag and drop, 859–862
  MotionEvent object, 845–857
  recycling, 857
  velocitytracker, 857–859
Motorola XOOM, 5
mouse click event callbacks, widget view, 722
moveToFirst( ) method, 102–103
moveToNext( ) method, 103
moveToPosition( ) method, 181
Movie class, 15
multi-pane mode, 1032
multi-touch, 862–871
  gestures, 883
  post version 2.2, 871
  prior to version 2.2, 863–870
MultiAutoCompleteTextView control, 156–157
MultipartEntity, 312
Multipurpose Internet Mail Extensions types. *See* MIME types
multithreading issues, consuming HTTP services, 315
Murphy, Mark, 445
Music application, 18
Musical Instrument Digital Interface (MIDI), 591
music_file.mp3, 585
mVMatrix variable, 688
My Downloads, 1011
my_column, 821
MyContactsContentProvider, 707
MyContactsProvider class, 701, 703, 707
MyContactsProvider code, 703
MyContactsProvider.java file, 700, 703–707
MyCursor.java file, 700, 708
MyDialogFragment class, 1045
MyFragment class, 1019
MyLocationDemoActivity.java file, 549
MyLocationOverlay class, 549–553, 871
my_menu.xml file, 239
MySMSMonitor class, 564

N

n command, 38
name attribute, 196, 734
NAME field, 706, 735
name property, 65
nameContainer object, 148–149
NameValuePair objects, 310
navigation modes, 1079–1080
Near Field Communication sensors. *See* NFC sensors
near point, 636
nesting PreferenceScreen elements, 281
net package, 18
net.ssl package, 18
NETWORK_PROVIDER, 552
NETWORK_WIFI, 334
New Android Project button, 31
New Android Project dialog box, 31
New Android Project wizard, 572
New live folder option, 696–697, 701
New Project dialog box, 31
New Project Wizard, 31–32
newInstance( ) method, 319, 573, 1019, 1030–1031, 1044–1045, 1057–1058, 1060
Nexus S phone, 999
NFC (Near Field Communication) sensors, interpreting data from, 923
  enabling, 925
  reading tags, 933
  testing with NFCDemo, 934
nio buffers, 629, 641
nio package, 18, 626
nio.channels package, 18
nio.channels.spi package, 18
nio.charset, security, security.acl package, 18
No Search Activity option, 767
NO_MATCH, UriMatcher class, 118
noncompiled resources, 70
nonsticky services, 456–457

normalized texture coordinates, 669
NoSearchActivity, 757, 766–767
not-runnable state, 413
Notepad application, 42–51
  dissecting, 44–51
  loading and running, 42–43
Notepad class, 46
NotePadProvider class, 49–50
NotePadProvider database, 97
Notes class, 46
NotesList activity, 44, 47
NotesList application, 43
NotesList class, 46
NotesList.onCreate( ) method, 45
notification value, 280
Notification.FLAG_NO_CLEAR, 341
NotificationManager, 341
NotificationReceiver.java file, 462
notifications, from broadcast receivers, 434–440
  monitoring through notification manager, 435–437
  sending, 437–440
Notifications icon, 437
notifyChange method, 117
notifyDataSetChanged( ) method, 174, 178
null value, 272
Nvidia Tegra2, 5

O

ObjectAnimator class, 1064–1067, 1131
<objectAnimator> tag, 1034, 1066–1067
obtain( ) method, 857–858
obtainMessage( ) method, 407
onAccuracyChanged( ) method, 897–898, 903
onActivityCreated( ) method, 1018, 1022, 1040
onActivityResult( ) method, 140, 142, 543, 616, 618, 829, 841, 925, 1064
onAttach( ) method, 1020, 1057
onBind( ) method, 338, 341, 346, 350–351, 355
onCallStateChanged( ) method, 570
onCancel( ) method, 1048, 1058
onCheckedChanged( ) method, 165
OnCheckedChangeListener interface, 161, 163
OnCheckedChangeListener method, 165
onClick action, 1118
onClick area, 723
onClick behavior, 1118
onClick events
  handler, 1110–1112
  responding to, 1112–1113
onClick intent, 1110, 1120
onClick( ) method, 158, 161, 252, 829, 857, 1062
onClickHook method, 258, 261
onContextItemSelected( ) method, 234
onCreate( ) method, 45, 786–787, 812, 1020–1021, 1107
onCreateContextMenu( ) method, 232–234
onCreateDialog( ) method, 253–254, 1046–1047, 1062
onCreateMethod method, 255
onCreateOptionsMenu( ) method, 219, 225, 231–232, 235
onCreateView( ) method, 1018, 1021, 1023, 1031–1032, 1040, 1046, 1058, 1060, 1129
onDataSetChanged( ) callback method, 1109
onDelete( ) method, 722, 728, 730
onDeleted( ) method, 720
onDestory( ) method, 342, 419, 456, 557, 830, 903, 905, 1023, 1107–1108
onDestroyView( ) callback, 1023
onDetach( ) callback, 1023
onDialogDone( ) method, 1053, 1058
OnDialogDoneListener interface, 1053–1054, 1057
OnDialogDoneListener.java file, 1050
onDisable( ) method, 722, 728
onDisabled( ) method, 720, 730
onDismiss( ) method, 1048, 1058, 1062
onDrag( ) method, 1129–1132, 1136
onDraw method, 651–652
onDrawFrame( ) method, 638–639
onEnable( ) method, 728
onEnabled( ) method, 719–720, 730
onError( ) method, 613
OnErrorListener interface, 607
OneShot parameter, 497
onGesturePerformed( ) method, 889
onGesturePerformedListener interface, 889
onHandleIntent( ) method., 442
onHandleIntent( ) method, 443–446
onHandleIntent(Intent) method, 442
onHandleMessage( ) method, 444
onInflate( ) method, 1018, 1020
onInfo( ) method, 613
OnInfoListener interface, 607
onInit( ) method, 830–831, 840
OnInitListener class, 830
onItemClick( ) method, 178
onListItemClick( ) method, 47–48, 1040
onLoadComplete( ) method, 590
onLoadCompleteListener interface, 590
onLocationChanged( ) method, 545, 547
onMeasure( ) method, 1136
OnMenuClickListener interface, 221
onMenuItemClick( ) method, 221–222
onNewIntent( ) method, 784, 786–787, 790, 793, 807, 812, 823
onOptionsItemSelected( ) method, 219, 221–222, 227, 234, 240, 1083
onPause( ) method, 53, 419, 545, 570, 603, 608–609, 897, 920, 1022
onPostExecute( ) method, 323–324, 326–327
onPreExecute( ) method, 323–324, 331
onPrepare method, 259
onPrepareDialog( ) method, 253–254
onPrepareOptionsMenu method, 238
onProgressUpdate( ) method, 323–324
onProviderDisabled( ) method, 548
onProviderEnabled( ) method, 548
onReceive( ) method, 335, 427, 440–441, 564, 730, 899, 905, 1110, 1112
onRestart( ) method, 53
onResume( ) method, 53, 419, 545, 571, 603, 608, 897, 903, 920, 1022

onRetainNonConfigurationInstance( ) method, 327–328
onSaveInstanceState( ) method, 1020, 1036–1037, 1058
onScale( ) method, 881
onScaleBegin( ) method, 881
onScaleEnd( ) method, 881
onSearchRequested( ) method, 765–766, 769, 778, 821
onSensorChanged( ) method, 897, 903, 913
onServiceConnected( ) method, 354, 364
onServiceDisconnected( ) method, 354
onStart( ) method, 53, 339, 341, 419, 441, 444, 456, 903, 1022
onStartCommand( ) method, 342–343, 345–346, 441, 444, 450, 455–457
onStartCommand( ) version, 341
onStatusChanged( ) method, 548
onStop( ) method, 53, 419, 903, 1022
onSurfaceChanged( ) method, 639
onSurfaceCreated( ) method, 638, 671
onTap( ) method, 872, 874
onTouch( ) method, 846–847, 851, 853–857, 872
onTouchEvent( ) method, 846–847, 854–856, 858, 861, 872, 877, 881
onUpdate( ) method, 719–722, 726, 730, 1101, 1104, 1106, 1114
onUtteranceCompleted( ) method, 831, 840
OnUtteranceCompletedListener interface, 831
Open Handset Alliance, 4, 18
open( ) method, 614
OpenCORE, PacketVideo, 7
OpenGL
  camera and Coordinates
    glFrustum and viewing volume, 636–637
    gluLookAt and camera symbolism, 634–635
    glViewport and screen size, 637
  drawing multiple figures, 674–678
  glClear, 632–633
  glColor, 633
  glDrawElements, 630–632
  glVertexPointer and specifying drawing vertices, 628–630
  history and background of, 624–627
  M3G, 626–627
  resources, 690–691, 710
  shapes
    animating RegularPolygon shapes, 666–668
    implementing RegularPolygon shapes, 657–664
    rectangles, 653–655
    RegularPolygon class, 656–657
    rendering square using RegularPolygon class, 664–665
  textures
    abstracting common handling, 669–672
    drawing with, 672–673
    normalized coordinates, 669
    overview, 668–669
OpenGL ES
  drawing with, 628–633
  interfacing with Android
    AnimatedSimpleTriangleRenderer, 652–653
    animating simple triangle, 651–653
    changing camera settings, 647–648
    drawing triangle with test harness, 641–647
    GLSurfaceView and related classes, 638
    renderer for, 638–641
    using indices to add another triangle, 649–650
  Java ME, 626
  overview, 625
OpenGL ES 2.0, 678–689
  java bindings for, 678–682
  rendering in, 682
  shaders, 682–685
    accessing program variables for, 685
    compiling into program, 684
  simple triangle in, 685–689
OpenGL library, 7
OpenGL Programming Guide (book), 625, 690
openRawResourceFd( ) method, 586
option key, 273
option value is 1 (# of Stops) message, 271
Options menu, 1071
organizing preferences, 280–282
org.apache.http.*, 18
org.json, 18
org.w3c.dom, 18
org.xmlpull.v1, 18
org.xml.sax, 18
orientation attribute, 199
orientation property, 199
orientation sensors, interpreting data from, 915–922
orthographic projection, 636
OS version 1.6, Android, 5
out-of-process broadcast receivers, project for, 433–434
OvalShape, 15
Overlay class, 531, 871–872
overlays
  MyLocationOverlay, 549–553
  overview, 528–533

P

p command, 38
Package Manager, 14
package name, 1006
PackageInstaller application, 18
PackageManager class, 136
PackageManager method, 1005
PackageManager.SIGNATURE_MATCH, 1005
packagename application, 838
packages, 377–398
  deleting through package browser, 379
  and library projects, 384–397
    adding as dependencyto package, 390–397
    creating, 387–390
    defined, 384
    facts about, 385–387
  listing installed, 378–379
  and process name, 378
  sharing data among, 382–384
    code pattern for, 383–384
    and shared user IDs, 382–383

signing of, 379–382
overview, 380
and PKI certificates, 381–382
and public and private keys, 381
specification details of, 377–378
Paint class, 15
PaintDrawable class, 79
Palette.java file, 1126
palette.xml file, 1125, 1138
parameters, for SoundPool, 590
params HashMap, 839–840
Parcel class, 357
Parcelable class, 357–358, 365
Parcelable interface, 356–357
parentActivity variable, 405
parentContainer, 149
Path class, 15
PATH variable, 25
PathShape, 15
path_to_/JDK_directory, 23
pause( ) method, 584, 592–593, 595
Pause Player button, 584
penaltyDeath( ) method, 58
pending intents, 142–144
Pending.getActivity( ) method, 143
PendingIntent class, 467–468, 556
People class, 101–102
People table, 101
period character, 831
permissions
custom, 297–303
declaring and using, 295–297
URI, 303–306
in content providers, 304–305
passing in intents, 303–304
permitDiskReads( ) method, 60
persistentDrawingCache tag, 504
Person class, 358, 360–361, 364
Person.aidl file, 357
Person.java file, 357–358
perspective projection, 636
Phone application, 18
PhoneNumberUtils class, 16
PhoneStateListener, 570
photo setting screen, contacts API, 948–949
PICK intent, 141
Pico engine, 827, 837–838, 843
Pico Text To Speech engine, 13
pinch gesture, 875–878
pixels, 205
PKI (public key infrastructure) certificates, and signing of packages, 381–382
pkzip file, 19
planets.xml file, 186
platforms
adding to Android SDK, 24
on Android, 3
platforms\android-1.6\samples folder, 43
Play button, 612, 834, 837
play( ) method, 590, 592
playAudio( ) method, 584
playbackPosition integer member, 584
playEarcon( ) method, 840
playing audio content, 581–585
playing video content, 593–595
playRecording( ) method, 612
playSilence( ) method, 840, 842
PluralRules.java resource code, 74
plurals, 73–74
Plurals resource, 71
pname, 1006
pointer Id, 864
points, 205
populate( ) method, 531–532
populating context menus, 233–234
portrait mode, 1042
postInvalidate( ) method, 552
postTranslate method, 513, 516
PowerManager class, 16
PREFERENCE, 274
preference screen view, 267
PreferenceActivity class, 16, 271, 273–275, 283
PreferenceCategory element, 280, 282
preferences
framework, 265–286
CheckBoxPreference, 275–277
EditTextPreference, 277–278
ListPreference, 266–275
manipulating programmatically, 283–284
RingtonePreference, 278–280
saving preferences, 284–286
organizing, 280–282
preferences activity, 827
Preferences dialog box, Eclipse, 28
preferences Editor, 285
Preferences window, Eclipse, 576
PreferenceScreen element, 267, 278, 280–282
prepare( ) method, 584–585, 592, 612
pressure sensors, interpreting data from, 907
pressure value, 852
preTranslate method, 513, 516
primitive shapes, 628
printCursorColumnNames( ) method, 970
PRIORITY parameter, 590
PrivActivity class, 298–299, 303
privileged activities, 298
process boundary, 295
process lifetimes, 418–421
of activities, 418–419
of providers, 421
of receivers, 420–421
of services, 420
process name, and packages, 378
.profile file, 23, 25
ProgressBar control, 194
ProgressBar view, 718
ProgressBar widget, 17
ProgressDialog, 264
Project option, Android, 42, 422
project properties screen, 385
Projection interface, 872
projection maps, 110, 119
projection parameter, managedQuery( ) method, 47
projections, 102, 116

prompt dialog
designing, 246–251
creating and showing, 249
PromptListener class, 249
setting up alert-dialog builder with user view, 248
setting up buttons and listeners, 248
XML layout file for, 247
rearchitecting, 252
PromptDialogFragment dialog fragment, 1054–1058
PromptDialogFragment.java file, 1050
PromptListener class, 248–250, 252
promptReply field, 249
properties context menu, 389
properties dialog, 389
properties window, 385
provider class, 108
provider declaration, 701
Provider projects, 19
<provider> tag, 304–305
providers, life cycles of, 421
proximity sensors, interpreting data from, 906
ProximityReceiver class, 557
Proxy class, 349
ptrId, 870
ptrIndex, 870
public and private keys, and signing of packages, 381
public key infrastructure (PKI) certificates, and signing of packages, 381–382
public Map<String,String> getPrefsToSave( ) method, 735
public static identifier, 47
public String getPrefname( ) method, 735
public void setProjectionMap(Map columnMap), 119
public void setValueForPref method, 735
Publish button, 1010
publisher, becoming, 994–1001
publishProgress( ) method, 323, 331
putExtras, 131
putFragment( ) method, 1036–1037

Q

QSB (Quick Search Box), 771, 773, 776, 791–793, 814–815
quantity attribute, 74
queries, passing to suggestion provider, 802–804
query( ) method, 108, 110, 116–117, 337, 707, 788–789, 797, 802
query string, 806
queryActionMsg attribute, 820
queryActionMsg value, 820
queryAfterZeroResults attribute, 788, 805
QueryBuilder class, 119
queryString, 782
QUEUE_ADD intent, 829, 831
QUEUE_ADD mode, 840
QUEUE_FLUSH intent, 829–831
queues, sending message objects to, 407–408
queueSound( ) method, 591
queuing mechanism, 840
Quick Search Box (QSB), 771, 773, 776, 791–793, 814–815
Quick Search Box tab, 755

R

R class, 47
Radio Frequency ID (RFID), 923
RadioButton control, 162–165
RadioButton widget, 17
RadioGroup class, 162–164
RadioGroup widget, 17
Rasterizer class, 15
RatingBar control, 194
RatingButton widget, 17
raw assest, arbitrary, 72
raw contacts, 977–985
raw directory, 70
raw files, 70, 72
raw folder, 41
raw resources, 82
RawContact object, 981
RawContactEntity view, 984
RawContactFunctionTester.java, 977
raw_contact_id, 955
RawContact.java file, 977–978
ray, 636
R.draawable.robot icon, 438
R.drawable.frame_animation resource, 497
readFromParcel( ) method, 357
README.TXT file, 1067
Receiver class, 426
receiver element, 428
receiver node, 725
receivers
life cycles of, 420–421
setting up for simple alarm, 467
RecentSearchSuggestionProvider, 795
recognize( ) method, 889
Record button, 834
recording
audio
with AudioRecord, 600–604
required permission for, 296
using intent, 615–618
video, 605–614
RECORDING message, 606, 612
recordoutput.3gpp file, 600
records, inserting in content providers, 106–107
RectShape, 15
recycle( ) method, 858
recycling MotionEvents, 857
red book, 625, 690
redeliver intents mode, 457
Reduced Instruction Set Computer (RISC), 9
reference syntax for resources, 67
References tab, 1099
refunds, 996
registerDialogs( ) function, 259
registerForContextMenu method, 233
registering view for context menus, 233
registerListener( ) method, 897

RegularActivity class, 758, 761, 770, 775, 777–778
RegularActivity.java file, 757, 766, 770, 775
RegularPolygon class
overview, 656–657
rendering square with, 664–665
shapes
animating, 666–668
implementing, 657–664
RelativeLayout, 198, 206–208, 527, 718, 848
release( ) method, 584, 593
releaseCamera( ) method, 609
release.keystore file, 289
releaseRecorder( ) method, 609
remapCoordinateSystem( ) method, 922
remote services, 30, 337–338
remote views, 1098–1113
factory, 1118–1120
layout
loading, 1104–1105
preparing, 1101–1104
onClick events
handler, 1110–1112
responding to, 1112–1113
RemoteViewsFactory interface, 1106–1109
constructor, 1107
getCount( ) callback method, 1108
getItemId( ) callback method, 1109
getLoadingView( ) callback method, 1108–1109
getViewAt( ) callback method, 1108
getViewTypeCount( ) callback method, 1109
hasStableIds( ) callback method, 1109
onCreate( ) callback method, 1107
onDataSetChanged( ) callback method, 1109
onDestroy( ) callback method, 1107–1108
RemoteViewsService class, 1105–1106
service, 1120
RemoteView interface, 1099
RemoteViews class, 711, 718–719, 721, 740–743, 1098
RemoteViewService class, 1106
RemoteViewsFactory class, 1100
RemoteViewsFactory interface, 1106–1109
constructor, 1107
getCount( ) callback method, 1108
getItemId( ) callback method, 1109
getLoadingView( ) callback method, 1108–1109
getViewAt( ) callback method, 1108
getViewTypeCount( ) callback method, 1109
hasStableIds( ) callback method, 1109
onCreate( ) callback method, 1107
onDataSetChanged( ) callback method, 1109
onDestroy( ) callback method, 1107–1108
RemoteViews.RemoteView interface, 1099
RemoteViewsService class, 1100, 1105–1106
RemoteViews.setOnClickFillIntent( ) method, 1100
RemoteViews.setPendingIntentTemplate( ) method, 1100
remove( ) method, 1035
removeData( ) method, 730
removePrefs( ) method, 729–730
Renderer interface, 638–641
RENDERMODE_CONTINUOUSLY, 651
RENDERMODE_WHEN_DIRTY, 651
replace( ) method, 1034–1035
reportBack( ) method, 1073–1075
ReportStatusHandler class, 411–412, 417
ReportStatusHandler.java class, 413
reportTransient( ) method, 964, 1073
REpresentational State Transfer (REST), 89
requery, 703, 707–708
requestCode, 140, 143
requestLocationUpdates( ) method, 545, 548
ReqularActivity.java, 765
/res/anim/alpha.xml file, 504
/res/anim subdirectory, 498, 503
/res/anim/translate_alpha.xml file, 505
/res/animator directory, 1066
res/drawable/box1.xml file, 723, 1120
/res/drawable folder, 159, 230, 438, 493, 531, 727, 1103
/res file, 1002
res folder, 40–41, 47, 70
res/layout/bday_widget.xml file, 723
/res/layout directory, 126, 1031
/res/layout file, 1002
res/layout folder, 187
/res/layout-large file, 1002
res/layout/local_search_enabled_activity.xml file, 757
/res/layout/main.xml file, 273, 332, 368, 462, 757
/res/layout-normal file, 1002
res/layout/no_search_activity.xml file, 757
res/layout/search_activity.xml file, 757
res/layout/search_invoker_activity.xml file, 757
/res/layout subdirectory, 493, 960
\res\layout\test_list_widget_layout.xml file, 1120
/res/menu/main_menu.xml file, 273, 414, 462, 643, 758
res/menu/search_invoker_menu.xml file, 758
/res/raw folder, 585–586, 838, 840, 888
/res/values/arrays.xml file, 271, 368
/res/values directory, 1004, 1135
/res/values folder, 151
/res/values-fr folder, 1003
/res/values/planets.xmlfile, 174
/res/values/strings.xml file, 155, 186, 272, 301, 368, 758, 780
/res/xml/, 267
res/xml/bday_appwidget_provider.xml file, 723
\res\xml\ test_list_appwidget_provider file, 1121
reset( ) method, 592
ResolveInfo API, 136
ResolveInfo class, 237
resource-reference syntax, 67
ResourceCursorAdapter adapter, 174
Resource.drawable.frame_animation resource ID, 496
resources, 63–88
arbitrary XML resource files, 80–81
assets, 82
color, 76
color-drawable, 79–80
compiled and noncompiled, 70
and configuration changes, 83–87
defining IDs for, 69

dimension, 77
directory structure, 83
image, 78–79
key Android, 71–80
layout, 66–67
plurals, 73–74
raw, 82
reference syntax for, 67
string, 64–66, 74–76
string arrays, 73
Resources class, 14
<resources> tag, 65, 159
Resources.java resource code, 74
respondToMenuItem( ) method, 405
ResportStatusHandler class, 410
REST (REpresentational State Transfer), 89
Restart Player button, 584
RESULT_CANCEL constant, 141
RESULT_FIRST_USER constant, 140–141
RESULT_OK constant, 141, 829
retrieveData( ) method, 730
retrievePrefs( ) method, 729–730
returns false button, 853–856
returns true button, 854–856
RFID (Radio Frequency ID), 923
R.id.menu_library_activity menu item, 392
R.id.mid_si_search, 769
R.id.text constant, 69
Ringtone class, 15
ringtone value, 280
RingtonePreference view, 275, 278–280
ringtoneType attribute, 280
RISC (Reduced Instruction Set Computer), 9
R.java constants file, 220
R.java file, 10, 64–65, 68, 84, 385, 395–397
R.java namespace, 77
R.layout class, 66
R.layout.details resource, 1031
R.layout.list_layout ID, 501
RootElement class, 16
rotate animation, 498
rotation vector sensors, interpreting data from, 923
RotationAnimation class, 17
RoundRectShape, 15
RPC service. *See* remote services
Rubin, Andy, 4
rules for becoming publisher, 994
run( ) method, 411–412, 540
RunHelloWorld configuration, 33
Runnable class, 495
runnable state, 413
runOnFirstFix( ) method, 552
runtime security checks
custom permissions, 297–303
declaring and using permissions, 295–297
process boundary, 295
URI permissions, 303–306
in content providers, 304–305
passing in intents, 303–304

S

Save button, 1058
saveRecentQuery, 788
scale animation, 498
scale-independent pixels, 206
ScaleAnimation class, 17
scale.xml file, 503–504
scanFile( ) method, 620
Screen Capture button, 1008
screen sizes, supporting, 1001–1002
screenshots, 1008
Scroller widget, 17
ScrollView control, 194, 1080
ScrollView widget, 17
SD (Secure Digital) cards, 575–580
sdcard folder, 577, 885
/sdcard/gestures file, 888
sdcard.img file, 576
SDK Manager, 28
SDK/platforms/<version>/data/res/drawable folder, 342
SDK (Software Development Kit), 2, 22, 145, 742
search
disabling, 766–767
invoking through menu, 767–771
SEARCH actions, 774, 804
search activity for custom suggestion provider
finishing, 812
layout, 811
responding to ACTION_SEARCH and ACTION_VIEW, 810–811
responding to onCreate( ) and onNewIntent( ), 812
responsibilities of, 807
SearchActivity invocation, 809–810
source code, 808–809
strings.xml, 811
search activity for simple suggestion provider, 784–789
Search Activity screen, 792
search box, 746
search framework, 746–822
action keys in Android search, 818–821
activities and search key interaction
disabling search, 766–767
enabling type-to-search, 777–778
invoking search through menu, 767–771
local search and related activities, 771–777
overview, 757
regular activities, 758–765
application-specific search context, 821–822
custom suggestion provider, 796–818
manifest file, 813–814
planning, 796
SuggestURLProvider class, 797–807
SuggestURLProvider project implementation files, 796–797
user experience, 814–818
global search, 746, 753, 757
simple suggestion provider, 778–795
implementation files, 779–780
planning, 779

search activity, 784–789
search invoker activity, 789–790
SimpleSuggestionProvider class, 780–784
user experience, 791–795
search icon, 752–753, 771, 773, 796, 815
Search Invoker Activity, 770–772
search metadata XML file, 774
Search option, 755, 771
search query method, 810
Search Recent Suggestions API, 823
search results activity, 772
Search settings application, 755, 814
search suggestions, 750–751
search URI, 797, 801
Searchable items option, 755
searchable.xml file, 801, 803
SearchActivity class, 784–789, 796–797, 804, 807
SearchActivity.java file, 757, 779, 796, 807
search_activity.xml file, 780
SearchEanabledActivity, 775
SearchInvokerActivity class, 767, 770
SearchInvokerActivity XML, 769–770
SearchInvokerActivity.java file, 757
SearchInvokingActivity, 773
SearchManager class, 801–802, 805, 820, 823
SearchManager.APP_DATA, 822
SearchManager.QUERY, 786
SearchRecentSuggestionsProvider
database modes, 781–783
saving query with, 787–788
searchSuggestAuthority attribute, 788
searchSuggestIntentAction attribute, 804
searchSuggestIntentData attribute, 804
searchSuggestPath attribute, 804
searchSuggestSelection attribute, 788, 803–804
searchSuggestThreshold attribute, 804
Sears, Nick, 4
Secure Digital (SD) cards, 575–580
Secure Sockets Layer (SSl) library, 7
security
model, 294
overview, 287–288
runtime checks
custom permissions, 297–303
declaring and using permissions, 295–297
process boundary, 295
URI permissions, 303–305
signing applications for deployment, 288–294
aligning applications with zipalign, 293–294
generating self-signed certificate with Keytool, 288–291
updating and signing applications, 294
using Jarsigner tool to sign .apk file, 292
security.auth package, 18
security.auth.callback package, 18
security.auth.login package, 18
security.auth.x500 package, 18
security.cert package, 18
SecurityException, 571
security.interfaces package, 18
security.spec package, 18
seekTo( ) method, 584, 593, 595
select argument, 797
Select root directory option, Eclipse, 421, 461
selected_flight_sort_option argument, 273
selected_flight_sort_option string, 272
selected_flight_sort_option value, 274
selectInitialQuery argument, 769, 822
selection argument, 105, 802–804
selection parameter, managedQuery( ) method, 47
selection string, 788
selectionArgs argument, 802–803
selectionArgs parameter, managedQuery( ) method, 47
self-signed certificates, 288–291
sendBroadCast( ) method, 425–426, 432–433
sendDataMessage( ) method, 562
sendMessage( ) method, 407–408, 422
sendMessageDelayed( ) method, 407–408
sendMultipartTextMessage( ) method, 563
sendSmsMessage( ) method, 562
sendTextMessage( ) method, 562–563
SensorEventListener interface, 897
SensorManager class, 906, 922
sensors, 891–935
detecting, 892
interpreting data from
accelerometers, 908–914
gravity sensors, 923
gyroscope sensors, 907–908
light sensors, 905–906
linear acceleration sensors, 923
magnetic declination and GeomagneticField class, 922
magnetic field sensors, 914–915
NFC sensors, 923
orientation sensors, 915–922
pressure sensors, 907
proximity sensors, 906
rotation vector sensors, 923
temperature sensors, 907
issues with events for, 895–905
no direct access to sensor values, 898
onAccuracyChanged( ) method, 898
sensor values not sent fast enough, 898
sensors turn off with screen in Android 2.1, 899–905
querying information about, 892–895
Service class, 30
service components, of Android, 13
service flags, specifying in OnStartCommand method, 457
Service object, 341
<service> tag, 345, 351
ServiceConnection interface, 354
services
AIDL in, 346, 349–351
consuming HTTP
exceptions, 313–315
multithreading issues, 315
overview, 307–308
timeouts for, 318–319
using AndroidHttpClien, 319–320
using AsyncTask, 320–331

using DownloadManager, 331–337
using HttpClient for HTTP GET requests, 308–310
using HttpClient for HTTP POST requests, 310–312
using HttpURLConnection, 319
defining interface in Android Interface Definition Language (AIDL), 347–349
external components, 401
Google Translate example using, 366–375
interprocess communication
calling services from client applications, 351–355
passing complex types to services, 355–366
JSON support, 313
life cycles of, 420
local, 339–346
overview, 337–339
setting up development environment, 30
SOAP support, 312–313
Service.START_NOT_STICKY flag, 456
Service.START_REDELIVER flag, 457
Service.START_STICKY flag, 457
ServiceWorker class, 342
Session Initiation Protocol (SIP), 559, 571–574
Set Package Name option, 278
Set Ringtone Preference option, 280
<set> tag, 1067
setAdapter( ) method, 156
setAlpha( ) method, 1065
setArguments( ) method, 1020
setAutoLinkMask( ) method, 153
setBounds( ) method, 532
setBuiltInZoomControls( ) method, 527
setCenter( ) method, 533
setChecked( ) method, 161, 163
setClickable(true) method, 526
setConsiderGoneChildrenWhenMeasuring( ) method, 209
setContentView( ) method, 148, 151, 181, 439, 1042
setContext( ) method, 331
setCustomAnimations( ) method, 1034, 1065
setData( ) method, 344, 407
setDataSource( ) method, 581, 585–586, 595
setDataSource(FileDescriptor desc), 586
setDestination*( ) methods, 336
setDropDownViewResource( ) method, 187
setEdgeFlags( ) method, 853
setEngineByPackageName( ) method, 840
setEntity( ) method, 310, 312
setEntries( ) method, 284
setGroupCheckable method, 220
setGroupEnabled method, 220
setGroupVisible method, 220
setHint( ) method, 155
setIcon method, MenuItem class, 229
setImageInView( ) method, 328, 331
setImageResource( ) method, 159, 166
setIntent( ) method, 222
setLanguage method, 841
setLatestEventInfo( ) method, 364, 439–440
setListAdapter( ) method, 175, 1040
setLooping( ) method, 592
setMarker( ) method, 532
setMaxDuration(int length_in_ms) method, 600
setMaxFileSize(long length_in_bytes) method, 600
setMediaController( ) method, 595
setMovementMethod( ) method, 1081
setOnCheckedChangeListener( ) method, 161, 163
setOnClickFillIntent( ) method, 1112
setOnClickListener( ) method, 158
setOneShot( ) method, 496
setOnTouchListener( ) method, 846, 871
setOnUtteranceCompletedListener( ) method, 830
setOptionText( ) method, 273–274
setPendingIntentTemplate( ) method, 1111
setPitch method, 842
setProfile( ) method, 614
setProgress( ) method, 331
setRemoteAdapter( ) method, 1106
setResult( ) method, 141
setRetainInstance( ) method, 1023, 1036
setRotate method, 516
setRotation( ) method, 1065
setScale method, 512, 516
setSkew method, 516
setSpeechRate method, 842
setTabListener( ) method, 1080
setTargetFragment( ) method, 1064
setText( ) method, 195
setThreadPolicy( ) method, 58
Settings application, 16, 18
settings page, Android, 754
Settings screen, 825
SettingsProvider project, 19
setTokenizer( ) method, 156
setTransition( ) method, 1034
setTranslate method, 516
setupMatrices function, 688
setValue( ) method, 734
setValueForPref( ) method, 731
setVideoPath( ) method, 595
setVideoURI( ) method, 595
setVolume( ) method, 592
setX( ) method, 1066
setZoom( ) method, 533
SGI (Silicon Graphics, Inc.) Open GL. *See* OpenGL
Shader class, 15
Shakespeare class, 1032
<shape> tag, 72, 79–80
shared user IDs, 382–383
SharedPreferences class, 16, 274, 742
SharedPreferences file, 734
SharedPreferences.Editor class, 734, 743
SharedPrferences facility, 732
sharing data, among packages, 382–384
code pattern for, 383–384
and shared user IDs, 382–383
shell command sets, 93
Short Message Service. *See* SMS
shortcut URI, 801
shortcut_id, 806
SHORTCUT_MIME_TYPE, SearchManager class, 802
show contact detail screen, contacts API, 945
show contacts screen, contacts API, 944

Show Me! button, 921
show( ) method, 251, 256–258, 1034, 1047, 1049, 1053, 1058
showAllRawContacts( ) method, 981
showAsAction tag, 1083
showDetails( ) method, 1027, 1032, 1040–1041
showDialog method, 254
showRawContactsCursor( ) function, 981
showRawContactsDataForRawContact( ) function, 988
showSilent attribute, 280
shutdown( ) method, 830
sides variable, 667
signing
  applications for deployment, 288–294
    aligning applications with zipalign, 293–294
    generating self-signed certificate with Keytool, 288–291
    updating and signing applications, 294
    using Jarsigner tool to sign .apk file, 292
  of packages, 379–382
    overview, 380
    and PKI certificates, 381–382
    and public and private keys, 381
silence, playing with TTS APIs, 840
Silicon Graphics, Inc. (SGI) Open GL. *See* OpenGL
SIM card, 998
SIM (Subscriber Identity Module) serial number, 16
simple suggestion providers, 778–795
  implementation files, 779–780
  planning, 779
  search activity, 784–789
  SimpleSuggestionProvider class, 780–784
    declaring in manifest file, 783–784
    responsibilities of, 780–781
    source code for, 781
  user experience, 791–795
SimpleAdapter adapter, 174
SimpleCursorAdapter adapter, 47, 171–172, 174
simple_list_item_1.xml file, 173
SimpleMainActivity.java file, 779
SimpleSpinnerArrayAdapter java file, 1084–1085
SimpleSuggestionProvider class, 780–784
SimpleSuggestionProvider.java file, 779
SimpleTriangleRenderer class, 639, 642
SimpleTriangleRenderer2 class, 650
SingleAbstractTextureRenderer class, 670
singleLine property, 155
singleTop mode, 784, 787, 807, 823
SIP (Session Initiation Protocol), 559, 571–574
SipManager object, 573
Skia library, Google, 8
SkMatrix.cpp file, 19
sleep( ) method, 402, 404, 411
slide_out_down.xml file, 1067
SMS (Short Message Service), 559–568
  e-mail, 567–568
  folders, 565–567
  monitoring incoming messages, 563–565
  sending messages, 559–563
SmsManager class, 562–563, 565
SmsManager.sendTextMessage( ) method, 562
SmsMessage object, Android, 565
SmsMessage.createFromPdu( ) method, 565
SOAP, support for, 312–313
soft keyboard, 750
Software Development Kit (SDK), 2, 22, 145, 742
software stack, 6–8
Software Updates, Eclipse. *See* Install New Software...option, Eclipse
SomeHandlerDerivedFromHandler handler, 405
some_view layout, 126
sort option, 271
sortOrder parameter, managedQuery( ) method, 47
soundFileResourceId, 838
SoundPool class, 587–591
SoundRecorder application, 18
source code
  example that defers work, 405–406
  standard navigation, 1090–1091
  taking advantage of, 18–19
source variable, 684
sourceid field, 954
Spare Parts application, 750
Speak button, 831, 834, 837
speak( ) method, 829–830, 837–840
specification details, of packages, 377–378
speech synthesis engine, Pico, 827
Spinner class, 186
Spinner control, 185–187
Spinner widget, 17
SpinnerAdapter interface, 1085–1086
spinner_while_refreshing, 806
sql package, 18
SQLite database library, 7, 952–953
SQLite, primer on, 95
sqlite3 commands, 94
SQLiteCursor class, 15, 707
SQLiteDatabase class, 15, 117
Sqliteman tool, 95
sqlite_master table, 95
SQLiteOpenHelper class, 50
SQLiteQuery class, 15
SQLiteQueryBuilder class, 15, 105, 116, 119
SQLiteStatement class, 15
sqllite database, 721
src folder, 33, 40, 61, 723
SRC_QUALITY value, 590
SSl (Secure Sockets Layer) library, 7
stand-alone BCR files, 462–463
stand-alone BCR project, 461
StandaloneReceiver.java file, 433, 462
standard navigation, 1090–1095
  AndroidManifest.xml file, 1092
  BaseActionBarActivity class, 1091–1092
  examining, 1092–1095
  source code, 1090–1091
StandardNavigationActionBarActivity java file, 1090–1092
start event, 457
start( ) method, 496, 540, 584, 593, 595, 612
Start Playing Audio button, 584
startActicity( ) method, 48, 139, 222, 926, 1064

startActivityForResult( ) method, 48, 140, 616, 829, 1064
startDrag( ) method, 1135
startMethodTracing( ) method, Debug class, 55
startMyActivityDesc constant, 301
startOffset value, 503
startRecording( ) method, 604
startSearch( ) method, 765, 769, 822
startService( ) method, 342–343, 346, 352, 401, 420, 442, 444, 455, 457
static final property, 357
stickiness, 457–458
sticky services, 457
Stk application, 18
StockQuoteClient, 351
StockQuoteService project, 350
StockQuoteService.java class, 350
stop( ) method, 496, 584, 591, 593, 612, 830
Stop Recording button, 612
stopPlayback( ) method, 595
stopPlayingRecording( ) method, 612
stopRecording( ) method, 612
stopSelf( ) method, 444, 457
stopService( ) method, 343, 421, 456
StopWatch, 742
storepass argument, 289
storing values, 272
STREAM_ALARM audio stream, 839
STREAM_MUSIC audio stream, 839
STREAM_NOTIFICATION audio stream, 839
STREAM_RING audio stream, 839
STREAM_SYSTEM audio stream, 839
STREAM_VOICE_CALL audio stream, 839
Street button, 874
StreetView activity, 878
StreetView application, 872–874, 877, 921
StreetView mode, 877
stretchable images, 78
StrictModeWrapper class, 60
stride argument, 630
String arrays, 71, 73
string clause, 104
<string> element, 65
string resources, 64–66, 74–76
String type, 105
StringEscapeUtils, 374
Strings resource, 71
strings.xml file, 64–65, 68, 151, 272, 761, 763, 811–812, 1003
structure of Android applications, 39–42
Stub class, 349–350
styles, 194–197
styles.xml file, 197
submenus, 230–231
Subscribed FeedsProvider project, 19
Subscriber Identity Module (SIM) serial number, 16
substitutable values, 803
SUCCESS intent, 830
suggest URI, 797
suggestActionMsg attribute, 820
suggestActionMsg value, 820
suggestActionMsgColumn attribute, 820–821
suggestion columns, 751
suggestion cursor, 752, 820
suggestion list, 751
suggestion providers
  custom, 796–818
    manifest file, 813–814
    planning, 796
    SuggestURLProvider class, 797–807
    SuggestURLProvider project implementation files, 796–797
    user experience, 814–818
  enabling for global search
    in Android 2.2, 754–756
    in Android 2.3, 756–757
    overview, 753
  simple, 778–795
    implementation files, 779–780
    planning, 779
    search activity, 784–789
    search invoker activity, 789–790
    SimpleSuggestionProvider class, 780–784
    user experience, 791–795
suggestion rewriting, 752
suggestions cursor, 751
SUGGEST_MIME_TYPE, SearchManager class, 802
SuggestURLProvider class, 797–807
SuggestUrlProvider class
  getType( ) method and specifying Multipurpose Internet Mail Extensions (MIME) types, 802
  passing query to suggestion provider: selection argument, 802–804
  populating and returning list of columns, 806–807
  project implementation files, 796–797
  responsibilities of, 797
  search metadata for custom suggestion providers, 804–805
  source code, 798
  suggestion cursor columns, 805–806
  URIs, 801–802
SuggestUrlProvider.java file, 796
summary attribute, 267
summary property, 267
summaryOff attribute, 277
summaryOn attribute, 277
supporting different screen sizes, 1001–1002
<supports-screens> element, 1001
Surface Manager library, 7
Surface object, 605
Surface.Callback callbacks, 608
surfaceCreated( ) method, 609
SurfaceHolder.Callback interface, 607
SurfaceView, 680
suspended option, 957
SweepGradient class, 15
Swing, Java SE, 2
switch statement, 227
syh.permission.STARTMYACTIVITY permission, 299, 302
Sync application, 18
sync fields, 954–955
syncing contacts, impacts of, 989–991
synonyms, 110

synthesizeToFile( ) method, 837
system menus, 231
SystemProperties class, 614

T

t command, 38
T-Mobile G1, 4
t1_1_en_p string, 87
t1_1_en_port resource ID, 85
t1_enport resource ID, 85
t1_enport string, 87
t2 resource ID, 85
t2 string, 87
tab1, 1084
tab2, 1084
Tabbed Action bar, 1071
tabbed navigation, 1071–1084
  action bar and menu interaction, 1081–1083
    displaying menu, 1082
    menu items as actions, 1083
  assigning uniform behavior, 1075–1077
  base classes, 1073–1075
  examining, 1084
  manifest file, 1083–1084
  navigation modes, 1079–1080
  obtaining action bar instance, 1079
  scrollable debug text view layout, 1080–1081
  tabbed listener, 1077–1078
TableLayout layout manager, 198, 202–206
TableRow elements, 202–203
tablets, for Android, 5
TabListener.java file, 1072
Tabs area, 1071
TabWidget widget, 17
TED conference, 862
telephony APIs
  SIP, 571–574
  SMS, 559–568
    e-mail, 567–568
    folders, 565–567
    monitoring incoming messages, 563–565
    sending messages, 559–563
  telephony manager, 568–571
telephony components, of Android, 13–14
TelephonyManager class, 16, 568–571
TelephonyManager.getLine1Number( ) function, 570
TelephonyProvider project, 19
temperature sensors, interpreting data from, 907
TemperatureSensor project, 907
Terms of Service, 999
test harness
  creating for menus, 222–224
    adding regular menu items, 225–226
    adding secondary menu items, 226
    creating activity, 224–225
    creating XML layout, 224
    responding to menu-item clicks, 227–228
    setting up menu, 225
    tweaking AndroidManifest.xml file, 228–229
  planning for 2D layout animation, 499
Test List Widget Application widget, 1122–1123
test1 string, 792
Test60SecBCR.java file, 460, 463
Test60SecBCRService.java file, 460, 463
testAccounts( ) method, 962
TestAppActivity.java file, 390
TestBCR files, 461–462
TestBCR project, 461
TestBCRActivity.java file, 428, 461
TestContactsDriverActivity.java class, 965
TestContactsDriverActivity.java file, 960, 978, 982, 986
TestHandlersDriverActivity activity, 418, 422
TestHandlersDriverActivity.java file, 414
testing devices, different, 1001
TestLibActivity.class, 392
TestLibActivity.java file, 387
TestListWidgetProvider.ACTION_LIST_CLICK action, 1110
TestListWidgetProvider.java file, 1114
testport_port resource ID, 85
testport_port string, 87
TestReceiver.java file, 428, 430, 461
TestRemoteViewsFactory.java file, 1114
TestRemoteViewsService.java file, 1114
testSendBroadcast( ) method, 432
TestStandaloneBCR application, 463
teststring_all resource ID, 85
teststring_all string, 86
testThread( ) function, 409
TestTimeDelayReceiver.java file, 461
test.xml file, 81
text argument, 838
text controls, 152–157
  AutoCompleteTextView, 155–156
  EditText, 154–155
  MultiAutoCompleteTextView, 156–157
  TextView, 153–154
text messaging, 559
text package, 18
Text to Speech APIs. *See* TTS APIs
text1 constant, 67, 805
text_2 constant, 805
textColor attribute, 197
TextToSpeech class, 16, 825, 830, 842
TextToSpeech.LANG_AVAILABLE intent, 841
TextToSpeech.LANG_COUNTRY_AVAILABLE intent, 841
TextToSpeech.LANG_COUNTRY_VAR_AVAILABLE intent, 841
TextToSpeech.LANG_MISSING_DATA intent, 841
TextToSpeech.LANG_NOT_SUPPORTED intent, 841
TexturedSquareRenderer class, 672–673, 676
textures, OpenGL
  abstracting common handling, 669–672
  drawing with, 672–673
  normalized coordinates, 669
  overview, 668–669
TextView controls, 76, 148–149, 153–154, 195, 233, 273, 494, 880
TextView field, 1021
TextView view, 67, 718
TextView widget, 17

thefreewebdictionary.com, 806
\"Theme.Dialog.AppError\"styles, 198
themes, 197–198
themes.xml file, 198
this variable, 407
Thread object, 321
ThreadGroup class, 342–343
threading and components, 399–403
  content providers, 401
  external service components, 401
  main thread, 400–401
  thread pools, 401
  thread utilities, 401–403
ThreadPolicy method, 58
threads
  behavior of, 412–413
  pools, 401
  utilities, 401–403
  worker, 408–413
    communicating between main threads and, 410–412
    invoking from menu, 409–410
    thread behavior, 412–413
ThreadSafeClientConnManager, 317, 319
ThumbnailUtils class, 193
timeouts, consuming HTTP services, 318–319
TimePicker control, 167–168
TimePicker widget, 17
TimePickerDialog, 264
TimeUtils class, 17
Title area, 1071
title attribute, 267
title property, 267
TITLE value, 618
TitlesFragment class, 1037, 1040
TNF (Type Name Format), 931
TNF_UNCHANGED record type, 931
to parameter, 172
Toast class, 263, 563, 1073
Toast message, 885
toggle( ) method, 161, 163
ToggleButton control, 159–160, 590
Tools window, 577
toPixels( ) method, 872
touch events, 846
touches with maps, 871–874
touchscreens
  gestures, 874–889
    custom, 881
    GestureDetector class, 878–881
    and Gestures Builder app, 882–889
    pinch gesture, 875–878
  MotionEvents, 845–862
    drag and drop, 859–862
    MotionEvent object, 845–857
    recycling, 857
    velocitytracker, 857–859
  multi-touch, 862–871
    post version 2.2, 871
    prior to version 2.2, 863–870
  touches with maps, 871–874
toUri( ) method, 1110–1111
transaction fees, 999
transformation matrices, 516
transitions, FragmentTransaction objects, 1034–1035
translate animation, 498
Translate example, Google, 366–375
translate methods, 514
<translate> tag, 1034
TranslationAnimation class, 17
Translator.java code, 367
trouble words, 838
trueBtnTop, 851
TrueButton class, 848–849, 853
trueLayoutTop, 855
tryOneOfThese(activity), 128
TTS engine, 829, 831–832
TTS (Text to Speech) APIs, 842
  advanced features of TTS engine, 838–842
    earcons, 839–840
    language methods, 840–842
    playing silence, 840
    setting audio streams, 839
  audio files, 832–838
  overview, 825–830
  using alternative engines, 840
  utterances, 830–832
tv.getText( ) method, 195
tweening animation, 11, 17
Type Name Format (TNF), 931
type-to-search, enabling, 777–778
TYPE_AUTOMATIC, 989
TypeFace class, 15
TYPE_KEEP_SEPARATE, 989
TYPE_KEEP_TOGETHER, 989

U

udpateAppWidget function, 740
UI/Application Exerciser Monkey, 1001
UI framework, Android SDK, 2
UI (User Interface), 145–152
  advanced concepts, 11–13
  for Android, 9
  with code
    overview, 147–149
    and XML, 150–151
  with XML
    and code, 150–151
    overview, 149–150
unbindService( ) method, 354–355
uniform behavior, assigning for tabbed navigation, 1075–1077
Uniform Resource Identifiers. *See* URIs
Uniform Resource Identifiers (Android URIs), 14
uninstalling widget packages, 722
unlocked, 998
up vector, 635
update method, 108, 110, 117
updateAppWidget( ) function, 740
updateAppWidgetLocal( ) function, 740
Updater application, 18
updates
  of ADT, checking for, 27

of content providers, 108
updating and signing applications, 294
Upload Application screen, 1009
uploading applications, 1007–1010
Uri class, 15, 105, 568
URI parameter, managedQuery( ) method, 47
URIFunctionTester class, 969
UriMatcher class, 105, 111, 802
URIs (Uniform Resource Identifiers)
data, relationship to intents, 129
overview, 801–802
passing where clauses through, 104–105
permissions, 303–306
in content providers, 304–305
passing in intents, 303–304
reading data with, 100–102
structure of, 97–98
url field, 735
UrlEncodedFormEntity class, 310
Use as ringtone option, 280
Use with field, 837
user experience of Android market, 1010–1012
User Interface. *See* UI
User's Calendar Data, required permission for, 296
User's Contact Data, required permission for, 296
users' data protection, 996
User's Guide, Android, 944
<uses-configuration> tag, 1002–1003
<uses-feature> tag, 895, 906, 914, 933, 1002–1003
<uses-permissions> tag, 305, 599, 1002–1003, 1009
uT (micro-Teslas), 914
util package, 18
util.concurrent package, 18
util.concurrent.atomic package, 18
util.concurrent.locks package, 18
utilities, date-related, 737–738
util.jar package, 18
util.logging package, 18
util.prefs package, 18
util.regex package, 18
Utils class, 427, 970
Utils.java class, 413
Utils.java file, 427–428, 433–434, 461, 463, 969
Utils.logThreadSignature( ) method, 408, 411
Utils.logThreadSignature(tag) method, 432
util.zip package, 18
utterances, 830–832

V

v argument, 289
validity argument, 289
values
storing, 272
substitutable, 803
values directory, 41, 70, 85
values/strings.xml file, 797
variable length ID field, 931
variable length payload field, 931
variable length type field, 931
.vcf files, 950–951
VelocityTracker, 845, 857–859
video
playing content, 593–595
recording, 605–614
VideoView class, 594–595
VideoView component, 595
VideoView interface, 607
VideoView widget, 17, 593
VIEW action, 804, 807, 809
view animation, 2D, 507–516
adding animation to ListView, 511–514
AnimationListener class, 515–516
overview, 507–510
providing depth perception with camera, 514–515
transformation matrices, 516
View attributes, 196
View class, 17, 145, 194, 846
view groups, 9
VIEW intent, 130
View menu, 1008
view method, 810
View object, 158, 248, 846–847, 852, 854, 857
view point, 635
ViewAnimation class, 511
ViewAnimationActivity, 512
ViewAnimationListener class, 516
ViewGroup class, 17, 145, 1033
ViewHolder object, 192–193
viewing
live folders, 697
volume, 625, 629, 636
viewing box, 625, 629
View.OnTouchListener interface, 846–847
views, 9, 29, 146, 694
virtual keyboard object, 846
Virtual Machine (Dalvik VM), 6–8
VirtualJax application, 916
VirtualJaxWithRemap application, 922
vnd.android.cursor.item, 100
vnd.ms-excel subtype, 99
VoiceDialer application, 18
VOICE_RECOGNITION audio source, 599
v.onTouchEvent(event), 855

W

wake locks
abstracting with LightedGreenRoom abstraction, 449–455
controlling from two places, 458
WebKit library, 7
WebView class, 17, 194
web.xml file, 41
weight, in LinearLayout, 199–201
WHERE clause, 985
where clauses, 104–106, 116–117, 803
whereClause argument, 108
while loop, navigating through cursors using, 103
White, Chris, 4
widget background shape file, 727–728
widget configurator, 715–716
widget definition, 715, 717–719, 725
widget instance creation, 719–720

widget instance ID, 716
widget layout file, 726–727
widget layout-related files, 726–728
widget manager class, 743
widget model
  abstract implementation of, 732–734
  implementation for birthday widget, 735–737
  interface for, 731–732
  overview, 730
widget provider class, 712, 715, 728
widget providers
  metadata, 1121
  test, 1114–1118
widget view, mouse click event callbacks, 722
widgets
  code for, 743
  defining provider, 724–725
  defining size, 725–726
  description of, 146
  designing, 743
  extensions for, 742–743
  implementing configuration activity, 738–742
  implementing provider, 728–730
  lifecycle of, 716–722
    creating instance on home screen, 713–715
    deleting widget instance, 722
    onUpdate phase, 720–721
    uninstalling widget packages, 722
    widget definition phase, 717–719
    widget instance creation phase, 719–720
    widget view mouse click event callbacks phase, 722
  limitations of, 742–743
  main layout file, 1120
WiFi location information, required permission for, 296
WifiConfiguration class, 16
WifiManager class, 16
WorkerThreadRunnable class, 410–411, 413
world coordinates, 629, 634
wrapping cursors, 707
writeToParcel( ) method, 357

X

X component, 852
X coordinate, 856
x, y, z values, 628
XAL (Extensible Address Language), 15
Xml class, 17
xml directory, 70
XML (Extensible Markup Language)
  arbitrary resource files, 80–81
  layout files, for prompt dialog, 247
  menu tags
    checkable behavior tags, 241
    group category tag, 241
    menu enabling/disabling tag, 242
    menu icon tag, 241
    menu item shortcuts, 242
    menu visibility, 242
    to simulate submenu, 241
  UI development with, 149–151
XML files, 70, 72
xml folder, 41
xml/searchable.xml file, 757, 780, 797
xml\ test_list_appwidget_provider.xml file, 1114
xmlparsers package, 18
XmlPullParser, 81
XmlResourceParser, 81

Y

Y coordinate, 855
YourGLESRenderer class, 679

Z

zero suggestions mode, 749–750
ZIP files, creating projects from, 421, 461
zipalign tool, 293–294, 1007
ZoomButton widget, 17
zoomIn( ) method, 525
zoomOut( ) method, 525
  zoomToSpan( ) method, 5, 533

CPSIA information can be obtained at www.ICGtesting.com
Printed in the USA
LVOW111026110313

323665LV00002B/4/P